Egyptian Origin of the Book of Revelation

John H.C. Pippy

Egyptian Origin of the Book of Revelation

© 2011 by John H.C. Pippy
St. John's, Newfoundland, Canada

All rights reserved. Except for quotation of short passages for the purposes of criticism and review, no part of this publication may be reproduced, stored in a retrieval system, or transmitted, in any form or by any means, electronic, mechanical, photocopying, recording or otherwise, without the prior permission of the author.

Published by John H.C. Pippy
Printed by Lulu Enterprises Inc.
Raleigh, NC, USA

Second Edition, December 2011
Copyright 2009, 2010 and 2011 by John H.C. Pippy
All rights reserved

ISBN-13: 978-0-9812570-4-4

(ISBN-13 for hard cover edition: 978-0-9812570-3-7)

Reproduction of figures from *The Tomb of Ramesses VI* by PIANKOFF, ALEXANDRE; *EGYPTIAN RELIGIOUS TEXTS AND REPRESENTATIONS, VOL. 1.* © 1954 by Bollingen, 1982 renewed PUP Reprinted by permission of Princeton University Press.

Revised Standard Version of the Bible, copyright 1952 [2nd edition, 1971] by the Division of Christian Education of the National Council of the Churches of Christ in the United States of America. Used by permission. All rights reserved.

The Egyptologist hieroglyphic fonts in this book are used with permission from Deniart Systems, Toronto, Canada.

TABLE OF CONTENTS

Quick Reference Version
(See "Full Version" of the Table of Contents starting on next page)

PREFACE 33

PART I. BACKGROUND 37
Chapter 1. The Enigmatic Book of Revelation 39
Chapter 2. New Approaches 43

PART II. THE THRONE SCENE 57
Chapter 3. The Preeminent Deities 59
Chapter 4. Other Characters in Revelation 84
Chapter 5. The Word of God 101
Chapter 6. The Twelve Tribes of Israel (Rev. 7:4-8, Rev. 14:1-5) 116
Chapter 7. The Great Multitude (Rev. 7:9-17) 142
Chapter 8. Egyptian Parallels in the Seven Letters (Rev. 2-3) 154

PART III. THE AMDUAT SERIES (REV. 5-14) 195
Chapter 9. Opening of the Scroll (Rev. 5) 198
Chapter 10. Call to Arms (Rev. 6.1-17) 211
Chapter 11. Prelude to War (Rev. 7:1-15) 231
Chapter 12. Silence in Heaven (Rev. 8:1) 242
Chapter 13. Catastrophes 249
Chapter 14. From Catastrophe to Myth 281
Chapter 15. The Little Scroll (Rev. 10) 297
Chapter 16. The Two Witnesses (Rev. 11:1-13) 312
Chapter 17. The Woman in the Sky (Rev. 11:15-18, Rev. 12) 336
Chapter 18. The Beasts of Rev. 13 368
Chapter 19. Reaping of the Harvest (Rev. 14:6-20) 403

PART IV. THE BOOK OF GATES SERIES (REV. 15-22) 413
Chapter 20. The Song of Moses (Rev. 15:2-4) 415
Chapter 21. Seven Angels with the Wrath of God (Rev. 15:1,5-8) 425
Chapter 22. Armageddon (Rev 16:12b-16) 441
Chapter 23. The Harlot and the Kings (Rev. 17) 456
Chapter 24. The Millennium (Rev. 20:1-10) 475
Chapter 25. Resurrection and Judgment (Rev. 20:11-15) 497
Chapter 26. A New Creation (Rev. 21:1-8) 512
Chapter 27. The Holy City (Rev. 21:10 - Rev. 22:5) 529

PART V. CONSPECTUS 545
Chapter 28. Egyptian deities in the Book of Revelation 547
Chapter 29. Parallel Series of Scenes 555
Chapter 30. Literary Analyses 560
Chapter 31. Perspectives 568

BIBLIOGRAPHY & REFERENCES .... 575 & 583

APPENDICES 610

REVELATION INDEX & GENERAL INDEX .... 624 & 634

TABLE OF CONTENTS

Full version
(Also, see "Quick Reverence Version" on the previous page)

TABLE OF CONTENTS
   Quick Reference Version 3
   Full version 4

MAP OF ANCIENT EGYPT 16

MAP OF ANCIENT MIDDLE EAST 17

CHRONOLOGY OF ANCIENT EGYPTIAN
   DYNASTIES AND KINGS 18

PRONUNCIATION OF EGYPTIAN WORDS 20

LIST OF FIGURES 21

LIST OF TABLES 31

PREFACE 33

PART I. BACKGROUND 37

Chapter 1. The Enigmatic Book of Revelation 38
   Christian Perspectives 38
   Egyptian Perspectives 40

Chapter 2. New Approaches 42
   Studies on Style 45
      Subordination of Text to Image 46
      Translation Considerations 48
      Egyptian – the Divine Language 50
      Identification of Egyptian Gods 53
         Names in texts 53
         Heads of gods in illustrations 53
         Crowns, diadems and head-dresses 53
      Metaphors 53
   Conventions Used 54
      Abbreviations for Names of Egyptian Texts 54
      References to Egyptian Illustrations 54
      Quotations 55

Table of Contents

  References to Budge's (1920) Hieroglyphic Dictionary 56
  References to Plates in The Egyptian Book of the Dead 56
  Footnotes, Endnotes, and Appendices 56

PART II. THE THRONE SCENE 57

Chapter 3. The Preeminent Deities 58
 God on the Throne 58
  God's Apparel (Rev. 1:13) 60
  God's Radiance (Rev. 1:16, 21:10-11,23) 60
  God's Metallic Flesh (Rev. 1:15) 61
  God's Hair (Rev. 1:14) 61
  Truth (Rev. 3:7) 61
  The Sword from God's Mouth (Rev. 2:16) 62
   Word Power 62
   Punning 62
   Simple description of Hieroglyphics 63
  Water from the Throne (Rev. 22:1-2) 63
  Angels flying in midheaven (Rev. 8:13) 64
 The Lamb 66
  The Lamb of Re 66
 God *and* the Lamb 69
 The Amen 71
 Christ 73
  First-born of the dead (Rev. 1:5) 75
  Ruler of Earth (Rev. 1:5) 76
  The Anointed One (Rev. 1:1) 77
  The Morning Star (Rev. 22:16) 78
  The Faithful Witness (Rev. 1:5a) 79
  Freed by his Blood (Rev. 1:5b) 80
  A note on the name "Jesus" 80
  Conclusion 82
 Discussion 82

Chapter 4. Other Characters in Revelation 84
 Four Creatures before the Throne (Rev. 4:6-9) 84
 Seven Spirits of God (Rev. 1:4; 3:1; 4:5; 5:6) 88
 Twenty-four Elders (Rev. 4:4) 90
 Angels (Rev. 5:11) 93
 Satan, the Devil and the Ancient Serpent (Rev. 12; 13:2-4; 20:2-3) 95
 The Beast (Rev. 13) 97
 Discussion 100

Chapter 5. "The Word of God" (Rev. 19:11-21) 101
 Parallels with Thoth (Rev. 19:11-16) 102
  Thoth as judge (Rev. 19:11) 102
   Thoth – faithful, true and righteous (Rev. 19:11) 103
  Thoth as Warrior (Rev. 19:11, 14-16) 103
   Sword from the Thoth's mouth (Rev. 19:15) 104
 Parallels with Horus 106
  Horus as "The Word of God" 106

His name is on his robe and thigh (Rev. 19:16) 106
Horus as judge 107
Horus as witness 107
Horus as warrior 108
    Horus' horse (Rev. 19:11) 108
    Horus's red robe (Rev. 19:13) 109
Horus' army 110
    Uniforms of white linen (Rev. 19:11) 110
    Riders on white horses (Rev. 19:14) 110
Non-specific parallels 110
The leader's secret name (Rev. 19:12) 110
Eyes like flame of fire (Rev. 19:12) 111
Many crowns (Rev. 19:12) 111
    The crowns of Thoth 111
    The crowns of Horus 112
Discussion 112

Chapter 6. The Twelve Tribes of Israel (Rev. 7:4-8, Rev. 14:1-5) 116
Division into Groups of Twelve 117
Names of the Tribes of Israel (Rev. 7:4-8) 119
Names in the *Book of Gates* 119
Names in the *Amduat* 121
    Israel, Patriarch of the Tribes (Rev. 7:4) 127
Attributes of the Tribes of Israel 129
First Fruits for God and the Lamb (Rev. 14:4) 130
Once lived on earth (Rev. 14:3-4) 131
Truthfulness (Rev. 14:5) 131
Chaste, all-male composition (Rev. 14:4) 132
Followers of the Lamb (Rev. 14:4) 133
Owned by God (Rev. 14:3-4) 133
Father's name written on their foreheads (Rev. 7:3; 14:1) 134
Those who Praise (Rev. 14:2-3) 135
The 144,000 (Rev. 14:1):- 136
Discussion 137
The tribes as part of a parallel sequence 137
The all-male character of the tribes 137
Why do the names of the tribes seem to be hidden? 138
Implications of findings on the date of the Exodus 139
Earliest records of the tribes in Egyptian writings 140
Of Re and Yahweh 140
An Alternative Solution to the Tribal Identity Problem 140

Chapter 7. The Great Multitude (Rev. 7:9-17) 142
Attributes of the Great Multitude (Rev. 7:9-17) 142
Followers of the Lamb (Rev. 7:17) 142
Multiracial composition (Rev. 7:9) 143
Palm Branches in their hands (Rev. 7:9) 143
Clothed in white robes (Rev. 7:9) 145
Serve as priests (Rev. 1:5-6, Rev. 7:15, Rev. 5:10; Rev. 20:6) 146
Sheltered ones (Rev. 7:15) 147
Resting Ones (Rev. 14:13) 148

      Recipients of Food and Water (Rev. 7:15-17) 148
      Happiness (Rev. 7:17) 149
Unassigned Multitude 150
      Fight for God (Rev. 6:9,11; Rev. 11:18; Rev. 12:7,11; Rev. 19:19) . 150
Discussion 151

Chapter 8. Egyptian Parallels in the Seven Letters (Rev. 2-3) 154
    Parallel Elements in the Letters and Egyptian Texts 155
      I know ... (Rev. 2:2,9,13,19; Rev. 3:1,8,15) 155
      I know your dwelling place (Rev. 2:13) 155
      I know your works (Rev. 2:2,19; Rev. 3:1,8,15) 156
      I know those with false credentials (Rev. 2:2,9; Rev. 3:9) 156
      I know ... those who rebel (many references) 156
      Fornication and Eating Sacrificed Food (Rev. 2:14, 20) 158
      The Conquerors (Rev. 2:7,11,17,26; Rev. 3:5,12,21) 159
      Deceased is to be judged like the One on the Throne (Rev. 3:21) . . 161
      Confession of Deceased Before the Throne (Rev. 3:5) 161
      Deceased Claims Share in Throne (Rev. 3:21) 162
      Promise of No Second Death (Rev. 2:11) 162
      Gift of the Tree of Life (Rev. 2:7) 163
      Gift of White Garments (Rev. 3:5a) 164
      Maintain Name in the Book of Life (Rev. 3:5b) 165
      Become a pillar in the temple (Rev. 3:12) 165
      Eating in the presence of God (Rev. 3:20) 167
      Gift of hidden manna (Rev. 2:17) 167
      Gift of a white stone with a secret name (Rev. 2:17) 168
      Gift of the morning star (Rev. 2:28) 169
      An open door (Rev. 3:8) 170
      He who has an ear, let him hear ... (Rev. 2:7,11,17,29; 3:6,13,22) . 170
    Structural Parallels in the Seven Letters 171
      Letter to Philadelphia (Rev. 3:7-12)
          and Chapter 115 of the *Book of the Dead* 172
          A door is opened (Rev. 3:8b) 172
          "I know your works"(Rev. 3:8a) 172
          People with false credentials (Rev. 3:9b) 173
          Authority and Power (Rev. 3:9) 173
          Reference to Satan (Rev. 3:9a) 173
          Reference to Lies (Rev. 3:9a) 173
          Arrival of a Deity (Rev. 3:11) 174
          Deity rules against the adversary (Rev. 3:10) 174
          Stripping of Authority (Rev. 3:11) 174
          Conqueror becomes a pillar (Rev. 3:12a) 174
          The City of God (Rev. 3:12b) 175
          List of names (Rev. 3:12c) 176
      Letter to Thyatira (Rev. 2:18-28) and the
          5th Division of the *Book of Caverns* 177
          Woman assigned to a place (Rev. 2:20-23) 179
          Repentance (Rev. 2:21-22) 179
          Being thrown into tribulation (Rev. 2:22) 179
          Death Sentence (Rev. 2:23a) 180
          Searching the mind and heart (Rev. 2:23b) 180

Deep Things of Satan (Rev. 2:24) 181
No burden on faithful (Rev. 2:24) 182
"I come ..." (Rev. 2:25) 182
Rod of Power (Rev. 2:26-27) 182
Something is broken into pieces (Rev. 2:27) 183
"He who has an ear ..." (Rev. 2:29) 183
Comments on the Letter to Thyatira 183
Discussion 185
   Discussion on Parallel Elements 185
   Discussion on Structural Parallels 186
   Historical parallels – the end of the Hyksos occupation 186
      Rebellion against a deity 192
      War is Declared: 192
      Followers in the synagogue of Satan 192
      Faithful among enemies are spared in the conflict 192
      The "New Jerusalem" 193
      The "Hour of Trial" 193

PART III. THE AMDUAT SERIES (REV. 5-14) 195

Chapter 9. Opening of the Scroll (Rev. 5) 197
   Presentation of the Scroll (Rev. 5:1-2) 197
      No one worthy to open scroll (Rev. 5:2-4) 199
      The lion of Judah (Rev. 5:5) 200
      The slain lamb (Rev. 5:6-9) 203
   A Most Holy Scroll 203
      The House of Life in Rev. 5:3-11 204
   Discussion 208

Chapter 10. Call to Arms (Rev. 6.1-17) 211
   The Four Horsemen (Rev. 6:1-8) 212
      Colors of the Four Horses (6:1-8) 213
   War Cries (Rev. 6:1-8) 215
      Conquerors (Rev. 6:2) 216
      Removal of Peace (Rev. 6:4) 217
      Spoils of War (Rev. 6:5-6) 218
      Death by Sword, Pestilence & Beasts (Rev. 6:7-8) 220
   War in the *Amduat* (Rev. 6:2-11) 222
      Casualties of War (Rev. 6:2-8) 222
      Souls of Those Slain (Rev. 6:9-11) 223
   The Wrath of the Lamb (Rev. 6:12-17) 227
   Discussion 229

Chapter 11. Prelude to War (Rev. 7:1-15) 231
   The Four Angels and the Four Winds (Rev. 7:1-3) 231
   The New Conscripts (Rev. 7:4-8) 236
   Multitudes with Palm Branches (Rev. 7:9-10) 237
   Protection of the Faithful (Rev. 7:15) 238
   Discussion 239

Table of Contents

Chapter 12. Silence in Heaven (Rev. 8:1) 242
   Personal Silence 243
   Contemplative Silence 243
   Silence in Death 244
   Silence and the Renewal of Creation 245
   Conclusion 248

Chapter 13. Catastrophes 249
   The Revelation Account (Rev. 6,8,9,14,16,18,19) 250
      A Very High Mountain (Rev. 18:5) 251
      Warning to leave (Rev. 18:4) 251
      Sudden Fire, Smoke, Lightning, Noise and an Earthquake
         (Rev. 8:5,8; Rev. 9:2; Rev. 16:18-19; Rev. 18) 252
      Darkness (Rev. 6:12-13; Rev. 8:12; Rev. 9:2; Rev. 16:10) 252
      Hail of Death (Rev. 8:7; Rev. 9:2-11; Rev. 16:10,11,21) 253
      Poisonous Water (Rev. 8:9-11; Rev. 16:3,4,13) 255
      View from the Sea (Rev. 18) 255
      Discussion 256
   Egyptian Accounts 259
      Book of the Dead 260
         A Very High Mountain (Rev. 18:5) 262
         Sudden Fire, Smoke, Lightning, Noise, an Earthquake and Darkness
            (Rev. 8:5,8; Rev. 9:2; Rev. 16:18-19) 262
         Hail of Pain and Death (Rev. 8:7; Rev. 9:2-11; Rev. 16:10,11,21)
            262
         Poisonous Water (Rev. 8:9-11; Rev. 16:3,4,13) 266
         View from the Sea (Rev. 18) 266
         Mountainous Waves 266
         Discussion 266
      Book of the Divine Cow 267
      Prophesy of Neferrohu 269
      Admonitions of an Egyptian Sage 271
   Plato's Account 271
   A Modern Account 274
   Discussion 278

Chapter 14. From Catastrophe to Myth 281
   Sources and Probable Dates of the Catastrophes 282
   Dates of the Egyptian Accounts 283
   Thera's Eruption in Egyptian Mythology 284
   The Aegean Islands as a Parallel to Revelation's Babylon 290
   Discussion 293

Chapter 15. The Little Scroll (Rev. 10) 297
   Presentation of the Scroll (Rev. 10:1-4) 297
      An Angel in a cloud (Rev. 10:1) 299
      With a rainbow over his head (Rev. 10:1) 300
      His face was like the sun (Rev. 10:1) 300
      His legs were like pillars of fire (Rev. 10:1) 300
      He had a little scroll open in his hand (Rev. 10:2) 300
      His feet were on the sea and the land (Rev. 10:2) 301

　　　　He "Called Out Like a Lion Roaring" (Rev 10:3) 301
　　　　The Seven Thunders Speak (Rev 10:3-4) 301
　　　　Instruction not to Write (Rev 10:4) 302
　　Call for Immediate Action (Rev 10:5-7) 303
　　Ceremony of the Little Scroll (Rev. 10:8-11) 306
　　Discussion 310

Chapter 16. The Two Witnesses (Rev. 11:1-13) 312
　　The Temple of God (Rev. 11:1-2) 313
　　Story of Two Witnesses (Rev. 11:3-13) 315
　　　　The Two Witnesses (Rev. 11:3) 315
　　　　　　The Two Mourners (Rev. 11:3) 316
　　　　The Two Lampstands (Rev. 11:4b) 317
　　　　　　The fearful flaming ones 317
　　　　　　The flaming ones as lampstands 318
　　　　　　Power to Spit Fire 319
　　　　　　Power to Cause Plagues 319
　　　　　　Power to Shut up the Sky 320
　　　　The Two Trees (Rev. 11:4a) 321
　　　　Death of the Two Witnesses (Rev. 11:7-11) 321
　　　　　　Death by the Beast from the Bottomless Pit 322
　　　　Fate of the Two Witnesses (Rev. 11:8-12) 323
　　　　　　Display of their Bodies 323
　　　　　　Their Resurrection 324
　　The Great Earthquake (Rev. 11:13) 327
　　Discussion 329

Chapter 17. The Woman in the Sky (Rev. 11:15-18, Rev. 12) 336
　　The Woman 339
　　　　The Great Portent (Rev. 12:1a) 339
　　　　Clothed with the Sun (Rev. 12:1b) 339
　　Parallels in the *Book of Day* (Rev. 12) 343
　　　　Moon Under her Feet (Rev. 12:1c) 343
　　　　Crown of Twelve Stars (Rev. 12:1d) 343
　　Birth of the Child-God (Rev. 12:2-5) 344
　　Attack of the Dragon (Rev. 12:3-4) 345
　　Prophesy of Power (Rev. 12:5) 345
　　Falling Stars (Rev. 12:4) 346
　　Flight of the Mother (Rev. 12:6,14) 346
　　　　War in Heaven (Rev. 12:7-9) 347
　　　　Michael, Leader of the Army (Rev. 12:7) 348
　　　　Defeat of the Dragon (Rev. 12:8-9) 349
　　The Kingdom of God (Rev. 12:10-11) 350
　　Pursuit of the Woman (Rev. 12:15-16) 352
　　War on the Woman's Offspring (Rev. 12:17) 355
　　One Standing on the Sand (Rev. 12:17) 356
　　Parallels in the *Book of Night* (Rev. 11:15-18) 357
　　　　Arrival of the Kingdom of God (Rev. 11:15) 358
　　　　The Resurrection (Rev. 11:18) 359
　　　　The Nations Rage (Rev. 11:18a) 360
　　　　The Judgment (Rev. 11:18c) 360

Table of Contents

- Discussion 360
  - Merging of Egyptian Myths in Rev. 12 360
    - The Cosmic Cycle 361
  - Renewal of the Earth 362
  - Conclusion 364

- Chapter 18. The Beasts of Rev. 13 368
  - The First Beast:- from the Sea (Rev. 13:1-8) 370
    - Arrival of the 1st Beast (Rev. 13:1) 370
    - The beast's power and war (Rev. 13:2,7) 372
    - Blasphemous words of the 1st beast (Rev. 13:5) 373
    - The Forty-two Month Reign (Rev. 13:5-6) 374
    - Egypt's parallel to Revelation's 1st beast 375
      - Apophis and Seth 375
      - Seth's mortal wound 376
      - Seth as a pig 377
      - Additional evidence 377
  - Fate of the Faithful (Rev. 13:7-10) 377
    - The Book of Life 379
    - Separation of the faithful 380
  - The Second Beast:- from the Earth (Rev. 13:11-18) 381
    - Egypt's parallel to Revelation's 2nd beast (Rev. 13:11) 381
    - The "Image of the 1st beast" (Rev. 13:14-15) 384
      - The "shape created by Horus" 385
      - "Image by Horus himself" 386
      - "Image made by Horus" 387
    - Breath to the Image of the 1st beast (Rev. 13:15) 387
    - Authority of the Image of the 1st beast (Rev. 13:15) 388
    - Branding of the Beast's Followers (Rev. 13:16) 389
    - 666" – the Mark of the Beast (Rev. 13:17-18) 391
  - Discussion 392
    - Parallels to the Main Characters 392
    - Organizational Parallels 392
    - Historical Parallels 394
      - The Hyksos in the 2nd Intermediate Period 394
      - Parallels with the Hyksos Rule 395
      - Signs from Heaven 396
      - The Two and Ten Kings 396
      - The Forty-two Month Period 397
      - The False Prophet 397
    - Conclusion 400

- Chapter 19. Reaping of the Harvest (Rev. 14:6-20) 403
  - The Harvest (Rev. 14:14-18) 404
    - Arrival of Harvest Time (Rev. 14:6-7,15) 404
    - The Harvest Begins (Rev. 14:14-18) 406
  - The Judgment (Rev. 14:6-13,19-20) 407
    - Punishment of the followers of the Beast (Rev. 14:7-11) 409
  - Discussion 411

12   *Egyptian Origin of the Book of Revelation*

PART IV. THE BOOK OF GATES SERIES (Rev. 15-22) 413

Chapter 20. The Song of Moses (Rev. 15:2-4) 415
   Singers by the Lake of Fire (Rev. 15:2) 415
      The Singers' Harps (Rev. 15:2) 417
   The Song of Moses (Rev. 15:3-4) 418
      The Song in the *Book of Gates* 418
      The Song in the Victory Hymn of Thutmosis III 420
         A Song of Moses *and* the Lamb (Rev. 15:3) 421
         Moses, Servant of God (15:3) 422
         King of the Ages (Rev. 15:3) 423
         Great and Wonderful Deeds (Rev. 15:3-4) 423
   Discussion 423

Chapter 21. Seven Angels with the Wrath of God
         (Rev. 15:1,5-8; Rev. 16:1-12a, 17-21) 425
   The Egyptian Setting 425
   The Seven Angels 428
      Appearance of the Seven Angels (Rev. 15:6) 428
         Their Robes 428
         Their Collars 429
   Opening of the Temple (Rev. 15:5-7) 429
      The Bowls of Wrath (Rev. 15:6-7) 429
   Judgment against the Nations 431
      Waters turned to blood and consumed (Rev. 16:4-6) 433
      Praise for God's Judgment and his Eternal Nature (Rev. 16:5-7) ... 435
      Natural Phenomena in the Wrath of God (Rev. 16) 436
         Earthquakes (Rev. 16:18-20) 436
         Poisonous Waters (Rev. 16:3-4) 437
         Fire from the Sun (Rev. 16:8-9) 438
   Discussion 438

Chapter 22. Armageddon (Rev 16:12b-16) 441
      Armageddon in the *Annals of Thutmosis III* 442
      Cities of the Nations Fall (Rev. 16:19) 442
      "Coming like a thief"(Rev. 16:15a) 443
      Naked Enemy Soldiers (Rev. 16:15c) 443
   Armageddon in the *Book of Gates* 444
      Events at the Euphrates River (Rev. 16:12-14) 445
         A River Dries up (Rev. 16:12) 445
         The Dragon in the River (Rev. 16:13) 446
         The False Prophet (Rev. 16:13) 447
         Evil Spirits from the Dragon (Rev. 16:13-14) 447
      The Battle of Armageddon 449
         Nakedness of the Enemy (Rev. 16:15) 450
         Cities of the nations fall (Rev. 16:19) 452
   Discussion 453

Chapter 23. The Harlot and the Kings (Rev. 17) 456
   The Great Harlot 456

Table of Contents

The Beast Beneath the Woman (Rev. 17:3) 459
The Kings (Rev. 17:9-13) 460
    The Ten Kings (Rev. 17:12-13) 461
    The Seven Kings (Rev. 17:9-10) 462
    The Eighth King (Rev. 17:11) 463
War with the Lamb (Rev. 17:13-14) 464
    Opposition to the Harlot and the Beast (Rev. 17:15-18) 465
Discussion 466
    The Woman 466
    The Woman as a "Great City" 467
    Many Nations 467
    The Harlot 469
    The Seven Kings of Avaris 470
    The Ten Kings of Thebes 471
    Egypt's 2nd Intermediate Period 473

Chapter 24. The Millennium (Rev. 20:1-10) 475
Capture of the Ancient Serpent (Rev. 20:1-4) 475
    The Ancient Serpent 475
    The Angel 476
    The Hand 477
    The Great Chain 477
    The Binding of the Serpent 477
    The Pit 477
    Judgment of the Serpent and his Followers 478
The 1,000 Year Period (Rev. 20:2-7) 479
    1,000 as a very large number 479
    The 1,000 year link with a lifetime 479
    The 1,000 year Phoenix Period 481
    1,000 Year Periods in the *Book of Gates* 482
The First Resurrection 483
    Reign of the Lamb (Rev. 20:4-5) 483
    Reign of the Martyrs (Rev. 20:4) 484
    The Resurrected Made Priests (Rev. 20:6) 487
The Second Resurrection (Rev. 20:5) 490
Satan's Release from Prison (Rev. 20:7-10) 491
    Battle of Magog (Rev. 20:7-10) 492
Re-capture of the Ancient Serpent (Rev. 20:10) 495
Discussion 495

Chapter 25. Resurrection and Judgment (Rev. 20:11-15) 497
The Resurrection (Rev. 20:13) 498
    Resurrection of the Believers 500
    Resurrection of the Drowned (Rev. 20:13) 500
    Resurrection of the Enemies (Rev. 20:13) 501
The Judgment (Rev. 20:12-13) 503
    The Great White Throne (Rev. 20:11) 504
    The Great and the Small (Rev. 20:12) 505
    Opening of the Books (Rev. 20:12) 506
    Judgment of the Believers and the Drowned (Rev. 20:13,15) 508
Discussion 510

Chapter 26. A New Creation (Rev. 21:1-8) 512
   A New Heaven (Rev. 21:1) 514
   A New Earth (Rev. 21:1) 515
   The Sea is No More (Rev. 21:1) 516
   Arrival of the Holy City (Rev. 21:2-4) 517
      A City Prepared as a Bride (Rev. 21:2,9-10) 518
      Dwelling Place of God and Men (Rev. 21:3) 518
      The End of Mourning (Rev. 21:4) 520
   Renewal (Rev. 21:5-22:5) 521
      All Things Made New (Rev. 21:5) 521
      Truth of the Claim (Rev. 21:5) 522
   Alpha and the Omega (Rev. 21:6a) 522
   Reward of the Water of Life (Rev. 21:6b-7) 525
   Punishment of the Unrighteous (Rev. 21:8) 527
   Discussion 528

Chapter 27. The Holy City (Rev. 21:10 - Rev. 22:5) 529
   The City's Shape and Size (Rev. 21:16) 530
   Material Composition of the City (Rev. 21:18) 532
   The City's Walls and Gates (Rev. 21:12-14,16-21) 532
      Wall's Material and Foundation (Rev. 21:18-21) 532
      Height of the Walls (Rev. 21:17) 534
      Function of the Walls 534
      Number and Form of its Gates (Rev. 21:12,21) 535
      Names of the Twelve Gates (Rev. 21:12) 537
      The Angels at the Gates (Rev. 21:12) 537
      Location of the Twelve Gates (Rev. 21:13) 538
   The River (Rev. 22:1-2) 538
   The Tree of Life (Rev. 22:2) 539
   Light in the City (Rev. 21:11,23; Rev. 22:5) 541
   City's Temple is God (Rev. 21:22) 541
   The Dwelling Place of God (Rev. 21:3) 542
   Discussion 542

PART V. CONSPECTUS 545

Chapter 28. Egyptian Deities in the Book of Revelation 547

Chapter 29. Parallel Series of Scenes 555

Chapter 30. Literary Analyses 560
   Egyptian-Greek Substitutions 560
   Egyptian-Hebrew Translations 560
   Use of Word Play 562
   Use of Metaphors 564
   Special Numbers 565
   Discussion 566

Chapter 31. Perspectives 568

BIBLIOGRAPHY 575

REFERENCES 583

LIST OF APPENDICES 610

APPENDIX 1. Names of the Tribes of Israel in the *Book of Gates* 611

APPENDIX 2. Names of the Tribes of Israel in the *Amduat* 612

APPENDIX 3 Distribution of Attributes of the Multitudes
  in the Book of Revelation 614

APPENDIX 4. *Book of Aker*, Part B 616

APPENDIX 5. List of Selected Parallels 617

APPENDIX 6. GLOSSARY
  Egyptian Gods and Goddesses 620
  Egyptian Terms 622

INDEX TO BOOK OF REVELATION 624

GENERAL INDEX 634

MAP OF ANCIENT EGYPT

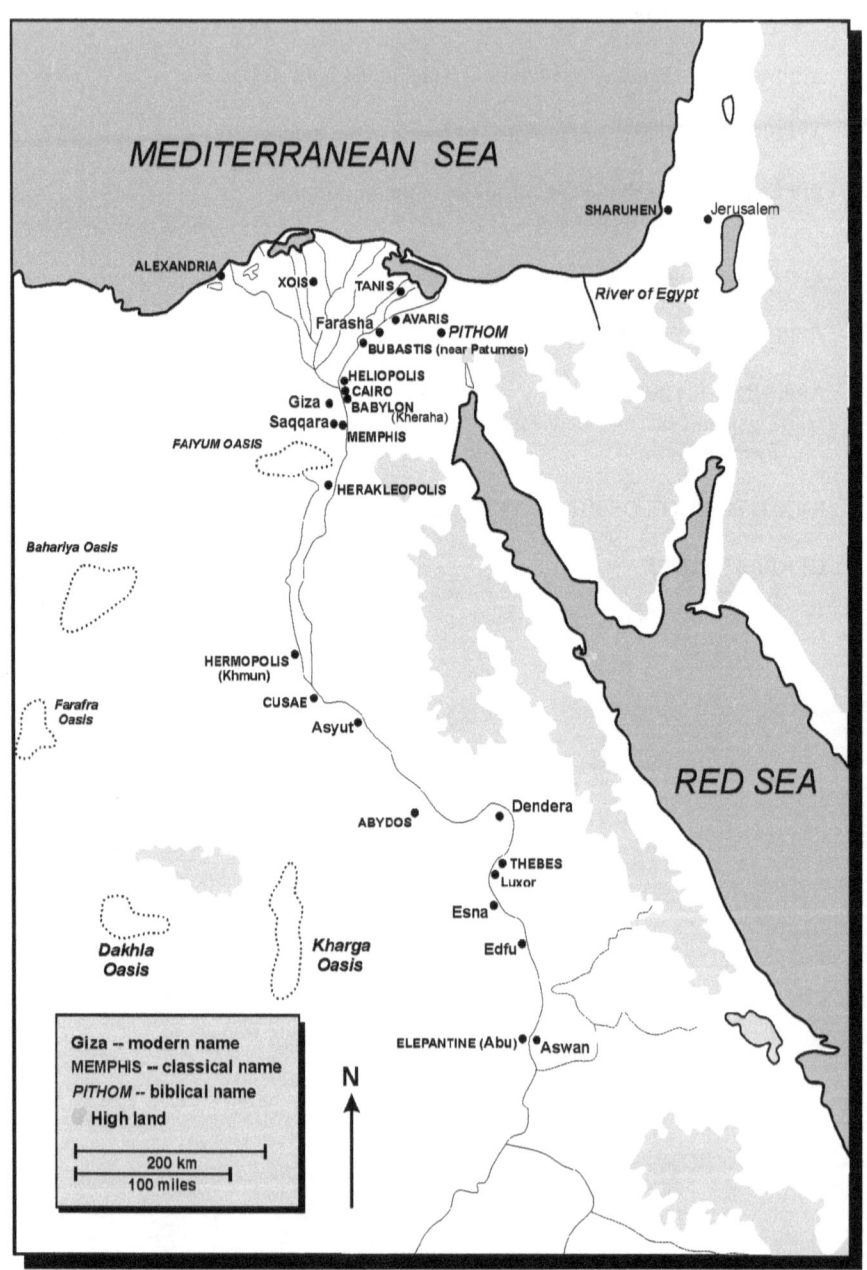

Figure 1. Map of ancient Egypt showing place-names mentioned in text.

MAP OF ANCIENT MIDDLE EAST

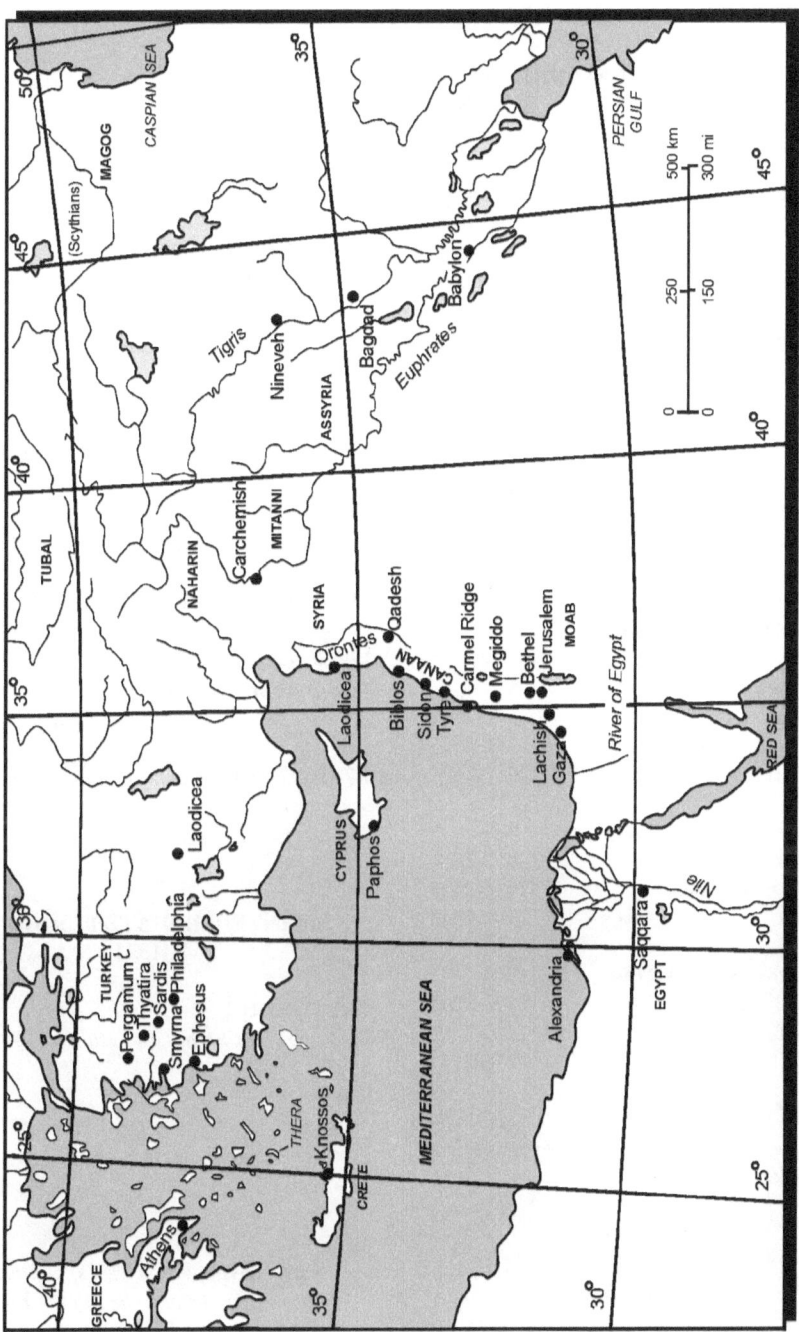

Figure 2. Map of Middle East and surrounding areas showing place-names mentioned in text.

CHRONOLOGY OF ANCIENT EGYPTIAN DYNASTIES AND KINGS

Chronology of ancient Egypt showing the names of some better known kings and including all kings referred to in this work. Primarily based on Baines and Malek's *Atlas of Ancient Egypt* (1980, pp. 36-37) with the addition of the 15th Dynasty material from Grimal (1992, pp. 185-195, 392). Dates known with precision are marked with an asterisk as in Baines and Malek. Note that all dates from the Late Predynastic Period to the 2nd Persian Period are BCE. Asterisks indicate dates are known with precision.

LATE PREDYNASTIC
c. 3000

EARLY DYNASTIC PERIOD
2920-2575

OLD KINGDOM 2575-2134

4th Dynasty, 2575-2465
Snofru — 2575-2551
Khufu (Cheops) — 2551-2528
Shepseskaf — 2472-2467

5th Dynasty, 2465-2323
Sahure' — 2458-2446
Neferirkare' Kakai — 2446-2426
Wenis — 2356-2323

6th Dynasty, 2323-2150
Teti — 2323-2291
Pepy I — 2289-2255
Pepy II — 2246-2152

7th/8th Dynasty — 150-2134
Numerous ephemeral kings, including Neferkare'

1st INTERMEDIATE PERIOD
2134-2040

9th/10th Dynasty (Herakleopolitan)
2134-2040

Several kings called Khety; Merykare'; Ity

11th Dynasty (Theban) — 2134-2040
(five kings)

MIDDLE KINGDOM 2040-1640

11th Dynasty (all Egypt) — 2040-1991
(six kings)
12th Dynasty *(8 kings)* — *1991-1783
13th Dynasty *(about 70 kings)*
— 1783 - after 1640

14th Dynasty *(A group of minor kings who were probably all contemporary with the 13th or 15th Dynasty.)*

2nd INTERMEDIATE PERIOD
1640-1532

15th Dynasty
(Hyksos; from Baines and Malek, 1980)
Salitis, Sheshi
Khian
Apophis — *c.* 1585-1542
(*'Awoserre'* and others)
Khamudi — *c.* 1542-1532

also:
   15th Dynasty *(Hyksos; alternate chronology from Grimal, 1992)*
   Salitis, Sheshi, Sharek(?)
   Yaqub-har, Yaqub-Baal
   Khyan

Apophis I	c. 1585-1542	Twosre	1198-1196
Apophis II, Khamudi			
Apophis III		**20th Dynasty**	**1196-1070**
		Ramesses V	1156-1151
16th Dynasty		Ramesses VI	1151-1143

Minor Hyksos rulers, contemporary with the 15th Dynasty

3rd INTERMEDIATE PERIOD 1070-712

21st Dynasty	1070-945

17th Dynasty	**1640-1550**

Numerous Theban kings; numbers give positions in the complete list

22nd Dynasty	945-712

Inyotef V #1	c. 1640-1635	23rd Dynasty	c. 828-712
Sebekemzaf I #3			
Nebireyeraw #6		24th Dynasty (Sais)	724-712
Sebekamzaf II #10			
Ta'o I (*Seqenenre Ta'a I*) #13		25th Dynasty	770-712
T' o II (*Seqenenre Ta'a II*) #14			
Kamose #15	c. 1555-1550	**LATE PERIOD 712-332**	

NEW KINGDOM 1550-1070

25th Dynasty	712-657
26th Dynasty	*664-525

18th Dynasty	**1550-1307**
Ahmose	1550-1525
Amenophis I	1525-1504

27th Dynasty (Persian)	*525-404

Tuthmosis I	1504-1492
Tuthmosis II	1492-1479

28th Dynasty	*404--399

Tuthmosis III	1479-1425
Hatshepsut (Q)	1473-1458

29th Dynasty	*399-380

Amenophis 11	1427-1401
Tuthmosis IV	1401-1391

30th Dynasty	*380-343

Amenophis III	1391-1353
Amenophis IV/Akhenaten	1353-1335

2nd Persian Period	*343-332

Smenkhkare' (= Nefertiti Q?)	1335-1333
Tut'ankhamun	1333-1323

GRECO-ROMAN PERIOD *332 Bc-395 AD

Aya	1323-1319	Macedonian Dynasty	332-304 BCE
Haremhab	1319-1307	Ptolemaic Dynasty	304 - 330 CE
		Roman emperors	***30 BCE-395 CE**

19th Dynasty	**1307-1196**
Ramesses I	1307 1306

(names found in hieroglyphic and demotic texts, down to the tetrarchy)

Sethos I (Seti or Sety)	1306-1290	Augustus	*30 BC - 14CE
Ramesses II	1290-1224	Nero	*54-68CE
Merneptah	1224-1214	Vespasian	*69-79CE
Sethos II	1214-1204	Titus	*79-81CE
Amenmesse		Domitian	*81-96CE

(usurper during reign of Sethos II)

Siptah	1204-1198

PRONUNCIATION OF EGYPTIAN WORDS

Approximate sound-values of transliterations of Egyptian hieroglyphic signs used by Budge (1920,) and Gardiner (1927, p. 27) and adopted in this work. NOTE: Hieroglyphs may be written from right to left or from left to right.

Budge	Gard.	Budge	Gard.	Approximate Sound-value
		a	3	the glottal stop heard at the commencement of German words beginning with a vowel, ex. *Der Adler*.
		ȧ	i	usually consonantal *y*; at the beginning of words sometimes identical with 3.
		i	y	y
		ā	a	a guttural sound unknown to English
		u	w	w
		b	b	b
		p	p	p
		f	f	f
		m	m	m
		n	n	n
		r	r	r
		h	h	*h* as in English
		ḥ	ḥ	emphatic *h*
		kh	ḫ	like *ch* in Scotch *loch*
		kh, kha	ẖ	perhaps like *ch* in German *ich*
		s	s	s
		sh	š	sh
		q	ḳ	backward *k*; rather like our *q* in *queen*
		k	k	k
		g	g	hard *g*
		t	t	t
		th	ṯ	originally *tsh* (*č* or *tj*)
		ṭ	d	d
		tch	ḏ	originally *dj* and also a dull emphatic *s*

LIST OF FIGURES

Sources of figures:
From Piankoff (1954), reprinted by permission of Princeton University Press: #2, 8-11, 14, 19, 20, 26, 28-34, 39-42, 44, 45, 48-53, 56-70, 72, 73, 76-79, 82-97, 100-108, 110-113, 116, 119, 121, 122, 124, 128.
From Budge (1904) Vol. I: #12, 13, 16, 23, 24, 109, 114, 115, 117, 120, 123, 125.
From Budge (1904) Vol. II: 15, 18, 36, 81, 99.
From Budge (1934), #17.
Erman (1907) #4, 5, 7, 22.
James (1960), #126 (reprinted with permission from JM Dent, a division of The Orion Publishing Group and GP Putnam's Sons of the US).
Figures by the author: #1, 3, 6 (upper picture based on Erman 1907, p92; lower picture based on Faulkner 1994, Plate 34B), 21, 27, 35 (based on Hornung 1990, p. 149), 37 (based on Hornung 1990, p. 61), 38, 43, 46, 47 (based on Wilkinson 1994, Fig. 98, p. 144), 54 (based on Wilson 1985, p.113), 55 (based on Wilson 1985, p.134), 58, 71and 74 (based on Hornung 1999A, Fig. 55, p. 104), 75, 96, 98, 118 (based on Hornung 1990, p. 124), 127 (based on Hornung 1990, p. 107), and 129-132.

Explanatory notes:
A. In order to conserve space, captions presented in this list are abbreviated versions of those in this book.
B. Locations of Egyptian texts and figures are at times given in the following format: Nd.r.p1-p2. This format is explained in the section dealing with *Conventions Used* in Chapter 1, *The Enigmatic Book of Revelation*.

Figure 1. Map of ancient Egypt showing place-names mentioned in text. 16

Figure 2. Map of Middle East and surrounding areas; place-names mentioned in text. . . . 17

Part I. Background

Chapter 2. New Approaches

Figure 3. A simplified, modern rendering of the middle register of the 7th Division of the *Amduat*. (This will assist readers unfamiliar with Egyptian literary styles.) 47

Figure 4. Portion of the middle register of the 7th Division of the *Book of Gates*. This figure is to assist readers unfamiliar with ancient Egyptian literary styles. 47

Figure 5. Percentiles of the second register of the 7th Division of the Egyptian *Amduat*; this figure explains convention used to site locations of drawings in Egyptian sources. 55

Part II. The Throne Scene

Figure 6. The scene of the Judgment of the Dead from Chapter 125 of the Egyptian *Book of the Dead* which parallels that in the Book of Revelation. 57

Chapter 3. The Preeminent Deities

Figure 7. Graphic comparison of the throne scene in the *Book of the Dead* with that in the Book of Revelation. 59

Figure 8. Two pictures of the throne of Osiris. The upper one clearly shows a stream or river of flowing water flowing from the throne as in Rev 22:1) 64

Figure 9. Life in the land of the blessed with its many canals showing water coming from three manifestations of the sun-god; a part of Egypt's holy city wherein the blessed live. 65

Figure 10. The ram-headed sun-god *stands* in his protective shrine – or throne – as in Rev. 5:6. (AM4.2.1-3) 67

Figure 11. The Egyptian symbol of the "lamb of Re" showing which is consistent with the lamb mentioned in of Revelation. 67

Figure 12. Representation of the birth of Re in his juvenile, "lamb" or ram-headed form as he rises into the morning sky at dawn. (BC6.1.Final Picture) 68

Figure 13. Unified Osiris and Re which parallels "God on throne" in Rev. 22:1-3. 70

Figure 14. Amen, the Egyptian "King of the Gods," wearing a crown made of a disk and plume. His attributes conform with those of *the Amen* in the Book of Revelation. 72

Figure 15. Horus, the Son of Osiris and of Re in human form with the head of a falcon. His attributes conform with those of Christ, "the anointed one" in Revelation. 75

Figure 16. Horus emerges from dead body of Osiris, a scene consistent with Revelation's Christ being the "first-born of the dead" as in Rev. 1:5. (BA.D.3[rd picture]) 76

Figure 17. King Seti I is anointed with the water of "life," thus assuming the title of "the anointed one" as does the Christ of Revelation. 78

Chapter 4. Other Deities in Revelation

Figure 18. The four sons of Osiris/Horus, each bearing the head of a different creature which parallel the four creatures before the throne in Rev. 4:6-9 and elsewhere. 86

Figure 19. An Egyptian "All-god" covered with eyes as described in Rev. 4:6 and 8. 87

List of Figures

Figure 20. An Egyptian "All-god" with six wings as described in Rev. 4:8. 87

Figure 21. Seven torches surround Osiris just as seven lampstands surround God on the throne in Rev 1:12-13 and Rev. 2:1. (AM2.3.4-6) 89

Figure 22. Twenty-four deities before the throne of the sun-god conform with the twenty-four elders described in Rev. 4:4 and elsewhere. (AM.9.1-3.1-5) 91

Figure 23. Apophis, the ancient serpent of Egyptian myths who is as old as creation parallels Revelation's "ancient serpent," Satan the devil. 96

Figure 24. The Egyptian god Seth which parallels the 1st beast of Rev. 13:18, ... 99

Chapter 5. "The Word of God"

Figure 25. The Egyptian god Thoth which parallels the word of God in Rev. 19:13 102

Chapter 6. The Twelve Tribes of Israel

Figure 26. Example of groups of 12 deities in Egyptian sources have characteristics which parallel those given for the twelve tribes of Israel in Rev. 7:4-8 and elsewhere. 118

Figure 27. The distribution of 25 names in groups of 12 in Egypt's *Amduat* with meanings which conform with those of Revelation's 12 tribes of Israel in Revelation 7:4-8. . 123

Figure 28. Cluster of names in the 7th division of the *Amduat* with meanings similar to those the names of the tribes of Israel. 124

Figure 29. The juvenile, ram-headed (lamb) form of the sun-god in his shrine as he is towed by his followers to emerge reborn to new life with him. (AM12.2.1-6). 131

Figure 30. Twelve followers of the sun-god carry the symbol of truth on their heads, a scene conforming with Rev. 14:5. (BG6.1.6-10) 132

Chapter 7. The Great Multitude

Figure 31. This scene showing a group carrying of palm branches signifying the endowment of long life upon the ruler as described in Rev. 7:9. (AM2.3.1-2) 144

Figure 32. Another scene showing a group carrying of palm branches signifying the endowment of long life upon the ruler as described in Rev. 7:9. (AM9.3.6-10) 144

Figure 33. Twelve deities seated on hieroglyphs for clothing illustrate their importance of pure white robes to the followers of their god, as in Rev. 7:9-13. (AM9.1.1-5) 145

Figure 34. A protective "Enveloper serpent" forms a protective tent (or shrine) over the sun-god and his followers parallels the scene in in Rev. 7:15. (AM11.2.1-8) 147

24 *Egyptian Origin of the Book of Revelation*

Figure 35. Followers of the sun-god rest in peace on their funeral biers. The accompanying text conforms with that of Rev. 14:13. (BG5.3.1-6) 148

Figure 36. A multitude of soldiers armed with javelins are ready to spear enemies enemy of the sun-god as do followers of the Lamb. (BG5.1.1-4) 151

Chapter 8. Egyptian Parallels in the Seven Letters

Figure 37. The lake of fire at the Osirian judgment symbolizes the Egyptian's second death, a parallel to the scene described in Rev. 2:11 and Rev. 20:14. 162

Figure 38. Egyptian scene showing the triumphant dead partaking of the water and food of the tree of life as in Rev. 2:7. 164

Figure 39. The *Pillar-of-His-Mother* Priest who performs his duties in the temple parallels the reference in Rev. 3:12 to the conqueror being a pillar in the temple. 166

Figure 40. Clustering of pictures in the 5th Division of the *Book of Caverns*; their associated text parallels that of the letter to Thyatira in Rev. 2:18-28. 178

Figure 41. *Shetait*, the "Mysterious One," a manifestation of *Nut*, the sun-goddess. (C5.1.1$^{st\ picture}$) 178

Figure 42. The attributes of the goddess called *The Butcher* parallel those of Jezebel in Rev. 2:20-23. (C5.3.1$^{st\ picture}$) 179

Figure 43. The Rod of Power over the enemies of the sun-god and the destruction of the enemies of the sun-god as in Rev. 2:26-27. 182

Figure 44. Those "who mount upon the earth without being weary" and who "rest in Re" correspond to those in Rev. 2:24. (C5.2.2^{picture}) 182

Figure 45. Map showing the distribution of the seven Hyksos fortresses in the Nile Delta whose attributes parallel those of the seven churches of Rev. 2-3. 191

Chapter 9. Opening of the Scroll

Figure 46. The scene in the middle register of the 6th Division of the *Amduat* which corresponds to that of the opening of the scroll described in Rev. 5. 198

Figure 47. The Lion of the Tribe of Judah of Rev. 5:5 as represented in the 6th Division of the *Amduat*. 200

Figure 48. Reproduction of an ancient diagram of the Egyptian *House of Life* in Abydos which has attributes which parallel those in Rev. 5:6. 204

Chapter 10. Call to Arms

Figure 49. Illustration of the rite of driving four calves with the same colors as the four horses of Rev. 6:1-8. 213

Figure 50. Casualties in war against Apophis (Revelation's Satan) and his followers depicted in middle register of the 7th Division of the Amduat and in Rev. 6:2-8). 222

Figure 51. Punishment of prisoners of war before the throne of Osiris in the upper register of the 7th Division of the Amduat as in Rev. 6:4-8. 223

Figure 52. The 8th Division of the Amduat contains scenes consistent with those described in Rev. 6:9-11 224

Figure 53. Souls of the beheaded soldiers who died for their god wear the gift of clothing as in Rev. 6:9-11. (AM8.2.6-10) 225

Figure 54. The vestibule of the 8th Division of the *Amduat* showing the souls of dead soldiers with their gifts of new clothing parallels the scene described in Rev. 6:9-10. 226

Chapter 11. Prelude to War

Figure 55. The *Schutzbild* scene shows four serpents (angels) which spit fire against four enemies representing the winds four winds has many similarities to Rev. 7:1-3. ... 232

Chapter 13. Catastrophes

Figure 56. Illustration showing how the eruption of the volcano on Thera in 1628 BCE would have been visible from Egypt's Nile delta. 276

Figure 57. A diagram demonstrating that the force of a tsunami originating at Thera could have reached Egypt without being blocked by intervening islands. 278

Chapter 15. The Little Scroll

Figure 58. The 5th Division of the *Amduat* which represents the secret cavern of Sokaris contains most of the elements mentioned in Rev. 10. 298

Figure 59. Scene showing the Egyptian equivalent of the "Mighty Angel" holding the scroll in Rev. 10:1-4; many parallels are evident between these two sources. 299

Figure 60. The two mourners at the "mound of darkness." (AM5.1.5-6) 299

Figure 61. Knowledge and wisdom is represented by the head of a baboon on a serpentine deity about to consume a copy of a sacred book as in Rev. 10:8-11. 307

Chapter 16. The Two Witnesses

Figure 62. The temple of Osiris with enemies outside (BA.D.1.1$^{st\ picture}$) conforms with the description of the temple of God in Rev. 11:1-2. 314

Figure 63. Two guardians stand with arms raised in front of the god Aker (BA.A.1.2$^{nd\ picture}$). Their attributes parallel those of the two witnesses of Rev. 11. 316

Figure 64. Scene at the start of the *Book of Aker* showing two deities morning over the body of Osiris; they parallel the two witnesses in Rev. 11:3. 317

Figure 65. Scene from the *Book of Aker* showing Egyptian parallel to the fire-breathing aspect of the two witnesses in Rev. 11:5 and Rev. 11:7-11. 318

Figure 66. Two fire-spiting uraeus serpents which parallel Revelation's two witnesses acting as "Lampstands," as in Rev. 11:4 (AM2.2.1-4). 319

Figure 67. In BA.D.4.1$^{st\ picture}$, as in Rev. 11:5, enemies are burned by fire which pours from the mouths of two deities. 320

Figure 68. Apophis, who parallels Revelation's ancient serpent from the bottomless pit, kills the two guardians, as in Rev. 11:7. (BA.D.4.3$^{rd\ picture}$) 322

Figure 69. Two bodies lie in coffins as in Rev. 11:9. (BA.A.4. 4$^{th\ picture}$) 323

Figure 70. Two bodies lying in boats (BA.B.4$^{th\ picture}$) parallel the display of the two witnesses whose "bodies lie in the street of the great city" in Rev. 11:8. 324

Figure 71. In BA.A.3.2$^{nd\ picture}$, two deities are lifted into heaven on after a period of three and a half days as described in Rev. 11:11-12. 324

Figure 72. The two guardians of the sun-god are resurrected and stand up as they rise into the heavens (BA.B.5$^{th\ picture}$) as described of the two witnesses in Rev. 11:11-12. 326

Figure 73. Scene showing 7,000 people killed by an earthquake at the end of the *Book of Aker* and which parallels that described in Rev. 11:13. 327

Figure 74. Scene showing the resurrection of multitudes of individuals adjacent to the resurrection scene the two guardians in the *Book of Aker* (BA.B.1$^{st\ picture}$) 330

Figure 75. Illustration depicting the death and renewal of the cosmos as depicted in Part D of the *Book of Aker* and which conform with events described in Rev. 11:13. 331

Figure 76. Pictorial summary of the *Book of Aker* in the lower register of Part A parallels the sequence of scenes described in Rev. 11:3-13. 333

Figure 77. Scenes in the *Book of Aker* which parallel those of Rev. 11:1-13. 335

Chapter 17. The Woman in the Sky

Figure 78. General arrangement of two views of Nut in the *Books of the Heavens* in the tomb of Ramesses VI used as basid for discussion of parallels with Rev. 12.. 348

Figure 79. Events in the final Hours of the *Book of Night* in wich the imminent birth of the sun-god parallels the birth scene in described in Rev. 12:2a. 340

Figure 80. The opening scene of the *Book of Day* parallels which parallels the rising into heaven of the child in Rev. 12:5. 341

Figure 81. The sunset and twilight portion of the *Books of the Heavens* depicting the swallowing of the river of water in Rev. 12:16 and one "standing on the sand" in Rev. 12:17. 342

Figure 82. Views of the Egyptian sky-goddess, Nut, showing here body decorated with a crown, the sun, moon and stars as in Rev. 12:1 343

Figure 83. The sky-goddess, Nut, her body adorned with the sun, moon and stars with a crown of twelve rays on her head. 343

Figure 84. The army of the sun-god stands ready to fight Apophis and his army in the 1st Hour of the *Book of Day* prior to the war in heaven described in Rev. 12:7-8, t. 348

Figure 85. Parallel in the 1st Hour of the *Book of Day* of the defeat of the dragon described in Rev. 12:8-9. 350

Figure 86. The Fields of Yaru, "the city of Re" and the "City of God" in the 1st Hour of the *Book of Day*, a parallel to the Kingdom of God referred to in Rev. 12:10. 351

Figure 87. The 12th Hour of the *Book of Night* showing flood of water onto the sky, a picture with parallels to parts of Rev. 12:13-16. 354

Figure 88. The judgment of the dead by Osiris in the 8th Hour of the *Book of Night*, a scene with parallels to the judgment scene in Rev. 11:12 and 18. 358

Figure 89. The resurrection scene in the third registers of the 2nd to 7th Hours of the *Book of Night* corresponding to that described in Rev. 11:18 and Rev. 20:13. 359

Figure 90. Flow of parallels scenes in the *Books of the Heavens* which parallel the flow of scenes Rev. 11:15 to Rev. 12:16. 362

Chapter 18. The Beasts of Rev. 13

Figure 91. The 4th Division of the *Amduat* replete with parallel scenes from the 13th chapter of the Book of Revelation. 369

Figure 92. Egyptian parallels found in AM4.3.1-7 to the arrival and enthronement of the 1st beast, his demonic activities and blasphemous words described in Rev. 13:1-8. ... 371

Figure 93. Scene in AM4.3.7-10 with array of symbols which parallel the 42 time periods Rev. 13:5 in which the 1st beast exercises authority over the saints for 42 months. 374

Figure 94. Events in AM4.2.5-10) which parallel those in Rev. 13:7-10 describing the 1st beast's authority and the gift of life to the faithful. 378

Figure 95. Egyptian parallel in AM4.2.8-9 symbolizing the separation of the saints from the followers of the 1st Beast in Rev. 13:7-10. 381

Figure 96. Sequence of scenes in AM4.1 which parallel those in Rev. 13:11-16. 383

Figure 97. Scene from in AM4.1.1-2 which parallels that describing the 2nd beast in Rev. 13:11 which "rose out of the earth.". 384

Figure 98. Egyptian parallel in AM4.1.3-5 to the worshiping of the image of the 1st beast in Rev. 13:12. 384

Figure 99. Scene in AM4.1.7-8 which parallels the branding of people in Rev. 13:16. . . 389

Figure 100. Parallel scenes from Rev. 13 in the 4th Division of the *Amduat*. 393

Figure 101. Egypt's parallel to the 2nd beast of Rev. 13; he is called "His Two Faces" and has two heads, "one bearing right and one bearing wrong." 399

Chapter 19. Reaping of the Harvest

Figure 102. Procession of grain boats traveling toward the fields to reap the harvest in AM2.2.3-10. This scene parallels the main theme of Rev. 14. 404

Figure 103. Left side of the lower register of the 2nd Division of the *Amduat* which contains parallels to several events which parallel those described in Rev. 14:14-18. 405

Figure 104. Parallel in the *Amduat* (AM2.3.6-10) to the scene describing reaping of the harvest in Rev. 14:14-18. 406

Figure 105. Parallel scene in the *Amduat* (AM2.1.4-10) to the judgment and punishment of the enemies of God in Rev. 14:7-11. 408

Chapter 20. The Song of Moses

Figure 106. Gods standing by a lake of fire in the *Book of Gates* (BG2.1.6-10) are clothed in garments similar to those surrounding the sea of glass and fire in Rev. 15:2. 416

Chapter 21. Seven Angels with the Wrath of God

Figure 107. Parallel in the second Division of the *Book of Gates* (BG2.2.5-7) to the seven angels with seven plagues in Rev. 15. 426

Figure 108. The entire scene in the middle register of the 2nd Division of the *Book of Gates* sets the scene for parallel events in Rev. 15. 427

Figure 109. The judgment scene in the *Book of Gates* showing Seth (= Revelation's 1st beast) conforms with the judgment scene in Rev. 15:4. (BG5/6) 432

Figure 110. This picture at BG3.1.3-10 conforms with Rev. 16:4-6 and shows four lakes of water and blood which the gods drink. 433

Figure 111. Seven gods at BG8.3 unleash fire from the mouth of a serpent to punish the sun-god's enemies in an act which parallels Rev. 16: 5-7. 436

Chapter 22. Armageddon

Figure 112. As in Rev. 16:12-14, goddesses stand by a serpent (dragon) lying in a dried-up river bed at BG3.2.7-10 and are told to stop the evil which come from it. 445

Figure 113. Nakedness of the enemies of the sun-god is displayed in this scene from BG6.2.4-10 and events associated with it conform with those in Rev. 16:15-16. 451

Chapter 23. The Harlot and the Kings

Figure 114. This scene at BG9.2.8-10 which shows a gaudily dressed woman and contains parallels element to most elements in Rev. 17:3-8. 457

Figure 115. This scene at BG9.1.1-5 depicts the rise and fall of ten kings as described in Rev. 17:9-13. 461

Figure 116. In BG9.2, military forces of the ram-headed sun-god (= Lamb) who stands in his shrine fight against the forces led by the devil as in Rev. 17:14. 464

Chapter 24. The Millennium

Figure 117. Apophis, Egypt's equivalent to Revelation's "ancient serpent" is captured and held in chains as described in Rev. 20:1-3. (BG10.1.3-10) 476

Figure 118. Pictorial representation of the rewards to dead warriors, including resurrection, a 1,000 year reign, and serving as priests as in Rev. 20:2-7. (BG10.2.8-9) 482

Figure 119. Groups of deities representing the faithful followers of the sun-god who are born with him into the morning sky in BG10.3; this scene parallels Rev. 20:4. 484

Figure 120. The resurrected faithful reign the ram-headed sun-god (the Lamb of Rev. 20:4) as he traveling across the day-time sky from one horizon to the other. 487

Figure 121. Pictorial representation of a military scene in the *Book of Gates* which parallels the Battle of Gog and Magog in Rev. 20:7-10. (BG10.2.9-10) 494

Figure 122. Apophis, Egypt's devil and Satan, reappears and is again captured and severely punished as in Rev. 20:7-10. (BG11.2.4-8) 495

Chapter 25. Resurrection and Judgment

Figure 123. One of "The burned ones" of the 6th Hour of the *Book of Night*. The symbolism in this picture describes an enemy being burned in a circular lake of fire. (BN6) ... 502

Figure 124. The judgment scene which parallels that in Rev. 20:11-12 showing the "great white throne" and the "great and small" before it, and the open book (BN8) 504

Figure 125. *Seshat*, the goddess of writing who maintained a record of the deeds of every person, a record which parallels the book of life in Rev. 20:12. 508

Figure 126. The "Weary Ones" and the "Drowned Ones" in the 9th Hour of the *Book of Night* are parallel those in Rev. 20:13 who were "given up by the sea." (BN9-10) 509

Chapter 26. A New Creation

Figure 127. Daily re-enactment of creation portrayed in the 12th and final Division of the *Book of Gates* conform with the new creation in Rev. 21:1-8. 513

Figure 128. Osiris is shown here as the earth from which plants grow when they receive life-giving water of the Nile. In this picture, Osiris plays the role of an earth-god. 516

Figure 129. The young sun-god is encompassed by a serpent with its tail in its mouth, a symbol representing the continuing cycle of the beginning and end of time. 524

Chapter 27. The Holy City

Figure 130. The celestial Yaru Fields beside the primordial river where the blessed dead go in the *Book of Day* resemble the scene described in Rev. 22:1-2. 540

Figure 131. Picture of the Yaru Fields in preceding figure showing its appearance when folded to represent fields on both sides of the river. 540

Chapter 28. Egyptian deities in the Book of Revelation

Figure 132. Collection of pictures of Egyptian deities with attributes similar to characters portrayed in the Book of Revelation. 550

Figure 133. More Egyptian deities portrayed in the Book of Revelation. 551

Chapter 29. Parallel Series of Scenes

Figure 134. In the tomb of Ramesses VI, the arrangement of parallel scenes conforms with the overall structure of the Book of Revelation. 558

LIST OF TABLES

(Captions in this list are abbreviated to conserve space.)

Table 4.1 Attributes of angels referred to in the Book of Revelation. 94

Table 4.2 Symbols from the Hebrew, Arabic and Syriac languages which may be related to the Egyptian parallel with the number 666 – the name of the 1st beast in Rev. 13:17-18. 98

Table 5.1 Comparison of weights of arguments for which of the Egyptian gods, Thoth or Horus, more closely parallels Revelation's "Word of God" described in Rev. 19:11-16. 115

Table 6.1 The names of 14 (42%) of 33 groups of twelve from the *Book of Gates* which conform to the meanings of 8 of the names of the twelve tribes of Israel. 120

Table 6.2 Names of deities in two groups of twelve in the 7th Division of the *Amduat* which have meanings similar to those of the Hebrew names of the tribes of Israel. 125

Table 8.1 Summary of the similarities between the 5th Division of the *Book of Caverns* and Revelation's Letter to Thyatira. 184

Table 9.1 Comparison of the description of *The House of Life* (the sacred library of the Osirian cult) with the scene of the opening of the secret book in Rev. 5. 205

Table 13.1 Attributes of volcanic eruptions described in Chapters 146, 149 and 150 of the *Book of the Dead* (BD) compared with passages from the Book of Revelation. 263

Table 13.2 Events which may be associated with a volcanic eruption in the *Book of the Divine Cow* which parallel events found in the Book of Revelation. 268

Table 13.3 Compilation of events from the *Admonitions of an Egyptian Sage* which may be related to a volcanic eruption. 272

Table 13.4 Comparison of the opening scenes of the *Book of the Divine Cow*, Plato's *Timaeus* and the Book of Revelation. 280

Table 14.1 Approximate earliest attestations of Egyptian writings which contain accounts of catastrophic events consistent with those of a volcanic eruption. 285

Table 15.1. Comparison of Rev 10:1-3 to text in the 5th Division of the *Amduat*. 298

Table 15.2. Comparison of Rev. 10:5-6,10 to text in the *Book of the Divine Cow*. 304

Table 17.1 Comparison of the sequence of the main themes in Revelation 12 with those of the Seth-Isis-Horus and the Python-Leto-Apollo myths. 337

Table 17.2 Comparison of the names of goddesses common to both the *Book of Night* and the portals in Chapter 146 of the *Book of the Dead* in relation to cosimic renewal. 365

Table 17.3 Comparisons among Rev. 12, the Egyptian *Books of the Heavens* and the main themes of the Python-Leto-Apollo myth; this shows closest affinity to Egyptian myths . 366

Table 18.1 Egyptian parallels to the Devil, Satan, the dragon, the two beasts, the false prophet, and the image of the beast in the Book of Revelation. 402

Table 20.1 Elements the *Book of Gates* which parallel those found in the Song of Moses (Rev. 15:3-4). 419

Table 24.1 Characteristics of and rewards to the dead who rejoice on the arrival of the sun-god in their parts of the Netherworld. 491

Table 25.1 Those before the judgment throne of Osiris in the *Book of Night* who parallel with "the dead, *great* and *small*" referred to in Rev. 20:12. 506

Table 28.1 Names of characters or deities in the Book of Revelation and their Egyptian parallels. 552

Table 28.2 Names of groups of beings in the Book of Revelation and their Egyptian parallels. References to Revelation and Egyptian sources are representative examples. 553

Table 28.3 Comparison the current findings and those identified by Egyptianby Massey (1907) showing that none are in complete agreement. 554

Table 29.1 Comparison of the order of the landmark scenes in the *Amduat* and the *Book of Gates* Series their counterparts in the Book of Revelation. 556

Table 30.1 Number of occurrences and proportionate usage of numerals and ordinals 2, 3, 4, and 7 in the Book of Revelation. 565

PREFACE

In spite of difficulties understanding parts of the Book of Revelation, modern Christians generally agree that most of the book conforms quite well with traditional Christian beliefs. Some of its passages are remarkably beautiful and moving and resonate strongly with the teachings of Christ recorded in other books of the New Testament. Such powerful elements have contributed a great deal to the idea that the Book of Revelation, as a whole, is a genuine Christian document and that the true meaning of its enigmatic passages and prophesies will some-day be unambiguously revealed. This commonly held Christian position has played a strong role in the steadfast belief that the book represents a legitimate part of the Christian canon.

During the twentieth century, several highly respected scholars examined the possibility that parts of the Book of Revelation were somehow linked to elements in other ancient religions and concluded that parts of the book may be of non-Christian origin. Nevertheless, most Christian theologians maintain that the similarities are neither common nor significant enough to warrant serious consideration. In support of a Judæo-Christian background they cite the many obvious allusions to Old Testament sources and apparent allusions to the beliefs and tribulations of the early Christian church; Most Christian scholars maintain that the book should be considered of Christian origin.

These conclusions are, however, based on the assumption that all available knowledge of non-Christian religions has been compared with the many and varied passages in the Book of Revelation. The truth is, however, that researchers have not yet critically compared the book with the religious beliefs of the ancient Egyptians, even though the doors to knowledge of this religion opened in about 1830 when Egyptologists first learned to decipher ancient Egypt's hieroglyphic texts. Remarkably, however, nearly two hundred years have passed without a single detailed critical comparison between the religious writings of these ancient texts and the Book of Revelation. Clearly, the time has come to conduct at least a preliminary comparison of the two.

This book presents the results of research on a wide range of possible parallels between ancient Egyptian religious texts and the Book of Revelation. Special efforts are made to avoid controversial areas of Egyptology by confining the study to works by highly respected Egyptologists, including their translations of original sources. Translations include mainstream works such as the *Egyptian Book of the Dead*, the *Amduat*, the *Book of Gates*, the *Book of Caverns*, the *Book of Aker* and the *Books of the Heavens*. Occasionally, less well-known books and minor texts are examined when necessary to seek parallels not found in better-known sources. In addition, and especially when interpreting difficult Egyptian texts, different translations of the same texts are consulted to explore translational differences or ambiguities. Reference books of a general nature were also used. These include books on the interpretation of Egyptian art and symbols as well as standard references to well-known Egyptian gods such as Re, Osiris, Horus and Seth. Extensive citations are presented to facilitate later critical, in-depth assessments of this work by Egyptologists and enquiring students. Furthermore, the book is organized to facilitate a gradual understanding of the religious beliefs of the ancient Egyptians by novices to the subject. It begins with an introduction to Egypt's main deities and goes from there to the religious beliefs of the ancient Egyptians. And it ends with detailed comparisons between their many gods, beliefs and religious texts with the characters, events and series of events which make up the Book of Revelation. References to popular, easily understood literature on the religion of the Egyptians are frequently provided to assist non-Egyptologists to understand some of the more difficult arguments.

Parallels to historical events in ancient Egypt were also included in this study. This, of course, is in keeping with the approach of biblical scholars in which specific passages of Revelation are interpreted in the light the past (for example, tribulations of the early Christian church) and the future (the apocalypse, Armageddon) as well as the present (wars, natural catastrophes, rise of specific personalities). It is clear from the vast number of different interpretations suggested for many passages that most of them are wrong; new interpretations of some seem to spring up annually. In contrast, in this research, whenever attempts are made to relate a given event in Revelation to some earthly event, only historical events associated with ancient Egypt are considered and these are selected from occurrences before the birth of Christ. It is possible – and even very likely – that some of the suggested parallels are weak and that such passages refer to some other historical event in Egypt. This, of course, contrasts with the traditional approach by many Christian scholars who consider all time – past, present and future – and the whole world to be a valid working base. The reader should therefore bear in mind that each suggested parallel is based on a specific time in a specific geographic area. Furthermore, what is important to realize here is that parallels to practically all significant events described in the Book of Revelation will be described and we need go no further in either time or location than ancient Egypt to seek valid historical parallels. Also, the reader should realize that alternative and more appropriate parallels for specific passages proposed by future investigators will in no way weaken the main conclusion of this work. Indeed, such findings will very likely further strengthen rather than weaken it.

To facilitate reasonable understanding of what may be to many readers a whole new field, this book is organized in very much the same way as the Book of Revelation. I first identify the main elements in Revelation's opening scene and establish their Egyptian parallels. Egyptian gods which parallel characters surrounding the throne, and others which play roles later in Revelation, are then compared with similar characters in Egyptian texts. From there I conduct a comparative analysis of the contents and form of the seven letters in Revelation with similar Egyptian beliefs and texts. With the opening of a special scroll in Revelation, a long series of events begins, events which are compared with similar events and series of events in Egyptian texts. Included here is the series of catastrophic, apocalyptic events leading up to the "end of the world." Identifications of additional parallels to other characters in Revelation are indicated and parallels between the main events in the two sources are compared. Finally, the observed parallels with Egyptian deities, events, scenes and series of scenes are summarized.

Many of the more obvious parallels with Egyptian texts were found during the early stages of this research. At the time, I considered a rather general, non-technical publication. As the research continued, however, it became increasingly clear that numerous additional and less obvious parallels were also present, including series of parallels within both short and long sequences of scenes. It also became apparent that there were certain words in the Book of Revelation which seemed to be based on homonyms of Egyptian words. This suggested that Egyptian puns should be included in the search for parallels, an added complexity which demanded more detailed analyses of the texts – and which resulted in the discovery of some rather surprising parallels which might otherwise have remained hidden.

In spite of my attempts to educate readers about both Egyptian and Christian literature, and in view of the inherent complexities of the task, I found it necessary to choose the more formal, academic approach as the best format for presenting the results of my research. Also, since not all of the many parallels found were of equal value (some were so obvious that there was no doubt about their similarities while others were less obvious and still others mediocre or even weak), I was faced with either including only the strongest and omitting the weaker parallels, or including all the observed parallels. The former approach would have the advantage of overall simplicity and readily perceived credibility; this would likely be more impressive and lead to less criticism. Its main disadvantage, however, would be that some readers familiar with the Book of Revelation, and especially those who have traditionally interpreted its passages within well-established Christian contexts, might assume there are no parallels for untreated parts of the book, i.e., that Egyptian parallels can be found only in parts of the book while the remainder of the book is free of parallels. The approach would thus be misleading and lead to a situation only marginally better than the status quo; it would merely serve to unnecessarily agitate Christian believers. On the other hand, presentation of the full range of parallels will provide readers with both a broad knowledge of the Book of Revelation to those who have little or no familiarity with the subject and an equally broad knowledge of ancient Egyptian beliefs and texts to those who know little of Egyptology. Perhaps more importantly, the latter approach facilitates critical analyses by scholars to determine which of the arguments are reasonable and which should be discarded as untenable. The more comprehensive scientific approach was therefore taken to present the results of this research.

One unexpected outcome of this work was the possibility that parts of the Book of Revelation may be useful in the interpretation of certain Egyptian texts. As the reader will see during the course of this study, many Egyptian texts are difficult to understand, primarily because of a lack of knowledge of the context in which they were written. Remarkably, the relatively simple language used to describe such events in the Book of Revelation can be used as a basis for straight-forward interpretations of some otherwise enigmatic Egyptian texts. This, of course, is because parallels work in two directions: just as enigmatic texts in the Book of Revelation were found to have perfectly logical meanings when viewed from an ancient Egyptian perspective, many difficult Egyptian texts took on straightforward meanings when examined from the point of view of parallel passages in Revelation. These types of parallels provided the basis for entirely new interpretations which at times shed light on possibly novel meanings of difficult (and sometimes simple) texts in both sources.

Most Egyptologists should have little trouble following the arguments presented here because they will already have a basic familiarity with the source material used from ancient Egypt. However, non-Egyptologists, including most Bible scholars and other interested readers might be confused by the many references to different Egyptian gods, groups of gods and strange religious beliefs in ancient Egypt. This, of course, would influence the non-initiated person's ability to fully comprehend certain arguments. For this reason, special attention is frequently given to supplying a fair amount of background information on some subject areas; while the amount may sometimes seem tedious to some, it will give others the background necessary to follow arguments leading to conclusions based on comparisons of specific passages from the two main sources.

While being a source of diversion and pleasure, this research – from its meager beginning when the first glimmers of parallels shone through the confusing mixture of images from the Book of Revelation and the Egyptian *Book of the Dead* – has been a lonely pursuit due to an almost complete lack of intellectual discussions and challenges with like-minded people in my home province, especially Egyptologists interested in the religion of the ancient Egyptians. My list of acknowledgments to those who have been helpful in this research is therefore woefully limited. My most important support for this work came from my wife Jane who, in spite of her strong Christian faith and belief in the Christian nature and origin of the Book of Revelation and her grave doubts about my findings and her frequent challenges to them, understood the need for in-depth research in all branches of knowledge. I am indebted to Professor Dr. David J. Hawkin of the Religious Studies Department of Memorial University of Newfoundland who read an early draft of this book and offered encouragement and valuable advice which I believe greatly improved the content, presentation and format of the final draft. I am also indebted to Professor Dr. Eric Hornung of the University of Basel, Switzerland, who gave generously of his time in 1997 to help me resolve several perplexing difficulties I was having with my interpretations of several ancient Egyptian concepts, texts and pictures relevant to this research. I am also pleased to acknowledge Rev. Dr. (Cand.) Andreas Marti of Zurich, Switzerland, Mr. Robert Youden of Chester, Nova Scotia, Canada, and my son Mark, all of whom faithfully encouraged me to complete and publish this work.

John H.C. Pippy
2011

PART I. BACKGROUND

The Book of Revelation is the last book in the Christian Bible and as such is the last book of the its New Testament. Readers with a general knowledge of the book already know of the multitude of different interpretations placed on its many enigmatic passages by Christian scholars, church leaders and lay people. In practically all cases, however, interpretations are based on the assumption that the book is of Christian origin and that it has a legitimate place in the Christian canon. This section provides a rationale for a re-interpretation of the book based, not on Christian beliefs, but on a sampling of our current knowledge of the religious beliefs and traditions of ancient Egyptians.

The first of its two chapters is entitled *The Enigmatic Book of Revelation* and is presented primarily for the benefit of those who have little or no knowledge of the Book of Revelation and its background. It gives a brief overview of some of the more obvious difficulties inherent in past and current interpretations of the book and outlines the initial doubts by the early Christian churches about its Christian nature before it was finally accepted by all the main groups of churches of the day.

Chapter 2, *New Approaches,* describes approaches taken to compare the book with ancient Egyptian religious texts. Oriented to non-Egyptologists, it describes a variety of special features of the ancient Egyptian language and writings which must be considered in a study such as this; the reader should realize it is important for non-Egyptologists to pay special attention to this chapter as it explains many complexities presented to ensure a better understanding of many parts of this book. Meanwhile, Egyptologists will benefit from this chapter because it describes several approaches not normally taken in past studies of ancient Egyptian texts.

The reader may also wish to take note of Figure 1 and Figure 2 which give the location of place-names mentioned in the text. Also, the *Chronology of Ancient Egyptian Dynasties and Kings* starting on page 18 will be useful to help orient the reader to many of the dates and periods of ancient Egypt's long history. Non-Egyptologists will also find the guide to the *Pronunciation of Egyptian Words* on page 20 helpful in understanding the background to some of the discussions on word play encountered in the ancient texts. Finally, a *Glossary* of commonly sited Egyptian gods and goddesses as well as certain specialized terms is presented in *Appendix 6*.

Chapter 1. The Enigmatic Book of Revelation[1]

"There are few primitive Christian writings which as a whole and in detail have received so much attention [as the Book of Revelation] and yet seem to remain untouched in regard to the secret to their meaning and history."
— Lohmeyer (1934)[2]

Christian Perspectives

The Book of Revelation has remained for centuries the most controversial document in the annals of Christian Literature. Fifty-one years after Lohmeyer published the above quotation, Fiorenza (1985) states that "Despite all scholarly efforts, no generally recognized or accepted consensus has been reached in regard to the composition and the theological interpretation of the book." She adds that the results of Lohmeyer's studies on Revelation remain true today.[3] And with respect to the book's references to future events she says that, "While serious scholarly works are rare, popular and fundamentalist writings abound. No wonder that Rev. is still considered to be the most difficult book in the NT [New Testament]. Scholars seem to have arrived at a consensus that the book does not provide us with any details of church – or world-history nor give us a calendar of future events, while popular interest still focuses on such information."[4] This discrepancy between the opinions of serious scholars and what some might call fundamentalists is not generally appreciated among many modern Christians, perhaps because of the complexity of the underlying interpretational problems which are seldom brought to the attention of the laity by local clergy and church leaders.

Indeed, modern-day difficulties with interpretation of the Book of Revelation are not new and echo those of the early years of Christianity. The first five hundred years of Christianity were accentuated by debates on whether or not the Book of Revelation was even a genuinely Christian document. Summaries of the often turbulent background leading to its general acceptance by the early churches are provided in the Oxford Companion to the Bible and Unger's Bible Handbook where we learn that among the earliest scholars who accepted or made reference to the book in their writings was the much quoted Irenaeus of Gaul (c. 140-203 CE), while those who rejected it included Ignatius, Bishop of Antioch (c. 116) and Polycarp, Bishop of Smyrna (c. 69-155). Through the next 250 years or so, the number of scholars who accepted the Book of Revelation gradually increased and included Athanasius of Alexandria (298-373) who first applied the term "canonical" to those books accepted as being the inspired word of God and therefore recognized as a valid part of the New Testament. After much debate, most churches of western Europe approved the Book of Revelation as authentic by 419 CE[5]. It was rejected, however, in the Canon of Constantinople and the Syriac Peshitta Canon (411-435) by the Syrian National Church which represented eastern churches, and it was not until about 508 CE, when the Syriac Peshitta was revised that the Book of Revelation was finally accepted by both the western and eastern Christian churches, thus bringing the debate to an uneasy conclusion.

In spite of this early acceptance into the canon, however, critical debate has continued. Among the most notable adversaries of the Book of Revelation were the leaders of the Reformation in the sixteenth century, namely Martin Luther, Ulrich Zwingli, and Desiderius Erasmus. These theologians followed Jerome (c. 340-420 CE) who believed the book should not be held as canonical in the early Christian church because it was not of apostolic origin and "lacked the heart and spirit of John the Divine." Fiorenza points out that even today, contemporary "scholarly discourse on Rev. still seems ... to reflect Luther's judgment that the book is not quite Christian."[6] She notes that "Critics of Rev. have pointed out that the book preaches vengeance and revenge but not the love of the Sermon on the Mount. It is therefore sub-Christian, the Judas of the NT."[7]

Disagreements on authorship of the Book of Revelation were an important part of the early debates and continue to be in modern times. Irenaeus (c 180 CE), for example, assumed that the author was John the Divine who wrote the Gospel and the letters of John. Some, like Dionysius of Alexandria (c.200-265 CE), questioned this identification because of differences in thought, style and language and suggested that there may have been two writers named "John" in Ephesus – as hinted by Papias (c. 80 - c. 155 CE). Still others felt the Book of Revelation was pseudonymous, that it was written by some anonymous writer with John's name appended to provide it with authority, a practice common with apocalyptic literature. Many of today's scholars attribute it to Johannine theologians[8] while some bible commentaries continue to assert it was written by John the apostle.[9] Collins (1984), who provides a modern in-depth overview and analysis of this problem,[10] however, maintains that "Sound judgment leads to the conclusion that it was written by a man named John who is otherwise unknown to us."[11]

The first ever record of the Book of Revelation was by Papias in the early part of the second century.[12] Since then, in each attempt to identify authorship, the basic assumption has been that the book was actually written during the first century, if not by one of the twelve apostles, then by someone who knew one or more of them. Given this general agreement on the range of possible writers of the Book of Revelation, efforts to refine the date of writing within this time frame seemed straightforward and these refinements were based on interpretations of internal evidence related to historical events. Irenaeus based his estimate of the date on the assumption that Emperor Nero was the false prophet of Rev. 16:13, Rev. 19:20 and Rev. 20:10 and concluded a date toward the end of the reign of Domitian (81-96 CE).[13] Practically all modern scholars assume that the Babylon mentioned in Chapters 14, 16 and 18 of Revelation is the beast with seven heads and seven horns of Rev. 17:7 and that it represents the ancient Roman empire; they assume that Rev. 17:6, Rev. 18:24 and

Rev. 19:2 describe the intense hatred by the early Christians of ancient Rome during the years 68-70 CE. On this basis, they demand a date close to the destruction of Rome by fire in 64 CE.

No one has seriously considered the possibility that the book may in fact have been written many years – perhaps even centuries – before the birth of Christ although some authors have pondered evidence that point to the more ancient time. For example, according to Fiorenza (1985), Hill "insisted that John is very much like the prophets of the OT."[14] She says that "the 'Jewish' character of the book leads to its classification with OT prophecy or Jewish apocalypticism"[15] and further quotes Hill as stating that "the words of John, and indeed his experience ... are so remarkably unlike those of other New Testament speakers or writers and so strikingly like those of Old Testament prophets that one may be justified in regarding him as unique: at the very least it is unwise to regard him as typical of New Testament prophets."[16] If comments such as these are seriously considered, one is tempted to place the writing of the Book of Revelation in Old Testament times. An important difficulty with such a dating is that we have no record of the book's existence prior to the birth of Christ. In the absence of such evidence biblical scholars rightfully avoided such a conclusion. Nevertheless, doubts continue.

Egyptian Perspectives

Wallis Budge was an Egyptologist who published in the late 19th and early 20th centuries and his work contains brief, almost incidental references to parallels between Egyptian texts and passages in the Book of Revelation. His 1904 book on *The Gods of the Egyptians* was among the first to draw attention to similarities between the Book of Revelation and the religious beliefs of ancient Egyptians. He felt the image of the seven-headed dragon in Rev. 12:3 and the beast in Rev. 13:1 had their origins in the seven-headed serpent mentioned in the *Pyramid Texts*.[17] He also pointed out that the horses in Rev. 9:17-19 which "had tails ... like serpents, with heads, and by means of them they wound" were similar to "a monster which inhabited one of the Pylons of the Ṭuat, had the body of a crocodile and a tail formed of a writhing serpent's body with a serpent's head for the tip of it."[18]

But it was the self-made scholar and mystic Gerald Massey who first seriously compared larger parts of the Book of Revelation with ancient Egyptian beliefs. This work formed the eleventh division or "book" of a larger study entitled, *Ancient Egypt: The Light of the World*[a] which was published in 1907. He called it, *Egyptian wisdom in the Revelation of John the Divine* and in it he refers to several Egyptian deities which he suggests are parallels to well-known Christian characters referred to in Revelation: Christ/Jesus, the Lamb and the dragon (Devil, Satan). He also suggests Egyptian parallels to Revelation's woman in the sky (in Rev. 12), the bride of the Lamb (in Rev. 21), the four creatures before the throne (Rev. 4), judgment day (Rev. 20) and others. He provides us with little or no detail on his rationale for his parallels,

---

[a] Only five hundred copies of Massey's two-volume book were originally published. It is now in the public domain and can be downloaded on line from *www.theosophical.ca*. It is also available in printed form from *Kessinger Publishing* (2002) and *Axum Publications* (2006).

however, so that it is impossible to critically evaluate his conclusions in the light of modern Egyptological publications – and in the light of the results of this work. Suffice it to say here that not all his parallels agree with those presented here, and those which do, agree for different reasons. As will be discussed later in this chapter, these differences likely result from the much larger knowledge base of Egyptian records available to this study as well as the fundamentally different approach used. In Massey's search for parallels, he used numerous beliefs and traditions in the Christian church to guide him and did not dwell in depth with the most relevant segments of the Book of Revelation.

There have been no attempts by modern researchers to follow through with Massey's ideas. Nevertheless, at least one modern Christian theologian conducted a study involving comparisons of a number of ancient myths with scenes described in the Book of Revelation. Collins (1976) reviewed the literature relating the combat myth in the Book of Revelation to a wide variety of myths and beliefs found in the religions of the Near East.[a] She noted that the Egyptian god Seth, who was red in color, could be equated with the Greek Typhon who was thought to be a dragon – as in Revelation 12. While she made observations on several parallels between Egyptian myths and images and scenes found in the Book of Revelation, she emphasized those found in Chapter 12 of Revelation. She points out that "The particular form of the combat myth which most closely resembles Revelation 12 is that exemplified by the myth of Seth-Typhon's attack on Isis and Horus and of Typhon's pursuit of Leto" and concludes that some images in Revelation have parallels in Egyptian and other mythologies. Her study of ancient Egyptian mythology, however, was limited in that it was based primarily on ancient Greek documents. This, and the wide range of myths from different ancient civilizations, severely limited her research on ancient Egyptian documents so that her conclusions with respect to Revelation were at best preliminary.

Such a paucity of studies is remarkable, especially in light of the large volume of published studies in both areas. It is as if Christian scholars and Egyptologists alike (with the notable exception of Dr. Collins, as above) have closed their minds to the possibility that the two fields might have a lot in common. Apparently, Egyptologists seldom read studies comparing ancient Egyptian beliefs with those of the early Christians while modern Christian theologians seldom bother to critically read Egyptological literature. This study, on the other hand, uses practically the entire text of the Book of Revelation as a basis for comparison with ancient Egyptian beliefs. Traditional, Christian interpretations of the Book of Revelation are seldom used. Also, only modern, mainstream Egyptological studies and translations of original Egyptian documents by well-known Egyptologists are used as a basis for Egyptological aspects of the study.

---

[a] In *The Combat Myth in the Book of Revelation* Collins (1976) compared images of certain scenes in the Book of Revelation with those from Ugaritic, Accadian, Greek, and Egyptian parallels and included myths concerning the Battle in Heaven in Accadian, Greek, Egyptian, Hittite, Ugaritic and Israelite-Jewish mythology.

Chapter 2. New Approaches[19]

This study begins with a detailed comparison of the many characters found in Revelation – its deities, angels, beasts and an array of the well known Egyptian gods. For example, the physical characteristics and functions of the central figure of God on the throne, the Lamb, Christ, and the four living creatures which surround the throne are discussed in relation to characters with similar characteristics in similar settings in Egyptian sources. The attributes and beliefs of both the faithful and rebellious followers of God described in Revelation's letters to the seven churches as well as the literary structure of the letters are compared with those attributed to certain followers of Osiris and those who rebelled against him. The attributes of other characters in the Book of Revelation, characters such as Satan, the Devil, the harlot, the 1st and 2nd beasts, the image of the beast, the false prophet and the Word of God are also compared with figures in the Egyptian pantheon. Finally, the characteristics of groups of characters such as the twelve tribes of Israel, the great multitudes of the blessed dead and the throngs of angels which surround the throne of God are all compared with similar groups of Egyptian deities.

Not only the characters, but also the scenes in which they appear are compared. For example, Revelation's judgment scene is compared with that of the judgment of the dead by Osiris as described in the *Eyptian Book of the Dead*. Also, attention is given to comparing major blocks of text in Revelation with similar texts in important Egyptian works such as the *Book of Gates*, the *Amduat*, the *Book of Aker* and the *Books of the Heavens* as well as parts of the *Book of the Dead*. In this way *sequences* of events in the Book of Revelation and the role of characters in them are compared with similar sequences of events and characters in Egyptian literature. Comparisons of short passages in Revelation with similarly short passages in the Egyptian literature are frequently accented.

Analyses of the possible use of Egyptian words and phrases in the text of the Book of Revelation are also included. These are based on the well-known Egyptian practice of word play (*paronomasia*) whereby Egyptian priests selected phonetically similar words and phases to enhance the magical qualities of their most important texts. These analyses are based only on those words defined in published English-Egyptian hieroglyphic dictionaries – dictionaries which are, in reality, barely adequate for this type of study. This aspect of the study must therefore be considered, at best, preliminary.

The destruction of Babylon in the Book of Revelation is also examined. These are compared with similar events and elements described in the Egyptian literature, including parts of the *Book of the Dead*, the *Admonitions of an Egyptian Sage*, and the *Prophesy of Neferrohu*. They are compared with scientific and historical

2. New Approaches   43

information available on volcanic eruptions in the eastern Mediterranean Sea, including their potential impacts on the Delta region of the Nile River. These analyses provide the basis for novel interpretations of many scenes and symbols found in the Book of Revelation, especially those which include references to apocalyptic events.

The enormous mass of material published on the religious beliefs of the ancient Egyptians has made it necessary to restrict arguments to the most widely accepted interpretations and expert opinions on Egyptian texts and beliefs. Only the works of some of the most highly respected Egyptologists in the field were used and publications on widely disputed topics were avoided. For example, it would be an impossibly long task to conduct an in-depth review of all the Egyptological literature on the physical characteristics of Osiris before comparing his characteristics with "God on the Throne" in the Book of Revelation. Similarly, parallels with specific elements, images, and story lines in Revelation are compared with the help of summaries by established authorities. Also, publications providing general overviews and summaries were used wherever possible to facilitate the understanding of this work by non-Egyptologists such as Christian theologians. For example, handbooks such as *An Illustrated Dictionary of the Gods and Symbols of Ancient Egypt* by Lurker (1980), *Reading Egyptian Art, A Hieroglyphic Guide to Ancient Egyptian Painting and Sculpture* by Wilkinson (1992) and *Symbol and Magic in Egyptian Art* by Wilkinson (1994) served as exceptionally useful guides to understanding and interpreting Egyptian texts and pictures in the context of the Book of Revelation. The wide availability and summary nature of these books will enable readers without an extensive background in Egyptology to quickly familiarize themselves with relevant subject matters using a minimum number of reference books.

As much as possible, English translations of Egyptian hieroglyphic texts by authorities in the field were used to as the basis of comparisons with English translations of Greek versions of the Book of Revelation. Egyptian texts were compared with the Revised Standard Version of the Book of Revelation, a version considered by many bible scholars to be among the best available. This version is available online at *http://quod.lib.umich.edu/r/rsv/browse.html* and a search engine is available for the RSV *at http://quod.lib.umich.edu/r/rsv/*. References are made to other English translations and at times transliterations of original Greek texts to help resolve specific interpretational difficulties.

The approach taken here is very different from that taken by Massey who examined the Book of Revelation in the light of general Judaeo-Christian traditions. Massey used a "broad brush" approach to identify Egyptian beliefs and deities among early traditional Christian beliefs, including those about characters such as Jesus Christ, the Lamb, the bride of Christ and a few others. From there, in his *Book XI: Egyptian Wisdom in the Revelation of John the Divine,* he compared only those beliefs and characters identified in ancient Egyptian records available at the end of the 19th century. He then applied the results of these studies to work on the Book of Revelation. This approach biased his study in favor of Judaeo-Christian traditions outside the purview of the Book of Revelation and contributed to an almost complete neglect of many important attributes of characters described in Revelation as well as details of particular scenes and series of scenes in which they appear. Much information available only in the Book of Revelation was therefore not considered so that his identifications fall far short of being acceptable by today's academic standards. In contrast, the current approach is based almost entirely on comparisons between the Book of Revelation and highly respected English translations of original Egyptian sources with relatively little emphasis placed on other ancient sources such as the Old Testament, other books of the New Testament and Christian traditions.

Unfortunately, because of a scarcity in his work of references to the literature he studied, it is almost impossible to critically analyze the logic of most of the parallels identified by Massey. This, and his use of now obscure names for ancient Egyptian deities and places, make it extremely difficult to follow some of his arguments and compare his results with those presented in this work; the best that can be done here is to provide simple comparisons of his results with those presented here. These are presented near the end of this book in Chapter 28, *Egyptian Deities in the Book of Revelation* (see Table 28.3).

The following is a list of works commonly consulted during the course of this study:

Book of Revelation
Revised Standard Version (RSV) and other versions consulted as required.
PC Study Bible, Version 1.7, 1994, by Biblesoft, Seattle, WA.
Reference sections used in *PC Study Bible* as follows:
Interlinear Bible
Browns-Driver-Briggs Definitions
Strong's Greek/Hebrew Dictionary
Thayer's Definitions
Vines Expository Dictionary
Interlinear translation of the Greek-English New Testament
by A. Marshall (1984).

English Translations of Egyptian Texts
Amduat: Piankoff (1954), *The Tomb of Ramesses VI.*
Book of Gates: Piankoff (1954), *The Tomb of Ramesses VI.*
Book of Aker: Piankoff (1954), *The Tomb of Ramesses VI.*
Book of the Dead: Faulkner (1994), *The Egyptian Book of the Dead, the Book of Going Forth by Day.*
Book of the Divine Cow: Piankoff (1954), *The Tomb of Ramesses VI*; (1955), *The Shrine of Tutankamon.*
Books of Night and Day: Piankoff (1954), *The Tomb of Ramesses VI.*
Coffin Texts: Faulkner (1973), *The Ancient Egyptian Coffin Texts.*
Pyramid Texts: Faulkner (1969), *The Ancient Egyptian Pyramid Texts.*
Miscellaneous shorter works in: Erman (1966), *The Ancient Egyptians, A Sourcebook of their Writings*
Writings of Thutmosis III: Breasted (1962), *Records of Ancient Egypt.*

Dictionaries and Grammar
Strong's Greek Dictionary, PC Study Bible
A Concise Dictionary of Middle Egyptian, Faulkner (1962).

Egyptian Grammar, Gardiner (1927).
An Egyptian Hieroglyphic Dictionary, Budge (1920).
The Ancient Egyptian Pyramid Texts, appended dictionary, Faulkner (1969).
The Ancient Egyptian Coffin Texts, appended dictionary, Faulkner (1973).

Both the chronology of the kings of ancient Egypt (see pages 18 and 19) and Egyptian place names and their locations referred to in this study, as presented in Figure 1, are based on Baines and Malek's (1980) *Atlas of Ancient Egypt*. Other place names mentioned in the text are shown in Figure 2.

Studies on Style

There are a number of reference books on the vocabulary and grammar of ancient Egyptian. Unfortunately, and in spite of the excellent quality of the above sited references, none are especially suited to a study such as this. The best sources assume the text to be studied is written in Egyptian hieroglyphics and are organized accordingly. For example, Faulkner's (1962) *Concise Dictionary of Middle Egyptian* does not have an English-to-Egyptian index which would assist in comparing English texts (such as the Book of Revelation) with possible Egyptian counterparts, a common task required throughout much of this work. Nor would it be wise to assume that all of the Book of Revelation could have been based on Middle Egyptian (used from about 2040 BCE) for there seem to be allusions in Revelation to Egyptian texts dated to the Old Kingdom (2575-2134). During the course of this study, no particular age is assumed for the possible sources of Revelation's many potential allusions to Egyptian texts although Middle Egyptian texts abound.

Comparison of the Book of Revelation with Egyptian sources also entails other difficulties, not the least of which is the rather unusual manner in which many Egyptian texts are dependent on accompanying illustrations. Comprehension is further frustrated by the ancient belief that Egyptian was a divine language; consequently, the use of puns (word play) became an essential component. For example, since the Egyptian word for "soul" has the same sound as that for "sheep," these were inextricably linked in the minds of the speaker and writer – and the ancient readers. Sometimes texts contain words which could be used as puns but where no pun was intended. For the reader to interpret texts with hidden puns, prior knowledge would be required of their intended meaning and function. Thus, in some Egyptian texts, especially religious ones, puns could be used as simple mnemonics to remind a priestly reader of the true meaning of a passage. Meanwhile, as in many ancient religious writings, metaphors are at times difficult to first detect and then properly interpreted because of a lack of relevant background knowledge.

The complex interplay of all of these factors in Egyptian religious compositions necessitates the reader have at least a basic understanding of when and how they were used in the ancient tongue. Only then can one get a reasonable understanding of the original meaning of a passage. Furthermore, in a study such as this we must at times examine the Greek versions as well as English translations of the Book of Revelation, bearing in mind the potential for additional parallels between specific Greek passages and ancient Egyptian texts, relationships which are practically impossible to detect from English translations. With this in mind, the various components mentioned above are expanded below to provide sufficient background to enable readers to appreciate approaches taken in this work.

Subordination of Text to Image

Many Egyptian religious writings, especially those written from the Middle Kingdom (2040-1640) forward, contain pictures along with text; this feature has likely contributed more than most to the failure of earlier research to recognize the possible parallels between passages in the Book of Revelation and ancient Egyptian sources. For this reason, it is imperative that readers have a basic understanding of how the Egyptian scribes married text to image to maximize the information provided in a document.

Perhaps the best way to understand the concept of combining text and image is to compare the design of modern comic scripts with the Egyptian approach. Simple examples given in Figure 3 and Figure 4 serve to illustrate the difference. Notice that the picture shown here does not tell the whole story but rather establishes a background against which the text is to be interpreted. In modern comic scripts, general comments and explanations of aspects of a scene are frequently placed in horizontal rectangles along the top or bottom of a frame. In addition, words spoken by characters in the scene are shown in speech balloons. It is only when all three of these elements (pictures, narratives and quotes) are viewed together that we get a full understanding of the scene; the picture tells a major part of the story but without the text, it falls far short of the entire message. Additions of explanatory notes and speech balloons greatly expand our understanding of a scene – and *vice versa*.

While the Egyptians used essentially the same technique as that for comic strips, they did not separate texts into rectangular boxes and speech balloons; instead, they placed masses of text around, above or below the various characters (see Figure 4). This ancient technique frequently led to difficulties. When documents were copied, scribes at times misplaced parts of the text, probably because of the constraints of limited space on sheets of papyrus or on tomb or temple walls. While this did not cause much of a problem for knowledgeable Egyptian priests who had been trained to properly read the text, modern Egyptologists at times find it difficult or impossible to associate important segments of text with their appropriate parts of the pictures. For this reason, different translators at times produce slightly different arrangements of segments of the translations and at times do not agree on which of the gods to assign a particular quotation.

Goelet (1994), citing the *Book of the Dead* as an example, explains one of the inevitable results of the Egyptian approach: "In the format of the BD the Egyptians display an attitude that the text was subordinate, a mere subtext. Over the centuries the visual predominance of image above text continued to grow until, during the final stages of the BD's development, the scribes used only as much text as could fit into the ever-diminishing space beneath the vignettes."[20] Furthermore, the text was not always aligned with the pictures so that, unless the reader was familiar with a passage, it could be very difficult to interpret the combined meaning of the text and image. Goelet suggests that such "displacements indicate that the vignettes alone evoked the

2. New Approaches

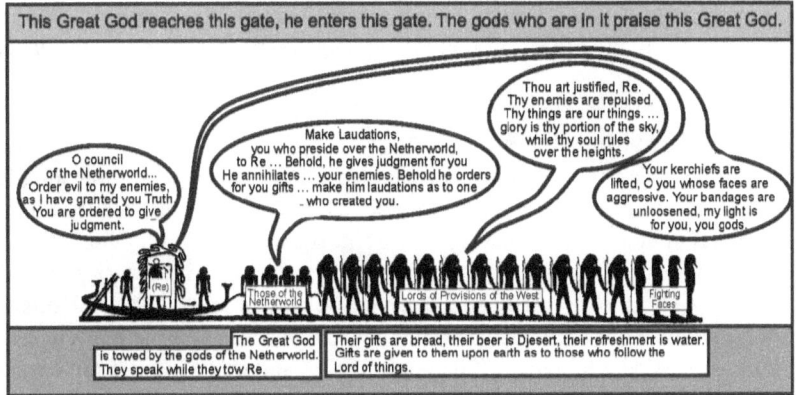

Figure 3. A modern, simplified rendering of the middle register of the 7th Division of the *Amduat*. In the original version (see Figure 4) the text is arranged in rows above the picture and at times it is difficult to follow who is saying what or to what part of the picture certain explanatory texts (boxed text above and below the picture) refer. This presentation of the register's picture and text enhances one's ability to understand the approach taken by the ancient Egyptian scribes. The text shown here is an English translation (by Piankoff, 1954) of extracts from the actual hieroglyphic text. (BG7.2)

Figure 4. Portion of the middle register of the 7th Division of the *Book of Gates*. The vertical columns over the drawing contains hieroglyphic texts give overviews of the main events, detailed verbal instructions from the sun-god and responses from his followers. All these literary aspects of the scene are intermixed to various degrees in the text and are dependant on the picture and the knowledge of the reader for a full understanding. This format is more difficult to follow and interpret than the modern format of comic strips.(BG7-2)

chapter's entire religious and ritual content; the images had an innate potency greater then the power of the text accompanying them." He adds that such approaches "have to do with why the BD is so frequently incomprehensible to us today." The same might be said for many other religious texts such as the *Amduat* and the *Book of Gates*.

Translation Considerations

Like all languages, Egyptian phonics and grammar varied with time and place. This, of course, complicates the study of possible Egyptian puns, especially when the original source material is written in Greek and subsequently translated into other languages. To further frustrate this study there are only a few dictionaries of ancient Egyptian, none of which is really adequate for the task. As noted above, Faulkner's *Concise Dictionary of Middle Egyptian* emphasizes words and grammar commonly used in Egypt's Middle Kingdom (2040-1640 BCE) and omits many from earlier or later periods. Gardiner's (1927) excellent *Egyptian Grammar*, which remains the best and most influential work on Egyptian grammar, similarly deals with Middle Egyptian while its accompanying dictionary contains even fewer words than Faulkner's. The only other dictionary comparable with Faulkner's is Budge's (1920) *Egyptian Hieroglyphic Dictionary* which, while containing a greater number of words, is not limited to any particular period in Egypt's history, nor does it explicitly identify periods to which particular words and phrases belong. Furthermore, some (and perhaps many) entries in Budge's work are considered inaccurate by modern scholars and the documentation he supplies with each word, when supplied, is often inadequate to evaluate in terms of his sources; the precise meanings and background of many words are thus not amenable to further study. For these reasons, the modern researcher is faced with just a few excellent dictionaries containing relatively few words – or a single, relatively inadequate dictionary containing many words.

The reader should also bear in mind that modern Egyptian dictionaries are not constructed in the same manner as their ancient counterparts; in fact, the ancient versions were not even dictionaries in the modern sense of the word. Modern versions provide us with definitions of individual words arranged according to strict protocols based on alphabetization of their component syllables as described by Gardiner (1927). Ancient versions, on the other hand, did not offer definitions but were simply lists of words arranged according to their general phonetic similarities to one another. One example of such a dictionary is the Papyrus Carlsberg No. VII which provides us with examples of how particular words might have been used. Clagett (1989) quotes several examples to illustrate this complicated approach, including the following entry for the word "day."

> I.e. The Day (*hrw*), I.e. Re in his rise in the morning, by means of whom everything is perceived. I.e. the Ennead The eye is called the Ennead. The sun-disk came into existence from the right eye of Re. It is the Vulture-Goddess who binds (?) the bows, and who binds ... It is Ta-tenen, the male one. The Uraeus came into existence from the right eye of Re; it is the crown of Lower Egypt who unites it with her body.[21]

2. New Approaches

Clagett says "It is evident in this treatise that we have no ordinary dictionary but rather a mythological exposition, which shows in part how the mythological associations originated in punning or the use of words that sounded like those being discussed." It is against this background that Greek (and hence English) words used in the Book of Revelation will be occasionally examined in relation to potential Egyptian words including those "related," or phonetically similar words that might have conceivably been used in word play.

Budge's, Gardiner's and Faulkner's dictionaries use different systems to transliterate hieroglyphic symbols into their phonetic equivalents. Budge's (earlier) work uses standard English word sounds and adds vowels wherever appropriate. Gardiner and Faulkner use internationally recognized phonemes and like the original Egyptian, does not usually include vowels; at times, vowels are added to facilitate pronunciation. Sometimes in this study it is helpful to the reader to compare phonetics and transliterations used in the different dictionaries. A background for such comparisons is provided in the table, *Pronunciations of Egyptian Words* (see page 20). While the rules in Budge's system are less critical, Gardiner's and Faulkner's dictionaries follow well-defined rules which may be used to compare pronunciation of certain words or phrases resulting from Budge's conventions. Gardiner summarizes the method used by modern translators as follows:

> The course usually adopted is to use the English vowel *e* in every case except where the consonants ꜣ and *a* occur; in those two cases *a* (pronounced as in French) is substituted for *e*. Thus the following pronunciations are obtained: *men* for *mn*, *djed* for *dd*, *sedjem* for *sdm*, *nefret* for *nfrt*; but *hena* for *hna*, *adja* for *adꜣ*, *weya* for *wꜣ* and *aa* for *aꜣ*. ... In order to help the beginner, vocalized transliterations of the kind just indicated have been added to the purely consonantal transliterations in the vocabularies accompanying the first two lessons. Thus '● ▲' *ḫt* ("chet") 'thing' must be understood as meaning the Egyptian word ● ▲, having the signification 'thing,' is to be transliterated in writing as *ḫt*, but may be pronounced conventionally as 'chet,' with 'ch' as in Scotch 'loch' ... .[22]

Gardiner adds that such vocalizations "are purely artificial makeshifts and bear little or no relation, so far as the vowels are concerned, to the unknown original pronunciations as heard and spoken by the Egyptians themselves." This comment is important to remember when the phonetics of different Egyptian words and phrases are discussed in this book. Many other differences in pronunciations are presented by the above authors and interested readers may wish to refer to Gardiner's, Faulkner's and Budge's publications to become better acquainted with the pronunciations of Egyptian words. Meanwhile, the information provided in the aforesaid table, *Pronunciations* and the above quotation is generally sufficient for the reader to get a general understanding of the arguments presented here.

In spite of the above difficulties, and because of a lack of suitable alternatives, it was decided to use the available dictionaries in this study, regardless of their limitations. It is hoped that sufficient probable parallels will be identified between the

Book of Revelation and ancient Egyptian texts to at least suggest areas of future research to either strengthen or negate specific conclusions reached here.

Egyptian – the Divine Language

The Egyptian language was considered to be as old as time itself; it existed even before creation. Indeed, it was through the use of the spoken "word" of the creator-god that all of creation came into existence. The language was believed to have been given to Egyptians through the god Thoth who was not only the inventor of hieroglyphic writing, but also the very "tongue of Re."[23] The Egyptian language, and especially the hieroglyphics which expressed it, were thus considered gifts from Re; it was through them that the sun-god often communicated with his people. This basic belief in the origin and nature of their language is intimately intertwined with other beliefs, ranging from cosmogony to a divine relationship between names and the objects they represent. Sauneron's (1957) excellent overview of the subject demonstrates how these beliefs influenced the Egyptian's perception of the power of the spoken word:

> The Egyptians never considered language – namely that which corresponds to the hieroglyphs – as a social tool. It always remained for them a sonorous echo of the essential energy which gave rise to the universe, in fact a *cosmic force*. Also the study of this language allowed them an "explication" of the world. This explication was the "play on words" which furnished it to them. From the moment that *one considers words as intimately tied to the essence of the beings or things they define, the resemblances of words could not be simply fortuitous but rather convey a relationship of nature,* a subtle rapport which the science of the priests will have to define. Names of places, names of divinities, terms designating sacred objects, all ought to be explicable by means of a phonetic etymology – and the door is open to the most extravagant fantasies.[24]

Word Play

For the above reasons, no search of Egyptian texts for parallels with the Book of Revelation is complete without attention of Egypt's age-old practice of word play. Goelet (1994) says that "One of the consequences of the Egyptians' belief that their language was a divine gift was a conviction that a similarity between words did not arise accidentally, but instead reflected an actual relationship which the gods themselves had intended to be discovered by people."[25] *Words which sounded similar were therefore related.* We may therefore assume, for example, that while Nut was the name of the sky-goddess, its homophone, *nut*, meant a city or town; hence the sky-goddess herself was believed to be associated with a city, or more specifically, a celestial city; Nut could even be considered to be a personification of it. While this simple example serves to illustrate the point, many variations of the principle are evident among the words and religious beliefs of the ancient Egyptians. Furthermore, words which had similar but not identical sounds could be related if their pronunciations were close enough. The use of puns therefore flourished, at least in religious settings. Goelet tells us that,

2. New Approaches

Egyptian puns seem heavy handed, but they were not intended to amuse. They created an alternate focus which could deflect the power in a word. One example involves the euphemistic substitution of the phrase *mi* "come" for *mut* "death." Most word play in the *BD* [Book of the Dead] either deflects enmity or gives power by a simple reworking of the name of a god or a place: ... 'Hermopolis (*Wenu*) is opened (*wenu*) ...' The intent is normally to manipulate a name so as to demonstrate the deceased's control over a person or thing in the beyond. Stating a name or merely threatening to do so was often sufficient means for gaining power.[26]

Budge also says that "Paronomasia was especially important as a means of revealing the hidden connections between this world and the next."[27] Budge (1904), like Goelet, gives an example from the *Book of the Divine Cow* wherein Re assigns Thoth as his messenger to the people: "And thou shalt be in my place (*ȧst*), and thou shalt be called *Ȧsti*, that is to say, the deputy of Re. And it shall be permitted to thee to send for thy messenger (*hab*), and at these words the ibis (*habi*), which is the envoy of Thoth, came into being."[28]

He furthermore gives a somewhat broader example of how similar sounding words shaped Egyptian mythology, affected understandings of the names of the gods, and influenced the details of their actions.

The name of the god Thoth, Teḥuti, appears to be derived from the supposed oldest name of the ibis in Egypt, i.e., *teḥu,* to which the termination *ti* has been added, with the idea of indicating that the king called Teḥuti possessed the qualities and attributes of the ibis. A derivation of the name which appears to have been favoured by the Egyptians connected it with the word *tekh,* "a weight," and in passages quoted by Lanzone we find the god actually called *tekh*. Now the determinative for the word *tekh,* a weight, is the sign for "heart," and we know that the bird called *tekh* or *tekhnu,* which closely resembled the ibis, the bird sacred to Thoth, was in the opinion of some ancient writers connected with the heart. Thus ... when the Egyptians wish to write "heart" they draw an ibis, for this bird was dedicated to Hermes (i.e., Thoth) as the lord of all knowledge and understanding.[29]

He also gives discrete examples of the use of word play in their religious texts. For example, in a *Hymn to Osiris* which describes the successful search of Isis for the body of Osiris we read that, "She [Isis] sought him without weariness, she went round about this earth in sorrow, not alighted she without finding him, she made light [*shut*] with her hair (or feathers) [*shut*] making to become wind with {her} wings, she made cries at the bier of her brother."[30] He also points out that in some passages it is difficult to decide whether the *ḥu* mentioned in the texts refers to the god of the sense of Taste, or to the divine food *ḥu*.[31]

In our study of the Book of Revelation we should have, under ideal conditions, an Egyptian language version of the book to seek evidence for such word play. Since we haven't, we are restricted to a Greek version which may or may not have been the original language in which it was written. Nevertheless, if we assume that the Book of Revelation is somehow linked to ancient Egypt's religious texts, the almost ubiquitous nature of word play in Egyptian sources would suggest it is unwise to assume that word play based on Egyptian words is absent in the book – and that we should not examine the possibility of its presence; clearly, the possibility of word play in the Book of Revelation should be a part of this study.

The approach taken in the study of Egyptian puns must therefore, of course, be different from the study of the same puns in original Egyptian texts. When studying Egyptian texts one looks for two or more similar sounding words with entirely different meanings used in close conjunction with one another, several examples of which are given above. When it is obvious that an Egyptian passage intends to make a conceptual connection between the words, the presentation of a pun may be suggested. Clagett (1989), in discussing an Egyptian book on the interpretation of dreams gives several examples of obvious punning:

> The dream of being "up a growing tree (*nht*) ... means his loss (*nhy*) of ... {something}" and a dream of "white (*ḥd*) bread being given to him ... means {that} something {will happen} at which his face will brighten up (*ḥd*)" and a dream of "uncovering his own backside (*pḥwy*) ... {means that} he will be an orphan later (*ḥr ḥwy*)."

Clagett also says that the

> Earliest doctrine concerning man's creation was that he was produced from the tears of Atum. ... This doctrine seems to have had its origin in the similarity between the word for human beings (*rmwṯ*) and that for tears (*rmwt*), another example of the role of punning in the creative process.[32]

In this study, we at times come across strange images in the Book of Revelation which might make sense in Egyptian hieroglyphics but have little meaning in a translated version. This type of confusion can be the result of a loss of the context of a passage. An excellent example of a possible loss of context is in our interpretation of the symbolism of the reference in Rev. 19:15 to the "sword coming from the mouth" of God. It is logical to assume that this should not be taken literally. In a Greek or English setting, we might rightly regard this as a simple metaphor for the power of the authoritative and commanding power of the words of God. Egyptian religious tradition, however, also offers an alternative. It will be shown in this work how this phrase may be interpreted to be a simple *description* of the hieroglyph for word "word" which is sometimes written as a picture of a *sword* next to a man pointing to his mouth. Numerous other examples of this and other types of potential Egyptian word play in the Book of Revelation will be demonstrated during the course of this study.

This is the exact opposite of that outlined by Clagett. Here, it is first assumed that a particular passage from Revelation is based on the Egyptian language, irrespective of which Egyptian document a given passage might have come from. One or more potential Egyptian puns for English words are then inserted in brackets after each grammatically important English word and the relative similarities of the sounds of these words are compared. This approach, as will be demonstrated throughout this study, indicates that some passages in Revelation clearly indicate the presence of possible Egyptian puns. In fact, some rather extensive passages suggest an even greater abundance of them than we might expect in normal Egyptian texts. The presence of such potential puns can be used as supporting evidence for other types of parallels. Remarkably, this approach sometimes suggests identification of parallel passages which would otherwise be difficult or impossible to identify.

Identification of Egyptian Gods

The following examples illustrate some of the more common approaches to determining the identity of Egyptian gods in illustrations. It is by no means exhaustive but simply serves to assist the reader's understanding of the more common approaches taken.

> *Names in texts:-* This is the simplest and most straightforward method of identifying a god; the name is simply mentioned in the text. It may stand on its own or be a reference in a scene to a nearby picture of an otherwise unidentifiable god. At times, a solitary hieroglyph represents the presence of a god.

> *Heads of gods in illustrations:-* Identifications of gods in illustrations devoid of captions or other textual support are usually based on differences associated with their heads which effectively served as their emblems. These emblems were usually heads of animals. For example, the gods Horus and Seker were frequently identified by a falcon's head, Sekhmet was typically identifiable as a goddess with the head of a lioness, Seth bore the head of a "Seth animal," Hathor that of cow, Thoth of an Ibis and so on. This system is not entirely foolproof, however, because some gods shared certain animal head emblems with other gods. For example, the head of a ram could be used to identify different deities such as Re and Tatenen; in such cases, final identifications are typically made on the basis of text, context, captions or symbols worn on their bodies or heads.

> *Crowns, diadems and head-dresses:-* The identity of many deities can also be determined by single symbols. For example, the goddess Isis usually wore the symbol for a throne (𓊨) on her head, Osiris typically wore the White Crown (𓋑), Maat and Shu both wore a single feather and Hathor wore a crown formed by a solar disk mounted between two cow's horns, Khons, a moon disc and crescent, and Seshat wore a crown consisting of a seven pointed star surmounted by a bow resembling a set of inverted cow horns (𓋇).

Metaphors

Metaphors abound in the religion of the ancient Egyptians, just as in all religions throughout time. The Book of Revelation is no exception. Indeed, the almost continuous barrage of metaphors in the book has contributed to its being the most difficult book in Christian literature to understand. When the age and context of a passage are unknown, metaphors can be misunderstood, confusing, enigmatic, and sometimes not even recognized as metaphors. It is therefore not surprising to read the statement by Lohmeyer (1934) that, "There are few primitive Christian writings which as a whole and in detail have received so much attention and yet seem to remain untouched in regard to the secret to their meaning and history."[33]

Because metaphors were so extensively used by ancient writers, especially in religious contexts, modern analysts are often quick to invoke their presence to explain otherwise incompressible passages. This practice can lead to especially misleading results when neither the context nor the composition date of a document is known. A simple example of possible misinterpretation in the Book of Revelation is found in the reference to Babylon. Practically all modern Christian scholars assume that Revelation was written during the early years of Christianity when Christians were being persecuted by the Romans so they assume that the Babylon of Revelation represents the power of imperial Rome. If, on the other hand, the Book of Revelation was composed at a time of actual conflict with ancient Babylon, invoking this metaphor would be entirely unnecessary. Is it not possible that Revelation's Babylon simply meant the ancient city of Babylon on the Euphrates River – or even some other city bearing the same or even a different name with a similar pronunciation? Many apparent metaphors in the Book of Revelation are traditionally interpreted in the context of early Christianity and are assumed to be related to the second coming of Christ, the final judgment or an array of cataclysmic events which are to mark the final days of life on earth. But when the context and date are dramatically changed, interpretations also change dramatically.

For this reason, and insofar as possible, all apparent metaphors in this study are purposely *not* treated as such, at least not initially. Initially, for example, it was assumed that when the author describes a "sword coming from the mouth" of God, this is exactly what is meant. No attempts were made to explain the phrase in terms of a metaphor but rather in terms of the existence of similar references found in the ancient Egyptian literature including Egyptian puns and physical descriptions of actual hieroglyphic symbols. This treatment does not mean that a particular phrase is not metaphorical, but rather, a simple report on what the author of Revelation was actually shown, what he read, or what was described to him. For example, when the author in Rev. 13: 1 and Rev. 13:11 describes a beast coming out of the sea and another coming out of the earth, "earth" and "sea" are not initially assumed to represent metaphors but are taken at face value and comparable story lines with images or descriptions of beasts associated with both the sea and land are sought in the Egyptian texts.

Attempts are seldom made to interpret possible metaphors found in either the Book of Revelation or ancient Egyptian texts. When it seems feasible, possible mythological and historical backgrounds to certain images are at times explored and discussed to clarify and illuminate the nature of potential parallels to otherwise confusing scenes in the Book of Revelation.

Conventions Used

Abbreviations for Names of Egyptian Texts:-

AM = *The Amduat*
BA = *Book of Aker*
BC = *Book of Caverns*
BD = *Book of the Dead*
BDY = *Book of Day*
BG = *Book of Gates*
BH = *Books of the Heavens*
BN = *Book of Night*
BDC = *Book of the Divine Cow*
CT = *Coffin Texts*
PT = *Pyramid Texts*

References to Egyptian Illustrations:- Special notations are used as abbreviations for Egyptian works which have more than one horizontal sections or "registers." Typically, these are parts of the *Amduat*, the *Book of Gates*, the *Book of Night* and the

2. New Approaches

Book of Caverns. The format is based on the formula: Nd.r.p1-p2, where N = abbreviation of the name of the Egyptian book (as in the above key), d = Division number of the book, r = register number (numbered from top to bottom), p1 = the starting percentile of a scene and p2 = the ending percentile of the scene. Figure 5, which shows the 2nd register of the 7th Division of the *Amduat* gives several examples of how this format is applied to the pictures of different parts of a register. All percentiles are based on illustrations in Piankoff (1954).

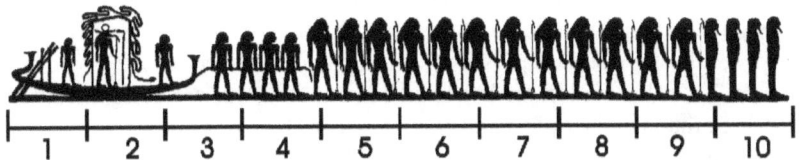

Figure 5. The ten percentiles of the second register of the 7th Division of the Egyptian *Amduat*.

Note the following locations in the figure:
    Entire register: AM7.2 (the entire *Division* would be AM7)
    Solar barque: AM7.2.1-3
    Four towers in front of barque: AM7.2.3-4
    Nine figures with scepters (↑): AM7.2.4-9
    Four bearded mummies: AM7.2.10

The *Book of Caverns* is treated differently and conforms with the format used by Piankoff (1954) which identifies texts with numbered pictures in numbered registers.

Example for *Book of Caverns*:

(BC5.2.3$^{rd\ Picture}$)

The scene referred to here is the third picture of the second register of the 5th Division of the *Book of Caverns*.

Quotations:- Where appropriate, the following changes are made in quotations:

    A. Place names, or names of deities which are shown in upper case print in the original material (common in works by E.A.W. Budge), are presented in lower case to conform with conventions used here.
    B. *Italicized print* is used for emphasis in quotations. If the italics are not present in the original text, text italicized by this author is immediately followed by a solid raised dot symbol (˙); the absence of a dot after an italicized portion of a quotation indicates the italics are in the original text. Such dots are not used in biblical quotations because italics do not appear in any of the texts quoted.

C. Brackets [...] and {...}: Square brackets [...] are used in quotations to indicate comments inserted by this author. When a quotation already contains square brackets, they are converted to curled brackets {...}. There are no brackets used in the English translations of the Book of Revelation used here and brackets in quotations used here are therefore those of the author.

References to Budge's (1920) Hieroglyphic Dictionary:- Words in Budge's dictionary are arranged on two-column pages. For ease of locating words with many homonyms, all references are provided with the page number followed by either an "a" or a "b." Words found in the left-hand column of a page are designated with an "a" and those found in the right-hand column with a "b." For example, a word quoted from the right-hand column of page 125 is sited as being located on "p. 125b" of the dictionary.

References to Plates in The Egyptian Book of the Dead:- Most of the plates and associated hieroglyphic text in Faulkner's (1990) translation of the *Egyptian Book of the Dead* are presented as two-page spreads. Text locations in these translation are designated as either plate number A or B where A = left-hand side of a plate and B = its right-hand side; eg., Plate 10B.

Footnotes, Endnotes, and Appendices:- Footnotes are used for brief explanatory notes and are designated with letters of the alphabet. Endnotes are used exclusively for references to publications listed in the *References* section. Some larger explanatory notes and tables are inserted as Appendices.

PART II. THE THRONE SCENE

The throne scene in the Book of Revelation is first mentioned in Rev. 1:12-16 while numerous other references are found in later chapters, especially Rev. 4-5 and parts of Rev. 19 and Rev. 22. In the first scene, a deity is described as sitting on a throne in the midst of seven spirits (Rev. 1:4), four different-looking creatures (Rev. 4:6-9) and a vast multitude of souls including the twelve tribes of Israel (Rev. 7:4-8,14:1-5). At times there is a Lamb (Rev. 5:6), a council of judges (Rev. 20:4), and a deity called Christ (Rev. 3:5, Rev. 22:16). Nearby, throngs of beings and a Lake of Fire (Rev. 20:14) stand ready to destroy all who have done evil. Revelation provides sufficient detail in its descriptions of these characters, scenes and circumstances to enable detailed comparisons with similar characters and scenes in the religious literature of ancient Egypt.

Descriptions of characters and situations in the Book of Revelation are usually unambiguous and for the most part, unique. For example, the deity on the throne is described as wearing a white garment which extends to his feet, has a golden collar, white hair, eyes like fire, feet like bronze and eyes that shine as brightly as the sun. One verse describes a river flowing from his throne while another describes a "sea of glass" in front of it. In the midst of another throne stands a light-emitting being called the "Lamb." Also, "The Amen" is associated with the throne and is worshiped through reverential repetition of his name, Christ is referred to as the "Morning Star." Another deity is described as having eyes of fire and wearing many crowns and a robe dipped in blood; his name is written on his thigh and he leads an army of righteous followers against the forces of evil, smiting them with a sword from his mouth. Remarkably, all these characteristics can be found among the gods of the ancient Egyptians, especially those we find closely associated with the throne of Osiris.

Egyptians envisaged the throne of Osiris to be located in the Netherworld where the dead were judged according to their deeds during their life on earth. Perhaps the best known version of the scene is found the *Book of the Dead* showing the judgment of the dead before Osiris (Figure 6). It is this scene which forms the basis of Part II comparisons of the many elements of the throne scene in the Book of Revelation with those of ancient Egyptian religious beliefs.

Figure 6. The scene of the Judgment of the Dead from the 125th Chapter of the *Book of the Dead* which parallels in many ways the judgment scene mentioned in various parts of the Book of Revelation.

Chapter 3. The Preeminent Deities[34]

This chapter compares five deities found in the Book of Revelation with similar deities in the Egyptian pantheon. We begin with one of the most popular Egyptian gods, Osiris, the god of the dead, ruler of the Egyptian Netherworld and the one who presides over the judgment of the dead. Osiris had the final word on whether individuals' lives on earth and knowledge of important magical spells justified admission to the Egyptian paradise (the coveted Fields of Rushes also known by other names such as the Fields of Yaru and the Field of Offerings) or were to be condemned to annihilation by fire or some other equally terrifying fate. A brief examination of the setting in which Osiris judges the dead reveals a remarkably similar setting to that found in the opening scene of the Book of Revelation. The Egyptian throne scene, so central to the hope of eternal like for the Osirian believer, is a natural starting point for our comparison of the characters and events found in Egyptian texts with those found in the Book of Revelation.

In later chapters, we shall see how many events and sequences of events associated with and involving these and other characters in the Book of Revelation parallel similar events and sequences of similar events in Egyptian sources.

God on the Throne

The Book of Revelation provides us with an extraordinarily detailed description of different aspects of the throne scene. The first of its attributes are found in Rev. 1 and Rev. 2, but, as will be made evident throughout this work, other parts of Revelation describe events associated with this same setting. These descriptions enhance our comparison between scenes in Revelation and those in with typical Osirian throne scenes such as the one from the *Book of the Dead* shown in Figure 7.

Although the throne scene is introduced in the first chapter of Revelation, the actual judgment of the dead associated with it appears much later in the book. The same is true for the Osirian throne scene which is typically placed at the beginning of the *Book of the Dead* even though events involving the judgment of the dead do not appear until much later. Discussion on the parallels referred to in Figure 7 will be presented next.

3. *The Preeminent Deities* 59

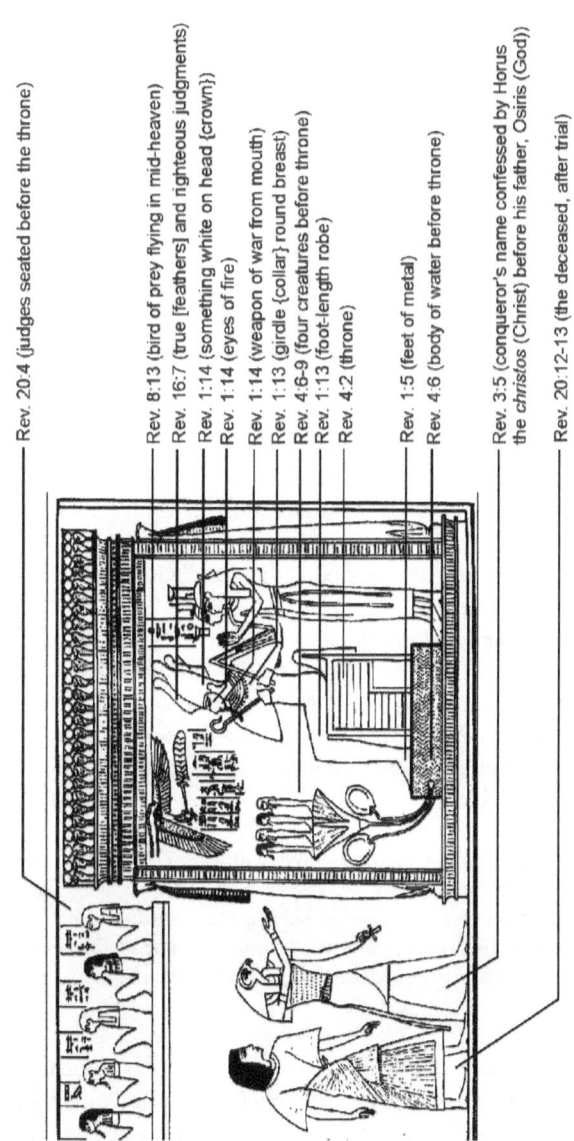

Figure 7. Graphic comparison of the throne scene in the *Book of the Dead* with that in the Book of Revelation demonstrating that many of its characteristics are common to both sources. In this scene, Osiris sits on his throne while his son Horus introduces the deceased to him after his having just been declared innocent (vindicated, conquered) before a panel of judges, some of which are seen in the upper left corner of the figure.

God's Apparel (Rev. 1:13)

Rev. 1:13 describes the deity on the throne as being "clothed with a garment down to the foot" (KJV). Osiris typically wears a similar garment,[a] as shown in Figure 7; he wears a long white garment extending from his neck to his ankles.[35] Also, the chests of both Revelation's God on the throne and Osiris are covered with what Revelation describes as "a golden girdle round his breast," a description which is similar to that of the Egyptian "broad collar." These were typically worn on special occasions and varied greatly in design and construction, being made of anything from flowers to precious stones to gold, the latter typically worn by the most high ranking officials. Osiris is seldom depicted without one and his regal position demanded a golden collar. This ensured that his collar was true to the nature of the hieroglyph used to represent it, ⌒, a hieroglyph for both the broad collar and gold itself. Any material other than gold around the neck of Osiris would not conform with its true nature (as dictated by the belief that hieroglyphic writing was a gift from the creator).

God's Radiance (Rev. 1:16, 21:10-11,23)

Revelation describes the face of the one on the throne as being "like the sun shining in full strength" (Rev. 1:16). In fact, it is so bright that it lights up the entire holy city described in Rev. 21:10-11 as "having the glory of God." Note that in Rev. 21:23 we are told that "the glory of God is its light." God's light is also described in Rev. 15:8 as filling his temple.

Similarly, Chapter 22 of the *Book of the Dead* refers to Osiris with the words, "Homage to thee. O thou lord of *Brightness*."[36] One Hymn to Osiris says that the "*brilliance*' of the turquoise encircleth thee,"[37] words reminiscent of the holy city in Revelation "having the *glory of God*, its radiance like a most rare jewel, like a jasper, clear as crystal." Hornung (1983) includes radiance among the characteristics of prominent Egyptian deities:

> A god may be sensed and seen not only in his attributes of fragrance, and power, but also and more forcefully in the way he affects men's hearts – in the love, fear, terror, respectful awe, and other feelings that his presence evokes. ... the invisible god may be grasped as a subjective reality, whereas he can be made visible to the believer only in images, *because his true appearance has no fixed contours and is suffused with blinding radiance.*'[38]

Not only did the body of the enthroned one in Revelation emit light, so did his eyes; Rev. 1:14 says that his eyes were "like a flame of fire." Flaming eyes were also common elements among Egypt's most powerful deities. For example, the *Book of the*

---

[a] Not all pictures of Osiris show him wearing a completely white garment, as noted by Budge (1934, p. 294). "The white body of Osiris [in the papyrus of Ani] is covered with a painted pattern, which some have described as 'scale work', but which probably represents a design made by tattûing, cicatrization, or painting." Goelet (1994, p. 156) suggests that "The pattern on the garment which Osiris wears may represent fish scales, a possible reference to the myth in which Osiris drowns and gets eaten by a fish."

Dead refers to the destructive aspect of flaming eyes used against evil doers. It says, "May the flame of the Eye of Horus go forth against you."[39] Concerning the very ancient god, Ptah, Budge (1895) says that, "As a solar god he is called 'Ptah, the Disk of heaven who illumineth the world by the fire of his eyes.'"[40] Most significantly, the *Pyramid Texts* describe Osiris with the words, "thy two eyes ... shine (again) in thy head."[41] Budge (1904) even says "there is little doubt that the Egyptians ... supposed the name of the god [Osiris] to mean something like the 'strength of the Eye,' i.e., the strength of the Sun-god Rā."[42] We may conclude that the fiery eyes of the Egyptian god Osiris parallel those described in Rev. 1:14 and Rev. 2:18. Clearly, Osiris who sat on the judgment throne of the ancient Egyptians emitted light just as did God on the throne in the Book of Revelation.

God's Metallic Flesh (Rev. 1:15)

Another attribute of the one on the throne is that "his feet were like burnished bronze, refined as in a furnace" (Rev. 1:15). This also conforms with Egyptian beliefs. Shining metallic flesh of Egyptian gods, especially their limbs, not only formed a part of Egyptian beliefs, but was also a hoped-for attribute for themselves in the afterlife. Hornung (1983) says that, "from the Middle Kingdom on ... the 'flesh' of the gods is of gold and their bodies of the most precious materials and the blessed deceased wishes to become "one body" with the god and hence to partake in his precious, radiant substance."[43] One hymn to Osiris reads, "Thy body is of bright and shining metal ... and the brilliance of the turquoise encircleth thee."[44] While Rev 1:15 says the feet of the one on the throne were made of burnished bronze, Egyptian sources say Osiris's limbs, were made of shining copper, gold, or some other precious metal or alloy. Like the bronze in Revelation, these are yellowish in color.

God's Hair (Rev. 1:14)

Rev. 1:14 says of the one on the throne: "his head and his hair were white as white wool, white as snow." White hair is universally associated with old age, and Osiris was among the oldest Egyptian gods. Indeed, in Chapter 175 of the *Book of the Dead*, the god Atum refers to conditions at the end of a cycle of time; he says, "The earth will return to its Primordial Water, to the surging flood, as in its original state. But I will remain with Osiris." In this version of the creation myth, Osiris is already present at the beginning of the next cosmic cycle so that both he and Atum may be considered the oldest of the gods. This creation story conforms with the interpretation of Rev. 1:14 concerning the age of the one on the throne. Another possible parallel is related to the White Crown of Upper Egypt which Osiris typically wears on his head; here we simply note the parallel of something white on the head of the one on the throne. Whether age-related white hair or a white crown, the color white is associated with his head in both sources. This attribute of Osiris can thus be considered a parallel to the description of the head of God in Rev. 1:14.

Truth (Rev. 3:7)

There are several references to the one on the throne being associated with truth. In Rev. 3:7, God on the throne says to the author of Revelation "To the angel of the church in Philadelphia write: 'The words of the holy one, *the true one.*' " And in Rev. 16:7, a voice from the altar near the throne cries out, "Yea, Lord God the Almighty, *true* and just are thy judgments!" The ancient Egyptians symbolized truth with an ostrich feather (𓆇), a symbol which also represented *Maat*, the goddess of truth and order.[45] This feather plays an important part in the judgment scene where we find it typically mounted on one of the pans of the scales of justice where it is weighed against the heart of the deceased. Also, Osiris' crown in Figure 7 has two ostrich feathers, symbols of the validity of his judgments. Associations of truth with Osiris go back as far as the *Pyramid Texts* where the Text §1520 calls him "Lord of Truth (Righteousness)."[46]

The Sword from God's Mouth (Rev. 2:16)

What appears at first thought to be a simple metaphor is found in the 1st, 2nd and 19th chapters of Revelation. In Rev. 1:16 we read that "from his mouth issued a sharp two-edged sword." Similarly, in Rev. 2:16, military action is threatened by God with "the sword of my mouth." In Rev. 19:15 it is said that "From his mouth issues a sharp sword with which to smite the nations" and in Rev. 19:21 people are slain by "the sword that issues from his mouth." At least three alternatives to this being a "simple" metaphor for a person's words may be found when these passages are compared with Egyptian sources, each of which ultimately involves the use of a more complicated approach to the metaphor, i.e., the use of puns. These will be dealt with separately.

Word Power:- Let us first examine the phrase common to each of the above quotations, "from his mouth issued a sharp two-edged sword." It seems absurd that these passages might imply an actual sword issuing from the mouth of God and it would be far more likely that what comes out of his mouth is a *command* that his enemies be killed by the sword or some other type of weapon, i.e., *words* alone are not sufficient to the kill God's enemies.

Nevertheless, smiting the enemy with words alone was by no means a foreign concept in Egyptian beliefs. Clagett (1989) points out that "abundant citation, has made clear that Thoth's epithet 'Lord of the Divine Word' implies not merely his invention of hieroglyphics but also authorship and control of cult-ritual and *magical formulae, in short, of creative words.*"[47] Powerful gods could use the creative power of the spoken word to affect any action whatsoever against their enemies, including killing them as if by a sword. As the "Lord of the Divine Word," i.e., of the personification of the word of the sun-god, Thoth's words had the same magical, creative and destructive power as the words of the sun-god. In fact they *were* the words of the sun-god (i.e., of Osiris or Re or both combined, as will be discussed later) and his words actually become a sword, if that was his intent. The reference to Revelation's god on the throne killing with a sword from his mouth thus conforms with the beliefs of pious ancient Egyptians. In this sense we may view Rev. 19:15 as if it said that "From his mouth issues all-powerful *words* to smite the nations."

Punning:- This interpretation suggests a brief examination of yet another aspect ancient Egyptian practice – punning. As discussed in the previous chapter, punning was a very real and important practice in Egyptian religious writings and beliefs. The Egyptian word for "word" is *mdw,*[48] and this is phonetically identical to the word for

3. The Preeminent Deities

"staff." Now the staff was, from prehistoric times, considered to be not only a walking stick, but also a weapon. The Egyptians recognized this in their language in the homonyms for "stick" and "strike," either of which may be pronounced *met*.[49] It is therefore not surprising that the similar word *meter*, meant "staff, stick, or *weapon*."[50] Since the staff was perceived as a weapon and the Egyptian word *mdw* could mean either "word" or "staff," we may conclude that an Egyptian equivalent to the phrase "From his mouth issues *words* to smite the nations" could be "From his mouth issues *weapons* (from *mdw* = "word" and "staff") to *strike* (*met*) the nations." This brief study not only reinforces the idea of the metaphor mentioned above but also suggests a rather interesting logic for it.

Simple description of Hieroglyphics:- There is still another possible parallel between Revelation's link between the spoken word and a sword; as noted above it is found in the *mdw*, Egyptian for "word." The hieroglyphic word for *mdw* is written as ▌━▶ ▶ ♣.[51] Note the first symbol, ▌; this is the symbol for staff, which as pointed out above, can be used as a weapon. Indeed, Budge (1920) interprets the word *meter*, which uses this symbol as its determinative, to mean "staff, stick, or *weapon*."[52] Note too that this symbol is pointed at the top and has a horizontal bar near the rounded bottom. It bears a remarkable resemblance to an inverted, archaic determinative for a dagger, ▮,[53] and to a lesser extent the later sign, ▮.[54] Thus, even the hieroglyph for "word," *mdw*, contains a suggestion for a weapon, and in particular, a dagger which apparently evolved into a sword and is therefore closely related to it. *Mdw* not only meant word, but contained in its hieroglyphs the idea of a weapon and in particular, a sword. Meanwhile, on the far right of the word ▌━▶ ▶ ♣ we find a picture of a kneeling man pointing to his mouth, a gesture which may be seen to link the symbol for the weapon with the mouth. The ▌ and ♣ symbols in this word may therefore be looked upon as a mnemonic for linking the idea of a *weapon* coming from the *mouth*, just as we see in the expression in Rev. 1:16 "from his *mouth* issued a sharp two-edged *sword*."

This additional Egyptian parallel with Rev. 1:16 suggests yet another approach to the examination of passages in the Book of Revelation for possible Egyptian parallels – parallels based on simple descriptions of hieroglyphic words and phrases.

Water from the Throne (Rev. 22:1-2)

An intriguing and peculiar aspect of the throne described in Revelation is that it has water flowing from it. The text describes it as "the river of the water of life, bright as crystal, flowing from the throne of God and of the Lamb" (Rev. 22:1-2). Like Rev. 22 which describes a celestial paradise, we also find pictures of the Egyptian paradise showing the throne of Osiris with water flowing from it; the water is typically called the "Efflux of Osiris." One such picture is found in Chapter 110 of the *Book of the Dead* shown here in lower part of Figure 8. The text describing the stepped throne says that "The god who is within is Osiris."[55] At least one version of this scene, shown in detail in the upper part of Figure 8 and in its original setting in Figure 9, emphasizes through the zig-zag pattern below the barque that the water is actually flowing from the throne; each of the three thrones in Figure 9 clearly show symbols of flowing water typical of those found in hieroglyphs of water-pots or libation vessels (see Figure 38). Note too that the water of life from the throne of Osiris is accentuated in Figure 7 where it is depicted as a rectangular pool filled with water (▥)⁵⁶ located directly underneath the throne and extending out in front of it. This too is consistent with the concept of water flowing from the throne of God in Revelation. This river of the water of life will be discussed in detail in Chapter 27, *The Holy City*.

The text associated with the lower half of Figure 8 refers to "The holy shore," a reference pertaining to the shoreline of the waterway through the Field of Offerings. This waterway is consistent with the idea of a street in the Holy City in Rev. 22:1-2 because waterways in the Egyptian paradise (see Figure 9) functioned as streets just as canals did in many of Egypt's cities and towns along the Nile River. (See also the section entitled *The River* in Chapter 27, *The Holy City*.

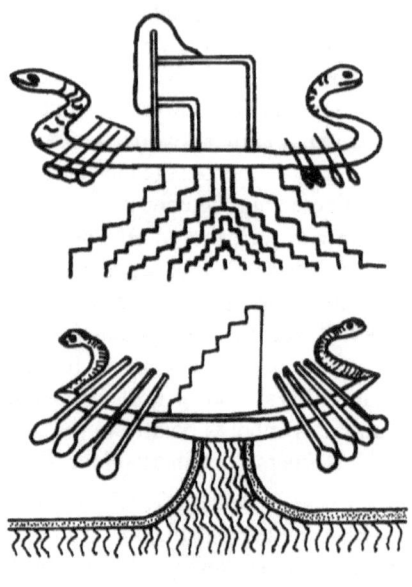

Finally, the reference in Rev. 22:1 to water flowing from the throne of God and the Lamb is consistent with the Egyptian concept of the oneness of *Osiris and Re* as expressed in the combined god called Osiris-Re. This will be discussed later in this chapter in the section entitled "God and the Lamb."

Figure 8. *Upper picture:* Water flowing from the throne of Osiris in the land of the blessed parallels the scene described in Rev. 22:1. *Lower picture:* This, more typical representation of the throne shows the throne on its barque which seems to be moored in a small inlet or bay. This picture is ambiguous with respect to the idea of water flowing from the throne.

Angels flying in midheaven (Rev. 8:13)

There are two references in the Book of Revelation to beings flying in midheaven and both involve announcements of judgment. In Rev. 8:13 we read that the author "heard an eagle crying with a loud voice, as it flew in midheaven, 'Woe, woe, woe to those who dwell on the earth.'" The second reference is in Rev. 14:6-7 where the author refers to an "angel flying in midheaven, with an eternal gospel to proclaim to those who dwell on earth ... and he said with a loud voice, 'Fear God and give him glory, for the hour of his judgment has come.'" In Egyptian sources, a vulture is quite often present flying in midheaven over pictures of Osiris seated on his judgment throne, as in Figure 7. The only difference between Rev. 8:13 and the Egyptian throne scene is the type of bird involved; in Revelation it is referred to as an eagle while Egyptian texts refers to a vulture. The vulture was associated with a number of female deities, especially Nekhbet, the goddess of Upper Egypt where the vulture was considered to be a "heraldic creature,"⁵⁷ a role consistent with that of the eagle in Rev.

Figure 9. The land of the blessed was envisioned as a heavenly land with many waterways (which acted as streets) surrounded by the primordial waters of the Nile River into which water flowed from three different manifestations of the throne (in this particular version) of the sun-god; in this setting, the form of the cental throne is typically considered to represent that of Osiris, i.e., "Revelation's God on the throne." The water flowing from the thrones parallel that described in Rev. 22:1. (BD110)

8:13 and the angel in Rev. 14:6-7. A large bird with crooked beak, large wings and sharp claws are present in both sources; the difference between the eagle in Revelation and the vulture in Egyptian throne scenes does not seem to be significant enough to negate the presence of the vulture in the judgment scene as a parallel to the eagle in the Book of Revelation (especially when one considered all other observed parallels to this scene, including those discussed above and those yet to be discussed).

The Lamb

The Lamb is another of the central characters in Revelation's throne scene, being mentioned twenty-nine times in the text. The name "Lamb" can be interpreted as meaning that his appearance was like that of a young sheep – i.e., a lamb. He is described as "standing" near, or even "on" a throne in Rev. 5:6; for example, some translations describe him as standing between the throne and four living creatures and among elders (RSV) while others describe him as "standing" in the center (NIV) or in the midst (KJV, ASV) of the throne.

We are also told that the Lamb emits light and that the holy "city has no need of sun or moon to shine upon it, for the glory of God is its light, and its lamp is the Lamb" (Rev 21:23). The following paragraphs demonstrate how each of these characteristics parallel those of the powerful Egyptian god, Re.

The Lamb of Re

An important aspect of the Egyptian concept of Re is intimately bound up with that of a male sheep. The 26th Invocation of *The Litany of Re* says, "Praise to thee, Re, with exalted power, with a raised head and great horns; surely thou art the Ram, Great of Forms (or Transformations) *(ḫprw).*"[58] The full-bodied picture of a ram in the hieroglyph 🐑 is usually referred to as a *ba* (*b₃*), a symbol also used as the determinative in words for sheep, especially those with long coiled horns,[59] and is frequently used to represent Re. On the walls of temples and tombs, Re is often depicted in his human-headed form while the ram-headed, human figure is more prominent in the *Book of Gates* and the *Amduat* (Figure 10). This association of the sun-god with a ram immediately suggests a parallel between the Lamb of Revelation and Re, the main difference between them being that a horned ram refers to a mature male sheep whereas a lamb is an immature one.

We might well enquire as to the extent to which an image of the mature ram of Egyptian mythology parallels Revelation's Lamb. The answer lies in the presence of the scarab beetle (*ḫprr* or *kheprer*) whose picture (🪲) is often placed next to that of the ram-headed form of Re, as in Figure 11. *Ḫprr* and its derivative *ḫpr* (🪲◇), means "to become, come into being, or change."[60] The scarab symbol is thus used to denote a juvenile form of something. For example, *ḫpr* is used to refer to young people as in the word *ḫpry*, 🪲◇𐤍𓏤 or 🪲◇𓀀𐩐, both of which simply mean "children."[61] Note that in the second expression, the idea of a "child" is expressed in relation to the hieroglyph for a mature man, 𓀀[62] while the juvenile stage is indicated by the beetle. Similarly, the idea of a juvenile sun-god is can be expressed as 🪲◇◇𓁛, *Ḫprr*, or

3. The Preeminent Deities

Figure 10. In this figure from the 4th Division of the *Amduat*, the ram-headed sun-god *stands* in his protective shrine – or throne (the Egyptian word for *shrine* being phonetically similar to that for *throne*) – as he passes through the Netherworld. In this sense, this scene conforms with the statement in Rev. 5:6 which says, "In the midst of the throne ... stood a lamb ..." (AM4.2.1-3)

Figure 11. The Egyptian symbol of the "lamb of Re" where the "lamb" is represented by a scarabaeus beetle (meaning "becoming") beside a mature ram-headed deity (Re), both of which are inside a circle (a solar disk and symbol of Re). Important aspects of the Egyptian lamb of Re are consistent with the "Lamb" of Revelation.

Khepri, which means the "young sun-god."[63] Also, the scarab symbol is frequently found combined with the hieroglyph for Re (◯ or ☉) and his ram-headed form (🐏, 🐏, 🐏 or 🐏) to create a hieroglyph which literally means "young ram" or "becoming a ram" – or simply, a "lamb." This form may thus be referred to as the "Lamb of Re" although this is not the translation Egyptologists usually apply to the hieroglyphs such as 🐏🐏 or 🐏🐏.

Nowhere is the idea of the "lamb of Re" more pronounced and more obvious than in the last scene of the *Book of Caverns* where we find a picture of a scarab beetle with the head of a ram in front of twelve deities who tow the solar barque (Figure 12). This picture shows a progression from right to left of different aspects, or transformations, of the sun-god as he is reborn in the sky at dawn. To the far right is the ram-headed form of the sun-god standing on his solar barque. Immediately in front of him is the beetle denoting his infancy, or as some Egyptologists say, his "prenatal" or "fetal" condition."[a] The goose standing in front of the beetle is an alternative symbol of the sun-god (especially in his form of the god Amen)[64] and probably serves to confirm the identity of the sun-god Re (in his name, Amen-Re). The egg on which the goose stands re-emphasizes the sun-god's incubating or fetal nature. The twelve who tow the sun-god acclaim that "Nut [the sky-goddess] has given thee birth,"[65] again emphasizing Re's infantile nature at this time. In front of the twelve towers a ram-headed beetle denotes and accentuates his infantile form as he begins his reign in the

---

[a] Egyptologists generally agree that as the ram-headed form of the sun-god passes through the Netherworld he is in fact the fetus of the sun to be later born in the sky each morning at dawn (in his Khepri form). In this book, both these forms (fetal and newborn/juvenile) are considered to be the "lamb" form of Re.

Figure 12. Representation of the birth of Re from his juvenile ram-headed, or "lamb" form (🐑) to the juvenile human form of sun-god as he rises into the morning sky at dawn. The ram-headed scarab beetle can be best translated as the "lamb" form of the sun-god. (BC6.1."Final Picture")

morning sky.[a] To the immediate left of the ram-headed beetle is a picture of the young child-god with its feet touching the disk of the sun as if to emphasize the process of his maturation from youth (the child, or lamb) to adulthood (symbolized in the sun-disk). The Lamb described in the Book of Revelation is entirely consistent with that of the juvenile, ram-headed form of sun-god Re, a form frequently encountered in Egyptian mythology, especially throughout his nightly journey through the Netherworld and his birth in the morning sky. Meanwhile, the text above the twelve towers says, "How great is He who has a throne in the Sky,"[66] a statement which conforms with Rev. 12:5 which says that the (holy) "child was caught up to God and to his throne."

Revelation's Lamb is similar to Re in other ways. For example, the Lamb in Rev. 21:23 is described as being a lamp, meaning he gives off light, an attribute which is, of course, the most prominent and obvious characteristic of the Egyptian sun-god. Indeed, the hieroglyph for Re's name is most often in the form of a disk of the sun (O or ☉) or as a man with a crown consisting of a solar disk encircled by two protective serpents (🜚).

One of the rather peculiar aspects of the Lamb in Revelation (and therefore an important consideration for assessing Egyptian parallels) is that he is described in the unusual situation of *standing in the midst of* a throne (RSV). This interpretation of the original Greek is consistent with a *transliteration* of the original text of Rev 5:6 which reads, "And I saw in {the} midst of the throne and of the four living creatures and in {the} midst of the elders, a Lamb standing ..."[67] (see also Rev. 7:17). That any deity should be described as standing in the midst of a throne is difficult to imagine. From an Egyptian perspective, however, such a statement is entirely consistent with two common homonyms: the Egyptian word *khent* can mean either "throne"[68] or "shrine."[69] A statement using the word *khent* may thus be used in the context of either a throne or a shrine (in which a deity may stand). This is important because Re is frequently shown standing in the midst of a shrine, as in Figure 10. In the absence of such a well-defined context, a simple description of Revelation's lamb may be interpreted from an Egyptian perspective to mean he is standing in the midst of a shrine – or a throne as we read in Revelation.

---

[a] This is but one of several versions of the myth of the birth of Re. Another is found in the *Books of the Heavens* and will be discussed in Chapter 17, *The Woman in the Sky* when the story of the birth of the child-god by a "woman clothed with the sun" (Rev. 12) is examined.

The above comparisons of Revelation's Lamb with Egypt's juvenile, ram-headed form of Re emphasize the most readily recognizable attributes common to both sources. They do not, however, compare *events* or *sequences of events* associated with the lamb. Such an approach is beyond the scope of this chapter and more properly belongs with detailed discussions of the sun-god's travels through the Netherworld depicted in the *Amduat* and the *Book of Gates*. The events involving the Lamb in Rev. 5:6 will be discussed as part of our examination of the *Amduat* in Chapter 9, *Opening of the Scroll*. Similarly, other situations, such as the one involving the Lamb standing on a mountain in Rev 14.11, his throne in the heavenly city in Rev 22.1, his relationship to his 144,000 followers mentioned in Rev 14, his death that people may live in Rev 5.9, his provisions and comforts afforded them in Rev. 7:17, and finally, his relationship to the bride in Rev. 19.7 will be examined in later chapters.

God *and* the Lamb

Included in the Book of Revelation are several, somewhat ambiguous references to either another deity or a combination of two deities. These include Rev. 7:10, Rev. 14:1, Rev. 21:22-23, and Rev. 22:1-3. The last one makes reference to "the throne of God *and* of the Lamb" and Rev. 21:22-23 is just as ambiguous. The temple of the holy city in Rev. 21:22 is defined as "the Lord God the Almighty *and* the Lamb" while Rev. 21:23 says "city has no need of sun or moon to shine upon it, for the glory of God is its light, *and* its lamp is the Lamb." These passages, Rev. 22:1-3 and Rev. 21:22-23, suggest a very close relationship between God and the Lamb in the Book of Revelation.

If we look closely at Rev. 22:1-3, we find three possible interpretations of the phrase, "God and the Lamb": (1) God and the Lamb share the same throne, (2) there are two thrones, one for each, or (3) God and the Lamb are one. From an Egyptian perspective, the last one is the most appropriate interpretation. Reasons for this will become obvious throughout the course of this book when we discuss how similar ambiguities appear during the daily course of the sun-god through the Egyptian heavens and the Netherworld where Osiris (who parallels God in Revelation) and Re (who parallels the Lamb) effectively lose their separate identities to become a single unified deity. Furthermore, it will be pointed out that the *circumstances* in which this dual form appears in Egyptian texts also conform with those described in the Book of Revelation. It will serve our purpose here to simply discuss the basic concept of Revelation's "God *and* the Lamb" and how it relates to ancient Egypt's similar – and important – concept of "Osiris *and* Re."

Hornung (1990) tells us that "shining images in the Books of the Netherworld and the Litany of Re relate the nocturnal encounter of two great gods, and their fusion into a single form, the 'Joint God.'"[70] He is speaking of Osiris and Re. Their union is not, however, viewed as simple syncretism of two different gods, but rather a temporary commingling in which each deity becomes one with the other to fulfil an important mythological function. A picture of this unified form of Osiris and Re, called *Osiris-Re* or *Re-Osiris* by Egyptologists, has been identified in a well-known relief in the

Figure 13. The united form of Osiris and Re, commonly referred to as *Osiris-Re*, with Nephthys and Isis in attendance. The mummified body signifies Osiris ("God on throne" in Revelation) while the solar disk and ram's head signifies Re (Revelation's "Lamb"). The accompanying text and the theological meaning of this picture conform with the idea in Rev. 22:1-3 of two simultaneously ruling deities.

tomb of Nefertari and shown here as Figure 13. Hornung (1983) comments on the ambiguity which is deliberately built into this figure. He says that it "shows a ram-headed mummy between Isis and Nephthys captioned 'this is Re when he has come to rest (*ḥtp*) in Osiris" and "this is Osiris when he has come to rest in Re'; it is thus deliberately left open which god has come to rest in the other."[71] Elsewhere, Hornung says that,

> The union of Re and Osiris was conceived as temporary rather than eternal however. Re continually takes up new forms: Khepri's beetle in the morning, Harakhty's falcon at midday, Atum's ram in the evening, and the form of Osiris in the deepest night. He thus achieves sovereignty in the realm of the dead, and the deceased pharaoh may partake thereof, in his role as son of Re and heir of Osiris.[72]

In the New Kingdom the main thrust of worship shifted from Re in the sky to Osiris in the Netherworld, Re's role as the sun-god's soul, or *ba*, dominated the daytime sky and was seen to commingle with his body (represented by Osiris) in the Netherworld during his sojourn through the darkness of night. At times, this union was seen as extending into the daytime sky as is apparent in Chapter 119 of the *Book of the Dead*:

> Hail to you, Osiris ...
> Raise yourself.
> Yours is the might in Rosetau,
> Yours the power in Abydos.
> Crossing the heavens, sailing with Re,
> You behold your people.[73]

Hornung (1990) says that this

> final verse may surprise us, as Osiris is doomed to remain in the Netherworld. But the god who emerges triumphantly before our eyes from the gates of the eastern horizon is in fact the *ba* [soul] of Osiris, which traverses the arc of the heavens with Re, and with Re the souls of the deceased remain eternally in the light of the sun.[74]

It is therefore not surprising that, as Hornung (1983) points out,

> In the *Book of the Dead* the two gods are felt to be a unity to such an extent that in many passages their names appear to be interchangeable, while in the *Amduat* the corpse of the sun god is at the same time the corpse of Osiris. At the judgment of the dead it is not clear which of the two entirely different gods properly should preside."[75]

The interchangeability of, and even unification of Osiris and Re thus conform with the ambiguity of Revelation's expression, "God *and* the Lamb." The concept of Revelation's "God and the Lamb" and Egypt's "Osiris-Re" thus parallel one another. During the course of this book, we will occasionally examine passages in the Book of Revelation which conform with this idea. And to further accentuate the parallel, it will be shown that sequences of such events in Revelation at times follow similar sequences of events in Egyptian sources.

The Amen

Rev. 3:14 speaks of "The words of *the Amen*, the faithful and true witness, the *beginning of God's creation*." The name of the Egyptian god, *'Imn* (Figure 14) has been variously transliterated into English as not only Amen, but also Àmen, Amana, Amon, Ammon, Amūn, and Amun. Amen was possibly the most revered and feared of Egyptian deities and was at times known as the "King of the Gods." His name is based on the word *'imn*, which means a "hidden person or thing" or "secret"[76] so that his name, *'Imn*, meant "the hidden one" and was usually understood to mean "Àmun, 'the hidden god' who is in heaven."[77] Hornung (1983) says that Amen was most often "shown with a tall crown of feathers; often in the form of [the god] Min, as well as ram and goose forms. ... From 2000 to 1360 BCE he is preeminent among the deities and combines in a single figure *all the characteristics of the creator* and sustainer of the world."[78] Amen was originally a local deity at Khmun in Middle Egypt until his cult reached Thebes. At Thebes, and to endow him with unrivaled power, the local princes who founded the Eighteenth dynasty associated him with the sun-god Re of Heliopolis;[79] he thus became known as the supreme deity Amen-Re and became the national god of Egypt.[80]

The name Amen is used in Rev. 3:14 where the speaker tells the angel of the church at Laodicea to write, "The words of the Amen, the faithful and true witness, the beginning of God's creation." This passage has a distinctly Egyptian ring to it. Indeed, it seems to be a precis of the opening words in one of the many Hymns to Amen-Re. For example, consider the following:

> This august god, Lord of all gods,
> Amon-Re, Lord of the Thrones of the Two Lands,
> He who is at the fore of Karnak.
> August Soul (*b3*), *who came into being at the beginning,*
> the Great God who lives on *Truth*,
> *the first primeval one* who fashioned the primeval gods,
> he out of whom every other god came into being.
> The Unique one, *who created what existed*,
> *who at the first time created the earth.* [81]

Figure 14. Amen (*'Imn*), the Egyptian "King of the Gods," wearing a double-plumed crown and carrying a *was* scepter. His attributes conform with those of *the Amen* in the Book of Revelation.

Note that, the concept of truth is central to both passages; Revelation's Amen is called a "true witness" while the Egyptian hymn refers to Amen as one "who lives on Truth." The concept of the beginning of creation is also found in both; while Revelation refers to him as "the beginning of God's creation," the Egyptian text refers to him as one "who came into being at the beginning" and calls him "the first primeval one" as well and the one "who created what existed, who at the first time created the earth."

Clagett (1989) says this hymn expresses the ideas found in other hymns to Amen-Re in that "it demonstrates Amun's position as the first primeval god from whom all others came into being."[82] Another Hymn to Amen-Re, as in Rev. 3:14, emphasizes the spoken word in relation to truth and the beginning of creation. "Hail to you, O Re, lord of *maat'* [truth]. ... Who gave commands (lit. decreed words) and the gods came into being. ... who made the people."[83] Part of this quotation, "who gave *commands*,'" is suggestive of the opening phrase of Rev. 3:14 – "The *words* of the Amen." Clagett also refers to Amen-Re's use of the creative spoken word in reference to the creative process mentioned in other hymns: "For example, notice how the doctrine of the creative word is expressed in the Ramesside hymn to Amon-Re-Atum-Harakhti, 'who spoke with his mouth and there came into being men, gods, cattle and all goats in their totality (and further) all that flies and alights.'"[a] The juxtaposition of references to Amen, his spoken word and its truth, and the link with the beginning of creation are common themes among hymns to Amen and represent, as a group, parallels to "the Amen" in Rev. 3 :14.[b]

Christ

The names of "Christ" and "Jesus Christ" in both ancient and modern versions of the Book of Revelation have played and continue to play a paramount role in the widespread belief in its Christian origin. Nevertheless, as will be demonstrated here, there are parallels between both these names and names in ancient Egyptian texts.

References to "Christ" in the Book of Revelation are based on the Greek word, *christos,* which means "anointed."[84] Some parts of the book include the definitive article *toú* before *christos* (Rev. 11:15; Rev. 12:10; and Rev. 20:4,6) and these can be translated as meaning "*the* anointed one." Other references to Christ do not include the article (Rev. 1:1,2,5,9 and Rev. 20:4). *Vine's Expository Dictionary of Biblical Words* explains the difference:

> As to the use or absence of the article, the title with the article specifies the Lord Jesus as 'the Christ'; the title without the article stresses His character and His relationship with believers. Again, speaking generally, when the title is the subject of a sentence it has the article; when it forms part of the predicate the article is absent.[85]

We may therefore say that even when *toú christos* is not used, "the anointed one" is implied.

---

[a] Clagett (1989, pp. 319-320) says this quote is a "slightly altered" translation by A.H. Gardiner's *Hieratic Papyri in the British Museum: Third Series, Chester Beatty Gift,* Vol. I (London, 1935), p. 32.

[b] The name Amen appears nine more times in other parts of Revelation (Rev. 1:6, Rev. 1:7, Rev. 1:18, Rev. 5:14, Rev. 19:4, Rev. 22:20, Rev. 22:21 and twice in Rev. 7:12) although in these cases, it seems *not* to be used as the name of a deity. Instead, and unlike extant Egyptian texts, it is used in much the same way as in many parts of the Old and New Testaments, i.e., in the Hebrew sense of commentary such as "true," "so be it!" "verily," or "truly." Moreover, the use of the word "Amen" in Rev. 19:4 is ambiguous with respect to the name of Egypt's Amen. The verse reads, "And the twenty-four elders and the four living creatures fell down and worshiped God who is seated on the throne, saying "Amen. Hallellujah!"

But Revelation also links the name "Jesus" to *christos* to form the name "Jesus Christ" (for example, in Rev. 1:1,2,5,9; Rev. 12:17 and Rev. 22:21). Few authorities express doubt about the validity of the inclusion of references to Jesus in the Book of Revelation and Christian theologians generally accept them without question. Nevertheless, there are reasons to question their validity. The first is that the many variants of the Book of Revelation exhibit very little uniformity in the use of the names, "Jesus," "Christ," or combinations thereof. For example, a remarkable variation is found in the first verse of Codex 4 of the Armenian Version translated by Conybeare (1907). In it, instead of the opening phrase (in the RSV) of Revelation stating that the book represents *"The revelation of Jesus Christ,* which God gave him to show to his servants what must soon take place ...," Codex 4 reads, "The *revelation of John the Evangelist,* which he saw. Blessed are they that hear and do the things therein written. For the time is near."[86] Thus, the Armenian version, unlike earlier versions of this verse, does not mention Jesus and can be interpreted to mean the revelation was that of John rather than of Jesus Christ. This, and the absence of references to Jesus in certain other parts of the original documents, suggests disagreement among at least some of the early scribes who copied the manuscripts. Furthermore, Ford (1975), in commenting on the references to "Jesus Christ" in Revelation, noted that most of them

> ... do not occur in the main body of the work but rather in the beginning and the end, which may be Christian additions. ... Further, "Christ" is never anarthrous, and could refer to any anointed one among the Jews, either priest, prophet, or king. ... but in Revelation this lordship is associated only twice with the name of Jesus (22:20,21). ... what few Christological references Revelation contains are ambiguous at best.[87]

We cannot, therefore, categorically state that the lost original copy of the Book of Revelation in fact contained references to the name "Jesus." It is against this brief background of uncertainties concerning the reference to "Jesus" and Christianity's "Christ" in the book that we may critically examine potential Egyptian parallels to the characteristics of Christ in the Book of Revelation.

Rev. 1:5 is the first verse to mention any of Christ's characteristics. It says that he is a "faithful witness, the first-born of the dead, and the ruler of kings on earth ... who loves us and has freed us from our sins by his blood." Perhaps the most informative element here is that Christ is called "the ruler of kings on earth." This same title was often applied to the king of Egypt who was believed to be the earthly incarnation of the god Horus. From the 4th Dynasty on, Horus was recognized as the "Son of Re"[88] or the "Son of Amen."[89] He was also referred to as the "Son of Osiris."[90] These titles applied whether to Horus of the Netherworld or Horus, the king of Egypt. But it is in the form of Horus the son of Osiris (Figure 15) that he most closely resembles the Christ of the Book of Revelation for it is Horus who, like the Christ of Christianity, was known as "the first born of the dead." Horus was also known as "the ruler of the kings of the earth" and played a pivotal role in a bloody struggle of good against evil so that the description of "he who freed us from our sins by his blood" may also be applicable to him.

3. The Preeminent Deities

The essence of the myth in which these various aspects of Horus is laid out with exceptional clarity is presented by Horning (1990), as follows:

> Osiris is not only murdered by his brother Seth, but actually dismembered, the pieces of his body thrown helter-skelter into the Nile and consigned to oblivion. The worst kind of death has overtaken him before he has been able to beget an heir who will ensure the continuity of his kingship. ... Loyalty beyond death achieves the miracle. Isis, the wife-sister of Osiris, gathers the various parts of his body with help from her friends, and supplies the missing phallus to assure her husband *a posthumous child by conceiving Horus from Osiris's dead body*.' Seth's scheme is thwarted: Horus' presence guarantees the victory of right and parentage, the transmission of the inheritance from father to son, which cannot be interrupted even by violence. Horus must still prove his mettle, but he triumphs in the end, using deceit and Isis's magical powers to overcome *Seth's reliance on unrefined violence*' [against Horus]. Ceremoniously, the divine magistrates at Heliopolis decide the matter: Osiris is given the Sovereignty of the depths into which he descended, and *Horus is made king of earth*' ... the ruling pharaoh.[91]

The attributes of Christ expressed in the Book of Revelation conform with those of Egypt's Horus, as follows:

First-born of the dead (Rev. 1:5):- A varient of the above story is found on the *Stele of Paris*. It says that Isis "made air to come into being by means of her two wings, and she cried the death cry for her brother [Osiris]. She made to rise up the inert members of him whose heart was at rest. She drew from him his essence, and she made therefrom an heir [Horus]."[92] Meanwhile, a dramatic and ingenious picture depicting the birth of Horus is found in the second register of the *Book of the Aker* and shown here as Figure 16. The text describing it says,

Figure 15. Horus, the Son of Osiris/Son of Re, is usually depicted in human form with the head of a falcon. His earthly incarnation was Pharaoh, King of Egypt and his attributes conform with those of the *christos*, the Christ, "the anointed one" in the Book of Revelation.

Figure 16. Isis and Nephthys stand at the foot and head of Osiris's body as his posthumous son, the hawk-headed Horus emerges from his body in the presence of Re, shown here as a solar disk (O). This scene is consistent with the *christos* of Revelation being the "first-born of the dead" as in Rev. 1:5. (B.A.D. 3rd picture)

The Great God is like this in his egg which is in the Netherworld. *Horus comes out of the body of his father,* and praises him who has procreated him while the two goddesses [Isis and Nephthys] join his body. This Great God [Re] speaks to him while he sees the rays of his disk.[93]

Hornung (1990) associates this concept with Chapter 18 of the *Book of the Dead* which says, "Horus came from the seed of his father when he was already putrid."[94] In this manner, the reference in Rev. 1:5 to Christ being "born of the dead" quite literally parallels this event in Egyptian mythology.

Ruler of Earth (Rev. 1:5):- Horus's destiny as the ruler of the earth was foreseen before his birth and announced by his mother shortly after she became pregnant. One version of this story says,

> The lightning flash strikes, the gods are afraid, Isis wakes pregnant with the seed of her brother Osiris. She is uplifted, (even she) the widow, and her heart is glad with the seed of her brother Osiris. She says: 'O you gods, I am Isis, the sister of Osiris, who wept for the father of the gods, (even) Osiris who judged the slaughterings of the Two Lands. His seed is within my womb, I have molded the shape of the god within the egg as my son who is at the head of the Ennead. *What he shall rule is the land, the heritage of his (grand-) father Gēb·* [the earth-god] ... .[95]

Horus, the posthumous son of Osiris, was reared up in secret by Isis and upon maturity sought retribution for the atrocities his uncle Seth had inflicted on his father. Seth had an overwhelming desire for the throne of Egypt and the two fought numerous battles over it until a stalemate was reached and the conflict was finally settled by a court of divine magistrates. Horus's claim to the throne was vindicated and many hymns were written to proclaim his victorious rise to power. One hymn to Osiris reads:

> Thy [Osiris'] son Horus is triumphant before the whole company of the gods.
> *Sovereignty over the world·* hath been given unto him,
> And *his dominion is in the uttermost parts of the earth.·* [96]

The 183rd Chapter of the *Book of the Dead* refers to this dominion in no uncertain terms:

> Horus is vindicated in the presence of the entire Ennead: the kingship over the land has been given to him ... *The throne of Geb (the earth) has been allotted to him,·* and the potent office of Atum has been confirmed in writing in a testament which has been

engraved on a block of sandstone, according as your father Ptah-Tatenen commanded from upon the great throne.[97]

Horus was believed to have two manifestations, one in the afterlife and the other on the earth. In the afterlife, in the Egyptian Tuat, he was known as "Horus of the Netherworld" while his earthly incarnation was Pharaoh, king of Egypt, son of Osiris (or the son of Re, depending on the context)[a] and the sun-god's sole representative on the entire earth. Near a picture of the king on a pillar in the Tomb of Ramesses VI the text reads, "I give thee the South as well as the North, the West as well as the East, all the foreign lands are under thy soles, *all the lands are at thy feet.*"[b] All Egyptians viewed their king, not only as ruler of Egypt, but as sovereign over all foreign lands. (In reality, of course, he did not always exercise this authority.)

Horus is the only Egyptian deity which can be readily and so consistently recognized as both the "first-born of the dead" (Osiris) and "ruler of kings on earth" as described for the Christ in Rev. 1:5. These two features alone lend strong weight to the parallel between Revelation's *christos* and Egypt's Horus.

The Anointed One (Rev. 1:1):- As noted above, *toú christos*, the Greek words used for "the Christ" in the Book of Revelation, means *the anointed one*. Three types of ancient anointing are typically recognized: the first is related to healing, the second to consecration, and the third to ordination. As healing, it was used to apply the power of natural and supernatural forces to the sick and thereby ward off the influences of diseases and demons. As consecration, it applied to people and sacred objects used for the pleasure of the divine in a holy place; sometimes weapons were dedicated to his service. As an act of ordination, anointing was used in rituals to dedicate certain men to positions of eminence. "In ancient Israel and various Christian cultures, the king was anointed during his coronation as the one chosen by God to rule over the people."[98] The Old Testament commonly uses anointing in the sense of setting apart an individual for an office or function. Elijah was anointed to be a prophet (1 Kings 19:16); more generally, kings were anointed to their office[99] (1 Samuel 16:12; 1 Kings 1:39). The reference to the "authority" of Christ in Rev. 12:10 suggests that, of these three possible uses of *the christos,* the act of ordination best reflects the original intention of the writer where he says that, "Now the salvation and the power and the kingdom of our God and the authority of his Christ have come." It is clear that *the christos,* "the anointed one" of Revelation is in reference to an individual being anointed to an office of authority.

Sawyer (1993) says that the main biblical usage of "anointed" is "virtually a synonym of 'king,' in particular David and his descendants, and it should be understood in the context of the royal ideology documented in the books of Samuel, Kings and Psalms, even when it is applied secondarily to priests and others."[100] We

---

[a] Two popular myths were generally accepted by the ancient Egyptians. The oldest was that Horus was the son of Osiris, as described above; the other was that he was the son of Re, the sun-god, a belief which developed as part of the Heliopolitan doctrines. (See Clagett, 1989, Section II, Chapter 2, *The World and Its Creation: Cosmogony and Cosmology*, p. 263 ff.)

[b] In the Tomb of Ramesses VI, Face D of Pillar III in Hall E; see Piankoff (1954), p. 23.

may conclude from this that the meaning of the word anointed (*christos*) in the Book of Revelation depends to a large extent on when the book was written. If it was written during the Old Testament period, for example, it would likely imply a king; after the postexilic period, (i.e., after about 536 BCE) it could mean a priest or a king, and by the end of the Old Testament Period it was used for the coming of a national savior or messiah to the Jews. After this, it came to mean the Christ of Christianity.

The use of *christos* throughout the entire Book of Revelation conforms with the meaning associated with a king or ruler. For example, in Rev. 1:5 we read that Christ is "the ruler of kings on earth," and in Rev. 11:15, "The kingdom of the world has become the kingdom of our Lord and of his Christ, and he shall reign for ever and ever." The "authority of Christ" is mentioned in Rev. 12:10 while in Rev. 20:4 the faithful are promised that they will "reign with Christ a thousand years." This latter promise is expanded in Rev. 20:6 to refer to "priests of God and of Christ," a phrase which the Hebrews during Old Testament times would have interpreted as being "priests of god and the king." It is therefore apparent that the simplest and most straightforward indication for the use of *the christos* in the Book of Revelation is that it almost always implies kingship.

The king of Egypt can be referred to as "the anointed one" simply because he was anointed king during his coronation. In Egypt, this involved a ceremonial purification as a main feature of the coronation of Egyptian kings, as shown in Figure 17.[a] If we interpret Revelation in an Egyptian context, we may conclude that *the christos* of Revelation parallels the king, the "son of the sun," the "son of Re," "the son of Osiris," and Horus, the King of Egypt. This conforms with a similar conclusion already made from the examination of Horus as being the first born of the dead (Osiris) and ruler of the world.

The Morning Star (Rev. 22:16):- Rev. 22:16 tells us that Jesus refers to himself as "the bright morning star." The ancient Egyptians believed that stars in general were living entities. The Morning Star, however, had special significance. Like Horus who leads the deceased to his father's throne in the final judgment, the Morning Star led the deceased into the glorious hereafter. Chapter 122 of the *Book of the Dead*

Figure 17. King Seti I is anointed with the water of "life" (☥) by the gods Seth and Horus as they participate in his coronation ceremony. The king thus assumes the title of "the anointed one" as does the Christ of the Book of Revelation.

---

[a] In the Middle East generally, the act of anointing typically involved the ritual application of oil or fat to the head or body of a person or to an object although both its implementation and substance used varied among the religions. Revelation does not state which substance is used, whether by oil, fat or water.

says, "the Morning Star has made a path for me, and I enter in peace into the beautiful West."[101] Moreover, a more ancient *Pyramid Text* (Ut. 519 §1207), refers to Horus as the Morning Star with the words, "*O morning star, Horus of the Netherworld,*' divine Falcon, w₃ḏ₃ḏ-bird whom the sky bore: Hail to you."[102] It is thus clear that the otherworldly Horus was, like Revelation's Christ, called the morning star. Meanwhile, Clagett (1989) says that "The king himself [i.e., the earthly incarnation of Horus] is sometimes seen as the Morning Star itself"[103] Egypt's description of Horus as the morning star is thus identical to Revelation's description of Jesus.

The Faithful Witness (Rev. 1:5a):- We have already observed that ancient Egypt was a theocracy ruled over by a king, the sun-god's representative on earth. As Horus, son of the sun-god, the king was considered by his subjects to represent the final word of authority in all matters of religion and state; he was thus the sun-god's mouthpiece and hence, his witness to the Egyptians. The 130th Chapter of the *Book of the Dead* refers to Horus as "having approached his lord, whose seats are secret, whose shrine is pure, messenger of the god to him whom he loved. I am one who takes hold of Maat [*truth*]."[104] Messengers, of course bear witness of those who send them and a faithful messenger is one who speaks the truth, i.e., they speak only those words instructed by the master. And they do so accurately, as in Rev. 1:5a. As the divine anointed one of the Great God, his wishes, words and commands were those of the sun-god himself. It is easy to imagine Horus having been viewed as the faithful witness of the sun-god who speaks for his father. It is just as easy to to see how this parallels the idea of a "faithful witness" mentioned in Rev. 1:5a.

But there is another aspect of Horus which conforms with the idea of a faithful witness – and it even more closely parallels that of Revelation's Christ. It involves what is perhaps Horus's most critical role on behalf of the deceased in the afterlife: Horus' introduction of the deceased to Osiris during the ceremony of the judgment of the dead. Judgment scenes typically show a balance with the heart of the deceased laid on one pan and the feather of truth *(maat)* on the other. "O my heart of different ages!" the deceased petitions his own heart, "Do not stand up as a witness against me, do no be opposed to me in the tribunal, do not be hostile to me in the presence of the Keeper of the Balance."[105] After the heart of the deceased is successfully weighed against the feather of truth, the deceased is brought before Osiris by Horus who then bears witness to the results of the trial (Figure 7). Chapter 30B of the *Book of the Dead* records his words:

> Thus says Horus son of Isis: I have come to you, O Wennefer [Osiris], and I bring *N* [the deceased] to you. His heart is true, having gone forth from the balance, and he has not sinned against any god or any goddess. Thoth has judged him in writing which has been told to the Ennead [who also served as judges], and Maat the great [the goddess of truth] has witnessed. Let there be given to him bread and beer which have been issued in the presence of Osiris, and he will be forever like the Followers of Horus.[106]

After this statement, Osiris accepts the deceased into his kingdom and land is granted to him "in the Field of Offerings as for the Followers of Horus."[107] Horus's role in the final judgment thus placed him firmly in the minds of the Osirian penitent as Horus, the final "faithful witness" of the dead before Osiris, in complete accord with the words of Revelation's Christ in Rev. 1:5.

Freed by his Blood (Rev. 1:5b):- Rev. 1:5 also tells us that Christ "has freed us from our sins by his blood." This statement is somewhat ambiguous if we try to interpret it in the context of Osirian beliefs for it is unclear as to whose blood it refers. For example, one might ask if it refers to the Christ mentioned in the first half of the verse, i.e., the one who parallels Egypt's Horus? Or does it refer to Osiris, his father who died before Horus was conceived and who was resurrected by his sister Isis (see above)? Different myths describe how both Osiris and Horus were horribly mutilated by Seth and we have already discussed the brutal dismemberment of Osiris by him. A brief review of Horus's conflicts with Seth is therefore instructive if we are to assume that Horus parallels Revelation's Christ referred to in Rev. 1:5.

Horus and Seth had numerous battles and legends abounded of terrible injuries received by Horus. In one myth, Horus is killed but "[Thoth] taught the goddess Isis spells whereby she ... expelled the poison from the body of her son Horus after he was stung by the scorpion sent by Seth."[108] Another myth says that Isis' son, Horus, "was killed by Titans who threw his body into the water, but having administered ... medicine to him, he not only came to life again but became immortal."[109] Still another tradition involves the famed "eye of Horus"; Chapter 17th of the *Book of the Dead* touches on this during its account of the fight between Horus and Seth on "the day when Horus fought with Seth when he inflicted injury on Horus's face."[110] Breasted (1912), reviews the details of the fight:

> The battle of Horus and Seth[a] ... waged so fiercely that the young god lost his eye at the hands of his father's enemy. When Seth was overthrown, and it was finally recovered by Thoth, this wise god spat upon the wound and healed it. ... Horus now seeks his father, even crossing the sea in his quest, that he may raise his father from the dead and offer to him the eye which he has sacrificed in his father's behalf. This act of filial devotion, preserved to us in the *Pyramid Text* ... made the already sacred Horus-eye doubly revered in the tradition and feeling of the Egyptians. It became the symbol of all sacrifice; *every gift or offering might be called a "Horus-eye."*[111]

Horus won the battle with Seth in spite of his wound and his victory meant that Egyptians were saved from domination by the evil form of Seth. In effect, Egyptians were "freed from Seth's dominion by the blood of Horus."

A note on the name "Jesus":- The above analysis does not critically examine the name "Jesus" which is at times closely linked with the name of Christ in the Book of Revelation. If we were to assume that the Book of Revelation was not originally a Christian document, one possibility for the presence of Jesus' name in it is that early Christian redactors mistakenly substituted or added the name Jesus to references to the *christos* found in the original Greek in order to add variation to the text or to

---

[a] Clagett (1989, p. 141), notes that this battle was associated with the town of *Kheraha*, "a kind of suburb of Heliopolis." "Kheraha" means "The Place of the Battle" and was called "Babylon" by the Greeks, a place-name which plays a major role in the Book of Revelation. This will be discussed in Chapter 13, *Catastrophes*.

3. The Preeminent Deities

accentuate its perceived Christian character. This type of change to ancient texts not only could happen, but in fact did happen and it is generally accepted among today's bible scholars as an explanation for the book's many variants. It also forms the basis of Ford's (1975) criticism on the disproportionate occurrence of the name "Jesus Christ" and "Jesus" in different parts of the Greek text.[a] A concrete example of how this could have happened to some of the old manuscripts is provided in Conybeare's (1907) analysis of nine different Armenian sources of the Book of Revelation.[112] "Jesus" was added to the text of Rev. 1:9b in two or more of the versions and "Jesus Christ," "Jesus," or "Christ Jesus" was added to verses in two or more of the sources. Similarly, "Jesus Christ" was added to Rev. 22:20-22 in two or more versions and "Jesus" was omitted from two or more versions of Rev. 19:10. The identification of *the christos* in some parts of the Book of Revelation with Jesus, the Christ of Christianity, is therefore suspect.

In spite of the above doubts as to the validity of the presence of the name Jesus in the original version of Book of Revelation, we are bound to examine its presence from an Egyptological point of view, particularly with respect to phonetic similarities with several Egyptian names for Horus and the Hebrew name for Jesus. If "Horus" was written in Egyptian as *Ḥeru-sa,* meaning "Horus, the son of..."[113] in the earliest drafts of Revelation, it could have been misinterpreted by early translators. *Ḥeru-sa* has a roughly similar sound to the Greek and Hebrew words for Jesus, *Iēsou* and *Iesoûs*[b] (the later of which is pronounced *ee-ay-sooce'*).[114] A related possibility would be that the original text made reference to the singing of praises to Horus using the Egyptian word *ḥessu,* meaning "praises, hymns of praise, songs" or "one who is praised,"[115] or a similar word, *ḥesiu,* meaning "singers and musicians."[116] In this possibility, the original text could have had a mixture of both Egyptian and Greek words which said something like *"ḥesiu christos."* This would have been translated by unwary or overzealous Christian redactors as "Jesus Christ, the one who is praised," where the name of Jesus would have been added for clarity. Of course it is difficult to say with any degree of certainty that such manipulations or misinterpretations of early manuscripts contributed to the inclusion of the references to the name Jesus. But,

---

[a] Ford (1975) points out that, "Disproportionate occurrence of the phrases 'Jesus Christ' and "Jesus" in chs. 1-3 suggests that these chapters are a later Christian addition. 'Jesus Christ' occurs only in Rev 1:1, 2, 5, and nowhere else in the whole of the text." He also says that there are variants which read 'Jesus Christ,' (for example, Rev 1:9) and says both the "variants 'Christ Jesus' and 'Jesus Christ'" and "Jesus" are prominent in this section, appearing five times in chs. 1-3, compared with eight times in the whole of the rest of the text. Chs. 4-11which probably comprised the first section of the original work contain not one occurrence of either 'Jesus Christ' or 'Jesus.' In chs. 12-22 the name 'Jesus' appears in 12:17, 14:12, 17:6, 19:10 (*bis*), 20:4, 22:16, 20."

[b] Errors involving the mixing of Egyptian, Greek and Hebrew words would be consistent with a situation where the original text was written in Greek by a Hebrew scribe who was not thoroughly familiar with the Greek translations of certain Egyptian words as he attempted to portray an Egyptian story in Greek.

considering the abundance of other Egyptian parallels in the Book of Revelation, it should be considered a possibility.

Conclusion:- The strongest argument in favor of Horus being an Egyptian parallel to Revelation's Christ is that he was both the "first born of the dead" *and* "the ruler of kings on earth." The earthly manifestation of Horus was recognized as the king, "the anointed one," an expression equivalent to the *christos* in our oldest Greek versions of the Book of Revelation. Revelation's *christos* also parallels Horus the fighter who sacrificed his eye, and hence his blood (Rev. 1:5b) in a great and terrible battle against his brother Seth, the powerful god of evil. And later, in the final judgment of the dead, it is Horus as a "faithful witness" who testifies before Osiris on behalf of the deceased, just as Christ does in Rev. 1:5a. When all the above pieces of evidence are considered together, we can readily see a particularly strong parallel between Egypt's Horus and Revelation's Christ.

Discussion

In this chapter, evidence was presented that Revelation's God on the throne parallels Osiris, the ancient Egyptian god of the dead while the Christ of Revelation was shown to parallel the Egyptian god Horus, the son of Osiris (or of Re) and the sun-god's representative on earth. The Egyptian counterpart of the Lamb was identified with the juvenile, ram-headed form of the sun-god Re which was believed to be in the fetal form as he passed through the Netherworld before being born into the morning sky. "The Amen" of Revelation paralleled the powerful sun-god, Amen or Amen-Re. Evidence for these parallels is generally straightforward and unambiguous. Furthermore, the fact that we find all four of these deities associated with the throne scene in both sources supports the individual arguments for their parallel nature.

As pointed out in Chapter 1, *The Enigmatic Book of Revelation,* Massy (1907) proposes an Egyptian origin for Revelation's God on the throne and for Christ and the Lamb. It is only after he establishes parallel characters within general Christian beliefs and traditions that he applies these observations to the Book of Revelation. In contrast, this study is restricted to a direct and dedicated comparison of text of the Book of Revelation with Egyptian beliefs and traditions; special effort is made *not* to let Christian interpretations and opinions of the book, which have developed since the dawn of Christianity, influence interpretations of specific names, events and passages in Revelation. Massey equates God on the throne with Horus who, he says, appears as the human form of his father Osiris and the God Atum. He also suggests that the Lamb of Revelation can be equated with Horus, basing this conclusion on the New Testament's Lamb being representative of Christ (as in 1 John 1:29,36; Acts 8:32; 1 Peter 1:19). His identification of the Lamb clearly differs from the current results which show that Revelation's Lamb parallels the juvenile ram-headed form of the sun-god, Re. While his parallel between Christ and Horus agrees in part with this work, his conclusion is based primarily on arguments which are difficult and at times impossible to follow. Other differences between the present results and Massey's conclusions will be presented in Chapter 28, *Egyptian Deities in the Book of Revelation*.

3. The Preeminent Deities

In summary, several parallels between important, mainstream Egyptian deities and those in the Book of Revelation have been demonstrated: (1) The deity who sits on the throne in the first and second chapters of Revelation parallels Osiris, the Egyptian god of the dead, (2) the "Lamb" of Revelation parallels the juvenile form of Re, the Egyptian sun-god as he travels in his juvenile form through the Netherworld to be reborn into the morning sky, (3) "God and the Lamb" conforms with the joint god, Osiris-Re, (4) Christ, "the anointed one" of Revelation conforms with Horus, the son of the god Osiris and (5) the Amen can be identified with the Egyptian god Amen (or Amen-Re). Further evidence for each of these conclusions will be presented in the context of numerous parallels between scenes and between sequence of scenes in Egyptian sources and the Book of Revelation.

The next chapter will describe general aspects of the throne scene and a number of beings and groups of beings in its vicinity; their descriptions will be compared with attributes of other important deities in ancient Egyptian beliefs.

Chapter 4. Other Characters in Revelation[117]

The previous chapter focused on five deities associated with the throne scene in the Book of Revelation. The central deity on the throne in the 1st chapter of Revelation was deemed to parallel Osiris, the Egyptian god of the dead who is quite often shown seated on a throne. Closely linked to him was the Lamb who was identified with to the juvenile form of the Egyptian sun-god, Re. Revelation's "God and the Lamb" paralleled Egypt's "joint god," Osiris-Re. "The Amen" conformed with the god Amen while Christ "the anointed one" of Revelation was similar to Horus, "the anointed," son of Osiris and perceived ruler of earth. Each of these deities are portrayed as benevolent deities in both the Book of Revelation and Egyptian sources.

This chapter extends the study on parallels to the characters around the throne to include several other deities, some of which may be considered benevolent and others, evil. For example, among those who support the one on the throne are seven spirits and seven "lampstands." There are also four creatures, each of which is described as having a different head and other distinctive features. Twenty-four seated elders, clothed in white, praise the one on the throne while an unspecified number of judges sit on thrones of their own and assist in the judging of the dead. Also, there are numerous references to angels, some of which are uncharacteristic of Judaeo-Christian beings. All these are presented as faithful followers of the one on the throne. Other beings around the throne are described as enemies of God; these include the devil, the beast and the false prophet.

All these will be compared with similar gods in the Egyptian pantheon to provide a logical background for later in-depth comparisons with the Revelation's numerous parallel events, scenes and sequences of scenes.

Four Creatures before the Throne (Rev. 4:6-9)

Four creatures are described in Rev. 4 which are of particular interest to this study because of their peculiarities and relevance to four Egyptian gods and beliefs and traditions associated with them. The Greek text uses the word *zoóa* to describe them,

4. Other Characters in Revelation

a word which literally means a "live thing" or "animal";[a] it is usually translated as "creature."[118] Revelation describes them with a bizarre assortment of animalistic characteristics. Each has a different head: one with the that of a lion, another an ox, one a man and one an eagle (Rev. 4:7). Each has six wings (Rev. 4:8) and is full of eyes "in front and behind, and all round and within" (Rev. 4:6 and Rev. 4:8). These four beings periodically appear throughout Revelation and are directly involved in the worship of God on the throne and overseeing tribulations unleashed upon the earth and its inhabitants. They are typically found either "round the throne," "on each side of the throne" or "before the throne" (Rev. 4:6, Rev. 5:6, Rev. 14:3 and Rev. 19:4).

The idea of a group of four living "creatures" being in such close proximity to an enthroned god is well documented in the Egyptian literature. In texts and paintings they typically stand before the throne of Osiris. And like Rev. 4:7, the *Book of the Dead* shows all four with the bodies of men or human mummies, three of which have heads of animals. In early times they were identified with the four cardinal points and were believed to hold up the four pillars of heaven; *Imsety* was visualized with the head of a man and represented the south, *Hapy* had the head of a baboon and represented the north, *Duamutef* had the head of a jackal and represented the east and *Qebehsenuef,* the north, bore the head of a hawk.[119] Some illustrations depict all four as completely human. They were typically referred to as the "four sons of Osiris" or, sometimes, the "four sons of Horus" (Figure 18).

The four sons of Osiris played several roles but it was as guardians or protectors of the dead that they were best known in ancient Egypt. Pictures of them, or simply their names, were at times used to guard the four corners of coffins.[120] The most revered of the dead, Osiris, had died and was later resurrected to become the Lord of the Dead so he too was given their protection; their presence before the throne of Osiris is therefore quite understandable. They were also depicted in the middle registers of the *Book of Gates* as human-form deities towing the sun-god's barque through the Netherworld where they are typically called "those of the Netherworld." As four human-form deities in the *Book of the Divine Cow*, they assisted in the emergence of Nut, the sky-goddess, into the heavens.

It is in their role as fighters against the enemies of the sun-god that they come closest to the functions of the four creatures before the throne in the Book of Revelation. In the 10th Division of the *Book of Gates* they are shown in totally human form as they capture the sun-god's enemies, the evil serpent Apophis and his followers, thus demonstrating their role as warriors of the sun-god whose "knives are planted into Evil Face [Apophis]."[121] In the *Book of Apophis,* Isis mentions how the four sons of Horus dealt with the evil one: "The four Sons of Horus smash thee with their blows, thou art destroyed by their violence."[122] And in the 17th chapter of the *Book of the Dead* reference is made to them with the words, "Imsety, Hapy, Duamutef

---

[a] Note that the "four creatures" are not described by the same Greek word as those called "beasts" elsewhere in Revelation. The Greek word used here and translated as "creature" is based on *zoóa* while that of "beast," used in Rev. 11:7, is based on *therion* which means a dangerous animal or a venomous or wild beast (Strong's Definition). While most translations follow this usage, the KJV does not distinguish between the two, referring to both *zoóa* and *therion* as "beasts."

Figure 18. The four sons of Osiris/Horus, each bearing the head of a different creature. In this figure they guard a funerary chest; elsewhere, they are frequently depicted as standing in front of the throne of Osiris (see Figure 7).

and Qebehsenuef. Hail to you, Lords of Justice, tribunal which is behind Osiris, who put terror into the doers of wrong, who are in the suite of Her who makes content and protects."[123] Thus, like the four creatures before the throne in the Book of Revelation (for example in Rev. 6 and Rev. 15:7-8 and others), they also fought against evil and were dispensers of the wrath of their god against the enemy; examples of the latter will be presented in detail in later chapters.

We next compare the four sons of Osiris/Horus with the four creatures described in the Book of Revelation; we begin with their appearance. In Revelation, the first living creature is "like a lion, the second living creature like an ox, the third living creature with the face of a man, and the fourth living creature like a flying eagle" (Rev. 4:7). The head of a lion in Revelation is somewhat similar to that of the baboon insofar as both are typically drawn or carved with heavy manes; some Egyptian pictures and carvings of baboons do indeed resemble lions. The head of another is that of a man which is, of course identical in both sources, and the head of an eagle, for practical purposes, is similar to that of a hawk. Thus, with respect to appearance, we find these three to be reasonable Egyptian parallels to three of the four of the creatures described in the Book of Revelation.

The remaining creature has the head of an ox; this bears no resemblance to the jackal-headed *Duamutef*. If there is a parallel between Egypt's jackal and Revelation's ox, we must therefore look beyond their physical appearance. We therefore briefly examine Egyptian words used for ox and note that the Egyptian word for ox is *áua*[124] (plural: *áuau*) while that for a jackal is the remarkably similar word, *áuau*.[125] Similarly, another Egyptian word for ox, *sāb*,[126] is also a close homophone of another word for a jackal, *sab*.[127] Recall that the use of puns was frequently used in the ancient Egyptian language so that these similarities enable the suggestion that the ox and the jackal were closely connected to each other in the minds of the Egyptians. Thus, while Revelation's ox may not physically conform with the Egyptian jackal, it may be considered a parallel from the point of view of phonetic similarities to their names.

This conclusion, of course, conforms with the parallels suggested for the descriptions of other three creatures so that we may now say that there are Egyptian parallels to all four of the creatures before the throne in the Book of Revelation.

But what of the other features of the four creatures in Revelation? We are told that all four are "full of eyes in front and behind ... each of them with six wings, are full of eyes all round and within" (Rev. 4:8). These features have not been recorded for the four sons. They do, however, conform with a certain type of Egyptian deity – the Egyptian *All-god*. Little is known about these gods except that, like the four sons, they were very powerful. They were usually associated with magicians who were supposed to have within themselves the powers and forms of ancient cosmic gods and so assumed the attributes of all the gods of heaven above and the Netherworld below.[128] Budge provides two illustrations of All-gods which have characteristics suggestive of the above characteristics of the four creatures in Revelation. One All-god (Figure 19) has eyes on its body, arms, and legs, thus conforming reasonably well with Rev. 4:8 which says they were "full of eyes in front, and behind," and "full of eyes all round and within." This particular All-god, however, has only four wings in comparison with six in Revelation. Another All-god which Budge calls the "God Comprehending All Gods"[129] (Figure 20) bears the requisite six wings[a] (plus the tail of a bird). When one combines the physical characteristics of the four sons of Osiris with those of Egyptian All-gods, almost all the unusual or even bizarre characteristics of the four creatures in Rev. 4 are accounted for in terms of Egyptian mythology. Furthermore, considering the importance of the four sons to the protection of Osiris (the very body of the sun-god), it is quite conceivable that these four possessed all the fantastic powers of the All-gods – even so much so that they sometimes physically resembled them, or possibly, that the four *were* at times, All-gods.

Figure 19. An Egyptian "All-god" covered with eyes as described in Rev. 4:6, 8.

Figure 20. An Egyptian "All-god" with six wings as described in Rev. 4:8. (The feathered tail in this All-god is quite elaborate so that, at first glance, it gives the impression of having more than six wings; see text.)

---

[a] Four of its six wings are shown as four ▬ symbols while the remaining two are shown as a single ⍦ symbol rotated 45° to the left and centered on the All-God's beetle-shaped body ●.

Seven Spirits of God (Rev. 1:4; 3:1; 4:5; 5:6)

To understand how the Seven Spirits of God in the Book of Revelation parallel spiritual beings in the Egyptian literature, it is prudent to render at least a basic account of the complexity of the Egyptian view of the spirit and other aspects of a person's being.[a] Egyptians believed that a person was made up of seven distinct parts, each of with had its own particular function and separate existence. The most obvious was, of course, the person's physical *body* (which not only served the person on earth, but in the afterlife as well). The next obvious part was the *shadow*, which had an intimate connection with the sun, and hence the sun-god, and was associated with a person being able to move "with the swiftness of a shadow." The *heart* was considered to be the seat of emotions and the intellect. A person's *name* was considered to be so vital a part of a person that its loss, through the ravages of time or the physical destruction of all written records containing it could annihilate the entire person. They believed that one way to gain power over another person or malevolent being was through the mere knowledge of his or her name. For this reason, in addition to their regular names, the Egyptians had secret names which only they knew. The last two parts of a person, the *ba* and the *ka* [k_3[130]], were related to one's spiritual existence. The *ba* was usually considered to be similar or identical to our modern concept of the "soul" and typically manifested itself only when the body died; at death, it was depicted as a bird with a human head, a *ba*-bird, which was free to fly wherever it pleased. The *akh* was that part which after death and a successful, safe journey through the Netherworld takes on the form of a solar or stellar being, thus becoming one of the "blessed dead."[131] The *akh* was therefore closely related to the *soul* which was at times also believed to be represented by the stars, or at times *were* stars. Finally, the *ka* was thought to represent the "vital energy" of human existence and could exist separately from a person's body while he or she was still alive; it's closest parallel in modern Christian beliefs would be the "spirit." But it was possible for a person to have more than one such spirit. This was especially so for powerful deities such as Re, Osiris or Hathor who could have many *kas*. It is this multiplicity of Egyptian *kas*, or spirits, which makes them particularly relevant to our discussion on the Seven Spirits of God described in the Book of Revelation.

The first reference to the seven spirits of God in the Book of Revelation appears in Rev. 1:4 where we read, "Grace to you and peace ... from the seven spirits who are before his throne." Later, in Rev. 4:5 the seven spirits are equated with seven torches: "before the throne burn seven torches of fire, which are the seven spirits of God." Still later, in Rev. 6:6 we are told that the seven spirits are eyes: "seven eyes, which are the seven spirits of God." We may therefore `conclude that the seven spirits of God can be represented by both torches and eyes. Interestingly, from an Egyptian perspective these representations of the spirit are phonetically very close. For example, another

---

[a] The following brief overview of the parts of a "person" is based primarily on that provided by Goelet (1994, pp. 150-152).

Egyptian word for spirit is $_3\underline{h}$ while that for both the *eye* (of god) and flame is $_3\underline{h}t$.[a,132] This means that spirits, flames (as torches) and eyes were all very closely related to one another in the mind of the ancient Egyptians (*cf.* discussion on *Word Play* in Chapter 2, *New Approaches*). This grouping of phonetically similar Egyptian words for spirit, eye and flame and the equating of spirits, eyes and torches in the text of Revelation is yet another parallel between the two sources.

But the parallels to phonetic similarities between Egyptian words and those used to describe the throne scene in Revelation do not end here. In Rev. 2:1 we read that the one on the throne "holds ... seven stars in his right hand, who walks among the seven golden lampstands." Understandably, the two phonetically similar Egyptian words *khabs*[133] and *khebs*[134] both mean star or lamp. Thus, just as the stars and the lampstands are linked in Revelation, stars and lamps were linked in the minds of the Egyptians.

There is still another parallel involving the seven stars. In the 2nd Division of the *Amduat*, Osiris (= Revelation's God on the throne) is shown surrounded by six deities (Figure 21) holding seven stars (two of the stars are held by one deity who carries them aloft on two long *censer* stands so that they act as torches). These stars may be described as being lamps, or even lampstands, as we read in Rev. 2:1. Indeed, the Egyptian word *stst* can mean both *censer* and lamp.[135] And since the Egyptian word *khabs* (and *khebs*) can mean both star and lamp, we may assume that all the stars in the figure can actually represent seven torches (functionally, lampstands) held in the hands of the deities. We may therefore conclude that in Figure 21 Osiris appears both in the midst of seven stars as in Rev 1:12-13, and seven lampstands as in Rev. 2:1. This mix of potential Egyptian homonyms and near homonyms thus conform closely with the throne scene in the Book of Revelation and represent yet another parallel with the Book of Revelation.

The Seven Spirits of God described in the Book of Revelation play major roles in a number of events. In Rev. 2-3, they are called angels and are instrumental in delivering messages to seven churches. These messages describe each of the churches

Figure 21. Seven torches (stars) surround Osiris in this scene from the *Amduat*, just as seven stars and seven lampstands surround God on the throne in Rev 1:12-13 and Rev. 2:1. (AM2.3.4-6)

---

[a] Gardiner (1927, §51 on p.48) tells us that the *t* ending on a word signifies the sense of the English neuter ('it,' 'thing')" and also expresses the Egyptian feminine.

as containing some who are faithful followers of God on the throne (e.g., Rev. 2:10) and others who have broken faith (e.g., Rev. 2:5) and elected to follow Baal or Satan (as in Rev. 2:24). These messages also promise rewards to the faithful while the unfaithful who do not repent are threatened with darkness (Rev. 2:5), war (Rev. 2:16), great tribulation (Rev. 2:22) and death (Rev. 2:11, Rev. 2:23). Later, in Rev. 8:1 to Rev. 11:19, the seven angels usher in a series of catastrophes which befall the earth and its inhabitants. The earth is bombarded with hail, fire and blood (Rev. 8:7) and something like a great mountain of fire falls into the sea, destroying a third of all life in it as well as a third of its shipping (Rev. 8:8-9). A great star, blazing like a torch falls to earth poisoning freshwater supplies (Rev. 8:10-11) while the sun, moon and stars dim, losing a third of their brightness (Rev. 8:12). Smoke rises into the air as if from a great furnace, causing darkness to cover the earth and dreadful calamities involving months of agonizing torment to the people (Rev. 9:1-12). War breaks out on the earth and a third of mankind ultimately dies (Rev. 9:13-18). The reasons given for these assaults by the seven angels are the immoral deeds perpetrated by the people, including demon and idol worship, murder, sorcery and theft (Rev. 9:20-21). The forces of benevolence prevail and God assumes control and power. The dead are judged for their deeds and the faithful who had feared the name of God and served him are rewarded (Rev. 11:15-18). The series ends with a graphic display of the deity's cosmic powers — lightning, "voices," thunder, an earthquake and heavy hail (Rev. 11:19). Thus, while the Seven Spirits of God are messengers (angels) to the seven churches in the second and third chapters, in later chapters they are heralds of great catastrophes, destruction and tribulation. As we shall see in later chapters, these functions of the Seven Spirits of God in the Book of Revelation parallel those of the seven spirits of Osiris.[a]

Twenty-four Elders (Rev. 4:4)

Rev. 4:4 tells us that around "the throne were twenty-four thrones, and seated on the thrones were twenty-four elders, clad in white garments, with golden crowns upon their heads." Groups of twenty-four deities can be readily identified in Egyptian throne scenes as two contiguous groups of twelve or as two separate groups of twelve arranged in the scenes so that they appear either on opposite sides of the sun-god or above and below him. Such two-dimensional portrayals can imply that they surround the central figure – as in Rev. 4:4.

An Egyptian scene comparable to Rev. 4:4 is located in the 9th Division of the *Amduat* (Figure 22). In it, we see twenty-four deities seated on thrones, 12 in human form in the upper register above the shrine of Re and 12 as serpents in the lower register below the shrine. They thus flank the central sun-god in a manner consistent with Rev. 4:4. Furthermore, each deity is seated on a throne represented by a clothing

---

[a] Details of Egyptian parallels to the powers and events which cause great tribulation among the doers of wrong in the Book of Revelation will be provided and thoroughly discussed in Chapter 13, *Catastrophes*.

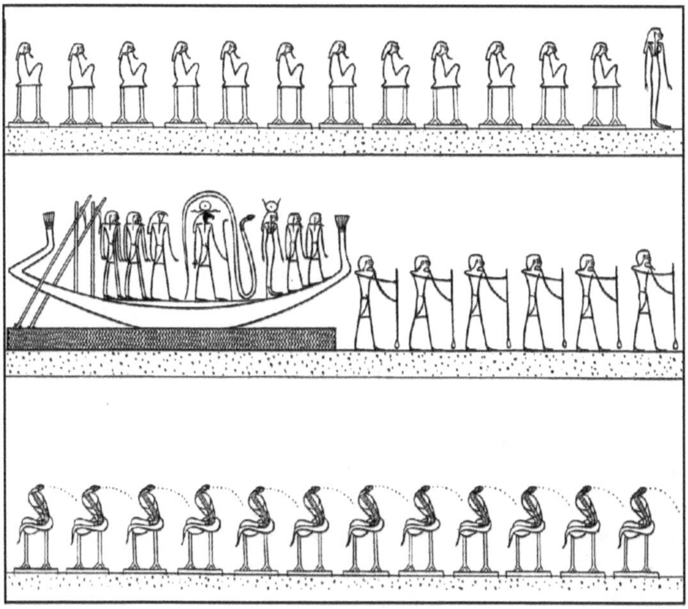

Figure 22. Twenty-four deities before the throne of the sun-god, depicted here as 12 human and 12 serpentine forms seated on thrones on the left-hand side of the upper and lower registers of the 9th Division of the *Amduat*. Each throne is formed by a hieroglyph for "clothing" (𓋳). Most of the characteristics of these deities conform with those of the twenty-four elders described in Rev. 4:4 and elsewhere. (AM.9.1-3.1-5)

sign, 𓋳,[a] indicating that they wear brilliant white robes similar to those worn by the elders in Rev. 4:4. This scene therefore contains almost all of the characteristics of the elders described in Rev. 4:4 – their position around the central deity, thrones, their clothing, and their number. They do not, however, wear crowns. Nevertheless, another representation of a group of twenty-four deities, this time in the 6th Division of the *Book of Gates*, wear either truth symbols (𓆄) or symbols of baskets full of grain on their heads (●), both of which may be considered to be special diadems or crowns (typical of many pictures of Egyptian deities) as described in Rev. 4:4. Also, in the 3rd register of the 7th Division of the *Amduat* we find twenty four deities wearing crowns (or diadems) formed by star hieroglyphs (★) denoting adoration or praise and standing before the throne of Horus of the Netherworld. These symbols of praise on the heads of the twenty-four thus conform the action of the twenty-four elders when

[a] In the Tomb of Ramesses VI this scene is modified so that the 12 human deities and the 12 serpent deities are flanked on either side of Horus of the Netherworld rather than above and below the ram-headed form of Re standing in his barque as we see in Figure 22. The significance of white clothing in Egyptian mythology will be discussed in Chapter 7, *Egyptian Beliefs in the Seven Letters*.

they fall on their faces in reverence before the throne of God in Rev. 4:10. Several other groupings of twenty-four deities associated with the sun-god are found in other locations of the *Book of Gates* and the *Amduat*.[a]

The ritual in which the twenty-four elders "fall on their faces" before the throne (Rev. 4:10, Rev. 5:8, Rev. 5:14, Rev. 7:11, Rev. 11:16 and Rev. 19:4) was quite common in ancient Egypt. It was not only practiced before the gods but used in the judiciary system and high government offices as well as by audiences before royalty. Lurker (1980) says that when hailing a deity, a priest "knelt and inclined himself to the ground which he touched with his nose and forehead, an attitude called 'kissing the ground.'"[136] Spence (1915) says that "Standing face to face with the god [in the Holy of Holies], he [the priest] prostrated himself."[137] And the *Great Hymn to Osiris* says that "Those in the dat (the Netherworld) kiss the ground, those on high bow down."[138] Other examples could be given but these are sufficient to illustrate the similarities between Egyptian rituals and those exercised by the twenty-four elders in the Book of Revelation.

The arrangement of the twenty-four around the throne in Revelation also conforms with ancient Egyptian rituals; encircling the throne of a deity was typical of Egyptian worshipers. For example, one of the *Pyramid Texts* (§§730-3) describes the newly deceased King Teti as becoming a member of the "elders who surround Re." Its full text reads, "Thou dawnest, O king Teti, in the royal hood; thy hand seizes the sceptre, thy fist grasps the mace. Stand, O king Teti, in front of the two palaces of the South and the North. Judge the gods, (for) *thou art of the elders who surround Re,* who are before the Morning Star."[139] This passage is particularly applicable to the first part of Rev. 4:4.

An interesting aspect of the above text is that one of the functions of the Egyptian elders was to act as judges. Similarly, in the 7th division of the *Book of Gates* there are twenty-four judges identified as two groups of twelve, one standing before the ram-headed sun-god in the 2nd register and the other below him in the 3rd register. The sun-god says to the twelve in the 2nd register, "O Council which is in the Netherworld, lords of things in the West, as I have granted you Truth. You are ordered to give judgment." To those in the 3rd register, he says, "Hail, Council of Judges, who judge the dead, who protect the souls! The Divine One is placed upon his throne, Truth is yours, O you gods."[140] The number of judges, or assessors in the Egyptian texts, was not, however, fixed at twenty-four and could vary from nine to forty-two. For example, fourteen are shown in the throne scene along the top left two thirds of Figure 6 and seated on (invisible or implied) thrones as they listen to the pleas of the deceased who kneels on one knee in front of them. Rev. 20:4 describes an undefined number of judges in the throne scene, as follows: "Then I saw thrones, and seated on them were those to whom judgment was committed." It seems reasonable to assume that, as in

---

[a] These are as follows: BG1.1.1-6-10, BG2.1.1-10, BG3.1.1-7, BG4.1.1-9, BG5.1.1-7, BG5.3.1-10, BG6.1.1-10, BG7.1.1-10, BG10.3.1-8, AM9.1.1-10 and AM12.1.1-10. In addition to these unambiguous groupings of twenty-four deities, two other possible groups of twenty-four may be identified. These are arranged as two groups of twelve, each located on a different register in BG3.2.7-10 & BG3.3.5-8 and BG4.2.7-10 & BG4.3.5-8.

the Egyptian texts, the judges on the thrones in Rev. 20:4 are the same individuals as the elders (also described as being on thrones) identified in Rev. 4:4.

Descriptions of twenty-four elders in the Book of Revelation thus parallel those of groups of twenty-four deities in both the Egyptian *Book of Gates* and the *Amduat*. They are both twenty-four in number, wear white clothing and crowns, are committed to truth, are arranged "round the throne" of their god, are followers who praise their god by bowing or falling down to the ground, and are involved in the judgment of the dead. Many of them seem to relate to Re rather than Osiris (who parallels god on the throne in Revelation) but this difference disappears when one considers that Osiris and Re were considered to represent different aspects of the sun-god and at times were even found within one another (see discussion on "Osiris-Re," *God and the Lamb*, in Chapter 2, *The Preeminent Deities*).

Angels (Rev. 5:11)

There are numerous references to angels in the Book of Revelation. They do not, however, form a homogeneous group for they vary in both appearance and function. One angel, for example, is described as being so bright as to illuminate the earth as he descends from heaven (Rev. 18:1). Some are described simply as worshiping God on the throne (Rev. 7:11) while still others are prophets (Rev. 22:6) or guides who describe and interpret events (Rev. 17:1). Some announce catastrophic events on earth (Rev. 8:7) while others are soldiers who fight in heaven against the evil dragon and his angels (Rev. 12:7, 9), in which case angels are recognizable as warriors. They may also appear in multitudes as described in Rev. 5:11 where we read, "Then I looked, and I heard around the throne and the living creatures and the elders the voice of many angels, numbering myriads of myriads and thousands of thousands." The full range of characteristics and functions of the angels described in the Book of Revelation is outlined in Table 4.1.

Many of these groups of angels in the Book of Revelation do not conform with traditional Middle Eastern views of angels. The ancient Greek word for angel in the Book of Revelation is *angelos,* meaning a messenger (from *angello*, 'to deliver a message') sent by God, man or Satan. It was "also used of a guardian or representative."[141] In early and recent Middle Eastern religions (Zorastrianism, Judaism, Christianity, and Islam) angels were typically considered to be celestial or atmospheric spirits.[142] In Christianity, they acted primarily as envoys or messengers.[143] Angels who serve God were usually considered as benevolent beings while those who serve Satan were malevolent demons. Furthermore, angels in biblical times were both classified and ranked:

> In the New Testament, celestial beings were grouped into seven ranks: angels, archangels, principalities, powers, virtues, dominions, and thrones. In addition to these were added the Old Testament cherubim and seraphim, which with the seven other ranks, comprised the nine choirs of angels in later Christian mystical theology. Various other numbers of the orders of angels have been given by early Christian writers.[144]

Such groupings of spiritual beings were (and still are) common in most or all of the eastern and Middle Eastern religions, including Christianity.[a]

Generally speaking, ancient Egyptians did not have special names for spiritual beings with particular functions and characteristics such as those of the angels known in other parts of the Middle East. Instead, most spiritual beings were simply called

Table 4.1 Attributes of angels referred to in the Book of Revelation. Only those references which can be unambiguously classified are included.

General Attributes	Specific Attributes	References
Appearance	Masculine	Rev. 7:2, Rev. 18:2, Rev. 19:17, Rev. 22:6
	Ability to fly	Rev. 14:6 and possibly Rev. 8:13, Rev. 18:1, Rev 20:1
	Radiate Light	Rev. 18:1
	Many	Rev. 5:11
Ceremony	Fall on Faces	Rev. 19:4 and also Rev. 1:17, Rev. 5:8, Rev. 5:14, Rev. 7:11, Rev. 19:10, Rev. 22:8
	Encircling	Rev. 7:11, Rev. 5:11
	Ceremonial	Rev. 5:2, Rev. 8:5 Rev. 10:8, Rev. 11:1, Rev. 18:21
Messengers and Heralds	Messengers and Heralds	Rev. 1:1-2, Rev. 2:1, Rev. 2:8, Rev. 2:12, Rev. 2:18, Rev. 3:1, Rev. 3:7, Rev. 3:14, Rev. 5:2, Rev. 8:13, Rev. 10:6, Rev. 14:6, Rev. 16:17, Rev. 19:17, Rev. 22:16
	Heralds of Destruction	Rev. 7:3, Rev. 8:7, Rev. 8:8, Rev. 8:10, Rev. 8:12, Rev. 8:13, Rev. 9:15, Rev. 16:3, Rev. 16:4, Rev. 16:8, Rev. 16:10, Rev. 16:12
Prophets	Prophets	Rev. 22:6
Guardians	Guards	Rev. 21:12
	Soldiers	Rev. 12:7-8, Rev. 20:1
	Overseers	Rev. 1:20
	Earth Protectors	Rev. 7:1
Guides	Personal Guides	Rev. 17:1, Rev. 17:7, Rev. 21:9, Rev. 22:8

[a] In The *Oxford Companion to the Bible* (1993, p.28), Meir reviews the roles of angels in the lives of the ancient Israelites who in the early days considered them to be God's "divine assistants" or "messengers." They later became "divine mediators" as well. Only two were named; one of these, Michael, took on a combative role while the other, Gabriel, revealed future events. Meir also says that some angels acquired a personal, "protective" role. Zondervan's Dictionary (1963), which considers them from a purely Christian perspective, refers to them as spirits, beings who are not omniscient but who are stronger than men, who minister to Christ, who worship god, execute his will towards individuals and nations, guide the affairs of nations, protect and guide individuals, and assist in the interpretation of God's will. The PC Study Bible mentions the following characteristics of angels in Christianity: masculine gender, supernatural (spirit) messengers, messengers acting as diplomats or representatives of God to deliver terms of surrender, deliverers of destruction, and fulfilling the saving or protective function of guardians. Presumably, the references to terms of surrender, guardians and deliverers of destruction refer primarily to their roles the Book of Revelation.

neteru (singular: *neter*), a term usually translated as "gods."[a] Budge (1904), summarized his thoughts on the *neteru* and suggested they should be classified as angels:

> It is very unfortunate that the animals, and the spirits of natural objects, as well as the powers of nature, were all grouped together by the Egyptians and were described by the word *neteru*; which, with considerable inexactness, we are obliged to translate as "gods." There is no doubt that at a very early period in their predynastic history the Egyptians distinguished between great gods and little gods, just as they did between friendly gods and hostile gods, but either their poverty of expression, or the inflexibility of their language, prevented them from making a distinction apparent in writing, and thus it happens that in dynastic times ... the scribe found himself obliged to call both God and the lowest of beings that were supposed to possess some attribute of divinity by one and the same name, i.e., *neter*. ... Other nations of antiquity found a way out of the difficulty of grouping all classes of divine beings by one name by inventing series of orders of angels, to each of which they gave names and assigned various duties in connection with the service of the Deity.[145]

Furthermore, and as discussed above, many Egyptian deities, especially high ranking ones like Re and Osiris had multiple *bas* and *kas*. These could function as servants or messengers so that, just as the *neteru*, they too might be called "angels" in the same sense that *angelos* is used in the Book of Revelation. Similarly, since practically all the major and minor gods, and most of the spiritual beings of the Egyptian Netherworld were called *neteru*, many of the Egyptian *neteru* (like the *bas* and *kas)* can be described as angels. Indeed, Budge concluded that,

> A comparison of the passages in Rabbinic literature which [liken] ... angels, spirits, etc., of ancient Hebrew mythology with Egyptian texts shows that both the Egyptians and Jews possessed many ideas in common, and all the evidence goes to prove that the latter borrowed from the former in the earliest period."[146]

Budge felt the Hebrew *angels* and most of the Egyptian *"gods"* (or *neteru)* were practically identical.

Since Budge did not specifically consider the angels of the Book of Revelation, it is appropriate that the characteristics of the more important angels in Revelation be compared with those of particular Egyptian gods – or *neteru*. This will be done later during in-depth treatments of characteristics of specific "angels" in the context of particular passages and events in which they appear in the Book of Revelation. For now, we will highlight just a few of the more prominent ones.

Satan, the Devil and the Ancient Serpent (Rev. 12; 13:2-4; 20:2-3)

All of the above characters in Revelation may be considered to be on the side of good. This section will emphasize the evil "dragon, that ancient serpent, who is the Devil and Satan" (Rev. 20:2) and who is ultimately judged and thrown into a pit which is

---

[a] The plural, "gods," is *neteru (ntrw)* while the singular is *neter (ntr)*.

sealed over him (Rev. 20:3). As the first of the evil beings to be portrayed here and, as with the previous characters, his attributes in Revelation will be outlined before comparing him with specific Egyptian deities with similar characteristics.

Satan's main attributes are summarized in Rev. 12:3-9 as follows: "... behold, a great red dragon. ... And the great dragon was thrown down, that ancient serpent, who is called the Devil and Satan, the deceiver of the whole world – he was thrown down to the earth, and his angels were thrown down with him." We see here that Satan's most obvious features are that he is large, red, has the form of a dragon, is a deceiver, and lives on earth; his most peculiar attribute is that he is a serpent, is like a dragon and is ancient.

The Greek word used for "dragon" is *drakon,* a word typically defined as a "mythical monster, dragon, a large serpent,"[147] "a fabulous kind of serpent"[148] or "a serpent, a venomous snake."[149] The King James Version of the Bible translates it in four different ways – a dragon, sea-monster, serpent, or whale[150] depending on its context. The popular modern-day image of the dragon is typically that of a huge, bat-winged, fire-breathing, scaly lizard or snake with a barbed tail. The *Encyclopædia Britannica* says that,

> In the Far East, the dragon managed to retain its prestige and is known as a beneficent creature. The Chinese dragon, known as *lung,* appears as the national symbol and was the badge of the Imperial family. The Japanese dragon, known as *tatsu,* is capable of changing size at will even to the point of becoming invisible. Both Chinese and Japanese dragons, though regarded as powers of the air, are usually wingless. They are among the deified forces of nature in Taoism. ... in the Near Eastern world, where snakes are large and deadly, the serpent or dragon was symbolic of the principle of evil. Thus the Egyptian god *Apepi [Apophis], for example, was the great serpent of the world of darkness.*'[151]

As one might expect, Revelation's dragon conforms both in its ancient, evil nature and its dwelling place (the inner parts of the earth) with the great serpentine dragons of the Middle East. The same can be said of *Apophis* (also known as *Apep, Apepi, Aepep, Apopis* and other names), the Egyptian god of chaos. Nevertheless, Clagett (1989) informs us he was at times closely associated with the creator-god himself:

> The snake-form of the creator [Figure 23] is considered as an earlier form of him [Apophis], a form he shed and constantly combated when it was considered to be the primitive chaos. It was the snake Imy-Wahaf in Heliopolis or more widely, in later accounts, the serpent Apep [Apophis]. ... this image of the snake-creator was superceded [by the creator god, Atum] as [Egyptian concepts of] creation progressed.[152]

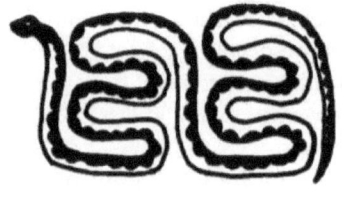

Figure 23. Apophis, the ancient serpent of Egyptian myths who is as old as creation. At times he is depicted with several arrows or spears penetrating his body.

A version of ancient Egyptian cosmology found on the walls of the Temple of Esna suggests that a creation goddess called Neith

4. Other Characters in Revelation

was directly involved in Apophis's origin. This ancestor goddess "thrust aside a wad of spittle from her mouth which she had produced in the Abyss, and it was transformed into a serpent of 120 cubits, which was named Apep [Apophis]. Its heart conceived the revolt against Re, its cohorts coming from its eyes."[a] Apophis' power of chaos"[153] conforms with his personification as the *god of chaos* and is consistent with Revelation's reference to the Devil being a *deceiver*.

With the above background in mind, Revelation's use of the term *ancient serpent* is especially applicable to Egypt's ancient Apophis. And Apophis is a good match for Revelation's Devil (Satan). The serpentine dragon of Rev. 20:2 bears the very specific names "Devil" and "Satan" which do not seem, however, to have Egyptian parallels; both are Hebrew terms which form important parts of both the Old and New Testaments. Additional evidence for the identification of Egypt's Apophis with Revelation's Devil with will be presented later in our discussion of the story of the beasts of Rev. 13 and the "binding of the serpent" in Rev. 20:1-3.

The 1st Beast (Rev. 13)

Another evil deity is mentioned in Rev. 13. It is called the "beast" or, more specifically, the "1st beast," a character which will be discussed in detail in Chapter 18, *The Beasts of Rev. 13* where we will also meet the 2nd beast. After judgment is passed upon the dragon, the beast shares the same fate: "And the beast was captured, and ... thrown alive into the lake of fire that burns with sulphur" (Rev 19:20).

The 1st beast in the Book of Revelation can be tentatively identified by solving the riddle presented in Rev. 13:18. We are told, that special knowledge is required to reckon, or understand, the number of his name: "This calls for wisdom: let him who has understanding reckon the number of the beast, for it is a human number, its number is six hundred and sixty-six" (Rev. 13:18). His name may thus be written as "666." Such a practice of assigning numbers to deities was common among Middle Eastern religions. Nevertheless, the question remains – Why 666? Why not some other number?

It is possible to answer these questions from an Egyptian point of view, especially if one bears in mind certain similarities in Egyptian to other Middle Eastern languages. The answer resides in the context of several characters common to various written languages in the eastern Mediterranean. The relevant symbols are shown in Table 4.2. The two Hebrew characters are called *wâw* and are vocalized as "w" or "u." Its numeric value is "6." As shown in the table, the Hebrew characters are analogous to characters in Syrian and Arabic which are also called *wâw* and have the same pronunciation. Two similar symbols are found in the Egyptian language: ℚ and ⸢ (which can be written in the opposite direction). The first (ℚ) is similar to the Hebrew, Arabic and Syriac symbols and has the same phonetic value. The second ⸢,, depending on the direction of the text also has a similar shape, especially to the Arabic *wâw* sign but has a different phonetic and numeric value; ⸢ has the phonetic value *št*

---

[a] From the *Cosmogonies at the Temple of Esna, Neith*; translation by Clagett (1989), Vol. I, p. 580-581.

Table 4.2 Compilation of symbols from the Hebrew, Arabic and Syriac languages which correspond to the number 6 and the Egyptian symbol for 100. This forms the basis for an Egyptian parallel with the number of the name of the 1st beast (666) in Rev. 13:17-18.

Origin	Symbol	Name of Character	Phonetic Value	Numeric Value	Reference
Hebrew	ו or ן	wâw	w, u	6	Budge, p. cxlix
Arabic	و	wâw	w, u	6	Budge, p. cli
Syriac	ܘ	wâw	w, u	6	Budge, p. cl
Egyptian	ꜥ	—	w	—	Gardiner, p. 537
Egyptian	ꜥ	št	št	100	Gardiner, pp. 191-192, 521-522

and the numeric value "100." The visual similarity of ꜥ to the ꜥ symbol suggests the two symbols could, under certain circumstances, be used as visual puns for each other – or at times even be confused with each other.[154] For example, the Egyptian ꜥ (št = 100) symbol could be used as a visual pun for ꜥ (w) in which št could represent w and vice versa. It is entirely possible that if a Hebrew, Syrian or Arabic scribe read an Egyptian text and encountered the št symbol, he could perceive it a pun on their number "6" (wâw) and hence read it as a "6." This observation does not completely explain the likely background to the number "666" in Rev 13:18, as we shall see next.

The two most prominent gods of evil in the Egyptian pantheon are Apophis and Seth. Apophis has already been discussed and likened to Revelation's Devil but attempts to reconcile the number 666 with his name were unsuccessful. When Seth's name was critically examined, however, it was indeed possible to link him with the number 666. The following outlines the method used to derive the name of the Egyptian god Seth from Revelation's number 666. We begin with the ꜥ symbol in Table 4.2 which has the phonetic value of št. A similar hieroglyph is formed by placing a door bold across the symbol to form the similar hieroglyph, ⤢, which has the phonetic value of st (śt).[155] This symbol can be tripled to form ⤢⤢⤢[156] or ꜥꜥꜥ[157] to yield the sound śt in parts of words such as Rstзw (Rosetau). Budge (1920) gives ꜥꜥꜥ the sound-value of —•— ⬬ or set.[158] Śt or set, of course, sounds similar to the name of the god Seth (which Gardiner (1927) says was written as —•— ⬬ ⟜ 𓊽 and ☥ ⬩ ⬬ ⟜, and vocalized as Stẖ and St respectively[159]). One can therefore readily understand how a Hebrew, Syrian, and especially an Arabic scribe, recognizing the similarity of the constituent parts of ꜥꜥꜥ to their number "6," might choose to assign the number 666 to Seth for mythological purposes as in the expression "the name of the beast [Seth, the Egyptian god of evil] or *the number of its name ... is six hundred and sixty six*" (Rev. 13:17-18). In this manner, we find a parallel between the Egyptian god Seth and the 1st beast of Rev. 13.

This parallel can be strengthened somewhat by a brief look at the close association between the 1st beast (Seth) and the Devil [Apophis] described in Rev. 13:2 – "And to it [the 1st beast] the dragon [Apophis] gave his power and his throne and great authority." Seth was also considered to be such a close associate of Apophis that he was at times considered his equivalent.[160]

There are other parallels between the 1st beast of Revelation and the god Seth, not the least apparent is that he might be referred to as a "beast." It relates to the age-old mystery of exactly what kind of animal the Egyptians used to represent him in their pictures and writings. Wilkinson (1992) outlines the problem:

> The iconography of Seth shows an interesting development, and while the god was later represented in anthropomorphic form as an animal-headed deity [Figure 24], he was originally depicted as an animal with a curved head, tall square-topped ears, and erect arrow-like tail. The exact species represented by the Seth animal has never been determined, however, and while suggestions have ranged from the ardvaark, jackal, antelope, okapi, pig, and ass, it is just as possible that the animal was a fabulous creature like the griffon.[161]

Figure 24. The Egyptian god Seth bearing the head of an unknown, perhaps non-existent animal, parallels the 1st beast of Rev. 13:18 and "the number of his name," 666, in several Semitic languages.

It is entirely possible, of course, that the Egyptians themselves did not know what kind of animal, or animals, was represented in the iconography of Seth. If so, then it would be reasonable to assume that the Egyptians unofficially called him something akin a beast.

It should be noted, however, that Seth's position was not always considered inimical for he was often held to be cunning and of great strength and admired by many of Egypt's kings; some even called themselves "Beloved of Seth." Wilkinson (1992) summarizes his ever-changing status:

> By the Middle Kingdom Seth was assimilated into solar theology as the god who stood in the bow of the sun god's barque to repel the cosmic serpent Apophis. In the Hyksos Period he seems to have risen to considerable popularity, and in the Nineteenth and Twentieth Dynasties the god became important as the patron deity of the Ramesside kings. But evidence for Seth declines after the Twentieth Dynasty, and his role as god of the desert and foreign lands led to his association in the later periods with Egypt's hated foreign overlords [the Hyksos].[162]

Looking back from the 20th Dynasty, Seth had changed from the murderer of his father and enemy of Horus to a beloved benefactor of many famous kings – and then back to a villainous creature, or beast, again. Nevertheless, for a great deal of Egypt's history, he was considered to have a violent and evil nature, the same as Revelation's 1st beast.

Additional Egyptian parallels with Revelation's 1st beast will be presented in Chapter 18, *The Beasts of Rev. 13* where it will be discussed in relation to a dramatic parallel sequence of events described in Rev. 13; Chapter 18 will also demonstrate Egyptian parallels to the 2nd beast described in Rev. 13:11-17, the "image of the beast" mentioned in Rev. 13:14 and Revelation's "false prophet."

Discussion

This chapter and the previous one have shown how the main characters around the throne in the Book of Revelation conform with well-known Egyptian deities, both good and evil. We have seen how the "four creatures" before the throne in Revelation parallel the four Sons of Osiris who are typically present before Osiris's judgment throne. The seven "spirits of god" parallel the seven spirits of Osiris described in the *Book of the Dead* while the "twenty-four elders" match two groups of twelve deities which appear in several scenes involving Re and Osiris, two different aspects of the Egyptian sun-god. The many physical and functional characteristics of the angels portrayed in the Book of Revelation conformed closely with those of numerous miscellaneous deities in the Egyptian literature. Other beings were discussed: the Devil and the beasts. The Devil, the ancient serpent of Revelation, parallels Apophis, the ancient Egyptian god of chaos who was present since the beginning of creation while the 1st beast conforms with Seth, the brother of Horus and killer of Osiris. Egyptians often considered Seth and Apophis to represent the same evil deity – in concert with the affinity between Revelation's Devil and the 1st beast. At this stage in the study we may say that, when these parallels are combined with those described in the previous chapter, most of the more prominent characters in the Book of Revelation have significant parallels in the Egyptian pantheon.

The next chapter will deal with what has been the most difficult deity to identify i.e., Egypt's parallel to Revelation's "Word of God."

Chapter 5. "The Word of God" (Rev. 19:11-21)[163]

Rev. 19:11-21 describes a series of events beginning with the introduction of one called "Faithful and True" (Rev. 19:11) and "The Word of God" (Rev. 19:13). He leads a great army of the faithful against the "beast" and the kings of the earth (Rev. 19:19) and their followers (Rev. 19:21) who have gathered together to make war against him. We are told that his army unleashes "the fury of the wrath of God the Almighty" upon the enemy (Rev. 19:15). The enemy is defeated and the beast and one called "false prophet" are thrown into the lake of fire while their followers are "slain with the sword" (Rev. 19:21). In this chapter we will examine the attributes of "The Word of God," the leader of this army, and show that he closely resembles two Egyptian gods, Thoth and Horus, one of which is marginally closer to Revelation's "Word of God."

It is important to realize that the concept of the *word of god* was well developed in ancient Egypt. Clagett (1989) points out that Thoth's "epithet 'Lord of the Divine Word' implies not merely his invention of hieroglyphics but also his authorship and control of cult-ritual and magical formulae."[164] Like Re, Osiris and Ptah, Thoth could bring something into existence by merely speaking its name, an aspect of the Egyptian language referred to as the "creative word" and discussed in Chapter 3, *The Preeminent Deities* in relation to the attributes of Amen.

But more to the point of the one called "Word of God" in Rev. 19, Budge (1904) tells us that Thoth "was held to be both the heart and *tongue* of Ra, that is to say, he was the reason and the mental powers of the god, and also the means by which their will was translated into speech; from one aspect he was speech itself."[165] Elsewhere, Budge (1934) tells us that Thoth was known as the "Word-god" and was "the mind and tongue of Rā,"[166] a point emphasized by Clagett (1989)[167] and echoed by Lurker (1980).[168] This evidence alone suggests that Thoth, as the personification of "the word of Re," is an obvious Egyptian parallel to Revelation's "Word of God."

On close examination of Rev. 19:11-21, however, Thoth may not be the only candidate for a parallel. Indeed, several attributes of the "The Word of God" in Revelation suggest that it is Horus who parallels Revelation's "Word of God." This dual possibility complicates the identification of the Egyptian parallel and necessitates a detailed comparison of the attributes of Thoth and Horus before coming to a conclusion on the matter. To begin this comparison, the relevant parallels of the two Egyptian deities will first be considered separately and then compared.

Parallels with Thoth (Rev. 19:11-16)

Thoth as judge (Rev. 19:11)

We are told in Rev. 19:11 that "The Word of God" acts as a judge: "In righteousness he judges." Thoth also acted as a judge. Indeed, he was considered to be the most important – and most popular – judge in the Egyptian pantheon and was well known for his role as the presiding judge at the judgment of the dead. His status as a judge is well documented in the *Book of the Dead*. "I am Thoth, Lord of Justice,"[169] says the text in the 183rd chapter (Figure 25). Thoth possessed the ability to settle divergent opinions and heated arguments, and his judgments acted as models for future cases. In the 182nd chapter we are given an example of the fairness of his judgment in disagreements between people of unequal means or social standing. The text reads, "I am the Lord of Justice, one truly precise to the gods, who judges a matter so that it may continue in being; who vindicates him whose voice is hushed; who dispels darkness and clears away the storm."[170] And in the 123rd chapter we read that Thoth acted as judge in the feud between Horus and Seth: "Hail to you, Atum! I am Thoth who judged between the Rivals. I have stopped their fighting ..."[171]

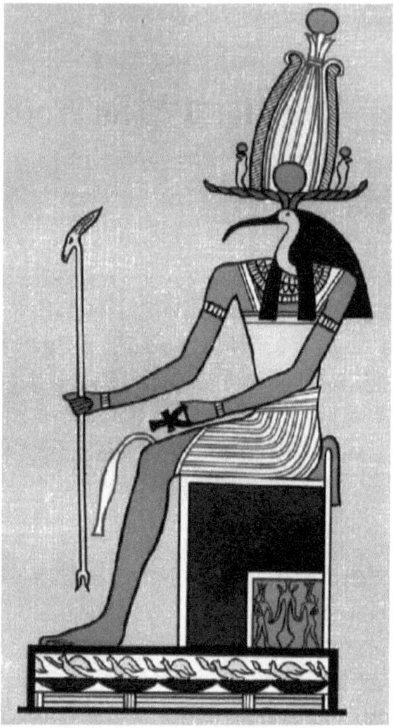

Figure 25. The Egyptian god Thoth wearing his many crowns (Rev. 19:12) indicating his many functions. Thoth's parallels in Revelation include the Word of God (Rev. 19:13), the Lord of Truth (Rev. 19:13), a warrior against the enemies of his god (Rev. 19:11), a judge (Rev. 19:11) and one who maintained a written record of the proceedings of the final judgment before Osiris.

Thoth's ultimate role in the judgment of the dead is nowhere more pronounced than in the *Book of the Dead*. Budge (1934) points out that, over time, "the judgement of the dead had practically passed from the hands of Osiris to Thoth. It is Thoth who is the Warden of the scales [of judgment], and the Overseer of the Scales, and the examiner of the beam of the scales whilst Osiris sits motionless."[172] He goes on to say that "It was Thoth who decided that the heart [which was being weighed] in the Scales was righteous, and it was the Great Company of Gods who accepted his report and decreed the reward which the *ba* (i.e., soul) of the deceased was to receive in the Field of Offerings."¹⁷³ Thoth presided over the weighing with pen and writing palette in hand and recorded the result.¹⁷⁴ "The Scales showed that the heart of the deceased counterbalanced exactly the feather of Maāt [truth], and Thoth, the righteous scribe of the gods, who also had been watching the weighing of the heart, was satisfied that *N* [the deceased] was a man without sin, and he [Thoth] reported this fact to the 'Great Company of the Gods' who are before Osiris, saying 'Hear ye this word (i.e., decision)."¹⁷⁵ "And it was his verdict of 'Maā Kheru', i.e. 'True of voice (or word)' which was accepted by the jury of the gods."¹⁷⁶ In this case, it is Horus who reports the results of the trial to Osiris, and in so doing, acknowledges Thoth's contribution as a judge:

> His heart is true, having gone forth from the balance, and he has not sinned against any god or any goddess. *Thoth has judged him in writing'* which has been told to the Ennead, and Maat the great [representing "truth"] has witnessed. Let there be given to him bread and beer which have been issued in the presence of Osiris, and he will be forever like the Followers of Horus."¹⁷⁷

Thoth – faithful, true and righteous (Rev. 19:11):- Thoth's faithful recording of the results of each trial armed the Osirian believers with assurance for a fair judgment. Several examples may be sited from the *Egyptian Book of the Dead*. Chapter 30B quotes the Great Ennead in Hermopolis as saying to Thoth, "This utterance of yours is true."¹⁷⁸ In Chapter 183, Thoth characterizes himself as one who detests falsehood with the words, "I am Thoth ... who writes what is true, who detests falsehood."¹⁷⁹ Budge tells us that he was known as "lord of Maat" (i.e., of truth) and was "a great righteous witness" at the judgment of the dead.¹⁸⁰ In this scenario, Thoth's role in the judgment is that of a truthful witness and secretary who faithfully reports the conclusions of the trial to Horus who in turn presents it to Osiris. The innocense of the deceased is ultimately accepted and he receives the promise of riches, blessings and all the privileges of the Egyptian afterlife.

Thoth as Warrior (Rev. 19:11, 14-16)

In addition to telling us that "The Word of God" is a judge, Rev. 19:11 also says he is a warrior: "in righteousness he judges and makes war." Rev. 19:14-15 elaborates upon this by saying that "the armies of heaven, arrayed in fine linen, white and pure, followed him on white horses" and that "a sharp sword" issues from his mouth "to smite the nations." A heavenly war is also mentioned in the *Book of the Dead*. In Chapter 17 of the book we read that the "Children of Impotence ... entered into the east of the sky, and war broke out in the entire sky and earth."¹⁸¹ Elsewhere, in Chapter 18, we read an address to the god Thoth praising his role in the war against Seth and his followers:

> O Thoth, who vindicated Osiris against his enemies ... on that night of battle ... and on that day of destroying the enemies of the Lord of All. ... the destruction of the gang of Seth when he repeated his offenses¹⁸² ... on that night of making an accounting of their dead. ... on that night of hacking the earth with their blood ... when they were sacrificed in the

presence of these gods, and the blood which dropped from them was captured and was given to those who are counted among the ones of Busiris.[183]

There are many other Egyptian texts which make reference to Thoth's struggle against Seth and his followers. For example, in one of the *Pyramid Texts* we read: "Horus hath come that he might embrace thee [Osiris]. He hath caused Thoth to turn back the followers of Set before thee."[184] The first chapter of the *Book of the Dead* describes Thoth as a fighter:

> Hail to you, Bull of the West [Osiris] – *so says Thoth,*' the king of Eternity, of me. I am the Great God, the protector. *I have fought for you,*' for I am one of those gods of the tribunal which vindicated Osiris against his foes on that great day of judgment ... "I belong to your company, O Horus, *I have fought for you*' and have watched over your name; *I am Thoth who vindicated Osiris against his foes*' on that day of judgment in the great Mansion of the Prince which is in Heliopolis."[185]

There is a less well known passage which is perhaps more relevant to the events described in Rev. 19:11, 14-15. It was found in the Temple of Esna and entitled by Egyptologists, "Text 206: Neith," and deals primarily with the origin of the gods but includes a reference to the revolt by the followers of the sun-god. It is relevant to Rev. 19:11 because it makes reference to Thoth being called both the "Lord of the Word of God" and to his status as a warrior in charge of the god's army. Clagett (1989) quotes the text as follows:

> They {the ancestor gods} thrust aside a wad of spittle from her mouth which she had produced in the Abyss, and it was transformed into a serpent of 120 cubits, which was named Apep [Apophis]. Its heart conceived the revolt against Re, its cohorts coming from its eyes.
> Thoth emerged from his {i.e. Re's} heart in a name of Thoth ($\underline{d}hwty$), which accounts for his name of Thoth {$\underline{d}hwty$}. He speaks with his father, who sent him against the revolt, in the name of *Lord of the Word of God*.' And this is how Thoth, Lord of Khmun, came into being.[186]

We see here that it was the god Thoth who was sent out to lead Re's army against rebels led by Apophis, the ancient god of chaos. Like the "Word of God" in Rev. 19:11, Thoth made war against the enemies of his god.

Sword from the Thoth's mouth (Rev. 19:15):- There are a number of references concerning the sword of Thoth in Egyptian sources. For example, in the 95th chapter of the *Book of the Dead*, we read,

> I am he who gave protection in the tumult, who guarded the Great Goddess in the war. I smote with my knife [sword], I calmed Ash, I acted on behalf of the Great Goddess in the war. I made strong the *sharp knife which was in the hand of Thoth*' in the tumult.[187]

Frankfort (1948) discusses the nightly and early dawn conflict with the sun-god's enemy, the "darkness, symbolized by the snake Apophis" in which victory is always achieved. He quotes a hymn sung at dawn to the sun-god, here "father of fathers of all gods," as follows:

> *Thoth puts him to the sword and destroys him.'*
> How beautiful is Re in his boat [the celestial barque]. ...
> Apophis fell before him,
> His followers rejoice.[188]

It is obvious among these texts that both Revelation and the Egyptian sources mention the sword of the leader of the heavenly army. In spite of these similarities, it is clear from the account given in the *Book of the Dead* that Thoth held his sword in his hand and not in his mouth as is described in Rev. 19:15.

Nevertheless, the idea of a sword coming from the mouth of Thoth does indeed conform with what we know of him. In Chapter 3, *The Preeminent Deities*, we discussed the references to a sharp sword which issued from the mouth of God (in Rev. 1:16 and Rev. 2:16). In each of these cases it was pointed out that the phrase, "sword from the mouth," referred to the mouth of Revelation's "God on the throne." It was also noted that the reference to this sword paralleled the graphic representation of the Egyptian hieroglyph for the "word" which contains a picture of a sword and a man pointing to his mouth. Now, in Rev. 19:15 we find a similar phrase which refers to "The Word of God" and says, "From his mouth issues a sharp sword with which to smite the nations." It is clear, therefore, that the earlier discussion on the concept of the sword from the mouth of God on the Throne should be examined with the possibility that it also applies to Thoth.

Clagett (1989) provides us with the necessary information to interpret Revelation's reference to the sword in the mouth of the "Word of God." He explains Egyptian *ḥike* (magic) and quotes Boylan's (1922) comments on it in relation to Thoth.

> Looking at the use of the word *ḥike* generally, we find that it seems to include the whole field of what might be called magical. It is a sort of mysterious power which can produce effects beyong the sphere of man's achievements: ... it is something before which demons of sickness, and of poison – evil demons in general, must give way. Hence the uraeus serpents, the deities who guard the king, are "great in *ḥike*." Isis and Nephthys, as protectors of Osiris, are also "Great in *ḥike*." Thus *ḥike* seems to include the whole sphere of magic and to extend beyond it ... Thoth then, when he is called "Great in *ḥike*" {himself}, appears as a god of magic."[189]

Just as Osiris could threaten to use powerful magic in his words to strike against his enemies, Thoth could use this same magical power to defeat both his own enemies and those of the sun-god. An example of Thoth's magic power is provided by Borghouts (1978) in a situation where it is used against the "evil eye":

> Sekhmet's arrow is in you, *the magic {ḥk₃} of Thoth is in your body,'* Isis curses you, Nephthys punishes you, the lance of Horus is in your head. They treat you again and again, you are in the furnace of Horus. ... You will be slain like Apap, you will die and not live for ever.[190]

The 182nd chapter of the *Book of the Dead* speaks of Thoth's magical power, even including the giving of the breath of life to the dead.

> I am Thoth who made Osiris triumphant over his enemies. I am Thoth . ... I give breath to him who is in the secret places by means of the power which is on my mouth, and Osiris is triumphant over his enemies.[191]

While there seems to be no specific reference to a sword issuing from the mouth of Thoth in documents examined in this study, it is obvious that the Thoth's magical powers were more than capable to destroy the enemy with his own "creative words." The mention in Rev. 19:15 of the power to destroy with a sword from the mouth conforms with the well-known magical powers of Thoth rather than an explicit reference to a sword from his mouth.

Parallels with Horus

As pointed out above, there are also parallels between the attributes of Revelation's "Word of God" and ancient Egypt's Horus while some of the attributes of "The Word of God" parallel those of Thoth; others parallel those of Horus while still others seem to apply to both of them. The parallels with Horus will be dealt with next. Later, in the *Discussion,* they are compared with those of Thoth

Horus as "The Word of God"

As the son of Re and the incarnation of the spiritual Horus of the Netherworld, the king of Egypt represented Re on earth; when he spoke, his words represented those of the sun-god. In Egypt, therefore, the king's word was effectively the "word of Re," i.e., of the sun-god, or simply "of God." This parallel is not as strong as the same element for Thoth; the case for a parallel with Thoth is stronger because Thoth was explicitly called *the word of the sun-god* – and the religious literature frequently refers to him as such.

His name is on his robe and thigh (Rev. 19:16)

Rev. 19:16 says, "On his robe and on his thigh he has a name inscribed, "King of kings and Lord of lords." Recall from Chapter 3, *The Preeminent Deities*, that Horus, the king of Egypt was called the "king of the earth." Furthermore, as we shall see next, the reference to the king's name being written on his thigh in Rev. 19:16 bears a remarkable resemblance to an Egyptian belief about their kings.

The first reference to the king of Egypt having his name written on any of his limbs comes from the 5th Dynasty. David (1980), tells us that "One of the most interesting legends found in Egyptian literature recounts the events which are supposed to have occurred immediately before the rise of the solar cult [in Heliopolis] in the Fifth dynasty." She says that "The kings of the Fifth dynasty are portrayed as religious rulers whom the god has begotten, whereas the kings of the Fourth dynasty, especially Cheops, have been represented as tyrants in later legends."[192]

At about this time a simple tale written in the popular language (and recorded in the Westcar Papyrus) emerged that it was the sun-god himself who created the rulers of the 5th Dynasty and this story set the stage for practically all later beliefs that the king of Egypt was in fact the son of the sun-god, i.e., the Son of Re. The tale speaks of the wife of a priest of Re who conceived three children by him so that each was of divine origin. The part of the story most pertinent to Rev. 19:11 deals with the birth of the first of the divine triplets. Four deities, including Isis and Mesekhent, assist in his birth. The story goes like this:

> The goddesses hasten the birth of the first child; Isis says, "Be not hasty in her womb, as truly as thou art named User-ref." This child then slipped forth on to her hands, a child of one cubit with strong bones; *the royal titulary of his limbs*' was of gold and his head-cloth of true lapis-lazuli. They washed him, cut is navel string, and laid him upon a sheet on a brick. And Mesekhent drew near to him and she said: "A king that will exercise the kingship of the entire land." And Khnum gave health to his body.[193]

David goes on to tell us that all three of "the children are born wearing the royal head cloth, and *the titulary which was usually assumed on reaching the throne is already present on their limbs*,' inlaid in gold."[194] She points out that the story was "successful in conveying the information that the power of the Heliopolitan sun-cult was growing rapidly, that the sun-god had created the rulers of the Fifth dynasty, and (a fact which is borne out by other evidence) that these rulers venerated Re."[195] The belief that the king of Egypt was the son of the sun-god was thus born, and associated with it was the idea that he was born already wearing the royal head cloth and bearing his royal title on his limbs. We thus find yet another parallel: both Rev. 19:16 and Egyptian tradition describe the name of the king on his limbs *and* this is mentioned in conjunction with part of his apparel (his "robe" in Revelation and the "royal head cloth" in the Egyptian tradition).

Horus as judge

As in all countries throughout history, Egypt had its own judges, each operating within his own jurisdiction under Horus the king. In Egypt it was possible to appeal the decision of a local judge and ultimately bring one's case all the way up to the level of the king. An example of such a case is found in the Egyptian story of *The Complaints of the Peasant*[196] in which a lowly peasant is harassed by a landowner, finds no justice from lower-ranking judges, and ultimately brings his case all the way up the king himself. The king, of course was, Horus, Re's representative on earth and as such was the *de facto* judge of the land. As the son of Re, the sun-god, he also forcefully exerted his powerful influence over other countries, especially in the Levant, where he, at times, effectively ruled as king – and judge – over these places as well.

Horus as witness

This topic has been discussed in relation to Rev. 1.5 in Chapter 3, *The Preeminent Deities*.

Horus as warrior

Much has been written about Horus as a warrior who fought against his evil brother Seth to avenge the murder his father Osiris. Spence (1915) points out that Horus was originally a sun-god who later became Re's chief warrior:

> But in time the two gods came to be regarded as separate and distinct personages, Ra being the highest, and Horus serving him as sort of *war-captain*.' The winged disk [a symbol of the sun-god], therefore, and all his train represented the powers of light, while the wicked Set and his companions symbolized darkness. Thus it is that Horus was always victorious over his enemies.[197]

Some texts tell us that Horus (of the Netherworld), like Thoth, was the leader of the sun-god's celestial army. Utterance #301 of the *Pyramid Texts* tells us that "The Armed Fighter Horus, who is over the gods of the Sky, is he who vivifies Re every day."[198] Budge (1904) tells us that

> Ḥeru-Beuet ... is one of the greatest and most important of all the forms of Horus, for he represents that form ... which prevailed in the southern heavens at midday, and as such typified the greatest power of the heat of the sun. It was under this form that Horus waged war against Set or Typhon, and the inscriptions are full of allusions to the glorious victory which the god of light gained over the prince of darkness and his fiends.[199]

As "The Armed Fighter" and Re's war-captain, Horus certainly qualifies, like Thoth, to be a parallel to the leader of the heavenly army referred to in Rev. 19:14.

There is an interesting association between the mention in Rev. 19:16 that the name of the leader of the heavenly army was on his thigh ("On his ... thigh he has a name inscribed...") and the Egyptian word for "fighter." Budge (1934) tells us that the constellation of the Great Bear was called *Mesekhti* (Pyr. §458), i.e., the 'Fighter.' ... Later it was called the 'Thigh' and was depicted as an oval, bull-headed object or by a whole ox."[200] It therefore seems that, because of their belief in the magic of puns (see Chapter 2, *New Approaches*), the Egyptians envisioned a conceptual link between the thigh and a fighter, a link which conforms with the roll of their king (Horus) as a warrior and the tradition that his name was written on (at least) one of his limbs. Of course the earthly incarnation of the heavenly Horus was no less a warrior. As king and the son of Re he led Egypt's army into battle against Egypt's enemies, all of whom were considered to be enemies of the sun-god.

Great battles were fought by the Egyptian armies in the Levant and surrounding areas, but there seems to be no reference to a king destroying the enemies by the mere power of his spoken word (as discussed above). While this aspect of the earthly Horus does not exactly correspond with Rev. 19:15, it is entirely possible that as the son of Re and their leader in battle, many Egyptian soldiers believed he was capable of such magic.

Horus' horse (Rev. 19:11):- This verse says that "The Word of God" sat on a white horse. Similarly, Horus the king typically rode a horse at the head of his army at least up until the time that chariots were adopted by the Egyptians in the 2nd Intermediate Period. There seems to be little written about the preferred color of

Horus' horse(s) although, it may very well have been white, the color of purity. Wilkinson (1994) tells us that this color was "best suited to denote cleanliness and thus ritual purity and sacredness, white was almost invariably used to depict the clothing of most Egyptians and was especially symbolic in regard to the priesthood."[201] The color of the horse thus conforms with an attribute of Horus, the king of Egypt for he was symbolically cleansed of his impurities each day in the temple where he (or his chief priest acting on his behalf) served as the chief priest of the sun-god. And there can be little doubt that Horus typically wore white as he rode high on his horse or chariot before his army.

Horus's red robe (Rev. 19:13):- This verse says that he, "The Word of God" "is clad in a robe dipped in blood." Since it would be highly unlikely that the leader of an army would wear a robe which had been dipped in blood, this statement should not be taken literally. It seems to be a metaphor for the leader's ability to destroy the enemy with great shedding of blood. While this may well be the case, this metaphor can be interpreted from an Egyptian perspective to yield a more in-depth meaning, a meaning based on the symbolism of color "red."

Wilkinson (1994) says that the color red was "associated with fire and with blood ... Red could thus be used to signify anger, destruction, and death."[202] Perhaps, more relevant to Rev. 19:13 is the comment by Lurker (1980) that, among other things, the color symbolized victory.[203] He adds that "Red was also the color of all-destructive fire," a symbolism which leads to an expansion of the parallel between the color of the robe in Revelation and the wearer's position as leader of the army. In the *Annals of Thutmosis III* where the king leads his army against the enemies of the sun-god in the Levant, the text tells us that,

> The king himself, he led the way of his army, mighty at its head, *like a flame of fire,*' the king who wrought with his sword. He went forth, none like him, slaying the barbarians, smiting Retenu ... bringing their princes as living captives, their chariots wrought with gold, bound to their horses.[204]

Since a flame is associated with the color red, we can be reasonably certain that the color of the Thutmosis' robe – or more likely, his cape – was red, a color in stark contrast with the bright white uniforms (to be discussed next) of the army he led. Since the annals of Thutmosis III served as a model for Egyptian military practices in subsequent years, we might well assume that most or all the kings of Egypt wore such capes as they led their armies into battle.

As indicated above, the king of Egypt was considered to be the earthly incarnation of the divine Horus. We may therefore assume that, since the Egyptians viewed the spiritual world as a reflection of the earthly world (and *vice versa*), the spiritual Horus also wore a red robe. We may also assume that the red color of the robe of "The Word of God" in Rev. 19:13 parallels the color of the cape (or robe) of both Horus of the Netherworld and Horus the king of Egypt when they led the sun-god's army against the enemies of Re.

Horus' army

Egyptians took pride in their traditional clothing of fine white Egyptian linen. This pride is reflected in the *Admonitions of an Egyptian Sage* where the writer describes the sad state of affairs which accompanied what seems to be a great natural disaster in Egypt in which parts of Egypt were apparently covered by a layer of grey dust (see Chapter 13, *Castastrophes*). The author tells us that "men look like gem-birds [presumably because they are covered with dust]. Squalor is throughout the land. *There is none whose clothes are white in these times.*'"[205] This pride in pure, white linen went far beyond that of every-day dress; it was especially important in the army.

Uniforms of white linen (Rev. 19:11):- Unlike the leader of Revelation's heavenly army who wore a red robe, the troops who followed him were "arrayed in fine linen, white and pure" (Rev. 19:11). Similarly, Egyptian troops were internationally known for their uniforms of white linen. And, as will be discussed in detail in Chapter 7, *The Great Multitude,* those who "fight for their god" are described as wearing white robes. Each Egyptian soldier knew that if he should be killed in battle, his once pure, white garment soiled with blood or torn in battle would be replaced with new white garments in the hereafter. This topic will be continued in some detail in Chapter 10, *Call to Arms* with respect to Rev. 6:9-11 which deals with the presentation of new white robes (Rev. 6:11) to those who had been slain for "the word of god."

Riders on white horses (Rev. 19:14):- Rev. 19:14 tells us that the armies of heaven followed their leader on "white horses." While the king and his guards rode into battle on horseback in the early days and on chariots in later times, this description does not conform with what we know of an entire Egyptian army – or for that matter, any armies in either ancient or modern times. Most members of the Egyptian army were foot soldiers rather than horseback riders; a relatively small portion of the army fought on horseback or from chariots because of the high cost of maintaining this part of the army. It therefore seems that, if we are to draw any parallel to the reference to horses in Rev. 19:14 it would apply to only a relatively small segment, albeit an extremely important segment, of the Egyptian army. With respect to the color of the horses, it is also unlikely that all the Egyptian horses would be white; such horses would very likely be reserved for use by the king and his most trusted bodyguards. A parallel, if any, to the white horses of Rev. 19:14 would probably apply only to the king, his bodyguards and high-ranking officers.

Non-specific parallels

This section discusses Egyptian parallels which are not unique to either Thoth or Horus.

The leader's secret name (Rev. 19:12)

Rev. 19:12 tells us the leader of the heavenly army had "a name inscribed which no one knows but himself." The importance of a secret name among the Egyptians and their gods will be discussed in Chapter 7, *Egyptian Beliefs in the Seven Letters,* in relation to Rev. 2:17 which deals with the gift to the believers of a stone with a secret name. As we shall see then, secret names protected individuals from any harm others might wish to bring against them, especially evil spells. A secret name for the leader of the army in Rev. 19 is therefore quite understandable in the context of ancient Egyptian beliefs; it ensured his protection against all forms of magic and danger. Since the tradition of having a secret name was common in ancient Egypt, this particular attribute of Revelation's "Word of God" cannot be used as a parallel to help identify the "Word of God" in Rev. 19:12. Nevertheless, insofar as the practice of having one was common among the Egyptian gods and the Egyptians themselves, it remains a valid parallel to Revelation's mention of such a name.

Eyes like flame of fire (Rev. 19:12)

The reference to the leader's eyes being like fire in Rev. 19:12 is consistent with Egyptian beliefs about most of their more powerful deities so that, like the secret name mentioned above, this characteristic is not unique to either Thoth or Horus. This topic has been covered in Chapter 3, *The Preeminent Deities*, in relation to the parallel between the eyes of God on the throne (in Rev. 1:14 and Rev. 2:18) and those of Osiris. As with the secret name discussed above, this attribute does not provide us with a parallel unique to either Thoth or Horus. Nevertheless, and again, its presence in Revelation conforms with Egyptian beliefs about the fiery eyes of a variety of their gods.

Many crowns (Rev. 19:12)

Rev. 19:12 tells us that "The Word of God" wears "many diadems." Diadems, of course, are crowns so we must examine this verse accordingly. To begin with, it should be pointed out that practically all of the most important Egyptian gods wore more than one crown, each signifying a different function. We will deal with the crowns of Thoth and Horus separately to give the reader an idea of the number of crowns attributed to each, and hence some idea of the degree to which the reference to the "many crowns" of the "The Word of God" is applicable to both these deities.

The crowns of Thoth:- Budge (1904) tells us that, "When [pictured] in human form Thoth holds in his hands the sceptre and emblem of 'life' common to all gods, but his headdress varies according to the particular form of the god in which the artist wishes to depict him."[206] Elsewhere, he tells us that, "as a chronographer he wears the full lunar disk and a crescent [☉]; as a god of the dead (Osiris) he wears the *Atef* crown with horns, cobras, solar disk, &c."[207] (Figure 25). Also, Thoth sometimes wears the "the united crowns of the South and the North [ ]."[208] In addition, his sovereignty in other areas is revealed in simple titles. Lurker (1980) points out that he was "lord of the moon, lord of time ... protector of scribes, protector of Osiris, helper of the dead and inventor of writing.[209] Budge adds that he was the god of equilibrium, head of the Company of the Gods at Hermopolis, pacifier of the gods, the author of the forty-two *Books of Thoth*, and lord of books. Such a wide range of attributes certainly parallels Revelation's reference to the one called "The Word of God" wearing "many diadems."

The crowns of Horus :- This topic has already been addressed in Chapter 3, *The Preeminent Deities*. Suffice it to reiterate here a portion of the second to last paragraph of the section dealing with Horus as the ruler of the earth: "Near a picture of the king on a pillar in the Tomb of Ramesses VI the text reads, 'I give thee the South as well as the North, the West as well as the East, all the foreign lands are under thy soles, all the lands are at thy feet.' All Egyptians viewed their king, not only as ruler of Egypt, but as sovereign over all foreign lands." In this context, one can readily understand how Horus, the son of Re and king of Egypt might also be considered a ruler with many diadems, as described in Rev. 19:12.

Discussion

At first glance, it seems that the more likely parallel to Revelation's "Word of God" is Egypt's Thoth. The reason for this is the greater number of attributes which conform with those of "The Word of God." There are numerous references in the Egyptian literature to Thoth being associated with the words of the sun-god, including one which says he personified the very *tongue* of Re. Thoth was also renowned for his ability to use the "creative word" for magical purposes, including the killing of his foes at a distance. He was the *leader of Re's heavenly army* which fought against Apophis and his army. Thoth also acted as *judge* before Osiris at the judgment of the dead, a role which firmly established him as a faithful and true witness before Osiris.

It is also obvious that many of the attributes of Thoth can also be attributed to Horus, either in his spiritual form as Horus of the Netherworld or as Horus, king of Egypt. Horus was generally believed to possess magical powers which may very well have included the "creative word" and the capability of performing supernatural acts; he certainly possessed the power over life and death in Egypt. And in the judgment of the dead, Horus of the Netherworld became, over time, an even more popular *witness at the judgment* than Thoth; he replaced Thoth in reporting the results of the trial to Osiris at the final judgment. Nevertheless, the attributes of Revelation's "Word of God" do not seem to conform to Horus quite as well as they do to Thoth. For example, in order to establish one parallel, we must infer that, as king of Egypt and the son of Re, Horus was considered to be Re's representative on earth and therefore his word was considered to be the "word of Re." With respect to Thoth, the title "word of Re" actually appears in the religious texts.

But perhaps the best way of comparing the parallel attributes of Thoth and Horus is to combine them in a single table and classify them as either being explicitly or implicitly mentioned in the Egyptian texts. This method is presented in Table 5.1 which compares the various attributes of Revelation's "Word of God" with those of Egypt's Thoth and Horus. Note that the table is divided into three sections, the upper one shows the attributes which do not favor either Thoth or Horus. The middle one presents those which better fit Thoth while the lower one contains characteristics which conform better to Horus. In order to determine which of the two Egyptian deities better conform with Revelation's "Word of God," we begin with the top section, very briefly discussing each of the three sections in turn.

5. The Word of God

Attributes which apply equally to both:- Note that the first five attributes in this section are classified as being explicitly mentioned. The remaining two are considered to be only implicitly mentioned in the texts but like the first five, cannot be used to favor either Thoth or Horus.

Attributes which favor Thoth:- Revelation's name, "Word of God" parallels the explicitly stated descriptive name of the Egyptian god Thoth. (This cannot be said for Horus, except as it applies to the king of Egypt who, as son of the sun-god, represented his father; we may imply from his status as king that his word represented the word of his father, i.e., the king's word was considered to be the "word of Re.") Similarly, Thoth is explicitly described as a "judge" of the fight between Horus and Seth and he was a judge in the judgment of the dead. (The best we can say about Horus is that he acts as the chief judge and arbiter among the people of Egypt – and the nations.)

Attributes which favor Horus:- The first attribute, that the "Word of God" had his name inscribed on his thigh is by far the most prominent feature to distinguish between the two potential candidates. We have discussed texts describing the case for Horus, king of Egypt who was said to have been born with his name already present on one of his limbs; but there is no such evidence for Thoth. The second attribute, that the Egyptian king's army wore white clothing is well known from drawings and carvings of the king's soldiers. Finally, we may infer from the writings of king Thutmosis III that the color of Thutmosis' robe (or cape) was red, and from tradition, that his horse was white. There seems to be no reference, either implied or otherwise, to the color of Thoth's robe or his horse in any of the documents examined here.

When the relative weights of all these attributes are presented in this manner, it seems that a better argument for the Egyptian parallel to Revelation's "Word of God" can be made for Horus as the king of Egypt, the most important characteristic being the belief that the name of the king of Egypt was already inscribed on one of his limbs at birth, a belief which conforms with Rev. 19:16 which says that "on his thigh he has a name inscribed."

Regardless of this conclusion, Table 5.1 presents us with many attributes, most of which are or seem to be applicable to both Horus and Thoth. It is therefore natural that we might wonder if these two gods might be one and the same; they certainly seem to be almost identical in the table, except for the reference to his name being written on one of his limbs. This similarity is, however, an illusion because only those attributes of Revelation's "Word of God" are considered. In fact, there are many differences between the two Egyptian gods. For example, the following attributes of Thoth do not apply to Horus: Thoth is typically represented in drawings as an ibis or a crouching baboon called the lord of the moon, the lord of time and "reckoner of years." He was also the inventor of writing. In contrast, the following attributes of Horus do not apply to Thoth: Horus was initially a sky god represented by a falcon with outstretched wings and whose eyes represented the sun and moon; the falcon was the symbol for his name, some myths describe him as the son of Re while others, as the son of Osiris, his earthly incarnation was the king of Egypt, the "son of Re"; and finally, the sun-god's sole representative on earth as well as the perceived ruler of all the world. All these are important and well-recognized differences between Horus and Thoth and are not considered in Table 5.1. It is therefore clear that while Horus and Thoth may be different in several rather minor respects, the attributes listed in the table indicate a simple overlap of practically all the characteristics except for the reference to the king's name being written on one of his limbs. It is this most unusual attribute of Horus, the son of Re and king of Egypt which establishes him as being closer to Rev. 19's "Word of God" than Thoth.

Horus and Thoth were undoubtedly different deities about which many different myths developed through Egypt's dynastic period and it is clear that aspects of these myths sometimes overlapped. An important overlap is that both deities were at times considered to be leaders of the sun-god's army in the fight against his enemies. Sometimes – but not always – Thoth fought for Re against Apophis while Horus fought for Osiris against Seth although during the course of Egyptian history Apophis and Seth were frequently considered to be practically the same god. Thus, both Horus and Thoth could be considered to have fought for different aspects of the sun-god (Re and Osiris) against different aspects of the personification of evil.

In the next two chapters we leave our analyses on individual deities and move on to two large groups described in the Book of Revelation: *The Twelve Tribes of Israel* and *The Great Multitude*. The same approach will be used to identify Egyptian parallels to these groups as for individuals in this and the previous two chapters.

Table 5.1 Comparison of weights of arguments for which of the Egyptian gods, Thoth or Horus, more closely parallels Revelation's "Word of God" described in Rev. 19:11-16. "Implicit" means that no actual texts were found in any of the sources examined which explicitly state that a given attribute applied to Thoth or Horus but that reasonable arguments can be made for the presence of a particular attribute; "Explicit," means that an attribute is explicitly mentioned.

Attributes in Book of Revelation	Weight in Egyptian Sources	
	Thoth	Horus
Attributes not favoring either Thoth and Horus		
Faithful and true (Rev. 19:11)	Explicit	Explicit
Makes war (Rev. 19:11)	Explicit	Explicit
Rides at the head of an army (Rev. 19:11, 14)	Explicit	Explicit
Eyes like flame of fire (Rev. 19:12)	Explicit	Explicit
Many crowns (Rev. 19:12)	Explicit	Explicit
Has a secret name (Rev. 19:12	Implicit	Implicit
Soldiers ride white horses (Rev. 19:14)	Implicit	Implicit
Sword from mouth to smite the nations (Rev. 19:15)	Implicit	Implicit
Attributes favoring Thoth		
Name is "The Word of God" (Rev. 19:13)	Explicit	Implicit
Judges (Rev. 19:11)	Explicit	Implicit
Attributes favoring Horus		
Is inscribed with his name (Rev. 19:12,16)	No	Explicit
Army wears white clothing (Rev. 19:14)	Implicit	Explicit
Wears a red robe Rev. (19:13)	?	Implicit
Rides a white horse (Rev. 19:11)	?	Implicit

Chapter 6. The Twelve Tribes of Israel
(Rev. 7:4-8, Rev. 14:1-5)[210]

Two multitudes are mentioned in the seventh and fourteenth chapters of the Book of Revelation, one much smaller than the other. The smaller group is mentioned twice, once in Rev. 7:4-8 which describes 144,000 souls belonging to the "twelve tribes of Israel" and once in Rev. 14:1-5 which in Rev. 14:1 refers to "a hundred and forty-four thousand who had his (the Lamb's) name and his Father's name written on their foreheads." The larger group is unambiguously mentioned only once and is described as "a great multitude which no man could number, from every nation, from all tribes and peoples and tongues" (Rev. 7:9). Both these groups are of particular interest from an Egyptological point of view because they have a number of important characteristics in common with groups of twelve deities found in the *Amduat* and the *Book of Gates*.

This chapter will deal primarily with three attributes of the tribes of Israel. Firstly, the number of tribes involved, then the names of the tribes, and finally their attributes as provided in Rev. 7:4-8. Before addressing the nature of these parallels we will review a few particulars about the tribes of Israel to help orient the reader to this aspect of the study. Whybray (1993) summarizes their history as follows:

> The Hebrew Bible in its final form takes it for granted that the Israelite people are descended from the twelve sons of Jacob [who is later named Israel], each being the ancestor of the tribe named after him (1 Kings 18.31). This tradition has persisted into later times. The book of Genesis records the births of Jacob's twelve sons (chaps. 29-35), and then provides a list of them arranged under the names of their mothers . ... After Joseph brought his family from Canaan (Gen. 46-47) to Egypt the twelve brothers and their families continued to reside in Egypt where they increased in numbers, becoming the people of Israel, literally the "sons of Israel" (Exod. 1.1-7), Jacob's name having been changed by God to Israel (Gen. 32.28; 35.10). This united people, after many vicissitudes, took possession of the land of Canaan and established their home there, with each tribe assigned its own territory (Josh. 13-19).[211]

Genesis 49:1–28 lists the names of the tribes as Joseph, Gad, Naph'tali, Is'sachar, Levi, Simeon, Benjamin, Asher, Zeb'ulun, Judah, Reuben and Dan. In contrast, the list of names given in Rev. 7:4-8 omits Dan and instead, includes Manas'seh, one of

Joseph's sons. The resolution of this problem preferred by Glasson (1965) is that "a scribe's error turned Dan into Man and this was later taken to be an abbreviation (Man.) and was expanded into Manas'seh."[a, 212] In order to accommodate this possibility, we will tentatively include the name of Dan as a alternative to Manas'seh in the list of names to be compared with those in the Egyptian records; we will see that Glasson's resolution conforms with the results of this study.

In this section, we divide our analyses into three main themes, as follows.

1. The multitudes in groups of twelve
2. The names of the tribes of Israel (Rev. 7:5-8)
3. Attributes of the tribes of Israel

Division into Groups of Twelve

Rev. 7:4 states that each of the twelve tribes contains 12,000 people (i.e., a total of 144,000 members). Neither the *Amduat* nor the *Book of Gates*, however, explicitly refers to this number. Nevertheless, that such a large number of individuals can be represented by the twelve deities in the Egyptian texts may be illustrated by a brief look at several Egyptian numerical conventions. We begin with the idea of duality. Duality was expressed in its hieroglyphic form by two simple strokes or pictures; two gods could be represented by a picture of a single god accompanied by two strokes, or simply by two pictures of the same god. Three such symbols, however, usually meant three or more, and quite often meant "many." Groups of two and three could be combined to represent even greater numbers. For example, two groups of three could mean "many many" or "very, very many."[213] A group of four represented a very large number, or "multitude." For example, in the 4th Division of the *Book of Gates* we find a group of four Negroes with the accompanying text, "I was pleased with the *multitude*' which came out of me in your name of Negroes."[214] Also, in the 10th Division of the same book we see four deities towing the barque of the sun-god; that these four actually represent many more than four is evident in the belief that the sun-god's barque was envisioned to be about 310 cubits long, large enough to carry thousands of faithful souls; it would take a multitude of rowers to row such a large boat and even more towers to move it through shallows and over sandbanks. In the register above the four towers, the sun-god's army is represented by three groups of four warriors, two in front of and one behind, i.e., "many multitudes" of soldiers (their number being derived from multiplying three (= many) by four (= multitudes)). The multitude of Apophis' followers is shown on the far right-hand side of the same register as four captive serpents; the head of a fifth serpent, shown emerging from the

---

[a] Our understanding of the exact number and names of the tribes is not without its difficulties. Whybray (1993: pp. 778–779) tells us that "The Bible is ... not consistent with regard to either the number or the names of the tribes. In the numerous tribal lists found in the various books of the Bible, the number varies from eleven to thirteen." For example, some lists include Ephraim and Manas'seh (Gen. 48.8–20) as separate tribes and one includes Machir (Josh. 17.1). Also, for various reasons, certain names are added or dropped in the lists so that a total of fifteen names can be accounted for.

ground, is shaped like the hieroglyphic symbol ⟩ which represents the number 10,000. This gives some idea of the number of foes in the multitude: 40,000 (from 4 x 10,000). Groups of twelve in the Egyptian literature (3 groups of 4, i.e., many multitudes) clearly represented many thousands of individuals, possibly as many as the 144,000 members of the twelve tribes of Israel described in the Book of Revelation.

Nowhere is the strong connection between the multitudes and the number twelve felt more strongly than in the opening scene of the *Book of Gates*. In the book's prologue (Figure 26) we find two groups of twelve deities, one in the upper part of the scene and one in the lower part. They flank the evening sun-god as he sets with his solar barque into the western desert (the entrance to the Egyptian Netherworld where he will be rejuvenated) and are described in the text as being special to him.

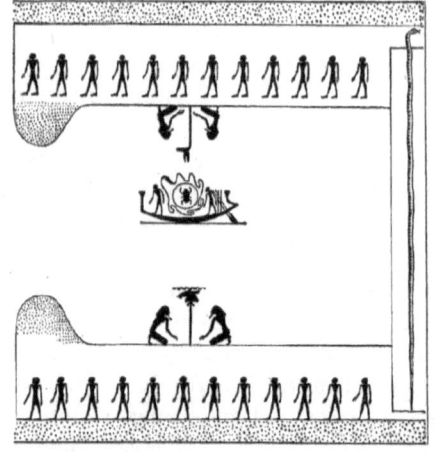

> Those who came into being from Re, from his Glorious Eye, who came forth out of his Eye. He grants them their hidden seat, the Desert (Necropolis) to which are brought together men, gods, all cattle, all worms, which are created by this Great God. This god takes measures concerning them after having mounted upon earth (which) he has created from his right eye."[215]

Figure 26. Twenty-four deities flanking the sun-god (shown here as a beetle inside a disk encircled by a protective serpent) as he enters the Netherworld in his solar barque. These two groups of twelve effectively introduce the many groups of twelve in the book of Gates who may represent the twelve tribes of Israel described in Rev. 7:4-8 and elsewhere in the Book of Revelation. (BG^{Prologue})

The text also describes this part of the desert as being "bright ... filled with the chosen ones of the gods."[216] This special nature of the groups of twelve surrounding the sun-god sets the tone for the appearance, arrangement, and function in the rest of the groups of twelve in the *Book of Gates*. Remarkably, we learn that special attention is given to them in all but the last two divisions.

Fortunately, the groups of twelve in the *Amduat* and the *Book of Gates* have very well defined attributes which can be readily compared with those of the twelve tribes of Israel in the Book of Revelation. In the following paragraphs, the names of these groups in the two books (or of individual gods in the groups) will be compared with those of the twelve tribes in the Book of Revelation. It will be shown that the two sources agree quite well with one another.

Names of the Tribes of Israel (Rev. 7:4-8)

Rev. 7:4-8 lists the names of the twelve tribes of Israel as Judah, Reuben, Gad, Asher, Naph'tali, Manas'seh, Simeon, Levi, Is'sachar, Zeb'ulun, Joseph and Benjamin. The most straightforward approach to identifying the names of the tribes of Israel in ancient Egyptian records is to examine the records for the same or similar sounding names. Past studies by a number of scholars using this method have consistently failed so that there are no published accounts of such records in ancient Egypt. The approach taken here, however, has resulted in more encouraging results.

The following study is based on the *meanings* of the names rather than the names themselves. In it, the meanings of Egyptian names are based on English translations of the original hieroglyphic texts by Piankoff (1954). Since there are literally hundreds of names recorded in Egyptian texts, it quickly became obvious that comparisons with all of them would be simply impractical. To make the task more manageable and meaningful, the only names considered were those associated with groups of twelve deities. The *Amduat* and the *Book of Gates* were subsequently selected for study because they contain many such groups.

Meanings of the Hebrew names of the tribes referred to in Revelation were obtained from a variety of sources (see notes below Table 6.1). It was noted that while the meanings of some of the Egyptian names bore remarkable similarities to those of the Hebrew names, others were not as similar and still others were doubtful. Accordingly, each possible match was ranked from 1 to 3 as follows: Rank 1 was applied to Egyptian names which were reasonably *good matches* for a Hebrew name, Rank 2 names were *reasonable matches*, and Rank 3 names were *poor matches;* Egyptian names which could not be matched with Hebrew names were not assigned any rank. This system enabled a more informative means for comparing names than one based on simple agreement or non-agreement, particularly in view of the difficulties inherent in translating Egyptian names (see chapter entitled *Names and Combinations of Gods* in Hornung's *Conceptions of God in Ancient Egypt* (1983).

Names in the *Book of Gates*

There are 34 groups of twelve in the *Book of Gates* (Appendix 1). Of these, 33 groups are identified by name[a] and 14 of these (42%) have names which match eight (67%) of the 12 names of the tribes of Israel (Table 6.1); twelve (36%) of the matching names were classified as being *good* matches, one (3%) as a *reasonable* match and one (3%) as *poor*. Nevertheless, of these 14 matching names, only eight conformed with those of the tribes because of similar names (included Manas'seh, whose name, as mentioned earlier, is considered to represent Dan (to judge)). It is remarkable that the names of from 36% to 42% (from 36%+3%+3%) of the 33 groups of deities could

---

[a] Locations in the *Book of Gates* of the 34 groups of twelve not matched to Hebrew names are as follows: at BG- Prologue/upper register, BG-Prologue/lower register, BG1.1a, BG1.1b, BG2.1a, BG2.1b, BG3.1a, BG3.1b, BG3.1c, BG3.2, BG3.3, BG4.1a, BG4.1b, BG4.2a, BG4.2b, BG4.3, BG5.1a, BG5.1b, BG5.1c, BG5.2, BG5.3a, BG5.3b, BG6.1a, BG6.1b, BG6.3, BG7.1a, BG7.1b, BG7.2, BG7.3a, BG7.3b, BG8.1, BG10.1, BG10.3a, and BG10.3b.

be matched to varying degrees with the meanings of Hebrew names of the tribes of Israel. These percentages seem significant, especially when similarly good matches are by no means as common among the hundreds of names of deities examined elsewhere in the same book. Unfortunately however, there is no way to statistically compare these data on matching names of groups with those of individual deities elsewhere in the *Book of Gates* so it is impossible to estimate the degree of similarity between these two categories and the names of the groups of twelve in Revelation. This restriction, however, is not so for names within groups of 12 in the *Amduat*, as we shall see next.

Table 6.1 The names of 14 of 33 (in the right-hand column) groups of twelve from the *Book of Gates* which conform to the meanings of eight of the names of the twelve tribes of Israel. Note that the meanings of some Hebrew names match those of Egyptian names of more than one group. No matches were found for *Benjamin* (son of the right hand [Y]), *Naph'tali* (wrestling,[Y] wrestler,[O] I have fought[D]), *Reuben* (behold a son,[Y] see ye a son[S]) and *Simeon* (hearing,[SY] call (gather) together[Jr]).

Hebrew Name	Meaning of Hebrew Name	Translation of Names of Groups in the Book of Gates	Location of Group
Good matches			
Asher	a) happy,[Y] to be blessed,[J] women will call me happy [D]	a) Those who are *in peace* who worship Re[217]	BG1.1.1-6*
		Those who are *in peace*. Those who create (?) the gifts of the just[218]	BG6.1.1-5**
	b) Asherah (Canaanite goddess; a consort of Ba'al)[D]	b) —	
Dan	judge[Y] or to judge [D]	*The Council who Judges*[219]	BG7.3.7-10
		Lords of Provisions of the West ... *judge me your judgment* ...[220]	BG7.2.4-8
Gad	a) troop,[B] *to crowd upon i.e., attack,*[Sr] *to penetrate,*[D]	a) The gods[b] who cut the throats [and *overthrow* the evil god Apophis].[221]	BG10.1.5-7
	b) fortune,[Y] fortune, luck [D] good fortune,[L] fortunate [G]	b) —	
Is'sachar	a) *he will bring* a reward [S]	a) Those who are in peace. Those who *create (?) the gifts* of the just[222]	BG6.1.1-5**
	b) *bearing* hire,[Y]	b) —	
Judah	praise,[YJr] worship (with extended hands),[Sr] to hold out the hand [Sr]	Those who *acclaim* in the Netherworld[223]	BG4.1.1-4
		Those who are in peace who *worship* Re[224]	BG1.1.1-6*

6. The Twelve Tribes of Israel

Hebrew Name	Meaning of Hebrew Name	Translation of Names of Groups in the *Book of Gates*	Location of Group
Levi	joined,[Y] attached,[S] *to twine*,[Sr] to join[O]	Those who carry the *cord* in the fields of the Netherworld[225]	BG4.1.4-8
		Those who carry *the twisted cord* which comes out of the stars[226]	BG5.1.7-10
		Those who carry *the twisted serpent rope* and create the hours[227]	BG7.1.6-10
		Those who carry the *[twisted] rope* and create the mysteries[228]	BG7.1.1-5
Reasonable matches			
Joseph	increase,[r] let him add,[S] may God *give increase*[O]	Gods who carry the swallower *from whose coils issue heads [i.e., people]*[229]	BG5.1.4-7
Poor matches			
Zeb'ulun	dwelling,[Y] *to reside*,[JrSr] to enclose[Sr]	(*Those of the) hole* in the hard earth[230]	BG5.3.7-10

Key to both Table 6.1 and Table 6.2:
   B = *Brown Driver & Briggs Hebrew Lexicon*.
   C = *The Complete Who's Who of the Bible* by Gardener (1995).
   D = *Dictionary of Proper Names and Places in the Bible* by Odelain and Séguineau (1981).
   O = *The Oxford Guide to People & Places of the Bible* by Bruce and Coogan (2001).
   r = from root word(s).
   S= The New *Strong's exhaustive concordance of the Bible* by Strong (1996).
   T = Thayer's definitions.
   U = (Usage in the King James Version).
   Y=*Young's Analytical Concordance to the Bible* by Young (1982).

Names in the *Amduat*

There are ten groups of twelve gods in the *Amduat*.[a] Unlike the groups in the *Book of Gates*, however, all except one group contain the names of individuals to which we must pay specific attention (this group will be identified later).

Of the 120 deities among the groups of twelve, 110 or 92% are assigned names. When the meanings of these names were compared with those of the tribes of Israel given in Rev. 7:4-8, 25 (or 23%), 110 names could be matched with names of the tribes of Israel. These are given in Appendix 2 along with those names which did not match those of any of the tribes. Of particular interest to us at this point in our examination are the matches made with the names found in two specific groups of twelve in AM7.3; these matches are shown in Table 6.2. Before critically examining these matches, however, a few explanatory notes on two of the matches are in order.

---

[a] The 10 groups of twelve in the *Amduat* are located at AM7.3a, AM7.3b, AM9.1a, AM9.1b, AM9.2, AM9.3, AM11.2, AM12.1a, AM12.1b and AM12.2. Only the one at AM9.1a is named.

The first explanatory note pertains to the tribe of Dan. The name Dan is not mentioned in Rev. 7:4-8 although Manas'seh is present in the list; it seems the two names refer to the same tribe. In consideration of this omission of Dan, a name present in all other Old Testament lists of the tribes of Israel, Glasson (1965) suggests the possibility that "a scribe's error turned Dan into Man and this was later taken to be an abbreviation (Man.) and was expanded into Manas'seh."[231] For this reason, the name Dan rather than Manas'seh is used in the current comparison of the meanings of the names of the tribes.

A second comment on Table 6.2 involves the matching of the name Gad with "He who lifts his arm." Again, examining the names from an Egyptian perspective reveals a possible link. The raised arm is often an Egyptian symbol of power when presented in a threatening manner as when one arm is lifted high behind one's head in the act of striking a foe; the stance is even incorporated as a hieroglyph in its own right (𓀠). A well-known example is the "royal smiting motif" known from the earliest dynasties in which the king is shown in the act of smiting an enemy. In this manner, the meaning of the Egyptian name conforms with that of Gad which is believed by some to involve an action by troops such as "to attack."

With the above background in mind, we begin our critical examination of matching names. We first focus on the matches found in the two groups of 12 in the lower register of the 7th Division of the *Amduat* as shown in Table 6.2. The number of matches found (13) was evaluated according to the degree to which they resemble the meanings of the Hebrew names in Revelation, as follows: eight (61%) of the 13 matches in the two groups of 12 are considered *good* matches, four (31%) are *reasonable* and one (8%) is considered a *poor* match. Three of the matches were especially close: Dan (*the judge* – and hence Manas'seh as discussed above) which matches *The Opener*, Levi (*to twine*) which compares well with the goddess called *The Weaver*, and Benjamin (*son of the right hand*) which is almost identical with *The One of the Right Hand*. The close agreement of the meanings of these three names is a strong suggestion that this particular grouping of 24 deities may be of special interest.

When we look at the distribution of matching names of individuals in groups of twelve throughout the *Amduat* the pattern is basically the same, as illustrated in Figure 27A. It is apparent from this figure that 13 (52% of 25) matching names are clustered in a single scene in the lowermost register of the 7th Division while the remaining 12 (48%) are distributed somewhat unevenly through the other 3 divisions where they constitute 14% of the remaining 86 named deities. The 7th Division is also unusual in that the 13 matching names are found here mixed among two contiguous groups, one male and the other female (see Table 6.2). In the details of the similarities between these names and those in Rev. 7:4-8 note that only 11 of the twelve tribes are identified even though 13 of the Egyptian deities have matching names; this apparent discrepancy is caused by the fact that the Egyptian names of four of the deities (1st goddess plus the 8th god and 5th & 6th gods) conform with the names of only two of the tribes (Judah and Simeon). This is shown graphically in Figure 28.

6. The Twelve Tribes of Israel

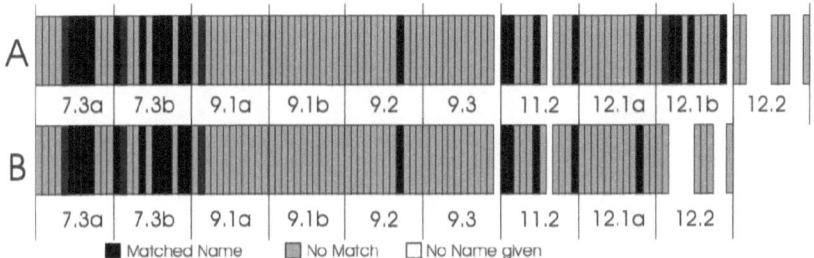

Figure 27. The distribution of 25 names (one name not shown here is a group name) in groups of 12 in the *Amduat*. The meanings these names conform with those of the names of the twelve tribes of Israel given in Revelation 7:4-8. Numbers refer to division numbers in the *Amduat*. Part A contains all the names and AM12.1b is omitted in Part B to illustrate the overall effect of this anomalous (see text) division. See Appendix 2 for details.

This apparent grouping of the 13 matching names in AM7.3 is shown graphically in Figure 27A. A legitimate question concerning the apparent difference between the proportions of names shown in the figure (54%) and those in the remaining 8 groups of twelve (14%) is: "Is this grouping of 13 matches in the 7th Division fortuitous?" In other words, "Is the grouping a meaningful clustering of Egyptian names which have meanings similar to those of the tribes of Israel in Rev. 7:4-8?" "Is the observed grouping of names in AM7.3 statistically significant or is it simply random?" To answer this question, Fisher's Exact Test of Proportions was used to compare the proportion of matching names in AM7.3 (Table 6.2 and Figure 28) to that of matching names in the remaining eight groups of 12. In this scenario, the proportion in the remaining eight groups is considered to be a background level against which the proportion in the 7th Division can be compared. The two proportions compared in this case are .54 of 24 and .14 of 86. The results of these analyses indicate the difference between the two proportions is statistically significant at the p = .0001 level of significance; in other words there is only about one chance in 10,000 that the two proportions are the same. This means that the clustering of names in AM7.3 which match those of the tribes of Israel in Rev. 7:4-8 is very likely *not* due to chance.

There is one potential bias in this statistical approach and it is related to the group of twelve in AM12.1b. Five of the 11 translated names in this group conform with the meaning of the name of Judah (see Figure 27A and Appendix 2), a situation which is different from any of the other groups in the *Amduat*. The reason for this is related to the apparent function of all the deities in this group, i.e., to give praise to their god (this is evident in the manner in which all twelve of them stand – they all stand with their hands raised in a stance (𓀀) which forms the hieroglyph for *praise*).[232] In other words, the stance of all 12 deities in this group can be said to conform with the name Judah. For this reason, this group of 12 is atypical and may be omitted from the statistical analysis. This means that the number of possible deities represented in places other than AM7.3 is 11 less than the 86 used in the earlier analysis, which

124   *Egyptian Origin of the Book of Revelation*

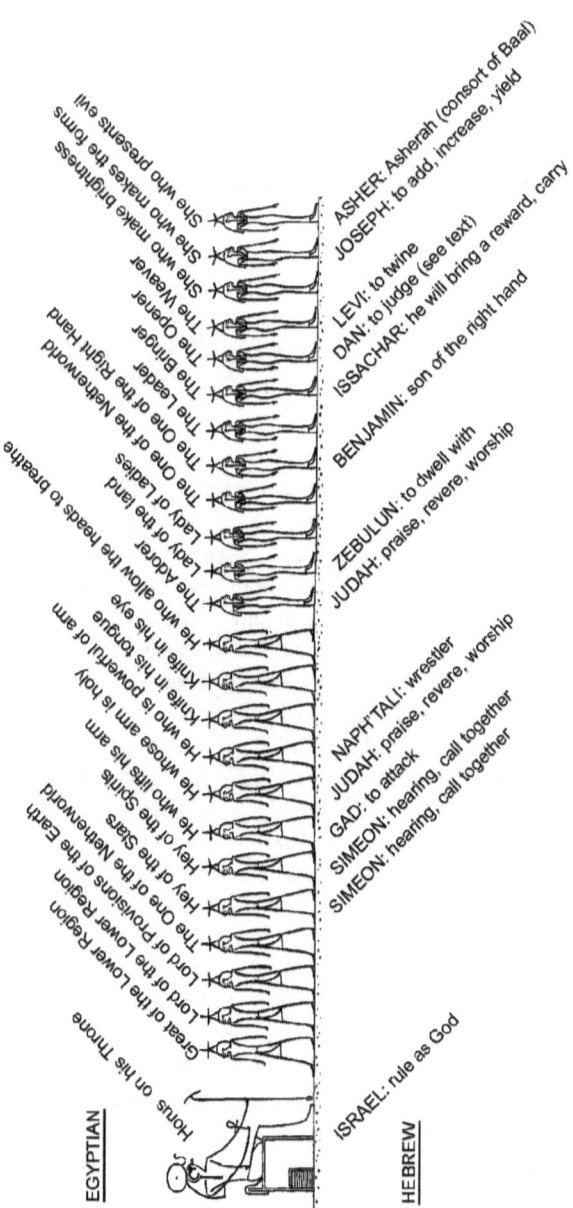

Figure 28. Cluster of names in the *Amduat* (AM7.3) with meanings similar to those the names of the tribes of Israel, including Israel himself. Translations of the meanings of the Egyptian names (by Piankoff (1954), p. 283) are shown above while the meanings of comparable Israelite names are below. Also, see Table 6.2.

6. The Twelve Tribes of Israel

Table 6.2 Comparison of the meanings of the names of deities in two groups of 12 in the third register of the 7th Division of the *Amduat*. Note that the names of 7 of the 12 tribes may be considered "good matches" while three may be considered as "reasonable matches" and one as a "poor match" for a total of eleven possible matches; no match was found for Reuben. Translations of Egyptian names are from Piankoff (1954, p. 283). (See Table 6.1 for the key to sources of Hebrew names.)

Hebrew Name	Meaning of Hebrew Name	Translation of Names in the Group of 24 Deities in AM7.3	Location of Deity
Good matches			
Asher*	a) Asherah (Canaanite goddess; a consort of Ba'al)^D	a) She *who presents evil*	12th goddess
	b) happy,^{Y} *to be blessed*,^{J} *women will call me happy*^{D}	b) —	
Benjamin	*son of the right hand*^{Y}	*The One of the Right Hand*	5th goddess
Dan	*judge*^{Y} or *to judge*^{D} (see text for discussion on the name "Manas'seh")	*The Judge* (= *The Opener* in figure, see text)	8th goddess
Gad	a) troop,^{B} *to crowd upon i.e., attack*,^{Sr} *to penetrate*,^{D} *gather (selves together in troops)*^{J}	a) He who *lifts his arm*	7th god
	b) fortune,^{Y} *fortune, luck*^{D} *good fortune*,^{L} *fortunate*^{G}	b) —	
Is'sachar*	a) *he will bring a reward*^{S}	a) *The Bringer*	7th goddess
	b) *bearing hire*,^{Y}		
Judah	*praise*,^{YJr} *worship* (with extended hands),	*The Adorer*	1st goddess
	^{Sr} *to hold out the hand*^{Sr}	*He whose arm is holy*	8th god
Levi	*joined*,^{Y} *attached*,^{S} *to twine*^{Sr} *to join*^{O}	*The weaver*	9th goddess
Reasonable matches			
Joseph	*increase*,^{Y} *let him add*,^{S} *may God give increase*^{O}	She who *makes the forms*	11th goddess
Simeon	*hearing*,^{SY} *call (gather) together*^{Jr}	*Hey* of the Stars *Hey* of the Spirits	5th god 6th god
Naph'tali	*wrestling*,^{Y} *wrestler*, ^{O} *I have fought*^{D}	He who is *powerful of arm*	9th god
Poor matches			
Zeb'ulun	*dwelling*,^{Y} *to reside*,^{JrSr} *to enclose*^{Sr}	*Lady of the Land*	2nd goddess

* See Table 6.1 for key to references B, C, D, etc.

yields a new total of 75. We should therefore compare 13 (or 54%) of the 24 at AM7.3 with 7 (or 9%) of the 75 deities in the remaining groups shown in Figure 27B. The two proportions to be compared in this case are 0.54 of 24 and 0.09 of 75 and the difference between them is significant at about the .00001 level of significance; in other words, the two proportions, 0.54 and 0.09, are even more different than that observed in the previous analysis (0.54 and 0.14); in this case, there is only about one chance in 100,000 that they are the same. The removal of this bias accentuates the difference and increases the statistical significance of the grouping of matched names in AM7.3.

One might enquire what happens if we eliminate the poorly matched name, Zebuluin, in Table 6.1 and consider only the *good* and *reasonable* matches? Such an analysis would be based on 12 (or 50%) of 24 in AM7.3 and 12 (or 14%) of 86 (the worst case scenario) in all the remaining groups. The results of this analysis indicate a significant grouping of recognizable names in AM7.3 at the .0005 level, thus conforming with the earlier conclusion in which Zeb'ulun (and the group at AM12.1b) is included.

These analyses suggest the clustering of matching names in AM7.3 is not mere coincidence and may be interpreted to mean that the grouping of Egyptian names with meanings similar to those of the tribes of Israel represents a valid parallel with the names of the tribes given in Rev. 7:4-8.

There is one rather perplexing aspect of the findings presented in Table 6.2 and Figure 28; it involves the possible implications of several duplicate matches. There are duplicates of names matching Simeon and Judah. Simeon's name is represented in two adjacent deities, *Hey of the Stars* and *Hey of the Spirits* while Judah is represented by *The Adorer* and *He whose arm is holy*. Thus, four of the twenty-four deities in this scene account for the names of two tribes. In addition to these duplicates, the Egyptian equivalent of Israel, the leader of the tribes, appears once as *Horus on his Throne* and once as *The Leader* (not labeled as "Israel" among the Hebrew names in Table 6.2 but identifiable as the 6th goddess in Figure 28). The reason for these duplications is unclear although one of the duplications could involve a misidentification of the two deities labeled *Hey of the Stars* and *Hey of the Spirits*; it is possible that neither of these is a match for any of the names of the tribes. Nevertheless, as pointed out above, an error involving so few names would not significantly change the main conclusions made from the statistical analyses.

In addition to the above, of the eleven deities which could not be specifically identified with any of the tribes, four may be otherwise explained. These are the 1st, 2nd, and 3rd gods called *Great of the Lower Region*, *Lord of the Lower Region* and *The One of the Netherworld*, and the 4th goddess called *The One of the Netherworld*. All of these (with the possible exception of the last one) can be readily identified with Osiris who rules the Netherworld and who is identified as Revelation's God on the throne in Chapter 3, *The Preeminent Deities* (such duplication of deities in a single group is common in Egyptian religious literature). Four of the remaining deities have names of note; they are *Knife in his tongue* (10th god), *Knife in his eye* (11th god), *He who allows the heads to breath* (12th god), and *Lady of Ladies* (3rd goddess). It might be argued that *Knife in his tongue* corresponds with the Hebrew name of Manas'seh, which means "to forget." Nevertheless, if we assume that *Knife in his eye* refers to a blind person then *Knife in his tongue* might not refer to the forgetfulness suggested by Manas'seh's name, but rather, that this god simply cannot speak. These four are therefore more difficult to identify with names of the tribes of Israel and their function in Figure 28 is unclear. It seems that Figure 28 represents more than a simple display of the tribes of Israel. Detailed analyses of the original Egyptian hieroglyphic text may be enlightening in this area. In spite of this difficulty the main conclusion is still valid – that this scene in AM7.3 contains references to most of the names of the tribes of Israel provided by Rev. 7:4-8.

Israel, Patriarch of the Tribes (Rev. 7:4)

But what of Israel, the patriarch of the twelve tribes? Does he too have a parallel in this part of the *Amduat*? To answer these questions, we turn our attention to a 25th deity in Figure 28. He is prominently figured on the far left of the figure, seated on a throne and carrying a scepter in one hand ( ) and an *ankh* symbol in the other. He is called *Horus on his Throne,* a name indicating he rules over the two groups of 12 in front of him in this part of the Netherworld. That Horus should rule as if he were Osiris was a belief among Osirian believers; the *Legend of the Contendings of Horus and Seth* says that, after the trial to determine who had the right to the throne, "Horus was brought forth forthwith, and the White Crown was placed on his head, and he was set in the place of Osiris."[233] Also, referring to *Pyramid Text* §219, Breasted (1912) says that "the dead king [Horus] receives the throne of Osiris, and becomes, like him, king of the dead."[234] Furthermore, recall that Egypt's Osiris parallels Revelation's God on the throne so that, at times, Osiris on his throne is indistinguishable from Horus on his throne. Indeed, Hornung (1990) points out that at times the sun-god Re takes on the role of Horus of the Netherworld: "Being dead, Osiris is always in danger and requires the aid of the sun god on his nightly voyage. Re thus fulfills the role of the loyal son Horus, forcing his way against all odds to his father in the Netherworld, and the texts of the Beyond identify him as 'Horus of the Netherworld.'" Thus, when Re entered the Netherworld over which Osiris ruled, he ruled with Osiris – as Horus. The interpretation that "Horus rules with Osiris" can therefore, in the context of the Book of Revelation, be said to mean "Horus rules with God." This interpretation thus corresponds with Strong's (1966) and Young's (1982) meanings of the Hebrew name *Israel* as "ruling with God" and "prevail" or "rule as God." In Figure 28 *Horus on his throne* rules with Osiris in the Netherworld just as Israel *ruled with God* on earth. Of course, from an earthly perspective, it is Horus, king of Egypt who rules on earth and his name seems to have taken the place of Israel in Figure 28. Not only do the 24 deities in AM7.2 conform with the twelve tribes of Israel, but the meaning of the Egyptian name of their ruler also conforms with the meaning "Israel," the patriarch of the twelve tribes if we accept that Horus was their earthly ruler in Egypt..

On first read, the hieroglyphic text associated with Figure 28 does not seem to conform with either the above analyses or our general knowledge of the tribes of Israel; it seems to have nothing to do with them. A new interpretation emerges, however, when ancient Egyptian techniques of ambiguous terminology, symbolism, and visual and verbal punning is used to read the text. In the latter technique, homonyms, near homonyms or non-explicit symbols may be substituted for key words to hide or otherwise distort the original intent of a passage, an encoding technique (called *paronomasia*) discussed earlier. Three reasonable substitutions present themselves for consideration in the text associated with Figure 28. The substitutions themselves will be discussed before we present their possible impact on our understanding of the text. They involve references to *Horus on his Throne*, the *stars*, and the *Hours* and involve the following substitutions:

> *Horus on his Throne = Israel:-* This substitution has been discussed above; the title of the deity on the throne in the scene may thus be interpreted to mean "Israel."
>
> *Stars = souls:-* The text in the bottom register informs us that Horus "speaks to these gods and to the stars," suggesting the stars are living entities which can understand what is being said to them. Indeed, the Egyptians believed that stars represented the souls, or at times, the dwelling place of the souls of the faithful dead. The stars above the heads of each of the twenty-four deities in Figure 28 and the references to them in the accompanying text may therefore reasonably be considered to represent the *souls* of the faithful followers.
>
> *Hours = priesthood:-* The Egyptian word used for *hour* in the text of the seventh division is pronounced *wnwt*. Another Egyptian word which is pronounced the same means "priesthood." For this reason, we may assume a pun and apply the word "priesthood" to the word *wnwt*.

Note that the substitutions for *stars* and *hours* result in possible attributes of the tribes of Israel. Although seeming insignificant, when incorporated into the original text they contribute to several well-known aspects of the exodus of the Israelites from Egypt. The revised text associated with Figure 28 reads:

> This image (represents) *Israel*. This image is like this. What it does in the Netherworld is to set the *souls* in motion, to make the *priesthood* stop (?) in the Netherworld.
>
> The majesty of *Israel* speaks to these gods and to the *souls*:
>
> May your flesh be right, may your forms come into being, you are satisfied with your *souls*! Stand up before Re, He of the Horizon, who is in the Netherworld every day. You are in his following while your *souls* are before him to let him pass through the beautiful West in peace. You are indeed those who stand in the land. O you, your *souls* belong to me(?), I who am in Heaven! He is satisfied indeed, the Lord of the Horizon.
>
> The majesty of the *Israel* of the Netherworld speaks to the *priesthood* who are in this city:
>
> O *priesthood* who become, O *priesthood of souls*, O *priesthood* who protect Re, who fight on behalf of He in the Horizon. Take your forms [prepare to leave Egypt?], carry your images [the Ark of the Covenant?], lift up your heads, while you lead this Re [= Yahweh[a]] who is in the horizon toward the beautiful West [the Promised Land?] in peace.
>
> These gods and goddesses [Israelites?] conduct this Great God [Yahweh, whose presence is represented by the Ark of the Covenant?] toward the mysterious road of this city [the Promised Land?].

---

[a] Budge (1934: 16–8, 380–381) presents a list of 15 ancient Egyptian passages describing the power and attributes of Amen, Ptah and Amen-Ptah, their "God, the One God, the creator of the universe" and notes that they conform with the attributes of Yahweh, the ancient supreme god of the Hebrews.

The deities who "stand up before Re" are "in his [Re's] following," i.e., in the following of the one who is "in heaven" just as the Hebrews followed Yahweh who is in heaven. These also "belong to" Re just as the Israelites belonged to their god, Yahweh (for example, I Kings 6:13); the Egyptian text says, "O you, your souls *belong to me*' (?), I who am in Heaven!" Furthermore, they are referred to as "those who stand in the land" in much the same way as the Israelites stood on their new land ("the promised land") after their sojourn in the desert. And just as the Israelites were instructed to carry the Arc of the Covenant ahead of them in the wilderness during their trek to the promised land, the deities in the *Amduat* are told to "Take your forms, carry your images, lift up your heads, while you lead this Re who is in the horizon toward the beautiful West in peace. These gods and goddesses conduct this Great God toward the mysterious road of this city."

One interpretation of the last two paragraphs in the above revised quotation may be of particular interest to some readers. In it, the "Israelites" seem to be instructed to prepare to leave Egypt and to take with them their most sacred religious symbol, "the Ark of the Covenant." Here, it seems that those who "carry your images" (the Ark of the Covenant) are placed in juxtaposition with the priesthood "who fight on behalf of He in the Horizon" just as the Ark of the Covenant went into battle before the Israelites.

The apparent reference to the *souls* of Israel being a *priesthood* also warrants comment. It conforms with the statement in Exodus 19:6, which provides us with some details of the Sinai event; we read here that Yahweh declares the Israelites "shall be for me a priestly kingdom and a holy nation." The suggested reference to the souls being a priesthood in this part of the *Amduat* is therefore consistent with Hebrew tradition.[a]

This analysis of the hieroglyphic text associated with Figure 28, although not at all conclusive in its own right, lends support to the above matching of Egyptian names in the figure. It conforms with Revelation's version of the tribes of Israel as well as other events found in the Old Testament and Jewish traditions. More research is needed in this area.

Attributes of the Tribes of Israel

Revelation provides us with several attributes of the tribes of Israel. In this section these attributes will be compared with those of the groups of twelve in the *Book of Gates* and the *Amduat*. Most of our discussion in this area will be concentrated, however, on parallel attributes found in the *Book of Gates* where most of the groups of twelve are found. A comparative listing of the parallel attributes is provided in

---

[a] The nation was thus a theocracy in which every person was a priest and Yahweh their king. Such an ideal was less than practical, however. Hence, a representative principle was established in which the firstborn son of each family became a priest who represented the family (Lev. 13:2,13; 22:29). Later, in Num. 3:12, we read that Yahweh had appointed the Levites to serve in place of the first born sons: "Behold I have taken the Levites from among the people of Israel instead of every firstborn that opens the womb among the people of Israel."

Appendix 3 and the following subsections discuss the criteria on which this appendix is based. As we shall see, Revelation's attributes of the tribes of Israel conform quite well with those of the deities within the groups of twelve, and the general attributes of the groups themselves in the two sources.

First Fruits for God and the Lamb (Rev. 14:4):- Rev. 14:4 states that the twelve tribes of Israel are the "first fruits for God and the Lamb," a statement which warrants some interpretation before comparing it with Egyptian texts. One might very well be mystified by the expression "*for* God and the Lamb" and is tempted to interpret it as meaning "*of* God and the Lamb." We should therefore make a brief reference to other translations of the same passage. At least three of the more common bible translations use words which are similar in form to the Revised Standard Version quoted above.

The King James and the American Standard Versions interpret the original as saying "unto God" while the New International Version translates it as "to God." Thus all four translations suggest that the members of the twelve tribes of Israel were born not *of* God but *for* or *unto* Him – as if to fulfill some purpose. That the reference to them being the first to be born, not *by* God or *of* Him, but *for* God, is therefore generally agreed. As we shall see next, this interpretation conforms with Egyptian beliefs concerning the groups of twelve, especially as they accompany the sun-god into the sky at dawn.

In the *Amduat*, Re's rebirth in the morning sky is described in the upper register of the 12th Division. His birth is proclaimed with the words, "Born is he who is born, came to being, he who has come to being. Glory of the earth, Soul of the Lord on High. The sky is for thy soul that it may rest in it. ... Thou has taken the horizon ... Hail to thee, soul which is in the sky!"[235] In the register immediately below this we read that the rebirth itself results from the sun-god having been towed through *the inside* of the giant serpent called, "The Great *Ka,* Life of the Gods,"[236] a name befitting of its function – to renew life to the sun-god and his entourage as they pass through it (see Figure 29). The text says these are they

> who are honoured by Re, who are in his following and who are before him, their births take place upon earth every day *after* this Great God is born before them in the East of the Sky. They enter this mysterious image of the serpent, Life of the Gods, as the honoured ones. They come out as the Youths of Re every day.[237]

Their births take place *after* the sun-god is born. They are thus the first to be born *after* Re's appearance as the sun-god of the morning sky. And since they are in the "following of the Great God," they must be considered to have been born first *for* some purpose, a topic which will be discussed later. Meanwhile, since these followers are the first of his followers to pass through the "Life of the Gods" serpent, they also conform with the part of Rev. 14:4 which states that the twelve groups were born "as *first* fruits for God."

But Rev. 14:4 also states that the tribes of Israel were born for God *as well as* for the Lamb. Since the Egyptians considered both Osiris and the ram-headed form of Re to be two different aspects of their sun-god, this group of twelve may be considered to be the first-born for *both* Osiris and Re (see discussion on Osiris-Re in Chapter 3, *The Preeminent Deities*) as they emerge from the mouth of the serpent – or, as Revelation states it, the "first fruits for God *and* the Lamb."

Figure 29. The juvenile, ram-headed (lamb) form of the sun-god stands in his shrine as he is towed by his twelve followers through the body of a magical serpent, *The Great Ka, Life of the Gods*. They and the sun-god emerge from the serpent reborn to new life with their god. (AM12.2.1-6)

Once lived on earth (Rev. 14:3-4):- Perhaps the most fundamental of the attributes of the groups of twelve Tribes of Israel is that they are those "who had been redeemed from earth" (Rev. 14:3), i.e., "from mankind" (Rev. 14:4). Similarly, the Egyptian text emphasizes five groups of twelve deities in the *Book of Gates* which are described as having once lived upon earth. For example, two groups in the 1st Division are described as being "Those who worshiped Re *upon earth*. ... You are indeed those who adore (me)" and "Those who spoke truth *upon earth*."[238] One group in the 4th Division "knew Re *upon earth*"[239] while another is similarly described as "Those who have spoken the truth *upon earth*."[240] Finally, a group in the 6th Division is described as "Those who have acted according to justice while *on earth*."[241] The *Book of Gates* obviously emphasizes this aspect of the groups of twelve, just as we read in Rev. 14:3.

Truthfulness (Rev. 14:5):- Truthfulness among the tribes of Israel is first mentioned in Rev. 14:5 where we read, "in their mouth no lie was found, for they are spotless." As in Revelation, this same attribute is mentioned in juxtaposition with the mention of those who lived on earth; this is obvious in several of the quotations in the previous paragraph. Meanwhile, Revelation also emphasizes truthfulness elsewhere where we read that the Holy City was off limits to "any one who practices abomination or falsehood" (Rev. 21:27) or to any one "who loves and practices falsehood" (Rev. 22:15). This lofty, moral standard is also emphasized in the *Book of Gates* for groups of the twelve followers of the sun-god. For example, in the 1st Division, we read that they "they live on truth." "Truth is yours that you may live," they are told. "Your bread is destined for you. O Truthful Ones."[242] But nowhere in the *Book of Gates* is the truthfulness of the twelve emphasized more than in the 6th Division (Figure 30); here the twelve wear crowns of the very symbol of truth itself – an ostrich feather (↓). They are called, "Those who carry truth" and Osiris says to them, "I have decreed for you a complete existence under truth, to which evil does not come."[243] These references to the truthfulness of the twelve followers of the sun-god represent an important part of the array of parallels to the attributes of the twelve tribes of Israel in the Book of Revelation.

Figure 30. Twelve followers of the sun-god shown with their arms raised in adoration, each bearing an ostrich feather, the symbol of truth (↓, *maat*) on his head. The text describes them as soldiers who "carry truth." This figure conforms with Rev. 14:5. (BG6.1.6-10)

Chaste, all-male composition (Rev. 14:4):- Rev. 14:4 says, "It is these who have not defiled themselves with women, for they are chaste," a clear reference to them being all-male. Similarly, thirty of the thirty-two groups of twelve deities the *Book of Gates* are entirely male.[a] Texts concerning the groups of twelve in the Netherworld describe a concept of purity similar to that of priests and closely parallel the chasteness of Revelation's tribes of Israel. For example, the second group of twelve deities in the 1st Division of the *Book of Gates* is described as "Those who do not approach the expelled ones,"[244] indicating they had separated themselves from unworthy inhabitants of the Netherworld. One might ask, "Who are these expelled ones?" and "Do they include those who are not celibate?" A possible answer is found in the rubric at the end of Chapter 64 of the *Book of the Dead* after the deceased has finished speaking to the Ennead of judges, presumably before the judgment throne of Osiris. It says this chapter "should be recited while one is pure, without going near women."[245] It seems that in certain cases, at least male chastity was associated with purity. This reference to chastity among ancient Egyptians conforms with the text in

---

[a] The two remaining groups, found at BG10.3.5-7 and BG3.2.7-10, are composed of females. The first group is called *Goddesses of the Hours* and, like the members of the twelve tribes of Israel, these are clothed in white. Their function is to eradicate the hours as they emerge from the serpent Hereret, an attribute not consistent with those of the twelve tribes. The second group is not specifically named but appears to also represent the Goddesses of the Hours, their function being to "establish the periods of life, and the years of those among whom you are." In this quotation, the expression, "those among whom you are" may be interpreted as being the group of twelve male deities standing to their immediate left (at BG10.3.1-5), indicating that the function of the twelve goddesses in this register is to ensure long life in the hereafter to the nearby male followers of the sun-god. This second group of goddesses also assists in the towing of the solar barque as it carries the sun-god and his faithful followers through the difficult shallow parts of the primordial river which flows through the Netherworld; the text quotes the sun-god as saying to them, "You tow my followers toward the heights of heaven and lead me toward your ways." This group clearly contains goddesses in charge of the passage of time while the only attributes they have in common with the other groups of twelve are that they are all dressed in white and total twelve in number. The number twelve in these cases thus represents the twelve hours of the day and night rather than the multitudes represented by the all-male groups of twelve.

Rev. 14:4-5 which describes the twelve tribes of Israel as those "who have not defiled themselves with women, for they are chaste ... for they are spotless." The reference to them being spotless may, of course, be interpreted as meaning overall cleanliness, purity, holiness and high moral standards in addition to chastity. These same attributes were also applicable to the Egyptian blessed dead as is evident in texts from a variety of sources. Furthermore, it is clear that purity, and especially ceremonial purity, was a fundamental requirement for participation in certain religious rituals. It seems that, while there is no specific mention among the groups of twelve to male chastity their service as soldiers who go to battle for him might have required it. For this reason it is entirely possible, perhaps even likely, that "the expelled ones" in the 1st Division refer to those who were not chaste.

Followers of the Lamb (Rev. 14:4):- We read in Rev. 14:4 that the twelve tribes of Israel "follow the Lamb wherever he goes." Recall from Chapter 3, *The Preeminent Deities*, that the juvenile form of Re parallels the Lamb of Revelation. We now see that all the groups of twelve are shown in close association with the lamb form of Re, either before him in the center register or standing on the banks of either side of the river as he sails along the central river of the Netherworld; their presence in nine of the twelve divisions of the *Book of Gates* emphasizes their presence during practically all of the sun-god's voyage through the Netherworld. The numerous texts describing their deeds and rewards leave absolutely no doubt that they are followers of the sun-god (i.e., in either his ram-headed (lamb) form or his Osiris form in the Netherworld, or both, as in Osiris-Re). Indeed, there are two written references to them being followers, one in each of the *Book of Gates* and the *Amduat*. The first is in the lower register of the 3rd Division of the *Book of Gates* where Horus describes a group of twelve as those "who are in the following of He at the Head of the Westerners [i.e., Osiris]."[246] The second is in the upper register of the 12th Division of the *Amduat* where we read that "They are in the following of this god [i.e., Re]. ... They cross the sky in his following, (having taken) their places in the Morning Barge."[247] Note that in this instance, they are in the following of the sun-god in the morning, i.e., at the time when the sun-god would be newly born, and now visible in his young "lamb" form. As followers of the sun-god (mostly of Re but sometimes of his Osiris form), the groups of twelve clearly parallel the "followers of the Lamb" of Rev. 14.

Owned by God (Rev. 14:3-4):- Note that Rev. 14:3-4 also states that those members of the twelve tribes of Israel had not only once lived on earth but had also been *redeemed* from earth. There does not seem to be any reference to redemption in the Egyptian religious literature – or even in the Egyptian language – so one is tempted to say that there is no clear parallel to this statement in the Book of Revelation. Nevertheless, since the word "redeemed" implies ownership of the person or thing redeemed, we might consider a brief examination of the text associated with one group of twelve in the 3rd Division. In an oblique reference to ownership of the twelve, Horus says, "You are *assigned to me*,' you gods who are in the following of He at the Head of the Westerners!"[248] In this case, the twelve who once lived on earth and who follow the sun-god (in this case, Osiris) are *assigned* to the god Horus. They would, of course, have to have been owned by the sun-god for him to assign them to Horus.

This is by no means, a strong argument in favor of a parallel with Revelation's reference to redemption but, considering that the Egyptians apparently did not have a word for redemption and the fact that the groups of twelve are all followers of the sun-god, their "ownership" by the god may very well be implied. More research on this topic is required.

Father's name written on their foreheads (Rev. 7:3; 14:1):- There are two references in the Book of Revelation to members of the twelve tribes having distinguishing marks of some kind on their foreheads. The first is in Rev. 7:3 where we are told that certain catastrophic actions against the earth are not to take place until the twelve tribes are protected against them, i.e., until *"we have sealed* the servants of our God upon their foreheads." Such an association of the sun-god's followers being sealed against harm is also found in the 3rd Division of the *Book of Gates* where the sun-god says to a group of twelve, "You are in peace while your enemies are annihilated. They shall not exist. Your spirits are destined for their seats while *your souls are to be sealed up.*"[249] Rev. 14:1 provides us with the nature of the seal on their foreheads; it says that they "had his name (the Lamb's) and his Father's name written on their foreheads." This concept of bearing the name of a god on the forehead is also demonstrated in Figure 30. Here, the twelve followers of the sun-god have ostrich feathers on their heads. As mentioned above, this is the symbol of the Goddess *Maat,* one of the sun-god's chief personifications of truth, justice, righteousness and order. Furthermore, the name of the sun-god himself is at times directly associated with *maat*, as we read in the following excerpt from a hymn to Amen-Re:

> Hail to you, Amon-Re,
> ...
> *Lord of Maat* [of truth or order], father of the gods,
> Who made mankind and created beasts,
> Lord of what is, who created the fruit tree (or the plants of life),
> who made herbage and caused cattle to live.
> ...
> Hail to you, O Re, *lord of maat,*
> whose shrine is hidden, lord of the gods,
> ...
> Hail to you, who made all that is,
> *Lord of Maat,* father of the gods,
> Who made man and created beasts,
> Lord of the grain,
> Who made nourishment for the beasts of the desert.[250]

In this passage we note that Re (Amon-Re) is called the *Lord of Maat*, an expression translated from the Egyptian word, *Nebmaat,* one of the sun-god's titles (and a title adopted by certain kings).[a] The ostrich feathers on the heads of the twelve

---

[a] The popularity of the attribute of truth among the kings of Egypt is expressed by Clagett (1989, p. 282) who says that the Horus name of Sneferu, the first king of the fourth dynasty was "*Nebmaat* ('Lord of Order')," i.e., of truth, justice and righteousness. "Also, one of the epithets

followers in Figure 30 can therefore be interpreted as representing a title of the sun-god, or even his name, so that this twelve may represent not only the truthfulness mentioned in Rev. 14:5 but also the name of their god on their foreheads as in Rev. 14:1.

If Revelation's Lamb parallels the ram-headed form of the juvenile sun-god, who then parallels the "*Lord of maat*," father of the gods" in the above poem? According to the creation myth in the *Book of the Divine Cow* the father of Re was the earth-god Geb. If we carry this parallel further, Rev. 14:1 can be interpreted in different ways, as follows:

> Then I looked, and lo, on Mount Zion stood the Lamb (Christianity's Christ and Egypt's juvenile Re), and with him a hundred and forty-four thousand who had his name (Christianity's Christ and Egypt's juvenile Re) and his Father's name (Christianity's God and Egypt's Geb) written on their foreheads.

But there seems to be no reference, either pictorial or textual, to the name of Geb being placed on the heads of the followers of Re. This part of Rev. 14:1 therefore remains an enigma from the point of view of a possible parallel to this particular Egyptian text.

Those who Praise (Rev. 14:2-3):- The theme of Rev. 14:2-3 is one of *praise* to the one on the throne:

> ²And I heard a voice from heaven like the sound of many waters and like the sound of loud thunder; the voice I heard was like the sound of harpers playing on their harps, ³and they sing a new song before the throne and before the four living creatures and before the elders. No one could learn that song except the hundred and forty-four thousand who had been redeemed from the earth.

The element of praise is, of course, quite common in the religious texts of ancient Egypt so that the general significance of these verses in Revelation can be readily explained within the context of Egyptian sources where the manner in which praise is accentuated in the writings and parts of the pictures themselves. For example, two groups of twelve in the 1st register of the 6th Division of the *Book of Gates* have their hands raised over their heads ($\text{\textyen}$) in a gesture meaning to "be high," rejoice, joy, or exult.[a] And in the 3rd register of the 10th Division of the *Book of Gates* and the 7th Division of the *Amduat*, twelve deities have stars drawn ($\star$) over their heads, a hieroglyphic meaning "to adore" or "to pray."[b] Finally, in the 1st register of the 12th Division of the *Amduat*, twelve deities stand with hands raised before them ($\text{\textyen}$) in an

---

of the solar god under his name of Reharakhti (Re-Horus of the Horizon) was *Nebmaat* at the solar temple built in Abu Ghurab by the fifth-dynasty King Niuserre."

[a] See either Faulkner (1927), p. 445, character #A28, or Budge (1920), p. xcvii, character #8 for hieroglyphic determinative meaning to "be high," rejoice, joy, or exult.

[b] See either Faulkner (1927), p. 487, character #N14, or Budge (1920), p. cxxv, character #35 for the ideograph or determinative of meaning "to adore," or "pray."

explicit gesture of "praise."[a] It is clear that one of the main activities of the twelve followers in both the *Book of Gates* and the *Amduat* was to praise and pay homage to the sun-god in a manner similar to the theme of Rev. 14:2-3.

The 144,000 (Rev. 14:1):- But what can we make of the actual number referred to in the Book of Revelation? Is there a reference to the number 144,000 in the *Book of Gates*, the *Amduat*, or any other ancient Egyptian source? The answer to this question is, "Maybe." We find the closest contender (in the literature examined) in the 64th Chapter the *Book of the Dead* where there is a reference to a group of 1,200 souls of the blessed dead as part of a much larger multitude. The text, is difficult to understand and reads:

> I know the depths and I know your name. You have made the portions of *the blessed dead – who are millions and hundreds of thousands more* – and *1,200 things moreover*' than those things of theirs. The eddies are more than the hours of the day. That which is upon the shoulders of Orion is examined, *being one-twelfth strewing out what is united,*' as what one gives to another among them. It is one-sixth which is due therein which is preeminent, namely the hour of overthrowing the rebel and returning therefrom vindicated. It is these who are in the opening of the Duat [a reference to the two groups of twelve in the opening scene of the *Book of Gates*?], it is these who are provided for by Shu.[251]

The exact meaning of the expression, "and 1,200 things moreover," is unclear although the reference to the "things" being on the shoulders of Orion suggests they are the souls of the dead manifested as stars and/or possibly a constellation of stars above the constellation of Orion in the night sky. It seems that the 1,200 represents a portion of the great multitude of "millions and hundreds of thousands more" of the blessed dead mentioned earlier in the same sentence in the text. This is consistent with the juxtaposition of the scene describing the numbers in the tribes of Israel in Rev. 7:5-8 with the scene in Rev. 7:9 describing the "great multitude which no man could number, from every nation, from all tribes and peoples and tongues." The "one-twelfth strewing out of what is united" would parallel the division in Rev. 7:4-8 of the Israelites into twelve tribes of equal size. However, if 1,200 represents one-twelfth of the total, then the total is 14,400 rather than 144,000, the number cited in Revelation; the sense of the number (a multiple of 1,200) is correct, but the implied number (14,400) does not agree with the 144,000 mentioned in Rev. 14:1. Nevertheless, these partial parallels with the Book of Revelation are tantalizing but not definitive and alternative interpretations of the Egyptian text are certainly possible. Unfortunately, there seems to be no clear understanding of this passage in the *Book of the Dead* and more research is necessary before a definitive statement can be made on the possibility of such a parallel.

---

[a] See either Faulkner (1927), p. 445, character #A30, or Budge (1920), p. xcvii, characters #3 and #4 for hieroglyphic determinative meaning to praise, adore, pray, worship, or entreat.

Discussion

It appears that practically all the attributes of the tribes of Israel provided in the Book of Revelation have parallels in the Egyptian *Amduat* and the *Book of Gates*. This includes their all-male makeup, chasteness, truthfulness, and even references to them having once lived on earth. These and other characteristics parallel those of the tribes of Israel only when the groups of twelve were considered as a single group. In other words, attributes which Revelation describes as being applied to only one tribe were typically found in one or more – including all the groups – of twelve in the Egyptian writings. While this difference between the two sources is striking, it is not considered critically important; the critical indicator is that the attributes associated with all the groups of twelve considered together, parallel those outlined in Revelation.

There are other groups of deities in the *Amduat* and *Book of Gates* which have more or less than twelve members. None of these, however, contain the same high density of relevant attributes as the groups of twelve followers of the sun-god, a feature which suggests special status of these groups. This, and the arguments presented in the previous paragraphs, suggest the groups of twelve in the *Book of Gates* and the *Amduat* contain important parallels to Revelation's twelve tribes of Israel.

The tribes as part of a parallel sequence:- In addition to the specific parallels presented in this chapter, there is another general parallel which should be mentioned. It involves the placement of Rev. 7:4-8 in the Book of Revelation – its place in the sequence of events in Revelation conforms with those in the *Amduat* Series – the tribes of Israel are mentioned in Rev. 7:4-8 *after* Rev. 5:1-4 (which describes the offering of the scroll, the lion of Judah, and the slain lamb, a scene which conforms with scenes in the 6th Division of the *Amduat*), and *before* Rev. 7:9 (which deals with the great multitude carrying palm branches which is found in the *Amduat's* 9th Division, (to be discussed in Chapter 7, *The Great Multitude*). The three scenes thus appear in the same order in the Book of Revelation as their counterparts in the *Amduat*. In Chapter 29, *Parallel Series of Scenes*, this aspect the twelve tribes will be placed in the much broader context of other scenes in the *Amduat Series*.

The all-male character of the tribes:- It is remarkable that the attributes of the tribes of Israel in the Book of Revelation are not explicitly mentioned or listed in Old Testament descriptions as they are in Revelation. An important exception is the list of attributes provided in Gen 49:16-27 which tends to emphasizes the military activities of the tribes, as follows: "Dan shall be a serpent in the way, a viper by the path, that bites the horse's heels [horses were weapons of war] so that his rider falls backward" (vs.17), "Raiders shall raid Gad, but he shall raid at their heels" (vs. 19), "The archers fiercely attacked him, shot at him, and harassed him sorely" (vs. 23), and "Benjamin is a ravenous wolf, in the morning devouring the prey, and at even dividing the spoil" (vs. 27). In addition to these, there are many references in the Old Testament to the Israelites going into battle against the inhabitants of the "promised land" after they left Egypt. These soldiers were, of course, men – just as most of the groups of twelve in the Egyptian texts are portrayed as being men.

Why do the names of the tribes seem to be hidden? - Parallels between the names in the two sources are especially intriguing, especially since they have a very specific nature: parallels to their *meanings* were found in the Egyptian texts rather than the names themselves. This suggests some kind of relationship between the names of the tribes of Israel and groups of twelve in the Egyptian texts. It also seems as if Egypt's priestly writers intentionally hid the references from everyone except those who had knowledge of how to interpret the texts. One might therefore ask, "If the deities identified in the middle register of the 7th Division are indeed associated with the tribes of Israel, how might we explain their apparent concealment in the Egyptian record?"

A possible answer to this question is that the Egyptians were upset by the exodus of the Hebrews from Egypt, perhaps even embarrassed because of their lack of control over them. The Egyptians were extremely nationalistic, and like their religious beliefs, were profoundly self-centered and hardly ever gave overt historic recognition to unfavorable events involving non-Egyptian people living among them. They also did not like to be reminded of events which showed them in a bad or less than perfect light. For this reason their records frequently mention glorious victories over the enemy but almost never mention their defeats (about which we typically learn from non-Egyptian sources). It would be very "un-Egyptian" to describe activities of the Hebrews in a manner which would embarrass Egypt – and especially the king, the illustrious son of the sun-god.

This situation would be particularly relevant to Egypt's 2nd Intermediate Period when many people of non-Egyptian descent (including the "Hyksos") lived in the Nile delta. Near the end of that period, war broke out between the Egyptian kings in Thebes and the invaders in the delta. It is possible that a portion of the non-Egyptians in the delta elected to fight for Thebes; if so, it is also possible that such individuals were especially represented in the groups of twelve in the *Amduat* and the *Book of Gates*. It is even possible, or even likely, that a portion of these people from the Levant belonged to the Tribes of Israel.

If a portion of the Hebrews fought against their brethren in the delta, this might well have not been recorded in the Jewish records. Furthermore, it seems likely that the Egyptian kings would have sought to strengthen Egypt's pride in their own soldiers who fought to drive the invaders out of the delta by downplaying the role of the Hebrews who also fought for the Egyptian cause. They may therefore have elected to conceal the identity of the Hebrews in this part of the *Amduat* by not revealing the correct Hebrew tribal names, electing instead to present them with Egyptian names based on the meanings of the Hebrew names. In this manner, the authors of the *Amduat* could make "encrypted" references to historic events involving the Hebrews which would be available only to a select group of priests; this would have ensured that the document imposed as little a strain as possible on Egyptian nationalistic and religious sentiments.

In spite of the above, it would be folly to suggest that all the groups of twelve in the *Amduat* and the *Book of Gates* are parallels to the tribes of Israel. It is possible, for example, that the two groups of twelve deities illustrated in the opening scene of the *Book of Gates* merely introduce the many groups of twelve in the book rather than actually represent them; the text does not describe any of their characteristics which might be used to identify them with the tribes of Israel. (Nevertheless, for completeness, they are included in our discussions on the groups of twelve in the Book of Gates.)

Implications of findings on the date of the Exodus:- The current recognition of possible references to the names of the tribes of Israel in an Egyptian source enables speculation on the dates during which they were in Egypt. For example, they had to have been present sometime before the *Amduat* was written. While some scholars have suggested that of the *Amduat* underwent various stages of composition possibly going back to the Old Kingdom (2575–2134 BCE), Hornung's (1999) view is that, because of the vividness of the description of the Netherworld along with its many detailed illustrations, it is unimaginable for the Old Kingdom, or even the Middle Kingdom (2040–1640 BCE) to have produced such a work. Furthermore, he says that our oldest fragments of the *Amduat* are from the early years of Queen Hatshepsut (1473–1458) who co-reigned with Thutmosis III (1479-1425) during the early part of his reign. Indeed, our earliest complete copies come from the tombs of Thutmosis III and Useramun, the first of his viziers.[252] It is therefore likely that the *Amduat* was composed in the early part of the New Kingdom (1550–1070 BCE) and certainly prior to the end of the reign of Thutmosis III and the writing of his annals. This limitation on the latest likely date of composition of the *Amduat* provides the basis for a comment on the pre-Exodus status of the tribes of Israel in Egypt.

It seems that, at the time the *Amduat* was composed, not only were the Israelites well established in Egypt but they were recognized by the Egyptians as a people whose demands were to be taken seriously. Many generations must have passed for the population of the Israelites to have reached numbers significant enough for them to have played such substantive roles in Egypt that the Egyptian priests included references to them in the *Amduat*. The evidence presented above suggests the tribes were already recognized as important groups in Egypt for many years prior to the beginning of the reign of Thutmosis III in 1479 BCE.

Coogan (1993) informs us that "The first mention of Israel in a source other than the Bible is in an inscription written to commemorate a victory of the Egyptian Pharaoh Merneptah [1224-1214 BCE] at the end of the thirteenth century BCE; there, Israel is associated with places in Canaan rather than Egypt." This is therefore likely to be a reference to a post-Exodus event since the latest date ascribed for the Exodus by many biblical scholars is roughly 65 years earlier, during the reign of Ramesses II (1290-1224 BCE). If the current recognition of a record of the tribes of Israel in Egypt is valid, then 1479 BCE (i.e. the beginning of the reign of Thutmosis III) as the earliest date on record for the recognition of the Israelites predates the reign of Ramesses II by roughly 135 to 189 years.

The date of 1479 brings the date closer to that accepted by most modern scholars who prefer a date of the exodus being just after the end of Egypt's 2nd Intermediate Period (1640-1532) to the beginning of the reign of Pharaoh Ahmose (1550-1525) who drove the Hyksos out of Egypt in *c*. 1550 BCE. Indeed, it was Josephus (CE 37 – *c*. 100) who first suggested the time of *c*. 1550 BCE for the Exodus, basing his opinion on the figure of 480 years from the Exodus to the dedication of the Temple by Solomon (I Kings 6:1). Since then, a large number of archeological studies have supported his view.[a]

Earliest records of the tribes in Egyptian writings:- A positive identification of an Egyptian text containing possible references to the names of the tribes of Israel is important in its own right. Written evidence for their presence in Egypt has been sought by bible scholars and archeologists for centuries and by Egyptologists since the hieroglyphics were first deciphered in the early 1800's. If supported by further study, the current findings represent the first time records of the tribes have been identified in any ancient Egyptian writings. More research is therefore advisable on the names of the deities in the seventh division and among the other groups of twelve in the *Amduat* – and possibly those in the *Book of Gates* as well – especially since the study of Egyptian names is notorious for its numerous difficulties (problems with translation of names are emphasized by Hornung, 1983).[253]

Of Re and Yahweh:- Another aspect of the identification of Egyptian parallels to the names of the tribes of Israel begs comment; it involves the obvious importance of the groups of twelve in the *Amduat* and the *Book of Gates*. It is glaringly obvious that the groups are identified both in pictures and writings as followers of the Egyptian sun-god and not of Yahweh, the god of the Hebrews as we might expect if they represented the Israelites. This brings to mind the writings of Budge (1934) who felt strongly about the possibility of a link between the god of the Christians and Egypt's creator-god Ptah. Ptah was a protagonist of the Theban god Re, whom the priests of Memphis endowed with all the characteristics of the Egyptian sun-god.[254] Budge commented on this parallel: "That such spiritual conceptions were evolved by the priests of Memphis about 4,000 years before the Christian Era is a matter for wonder."[b, 255] It would seem that the groups of twelve in the *Amduat* and the *Book of Gates* were followers of a god with essentially the same characteristics of God almighty of the Judaeo-Christian beliefs. The link here is intriguing and requires more research and open discussion.

An Alternative solution to tribal identity problem:- Notwithstanding the entire range of evidence for the appearance in the Egyptian record of names which parallel those of the twelve tribes of Israel, the above findings remain to be some of the more perplexing ones of this study. We may well ask, "Why do the apparent tribes of Israel seem to be so prominently featured in the *Amduat*, one of ancient Egypt's more important religious compositions?" The "knee-jerk" reaction to this question is that

---

[a] The most important of these studies are summarized and critically evaluated by Manning (1999).

[b] In a footnote to this comment Budge (1934) writes on page 16, "In a large edition of the *Westminster Catechism* the attributes of God are enumerated together with Bible references as authorities. Thus we have: His infinity Exod. iii. 14; Job xi. 7-9; glory Acts vii. 2; blessedness I Tim. vi. 15; perfection Matt.v. 48; all-sufficiency Gen. xvii. 1; eternity Ps. xc. 2; unchangeableness Mal. iii. 6; incomprehensibility I Kings viii. 27; ubiquity Ps cxxxix. 1-13; almightiness Rev. iv. 8; Omniscience Heb. iv. 13; wisdom Rom. xvi. 27; holiness Isa. v. 24; justice Deut. xxxiv. 4; mercy and graciousness Exod. xxiv. 6; unity Deut. vi. 4; I Cor. viii. 4. The great hymn of Ptah at Berlin shows that the same attributes were ascribed to him."

the names of the gods in the 7th Division have been mis-classified in this research; but this answer may be an oversimplification of the issue. More research is obviously needed on this particular complication.

A simpler explanation for the presence of the parallel names is that the names originally had nothing to do with the tribes of Israel. For example, it is conceivable that the parallel names were simply those of twelve subdivisions of the four main divisions of the Egyptian army (recall that the groups of twelve Egyptians contained practically all men who fought for their god). In this scenario, the Egyptian names became a part of the memory of a segment of the Hyksos invaders which occupied the Nile Delta during Egypt's 2nd Intermediate Period and were expelled at the end of this period; over time, the memory of these names was incorporated into the group memory of the Israelites. This explanation is somewhat similar to and conforms with part of an interview with Israeli archaeologist Israel Finkelstein who in a recent issue of *Biblical Archeology Review* paraphrased a colleague's (Donald Redford's) sentiment on other problems with the Biblical account of the Exodus:

> ... perhaps the expulsion of Canaanites {the Hyksos} from Egypt in the 16th century {B.C.E.} could have left a memory and that memory became some sort of myth that later found its way into the Biblical text in a process that we cannot fully reconcile. And even this is a simplistic answer [to the Biblical account of the Exodus]. ... Some scholars suggest that there was a group of people who came from Egypt with egalitarian ideas different from the local belief or faith in Canaan, and that these were the nucleus for the people in the Canaanite highlands who became Israel.[a]

The reader is also referred to the concluding section of Chapter 7, *The Great Multitude*, for additional material on this topic. Meanwhile, this alternative solution is undoubtedly not the only one possible and a great deal more research in this area is warranted.

---

[a] From an interview with Israel Finkelstein published in *Biblical Archeology Review*, May/June 2010, Vol. 36 No 3, pp.48-58. (See also Chap. 8, *Egyptian Parallels in the Seven Letters*.)

Chapter 7. The Great Multitude (Rev. 7:9-17)[256]

In the last chapter we dealt with the smaller of two multitudes mentioned in the Book of Revelation; the smaller is described as having 144,000 members and is called the "twelve tribes of Israel" (Rev. 7:4-8). The larger group is referred to in the remaining half of Rev. 7 and is described as "a great multitude which no man could number" (Rev. 7:9); this is the only place in Revelation where this latter group is unambiguously identified. There are, however, other groups identified in Revelation which seem to be associated with either the tribes of Israel or the Great Multitude; these are designated in this chapter as the "Unassigned Multitudes" and will be dealt with separately near the end of this chapter. Unlike the tribes of Israel which are close to the throne, the Great Multitude seems to fill the entire outer ring around the throne of God. As with the tribes of Israel in the previous chapter, attributes similar to those of the great multitudes of Revelation may also be found in Egyptian texts.

Attributes of the Great Multitude (Rev. 7:9-17)

The Book of Revelation describes a "great multitude," and points out that it is multinational and multiracial in scope (Rev. 7:9). Its members are described as followers of the lamb, belong to many races, hold palm branches in their hands, are clothed in white robes, are sheltered by God, rest from their labors, receive food and water, and are happy. They also fight for their God. The following paragraphs discuss these attributes.

Followers of the Lamb (Rev. 7:17):- Like the possible reference to the twelve tribes of Israel in Rev. 7:4, the Great Multitude of Rev. 7:17 is portrayed as being guided by the Lamb: "the Lamb in the midst of the throne will be their shepherd, and he will guide them ..." Similarly, the belief that the Egyptian sun-god acted as a shepherd to his followers goes back at least as far as the Ramesside period (1295-1069 BCE) where we find a eulogy to Amon in which he treats his cattle as would a herdsman.[257] Breasted (1912) says that the origin of this notion appears to be related to the idea that "The Pharaoh was the 'good shepherd' or 'good herd-man,' and this figure of the paternal and protecting sovereign had been transferred to Re. Re had thus gained wondrously in qualities of humane and paternal sympathy."[258] This sentiment reverberates in Lurker (1980) where he says that Re "'acts as shepherd in his herbage,' and men and animals breathed the air and drank of the water which he gave them.'"[a, 259] In this manner, the ram-headed form of Re, who stands in the midst of his shrine, or throne, parallels the one described in Rev. 7:17 as a "shepherd."

Multiracial composition (Rev. 7:9):- In Rev. 7:9 we read that the great multitude which no man could number was "from every nation, from all tribes and peoples and tongues." Similarly, the Egyptian Netherworld was at times viewed as being multiracial. The *Book of Gates* (BG4.3.1-5) contains four groups of four deities (i.e., 4 x 4 = a "multitude of multitudes") who belong to different races. The text labels them as "Men" (i.e., Egyptians), "Asiatics," "Negroes" and "Libyans." Hornung (1990) comments on this from the perspective of Egyptians during "the cosmopolitan period at the end of Dynasty 18 and the beginning of Dynasty 19 [about 1,300 BCE], when the royal family made diplomatic marriages with the ruling houses of Egypt's traditional enemies."[260] He says that,

> In the commoners' Book of the Dead, the departed must content themselves with a bit of land or an honored place in the solar bark, as available space must be shared with the millions of dead who preceded them. That all nations, including even the ancient foes of Egypt, are present in the Beyond is shown in scene 30 of the Book of Gates. ... They ... are attended to and provided for, receiving places in the Realm of the Dead.[261]

Both the "millions of dead" and the "multitudes of multitudes" in the *Book of Gates* conform with the concept of a "great multitude which no man could number" mentioned in Rev. 7:9 although it is not, like the other parallel attributes, explicitly mentioned in texts associated with groups of twelve.

Palm Branches in their hands (Rev. 7:9):- We are told that the Great Multitude of the Book of Revelation stood before the throne carrying palm branches in their hands (Rev. 7:9). To the Egyptians, a palm branch, and its hieroglyph, ⌠ (a palm branch stripped of leaves),[262] had several meanings, most of which are relevant to this verse in Revelation. Gardiner (1927) describes its determinative form as meaning to "be young" or "vigorous," or ideographically, meaning a "year."[263] It was also an ideograph for "time" or "season," especially when planted in the ⊙ symbol to form ⌠. The image of the Great Multitude standing before the throne holding palm branches in their hands thus exhorted, in Egyptian terms, that the one on the throne be *young and vigorous* while the presence of a multitude of branches signify that he should reign for many years. Lurker (1980) describes the significance of palm branches in the hands of admirers in a way most befitting of events described in Revelation.

> A door in the temple of Medamud ... shows Senusret III receiving a palm branch, a token of long reign, from Horus and Seth, respectively, the national gods of Upper and Lower

---

[a] Lurker (1980, p.62) goes on to say that this aspect of Re was adopted by his son, the king of Egypt. He says, "It is obvious that the king who led his people was viewed as a shepherd, rather as in Mesopotamia. Pharaoh's insignia originated, via Osiris, from the ancient royal god Anedjti who, at the same time, had the characteristics of a divine shepherd. The crook was originally a shepherd's crook."

Egypt." Occasionally, a tadpole, the symbol for 100,000, was attached to the lower end of the palm leaf. In one relief on the outer wall of the first pylon at Medinet Habu, Amun, enthroned, hands the king a fourfold ideogram for heb-sed, a great jubilee celebration which was usually held for the first time after thirty regnal years, and was then repeated at shorter intervals. The palm leaf, worn on the head or held in the hand, was an attribute of the god Heh, the personification of eternity.[264]

Figure 31. A scene showing a group carrying of palm branches, ſ, which signify the endowment of long life for the ruler – as described in Rev. 7:9. (AM2.3.1-2)

There are scenes in both the *Amduat* and the *Book of Gates* which explicitly show the followers of the sun-god carrying palm branches.[a] There are three in the *Amduat*; the first involves a group of three at the far left-hand side of the 3rd register of the 2nd Division and shown here as Figure 31; each holds a palm (ſ) stripped of leaves and notched to serve as a tally of the years.[265] The accompanying text says, "These gods are like this, they acclaim this Great God with the symbols of the year. They acclaim him with branches which they hold in their hands. ... They call him, and live through the voice of the Great God."[266] The second group consists of nine gods on the right side of the 3rd register of the 9th Division and shown here in Figure 32. Their number suggests they represent "many, many, many" (3 x 3 x 3) or possibly a "great multitude." The text accompanying them tells us that,

> These are ... the lords who carry the sign of life as well as their scepters. They are like this. They stand carrying the signs of life, leaning on their scepters, while this Great God calls out to them. It is they who communicate the words of the gods who are in the Netherworld in this city.[267]

Piankoff (1954) identifies their scepters as "palm scepters,"[268] an observation conforming with Rev. 7:9. This group of nine gods is unique in that it is found in a division in which there are no less than four large groups of deities – each of which contains twelve (3 x 4) members. One might interpret this to mean that this group of

Figure 32. This scene shows nine (suggesting a great many) gods holding palm branches in their hands in the lower registers of the 9th Division of the *Amduat*. It conforms with that described in Rev. 7:9. The god Horus "presides" in front of them. (AM9.3.6-10)

---

[a] There are no deities carrying palm branches in any of the other books examined in this study.

nine is closely related to the groups of twelve and that they represent at least a part of "the great multitude." It is therefore reasonable to say that Figure 32 parallels Rev. 7:9 in that we have find here a component of a great multitude of the faithful carrying palm branches. Certainly, we see that the group of "many, many" gods carrying palm branches is closely associated with the larger groups of twelve in the same division.

Clothed in white robes (Rev. 7:9):- "... behold, a great multitude ... clothed in white robes." The Egyptian word for clothing is *menkhet* and its hieroglyph is 𓎛. Numerous illustrations in the *Book of the Dead* show the blessed dead wearing bright, white clothing symbolized by this hieroglyph. In Chapter 171, the *Chapter for Donning a Pure Garment,* the deceased pleads for special clothing from the gods: "May you give this pure garment to the worthy spirit of *N* [the deceased]. ... As for this pure garment for *N*, may it be allotted to him for ever and ever, and may you remove the evil which is upon him."[269] In the 169th chapter the deceased is told, "You shall be adorned with gold, your vestment being of fine linen."[270] Wilkinson (1992) reviews the significance to the Egyptians of this special clothing:

> Fine clothing was considered an important commodity for the afterlife, and linen is commonly included in mortuary offering lists along with "bread, beer, oxen, fowl, and alabaster jars (of oil). *Menkhet* seems, therefore to have been regarded as an important staple rather than a luxury item. In the eighth "hour" [of the *Amduat*] it [*menkhet*] is depicted next to figures of gods and spirits who have been properly mummified and who are apparently suitably provided with funerary linen. The sign also appears next to the enigmatic symbols of "followers" of the gods and as a kind of seat upon which various deities sit [as in Figure 33] – both here and in other "hours" [i.e., in other divisions of the *Amduat*]. The prevalence of these signs underscores the importance of proper clothing in these religious ideas.[271]

Figure 33. Directly above Re in his shrine, twelve deities seated on clothing signs, 𓎛, illustrating the importance of gifts of pure white robes to the followers of the sun-god. This conforms with the reference in Rev. 7:9-13 to a Great Multitude clothed in white robes before the throne of the Lamb. (AM9.1.1-5)

Clothing signs in the 9th Division of the *Amduat* are clearly associated with the twelve followers of the sun-god; as in Figure 33 from the upper register where the 𓎛 symbols represent a throne, twelve other gods (in the form of uraeus serpents) in lower register are also seated on *menkhet* symbols. The text above the twelve in the upper register says, "They are like this in the Netherworld, firmly established upon their clothing in their forms, and in their images made by Horus. Re speaks to them: You are provided with your cloth, your glory [light] is your garments. Horus has clothed you there as he did his father in the Netherworld which hides the gods."[272] The presence of twelve deities above and twelve below the shrine of the sun-god in this division is consistent with the statement in Rev. 7:9 that a great multitude clothed in white robes were before the throne of the Lamb.

Similarly, the text associated with a group of twelve in the lower register of 7th Division of the *Book of Gates* says, "Receive your garments, be bright in the light, for the Region of Silence is open to you."[273] Spence suggests that light was even emitted by the garments of the faithful dead: "Those happy enough to gain the heaven of the sun-god were clothed in light, and their food was described as 'light.'"[274] It is obvious that the wearing of special garments in the hereafter was of great importance to the ancient Egyptians, especially to the followers of the sun-god. In view of the above, it is clear that the reference to clothing of the great multitude before the throne in Rev. 7:9-13 closely parallels Egyptian beliefs.

Serve as priests (Rev. 1:5-6, Rev. 7:15, Rev. 5:10; Rev. 20:6):- We are told that the Great Multitude is "before the throne of God, and serve him day and night within his temple" (Rev. 7:15). Service in the temple indicates these are priests, a conclusion conforming with Rev. 1:6 which says that, "To him who ... made us a kingdom, priests to his God and Father." Rev. 5:10 says that the Lamb "hast made them a kingdom and priests to our God," and Rev. 20:6 says that those over which "the second death has no power ... shall be priests of God and of Christ." Such references have many parallels in Egyptian writings. For example, as in Rev. 7:15, the sun-god says to one of his groups of twelve followers in the 7th Division of the *Amduat*, "the Region of Silence is open to you, while you enter the holiness of Osiris"[275] – a clear reference entering the temple of Osiris.

The priesthood of ancient Egypt represented an elite group of scribes whose function was not only to participate in ecclesiastical functions of the state religion but also to perform the duties of the civil service. As civil servants, they were stewards of society whose work included administration and maintenance of public records. Some, such as judges or magistrates, assumed positions of special authority. A particularly gifted person might even rise to the position of vizier, the highest administrative position in the land next to the pharaoh himself (an example is the well-known story in Genesis 41:39-44 of Joseph's rise to power in Egypt). In contrast to the life of the illiterate, common laborers of the massive workforce in Egyptian society, the life of a priest was coveted by all who were capable and ambitious. As the servants of Re's representative on earth, the priests assisted the pharaoh in ruling Egypt.[a]

It is well understood that the Egyptians extended their earthly customs and traditions to the afterlife where the blessed dead served like gods in the priesthood of Osiris. We find an example of this in the 7th Division of the *Book of Gates* in reference to the twelve followers of the sun-god being made like gods: "O Council which is in the Netherworld, lords of things in the West, judge me your judgment, order evil to my enemies, as I have granted you Truth. You are ordered to give judgment, (you whom) *I have made like gods*"[276] When we compare this scenario with that outlined in Rev. 5:10, the parallel is clear. Egyptian priests in the Netherworld are "ordered to give judgment" while those in Revelation they "shall reign on earth;" the difference

---

[a] Pharaoh himself was considered to be the chief priest of the cult because he was the divine son of the sun-god, the "anointed one" (*the christos*).

between the two is not particularly significant, especially when viewed from an Egyptian perspective.

Additional parallels to the faithful serving as priests will be discussed in Chapter 24, *The Millennium* in the context of the resurrected being made priests during the millennium described in Rev. 20:4-6.

Sheltered ones (Rev. 7:15):- This verse says that "he who sits on the throne will spread his tent over them" (NIV). The New International Version, in contrast to the Revised Standard Version, is closer to the literal translation of the Greek text. A note in the *New Oxford Annotated Bible* says that the literal translation reads, "spread his tabernacle over them."[277] Hayes (1993), describes the Hebrew tabernacle as a

> portable sanctuary constructed by Moses at Sinai and primarily associated with the people's wilderness wandering. Various expressions are used in referring to this sanctuary – "tent of meeting," "tabernacle," "tabernacle of the testimony [NRSV uses the word, *covenant*]." Conceived as a movable shrine, the tabernacle was constructed so that it could be assembled, dismantled, and reassembled as the people moved from one place to another.[278]

A similar idea to Revelation's Great Multitude being sheltered by a tent, or tabernacle, is found in both the *Book of Gates* and the *Amduat*. In the *Book of Gates*, it is used in the description of one group of twelve followers called, the "Perfect Spirits, accomplished spirits" who are being resurrected. They are ordered to rise up from their rest on their funeral biers. The text says, "May you stand under the canopy [tent] which elevates the spirit of the One of the Horizon [the sun-god]!"[279] The concept of a protective canopy or tent is emphasized in the illustration found in the 11th Division of the *Amduat* (Figure 34). In it, the ram-headed sun-god travels within a shrine formed by a large protective serpent called "The Enveloper," otherwise known as the *Mehen* serpent, the special protective serpent which shields the sun-god against the ever-present dangers of the Netherworld. In front of the sun-god, his twelve followers who walk before the sun-god carry a second manifestation of the *Mehen* serpent on their heads. The scene here is very similar to that described in Rev. 7:15; the Egyptian text says,"They are like this in front of the Great God. They carry the Enveloper on their heads toward this city."[280]

Figure 34. On the solar barque, the protective Enveloper (*Mehen*) serpent covers the sun-god and forms a protective tent (or shrine) over him. In front of him, his twelve followers are shown to be similarly shielded as they carry a second manifestation of the same serpent on their heads. This illustration conceptually and graphically parallels the text of Rev. 7:15. (AM11.2.1-8)

That the Enveloper serpent was indeed related in the minds of the Egyptians to a tent, shrine or portable tabernacle is evident in an array of similar sounding words representing serpents, tents, and shrines. For example, an Egyptian word for "serpent" is *āanh*[281] (*aany*)[282] sounds similar to *āan*, a word for "tent."[283] Similarly, *qerh*[284] is a name for "serpent" while the similar word, *qeh* can represent a "shrine."[285] Also, *hetch* means "shrine"[286] and the close homonym *hetch-t* is the name of a special royal serpent.[287] Another relevant set of near homophones is *tcheri-t* which means "shrine"[288] while *tcher* means "to envelop"[289] and *tchetf-t* means "serpent."[290] Finally, the reference to the tent of God in Rev. 7:15 is consistent with the Egyptian concept of a shrine or tent formed by the giant Enveloper serpent *(Mehen)* to protect both the sun-god and his faithful followers in Figure 34; the similarity to the text in Revelation is striking.

Resting Ones (Rev. 14:13):- In Rev. 14:13 the dead are described as resting: "'Blessed are the dead' .... 'Blessed indeed,' says the Spirit, 'that they may *rest* from their labors, for *their deeds* follow them!' " Note that the deeds of the blessed dead are thus linked to their resting state. This conforms with a picture in the 5th Division of *Book of Gates* showing twelve followers of the sun-god resting on their funeral biers (Figure 35). The text accompanying this picture says, "Hail, O you spirits! Hail, inhabitants of the Netherworld! ... May your souls be *happy*' ... May you *rejoice*,' you souls, *you (who) are accomplished!*' ... Hail to you, spirits, you who are on your places, who *sleep*' on your couches!" Here we find a similar juxtaposition of the three images. The statement, "May your souls be happy," and "May you rejoice," of course, parallels "Blessed are the dead" of Rev. 14:13. The reference to the spirits "who sleep on your couches," parallels Revelation's statement "that they may rest from their labors." And "you (who) are accomplished" corresponds to the statement, "their deeds follow

Figure 35. In the 5th Division of the *Book of Gates*, twelve followers of the sun-god rest in peace on their funeral biers cushioned by the body of *Nehep*, a large, protective serpent. The accompanying text conforms with that of Rev. 14:13. (BG5.3.1-6)

them." The concept of a group of twelve of the dead resting in a state of happiness after accomplishing certain deeds is therefore at least as prominent in the *Book of Gates* as it is for the Great Multitude in the Book of Revelation.

Recipients of Food and Water (Rev. 7:15-17):- We read in Rev. 7:15-17 that "They shall hunger no more, neither thirst any more ... and he will guide them to springs of living water." Similarly, the necessity for food and water was among the basic necessities of Egyptians as projected from their earthly domain to the afterlife. Such references go back at least as far as the Pyramid Age. Bodily sustenance for the blessed dead in the afterlife was later emphasized in the *Book of the Dead* where it is first mentioned in the *Introductory Hymn to Osiris*.[a]

The importance of food and water to the Egyptian dead is clearly emphasized in this hymn: "May there be given to me bread from the House of Cool Water and a table of offerings from Heliopolis. ... May the barley and emmer which are in it belong to the Ka of the Osiris *N*."[291] It is therefore not surprising to find similar references to the need for food and drink in the *Book of Gates*. Food and drink are especially prominent at the conclusions of three different scenes with groups of twelve deities:

> Their gifts are bread, their beer is *Djesert*, their refreshment is water. Offerings are given to them upon earth as to those who are in peace like them. (BG4.2.7-10)[292]

> Their refreshment is water, the serpent Nehep guards their bodies while their souls pass on to the Fields of Yaru that they may receive their libations. The Protector of the Earth reckons for them their flesh. Their gifts are bread, their beer is *Djesert*, their refreshment is water. They receive offerings upon earth as the Noble One, He who rests upon his seat. (BG5.3.1-6)[293]

> May wind be for your nostrils, and the perfume of your unguent be sweet! May your bandages be loosened, may you walk! May you go to take the refreshments! May you rejoice, you souls, you (who) are accomplished! May you take the food, and be satisfied with the offerings! Your refreshment is offered to you from the lake of the corner of the Netherworld! ... Their offerings are bread, their beer is *Djesert*, their refreshment is water. Gifts are given to them upon earth as to the perfect souls who have power over their shadows. (BG7.3.2-7)[294]

These examples unambiguously demonstrate the importance of food and water to the deceased in the Egyptian afterlife just as we find for the members of the Great Multitude of followers in the Book of Revelation.

Happiness (Rev. 7:17):- Rev. 7:17 says that "God will wipe away every tear from their eyes." There are no explicit references to tears in either the *Amduat* or the *Book of Gates* (except possibly for that found in the scene with the Lion of Judah in Figure 47. Nevertheless, since tears can imply sadness, we may conclude that this text means there will be "no more sadness" and that God will cause happiness among his people. It is not surprising that we find references to happiness in three of the 32 groups of twelve in the *Book of Gates*. For example, the text describing the group at BG5.2.4-8 says, "Happy are you, you towers"[295] and the group at BG7.3.2-7 declares, "May your souls be happy."[296] A third text, located at BG6.1.6-7 is related to the those "who are convoked to the place (called) the Gladness of Earth," a phrase which implies

---

[a] The *Introductory Hymn to Osiris* is actually part of the book's conclusion rather than the beginning but is placed at the beginning because of its importance. For more examples of references to food and drink in the *Book of the Dead*, see Chapters 1, 30B, 58, 83, 99, 110, 117, 127, 136A, 148, 153, 168, and 178.

happiness(although its meaning here may not be exactly the same as in the previous two examples).[a]

Unassigned Multitude

While the previous section dealt with groups which could be assigned to the Great Multitude, this section deals with a group which is not easily assigned to any particular multitude although it is quite possible that its members belong to the Great Multitude or the tribes of Israel, or both. It is characterized by those who fight for their god.

Fight for God (Rev. 6:9,11; Rev. 11:18; Rev. 12:7,11; Rev. 19:19):- There are several references in the Book of Revelation to the followers of God being involved in mortal conflicts (Rev. 6:9,11; Rev. 11:18; Rev. 12:7,11; 19:19). In Rev. 12:7, war is mentioned in which the followers of God fight against the forces of the dragon; we are told that the dragon made war "on those who keep the commandments of God." And in Rev. 19:19, "the beast and the kings of the earth with their armies gathered to make war against him who sits upon the horse and against his army." Many die in the battles between good and evil. Remarkably, these battles include those fought on earth, for we are told in Rev. 6:9-11 that the writer of the Book of Revelation,

> saw under the altar the souls of those who had been slain for the word of God and for the witness they had borne; they cried out with a loud voice, "O Sovereign Lord, holy and true, how long before thou wilt judge and avenge our blood on those *who dwell upon the earth*?" Then they were ... told to rest a little longer, until the number of their fellow servants and their brethren should be complete, who were to be killed as they themselves had been.

Elsewhere, in Rev. 11:18 we read that those who fought in the great battles were rewarded after the "nations raged" and the time came "for rewarding thy servants ... for destroying the destroyers of the earth." After the war mentioned in Rev. 12:7 where the enemy is said to have been "thrown down," those who died in the conflict were given special mention: "they have conquered him ... for they loved not their lives even unto death. Rejoice then, O heaven and you that dwell therein!"

The 6th Division of the *Book of Gates* contains a similar reference to a group of twelve followers of the sun-god who fight for him. It pertains to the same twelve deities mentioned in the previous chapter as having symbols of truth (𓏴) on their heads in Figure 30 and who, it was suggested, parallel the tribes of Israel. They are described as "Those who have acted according to justice while on earth, who fight for their god, who are convoked to the place (called) the Gladness of Earth."[297] Also, in the 1st Division of the *Book of Gates* a group of twelve described as having worshiped Re upon earth is described as having "enchanted Apopis. ... You are indeed those who adore (me) and repulse Apopis from me."[298] In the 5th Division, another twelve followers bear javelins to fight the evil serpent (Figure 36); they say, "Our javelins,

---

[a] An alternative and possibly more likely interpretation of this particular passage will be presented in Chapter 21, *Seven Angels with the Wrath of God*.

O Re, are in the serpent Mamu! We spear the evil serpent, O Re!" Still another example is from the 9th Division of the *Amduat* where twelve cobra-form followers of the sun-god are shown seated on clothing signs (𐦀) as they spew fire from their mouths. The text says that, "The flames of their mouths cause the overthrow of the enemies in the Netherworld."[299]

In Chapter 17 of the *Book of the Dead* we read that, "As for that night of making war, it means that they entered into the east of the sky, and war broke out in the entire

Figure 36. The great multitude of followers of the sun-god represented as twelve soldiers carrying javelins with which to spear the enemy of the sun-god. This scene is reminiscent of several in the Book of Revelation which describe the followers of the Lamb fighting against evil. (BG5.1.1-4)

sky and earth."[300] Fearing death at the hands of the adversary in the sky, Egyptian warriors plead with the sun-god: "*Save me from those who deal wounds, the slayers whose fingers are sharp, who deal out pain, who decapitate those who follow after Osiris.*"[301] Thus, in spite of statements suggesting the practically invincible nature of the sun-god's army, this heavenly war was not without risk, and some – or even many – would be killed in battle. The same is undoubtedly true for the war which arose in heaven where Michael and his angels fought against the dragon and his angels (Rev. 12:7). War inevitably causes death on both sides, whether in heaven or on earth.

Discussion

The distribution of the attributes of members of the groups of twelve in the *Book of Gates* is by no means uniform and one wonders just how uniform it really is. It's variation is shown graphically in Appendix 3 which presents a simplified comparison between Revelation's three multitudes (the tribes of Israel, the Great Multitude and the Unassigned Multitude) and the attributes of the groups of twelve in the book. The reader should realize that there are several universal, parallel attributes which are not shown in this appendix.[a] It is evident from Appendix 3 that the remaining attributes

---

[a] The first is that they are all followers of their god, an attribute obvious from all the texts pertaining to each group although it is explicitly stated for only two (at BG3.3.5-8 and BG6.1.6-10). The second is that they are practically all male (excepting the group of female gods at BG10.3.1-5 and possibly the group at BG3.1.7-10 which consists of twelve uraeus serpents of unknown sex). The third is that they are practically all clothed in white robes (based primarily on the color of their garments in pictures which illustrate them in human form). To this we might add the multiracial element which, although not specifically mentioned among any of the groups of twelve in the *Book of Gates*, is generally accepted as a characteristic of the multitudes of the dead in the Egyptian Netherworld (at least during parts of Egypt's Dynastic Period).

are not quite randomly distributed among the various groups of twelve: many seem to be concentrated in groups found in the first four divisions. A closer look at the contents of Appendix 3 is in order, as follows.

Before looking at the broader picture, we begin our examination with the first group of twelve found in the 1st Division at BG1.1.1-6 and presented in column C of the Appendix. Note that apart from the universal attributes mentioned above, this group has two attributes of Revelation's tribes of Israel. The first is that they once lived on earth and the second that they praise their god. But this same group has two more attributes and these are identified with the Great Multitude; "the resting ones" and those who receive food and water. Furthermore, column C also contains those who fought for their god.[a] Now, if we are to assume from the examination of the distribution of the attributes that this group of twelve belongs to representatives of the tribes of Israel, we may also conclude that it also belongs to the Great Multitude, and to those who fight for their god. We may therefore conclude that this group of twelve conforms with Revelation's tribes of Israel which at the same time may be identified as a subgroup of the Great Multitude and those who "fight for their god." A similar line of reasoning may be followed for a number of the remaining groups of twelve (described in columns D, F, G, J, K, M, V, and c)[b] where it is apparent that the groups with attributes similar to those of the tribes of Israel also represent sub-groups of the Great Multitude. This conclusion conforms with the opinion of most bible scholars that Revelation's 144,000 members of the tribes of Israel belong to the much larger multitude containing millions more.

On a different note, the Prologue of the *Book of Gates* is rather interesting in that a part of its text can be interpreted to apply to the wanderings of the Israelites in the desert. As noted near the beginning of the previous chapter, there are two groups of twelve deities flanking the sun-god as he sinks into the western desert (the entrance to the Netherworld) from his position in the evening sky (see Figure 26). Re says,

> The desert is bright. I give light with what is on me. (O thou) who destroyest men, who art filled with the *chosen ones*' of the gods. Breath be given to you, among whom I am. Let there be rays for you, dwellers of the Region of Offerings, My Glorious Eye is for you, I

---

[a] This suggests that, from an Egyptian perspective, those who in Rev. 19:19 who fight in the army led by the one called the "Word of God" may also be a part of what Revelation calls the tribes of Israel.

[b] When all the groups of twelve are considered as a single body, we can say that most if not all the characteristics of the tribes of Israel, the Great Multitude and the Unassigned Multitude in the Book of Revelation have attributes similar to those of groups of twelve in the *Book of Gates*. Note that they all wear white clothing and except for the almost universal mention of the groups being followers of the sun-god (either explicitly expressed or implied), they are almost all male – although not one group has all the characteristics mentioned in Revelation. Instead, individual groups are described as having one or more of the attributes. This is as one would expect since it would be most cumbersome to ascribe all the attributes to each of the tribes separately in any literary composition written in the style of the Book of Revelation. We may therefore assume that practically all groups do indeed have most or all the attributes examined here.

have ordered their destruction, destruction is for all of them. I have hidden you from those upon earth, you to whom the diadem is restored in the Desert.[302]

We see here an apparent reference to hiding the "chosen ones" in the desert. At first glance, this statement seems to refer to the dead being buried in the desert away from human habitation and those who might destroy their bodies. This may well be so. But it should be pointed out that the statement also parallels a very prominent aspect of Jewish history – the wandering of the Israelites, "the chosen ones" (see I Chronicles 16:13) in the Sinai Desert after the Exodus. When examined from a purely Hebrew point of view, the passage seems to echo Hebrew traditions concerning events after the Exodus.

This later conclusion is similar to and conforms with the suggestion made at the conclusion of Chapter 6, *The Twelve Tribes of Israel* where, under the heading of *An Alternative Solution to Tribal Identity Problem* it is pointed out that the names and attributes of the twelve tribes could themselves be an echo of memories of the structure of the Egyptian army brought out of Egypt by a segment the Hyksos who left Egypt at the end of its 2nd Intermediate Period.

Chapter 8. Egyptian Parallels in the Seven Letters (Rev. 2-3)[303]

The second and third chapters of the Book of Revelation are in the form of seven letters, each addressed to a "church" in a particular town or city (Ephesus, Thyatira, Pergamum, Sardis, Smyrna, Laodicea, and Philadelphia). These letters are quite short, ranging in length from 186 to 287 words each (in the RSV) with an average length of 208 words. Their mention of Jews (Rev. 2:9; Rev. 3:9), synagogues (Rev. 2:9; Rev. 3:9), Balaam (Rev. 2:14), Jezebel (Rev. 2:20), Satan (Rev. 2:9; Rev. 2:13; Rev. 2:24; Rev. 3:9), the "key of David" (Rev. 3:7), and the "new Jerusalem" (Rev. 2:12) gives them a decidedly Jewish flavor, a fact which has undoubtedly influenced biblical scholars since the early days of Christianity. Early Christian scholars believed these churches were located in cities in Asia Minor,[a] an area visited and written about by the apostle Paul (even though Paul's letters in the New Testament fail to mention four of them: Pergamum, Sardis, Smyrna and Philadelphia). To ensure as complete as possible a comparison with Egyptian texts, the contents of the seven letters are included in this study. Indeed, as will become clear by the end of this chapter, the parallels between beliefs described in the letters and those of the Egyptians are quite striking.

In the second part of this chapter, we will examine equally striking parallels between the *structure* of two letters and certain Egyptian texts. Until then, a basic understanding of their structure and general content is helpful. Fiorenza (1985) notes that the seven letters follow a definite pattern, each consisting of five sections: an Introduction; a Messenger Formula; "I know ..." Formula; a Call to Hear and an Eschatological Promise.[304] The phrase "I know ..." states either the addressee's activities (as in Rev. 2:2, Rev. 2:19, Rev. 3:1, Rev. 3:8 and Rev. 3:15), tribulations (Rev. 2:9), or their dwelling place (Rev. 2:13). These are usually followed by positive comments coupled with negative ones – and warnings. The call to hear and heed is then made and an eschatological promise guarantees rewards to the faithful, i.e., "to him who conquers."

---

[a] For the traditionally assumed locations of the seven churches mentioned in Revelation, see any modern commentary on the Book of Revelation, such as *The Oxford Companion to the Bible,* 1993, p. 652 or the *Zondervan Pictorial Bible Dictionary,* 1963, pp. 721-722.

8. Egyptian Parallels in the Seven Letters 155

By way of introduction, it should be noted that the speaker who dictates the seven letters is identified in Rev. 1:17-18 as "the first and the last, and the living one; I died, and behold I am alive for evermore," characteristics which conform with the attributes of Osiris (see Chapter 3, *The Preeminent Deities*). In this chapter, strengthening evidence for this parallel will be demonstrated with references to the granting of special rewards to the "conquerors" (in Rev. 2:7, Rev. 2:11, Rev. 2:17, Rev. 2:26, Rev. 3:5, Rev. 3:12, and Rev. 3:21) as well as to the condemnation of doers of evil.

Parallel Elements in the Letters and Egyptian Texts

The following sub-sections compare each of the letters' main elements with well-known ancient Egyptian beliefs.

I know ... (Rev. 2:2,9,13,19; Rev. 3:1,8,15): - As mentioned above, one of the recurring formulas in the seven letters involves the phrase, "I know ..." It is used seven times in the Book of Revelation, each time referring to knowledge about a particular group of people, where they live (Rev. 2.13), their activities (Rev. 2.2, Rev. 2.19, Rev. 3.1, Rev 3:8, Rev 3:15), their strengths and weaknesses (Rev. 2.2, Rev. 2.9, Rev. 2.19,), and their faith and moral standards (Rev. 2.2, Rev. 2.19, Rev 3:8, Rev 3:15).

An equivalent phrase is common in Egyptian religious literature, especially in the *Book of the Dead* where we find a group of eight chapters devoted to having *knowledge* of the actions of seven different groups. The eight chapters of *"Knowing the Souls of ... ."* are as follows: Chapter 107, called *The Chapter of going into, and of coming forth from, the gate of the gods of the west among the followers of the god, and of knowing the souls of Amentet;* Chapter 108, called **The Chapter of knowing the souls of the West;** Chapter 109 is *The Chapter of knowing the souls of the East;* Chapter 112 is *The Chapter of knowing the souls of Pe;* Chapter 113, **The Chapter of knowing the souls of Nekhen;** Chapter 114, called *The Chapter of knowing the souls of Khemennu (Hermopolis);* Chapter 115 is called *The Chapter of coming forth to heaven, of passing through the hall of the tomb, and of knowing the souls of Ȧnnu [Heliopolis];* and Chapter 116 is called, *(The Chapter of) knowing the souls of Ȧnnu [Heliopolis].*[305] Note that Chapters 115 and 116 both involve knowing the souls of Ȧnnu and therefore acount for only one location, bringing the total number of localities mentioned to seven – the same number as that of the churches addressed in Rev. 2-3; the number is thus similar while the names are different. The main parallel here is the repetition of the phrase "I know ..." in conjunction with statements of information about the souls living in seven locations.

I know your dwelling place (Rev. 2:13):- Rev. 2:13 says, "I know where you dwell, where Satan's throne is; you hold fast my name and you did not deny my faith." There is at least one passage in the Egyptian literature where the phrase "I know where you dwell" is used in a manner similar to that in Revelation's letter to Pergamum. In the upper register of the 1st Division of the *Book of Caverns* the sun-god says to the faithful, *"I know your place*' in the Netherworld."[306] In a manner similar to some of the phrases in the seven letters the Egyptian text goes on to say,

"Behold, I know your names, your caverns, your secrets." Furthermore, just as Rev. 2:13 refers to knowledge of the place where Satan's throne is located, the sun-god continues by saying several times that he will "greet those who are in" Osiris but "set his enemies in their place of execution," indicating that the presence of enemies of Osiris along with the faithful in this same part of the Netherworld just as the faithful co-existed with the followers of Balaam in Pergamum.

I know your works (Rev. 2:2,19; Rev. 3:1,8,15):- There are many similar examples of this phrase in the *Book of the Dead*. One is in Chapter 32 where the speaker invokes magic powers against crocodiles (enemies) by claiming knowledge of their "lives," in other words, claiming knowledge of their behavior, deeds – or works. The speaker says, "I know them by their names and their *lives,*' and I save my father from them."[307] A more pertinent example is found in Chapter 115 of the *Book of the Dead*. Here we find a statement referring to the occupants of Heliopolis: "I know the souls of Heliopolis . .... (I know) the hostile *acts*' by Him who would destroy the heirs of ... ." The similarity between Revelation and the Egyptian source is irrefutable – knowledge of the works, acts, deeds or activities of groups of individuals is mentioned in both sources and is prefaced by the phrase, "I know. ..."

I know those with false credentials (Rev. 2:2,9; Rev. 3:9):- Three of the seven letters in Revelation contain references to people with false credentials. In the letter to Ephesus they are referred to as "those who call themselves apostles but are not, and [I] found them to be false" (Rev. 2:2), while in the letters to Smyrna and Philadelphia, they are described as "those who say that they are Jews and are not" (Rev. 2:9, Rev. 3:9). A similar reference to false credentials is found in Chapter 115 of the *Book of the Dead* where we read about the hostile acts of the "High-priest of Heliopolis who was not initiated through revelation."[308] The concept of false credentials is thus found in the *Egyptian Book of the Dead* and in three verses in Rev. 2-3.

I know ... those who rebel (many references):- One component common to all seven letters is the reference to interpersonal conflicts between the faithful and the unfaithful. In the letter to Ephesus, for example, while the speaker is pleased with the peoples' patient endurance (Rev. 2:3), he is displeased with the abandonment by some of an earlier love (or allegiance) to him (Rev. 2:4). He calls for repentance and threatens the guilty with darkness (death?) if they refuse (Rev. 2:4). In Smyrna we read of ongoing tribulation of the faithful, including poverty, slander and imprisonment by the followers of the Devil (Rev. 2:9-10). In Pergamum, we learn that some had dissented and crossed over to the enemy (Rev. 2:14) while Antipas, a faithful follower, was killed because of his steadfast allegiance (Rev. 2:13). Most of those in Sardis were accused of being "dead" (Rev. 3:1) while a few remained faithful (Rev. 3:4). In Philadelphia, the faithful followers are weak (Rev. 3:8) compared with their rivals in the synagogue of Satan (Rev. 3:9). Meanwhile, in Laodicea, most are accused of having only a "lukewarm" attitude (Rev. 3:15-16) and are counseled to establish (or re-establish?) commercial ties with the speaker (Rev. 3:18). In each case, except in the letter to Smyrna, the faithful are characterized as being "conquerors" and offered rewards for their loyalty ((Rev. 2:7, Rev. 2:11, Rev. 2:17, Rev. 2:26, Rev. 3:5, Rev. 3:12, Rev. 3:21) while the unfaithful are threatened with punishment (Rev. 2:5, Rev. 2:16, Rev. 2:22-23, Rev. 3:3, Rev. 3:9-10, Rev. 3:16). Rewards to the faithful are promised in Rev. 2:17 while dissenters in Rev. 2:16 are threatened with military action. Followers of Jezebel in Thyatira are to be thrown into great tribulation, including death (Rev. 2:20-23) while the faithful are promised ultimate dominion and power over the evil ones (Rev. 2:25-27).

The distribution of rewards and punishments in this part of Revelation is similar to events concerning the sun-god when he encounters both his faithful followers and his enemies as he passes through the Netherworld. There, he rewards the faithful and punishes the unfaithful. Indeed, many Egyptian texts contain the same general formula as in Revelation; they mention conflicts, rewards and punishments.

Especially striking parallels between the letters and Egyptian texts are found in the *Book of Caverns* where each division clearly separates the sun-god's rewards to the faithful from the punishments of the wicked; scenes dealing with rewards are typically placed in the upper registers while those which deal with punishment are located in the lower ones. Also, the text of the 1st Division of the *Book of Caverns* clearly indicates that the followers of the sun-god coexist with his enemies, just as in Revelation; when he enters this cavern, one of his first acts is to separate the righteous from the unrighteous: "Behold, I enter into the land of the fair West to take care of Osiris, to greet those who are in him. I set his enemies in their place of execution."[309] He then rewards his followers. His words and phrases are not very dissimilar to those used in the seven letters:

> Behold, *I know your names, your caverns, your secrets;* I know from what you live, when the One of the Netherworld [a title for Osiris] orders you *to live. Your throats breathe* when *you listen* to the words of Osiris. When I pass through the Netherworld, when I take the roads of the West, you are in peace, your souls are mighty, *you are powerful* in your caverns. *You hear my voice.* I call to you by your *names.*[310]

Here, we find the same basic elements as in Revelation (indicated by italics): "*I know ...*" (as in Rev. 2.2, Rev. 2.9a and Rev. 2:9b, Rev. 2.13, Rev. 2.19, Rev. 3.1, Rev 3:8, Rev 3:15) and "*You hear my voice ...*" (as in Rev. 2.7, Rev. 2.11, Rev. 2.17, Rev. 2.29, Rev. 3.6, Rev. 3.13, Rev. 3.22) are observed in each of the letters to the churches. Knowledge of *names* (as in Rev. 3:1, Rev. 3:5), *caverns* (i.e., dwelling places in Rev. 2:13) and *secrets* (i.e., works, as in Rev. 2.2, Rev. 2.19, Rev. 3.1, Rev 3:8, Rev 3:15) are also mentioned in this example. Rewards include the gift *to live* ("of life" is used in Rev. 2:7 and Rev. 2:10) and *power* (as in Rev. 2:26-27, Rev. 3:21).

We read in Rev. 2:5 that those of the church in Ephesus are advised to repent because *they did not do the works they did at first*. And in Rev. 2:20-22, unfaithful servants in the church at Thyatira rebelled by immorally eating food sacrificed to idols and are warned that they will be thrown into great tribulation if they refuse to repent of their deeds. Similarly, evil and discord in the Egyptian Netherworld is clearly due, at least in part, to rebellion against the sun-god. The 1st and 3rd Divisions of the *Book*

158   *Egyptian Origin of the Book of Revelation*

of Caverns contain examples of how the doers of evil in the Netherworld create discord among the sun-god's followers.ª The sun-god confronts them with the words,

> *It is you who cause the evil, who create the discord in the Netherworld.*' It is Osiris, He at the Head of the West, who delivers you to your retribution and who consigns you to the Place of Destruction, in accord with what has come from my mouth against you.[311]

He then declares, "You are *the enemies of Osiris who spread evil*' in the Hidden World,"[312] and then condemns them to great tribulation:

> I have committed you to the Sons of Earth so that you may not escape their guard. ... I deliver them to the Place of Destruction. O those who must be *annihilated,*' O those who must be *beheaded,*' enemies of Osiris, whose heads are cut off, who have no longer their necks, who *have no longer their souls,*' whose *corpses are annihilated.*' Behold, I pass by you; *I deliver you to your evil;*' I consider that you *exist no longer;*' you are those who are *overwhelmed with evil,*' you are *in the place of annihilation.*'[313]

The *Book of the Dead* also makes reference to the negative impact of the wicked on the followers of the sun-god in the Netherworld. Chapter 175 begins with,

> O Thoth, what is it that has come about through the Children of Nut? They have made war, they have raised up tumult, they have done wrong, *they have created rebellion,*' they have done slaughter, *they have created imprisonment,*' they have reduced what was great to what is little in all that we have made; ... they have done hidden damage to all that you have made.[314]

This passage includes a reference to imprisonment of the followers of the sun-god which conforms with the reference to imprisonment of the faithful in Rev. 2:10. It illustrates yet another parallel between Egyptian writings and the letters to the churches.

Fornication and Eating Sacrificed Food (Rev. 2:14, 20):- These verses provide an interesting juxtaposition of seemingly unrelated images – fornication and eating food; it occurs twice in the Book of Revelation. In Rev. 2:14, written to the church at Pergamum, the speaker says that he is against those who "eat things sacrificed unto idols, and ... commit fornication" (KJV, but the RSV uses the word "immorality"). In the second passage, written to the church at Thyatira, he is against those who seduce his servants "to commit fornication, and to eat things sacrificed unto idols" (Rev. 2:20, KJV). Note that the order of the main elements of Rev. 2:14 (eating and fornication) is reversed in Rev. 2:20 (fornication and eating). Remarkably, in the part of Chapter 125 of the *Book of the Dead* where unacceptable conduct is also mentioned we note the same reversal in the order of the same or similar pertinent elements. The

---

ª Division 5 of the *Book of Caverns* is another good example of the coexistence and interactions between the faithful followers and enemies of the sun-god. This division is a special case, however, since it is similar to the letter to Thyatira in several other significant ways; it will therefore be dealt with in more detail in the next section (*Structural Parallels in the Seven Letters*) which correlates entire chapters of Egyptian texts with specific letters in Revelation.

text reads, "I have not *lessened the food-offerings*' in the temple, I have not destroyed the loaves of the gods, I have not taken away the food of the spirits, I have not *copulated*,' I have not *misbehaved*,' I have not *lessened food-supplies*.' "[315] Such juxtapositions and reversal of seemingly unrelated deeds in both sources suggest a parallel between this part of Chapter 125 of the *Book of the Dead* and Rev. 2:14 and Rev. 2:20.

The Conquerors (Rev. 2:7,11,17,26; Rev. 3:5,12,21):- Near the end of each letter, Revelation makes a rather peculiar use of the Greek word *nikao* which is typically translated as "conquerors." Indeed, the manner in which *nikao* is used in the letters is similar to that used in Rev. 20 and Rev. 21 to describe one's success in the final judgment of the dead. In Rev. 21:7-8 it is used to introduce rewards to those who have been victorious in the judgment and punishment of those who are not; we read that "He who *conquers* shall have this heritage ..." and those who do not succeed in the judgment are destroyed in "the lake that burns with fire and sulfur." This juxtaposition of conquerors and judgment suggests the conquerors in the letters may be related to, or even the same as, those who are successful in the final judgment.

An Egyptian word used in a similar way to Revelation's *nikao* is *ma'a-kheru*, the exact meaning of which has been debated by Egyptologists since hieroglyphics were first deciphered in the early 1800's. Anthes (1954) conducted an in-depth study on *ma'a-kheru* and concludes it was originally a legal term meaning something like, "the acclamation given to him is 'right,'" "he is called right," or, "he is acknowledged as right by means of acclamation." The author also suggests that "he is justified" should be retained, and in certain cases "he is acknowledged as right(eous)" might be preferable.[316] The literal translation of *ma'a-kheru* traditionally accepted by many modern authorities is "true of voice," "true of statement," or "true of claim."[317] Meanwhile, Faulkner (1994), translates it as "vindicated" while Clagett (1989) prefers "acclaimed right"[318] or, when applied to moral or legal issues in a tribunal, "acclaimed just [i.e. vindicated before the tribunal]."[319] Used as an adjective, *ma'a-kheru* was "one of the most common words in Egyptian [funerary literature] since it was added to the name of every deceased person from the Middle Kingdom on"[320] to describe one's successful trial in the final judgment.

Zeller (1969), who studied the early Coptic (Egyptian Christian) versions of the Book of Revelation written in the southern Egyptian dialect, translated the Coptic word used in the letters to mean "they who shall be found *victorious*,"[321] thus paralleling allusions to success in the judgment of the dead. The Coptics apparently saw little or no difference between the words for *conquerors* and for those who were *victorious* – and they used them in much the same way as their non-Christian, Osirian counterparts in the judgment of the dead.

It was during the pre-dynastic period and the emergence of a story about a dispute between Osiris and his brother Seth that *ma'a-kheru* was first used in a legal setting. Seth, hoping to gain the throne of Egypt, lodged charges against Osiris and entered a tribunal against him in Heliopolis.[322] A court concluded his charges were false while the defense of Osiris was true; Osiris was found to be *ma'a-kheru* and the tribunal decreed that "the thrones of Geb [the earth-god] should revert to him."[323] Osiris's rewards were manifold. Breasted (1912) quotes from and comments on several passages in the *Pyramid Texts*:

> "The sky is given to thee, the earth is given to thee, the fields of Rushes are given to thee, the Horite regions, the Setite regions, the cities are given to thee. The nomes are united for thee by Atum. It is Geb (the Earth-god) who speaks concerning it" [*Pyramid Text* §961]. Indeed, Geb, the Earth-god and father of Osiris, "assigned the countries to the embrace of Osiris" [*Pyramid Text* §1033]. ... After his death, one of the oldest sources says of him: "He entered the secret gates in the (splendid) precincts of the lords of eternity, at the goings of him who rises in the horizon, upon the ways of Re in the Great Seat" [Brit. Mus. Stela 797m k, 63]. ... It was a subterranean kingdom of the dead over which Osiris reigned, and it was as champion and friend of the dead that he gained his great position in Egyptian religion.[324]

As will be discussed in the next section, just as Osiris received rewards as a result of his victory (*ma'a-kheru*) over Seth, the Osirian believer expected no less when he too was declared to be *ma'a-kheru* – "acclaimed just," "vindicated," "victorious" and a *conqueror*.

The legal battle between Osiris and Seth and the results of the trial are mentioned in passing many times in the *Book of the Dead*, especially when the deceased faces the final judgment. Here, the deceased stands before a group of deities called the divine Ennead and makes a *Declaration of Innocence*, the text of which is recorded in Chapter 125; he concludes with a statement concerning his own truthfulness and purity. His heart, being the seat of his intellect, is called as a witness to his earthly deeds and sinlessness and is placed on one pan of the "great balance" while a feather, the symbol truth, or *maat*, is placed on the other. Thoth, the same judge and keeper of the written record of the dispute between Osiris and Seth, examines the position of the pointer on the balance and declares to the Ennead, "His deeds are righteous in the great balance, and no sin has been found in him." The Ennead confirms the judgment by saying, "This utterance of yours is true. The vindicated [*ma'a-kheru*] ... is straightforward, he has no sin, there is no accusation against him before us." The deceased is then introduced to Osiris by Horus who recommends he be rewarded "forever like the followers of Horus."[325] Then, with a triumphant attitude, the deceased proudly says to Osiris, "Here I am in your presence, O Lord of the West. ... vindicated [*ma'a-kheru*] before Osiris."[326]

Another interesting parallel with Revelation's *conquerors* is that the Egyptian phrase, "... vindicate the Osiris *N* ... against his enemies ... in the presence of the Great Council," is repeated ten times the 18th Chapter of the *Book of the Dead* while the parallel phrase, "To him who conquers ..." is mentioned seven times in the 2nd and 3rd Chapters of Revelation. Although the number of times the phrase is repeated is slightly different, the act of repetition itself of the phrase is present in both sources.

While the concept of *"conqueror"* or those "found victorious" is common to all seven letters in Revelation 2-3, the rewards promised the conquerors differ from letter to letter – just as the rewards differed among different penitents who stood before the throne of Osiris.

Nikao is also used in the Book of Revelation in the sense of vanquishing the foe. Similarly, the *Book of the Dead* does not restrict the use of *ma'a-kheru* to the results of tribunals. We also find it in the context of physical conflicts with enemies where it more closely corresponds with the traditional meaning of "triumph" or "conquest." For example, in Chapter 134 we read, "... they fall on their faces when Ani is 'triumphant' [*ma'a-kheru*] over his enemies in the Upper Sky and the Lower Sky."[327] Similarly, other uses of *nikao* in Revelation refer to acts of physical conquest or triumph over the enemy (as in Rev. 6:2, Rev. 11:7, Rev. 13:7 and Rev. 17:14), just as *ma'a-kheru* is sometimes used in the *Book of the Dead*. The *range* of ways in which *nikao* is used in the Book of Revelation therefore also parallels that of the use of *ma'a-kheru* in Egyptian literature.

Deceased is to be judged like the One on the Throne (Rev. 3:21):- The one on the throne in Rev. 3:21 refers to "*he who conquers ... as I myself conquered* and sat down with my Father on his throne." Similarly, it was the desire of every Osirian believer to be "vindicated" before Osiris just as Osiris was vindicated before his father Geb and the divine tribunal. This is nowhere more obvious than in the 18th chapter of the *Book of the Dead* where, as noted above, the deceased addresses the trial judge ten times with the words, "*O Thoth, who vindicated Osiris ...* [also] *vindicate the Osiris N ... in the presence of the Great Council.*"[328] The parallel between this statement and Rev. 3:21 is striking although there is a different speaker in each case; in the Book of Revelation it is the one on the throne who speaks while in the Egyptian version it is the deceased who is speaking. In both cases, however, the deceased is victorious just as the one on the throne was victorious (in his trial against Seth); the deceased claimed a victorious judgment even as Osiris was judged victorious – just as in Rev. 3:21.

Confession of Deceased Before the Throne (Rev. 3:5):- The latter part of Rev. 3:5 says, "I will confess his name before my Father and before his angels." This statement parallels in just a few words one of the most treasured tenets of the Osirian believer wherein Horus stands before the throne of Osiris and speaks on behalf of the deceased. In the Egyptian equivalent of this verse, the speaker is Horus rather than the one on the throne. Nevertheless, the scenario is essentially the same; after the deceased is judged before the tribunal, Horus personally introduces the deceased to his father (Osiris).

This act was so important that a picture of the event (Figure 7) was placed near the beginning of the *Book of the Dead* even though the details of the judgment process itself appear later (in much the same way as the cover of a modern book might bear an illustration of one of its more important scenes).[a] Details are provided in Chapter 30B of the *Book of the Dead* where Horus is described as standing before the throne as he presents the deceased to Osiris with the words, "I have come to you, O Wennefer [Osiris], and I bring *N* [the *name* of the deceased] to you." He then bears witness to Osiris concerning the results of the hearing before the tribunal of judges (angels in Revelation) with the words,

---

[a] See also the discussion on the judgment scene in Chapter 3, *The Preeminent Deities*.

His heart is true, having gone forth from the balance, and he has not sinned against any god or any goddess. Thoth has judged him in writing which has been told to the Ennead, and Maat the great [representing "truth"] has witnessed. Let there be given to him bread and beer which have been issued in the presence of Osiris, and he will be forever like the Followers of Horus."[329]

As in Revelation, the deceased has been judged and has gone forth from the judgment process vindicated – a conqueror before the throne of Osiris. And like the conquerors in Rev. 2-3, he is rewarded for his faithfulness (parallels to the gifts presented as rewards will be discussed later in this chapter).

Deceased Claims Share in Throne (Rev. 3:21):- We learn in this verse that the conqueror will be granted "to sit with me on my throne, as I myself conquered and sat down with my Father on his throne." Similarly, as part of his reward for having conquered, been vindicated before the throne of Osiris, the pious Egyptian believer expected to share in Osiris' glory by actively participating in ruling his kingdom, the Netherworld.[330] A funerary document from the VIth Dynasty reads, "Hail Unàs. Not hast thou [the deceased] gone, behold, (as) one dead, thou hast gone (as) one living to sit upon the throne of Osiris."[331] And on a wall in the pyramid of Pepi I, we read, "thou has found Rā and he watcheth over thee, he hath taken thee by thy hand, he hath led thee into the two regions of heaven, and he hath placed thee on the throne of Osiris."[332] Also, at the conclusion of the 146th chapter of the *Book of the Dead*, the deceased says, "[I have] received my crown at my rising, and I have power to sit upon the throne, upon the throne of my father and of the great company of the gods."[333] While Osiris was awarded the throne after he was judged by the divine Ennead, the deceased, having shared a similar victory before the tribunal, claimed the same right to participate in the authority of the throne. The parallel between Revelation and Egyptian beliefs is striking.

Promise of No Second Death (Rev. 2:11):- This verse says that "He who conquers shall not be hurt by the second death." It is not until much later in Revelation that the nature of this second death is defined. Rev. 20:14-15 says, "This is the second death, the lake of fire; and if any one's name was not found written in the book of life, he was thrown into the lake of fire." Note that the reference to the judgment is clearly associated with being "thrown into the lake of fire." Elsewhere, we read that "The beast was

Figure 37. Scene showing the Lake of Fire which threatens all doers of evil in the final judgment. The deceased bows before Osiris while the rectangular Lake of Fire lies in wait for him (the "second death") should he fail to vindicate himself. The lake is surrounded by six fire symbols (🜂). This scene parallels those described in Rev. 2:11 and Rev. 20:14.

8. Egyptian Parallels in the Seven Letters

captured, and with it the false prophet ... were thrown alive into the lake of fire that burns with sulphur" (Rev. 19:20). And "the devil who had deceived them was thrown into the lake of fire and sulphur where the beast and the false prophet were, and they will be tormented day and night for ever and ever" (Rev. 20:10). The association between the Egyptian judgment and the lake of fire is graphically shown in Figure 37. Hornung (1990) comments on this extreme act of violence against the offender: "Consignment of the body to flames symbolized the absolute negation of existence – the hardest imaginable sentence on earth. ... At the center of the infernal punishments was the Lake of Fire, whose very water is fire."[334] Its location in the Netherworld is given in the 5th Division of the *Amduat* where we learn of "the secret cave of Sokaris, a secluded spot guarded by the earth god Aker in the form of a double sphinx [🐾]. ... At its heart lies the Lake of Fire, whose red waves portend one of the most refined places of punishment reserved for those condemned at the Judgment of the Dead."[335]

The second death is mentioned several times in the *Book of the Dead* and was such a terrifying prospect to the ancient Egyptians that three chapters in the book are devoted to the theme of "not dying a second time." Chapter 44 is entitled the *Chapter for Not Dying Again in God's Domain*. Chapters 175 and 176 are both entitled *Chapter of Not Dying Again*. Also, the rubric at the conclusion of Chapter 135 states that "As for him who knows this chapter, he will be a worthy spirit in the God's Domain, and *he will not die again*' in the realm of the dead, and he will eat in the presence of Osiris."[336] This promise of not dying again closely parallels the text of Rev. 2:11.

Other forms of punishment, including the destruction of the body and separate parts of the dead were recognized forms of dying a second time. One form is implied by the presence of a monster hungrily waiting beneath the lake of fire in Figure 37. But destruction in the Lake of Fire was by far the most feared.

Gift of the Tree of Life (Rev. 2:7):- Rev. 2:7 refers to the conqueror being granted "to eat of the tree of life, which is in the paradise of God." Many Osirian believers had a strong religious fascination with trees and shared the same belief. Various deities were even said to have come forth from trees. For example, as Lurker (1980) points out, the god Horus came

> from the acacia, Re from the sycamore and Wepwawet from the tamarisk. According to Theban temple inscriptions the sky goddess Nut bore Osiris under the *kesbet* tree. ... Tree cults were widespread in the Nile valley. An acacia was venerated in Heliopolis in which 'life and death were decided' and it, therefore, paralleled the *ished*-tree. ... Two Upper Egyptian nomes had sacred trees as their signs, the 'sycamore nome' ... and the 'tree nome' ...[337]

But more to the point of Rev. 2:7, we note that Lurker also says the Egyptians frequently referred to a tree of life (Figure 38) which promised abundance of food and drink in the hereafter:

> As the living found refreshment in the shade of a tree so the souls of the dead also alighted on trees. Again and again images show female tree spirits, who were thought of as the sky goddess Nut or Hathor, giving water and handing fruit to the soul of the deceased who was

in bird form. The tree, especially the date palm and the sycamore, was therefore a *tree of life.'* Whoever drank of the water of life and ate of the celestial fruits lived on after death.[338]

Figure 38. Served by the tree goddess, the triumphant dead and his soul (the *ba*-bird) partakes of the water and food of the *tree of life*. The scene conforms with Rev. 2:7 which says, "To him who conquers I will grant to eat of the tree of life, which is in the paradise of God."

Chapter 68 of the *Book of the Dead* says that the blessed dead will "sit under the branches of the tree of Hathor"[339] and Chapter 189, which describes a conversation between the deceased and the gods and spirits, provides us with a god's question to the deceased: "Where is it granted you to eat?" The deceased replies, "I will eat under that sycamore of Hathor. ... Under the branches of the *Djebat-nefret* tree ... to which I have been taken."[340] Hornung (1990) notes that in many private tombs, a tree goddess grows out of the tree and offers "the deceased and his *ba* (soul) cool water and food. ... The tree offers shade, moisture, and sustenance. ... The tree goddess offers a stream of life that does not cease in the Beyond."[341] Budge (1895) describes the blessed dead as going "in the midst of the Field of Peace whereon the great gods sit; and these great and never failing gods give unto him (to eat) of the *tree of life'* of which they themselves do eat that he likewise may live. ... He suffers neither hunger nor thirst."[342] Thus, like Rev. 2:7, the Tree of Life offered all Egyptians fortunate enough to enter paradise, an everlasting supply of life-sustaining nourishment.

Gift of White Garments (Rev. 3:5a):- References to white garments in the hereafter have been discussed in the previous chapter. Suffice it to now illustrate its importance to the deceased in relation to his having victoriously emerged from the final judgment: "He who conquers shall be clad thus in white garments" (Rev. 3:5). The essence of the Egyptian desire to receive a white garment is found in Chapter 171 of the *Book of the Dead*, aptly entitled the *Chapter for Donning a Pure Garment*. The victorious dead first addresses several important Egyptian gods, including the Greater and Lesser Enneads (important groups of gods), and then respectfully makes his request: "... may you give this pure garment to the worthy spirit *N;* may you grant that it be beneficial to him; As for this pure garment for *N*, may it be allotted to him for ever and ever, and may you remove the evil which is on him."[343] In the following chapter (#172) we read an account which is even closer to the brief passage provided in Revelation. Here, the victorious dead, having triumphed in the judgment, receives instructions to "don the pure garment ... you receive the loin-cloth of fine linen . ... may you proceed on the paths ... being clad in fine linen every day and being guided by the god to the portals of the Great Mansion."[344] The parallel between Rev. 3:5 and such Egyptian beliefs is obvious.

Maintain Name in the Book of Life (Rev. 3:5b):- In the next part of Rev. 3:5, the one on the throne says, "I will not blot his name out of the book of life."[a] As in the Book of Revelation, books were used during the Osirian judgment process (see Chapter 25, *Resurrection and Judgment* for details) and this is obvious in the *Introductory Hymn to Osiris* in the *Book of the Dead* (Figure 6) where we find a reference to the name of the deceased being recorded: "... *may my name ... be found at the board of offerings.*"[345] And like the book in Revelation, this book could be revised by removing names from it. Such a book is mentioned in Division 5 of the *Book of Caverns*. In it, the deceased are referred to as "the veiled ones, O the veiled ones ... I call you by your names ... Mysterious Book, first apparitions, *great revision.*"[346] The meaning of a "great revision" is obvious; it implies the possibility of having one's name removed (blotted out) in the final judgment, just as we read about in Rev. 3:5. Elsewhere, in the same Division of *Book of Caverns* the sun-god says, "I have counted [i.e., recorded] them, I have established their bodies, I cause them to be in peace."[347] We cannot be certain, of course, if this "Mysterious Book" is a precise parallel to Revelation's "Book of Life," nor can we be certain that it is the same one which contains the records written by Thoth, the secretary and overseer at the tribunal. Nevertheless, both books seem to accomplish the same purpose.

Become a pillar in the temple (Rev. 3:12):- This verse explicitly says of the conqueror, "I will make him a pillar in the temple of my God; never shall he go out of it." When we think of ancient temples, we also think of the importance of massive pillars used to support their roofs. Or we might think of a person who is a stalwart, dependable, most worthy member of the temple staff. But when we think of Rev. 3:12 from a purely Egyptian perspective, an alternative meaning comes to the fore: references to pillars in Egyptian temples can also apply to priests. One type of priest which was especially prominent in some ceremonies – including the judgment of the dead – was the *Iunmutef* priest; his name literally meant "Pillar of his mother." This priest symbolized the eldest son of the deceased and is typically illustrated with

---

[a] There are five different types of "books" mentioned in the Book of Revelation, each of which appears to have a different function. The first one is the Book of Revelation itself (first mentioned in Rev. 1:11, but also referred to in Chapter 22 (Rev. 22:7, Rev. 22:9, Rev. 22:10, Rev. 22:18 and Rev. 22:19). The second book has the seven seals (Rev. 5:1, Rev. 5:2, Rev. 5:3, Rev. 5:4, Rev. 5:5, Rev. 5:7, Rev. 5:8 and Rev. 5:9) and contains references to seven plagues. The third is a "small book" eaten by the author (Rev. 10:2, Rev. 2:8-10) which is apparently an edible version of a book containing certain prophesies. The forth (Rev. 20:12) is in fact several books which are opened at the time of the final judgment; these contain information related to the deeds of individuals (Rev. 20:12), information necessary for the judgment of the deceased. Finally, there is a fifth book, the *Book of Life* which, according to Rev. 3:5, Rev. 13:8, Rev. 17:8, Rev. 20:15, and Rev. 21:27, contains the names a select group of people created since the world began (as stated in Rev. 13:8, Rev. 17:8 and Rev. 20:15); the names of others are not found in this book.

the youthful side-lock and wearing a panther skin as in Figure 39. His name "was intended to signify the god *Iunmutef* himself as the model for the priest carrying out functions of a filial nature, such as the care of the mummy of a father."[348] In the introduction to Chapter 18 of the *Book of the Dead* we read that as part of the judgment process, the *Iunmutef* priest introduced the deceased to the divine council. Faulkner (1994) translates the relevant section as, "Words spoken by the Pillar-of-his-Mother Priest, he says: I have come before you, O Great Councilors who are in the sky, earth, and the God's Domain, I have brought to you Osiris, *N* [the deceased] who is blameless before all the gods, let him be with you every day."[349]

An alternative but somewhat similar parallel to the "pillar" in Revelation is that of the "noble *djed*," a signification based on the *djed* pillar (☥), an important Egyptian symbol meaning "stability." In the Old Kingdom at Memphis there were priests of the 'noble *djed*,' including the chief Memphite god, Ptah, who was himself called 'the noble *djed*.'"[350] The important role in temple rituals of both the *Iunmutef* priest in the judgment of the dead, and the "noble *djed*," or the noble pillar-priest in Memphis, was undoubtedly the ultimate focal point of aspirations of many scribes. It is entirely possible – even probable – that these priests and the *Iunmutef* priests were thought of a "pillars" in the temple, just as we read about in Rev. 3:12.

Rev. 3:12 also promises the conqueror that he shall never leave the temple. Such a promise would have special meaning to scribes and other professional workers in Egypt's theocratic society where the priesthood and the civil service were tightly integrated and the amount of time served as a priest in the temple could be limited. While some priests held permanent positions in the temple, David (1980) says that the priesthood,

Figure 39 The *Iunmutef* priest, or *Pillar-of-His-Mother* Priest, shown here as he performs his duties in the temple. His name parallels the reference in Rev. 3:12 to the conqueror being a pillar in the temple.

was usually a secondary profession, held on a hereditary basis by members of certain families. These men might be lawyers, doctors or scribes, and they would hold priesthoods related to their original profession. In addition to their other duties, they would enter the temple each year as temporary personnel. They were divided into four groups, each of which worked continuously for one month at the temple; in one year, each man would thus have completed three months of duty. For the reminder of the year, they would continue their main occupations outside the temple.[351]

Such assignments would very likely be a welcome change from the possibly more stressful day-to-day responsibilities of a civil servant. Also, the greater prestige in the temple would enhance one's reputation and stature in the eyes of his family, peers and the general populace. This sentiment is captured near the end of Chapter 115 of the *Book of the Dead* where we read that "the heritage of the heir came into being, and great will be he who shall see it; *he will become High-priest.*"[352] The High-priest was, of course, a permanent position in the temple hierarchy. To be permanently assigned a priestly position in the temple was obviously coveted and in this sense conforms well with the words of promise to the conqueror in Rev. 3:12.

Eating in the presence of God (Rev. 3:20):- The conqueror in Revelation is promised a repast with the one on the throne. The text says, "I will come in to him and eat with him, and he with me." Similarly, the Osirian faithful believed they would have a similarly special relationship with Osiris. In Chapter 136A, we read that the deceased *"will eat and drink in the presence of Osiris"* every day."[353] In fact, the deceased even expressed the desire to be a personal friend of Osiris just as other gods in the Netherworld; he says to these gods, "May I be like one of you, a friend of the Lord of Eternity [Osiris], may I walk like you walk, may I stand like you stand, may I sit like you sit, may I speak like you speak before the Great God, Lord of the West [Osiris]."[354] Many such expressions of the desire of the deceased to eat and socialize with Osiris are found in the *Book of the Dead*.[a] Indeed, when Horus introduces the deceased to Osiris after the judgment process, he says, "Let there be given to him bread and beer which have been issued *in the presence of Osiris,* and he will be forever like the Followers of Horus."[355] Elsewhere the deceased says, "... I have eaten and *I have swallowed in his presence.*"[356]

Gift of hidden manna (Rev. 2:17):- "To him who conquers I will give some of the hidden manna." The Greek word used for "hidden" in this verse is *krupto*, "to conceal." In addition to "conceal," the King James Version variously translates it as "to hide (self), keep secret, secret(ly),"[357] concepts which had special meanings in the Osirian cult. Many temples and practically all tombs were accessible only to a select few; Goelet (1994) says that, "All modern reconstructions of Egyptian temples and their priestly staffs have noted that not only were the temple complexes divided into public and restricted sections, but also that levels of access within the priesthood itself were differentiated. Only the upper level of the permanent priesthood seems to have been allowed to come in close contact with the divine image [of the god], for example."[358] To eat in the presence of a great god such as Osiris could therefore only be carried out in the inner sanctum of a temple by a high priest. Since much of the structure of the Netherworld was patterned after realities in Egypt, the privilege of dining in the presence of Osiris in the Netherworld would be granted to only a few – but included all who had become priests as a reward for being victorious at the judgment (see above discussion on Rev. 3:12). In the *Introductory Hymn to Osiris* near the beginning of the *Book of the Dead*, the deceased expresses the expectation to eat from offerings: "May there be given to me bread from the House of Cool Water and a *table of offerings'* from Heliopolis."[359] Just as the high priests partook of offerings presented in especially holy and hidden areas of the temples of Egypt, the deceased would partake of them with Osiris in the hidden sanctuaries of the Netherworld – in complete agreement with the text of Rev. 2:17.

---

[a] For example, see the following passages translated by Faulkner (1994): BD-*Introductory Hymn to Osiris*, Plate 1; BD30B, Plate 2; BD83, Plate 27; BD135, p. 118; BD153B, p. 124.

Gift of a white stone with a secret name (Rev. 2:17):- This verse promises a reward which would be unusual and meaningless in most modern contexts. Perhaps, this is why Egyptologist Wallis Budge (1904) so readily associated this verse with ancient Egyptian beliefs. Indeed, this is one of the very few parts of the Book of Revelation Budge mentions in his writings; he says,

> We may note in passing that one of the greatest gifts which was to be given to the true believers of the Church of Pergamos was "a white stone, and in the stone a new name written, which no man knoweth saving he that receiveth it" (Rev. ii. 17). Here is a direct allusion to the old belief in the efficacy of an amulet which was made of a certain stone, and inscribed with a name, by and through and in which its owner would enjoy life and happiness.[360]

He also provides us with a rationale for the custom:

> Every god and goddess and supernatural being were believed to possess a hidden name by, and through, and in which he or she lived. The man who could find out these names was able to command the help of the gods who bore them, and the man who could obtain by any means a hidden name for himself thought he would be the equal of the gods. On the other hand, to destroy or "blot out" a name was to wipe out of existence the being who bore it, and it was for this reason that in the earliest days of civilization in Egypt services in which the name, or names, of the dead were commemorated, and were mentioned with laudatory epithets, were established.[361]

Much has been written about amulets since the early days of modern Egyptology. Lurker (1980) says that, "The most important forms of amulets are of divine figures (e.g. Osiris, Bes, Taweret), animal figures (e.g. lion, ram, scarab), parts of the human body (*wedjat*-eye, hand), royal insignia (especially crowns) and actual symbols such as the *ankh* and *djed* pillar."[362] These amulets were probably originally hung around the neck as jewelry while most, in addition to decorating, were worn to protect the wearer from evil. Today the "wearing of amulets or talismans is a world-wide phenomenon, even in the strictest monotheistic cultures."[363] Because they were so common in Egypt for millennia and were made of such a durable material these artifacts can even be purchased in the thousands by tourists visiting modern-day Egypt.

Goelet (1994) explains that the protective power of these amulets can most easily be understood as a type of magic "to gain control over supernatural forces and irrational forces. ... to coerce gods and supernatural beings to perform the will of the deceased."[364] Their power was enhanced by inscribing them with mottos, important religious passages, or the names of powerful kings or deities. The durability of the material of which they were made, usually glazed steatite (soapstone, talc), ensured their survival over time.

Secret names, however, held special significance. For example, according to one popular legend, it was by tricking Re into telling her his secret name that the goddess Isis gained power over him.[365] While many amulets were manufactured with the owner's name already inscribed, others were made and sold with a blank space so that the owner's name could be added later.[366] At least this is one possible explanation for the blank space. Could not the blank spaces sometimes been reserved for invisible, secret names as in Rev. 2:17? It is entirely reasonable to assume that some owners envisaged their secret, invisible name being present in the otherwise blank space, thereby rendering the amulet especially powerful.

But what of the stone's color? The most important type, the heart scarabs, which were used as funerary amulets, were ideally made of green basalt.[367] According to the rubric of Chapter 30B of the *Book of the Dead*, one type was to be inscribed with Chapter 30B "on a scarab made of nephrite [which is green], mounted in fine gold, with a ring of sliver, and placed at the throat of the deceased."[368] Thus, heart scarabs were not usually white in color as described in Rev. 2:17. Typically, these stones would be manufactured with engravings of parts of Chapter 30B while blank spaces would be left for the name of the deceased to be added by his or her survivors. In spite of the dictates of the *Book of the Dead*, the stone most used for scarabs, as indicated above, was steatite, a stone which is usually light grey in color. The beetle (*Scarabaeus sacer*) was usually black and "the craftsman covered the natural color of the stone with some kind of dark wash or pigment, and later with green or blue glaze."[369] The light grey color of the unadulterated steatite might, of course, have been considered to be white or near white in a relative sense so that such stones would conform with the color of the one referred to in Rev. 2:17.

At least one white scarab is known to exist, however; it is described by Budge (1893) who states that the scarab bearing the British Museum reference number 7917 "shows that the heart scarab was sometimes made of material other than green basalt. This example is in white limestone, and was made for a Sem priest, who was also the high-priest (*Ur-kherp-hem*) of Ptah." Budge comments on its unusual color with the words, "It is surprising to find that the relatives of such a high ecclesiastical official should have disregarded the direction of the Rubric of Chapter XXXB."[370] It would, nevertheless, appear that the practice existed, however rare, in using white stone for scarabs. Since white was considered the color of purity,[371] this could be a natural extension of Egyptian beliefs; the idea of a white or near white scarab stone representing the purity which every Egyptian wished to be revealed in the final judgment would certainly conform with Rev. 2:17.

Gift of the morning star (Rev. 2:28):- References to individuals receiving a star as a gift appear in Egyptian beliefs just as we read in Rev. 2:28. Chapter 164 of the *Book of the Dead* says, "His flesh and bones shall be found like one who does not die. He shall drink water from the river; land shall be given to him in the Field of Reeds," and finally, "*a star of the sky shall be given to him.*"[372] During the final judgment and after Horus introduces the "conqueror" to his father Osiris and leads him into the hereafter, the deceased comments on the personal value of the star:" The Morning Star has made a path for me, and I enter in peace into the beautiful West. I belong to the garden of Osiris, and a path is made for me so that I may go in and worship Osiris."[373] Another text explains, "Thou (O Morning Star) makest this *N* to sit down because of his righteousness and to rise up because of his reverence."[374] A gift of the Morning Star thus had an immense appeal to the ancient Egyptian believer who longed for a safe, peaceful and blessed existence in the hereafter. Revelation's reference to it being a gift to the conqueror is an excellent parallel with Egyptian beliefs.

The star's value in the afterlife seems to have been recognized in Egypt since the earliest times and gradually grew in sophistication. As mentioned in Chapter 3, *The Preeminent Deities,* the Morning Star was also identified with Horus of the Underworld[375] (as well as the soul of Osiris).[376] Clagett (1989) says that the king himself (Horus, the *christos*) was sometimes seen as the Morning Star[377] while Budge (1934) says that the "Morning Star was the ferryman of Osiris, or the Soul of Osiris, i.e., the [sacred] Benu bird."[378] Budge (1904) also notes that Osiris himself was "made like the morning star."[379] Breasted (1912) says that one of its roles in the afterlife involved the protection of the dead, the resurrection of the body, and eternal life: "Life comes to thee, but death comes not to thee. They (Orion, Sothis, and the Morning Star) save thee from the wrath of the dead who go head downward. Thou art not among them. Rise up for life, thou diest not; lift thee up for life, thou diest not."[380] The importance of the morning star to the ancient Egyptians certainly conforms with the promise of a gift to the faithful in the letter to the church in Thyatira (Rev. 2:28).

An open door (Rev. 3:8):- Rev. 3:8 says, "I have set before you an open door, which no one is able to shut." Similarly, the concluding sentence of one paragraph in Chapter 64 of *The Book of the Dead* says, "It is these who are in the opening [of the door/gate] of the Duat [the Netherworld], it is these who are provided for by Shu [the god of (life-giving) air]."[381] The parallel between the two sources is obvious, especially when we consider that the "opening," or first door into the Netherworld is death itself, something which no one on earth can avoid, or as Revelation puts it "an open door, which no one is able to shut."

Supporting evidence for this parallel is found in the opening sentence of the same paragraph in the *Book of the Dead.* It says, "*I know*' the depths and I know your name. You have made the portions of the blessed dead."[382] This opening statement, of course parallels the common phrase "I know ..." in the seven letters as discussed above – and which forms the opening phrase of Rev. 3:8 – thus introducing the reference to the open door. The juxtaposition and similar sequence of these two parallels strengthen the validity of each of the two separate parallels to Rev. 3:8.

He who has an ear, let him hear ... (Rev. 2:7,11,17,29; 3:6,13,22):– The phrase in Revelation, "He who has an ear, let him hear what the Spirit says to the churches," has identical form in each of the seven letters to the churches.[a] It also has a distinctly Egyptian ring to it. The Egyptians believed that our "ears ... alluded to the goodwill of the gods," and "images of huge ears ... were thought to be a magical pledge that the prayer would be brought before the gods."[383] Also, they believed "the ear referred symbolically to the readiness of the mind to be receptive to that which it had heard,"[384] an idea conceptually identical with that expressed in Rev. 2-3. They also paid particular attention to the words of their sages, one of whom was Ptahotep, a well-known, ancient Egyptian philosopher. Ptahotep explained the relationship between the love of God and hearing words of wisdom: "He whom God loves, hears, but he whom God hates, hears not. It is the heart that makes the owner into one that hears or one

---

[a] The first half of the phrase, "He who has an ear, let him hear," is also similar to an instruction in Rev. 13:9 concerning the war against the saints. The possible significance of this similarity will be discussed in Chapter 18, *The Beasts of Rev. 13.*

that hears not. His heart is a man's fortune. ... As for a fool that hears not, he can do nothing at all."[385]

It is also relevant that the expressions "He who has an ear ..." in Revelation immediately precedes promises of rewards to the faithful and punishment for others. For example, in letter to Sardis, those who have "not soiled their garments" are rewarded with white garments and the promise that their name will not be removed from the Book of Life, but those whose works are not perfect are advised to repent or they will not know what hour their punishment will come. In the letter to Ephesus, those who do not "repent" of their deeds will have their lampstands removed while those who "conquer" will be spared a second death in the lake of fire. Other examples are apparent in the remaining letters. Similarly, in the Egyptian Netherworld the faithful dead anxiously await the arrival of their sun-god during his nightly journey where he speaks to them and rewards them for their deeds – while his enemies, who do not hear his voice, are severely punished for their deeds. This dichotomy is especially evident in the *Book of Caverns* where the followers of the sun-god are said to listen to and hear his voice. "I know from what you live, when the One of the Netherworld orders you to live. Your throats breath when you listen to the words of Osiris. ... You hear my voice. I call you by your names."[386] But the evil ones in the Netherworld, who do not hear the words of the sun-god, are severely punished. The text describes them with the words, "This is how they are ... those who do not hear his words ... Re causes them tribulation after he has passed near them."[387] Another text says, "I act against you, I punish you ... whose nature is bad, whose souls do not go forth from earth ... who do not hear the words of this Great God as he passes near to their cavern."[388]

Structural Parallels in the Seven Letters

Fiorenza (1985) indicates the seven letters of Rev. 2-3 follow a definite pattern, each consisting of five sections, or formulae, as follows: (1) an Introduction, (2) a Messenger Formula, (3) an "I know ..." Formula, (4) a call to Hear and (5), an Eschatological Promise. We have already discussed the "I know ..." phrases which include knowledge of the addressee's activities (Rev. 2:2; Rev. 2:19; Rev. 3:1; Rev. 3:8; Rev. 3:15), tribulations (Rev. 2:9), and dwelling places (Rev. 2:13) and are generally followed by positive comments about the churches followed by lists of negative attributes and warnings. The "call to hear" is then made and the eschatological promise guarantees rewards to the faithful, or more specifically, "to him who conquers."

It is suggested in this chapter that the general content and structure of two of the seven letters to the churches parallel two Egyptian texts. The structure and content of the letter to the church in Philadelphia is similar to that of Chapter 115 of the *Book of the Dead* while that to Thyatira parallels the arrangement of important aspects of the 5th Division of the *Book of Caverns*. Alternative locations of the seven churches, which modern scholars believe were located in Asia Minor, will be presented in the *Discussion* section of this chapter.

172 Egyptian Origin of the Book of Revelation

Letter to Philadelphia (Rev. 3:7-12) and Chapter 115 of the *Book of the Dead*

The title of Chapter 115 of the *Book of the Dead* is *The Chapter of Ascending to the Sky, Opening up the Tomb, And Knowing the Souls of Heliopolis*. At first reading, parallels between it and Rev. 3:7-12 are not immediately apparent. It appears to concern a dispute among the gods of Heliopolis; the passage in the Book of Revelation, on the other hand, concerns a moral judgment on the activities of the members of the church in Philadelphia. Nevertheless, when both sources are broken down into a series of discrete elements, a total of at least twelve parallels comes into focus. These parallels are highlighted in italics and numbered 1 to 12 in the following translation of the Egyptian source by Faulkner (1994):

> I have spent yesterday among the great ones, I have become Khepri, I have cleared the vision of the Sole Eye, [1] *I have opened up the circle of darkness*.' I am one of them, [2a] *I know* the Souls of Heliopolis, [3] into which *the High-priest of Heliopolis was not initiated through revelation;* [2b] *(I know) the hostile acts by Him who would destroy the heirs of Heliopolis;* [4] *I know why a braided lock is made for a man.*'
>
> Re disputed with [5] *the serpent, 'Him who is in his burning',* and [6] *his mouth was injured, and that is how the reduction in the mouth came about.*' He said to the serpent: 'I will take my harpoon, which men will inherit,' and that is how the harpoon came into being. The serpent said: 'The Two Sisters will come into being', and that is how [7] *Re's passing came into being.*'
>
> It so happened that [8] *He of the red cloth heard, and his arm was not stopped.*' He transformed himself into a woman with braided hair, and that is how the priest of Heliopolis with braided hair came into being. It so happened that [9] *the mighty one was stripped in the temple,*' and that is how the stripped one of Heliopolis came into being, [10] and great will be he who shall see it; *he will become High-priest of Heliopolis.*'
>
> I know the Souls of [11] *Heliopolis;* they are [12] *Re, Shu, and Tefnut*.' [389]

The following discussion on the twelve elements is based on the order in which they appear in the *Book of the Dead* to facilitate comparison with their order in the Rev. 3:7-12 (as indicated by the verse numbers in which they are found).

1. A door is opened (Rev. 3:8b):- In Rev. 3:8b the speaker says that "I have set before you an open door." Similarly, Chapter 115 of the *Book of the Dead* begins with something being opened. It says, "I have opened up the circle of darkness." While Egypt's circle of darkness seems to refer to Heliopolis, Rev. 3:8b is not clear about which "door" has been opened, or even if it is a real, material door or an expression suggesting choices to be made. It is possible, of course that the door in Revelation figuratively leads into Philadelphia in much the same way as the metaphorical "door" in the Egyptian text seems to lead into Heliopolis, apparently called "the circle of darkness" in this particular passage. Regardless of which interpretation is correct, elements parallel to the opening of an entrance can be readily identified in both sources.

2a & 2b. "I know your works"(Rev. 3:8a):- The speaker says to those in the church at Philadelphia, "*I know* your *works*." Similarly, in Chapter 115 of the *Book* *of the Dead*, the speaker in #2a makes a statement concerning knowledge of a group of people containing the words, "*I know*' the souls of Heliopolis," and perhaps more to the point, shortly thereafter in #2b, he says, "(I know) the hostile *acts* ' by Him who would destroy the heirs of Heliopolis." The parallel here is obvious – adversarial deeds of a group of individuals are mentioned in both sources and they are both introduced with the words, "I know."

3. People with false credentials (Rev. 3:9b):- This passage makes reference to "those of the synagogue of Satan who say that they are Jews and are not, but lie." While this topic has already been discussed in the previous chapter, it is of special interest here because of its rather specific nature: it deals with those who are accused of falsely characterizing themselves. This accusation parallels the statement in the *Book of the Dead* (element #3) concerning a High Priest who claims an office for which he "was not initiated through revelation." The main difference between the two is minor – Revelation mentions several with false credentials while the *Book of the Dead* refers to only one.

4. Authority and Power (Rev. 3:9):- The allusion to power in Rev. 3:9 is an obvious reference to authority. The church in Philadelphia is told that the adversary will be made to "come and bow down before your feet." The *Book of the Dead* does not mention anyone bowing down before the feet of another although it does imply a person of great authority in the reference to "why a braided lock is made for a man." As shown in Figure 39 the braided lock was worn by the powerful *Iunmutef* priest who was discussed in the previous chapter in reference to Rev. 3:12 and one being made "a pillar in the temple." Such a priest must have had great authority and power over the people. In this manner, the reference to the assignment of this level of authority to the angel of the church – or the church itself – in Philadelphia is similar to and parallels that implied in the promise to the faithful in Rev. 3:9, "I will make them come and bow down before your feet." This parallel with authority is admittedly a rather poor one but it is included here simply to bring it to the reader's attention. Meanwhile, the parallel with an *Iunmutef* priest will be discussed below in element #10 in relation to the conqueror becoming a pillar (priest).

5. Reference to Satan (Rev. 3:9a):- This part of the verse also identifies a dispute in the synagogue of Satan involving those who falsely represent themselves as Jews: "Behold, I will make those of the synagogue of Satan who say they are jews and are not, but lie – behold, I will make them ..." Recall from Chapter 4, *Other Characters in Revelation*, that Revelation's Satan (also called the Devil) parallels Apophis, ancient Egypt's serpentine god of evil and chaos. This finding indicates that the reference to Satan in this verse applies to the Egyptian god Apophis, the "ancient serpent" who was ultimately destroyed by fire. In this manner the relative location of the reference to "the serpent, 'Him who is in his burning'" (in #5) parallels that of the reference to Satan in Rev. 3:9.

6. Reference to Lies (Rev. 3:9a):- While Rev. 3:9 accuses those in the synagogue of Satan (= Apophis) as lying, the Egyptian text says that "his [Apophis'] mouth was injured, and that is how the reduction in the mouth came about." This statement can be interpreted to mean that Apophis was a liar, just as the followers of Satan (Egypt's

Apophis) also lied. The relative position of this text in Rev. 3:9 parallels that of the reference to falsehoods in this part of the *Book of the Dead*.

7. Arrival of a Deity (Rev. 3:11):- With the expression in Rev. 3:11, "I am coming soon," the reader's attention is focused on the arrival of a deity. Similarly, in the Egyptian text, and after a brief statement that the two sisters (Isis and Nephthys) will come into being, we are told that "Re's passing came into being." This association of the two sisters with Re's coming into being is very likely related to their role in the birth of Re (this will be discussed in detail in Chapter 17, *The Woman in the Sky;* see Figure 80). The only practical difference between the two sources which needs to be addressed here is the tense; in Revelation, the coming of the deity is declared in the future tense while in the *Book of the Dead* it is in the past tense. This difference becomes irrelevant, however, if one considers the cyclical nature of the birth of the sun-god which will also be discussed in *The Woman in the Sky*. Furthermore, the reader should note that in both sources the reference made to the passing or arrival of a deity is placed in juxtaposition with a comment on action taken against adversaries, to be discussed next.

8. Deity rules against the adversary (Rev. 3:10):- We read in Rev. 3:10 of an "hour of trial which is coming on the whole world, to try those who dwell upon the earth." An exception is made, however, for the faithful who "kept my word of patient endurance"; they will not suffer the "hour of trial." Similarly, in the *Book of the Dead* we read of action taken by "He of the red cloth" against an adversary. We are told that "his arm was not stopped," a phrase which parallels the making of a decisive move against an enemy, as in Rev. 3:10. (It is interesting to note here that, following this statement in the *Book of the Dead*, we have yet another reference to the initiation of a powerful priest, one who is associated with braided hair such as we find on the head of the *Iunmutef* priest. The reference to his arm not being stopped conforms with the power inherent in this priest).

9. Stripping of Authority (Rev. 3:11):- Rev. 3:11 advises the faithful to maintain their own authority by "holding fast what you have, so that no one may seize your crown." Apparently, this action is to be taken against the liars in the temple who hold false credentials. The Greek word used for "crown" here is *stephanos* and although most Bible versions (if not all) translate *stephanos* as "crown," the passage can also signify a threat to "authority." Similarly, the *Book of the Dead* describes a scene wherein an imposter, "the mighty one was stripped of authority in the temple." The words are different in the two sources but the idea is the same: an imposter in the temple is stripped of authority.

10. Conqueror becomes a pillar (Rev. 3:12a):- Immediately after advising some to hold fast to what they have, a reward is offered. "He who conquers, I will make him a pillar in the temple." It seems that, in this case, the phrase "He who conquers" refers to victory of the faithful over imposters in the temple. Similarly, and almost immediately after the reference to the stripping of authority in the temple (in #9), it says that he who witnesses this action will become an important priest in Heliopolis: "great will be he who shall see it; *he will become High-priest*˙ of Heliopolis." Since, as mentioned above, the "pillar" in the temple parallels the authoritative *Iunmutef* priest, the phrase "He who conquers, I will make him a pillar in the temple" seems to suggests that he who defeats the imposters (i.e., the followers of Satan, the Devil) is promised a position as a high priest in the temple.

11. The City of God (Rev. 3:12b):- This part of Rev. 3:12 extends the gift to the faithful at Philadelphia to include their identification with "the name of my God, and the name of the city of my God." Note first that a similar manner, the next part of the passage in the *Book of the Dead* concludes with the statement, "great will be he who shall see it; *he will become High-priest of Heliopolis.*" Then note that in both cases, the promise of becoming a priest (in Rev. 3:12a) is immediately followed by the name of a city; in Revelation, it mentions the "city of my God" while the Egyptian text refers to Heliopolis.

There is a broader argument in favor of Revelation's "City of my God" being a parallel to Egypt's holy city. Egypt's "City of God" was envisioned as being located in the sky and was replete with celestial equivalents of major Egyptian centers – including the capital of Lower Egypt which the Greeks called Heliopolis, "The City of the Sun," which, of course, meant the "City of Re" which can be interpreted to mean, "City of God."

Also, Rev. 3:12b also says that the "city of my God ... comes down from heaven." Egyptians frequently used the similar phrase, "City of God," to describe their heavenly city. Chapter 110 of the *Book of the Dead* refers to the Field of Offerings, the coveted paradise of peace in which the blessed dead live:

> ... there is no shouting in it, there is nothing evil in it. ... he [the deceased] partakes of a meal in the birth-place of the god [i.e., in the sky]. ... I plow and I reap, and I am content in the *City of God.*' I know the names of the districts, towns, and waterways which are in the Field of Offerings and of those who are in them; I am strong in them and I am a spirit in them; I eat in them and travel about in them. I plow and reap in the Field; I rise early in it and go to rest in it. I am a spirit in it ... I shoot and travel about in it. ... I arrive at its towns, I row on its waterways, I traverse the Field of Offerings as *Re who is in the sky.*"[390]

It is apparent that the location of the Revelation's "city of my God ... which comes down ... from heaven" conforms with that of the ancient Egypt's celestial home of the blessed dead which is with Re in the sky..

Budge (1904) describes some of the background to the obvious connection between Heliopolis and the heavenly abode of the faithful followers of the sun-god. The earthly Heliopolis was "the home and center of worship of Re in Egypt during dynastic times" and Egyptians "believed that Re bathed each day at sunrise in a certain lake or pool which was in the neighborhood."[391] Heliopolis was also generally considered to have been the main center of the earth-god, Geb, who with his female counterpart, Nut, the sky-goddess, "produced the great Egg whereout sprang the Sun-god under the form of a phoenix."[392] According to those who lived there, Heliopolis was particularly special because the work of creation was believed to have begun there and it was the birthplace of the company of the gods;[393] it was believed to be the first place on earth where the sun-god stood on dry land. Heliopolis was thus the most sacred city in Egypt. This, and its very special name, made it the ideal template for Egypt's heavenly city, the "City of God."

There is one other aspect of Rev. 3:12b that should be mentioned here and that is its reference to the "city of my god" being called the "new Jerusalem." In the *Discussion* part of this chapter, however, it will be shown the "new Jerusalem" of Rev. 3:12b closely parallels a post-war, rebuilt version of the Egyptian city of Heliopolis in the Nile Delta.

12. List of names (Rev. 3:12c):- This is the final concept presented in the letter to Philadelphia. Rev. 3:12c refers to three names, "[1] the name of my God, and [2] the name of the city of my God, ... and [3] my own new name." Similarly, Chapter 115 concludes with a list of three names; a brief examination of them suggests they too may parallel those mentioned in Revelation. The Egyptian names are Re, Shu, and Tefnut. Each name will be discussed in turn.

> **a) Re** - Re was the sun-god, the supreme Egyptian deity, especially at Heliopolis, "the city of the sun." The deity's name is implicit in "Heliopolis" so that it conforms with Revelation's "name of my God" as discussed above.
>
> **b) Shu** - It so happens that the name of Shu, is one of the 75 forms (names) of Re given in *The Litany of Re*.[a] Thus, the name Shu may be said to conform with Revelation's "new name," i.e., an alternative name for Re.
>
> **c) Tefnut** - Tefnut conforms with the reference to "the city of my god" from the point of view of its phonetic characteristics. The meanings of the two syllables of Tefnut are germane: *tef* means "to spit, to eject anything from the body" and is closely related to *teftef* which means "to pour out."[394] The Nile River itself was viewed as the water of Osiris, the bodily form of the sun-god. The word *tef* can thus apply to a "river." The next syllable, *nut,* means "city." Thus, a literal translation of *tef-nut* is something like "flowing city" or "river city," i.e., a city with a river running through it – or at least a city located by a river, a concept which conforms with the idea of the celestial city of the Egyptians through which the celestial Nile flowed (see Chapter 27, *The Holy City*). In this manner, the name "Tefnut" can be seen to be related to the phrase, "the city of my God" in Rev. 3:12. This latter argument for a parallel is not particularly strong. But it should not be entirely overlooked, especially since it conforms with the grouping of three names, Re, Shu, and Tefnut.

It seems that two, and possibly all three references to names at the end of the letter to Philadelphia may be considered parallels to the names of the gods mentioned at the end of Chapter 115 of the *Book of the Dead*. As we read in #12 above, "They are Re [the name of my God], Shu, [my own new name] and Tefnut [Egypt's celestial city of the sun-god and Revelation's "city of my god?]"

Comment:- In addition to the above twelve parallels it is important to note that their *sequence* of the twelve elements is practically the same in both sources.

---

[a] See Figure II.48 of Clagett, 1989, p. 858.

Letter to Thyatira (Rev. 2:18-28) and the 5th Division of the *Book of Caverns*

Like the letters to Philadelphia, the letter to Thyatira speaks of conflicts between good and evil. The letter to Thyatira involves a woman called Jezebel, a "prophetess" who lures the righteous with her immoral ways and teachings about the "deep things of Satan."[a] Those who associate with her must share in the tribulations of her punishment. The relevant text says,

> But I have this against you, that you tolerate the woman Jezebel, who calls herself a prophetess and is teaching and beguiling my servants to practice immorality and to eat food sacrificed to idols. I gave her time to repent, but she refuses to repent of her immorality. Behold, I will throw her on a sickbed, and those who commit adultery with her I will throw into great tribulation, unless they repent of her doings; and I will strike her children dead. (Rev. 2:20-23)

Similar events, especially those concerning the destruction of her followers as punishment for their association with the things of Satan, are comparable with events described in the 5th Division of the *Book of Caverns*.[b] This division is arranged in five horizontal registers while its text is arranged in vertical columns which are not necessarily close to the illustrations to which they refer (Figure 40). Unfortunately, there is no clear understanding of the order in which the various pictures and texts should be read. Piankoff's translation starts with the text in the upper the right-hand side of the division and proceeds left to the large picture of a standing woman (Shetait, Nut) with a disk in her left hand (see Figure 40). From there it moves downward through the remaining registers, moving from right to left in each. This same right to left and top to bottom direction of text is followed throughout. Unlike our treatment of the previous two letters, and because of the uncertainty of the proper sequence of images and texts in this part of the *Book of Caverns*, our treatment of the letter to Thyatira is organized according to verse numbers in the Book of Revelation rather than to features of the Egyptian document.

There are two pictures of standing goddesses located in the right-hand third of the 5th Division; they are enlarged here as Figure 41 and Figure 42. Figure 41 is of *Shetait*, the *Mysterious One* identified by Piankoff (1954) as the sky-goddess *Nut*.[395] She holds a small ram-headed figure in her right hand and a solar disk in her left. The

---

[a] The mention of the name Jezebel and the events surrounding her are apparently allusions to the biblical Jezebel of ancient Tyre portrayed in I and II Kings.

[b] The translation of the *Book of Caverns* used for this part of the study is based on the version found in the Tomb of Ramesses VI and translated by Piankoff (1954, *The Tomb of Tomb of Ramesses VI*, pp. 45-135). According to Piankoff, the only other complete editions of the *Book of Caverns* are found in the Osirion at Abydos, constructed under Merneptah, and the tomb of Pedemonopet which was constructed in the Late Period. A few extracts of the text are found on Sarcophagus 29306 of the Cairo Museum and in a monument near the Nilometer of Rodah while some of its illustrations are found in the *Papyrus of Queen Netchemet*.

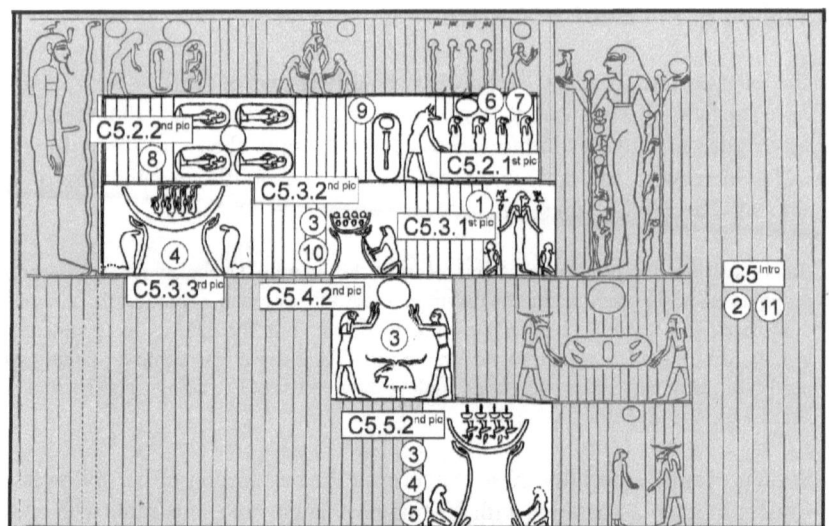

Figure 40. General layout of the 5th Division of the *Book of Caverns*. The central area shows the clustering of those pictures which parallel the text of the letter to Thyatira found in Rev. 2:18-28. Labels in rectangles represent picture numbers from Piankoff (1954); numbers in circles represent numbered comments in the current text.

goddess in Figure 42 is situated in front of and near the feet of Nut and holds two scepters in her hands; two bound enemies kneel before her.

The picture of Shetait sets the stage for the events described in the remainder of the division. The two sets of smaller figures in front of and behind her legs represent different aspects of the age-old conflict between the sun-god and his enemies. Behind her are four crocodiles representing enemies of the sun-god,[396] each pursuing a different manifestation of him. In front of her is another series of manifestations of the sun-god, all facing downwards toward the open arms of the earth-god Geb. Leaning against her arms are two serpentine staffs with eyeless human heads, possibly representing the ever-present danger of the evil serpent Apophis; the text in front of Shetait reads, "*Unty*, the Apopis, of the wicked eye (He is blind!). He is like this on the arms of the *Mysterious One* of forms."[397] The two serpents, the crocodiles, and the small figures of the sun-god represent the struggle of the forces of evil against the sun-god and his followers as he travels across the body of Nut (Shetait), the sky.

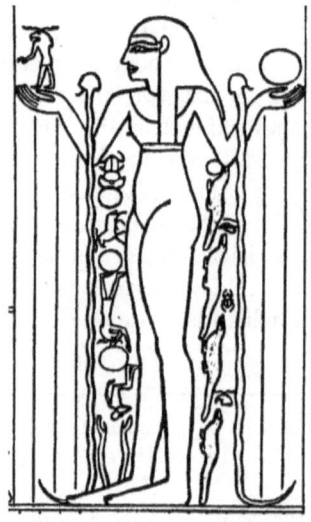

Figure 41. The goddess *Shetait*, here called the "Mysterious One," and a manifestation of *Nut*, the sky-goddess. (C5.1.1^{st picture})

As we shall see, a fair number of events in this division parallel those described in the letter to Thyatira in Rev. 2:18-27. These parallels will be described in a series of numbered subsections corresponding to the circled numbers in Figure 40 and summarized in Table 8.1.

We begin with the scene at the right end of the third register and immediately in front of the *Shetait's* feet. This scene (Figure 42) is closely connected with the fate of the sun-god's enemies and therefore of particular interest to us in the context of the letter to Thyatira.

1. Woman assigned to a place (Rev. 2:20-23):- There are several aspects of "The Butcher" in Figure 42 which correspond to Jezebel of Rev. 2:20. Firstly, Revelation calls her an adulterous woman who professes to be a prophetess and is "thrown on a sick-bed." Her associates are thrown into "great tribulation." Similarly, in the *Book of Caverns* we read that The Butcher is put in a place of tribulation called the Place of Destruction: Re says in C5.3.1[st picture], "O she who remains in this mysterious place ... to which are assigned my enemies."[398] Next, like Jezebel in Rev. 2:22, The Butcher accompanies the enemies of the sun-god: "(Thou) has tied (them) with thy two arms when thou has taken them for thee (to) the poles in the earth to which are assigned my enemies."[399] The parallel in this case is that, like Revelation's Jezebel who is thrown on a sick-bed along with her sinful associates, both The Butcher and the sun-god's enemies are put in and remain in a place of tribulation. (The *Book of Caverns* is silent on the question of whether these enemies are her followers or her victims).

Figure 42. The goddess called *The Butcher* presides over the enemies of the sun-god. Her attributes are similar to those of Jezebel in Rev. 2:20-23. (C5.3.1[st picture])

2. Repentance (Rev. 2:21-22):- The letter to Thyatira also says "those who commit adultery with her [Jezebel] I will throw into great tribulation unless they repent of her doings" (Rev. 2:22). Similarly, in the introductory text to this division, Re says, "I address those who are in it. ... Behold, the path which lies in it (the place of mystery) has made the gesture of submission before me."[400] The expression "gesture of submission" may be interpreted as being loosely similar in meaning to Revelation's reference to repenting. The context of this statement suggests Re is speaking to all the inhabitants of this cavern so that this particular parallel should be considered a weak one. Nevertheless, this scene in Revelation may be applicable to that involving The Butcher and those with her in Figure 42.

3. Being thrown into tribulation (Rev. 2:22):- Rev. 2:22 emphasizes the verb *to throw* in relation to the casting of the damned into tribulation with Jezebel. Similarly, the 5th Division of the *Book of Caverns* describes how *The Butcher* enters the special place where tribulation is "thrown" or "hurled" at those with her. We read in the third and forth registers that "the Lord of the Flame, *throws*' the fire against you who are (in) the caldron"[401] (C5.3.2nd picture) and "I am Re. ... I *hurl*' tribulation at my enemies"[402] (C5.4.2nd picture). In the 5th register, the sun-god urges his followers to "*Hurl*' your flame and your fire among the enemies of He Whose Name is Hidden"[403] (C5.5.2nd picture). Tribulation is also thrown or hurled at captives of *The Butcher*. The text says,

> This Great God ... sends tribulations to those who are in it, among the enemies of the Region of the Netherworld. ... *Throw*' your flame, light your fire under the caldron in which are found (?) the enemies of Osiris! O the empaled ones, guarded by the poles, you are these burned ones, enchained in their misery, kept in the concealed (place) of the Great God![404] (C5.3.1st to 3rd pictures)

This reference to "throwing" tribulation emphasizes the tribulation caused to the enemy in the *Book of Caverns* just as in Rev. 2:22 which says, "I will *throw* her on a sickbed, and those who commit adultery with her I will *throw* into great tribulation." There is a slight difference in the two circumstances, however. In Revelation, it is the followers of Jezebel who are thrown into tribulation while in the *Book of Caverns* it is tribulation itself which is thrown against the evil doers. This difference is of little if any significance, however, and the two remain compatible,

4. Death Sentence (Rev. 2:23a):- In Rev. 2:23a we read that the ultimate fate of the woman's children is death. This parallels descriptions and pictures found in the *Book of Caverns*:

> These enemies of Osiris who are in *the place of annihilation*,' judged by the great tribunal which is in the Mysterious One [Nut, the sky-goddess], their affairs being before Osiris. He assigns them their evil posts in the *Place of Destruction*' for their acts which they have committed in the mysterious chamber.[405] (C5.5.2nd picture)

Elsewhere we read that, "As you are the enemies of Osiris, your bodies are chopped, your heads are separated! ... your souls are sent away, you blood is spilled! Your shadows are sent away, your forms have ceased to exist! ... you are annihilated, your forms are punished!"[406] – and so on and on (C5.5.2nd picture). Also, as pointed out above, those in control of the fire are to "Throw your flame, light your fire under the caldron in which are found (?) the enemies of Osiris! O the empaled ones, guarded by the poles [see Figure 42], you are these burned ones, enchained in their misery, kept in the concealed (place) of the Great God!"[407] (C5.3.3rd picture). The ultimate end of the rebellious enemies is revealed where the sun-god declares they have been "massacred in the Place of Destruction, you whose souls and whose shadows are annihilated"[408] (C5.3). Annihilation of their souls amounts to the total annihilation of the entire person.

5. Searching the mind and heart (Rev. 2:23b):- To understand how the phrase "I am he who searches mind and heart, and I will give to each of you as your works deserve" (Rev. 2:23b), conforms with the text of the *Book of Caverns*, it is necessary to reflect momentarily on the original meaning of certain words used in the Greek text of the Book of Revelation. The Greek word used for "searches" (*ereunao*) means "to examine into"⁴⁰⁹ or, through the idea of inquiry, "(figuratively) to investigate."⁴¹⁰ The concept expressed here therefore conforms with some aspect of a judgment process. Such references to mind and heart are also found the Egyptian judgment scene.

The involvement of the heart in the Osirian judgment has already been discussed (see discussion on "The Conquerors" in Chapter 7, *Egyptian Beliefs in the Seven Letters*). The reference to the mind, however, is a special case which demands comment. The Greek word which the King James Version translates as "mind" is *nephros*, a "word used to designate the *inward parts*."⁴¹¹ At times it was used to specifically indicate "kidneys." The Hebrew equivalent of kidney was *kilyah* which was "thought by the Israelites to be the seat of the emotions"⁴¹² and hence the translation from the Greek *nephros* into "mind." In fact, some bible translations, such as the American Standard Version, more closely adhere to the original Greek and translate it "reins," a little used English word meaning "kidney."ᵃ

It is the translation of *nephros* as "inward parts" which comes closest to the Egyptian text. The third and fifth registers of the 5ᵗʰ Division contain pictures of the destruction of rebels where we see representations of the headless bodies, heads (), hearts (), flesh (), shadows (), and souls () of the enemies of the sun-god being destroyed in cauldrons (Figure 40 and Figure 43). The text associated with the lowermost picture (C5.5.2ⁿᵈ ᵖⁱᶜᵗᵘʳᵉ) describes two "goddesses of the great flame, of powerful fire, who stir their caldrons with the bones of strangers, who burn the souls, the bodies, *the members*, and the shadows of my enemies"⁴¹³ (C5.5.2ⁿᵈ ᵖⁱᶜᵗᵘʳᵉ). Two other versions of the *Book of Caverns*, one found on the walls of the Osireion at Abydos and constructed under king Merneptah, and the other found in the tomb of Pedemenopet,⁴¹⁴ provide insight into the meaning of "bodies" and "members" mentioned here. They describe the contents of the cauldrons as "... the souls, the bodies, the shadows of the enemies of Re and Osiris, the rebels, the heads," and most significantly in this case, "*their cut-away parts*"⁴¹⁵ (C5.5.2ⁿᵈ ᵖⁱᶜᵗᵘʳᵉ). The English translation of the Egyptian text as "their cut-away parts" corresponds well with the English translation of the Greek word *nephros* being "inward parts." In this manner, these pictures and texts dealing with the heart and the inward parts in the Egyptian judgment parallel the "heart" and "mind" mentioned in this part of the Book of Revelation.

6. Deep Things of Satan (Rev. 2:24):- The reference to not learning the "deep things of Satan" found in Rev. 2:24 is reminiscent of a situation found in the *Book of Caverns*. Like the inhabitants of Thyatira, those of the 5ᵗʰ Cavern are also forbidden to learn certain secrets. Here, the restriction is associated with an image of the *Sekhem* scepter of power (in Figure 43). The relevant text says, "O this *Sekhem*' whose image is great, created by the Netherworld, engendered by the silent Region, he whose image is *unknown, unique mystery hidden from the inhabitants of his cavern*"⁴¹⁶ (C5.2.1ˢᵗ ᵖⁱᶜᵗᵘʳᵉ). The parallel between the two sources is obvious: in the Book of Revelation there is emphasis on the "deep things of Satan" which should not be learned; in the *Book of Caverns* it is secret knowledge of the *Sekhem* scepter. In each case, knowledge of

---

ᵃ Webster (p. 993) defines "reins" as, "1a: kidneys b: the region of the kidneys: loins. 2: the seat of feelings or passions."

something with power is forbidden. (Also, see discussion on the *Sekhem* ⸸ symbol in #9 below).

7. No burden on faithful (Rev. 2:24):- Another interesting parallel between this verse and the Egyptian text relates to the faithful in Figure 43. Rev. 2:24 states that "I do not lay upon you any other burden." The Egyptian text says that "These gods are like this, they mount upon the earth without being weary"[417] (C5.2.1st picture). The connection between the words "burden" and "weariness" is obvious, although, as with all other parallels with Egyptian texts, this is not a direct translation of the Egyptian. But it is a parallel to it. Furthermore, in the 2nd picture of the same register (Figure 44), the sun-god says, "Behold, ... you are in peace in your places, I have caused you to rest in me ..."[418]

8. "I come ..." (Rev. 2:25):- In Rev. 2:25 the faithful are advised to "hold fast what you have, until *I come*," a phrase which contrasts with the awful fate of the unfaithful mentioned in Rev. 2:23 (see #4 and #5 above). The 5th Division of the *Book of Caverns* also greets his followers on his arrival. For example, the text quotes the sun-god as saying, "O Behold, *I pass*· near you, I have placed Anubis as your guardian. I give you light, I disperse your darkness, I speak to those who are in your following" (C5.2.1st picture), and "Behold, *I pass*· near you. I call your souls."[419] (C5.2.2nd picture).

Figure 43. The Rod of Power (⸸) rules over the enemies of the sun-god as in Rev. 2:26-27. Below it, the heads (🝗) and hearts (♥) of the enemies of the sun-god are destroyed in a cauldron. (C5.2.1st picture)

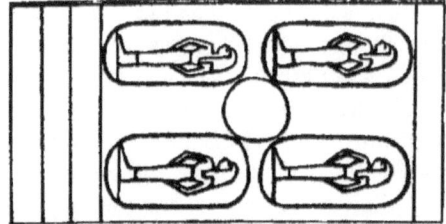

Figure 44. This scene is adjacent to the previous figure and parallels Rev. 2:24 which says, "I do not lay upon you any other burden." The Egyptian text says, "You are in peace in your places, I have caused you to rest in me." (C5.2.2nd picture).

9. Rod of Power (Rev. 2:26-27):- We are told in Rev. 2:26-27 that the conqueror will receive "power over the nations, and he shall rule them with a rod of iron ... even as I myself have received power over the nations." It should be noted that this "rod of iron" may be interpreted in the literal sense as being a scepter as well as in a metaphorical sense in which case it can suggest a strong authoritative rule. Receipt of such power was part of the Egyptian's hope for the afterlife, especially, for example, after ascending to the throne of Osiris (see discussion on Rev. 3:21 above. Such a scepter, called the *Sekhem,* is briefly mentioned in #6 above and shown graphically in Figure 43 where it is represented by the hieroglyph, ⸸, inside a vertical oval.

Wilkinson (1992) says that the *sekhem* scepter "denotes the concept of 'power' and 'might.' ... From the Third Dynasty on, the *sekhem* appears in the royal names

8. Egyptian Parallels in the Seven Letters

of kings, and later in the titles of queens and princesses also."[420] Meanwhile, just as the reference to the rod in Revelation refers to the supreme deity's power, the label accompanying the scepter in Figure 43 refers to it as, "The *rod of power*' (?) of Atum."[421] (Lurker notes that Atum was the powerful "creator god of Heliopolis. ... 'who came into being of himself' before heaven and earth were separated he was the 'Lord of all.' "[422]) The term "rod of iron" in Revelation closely parallels the *sekhem* scepter, which is called the "The rod of power of Atum" in the *Book of Caverns*, even to the point of alluding to its power coming from the "Lord of all," an Egyptian equivalent to Revelation's God on the throne in Rev. 2:26-27.

10. Something is broken into pieces (Rev. 2:27):- Immediately below the picture of "The rod of power" in Figure 43 is a scene (C5.3.$2^{nd\ picture}$) showing a serpent-headed god stoking the fire beneath a large cauldron containing the heads (🝆) and hearts (♥) of the enemies of the sun-god. Two other similar cauldrons are shown in this Division, one to the immediate left in C5.3. $3^{rd\ picture}$ and the other in the bottom register in C5.5. $2^{nd\ picture}$ (see Figure 40). Egyptian cauldrons were earthen-ware vessels as are the pots mentioned in Rev. 2:27. We now have a juxtaposition of two images in both sources; the first is the scepter (see #9) while the other image is of these earthen pots. We are told in Rev. 2:27 that earthen pots are broken into pieces, a point not made in the text of the *Book of Caverns*. But here, instead of broken pots we find images of dismembered body parts of the enemy inside pots. In the sense that "pieces" of something are referred to in both sources, all three images can thus be found in both sources, all in juxtaposition to one another – the rod of power, earthen pots, and something broken into pieces.

11. "He who has an ear ..." (Rev. 2:29):- This phrase is a repetition of those found in each of the other letters: "He who has an ear, let him hear what the Spirit says to the churches." The sun-god makes a somewhat similar statement in the introduction to the 5th Division, he concludes with the phrase, "I have called you." The text say,

> Taking the fair road by this Great God, entering into the mysterious caverns of the West, entering by these great gods the Cavern of Mystery of the great gods, *he says to those who are in them:*' O gods, these great gods in the cavern in the following of Osiris in this place of mystery. You are hidden, you rejoice yourselves in me as *I have called you.*'[423] (C5^{Introduction})

This introductory remark to the faithful present in the 5th Cavern can therefore be considered a reasonable parallel to Rev. 2:29 where God calls upon the faithful to hear him.

Comments on the Letter to Thyatira:-A summary of the parallels between the events in the letter to Thyatira and those in the 5th Division of the *Book of Caverns* is given in Table 8.1. Unfortunately, as indicated in the introduction to this letter, the exact order in which the Egyptian text was meant to be read is unknown so that a comparison of the order of events in the two sources is not possible. Nevertheless, a crude analysis of the general layout of the texts is possible. Locations of these parallels are illustrated in Figure 40; note that they are clustered inside an area, roughly the shape of a triangle, bounded by the three scenes, C5.2.2$^{\text{2nd picture}}$, C5.2.1$^{\text{st picture}}$ and C5.5.2$^{\text{nd picture}}$. Apart from the parallel content of the passages, all three Egyptian scenes are clustered in the central part of this Division. This further strengthens the evidence for a general Egyptian parallel to this letter.

That the letter to Thyatira should parallel a part of the *Book of Caverns* is of particular interest from a moralistic point of view. The upper registers of each Division are devoted to the praising of the deity and the rewards to the faithful while the lowermost registers are devoted to the punishment of the enemies of the sun-god. Piankoff (1994) points out that Champollion was the first to note the highly psychological conception of this composition, and in one of his letters from Egypt he describes it:

> This double series of tableaux therefore gives us the Egyptian psychological system in these two most important and most moral points, the rewards and punishments. In this way everything that the ancients said of the Egyptian doctrine of the immortality of the soul and the positive objective of human life is completely shown.[424]

Similarly, practically all modern Bible scholars look upon the letters to the seven churches as presenting important information on the moral background of the churches.

Table 8.1 Summary of the similarities between the 5th Division of the *Book of Caverns* and Revelation's letter to Thyatira. Events are arranged in the order in which they appear in the Book of Revelation while references to the *Book of Caverns* show their locations in the division. All these events are clustered in the center of the Division (see Figure 40).

	Letter to Thyatira Rev. 2:18-28		Book of Caverns 5th Division		Parallel
	Event	Verse	Event	Location	
1	Behold, I will *throw her on a sickbed*,	2:22a	... O she ... whom *I have placed to remain there* ... who does not go forth from the darkness.	C5.3.1$^{\text{st picture}}$	- woman assigned to a place
2	unless they *repent* of her doings	2:22c	make a *gesture of submission* before me, withdraw your arms	C5 (intro.)	- repentance
3	I will *throw her on a sickbed*, and those who commit adultery with her I will *throw into great tribulation*	2:22a,b	... the Lord of the Flame, *throws* the fire against you who are (in) the caldron I am Re, the god who speaks to the bodies. ... *I hurl tribulation* at my enemies Hurl your flame and your fire among the enemies of He Whose Name is Hidden	C5.3.2$^{\text{nd picture}}$ C5.4.2$^{\text{nd picture}}$	- tribulation associated with something thrown or hurled
4	and I will *strike her children dead*. ... and I will give to each of you as your *works* deserve.	2:23a,c	He *assigns them their evil posts in the Place of Destruction for their acts* which they have committed in the mysterious chamber	C5.5.2$^{\text{nd picture}}$	- death or destruction as punishment for deeds.

	Letter to Thyatira Rev. 2:18-28		Book of Caverns 5th Division		Parallel
	Event	Verse	Event	Location	
5	... I am he which searcheth the *reins and hearts* ... (KJV)	2:23b	... the souls, the bodies, the shadows of the enemies of Re and Osiris, The rebels, the heads, *their cut-away parts*.	C5,5,2nd picture	- separate body parts
			... your *bodies are chopped, your heads are separated!*	C5,5,2nd picture	- separate body parts
6	who have *not learned* what some call *the deep things of Satan*	2:24b	he whose image is unknown, unique *mystery hidden from the inhabitants of his cavern*.	C5,2,1st picture	- hidden knowledge
7	I do *not lay upon you* any other burden	2:24c	they mount upon the earth *without being weary*	C5,2,1st picture	- no impedance
8	hold fast what you have, until *I come*	2:25	Behold, *I pass near you*	C5,2,2nd picture	- arrival of deity
9	I will give him *power* over the nations, and he shall *rule them with a rod* of iron	2:26b 2:27a	The rod of power ... O this *Sekhem* whose image is great	C5,2,1st picture	- rod of power
10	earthen pots are broken in pieces,	2:27b	(picture of large cauldron containing the heads and hearts of the enemies of the sun-god)	C5,3,2nd picture	- something broken into pieces
11	let him hear what the Spirit says	2:25	*he says to those* who are in them ... rejoice yourselves in me as *I have called you*	C5 Intro	- deity speaks to followers

Discussion

Discussion on Parallel Elements

The seven letters in the Book of Revelation are fertile ground for parallels with ancient Egyptian beliefs. These similarities are, in part, associated with the rewards to the "conquerors" in Revelation and rewards to Osirian penitents who are "victorious" in the final judgment. The reliance upon the advocate before the judgment throne, a variety of gifts, the deceased claiming a share in the throne, the promise of no second death, the gift of the tree of life, white garments, the maintaining of one's name in a Book of Life and on a small stone, being made a "pillar" in the temple, the eating of hidden manna in the presence of God, and the gift of the morning star together contribute to a coherent body of parallels with Egyptian religious beliefs and teachings. Furthermore, the *unusual* nature of some of the offences discussed in the letters represents especially strong supporting parallels with the Egyptian texts. For example: those with false credentials in the temple, the association of fornication with the eating of sacrificed food, lies, and the stripping of authoritative power in the temple.

The above parallels can be strengthened even further if they appear in both sources, either in the same order or with similar groupings. This idea will be explored in the next section.

Discussion on Structural Parallels

The structure of the letters to Philadelphia and Thyatira were found to parallel that of two Egyptian texts. Apart from a few minor displacements in the flow of images in the letter to Philadelphia, and the weak nature of some of the parallels, the main elements follow a sequence similar to those in Chapters 115 of the *Book of the Dead*. Nevertheless, it is quite clear that the text of Revelation is not a direct translation of these texts; it seems to be either an allusion to or simply a précis of it.

While parallels to all the main elements in the letter to Thyatira were found in the 5th Division of the *Book of Caverns*, a comparison of the flow of these elements between the two sources could not be made because of uncertainty about the correct flow of the text in the Egyptian source. And when one looks closely at the location of the encircled comment numbers in Figure 40 it is obvious that a consecutive flow of parallel scenes in the two sources is practically impossible. It may be said, however, that all of the parallel elements were found to be clustered in a well-defined area near the center of the 5th Tableau (the un-shaded part of Figure 40).

The apparent absence in Egyptian texts with parallel structures to the five remaining letters does not necessarily mean that there never was such a text in ancient Egypt; such texts could have existed but are now lost or simply were not a part of the investigated material. Indeed, an intensive search of the many Egyptian sources studied here (see Chapter 2, *New Approaches*) did not reveal any other similarly structured parallel texts or scenes for the remaining five letters with the possible exception of the letter to Pergamum; this letter seems at first glance to have a parallel sequence with possibly as many as eight elements similar to those in Chapter 108 of the *Book of the Dead*. Although a parallel structure between these two sources could not be clearly defined, there is at least a possibility that they have a significant parallel structure; more research on this possibility may be fruitful. Regardless of the results of such studies, the remaining structural parallels are striking, especially when considered along with the parallels to specific elements as described in the first part of this chapter. The above combined parallels involving both specific elements and organizational structures strengthen the suggestions of the parallel structural nature between at least two Egyptian texts.

Historical parallels – the end of the Hyksos occupation

One naturally questions why the seven letters were written and included at this point in the text of Revelation, especially considering that their content and style are so different from the rest of the book. The response to this question, of course, relates to their purpose. Each letter identifies a certain geographic area and makes a statement as to whether some or all those who live there are faithful followers of the one on the throne. Several warn of impending acts of war against them if certain conditions are not met. For example, those living at Pergamum are told to either repent for having followed Balaam (a god which is similar to Egypt's Seth) or war will be declared against them. In Rev. 2:15-16 the addressees are told, "So you also have some who hold the teaching of the Nicolaitans. Repent then. If not, I will come to you soon and war against them." And in Rev 2:21-23 we read, "I gave her time to repent, but she refuses. ... Behold, I will throw her on a sickbed, and those who commit adultery with her I will throw into great tribulation ... and I will strike her children dead." Rev. 3:2-3 also insinuates violence with the words, "I have not found your works perfect in the sight of my God. Remember then what you received and heard; keep that, and repent. If you will not awake, I will come like a thief, and you will not know at what hour I will come upon you." This last quote seems to be a warning of a surprise attack against the church at Sardis. Indeed, when the content and tone of all seven letters are viewed as a whole one does not have to think very hard to arrive at the conclusion that, as a group, they almost certainly constitute a *declaration of war*. The declaration seems to be addressed to sites in an area containing at least seven cities or city-states in which some or all of the inhabitants are rebellious against the one on the throne; some remain faithful to him.

We might therefore ask where the most likely location for such a war might have been. Bible scholars universally assume that the seven churches of Rev. 2-3 were located in Asia Minor where there are cities and towns with names that match those of the seven churches. They also assume that the conflicts mentioned in the letters can be interpreted to refer to those between the early Christians and their Roman masters. No such assumption is made in this study for the simple reason that this study is set up to examine the Book of Revelation from the perspective of ancient Egypt; Asia Minor does not conform with what we know of Egyptian influences and military activities in Asia Minor are not consistent with those mentioned in the seven letters or elsewhere in the Book of Revelation. While Egyptian kings frequently led military campaigns into the Levant, at times passing as far as the Euphrates River and beyond, they only rarely ventured into the heart of Asia Minor, and even then, they did not establish any suzerainties in the area. It therefore seems that, from an Egyptian point of view, Asia Minor is not a likely candidate for the location for the seven churches mentioned in the Book of Revelation.

In fact, it was the Levant which bore the brunt of most of Egypt's military might. It is therefore reasonable to ask if the seven churches might have been located in this area rather than Asia Minor? The answer to this question is a doubtful "Possibly" for it so happens that there were at least two cities in the area with names similar to the seven given in Revelation. One is the ancient city of Laodicea in the Levant and the other is Philadelphia (= ancient Rabbath Ammon and known today as Amman, Jordan).[425] But good matches cannot be made for the remaining names although the names of some bear phonetic similarities to cities or city-states in the Levant. Smyrna, for example, sounds very much Simrya and Thyatira sounds much like Tyre, the ancient fortified city on the Mediterranean coast. Supporting evidence that Thyatira represents the ancient city of Tyre is found in Rev. 2:20 which tells us that Jezebel is "a prophetess [of Thyatira] and is teaching and beguiling my servants to practice immorality." Jezebel was the daughter of a king of Tyre[a] and her evil deeds are discussed at some length in the Old Testament.[b] The next city with a somewhat similar sounding name is Sidon. This name could have been mistakenly translated as "Sardis" by ancient scribes eager to locate the city in Asia Minor where the apostle Paul preached. The name Pergamos is more difficult to place although the name (very) roughly resembles Per-Kanen in southern Palestine. Ephesus is probably the most difficult city to place outside of Asia Minor but the sound of the name has the ring of the name of the ancient city of Pathos on the southern shore of Cyprus, an island with which the Egyptians also had dealings. It seems that only two or three Levantine names (Laodicea, Philadelphia and Thyatira) are reasonably good matches while the others are less similar to the names of the seven churches.[c] This similarity of names, along with the knowledge that Egyptian kings frequently led military campaigns into the Levant is perhaps the only historical evidence available which might support the suggestion for parallels to the seven churches in Rev. 2-3 in the Levant (and Cyprus).

There is, however, another possible source of parallels to the seven churches which seem to have greater potential as a possible location. We find this one within Egypt itself. As we shall see next, there are good reasons to suspect the Nile Delta may actually be the best locale, especially if we consider more than just the names themselves - or more appropriately, not consider the names at all but the number.

The remains of seven notable fortifications have been identified in the Nile Delta where archeologists have found evidence of occupation by people of Asian decent; the Egyptians called these people the *aamu*,[426] The *aamu* are believed to have been of Syro-Palestinian origin who, apparently, originally entered the area during the latter part of the Middle Kingdom (perhaps from about 1710 BCE on). They spread throughout many areas of the Delta and later established their own dynasties (the 15th and 16th) during what is called Egypt's 2nd Intermediate Period (*c.* 1640-1532 BCE).

---

[a] I Kings 16:31says that Jezebel was "the daughter of Ethbaal king of the Sidonians, and went and served Baal, and worshiped him." Hackett (1993), tells us that "Sidonians" is a biblical term for Phoenicians in general and that Ethbaal was the king of Tyre.

[b] For example, see I Kings 18:13, I Kings 21:14, I Kings 21:23-25; II Kings 9:7 and II Kings 9:22.

[c] There is another tantalizing possibility for a relationship with the ancient cities of the Levant. We find it in the Chapter 115 of the *Book of the Dead* discussed above. It is apparent from the last sentence of this chapter that it pertains to a city called Heliopolis: "I know the Souls of Heliopolis; they are ..." There can be no doubt that the Heliopolis referred to here was located in Egypt and is now a suburb of the modern city of Cairo. Nevertheless, the modern city of Baalbek, located northeast of Beirut in eastern Lebanon, was also called Heliopolis during the Seleucid (323 - 64 BCE) and Roman (64 BCE - 312) periods. If we assume that the seven letters in Revelation are based in part on writings such as the *Book of the Dead*, it is possible that the Heliopolis of the Levant was referred to in the original text of Revelation and for some reason the name of Philadelphia was substituted for it by later redactors. This would bring the number of matching names of places visited by the apostle Paul in the New Testament from three up to four.

8. Egyptian Parallels in the Seven Letters

The kings of the 15th and 16th Dynasties ruled concurrently and were called Hyksos, a name based on "the Egyptian epithet *hekau khasut*, 'rulers of foreign (lit. mountainous) countries' and which applied only to the rulers of the Asiatics."[427] (The Asiatics, of course, included the peoples of the Syria-Palestinian area). The Hyksos followed the administrative model set up by 12th Dynasty Egyptian kings, presumably to establish a lasting entrenchment of their rule. They incorporated Egyptian organizations and practices and even employed Egyptian civilians, priests, civil servants – and soldiers – in their ranks. Their center of administration and power was concentrated in the heavily fortified city of Avaris in the eastern part of the Delta (see map, Figure 45). Bourriau (2000) informs us that "The ruler of Avaris claimed to be King of Upper and Lower Egypt, although from the stelae of Kamose (a king of Thebes during the 17th Dynasty) we know that Hermopolis marked his theoretical southern boundary and Cusae, a little further south, the specific border point."[428] In spite of this claim of kingship over all of Egypt, the border between Upper and Lower Egypt was strictly controlled, especially during the reign of Kamose, who eventually rebelled against Hyksos authority. It seems that a fortress (Qua el-Kebir) south of Mostagedda on the east side of the Nile controlled shipping for the Theban kings of Upper Egypt while, on the opposite side of the river, another fortress (Dier Rifa) just south of Asyut controlled shipping for the Hyksos in Lower Egypt.[429]

In addition to Avaris, the remains of six other Hyksos fortresses have been identified in the eastern part of the Delta bringing the total in that area to seven (note that this is the same number of "churches" mentioned in Rev. 2-3). Their modern names are (1) Tell el-Dabᶜa (Avaris), (2) Tell Fauziya, (3) Tell Geziret el-Faras, (4) Farasha, (5) Tell el-Yahudiya (Egyptian, *Nay-ta-hut*; Greek, Leontopolis),[a] (6) Tell el-Maskhuta (Pithum) and (7) Tell el-Habra (Figure 45).[b, 430] These fortresses were commanded by Egyptians, presumably to facilitate their acceptance by the local native Egyptians (*cf.* the earlier mention of traitors among the members of the seven churches of Revelation – this will be discussed shortly).

The Hyksos adopted many Egyptian gods and kingly titles. For example, like the Egyptian kings in Thebes, each Hyksos king called himself the "Son of Re." Nevertheless, they rejected Re as their national deity and established a variant of the Egyptian god Seth which combined many of the attributes of their Syro-Palestinian

---

[a] Tell el-Yahudiya (Egyptian, *Nay-ta-hut*; Greek, Leontopolis), which means "The Mound of the Jews" was located in the ancient 13th (Heliopolitan) nome, a little north of Heliopolis. Baines and Malek (1980, p. 174) indicates it resembled "the so-called 'Hyksos Camp,'" and is "usually interpreted as fortifications and dated to the late Middle Kingdom or the 2nd Intermediate Period. ... builders of the enclosure have been sought outside Egypt, the immigrants from northwest Asia during the Hyksos Period being the obvious choice. There is, however, a strong possibility that the structure is of a religious rather than military character." If the letter is true, this does not rule out the possibility that it also acted as a fort for a time, as most Egyptologists believe.

[b] Bourriau (2000, p. 195) says that two of these sites "Tell el-Maskhuta and Tell el-Yahudiya, had come to an end before the period represented by the last Hyksos statum (D/2) at Tell el-Dabaa." These sites may therefore have been the first to later fall at the hands of Theban Kings.

storm-god, Baal-Reshef and the Hittite god, Teshub.[431] Seth (or perhaps more accurately, Seth-Baal) thus became the god of Lower Egypt (*cf.* the reference to the worship of Baal among members of the seven churches). Bourriau (2000) tells us that "the cult of Seth, retaining the attributes of a Syrian storm-god, continued and even expanded during the New Kingdom."[432]

Of course, the adoption of Seth as Lower Egypt's national god meant that many of the native Egyptians had to more or less reject Re's supremacy and follow the corrupted Hyksos version of the god Seth. It seems reasonable to speculate that when Kamose, the last pharaoh of the 17th Dynasty, and Ahmose, the first king of the 18th Dynasty, took up arms against the Hyksos, they considered the native Egyptian commanders and troops to be Egyptian traitors, not only against their native Egypt but against Re. Also, it is likely that before the Egyptian troops attacked the Hyksos,[a] the Theban kings would have offered the native Egyptians commanders and other Egyptians among the *aamu* troops the chance to switch allegiance back to native Egyptian kings and gods. It would also make sense that, when the *aamu* and their Hyksos leaders were defeated and finally driven out of Lower Egypt by Ahmose, those Egyptians who had switched their allegiance from the then ruling Hyksos king (Kamudi or Apophis II) received pardons and possibly even rewards (*cf.* the rewards in the seven letters).

This scenario conforms quite well with the above suggestion that the seven letters of Revelation are declarations of war against seven settlements of some kind, possibly fortresses. And if we assume that Revelation's letters parallel declarations of war by a Theban king against the Hyksos, we should examine the observed Egyptian parallels in the letters with the view they may refer to actual historical events.

To do this, we assume the names of the "churches" provided in Rev. 2-3 and 3 are not the original names and that overly enthusiastic Christian scribes imagined the

---

[a] In his brief review of the defeat of the Hyksos, Bourriau (2000) tells us that, "The strategy of Ahmose seems to have been to bypass Memphis to take Heliopolis and then, three months later, in mid-October (after the water level of the inundation had begun to fall and men in chariots could move again in the valley), to attack Tell el-Habra, which had the effect of cutting of the Hyksos from a retreat across northen Sinai to Palestine. The assault on Avaris followed." Ultimately, the Hyksos were driven out of Egypt, an event which was described by Josephus. Bourriau (2000) goes on to say that, "Because Josephus considered the Hyksos to have been the founders of Jerusalem, his version of Manetho [a well-known Egyptian priest who lived during the 30th Dynasty (380-343 BCE) and was commissioned by Ptolemy I to write a history of ancient Egypt which he did by accessing a vast number of writings from temple archives], includes a detailed account of events after they were driven out of Egypt by Ahmose. On the siege of Avaris he says: 'They {the Hyksos} enclosed {Avaris}with a high strong wall in order to safeguard all their possessions and spoils. The Egyptian king attempted by siege to force them to surrender, blockading the fortress with an army of 480,000 men. Finally, giving up the siege in despair, he concluded a treaty by which they should all depart from Egypt.'" Bourriau (2000) also makes reference to a written account of one of Ahmose's soldiers which reveals events after the defeat of Avaris. His speaks of another campaign to southern Palestine during which Sharuhen was taken. Bourriau adds that, "We do not know whether the intention was to destroy the remnants of the Hyksos or to exploit the vacuum they left to push on into Palestine and even as far as Lebanon."

8. Egyptian Parallels in the Seven Letters

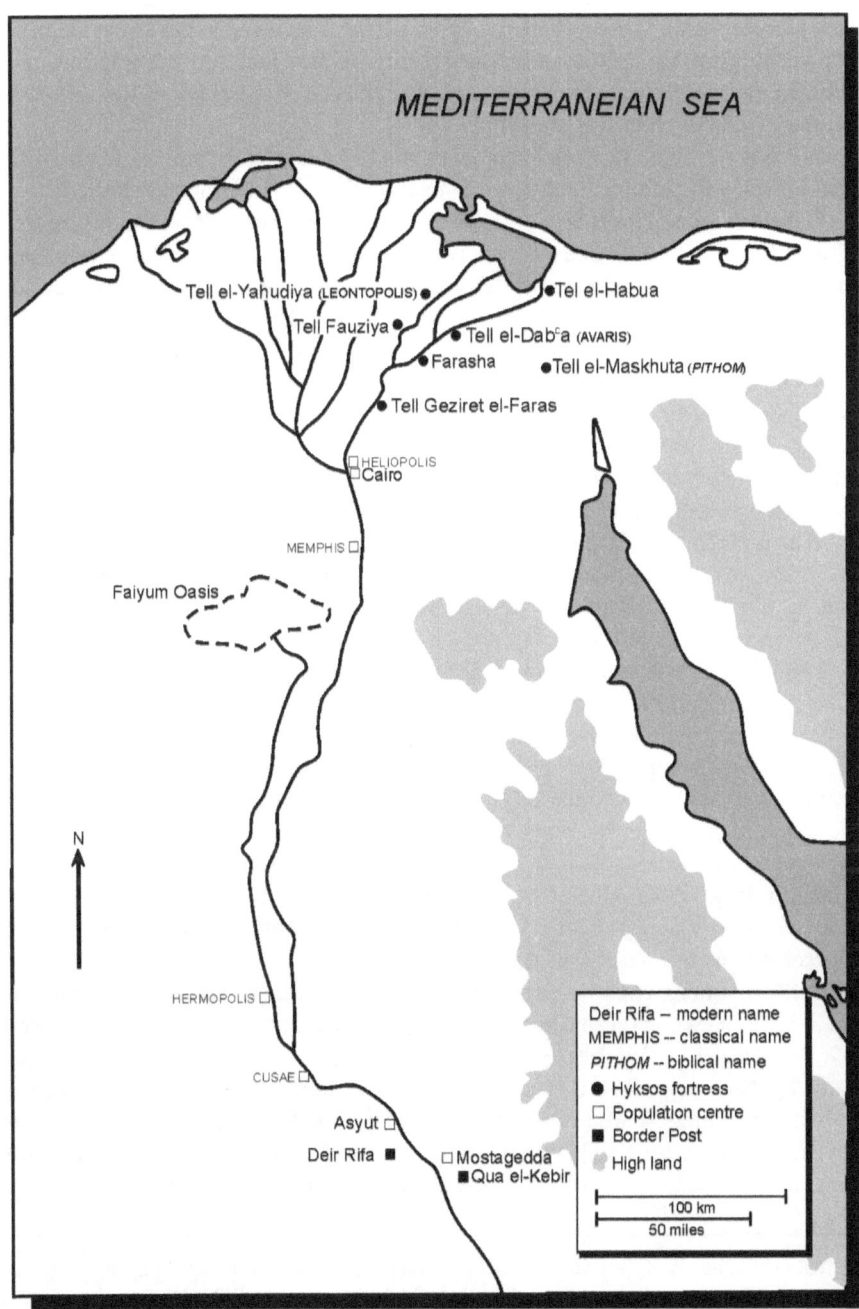

Figure 45. Distribution of the seven Hyksos fortresses in the Nile Delta. Important attributes of these fortresses parallel those of the seven churches of Rev. 2-3. Map is based mainly on Bourriau (2000, p. 200) and Baines and Málek (1980, pp. 109, 121).

difficult, foreign names in early copies of Revelation bore some mystical relationship to the places in Asia Minor which the apostle Paul is believed to have visited during his preaching in the early days of Christianity. In this manner, the original, then unknown names of the seven fortresses were replaced in the Book of Revelation by names of towns or cities in Asia Minor.

We thus turn our attention to comparisons of some of the elements found in the seven letters with parallels found in the history of the 2nd Intermediate Period:

Rebellion against a deity:- Two of the seven churches in Revelation (see Rev. 2:4 and Rev. 2:14) are accused of having among their number those who have switched allegiance. Similarly, Egyptian records tell us that Egyptian commanders in the Delta reported to Hyksos[433] rulers rather than Egyptian-born kings as tradition demanded. Also, many native Egyptians served as regular soldiers in the Hyksos army. This suggests that some of the Egyptians in the area controlled by the Hyksos rejected Re in favor of Seth-Baal (or at least were perceived as rejecting him), a situation which parallels the rebellious nature outlined for the churches in Ephesus and Smyrna (Rev. 2:4 and Rev. 2:14). Of course Egyptian soldiers in the Delta would have been perceived as rebelling against the king of Thebes – and Re.

War is Declared:- War or warlike actions are threatened against the churches in Rev. 2:16, Rev. 2:9-10, Rev. 2:22-23 and Rev. 3:3. Similarly, kings Kamose and Ahmose of Thebes took military action against the Hyksos and waged war against their seven fortresses in the Delta.

Followers in the synagogue of Satan:- It was suggested in Chapter 4, *Other Characters in Revelation,* that Revelation's Satan (or Devil) was another name for the Egypt's Apophis who was often considered to be represented by Seth. The reference to followers of Satan in Rev. 3:9 may thus be extended to parallel "followers of Egyptian god, Apophis." Remarkably, "Apophis" was also the name of several Hyksos kings,[a] and in particular, the names of the two kings in power at the time the Theban kings waged war against the Hyksos, i.e., Apophis I and Apophis II.[434] The reference to Satan in Rev. 3:9 can thus, from a historical perspective, be considered a parallel (or an allusion) to Apophis, the Devil who took the form of Apophis I and II, two Hyksos kings whose center was Avaris.

Faithful among enemies are spared in the conflict:- The declaration of war in Rev. 2-3 promises that those who remain faithful (Rev. 2:4, Rev. 2:7, Rev. 2:11, Rev. 2:17, Rev. 2:26, Rev. 3:4, Rev. 3:5, Rev. 3:12, Rev. 3:21), in spite of the way they are treated by the enemy (Rev. 2:10), are to be spared during the conflict and rewarded for their faithfulness. Those who rebelled and followed the enemy are to be punished (Rev. 2:20-23). Those who joined the ranks of Apophis' army would, upon capture, be made subservient to the local Egyptians who had remained faithful to the sun-god

---

[a] Grimal (1992, pp. 194) indicates "The chronology of the last two Hyksos kings is somewhat confused. ...The name of one of them, Aazehre, the last king of the Fifteenth Dynasty appears on an Obelisk at Tanis – he probably corresponds to Manetho's Asseth and the Turin Canon's Khamudy. The other, Apophis III, was the last of the Sixteenth Dynasty Hyksos vassal kings, and his name appears on several monuments, including a dagger from Saqqara. No textual source can supply the least detail on the final phase of Hyksos rule." Grimal (p. 392) equates Khamudy with Apophis II, the last king of the 15th Dynasty.

and his Theban king. This would conform with the last part of Rev. 3:9 which says, "I will make them (the false Jews, the Hyksos and their Asiatic followers) come and bow down before your feet, and learn that I have loved you."

The "New Jerusalem":- In the letter to Philadelphia, Rev. 3:12b says that "the city of my God, the New Jerusalem" will be written on the conquerors. As indicated above, "the city of my God" conforms with the name of Egypt's Heliopolis, i.e., "City of the Sun" or the "City of Re." One of the seven Hyksos sites mentioned above, was located north of Heliopolis in the 13th (Heliopolitan) nome and is now known as Tell el-Yahudiya, meaning "The Mound of the Jews." Baines and Malek (1980)[435] indicates it resembles a "so-called 'Hyksos Camp,'" and is "usually interpreted as fortifications and dated to the late Middle Kingdom or the 2nd Intermediate Period. ... builders of the enclosure have been sought outside Egypt, the immigrants from northwest Asia [the *aamu*] during the Hyksos Period being the obvious choice." As an important fortress in the Delta, Tell el-Yahudiya was undoubtedly associated with the protection of Heliopolis so that the "*New* Jerusalem" in Rev. 3:12b might just conceivably be a reference to plans by king Ahmose to rebuild Tell el-Yahudiya after its defeat (and likely destruction).

Another possibility is that the "New Jerusalem" could refer to the Jerusalem in Palestine toward which the *aamu,* the Syro-Palestinians, traveled during their escape back to their place of origin. Finally, and from a more straight-forward point of view, it might well refer to Egypt's "City of Re" (see Chapter 27, *The Holy City*), Heliopolis, the "City of the Sun." The original text of Revelation would then be understood that Heliopolis itself would be rebuilt after the war. In later versions of the Book of Revelation which were copied and edited by Hebrew scribes and teachers, the *New* City of Re became the "New Jerusalem." While it seems there is an Egyptian parallel to Revelation's "New Jerusalem" here, it's exact nature is questionable; but the best parallel seems to be Heliopolis.

The "Hour of Trial":- In the message to the people of Sardis, Rev. 3:10 says, "Because you have kept my word of patient endurance, I will keep you from the hour of trial which is coming on the whole world, to try those who dwell upon the earth" (Rev. 3:10). This statement does not necessarily mean that man-made tribulations would be invoked; military intervention was not the only means of applying pressure on and maintaining loyalty among Egypt's suzerainties. The Egyptian king, as the incarnation of Horus, the "son of Re," was believed to possess all the supernatural powers of the sun-god, including the power to cause natural disasters and phenomena such as storms, famine, pestilence, earthquakes and other natural catastrophes. At times the king could call upon the wrath of the sun-god to wreck such havoc among his enemies. Indeed, the pharaoh often took credit for natural disasters which had earlier decimated enemy states and armies to reinforce this belief.

The Book of Revelation mentions the dissemination of the dreadful wrath of God on the nations of the world, including many catastrophic events and several chapters are devoted to describing their devastating effects. For example, Rev. 3:10 could mean that faithful Egyptians in the Delta would not have to suffer along with the Hyksos. Later in this book we will examine in detail the awful extent of this "hour of trial which is coming on the whole world," the first indications of which are found in the part of the throne scene described in Rev. 6:12-17, as follows:

> ... there was a great earthquake; and the sun became black as sackcloth, the full moon became like blood, [13]and the stars of the sky fell to the earth as the fig tree sheds its winter fruit when shaken by a gale; [14]the sky vanished like a scroll that is rolled up, and every mountain and island was removed from its place. [15]Then the kings of the earth and the great men and the generals and the rich and the strong, and every one, slave and free, hid in the caves and among the rocks of the mountains, [16]calling to the mountains and rocks, "Fall on us and hide us from the face of him who is seated on the throne, and from the wrath of the Lamb; [17]for the great day of their wrath has come, and who can stand before it?"

Since the unleashing of the wrath of God on the wicked of the world is an integral part of the throne scene, and since its repercussions are manifest in and integral to many different parts of the Book of Revelation, discussion on this will be presented in the two chapters, Chapter 13. *Catastrophes* and Chapter 14, *From Catastrophe to Myth*.

Evidence for the conclusion that the Nile Delta best corresponds to the location of the seven "churches" in Revelation will, during the course of this work, be supported by Egyptian parallels to many other passages and scenes in the Book of Revelation. These parallels will occasionally be identified in their proper contexts and serve to broaden the sense of correspondence between characters and events in Revelation and those involving Egypt's religious beliefs and its historic role among the nations of the ancient Middle East.

PART III. THE AMDUAT SERIES (REV. 5-14)

Recall that one of the main objectives of Part II was to provide an Egyptological background against which the many scenes in the Book of Revelation could be compared. In it, we identified the main cast of characters associated with the throne scene in Revelation as well the much larger cast of lesser deities and multitudes which surrounded the throne. It was also suggested that the letters to the seven churches in Rev. 2-3 could be viewed as dire warnings – even declarations of war – against rebellious factions in the Nile Delta. The throne scene with its preeminent deities and warnings, especially to the unfaithful, sets the stage for the remainder of Revelation which contains many parallels to characters and events in the *Amduat*.

The *Amduat* is a funerary work describing the voyage of the sun-god from his entry as an aged deity into the Netherworld to his sailing with his entourage along the primeval river-banks which are populated by beings, both friend and foe, depending on his location along the river. In the Netherworld, the sun-god's form is that of a fragile, juvenile, ram-headed entity which some Egyptologists describe as the "fetal," lamb form of the ram-headed sun-god. At the end of the *Amduat* he emerges in the eastern sky as a rejuvenated, newly-born sun-god, which, as pointed out in Chapter 3, *The Preeminent Deities*, parallels Revelation's Lamb.

The sun-god's safety in the Netherworld is ensured by the powerful magic of his entourage. The *Amduat* informs us of the many dangers and pitfalls awaiting them in the afterlife and offers assurance that those who have been faithful to the sun-god will receive new life, food, light and bright white clothing in the presence of their god.

The *Amduat* was typically painted on the walls of royal tombs. The oldest known fragments of it are from the tomb of Thutmosis I (1504-1492 BCE) although it seems these actually belong to the early years of Queen Hatshepsut (1473-1458 BCE).[436] The earliest complete copies are from the tomb of Thutmosis III (1479-1425 BCE) and that of Useramun, the first of his visors.[437] Clagett (1989) points out that the presence of the book in the royal tombs was to "ensure the king's rebirth like that of his father Re."[438]

The *Amduat* is divided into twelve parts corresponding to the twelve hours of the night. These are variously referred to as "Divisions" or "Hours." The term "Division" will be used throughout this book. Each division is typically divided into three horizontal registers with the solar barque and Re's entourage always occupying the center one; each register typically contains a series of pictures, or scenes, with hieroglyphics written beside or above them. The sun-god is usually depicted in his ram-headed form standing in a protective shrine on his barque as he sails through each of the divisions in turn to finally emerge reborn into the morning sky in the 12th Division.

Most of the scenes and events in the 5th to 14th chapters of the Book of Revelation are well defined and, as we shall see, contain numerous scenes and events similar to those found in the religious – and in some cases secular – texts of ancient Egypt. Unlike the parallels identified in Part II, many of the scenes, and at times, events within the scenes in the *Amduat* follow the same order as parallel events in the Book of Revelation. Occasionally, orderly sequences of parallels are interrupted by parallels from other Egyptian texts, including the *Book of the Dead*, the *Book of Aker* and the *Books of the Heavens*. At times, secular documents and general historical references are used to identify additional parallels. Most scenes and events are discussed in essentially the same order as they appear in the Book of Revelation, regardless of the order in which their parallels appear in the Egyptian texts. To the above will be added two chapters dealing with Egyptian parallels to practically all the apocalyptic scenes and events described in the Book of Revelation.

Later, in Part IV, *The Book of Gates Series*, events in the remaining chapters of Revelation will be compared with those found in the *Book of Gates* and other important documents.

Chapter 9. Opening of the Scroll (Rev. 5)[439]

We begin our survey of the *Amduat* Series with the 5th chapter of the Book of Revelation and the description of God on his throne provided in Rev. 5:1-6. The main characters here are God on the throne, the Lamb, the four living creatures and a group of elders. The central deity holds in his right hand a sealed scroll the contents of which are secret. Around him and his attendants are "many angels, numbering myriads of myriads and thousands of thousands" (Rev. 5:11). In spite of the size of this multitude, the only one worthy to open and read the scroll is the Lamb (Rev. 5:9) who is also called "the Lion of the tribe of Judah, the Root of David" (Rev. 5:5). While these are the main elements of this scene, there are others which seem to be of relatively minor importance; these will be included in our analysis simply because some of their unique aspects are also found in the *Amduat* and other Egyptian records.

Presentation of the Scroll (Rev. 5:1-2)

The scene of the presentation of the scroll in Rev. 5 is introduced in the last three verses of the previous chapter, Rev. 4:9-11 where the twenty-four elders are described as falling down and worshiping God on his throne. Rev. 5 then begins with a description of a book which God holds in his hand. This opening scene bears a remarkable resemblance to portions of the 6th Division of the *Amduat* so our discussion will move directly to those parts of the 6th Division which are most similar to the events described in Revelation.

The opening scene is of the ceremony which begins with the words, "And I saw in the right hand of him who was seated on the throne a scroll ..." (Rev. 5:1). This corresponds to the scene in the middle register shown in Figure 46. The seated baboon-headed deity holds in his extended hand the sacred ibis (, a symbol of the god Thoth) which the text identifies as "Thoth, who stands before the Lord of those who are in the Netherworld [i.e., Osiris]."[440] The baboon is also a symbol of Thoth so that the baboon-headed form of Osiris emphasizes the symbol in his hand – i.e., knowledge and wisdom. Thoth was the well-known patron deity of scribes who was credited with the invention of Egyptian hieroglyphic writing.[441] He was also the god of learning[442] and the personification of the very "word of god" (see Chapter 5, *The Word of God*). Thus, Figure 46 shows Osiris seated on his throne and holding the symbol of knowledge and of the "Word of Re" in his hand. In this manner, the image

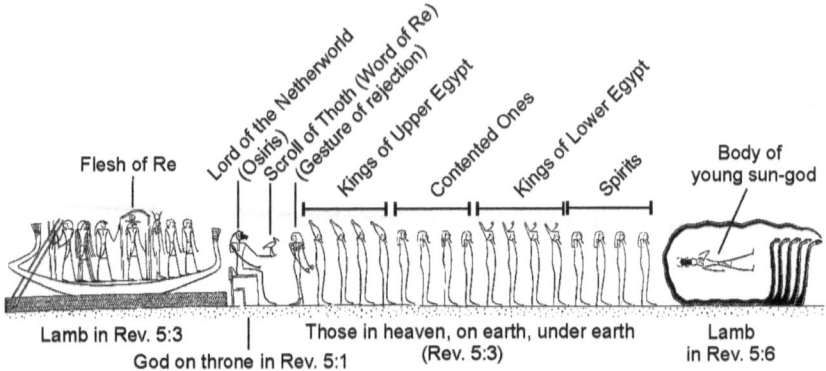

Figure 46. The middle register of the 6th Division of the *Amduat*. This register, contains most of the elements found in Rev. 5. On the far left, Re (Revelation's Lamb) stands in his shrine; in front of him, baboon-headed Osiris (= Revelation's God on the throne) sits on his throne (Rev. 5:1) and holds out a scroll (represented by an ibis, 🦤). The scroll is rejected both by the goddess who holds her hands behind her back and by the group of sixteen deities standing behind her (Rev. 5:3). To the far right is the dead body of Re (the slain Lamb of Rev. 5:6). (AM6.2)

produced here conforms with that in Rev. 5:1 of God on the throne holding out a very important book in his hand.[a]

Thoth is credited with writing the words of Re in a book which was known as the *Book of Thoth*. Unfortunately, there are no extant copies of this book so we must rely on ancient references to it to learn of its content and importance. The *Onomasticon of Amenope* says that it refers to "all things that exist; what Ptah created, what Thoth copied down, heaven with its designs, earth and what is in it, what the mountains belch forth, what is watered by the flood, all things upon which Re has shone, all that is grown on the back of earth."[443] The deceased was promised access to this book in the Netherworld: Chapter 64 of the *Book of the Dead* says, "You shall sit under the branches of the tree of Hathor who is preeminent in the wide solar disk when she travels to Heliopolis bearing the script of the divine words, the *Book of Thoth*. You shall have power."[444] Chapter 94 of the same book refers to the *Book of Thoth* in its opening sentence: "O you great one who see [*sic*.] your father, keeper of the *Book of Thoth*, see, I have come spiritualized, besouled, mighty, and equipped with the writings of Thoth."[445] The *Book of Thoth*, which consisted of forty-two volumes, was the ultimate word of Re and its wealth of knowledge was available only to a select few of the priesthood. That Osiris is depicted with the head of a baboon, an Egyptian symbol of wisdom and learning, is further evidence that what is being presented in his outstretched hand is knowledge – knowledge which dates back

---

[a] Figure 46 shows the book on the left rather than the right as described in Rev. 5:1. This is irrelevant, however, because the hand seen to hold the book depends on whether a particular version of the *Amduat* was written to be read from left to right or from right to left.

9. Opening of the Scroll

to the very beginning of time. It's importance thus parallels that of the scroll referred to in Rev. 5:1.

No one worthy to open scroll (Rev. 5:2-4)

We read in Rev. 5:3 that "no one in heaven or on earth or under the earth was able to open the scroll or to look into it." A similar concept is emphasized in Figure 46 where we see, in front of the throne of Osiris and immediately before the ibis bird, a goddess holding two offering vessels behind her. Also behind her are sixteen deities, each standing with their backs toward her and the throne, a gesture which may be interpreted as a rejection of that which is being held out by Osiris.

The symbolism in the gestures of Osiris, the woman, and the sixteen deities in this scene thus give the same sense of events as those outlined in Rev. 5:2-3. Osiris's gesture is self-evident; he is offering to those in front of him a book of wisdom (represented by the ibis, the symbol of Thoth, as above). The goddess standing before him holds both hands behind her back in a gesture similar to the hieroglyphic, $\cancel{k}$, a the determinative of the action to "turn away" from something.[446] She holds two ● symbols, pronounced *nu* (*nw, nìw,* or *nì*).[447] Note that the word *nì,* can mean to "reject."[448] And the pronunciation of the ● symbol is similar to that of the word, *niu,* meaning "to turn away."[449] Rejection is also implied in a visual pun based on the ● symbol itself because the somewhat similar words, *nu* and *nn* may also represent simple particles of negation "not and no"[450] or *nn* can simply mean "not."[451] It is therefore reasonable to interpret her stance to mean that she is rejecting the scroll ($\cancel{k}$) and offering it in turn to the sixteen deities standing behind her.

But the sixteen deities behind the goddesses have their backs turned toward her, a gesture which can be interpreted to mean that they also reject the offer.[a] The *identity* of those rejecting the offer in Figure 46 also conforms with Rev. 5:4. This verse says that "no one in heaven or on earth was able to open the scroll." Four of the eight deities without crowns are identified in the text as "Spirits" of the dead while the other four are called "Those in peace,"[452] a phrase implying the resting dead. These two groups of four represent the multitudes of spirits in the afterlife. The remaining eight deities wear crowns of Egypt, four representing Upper Egypt ($\triangle$) and four Lower Egypt ($\cancel{y}$) so that on earth, even the kings of Egypt who ordinarily might be considered the most worthy to accept the scroll, could not accept it – just as we read in Rev. 5:3 – that "no one was found worthy to ... look into it." Meanwhile, as noted above, these sixteen deities are all turned away from the ibis, a gesture which conforms with Rev. 5:4. The overall meaning of the scene showing the sixteen deities, both kings and spirits, standing with their backs toward the goddess who is also rejecting the scroll from Osiris is that there is no one in heaven or on earth to accept it, including the kings, just as we read as in Rev. 5:4.

---

[a] Note that the first four deities wear the White Crown of Upper Egypt ($\triangle$), sometimes called a *stà,* a word phonetically similar to *stah* which means "to reject" (see Budge 1920, p. 628b). The proximity of these particular crowns to the double ● ● symbols may be considered to have been visual puns to learned Egyptian priests to remind them that the scroll was being rejected by the group of sixteen, a concept which parallels that described in Rev. 5:2-4.

The lion of Judah (Rev. 5:5)

In Rev. 5:5, one of the elders says, "Weep not; lo, the Lion of the tribe of Judah, the Root of David, has conquered, so that he can open the scroll and its seven seals." An unambiguous reference to a lion is also found in this same Division of the *Amduat*. It is centrally located in the upper register (on the far left in Figure 47) and immediately above the sixteen standing deities discussed above; it is a picture of a recumbent lion, .

Before proceeding with a detailed discussion of Revelation's "Lion of Judah" we should briefly examine the reference by the author of the book in Rev. 5:5 to weeping when no one was found worthy to open the scroll. An Egyptian word for lion is *rema*, and this is phonetically similar to *remu*, meaning "weeper" or "mourner."[453] The idea of weeping is reinforced in the hieroglyphs above the lion where we see a single symbol below two eye symbols. These eye symbols are normally associated with the right and left eyes of the sun-god, Re, while according to Budge (1920) the symbol which Budge (1920) suggests is the "tear-drop of the divine eye."[a] This scene of the lion with its phonetic association with weeping and the weeping eye symbol above it is therefore consistent with the reference to weeping in Revelation. Finally, the juxtapositions of those rejecting the scroll in the middle register immediately below this scene strengthen the suggestion that this part of the 6th Division conforms with the image presented in Rev. 5:5.

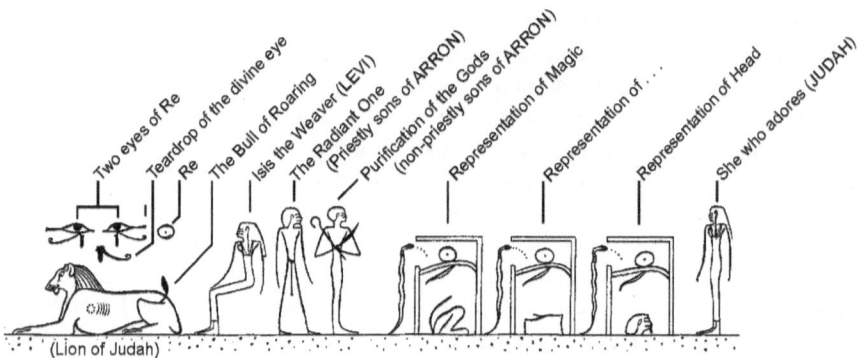

Figure 47. The Lion of the Tribe of Judah of Rev. 5:5 as represented in the 6th Division of the *Amduat*. The symbol above the lion represents the weeping mentioned in this verse while the deity on the far right represents Judah and the three deities immediately behind the lion represent Levite priests associated with the Judah (see text). (AM6.1.6 -10)

In Egypt, the lion was considered to be a manifestation of the sun-god. In the 62nd Chapter of the *Book of the Dead*, the deceased, who seeks to identify himself with the sun-god, says, "I am he who crosses the sky, I am the Lion of Re."[454] Lurker informs us that, "Under the name Herakhty, Horus assumed a lion's head as god of the morning sun"[455] so that, in this particular case, Horus assumes the role of the juvenile

---

[a] The concept of a "teardrop of the divine eye" is expressed by Budge (1920) p. cvi. Gardiner (1927), p. 452, sign #D17, says is the ideograph or determinative of "figure" or "image," as well as "the markings of a falcon's head" on p. 450, sign D10.

sun-god Re which we have identified in Chapter 3, *The Preeminent Deities*, as being a parallel to the Lamb of Revelation. But the earthly Horus was also recognized as the Lion of the people of Egypt; this, of course, included being the Lion of immigrants from the Levant such as the generations of the children of Israel. Even Ezekiel 32:2 says that outside Egypt the Pharaoh was recognized as "a lion among the nations," a phrase which would include the tribe of Judah. Thus, reference to the Lion of the Tribe of Judah, in an Egyptian context, is also consistent with our knowledge of Egyptian beliefs concerning Egypt's dominance or authority over Judah.

One might enquire if there is any evidence that the lion in this part of the *Amduat* is specifically connected in any way to the Tribe of Judah in either the pictures or text. The answer is "Yes," for the following reason: The name, "The Adorer," was found among the groups of twelve identified with the Tribe of Judah while a practically identical name is given for the goddess at the far right of the register, a position often reserved for deities with special functions related to the events extending for some distance across a register. Her name is "She who *adores*"' and she faces left toward the lion in the center of the register. We may infer from this that she represents the tribe of Judah and her favored position in the register conforms with the idea that the central lion parallels the "Lion of the tribe of Judah" mentioned in Revelation.

Support for this suggestion is found in the names of the three deities immediately behind the lion. The name of the one seated on an invisible throne immediately behind the lion is "Isis, the Weaver" who as indicated in Figure 47 (and Figure 28) can be identified with the name Levi which means "to twine." Thus, an allusion to Revelation's tribe of Levi can also be found in this scene. Also, it is germane that the members of the tribe of Levi were special among the twelve tribes. They consisted of two groups, the priests and the non-priests, as follows:

> The Mosaic legislation made a sharp distinction between the priests and non-priests or ordinary Levites. 1. The priests must belong to Aaron's family; the Levites belong to the larger family of *Levi*.' A priest was a Levite but a Levite was not necessarily a priest. 2. Priests were consecrated (Exod. 29:1-37; Lev. 8); Levites were *purified*' (Num. 8.5-22). 3. Levites were considered a gift to *Aaron*' and his sons (Num. 3:5-13; 8:19; 18:1-7). 4. The fundamental difference consisted of this: only the priest had the right to minister at the altar and to enter the most holy place (Exod. 28:1; 29:9; Num. 3:10,38; 4:15, 19f; 18:1-7; 25:10-13).[456]

A means of identifying parallels in the remaining two deities behind the lion in Figure 47 lies in this knowledge that the only Levites which could become priests were the sons of Aaron. Note that the name, Aaron, means "light bringer,"[457] a meaning consistent with "The Radiant One" who stands behind the seated "Isis the Weaver," (= the tribe of Levi). "The Radiant One" thus parallels Aaron and his priestly sons. Meanwhile, the deity called "Purification of the Gods" who holds a crook and sword across his chest parallels the "purified," non-priestly descendants of Levi. In summary, we find in this scene four deities whose names have meanings which parallel those of the Mosaic tradition:

1. *She Who Adores* parallels Judah (whose name means "to praise, revere, or worship"), the father of the Tribe of Judah.

2. *The Weaver* parallels the Tribe of Levi (meaning "to twine").

3. *The Radiant One* parallels Aaron (the "light bringer") the son of Levi and father of the Levite priests.

4. *Purification of the Gods* parallels the "purified sons of Levi," who were not priests.

Also, all three of the deities behind the lion are apparently the followers of Horus (Re's representative as the lion of Egypt and the king of kings on earth) just as are the slain soldiers of Horus (conquerors) whose body parts are located in three symbolic "Castles."[458] That all these are followers of Re is indicated by the preferred location of *She Who Adores* (Judah); her location encloses the groups of three solitary deities and three coffers behind the lion. From an Egyptian perspective, then, Horus the lion may be said to be king over *She who Adores,* i.e., over Judah, or metaphorically, it is the Lion of the tribe of Judah – as in Rev. 5:5.

Finally, the statement in Rev. 5:10 referring to the making of "a kingdom and priests to our God" is consistent with the text above the group of sixteen kings and spirits in the middle register (Figure 46). The idea of a kingdom being assigned to these deities is clearly expressed with the following words:

The majesty of *this god established this city* in the Netherworld *for these gods.*'
Re says to this god:
  May thy acts be established, may thy spirits be stable! The West leads thee to thy field in secret, she has hidden the hidden, thy hands have hidden their nakedness.
  The majesty of this Great God speaks to the Kings of Upper Egypt, to Those in peace, to the Kings of Lower Egypt, and to the spirits who are in this city: Your *kingdoms*' are yours, O Kings of Upper Egypt. Take you your White Crowns, your heads are your contentment, O Contented Ones. Your Lower Egyptian Crowns are yours, Kings of Lower Egypt. Your spirits are yours, O Spirits, your divine offerings are yours. May you be satisfied, may you be *powerful!*' Your souls are your glory, *your kingdom is your city.*' [459]

This text tells us that upon the sun-god's arrival in this part of the Netherworld he establishes a city-kingdom for all who serve him (i.e., the "Weaver," the kings, the "Contented Ones," the spirits, the "Radiant One," "Purification of the Gods" and his own soldiers). The text also emphasizes the purpose of his visitation to this part of the Netherworld. "This Great God travels in this city. ... The majesty of this god established this city in the Netherworld for these gods."[460] Re also says that "*your kingdom*' is your city," thus equating the new, celestial city with their kingdom, just as Rev. 5:10 refers to the making them "a *kingdom* and priests to our God." The deities in the upper register apparently represent those who administer, or rule over a kingdom so that the reference to a kingdom in Rev. 5:10 is compatible with this aspect of the 6th Division of the *Amduat*. Also, the reference to these deities being powerful in their city could very well indicate they hold priestly titles.

The slain lamb (Rev. 5:6-9)

Rev. 5:6 describes a peculiar circumstance which helps identify another parallel scene in this part of the *Amduat*; it describes "a Lamb standing, as though it had been slain." This statement seems to have an inherent contradiction – a slain lamb cannot stand up. But if we look at the right-hand side of Figure 46, we see exactly this. Khepri, the juvenile sun-god is clearly identifiable by the beetle sign 🪲 above his head and the text says, "This is the body of Khepri [the parallel of Revelation's Lamb] in his own flesh." The term "in his own flesh," is used to label the recumbent figure and suggests he is dead. Nevertheless, his legs are apart as if standing and he extends one arm upwards as if he were alive. Indeed, the text says, "the images [i.e., of Khepri and the human-form figure] in it [the five-headed serpent] *walk*."[461] This scene is therefore consistent with the idea of resurrection – and especially with Revelation's "Lamb standing." In this picture, his youthful, lamb-like vulnerability is protected by the encircling body of "Many Faces," the serpent.

Like Rev. 5:6, the Egyptian text focuses the readers' attention on an important theme of the two registers – the dead body of the slain sun-god and its resurrection. His presence as a prostrate deity in the process of being resurrected conforms quite well with Revelation's enigmatic description of a "Lamb standing, as though it had been slain." The parallel here is quite dramatic.

A Most Holy Scroll

If we look at Revelation's scene describing the opening of an important secret scroll from a purely Egyptian point of view, we might consider that this particular scroll could be in our possession today or is one mentioned in other Egyptian texts. Such a document may well have resided in Egypt's most holy temples where revered texts were protected against the eyes of unworthy persons, just as suggested about the scroll in Rev. 5:3 – "no one ... was able to open the scroll or to look into it." For these reasons, it is reasonable to extend our examination of Rev. 5 to include the possibility of the existence of such a mysterious book in ancient Egypt. We therefore turn our attention to a description of what the Egyptians referred to as the "ideal" temple library, its most sacred contents, and the special authority needed to enter its inner precincts.

There is a fairly short composition, dated to the Egypt's Ptolemaic Period, which describes the form of the sacred Egyptian *House of Life*, a facility which is best described in modern terms as a "central library."[a] This document is found in the British Museum where it is identified as artifact #10051. It describes the library in Abydos as having the ideal physical layout for other such libraries. It also describes some of its functions. Of particular interest to us here is its reference to the matter of authorization for access to various parts of the building and hence to its cult documents, many of which, like that of Rev. 5, were so highly secret that only

---

[a] Clagett (1989, p. 34) quotes P. Derchain (in *Le Papyrus Salt 825 (B.M. 10051) rituel pour la conservation de la vie en Égypte,* Académie Royale de Belgique, Classe des Letres, Mémoires, Vol. 38 (Brussels, 1965) as saying, "In a word, one ought to find there [in the *House of Life*] a complete totality of all the philosophic and scientific knowledge of the Egyptians."

select high priests had access to them. And, as in Rev. 5:5 and Rev. 5:9 which say that only the Lamb is permitted to read the contents of a certain book, only the sun-god Re (Revelation's Lamb) is permitted to look upon the writings located in its central repository. An English translation of the text is provided by Clagett (1989)[462] and reprinted here in the left-hand column of Table 9.1.

The House of Life in Rev. 5:3-11

The text begins with a physical description of the ideal House of Life. This is easier to understand when accompanied by the drawing originally published by Gardiner (1938).[a] The interior body, or main chamber of the House is roughly square and contains a centrally located shrine called *the Living One* which houses a statuette of Osiris (Figure 48). Each of the four sides of the outer courtyard opens into a smaller room named after one of the four deities Isis, Nephthys, Geb and Nut (or Horus and Thoth). A second door in each of these rooms opens to the outside. The ground floor is called Geb (the earth god) and the ceiling, Nut (the sky-goddess). Although the side chambers are small in the figure, they were likely relatively larger in the actual temple, their smaller size in the picture probably indicating their lesser importance than the chamber holding the central shrine (relative size corresponding to relative importance).

Figure 48. Reproduction of an ancient diagram of the House of Life in Abydos. In the middle of the central chamber Osiris stands on an egg containing a goose, a symbol of the sun-god Re, and in this case, an unhatched or fetal form of Re, i.e., a parallel to Revelation's Lamb (as in Rev. 5:6). The outer chamber is surrounded by four others oriented to the four cardinal points.

We will now make a detailed comparison of specific aspects of this House of Life with those given in the scene of the opening of the scroll in Rev. 5:3-11. These parallels, which correspond to the numbered elements in Table 9.1, will be discussed separately in the following paragraphs:

1. The elders (Rev. 5:6a):- Rev. 5:6 describes "elders" being present before the throne. Similarly, four rooms surrounding the centrally located throne in Figure 48 bear the names of six deities (Isis, Nephthys, Geb, Nut, Horus and Thoth). These deities are among the oldest and most revered in Osirian beliefs so it is reasonable to

---

[a] Original published by Gardiner, "House of Life" p. 169 and reproduced here from Clagett, 1989, p. 768, Figure I.30.

suggest they should parallel the "elders" of Rev. 5:6. Also, just as these gods share the courtyard with the four sons of Osiris, the throne area in Rev. 5:6 is occupied by both the elders and the four creatures (see # 3 below).

2. The hidden one (Rev. 5:6b):- The reference to the "hidden one" in the Egyptian text suggests that the "Great God" who rests within is Amen "the hidden one" (whom the Egyptians equated with Re and Amen-Re, as discussed in Chapter 3, *The Preeminent Deities*) and who loosely parallels the Lamb of Revelation. In Figure 48 Re is represented by a goose standing inside the egg (see Figure 12 and associated text) on which Osiris stands. Of course, Re's presence inside the egg also indicates his juvenile or pre-birth status so that this part of Figure 48 represents the sun-god's "lamb" stage, just as is described in Rev. 5:6, "And between the throne and the four living creatures and among the elders, *I saw a Lamb standing*." (This is emphasized in Figure 48 by the intimate proximity of Re to Osiris, suggesting the presence of the joint god Osiris-Re or Revelation's "God and the Lamb" as discussed in *The Preeminent Deities*.)

Table 9.1 Comparison of the description of *The House of Life* (the sacred library of the Osirian cult) with the scene describing the opening of a secret book in Rev. 5. The most notable parallels are in italics and are discussed in the text. The table is arranged in the same order as the Egyptian text so that the relative location of comparable elements in the two sources can be easily seen. The translation of *The House of Life* is from Clagett (1989, pp. 30-32) who bases his text on Derchain (1965).

The Egyptian *House of Life*	Book of Revelation
1. The House of Life. It shall be in Abydos and composed of four {side} bodies and an interior body {made} of covered reeds. *The four {bodies called} Houses and the {central body called} the Living One.* The Living One is Osiris, while the four Houses are *Isis, Nephthys, Geb, and Nut* ' (! Horus or Thoth?). Isis is on one side and Nephthys is on the other. *Horus is on the third side and Thoth on the last one.*' These are the four corners. Geb is the ground floor of it (the House of Life) and *Nut is its ceiling* '.	Rev. 5:6a And between the throne ... and *among the elders* ...
2. The *hidden one* who rests within it is the Great God. [italics from Clagett, 1989]	Rev. 5:6b ... *I saw a Lamb* [Re] standing, as though it had been slain
3. The four outer bodies are of stone which is from the Two Houses (?). The ground floor is of sand. The exterior is pierced in all four doors (two times): *one to the south, another to the north, a third to the west, and a fourth to the east.*'	Rev. 5:6a And between the throne and *the four living creatures* ... Also: Rev. 5:11a Then I looked, and I heard around the throne and *the living creatures* ...
4. *It shall be very, very, secret,*' not known and *not seen.*'	Rev. 5:3 And *no one* in heaven or on earth or under the earth *was able to open the scroll or to look into it*, Rev. 5:4 and I wept much that *no one was found worthy to open the scroll or to look into it.*

The Egyptian *House of Life*	Book of Revelation
5. *It is only the solar disk [Re] which looks upon its mystery.'*	Rev. 5:9b... *"Worthy art thou [the Lamb who parallels Re] to take the scroll and to open its seals,* for thou wast slain and by thy blood didst ransom men for God from every tribe and tongue and people and nation,
6. *The people who enter into it are the staff of Re: and they are the scribes of the House of life. The people who are inside it are (1) the "Shaven-headed Priest" who is Shu;'* (2) the *"Slaughterer",* who is *Horus,* who slays those who rebel against his father Osiris; (3) the "Scribe of the Sacred Book(s)," who is *Thoth,'* who recites the {ritual of} of glorification every day, without being seen or heard. {Properly} silent of mouth, their mouths and bodies covered, they are far removed from any repulsive violence. ...	Rev. 5:10a and hast *made them a kingdom and priests to our God,*
7. *No Asiatic* {i.e., foreigner} *will be allowed to enter there; he shall not see it and you will be far removed from it.*	Rev. 5:3 And no one in heaven or on earth or under the earth was able to open the scroll or to look into it,
8. *The books which are inside [the House of Life]* are the "Emanations of Re," wherewith to keep alive the god* ' *and to overthrow his enemies.*	Rev. 5:9a and *they sang a new song,* saying,
9. *The staff of the House of Life, who are in it, are the "Followers of Re" who protect his son every day.* ... *They (the gods or their priestly representatives at the House of Life) are personally occupied in protecting the god,' in defending the king in his palace, and in overturning those who rebel against him.'*	Rev. 5:10b ... *and they shall reign on earth."*

* These square brackets are in Clagett's original quotation of Derchain's translation.

3. The four creatures (Rev. 5:6a):- The centrally located shrine in which Osiris stands (in Figure 48) can be referred to as the throne area (*cf.* discussion on *The Throne Scene* in Chapter 3, *The Preeminent Deities*). The courtyard surrounding the throne has four doors which open to the outside and are oriented to the cardinal directions; the doors are labeled with the names of the four sons of Osiris, *Hapi, Imsety, Duamutef* and *Quebsennuef* who personify the cardinal directions. These are the same four beings identified in Rev. 4:6-9 (Chapter 4, *Other Characters in Revelation*) as being parallels to the four creatures before the throne of God; their location around the central throne in this picture thus conforms with Rev. 5:6a which describes them being in the vicinity of the throne. (See also #1 above.)

4. A very holy book (Rev. 5:3-4):- Rev. 5:4 states that "no one was found worthy to open the scroll or to look into it." This statement unambiguously tells us that this scroll in Revelation was of a highly secretive or "mysterious" nature. Similarly, the Egyptian text states that the House of Life "shall be very, very, secret, not known and *not seen.'*" We can readily see here that the description of the scroll in Rev. 5:2-3 closely parallels the secretive nature of the scrolls contained within the House of Life where the most secret, ancient and holy writings were stored.

5. Only the Lamb is worthy (Rev. 5:9b):- This verse says, "Worthy art thou [the Lamb] to take the scroll and to open its seals." Likewise, the Egyptian text says that "It is only the solar disk which looks upon its mystery." The solar disk, of course, represents the ram-headed sun-god Re whose juvenile form parallels Revelation's Lamb. Hence, Rev. 5:9b conforms with this part of the House of Life document; it is only Egypt's Re – or Revelation's Lamb – who is worthy to look upon the writings contained therein.

6. The presence of priests (Rev. 5:10):- We are told in Rev. 5:10 that the Lamb "made them a kingdom and priests to our God." Similarly, the Egyptian text places great emphasis on the presence of priests in the House of Life: "The people who enter into it are the staff of Re: and they are the scribes of the House of life." These would be those priests who maintained the temple and its library. Also, as indicated in Table 9.1 the only ones allowed entry into the inner shrine are (the priest of) Shu, Horus (the son of Re and the chief priest of the cult) and (the priest of) Thoth (an office usually held by Horus, the king). The parallel between this observation and the text of Rev. 5:10 is obvious: both sources mention the presence of priests in the vicinity of a central deity. The Egyptian text tells us it is Thoth who recites rituals from the book, an observation which leads us to the next point.

7. Those not worthy to see book (Rev. 5:3):- Rev. 5:3 says that "no one in heaven or on earth or under the earth was able to open the scroll or to *look into it*." The corresponding Egyptian text says "No Asiatic {i.e., foreigner} will be allowed to enter there; *he shall not see it*.'" Both sources thus prohibit outsiders from seeing the book's contents. The main difference between the two sources is that the Egyptian text disallows foreigners from coming near the sacred writings while Revelation says that no one (other than the Lamb) is able to look at or open the scroll. Nevertheless, note #6 above indicates that only Thoth, the "Word of Re" and hence an extension of Re, was privy to the contents of the book. The difference between the two texts is surely minor, especially when one considers that neither this nor any other passage in Revelation considered here is a direct translation of any particular Egyptian text.

8. A new song (Rev. 5:9a):- The parallel between the text in Rev. 5:9a and that of the document of Egyptian *House of Life* is somewhat less forceful than those sited above. Revelation refers to a group singing praises to the Lamb (i.e., Egypt's Re) while the Egyptian document says that the "Emanations of Re" were contained within books. The difference disappears, however, if we assume that the "Emanations of Re" refer to hymns to the sun-god in the sacred books, in which case the "Emanations of Re" would be hymns to Re written by Thoth. Such references to hymns would parallel the "song" being sung to the Lamb in Rev. 5:9a. Unfortunately, copies of the *Book of Thoth* have never been found so it is impossible to verify this aspect of the hymns – which it no doubt contained.

9. Priests as rulers (Rev. 5:10):- Rev. 5:10 tells us that the priestly followers of the Lamb "*shall reign on earth.*" This indicates that, in addition to being priests, they would be responsible for the daily government of the people (in a theocratic system). This sentiment can certainly be viewed as a parallel to the Egyptian text which says that "They (the gods or their priestly representatives at the House of Life) are personally occupied in protecting the god, in defending the king in his palace, and in overturning those who rebel against him." Since the Egyptian priests bore responsibility for Egypt's temples and bureaucracy as well as the army, they may be considered to have effectively ruled Egypt on their king's behalf, i.e., they would be rulers on earth, as in Rev. 5:10.

Discussion

In this chapter we have explored the degree to which Rev. 5 conforms with two separate Egyptian sources: (1) the text and pictures of the 6th Division of the *Amduat*, and (2) the ancient description of the ideal Egyptian House of Life, the central repository of Egypt's most sacred books.

As discussed in the introduction to *The Amduat Series*, the *Amduat* is composed of twelve parts, or Divisions. We have seen how our interest in Rev. 5 was quickly drawn to a scene in the middle register of the 6th Division. This register contained of a ceremony involving the opening of a book, most likely sacred writings called the *Book of Thoth*. This scene parallels Revelation's ceremony of the opening of the scroll in Rev. 5 while the scroll mentioned in Revelation parallels Egypt's *Book of Thoth* as suggested by the brief study of the document on the House of Life.

It seems odd that the *Amduat* Series of parallel images should begin half way through the *Amduat* rather than at it's beginning. But, as will become evident later in this work, not all scenes in Revelation follow exactly the same order we find in similar Egyptian texts; sometimes they closely follow a block of Egyptian texts only to suddenly change to an entirely different Egyptian source and later return to the original to continue with the flow of the previous sequence. In at least one case, the flow of images in Revelation switches into the reverse of those in the Egyptian texts. Patterns of switching from one Egyptian source to another will be shown to be especially prevalent in the *Amduat* Series where sub-series of parallel scenes may come from other sources such as the *Book of the Dead*, the *Book of Aker* and the *Books of the Heavens*. The reason for this apparently random switching among different sources is as yet unclear, although it is possible that an Egyptian source or sources with similar mixes of scenes and series of scenes from different texts exists. (See *Chapter 29, Parallel Series of Scenes*).

The most obvious difference between the *House of Life* document and this part of Revelation is that the parallels do not appear in the same order in both texts. Another difference is that the Egyptian document emphasizes both the physical arrangement and ceremonial protocols for the library while Revelation emphasizes only the ceremony so that ceremonial protocols must be inferred. The observed similarities, including the clustering of nine similar elements in the two sources nevertheless suggest a strong parallel between the settings of the two sources.

We also saw how Revelation's God on the throne corresponds not only with Osiris in 6th Division of the *Amduat*, but also with the centrally located statue of Osiris in the most secret room in the Egyptian *House of Life*. And like Revelation, the juvenile form of Re (Revelation's Lamb) is closely associated with Osiris (Revelation's God on the throne) in a picture of the House of Life and a short text describing it. The doors to the four rooms around the shrine are named after the four sons of Osiris, the same four "living creatures" which surround the throne in Revelation; and the elders

9. Opening of the Scroll

in Revelation correspond to important deities in the Egyptian pantheon identified in the text associated with the *House of Life* in Figure 48. Priests are identified as important elements in both sources and in each case are portrayed in the context of having great authority. Finally, in both sources only one deity has ultimate authority to look into its most sacred books and that person is symbolically identifiable with a male sheep. From the above observations we may conclude that this setting in this part of the Book of Revelation parallels that found in the Egyptian document called the *House of Life*.

The *Book of Thoth* which parallels the scroll in Rev. 5 was of extraordinary importance to the ancient Egyptians and although no copies of it are known to have survived, at least one must have survived until the early centuries of Christianity. It contained a vast collection of secret Egyptian knowledge and wisdom, including accounts of some of Egypt's most memorable historical events. We know this because one of the fathers of the early Christian church, Clemens Alexandrinus (the Greek, T. Falvius Clemens, c.150-220 CE), refers to it in his writings. Budge (1904), summarizes Clemens' comment as follows:

> ... the "Books of Thoth" were forty-two in number, and they were divided into six classes; books i.-x. dealth with the laws and the gods, and the education of the priests; books xi.-xx. treated of the services of the gods, i.e., sacrifices, offerings, forms of worship, etc.; books xxi.-xxx. related to the history of the world, geography and hieroglyphics; books xxxi.-xxxiv formed treatises on astronomy and astrology; books xxxv.-xxxvi. contained a collection of religious compositions; and books xxxvii.-xlii. were devoted to medicine.[463]

One interesting aspect of Clemens' commentary is that it was written well over a century after Christ. This late date suggests the book was available to non-Egyptians, and more significantly, to early Christians. In spite of its revered status, the book had shed its secret character and became known to at least some Christian scholars during the early years of the Christianization of ancient Egypt.[a]

The above outline of the *Book of Thoth* indicates that it contained much information on "the history of the world." This observation provides us with evidence that, in addition to religious themes which of course permeated almost everything Egyptian, history as viewed by the Egyptians was an important subject in the *Book of Thoth*. Since the book contained references to historical events, it is very likely that it was a source of information on Thera's eruption and its devastating effects on Lower Egypt and the rest of the eastern Mediterranean.

Past events were of particular importance to the Egyptians because they believed time and events had cyclical natures; they were firm believers in what is commonly meant by the modern phrase, "history repeats itself." Today this phrase is usually a metaphor while in ancient Egypt it was taken literally; to look into the past was equivalent to looking into the future; just as the sun-god rose into the heavens this morning, he will rise again tomorrow morning, and just as the earth and its

---

[a] Christianity gradually overtook much of Egypt so that by 313 CE, the emperor Constantine I (306-337) granted tolerance to the Egyptian Christians and gave impetus to the development of a formal Egyptian church that soon vied with that of Constantinople (see *Encyclopædia Britannica, Macropædia*, 1976, Vol. 6, p. 487).

inhabitants were created long ago, they will be created again (renewed) in the future. And Horus, the son of the sun-god who was born to be Pharaoh, the king of Egypt, lived and died to become one with Osiris, the ruler of the Netherworld while the new king became the next incarnation of Horus. Egypt was thus ruled by the same Horus, the son of the sun-god, even when the person of the Pharaoh changed from reign to reign. The cycles, of course, applied to political and military strategies and events whereby one pharaoh after another established and re-established Egypt's authority over its neighbors, over the Negro races to the south and the mix of Semitic groups to the north, especially the Levant. Annual military campaigns were thus taken to the South and North to conquer (and re-conquer) Egypt's enemies, establish new alliances or renew old ones, especially in the early years of the reign of a king.

Newly crowned kings often sought to outdo their predecessors by claiming increased power and new foreign territories for Egypt. As son of the sun-god, some kings even called upon the unlimited forces of nature to assist them; they threatened storms, earthquakes and plagues upon those who opposed them, conjuring up memories of past catastrophes as examples of what would happen to those who would resist. We can be sure that records of such events, from natural catastrophes to political and military campaigns, were maintained in the sacred House of Life, and formed an important part of the *Book of Thoth*. We may therefore assume that a ritual employing the opening and reading of the book containing details of great deeds of past kings would provide the basis of a wide range of actions a Pharaoh might take against Egypt's enemies. In the next chapter, *Call to Arms*, one such scenario will be explored. It draws on experiences of a previous king of Egypt (who was, as pointed out above, just another incarnation of Horus, the son of the sun-god) to launch a vast array of the horrors from past wars and natural catastrophes on all those who would be unfaithful to him and his god and on any who would resist his authority to rule.

Chapter 10. Call to Arms (Rev. 6.1-17)[464]

An Egyptian perspective on Rev. 6 enables a rather simplistic view of the events described in it; this is especially so when these events are viewed in relation to already established parallels found in the seven letters in Rev. 2-3. Recall that the seven letters can be interpreted as military dispatches to the leaders and people living in seven different areas, areas which may, from an Egyptian perspective, may be found in the Levant – but more likely, in the Nile Delta. Recipients of the dispatches were warned to change their ways: "I have not found your works perfect ... repent. If you will not awake [to my unfavorable judgment of your ways], I will come like a thief, and you will not know at what hour I will come upon you" (Rev. 3:2-3); "Repent then. If not, I will come to you soon and war against them with the sword." (Rev. 2:16); "and I will strike her children dead. And all the churches shall know that I am he who searches mind and heart, and I will give to each of you as your works deserve" (Rev 2:23).

Military conflicts are frequently mentioned in the Book of Revelation. Almost all of them describe the followers of God in great conflicts (Rev. 11:18; Rev. 12:7,11; Rev. 19:19). In Rev. 12:7, war is explicitly mentioned when the faithful fight against the forces of the evil dragon. In Rev. 12:17, we are told that the dragon made war "on those who keep the commandments of God," and in Rev. 19:19, "the beast and the kings of the earth with their armies gathered to make war against him who sits upon the horse and against his army." As with all wars, many die, a fact which conforms with Rev. 6:9-11 where we read about the souls of those who died in battle. Elsewhere, in Rev. 11:18, we read of those who fought in the battles when the "nations raged" and of a time "for rewarding thy servants ... for destroying the destroyers of the earth." And after the war spoken of in Rev. 12:7 where the enemy is "thrown down," those who died in the conflict receive special mention: "they have conquered him ... for they loved not their lives even unto death," the text declares. "Rejoice then, O heaven and you that dwell therein!" War plays an important part in the Book of Revelation and as in all wars, many die on both sides of a conflict. In Egyptian beliefs, this included those who died in wars in the celestial sphere and in the Netherworld.

War also plays an important part in the religious writings of ancient Egypt. For example, in the Egyptian texts, and especially in the 6th Division of the *Book of Gates*, we read about a conflict involving the followers of the sun-god who have symbols of truth (⸸) on their heads (Figure 30) and are described as "Those who have acted according to justice while on earth, who fight for their god, who he convoked to the place [called] the Gladness of Earth."[465] In the 1st Division of the *Book of Gates*, the same or a similar group of twelve is described as having worshiped Re upon earth and "enchanted Apopis. ... You are indeed those who adore (me) and repulse Apopis from me."[466] There is also a picture of twelve followers in the 5th Division of the *Book of Gates* bearing javelins to fight the evil serpent (Figure 36); the Egyptian text quotes them as saying, "Our javelins, O Re, are in the serpent Mamu! We spear the evil serpent [Apophis], O Re!" The text goes on to say that they "repulse Apopis in the sky while on their way to the Netherworld. They repulse Apopis from Re in the West."[467] And in the 9th Division of the *Amduat*, where twelve cobra-form followers of the sun-god are shown seated on clothing signs ( ) and spewing fire from their mouths, the text tells us that, "The flames of their mouths cause the overthrow of the enemies in the Netherworld."[468] Thus, the Egyptian literature is similar to the Book of Revelation in that it describes soldiers who fight for their god against the army of Apophis (= Revelation's Devil and Satan).

After Revelation's description of the throne scene (Rev. 1,4) and the letters admonishing the members of the seven churches and the declaration of war against rebellious factions within them (Rev. 2-3), we find a description of a ceremony in which a book of secret knowledge (Egypt's *Book of Thoth*) is opened (Rev. 5). Next, in Rev. 6, we find one of the better-known scenes in the Book of Revelation – the appearance of what is commonly referred to as the "four horsemen of the apocalypse." As discussed in Chapter 7, *The Great Multitude*, the number four when used symbolically in many Egyptian pictures and texts can represent a "multitude." Thus, from an Egyptian point of view, the four horsemen in Rev. 6 could represent a multitude of horsemen just as easily as it could simply represent four horsemen. Indeed, it will be shown in this chapter that the number four in the context of the horsemen can mean either four horsemen or a multitude – *or both*. Also, it will be shown that the main action described in Rev. 6 can be interpreted as a *call to arms*, i.e., a military draft, and a rousing battle cry to boost the courage of the draftees. To enhance this call to arms, the general tone of Rev. 6 emphasizes the coming retribution against the rebels.

Since these events follow the declaration of war (in Rev. 2-3) and the opening of the secret scroll in Rev. 5, we may assume that Rev. 6 describes different aspects of preparations for this war. The announcement of the four horsemen and their military mission in Rev. 6:1-8 is followed by a statement that many had already been killed in earlier battles and still more would be killed (Rev. 6:9-11) in battles to come. Finally, in a fashion reminiscent of modern-day "softening up" of enemy positions by massive bombing strikes against important strategic positions, the announcement is made that natural disasters will be launched against the enemy (Rev. 6:12-17). The following paragraphs will compare the events described in Rev. 6 with similar events recorded in both religious and secular writings of ancient Egypt.

The Four Horsemen (Rev. 6:1-8)

Each of the four horses and their riders in Rev. 6:1-8 are introduced with the thunderous call to "Come!" Then, one by one they are dispatched to conduct their appointed tasks. The first is to conquer (Rev. 6:2), the second to create civil war (Rev. 6:4), the third to secure the crops, presumably those belonging to the conquered (Rev.

6:5-6), and the fourth to kill or otherwise cause havoc among the inhabitants of the earth (Rev. 6:7-8). They ride horses, animals which in ancient times were used almost exclusively as instruments of war in the Middle East. The first two riders are armed, one with a bow and the other a sword – clear evidence of their mission. We may therefore reasonably assume, for the purposes of further analysis, that the calls for the four horsemen to "Come!" were *war cries* meant to energize captains and their troops prior to an important military campaign. The idea of many troops involved in this action is supported by the presence of *four* riders, possibly each rider representing one of four divisions of soldiers in the Egyptian army, or more specifically, each rider would be in charge of one of the army's four divisions.[a]

The colors of the four horses – white, red, black and grey – provide us with support, from an Egyptian perspective, for the idea that an entire army is represented by these four horsemen.

Colors of the Four Horses (6:1-8):- The colors of the four horses – white, red, black and grey – would have special significance to the ancient Egyptians in that they would remind them of the annual ritual of the driving of the calves, the mythological background of which is presented in Figure 49 from Egypt's 18th Dynasty. Wilkinson (1994) informs us that,

> The rite of driving the calves, which is represented in a number of New Kingdom temples ... shows the king driving four calves (specified as red [ ], black [ ], white [ ] and speckled [ ]) before the statue of a deity. The calves represent one of each kind of coloration naturally found in cattle and thus *signifying the totality or completeness of the action which they perform.*[469]

Figure 49. Illustration of the rite of driving the calves in which the king drives four calves which have the same colors as the four horses of Rev. 6:1-8. The colors are written in hieroglyphics in front of each of the calves.

Note that the colors of the first three calves, red, black and white, conform with those of the first three horses in Revelation. The *speckled* color of the fourth calf, however, requires a closer examination before the same can be said of it.

Gardiner (1927) tells us that the Egyptian word for "speckled" means something like "dappled" or "variegated."[470] Oxford (1991) defines "dapple" as "mark with spots or rounded patches or shade ... a dappled effect ... a dappled animal, esp. a horse."[471] And it defines "variegate" as "mark with irregular patches of different colors." Meanwhile,

---

[a] Hornung (1983, p. 220) says that "The four main divisions of the Egyptian army, with which Sethos I (1304-1290 BCE) and Ramesses II (1290-1244 BCE) conduct their campaigns in the Near East, are now named after these four gods." i.e., Amun, Re, Ptah, and Seth.

The Greek version of Revelation refers to the fourth horse as being *chloorós*, a word meaning green, greenish, yellowish-pale, or *dun-colored*."[472] Webster describes the word "dun" colored as it is used in relation to a horse as, "exhibiting reduced hair pigmentations *usu., accompanied by black points and a dorsal stripe so that a basically black coat becomes pale grayish*,' a bay become yellowish, a sorrel becomes pale and drab"[473] Note that it is the distinct, two-colored nature (pigmentations usu., accompanied by black points and a dorsal stripe) of the hair pigmentations which gives the horse a pale color. In this manner the two colors combine in one's eye and mind to create a single pale color when such a horse is seen from a distance. The same effect applies to calves so that when looking at the animal up close one would see a "variegated" color – and from a distance, a "pale" one. Thus, if Gardiner is correct, that the Egyptian word for "speckled" means something like "variegated," we may conclude that the dun-colored or ashen translation is a reasonable match for the Egyptian "speckled" color of the fourth calf – and the Greek equivalent of a dun- or pale-colored horse. With this proviso in mind, all four colors of the horses in Rev. 6:1-8 can be said to parallel those of the four calves in Egypt's ritual of the Driving of the Calves.

These four colors were of special significance and had deep symbolic meaning to the Egyptians, meanings which become clear on a close examination of the scene of the driving of the calves shown in Figure 49. This picture depicts the annual herding of cattle to their feeding grounds after the annual flood waters of the Nile recede and the banks of the river are turning green with fresh, succulent vegetation. Note that it is the king himself who is driving the cattle. While action depicted here is clearly symbolic and usually relates to an annual agricultural ritual, this same picture and its imagery had religious overtones and evoked a long-held pride in the belief of the Egyptians that they were special creations of their sun-god. While the Egyptians believed themselves to have been created as "Men" from the tears of Re, they also considered themselves to be the "cattle" of Re. The last chapter from the *Book of Gates* is particularly clear on this point:

> You are happy, *cattle of Re*' who are in the Netherworld, Egypt, and the red country: You are happy, *cattle of Re*,' who were created from the Great One who is in heaven. Let there be breath for your nostrils and let your bandages be loosened. For you are the tears of my Glorious Eye in your name of Men.[474]

Other people were called names consistent with their race, national identity, ethnic grouping. This claim of the sun-god's special loyalty to Egyptians provides us a conceptual stepping-stone to equate the cattle in Figure 49 with the Egyptian people themselves. In this way, the figure can be understood as a metaphor which not only shows the king leading the cattle to provide food for his people but also shows him offering his protective care when leading them in battle. The similarity between the colors of the four calves, which represent the Egyptians themselves, and those of the four horsemen in Revelation certainly conforms with this idea. It also conforms with the idea that the four riders in Rev. 6:1-8 are leaders of Egypt's four-division army.

War Cries (Rev. 6:1-8)

It is also likely that the descriptive introductions of the four riders in this passage represent four war cries. A quick look at the text certainly conforms with this idea, especially if they relate to an army with four divisions, each with its own mounted leader. In this scenario, the dramatic appearances of the four riders precede battle cries of each of the four divisions. It behooves us, therefore, to explore in greater depth the imagery contained in Rev. 6:1-8 for evidence of similar war cries in the annals of Egyptian military exploits.

We will begin by clearly defining the nature of the cries in Revelation and in particular, the command which is common to each – "Come!" – and include an examination of the instructions to take certain action against those who live on earth. The specific commands to be compared with Egyptian sources are as follows:

> 1. *"Come!"* And I saw, and behold, a *white horse*, and its rider had a bow; and a crown was given to him, and he went out *conquering and to conquer*. (Rev. 6:1-2)

> 2. *"Come!"* And out came another *horse, bright red*; its rider was *permitted to take peace from the earth, so that men should slay one another*; and he was given a great sword. (Rev. 6:3-4)

> 3. *"Come!"* And I saw, and behold, a *black horse*, and its rider had a balance in his hand; and I heard what seemed to be a voice in the midst of the four living creatures saying, *"A quart of wheat for a denarius, and three quarts of barley for a denarius; but do not harm oil and wine!"* (Rev. 6:5-6)

> 4. *"Come!"* And I saw, and behold, a *pale horse*, and its rider's name was Death, and Hades followed him; and they were given power over a fourth of the earth, *to kill with sword and with famine and with pestilence and by wild beasts* of the earth. (Rev. 6:7-8)

Similarities to these cries are found in what is known today as the *Victory Hymn of Thutmosis III*, a hymn found on a black granite tablet in a chamber northwest of the main sanctuary room of the great temple in Karnak.[475] This hymn consists of twenty-five lines of hieroglyphic text and was so well known and respected in ancient Egypt that several kings extracted portions of it for their own. The text gives a glowing overview of Thutmosis' military campaigns into the Levant in the north, Libya in the west, and Nubia in the south; it even includes a reference to threats against people living in Crete and Cyprus. Ten different cries are recorded in the hymn. The first four are presented here to give an idea of their form and variation in content. It is the sun-god who is speaking.

1. ^{13}*I [Amon-Re] have come,*' causing thee [Thutmosis III] to smite the princes of Zahi;
   I have hurled them beneath thy feet among their highlands.
   I have caused them to see thy majesty as lord of radiance,
   So that thou has shone in their faces like my image.[a]

2. ^{14}*I have come,*' causing thee to smite the Asiatics,
   Thou hast made captive the heads of the Asiatics of Retenu.
   I have caused them to see thy majesty equipped with thy adornment,
   When thou takest the weapons of war in the chariot.

3. ^{15}*I have come,*' causing thee to smite the eastern land,
   Thou hast trampled those who are in the districts of God's-Land.
   I have caused them to see thy majesty like a circling star,
   When it scatters its flame in fire, and gives forth its dew.

4. ^{16}*I have come,*' causing thee to smite the western land,
   Keftyew [Crete] and Cyprus are in terror.
   I have caused them to see thy majesty as a young bull,
   Firm of heart, ready-horned, irresistible.[476]

In each, cry, Amen-Re announces that he has "Come," a proclamation very similar to the introduction to each of the four horsemen presented in Revelation. Also, like Revelation, the king is then told ("causing thee to ...") to wage war against his enemies and to conquer them. These similarities are, of course, related more to structure than to parallel passages so it is not possible to identify specific parallels between the four war cries in Revelation and the first four of ten cries found in the Egyptian hymn. It is possible, however, to show that most of the elements in Revelation's text parallel elements found in this famous hymn. Each of these elements will be dealt with separately.

Conquerors (Rev. 6:2):- The rider of the first horse "had a bow; and a crown was given to him, and he went out conquering and to conquer" (Rev. 6:2). The presence of the crown suggests this rider is a king while his bow suggests he going to war. This description conforms with the fact that the kings of all ancient Middle Eastern countries traditionally led their armies in a war cry from high on the back of a horse as he led them into battle. This, of course, also conforms with the main theme of the hymn to Thutmosis III which involves the king's military campaigns into the Levant and which abounds with general and specific references to conquering the foe. Suffice it to highlight a few of them here.

The general introduction in the hymn elaborates on Amon-Re's assistance to Thutmosis III to conquer his foes during his campaigns:

---

[a] Super-scripted numbers at the start of each Egyptian war cry (and also below in quotations from the hymn) indicate column numbers in the original hieroglyphic texts (from Breasted, 1962).

> [1]I [Amon-Re] shine for love of thee,
> My heart is [2]glad at thy beautiful comings into my temple;
> ...
> [3]I have worked a marvel for thee;
> *I have given to thee might and victory against all countries,*
> I have set thy fame (even) the fear of thee in all lands.
> Thy terror as far as the [4]four pillars of heaven;
> I have magnified the dread of thee in all bodies,
> I have put the roaring of thy majesty among the Nine Bows [the enemies of Egypt].
> The chiefs of all countries are gathered in thy grasp,
> [5]I myself have stretched out my two hands,
>
> I have bound them for thee.
> I have bound the Nubian Troglodytes by tens of thousands and thousands,
> The Northerners by hundreds of thousands as captives.
> [6]I have felled thine enemies beneath thy sandals,
> Thou hast smitten the hordes of rebels according as I commanded thee.
> The earth in its length and breath, Westerners and Easterners are subject to thee,
> [7]Thou tramplest all countries, thy heart glad.[477]

Further along the text reads,

> [14]Thou has made captive the heads of the Asiatices of Retenu.
>   When *thou takest the weapons of war* in the chariot.
> [19]The isles of the Utentyew are (subject) to the might of thy prowess.
> [20]I have come, causing them to smite the utmost ends of the lands,
>   The circuit of the Great Circle (Okeanos) is inclosed in my grasp.

Note that the reference to taking "weapons of war in the chariot" in line 14 parallels the first horseman (a king as discussed above) in Rev. 6:2 who wielded a bow, a weapon of war, as he "went out conquering and to conquer." Elsewhere, in *The Annals of Thutmosis III*, and in a purely historical vein, we read of Thutmosis' intent to conquer his enemies as he left Egypt on his first Asian military campaign:

> {Year 23} first month of the third season (ninth month), on the fifth day; departure from this place in might, – – in power, and in triumph, to overthrow that wretched foe, to extend the boundaries of Egypt, according as his father, Amon-Re, commanded – – that he seize.[478]

It is clear from the above parallels that, not only does the introduction to the four battle cries in Rev. 6:1-8 ("Come!") parallels similar to the introductions used in the Victory Hymn of Thutmosis III but the military intent of Revelation's first horseman (to conquer) parallels that of the theme of the hymn.

Removal of Peace (Rev. 6:4):- The second horseman "was given a great sword" (Rev. 6:4), a continuation of the military theme set by the first rider. It is therefore not surprising that his role is to "take peace from the earth." What is unusual, however, is the manner in which this peace is to be removed: we are told that "men should slay one another." This suggests action in the form of the creation of internal strife among the enemy rather than by direct military action. It is in his *Annals* that we find a direct reference to rebels fighting against one another – a conflict with a form remarkably similar to that described in Rev. 6:4 which says that "men should slay one another." The parallel text in the *Annals* tells us of events during Thutmosis' first Campaign:

> Now, (at) that period *{the Asiatics had fallen into} disagreement, each man {fighting} against {his neighbor}'* ——. Now it happened {that the tribes} —— the people, who were there in the city of Sharuhen; behold, from Yeraza to the marshes of the earth, (they) had begun to revolt against his majesty."[a,479]

Rebellion, either within one nation or among several united nations is a form of internal strife which conforms with Revelation's scenario. Interestingly, this approach is similar to the international strife outlined in both the *Victory Hymn of Thutmosis III* and the *Annals of Thutmosis III*. In Thutmosis' *Victory Hymn* we read that at least part of his military campaign was focused on nations who rebelled against his authority: "[6]Thou hast smitten the hordes of rebels according as I commanded thee," the hymn says of the king. And "[11]There is no rebel of thine as far as the circuit of heaven."

Spoils of War (Rev. 6:5-6):- In the absence of a reasonable context, Rev. 6:5-6 is somewhat difficult to understand. The third rider is described as having a balance in his hand and is introduced with the enigmatic statement, "A quart of wheat for a denarius, and three quarts of barley for a denarius; but do not harm oil and wine!" It seems that the balance is mentioned in reference to payment (denarius) for wheat and barley. But what could this have to do with a war cry? And how might it relate to the command not to harm oil and wine? The answers to these questions are straightforward when considered in the context of a call to arms and war cries, and especially in the context of Thutmosis' military campaigns as outlined in his *Annals*.

After the surrender of the opposing forces at Megiddo the Egyptians took possession of, not only the golden chariots, bronze armor, bows, wooden poles wrought with silver, household goods, artifacts of gold and silver and costly wood, clothing, and many prisoners and slaves, but also of the abundant natural resources and crops in the area.[480] Thutmosis and other Egyptian kings almost always claimed as tribute a portion of the crops of the lands they conquered. Crops not destroyed in

---

[a] The background to this event is interesting. Unchecked by the pacifist policies of Queen Hatshepsut (Thutmosis III's, aunt, co-regent and stepmother), a dangerous coalition of native princes in Syria had rebelled against Egypt's authority and rallied around the prince of the city of Qadesh and sided with the rising power of the Mitanni east of the Euphrates. By the time Thutmosis III came to the throne, all of Syria and a large part of Palestine had rebelled and turned away from Egypt. The combined forces of the rebels were on the move, threatening the last Egyptian bases on Asiatic soil (Hornung, E., 1999, p. 88). The relative peace and stability in the Levant had thus disintegrated to the point that there was infighting among the people, just as described in Rev. 6:4. It was against this backdrop that Thutmosis moved into Palestine in 1457 BCE and attacked the coalition which had prepared for battle near Megiddo. The period of relative peace brought about by Hatshepsut's pacifist policies had come to an end.

10. Call to Arms

battle were harvested and divided among the troops as pay while the remainder was claimed by the king and brought back to Egypt for distribution among all his people. The olives and grapes fell into a different category because these crops had to be processed into oil and wine before being transported to Egypt. Details of these activities are provided in the *Annals*.[a]

> ... the cultivable land was divided into fields, which the inspectors of the royal house ... calculated, in order to reap their harvest. Statement of the harvest which was brought to his majesty from the fields of Megiddo: 208,200(+x) fourfold heket [a measure] of grain, besides that which was cut as forage by the army of his majesty.[481]

This statement has several elements in common with Rev. 6:5-6, the most pertinent of which is the reference to quantifying the amount of grain harvested. Thutmosis III's inspectors measured the grain and divided it up between the royal coffers and the soldiers.[b] The scene parallels that of the rider in Rev. 6:5-6 who holds a balance (a universal symbol of measurement or the act of measuring) in his hand while a voice calls out to say how much grain is to be paid for services rendered. Egyptian soldiers were not normally paid in coin as might be inferred from Rev. 6:6 but rather in grain (note the last sentence of the above quotation, "grain ... which was cut as forage by the army"). In this sense, it may be significant that the Egyptian word for "balance" is iwsw^{482} while that for "gruel," a meal made with grain, is the rather similar word, $\mathit{iwšš}$.[483] Such a phonetic relationship between a balance and grain would have linked the two in the mind of the Egyptians. Meanwhile, different translators of the Book of Revelation assign different values to the denarius (RSV) referred to in Revelation, including the penny (KJV), shilling (ASV), or even "a day's wages" (NIV), the latter being close to the meaning one might place on its use Rev. 6:6 where we can equate an allowance of grain to a day's wages for the soldiers in Thutmosis' army.

In stark contrast to the reference to wheat and barley, Rev. 6:6 also speaks of an instruction: "Do not harm oil and wine!" This is exactly as one might expect among instructions to a conquering army. It would be folly to remove or destroy such valuable resources[c] before they were processed into olive oil and wine in just the right season and time using processes involving local labor and specialized regional techniques;

---

[a] The harvest of the fields at Megiddo is also discussed in detail in Chapter 19, *Reaping the Harvest*.

[b] Breasted's (1962) translation of the Annals of Thutmosis III indicate he harvested of crops of the enemy during his 1st (§437 p. 189 and §434 p. 186), 5th (§461, p. 196), 6th (§465, p. 198), 7th (§475 p. 201 and §473 p. 200), 9th (§494 p. 207), 13th (§510 p. 210 and §514 p. 211), 14th (§519 p. 212), and 17th (§530 p. 215 and §535 p. 216) campaigns.

[c] There are also ample records of the removal of trees from enemy territory by the armies of Thutmosis III and wood from many of these was brought back to Egypt. Breasted's (1962) translation of the Annals of Thutmosis III record the cutting down of trees in his 1st (§433 p. 185), 5th (§461, p. 196 and §465 p. 198,), 7th (§471 p.199), and 9th (§492 p. 206) campaigns.

to destroy olive groves and vineyards would be tantamount to destroying the flow of future tributes of oil and wine into Egypt for many years to come. Grains, such as barley which were not destroyed in battle could, however, be harvested when ripe and either eaten or transported directly to Egypt.

Thutmosis' army was therefore not permitted to destroy the olive trees and vineyards and there are many references in the *Annals* to Thutmosis receiving tribute of oil and wine,[a] the number itself illustrating their importance to Egypt. This interpretation of the command not to harm the oil and wine in Rev. 6:6 is clearly in keeping with the militaristic interpretation of the scene set by the battle cries in Rev. 6:1-8, while at the same time demonstrates a parallel between this passage and texts documenting the military campaigns of Thutmosis III – campaigns which were almost certainly duplications of campaigns by earlier – and later – Egyptian kings who for centuries asserted their dominance in the Levant.

Death by Sword, Pestilence & Beasts (Rev. 6:7-8):- Ancient practices in war are especially evident in Rev. 6:7-8 with the fourth horse and its sword-carrying rider being preeminent. The second war cry of Thutmosis III (see above) refers to weapons which the king carries in his chariot: "¹⁴I [Amen-Re] have caused them to see thy majesty equipped with thy adornment [uniform and armor], when thou takest the weapons of war in the chariot." Death to the enemy is the main opening theme of each of Thutmosis' war cries; each begins with the refrain, "I have come, causing thee to smite the [enemy] ..." After battles ended, the conquered areas immediately entered the next phase typical of so many wars – that of subsequent death and suffering which was at least as terrible as that from the sword. Famine followed crop losses followed by disease and pestilence from bacteria, parasites and rodents because of the inevitable destruction of buildings and the degradation of personal hygiene and social institutions. While there are no specific references to "famine and pestilence" in Thutmosis III's *Victory Hymn* or his *Annals* as there is in Revelation, there can be no doubt that these afflictions followed his campaigns when crops were harvested as the army marched through the land.

The reference in Rev. 6:8 to death by "wild beasts of the earth" is somewhat more difficult to rationalize from the point of view of military action. It is possible, of course, that wild animals did in fact play a role after the destruction of homes in remote villages and farms which normally protected the residents from such animals. But this is not necessarily the only possible parallel – references to wild beasts are clearly mentioned in the context of the war cries in Thutmosis' *Victory Hymn*. Five of the ten battle cries claim that Amon-Re caused the enemy to see Thutmosis III and his army as wild animals rampaging across the landscape spreading fear and death. The text says:

> ²¹I have caused them to *see thy majesty as a southern jackal*,' steady of running, stealthy-going, who roves the Two Lands.

---

[a] Breasted's (1962) translation of the *Annals of Thutmosis III* indicate Thutmosis recieved tribute of oil and wine from his enemies during his 1st (§434 p. 186 §447, p. 191), 5th (§461, p. 196 and §462, 197), 7th (§472 p. 200), 8th (§482 p. 203), 9th (§491 p. 206), 10th (§501 p. 208), 13th (§509 p. 210 and §510 p. 210), and 14th (§518 p. 211 and §519 p. 212), campaigns.

¹⁶I have caused them to see thy majesty as a *young bull*,· firm of heart, ready-horned, irresistible.

¹⁷I have caused them to *see thy majesty as a crocodile*,· Lord of fear in the water, unapproachable.

²⁰I have caused them to *see thy majesty as a lord of the wing*· [a falcon?], who seizeth upon that which he seeth, as much as he desires.

¹⁹I have caused them to *see thy majesty as a fierce-eyed lion*,· thou makest them corpses in their valleys.

...

There is an interesting difference between the four war cries of Rev. 6:1-8 and their Egyptian counterparts: Rev. 6 begins each cry with the expression "Come!" whereas the Egyptian text starts with "I have come." Remarkably, while these two parallel each other, they also compliment one another in a manner suggesting they could be different facets of the same event. Indeed, when we combine the cry from Rev. 6:1-2 with that from Thutmosis' hymn, we can envisage a ceremony in which Revelation's war cry, "Come!" is answered by an Egyptian response "I have come." A ceremony incorporating facets from both Revelation and the hymn of Thutmosis is easily imagined to sound something like the following:

A loud call to "Come!" is given.

Rev. 6:1 — "I saw when the Lamb opened one of the seven seals, and I heard ... as with a voice of thunder, *"Come!"*"

A rider on horseback appears.

Amun-Re — "*I have come.*"

Rev. 6:2a — "And I saw, and behold, a white horse, and its rider had a bow."

The rider is crowned.

Rev. 6:2b — "And a crown was given to him."

Amun-Re — "I have caused them to see thy majesty equipped with thy adornment [crown]. ... smite the Asiatics. ... thou takest the weapons of war in the chariot."

The horse and rider leave.

Rev. 6:2c — "and he went out conquering and to conquer."

Amun-Re — "Thou hast made captive the heads of the Asiatics of Retenu."

This arrangement of the two texts clearly demonstrates their parallel nature.

War in the *Amduat* (Rev. 6:2-11)

We now switch to a comparison of the same text in Revelation with that of the *Amduat*. It should be noted at the outset that there are no explicit references to four horses and heir riders in any part of the *Amduat*. Nevertheless, there are descriptions of acts of war which parallel those associated with the four horsemen of Revelation. Also, bear in mind that the enemies of the sun-god were considered to be enemies of Egypt and references in the *Amduat* to acts of war against the enemies of the sun-god, while being set against the background of the Egyptian Netherworld, were very likely based on actual events on earth. Texts describe punishment of large numbers of the sun-god's enemies while pictures typically illustrate captives being decapitated or otherwise punished before the throne of Osiris. In the following paragraphs, attention will focus on those scenes in the *Amduat* which most closely parallel those in Rev. 6:2-11.

Casualties of War (Rev. 6:2-8):- There are two separate groups of four in the middle register of the 7th Division. These are shown in Figure 50 as four female deities holding swords and standing behind the slain body of Apophis, and behind them, four coffers, each surmounted by a sword and two bodiless heads (most likely "four" when coffers are viewed in three dimensions). The text tells us that the "goddesses chastize Apopis in the Netherworld, they repulse the enemies of Re. They are like this, they carry their knives [swords] and they chastise Apopis in the Netherworld, every day."[484] It is interesting to note that the names of three of these goddesses ("The Chastiser," "The Destroyer" and "She who cuts") conform well with the orders given to the four horsemen in Revelation (to remove peace, kill with the sword and conquer) – all three are associated with acts of war. The name of the fourth goddess, "She who unites," can also be interpreted in the context of war in the sense that the followers of the sun-god conquer the enemy, thereby uniting them under Re, or, in the case of an earthly war, under the king of Egypt. The functions of all four deities as a group can thus be seen to parallel those of the horsemen described in Rev. 6:2-8. Meanwhile, the four coffers with their swords and heads may be seen to represent the faithful followers of the sun-god (in the four army divisions) who gave their lives (especially by beheading) during the conflict.

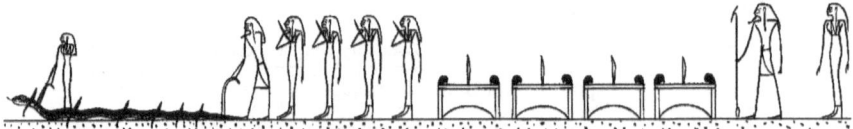

Figure 50. Casualties of the war against Apophis and his followers depicted in the middle register of the 7th Division of the *Amduat*. The many swords driven into the serpentine body of Apophis represent his followers who were killed in action and the four coffers with swords and heads represent the members of the four divisions of the sun-god's soldiers killed in action. (AM7.2.4-10)

In the register immediately above the four goddesses is a scene showing the fate of Apophis' followers who had been captured in battle (Figure 51). They are bound, presented to Osiris who sits on his throne, and decapitated just as the sun-god's soldiers were by Apophis' army. As with Rev. 6:4 and Rev. 6:8, a sword is mentioned in the text along with certain death before Osiris. The text describes the scene:

> Thy enemies are fallen beneath thy feet, thou hast prevailed over those who acted against thee. The flame of this serpent, Life of Forms, is directed against them, he burns them, he rages with his knife among them, they are his portion, they are his roast. Flesh is disposed of every day ... . You who acted wickedly against Osiris, who rebelled against He at the Head of the Netherworld, may your arms be chained, your ropes fastened, may your souls be annihilated, your shadows confined! The Chastiser chastises you with his knife, you will never escape from his restraint. (AM7.1.1-7)[485]

Notice that the enemies mentioned here are said to have acted wickedly against Osiris and rebelled against him. The reference in this text to "The Chastiser," a horned male in Figure 51, links this scene with one of the four goddesses in Figure 50 who is also called "The Chastiser," in Figure 50. Together, these figures emphasize death by the sword, just as in Rev. 6:4-8.

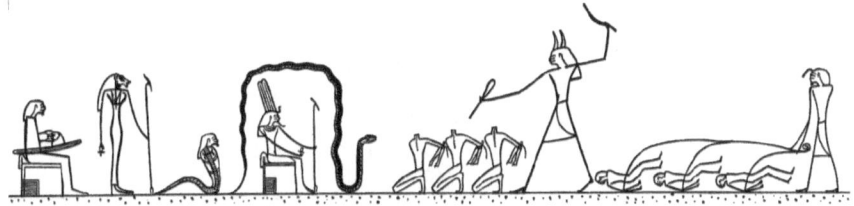

Figure 51. Punishment of the captives of war before the throne of Osiris in the upper register of the 7th Division of the *Amduat*. Many (3) captives are shown bound and then decapitated before Osiris. (AM7.1.1-7)

Souls of Those Slain (Rev. 6:9-11):- After the introduction to the four horsemen, the scene in Revelation suddenly shifts from war cries *per se* to the cries from those who had already died in battle "for the witness they had borne" (Rev. 6:9) and who now call for revenge against their slayers (Rev. 6:10). Such a cry could not have come from a more persuasive source, the very souls of the slain, souls who do not want to wait any longer for revenge. "O Sovereign Lord, holy and true," they cry, "how long before thou wilt judge and avenge our blood on those who dwell upon the earth?" Their cries are answered with gifts of white clothing and a promise; they are "told to rest a little longer" (Rev. 6:11) before their wishes are met.

Several rather unusual images are rendered in Rev. 6:9-11 which help identify its parallel in the 8th Division of the *Amduat*. These are the cries of the souls of those slain, the gifts of white robes, and the instructions for the dead to wait a while. Indeed, this parallel scene in the *Amduat* is of such great importance at this point in the *Amduat* that an entire division is devoted to it.

We begin our comparison with a reference to the slain followers of the sun-god. As with all the other divisions of the *Amduat*, the sun-god is depicted in the central register as he passes through the Netherworld in his barque (Figure 52). In front of the

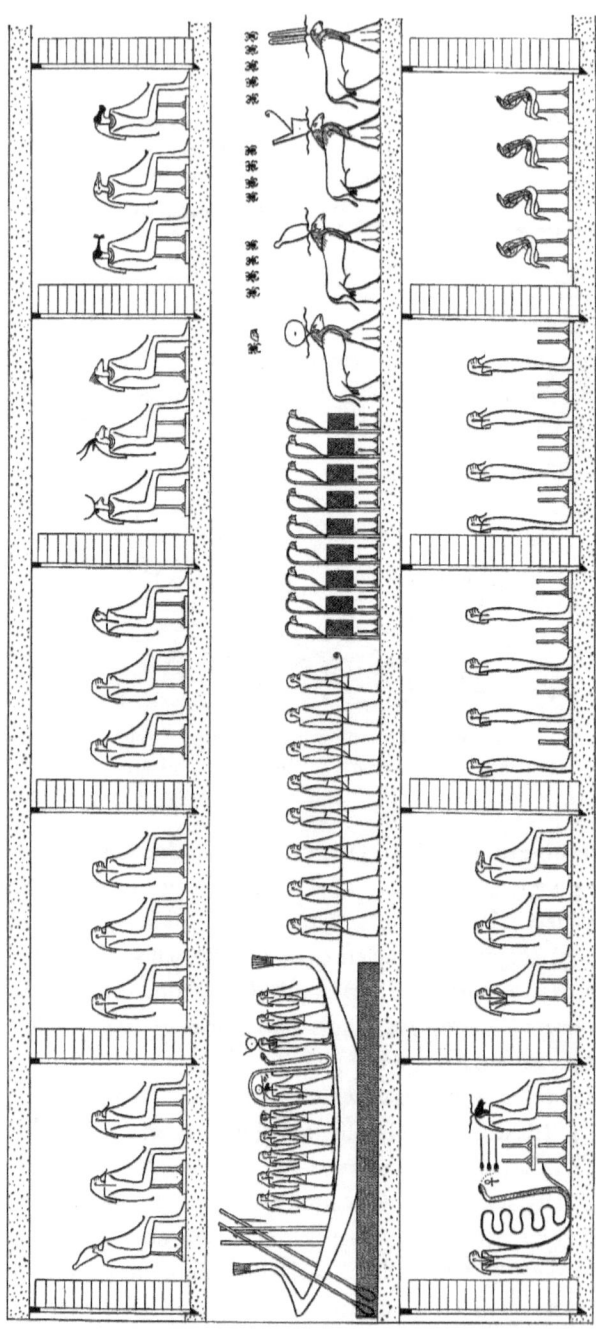

Figure 52. The 8ᵗʰ Division of the Amduat which contains scenes consistent with those described in Rev. 6:9-11.

barque and its eight towers are symbols, representing the souls of nine "followers" (𝍖 in Figure 53). The text clearly identifies them as soldiers for we are told that "What they do is to put to the sword the enemies of Re near this holy city which they conquer." Gardiner (1927) suggests that the rectangular package in the 𝍖 symbol "depicts the equipment of an early chieftain's attendant," but it may also be "an instrument for the execution of criminals."[486] Note, however, the presence of the head and sword (🜛🗡) attached near the top of the crook in these symbols, in the context of Rev. 6:9, they indicate that these followers represent the sun-god's soldiers slain by beheading. Direct evidence for this interpretation is the textual promise of resurrection and reunion with their heads: "When this Great God calls to them, what is in them becomes alive, and the heads come out of their knives when the god calls them by their names."[487] Also, and of particular significance to Rev. 6:11, the pictures and text indicate that they receive the coveted gift of the new clothing of the gods (⚏): "They are like this on the road by which this god is being towed, their clothing is before them in the forms of those of the god himself." This central scene thus conforms with the idea of slain followers of God expressed in Rev. 6:9-11.

Figure 53. Souls of the beheaded (🜛🗡) followers (𝍖) of the sun-god wear the gift of clothing (⚏) as in Rev. 6:9-11. The four crowned rams with gifts of clothing suggest those soldiers who died on earth for their god and king. (AM8.2.6-10)

Rev. 6:10 suggests that the souls which cry out to their "Sovereign Lord" are those of soldiers who died in battle on earth. They cry, "how long before thou wilt judge and avenge our blood on those who dwell upon the earth?" This reference to the earth conforms with the presence of the four crowned rams on the right half of Figure 53. The four rams are symbolic of the ancient earth-god, Tatenen,[488] suggesting the nine souls belong to soldiers who once fought and died on earth. Furthermore, the crowns on the heads of the first and last rams represent the sun-god (Amen and Re) while those of the two central rams bear the crowns of Upper and Lower Egypt; this can be interpreted to mean that the soldiers fought for both the sun-god and the king of both Upper and Lower Egypt, the son of the sun-god, while on earth (*cf.* Tatenen). And the gifts of new clothing underneath each ram confirm that these rewards are for deeds done while on earth.

But the parallels between this division and with the Revelation account do not end here. Above and below the followers of the sun-god shown in Figure 53 is a representation of a large tomb complex, a place called the "Sarcophagi of his Gods."[489] This tomb is divided into chambers each containing the bodies of deities. The vestibule and examples of two of the tomb's nine burial chambers are shown in

Figure 54. The vestibule of the tomb is shown at the far left of the figure and is guarded by the powerful "Enveloper of the Earth" serpent, a "girl," and a seated, ram-headed overseer called "Lord of the Subjects." The material contents of the vestibule indicate that this complex of tombs contains the souls of soldiers, presumably those slain in battle. A multitude (4) of gifts of clothing (⊥⊥⊥⊥) are present in this chamber as well as many (3) arrows (←←←) which are no longer needed for their soldierly duties to their god and king. The text in the vestibule emphasizes their gifts of clothing: "They are like this upon their clothing in the hidden forms of Horus, the Heir of Osiris."[490] Each of the nine burial chambers contains three or four (= many or multitudes of) occupants the names of some of which refer to their gods[a] while others, especially those in the lower register bear names reminiscent of war heroes.[b] The names of some chamber doors also reveal the warrior-like character of the occupants, each being prefaced by the phrase, "Knife [sword] of ... [the soldier's name]."[c] Also, some of the chambers themselves bear names suggesting warfare.[d] This array of names confirms that the occupants of this tomb were soldiers who died in battle, like the souls in Rev. 6:10 who cried out for revenge.

Figure 54. The tomb vestibule (with 3 protective gods and weapons of war) and two of nine chambers showing the mummies and souls of dead soldiers with gifts of new clothing (⊥). This part of the *Amduat* parallels the scene described in Rev. 6:9-10. (AM8.3.1-6)

In Rev. 6:9-10 we are told that the *"souls"* of the dead *"cried out with a loud voice, 'O Sovereign Lord ...'"* while Rev. 6:11 tells us that they are told to wait "until the number of their fellow servants and their brethren should be complete, who were to be killed as they themselves had been." The many occupants of the tomb in the 8th Division of the *Amduat* also cry out to their god; the text tells us "there are heard

---

[a] For example, in the upper register: "The Form of Osiris," "The Form of Isis," and "The Form of Horus."

[b] For example, "The Slaughter," "Hacking of the Earth," "The Roaring One," "The Coiled One," "The Flame," and "The Quick One."

[c] For example, "Knife of the One who repulses his enemies, ... Knife of Extinguisher of Souls, ... of the One who repulses his enemies ... of one whose forms are powerful," and "... Sharp of Flame."

[d] For example, "Annihilation of the Evildoers" or names which can be related to death on the battle field, such as "Grave of the Gods," "The Mourner" and "Rest of her Lord."

voices ... . when *their souls cry out to Re*·."[491] The text does not tell us what they are crying out for but it describes the sound of their cries as being like of a multitude of men, and animals, and nature itself, all crying out at the same time. The text for the second chamber in the upper register tells us the mood of their cries; its says that the voices of those in this cavern sound "*like (the voices) of men who lament when their souls cry out to Re.*"[492] The text thus provides us with the overall tone or significance of the cries of the multitudes of souls represented in this division. Their cries are laments to their god, just as the cries of the souls in Rev. 6:10 are laments to their Sovereign Lord.

In the Egyptian text, the potent lament of the multitudes of souls in this division all crying out at the same time sounds like the cries of thousands of thousands of different kinds of animals in the midst of the tumult of a rain storm and the collapsing of river banks. Piankoff (1954) emphasizes that the Egyptian text describes their cries are like those of the hum of bees, the voices of men who lament, the lowing of mating bulls, the sound of rain the fury of which is great, male cats, the roar of the living, the sound of a bank falling into the flood, the cry of a divine hawk, and a nest full of birds.[493] The basic nature of the cries of the souls of warriors who died in the service of the sun-god are consistent with the pleas of the souls of the slain in Rev. 6:10 who cry out, "how long before thou wilt judge and avenge our blood on those who dwell upon the earth?" Unfortunately, the text does not explicitly tell us why they are crying out to their god and we can only speculate on what their cries might mean and that they conform with Revelation's text. We do know, however, that as in Rev. 6:10, they are the souls of slain followers of their god to whom they make a mournful lament, and in the end, are each given gifts of clothing (𓊾) as in Rev. 6:11. The juxtapositions of these two similar elements in both sources support the suggestion of a parallel between the two sources.

The Wrath of the Lamb (Rev. 6:12-17)

Next, the text of Revelation abruptly switches from traditional war cries and promises of rewards after death in Rev. 6:1-11 to a description of a natural catastrophe of cosmic proportions. Rev 6:12-14 tells us "there was a great earthquake; and the sun became black as sackcloth, the full moon became like blood, and the stars of the sky fell ... the sky vanished ... and every mountain and island was removed from its place. Then ... everyone ... hid in the caves and among the rocks of the mountains." To the modern reader, this switch might seem out of place, having nothing whatsoever to do with preparations for war. From an Egyptian perspective, however, it would be entirely in keeping with traditional beliefs about their king, the earthly manifestation of the god Horus, the Son of Re the sun-god. Egyptians believed their king had the power and authority to call upon the forces of nature to lash out against his enemies. And he sometimes did just that.

We have already noted parallels between the military feats in the writings of Thutmosis III and those of parts of Rev. 6:1-11. We will now explore the similarities between some of the natural catastrophes mentioned in Rev. 6:12-17 and the Victory Hymn of Thutmosis III. We begin near the start of the hymn.

> [8]I have decreed for thee that *they hear thy roarings and enter into caves;*
> I have *deprived their nostrils of the breath of life.*
> [9]I have set the terrors of thy majesty in their hearts,
> My serpent-diadem upon thy brow, it [its fire] consumes them,
> It makes captive of the hair the Kode-folk,
> [10]*It devours those who are in their marshes* with its flame.
> Cut down are the heads of the Asiatics, *there is not a remnant of them;*
> *Fallen are the children of the mighty ones.*
> [11]I have caused thy victories to circulate among all lands,
> My serpent-diadem gives light to thy dominion.
> *There is no rebel of thine as far as the circuit of heaven.*
> They come, bearing tribute on their backs,
> [12]Bowing down to thy majesty according to my command.
> *I have made powerless the invaders* who came before thee;
> *Their hearts burned, their limbs trembling.* [494]

This portion of the hymn begins with a loud noise ("[8]thy roarings") and the seeking of refuge in caves (they "[8]enter into caves"); together, they are consistent with people seeking refuge in caves in Rev. 6:15 where we are told that people "hid in the caves and among the rocks of the mountains." Also, they find it difficult or impossible to breath ([8] "I have deprived their nostrils of the breath of life," a phenomenon consistent with large amounts of suffocating dust or some other material in the air which could cause the sun and moon to darken as we read in Rev. 6:12, "the sun became black as sackcloth, the full moon became like blood." The Egyptian text says that workers in the fields die along with their overlords, "[10]It devours those who are in their marshes" and "[10]Fallen are the children of the mighty ones," an event conforming with that described in Rev. 6:15 where we read that "the kings of the earth and the great men and the generals and the rich and the strong, and every one, slave and free, hid in the caves." The Egyptian text says that "[10]there is not a remnant of them," and later goes on to say that "[11]There is no rebel of thine as far as the circuit of heaven" and "[12]I have made powerless the invaders ... Their hearts burned, their limbs trembling." These statements conform with Rev. 6:17 which says that "none can stand against it." These are all unmistakable parallels between this part of the Book of Revelation and the opening lines of the Victory Hymn of Thutmosis III.

The events outlined in Rev. 6:12-17 are quite remarkable in that they describe a series of events one might expect downwind of a volcanic eruption. Major volcanic eruptions are usually preceded by violent earthquakes (as in Rev. 6:12). During the eruption large plumes of smoke and ash rise into the atmosphere blocking much of the light of the sun by day and the moon and stars by night. The sun and the moon can turn red in the daytime sky. And if an eruption is close enough, and especially if it is on an island, high mountains can slide into the sea, reshaping the islands or causing them to disappear altogether (as in Rev. 6:14). These and other events are described in detail in Chapter 13, *Catastrophes* and Chapter 14, *From Catastrophe to Myth*, which discuss events described Rev. 8 and Rev. 9 and suggest how those mentioned in Rev. 6 and elsewhere relate to other natural catastrophes described in the Book of Revelation.

Reasons why an Egyptian king might call upon powerful forces to help fight a war were as obvious centuries ago as they are today. These days, commanding officers call upon air strikes to destroy an enemy's supply lines, gun emplacements, troop concentrations and overall army infrastructure prior to sending ground troops into enemy-held territory; the main purpose of this action is to both reduce the enemy's ability to defend itself and to destroy their morale. There is evidence that the Egyptians had records of at least one great ancient disaster involving a volcanic eruption so we know they were well aware of the power of such an event – and they believed the king at the time of the eruption had the power to control it. This will be discussed in detail in Chapter 13, *Catastrophes*. For the time being, suffice it to say that, if past Egyptian kings could call upon the great power of Re to unleash devastating forces of nature against the enemy, any other Egyptian king should be able to do the same. Such action would greatly boost the morale and confidence of the troops prior to leaving Egypt to go to war.

Discussion

In this chapter we have demonstrated that the scene involving the four horsemen of Rev. 6 parallels a well-documented call to arms by one of Egypt's best known warrior kings, Thutmosis III. The cry, to "Come!", which is used to introduce each of the horsemen parallels the introductory phrase used in the Egyptian war cries used by Thutmosis. The colors of the four horses were shown to parallel those of the cattle in the annual drive of the Egyptian cattle to their feeding grounds, and metaphorically, to new army conscripts who were reminded that they were affectionately called the *cattle of Re* who consequently would protect them in battle. The reference to the sharing of wheat and barley was shown to parallel references to the feeding and payment of the troops while the command not to harm the oil and wine parallel the need to preserve olive groves and vineyards in conquered lands to ensure continued tribute in the form of oil and wine. All these parallels were clearly identified in the well-known writings of Thutmosis III.

Parallels to most other scenes and events in Rev. 6 were found in the *Amduat*, especially the 7th and 8th Divisions where casualties of both sides of warring factions are described in writing and visualized in pictures. These included the capture and execution of enemy troops – as well as the slaying, especially by decapitation, of Egyptian soldiers by the enemy. As in Revelation, troops who died in previous battles are described as having received rewards of sacred garments of the gods and rest in the hereafter. And like those who had been killed in previous battles, fresh army conscripts who followed their king into battle were promised the same rewards. If we assume year-to-year casualties during annual campaigns to assert and maintain Egypt's dominance over the nations in the Levant, we can readily visualize a parallel between them and the cries for revenge by the faithful who had been killed during earlier campaigns.

Meanwhile, the wrath of Re in the form of natural catastrophes was promised against the enemy to reduce their capacity to defend themselves. Such promises of preliminary slaughter of the enemy by Re would ease the natural fears of new recruits and facilitate the conscription process. In fairness to all regions of Egypt, the conscripts would be selected from all the main areas and ethnic groups and, as will be discussed in the next chapter, these groups include those which parallel the "tribes of Israel" in the Book of Revelation and discussed in Chapter 6, *The Twelve Tribes of Israel*.

Chapter 11. Prelude to War (Rev. 7:1-15)[495]

Rev. 6 began with a declaration of war against an enemy. This is dramatically presented in the parade of four horsemen accompanied by war cries and the call for the troops to rally against the enemy (Rev. 6:1-8), an enemy which had already caused the death of many of the soldiers' comrades (Rev. 6:9-11). The souls of the deceased cry out for vengeance but are each "given a white robe and told to rest a little longer, until the number of their fellow servants and their brethren should be complete, who were to be killed as they themselves had been" (Rev. 6:11). Interpreting the latter verse from a militaristic point of view, we conclude that it is the souls of the dead soldiers who are told to wait until preparations for war are completed and the army is ready to march. Meanwhile, the wrath of the Lamb is to fall upon the enemy in the form of natural catastrophes to kill (Rev. 6:12-14) or and otherwise demoralize them (Rev. 6:14,17).

Rev. 7 continues in the same vein but begins with a statement which appears to be more metaphorical than real. It refers to "four angels standing at the four corners of the earth, holding back the four winds of the earth, that no wind might blow on earth or sea or against any tree" until "we have sealed the servants of our God upon their foreheads" (Rev. 7:1,3). This passage obviously refers to a threat of war from the distant gathering of enemy forces. Soldiers would have to be conscripted into the army, including members of the tribes of Israel (Rev. 7:4-8) who are especially identified and promised rewards for gallant deeds in the forthcoming battles just as those who had gone on before them (Rev. 7:10-17). Detailed examination and discussion of these events follows.

The Four Angels and the Four Winds (Rev. 7:1-3)

As indicated above, in the first three verses of Rev. 7 destructive forces gathering on distant horizons are to be held back by four angels. From a militaristic point of view, this entire scene is about protection, about holding back the "enemy" (= wind, as will be shown later) until the required number of soldiers can be recruited, until the full size of the army is reached. This is most evident when we read the passage as a whole:

> [1]After this I saw four angels standing at the four corners of the earth, holding back the four winds of the earth, that no wind might blow on earth or sea or against any tree. [2]Then I saw

another angel ascend from the rising of the sun, with the seal of the living God, and he called with a loud voice to the four angels who had been given power to harm earth and sea, ³saying, "Do not harm the earth or the sea or the trees, till we have sealed the servants of our God upon their foreheads." (Rev 7:1-3)

An Egyptian parallel to this passage is found in Figure 55, the only extant copy of which is found in the tomb of Ramesses VI. Darnell (2004), who has recently translated practically all of its hieroglyphic text (written in "enigmatic" text," a coded form of hieroglyphics), introduces it as a *Schutzbild* scene, a name applied to it and other somewhat similar scenes by the two Egyptologists, F. Abitz and E. Hornung. Both Abitz and Hornung as well as Darnell interpret it as a protective scene because "it protected the tomb of Ramesses VI from the entry of hostile demons and any miasmic clouds which might waft through the break into the tomb of Ramesses VI and disturb the voyage of the dead king."[496] Notwithstanding their mystical interpretation, the protective theme of the scene and several of its separate features make it a prime candidate for a possible parallel to Rev. 7:1-3.

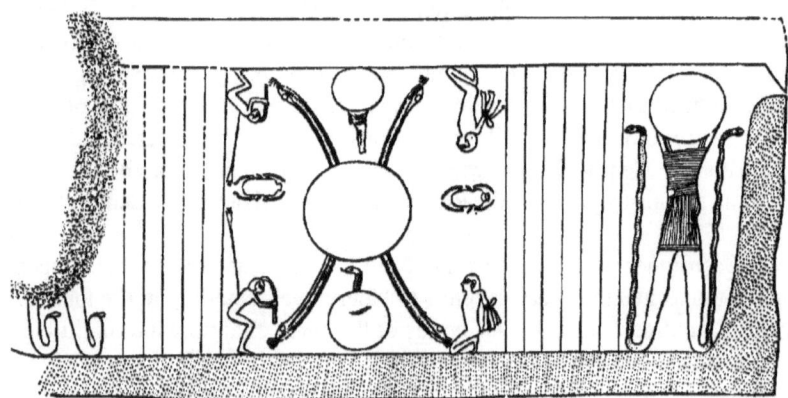

Figure 55. The *Schutzbild* scene shown here is similar to that described in Rev. 7:1-3. Four serpents (angels) spit fire against four enemies (🖑 and 🙢) which represent the four winds. The time of day is illustrated by the presence of the solar disk (○) at dawn (●○●). The head of the standing figure (angel) on the right bears the symbol for the name, or seal, of the sun-god (○).

Our examination of this *Schutzbild* scene begins with a general description of its main components. Its right-hand side is occupied by a large figure of a deity with a sun-disk for a head while his legs are in the form of two serpents; no arms are visible. The accompanying text tells us that he does, in fact, have two arms which represent the "Two Sisters" (i.e., the goddesses Isis and Nephthys): "his two arms remaining in the solar disk."[497] On the left-hand side we see the remains of what appears to be a somewhat similar figure; the text in this area of the original painting is badly damaged.[498] The identity of this deity is described by Darnell who concludes that he is "the Netherworld sun and the ram-headed god at the moment of his rejuvenation

– his appearance in the glory [i.e., at dawn]."[499] Darnell also says that, "Both the *Schutzbild* anquipede and the goddess-armed deity in the solar bark on the dropped portion of Corridor G ceiling [in the tomb of Ramesses VI] are presentations of the giant god at the eastern horizon, Re and Osiris at the time of their union."[500] This deity is therefore Osiris-Re, the one who is identified in Chapter 2, *The Preeminent Deities,* with phrases referring to "God and the Lamb" in the Book of Revelation.

The text associated with Osiris-Re in the *Schutzbild* tells us that "It is against one who is evil that he shoots (light/flame)."[501] It also provides us with what appears to be a reference to a call from Osiris-Re for the serpentine sisters (Isis and Nephthys) to come forth to provide protection by holding back this evil from damaging the earth. It says,

> 4) ... It is the deity who will call, in order that they might come forth from their cavern,
> 5) in order to perform *sḫne*-protection. It is this god who has made the burial pits. *When he calls, the damager of the earth is held back,*
> 6) *they coming forth.*'[502]

Note the resemblance to Rev. 7:3 where we read that the angel which ascends from the rising sun (Osiris-Re in Figure 55) says, " *Do not harm the earth* or the sea or the trees." Darnell identifies this scene with events at dawn, the same time frame mentioned in Rev. 7:1: "I saw another angel ascend from *the rising of the sun."*

Another parallel in the *Schutzbild* scene has to do with the reference to "the seal of the living God" in Rev. 7:1. This statement indicates the angel in Rev. 7:2-3 not only bore the name of God, but that he also bore the name of the *living* God. Osiris was, of course, the god of the dead and was frequently envisioned as the dead body of the sun-god while Re was the sun-god's living soul. In Figure 55, the snake-legged deity on the right-hand represents Osiris's physical body while the solar disk (○), represents the hieroglyphic form of the name of Re, or rather, the living soul of Re. This is consistent with the reference in Rev. 7:2 to the angel (in this case, the body of Osiris), "with the seal [i.e., name] of the living God (Egypt's Re). The combined body of Osiris and the symbolic head of Re constitute the form of Osiris-Re.[a] Recall that, when Re, the living soul of the sun-god merged each morning at dawn with Osiris, the sun-god's body, he became Osiris-Re, the living sun-god. This form parallels Revelation's descriptive phrase, *living god,* or in Egyptian terms, the sun-god's combined body and soul.

Also note the last sentence of the above quotation from the *Schutzbild* scene where Osiris-Re calls to his serpentine limbs (the two arms, Isis and Nephthys, and the two legs). The pertinent text says, "It is the deity who will call ... in order to perform *sḫne*-protection.... When *he calls, the damager of the earth is held back,'* they coming forth." This text closely parallels Rev. 7:2-3 which says that he *"called with*

---

[a] See also Figure 13 in Chapter 3, *The Preeminent Deities* where this deity is identified with Revelation's "God and the Lamb."

a loud voice to the four angels ... saying, 'Do not harm the earth or the sea or the trees.'"

Execution of this command is illustrated in the central square of the *Schutzbild* scene. Here we find a large, centrally located solar disk (O) representing the sun-god. It is flanked by two beetles (●O●) suggesting the sun-god is in his juvenile form. Two other manifestations of Re are located above and below the central disk; the upper one has the head of a protective crocodile extending from it while the lower one has the head of a protective serpent. Extending from the central solar disk are four serpents, presumably representing the arms of Isis and Nephthys which form the arms of Osiris hidden inside the solar disk (i.e., in the head of the large figure with serpentine legs on the right (and possibly the left) side of the figure, as discussed above. These four serpents spit fire at four enemy figures, two of which are bound with their hands tied behind their backs (𓀨, a hieroglyph symbolizing "enemy" or "rebel"[503]) and two have arrows (|)[504] in their backs and blood streaming from their heads (𓁇) thus signifying death and dying of "enemies."[505] All this is framed on either side and the bottom by a symbol consisting of two mountains with a valley between them (⌒). The central disk combines with the ⌒ symbol to complete a stylized form of the 𓈌 hieroglyph, a symbol known as an *akhet* which refers to either the horizon or the rising and setting sun.[506] The events in this scene therefore happen during dawn or sunset. Darnell (2004) concludes that "The texts and iconography of the various elements of the Corridor G treatise [in the tomb of Ramesses VI] emphasize the sun at the eastern horizon [i.e., at dawn]"[507] so that his conclusion is consistent with the statement in Rev. 7:2 that the angel is seen ascending "from the rising of the sun." Above and resting on the tops of the mountains of the 𓈌 hieroglyph is a *pt* symbol (▬) representing the sky. This suggests the events alluded to in this scene happened on earth.

With respect to the two smaller disks in Figure 55, Darnell suggests the crocodile and the serpent are emissaries sent out from the sun to root out and punish evil in the Netherworld. Darnell also says that the four "fire-breathing serpents spew flames onto bound enemies, the crocodile and the snake represent the solar deity's aggressive hatred of evil."[508] He concludes that, "The treatise ... emphasizes the importance of ... the need to keep the damned down in the bowels of the flaming east."[509] Meanwhile, the fire from the serpents' mouths is accentuated by the presence of the *akhet* hieroglyph, 𓈌, which was also, at times, "used not to suggest the rising sun, but as a visual metaphor referring to the related concepts of fire and heat."[510] Note too that the heads of the serpents extend outwards toward the four corners of a square where the figures of the enemies are located; this suggests the action of the four serpents focus on the four cardinal points, or at least on the distant horizons in all directions. This situation is similar to that described in Rev. 7:1 which describes "four angels standing at the four corners of the earth holding back the four winds," the only difference being that four serpents hold back *enemies* at the four corners of the earth in the *Schutzbild* while in Revelation four angels hold back the four *winds*.

The difference between the reference to *enemies* in the *Schutzbild* and *winds* in Revelation does not appear to be particularly significant in light of the possibility of a visual pun in the drawing of the four enemies in the figure. An Egyptian word for "wind" is *athu*[511] while a very similar sounding word, *atu*, can mean "enemy."[512] This phonetic similarity between the Egyptian words for "wind" and "enemy" could very well indicate the presence of a visual pun in which the "four winds" are illustrated as "four enemies." In this manner, the four fire-spitting serpents (angels) holding back the four enemies of the earth in Figure 55 closely parallel four angels holding back the four winds in Rev. 7:1.[a]

The severely damaged left-hand side of the *Schutzbild* is also germane to this discussion, especially as it relates to a series of events introduced near the beginning of the next chapter of Revelation. Only a small portion of the Egyptian text remains:

> 1) Khepri is one whose realization are come into being.
> 2) the one who is evil (Apep) ... . the little ones (?),
> 3) ... to endow
> 4) ... the West ... this flame therein
> As for the seven (Apep) punishing deities, th{ey} shoot {...}[513]

As with the Osiris-Re figure on the right side of Figure 55, the birth of the sun-god (as Khepri) is prominent (in line 1) and this is mentioned in close association with the evil serpent Apophis and his followers, "the little ones" (in line 2). The text goes on in line four to mention "seven punishing deities" who punish Apophis by shooting something, presumably, "this flame from therein" at Apophis and his followers. The "seven punishing deities" are of particular significance in this passage for it so happens that very early in the next chapter of Revelation (Rev. 8:2) we are introduced to seven angels whose destructive activities continue on through subsequent chapters of Revelation until they are concluded in Rev. 11:18. Thus, we find in the *Schutzbild* scene an apparent Egyptian parallel to the seven angels of Rev. 8-11. Furthermore, the placement of what seems to be a reference to the *Schutzbild* scene in the Book of Revelation is consistent with the relative locations of other, nearby parallels in the text of Revelation.

In addition to the above parallels between the two sources, the literary form of the description of events in Rev. 7:1-3 is reminiscent of an entirely different Egyptian source – Chapter 32 of the *Book of the Dead*. This chapter is an incantation against dangerous crocodiles which threaten spirits in "God's Domain." The speaker is empowered by the dreaded *Nau*-serpent which he harbors in his belly to drive back the enemy crocodiles located at each of the four corners of the earth. It contains four spells, each with a similar structure, each directed against one of the four crocodiles.

> Get back, you crocodile of the West, who lives on the Unwearying Stars! Detestation of you is in my belly, for I have absorbed the power of Osiris, and I am Seth. Get back you crocodile of the West! The *Nau*-snake is in my belly, and I have not given myself to you; your flame will not be on me.

---

[a] There is, however, a possible problem with this interpretation. The near homonyms referred to here are based on Budge's 1920 *Egyptian Hieroglyphic Dictionary* but these same words are not included in Faulkner's 1962 *Concise Dictionary of Middle Egyptian*. The reason for this is unclear so that this particular possibility of a visual pun in the *Schutzbild* scene in the Tomb of Ramesses VI requires further research.

> Get back, you crocodile of the East, who lives on those who are mutilated! Detestation of you is in my belly, and I have gone away, for I am Osiris. Get back you crocodile of the East! The *Nau*-snake is in my belly, and I have not given myself to you; your flame will not be on me.
>
> Get back, you crocodile of the South, living on feces, smoke and want! Detestation of you is in my belly, and my blood is not in your hand, for I am Sopd. Get back you crocodile of the South! for I become a Bebet-herb, and I have not given myself to you.
>
> Get back, you crocodile of the North, living on the ... which is in the midst of the stars! Detestation of you is in my belly, your poison is in my head; I am Atum. Get back you crocodile of the North! A scorpion is in my belly but I will not give it birth.[514]

Note that the phrase, "Get back, you crocodile," is repeated in each spell. Remarkably, we find in the reference to the crocodiles in this scene, yet another potential pun. Faulkner (1962) gives *mryt* as a word for crocodiles[515] and *mhyt* as a word for the north *wind*;[516] these words are thus close homonyms of one another. If one assumes a pun in this quotation from the *Book of the Dead*, an alternative interpretation of the phrase "Get back, you *crocodile*," could very well mean "Get back, you *north wind*." And when this phrase is repeated for each of the four cardinal directions, we note the remarkable similarity to the phrase in Rev. 7:1, "Holding back the four winds of the earth." In the Egyptian text, it is four enemy crocodiles which are held back while in Revelation it is the four winds.

But notice that in the second spell the speaker is protected against the crocodile by "the *nau*-snake ... in my belly." Budge (1920) says that this (*Nāáu*) serpent is "a benevolent god, a foe to the crocodiles."[517] He also says that *nau* (or *náu*) means "wind"[518] so that, if we assume a pun, its name may be interpreted to mean "wind snake." In this manner the magic of a pun would strengthen the serpent's power against the wind (crocodile) – a situation which also conforms with Rev. 7:1. It therefore seems that, as in Figure 55, similar ingredients may be found in both Chapter 32 of the *Book of the Dead* and Rev. 7:1.

The New Conscripts (Rev. 7:4-8)

If we assume that Rev. 7:1-3 means holding back distant enemies in a manner similar to that found in the above Egyptian parallels to this passage, we may conclude that the purpose of identifying the 144,000 members of the tribes of Israel in Rev. 7:4-8 is to enroll them in an army to fight against enemies found at the four corners of the earth. And as with any army, its soldiers would have to be clearly distinguishable from the enemy; each would be given a distinctive uniform and possibly an identification mark akin to today's "dog-tags" used to identify individual soldiers.

This interpretation would conform with Rev. 7:3 which describes the servants (conscripts) as being identified with the "seal of the living god" (Rev. 7:1) "upon their foreheads" (Rev. 7:3). In a modern sense, a seal is an engraved device which makes an impression on some relatively soft substance such as clay, wax, paper, etc., usually to ensure an item's authenticity. In antiquity, seals were used as official marks of a manufacturer to identify a product such as wine, to indicate ownership, or simply to denote authority (for example, a king may give his signet ring to one of his officers as a sign of the authority delegated to him). Simply put, seals were used as a means of identifying origin, authority, ownership, or allegiance to a master. In a military sense, being "sealed" could mean being identified by name or simply by the division to which he was assigned in the Pharaoh's army. One aspect of being "sealed" in the Egyptian military sense seem to have been the assignment of new uniforms of bright white linen for which the Egyptian army was famous in the ancient world. Another may have been the painting of a hieroglyph of the name of Re (O or ☉) somewhere on the soldier's body, such as the head (this may even be an explanation for why some pictures of gods show solar disks for heads, indicating they are followers of the sun-god). Regardless of the type of identification, we may be confident that such draftees would have been clearly identified or "sealed" prior to going to war – all 144,000 of them. In a theocracy such as ancient Egypt, such marks would likely refer to either the sun-god or his son/representative – Horus, the king.

Another possible purpose of a mark on the forehead of the sun-god's soldiers will be discussed later in this chapter in the section on the *Protection of the Faithful*.

Multitudes with Palm Branches (Rev. 7:9-10)

The remaining verses of Rev. 7 refer to "a great multitude which no man could number, from every nation, from all tribes and peoples and tongues, standing before the throne and before the Lamb, clothed in *white robes*, with *palm branches* in their hands, and crying out with a loud voice, 'Salvation belongs to our God who sits upon the throne, and to the Lamb!'" (Rev. 7:9-10).

As discussed in Chapter 7, *The Great Multitude*, bright new clothing is emphasized in parts of the 9th Division; we also discussed the nine deities in the same division (at AM9.3.6-10, Figure 32) who carry palm branches as scepters. Elsewhere (in AM9.1.1-5) rewards are mentioned in relation to the war against the enemies of the sun-god. The text makes it clear that bright "uniforms" are given to them prior to their battle against the enemies of Osiris. For example, one passage says,

> *You are provided with your cloth, your glory* [i.e., brightness] *is your garments.*' Horus has clothed you there as he did his father in the Netherworld which hides the gods. ... Perform what you have to perform for Osiris. *Praise the Lord of the Netherworld.*' Make him justified against his enemies every day.
>
> ...
>
> This is the Council of the Gods who avenge Osiris every day. This is what they do in the Netherworld: *(they) overthrow the enemies of Osiris.*' (A9.1.1-5)[519]

Meanwhile, the text associated with the twelve uraeus serpents seated on clothing signs to the immediate right of the nine figures holding palm scepters also speaks of war against the enemies in the Netherworld. It says,

> They are like this in the Netherworld, *firmly established upon their clothing*' [uniforms] in their own flesh. It is they who light up the darkness in the chamber which contains Osiris. *The flames of their mouths cause the overthrow of the enemies in the Netherworld.*'
>
> It is they who ward off all the serpents of the earth, whose forms the One of the Netherworld does not know. *They live on the blood of those whom they slaughter every day.*' (A9.3.1-5)[520]

These multitudes of deities clearly acted as soldiers in the service of their god. Since the palm branches were associated with time and longevity and was also the symbol of the god *Heh*, the personification of eternity, its use in the context of defending their god seems to suggest that the god whom they honor with the palm branches is to live forever in spite of the evil which threatens him, and very likely, that those among them who die in his service will receive eternal life.

Protection of the Faithful (Rev. 7:15)

In Rev. 7:15, we find an interesting reference involving the protection of those who serve the one on the throne. It says they are *"before the throne of God* ... and he who sits upon the throne will *shelter them* with his presence." On close inspection, this verse describes a scene very similar to that found in the middle register of the 11th Division of the *Amduat*. The relevant text refers to the picture shown in Figure 34 and is translated by Piankoff (1954): "They are like this *in front of the Great God*. They *carry the Enveloper on their heads* toward this city."[521] The similarity between the two sources may not be readily apparent so an explanation is advisable.

To properly compare Rev. 7:15 with Figure 34 it is important to first of all have a working understanding of the original meaning of the phrase which is translated in the Revised Standard Version as, "he ... will shelter them with his presence." Through the years, this phrase has been translated in a variety of ways. The King James Version and the New King James Version translates it as "he that sitteth on the throne shall dwell among them." Some modern translations, however, refer to it in the sense of God providing his people with protection by spreading his tent or tabernacle over them. For example, the American Standard Version translates the original Greek as "He who sits on the throne will spread His tabernacle over them," while the New International Version expresses it with the words, "he who sits on the throne will spread his tent over them." This last translation is closest to the original Greek; the two original Greek words used here are *skeenoósei*, which refers to a tabernacle, tent or dwelling, and *ep*, which refers to the manner in which the dwelling is to be used; it is usually translated as "upon, on, or over." A literal translation of the original text would therefore read something like "setting one's tabernacle (or 'tent') over (or 'on') them." It is the latter interpretation of Rev. 7:13 which best applies to the Egyptian text quoted above, "They carry the Enveloper on their heads," as we shall see next.

Egyptians believed that the "The Enveloper" or *Meḥen* serpent, the same one which protected the sun-god as he passed through the dangerous parts of the Netherworld during night, could also protect them in battle. The Egyptian word, *meḥen*, means "a covering"[522] and *Meḥen* was the name of the serpent deity[523] whose body is often pictured forming a protective canopy or shrine covering or surrounding important deities such as Re in Figure 34. Most modern translators therefore translate the name of this serpent as the "Enveloper," as does Piankoff. The use of the *meḥen* serpent as a protective shrine by the sun-god clearly alludes to portable tent-shrines used by the ancient Egyptians, and in particular, the one which houses the sun-god during his voyage through the Netherworld. Meanwhile, the text in the *Amduat* is quite clear as to the identity of the serpent being carried over the heads of the group of twelve deities in the middle register of the 11th Division – it is the same protective serpent which forms a protective canopy over Re in Figure 34. As stated above, the text says, "They carry the *Enveloper*' on their heads toward this city." The twelve followers of Re in Figure 34 are thus provided the same shelter and protection against evil as is their god, a situation similar to that spoken of in Rev. 7:15 which the New International Version translates as, "he who sits on the throne will spread *his* tent over them." Both the figure and the text therefore parallel the literal translation of the original Greek text, "setting one's tabernacle (or 'tent') over (or 'on') them."

There is, however, one aspect of this scene which does not conform with Rev. 7:15. It is related to the suggestion in Chapter 3, *The Preeminent Deities*, that in the Netherworld the god Re parallels the Lamb of Revelation and not Osiris who represents Revelation's "God on the throne." Thus, in Figure 34 we see that the twelve deities under the protective Enveloper serpent stand before Re (the Lamb) and not before the throne of "God" as in Rev. 7:15. This may or may not be an important difference, especially in view of the fact that Osiris and Re were often considered to represent the united one, Osiris-Re, in the Netherworld. This is discussed in *The Preeminent Deities*.

Discussion

From an Egyptian perspective, Rev. 7:1 can be interpreted to mean the holding back of enemies in some distant location(s) rather than holding back the winds at the four corners of the earth. This makes sense if we assume that this scene in Revelation involves preparations for war, including the conscription of soldiers and the invoking of supernatural powers to protect troops already fighting in the area (Rev. 7:2-3) until new recruits can be identified, registered and dispatched (Rev. 6:11 and Rev. 7:4). In Rev. 7:4-8 we learn that the new recruits are to come from a much larger population which Revelation calls "the twelve tribes of Israel," 12,000 from each tribe. After the army of 144,000 has been fully prepared, (i.e., its soldiers enroled, trained, and "sealed") they are to march to the distant battlefront at the "four corners of the earth" to assist existing troops in their fight against the enemy. Soldiers of other nationalities are added to the troops (Rev. 7:9) and a vast army of soldiers and support personnel is mustered. Special rewards and supernatural protection are promised to the select group of fighters who represent the tribes of Israel (Rev. 7:15-16).

With respect to the supernatural protective powers, there is one noteworthy difference between the text of Revelation and the attributes of the *mehen* serpent in the 11th Division of the *Amduat*, a difference which seems to be relevant to understanding events described later in Revelation: while the body of the *mehen* serpent completely surrounds the deity to protect him from evils coming from any direction, the *mehen* which covers the twelve followers covers only the head and therefore protects the soldiers from evil coming only from above. One wonders if this is merely a simple limitation in the visual metaphor describing the protective powers of the serpent to cover the large number of soldiers or if it represents something of much greater significance – such as a danger coming from the sky and thus threatening the faithful as well as the enemy. As we shall learn in later chapters, both Revelation and the Egyptian texts imply that while the same scorching heat threatens the faithful as well as the enemy, only the faithful are protected from it.

Rev. 7:4 indicates that those sealed came "out of every tribe of the sons of Israel." This topic was discussed in detail in Chapter 6, *The Twelve Tribes of Israel,* where the tribes were found to parallel groups of twelve deities described in the *Amduat* and the *Book of Gates*. This parallel included attributes which would be applicable to soldiers conscripted for battle against the enemies of Egypt (and hence the sun-god): they are those who once lived on earth (Rev. 14:3-4), were owned by God (Rev. 14:3-4), were followers of the Lamb (Rev. 14:4), and had their father's name written on their foreheads (Rev. 7:3, Rev. 14:1); also, and especially significant when considered in their role as soldiers, they were all male (Rev. 14:4).[a] As already pointed out, it was in the *Amduat* where exceptionally well circumscribed groups of twelve are found with characteristics similar to those of the tribes of Israel. In the 7th Division, for example, two contiguous groups of twelve contain individual deities bearing Egyptian names with meanings similar to those of the names of the tribes of Israel; also, the name of the leader of the two groups in this scene and that of the twelve tribes of Israel in Revelation share a similar meaning.

The relative location of the reference to the tribes of Israel at this point in the Book of Revelation is also a significant parallel. As noted in the previous chapter, the call to arms identified in Rev. 6 partially parallels pictures and text found in the 7th Division of the *Amduat*. We can now say that not only do listings of parallel Hebrew and Egyptian names occur in the same division of the *Amduat* but they also appear in adjacent chapters in the Book of Revelation. The finding that the most important list of names occurs in practically the same relative position in the flow of images in both sources is supporting evidence for a parallel nature of the two sources.

---

[a] Recall that we used the literal interpretation of Rev. 14:4 to conclude that the 144,000 were all male. Rev. 14:4 says that, "It is these who have not defiled themselves with women." The "all male" interpretation of this verse has led many New Testament scholars to assume that a literal interpretation of this verse is incorrect. For example, Fiorenza (1985) says that, "To assume that either the heavenly or the eschatological followers of the Lamb are a class of exclusively male ascetics seems to be unfounded in the overall context of the book [of Revelation]." When this same verse is viewed from an ancient Egyptian perspective, however, it is unnecessary to assume that the literal sense of the verse is incorrect; soldiers were male.

In the next chapter we examine, from an Egyptian point of view, the likely meaning and significance of the half hour of silence described in Rev. 8:1. We shall see how it parallels a particularly important period of silence mentioned in the Egyptian texts, a silence with introduces a dramatic series of cataclysmic events. And in the following two chapters we will examine Egyptian parallels to the "apocalyptic visions" which have contributed so much to making the Book of Revelation so very popular among certain groups of Christians.

Chapter 12. Silence in Heaven (Rev. 8:1)[524]

The 8th Chapter of Revelation begins with a verse which at first seems unrelated to anything which happens either before or after it. It simply says, "There was silence in heaven for about half an hour." This is an abrupt change from the dramatic beginning of the throne scene in which a great flurry of announcements is described, starting with a declaration of war on those who have rebelled, a call to arms, a promise that the wrath of the Lamb will send the enemy scurrying for protection into caves, and finally, the identification and conscription of those who are to fight for their god in the coming war. In this chapter, we will learn how, from an Egyptian point of view, the silence referred to in Rev. 8:1 appears exactly where it is in the Book of Revelation for an important mythological reason.

But we should first examine the half hour of silence from a very general perspective to take into account the full range of meanings of the concept of silence to the ancient Egyptians. As is common practice in modern times, the Egyptians divided both the day and night into twelve hours so we can assume that the time period given is comparable to modern standards.[a] The drama of a full half hour of absolute silence in the great court containing many hundreds of thousands, if not millions of souls, gives the feeling of a solemn and awesome spectacle; this would be especially dramatic if those present anticipated the events which were to follow. Bible scholars have variously described it with words such as "the ominous calm before a terrific storm,"[525] as "the lull after a preceding tempest and the prelude to a more terrible one,"[526] or as "A silence of expectation."[527] A comment in the *New Oxford Annotated Bible* suggests that "The sight of the unsealed scroll [in Rev. 8:1] leads to reverential silence."[528] Whether a "calm before a storm," "reverential silence" or some other reason, this period of silence marks a powerful and awe-inspiring interlude during the already dramatic events surrounding the throne.

To the Egyptians, personal silence was a virtue honored by everyone from common peasants to temple priests and on up to the king himself. It implied a variety of closely related qualities; to the individual, it might mean the quiet contemplation of a wise person during discussions involving conflicting passions, or it could simply mean not being rowdy or "loud-mouthed"; silence in the temples was viewed as a

---

[a] Although during the early days of Egyptian civilization the length of each hour of the night and day varied with the seasons, the daily average length was the same as in modern times.

token of respect for the gods. Meanwhile, some creation myths and entire cosmogonies were punctuated by a period of silence which permeated the primordial abyss before the act of creation transpired. The Egyptians even had a goddess personifying silence itself; her name was Mertseger which means *She who loves silence.* She was the goddess of the Valley of the Kings where many famous Egyptian kings lay entombed.[529] Also, the necropolis, the place of the dead to which everyone must ultimately go was devoutly called the "land of silence."

In the following paragraphs, the various forms of silence recognized by the ancient Egyptians are described to ensure that the reader understands the basis of the final decision on the type which best describes the silence mentioned in Rev. 8:1. And as we shall see, the type of silence which conforms best to the context of this verse is one which is ideally suited as an introduction to the events which follow, events which will be discussed in detail in Chapter 13, *Catastrophes*.

Personal Silence

Frankfort (1948) tells us that the teachings of the Egyptian sages distinguished two temperaments of man: the "passionate man" and the "self–disciplined" or so-called "silent man," each of which were desirable personality traits in the social norms of many Egyptians. The passionate man is garrulous, quarrelsome, grasping, arbitrary, overweening. "The silent man is patient, modest, calm, up to a point self-effacing, but above all master of himself under all circumstances."[530] "The silent man is pre-eminently the successful man. High officials describe themselves as 'truly silent.' ... true wisdom is true power; but it means mastery over one's impulses, and silence is a sign not of humility, but of superiority."[531] Frankfort points out that the sage, "Ptahhotep, like Amenemope who lived two thousand years later, represents silence not as a quality of the timid, the humble, or the meek, but of a superior man, whose mastery over himself constitutes an achievement acknowledged by all."[532] He quotes a memorable proverb which likens the superiority of one's silence to that of the fearsome crocodile.

> Put thyself in the hands of God
> and thy tranquility shall overthrow them (the enemies).
> In fact, the crocodile which gives no sound,
> of him above all fear is inveterate.[533]

Contemplative Silence

Silence was also desired by the gods. To illustrate this, Frankfort presents a prayer to Amen by an especially humble man:

> Thou art, the Lord of him that is silent;
> Who comest at the voice of the humble man.
> I call upon thee when I am in distress:
> And thou comest that thou mayest save me;
> that thou mayest give breath to him that is wretched;
> That thou mayest save me that am in bondage.[534]

Reverential silence was so important to the ordinary Egyptian that Breasted (1912) devoted a substantial portion of his chapter on *The Age of Personal Piety* to the subject. Here is an extract from this chapter:

> ... even in the opinion of the sages, who are wont to compromise with traditional customs, the most effective means of gaining favor of God is contemplative silence and inner communion. 'Be not of many words, for in silence shalt thou gain good. ... As for the precinct of God, his abomination is crying out; pray thou with a desiring heart whose every word is hidden, and he will supply thy need, and hear thy speech and receive thy offering.' .... This attitude of silent communion, waiting upon the gracious goodness of God, was not confined to the select few, nor to the educated priestly communities. On the humblest monuments of the common people Amon is called the god "who cometh to the silent," or the "lord of the silent."[535]

The link between an individual's silence and worship of his or her god found its ultimate expression in temples where ancient rituals were most highly cultivated. Here, the *Maxims of Ani* and the *Teachings of Amen-em-apt* were aptly incorporated into special religious celebrations. Budge (1934) tells us that men were advised "to assist regularly at the appointed festivals of God, to present to him gifts and offerings, to frequent his temple and to sit therein and pray to him with a fervent heart, but with few words."[536] Budge points out that, "During the days of the great celebration of the 'Mysteries' no man or woman might play a tambourine (or drum) or flute, or sing to the harp. Furthermore absolute silence was to be maintained, and no shouting or noise caused by any man's voice was permitted to be heard."[537] It is quite evident that, as with most or all other religions, the element of silence was a very real part of the religious ceremonies of the ancient Egyptians.

Silence in Death

Earthly practices of silence were extended into the afterlife where the land of the dead was known as the "Silent Land" or the "Land of Silence." On arrival in the hereafter, the deceased says in the 125th chapter of the *Book of the Dead* that "I have come here to bear witness to truth and to set the balance in its proper place within the Silent Land."[538] And in the 180th chapter the deceased says "I am one who is at peace in the Silent Land, I have made for myself offerings in the West with the souls who are among the gods."[539] In the *Introductory Hymn to Osiris* we read, "Hail to you, King of Kings, Ruler of Rulers, who ... rules the plains of the Silent Land."[540] Silence is especially conspicuous in certain parts of the Netherworld. For example, in the 110th Chapter it says that shouting is evil, "This is Horus. ... He does everything in it as it is done in the Island of Fire; there is no shouting in it, there is nothing evil in it."[541] Many other such references to silence in the Netherworld and ceremonies can be found throughout the *Book of the Dead*.[a] In the *Book of Gates* twelve deities in the 7th Division who recline on their funeral biers are addressed with the words, "Hail, O you spirits! Hail, inhabitants of the Netherworld! ... Receive your garments, be bright in the light, for the Region of Silence is open to you."[542] Hornung (1990) says that as the

---

[a] For more examples of silence, see the following chapters of the *Book of the Dead*: 24, 78, 106, 125, 127, 178 and 183.

sun-god passes on his nightly journey through each gate to enter the next region of the Netherworld, "Darkness drops over the region and the doors clang to a last wail before all the creatures resume the sleep of the dead. The jubilation and a dialogue with the god are followed by silence, another symbol of the Realm of the Dead and its divine Ennead, 'with heavy silence in the west.' Deathly silence, the silence of the beginning [of creation]."[543]

Silence and the Renewal of Creation

This is the last type of silence to be discussed here and it is probably the closest and most appropriate parallel to the silence described in Rev. 8:1.

"Deathly, silence, the silence of the beginning" was a hallmark of the creation story developed in the Egyptian city of Hermopolis and subsequently spread throughout much of Egypt. Hermopolis' priests envisioned the beginning of time as void of everything except a vast primordial ocean or abyss. Nothing else existed and pure, unaltered silence reigned in the darkness. Then the "sole god" appeared in the midst of the abyss and broke the silence with the cackle of a great goose. The 19th chapter of a hymn to Amen-Re explains it this way:

> His form (the sun-god) shone at the first time. *Everything was silent* on account of his majesty. {Then} he cackled, being the Great Cackler, in the place where he was created, he alone. He began to speak in the midst of silence. He opened all eyes and made them see. He commenced to cry when the earth was inert. *His cry spread about when there was no one else in existence but him.* He brought forth all things which exist.[a]

The creator god thus became known as the Great Cackler who initiated the original creation by breaking the primordial silence with the sound of his voice.[544] So it was that a period of absolute silence was associated with a noise, and presumably, it was a great noise – as we shall soon see. If the silence of Rev. 8:1 is also associated with the renewal of creation, we should expect to find parallels among other aspects of Egypt's creation mentioned in Revelation. To explore this possibility we look more closely at some of Egypt's ancient myths on the subject.

Hornung (1990) tells us that contemporary Egyptians "realized that powers predating creation contend with powers that maintain and cleanse creation. These powers were unstable and destructive forces inherent in the very idea of creation."[545] They believed that creation was periodically cleansed and renewed, an act accomplished by powerful forces which destroyed past evils to make way for a new beginning. Hornung (1993) quotes a passage from the *Book of Two Ways* describing the social and physical upheaval of change and devastation of this time: "Then I shall dwell with him [Osiris] in one place. Mounds will become cities and cities mounds, and estate will destroy estate." Meanwhile, the destruction of the entire world is explicitly mentioned in the 175th Chapter of the *Book of the Dead* where, after the creator god affirms that the blessed dead will live for millions of years in the afterlife, he says, "I will dispatch the Elders and destroy all that I have made; the earth shall

---

[a] This translation is provided by M. Clagett (1989, p. 563), who indicates in a note (on p. 550) that it is a modified version of that originally made by A.H. Gardiner in "Hymns to Amon from a Leiden Papyrus, " ZÄS, Vol 42 (1905), pp. 12-42.

return to the Primordial Water, to the surging flood, as in the original state."[546] Silence is re-established and ultimately broken when the act of creation is renewed with the cry of the Great Cackler. Eventually, evil abounds again and yet another cleansing of creation is required. Each time, Re, Osiris and other gods are reinstated, as we are told in Chapter 175 of the *Book of the Dead*: "How good is what I have done for Osiris, even more than for all the gods! I have given him the desert, and his son Horus is the heir on the throne which is in the Island of Fire."[547]

The most relevant point to note in the above background is that a period of profound silence was associated in the minds of the ancient Egyptians with a great noise, that of the renewal of creation. And each renewal of creation was associated with a period of utter destruction. A period of silence thus associated with the dramatic destruction of the previous creation may be likened to the event described in Rev. 8:2-5 when the half hour of silence in Rev. 8:1 is broken by the crashing to earth of fire and the sounds of peals of thunder, voices, flashes of lighting and an earthquake. To these are added a series of terrible events announced by seven trumpets in Rev. 8:6; events associated with them are described from Rev. 8:7 to the end of Rev. 11. Great catastrophes are loosed upon the earth, including hail and fire from the sky (Rev. 8:7), a fiery mountain falling into the sea (Rev. 8:8), waters turning to blood and becoming undrinkable (Rev. 8:8), darkness during both day and night (Rev. 8:12, Rev. 9:2), torturous plagues (Rev. 9:4-6) and a great earthquake which kills thousands (Rev. 11:13). Cosmic silence is thus closely linked to the sound of re-creation.

In addition to the above, the images in Rev. 8:1-5 – the silence, fire from the incense container, and the incense itself – conform with two groups of Egyptian homonyms or near homonyms. The first group contains *ger,* an Egyptian word for silence[548] and the close homonym, *ga,* which means "unguent" or a censer or "unguent pot,"[549] while another, *gerut,* is a word for incense, or "scented unguent."[550] And with respect to the breaking of the silence, *gaga*[551] means the cry of a bird, or "to cackle" The ideas embedded in these words are thus comparable to the silence of Rev. 8:1 and the cacophony of noises described in Rev. 8:5 – "Then the angel took the censer and filled it with fire from the altar and threw it on the earth; and there were peals of thunder, voices, flashes of lightning, and an earthquake." The selection of words and images used to describe the scene in Rev. 8:1-5 thus conform with two groups Egyptian words: one which begins with the similar syllables, *ga* and *ge*[a] and the other containing the words *ger* and *ga*. His selection of close

---

[a] An even richer grouping of Egyptian homonyms, based on 8:1-5 and also related to *ge* and *ga* sounds, is possible and this argues for more in-depth investigation. The following are potential homonyms or near homonyms (from Budge, 1920) in the selection of words used in Rev. 8:1-5. "When the Lamb opened the seventh seal, there was silence [*ger* = to be still, silent p. 810a] in heaven for about half an hour. ²Then I saw [*ga* = to see, to look p. 801a] the seven angels [*N[ḥ] egeb* = a water-god p. 398b] who stand before God, and seven trumpets were given to them. ³And another angel [*Gai* = a god in Tuat VI p. 801a] came and stood at the altar with a golden censer [*ga* = unguent or unguent pot p. 800b]; and he was given much [*ngesges* = to be heaped up full with something, to overflow p. 398b; *neges* to overflow p. 398b] incense [*gerut* = scented unguent p. 810a; *nāgu* = dust, powder Budge, p. 347b.] to mingle with the prayers of all the saints upon the golden altar [*gerr* = burnt sacrifice, offering p. 810a] before the throne [*gaà-t* = shrine, chapel p. 801a]; ⁴and the smoke [*gerr* = burnt sacrifice, offering p. 810a] of the incense [*gerut* = scented unguent p. 810a] rose with the prayers of the saints from

12. Silence in Heaven

homonyms is consistent with the ancient Egyptian practice of word-play discussed in Chapter 2, *New Approaches*.

Furthermore, and with similar reasoning, we note Revelation's choice of words involving silence, conflict and warfare. We find it in Egyptian words which sound similar to the word for "silence," *sgr;* while *sgr* means "silence,"[a] a similar word, *skr*, means "strike, as in strike down foes."[b] In this way "silence" – or *sgr* – would, in the minds of the ancient Egyptians be closely linked to *skr*, to strike down foes, a concept associated with warfare, even cosmic warfare. With this in mind, the dramatic ending of a half hour of silence in Rev. 8:5 can be considered a parallel to the unleashing of the wrath of the Lamb described in the verses which follow, especially where it says,

> [7]... and there followed hail and fire, mixed with blood, which fell on the earth; and a third of the earth was burnt up, and a third of the trees were burnt up, and all green grass was burnt up. [8]... and something like a great mountain, burning with fire, was thrown into the sea; [9]and a third of the sea became blood, a third of the living creatures in the sea died, and a third of the ships were destroyed. (Rev. 8:7-9)

Such destructive events continue with great fury through Rev. 9 while related events are mentioned in other chapters in the Revelation and will be discussed later.

The symbolic establishment of world order was reenacted each day at dawn. In the lower register of the 11th Division of the *Amduat*, and just before we see the picture of the newly born sun-god rising above the horizon at dawn in the 12th Division, the souls and shadows of the enemies are punished in their pits as "decreed every day by the Majesty of Horus of the Netherworld." These are "The overturned ones" and those who are in "The valley of the overturned ones." Horus says to them:

> You are fallen into the pits of fire, you will not escape. You will not avoid it. The fire of the serpent, She who sets millions ablaze, is against you. The heat of She who presides over her Caldrons is against you. The fire of She who is above her Pit of Flame is against you. The glare coming out of the mouth of She who presides over her Slaughtering Block

---

the hand of the angel before God. [5]Then the angel took the censer and filled it with fire from the altar and threw [*ga* = throw-stick, boomerang p. 800b; ***negengen*** to destroy, to break in pieces p. 398b; *negebgeb* = to break p. 398b; *negeb* = to break, to be destroyed, to come to an end p. 398b] it on the earth; and there were peals of thunder, voices [*gaga* = to cry (of a bird), to cackle p. 800b; ***nāgga*** = to cackle (of geese) Budge, p. 348a; *neg* = to cackle p. 398a; *negg* = to cackle, to quack p. 398a; ***negaga*** = to cackle, to quack p. 398a], flashes of lightning, and an earthquake."

[a] *Sgr* = "silence" in Faulkner (1962), p. 252. See also *s-ger* = "to make silent, to still, to hush, to silence" in Budge (1920), p. 706a and *s-ger* = "to make silent, to still, silence, rest" on p. 627b.

[b] *Skr* = "strike, as in strike down foes" or "wound, injury" in Faulkner (1962), p. 250. See also, *seger* = "to strike, to fight" in Budge (1920), p. 627b and *sger* = "fort, fortress, a strong enclosed place," p. 706a.

is against you, she cuts you to pieces, she slaughters you. You will never see the living on the earth.[552]

This slaughter is accompanied by earthquakes as indicated in the name, "Earthquake"[553] which appears among a group of twelve in the upper register. And in the lower register, punishment by fire is indicated in the name of "He who sets millions ablaze.[554] Thus, the silence before dawn, then earthquakes, fire, and punishment of the enemies of the sun-god are all suggested in this symbolic re-creation of the world at the rising of the newly-created, juvenile sun-god at dawn.

The *Book of the Dead* does not explicitly state how the destruction of the world is to take place; we are simply told only that the sun-god dispatched the elders to destroy all that he had made. Nevertheless, there can be no doubt that the cleansing of his creation was envisioned as a manifestation of his wrath and involved the unleashing of extremely great and terrible destructive powers of cosmic proportions. His action was viewed as a cosmic war against the evil which had overtaken the old world order; all evil had to be destroyed and the world re-created in which the enemies of the sun-god no longer existed. We read of one aspect of his wrath in the 17th Chapter of the *Book of the Dead* where "war broke out in the entire sky and earth."[555] Elsewhere in the book (Chapters 146 and 149) we find references to events which suggest that, during at least one point in Egypt's history, Egyptians very likely believed that events leading to the end of the world had already started.

Conclusion

To the Egyptians, silence and its many connotations was considered a great virtue; it not only gained high respect when expressed in the daily lives of the Egyptians but it also formed a component of their cosmogony – especially in the cleansing of the world and its symbolic re-creation at the dawn of each new day as well and the periodic total destruction and renewal of the world. Since the reference to the period of silence in Rev. 8:1 appears in juxtaposition with images in Rev. 8:7-13 of cosmic upheaval, we may assume that, from an Egyptian point of view, the silence in Revelation is more closely associated with the Egyptian story of the act of re-creation than to any pious act of personal or reverential silence, the silence of death, or that of the necropolis and certain parts of the Netherworld.

The awesome destructive forces unleashed in Rev. 8:7-13 will be discussed in detail in the next chapter, *Catastrophes*, where they will be linked closely to the full range of apocalyptic events described in Rev. 8 and similar events described in other chapters in Revelation. *Catastrophes* will be followed by Chapter 14, *From Catastrophe to Myth* which presents the likely geophysical and historical background to the broad spectrum of apocalyptic events described in the Book of Revelation.

Chapter 13. Catastrophes[556]

Descriptions of catastrophic events are interwoven through the very fabric of the Book of Revelation. As discussed in the previous three chapters, Revelation speaks of powerful winds, earthquakes, darkness and falling stars in Rev. 6:12-17, four angels with the "power to harm the earth and the sea" in Rev. 7:1-3, and after a period of silence described in Rev. 8:1, it introduces "seven angels who stand before God" in the midst of "thunder, voices, flashes of lightning, and an earthquake" in Rev. 8:2-6. The role of these angels is to announce the wrath of God on the earth. Catastrophes begin in Rev. 8:7 when the first angel blows his trumpet, and "hail and fire, mixed with blood ... fall on the earth." Then, in the next three chapters of Revelation, the remaining six angels deliver their devastating plagues of death and destruction. Additional disasters are described in Rev. 18 and parts of Rev. 14 and 16.

At first glance, the different kinds of disasters seem to be *unrelated* to one another for they include such diverse events as the darkening of the sun, moon and stars, fire and hail falling from heaven, lightning, earthquakes, a sinking island, pestilence and plagues. And many people, animals, plants and fish in the sea die. Bible scholars have typically associated these disparate events with the end of the world. Few if any, however, have considered them to be different aspects of a single natural event. When considered together, however, their true nature becomes obvious; taken as a whole, they suggest the most powerful of all natural phenomena on earth – a cataclysmic volcanic eruption.

This chapter documents the basis for this conclusion and identifies similarities between Revelation's apocalyptic events and those found in ancient Egyptian, Greek, and even modern literature. According to Rev. 18, the main focus of the events is a place called Babylon which bible scholars typically assume was the ancient city of the same name on the Euphrates River in modern-day Iraq. New evidence presented here points to a more likely location among the Aegean islands in the Mediterranean Sea. We will discuss how catastrophic events associated with the eruption of the volcano on the island of Thera (Santorini) in the 17th century BCE likely inspired the writing of certain Egyptian texts and influenced Egyptian views of the end of the world – and subsequently, the creation of a new heaven and a new earth (as in Rev. 21-22, and discussed later in Chapter's 26 and 27, *A New Creation* and *The Holy City*).

To simplify the arguments used, this chapter follows a slightly different format from the previous chapters. We first identify evidence in the Book of Revelation which conforms with events normally associated with a volcanic eruption. Next, we compare these events in Revelation to similar events described in the Egyptian literature. We then compare both of these sources with historical documents from ancient Greece, and finally, we wrap up all this evidence with a comparison with modern scientific records and investigations of ancient volcanic eruptions in the Mediterranean Sea.

The Revelation Account (Rev. 6,8,9,14,16,18,19)

The Book of Revelation informs us that a major catastrophe occurred in a place called "Babylon." This Babylon is introduced with description of its having had a thriving economy involving international trade in "gold, silver, jewels and pearls, fine linen, purple, silk and scarlet, all kinds of scented wood, all articles of ivory, all articles of costly wood, bronze, iron and marble, cinnamon, spice, incense, myrrh, frankincense, wine, oil, fine flour and wheat, cattle and sheep, horses and chariots, and slaves" (Rev. 18:11-14). Revelation also describes Babylon as an island or group of islands (Rev. 16:20) which is rich, "clothed in fine linen, in purple and scarlet, bedecked with gold, with jewels, and with pearls!" (Rev. 18:16) and filled with "dainties and splendor" (Rev. 18:14). We are also told that it was frequented by "shipmasters and seafaring men, sailors" (Rev. 18:17), a place where ship owners and merchants grew rich from trade (Rev. 18:3,19). Clearly, Revelation's Babylon was a prosperous, well populated area involved in the sea trade.

Rev. 18:21 later tells us that this Babylon experiences a sudden and great disaster: "a mighty angel took up a stone like a great millstone and threw it into the sea, saying, 'So shall Babylon the great city be thrown down with violence, and shall be found no more.'" She is destroyed by fire and "all shipmasters and seafaring men, sailors and all whose trade is on the sea, stood far off. ... crying out, 'Alas, alas, for the great city'" (Rev. 18:17,19). "Her plagues come in a single day, pestilence and mourning and famine, and ... fire" (Rev 18:8). Nearby, "every island fled away, and no mountains were to be found" (Rev. 16:20). This very brief description of the disaster suggests an eruption of a volcanic island and as we shall see in the following discussion, there are many other references in the Book of Revelation which support this conclusion.[a]

While references which parallel events associated with a volcanic eruption are found in several places in the Book of Revelation, detailed accounts are concentrated

---

[a] References to events in the Book of Revelation which may be associated with a volcanic eruption are as follows:- Suddenness of event – Rev. 18:8,10 / Mountain of Fire – Rev. 8:8; Rev. 18:5 / Fire and smoke – Rev. 8:4,7; Rev. 14:10,11; Rev. 9:2,17; Rev. 18:9 / Loud noises, thunder, etc. – Rev. 8:5; Rev. 9:9; Rev. 16:18 / Earthquakes – Rev. 6:12,14; Rev. 8:5; Rev. 16:18; Rev. 16:18,19 / Lightning – Rev. 8:5 / Darkness – Rev. 6:12,13; Rev. 8:12; Rev. 9:2; Rev. 16:10 / Hail – Rev. 8:7; Rev. 16:21 / Heat – Rev. 16:9 / Islands/mountains disappear – Rev. 16:20 / Ships at sea destroyed – Rev. 8:9 / Event viewed from a safe distance – Rev. 18:10,15,17 / Toxic materials from smoke – Rev. 9:3-6 / Waters poisoned – Rev. 8:9,10,11; Rev. 16:3,4 / People evacuated – Rev. 18:4 / Cities destroyed – Rev. 16:19, Rev. 18:17,20,21 / Famine – Rev.18:8. Some references, such as Rev. 6:12-15, Rev. 8:4-13, and Rev. 9:2-18 contain a higher degree of apparent mythologization than usual and their true nature of is less certain.

in four parts of the book: Rev. 14:7-12, Rev. 16:1-10, Rev. 17:21, and all of Rev. 18. If we assume that the Revelation account is based upon some past event, we should consider it natural for people living in the area to believe that an eruption of a volcano, the most potent, fearsome and awesome force known on earth, would represent the wrath of God sent to punish people of their evil deeds; indeed, many people who live near volcanoes today believe the same.

The following paragraphs present specific reasons for suggesting that most of the apocalyptic events in the Book of Revelation are attributable to a volcanic eruption. This information enables a realistic, natural explanation for many of the disasters described in Revelation:

A Very High Mountain (Rev. 18:5):- Rev. 18:5 says that Babylon's "sins are heaped high as heaven, and God has remembered her iniquities." To some, this might seem metaphorical but on close inspection of the original Greek and in the context of a volcano, we note this is not necessarily the case and that a metaphorical interpretation is not the only way of interpreting the scene. The word used for "sin" is *hamartíai*, a word which can mean "that which is done wrong ... an offence, a violation of the divine law in thought or in act."[557] Note too that the reference to "iniquities" at the end of the verse uses the Greek word, *adikeémata* which is based on *adikeo* which can mean to "hurt, injure, be an offender, be unjust, or to (do, suffer, take) wrong."[558] It is quite logical to assume that violent volcanic activity would be viewed as an act of retribution of the earth-god himself. The iniquities of Revelation's Babylon were *heaped* as high as heaven, i.e., they reached from the earth to high into the sky. The word "heaped" certainly conforms with the idea of a volcanic cone increasing in height over the years as molten magma from deep within the earth rises to the surface. We may therefore tentatively conclude that this verse in Revelation describes "offensive" and "injurious" influences which accumulate, i.e., are "heaped" over time to reach into the sky. In this context, Rev. 18:5 can be seen as a straightforward description of what we in the 21st century would call the emergence of a potential dangerous volcanic dome created by subterranean pressures pushing upwards from deep within the earth's crust. It is not necessary to characterize the description as metaphorical; Revelation's Babylon could have been situated near – or even on the side of – an ever-growing and ever-threatening volcanic mountain.

Warning to leave (Rev. 18:4):- It is natural for people living near a volcano to be concerned about frequent earth tremors as the volcanic dome slowly expands upwards to the sky. Active fissures along its sides spew steam, smoke, ash and poisonous gases into the atmosphere while rivers of hot lava flow down its slopes. Old, verbal accounts of stories of previous eruptions of the mountain renew latent fears in populations who live near the dome. The mountain is beginning to awaken. In Revelation, the people of Babylon are warned: "Come out of her, my people, lest you take part in her sins, lest you share in her plagues" (Rev. 18:4). Increasing frequency of easily recognizable seismic warning signs cause those living closest to the mountain to fear for their lives and, as conditions worsen, to leave.

When a volcano is far inland, people can at times move to a safe distance away. But when it is on a small island, inhabitants of that island must either leave by boat or seek the best refuge they can find as far away from the mountain as possible, i.e., along the shore, with choice places being caves to provide protection against falling ash and lava bombs. History has shown that prolonged minor eruptions typically drive most people from such islands before a catastrophic eruption occurs. "Come *out* of her," is the warning call in Revelation. Note the use of the word, "out," which implies that the threat was surrounded by some limiting feature such as a city wall, a mountain range or, in the case of an island, the ocean. Those who choose not to leave certainly "share in her plagues" as we read in Rev. 18:4. Such warnings would be consistent with the gradual buildup of more and more frequent and threatening seismic activity.

Sudden Fire, Smoke, Lightning, Noise and an Earthquake (Rev. 8:5,8; Rev. 9:2; Rev. 16:18-19; Rev. 18):- Rev. 9:2 describes a shaft of a "bottomless pit, and from the shaft rose smoke like the smoke of a great furnace." Elsewhere, in Rev. 8:8, the magnitude of the event is emphasized in the statement that "something like a great mountain, burning with fire, was thrown into the sea." The abruptness of the event is emphasized in Rev 18:8 where we read, "so shall her plagues come in a single day" while in Rev. 18:10 we read that, "In one hour has thy judgment come" and Rev. 18:17 says "In one hour all this wealth has been laid waste." We have here the vision of a high mountain burning with fire, falling into the sea and rapidly destroying everything near it. Merchants who watch from afar lament with the words, "What city was like the great city?" (Rev. 18:15). Other islands in the area are affected, some entirely disappearing for we read that "every island fled away [sank into the sea], and no mountains were to be found" (Rev. 16:20). This description of the destruction of Babylon conforms quite well with an eruption of a volcanic island in the midst of several other islands in the sea and the subsequent total destruction of low-lying islands by the inevitable earthquakes and tsunamis generated from a huge portion of a mountain falling into the sea. But such parallels with volcanic eruptions do not end here; other events described in Revelation confirm its volcanic nature beyond the shadow of a doubt.

Rev. 8:5 says "There were peals of thunder, voices, flashes of lightning, and an earthquake." The magnitude of this earthquake is emphasized in Rev. 16:18-19 where it is described with the words, "such as had never been since men were on the earth, so great was that earthquake. The great city [Babylon] was split into three parts" (Rev. 16:19). While some of the noise could have been caused directly by earthquakes and the sound of a cataclysmic blast, thunder could have been caused by the frequent and powerful lightning flashes which typically ravage the plumes of gas, smoke and ash thrown up into the atmosphere.

Darkness (Rev. 6:12-13; Rev. 8:12; Rev. 9:2; Rev. 16:10):- Another revealing feature of a major volcanic eruption is all-encompassing darkness. Revelation tells us that after the "bottomless pit" was opened and "from the shaft [the main conduit of the volcano] rose smoke like the smoke of a great furnace ... the sun and the air were darkened with the smoke from the shaft" (Rev. 9:2). Daytime darkness is a common element of every major eruption because airborne clouds of smoke, gases and ash block the light of the sun; these plumes can be so large and dense and high that they completely block the light from the sun in areas close to the eruption and greatly reduce it in areas for quite some distance downwind. Wilson (1985) describes the widespread darkness which accompanied the modern day eruptions of Krakatau and Mount St. Helens:

> In the case of Krakatau, although most of the ash cloud passed over the sea, ships like the *Berbice,* hove-to south of the Sunda Straits, reported no daylight from 6 am on the Sunday evening through to 8 am on the Tuesday morning. When, in 1980, parts of the states of Washington, Idaho and Montana were plunged into darkness by Mount St. Helens, a photograph taken 130 miles from the volcano at Richland, eastern Washington, vividly conveys the ash cloud's appearance moments before it engulfed the area and made it so dark that further photography was impossible.[559]

Ancient writers describe similar experiences. When Pompeii was destroyed by the eruption of Vesuvius in 79 C.E., Pliny the Younger, a Roman, was twenty miles away at Misenum when he saw "a horrible black cloud ripped by sudden bursts of fire, then, in what should have been broad daylight, impenetrable darkness ... . we were enveloped in night - not a moonless one or one dimmed by cloud, but the darkness of a sealed room without lights ... darkness and ashes, thick and heavy."[560]

Similarly, accounts of the catastrophic event described in the Book of Revelation include descriptions of darkness. The darkness mentioned in Rev. 9:2 is unmistakably associated with the smoke thrust up into the atmosphere which blocks out the light of the sun. "And the sun became black as sackcloth, the full moon became like blood." The light from the sun, moon and stars was dimmed so that both day and night were affected: "a third of the sun was struck, and a third of the moon, and a third of the stars, so that a third of their light was darkened; a third of the day was kept from shining, and likewise a third of the night" (Rev. 8:12). Similarly, when "The fifth angel poured his bowl on the throne of the beast ... its kingdom was in darkness; men gnawed their tongues in anguish" (Rev. 16:10). This association of darkness with the dimming of the sun is just as one would expect if the smoke from a volcano partially blocked the light from it. The reference in Rev. 6:13 to stars falling from the sky in Rev. 6:13 may be interpreted as meaning that the stars also disappeared from view because of the dense cloud. And this darkness is accompanied by an earthquake: for we read that at the time "there was a great earthquake" (Rev. 6:12); earthquakes are ever-present threats near active volcanoes and they invariably strike during an eruption.

Hail of Death (Rev. 8:7; Rev. 9:2-11; Rev. 16:10,11,21):- Revelation says that "there fell upon men a great hail out of heaven, every stone about the weight of a talent." (Rev. 16:21, KJV). The exact weight of an ancient talent is unknown although authorities suggest it weighed about 33 kg. (73 lbs) and varied from 20 to 40 kg (44 lbs to 88 lbs) depending on the era and their nationality. Regardless of which measure we use, the hailstones mentioned here were much heavier than normal ones made of ice and it is probably for this reason that the KJV of the book chose the simple word "stones" to describe them rather than "hailstones" used in other versions such as the Revised Standard Version. Another argument against ice-based hail is that we read in Rev. 8:7 that it was hot enough to burn anything on which it falls: "... and there followed hail and fire, mixed with blood [i.e., it was red hot, the color of blood], which fell on the earth; and a third of the earth was burnt up." Elsewhere we read of something falling out of the smoke which issued from a shaft deep in the earth (Rev.

9:2). When it fell to the ground it made a loud noise and killed many: "Then from the smoke came locusts [an obvious metaphor] on the earth" (Rev. 9:3). They sounded "like the noise of many chariots with horses rushing into battle" (Rev. 9:9). Revelation also says that "By these ... plagues a third of mankind was killed" (Rev. 9:18) and many survivors of the hail are left with horrible wounds (Rev. 9:19) – conditions undoubtedly made worse by the inevitable accompaniment of societal chaos and lack of medical assistance typical of such disasters.

The only natural phenomenon which can account for such a dense rain of heavy, hot stones from a cloud is a volcanic eruption in which hot lava is thrown high into the air where it partially cools to form red-hot rocks which fall back to the earth from a cloud of volcanic smoke and ash. When they hit the ground, they sometimes explode or flatten out, melding with others as they cool further. Such chunks of magma are known to range from fairly small to very large, depending on the nature and violence of the eruption. In some volcanoes, such as Mount Etna and Vesuvius, red hot fluid lava fragments varied from small, 8-10 cm. diameter bombs, to exceptionally large ones, reaching a diameter of some 50 centimeters. Much of the power which hurls them into the air comes from subterranean heat which turns subterranean water into steam to create, along with the upward pressure of the magma, such extremely high pressures that the magma itself is blasted out of the volcano's shaft as projectiles of tephra which are appropriately called "volcanic bombs" or "lava bombs." While the smaller bombs can seriously harm or kill anyone they hit, larger ones can destroy entire homes and their occupants. Sudden, violent eruptions emit great numbers of these lava bombs, killing many or all who cannot find adequate shelter in such places as caves and overhanging rock faces. In extremely violent eruptions, there may be a continuous rain of lava bombs, some of which may weigh several tons and hurled several kilometers.[561]

There is another aspect of a volcanic eruption which can accompany the lava bombs causes survivors great pain although it sometimes kills neither people nor vegetation. Volcanic ash and dust can be very toxic and cause severe burns on one's flesh. We read of a similar phenomenon in Rev. 9:3-6, as follows:

> Then out of the smoke came locusts ... with the power of scorpions ... they were told not to harm the grass of the earth or any green growth or any tree, but only those of mankind who have not the seal of God upon their foreheads [i.e., those who were protected from falling ash]; ... allowed to torture them for five months, but not to kill them, and their torture was like the torture of a scorpion, when it stings a man. And in those days men will seek death and will not find it; they will long to die, and death will fly from them.

Similar events are described in Rev. 16 – "... foul and evil sores came upon the men" (Rev. 16:2) and "men gnawed their tongues in anguish and cursed the God of heaven for their pain and sores" (Rev. 16:10-11). This scenario is consistent with conditions far enough away from a volcanic eruption to avoid its direct impacts (fire, heat, the force of the blast, the intense toxicity of the gasses and the rain of lava bombs) but close enough to experience thick blankets of toxic ash. This toxicity is exacerbated by sulfuric acid which forms in the atmosphere when sulfur and its compounds react with hot steam. Also, like those who were protected by the seal of God on their foreheads in Figure 34, individuals who hide in houses or caves or underneath some other type of shelter would not be burned by this type of ash.

When Washington state's Mount St. Helens erupted in 1980, falling ash blistered paintwork on cars as far away as Wyoming. Similarly, ash from the Theran volcano in the Aegean Sea is so toxic that even today, ash from earlier eruptions is known for causing skin irritations.[562] In this manner, just as described in Rev. 16:2, many people downwind of a volcanic eruption suffer severe skin conditions for many months afterwards. The comment by Luce (1969) on the toxicity of the ash from modern-day Thera is germane:

> The story of Thera eruptions continues into the present century. ... Conditions have sometimes been most unpleasant for the inhabitants of Thera and the neighbouring islands. 'Bombs' and blocks have been hurled at them from the vent of the volcano. Gaseous vapours have provoked fainting, headaches, vomiting, even led to suffocation. The white walls of houses in contact with the vapours have turned green or rust-red. ... Vegetation has been badly affected, acid-laden dust has induced conjunctivitis, and sulfurated hydrogen vapour has been responsible for angina and bronchitis. In certain wind conditions suffering has been caused as far away as Ios, Anaphi and Sikinos.[563]

This scenario is not entirely unlike the breath of fire and smoke and sulphur which issued from the mouths of horses in Rev. 9:17. Furthermore, in areas which do not receive very heavy ash-fall, most vegetation will survive, as in Rev. 9:4 where the "locusts" are "told not to harm the grass of the earth or any green growth or any tree."

Poisonous Water (Rev. 8:9-11; Rev. 16:3,4,13):- But toxic effects of Revelation's catastrophes are not limited to people and plants living on the land; both fresh and marine waters are also contaminated and many aquatic species are affected. In referring to fresh water supplies, Rev. 8:11 says that "A third of the waters became wormwood, and many men died of the water, because it was made bitter." And with respect to the ocean, Rev 16:3 says that "the sea ... became like the blood of a dead man, and every living thing died that was in the sea." Similarly, Wilson (1969) says that "Submarine exhalations [from modern Theran eruptions] have poisoned large quantities of fish."[564] In a more specific vein, he describes a bay in one of the area's two Kameni islands in which

> water is stained a deep reddish-brown [*cf.* Revelation's "sea ... became like blood]. Its temperature is bath-water warm, and at times when there have been minor eruptions (which today centre on the Kameni islands) the staining has stretched for many miles around the islands. All marine life within a twenty-five-mile radius has died when eruptions and staining of the water have occurred, apparently as a result of the presence of sulphuric acid.[565]

There are numerous records of such extensive fish kills associated with toxicity and discolored water in the vicinity of active volcanos. The reports of poisonous waters in Rev. 8:9-11 and Rev. 16:3-4 are therefore entirely consistent with the effects of a volcanic eruption on surrounding areas.

View from the Sea (Rev. 18):- We are told that Babylon will be "burned with fire" (Rev. 18:8) and survivors "will weep and wail over her when they see the smoke of her burning" (Rev. 18:9). This text refers to "merchants" (Rev. 18:15), "shipmasters and seafaring men, sailors and all whose trade is on the sea" (Rev. 18:17) as they watched her destruction from a great distance. A vivid image is thus presented of survivors standing on the decks of ships watching as their city is destroyed by fire. Those too close to the inferno are "scorched by the fierce heat" (Rev. 16:9) and "a third of the ships ... destroyed" (Rev. 8:9); those who stand "far off" at a safe distance survive (Rev. 18:17, Rev. 18:10,15) while those without ships or boats perish. The fact that the sailors in Revelation had to stand a "great distance" away from the fire indicates that this was no ordinary burning of a city. This description is entirely consistent with the destruction by a volcanic eruption on a heavily populated island in the sea.

Discussion:- We can conclude from the above that practically all the cataclysmic events described in the Book of Revelation can be explained in terms of a volcanic eruption. Perhaps the most telling evidence is the suddenness and extent of the event: "so shall *her plagues come in a single day*, pestilence and mourning [an obvious reference to death] and famine, and she shall be *burned with fire*" (Rev. 18:8; see also Rev. 18:10). We read of smoke and fire (Rev. 8:4,7,8; Rev. 9:2,17; Rev. 18:5,9) coupled with a thundering noises (Rev. 8:5; Rev. 9:9; Rev. 16:18), earthquakes (Rev. 6:12,14; Rev. 8:5; Rev. 16:18,19), and lightning (Rev. 8:5), all of which can be caused by an eruption. Darkness falls over the land underneath a huge, dense cloud of volcanic ash, smoke and gas (Rev. 6:12,13; Rev. 8:12; Rev. 9:2; Rev. 16:10) while lava bombs hail down from the cloud to the ground (Rev. 8:7; Rev. 16:21), killing everyone within range. Searing heat (Rev. 16:9) and toxic gases kill everything downwind of the blast, both on the land and in the water (Rev. 9:3-6; Rev. 8:9-11; Rev. 16:3-4). But those who had heeded the warning signs (Rev. 18:4) escaped in ships and watch the spectacle from afar (Rev. 18:10,15,17) while those not far enough away to escape the fury of the blast died (Rev. 8:9). Cities and towns for many kilometers around are destroyed by earthquakes or buried by the rain of hot lava bombs and ash (Rev. 16:19, Rev. 18:17,20,21). Islands disappear beneath the sea as the seabed drops (Rev. 18:21). And after the eruption, when the volcanic clouds are sufficiently cleared, survivors see that entire islands in the area have vanished (Rev. 16:20). The once mountainous volcanic dome is gone and the island itself has been split into three parts, her cities and towns utterly destroyed (Rev. 16:19). The aftermath is also devastating: many survivors suffer from broken bones, burns, and painful skin conditions caused by lava bombs, lingering toxic dust and ash-fall (Rev. 9:3-8) – ash-fall which covers much of the land, killing plants and causing widespread famine, including disease and death (Rev. 18:8).

Revelation's description of a volcanic eruption takes on added realism when viewed as a whole and its mythologizations are stripped from the text and scenes not directly related to catastrophic events are removed. The following annotated compilation of the remaining text, along with extracts from the above explanatory paragraphs, demonstrate and consolidate the high drama of the early accounts of the event:

> **Rev. 6:12** ... behold, there was a great earthquake; and the sun became black as sackcloth [from the smoke and volcanic ash spewed into the atmosphere during the

13. Catastrophes 257

eruption], the full moon became [red] like blood [because of the effect on its light by smoke, airborne ash and dust], [13]and the stars of the sky fell to the earth ["died," or became invisible] ... [14]the sky vanished [was no longer visible] ... and every mountain and island was removed from its place [shaken, enlarged or shrunken by the earthquake]. [15]Then the kings of the earth and the great men and the generals and the rich and the strong, and every one, slave and free, hid in the caves and among the rocks of the mountains [for protection against volcanic debris and lava bombs falling on them],

Rev. 8:4 ... the smoke [from the eruption] ... rose [into the sky] ... [5] ... and there were peals of thunder [noise from the eruption and the lightning produced in the volcanic plume], voices [noises], flashes of lightning, and an earthquake [a normal phenomenon during eruptions]. [7] ... and there followed hail [of lava bombs and rocks] and fire [red-hot lava bombs], mixed with blood [red-colored ash and dust from the volcano?], which fell on the earth [from the plume]; and a third of the earth [in the affected area near the eruption] was burnt up [by the heat, lava bombs flaming through the air, hot ash and dust], and a third of the trees were burnt up [by the heat, lava bombs, hot ash and dust], and all green grass [in the area] was burnt up [by the heat, lava bombs, hot ash and dust]. [8]and something like a great mountain [the volcano's towering dome], burning with fire [from the eruption], was thrown into the sea [i.e., much of the volcanic dome was ejected into the sky and fell into the sea while parts of the island simply collapsed and slid down the slopes into it]; [9]and a third of the sea became [the color of] blood [from the red ash which fell into it], a third of the living creatures in the sea died [from boiling hot water or the toxicity of dust and sub-sea gasses in the immediate vicinity of the volcano], and a third of the ships were destroyed [from the fiery heat and toxicity of the dust and gases from the eruption]. [10] ... and a great star [an extremely large portion of the mountain?] fell from heaven, blazing like a torch [on fire], and it fell on a third of the rivers and on the fountains of water [in the vicinity of the eruption]. [11] ... A third of the waters became wormwood [undrinkable], and many men died of the water, because it was made bitter [poison]. [12] ... and a third of the [light of the] sun was struck, and a third of the [light of the] moon, and a third of the [light of the] stars, so that a third of their light was darkened; a third of the [light of] day was kept from shining, and likewise a third of the [brightness of the moon and stars at] night. [13] ... "Woe, woe, woe to those who dwell on the earth [within the far-reaching range of the effects of the eruption, which, in the case of extremely large eruptions, may extend around the entire globe]."

Rev. 9:2 ... the shaft of the bottomless pit [the depths of the earth], and from the shaft [of "the bottomless pit," i.e., from the depths of the earth; the main conduit of the volcano] rose smoke [from the volcano] like the smoke of a great furnace, and the sun and the air were darkened with the smoke from the shaft [as is typical during volcanic eruptions]. [3]Then from the smoke came [fell] locusts [plagues, torment, etc. from hot lava bombs and toxic dust particles] on the earth, and they were given power like the power of scorpions [to burn or irritate the skin of the people] of the earth; [5]they were allowed to torture them for five months, but not to kill them, and their torture was like the torture of a scorpion, when it stings a man [burning inflamation, infection, high fevers, and etc.]. [6]And in those days men will seek death and will not find it; they will long to die [from these afflictions], and death will fly from them [because they are not mortally afflicted].[9] the noise [of the falling tephra and lava bombs]... was like the noise of many chariots with horses rushing into battle. [17] ... and fire and smoke and sulphur [which forms sulphuric acid when combined with steam] issued [from the gasses and lava bombs] [18]By these ... plagues a third of mankind was killed, by the fire and smoke and sulphur ....

Rev. 16:3 ... the [surrounding] sea, ... became [red from the red ash] like the blood of a dead man, and every living thing died that was in the sea [i.e., a massive fish kill occurred]. [4] ... the rivers and the fountains of water ... became [red like] blood [from the red-colored rock, ash and dust]. 9. men were scorched by the fierce heat [of the hot gasses from the eruption] ... ¹⁰The ... kingdom [of the people in the surrounding area, and especially the area enveloped by the dark cloud of volcanic debris and toxic gases] was in darkness; men gnawed their tongues in anguish ... ¹²... the great river Euphrates, and its water was dried up [because of earthquakes which caused parts of the land to raise while others dropped so that the river changed its course – a common phenomenon associated with earthquakes] ... ¹⁷... the [toxic gases in the] air, and a loud voice [noise] came out [from the volcano] ... ¹⁸And there were flashes of lightning [from within and around the volcanic plume], voices [noise], peals of thunder [associated with the eruption and the lightning], and a great earthquake such as had never been since men were on the earth, so great was that earthquake [associated with the eruption]. ¹⁹The great city [the volcanic island and its complex of cities and towns] was split into three parts, and the cities of the nations [city-states] fell [were destroyed], ... ²⁰And every island [in the vicinity of the eruption] fled away [sank into the sea or became invisible in the darkness of the volcanic ash and debris in the atmosphere], and no mountains were to be found [because the dust obliterated them from view, or they had sunk beneath sea level]; ²¹and great hailstones [lava bombs], heavy as a hundred-weight [lava bombs are known to exceed this weight], dropped on men from heaven [where the volcano's plume filled the sky], till men cursed God for the plague of the hail [lava bombs], so fearful was that plague.

Rev. 18:4 ... "Come out of her [evacuate the area], my people, lest you take part in [experience] her sins [dangers, evils, and harm], lest you share in her plagues [destructive actions]; ⁵for her sins [evils and potential for harm] are heaped high as heaven [in the form of a volcanic dome and/or the plume which could have extended more than 30 kilometers up into the atmosphere] ... ⁸so shall her plagues come in a single day [during her final cataclysmic eruption], pestilence [from the direct and indirect effects of the volcano] and mourning [death] and famine [with the destruction of crops and food supplies], and she shall be burned with fire [the fiery blast from the eruption and the hot, falling ash]; ... ⁹And the kings of the earth [diplomatic and trade representatives of the many nations' kings who had evacuated the area by ship] ... will weep and wail over her when they see the smoke of her burning; ¹⁰they will stand far off [on the decks of their ships], in fear of her torment [danger from the eruption], and say, "Alas! alas! thou great city, thou mighty city [group of cities or city-states], ... In one hour has thy judgment [destruction] come." ¹¹And the merchants of the earth [who did business in the area] weep and mourn for her, since no one buys their cargo any more, ¹²cargo of gold, silver, jewels and pearls, fine linen, purple, silk and scarlet, all kinds of scented wood, all articles of ivory, all articles of costly wood, bronze, iron and marble, ¹³cinnamon, spice, incense, myrrh, frankincense, wine, oil, fine flour and wheat, cattle and sheep, horses and chariots, and slaves, that is, human souls. ¹⁴"The fruit [special, coveted fruit products] for which thy soul longed has gone from thee, and all thy dainties and thy splendor are lost to thee, never to be found again!" ¹⁵The merchants of these wares, who gained wealth from her, will stand far off [on the decks of their sea-going ships], in fear of her torment, weeping and mourning aloud, ¹⁶"Alas, alas, for the great city that was clothed in fine linen, in purple and scarlet, bedecked with gold, with jewels, and with pearls! ¹⁷In one hour all this wealth has been laid waste." And all shipmasters and seafaring men, sailors and all whose trade is on the sea, stood far off [onthe decks of their ships] ¹⁸and cried out as they saw the smoke of her burning [eruption], "What city was like the great city?" ¹⁹And they threw dust on their heads, as they wept and mourned, crying out, "Alas, alas, for the great city where all who had ships at sea grew rich by her wealth! In one hour she has been laid waste. ²¹Then ... a stone like a great [mountainous] millstone ... [was ejected] into the sea [in the final cataclysmic eruption which caused the destruction or sinking of most of the island], ... "So shall ... the great city be thrown down with violence, and shall be found no more; ²²and the sound of harpers and minstrels, of flute players and trumpeters, shall be heard in thee no more; and a craftsman of any craft shall be found in thee no more; and the sound of the millstone shall be heard in thee no more; [23]and the light of a lamp shall shine in thee no more; and the voice of bridegroom and bride shall be heard in thee no more; ... [24]And in her was found the blood [death] of prophets and of saints, and of all who have been slain on earth [from the eruptions].

We find in this treatment what can only be interpreted as a vivid account of an eruption of a volcano on or near a densely populated island. As we shall see in the next section, many of these catastrophic events have parallels in ancient Egyptian texts. In later sections, we will explore accounts of similar events in ancient Greek and modern sources.

Egyptian Accounts

Egyptian literature mentions volcanic eruptions although no mention is made of the names of the volcanoes or when they might have erupted. Before discussing specific cases, a general comment should be made about ancient Egypt's depth of knowledge on the subject; it seems that it was imported from elsewhere, most likely from the mid-Mediterranean area, where there are several active volcanoes, and from deep within the African continent. One source of our understanding of the general state of knowledge in ancient Egypt is the *Onomasticon of Amenope*. This document has been an important adjunct to our understanding of Egyptian cosmology and contains some of Egypt's fundamental ideas about the creation of the earth. It is therefore a meaningful starting point for a discussion on volcanoes.

The *Onomasticon* is, as Clagett (1989) puts it, "a sober listing of all the categories of existence which the author thought his readers should know. No doubt if he had wished to describe the entries in addition to listing them, he [Amenope] would have resorted to mythological descriptions, as his remarks concerning Ptah and Thoth suggest."[566] The opening of this document provides us with a general comment on volcanoes; it says:

Beginning of the teaching for clearing the mind for instruction of the ignorant, and for learning all things that exist: what Ptah created, what Thoth copied down, heaven with its designs, earth and what is in it, *what the mountains belch forth*,˙ what is watered by the flood, all things upon which Re has shone, all that is grown on the back of earth, excogitated by the scribe of the sacred books in the House of Life, Amenope, son of Amenope. He said: ...[567]

Unfortunately, apart from this, there are very few if any other explicit references to volcanic activity in the Egyptian literature. Nevertheless, a brief survey of the best known religious sources in ancient Egypt reveals several closely related passages which, when mythologizeations are stripped, can be viewed as referring to one or more volcanoes. These references are most obvious in Chapters 146, 149, and 150 of the *Book of the Dead* and another source called the *Book of the Divine Cow*.

These three chapters from the *Book of the Dead* are unusual in the annals of Egyptian literature in that they emphasize a series of catastrophic natural phenomena. Each chapter is divided into short sections referred to as either "portals" in the case of Chapter 146 or "mounds" in the case of Chapter 149; Chapter 150 is simply a list of descriptive (or alternative) names of the mounds described in Chapter 149. Also, Chapters 146 and 149 seem to be temple rituals in which the participant is meant to walk from station to station as he recites a passage concerning events at each portal or mound. This purpose is more evident in Chapter 146 where each passage is prefaced by a statement something like: "What is to be said by N [the deceased] when arriving at the eighteenth portal." In Chapter 149 such prefaces are implied rather than explicitly stated. The similarities between the descriptions of events at the portals and mounds suggest these two chapters likely reflect the same events; they seem to be slightly different versions of a single source.

Two other documents, of a secular rather than religious nature, are also germane to the subject; these are typically called the *Prophesy of Neferrohu* and the *Admonitions of an Egyptian Sage*. They describe a period of physical devastation in Egypt, especially in the Delta region. Events described are usually attributed by modern Egyptologists to a period of social unrest during the Hyksos dominion in 2nd Intermediate period (1640-1532 BCE). But they also contain references to earthquakes, unusual darkness, dramatic environmental changes, death and local infighting; they make no mention of warfare as a contributing factor to the events.

Significantly, several of the seemingly volcanic-origin phenomena mentioned in these documents, like some of those in the Book of Revelation, are typically experienced many kilometers downwind of an eruption. This observation conforms with the fact that there is no volcano in Egypt, nor have there been any there for many thousands of years, and certainly not during the period in which our interest lies.

Book of the Dead

The mounds in Chapter 149 are described as having fields, hills, plateaus, mountains and lofty cliffs as well as cities and towns.[568] For example, the 1st mound is described as a pleasant place to live where "men live on Shens-loaves and jugs of beer" while the 2nd emphasizes fertile farmland. The 4th boasts of a very high mountain. The 8th, 11th and 14th describe plateaus while the 7th to 14th mention towns and harbors.[a] The exact locations of these towns are not given although the 14th, called Kheraha, is described as a shipping port and is usually assumed by Egyptologists to be the area now known as "Old Cairo" which lay just outside the ancient city of Heliopolis near modern-day Cairo. (This assumption may not be valid; the Kheraha of Chapter 149 will be discussed in the next chapter.) Another mound (the 7th) is described as being "far out of sight" while another (the 8th) is associated with high and mighty waves, suggesting that a large expanse of ocean is involved. The overall picture painted in Chapter 149 is thus one of a mountainous or hilly land spotted with fertile farms and shipping ports located somewhere beyond a large expanse of water.

---

[a] The names of the towns of the 7th through 14th (excluding the 13th) are Ises, Hahotep, Ikesy, Qahu, Idu, Wenet and Kheraha respectively; the 13th is described as having a harbor with the descriptive name of "He who opens his mouth, a basin of water." (See Faulkner, 1994, p. 122).

But Chapter 149 also paints pictures of places with disturbing and terrifying characteristics. The 3rd mound, for example, is described as having "Spirits whose faces are downcast," the 5th as a "Mound of Spirits by which men do not pass," the 7th has "breath of fire," the 8th describes "waves over the water in which none have power, because so great is the height of its roar." The 9th "opens with fire, and its breath is destruction to noses and mouths," the 12th is considered so dangerous that even "the gods cannot get near it, the spirits cannot associate with it," and the 13th is described as a "Mound of Spirts over which no one has power, its water is fire, its waves are fire, its breath is efficient for burning" people. The mounds of Chapter 149 are therefore described as being a very desirable place to live on the one hand, and on the other, an extremely dangerous place. Meanwhile, the naming of each of the stations as "mounds" is consistent with the concepts of them actually representing many islands in a coastal area – or different aspects of a single island, a descriptive technique frequently used by Egyptian priests.

Chapter 146[569] is similar to 149 except that it is almost entirely devoted to events associated with the destructive nature of a mountain of fire. Its fiery, destructive nature is revealed among the multitude of names associated with its various "portals." The 1st portal, for example, is called "Mistress of trembling, lofty of enclosure wall, chieftainess and Mistress of Destruction" while its gatekeeper is called "Terror." The 5th portal is called "Mistress of Heat," the 6th, "Lord of Shouting," the 8th is referred to as "Heat of Flames ... the one who kills without warning," the 14th is "Mistress of Wrath," and the 16th, "The Terrible One, Lady of Pestilence who casts away thousands of human souls." And the 21st describes one "who acts the slayer, who descends in her own flame." In a setting of a mountain of fire, so many references to trembling land, fire, heat, death, and destruction, the reader is left with a vision of a high, quaking mountain of fire dispensing death and destruction to everyone and everything within its reach – in short, it has the characteristics of an active volcano. Meanwhile, the naming of each of the stations as "portals" is consistent with the presence of harbors so at least a part of the area appears to be coastal. (This, of course, conforms with the coastal location of most ancient towns and cities.)

The overall impact of the descriptions of many mounds (islands) and portals (harbors) in Chapters 146 and 149 is that, rather than each mound and portal belonging to different areas, they represent different aspects of the same general area. The vision one gets is of pleasant communities (towns and cities) in Chapter 149 on a single island or distributed among a group of islands. But we are also given visions of wide-spread destruction and a mountain of fire which strongly suggest that these chapters (Chapters 146, 149 and 150) are closely related. Indeed, we may reasonably propose that they both deal with essentially the same theme – the destruction of many people living among a group of islands in the sea and that one looks like an enormous mountain of fire, i.e., an active volcano; this, of course, conforms with the conclusion reached in the preceding section concerning parallels found in the Book of Revelation.

We will next explore the extent to which events described in these three chapters of the *Book of the Dead* parallel events described in the Book of Revelation. These events are presented in Table 13.1; while most parallels outlined in the table are self-explanatory and require no elaboration, several items in the table warrant discussion, as follows:

A Very High Mountain (Rev. 18:5):- In Table 13.1 we find in the column which reports the content of Egyptian texts, a reference to a "very high mountain ... on which the sky rests." It is described as a woman, a "Mistress of Power" and a "devourer," a "Mound of Spirits over which no one has power." This mountain is greatly feared and "towering" in its majesty and is called, "One who Made Himself," a phrase which could refer to the way in which a volcanic dome gradual increases in height from subterranean pressures pushing upwards and the lava which pours out, cools and accumulates on its slopes. The latter suggestion is supported by the text which says "its water is fire, its waves are fire," and this "water" is undrinkable – a possible description of rivers of hot lava running down the mountain side. The mountain emits extremely hot gasses, for we are told that "its breath is efficient for burning." And like a volcano, it makes loud noises for it is also called "Lord of Shouting," a name which could refer to the thunderous roar of its activity. Furthermore, when shrouded in a vast cloud of smoke, volcanic ash and steam, its "length and breath cannot be known," and its shape is "mysterious," i.e., hidden or secret, and its "nature has not been understood since her beginning." Finally, this mountain is a long way from Egypt for, in spite of its great height, it is described as being "far out of sight." These aspects alone suggest an active volcano; and its terrifying, ever-increasing size parallels Rev. 18:5 where it says "her sins [the dangerous, evil powers within her] are heaped high as heaven."

Sudden Fire, Smoke, Lightning, Noise, an Earthquake and Darkness (Rev. 8:5,8; Rev. 9:2; Rev. 16:18-19) :- The volcano erupts unexpectedly at dawn; we are told that it is "She who announces the dawn in her time." The phrase "in her time" is usually interpreted as meaning that "she selects her own time" to make her announcement to the world. The Egyptian record calls her, the "Lord of Shouting." Her announcement, of course, involves sound – the thunderous noise of a "flaming hot" eruption which "kills without warning" for she is the "Fiery One, Mistress of Heat," "Lover of Heat" and "Mistress of Fire," and she "burns up the rebellious" ones who refuse to leave or are unable to escape the reach of her destructive power. The noise of the eruption and the accompanying earthquake conforms with Revelation's "voices" and "peals of thunder" (Rev. 16:18). She is also called, "Mistress of Darkness." This darkness conforms with the statement that "the sun and the air were darkened with the smoke from the shaft" (Rev. 9:2). As described above and in the Revelation account, darkness conforms with the blocking of sunlight by the plume of volcanic gasses, ash and debris which are thrust high in the sky above and in the vicinity of the eruption; it is emphasized in the Egyptian text with the descriptive name: " 'Mistress of every portal, to whom acclamation is made on the *day of darkness*' is your name.'" These Egyptian names thus have distinct parallels with events described in the Book of Revelation.

Hail of Pain and Death (Rev. 8:7; Rev. 9:2-11; Rev. 16:10,11,21):- Everyone within range who have not sought shelter are showered by lava bombs, swirling blobs of molten to semi-hardened rock, some the size of large boulders. This hail descends from the darkness of the volcanic plume; the Egyptian text describes the phenomenon as an aspect of a goddess "who descends in her own flame." The text also says that "She is under secret governance," a phrase which could refer to the mountain being

13. Catastrophes   263

Table 13.1 Attributes of volcanic eruptions described in Chapters 146, 149 and 150 of the *Book of the Dead* (BD)[570] compared with similar passages from the Book of Revelation. P = portal number and M = mound number in Chapters 146 and 149 respectively.

Attribute	Book of Revelation	Egyptian Text	Egyptian Source
Very high volcanic mountain	for her sins are heaped high as heaven, and God has remembered her iniquities. (Rev. 18:5)	- The Very High Mountain - as for the *very high mountain*' which is in God's Domain, *on which the sky rests*' ... - Mistress of Power, large size, devourer. 'O Foremost One, Mistress of Power, ... the *devourer*', the mistress of everyone.' ... 'One who Made Himself.' - 'Lord of Shouting,' whose length and breath cannot be known, whose nature has not been understood since her beginning. - the *Mound of Spirits over which no one has power*', its water is fire, its waves are fire, its breath is efficient for burning, in order that no one may drink its water to quench their thirst, that being what is in them, because their fear is so great and so *towering*' is its majesty.	BD150 B149/M4 BD146/P9 BD146/P6 BD149/M13
Fire, heat and Smoke	... a great mountain, burning with fire, was thrown into the sea; (Rev. 8:8) ... a third of mankind was killed, by the fire and smoke and sulphur ... (Rev. 9:18) ... her plagues come in a single day, ... she shall be burned with fire ... (Rev. 18:8)	- The mountain ... which is far out of sight, its breath is fire ... - none goes in or out ... it opens with fire - As for that mound of Wenet ... its breath is fire, and the gods cannot get near it, the spirits cannot associate with it ... - O Fiery One, Mistress of Heat' - O Heat of Flames ... sharp of flames ... the one who kills without warning, the one whom no one passes because of the fear of her pain. - She who ... burns up the rebellious ... - She who dances in blood ... Mistress of Fire.' - Lover of heat - She who announces the dawn in her time, flaming hot	BD149/M7 BD149/M9 BD149/M12 BD146/P5 BD146/P8 BD146/P11 BD146/P17 BD146/P18 BD146/P19
Darkness	... its kingdom was in darkness; men gnawed their tongues in anguish (Rev 16:10)	- 'Mistress of Darkness, Lord of Shouting,' - 'Mistress of every portal, to whom acclamation is made on the day of darkness' is your name.	BD146/P6 BD146/P11

Attribute	Book of Revelation	Egyptian Text	Egyptian Source
Viewing from a distance	they will stand far off, in fear of her torment ... (Rev. 18:10) The merchants ... will stand far off, in fear of her torment (Rev 18:15) ... and all whose trade is on the sea, stood far off and cried out as they saw the smoke of her burning (Rev. 18:17-18)	- Hahotep; it is he who guards it in order that none may come near it.	BD149/M8
		- none goes in or out ... its breath is destruction to noses and mouths. ... He has done it against those who are in it in order that none may come near it except on the day of great celebration.	BD149/M9
		- its breath is fire, and the gods cannot get near it, the spirits cannot associate with it.	BD149/M12
		- its water is fire, its waves are fire, its breath is efficient for burning, in order that no one may drink its water to quench their thirst, that being what is in them because their fear is so great and so towering is its majesty. ... Gods and spirits see its water [i.e., its fire] from afar ...	BD149/M13
Noise	Rev. 16:18 And there were flashes of lightning, voices, peals of thunder, and a great earthquake ... (Rev. 16:18)	- Lord of Shouting	BD146/P6
Lava Bombs	and great hailstones, heavy as a hundred-weight, dropped on men from heaven, till men cursed God for the plague of the hail, so fearful was that plague. (Rev. 16:21)	- O Mighty of Knives ["knife"is a homophone of "large stone"] ... the one who smashes the enemies	BD146/P4
		- She who bears knives [large stones], who burns up the rebellious.	BD146/P11
		- 'The terrible One, Lady of Pestilence, who casts away thousands of human souls, who hacks up human dead, who decapitates them who would go out, who creates terror.'	BD146/P16
		- 'Sharp of knife [large stones?] ... who acts the slayer, who descends in her own flame.	BD146/P21
Destruction	They have as king over them ... he is called Apol'lyon. [translation: The Destroyer] (Rev. 9:11)	- O Mistress of trembling, lofty of enclosure wall, chieftainess and Mistress of Destruction.' ... The name ... is 'Terror.'	BD146/P1
		- who destroys those who come at dawn	BD146/P12
Tsunami	Then a mighty angel took up a stone like a great millstone and threw it into the sea, saying, "So shall Babylon the great city be thrown down with violence, and shall be found no more; (Rev. 18:21)	- as for Hahotep, great and mighty, with waves over the water in which none have power, because so great is the terror of the height of its roar ...	BD149/M8
		- May I have power over the water in the flood like that god who is in the Mound of Water. ... Hail to you, you god in the Mound of Water!	BD149/M13

13. Catastrophes

Attribute	Book of Revelation	Egyptian Text	Egyptian Source
Fish kills	... and every living thing died that was in the sea. (Rev. 16:3)	- the god who is in it is called 'feller of the adju-fish.' ... The Feller of the adju-fish shall not have power over me.	BD149/M6
		- The god who is in it is Feller of Fish	BD150
Death	And in her was found the blood of prophets and of saints, and of all who have been slain on earth. (Rev. 18:24)	- Mistress of wrath, who dances in blood	BD146/P14
		- The terrible One, Lady of Pestilence, who casts away thousands of human souls, who hacks up human dead, who decapitates them who would go out, who creates terror.	BD146/P16
		- The god who is in it is Destroyer of Souls	BD150

made invisible because of the presence of its volcanic plume." But it is in her titles of "Mighty of Knives' [or large stones]"[a] and "... the one who smashes the enemies" which relates best to a hail of lava bombs on the heads of her victims. She "destroys those who come [within the range of her destructive power] at dawn," and "dances in [the] blood" of her victims. This interpretation parallels the event described in Rev. 16:21 as "great hailstones, heavy as a hundred-weight, dropped on men from heaven, till men cursed God for the plague of the hail, so fearful was that plague."

Chapter 150 of the *Book of the Dead* says that "The god who is in it [the 10th Mound] is a Destroyer of Souls." This compares with Chapter 146 which reports on the death of many who fall victim to "The terrible One, Lady of Pestilence, who casts away thousands of human souls, who hacks up human dead, who decapitates them who would go out, who creates terror." These texts have a ring similar to that of Rev. 11:13 which says that, "at that hour there was a great earthquake, and a tenth of the city fell; seven thousand people were killed in the earthquake, and the rest were

---

[a] The Egyptian word used in the 4th Portal of the 146th Chapter of the *Book of the Dead* is usually translated as "knives" rather than "large stones." In fact, the original text is ambiguous, especially in the *Papyrus of Ani*. The relevant Egyptian word for "knife" is *tes*, written as [hieroglyphs] or [hieroglyphs] (Budge, 1920, p. 888a) while the plural, "knives," is *tesu*, written as [hieroglyphs] where the [glyph] and [glyph] (or [glyph]) symbols are determinatives for knifes (Gardiner, 1927, Symbol T30, p. 514). Alternatively, the word for flint-stone is *tes*, usually written as [hieroglyphs] (Faulkner, 1962, p. 316) and that for "large stones" is *teseru*, written as [hieroglyphs] (Budge, 1920, p. 888b) where the [glyph] symbol in each is the determinative for stone (Gardiner, 1927, Symbol N37, p. 491). In the *Papyrus of Ani*, the word used in the 4th Portal is pronounced the same as *teseru* and written as [hieroglyphs] (from Faulkner, 1994, Plate 11) with a knife ([glyph]) as the determinative rather than a stone ([glyph]). The word enables a pun; it is written as "knives," but its vocalization can mean "large stones." Moreover, note that the similar word, *tesheru*, written as [hieroglyphs] (Faulkner, 1962, p. 316), means "blood," or when written as [hieroglyphs] means the 'red ones,' i.e., the wicked gods who were associated with Seth" (Budge, 1920, p. 889b). In this way we can see how red-hot molten lava bombs might be envisioned as "large red stones" or "knives," both of which can kill. This interpretation lends new meaning to the name translated by Faulkner (1992, p. 121) in the 11th Portal: "She who bears knives, who burns up the rebellious."

terrified." While the Egyptian text refers to the mountain as the "Mistress of wrath, who dances in blood" and says that "the god who is in it is a Destroyer of Souls," the Book of Revelation says that "in her was found the blood of prophets and of saints, and of all who have been slain on earth (Rev. 18:24).

Poisonous Water (Rev. 8:9-11; Rev. 16:3,4,13):- When eruptions occur in coastal areas or on small islands, marine fish in the area typically suffer high mortality rates. The *Book of the Dead* says that the god in the mountain is a "Feller of Fish," a descriptive phrase in keeping with massive die-offs of fish usually associated with volcanic eruptions. This parallels the text of the Book of Revelation where we read that the "sea ... became like the blood [from toxic, red volcanic ash] of a dead man, and every living thing died that was in the sea" (Rev. 16:3).

View from the Sea (Rev. 18):- Hot ash and toxic fumes are spewed from all eruptions. The Egyptian text says, "its breath is fire, and *the gods cannot get near it,* the spirits cannot associate with it" and "no one passes because of the fear of her pain." Similarly, we read in Rev. 18:17-18 that "all shipmasters and seafaring men, sailors and all whose trade is on the sea, *stood far off'* and cried out as they saw the smoke of her burning." It may be significant that this same theme is repeated four times in Chapter 149 of the *Book of the Dead* (at mounds 8,9,12,13) and as many as three times in Rev. 18 (at Rev. 18:10,15,17); this repetition in both sources also represents a parallel.

Mountainous Waves:- Egyptian records describe abnormally high seas: "great and mighty, with waves over the water in which none have power, because so great is the terror of the height of its roar." They even assign a god to the mountain of water which swept over the sea; at one station in the ritual, the priest claims "power over the water in the flood like that god who is in the Mound of Water. ... Hail to you, you *god in the Mound of Water!*'" Volcanic eruptions can create mountainous oceanic waves called *mega-tsunamis*, a name based on the name *tsunamis* given to high oceanic waves caused by undersea earthquakes. Mega-tsunamis are created when the walls of a volcanic dome suddenly collapse, sending huge sections of one or more of its sides sliding into the sea. The mass of such landslides can at times be as great as that of an entire mountain (an event which would parallel the statement in Rev. 8:8 that "a great mountain, burning with fire, was thrown into the sea"). Mega-tsunamis can rise up to hundreds of meters in height and are extremely devastating in heavily populated coastal areas. They spread rapidly from the eruption site and strike the shoreline of neighboring islands and distance coasts with devastating force. This single attribute of volcanic eruptions on small islands may cause more damage and loss of life than all others combined. Such mountains of water, can destroy an entire multi-island civilization, an event which parallels the one described in Rev. 18:21, "Then a mighty angel took up a stone like a great millstone and threw it into the sea, saying, 'So shall Babylon the great city be thrown down with violence, and shall be found no more.'"

Discussion:- The names and descriptions of many of the mounds and portals in Chapters 146, 149 and 150 of the *Book of the Dead* suggest these chapters represent a mythologized account of a set of catastrophes which beset a group of islands in the sea. The combined characteristics of these catastrophes strongly suggest that they resulted from a major volcanic eruption involving a group of islands – just as were those discussed in the Book of Revelation. Since the only well-known, documented group of islands in the Egyptian literature lies in the Aegean Sea, we may conclude that these chapters in the *Book of the Dead* refer to the eruption of the Aegean volcanic island of Thera in about 1628 BCE.

Book of the Divine Cow

This book is of special interest because it begins with what Budge (1934)) refers to as the "Legend of the Destruction of Mankind."[571] The legend gives a brief outline of the decimation of the human race on earth and begins at a time when Re lived on earth "as king of men as well as of the gods." But when he grew old, "men began to devise evil plans against him." So Re secretly called for his attendants to advise him on the rebellion and the best way to punish them. They said, "May thy Eye go out and catch (?) for thee those who conspire (against thee). There is no Eye more fit to strike them for thee. Let it come down as Hathor!" This *Eye* was Re's own fiery eye with which he smote his enemies. He then dispatched the goddess Hathor against the rebels who had escaped his wrath by fleeing into the desert; Hathor's action was so horrendous that one goddess even "waded in their blood."[572]

The legend continues, although apparently not in chronological order. It mentions events typical of a volcanic eruption and found here to be similar to events described in Revelation. Some of the more readily identifiable events mentioned in both the *Book of the Divine Cow* and the Book of Revelation are listed in Table 13.2 where they are organized according to what one might expect if they were related to an eruption; the correct or hidden sequence of events in the earliest Egyptian version is as yet unknown.

The *Book of the Divine Cow* goes on to describe the destruction of the old order, including several parallels to catastrophic events in the Book of Revelation. One segment of the *Book of the Divine Cow* describes a series of events which closely parallel those described in Rev. 10:5-6 and these will be discussed in Chapter 15, *The Little Scroll*. As we shall see there, these events also parallel those found in the *Book of Aker* which describe events at the end of the world and the re-creation of the cosmos. Some of the more pertinent ones mentioned in the *Book of Aker* will be discussed in the next section. Also, details of the *Book of Aker* will be discussed in Chapter 16, *The Two Witnesses* which deals with the text of Rev. 11:1-13.

Book of Aker

Scenes which parallel those in the Book of Revelation will be discussed in detail in Chapter 16, *The Two Witnesses*. Of particular interest here is the great earthquake mentioned in Rev. 11:13 and referred to in Table 13.2; the entire verse reads, "And at that hour there was a great earthquake, and a tenth of the city fell; seven thousand people were killed in the earthquake, and the rest were terrified and gave glory to the God of heaven." As will be discussed in *The Two Witnesses,* Egyptian parallels to this scene, including the death of 7,000 people, are found in the 2nd, 3rd and 4th registers of Part A (Figure 73). This scene represents only one of many events associated with the end of time (and the earth) and the beginning of a new creation; the entire concept is condensed into a single scene (Figure 75) in Part D of the *Book of Aker* where we see representations of the death of the sky, water, air, the earth, and even of life and death itself. As we shall see, these are all found in juxtaposition with symbols representing the renewal of life and power to the sun-god at the dawn of a new creation.

Table 13.2 Events which may be associated with a volcanic eruption in the *Book of the Divine Cow* which parallel events found in the Book of Revelation. Events are organized according to what one would expect if they were related to an eruption. The English translation is by Piankoff (1955); page numbers are supplied with the letters "a" to "d" to indicate their relative location in Piankoff's translation (Pi55; from "a" at the top of a page to "d" at the bottom).

Divine Cow	Book of Revelation
Then Nut [the sky goddess] began to shake owing to the height. (Pi55 p. 30c)	Rev. 11:13a And at that hour there was a great earthquake, and a tenth of the city fell. Rev. 11:19c ... and there were flashes of lightning, voices, peals of thunder, an earthquake [mountains come into being], and heavy hail.
And the earth was in darkness.	Rev. 16:10 The fifth angel poured his bowl on the throne of the beast, and its kingdom was in darkness;
Then they said before his majesty: May thy Eye go out and catch (?) for thee those who conspire (against thee). There is no Eye more fit to strike them for thee. Let it come down as Hathor! (p. 28a)	Rev. 8:6 Now the seven angels who had the seven trumpets made ready to blow them.
Then the massacre (came into being) among men.	Rev. 8:7 The first angel blew his trumpet, and there followed hail and fire, mixed with blood, which fell on the earth; and a third of the earth was burnt up, and a third of the trees were burnt up, and all green grass was burnt up. Rev. 8:8 The second angel blew his trumpet, ... Rev. 15:1 Then I saw another portent in heaven, great and wonderful, seven angels with seven plagues, which are the last, for with them the wrath of God is ended. ... .
Red ocher (?) was poured [into this beer,] and it looked like the blood of men, and made 7000 jars. (p. 28c) ... the land inundated.	Rev 11:6 ... they have power over the waters to turn them into blood, and to smite the earth with every plague. Rev. 11:13 ... seven thousand people were killed. Rev. 14:20 ... and blood flowed from the wine-press, as high as a horse's bridle, for one thousand six hundred stadia. Rev. 16:4 The third angel poured his bowl into the rivers and the fountains of water, and they became blood.
Then the majesty of Re said: Behold, they have escaped into the desert land, their hearts being afraid that I speak to them (p. 27d)	Rev. 6:15 Then the kings of the earth and the great men and the generals and the rich and the strong, and every one, slave and free, hid in the caves and among the rocks of the mountains,
Then this goddess came back after having *killed men* in the desert land. (p. 28a)	Rev. 6:16 calling to the mountains and rocks, "Fall on us and hide us from the face of him who is seated on the throne, and from the wrath of the Lamb;

Divine Cow	Book of Revelation
Then the majesty of Re said to this goddess: Is there a burning pain of sickness? And the period of sickness came into being. Then the majesty of Re said: As true as I live, my heart is weary to remain with them. I keep on killing them to the last one – the small remainder is not my gift!(p. 29a-b)	Rev. 9:5 they were allowed to torture them for five months, but not to kill them, and their torture was like the torture of a scorpion, when it stings a man. Rev. 9:6 And in those days men will seek death and will not find it; they will long to die, and death will fly from them. Rev. 16:10 ... men gnawed their tongues in anguish Rev. 16:11 and cursed the God of heaven for their pain and sores

Prophesy of Neferrohu

This section examines effects some distance away from a volcanic eruption. While such events may be less violent than those nearby, they can still be quite dramatic. Several such phenomena are known to reach considerable distances downwind of an eruption. As mentioned earlier, a volcanic plume may extend high enough into the atmosphere to block much of the light from the sun, moon and stars, turning daylight into twilight or darkness and the nighttime into total darkness over large areas. Ashfall on fields, trees and rivers can also have dramatic effects. Earthquakes too can be quite devastating even hundreds of kilometers away from an eruption, the amount of devastation depending on the size of the eruption and other factors involving the geographic distribution and dynamics of the tectonic plates involved. The magnitude of the atmospheric effects varies with the size of the eruption, the distance away from it and atmospheric conditions; in extreme cases, they may be experienced around the entire globe.

Reasonably good evidence for distant effects of a volcanic eruption is found in a fairly short Egyptian document called *The Prophesy of Neferrohu* translated by Erman (1927).[573] While this document does not refer to a mountain of fire or any such phenomenon which can be seen close to an eruption, it does refer to what seem to be volcanic effects normally experienced a long way from an eruption, in this case, the Nile Delta. Neferrohu says, "I show thee a land in lamentation and distress; that which has never happened (before) hath happened." Events are then described which involve greatly diminished sunlight, sometimes so great that the sun is not visible in the sky as during a storm so that it is impossible to tell if it is noon or some other time of day. At other times the sun resembles the moon in the sky, so dim that one can look directly at it without irritating the eyes. Of this widespread darkness the prophet says:

> How fareth this land? The sun is veiled and will not shine that men may see. None will live when the storm veileth (it); all men are dulled (?) though the want of it.
> .... .
> The sun separateth himself from men; he ariseth when it is the hour. None will know that it is midday, and his shadow will not be distinguished. No face will be bright that beholdeth thee, and the eyes will not be moistened with water. He is in the sky like the moon, and yet he deviateth not from his accustomed time.[574]

The effects described here are not unlike those described in Rev. 8:12 – "a third of the sun was struck, and a third of the moon, and a third of the stars, so that a third of their light was darkened." One might argue, however, that these words in fact simply describe heavy overcast.

But the Egyptian text goes on. Dramatic changes in the Delta result in destruction of the nesting habitat of marsh birds so that they are forced to nest uncharacteristically close to humans. "The birds no longer hatch their eggs in the swamps of the Delta, but the bird hath made her nest nigh unto men and letteth them approach her in her necessity."[575] This unusual behavior may have been related to changes in elevations and flow patterns in different parts of the Delta for we are told that "The land is taken away and added to, and none knoweth what the issue will be."[576] Changes in flow of at least one river are reported as far away as the River of Egypt in the Levant and these are reminiscent of the drying up of the Euphrates River in Rev. 16:12. The prophet says, "The River of Egypt is empty, men cross over the water on foot. Men shall search for water upon which the ships may sail; its road is become a bank and the bank is become water."[577] Such changes in the land and river flow patterns of rivers are typical effects of earthquakes where the elevations of river-beds and their surroundings may raise or fall dramatically, thus changing the courses of their flows. They may have also caused fish ponds to dry up: "those good things are ruined, the fishponds (?) where were slittings [fish processing], which shone with fish and wild fowl."[578] Further inland, wild animals are forced to change their drinking habits, made easier by an apparent decimation of humans near the river banks. "The wild beasts of the desert shall drink from the rivers of Egypt, in order that they may cool themselves upon their banks, for that there is none to scare them away (?)."[579] The entire landscape has changed and "That which was made is as if it were never made, and Rē might begin to found (anew) [i.e., re-create]. The whole land has perished, there is nought left." The prophet obviously believes that these events are signs of the end of the world prior to its re-creation.

These physical changes in the land and patterns of water flow in the Delta are accompanied by formidable social upheaval, just as one might expect in an area dependant on farming. The text says,

> Men shall take up weapons of war, that the land may live on uproar [in the prevailing distress, many live by robbing from others]. Men shall fashion arrows of copper, that they may beg for bread with blood. ... one slayeth another. I show thee the son as a foeman, and the brother as adversary, and a man murdereth his father. ... All good things have departed. ... Men take the goods of a man (of high estate) from him and give them to one from without. I show thee the possessor in deprivation, and him that is (from) without contented.[580]

People in all affected areas seek refuge in distant places. Large numbers of people who heeded the warning signs from the volcano may well have escaped from the Aegean Sea area (see discussion above on Rev. 18:4) and moved to the Levant and from there to Egypt. In the Levant, water shortages (because the water was contaminated with volcanic fallout) and food shortages (because crops were damaged) forced many people to move south into Egypt where conditions were believed to be better. Also, many previously permanent inhabitants of the Levant undoubtedly migrated *en mass* with their cattle from the Levant into Egypt. Neferrohu says, "They beg (again) for water, after their accustomed wise, that they may be able to give their cattle to drink."[581] Some come as enemies, "Foes are in the East, Asiatics are come down into Egypt. ... 'By night one will suddenly be fallen upon (?); men shall force their way into houses."[582] Such famine, infighting, confusion, mass migrations, and social upheaval in the absence of warfare are typical outcomes of widespread natural catastrophes – and conform with events normally associated with a volcanic eruption.

Admonitions of an Egyptian Sage

Like the *Prophesy of Neferrohu,* the *Admonitions of an Egyptian Sage* give an account of dramatic environmental and social upheaval. The *Admonitions,* a much longer work than the *Prophesy,* consists of a set of six poems. It gives a fairly detailed account of a terrible calamity in Egypt involving an unusual, or even unique, "plague" in which many people die, crops are destroyed, and social unrest becomes widespread. The first of the six poems deals primarily with what appears to be a natural catastrophe while most of the remaining five deal primarily with the social aftermath. For brevity, and in light of the background information already discussed above, references to events in the *Admonitions* which may relate only to a volcanic eruption are presented here in tabular form (Table 13.3). These parallels are not as convincing as those described for the *Prophesy* because of their ambiguity and lack of detail. When considered in the more general context of the poem and in the context of a great natural disaster, however, one is reminded of a volcanic eruption.[a]

Plato's Account

Since Champollion first discovered the key to deciphering Egyptian hieroglyphics in the early 19th century many Egyptologists have attempted to find the story of the legendary Atlantis which Plato said was located in Egyptian temples, a story passed down to him from Solon, a relative and close friend of his grandfather. It seems almost incredible that, if Solon was correct about there being records of a major catastrophe in the Aegean area, none have yet been identified. Surely, references to such a catastrophic event would have found their way into the religious literature of the time. Might it have been that the story of the eruption was considered to be of such great religious significance that references to it were purposefully concealed in mythological images and jargon? Without some independent, ancient document to guide us, it would be very difficult indeed to find such references, if for no other reason than that we would be unaware of the particular literary conventions and symbolism used in such compositions. This situation changes with the above finding

---

[a] When viewed in the context of major economic and social upheaval resulting from an invasion of foreigners, entirely different interpretations can result. Indeed, practically all students of this poem (and of the *Prophesy of Neferrohu*) assume this social upheaval to have been the cause rather than a symptom of widespread turmoil. For this reason, the possible context of a volcanic eruption for the *Admonitions* may have gone unnoticed by previous researchers.

Table 13.3 Compilation of events from the *Admonitions of an Egyptian Sage* (translation by Erman, 1927[583]) which are consistent with those of a volcanic eruption. Taken as a group, they describe conditions one might expect to find downwind of an eruption. Brief explanatory comments on individual elements in the table are identified with square brackets [...] in the right-hand column; references to parallel events in the Book of Revelation are given in the left-hand column. Bracketed numbers *(I)* and *(II)* refer to first and second poems of the *Admonitions*.

Volcanic Event	Admonitions of an Egyptian Sage
Fire (Rev. 14:10-11)	- the fire will mount up on high. [view of a volcano from a distance?] Its burning goeth forth against the enemies of the land. *(II)*
Ash Fall (Rev. 9:3-4)	- ... men look like gem-birds [covered with volcanic dust, they have taken on the same color as certain birds]. Squalor is throughout the land. There is none whose clothes are white in these times. *(I)*
Earthquake (Rev 16:18)	- Oh that the earth would cease from noise and strife be no more! *(I)* - ... the land turneth round as doth a potter's wheel. *(I)* - The towns are destroyed ... *(I)* - ... the secrets of the land, whose limits were unknown, is divulged. The Residence [Egypt's capital city in the delta] is overturned in an hour. *(II)* - gates, columns, and walls are consumed with fire ... [local effects of earthquakes] *(I)*
Poisoned water (Rev. 8:11)	... the river is blood [red with red volcanic dust]. Doth a man drink thereof, he rejecteth it as human, (for) one thirsteth for water. *(I)*
Hunger (Rev. 18:8)	- The storehouse is bare, and he that kept it lieth stretched out on the ground [dead]. *(I)* - No fruit nor herbs are longer found for the birds, and the offal (?) is robbed from the mouth of the swine, without it being said (as aforetime): This is better for thee than for me," for men are so hungry. *(I)*
Death (Rev. 6:8)	- Plague stalketh through the land and blood is everywhere. *(I)* - ... many dead men are buried in the river. The stream is a sepluchre ... *(I)* - ... the crocodiles (are glutted with) what they have carried off. Men go to them of their own accord ... *(I)* - He that layeth his brother in the ground is everywhere (to be seen) ... *(I)*
Collapse of trade (Rev. 18:11)	- Men do not sail to Byblos [a town in the Levant] to-day. What can we do to get cedars for our mummies? Priests are buried with their produce, and princes are embalmed with their resin, as far as the land of Keftiu [Crete], and now they come no more. *(I)*
Mass migrations (Rev. 18:4)	- the Red Land is spread abroad throughout the country [Erman's interpretation is, "everywhere one encounters foreigners"]. ... The strange people from without are come into Egypt. *(I)*

such a catastrophic event; a fresh look at Plato's work from the point of view of the Book of Revelation is now feasible.

The first reports of the existence in Egypt of written accounts of a major volcanic eruption are found in Plato's *Timaeus* where he tells us that while he was still quite young he heard of a great calamity which befell Athens while it was still very much in its infancy. This story had been brought back to Egypt by a famous Greek relative called Solon who learned of it during an extended visit to Egypt lasting several years, beginning in *c.* 629 BCE. Solon, a Greek poet and statesman known today as the founder of modern democracy was highly honored by the Egyptian priests who told him that both he and all his countrymen were almost entirely ignorant about their distant past.[584] Plato writes: "The story is a strange one, but Solon, the wisest of the seven wise men, once vouched for its truth. ... It relates the many notable achievements of our city long ago, which have been lost sight of because of the lapse of time and destruction of human life."[585]

Plato, tells us that the Egyptian priests told Solon that they had preserved in their "temples from earliest times a written record of any great or splendid achievement or notable event which has come to our ears whether it occurred in your part of the world or here or anywhere else."[586] These then already ancient records told of "earthquakes and floods of extraordinary violence, and in a single dreadful day and night all your [Greek] fighting men were swallowed up by the earth," and an island "was similarly swallowed up by he sea and vanished."[587] Solon was also told that he and his fellow Greeks were "descended from the few survivors that remained, but you know nothing about it because so many succeeding generations left no record in writing,"[588] for "the survivors of this destruction were an unlettered mountain race. ... for many generations they and their children were short of bare necessities, and their minds and thoughts were occupied with providing for them, to the neglect of earlier history and tradition."[589]

Solon started writing an account of the event while still in Egypt but failed to finish it either there or on his return to Athens. Plato tells us that "My father had his manuscript, which is now in my possession, and I studied it often as a child."[590] Many years later, Plato himself began to write his now famous story of the lost city of Atlantis which he claims was based on fact. But alas, Plato's rendering of Solon's account was never finished either. It ends in mid-sentence after describing the inhabitants of the land as being

> at the height of their fame and fortune. And the god of gods, Zeus, who reigns by law, and whose eye can see such things, when he perceived the wretched state of his admirable stock, decided to punish them and reduce them to order by discipline.
>
> He accordingly summoned all the gods to his own most glorious abode, which stands at the center of the universe and looks out over the whole realm of change, and when they had assembled addressed them as follows ...[591]

Plato's incomplete account of the island that sank beneath the sea has been the subject of numerous discussions, speculations and publications over the past two millennia. Nowadays, it is generally accepted that the event which formed the basis of his story of Atlantis was the massive volcanic eruption that occurred on the Aegean island of

Thera sometime near the middle of the second millennium BCE. This view is held by practically all modern historians as is evident in entries in highly respected encyclopedias such as *The Encyclopedia Britannica*. The most important elements of Plato's account conform closely with the above notion of the eruption of a volcano and its effects on the sun, moon, stars, the sky, land, islands, the sea and mankind, as outlined above. And they conform with the above Revelation and Egyptian accounts.

A Modern Account

The volcanic island of Thera has a long history of eruptions the most massive having occurred in *c.*1628 BCE. Lentz (1999) tells us that the earliest *recorded* eruption occurred in 197 BCE when "the world's first documented 'new island' was created."[592] Many minor eruptions have occurred since then, the most recent in 1950 CE when the northern island, Anea Kameni, hosted minor eruptions for about a month.

But it was during Thera's most powerful eruption in 1628 BCE that an entire area was laid to waste and the Minoan civilization in the eastern Mediterranean changed abruptly and dramatically. All cities and towns on the island were totally destroyed and there were no survivors among those who dared stay on the island – or who, for whatever reasons, could not leave, in spite of the numerous seismic warnings from the mountain itself. One hundred ten kilometers south, on the northern coast of Crete, the Minoan city of Knossos was struck by violent earthquakes, blanketed by a thick layer of volcanic ash – and hit by a mega-tsunami. The tsunami spread in all directions, demolishing low-lying coastal towns, sweeping over nearby low-lying islands, smashing boats and destroying shipping throughout the Aegean Sea. The administrative hub of the Minoan empire perished in an hour and its population was decimated. An article in the *Encyclopædia Britannica* describes it this way: that parts of the Book of Revelation contain recognizable, mythologized accounts of

> ... the volcano on the island of Thera, long, it seems, quiescent, erupted to bury the settlements there under many feet of pumice ash. The story of Atlantis, if Plato did not invent it, may reflect some Egyptian record of this eruption, one of the most stupendous of historical times. Knossos [on the northern shore of Crete] was shattered by a succession of earthquakes that preceded or accompanied the eruption, while great waves resulting from it appear to have damaged settlements along the northern coast of Crete. ... Some Cretan settlements might have been wrecked by blast from the eruption, although Thera lies about 70 miles (110 kilometers) away from Crete. ... The settlements on Thera ... lay buried deep in pumice, and the largest of these, at Akrotiri, opened by excavations since 1967, offers a unique picture of a Bronze Age town, the walls of the houses standing in places two stories high.[593]

At the time, survivors of the catastrophe undoubtedly thought they were witnessing the end of the world and their stories must have been told and retold.

As noted above, Thera's eruption was "one of the most stupendous of historical times." Indeed, the available evidence suggests it was larger than any experienced in the last 5,000 years – so big that many people today would find it impossible to imagine the physical dimensions and the extent of its awesome, destructive power.

Nevertheless it is possible to compare its approximate size with some of the more recent and familiar eruptions. One such comparison is based on estimated volumes of ash and other volcanic debris ejected. Because of the enormous volumes involved, such estimates are given in cubic kilometers; for example, the infamous Krakatau which erupted in Indonesia in 1883 ejected some 6 cubic kilometers of ash and debris into the atmosphere. Tambora, on the other hand, ejected about 50 cubic kilometers in 1815, more than eight times that of Krakatau. By comparison, the well known eruption of Mount St. Helens in 1980 measured less than one half of one cubic kilometer. Estimates of the size of Thera's eruption vary widely in part because we cannot be sure of the size of the island before it erupted; nevertheless, they range between 60 and 240 cubic kilometers, the lower limit already being greater than any subsequent eruption anywhere on earth.

But, considering the vast distance between Thera and Egypt, we may ask, "Was the eruption of Thera visible from Egypt?" The answer is a categorical, "Yes." More powerful eruptions send ejecta higher into the atmosphere than less powerful ones and in Wilson's (1985) comparison of Thera's eruption with that of Bezymianny in 1956, he says:

> In classic picture-book style a column of cloud and fire [from Thera] belched heavenwards. Although the exact height has inevitably gone unrecorded, it is possible to calculate that, allowing for the curvature of the earth, anything over thirty miles [48 km.] high would have been visible from the Nile Delta, five hundred miles across the Mediterranean. Since the much smaller Bezymianny eruption of 1956 reached a recorded height of forty miles [64 km.], and Krakatau's plume has been estimated at between fifty and a hundred miles high [80-161 km.], there can be little doubt that the Thera eruption would have been visible from Egypt.[594]

Wilson's rationale for this conclusion is summarized in Figure 56. This figure provides a visual explanation for the description of the 7th Mound in Chapter 147 of the *Book of the Dead*: "As for the town of Ises, *which is far out of sight*,' its breath is of fire and a snake is in it. ... you shall not come against me. ... Fall! Lie Down! May your hot rage be in the ground." If one assumes that Ises is an alternative or descriptive name for Thera or some other place in the Aegean Sea, then its location beyond the horizon conforms with Thera and the sight of its plume of smoke by day and the glow of fire at night from the Nile Delta is understandable. Furthermore, if Thera's plume was 60 miles [97 km.] high or higher, similar calculations show that it would also have been visible from places as far away as Sidon, Tyre, and Byblos in the Levant. The sight of such a gigantic column of smoke by day and fire and smoke by night reaching so high into the sky would also conform with Revelation's statement that "her sins [in this case, the volcanic plume] are heaped high as heaven" (Rev. 18:5).

The geographic extent of the impact of Thera's eruption was even more dramatic than the size and height of its plume might suggest. To get some feeling for this we need only review events following a few of the more recent and less violent eruptions. When Mt. St. Helens erupted in 1980, parts of the nearby states of Washington, Idaho and Montana were plunged into darkness. When Krakatau erupted in 1883, most of the ash cloud passed over the sea and ships had to heave-to south of the Sunda Straits, reporting no daylight from 6 am on the Sunday evening through to 8 am on the Tuesday morning.[595] After Tambora erupted, some 483 kilometers (300 miles) away there was, "An unusual thick darkness ... all the following night and the greater part of the next day. ... At Gresik and other districts more eastward ... this saturated state of the atmosphere lessened as the cloud of ashes passed along and discharged itself along the way."[596] Longer term effects can be equally dramatic because of the gasses and dust particles thrown high into the atmosphere. When the particles reach into the stratosphere, they can remain there for weeks and months before finally settling. The Tambora eruption of 1815 spewed smoke and ash high enough into the stratosphere to completely encircle the globe, causing average temperatures to drop and crop failures and famine in North America and Europe for two years afterwards.

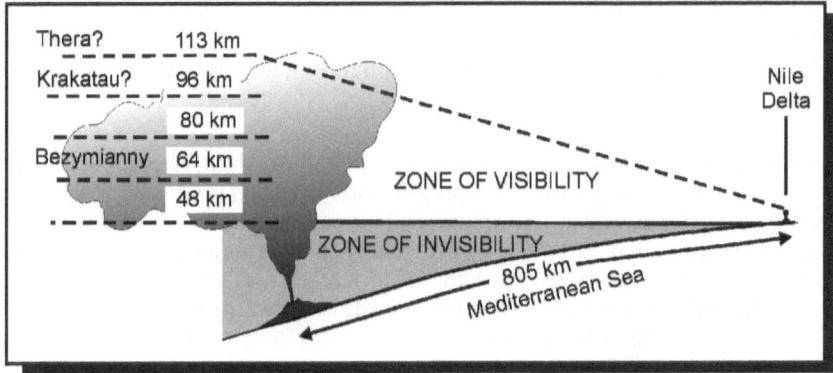

Figure 56. Illustration (not to scale) showing how the Thera eruption of 1628 BCE would have been visible from Egypt's Nile Delta. Based on a figure by Wilson (1985), *Exodus, the True Story*, p. 113.

Wilson (1985) provides a comparison of Thera's fury with that of its only rival, Tambora. While every volcanic eruption is different, there being no easy rule-of-thumb method of calculating scale by crater size, volume of ejecta, far-reaching effects, number of persons killed, or other criteria, it is only with Tambora's 1815 eruption that we have an eruption approaching in scale that of Thera's 1628 event. Indeed, Thera may have been substantially greater, its crater size, for instance, being twice that of Tambora's. Also, Thera's effects may have been exacerbated by its geographical location. While Tambora's ash could be washed away by tropical rains and lost in the wide expanses of the surrounding ocean, land in the eastern Mediterranean area is relatively arid and surrounded on three sides by areas which were quite densely populated even three and a half millennia ago.[597]

Untold thousands died as a direct result of Thera's fiery blast, hot ash, and earthquakes while evidence for the ash cloud from the eruption has been found in the eastern Mediterranean as far north as Turkey[598] and the Black Sea,[599] as far south as the Nile Delta[600] and as far away as Greenland and North America.[601] In badly affected areas, day turned to blackest night while in others the sun and moon were greatly dimmed. Volcanic ash covered everything – wildlife, fish, livestock, crops, and

13. Catastrophes

people, killing many in the worst affected areas. The worst, however, was undoubtedly the huge mega-tsunami spawned by the collapse of the mountain itself into the Aegean Sea.

After describing Krakatau's four initial massive explosions in 1883 which killed many and could be heard some two thousand miles away in the Northern Territory of Australia, Wilson (1985) says that, "Far worse was the death toll among hundreds of Java's coastal villages. Three of the four explosions triggered terrifying *tsunami*, giant sea waves that in the case of Krakatau reached heights of more than 100 feet [30 m.], slamming on to coastal shores with such force that 165 villages were simply swept away, together with more than 35,000 human lives."[602] In regard to Thera's eruption, Luce (1969) suggests a scenario which was likely far worse than Krakatau's.

> There is also some indication of a tidal wave over 200 m. high on nearby Anaphi [23 km away]. ... We do not know what happened on Crete and on the islands and coasts of the Aegean, but I consider it a safe guess that the loss of life and damage to property was no less [than that to Krakatau in 1883]. They may well have been many times as great. We can say with reasonable assurance that Crete had ceased to be a great maritime power."[603]

Wilson (1985) points out that, "It would have been perfectly possible for a tsunami from Thera to have reached Egypt for, while the effects of tsunami vary widely from one part of the coast to another, a map reveals that a dead straight line can be drawn between Thera and the eastern Nile Delta without a single island to interrupt its path [see Figure 57]."[604] He reports on researches of the Japanese geophysicist Yokoyama, who made calculations from quantities of sea-borne pumice found 150 feet [46 m.] above sea level on Thera's neighboring island of Anaphi, and fifteen feet [4.6 m.] above sea level on the seashore north of Tel Aviv, Israel. The tsunami struck the coast of Egypt about 80 minutes after it left Thera (from Figure 57) and although the height it reached in the Delta is unknown its effect on settlements, crops, people and shipping in the area must have been devastating. Extensive damage may well have extended far upstream along the main branches of the Nile in the form of massive *solitons,* waves that can travel through channels and tributaries for great distances without losing significant amounts of energy.[605] The impact of the tsunami on the low-lying Nile Delta would therefore have been at least as devastating as the direct effects of the ash-fall and the earthquakes associated with Thera's eruption. Thousands undoubtedly died in the heavily populated Delta and many towns along the sides of its many tributaries would have been destroyed; social upheaval and chaos among the survivors would have followed.

Egypt's first sign of the eruption would have been the view of the column of smoke and ash mixed with fire rising over the northwestern horizon. This was accompanied shortly thereafter by earthquakes, and a little later still, by the thunderous blast of the explosion. Then the tsunami struck the low-lying Delta and the resulting solitons invaded its many tributaries, killing many. Finally, an ash cloud blocked the full light of the sun and moon and the land was covered with choking dust which killed vegetation and destroyed marshes, wildfowl and fish. Physical evidence for this has been found by Daniel and Shen (1986) who demonstrated volcanic shards from Thera's eruption in the upper Minoan ash in the Nile Delta. Chaos reigned in the land and many undoubtedly thought that they were witnessing the end of the world. In time, new myths emerged to explain the awful events.

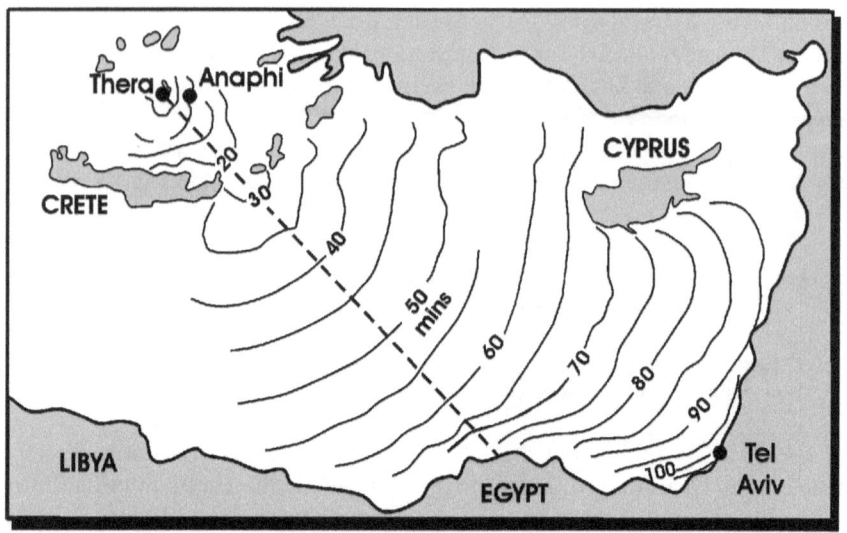

Figure 57. A refraction diagram based on figure in Wilson (1985, p. 134) demonstrating that the force of a tsunami originating at Thera could have reached Egypt within 80 minutes without being blocked by intervening islands.

Discussion

Plato tells us that his story was based on a poem started by Solon to be entered in a festival for the goddess Apatouria. He says "if he [Solon] had finished the story he brought back from Egypt, and hadn't been compelled to neglect it because of class struggles and other evils he found here [in Athens] on his return, I don't think any poet, even Homer or Hesiod, would have been more famous."[606] Plato never completed his draft of the story either, succeeding only in writing the introductory part.

The poem's setting is remarkably similar to the opening scenes of the Book of Revelation (especially Rev. 1 and Rev. 4) which describes a great assembly and "The revelation ... [which] must soon take place. ... and all tribes of the earth will wail ..." (Rev. 1:1-7). In Rev. 2-3, dire warnings are given to those who have rebelled against the one on the throne and later chapters describe the awful catastrophes which befall the human race. Also, the throne-scene setting in the Book of Revelation and that described by Plato and that both have quite remarkable similarities to the opening paragraphs of the Egyptian *Book of the Divine Cow*. Some of the more succinct and self-evident parallels in the *Book of the Divine Cow*, Plato's *Timaeus,* and the Book of Revelation, are presented in Table 13.4.

13. Catastrophes

When the obviously mythological aspects of the catastrophic events described in the Book of Revelation are removed from the text, and when many of these apparently disparate events are viewed as a whole, it is evident that they represent different aspects of a single type of natural phenomenon – a massive volcanic eruption. Similarly, when the same treatment is afforded many of the names and events described in Chapters 146, 149 and 150 of the *Book of the Dead*, a volcanic eruption can also be identified. And many events described in the two secular Egyptian writings, the *Prophesy of Neferrohu* and the *Admonitions of an Egyptian Sage*, also conform with those typically associated with those of a more distant volcanic eruption. Furthermore, important passages in the religious compositions, the *Book of Aker* and the *Book of the Divine Cow* (to be discussed in detail in Chapter 16, *The Two Witnesses* and Chapter 10, Call to *Arms*) which are associated with events at the end of time, the end of the world, and the re-creation of the world, contain allusions to similar catastrophic events. Taken individually or as a group, they closely parallel those found in the Book of Revelation; they all seem to be describing different aspects of the same natural phenomenon.

Modern volcanologists now believe that Plato's account of the catastrophe describes the devastating events associated with the eruption of the island volcano of Thera which in about 1628 BCE decimated the coastal population in the Aegean Sea area and reached all the way to Egypt and the Levant. It has been shown here that Plato's report of earthquakes and floods of extraordinary violence conform with those found in several ancient Egyptian sources as well as the Book of Revelation. This strongly suggests that all of these sources point to the same devastating event.

In the next chapter, *From Catastrophe to Myth*, we explore several of the more pertinent Egyptian myths from the point of view of how they might have evolved from stories which survived the many catastrophes associated with the eruption of Thera.

Table 13.4 Comparison of the opening scene of the *Book of the Divine Cow*, Plato's *Timaeus* and the Book of Revelation. Note the parallels involving references to an assembly of divine beings around the throne of an all-powerful deity to decide on action against rebels for their evil deeds.

Book of the Divine Cow	Plato's Timaeus	Book of Revelation
Then it came to pass that the majesty of Re ... having been king of men as well as of the gods. ... Now his majesty had learned about the plans which men were devising against him. ... Call to me my Eye, Shu, Tefnut, Geb, and Nut, together with the fathers and mothers who were with me when I was in the Watery Abyss, as well as the god of the Watery Abyss. Let him bring his attendants with him (but) bring them secretly, lest men see, and their hearts escape (?). ... These gods were brought, and these gods were (standing) on both sides with heads inclined toward the earth before his majesty, in order that he might speak his words	And the god of the gods, Zeus, who reigns by law, and whose eye can see such things, when he perceived the wretched state of this admirable stock, decided to punish them and reduce them to order by discipline. He accordingly summoned all the gods to his own most glorious abode, which stands at the center of the universe and looks out over the whole realm of change, and when they had assembled addressed them as follows: ... . [Plato's text ends here]	Rev. 4:2-11 ... and lo, a throne stood in heaven, with one seated on the throne! [4]Round the throne were twenty-four thrones, and seated on the thrones were twenty-four elders ... [5]and before the throne burn seven torches of fire, which are the seven spirits of God ... .[11]Worthy art thou, our Lord and God, to receive glory and honor and power, for thou didst create all things, and by thy will they existed and were created." Rev. 1:19 Now write what you see, what is and what is to take place hereafter. Rev. 2-3 (Action to be taken against the churches for their rebellious state. See Chapter 7, *Egyptian Beliefs in the Seven Letters*)

Chapter 14. From Catastrophe to Myth[607]

In the previous chapter, we examined parallels between images of catastrophic events in the Book of Revelation and those of ancient Egyptian, Greek, and modern science. It was concluded that these disparate catastrophes could be readily explained in terms of a single cause, a cataclysmic volcanic eruption; and more specifically, one which happened on an island in the midst of other islands in the sea; this conclusion was facilitated by removing obviously mythological elements from apparently relevant descriptions in Revelation, thereby reducing descriptions to their bare essentials. From this it became obvious that most of the catastrophes should not be considered independent events but rather different aspects of the same event – a major volcanic eruption. Similarly, it was shown that certain events described in the *Book of the Dead* conformed with those which normally occur close to an eruption while others conformed with more distant events described in the *Prophesy of Neferrohu* and the *Admonitions of an Egyptian Sage*. The overall setting for all these catastrophes conformed with that of the so-called "Legend of the Destruction of Mankind" which forms the opening scenes of Egypt's *Book of the Divine Cow*. Egyptian accounts also conformed with Plato's description of a great natural catastrophe which caused the almost complete destruction of a fledgling Greek civilization many hundreds of years BCE, an event which modern geophysicists believe was caused by the catastrophic eruption in about 1628 BCE of a large volcano on island of Thera (modern-day Santorini) in the Aegean Sea.

The Book of Revelation does not specifically mention the name of Thera in conjunction with its descriptions of these events. Instead, it refers to a place called "Babylon" which modern biblical scholars believe to be the ancient city of Babylon on the Euphrates River, and metaphorically to Rome, the main center of intolerance to the fledgling Christian community in the ancient world. If the catastrophic events described in Revelation in fact represent those associated with the eruption of Thera, how then might we explain the explicit references to the destruction of "Babylon" in the Book of Revelation? And why does Revelation's description give the impression of a catastrophe so great that it was believed to signal the end of the world? And how does the time of Thera's eruption correspond with the dates of events described in the Egyptian texts? This chapter will provide some insight into possible answers to these and several related questions.

The following paragraphs summarize and explain how many of the seemingly unrelated events described in the different sources conform with an the eruption of Thera's volcano. Also, how and why events associated with the eruption may have been incorporated into the mythology of the ancient Egyptians. Later, the extent to which these historic events parallel the natural catastrophes described in the Book of Revelation will be discussed.

Sources and Probable Dates of the Catastrophes

As mentioned earlier, the catastrophes described in the Book of Revelation best conform with those associated with a volcanic eruption, and in particular, an eruption which occurred either in a coastal area, on an island, or both. Since there have been no active volcanoes along the Nile River in Egypt for many thousands of years we may conclude that the Egyptian texts refer to, not only a relatively recent volcanic event, but also to one which happened outside Egypt's borders and was yet close enough for its effects to have been felt in Egypt. The maritime nature of the eruption described in both the Book of Revelation and the Egyptian records strongly suggests the possibility of volcanoes either in the Aegean Sea east of the Greek mainland or into the Tyrrhenian Sea west of Italy. Given these constraints, two possible locations emerge: one is the well known Mount Vesuvius and the other is Thera. We can quickly rule out the eruption of Vesuvius in 79 CE as being the source of the stones from the sky because it erupted far to late in history to have been included in the *Book of the Dead*. This leaves us with Thera, an island located about 120 kilometers north of Crete and about 720 kilometers northwest of Egypt's Nile Delta.

Thera's volcano is known to have erupted many times. The earliest eruption is believed to have happened about 10,000 years ago and numerous eruptions have occurred since then. Eruptions are known to have occurred in 197 BCE and as late as 1950 CE.[a] Eruptions since 1628 BCE are well outside the period during which the *Book of the Dead* was composed. The 1628 eruption, however, occurred during the early part of Egypt's 2nd Intermediate Period (1640-1532 BCE) when many chapters of the *Book of the Dead* already existed. Also, as will be discussed later, this 1628 date does not preclude its being recorded in the *Prophesy of Neferrohu* and the *Admonitions of an Egyptian Sage*, both of which contain, as discussed in the previous chapter, descriptions of what may well be events associated with a volcanic eruption.

The date of 1628 BCE is not accepted by all authorities. Some hold that the eruption occurred as late as the middle of the 15th century BCE. Luce (1969), for example, argues in favor of a date around 1470 BCE, an argument based primarily on archeological, historic, and mythological evidence. Manning (1999) champions a date of about 1628 BCE and bases his conclusion on the same evidence as that used by Luce but with additional evidence from modern scientific analyses, including studies on tree rings (dendrology) as well as a variety of studies on ice cores from the Greenland ice cap in which Theran ash deposits were found, and on ratios of trace elements in artifacts (using carbon dating methodologies) from the time of the eruption. Manning's study is a more thorough assessment of the problem and his date

---

[a] Known dates of eruptions of Santorini are as follows: 1628 (discussed here) and 197 BCE, and since then, 46, 726, 1570-73, 1650, 1707-11, 1866-70, 1925, 1928, 1939-41 and 1950 CE.

of about 1628 BCE may well be the one finally agreed upon by the majority of researchers in the field. A detailed critical examination and comparison of both Manning's and Luce's work along with additional research will ultimately, we hope, come up with an indisputable date. With this background in mind, 1628 BCE will be used as a working date for our discussions.

Dates of the Egyptian Accounts

In order to place the Egyptian accounts of the catastrophes in a time frame comparable with Plato's writings and modern accounts of Thera's eruption, it is important to consider the earliest dates associated with these texts. Table 14.1 presents a list of the relevant Egyptian texts for consideration. As noted previously, relevant references in the *Book of the Dead* are concentrated in Chapters 146, 149 and 150. Also, parts of the *Book of the Divine Cow* and the *Book of Aker* place emphasis on the destruction and renewal of the earth, involving great natural catastrophes. Accounts of disasters in the *Amduat* and the *Book of Gates* tend to be spread throughout these compositions where they are, for the most part, shrouded in allusions rather than explicit descriptions. On the other hand the *Admonitions of an Egyptian Sage* and the *Prophesy of Neferrohu*, both of which are secular documents, present vivid details of catastrophic events in the Delta. Table 14.1 shows at a glance that our earliest knowledge of these possible references to a volcanic eruption date from not earlier than the 2nd Intermediate Period (the *Pyramid Texts* and *Coffin Texts* contain few if any such references and are not included in the table).

Erman (1926) believes the *Admonitions of an Egyptian Sage* originated between the Middle and New Kingdoms, i.e., in the 2nd Intermediate period (1640-1532 BCE). More recently, in the introduction to the 1966 printing of Erman's book, Wm. Simpson says of the *Admonitions*:

> Traditionally regarded as a description of the anarchy following the end of the Old Kingdom, the text has recently been set in Dynasty 13 by J. Van Seters, JEA 50 (1966), 13-25, where evidence is marshaled for considering the text as a description of the time following the end of the Middle Kingdom and the advent of the Hyksos.[608]

It seems likely that the *Admonitions of an Egyptian Sage* were written during the time of the Hyksos rule in Egypt, i.e., during the 2nd Intermediate Period (1640-1532 BCE). This time frame includes the favored 1628 BCE date for the eruption of Thera.

The *Prophesy of Neferrohu* is known to us from a papyrus dating from the time of Thutmosis III (1479-1425 BCE) and from a few writing-boards and ostraca later in the New Kingdom (1552-1070 BCE). It concerns a period of natural catastrophes and chaotic social conditions when the sun did not shine, crops were destroyed, water became undrinkable, and anarchy spread throughout the Delta. The text speaks of a prophesy made to Snefru, the first king of the 4th Dynasty (which began in about 2575 BCE) concerning a later king, Amenemhet I (1991-1962 BCE), who was to begin his reign more than 600 years later during the 12th Dynasty (1991-1783 BCE). It is highly unlikely that the *Prophesy of Neferrohu* was actually written in the 4th Dynasty and it is even likely that it was written, not in the reign of Snefru as suggested in the text, but rather many years later during or even after the reign of Amenemhet I, possibly as late as the reign of Thutmosis III himself when we first find it in the records. In this scenario, the names of the kings and the events which it describes would be displaced back in time by the writer to produce the appearance of it being genuine prophesy. Since many of the events described in the *Prophesy of Neferrohu* are consistent with those of a volcanic eruption, serious consideration should be given to the possibility that all or parts of it were composed some time *after* both the reign of Amenemhet I and the eruption of Thera, i.e., after either 1962 or 1628 BCE).[a]

A date for the writing of the *Book of the Dead* is more complicated for it has its origins in the ancient *Coffin Texts* which were themselves based to varying degrees on the more ancient *Pyramid Texts* (written during the Old Kindom, 2575-2134 BCE). Indeed, the *Book of the Dead* is in fact a compilation of many different texts written over hundreds or even thousands of years. Thus, not all chapters of the *Book of the Dead* are found in the earliest chapters, including Chapters 146, 149 and 150. While some parts of these chapters have been found in the *Coffin Texts*, segments which deal with a mountain of smoke and fire and other natural phenomena conforming with a volcanic eruption are first noticed in versions from the 18th Dynasty (1550-1307 BCE).[609] This suggests the original versions of these chapters were written either during 18th Dynasty or, perhaps more likely, during the 2nd Intermediate Period (1640-1532 BCE).

Practically all of these dates are, of course, later than Manning's 1628 BCE date for Thera's great eruption and in this way do not preclude the mention of a mountain of smoke and related events in the *Book of the Dead* having originally been based on accounts of Thera's eruption. The same can be said for Luce's 1470 BCE date for the eruption although the most likely time frame for the events falls closer to Manning's 1628 BCE date, the preferred date used in this study. Bearing this in mind, it evident from Table 14.1 that, *The Book of the Dead* (specifically Chapters 146, 149 and 150), *Admonitions of an Egyptian Sage, The Amduat, the Prophesy of Neferrohu, The Book of the Divine Cow, TheBook of Gates and The Book of Aker* were all composed *after* Thera's eruption of 1628 BCE. These dates do not, therefore, preclude allusions of Thera's eruption in any of these texts.

Thera's Eruption in Egyptian Mythology

As noted above, when Thera erupted, Egypt was most likely in the 2nd Intermediate Period (1640-1532) in the case of a 1628 date (or less likely, during the reign of Thutmosis III (1479-1425) in the case of a 1470 date). Prior to the 2nd Intermediate Period, the Egyptians believed the cosmos was stable. Each day their sun-god rose in the form of a disk into the morning sky, grew brighter and stronger throughout the day to finally weaken in the evening and die at sunset. Early Egyptian myths thus reflected this natural daily cycle of the sun in which it was portrayed as being born anew each morning, maturing to adulthood, and slowly fading and dying of old age in the evening. At sunset, the sun-god entered the Netherworld where he was rejuvenated, reborn, and rose again the next morning to once again reign in earth's daytime sky.

---

[a] The dates and arguments presented here are based on information provided by Erman (1966) and Hornung (1999).

Table 14.1 Approximate earliest attestations (from Erman (1927) and Hornung (1999)) of Egyptian writings for the 2nd Intermediate Period (1640-1532 BCE) and later which contain accounts of catastrophic events consistent with those of a volcanic eruption. Dynasties and king names are from Erman and Hornung; dates are from Baines and Malek (1980).

Text	Period of Use	Earliest Attestation	Comment
Book of the Dead	2nd Intermediate Period (1640-1532) to Late Period (727-332)	17th Dynasty (1640 - 1550)	This book was based in part on the *Coffin Texts*, effectively replacing them, but included many new compositions.
Admonitions of an Egyptian Sage	2nd Intermediate Period to New Kingdom (1550-1070)	2nd Intermediate Period	Most likely older than New Kingdom, i.e., before 1550.
Amduat	New Kingdom (1550 - 1070)	Thutmosis I (1504-1492)	Some authors date this book to before the New Kingdom, despite the lack of a thorough rational. (e.g., Hornung, 1999, p. 28)
Prophesy of Neferrohu	New Kingdom	Thutmosis III (1479-1425)	Date of composition uncertain.
Book of the Divine Cow	New Kingdom	Tutankhamun (1333-1323)	The part presenting the "Legend of the Destruction of Mankind."
Book of Gates	New Kingdom	Haremheb (1319-1307), last king of 18th Dynasty.	Portions of book used sporadically after the New Kingdom.
Book of Aker	New Kingdom to Late Kingdom	Merneptah (1224-1214), in 19th Dynasty (1207-1196)	Uncertain if full document is available; almost all attestations are fragmentary.

The sun-god's sojourn across the daytime sky and descent into the Netherworld was fraught with danger, including battles with his arch enemy, Apophis, the personification of evil and darkness. But these conflicts always resulted in the defeat of darkness so that the battles had effectively no significant impacts on Egypt's religious beliefs and social stability. Up until the 2nd Intermediate Period (1640 -1532 BCE) such myths had stabilized and became firmly ingrained in the mythology of many parts of Egypt. This early period of stability came to an abrupt end during the 2nd Intermediate Period when Thera erupted. And it was Thera's eruption that a marked explosion of new myths, many of which expressed a greatly heightened awareness of the sun-god's vulnerability and his need to be protected by his followers during the inevitable cosmic conflicts with Apophis. Goelet (1994) describes the phenomenon:

> The expulsion of the Hyksos and the establishment of the Eighteenth Dynasty seems to have given rise to a great burst of creative activity in many fields, including the writing of funerary literature. The royal tombs of the Eighteenth and Nineteenth Dynasties contain a wide variety of texts whose purpose was to aid the king on his journeys through the

afterlife, as well as to put forth explanations of the cosmology of this world and the beyond: The *Litany of the Sun*, the *Amduat* (*What is in the Duat*), the *Book of Gates*, the *Book of Caverns*, the *Book of Aker* (the Earth), the *Book of Day and Night*, and the *Book of the Divine Cow*.[610]

Egyptologists usually associate this burst of creativity with national stresses associated with the invasion of the Hyksos and their occupation and rule over Egypt. But there can be little doubt that the dramatic events associated with the eruption of Thera also played a significant role. These will be discussed next.

Assuming an eruption date of 1628 BCE, the physical after-effects of the eruption would have greatly exacerbated any social unrest brought about by the presence of the Hyksos, especially in the Delta where they established their capital. Also, there can be little doubt that the Egyptian rulers and priests of this and at least some subsequent periods viewed the devastating impact of the tsunami, the toxic ash-fall, and the darkness which enveloped the Delta after Thera's eruption to be an expression of the sun-god's displeasure over the presence of the Hyksos on Egyptian soil. Near the end of this period, relationships with the Hyksos deteriorated further and military conflicts ultimately flared when King Kamose (1555-1550), the last king of the 17th Dynasty, actively campaigned against them and their expulsion from Egypt was finalized by the next king, Ahmose (1550-1525 BCE), the first king of the 18th Dynasty.

The dramatic natural phenomena in the Delta caused by Thera's eruption were recorded by Egyptian scribes in documents such as the *Prophesy of Neferrohu* and the *Admonitions of an Egyptian Sage*, as discussed earlier. But there can be no doubt that many other similar compositions existed for years after the catastrophe and these were subsequently lost. They would have included records of eyewitness accounts of the eruption brought to Egypt by survivors and traders. In them, distant islands whould have been reported to have disappeared beneath the sea as a great mountain spawned smoke and fire and massive earthquakes spread among the islands. At home in Egypt, enormous oceanic waves overwhelmed the Delta. Later, accounts of these events would have fueled the imaginations of the Egyptian priests of the early 18th Dynasty as patriotism associated with the expulsion of the Hyksos soared to new heights and priests struggled to explain the catastrophes in the context of their religious beliefs. Old cosmologies could not adequately account the dramatic events leading to the death of their sun (darkness). Consequently, they had to be reassessed and replaced by views more compatible with a new reality. Egyptian concepts of their sun-god and their relationship to him had changed. Very likely, these circumstances set the stage for the "great burst of creative activity in many fields, including the writing of funerary literature"[611] experienced after the Hyksos were driven out.

It is interesting to speculate on how the relatively great distance from Thera to the Nile Delta (733 km./456 miles) may have influenced the development of certain geographic features of the Egyptian Netherworld. Traditional beliefs held that the heavens were a celestial representation of earthly Egypt. The course of the Nile through Egypt was represented in the heavens by a celestial Nile while the souls of Egyptian dead were represented by the multitudes of stars on either side of the celestial river (the Milky Way). In this way, celestial Egypt mirrored earthly Egypt where the land and its people were considered to be the sun-god's special creations.

14. From Catastrophe to Myth

The Egyptians called themselves "the cattle of Re" on whom the sun-god lavished special favors. The celestial sphere was home to the living souls (the stars) of all who had been his faithful followers during their lives on earth. But just as the earthly Nile harbored dangerous creatures such as crocodiles, hippopotamuses and snakes, the celestial Nile harbored the evil, serpentine Apophis and his followers. These early concepts of the celestial sphere extended beyond the borders of Egypt, stretching from the western horizon to pass beneath the earth where they became the Netherworld which extended all the way up to Egypt's eastern horizon. And just as Re sailed in his boat along the celestial Nile to rule the earth in the daytime sky before growing old and passing beyond the western horizon into the Netherworld, the Egyptian Pharaoh, the "son of Re," periodically sailed along the Nile to exercise his sovereignty over his people. After death, he sailed along the Nile to his final resting place in a tomb in the earth. Prior to the 2nd Intermediate Period, their views did not, however, extend the celestial-Egyptian analogy to beyond the Delta and far out into the Mediterranean Sea.

New features of the cosmos revealed by the eruption of Thera must have greatly impacted on traditional views of the celestial sphere and Egypt's mirror image. Novel aspects of the Netherworld were influenced by the expansion of Egypt's perception of the Mediterranean Sea and its islands and shorelines; they now saw this distant area as an earthly representation of the Netherworld's more dangerous areas. Since they also believed that earthly events mirrored celestial ones, natural catastrophes and political and military events in the Mediterranean, including the cataclysmic eruption of Thera, were incorporated into new myths of the earthly Netherworld – and *vice versa* – thereby enhancing the impetus for the "great burst of creative activity in many fields."

Evidence for the incorporation of aspects of the geography of the Mediterranean Sea into the Netherworld can be found in the Egyptian literature where we read of certain large distances in the Netherworld which are most meaningful on a scale approaching the size of the Mediterranean; these are found in 1st, 2nd and 3rd Divisions of the *Amduat*. In the 1st Division we find a reference to an area of about 300 or 309 *itrw* in length, the latter dimension being also mentioned in the 2nd and 3rd Divisions. The relevant texts are as follows:

1st Division: The two goddesses Truth tow this God in the Nightbark, which passes through the gateway of this city. It is 120 *itrw* (*mistakenly,* 200) after that before he reaches Wernes, which is 300 (! 309?) *itrw* in length.[612] (AM1.2)

2nd Division: To rest in Wernes by the majesty of this god, to sail the fields on the Waters of Re. This field (i.e., region) is 309 *itrw* in length and 120 *itrw* in width. (AM2.Intro)[613]

3rd Division: This Great God rests in the Field of the Offering-dwellers and sails the Water of Osiris. This field is 309 *itrw* in length.[614] (AM3.Intro)

Since a distance of one *itrw* represents about 10.5 kilometers,[615] the length of the area described in the three divisions is about 3245 (or 3150?) kilometers, a distance approximating that from Levant to Gibralter (3390 kilometers), i.e., the east-west length of the Mediterranean Sea. The 2nd Division tells us that the width of this same area is 120 *itrw*, or 1260 kilometers, roughly the combined distance from the Nile Delta to the eastern end of Crete and from there to the northernmost part of the Aegean Sea in the vicinity of the island of Thasos; 1260 kilometers is also the approximate total distance from the Delta, along the coast to Byblos, from Byblos to the eastern end of Crete and from there to Thera. Although the northern Aegean is not the most northerly part of the Mediterranean (the Adriatic Sea extends further north), to the early Egyptians it was undoubtedly the most familiar and politically important part. The dimensions of the Waters of Re (or Osiris), or Wernes, described in the *Amduat*, therefore conform reasonably well with Egyptian perceptions of those of the Mediterranean Sea.

One might ask if the ancient Egyptians were aware of the actual size of the Mediterranean Sea. It is unlikely that such knowledge was obtained directly by the Egyptians of the 18th Dynasty (when the *Amduat* was composed) for the Egyptians were not well known for extensive sea-faring expeditions. The Mycneans, whose population centered on Crete, however, developed a fleet of sea-going vessels manned with well-trained crews and established trading partnerships with all the major powers in the eastern and southern portions of the Aegean as well as the Levant, Egypt and Lybia. They undoubtedly would have sent expeditions to explore commercial opportunities in the western reaches of the Mediterranean Sea and thereby amassed detailed knowledge of its size. Such knowledge would undoubtedly have found its way to Egypt through its trade links with Crete and the surrounding islands.[a]

That the Mediterranean Sea might be referred to in the 3rd Division of the *Amduat* as the "Waters of Osiris" is understandable in the light of Egyptian myths. The Nile River itself was considered to be the efflux of Osiris and since it flows into the Mediterranean it is only logical that the Egyptians would have considered the Mediterranean to be the accumulated efflux, or "Waters of Osiris" – and by the extension based on the Osiris-Re concept (discussed in Chapter 3, *The Preeminent Deities*), also of the sun-god, Re (as stated in the 2nd Division).

Hornung (1999) describes this part of the Netherworld in the first two divisions of the *Amduat* as, "a realm of abundance dominated by ... [a] watery expanse called *Wernes*."[616] (Other authors, such as Budge, Faulkner and Piankoff refer to it as *Urnes*.) While *Wernes* seems to reflect the afterworld's equivalent of the unusually productive areas of the Nile River system, literature dealing with the afterlife, works such as the *Book of the Dead* and the *Book of Gates* seem to place it somewhere

---

[a] We can be certain that the Egyptians of the 26th Dynasty (672-525 BCE) knew of the size of the Mediterranean because King Necho (610-595) had to have used such knowledge when he commissioned an exploratory expedition to circumnavigate the entire continent of Africa. A small fleet of ships manned by Phoenicians left the eastern part of the Nile Delta, traveled through a manmade waterway between the Mediterranean and the Red Sea, sailed through the Red Sea and then south along the eastern shores of Africa before rounding its southern tip and then north along its west coast to the Straits of Gibralter and then into the Mediterranean Sea and back to Egypt. The entire trip took three years. This expedition would likely not have been launched if the Egyptians did not prior knowledge of the western boundaries of the Mediterranean Sea. (See Gyles, 1959. *Pharaonic Policies and Administration, 663 to 323 BCE*, p. 28.)

beyond the Nile while descriptions in the *Amduat* suggest it may be patterned after an area of the Mediterranean Sea – an area which conforms with the Aegean area. It therefore seems wise to examine the Egyptian name *Wernes* for the possibility that it represents a descriptive term incorporating Egyptian knowledge of the volcanic nature of Thera.

To begin, the name *Wernes* is variously written as ⸺, ⸺, ⸺, ⸺, or ⸺, as well as others. The name can be broken down into the two syllables, *wr, wrr* or *ur (wer* or *ur)* and *ns (nes)* where *wr* can mean "great"[617] as well as "important"[618] and *ns* can mean "fire" or "flame"[619] so that *Wr-ns* can mean "great fire" or "great flames." Thus, a transliteration of the word Wernes can mean "great (or important) flames," a concept consistent with the place of fiery judgment by Re upon his enemies in the Netherworld (and hence the earthly Mediterranean). Hornung (1990) describes *Wernes* in the 5th Division of the *Amduat* as a place where "The gods, the blessed dead, and the damned do not wander on the paths of this region, filled with fire that Isis spews forth. At its heart lies the Lake of Fire, whose red waves portend one of the most refined places of punishment reserved for those condemned at the Judgment of the Dead."[620] Also, in the lower register of the 5th Division of the *Book of Gates* we find a picture of a circular, fiery pool described as a "holy pool." The text tells us that "the water of the pool is fire" and its fiery breath and fire "are directed against the souls who might come near to Osiris with bad intent. Thou art without lack! Ho, pool, there is no other (like thee), the gods who guard it have power over its waters."[621] This description conforms with an area close to a central, active volcano.

Finally, the "Water(s) of Osiris" and *Wernes* ("great fire") mentioned in the *Amduat* could very well represent the same area as the Netherworld in the *Book of Gates*; we find a description of the Lake of Fire in the *Book of Gates* which could very well be a lake of fiery lava inside Thera's boiling caldron;[a] it seems significant that the 5th Division of the *Book of Gates* shows the Lake of Fire as having a circular rather than the more traditional rectangular shape of the hieroglyph for a pool (▬). Hornung (1990) describes it as a "circular hole of fire."[622] This conforms with central lakes of boiling lava found in the caldera of active volcanoes. It therefore seems that, in addition to the earthly Mediterranean Sea representing the otherworldly part of the wide expanse of Re's journey through the Netherworld, the idea of a lake of fiery lava at Thera's core found its way into the deepest parts of the Netherworld where it conveyed an idea of the pitiless judgment and terrible wrath of the sun-god.

Egyptians undoubtedly linked the Theran disaster with their most powerful cosmic god, Re or Amen-Re, the creator of all, the "father of the gods" and the one who controlled light and darkness upon earth. Re's first act of creation was the solar disk which represented him as it emerged from the waters of the primordial ocean each morning. Rising into the morning sky, he gained strength throughout the day

---

[a] This statement assumes that either Egyptians or Minoans had ventured to the top of the volcanic dome and looked down upon the lake of lava; such excursions undoubtedly occurred just as they do on volcanic domes today, although the reasons for such trips up the mountain on Thera were probably more in line with religious beliefs rather than scientific study or feats of personal bravery.

only to die as a "bent and aged sun-god" who is swallowed up by the depths in the evening to reemerge fully rejuvenated into the sky the next morning. This and similar myths existed from very early times and were used to explain the sun's mysterious daily cycle, they were the central theme of texts and images on the ceilings of sarcophagus chambers in many of the tombs in the Valley of the Kings. Not all myths were embedded in such a peaceful setting, however, for many involved situations in which the sun-god was attacked by beings intent on destroying his power to shed light on the world of the living. Regardless of variations in the myths, the principal enemy of the sun was almost always the same – Apophis, the ancient serpent whose wicked purposes and followers pursue the sun-god throughout his course in both the earth's daytime sky and the darkness of the night in the Netherworld. Such myths seem to have influenced Egyptian perceptions and beliefs surrounding the eruption of Thera and especially its effects on the Egyptian Delta.

The Aegean Islands as a Parallel to Revelation's Babylon

The above explanation for the possible revamping of the Egyptian Netherworld does not, however explain the reference to "Babylon" in the Book of Revelation.

Bible scholars almost invariably assume that this Babylon has its origin in the ancient city of the same name on the Euphrates River in modern-day Iraq. Nevertheless, they assume that the reference to it in Revelation is purely symbolic, that Revelation's Babylon actually represents imperial Rome which was unsympathetic to the early Christians. This assumption is based primarily on its use as a symbol for Rome in Jewish writings, including, as pointed out by Collins (1984), the

> Apocalypse of Ezra (4 Ezra = 2 Esdras 3-14), the Syriac Apocalypse of Baruch (2 *Apoc. Bar*), and the fifth book of the *Sibylline Oracles*. In each case where it occurs in these three works, the context makes it abundantly clear why the name Babylon was chosen [in the Book of Revelation]. Rome is called Babylon because her forces, like those of Babylon at an earlier time, destroyed the temple and Jerusalem.[623]

The perceived moral degradation of ancient Babylon played an important role in its becoming a symbolic name for the Roman Empire at the time of its persecution of early Christians.[a]

Ancient Babylon was traditionally also considered an enemy of Egypt and many military campaigns were fought against it. Babylon was held responsible for the death of many Egyptian nationals, a fact that would have intensified Egypt's hostile attitude against it, hostility which was probably at least as vehement as that expressed in the Book of Revelation. There are, however, several logical difficulties with associating Iraq's Babylon with that of Revelation. In the first place, as already pointed out, Revelation's Babylon is described as being an island nation with many seaports, a description which does not conform with the Babylon on the Euphrates River.

---

[a] Collins (1984, p. 57) also points out that, "It is important to recognize that Babylon was not the obvious or only name that a Christian familiar with Jewish tradition might select as a symbolic name for Rome, to portray the city as the enemy of God's people. 'Egypt,' 'Kittim,' and 'Edom' appear along with the 'Babylon' in Jewish sources as symbolic names for Rome."

14. From Catastrophe to Myth

Secondly, Iraq's Babylon was situated on the eastern part of the Fertile Crescent, an area with no history of volcanic eruptions such as the one described in Revelation. Finally, there are no stories from this area, either in the form of legends or religious beliefs, of a catastrophic event involving a mountain of fire and earthquakes of the enormous and devastating proportions we find in Revelation. It therefore seems reasonably certain that the Babylon described in the Book of Revelation is not the ancient city located on the Euphrates River.

Before looking for Babylon among the Aegean islands it behooves us to first rule out the likelihood that Revelation's Babylon had a reasonable parallel within ancient Egypt itself. We might assume, for example, that the destruction of Babylon refers to the destruction of a town within Egypt itself, one with the same or a similar sounding name which could be misconstrued to mean Babylon.

We might well consider the town of Kheraha, a suburb of the ancient Egyptian capital of Heliopolis located in the eastern Delta near modern-day Cairo and known today as "Old Cairo." The ancient Greeks called it "Babylon." Egypt's Babylon is often mentioned in its religious literature, including the *Book of the Dead*. Nevertheless, the texts never speak of Kheraha with the same intense, negative tone we find for Revelation's Babylon. On this basis alone, it would seem that the Babylon of Egypt is not the Babylon spoken of in Revelation, although, as we shall see next, Kheraha may indeed have influenced the choice of names the Egyptians used to describe Thera.

Clagett (1989) tells us that the name *Kheraha* means "The Place of Battle," referring to "the battle between Horus and Seth."[624] Horus and Seth were sons of Osiris who engaged in a family feud following Seth's brutal murder of Osiris and the dismemberment of his body. After a series of battles, Horus defeated Seth and ascended to his father's throne while Seth was relegated to the desert. Legends about the event vary greatly with the oldest describing battles fought on both land and water and involving spears, chains, bows and arrows. During the 18th Dynasty, however, a new setting for the ancient battle was envisaged and the bulk of the battle was transferred to the celestial sphere where Seth was often considered a manifestation of the evil god Apophis. Some of the more dramatic aspects of the war found their way into the *Book of the Dead* where they are concentrated mainly in Chapter 17. Interestingly, this source describes the final battle as having extended not only through a day but also through a night. Night battles were seldom used in ancient warfare, especially major battles; most or all great battles were restricted to day-time clashes when visual signals could be used and troops performed at their best. But we are told in Chapter 17 that the light of the sun was darkened from the battle: "... the Sacred Eye [right eye of Re, i.e., the sun] ... had been injured on that day when the rivals fought." This turned a daytime battle into a nighttime one which lasted until dawn. This account describes Re as

> that Great Cat who ... on that *night of making war*' on behalf of those who warded off the rebels on that day in which were destroyed the enemies of the Lord of All. ... As for that *night of making war,*' it means that they entered into the east of the sky, and war broke out in the entire sky and earth. ... on that night of the flame against the fallen. ... The sky is encircled with the fiery blast of his mouth ... yet he is unseen. ... 'Swallower of Myriads'

is his name, and he dwells in the Lake of Wenet ... that Lake of Fire. ... As for Wadjet, Lady of the Devouring Flame, she is Re. ... She is the eye of Re. As for those few who approach her, it means that the confederacy of Seth are near her, because what is near her is burning.[625] (BD17)

We see here that the original terrestrial battle between Horus and Seth, became a celestial one wherein the enemies of the sun-god are destroyed by "the fiery blast of his mouth"; what was originally perceived as the Egyptian town of Kheraha where the historic battle of Horus and Seth was fought thus seems at first glance to have assumed cosmic significance, including a great fiery blast into the heavens from its mouth. There are no volcanoes which blast fire from its mouth in Egypt and this is reason enough to question whether Kheraha, Egypt's Babylon and the original "Place of Battle" between Horus and Seth in ancient Egypt is indeed the "The Place of Battle" described in Chapter 17 of the *Book of the Dead*.

As discussed elsewhere, the ancient Egyptians placed great importance on the meanings and sounds of names so that many names assigned to different places were frequently quite informative – just as they often are in all languages. In English, for example, we might refer to a particularly deep harbor by the name "Deep Harbor" or a picturesque and peaceful town by the name "Heart's Content." A breakdown of the various possible meanings of the name *Kheraha* is therefore appropriate. The hieroglyphic form of *Kheraha* is 𓈎𓂋𓄿𓀀𓏤𓊖,[626] the first part of the word, 𓈎𓂋, being pronounced *kher* and the latter, 𓄿𓀀, *āḥa*. Now the word *kher* can mean "evil or wickedness"[627] while *āḥa* can mean "to fight, to do battle, or wage war";[628] and 𓏤 means "strong"[629] while 𓊖 means a place such as a city or town.[630] Note that, when combined, these syllables form a word (a strong, evil, warring city) which expresses the idea found in the Book of Revelation that Babylon was the "dwelling place of demons, a haunt of every foul spirit" (Rev. 18:2), which has "drunk the wine of her impure passion" (Rev. 18:3) – and which was the sight of a great battle (Rev. 12:7 and Rev. 16:16).

But vocalization of the name *Kheraha* must have, in some circumstances, evoked additional images and emotions in the minds of the Egyptians. For example, the word *kerr*, which is phonetically similar to *kher*, meant "a burnt offering"[631] or an "offering by fire,"[632] while another phonetically similar word, *qerà*, meant "rainstorm, tempest, hurricane, or thunderstorm."[633] Words containing these sounds thus conjured up images of fire and tempest in the sky. *Ker* was also a type of earth-god[634] so that one might also associate these events with the earth itself, such as earthquakes. Meanwhile, words which were phonetically similar to the second part of the name *Kheraha* are equally informative. *Ha*, for example meant "to go to waste and ruin, to be destroyed"[635] as well as "to burn, to break into flame, heat, fire."[636] And *haha* meant "to flame, to burn up."[637] Another similar sounding word was *hh*, meaning a "blast of fire."[638] This latter group of homonyms or near homonyms conform with images of devastation and fire, images one might associate with a volcanic eruption. For these reasons, the phrase *kher-aha* (rather than the name) may be understood as a reference to a place of fire capable of causing destruction and ruin. To the Egyptians, then, the name *Kheraha* could simply mean either Egypt's own Kheraha and the place of the original battle between Horus and Seth, or some distant or mythical place known for its fire and destructive qualities. The latter view seems to be especially relevant in this discussion since the ancient Egyptians apparently did not have a word for "volcano" in their vocabulary.

There is another possible link between Kheraha and a place of almost unimaginable destruction. At the time of Thera's eruption, the island was known to the Greeks as "Calliste," which meant "Most Beautiful," a name consistent with some of the descriptions of Egypt's Wernes. But after the eruption, instead of using the parochial name for the island (if the Egyptians in fact knew it as Calliste), the Egyptians very likely assigned it a name which was more meaningful to their new view of the cosmos. Stories of Thera's eruption undoubtedly gave rise to many new myths about how the anger of the gods was expressed. This brought new meanings to old legends of the battle between the two brothers – and to the name of Kheraha itself. New images of a mountain of fire reaching up into the heavens enabled dramatic new cosmic phenomena to be incorporated into descriptions of Egypt's traditional Kheraha, the "Battle Place of the Gods" (Horus and Seth); these descriptions trumped Thera's original "Most Beautiful" place.

As discussed above, references to fiery mountains and their destructive powers, including fiery breath and rivers of fire are found in the 5th through to the 10th as well as the 12th and 13th mounds in Chapter 149 of the *Book of the Dead*. Gods are often described as living on or inside them. We might well ask if these texts describe different mountains or different aspects of the same mountain? The latter seems more likely, especially when we consider the Egyptian tradition of describing, with different names, the same deity from different points of view. Different attributes of the same god might be given different names which at times could even assume the properties or identities of entirely separate gods. Since it would be unlikely that more than one fiery mountain would be well known to the Egyptians (with the possible exception of Italy's more distant Mount Vesuvius), we may assume that any references to such a myth in Chapters 149 (and 146) relate to a single volcanic island in the midst of several other islands (as in the Book of Revelation). Meanwhile, elsewhere in the *Book of the Dead* and other sacred writings there are frequent references to the "Islands of the Sea" which modern scholars have identified with the Aegean Islands in the Mediterranean Sea.

Discussion

Egyptians may have believed that volcanic eruptions were the means by which the world was periodically cleansed of its accumulated evils in preparation for a new creation. As will be discussed in detail in Chapter 26, *A New Creation*, this cleansing and re-creation of the cosmos occurred at regular intervals, possibly as long as a thousand years each. Superimposed on these long term cycles were daily cycles during which the world was viewed as being re-created each morning at dawn when the newly born sun-god rose from the Netherworld to rule in the earth's daytime sky. Each morning a great battle was fought in heaven led by Apophis (sometimes Seth) and his forces to prevent the rebirth of the deity, and the sky turned red with blood (the redness of the sunset?) which flowed from the slain evil one. We have already mentioned this battle in reference to Rev. 7 which parallels the description in the 11th

Division of the *Amduat* where the followers of the sun-god are depicted as being protected by a large Enveloper Serpent against the evils sent against the forces of the enemy (see Chapter 11, *Prelude to War*). From there, Rev. 8 and Rev. 9 take us into a much greater battle, including apocalyptic visions of a volcanic eruption.

Descriptions of a mountain of fire in Egyptian texts conform with those of a volcanic eruption among a group of islands in the sea. The mountain itself is described as being very high and containing a lake of fire; this is most likely a centrally located lava lake. The mountain emits thunderous noises and its fiery blast kills everyone within its range while smoke, fire and ash rise up into the heavens from the exploding mountain – and seen from as far away as northern Egypt and the Levant. Only those who escape to a safe distance are spared, although even they are not immune to the harmful effects of toxic dust, gasses and ash-fall. Mid-day darkness, ash-fall and earthquakes are felt as far away as Egypt where tsunamis destroy many towns in the Delta, killing thousands of people. Eye-witness descriptions of the distant eruption reach Egypt indirectly through trade routes or directly from survivors arriving on ships seeking refuge in Egypt. At least one account of the eruption survived in the *Book of the Dead* while others survived to a lesser degree in other religious compositions such as the *Amduat*, the *Book of Gates* and the *Book of the Divine Cow*. Also, the effects of the eruption on the Nile Delta were described in the two secular compositions, the *Prophesy of Neferrohu* and the *Admonitions of an Egyptian Sage*.

During the years following the eruption, Egyptian priests struggled to explain the unprecedented events in the context of their prior understanding of order and stability of all things in nature, a concept known as *maat* which embraced the fundamentals of law, truth and order in the universe. *Maat* had failed. The sun, which graced the earth and sky with its warmth and beauty every day since time began, ceased to shine for days and terrifying darkness covered the earthquake-stricken land. Earlier myths of the dimming of the sun and moon had been associated with much less dramatic normal weather extremes or eclipses which had been attributed to periodic, localized actions by Seth and Apophis. These minor inconveniences paled in comparison with Thera's overwhelming power as old explanations failed to take into account the extraordinary events. New explanations were sought within the framework of the limited geophysical knowledge of the day and somehow had to be incorporated into the myriad of previously accepted mythologies. Hence, the relatively new Chapters 146, 149 and 150 of the *Book of the Dead* contain explicit references to a mountain of smoke and fire along with natural phenomena typically associated with a volcanic eruption.

After the tsunami struck the Egyptian Delta, surviving priests and those who lived upstream where it was not as destructive must have believed the regular daily attack of Apophis against the sun-god had met with unprecedented success. The sun and moon, the eyes of the sun-god himself, suffered great harm and ceased to shine. And the stars, the living souls of the dead, fell and died (i.e., disappeared) from the sky. The land was thrown into chaos as water supplies were poisoned by toxic fallout and irrigation canals were blocked with ash. Crops died from lack of sunlight or were destroyed by smothering ash. The situation in Egypt was made worse because the Nile Delta, which suffered most, was the main bread-basket of Egypt. Famine and social chaos spread upstream throughout the land and the Hyksos, who had entered Egypt from the Syria-Palestine area, quickly rose to power in the Delta.

This led to a separation of power between Upper and Lower Egypt; while Upper Egypt was ruled by native Egyptians, Lower Egypt was ruled by the Hyksos "chiefs of foreign lands." Avaris, the capital city of the Hyksos, situated in the eastern Delta, dominated Egyptian powers elsewhere in the Delta and as far up the Nile as Asyut. It was Kamose, the last king of the 17th Dynasty who declared all-out war against the Hyksos but his efforts effectively ended in a stalemate. Next, Ahmose, the founder of the 18th Dynasty finally defeated the Hyksos by literally driving them out of the Delta and deep into the Levant where the final stage of his conquest ended with a successful three-year siege of the fortified town of Sharuhen. And he re-united Upper and Lower Egypt under a single ruler.[639] Many of the 18th Dynasty's rulers understandably despised the memory of the Hyksos and looked upon them with disdain for their part in the turmoil and social instability, and for the disgraceful memory of their rule.

As details of events faded with time, the belief emerged that during the early part of the 2nd Intermediate Period the sun-god himself had been temporarily defeated with drastic consequences on earth. But Re had lashed out with unprecedented fury against the enemy, his wrath reaching all the way to the Delta where he punished the remaining Hyksos and their Egyptian supporters who had been "unfaithful" to him.

The literary evidence presented for parallels between events in the Book of Revelation and the devastation caused by a volcanic eruption may be difficult for some readers to accept. This is quite understandable in view of the mythological nature of the evidence and the possibility of alternative interpretations of the text. But these conclusions are reinforced by several similar parallels among different Egyptian religious and secular texts – as well as Plato's account of a similarly great catastrophe in the Aegean Sea. And further still, all the observed parallels are consistent with modern scientific conclusions on the magnitude and widespread effects of the eruption of Thera in the Aegean Sea $c.$ 1628 BCE. In Egypt, its dramatic sociological impacts led to the "great burst of creative activity in many fields," including the writing of a new branch of funerary literature" in the 18th Dynasty (for example, the *Amduat* and the *Book of Gates*).

In spite of the rather strong evidence that most of the apocalyptic imagery in the various sources conforms with a volcanic eruption, the parallels presented throughout this work and its final conclusion do not depend on the date of 1628 BCE; if future investigations on Thera's eruption suggest revising the date to some time after 1628 BCE and nearer the end of the 2nd Intermediate Period, they would likely have little if any effects on the main conclusions reached here.

Since many of the apocalyptic images in the Book of Revelation parallel those associated with volcanic eruptions, and since these are spread throughout many of its chapters, the background provided in this and the previous chapter facilitates understanding of many of the arguments for a host of additional Egyptian parallels to scenes in the Book of Revelation. For example, there are a number of scenes in Rev. 11 which parallel scenes and series of scenes found in the Egyptian *Book of Aker*. These scenes give a vivid description of a massive earthquake which kills 7,000 thousand people and apparently contribute to the book's account of events at the "end of time." Finally, in our examination of Rev. 12 (in Chapter 17, *The Woman in the Sky*), we will discuss another series of parallel scenes found in the well-known Egyptian *Books of the Heavens* which includes the end of creation, its rejuvenation – and the cyclical nature of time.

Chapter 15. The Little Scroll (Rev. 10)[640]

The 10th chapter of the Book of Revelation introduces the reader to what it calls a "little scroll." (Apparently, this is a different scroll from the one referred to in Rev. 5:2 which had seven seals and was likely larger.) The chapter can be divided into three parts, each of which has components similar to those found in Egyptian sources: The first (Rev. 10:1-4) describes a "mighty angel" coming down from heaven holding a "little scroll" in his hand, a scene which parallels one in the *Amduat*. The second part (Rev. 10:5-7) parallels a passage from the "legend of the destruction of mankind" found in the *Book of the Divine Cow*. The third part (Rev. 10:8-11) differs significantly from the others in the sense that it describes a ritual in which the author of Revelation eats the little scroll for the purpose of gaining the knowledge contained therein; it also parallels a scene in at least one chapter of the *Book of the Dead*. These three parts will be discussed separately.

Presentation of the Scroll (Rev. 10:1-4)

We begin our comparison of Rev. 10:1-4 with Egyptian sources with a passage from the beginning of third register of the 5th Division of the *Amduat*. This passage introduces the division and provides the basis for a close look at some fascinating parallels to events described in the Book of Revelation.

A side-by-side comparison of the two relevant texts is given in Table 15.1. It is clear from this table that while the text in Revelation is not a direct translation of the Egyptian, it contains a grouping of parallel images presented in the same order; the most obvious elements are highlighted in italics. These general parallels lead us to a more in-depth scrutiny of the 5th Division where we find additional textual and pictorial parallels between the two sources. Before addressing these, however, a brief overview of the illustration representing this division of the *Amduat* (Figure 58) will be given as a general background to the parallels.

Like other divisions of the *Amduat*, the 5th is divided into three registers. This division is different from the others, however, in that the bottom register, called the "mysterious cavern of Sokaris," protrudes up into the middle register to form an area of elevated land over which the sun-god must be towed in his barque. The barque is towed by seven male and seven female towers who are separated by the elevation

Table 15.1. Comparison of Rev 10:1-3 with the text at A5.3.5-6 of the 5th Division of the *Amduat*. The most obvious parallels are highlighted in italics; these and other parallels are discussed in the text. Also note that they are in the same order in both sources.

Book of Revelation	The Amduat
¹Then I saw another mighty angel coming down from heaven, *wrapped in a cloud,* with a rainbow over his head, and *his face was like the sun,* and his *legs like pillars of fire.* ²He had a little scroll open in his hand. And he set his right foot on the sea, and his left foot on the land, ³and called out with a loud voice, *like a lion roaring; when he called out, the seven thunders sounded.* (Rev 10:1-3)	The image is like this *(in) thick darkness.*˙ The egg which belongs to *this god is lighted up by the eyes in the heads* [sic] *of this Great God,*˙ his *flesh shines, the legs*˙ are inside in coils. The Great God keeps guard over this image. The noise is heard in the egg, after the Great God has passed by it, *like the sound of roaring in the sky during a storm.*˙ (A5.3.5-6)[641]

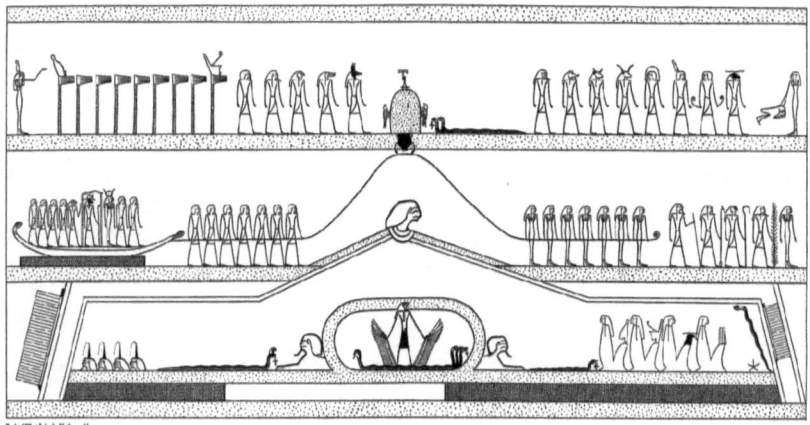

Figure 58. The 5th Division of the *Amduat* which represents the secret cavern of Sokaris. This division contains most of the elements mentioned in Rev. 10:1-4. (AM5)

while a scarab beetle pulls the rope upwards over it. This earthen mound is formed by the stylized shoulders of the god Sokaris whose head protrudes from it and whose stylized arms extend sideways from his chest out over most of the lower register (see Figure 59). Sokaris is also shown in the center of this register standing on a four-headed serpent inside his "egg" and holding the serpent's wings in his hands. His egg is flanked on either side by the forepart of the bodies of two human-headed lions which represent the so-called double-headed form of Aker ( ), a very ancient earth-god. In the center of the upper register is a second mound on the top of which is mounted a hieroglyph for "darkness" (Figure 60). Two birds, identified in the texts as "mourners," are situated one on either side of this mound of darkness thus conforming with the overall theme of death, darkness and dying in this division.

This theme is even more evident in the bottom register which, as noted above, features the god Sokaris. Sokaris, an ancient funerary deity and god of the dead who assumed the form of a divine falcon (hence the emphasis on wings in Figure 58). This part of the Netherworld is not meant for the faithful followers of the sun-god, however, but rather for the destruction of his enemies, depicted here as four burning heads behind the two-headed serpent on the left side of the lower register. As we shall soon see, Figure 58, along with the text of this division contains numerous images and events which closely parallel those described in Rev. 10:1-4. These will be dealt with separately below. To simplify understanding of some of these parallels, the locations of the relevant elements are shown in Figure 59.

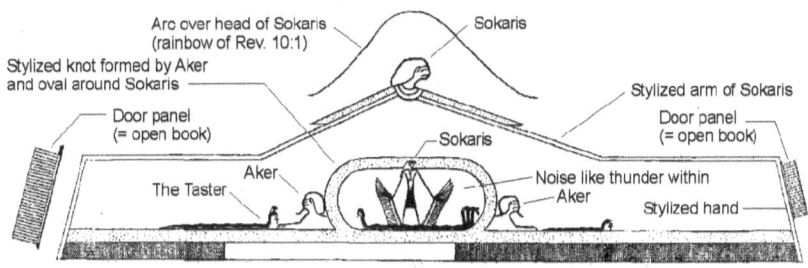

Figure 59. The main elements of the middle and lower registers of the 5th Division of the *Amduat* which are also found in the Rev. 10. The "Mighty Angel" of Rev. 10:1-4 is shown here as the god Sokaris who stands with legs apart inside an oval representing the knot which ties the string of a scroll (⸺). The two-headed lion-god Aker (⸺) identifies this scroll as the *Book of Aker* and also forms part of the stylized knot. (See text).

An Angel in a cloud (Rev. 10:1):- Revelation's description of an angel "coming down from heaven, wrapped in a cloud" is consistent with the picture of Sokaris shown standing as a hawk-headed figure holding two wings apart in his outstretched hands, an obvious reference to flight[642] in the heavens. The Egyptian text tells us he is "The Great God who opens his two wings, He of the Dappled Plumage,"[643] an obvious reference to Sokaris flying in his form as a hawk. It also says that "The image [of Sokaris] is like this (in) thick *darkness*'" Darkness, of course, is usually related to the night-time sky or the darkness under a storm cloud. It's determinative, 𓇳,[644] found at the exact center of the middle of the upper register (see Figure 58 and Figure 60) appears in the word *àgep* (*ỉgp*) which Budge (1920) translates as "cloud, fog, mist, the darkness of a storm" or "rainstorm"[645] and Faulkner (1962) translates simply as "clouds."[646] The prominent display of this symbol at the center of the upper register emphasizes its importance. Also, this location places it directly over the center of the arch formed by the tow rope of the sun-god's barque, which in turn is located directly over the head of Sokaris. In this manner, the textual reference to Sokaris being

Figure 60. Mound of darkness (𓇳) at the center of AM5.1.5. The two birds (Isis and Nephthys) are called "The Mourners," a name which associates the mound with death. (AM5.1.5-6)

"(in) thick *darkness*" is accentuated.[a] When these various elements are considered together we may conclude that, like the Revelation's angel which comes down from heaven in a cloud, the centrally located Sokaris is situated underneath or even inside a cloud in Figure 58. We may also say that he is associated with darkness since he is located under or in a cloud, as in Rev. 10:1, or as the Egyptian text says, "The image [of Sokaris] is like this (in) thick darkness."

With a rainbow over his head (Rev. 10:1):- In this verse the author of Revelation also says he saw the "mighty angel ... with a rainbow over his head." A bow, or arc over the head of Sokaris is also central in Figure 59. Here, we see a great arc created by the tow rope over Sokaris' head on top of the mound of sand in the center of the middle register. The rope also over the head of the second manifestation of Sokaris standing with outstretched legs in the center of the lower register. Furthermore, the upper half of the "egg" in which Sokaris stands in the bottom register can also be envisaged as forming an arc over his head, thus emphasizing the presence of an arc which of course, has the shape of a rainbow. These arcs in Figure 59 thus conform quite well with the idea of a rainbow over the head of the angel in Rev. 10:1.

His face was like the sun (Rev. 10:1):- This description parallels the text inside his oval-shaped egg. It says that "The egg which belongs to this god is lighted up by the eyes in the heads (*sic*) of this great god."[647]

His legs were like pillars of fire (Rev. 10:1):- Sokaris' legs are accentuated by his stance in the egg; he stands tall with legs apart. The text also accentuates them, making reference to their brightness with the words, "his flesh shines, the legs are inside the coils."[648] The brightness of the flesh of his legs parallels the expression in Rev. 10:1 where it describes his legs as "pillars of fire."

He had a little scroll open in his hand (Rev. 10:2):- There are no textual parallels to a scroll being held by Sokaris in the 5th Division of the *Amduat*. There are, however, two hidden references in the middle and lower registers. Figure 59 occupies almost this entire area and takes the form of the hieroglyph for a "papyrus-roll" (⌇) or "book"[649] wherein the two heads of the god Aker form a stylized knot in the string which seals the scroll.

That this part of the picture is indeed meant to represent a hieroglyph for a scroll is emphasized by the presence of a visual pun created by two hieroglyphs for door panels or leaves (⌇), one on each side of the scroll; the word; *ārt* is an Egyptian word for "book" as well as "two leaves of a door."[650] Significantly, one of these hieroglyphs is connected to Sokaris' stylized left hand at the end of his stylized left arm which extends outward from his stylized, sandy, right shoulder, suggesting he is holding a "book" in his hand, as in Rev. 10:2.

Rev. 10:2 says that the angel held a *little* scroll in his hand. The word "little" is, of course a relative term so that we may ask, "What is it's 'little' size relative to?" From an Egyptian perspective, note that the "scroll" in the hand of Sokaris is smaller than the one on the opposite (left) side of Figure 59. Thus, when the two "scrolls" are kept in mind, it is logical to refer to the one in Sokaris' hand as a "little scroll," just

---

[a] Piankoff (1954, p. 263) says that in versions other than the one from the Tomb of Ramesses VI (discussed here), the mound is called "night."

as described in Rev. 10:2. Identification of the door panel as a "book" in the hand of Sokaris is also entirely consistent with a certain apparently unique Egyptian idea about Sokaris. Budge (1934) describes Egyptian figures of Sokaris standing "on a pedestal on one side of which is a rectangular cavity which contains a small [little] roll of inscribed papyrus."[651]

Rev. 10:2 also says that the little scroll was "open" in his hand. On close inspection of Figure 59, we also find a parallel for the "open" status of the book. It so happens that the hieroglyph for a door panel ⟺ is also the determinative for the word "open" so that its presence on either side of the stylized scroll symbol in the figure can be readily interpreted as emphasizing that the scroll in Sokaris' hand is "open," just as described in Revelation.

Not unexpectedly, the stylized scroll shown in this part of the *Amduat* provides us with information not given in Revelation. As noted above, the double-headed symbol of the god Aker ( ) replaces the typical knot in the scroll's binding string. The scroll in the hand of Sokaris can thus be readily identified as the *Book of Aker* an important Egyptian religious text which will be discussed in some detail in the next chapter, *The Two Witnesses* and which contains many images parallel to those found in the next chapter of Revelation.

His feet were on the sea and the land (Rev. 10:2):- "And he set his right foot on the sea, and his left foot on the land. " In the 5th Division, Sokaris is called "He on his Sand," a title consistent with the deity in Revelation standing "on the land." Meanwhile, both land and water are mentioned in the text of the upper register near the five deities standing to the left of the central mound; it says, "May you land on the banks of the Great Flood! Your waters shall not dry up, may your banks [land] be high and not bare!"[652] We have here a picture of Sokaris stepping from a boat into the water and from there onto the land, a scene entirely consistent with Revelation's account of an angel coming ashore and, more specifically, at the moment when he has one foot on land while the other still in still in the water.

The theme of Sokaris' landing and standing on the bank of a river is quite evident in this division and conforms well with the description in Rev. 10:2 of an angel "setting his right foot on the sea and his left foot on the land."

He "Called Out Like a Lion Roaring" (Rev 10:3):- That Sokaris might be described as calling out like a roaring lion also parallels the presence of the double-headed *lion* figure which forms the knot of the central stylized book in the lower register. But the parallel in this part of the *Amduat* goes further; it also describes the sound of thunder within the egg.

The Seven Thunders Speak (Rev 10:3-4):- Rev. 10:3 says that when the angel called out like a lion roaring, "the seven thunders sounded." On both the left and right sides of the reclining two-headed lion is an inscription which ends with the statement that a "noise is heard in the egg, after the Great God has passed by it, like the sound of roaring in the sky during a storm."[653] The sound of thunder is thus mentioned in the Egyptian text in relation to Sokaris, the same deity which parallels the "angel who comes down from heaven wrapped in a cloud with a rainbow over his head." Revelation does not, however, inform us if the sound was that of atmospheric thunder or thunder from another source such as an earthquake; in the *Amduat*, the thunder comes from deep inside the Cavern of Sokaris (inside the earth), suggesting an earthquake.

Another way of comparing the reference to the sound of the seven thunders in Revelation to the scene in the *Amduat* is to assume that a pun is intended to suggest the word "thunders," as follows: Note that the number "seven" parallels the presence of seven male and seven female deities which *tow* the solar barque in Figure 58 (AM5.2.7-8). Meanwhile, the Egyptian word for "trembling" is *sdȝw*,[654] and trembling is conceptually related to earthquakes (especially in the sense that the name *Sṭa-ur* represented the "Great Quaker, a god of thunder and earthquakes").[655] But *sdȝw* also meant "dragging"[656] which, of course, is equivalent to "towing." And dragging (i.e., towing) a very large boat (310 cubits, i.e., over 450 feet long) over sand can cause a trembling sound or feeling beneath the feet, depending on the size and weight of the boat being towed, and composition of the object being pulled. Thus, "trembling" was conceptually related to towing in the minds of the Egyptians. This relationship ties the idea of the trembling sound of thunder or an earthquake to the towing the large solar barque over land (as is clear from the middle register where the towing rope loops up over the mound of sand). Thus, if we assume that a pun on the word towing is meant in the *Amduat*, either the seven male towers immediately in front of the barque or the seven female towers to the right of the head of Sokaris – both – may be described, as in Revelation, as "seven thunders" (i.e., seven *sdȝw*).

Instruction not to Write (Rev 10:4):- This verse tells us that after the seven thunders sounded, there came a voice saying, "Seal up what the seven thunders have said, and do not write it down." The above suggestion that the seven thunders may represent seven towers in the *Amduat* prompts a brief examination of the words of the *Amduat's* towers. Indeed, on close examination, as we shall see, the words spoken by them demonstrate a remarkable parallel with Rev. 10:4. Revelation's reference to "sealing up" what the seven thunders said and the instruction to the author not to write it down implies their words were secret. To understand the Egyptian parallel to this statement, we first take a look at the response of the seven male towers to the arrival of the sun-god:

> In peace, in peace! [Welcome!] Lord of Life! ... O Re! Thou speakest to Osiris, thou callest the Land of Sokaris, so that Horus on his sand may live. *Come to Khepri, O Re, Come to Re, O Khepri!* The towrope which you have brought, the towrope is lifted by Khepri that he may help Re, that he may make straight the mysterious [secret] ways of Re, Horus of the Horizon. (A5.2.3-4)[657]

The part of this response which has particular significance to the text in Revelation is presented in italics. After joyously welcoming the sun-god into the land of Sokar, the seven towers say, "*Come to Khepri, O Re, Come to Re, O Khepri!*"[a] As we shall see

---

[a] Note that in the 5th Division of the *Amduat*, Khepri (the sun-god's immature form) in the upper register is shown pulling the sun-god's tow rope up out of the earth (sand) suggesting the events portrayed here relate to the beginning of a new day – or a new creation. Meanwhile, Budge (1934) says that "Jéquier has pointed out rightly that originally the scenes of the Fourth and Fifth Hours formed a complete Book of the Ṭuat, and that the final scene in it was the sunrise." As noted in *Chapter 13, Catastrophes*, the catastrophic events included thunder and

next, these words embody one of the most secretive aspects of the sun-god's journey through time and of ancient Egypt's Osirian cult.

The 5th Division of the *Amduat* contains an unusual number of references to the mysterious nature of this part of the Netherworld. It is as if it contained a mention of some highly secretive event. For example, the cavern itself is called the *"mysterious* cavern of Sokaris"[658] within which occur the *"mysterious*' ways of the West ... the Holy Place of the Land of Sokaris."[659] The text says that this cavern contains "Knowledge [presumably in a book (the *Book of Aker*?)] of the souls who are in the Netherworld, what they do to those who are in the hours in accord with their *mysterious names, unknown, unseen, and imperceptible.*"[660] Also, it is here that we see "Sokaris guarding the *Mysterious Flesh*"[661] of the Netherworld. And the text immediately above the four gods near the far right of the third register identifies them as "Gods carrying the *mysterious symbols*' of Sokaris." It therefore seems that this part of the *Amduat* abounds with mysterious (i.e., secret) names and events which are unknown, invisible, and imperceptible.

The instruction in Rev. 10:4 for the author not to write down what the seven thunders say therefore conforms quite well with the secretive nature of events in this division. Indeed, this uniting of Re (the spiritual) and Khepri (his maturing physical body) forms of the sun-god in the Netherworld creates the form of the newly born sun-god each morning in his unified form as Osiris-Re. Hornung (1990) suggests that this unification creates a "new mysterious divine form uniting heaven and earth" and that *"this is the great mystery*' of the Netherworld."[662] This, of course, is the creation at dawn of the combined Osiris-Re deity discussed in Chapter 3, *The Preeminent Deities*. If we assume a relationship between this part of the *Amduat* and Rev. 10:4, the author may have been told not to record the phrase "*Come to Khepri, O Re, Come to Re, O Khepri!*'"

Call for Immediate Action (Rev 10:5-7)

After the introduction of the scroll (which as noted above, parallels the Egyptian *Book of Aker*), the angel raises his hand and swears by him who lives forever and ever that there should be no more delay in the fulfilling of the "mystery of God" (Rev. 10:5-7). Recall that the union of Re and Osiris took place at dawn, the time of the symbolic re-creation of the world, as discussed in Chapter 13, *Catastrophes* and elsewhere. It is this symbolism of re-creation of the cosmos that brings us directly to the next part of Revelation, Rev. 10:5-7, and its Egyptian parallel in the *Book of the Divine Cow*, a book which deals with the cleansing of the old world and the re-creation of a new one. As one might expect in translating such ancient hieroglyphics, English translations vary significantly. Nevertheless, it is apparent that the text in Revelation contains components which parallel those in the *Book of the Divine Cow*; these are

---

earthquakes believed to have been caused by the sun-god as part of the overall cleansing of the earth at its periodic renewal which was believed to happen symbolically each day just before sunrise, and in reality, near the end of each old and the beginning of each new cosmic cycle. Reference to thundering in the depths of the earth in this division of the *Amduat* from deep inside the earth at dawn is therefore consistent with this opinion.

included in Table 15.2 and will be discussed in the next paragraph as well as the following section.

Rev. 10:6d tells us "that there should be no more delay." Not all translations conform with this version, however. The King James Version, for example, says "that there should be time no longer." The latter translation more closely follows the original Greek in that the word *chronos* used here specifically means "time." When transliterated, the passage says, "that time no longer there should be." Clagett's parallel to this translation is found in the 89th column of the *Book of the Divine Cow* which reads: "Hail, thou lord of eternity (*nḥḥ*), thou creator of everlastingness (*ḏt*), who *causes the years of the gods to pass*' (lit. to be swallowed up)." Piankoff

Table 15.2. Comparison of Rev. 10:5-6,10 with columns 84-85 and 89 of the *Book of the Divine Cow* found in the tomb of Seti I (translated by Clagett, 1989, pp. 541-542 and Budge (1912, pp. 37-39)) and the tomb of Ramesses VI (translated by Piankoff (1953, pp. 225-226).

Book of Revelation	Book of the Divine Cow		
	Clagett	Piankoff	Budge
Rev. 10:5 And the angel ... lifted up his right hand to heaven	/84/ "Give praise	Let praise be given	Ascribe ye praise
Rev. 10:6a and swore by him who lives for ever and ever,	/84/ to the [truly] Eldest God (i.e. Nun),	the Eldest God,	to the god, the Aged One,
Rev 10:6b who created heaven and what is in it, the earth and what is in it, and the sea	/84/ [for] I have come into being /85/ from him. I have made the sky and stabilized [it].	As I came into being through him, I who created the sky, who established (earth)	from whom I have come into being. I am he who made the heavens, and I set in order (the earth
Rev 10:6c who lives for ever and ever, who created heaven and what is in it, the earth and what is in it, and the sea and what is in it.	/85/ I have made the sky ... in order that the *bas* of the gods might be set in it. I am with them an eternity.	to let the souls of the gods reside in it.	and created the gods, and)
Rev 10:6d ... that there should be no more delay, OR: Rev. 10:6d ... that there should be time no longer (KJV)	/85/ I am with them and eternity *(nḥḥ)*, which the years have formed. (p. 541)	I will be together with them in all eternity. The years are born ....(p. 225)	I was with them for an exceedingly long period; then was born the year and - - - - (p. 37)

Book of Revelation	Book of the Divine Cow		
	Clagett	Piankoff	Budge
Rev. 10:10 I took the little scroll from the hand of the angel and ate it; *it was sweet as honey in my mouth, but when I had eaten it my stomach was made bitter.*	(Not included in translation)	(Not included in translation)	/87/ Whosoever sayeth {these words} worketh his own protection by means of the words of power, "I am the god Ḥekau (i.e., the divine Word of Power [including prophesy]) and *I am pure in my mouth and in my belly.*'
		ALSO:	
Rev. 10:5-6a And the angel ... lifted up his right hand to heaven and swore by him who lives for ever and ever,	/89/ Hail, thou lord of eternity (*nḥḥ*), thou creator of everlastingness(*ḏt*),	O Lord of Eternity who created everlastingness,	Hail, thou lord of eternity, thou creator of everlastingness,
Rev 10:6d that there should be no more delay, OR: Rev. 10:6d that there should be time no longer (KJV)	/89/ who causes the years of the gods to pass (lit. to be swallowed up) (p. 542)	who abolished the years. (p. 226)	who bringest to nought the gods who came forth from Rā. (p. 39)

translates the same text as, "O Lord of Eternity who created everlastingness, *who abolished the years.*'" It is therefore reasonable to suggest that the King James translation of the Greek, "that there should be time no longer," is closer to the Egyptian record. From an Egyptian perspective, and as discussed in Chapter 13, *Catastrophes*, this period is related to the end of time and the beginning of a new creation where the "end of time" involves the (apparent) destruction of the world.

It was also proposed in *Catastrophes* that the destructive, cataclysmic events described in Revelation and the *Book of the Divine Cow* at the end of time conforms with events associated with the volcanic eruption of Thera in the Aegean Sea in the 17th century BCE. It would therefore be especially significant if we should find a reference to this same Aegean Sea disaster in the *Book of the Divine Cow*. In fact, we do. Indeed, it forms an important part of the book. In the 73rd column of the version in the Tomb of Seti I and translated by Clagett (1989) we read the phrase, "I shall cause thee to turn back the *Haunebu.*"⁶⁶³ According to a comment by Clagett (1955), *Haunebu* refers to "the isles of the Aegean Sea."⁶⁶⁴ This finding is all the more significant because the *Aegean Sea is the only explicitly mentioned geographic area in the Book of the Divine Cow.*[a] It therefore seems reasonable that many of the disasters mentioned in the Legend of the Destruction of Man in the *Book of the Divine Cow* may indeed be linked to Thera's eruption. Furthermore, as we shall see in the next chapter, *The Two Witnesses,* these disasters include a likely reference to the great earthquake described in Rev. 11:1-13 which kills thousands, an event for which there is a dramatic parallel found in the *Book of Aker* (also discussed in the next chapter).

Ceremony of the Little Scroll (Rev. 10:8-11)

This last part Rev. 10 is of special interest because it deals with a ceremony in which the author plays an active role. In Rev. 10:9, he receives the little scroll – the *Book of Aker* (as above) – and is told to "Take it and eat; it will be bitter to your stomach, but sweet as honey in your mouth." After eating it, he is told, "You must again *prophesy* about many peoples and nations and tongues and kings." As we shall see next, this scene parallels an Egyptian cult practice in which the participant eats food to gain new or mysterious (secret) knowledge, a purpose which conforms with the command given to the author to "prophesy about many peoples and nations and tongues and kings."

There is ample evidence in the Egyptian literature for belief in obtaining special powers through the ritualistic partaking of food. Goelet (1994) suggests that Chapter 124 of the *Book of the Dead* has "a hint of some manner of ritual concerned with food." Here, after the deceased puts "certain morsels of food in his mouth, he becomes one of the gods and thereby gains control over gods and situations that he may encounter in the beyond."⁶⁶⁵ The Egyptians believed they could obtain knowledge and power through the ritualistic eating of scrolls in which information or magical spells were written. Such spells were at times ostensibly placed in one's memory by writing them on papyrus and eating it; this would ensure that the person involved would remember the spell whenever it might be necessary to use it – as might well be the case during his sojourns in dangerous parts of the Netherworld. Also, the ritual was especially important to Egyptians who could not read. Goelet relates a simplistic story of such an approach given in a passage from the late Demotic tale known as *Setne Khauemwas and Naneferkaptah:*

> As I could not write – I mean, compared with Naneferkaptah, my brother, who was a good scribe and a very wise man – he had a sheet of new papyrus brought to him. He wrote on it every word that was in the book before him. He soaked it in beer, he dissolved it in water. When he knew that it has dissolved, he drank it and knew what had been in it.⁶⁶⁶

---

[a] The *Book of the Divine Cow* also mentions the "Field or Reeds," the "Island of the Double Soul" and the "Eastern Mountain" but these are mythical locations which do not correspond to known locations on earth.

Because a thorough knowledge of the writings in the *Book of the Dead* was required for the deceased to be victorious in the final judgment, such alternative, magical means of acquiring knowledge was at times necessary, especially for the illiterate.

The 5th Division of the *Amduat*, which introduces the "little" scroll, sets the stage for a sequence of ceremonial activities in which a scroll is consumed. Although such a ceremony is not specifically mentioned in the text of this division, it is implied through various symbols, both textual and graphic. The most prominent evidence for this is found in the name, position, and appearance of the two-headed serpent (Figure 61) to the immediate left of the two-headed lion (👁) lying on the stylized scroll (➰) in the lower register. The serpent's name is *The Taster*[a] and its location on the scroll suggests he is about to taste or eat the symbolized scroll.

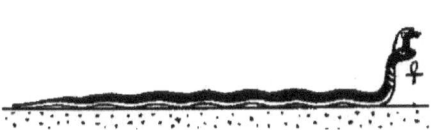

Figure 61 Knowledge and wisdom is represented by the head of a baboon on a serpent called *The Taster* who is about to consume a copy of the *Book of Aker*. (AM5.3.3-4)

The Taster's upper head is that of a baboon, an Egyptian symbol of wisdom and knowledge. An excellent and fitting example of the use of this symbol is cited by Wilkinson (1994):

> Another common example of this kind of visual metaphor may be found in many depictions of the sacred baboon. Because the baboon was a symbol of Thoth – the lunar god who was also god of writing and wisdom – its image could be used to represent those qualities commonly associated with that god. Thus, in both the written and hieroglyphic script, and in larger representational works, the baboon may signify wisdom, knowledge, judgment, writing, and even excellence.[667]

In the context of Rev. 10:8-11 then, the baboon's head emerging from *The Taster* represents knowledge and wisdom to be gained from the eating of the scroll (the *Book of Aker*) on which *The Taster* sits. Also, note the *ankh* sign (☥) immediately below the mouth of the serpent; Lurker (1980) says this sign "points to divine, i.e. eternal, existence."[668] Its presence in on the head of *The Taster* may therefore be interpreted to mean "eating eternal life," "eater of life," "consumer of life," or even one who receives "divine, eternal existence" by consumption.

Rev. 10:11 says that the eater of the scroll "must again prophesy about many peoples and nations and tongues and kings." Similarly, the text next to *The Taster* says that "He lives by the voice of the gods upon earth. He enters [the land of the living], comes out [of the land of the living, i.e., he returns], and reports ever day on the affairs of the living to this Great God, without being seen."[669] Note that the taster (or eater) of the scroll should report on the affairs of those living on earth while Rev. 10:11 says that the eater of the scroll should prophesy about many peoples. These two passages may be considered similar if one assumes that Revelation's "prophesy about"

---

[a] Piankoff, 1953 places a question mark after the designation of "The Taster," indicating some uncertainty in his translation.

and the Egyptian "reports on" have reasonably close meanings; for example, one can mean to "report on future events" while the other can mean to "report on current events." That the Egyptian text could also imply knowledge of future events is found in the effect of eating the scroll; "The Taster" would enter a "divine existence," a state likely consistent with the ability to prophesy, as in Rev. 10:11. The reference to the eating of the little scroll at this point in the Book of Revelation thus parallels, to a reasonable degree, events apparent in this part of the 5th Division of the *Amduat*.

In Rev. 10:8 the author is told to "Go, take the scroll which is open in the hand of the angel" and in Rev. 10:9 he goes to the angel and demands the scroll: "So I went to the angel and told him to give me the little scroll." Such requests of a deity for holy food were very much a part of Egyptian religious rituals. For example, we read in Chapter 124 of the *Book of the Dead* that the deceased asks for food to be placed in his mouth:

> Place bread in my mouth; I will go to the Moon-god [Thoth, the god of wisdom and knowledge], so that he may speak to me, that the followers of the gods may speak to me, that the sun [Re] may speak to me, and that the sun-folk may speak to me.[670]

The 126th Chapter describes a ceremony even more similar to the one described in Rev. 10 than the 124th Chapter; it not only mentions the presentation of divine food and the removal of the participant's sins, but is afterwards also then instructed (as in Rev. 10:11) to leave and go to a certain place or places. Here, the deceased makes a request to four baboons who sit at the prow of the solar barque.

> O these four ... (apes ...) who give divine offerings to the divine Ennead; who cause the sepulchral meals to appear for the spirits; who live upon truth; who swallow truth ... ; [whose abomination] is crime. Do away with the evil which is on me, in the name of Osiris, this King *N* the justified one. Annihilate his sins .... let him enter Ro-Setau by the mysterious pylons of the West! Let him be granted a cake and a jug! *(May) bread for the dead be given to him* even as that [given to the spirits] who enter and come out of Ro-Setau![671]

The baboons then give him a cake and jug which removes all sin from his body so realistically that it actually spills out onto the ground before him – presumably in the form of vomit. The baboons say,

> Come then, Osiris, this King *N*, the justified one. We have done away with the evil, *we have annihilated the sins. That which had to be cut off from thee is on the ground,'* we have removed all the evil which was on thee.[a]

This is an obvious parallel with Rev. 10:10 which quotes the author as saying, that while the scroll "was sweet as honey in my mouth ... when I had eaten it my stomach

---

[a] This translation is from Piankoff (1954). Faulkner's (1994, p. 116) translation is a little differently; it says, "The baboons reply: Come, so that we may expel your evil and grip hold of your falsehood so that the dread of you may be on the earth, and dispel the evil which was on you on earth."

was made bitter." The meaning of the phrase, "my stomach was made bitter" undoubtedly means that the recipient's stomach was upset after eating the scroll (as would be the case if it contained a suitable toxin). This effect could, if severe enough, cause him to vomit.

After the deceased vomits, the Egyptian text goes on to say that he is given the freedom to pass to and fro between the land of the dead (the West) and the earth. But he must return daily, presumably to report on events which transpired there:

> Enter Ro-Setau, pass by the mysterious pylons of the West! Go in and come out as thou wishest, as one of the spirits. Thou art called every day from the interior of the horizon, Osiris King N.[672]

This reference to being called every day "*from* the interior of the horizon" parallels the text of the next verse of Rev. 10 if we assume that the author of Revelation is instructed to go somewhere beyond the western horizon and, on his return, tell of events there and comment on how they might relate to future events (prophecy or knowledge of planned activities) among "many peoples and nations and tongues and kings" (Rev. 10:11) which lie beyond the horizon.

There is another aspect of this ceremony which parallels this part of Revelation. It relates to the specific choice of words used in Revelation to describe the *taste* of the scroll and its effect on the author's stomach. In Rev. 10:10 the author says that "it was sweet as honey in my mouth, but when I had eaten it my stomach was made bitter" (Rev. 10:10). A similar statement is found in the *Book of the Divine Cow* shortly after line /87/ (see Table 15:2) and should therefore be examined as a potential parallel. It says,

> Whosoever sayeth {these words} worketh his own protection by means of the words of power, "I am the god Ḥekau (i.e., the divine Word of Power [including prophesy]) and *I am pure in my mouth and in my belly.*'[673]

Note the similarity of the latter part of this statement (in italics) to Rev. 10:10 – both sources contain references to "my mouth" and "my belly" (i.e., my stomach).

This parallel continues in a way which is not obvious in Table 15:2. There is a parallel in the choice of words "I am pure in my mouth and in my belly." The Egyptian word for "something pure or holy" (*áb-t*)[674] is very similar to the word for "honey" (*ábá-t*).[675] Meanwhile, another word for "honey" (*bá-t* [676] or *bỉt*[677]) is very similar to or identical with a word for "loaf" or "cake" (*báa-t*[678] or *bỉt*[679]). From an Egyptian perspective therefore, the little scroll eaten by the author of Revelation could have been a honey-flavored loaf or cake in the shape or form of a scroll, hence the description of it tasting "like honey" in his mouth. The reference to it being "like honey" is thus explained in terms of a pun on the word for "pure." In this manner, the parallel between the two texts can be expanded to three words which closely follow each other in the same order, honey (pure), mouth, and belly. These observations and the fact that this similarity is found so close to the other parallels in the scene describing the eating of the scroll in Table 15.2 indicate a good parallel between the text in this part of the *Book of the Divine Cow* and that describing the eating of the scroll in Rev. 10.

Finally, and immediately following the above text in the *Book of the Divine Cow*, we find yet another parallel with the Revelation account. It is translated by Budge as follows: "{I am} Ra. ... When thou sayeth {this}, step forth in the evening and in the morning on thine own behalf if thou wouldst make to fall the enemies of Ra."[680] This is comparable with Rev. 10:11 where we read, "I was told, 'You must again prophesy *about* many peoples and nations and tongues and kings.'" Note, however, that this particular Egyptian text does not instruct the partaker of the scroll to speak *about* others as in Rev. 10:11 but rather to *do something* to make the enemies of the sun-god fall (for example, pray for the fall of the Re's enemies). This difference is reminiscent of differences among translations of Rev. 10:11. While the Revised Standard Version says that the partaker of the scroll must prophesy *about* others, the King James Version says that he "must prophesy again *before* many peoples." And the Armenian version of the Book of Revelation says that he shall "*prophesy unto* gentiles."[681] Another aspect of this parallel between Revelation and the Egyptian sources is less obvious and involves Revelation's reference to "many peoples and nations" and the phrase that the partaker of the scroll "wouldst make to fall the *enemies*˙ of Ra." Budge (1920) indicates that the hieroglyph 𓂝 means "prisoner, captive or foreigner"[682] while Gardiner (1927) suggests the same hieroglyph means "enemy."[683] Although this parallel between foreign "nations" in Revelation and "enemy" in the *Book of the Divine Cow* is not a particularly strong one, it should not be overlooked, especially when considered in the context of the parallels immediately before and after this part of the text in both sources.

Discussion

Parallels observed between the 10th Chapter of Revelation and Egyptian texts, especially the *Amduat*, the *Book of the Divine Cow* and the *Book of the Dead*, suggest a straightforward interpretation of the events in this otherwise confusing chapter of the Book of Revelation. From an Egyptian point of view, the "mighty angel coming down from heaven, wrapped in a cloud, with a rainbow over his head, and his face ... like the sun, and his legs like pillars of fire" in Rev. 10:1 corresponds to the Egyptian god Sokaris as portrayed in the 5th Division of the *Amduat*. And the "little scroll" he has open in his hand is the *Book of Aker*. After this introduction to the *Book of Aker*, Revelation pauses (in Rev. 10:5-6) and seems to make an allusion to the concluding paragraphs of the *Book of Aker* which contain a description of the violent and destructive cleansing of mankind's evil nature followed by a renewal of creation.

The author of Revelation then participates in a ceremony (Rev. 10:8-10) during which he consumes of a copy of a little scroll which, from an Egyptian perspective, is a copy of the *Book of Aker*. This ritual rids him of any evils he may possess, thereby enabling him to receive the secret knowledge contained within the scroll and the wisdom to understand it. He is finally told to prophesy about many peoples and nations (Rev. 10:11), a statement which, as we shall see in the next chapter, introduces us to yet another set of parallel scenes, this time from the *Book of Aker* itself which culminates in – and presents – a prophecy about the cataclysmic destruction of the world.

In conclusion, we may say that parallels to most of the images in Rev. 10 are evident in several Egyptian texts. Furthermore, Rev. 10:1-4 is an accurate description of the central theme of the 5th Division of the *Amduat* which emphasizes the activities of the Egyptian god Sokaris in his cavern deep within the body of the earth. Revelation's description of the "mighty angel" conforms with Sokaris while the "little scroll" he holds parallels the Egyptian *Book of Aker*. The seven thunders parallel seven deities who tow the sun-god's barque through this part of the Netherworld. Words spoken by them – words which are intentionally omitted in Revelation – are presented as a possible parallel, along with a likely reason why they might have been declared secret by the angel who instructed the author of Revelation not to write them down. Meanwhile, the reference to the ritualistic eating of the little scroll in Rev. 10:8-11 was also found in the 5th Division of the *Amduat* and other ancient temple rituals in which small copies of sacred books were eaten to enable participants to gain knowledge and wisdom from their revered contents. One of these, as in Rev. 10:11, concludes with instructions for the participant to leave and witness to or about other nations. Finally, the similarities between Rev. 10:5-9 and the *Book of the Divine Cow* indicate parallels with events described in the well-known *Legend of the Destruction of Mankind*. They also set the stage for a comparison of events described in the next chapter of the Book of Revelation with events described in the *Book of Aker*. These will be discussed next – in Chapter 16, *The Two Witneses*.

Chapter 16. The Two Witnesses (Rev. 11:1-13)[684]

The account of the two "witnesses" in Rev. 11 is introduced in a ceremony where the author of Revelation is told to measure "the temple of God and all who worship there" but not to measure the outer court because that area is relegated to "the nations" who "will trample the holy city for a period of forty-two months" (Rev. 11:1-2). Forty-two months is the same period mentioned in Rev. 11:3 where we are told that two "witnesses" or "prophets" clothed in sackcloth are given authority for 1,260 days (= forty-two months from a calculation based as 1,260 days ÷ 30 days per Egyptian month). The text then describes the two "witnesses" as two trees and two lampstands (Rev. 11:4). They are endowed with supernatural powers including the ability to spit fire from their mouths to kill the enemy, to cause drought and plagues, and to turn the waters into blood (Rev. 11:4-6). In spite of these great powers, however, they are both killed and their bodies put on public display (Rev. 11:7-8). After three and a half days they miraculously stand up and go up into heaven in a cloud (Rev. 11:11-12). Then, within an hour, a great earthquake strikes and kills 7,000 of the city's 70,000 occupants (Rev. 11:13).

The main elements in this story thus involve two authoritative and powerful individuals who are killed, put on display for all to see, and are resurrected just before a great earthquake which destroys the city in which they lived. When viewed from this simplistic point of view and compared with the range of ancient Egyptian documents examined, one book stands out above all the others as a likely parallel – the *Book of Aker*. This is particularly significant when one considers that, as pointed out in the previous chapter, it is this book which parallels the one used at the ceremony in Rev. 10:8-10 during which the author of Revelation took a little scroll (identified in the previous chapter as the *Book of Aker*) from the hand of an angel.

Revelation's telling of this story of is not, however, as straightforward as with many other passages in the Book of Revelation, perhaps because the *Book of Aker* is inherently more difficult to understand than most Egyptian texts. The search for parallels is especially complicated by the lack of general agreement among Egyptologists on where the book starts and ends as well as the proper order in which its many scenes should be read. One reason for the uncertainty among Egyptologists is that the only extant copies of the book are on the walls of sarcophagus chambers of royal tombs where, it seems, segments of it have been rearranged to suit the size and shape of the walls on which they were painted;[685] there are no copies available on papyrus to enable this study to pursue a linear examination involving an unambiguous sequence from beginning to end.

Hornung (1999) gives a description of the book and provides us with a set of figures showing its organization into four major parts designated as Parts A through D.[a] He comments on a disagreement among authorities regarding the order in which these four parts should be read and supports the suggestion by Abitz that it is "probable that Part D, with its praying king, represents the beginning of the book."[686] He also says that "Part A displays a clear central axis that has perhaps led to changes in the arrangement of the scenes"[687] and that some scenes may have been derived from a variety of other books. He suggests that "The lower register of Part A can be called a kind of concluding representation that summarizes the entire course of the sun."[688] As will be shown here, the sequence of the five scenes in this "summary register" closely parallels the sequence of similar scenes found Rev. 11 although it is difficult to relate this sequence to any sense of the order among parallel scenes found elsewhere in the book.

We begin with a comparison between the opening scene in Rev. 11 and the first scene (on the far right of the upper register) in Part D of the book, the part which Abitz suggests represents its beginning; we will conclude with the Hornung's so-called "summary" of the book found in the lower register of Part A.

The Temple of God (Rev. 11:1-2)

Rev. 11 begins with instructions of the writer of Revelation on what he should do in the temple of God; he is told to, "Rise and measure the temple of God and the altar and those who worship there, but do not measure the court outside the temple; leave that out, for it is given over to the nations, and they will trample over the holy city for forty-two months" (Rev. 11:1-2). This brief opening contains three elements which parallel the opening scene of the *Book of Aker*. The first is the temple itself, next, the description of an altar with worshipers, and finally, the area outside the temple which is occupied by foreigners, who, since they are to "trample over the holy city," must be considered to be enemies of God.

We must first assume that "God" in Rev. 11:1 parallels the god Osiris as discussed in Chapter 3, *The Preeminent Deities*. Given this assumption, the various parts of the scene shown in Figure 62 conform neatly with Rev. 11:1-2. This figure is from the extreme right-hand side of the upper register of Part D (i.e., at the book's presumed beginning, as discussed above). Osiris stands upright between two mounds in his shrine (⌂);[689] the text identifies the shrine as a "chapel."[690] Chapels and temples were closely associated with one another in the Egyptian language. For example, *r-pr* can mean both "temple" and "chapel"[691] and *ḥwt* can mean both "temple" and

---

[a] Graphic representations of Parts A through D are presented in three figures on pages 104-106 of Hornung (1999). Hornung also recognizes a fifth part, E, found on two sides of one pillar and one side of another in the front row of pillars in the sarcophagus chamber tomb of the Ramesses VI.

"funerary chapel."⁶⁹² We may therefore make a preliminary conclusion that the shrine, chapel or temple of Osiris in BA.D.1.1ˢᵗ ᴾⁱᶜᵗᵘʳᵉ parallels Revelation's "temple of God."

The Egyptian text tells us that as the sun-god Re passes by the chapel he speaks to Osiris with the words, "O this body whose role is mysterious, who resides in the Hidden Chamber, this great body of the One whose heart is darkened, whose chapel is guarded by those who are in the earth"⁶⁹³ (Figure 62). Inside, a "soul bird" faces him while standing on a mound and the upper part of a human figure emerges from the mound behind him; the arms of both figures are raised in worship. Below these two forms, two manifestations of the dog-headed god Anubis (one with a human head) adore a chest. Anubis was considered by Egyptians to be the guardian of the dead and in this scene he acts as the guardian of the body of Osiris in the chest. The text over the chest says it contains "The One over the Mysteries." All who are in the chapel are worshiping Osiris in this part of the scene; this parallels the introductory scene in Rev. 11 which describes the three main components as "[1] the temple of God and [2] the altar and [3] those who worship there."

Figure 62. The temple of Osiris with his enemies outside (BA.D.1.1ˢᵗᵖⁱᶜᵗᵘʳᵉ). This scene conforms with the description of the temple of God in Rev. 11:1-2.

The walls and roof of the temple are of particular significance because they contain serpents. The reason for their presence is well known – they protect Osiris and the worshipers from outside dangers. This conforms with the comment in Rev. 11:2 that there are enemies outside the temple. Furthermore, the Egyptian text describes the chapel as being a "Hidden Chamber," a phrase conforming with Rev. 11:2 which describes the special restricted nature of the temple into which foreigners (the nations) are forbidden to go. Indeed, both this picture and the accompanying text, like Revelation, emphasize this restriction.

In Revelation, those outside the temple are clearly considered to be enemies. In the Egyptian text we are told the "enemies are like this. They are punished outside the Hidden Chamber. ... These rebels are like this outside the Hidden Chamber. The god makes them suffer."⁶⁹⁴ Rev. 11:2 also says that the "nations" are outside the temple. In Figure 62, parallels to these "enemies" are depicted as six bound and beheaded enemies kneeling outside the temple wall (is the determinative for "enemy").⁶⁹⁵ Above them, their blood is drained into large caldrons containing their shadows and hearts (hieroglyphs and). The scene in Figure 62 therefore closely parallels practically all aspects of Rev. 11:1-2 except for the period of forty-two months, a topic to be discussed later in this chapter.

One might assume that in the Book of Revelation the description of events dealing with the temple of God in Rev. 11:1-2 forms a logical introduction to events described in the rest of the chapter. This does not seem to be the case. Instead, the next verse abruptly shifts away from the temple to what appears to be an entirely unrelated topic – the story of two witnesses. As will be discussed later, however, when the temple scene is considered in an Egyptian context we find an explanation for the juxtaposition of these two themes.

Story of Two Witnesses (Rev. 11:3-13)

The story of the two witnesses is summarized in the introduction to this chapter; in this section, it is examined in detail. The story has several conspicuous elements which enable a straightforward comparison with the text and pictures found in the *Book of Aker*. The first and most obvious is that there are *two* of them and that they are called *witnesses*. The second is that they wear sackcloth, indicating they are in *mourning*. Thirdly, they are described in terms of olive *trees* and *lampstands*. Fourthly, they have *supernatural powers* which include the ability to spew fire from their mouths, to cause drought and plagues and turn water into blood. And finally, they are associated with an *earthquake* which kills thousands. Egyptian parallels to these and other less conspicuous elements in the Book of Revelation will be described next.

The Two Witnesses (Rev. 11:3)

The *Book of Aker* contains an unusual number of scenes involving two individuals which are similar in several respects to those involving the two "witnesses" – or "prophets" – in Revelation. The Egyptian text, however, refers to them as "guardians" rather than "witnesses." Thus, and in order to properly set the Egyptian story in a context similar to that of the Revelation account, we should briefly examine the Egyptian word for "guardian."

The word, *s3w* not only meant "guardian or warden"[696] but also "magician."[697] Magicians by their very mystical nature were associated with prophecy, an attribute conforming with the prophetic nature of the two witnesses in Rev. 11:3. These two guardians appear quite frequently in scenes throughout the *Book of Aker* and, as we will see shortly, this phonetic association is but the first glimpse of many parallels between them and the two witnesses of Rev. 11.

The functions of the guardians in the *Book of Aker* will be dealt with first. These are provided in the Egyptian text near the central picture in the upper register of Part A (Figure 63). It refers to the two deities standing on the paws of the two-headed, lion-god Aker. The figure shows them holding their arms up in praise to the sun-god who stands in the center of the solar barque which Aker holds on his back. The text associated with BA.A.1.2[nd picture] tells us that,

> The two gods, the two great, the two powerful [*cf.* Rev. 11:3, "*power* to prophesy"], the two who are in Aker [the earth], they are mysterious when they turn toward the barge of

Re, and when they pass through the land of the One of the Horizon. When their feet are upon the earth [Aker], they guide the One of the Horizon. The guide who calls the gods, he guides Re on the mysterious ways. ... These gods are like this. *They guard·* the body of this god.[698]

Figure 63. The sun-god's barque on the back of Aker, the double-headed lion-god. The two guardians standing with arms raised in front of Aker's heads parallel the two witnesses of Rev. 11. (BA.A.1.2^{nd picture})

A somewhat similar scene is found on the far left of the upper register of Part D at BA.D.1.4^{th picture}. Here, the solar barque is held aloft by two uraeus serpents. As we shall see later, these serpents are manifestations of the two guardians found in many scenes elsewhere in the *Book of Aker*. In the scene, the sun-god says,

O behold, I [Re] pass through thy cavern, thou who art alone, [the two] who guardest the West, *for whom the inhabitants of the Netherworld lament,·* who art glad in hearing my voice. O [two] souls whom *I ordered to guard·* ... .[699]

These two guardians are shown in pictures and mentioned in the text throughout many parts of the *Book of Aker* although their appearance, sex, names and functions vary to conform with events in which they are depicted. They are also mentioned in prominent locations in the introductory parts of both the *Book of Aker* and Rev. 11. A similar scene found at the far left of Part D at D.4^{th picture} also emphasizes them in its accompanying text; they clearly play a key role in this book. Details of some of their parallel appearances and actions in pictures and texts follow.

The Two Mourners (Rev. 11:3):- The two witnesses in Rev. 11:3 are described as wearing "sackcloth" a tradition in the ancient Middle East indicating a state of mourning. Similarly, mourning themes appear in several scenes in the *Book of Aker*. For example, we find references to the two guardians in which they are described as those "who guardest the West, for whom the inhabitants of the Netherworld *lament,·* who art glad in hearing my voice. O souls whom I ordered to guard."[700] The lamenting theme is emphasized in the 1st picture of a series of scenes beginning at the lower right-hand corner of Part A (i.e., in the summary register). Here (Figure 64), a man and a woman, with raised arms stand by a mound on the top of which is a mummy. The mummy is "embraced"[701] by the two "Arms of Geb," the earth-god.

16. The Two Witnesses

At the far left of Figure 64 is a pair of deites with arms raised. Above them, a label reads *ḥ₃yt* which means "mourning"[702] (or "flood-waters"[703]) while the word between the two, *ḥ₃yty*, means "Two Mourners." Also, *ẖ₃yt*, a close homonym which sounds similar to *ḥ₃yt* and means "disease"[704] parallels the comment in Rev. 11:6 that the two witnesses have power "to smite the earth with every plague." The four ℓ figures in the mound indicate "flesh" or "body parts"[705] typically used to signify the various internal organs preserved separately during the mummification process. The overall theme of disease and mourning is accentuated by the symbol within the mound of the eye from which three tears flow (𓁿); this symbol is a determinative used in words such as "weep,"[706] an activity agreeing with an alternative meaning of *ḥ₃yt* – "flood waters" – so that the idea of profuse weeping seems to be implied here. This entire scene emphasizes the theme of mourning just as the sackcloth worn by the two witnesses in Rev. 11:3 signifies mourning.

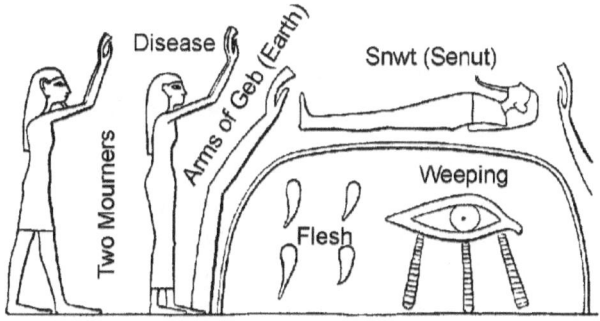

Figure 64. This scene of mourning, which represents the beginning of the *Book of Aker*, shows two deities standing over the body of Osiris. Like the two witnesses in Rev. 11:3, they are in mourning. (BA.A.4.1st picture)

The Two Lampstands (Rev. 11:4b)

The fearful flaming ones:- To the immediate left of Figure 64 is another scene (BA.4.2nd picture) shown here as Figure 65. This scene provides us with additional, pertinent characteristics of the two guardians. We begin with the two uraeus serpents in front of and behind a bearded man called "The Old One." His posture is readily identifiable with the hieroglyphic symbol 𓀢 which means "supplication" and is at times used as a determinative in words such as "adore."[707] The two uraeus serpents are forms of the two guardians for their names are "The Fiery One" and "The Flaming One," names typically associated with the guardians of the sun-god – and these serpents were renowned for their ability to spit fire at their enemies.[708] Their names in this part of the *Amduat* are thus consistent with the comment in Rev. 11:5 that "if any one would harm them (the two witnesses) fire pours out from their mouth and consumes their foes." In this way, these serpents also parallel the two witnesses described in Revelation.

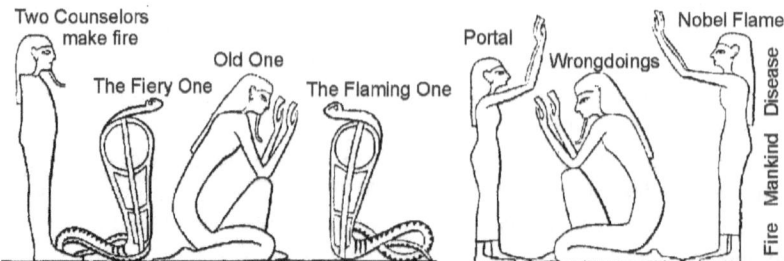

Figure 65. Scene from the first part of the story of the two guardians in the *Book of Aker*. Four manifestations of the guardians – the two fire-spitting uraeus serpents and the two gods called "Portal" and "Nobel Flame" – stand over enemies of the sun-god who kneel in supplication before them. Important elements of this scene parallel Rev. 11:5 and Rev. 11:7-11. (BA.A.4.2[nd picture])

The descriptive text in front of the bearded mummy says, "Two counselors make fires." Piankoff (1962) does not translate this text but instead, refers to the mummy by its assumed name, *Uanay* (*w₃w₃y*).[709] The entire text associated with the mummy, however, says *w₃w₃y kdkd ḫt* where the first segment conforms with Piankoff's footnote indicating the text as reading *w₃w₃*. But, Faulkner (1962) translates *w₃w₃* as "take counsel;"[710] the addition of *y* to it confers it with duality[711] so that this part of the text can actually mean "two counsels" or "two counselors." Meanwhile, Gardiner (1927) indicates the next hieroglyph, ↑, is a sign which "sometimes stands alone in the sense of a 'builder'" and is used in words such as *kd*, meaning "'build,' 'fashion (pots)' and related words."[712] In fact there are two such signs adjacent to one another in the text, a configuration which yields *kdkd*, suggesting that two of something is involved. The final hieroglyph is, ♄, which is pronounced *ḫt* and means fire. The full transliteration of the text then becomes "Two counselors make fire." The action of these two counselors obviously refers to that the two uraeus serpents sitting before it, "The Fiery One" and "The Flaming One," and as pointed out in the previous paragraph, they parallel the two witnesses of Rev. 11.

The flaming ones as lampstands (Rev. 11:4b):- Their fire-spitting ability also means that the two serpents can also be visualized as representing two *torches*, or as Rev. 11:4a describes the two witnesses, "two *lampstands* which stand before the Lord of the earth." To find an even more fitting parallel to this statement we leave the *Book of Aker* for a moment and go to the 2nd Division of the *Amduat* where two fire-breathing uraeus serpents, each of whom in this scene is called "Opener of the Ways," are positioned as look-outs at the bow of the solar barque (Figure 66) so that they light the way and guide the sun-god as he passes through the darkness of the Netherworld. Similarly, in the 4th and 5th Divisions of the *Amduat*, the bow and stern of solar barque itself is formed by the heads of the two serpents. Hornung (1990) provides us with a vivid description of their function in the latter scene. "Both the bow and stern are snake-headed, and the text describes how they spew bright fire before them, piercing the impenetrable, all-enveloping darkness."[713] The *Amduat* says that "This Great God sails by them in this way. The flames coming out of the mouth of his barge guides him

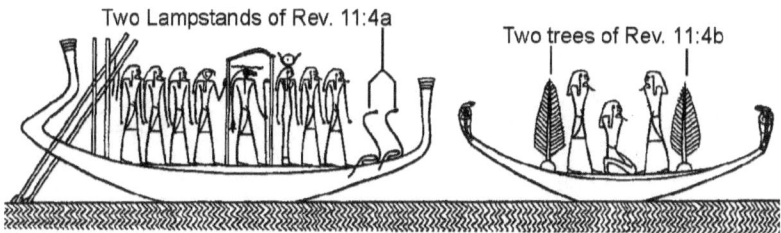

Figure 66. Two fire-spiting uraeus serpents (representing the guardians who parallel Revelation's two witnesses) acting as "Lampstands," as in Rev. 11:4, lighting the way of the solar barque through the darkness of the Netherworld. Note that the boat in front of the solar barque contains two trees which are also mentioned in Rev. 11:4. See also Figure 102. (AM2.2.1-4)

toward these mysterious ways."[714] This additional function of the two uraeus serpents thus also parallels the description in Rev. 11:5 of the two witnesses acting as "two lampstands which stand before the Lord of the earth."

Power to Spit Fire:- The ability of Revelation's two witnesses to spit fire has already been compared with the abilities of the fire-spiting uraeus serpents who act as protectors and light-bearers for the sun-god in the darkness of the Netherworld. This power to produce fire from their mouths (actions which conform with the aforementioned meaning of the word s_3w) enables them to punish the enemies of the sun-god just as we also read about in Rev. 11:5 which says that "fire pours out from their mouth and consumes their foes." This power is specifically referred to in the first scene of the bottom register of Part D, at BA.D.4.1$^{st\ picture}$, shown here as Figure 67. The figure shows the heads and body parts of the enemy being burned in cauldrons heated by streams of fire shooting upwards from the mouths of two deities whose bodies are not shown. The text describing the scene say:

> These gods are like this. (The arms) of the caldrons put the heads in the caldrons, the members and hearts in their pits of fire. The executioners take hold of their knives, while the goddesses attend to the severed members (?). These four arms of the god lift up their caldrons. The Great God lights up his fire, *the goddesses light up the fire.*˙ They hide their bodies [only their heads are visible above ground] when *they give forth their flame*˙ on their pits of fire.[715]

From the references in the text to the four arms, two heads, the two female deities standing over the centrally located heart and the two male deities cutting off the heads of the enemies, it is apparent that these the two fire-spiting heads are the same fire-breathing guardians of the sun-god illustrated in Figure 65 and Figure 66. They are also the two female deities in the center of Figure 67. In this manner, these vivid textual and graphic descriptions parallel the description in Rev. 11:5 of the two witnesses spewing forth fire from their mouths to consume their foes.

Power to Cause Plagues:- We read in Rev. 11:6 that the two witnesses "have power over the waters to turn them into blood, and to smite the earth with every

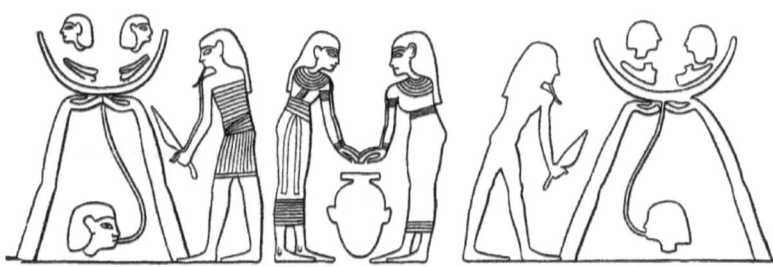

Figure 67. As in Rev. 11:5, enemies (in this case, their body parts) are burned by fire which pours from the mouths of two deities. (BA.D.4.1st picture)

plague, as often as they desire." Similarly, plagues affecting "mankind" are evident in the labeling of the picture at BA.A.4.2nd picture (Figure 65). At the far right of this picture is a short vertical strip of hieroglyphics which contains three words – "disease," "mankind" and "fire."[a] It is reasonable to assume that "mankind" in this Egyptian text has a meaning equivalent to all of mankind on "the earth" in Rev. 11:6 so that we have a juxtaposition of references to plague (disease) and mankind in both sources. The turning of water into blood (i.e., to red, the color of blood) mentioned in Rev. 11:6 parallels the color of the blood-red toxins in the water discussed elsewhere in Revelation (*cf.* Rev. 8:7-9 and Rev. 16:3-6 in Chapter 13, *Catastrophes*), it may also be a reference to the inclusion of the word "fire" on the far right of Figure 65.

Power to Shut up the Sky:- Rev. 11:6 says that they have power to "shut the sky," a possible reference to the bringing about of darkness or preventing rain from falling, or both. Similar text is found associated with BA.B.5th picture (Figure 72). This picture shows two deities standing upright in a vertical oval (a cloud)[b] with a solar

---

[a] The relevant text, ✗ ◇ ⚫ ♃, is not translated by Piankoff (1954) so that a note on the above transliteration is in order. The first character, ✗ is a very ancient determinative for words like "damage" and "break" (Gardiner, 1927, p.538) and was later replaced by the alternative, ✿, which Gardiner (p. 539) describes as "a morbid condition of the body," or "bodily growths or conditions, especially of the morbid kind," for example, "wound" and "disease." In the context of Rev. 11:6, the latter translation is germane . The second part of the text, ◇ ⚫, *rt*, means "mankind" (Faulkner, 1962, p. 150) while the last symbol, ♃, means "fire" (Gardiner, p. 500). Hence, we note from the transliteration that the text can refer to "disease," "mankind," and "fire" so ✗ ◇ ⚫ ♃ may be roughly translated as "disease, mankind and fire" or simply a "fiery disease of mankind – or a "fiery plague of makind. " – or simply a "Fiery plague on mankind.

[b] See footnote on page 326 about how the use of the word "cloud" is used to describe an oval in which a deity is situated.

disk over it while the text says, "These [two] gods are like this in their coffins[a] ... they are under the Eye of Re when it appears among them. *They stop the flame which is in the Eye of Re'* [i.e., the light of the sun]." In other words, they cause darkness.

The linking of the two witnesses with the shutting up of the sky also parallels a possible play on two phonetically similar Egyptian words, *mtr* and *mdr*. The former means to "shut out (storms)"[716] and the latter is obviously associated with the function of a witness for it means, "testify concerning."[717] Both these definitions parallel characteristics of the two witnesses provided in Revelation. Meanwhile, it should be noted that this same power to shut out the sky may be related to events outside the shrine of Osiris in Figure 62; the text near the shrine in that figure says, "These enemies are like this. They are punished outside the Hidden Chamber, *they are in darkness without light.*"[718]

The Two Trees (Rev. 11:4a)

Another rather remarkable aspect of Figure 66 (see also Figure 102) is the presence of two trees on a smaller boat in front of the sun-god's barque; it is especially remarkable because the two trees in this figure appear quite near the two serpents which serve as lights in the bow of the sun-god's barque as well as the fire-spitting uraeus heads on the front and rear of the boat with the trees – just as the two witnesses are described as both lampstands and trees in Rev. 11:4.

This association of two trees with the sun-god is well documented in Egypt's religious literature. For example, in the *Book of Two Ways*, the deceased confirms his knowledge of them with the words, "I know the *two sycamores of turquoise between which Re comes forth*,' which grow at Shu's sowing near the door of the Lord of the East through which Re comes forth."[719] The species of tree referred to here is different, but the idea of two trees is present in both sources. Nevertheless, the juxtaposition of the fire-breathing guardians and the two trees that are in front of the sun-god in this scene is an exceptionally good parallel to Rev. 11:4 which describes "two olive trees and two lampstands which stand before the Lord of the earth [i.e., Re, the ram-headed deity standing in the center of the solar barque]."

Death of the Two Witnesses (Rev. 11:7-11)

Rev. 11:7 tells us that "when they have finished their testimony, the beast that ascends from the bottomless pit will make war upon them and conquer them and kill them." The parallel to this event is found in the central picture of the bottom register of Part A (at BA.A.4.3[rd picture], Figure 76/Figure 77). It is at this point in the *Book of Aker* that the sun-god and his followers pass from the earthly sphere into the depths of the earth, the part which Revelation refers to as the "bottomless pit." It seems that

---

[a] Here we find a potential play on words for "cloud" and "coffin." Faulkner (1962 says that a word for "storm-cloud" is *krỉ* (p.280) and a word for "coffin" is *krsw* (p. 281); a pun by means of alliteration is possible .

the "beast" in this case is Apophis, the ancient god of chaos, and the ancient enemy of the sun-god and his followers.[a]

Death by the Beast from the Bottomless Pit:- The central portion of the bottom register of Part A of the *Book of Aker* has a picture (BA.A.4.3$^{rd\ picture}$) of the sun-god and his followers descending into the abyss, the bottomless pit, the domain of Apophis. This picture sets the scene for the very ancient encounter between the sun-god and Apophis. The book does not mention a war in which the two guardians are conquered or killed, such as we might expect from the text of Revelation. Instead, the aftermath of this encounter is presented and illustrated in BA.D.4.3$^{rd\ picture}$ (Figure 68). Here we see the bodies of the two guardians standing one on either side of a dome-shaped shrine containing the body of Osiris; their legs have disappeared beneath the surface of the ground into the Netherworld suggesting that they, like Osiris, are also dead. Outside, two ram-headed deities hold the slain body of Apophis which is stretched over them and Osiris. The accompanying text, which is difficult to understand, says,

> These gods [the three ram-headed deities] are like this. They guard the One who is in the earth, and the One in the coils of the serpent, the mysterious gods [the two guardians] who hide Khepri. Re summons them and gives orders to their souls. Then they [the souls of the guardians beneath Apophis] pass on after him while their bodies remain in their places."[720]

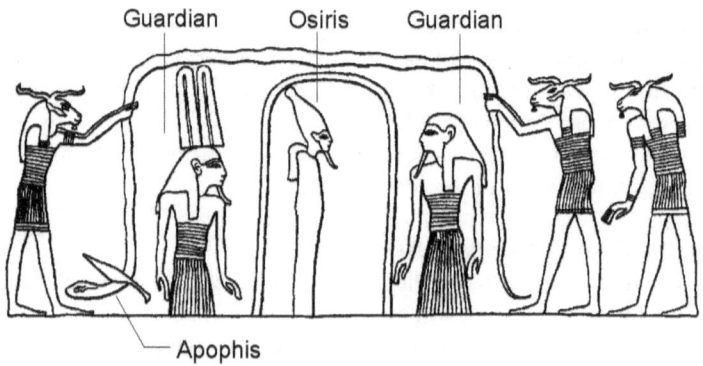

Figure 68. Apophis, who parallels Revelation's ancient serpent from the bottomless pit, kills the two guardians, as in Rev. 11:7. (BA.D.4.3$^{rd\ picture}$)

---

[a] Evidence will be presented in Chapter 18, *The Beasts of Rev. 13*, that references to "beasts" apply to either Revelation's 1st beast (a corrupted version of the god Seth) or the 2nd beast (a Hyksos king or kings in the Nile Delta). The suggestion that the beast in Rev. 11:7 is the god Apophis is therefore inconsistent with this nomenclature used elsewhere in Revelation. Nevertheless, it was Apophis who gave orders to the two beasts and thus was responsible for the two witnesses' death. This may be implied in Rev. 11:7.

The latter part of this passage indicates the souls of the dead guardians leave their bodies behind and join the sun-god. This event parallels Rev. 11:12 where we read that the two witnesses "went up to heaven." Greater detail of the guardians' ascent into heaven will be discussed in a later section dealing with an illustration (Figure 72) from Part B of the *Book of Aker*.

The central part of Figure 68 thus shows the bodies of the two guardians who seem to have been slain by Apophis. This interpretation conforms with the latter part of Rev. 11:7 which says that "the beast ... will ... conquer them and kill them."

Fate of the Two Witnesses (Rev. 11:8-12)

Display of their Bodies:- In the lower register of Part A (BA.A.4. 4th picture), and to the immediate left of the double-headed Aker shown in Figure 63, is a picture of two bearded deities lying face down in their coffins, being watched over by two armless figures (Figure 69). Their names, which are written above their bodies, are translated by Piankoff (1954) as "Hidden Arms" and "Mysterious Arms."[721] Note that both names refer to a mystery or secret of some kind.

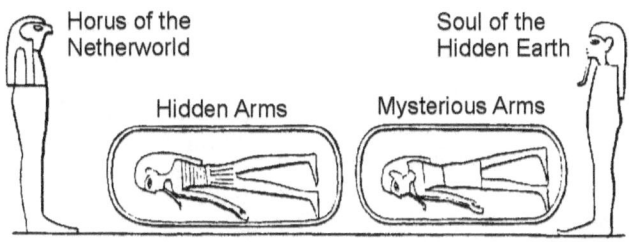

Figure 69. Two bodies lie in coffins as in Rev. 11:9. (BA.A.4. 4th picture)

We should bear in mind that the concepts of "mystery" and something being "hidden" were, very likely, closely related to the idea of a prophet or seer in the minds of the Egyptians. We find tentative evidence for this relationship in the two phonetically similar words, *tegai-t* and *tegaa; tegai-t* means "something hidden, or hidden"[722] while *tegaa* means "seer,"[723] a word implying a prophet. It therefore seems reasonable to suggest the two deities lying in the coffins are seers, or prophets, a suggestion which conforms with the description of the two witnesses as prophets in Rev. 11:3,6.

Rev. 11:8 says that the bodies of the two witnesses "will lie in the street of the great city." This statement conforms with the picture in Part B of the *Book of Aker* which is shown here as Figure 70. They parallel each other in at least one way, as follows: In the figure we see two bodies lying in boats, each accompanied by a standing goddess. The boats indicate the event depicted here involves a river or waterway, the functional equivalent of a street in ancient Egypt. Egyptians used tributaries and natural and manmade canals along the Nile for crop irrigation and to facilitate travel. Furthermore, Egyptian mythology includes a river flowing through the center of the great celestial city of Nut. It was along this sacred river that the sun-god sailed in his barque. In the Egyptian *Book of Two Ways,* the heavenly roadways and waterways are described as being functionally identical: "the roads to Rosetau on water and on land; these roads are those of Osiris, they are in the sky."[724] A reference to a "street" in place of a "canal" or "waterway" in Rev. 11:8 is also consistent with the text of Rev. 22:1-2 which says that "he showed me the river of the water ... flowing ... through the middle of the street of the city." Figure 70 is thus consistent with Rev. 11:8 which describes the bodies of the two witnesses lying in the street of the great city.

That the witnesses would be visible to the public for several days is also consistent with Egyptian funerary practices. We are told in Rev. 11:9 that "For three days and a half men from the peoples and tribes and tongues and nations gaze at their dead bodies." Egyptian funerary processions often followed the mainstream of the Nile and involved long upstream or downstream journeys to their final resting place while the general populace looked on from the banks. The time required for this journey would depend on the distance to the burial site so that a time frame of three and a half days mentioned in Revelation is not unreasonable.

Their Resurrection:- Rev. 11:11-12 says that "A breath of life from God entered them, and they stood up on their feet. ... And in the sight of their foes they went up to heaven in a cloud." There are at least two scenes in the *Book of Aker* which contain references to what seems to be the resurrection of the two guardians; the first is found at BA.A.3.2[nd picture] and the second at BA.B.5[th picture].

The resurrection scene in Part A is shown here as Figure 71. This scene shows the two guardians as they are lifted heavenwards toward the sun-god Re (O) while standing the hands of "the two destructive arms in the Place of Destruction." The arrangement of the two arms is of particular interest here because it

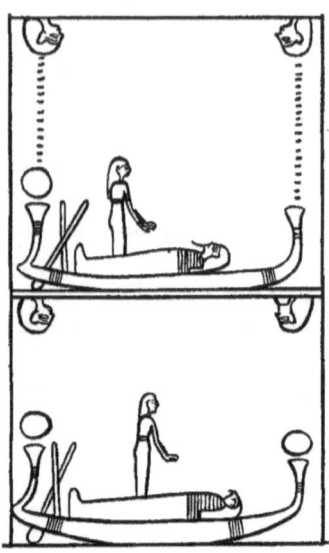

Figure 70. Two bodies lie in boats while Isis and Nephthys stand over them in Part B of the *Book of Aker*. This scene parallels the display of the two witnesses whose "bodies lie in the street of the great city" in Rev. 11:8. (BA.B.4[th picture])

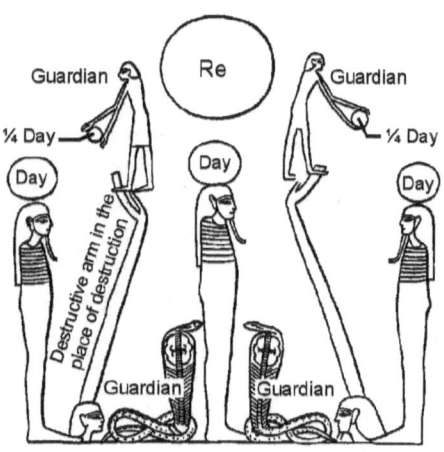

Figure 71. Two deities are lifted into heaven on the hands of "the two destructive arms in the Place of Destruction" after a period of three and a half days (indicated by the relative sizes of the five smallest disks) as described in Rev. 11:11-12. (BA.A.3.2[nd picture])

suggests the two deities are being lifted *away* from the place of destruction. The picture also conforms with the statement in Rev. 11:11-12 that the two witnesses "stood on their feet ... And ... . went up to heaven." The two arms reaching heavenward from the earth are usually interpreted to mean the "two arms of Geb," the earth-god. It is therefore interesting that *gb,* as the Egyptians likely pronounced his name,[725] is phonetically similar to the word *gp,* meaning "cloudburst." This similarity suggests the possibility of a visual pun in Figure 71, and if so, then one might interpret the raising into the heavens of the two guardians by the arms of Geb to mean that they were raised up in a "cloudburst."[726] Another Egyptian word which may be involved in the imagery presented in Revelation is *krỉ* which means both "storm-cloud" and to "draw-near."[727] With this one word, we can find the image of a cloud and the idea of the two witnesses being "drawn-up" to heaven in a "cloud," or as Rev. 11:12 puts it, "they went up to heaven in a cloud."

Note, however, that the puns also suggest the cloud is not an ordinary cloud as suggested in Revelation, but rather a "cloudburst" or a "storm-cloud." This would suggest their resurrection was not a peaceful ascent into the heavens. As suggested in reference to the "destructive" arms which holds them, a vision of an ascent *away* from some destructive event associated with the earth-god Geb is possible. This would conform with the statement in Rev. 11:13 that, "at that hour there was a great earthquake." In this way, the actions implied in this scene closely parallel those of Rev. 11:12-13 where the two witnesses go up to heaven and escape the devastation which unfolds beneath them.

As in Figure 65, two protective serpents in Figure 71 rear up near the lower center of the picture. This similarity, and the proximity of Figure 71 to Figure 65 in the *Book of Aker* (the latter being directly below the former in Part A), suggests these two cobras are the same ones identified earlier as the two guardians which parallel the two witnesses of Rev. 11. Their names in this picture are "He who assembles the forms" and "Rich in forms," names which agree with the idea that the two guardians in this story are shown in many different forms as in other parts of the *Book of Aker.* Two other manifestations of the guardians are found in this figure; they are those supported by the two destructive arms and are called "The Dancer" and "Devouring One." The name, "The Dancer," conforms with the action described in Rev. 12:10 which says that "those on earth will rejoice over them and make merry," while that of the "Devouring One" conforms with the reference to the thousands of victims of the earthquake in Rev. 12:13. This association of the "Devouring One" with an earthquake also conforms with the above-mentioned reference to the "the two destructive arms in the Place of Destruction." All these various names and pictorial allusions can thus be interpreted in the sense of Rev. 11:11-13.

Another rather interesting parallel may be found in Figure 71; it involves the three and a half days mentioned in Rev. 11:9 – "But after the *three and a half days*, a breath of life from God entered them." The large, central disk obviously represents the sun-god Re towards whom the two resurrected guardians are lifted. The remaining five disks in the figure apparently have different meaning; this is especially obvious in that the three on the heads of the bearded figures are bigger than the two in the hands of the two guardians. They are particularly significant because the "circle" is not only a symbol of Re but is also an ideograph or determinative in words for "day."[728] The combination of three larger disks can therefore be interpreted as meaning three days. Meanwhile, the two smaller disks can be interpreted as a quarter of a day each, so that, together, they represent a half day.[a] We may conclude that total time period indicated by the five disks below the central disk of Re means a period of three and one half days, the same period as stated in Rev. 11:11.

A second scene dealing with the resurrection is found in BA.B.5[th picture] and shown here as Figure 72. It is of particular interest because it provides us with a second parallel to the resurrection of the two witnesses and their ascent "up to heaven" in Rev. 11:12. We start our analysis with the left side of this figure. The upper, circular figure represents Re while the two standing deities inside the oval underneath the sun-god unambiguously parallel the two witnesses of Revelation; the text above the oval says, "They stop the flame [light] which is in the Eye of Re [the sun]," an expression which parallels Rev. 11:6 where we learn they have the power to "shut the sky." Furthermore, on the right side of Figure 72, we find a text underneath another symbol of Re which says, "When this god [Re] calls them they breathe,"[729] an obvious reference to the resurrection of two guardians; note that the words, "When this god [Re] calls them," conform quite well with Rev. 11:12 which says that "Then they heard a loud voice from heaven saying to them 'Come up hither!'" This command in Revelation and their subsequent rising into heaven "in a cloud" parallels the picture of the two deities inside the oval, which may be readily seen to represent a cloud[b] floating up into the heavens toward the sun. Also, this argument is strengthened by a potential pun on the words for "storm-

Figure 72. The two guardians of the sun-god are resurrected and stand up to rise toward Re (signified by his disk above the oval on the left side) who enables them to breath again (BA.B.5[th picture]) – as described for the two witnesses in Rev. 11:11-12.

---

[a] This suggestion is based on the ancient "Horus-eye notation" which uses different parts of the Horus-eye symbol, ☥ (according to legend, it was torn into fragments by the wicked god Seth). Gardiner (1927, pp. 197-198) informs us that the eyebrow, ⌒, represented ⅛, the inner part of the white of the eye, ◁, represented ½, and the "pupil," ○, represented ¼ of a *hekat*-measure of corn. In view of this brief analysis, the interpretation of the two smallest circles in Figure 71 as representing two ¼ parts, i.e., ½ of a day, is reasonable.

[b] The parallel between the "cloud" in Revelation and this oval in the Egyptian text is rather interesting in that we found a similar parallel in reference to Rev. 10:1. In that parallel, the cloud which "wrapped" the mighty angel coming down from heaven was found to be a parallel to the oval in which the god Sokaris stood (in the lower register of the 5th Division of the *Amduat*). (Not all references to clouds in Revelation conform with this convention.)

16. The Two Witnesses

cloud" and to "draw-near"; the Egyptian word ḳrỉ can mean both "storm-cloud" and to "draw-near."[730] The Egyptian text goes on to say that they then "*breath*," an event which parallels Rev. 11:11 which says that "*a breath of life* from god [in this case Re] entered them." In this single scene in Figure 72, we thus find a reference to the sun-god calling to the two guardians, and giving them the breath of life after which they stand up and ascend into the sky (or are "drawn-up" near to the sun-god Re) in what seems to be a cloud, just as described in Rev. 11:11-12.

The Great Earthquake (Rev. 11:13)

Revelation tells of a powerful earthquake which strikes in the same hour as the two witnesses rise into the sky: "at that hour there was a great earthquake, and a tenth of the city fell; 7,000 people were killed in the earthquake, and the rest were terrified and gave glory to the God of heaven" (Rev. 11:13). We should therefore enquire if the *Book of Aker* contains a reference to an earthquake in which 7,000 people were killed.

The *Book of Aker* does indeed contain a reference to what may be interpreted as a great earthquake. We begin with the evidence for the death of a number of people found in the 2nd, 3rd, and 4th registers of Part A of the *Book of Aker* and presented here as Figure 73. Note the seven burial mounds, each represented by the ∩ hieroglyph and each containing a body; the original of this version has hieroglyphic text over each mound. The exact form of this text over the mounds varies slightly from one mound to the other although Piankoff (1954) translates all seven of them as, "Nehep [*nhp*], He who is in his mound."[731] Piankoff does not translate *nhp* (𓈖𓊵𓏲) but in a later publication, Faulkner (1962) says that *nhp* means to "pulsate."[732] If we assume Faulkner's translation of *nhp* to be applicable, we may interpret the label over the

Figure 73. Illustration of 7,000 people killed by an earthquake on the left-hand side of the 2nd, 3rd and 4th registers of Part A of the *Book of Aker*. The two groups of deities on the right side of the 2nd and 3rd registers conform with those in Revelation who were terrified and give praise to God. This scene parallels that in Rev. 11:13.

mound to something like, "Pulsating. He who is in his mound." Piankoff apparently examined the word *nhp* solely in the context of the bodies lying in their mounds and, since he did not associate the word "pulsate" to any obvious representation of an earthquake in the text or the picture, he left *nhp* untranslated. It seems reasonable, however, to suggest that "pulsate" would be a reasonable translation of *nhp* if we assume an earthquake is involved, as in Rev. 11:13.

Another aspect of this text which seems to be related to an earthquake is found in the ideographic symbol ▲ used as a determinative in the phrase translated by Piankoff as, "He who is in his mound." Faulkner's dictionary indicates the ▲ symbol can refer to "ruin" as well as "mound."[733] Thus, when this symbol is used in a phrase associated with an earthquake, the phrase which Piankoff translates as "He who in his *mound*" may be more appropriately translated as "He who is in his *ruin*," especially if we consider the possibility that the ruination of an entire city may be involved – as described in Rev. 11:13. With this in mind, we might legitimately translate the phrasing of the hieroglyphic text above the seven mounds as, "*Pulsating*. He who is in his *ruin*" or more loosely, "*Trembling*. He who is in his *ruin*." In this way, the mummies in their mounds in Figure 73 may be interpreted to refer to those who died from the violent trembling, or "pulsating," of an earthquake, a situation not unlike that described in Rev. 11:13.[a]

We next turn our attention to the more obvious difference between the seven burial mounds in Figure 73 and the number of 7,000 people who died in the earthquake mentioned in Rev. 11:13. To arrive at the number 7,000 we would need to find within this figure three references to the number 10 which we might use as a basis for calculating the number 7,000 (from 7 x 10 x 10 x 10). The most obvious sources of the number 10 are found in two groups of ten deities whose heads protrude from the upper and lower edges of the middle register in the figure. Nevertheless, we need "three" indications of the number ten to complete the equation which yields 7,000 dead. This third number ten is little more difficult to find – but it is present and quite obvious to anyone who knows the numbering system used by the Egyptians. We see it in the *shape* of the seven mounds (∩). This same shape is used in hieroglyphic texts to designate the number "10"[734] In the context of the Revelation account, we may therefore assume that each of the seven mounds represents not one but 10 mummies. The number 7,000 can thus be obtained by simply multiplying the four numbers together (7 mounds x the number 10 x 10 heads x 10 heads). While there seems to be no clue in the text of this part of the book to indicate that such a calculation should be made, it is entirely possible that Egyptian priests used these numbers as mnemonics to remember the number of the dead in this part of the story. When one considers the many other parallels between Part A of the *Book of Aker* and Rev. 11 and the location of these various hidden symbols in the figure, it is difficult to accept that this arrangement is purely coincidental.

---

[a] The reader should bear in mind that such devastating natural catastrophes were associated with outbreaks of "disease" and "fire." This has already been discussed in some detail in Chapter 13, *Catastrophes* (*cf.* Figure 65) where it was pointed out that such events can be caused either directly or indirectly by earthquakes.

The upper group of ten heads have sunshades (☥) over them, hieroglyphs which indicate that they are the shadows of those who once lived;[735] the heads in the lower group raise their hands in praise. Also, there are two standing goddesses with arms raised in a gesture of praise at the rear of each of the two groups. It is possible to interpret the two groups of ten heads and two standing deities in the same sense of the statement in Rev. 11:13 which says that "a tenth of the city fell." All we need do is to view the 20 heads as those who died in the earthquake and the two standing goddesses as an indicator of the proportion represented by them. Thus, 7,000, the number who died in the earthquake, could represent 10% (from 2/20) of the people died, as in Rev. 11:13. Meanwhile, the gestures of praise by the two standing goddesses could represent those who survived who, according to Rev. 11:13, "were terrified and gave glory to the God of heaven." This is evident in the text over the lower group which says, "These gods are like this when they praise this Great God [Re]. ... The goddesses whose bodies are hidden praise (him) and show their heads."[736] The element of praise is a specially important feature of this scene – just as it is in Rev. 11:13.

We thus find in this part of the *Book of Aker* parallels to an earthquake ("pulsating"), 7,000 fatalities (those who are in their mounds) representing 10% of the people affected, and a group of people praising a deity, just as we read about in Rev. 11:13 which says that "seven thousand people were killed in the earthquake, and the rest were terrified and gave glory to the God of heaven."

Discussion

Neither the Book of Revelation nor the *Book of Aker* provides us with the names of the two witnesses/prophets/guardians although the Egyptian source gives us many to choose from; their names change from scene to scene, very likely in relation to their respective roles. For example, in Figure 64 they are called the "Two Mourners" and in other pictures they are called "guardians," "guides" or "counselors." Their true identities may not be entirely elusive, however, for we see them in Figure 65 unambiguously represented by fiery uraeus serpents. These serpents act as guides in Figure 66 where they are clearly identified as Isis and Nephthys, the devoted sisters who are well known for their role as protectors of the body of Osiris. The two sisters were also known affectionately to many Egyptians as *Ḥꜣyty* or *Ḥai-ti*,[737] meaning "mourners," who faithfully lamented the death of Osiris as in Figure 64. Thus, there is some evidence that the names of many of the individuals in the pairs of deities in the *Book of Aker* act as simple labels rather than names, *per se*. Nevertheless, it may be that not all pairs of deities represent the same deities and more research is needed in this area.

Revelation indicates that the beast which comes out of the bottomless pit kills only the two witnesses (Rev. 11:7) while the 7,000 other fatalities are victims of an earthquake which occurs three and a half days later (Rev. 11:11). At first glance, it seems that the death of the two witnesses was caused by something other than the earthquake. The two events, however, are not necessarily mutually exclusive. For example, the death of the witnesses by the beast from the "bottomless pit," i.e., from the depths of the earth, could very well mean death caused by an earthquake while the two witnesses could have been killed during a relatively minor fore-shock prior to the one which killed 7,000 people three and a half days later.

There is certainly an obvious connection between the death of the two guardians and mass mortality in the *Book of Aker*. It is in Part B (Appendix 4) just left of center where we found the picture of the two guardians lying in the "street" (Figure 70). In Figure 74, we see a relatively large (and hence important) picture of two groups of four mummies being resurrected, as indicated by their upright position in their mounds. These two groups of four imply a great many dead (multitudes of multitudes; from 2 groups of 4) an idea conforming with the death of 7,000 victims in Figure 73 and Rev. 11:13. The text above the coffins describes their resurrection:

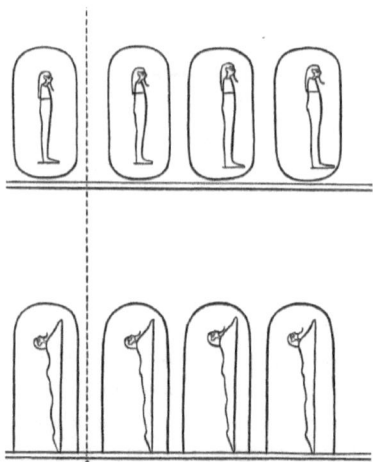

> These gods are like this. Their bodies are on their mounds while they show their heads from their mysteries. It is they who receive the light of Re and who breathe by his rays when their mounds are illumined by the voice of Re, as he calls them. Now after he has passed by them ... . Their bodies stand upright and they see ... These gods are like this in their mounds, standing upright in their coffins in the midst of their decomposition and putrefaction. This Great God calls their souls.[738]

Figure 74. Resurrection of multitudes (eight) of deities in Part B of the *Book of Aker*. This picture (at BA.B.1[st picture]) is adjacent to the overall resurrection scene which includes the two guardians in Figure 72.

Thus, in the Egyptian source, the bodies of a great many people (presumably earthquake victims) are resurrected, just as were the two guardians; Revelation is, however, silent on the resurrection of the masses who died in the earthquake. The lack of a clear indication of three and a half days (*cf.* Rev. 11:11) between the right and left scenes (BA.B.1[st picture] and BA.B.5[th picture]) in this part of the *Book of Aker* should not overshadow the reference to this period in Figure 71. The presence of the two scenes in the same part (Part B) of the book is evidence that they probably occurred either at the same time or fairly close to one another. In spite of the scene in Figure 74, it is evident in Part D that, just as in Rev. 11:13, not all who died in the quake were resurrected to be with their god; recall that one parallel in Figure 67 shows the enemies of the sun-god being subjected to terrible punishment, culminating their total destruction by fire.

There is nothing in the *Book of Aker* which explicitly mentions a volcano or its aftermath as discussed in Chapter 13, *Catastrophes*. Nevertheless, there is one quite remarkable scene in the book which can readily be interpreted as being an allusion to a volcanic eruption. It is found on the right side of the third register of Part D, at BA.D.3.1[st picture] and reproduced here as Figure 75. Significantly this picture is usually

16. The Two Witnesses 331

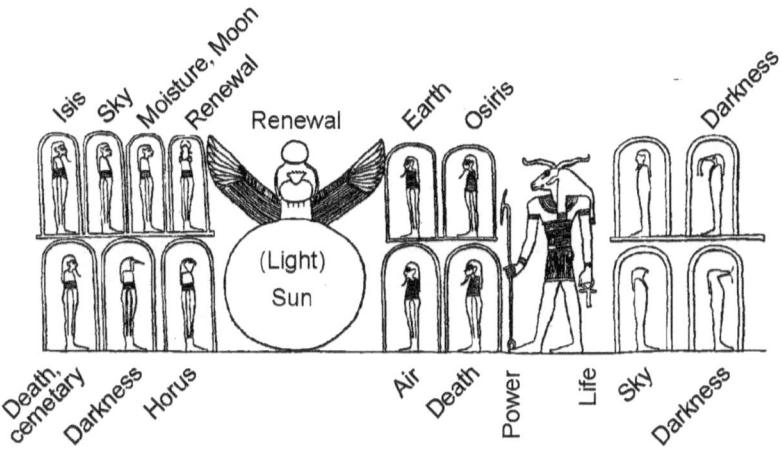

Figure 75. Death and renewal of the cosmos as depicted in Part D of the *Book of Aker*. This picture represents the renewal of previously destroyed parts of the old cosmos. Most labels here are not translations of the original text which contains the names of the various gods shown. Rather, they are interpretations of the names indicating the elements of nature they personify. The basis of these interpretations is provided in the text. (BA.D.3.1st picture)

interpreted by Egyptologists as a representation of the death and renewal of the world. It is here that we find references to the death or destruction of all of the main elements of creation. The earth, sky, sun, moon, water, atmosphere and even death itself, are expressed in terms of *corpses* of their respective Egyptian personifications.

Figure 75 shows a total of fifteen burial mounds. These mounds do not contain the usual bodies of the blessed dead or the enemies of the sun-god, but rather those of major cosmic deities. Their upright orientation indicates they are being resurrected. The two upper corpses in front of the ram-headed deity are the bodies of Osiris and Geb, both of which may be considered as earth-gods; their presence in this setting therefore suggests that the earth itself had died – or been destroyed – and is now being resurrected – or more accurately in this case and from an Egyptian perspective, being re-created. Below them is the corpse of Shu, god of the air, suggesting that the atmosphere above the earth had also come to an end. Next to Shu is the general designation of death itself, "The body of the One in his Coffin." On the other side of the large solar disk are seven more mummies. The upper four belong to Khepri (the god of renewal), Tefnut (the goddess of moisture, rain and the moon), Nut (the sky-goddess), and Isis (the protector of the body of Osiris which in this context would be the earth). The lower three corpses are those of Horus of the Netherworld (representing the Netherworld), Blind Horus (who dwells in darkness)[739] and Anubis (who guards the graves of the dead from evil forces in the darkness of night).[740] To the far right of the lower and upper registers of Figure 75 are two unnamed, shrew-headed mummies which symbolize darkness.[741] In front of the upper shrew-headed mummy is an unlabeled human-headed mummy which presumably represents unidentified common people. Finally, below this deity is an unnamed falcon-headed figure which could be another manifestation of the sky.[742]

Considered together, this assortment of corpses emphasizes the desolation of a cosmos in which the world is full of death and darkness without the sun, air, rain or any kind of moisture – even the sky itself; in other words, the death of all of creation as the Egyptians saw it. This picture does not present a mere earthquake, or even an extremely powerful and devastating one which kills thousands, but rather of a far more wide-spread and terrible event – one in which there is complete darkness without any hint of the sun or moon, one in which the land itself dies so that it will not support plant growth, and one in which the water is contaminated or dried up and the air is no longer breathable. The central emphasis on the death of the sun and moon and the overall emphasis on death itself conforms with the effects on the environment and people affected by a major volcanic eruption such as the one described in Chapter 13, *Catastrophes*.

Nevertheless, the vertical orientation of the mummies indicates the resurrection, or re-creation of all the gods who represent the natural elements of the cosmos; like the long-term aftermath of a volcanic eruption when the environment gradually recovers and the earth revitalizes itself, Figure 75 emphasizes the process of regeneration and renewal. Clear evidence for this is found in the midst of the desolation. Here stands a ram-headed god holding in his hands the promise of renewal of all life expressed in the symbolism of the *ankh* (life) and a *was* scepter (power and authority). And just to the left of center is the figure of the large solar disk from which emerges the winged beetle carrying a smaller disk, the well-known Egyptian symbol of rebirth and renewal – in this case, of Re, the sun-god himself. The central portion of Figure 75 is, in effect, an announcement of the re-creation of the cosmos as the Egyptians saw it and as defined by the natural elements symbolized in the figure.

When Figure 75 is viewed from the point of view of a large volcanic eruption and the reference to the death from an earthquake of some 7,000 people shown in Figure 73, we are led to the conclusion that the catastrophic earthquake described in Rev. 11:13 may well have been related to what seemed to the Egyptians to be a far more widespread and devastating event – the end of the world. Evidence for this is presented in Chapter 13, *Catastrophes* which describes fire and smoke on the distant horizon, a thundering noise, an earthquake the likes of which had never been experienced before, overwhelming darkness, suffocating ash fall and hot stones raining from the sky, tsunamis, starvation, and plagues of sickness and death. A general suggestion as to how these events probably evolved into such a myth is presented in Chapter 14, *From Catastrophe to Myth*.

In spite of the parallel nature of the scenes described in this chapter, the scenes in the *Book of Aker* do not all follow the same sequence as those found in the Book of Revelation. For example, to find references to the two witnesses spewing fire from their mouths (Rev. 11:5), we must go to the start of the lower register of Part D while the parallel to the comment that they have the power to shut up the sky (Rev. 11:6) is found in the 5th picture Part B. Also, reference to the death of the two witnesses by the beast which comes out of the bottomless pit (Rev. 11:7) is found in the 3rd picture of the lower register of Part D while their resurrection (Rev. 11:11-12) is emphasized in several places in Part B. Finally, parallels to the 7,000 people described in Rev.

11:13 as having been killed in an earthquake is depicted across the left side of the lowermost three registers of Part A. These differences in the sequence of events do, however, conform with the general disagreement among Egyptologists on the correct order of events in the *Book of Aker* as discussed at the beginning of this chapter.

There are, however, some important similarities in the sequence of similar events in the two sources. Hornung (1999) suggests that Part D is the first part of the book which begins on the upper register with "a schematic representation of the entire realm of the dead, with Osiris at its center."[743] And next to this scene, at the far right of the same register, is the temple scene (Figure 62), the first scene in Part D and the first significant parallel to events described at the beginning of the story of the two witnesses in Rev. 11. Finally, along the entire width of the lower register of Part A, which Hornung says is the last part of the book, is a set of scenes (Figure 76) whose order conforms quite well with that found for parallel scenes in Rev. 11, a finding which supports Hornung's conclusion that this register "can be called a kind of concluding representation that summarizes the entire course of the sun."[744]

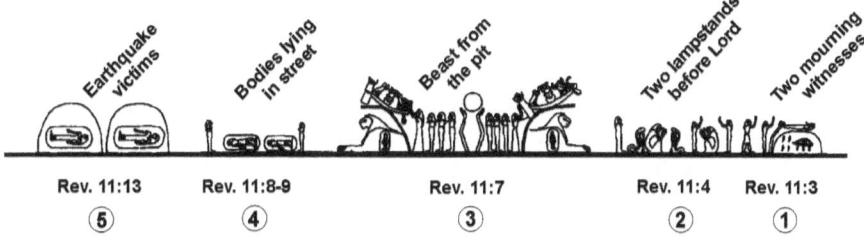

Figure 76. Pictorial summary found on the lower register of Part A of the *Book of Aker* (BA.A.4) which parallels a portion of the scenes described in Rev. 11:3-13. Other parallel scenes found in the Book of Revelation are absent in this summary and are discussed in the text and displayed together in Figure 77. (Only two of the seven mounds which account for the 7,000 dead in Rev. 11:13 are shown here while the remaining five are located in the two registers above this one; see Figure 77).

Figure 77 gives a graphic summary of the relative placements in the sequence of scenes in Figure 76 of all the major scenes discussed in this chapter; the figure shows lines drawn from each of the major scenes to their approximate position in Figure 76 (located at the center of Figure 77) based on the order in which they appeared in Rev. 11. Note that the labels beneath each of the scenes from Part B are designated as such but this label is switched from Part B to Part A along the long axis of the summary. The decision to do this was based on the statement by Hornung (1999) that Abitz concluded "Part B belongs to part A."[745] Using these alternate designations, the parallel scenes identified here fall into the following sequence:

Parts D→*A*→A→*A*→D→*A*→D→*A*→ A→A →A→*A*→A→D

It is obvious from this sequence that while most of the scenes in Revelation parallel those in Part A, i.e., the last part of the book, the remaining scenes resemble scenes in Part D, the book's first part. There is, however, no clear separation of parallel scenes in the first and last parts of the book from those in Part D; scenes from both parts are mixed. This seemingly random arrangement[a] of parallel scenes is as one would expect if the latter part of the book (Part A) referred back to events in the first part (Part D) in order to form a reasonably complete background on which to base the lowermost register in Part A, i.e., the summary shown at the center of Figure 76.

The Egyptians believed that practically all events in nature were cyclical so that significant past events were omens of the future. This view extended to the very nature of the cosmos so that long past catastrophes were believed to mark the end of the old and the beginning of the new or current cosmic cycle. The *Book of Aker* seems to be a compilation of diverse myths (or events) based on one such event – a catastrophic earthquake accompanied by darkness during the daytime hours and the death of many – and the eventual normalization of time and nature.

Remarkably, Egyptians seem to have been right in claiming that the observed catastrophes are cyclical. If we assume that the descriptions of catastrophic events in the *Book of Aker* are in fact mythologizations of actual events associated with the eruption of Thera in c. 1628 BCE, then the events most certainly will be repeated in the future. Then, for a time, people in the worst affected areas will once again believe they are experiencing the end of the world.

The location of parallel events in the *Book of Aker* at this point in the Book of Revelation (Rev. 11) seems a most appropriate place to introduce the even more dramatic series of parallels in the next chapter of Revelation (Rev. 12) which clearly illustrates the very nature of the ancient Egyptian's vision of the cyclical nature of time. This will be discussed in detail in Chapter 17, *The Woman in the Sky*.

As a final note, and in regard to the possible identity of the witnesses discussed in this chapter, one wonders if the two were Egyptians who lived in the Aegean area at the time of the eruption. For them to have been singled out for such attention in such an obviously important religious document they would have had to have been prominent dignitaries such as diplomats who died during the early stages of Thera's main eruption (i.e., three and a half days before it, as in Rev. 11:11?). This scenario, of course, is pure speculation as no evidence was found to support it in any of the documents studied here; nevertheless, it may be a reasonable avenue of further research by interested Egyptologists and historians.

---

[a] In the above sequence, Parts D→*A*→*A*→*A*→D→*A*→D→*A*→ A→A →A→*A*→A→D, letters in italicized/bold text represent scenes in the lower register of Part A while underlined scene letters (A) indicate the change from Part B to Part A according to an error correction by Abitz. Details of he sequence of parallel scenes in the *Book of Aker*, organized according to the Book of Revelation are as follows: (#1,D) BA.D.1.1$^{st\,picture}$, (#2,*A*) BA.A.4.1$^{st\,picture}$, (#3,A)/ BA.A.1.2$^{nd\,picture}$, (#4,*A*)BA.A.4.2$^{nd\,picture}$, (#5,D) BA.D.4.1$^{st\,picture}$, (#6,*A*) BA.A.4.3$^{rd\,picture}$, (#7,D) BA.D.4.3$^{rd\,picture}$, (#8,*A*) BA.B.4.4$^{th\,picture}$, (#9,A) BA.B.4$^{th\,picture}$, (#10,A) BA.B.5$^{th\,picture}$, (#11,A) BA.A.3.2$^{nd\,picture}$, (#12,*A*) BA.A.4.5$^{th\,picture}$, (#13,A) BA.A.2-4 (LHS)/BA.A.4$^{th\,picture}$, (#14,D) BA.D.3.1$^{st\,picture}$.

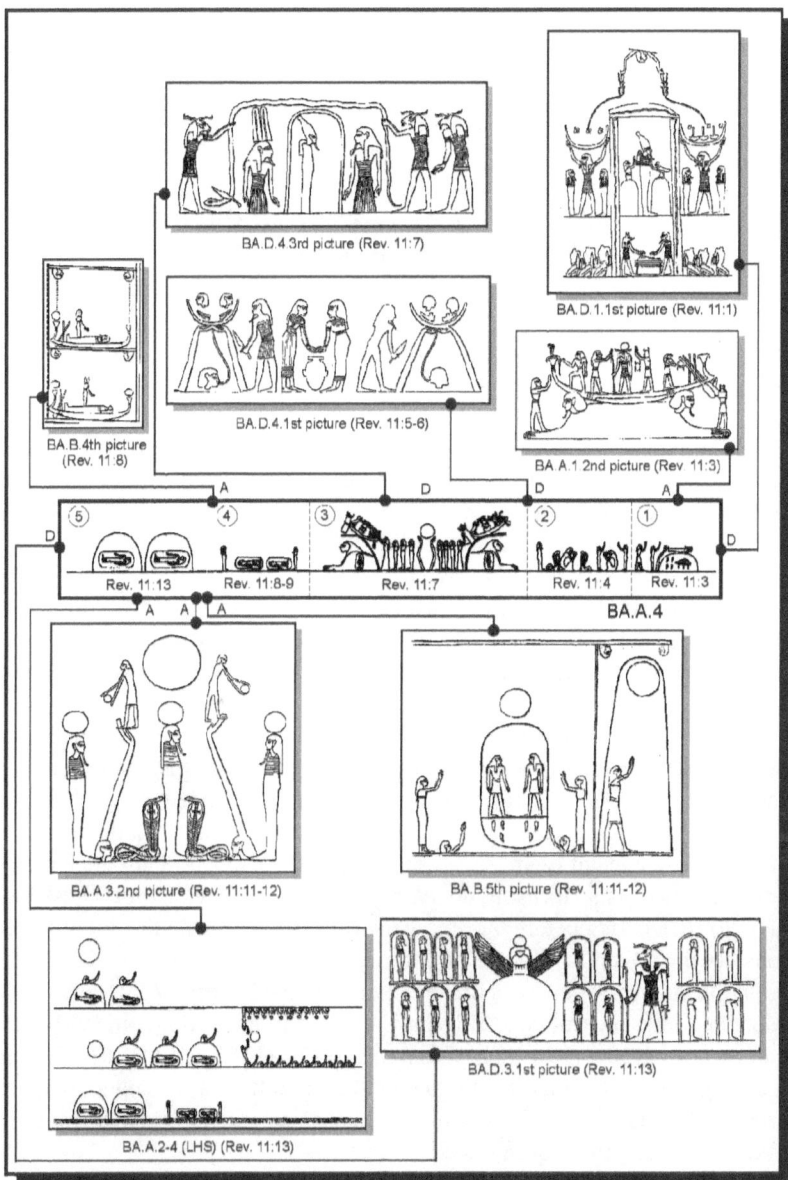

Figure 77. Scenes from the *Book of Aker* which parallel those in Rev. 11:1-13. The horizontal configuration of five scenes at the center of the figure is from Part A and is believed to be a summary of the *Book of Aker*. Individual parallel scenes are connected to this central array of five scenes at points corresponding to their relative positions in Revelation. See text for explanation for changing two of the scenes from BA.B to BA.A, i.e., from Part B of the book to Part A.

Chapter 17. The Woman in the Sky
(Rev. 11:15-18, Rev. 12)[746]

Rev. 12 distinguishes itself as perhaps the only chapter which at least one previous researcher has compared with ancient Egyptian myths. Collins (1976) compares the combat myth in Rev. 12 with similar myths in the Accadian, Hittite, Ugaritic, Greek, and Egyptian traditions and concludes that it most closely resembles the Python-Leto-Apollo myth of ancient Greece. The basis for her conclusion is the chapter's greater similarity in the sequence of themes to the Greek myth than to the Egyptian Seth-Isis-Horus myth (*cf.* Table 17.1). Collins suggests, "The similarity between the two narratives [Rev. 12 and the Python-Leto-Apollo myth] are too great to be accidental. They clearly indicate dependence. Since the Leto myth is the older of the two, we must conclude that Revelation 12 is at least in part an adaptation of the myth of the birth of Apollo."[747] Collins bases her analysis of Egyptian myths on a commentary by the Greek historian Herodotus and on the Metternich Stele (*c.* 378 BCE) and does not take into account the wider variety of versions of the myth known to have existed in ancient Egypt. Also, she does not take into account the fact that the earliest versions of Isis-Horus myths date at least as far back as the Old Kingdom (2700-2190 BCE), long before the emergence of Leto-Apollo myths. Finally, she did not consider the possibility that, in addition to Isis, the woman in Rev. 12 might *also* represent the goddess Nut who is first mentioned in the *Pyramid Texts* of Egypt's Old Kingdom and later presented in fully-grown myths in New Kingdom tombs such as those of Sethos I (1306-1290 BCE) and Ramesses VI (1151-1143 BCE). The current research expands on Collins' results by including additional in-depth comparisons with several English translations of original Egyptian texts, especially the *Books of the Heavens* and the *Book of the Dead*.

Recall from Chapter 16, *The Two Witnesses*, that the story of the two witnesses which begins at Rev. 11:1 and concludes with a great earthquake which kills thousands of people in Rev. 11:13, presumably as punishment for those who made war upon the two witnesses. After the account of the earthquake, the scene abruptly changes to one describing the arrival of "the kingdom of our Lord and his Christ" (Rev. 11:15-17) and then just as quickly goes on to the judgment of the dead and the rewarding of the saints (Rev. 11:18). As will be demonstrated in this chapter and in an Egyptian context, the arrival of the kingdom God, the judgment of the dead and

17. The Woman in the Sky

rewarding of the faithful have parallels in events described the Egyptian *Book of Night*, a book which makes up fully half of the *Books of the Heavens*. Other, even closer parallels, involve the story of the appearance of a woman in the sky described in Rev. 12; these are found in the *Book of Day*, the other half of the *Books of the Heavens*. Since the text of Rev. 11:12 to the end of Rev. 12 has parallels in the two *Books of the Heavens*, they will both be discussed in this chapter. Nevertheless, in spite of the fact that Rev. 11:15-18 comes before Rev. 12, examination of these parallels will begin with a comparison of Rev. 12 with the *Book of Day* because Rev. 12 provides us with a more remarkable series of parallels than Rev. 11:15-18. This approach also furnishes the reader with the background suitable to better appreciate the context of the parallels between the *Book of Night* and Rev. 11.

The best-known versions of the *Books of the Heavens* are found on the ceilings of the tombs of the 20th Dynasty kings; two are found on the ceilings of Tomb of Ramesses VI. One is in the sarcophagus chamber and its general layout is shown in Figure 78. This version shows the right and left sides of Nut's body with pictures and text underneath each half of her body. The other version is found on the ceiling of the outer hallway of the tomb and consists of a single picture of her body with illustrations

Table 17.1 Comparison of the sequence of the main themes in Revelation 12 with those of the Seth-Isis-Horus and the Python-Leto-Apollo myths. This shows a closer affinity of Rev. 12 to the Python-Leto-Apollo myth than the Seth-Isis-Horus one. (Based on Collins (1976, p. 66).

Book of Revelation (summary)	Seth-Isis-Horus myth (Colins's order #)	Python-Leto-Apollo myth (Colins's #)
—	1. Motivation of attack by Seth-Typhon on Osiris (kingship)	1. Motivation of Python's attack (possession of the oracle)
Rev. 12.2 Woman about to give birth	2. Isis pregnant by Osiris	2. Leto pregnant by Zeus
Rev. 12.4 Dragon intends to devour the child	3. Seth-Typhon persecuted Isis and child in order to kill child	3. Python pursues Leto with intent to kill her
Rev. 12.5a Birth of the child	5. Birth of Horus	5. Birth of Apollo and Artemis
Rev. 12.5b Kingship of the child	7. Kingship of Horus	—
Rev. 12.6 Woman aided by God Rev. 12.14 Woman aided by eagle Rev. 12.16 Woman aided by the earth	4. Isis aided by Ra and Thoth	4. By order of Zeus: North wind rescues Leto, Poseidon aids Leto
Rev. 12.7-9 Michael defeats dragon	6. Horus defeats Seth-Typhon	6. Apollo defeats Python
—	—	7. Apollo established Pythian games

and text belonging to both the *Book of Day* and the *Book of Night* underneath her. The pictures and text tell the story of the sun-god's journey through the daytime sky, his decent into the west in the evening, and his passage through the Netherworld at night.

The Egyptian word for sky was *pet (pt)*[748] and the personification of *pet* was a sky-goddess, *Nut (Nwt)*.[749] Her huge body was envisioned as stretching from one horizon to the other with her outstretched hands resting on one horizon and her feet resting on the opposite horizon as in Figure 78. Budge (1904) suggests "her legs and arms represent the four pillars on which the sky was supposed to rest, marking the position of the four cardinal points."[750] The general belief was that she gave birth to the sun-god Re each day at sunrise, that he passed over the exterior of her body during the day, disappeared into her mouth at sunset, and moved through the dark interior of her body at night to be revitalized and then reborn the following morning. The birth of Re and the events which occur during his travels across the daytime sky are documented in the *Book of Day* while events during his nighttime travel through the inside of her body are described in the *Book of Night*.

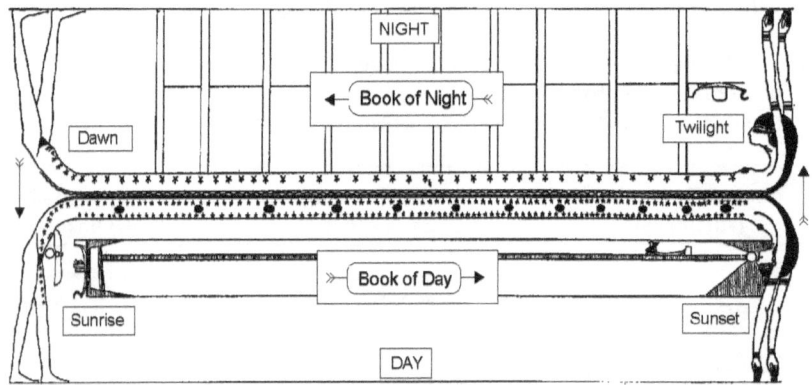

Figure 78. General arrangement of two views of Nut in the *Books of the Heavens* on the ceiling of the sarcophagus chamber in the tomb of Ramesses VI. The upper half represents the night and the lower half the day. The day begins with sunrise in the lower left corner and ends with the sunset in the lower right corner. The night begins with twilight in the upper right corner and ends with dawn in the upper left corner, thus completing a single day-night cycle. This figure also reflects the great cosmic cycle involving the creation of the universe (at sunrise), the voyage of the sun-god through time, the pre-dawn destruction of the cosmos, and it re-creation at the beginning of the next cycle. The story of the woman in Rev. 11:15-18 and through Rev. 12 contains parallels to many scenes found in these *Books of the Heavens*.

Two scenes, Figure 79 and Figure 80, summarize the dramatic events occurring from just before sunrise to just after sunrise, i.e., from just before the birth of Re until just after it; Figure 79 represents the final scene of the *Book of Night* while the opening scene of the *Book of Day* is shown in Figure 80. These scenes are usually placed close to Nut's thighs. Similarly, the final scene in the *Book of Day* in Figure 81 and the opening scene in the *Book of Night* summarize events occurring from sunset to the twilight hours of the night, i.e., during the sun-god's passing from the

17. The Woman in the Sky

daytime sky as an old man to his arrival at and the beginning of his rejuvenation in the Egyptian Netherworld. Many of the striking events described in Rev. 12 are depicted in pictures and text in the areas coinciding with these morning and evening periods.

Before going into details of the parallel events in these scenes, it is important to briefly review a few relevant aspects of the nomenclature of three related goddesses of ancient Egypt. One is Hathor who was also a sky-goddess and sometimes equated with Nut, although Hathor was usually portrayed as a much more violent deity. The second was Isis, the foremost goddess of Egypt who, significantly, was at times equated with Hathor and so from time to time was believed to have some of Hathor's attributes. As time went on, many of the myths concerning Nut, Hathor, and Isis became intertwined and stories about Isis were at times attributed to Nut and *vice versa*. For example, in one story Apophis sought to kill the infant Re as soon as he was born of Nut, and in another, Seth, an associate of Apophis sought to kill the infant as soon as he was born of Isis. Both mothers fled into the wilderness for protection. In this manner the story of the woman in the sky as told in Rev. 12 contains parallel events described in myths attributed to both Nut and Isis.

The Woman

The dramatic opening of Rev. 12 leads the reader to visualize the image of a woman described as a "great portent" appearing in the sky, who was clothed with the sun, the moon under her feet, and on her head a crown of twelve stars. There is only one deity in the ancient Egyptian pantheon which fully conforms with this description, it is the goddess Nut, the preeminent sky-goddess of ancient Egypt.

The Great Portent (Rev. 12:1a):- That the woman should be described as a "great portent" is consistent with the manner in which Nut was typically portrayed. Nut plays an important role, not only in events surrounding the daily birth of the sun-god at sunrise, but also in the sun-god's struggle against evil forces which strive to destroy him before he can complete his reign in the daytime sky, and in the evening, plunging into the darkness of the Egyptian Netherworld where he is regenerated before repeating the cycle. Because of its cyclical nature (see Figure 78), the many events included to this cycle not only speak of what has been, but also of *what is to come* during the next cycle – including the resurrection, the judgment of the dead, the rewarding of the faithful and punishment of evil doers. And just as it describes the day-night cycle, it also describes all time from the beginning of the world to its end and back to a new beginning (also, see Chapter 26, *A New Creation*). In this manner it parallels Revelation's "portent" of things to come.

Clothed with the Sun (Rev. 12:1b):- Egyptians typically portrayed their deities as fully clothed.[751] While Nut is sometimes depicted without clothes, she is only rarely completely naked, her body being typically decorated with cosmic symbols. Some pictures of Nut show her wearing a linear array of twelve sun-disks, one for each hour of the day as in Figure 78; others, such as Figure 82 and Figure 83 show her body decorated with stars and solar disks.

Figure 79. Events in the final Hours of the *Book of Night*. The fetal form of the sun-god (O) is lifted up toward the morning sky by the goddesses Isis and Nephthys. This scene announces the imminent birth of the sun-god, an event which parallels that described in Rev. 12:2a.

17. The Woman in the Sky

Figure 80. The opening scene of the *Book of Day* parallels that described in Rev. 12:2,5. Supported by the Shu (the god of the air which embodied the forces necessary for life – and not shown in the figure), the sky-goddess Nut gives birth to the sun-god Re who, depicted here as a lamb (a beetle with horns of a ram) ascends to heaven on wings to reign in the sky over the earth as a mature sun-god (O). This parallels the rising into heaven of the child in Rev. 12:5.

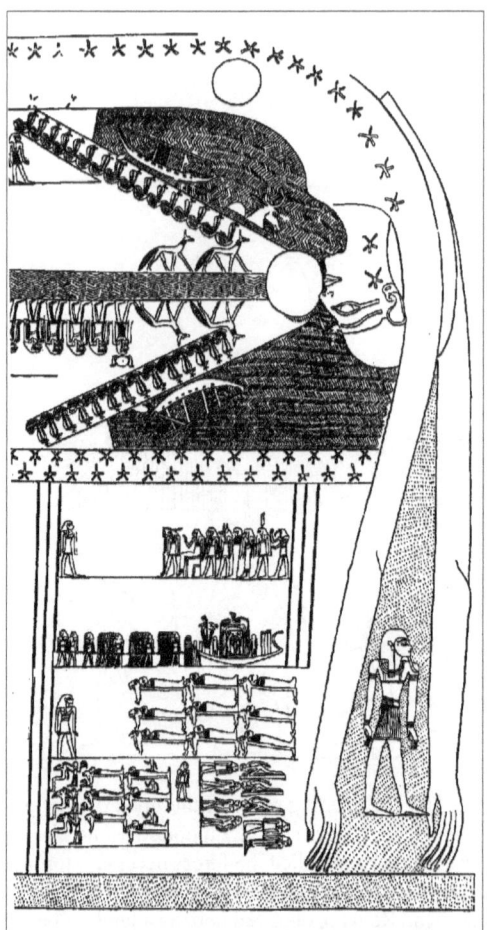

Figure 81. The sunset and twilight portion of the *Books of the Heavens*. The upper half represents the sunset depicted in the *Book of Day* while the lower half represents twilight in the *Book of Night* after the sun has set. In the final hours of the *Book of Day*, the primordial waters are swallowed by Nut along with the ageing sun-god (O) to enable him to make his nightly journey through the inside of her body. In the 1st Hour of the *Book of Night*, Horus (the king of Egypt) is seen standing on the sand (between the arms of the sky-goddess) as mentioned in Rev. 12:17.

17. The Woman in the Sky

Figure 83. Two views of Nut, one of the daytime sky and the other the nighttime sky. Her daytime body is decorated with sun-disks which parallel the reference in Rev. 12:1 to the woman's body being clothed with the sun. Nut's nighttime form bears a series of twenty-four smaller moons. Her two manifestations are supported by the earth god, Geb, who lies on his back underneath her nighttime form. Nut's crown bears a total of twelve distinct lobes (6+6) in this picture, the same as the number of stars mentioned in Rev. 12:1.

Figure 82. The sky-goddess, Nut, her body adorned with the sun, moon and stars. Her outstretched body is to be visualized so that her hands rest on the western horizon while her feet rest on the eastern horizon.

Parallels in the *Book of Day* (Rev. 12)

Rev. 12 opens with the appearance in the sky of a pregnant woman about to give birth (Rev. 12:1-2) and then quickly switches to a great red dragon which waits to kill the child as soon as it is born (Rev. 12:3-6). Its plot is foiled, however, when the child escapes up into heaven and the woman into the wilderness. Next, a celestial war against the dragon erupts in which he and his followers are defeated and exiled from heaven to earth (Rev. 12:7-11). The dragon then pursues the woman into a wilderness and, after failing to overcome her (Rev. 12:13-16), makes war on her offspring (Rev. 12:17). The following paragraphs compare details of these events with those of similar events found in the *Book of Day*.

Moon Under her Feet (Rev. 12:1c):- In addition to being adorned with a solar disk (O) Figure 83 shows a lunar disk (⊖)[752] on the lower part of Nut's abdomen, a position not entirely unlike that mentioned in Rev. 12:1c which describes "the moon under her feet." Many pictures of Nut are ambiguous on the exact position of these heavenly bodies, the ambiguity at times being due to confusion between the two symbols.

Crown of Twelve Stars (Rev. 12:1d):- Nut's body is at times decorated with many stars as shown in both Figure 78 and Figure 83. Indeed, Figure 83 shows almost her entire body covered with stars from her hands to her feet. Although she does not wear a crown of stars on her head in Figure 78, there is an allusion to such a crown in Figure 82 and Figure 83; Figure 83 shows an arrangement of what may be interpreted as twenty-four (=12+12) rays of light coming from 24 stars on her head; meanwhile, a very similar figure by Hornung (1990) shows 12 rather than 24 rays on her head.[753] Similarly, in Figure 82 the crowns on the heads of the day and nighttime manifestations of Nut total twelve (6 + 6) distinctly visible lobes which again associate the number 12 with a crown on her head. The numeric significance of the number 12 has been discussed in Chapter 7, *The Great Multitude* where it is pointed out that in Egyptian symbolism the number 12 can be represented by three 4's, where 3 represents "many" and 4 represents a "multitude." Nut's crown of 12 lobes or many rays may be said to represent many multitudes of stars, a number in keeping with the vast number of stars in the heavens and frequently shown in pictures of her.

Birth of the Child-God (Rev. 12:2-5)

In Rev. 12:2 the woman is about to give birth: "She was with child and she cried out in her pangs of birth, in anguish for delivery." The imminent birth of a child is depicted in a parallel scene found in the final hours of the *Book of Night* and presented here as Figure 79. This figure shows the infant sun-god just before birth, prophetically illustrated in his classic, mature form (O). After birth, he is assisted by the two goddesses Isis and Nephthys who transfer him from the barge of the night to the barge of the morning. The text describes a magical incantation to ensure his safe delivery into the morning sky:

> To come out of the Netherworld, to rest in the Morning Barge, to navigate the Abyss until the Hour of Re [his birth], She who sees the beauty of her Lord, to make transformations in Khepri [the young sun-god], to rise to the horizon, to enter the mouth, to come out of the vulva, to burst forth out of the Gate of the Horizon at the Hour, She who lifts up the Beauty of Re in order to make live men, all cattle, all worms he has created.[754]

A picture of the actual birth of the sun-god is found in the first Hour *Book of Day* (Figure 80). Nut is kneeling in the traditional Egyptian birthing position, ready to give birth to the infant sun-god, Re, who is visible inside her womb as a picture of a child with a finger in his mouth. The two sister-goddesses, Isis and Nephthys kneel on either side of her as they assist in the birth. Not shown in this figure is the newly born sun-god and his safe arrival into the outstretched arms of Shu, the god of the air, indicating the celestial nature of the event.

Rev. 12:5 tells us that "she brought forth a male child ... but her child was caught up to God and to his throne." The parallel to this is readily identifiable in Figure 80. Immediately after being born, the young sun-god rises into the heavens in the form of a winged scarab beetle (🪲) bearing the horns of a ram, symbolizing the young sun-god's future maturation[a] from a lamb into an adult ram; above the beetle, the mature sun-god (O) is shown as he assumes his position in the heavens as sovereign

---

[a] The hieroglyph for the 🪲 is an ideograph implying "to become" and derivatives. (See Gardiner 1927, p. 477).

over the earth. Nearby, the text abounds with praise at the birth of the god. Four jackals present at his birth are said "To praise, to adore Re by the inhabitants of the turquoise Country. To come out of the thighs of Nut when he appears in the door of the horizon. His apparition before the eyes of the people."[755] Then the gates of heaven open to accept the young sun-god: "The Spirits of the East are the four gods who worship Re. It is they who make Re rise and who open the doors of the four gates of the Eastern Horizon of Heaven ... They go before Re when Re rises, every day."[756] Other deities praise the arrival of the young god in the daytime sky with the words, "The sky is in fear of thy power, thou whose brow is adorned with horns [of a ram]! Hail to thee, Mysterious One who makes his manifestation as a child [lamb form of the ram], who appears in a mysterious way ... Thou crosseth the sky in peace."[a, 757]

Attack of the Dragon (Rev. 12:3-4)

But the birth of the child was fraught with danger; Rev. 12:4 tells us that "the *dragon* stood before the woman who was about to bear a child, that he might devour her child when she brought it forth." Recall that in Chapter 4, *Other Characters in Revelation,* it was concluded the dragon of Revelation is virtually identical with Apophis, the primeval Egyptian god of chaos. Apophis' attacks begin immediately afer Re's birth. One account which comes particularly close to the Revelation account is found in the 5th Division of the *Book of Caverns*. In Figure 41 we see the goddess Nut holding two images of the sun-god, the disk of the morning sun in her left hand and a ram-headed figure representing the mature evening sun in her right, symbolizing the passage of the sun-god across her body, the sky. Behind her, four crocodiles representing Apophis chase different manifestations of the sun-god in the sky (including Re's juvenile form, ●). Below the picture the text says that "He [Re] shines in the Eastern Mountain to repulse *Unty*, the Apophis of the wicked eye."[758] This version of the Nut myth thus conforms quite well with the account in Rev. 12:3-4 of the dragon (Apophis, called *Unty* in Figure 41) seeking to devour the newborn child. Details of the resulting battle with Apophis in the *Book of Day* will be discussed below in reference to the war in heaven (Rev. 12:7-9). Meanwhile, the two open arms in Figure 41 just below the figure of the child (♃) probably belong to the earth-god, Geb, thus signaling the beginning of the nighttime's fetal development of the rejuvenated sun-god to be born the following morning.

Prophesy of Power (Rev. 12:5)

Rev. 12:5 tells us that the child "is to rule all the nations." Similarly, in the *Book of Day* we read in the words of praise to the young sun-god, "The sky is in fear of thy power,"[759] while the *Egyptian Book of the Dead* praises the newborn deity and his kingship: "Homage to thee, O thou who has come as Khepera [Khepri], Khepera the creator of the gods [and the young sun-god himself]. Thou risest and thou shinest, and thou makest light to be in thy mother Nut [i.e., the sky]; thou art *crowned king of the gods*."[760]

---

[a] Recall from Chapter 3, *The Preeminent Deities* that the juvenile from of the ram-headed sun-god parallels the "Lamb" of Revelation.

Another version of the myth comes especially close to Rev. 12:5; it involves Isis who, as mentioned above, was at times considered to be one with Nut. The legend is called *The Wanderings of Isis in the Delta and the Birth of Horus*. In it, Isis receives counsel from the god Thoth concerning Horus who now assumes the place of his father Re. It takes the form of a prophesy similar to that described in Rev. 12:5, as follows:

> His members shall grow, and his strength shall become fully established, and it shall come to pass that he shall be set upon the throne of his father, whom he shall avenge, and the rank of Ruler (*Heq*) of the Two Lands (Egypt) shall be his.[761]

> ... O Rā ... be glad of heart, for thy son Horus is counted (among the) living. The face of this Child is the face of eternity (?). He shall oppose the faces and block the ways of the Sebau fiends [the followers of evil Seth], and shall take possession of the throne of the Two Lands.[762]

As discussed elsewhere, the king of Egypt was believed to be the incarnation of Horus, the son of Re. As such, he was considered to be king over the whole earth and Egypt.

No matter which version of the prophecy one considers, those involving the birth of Re or Horus, the newly born deity is endowed with the power to rule over the earth, just as in Rev. 12:5.

Falling Stars (Rev. 12:4)

Stars falling from the heaven are associated with the birth of the child in Rev. 12:4. The verse tells us that the dragon's "tail *swept down a third of the stars* of heaven, and cast them to the earth." A similar event is illustrated in Figure 78 where we see a group of stars flowing along Nut's back and down her left leg as far as the knee. In the version found in the outer corridor of the tomb of Ramesses VI the books are written underneath a single picture of Nut. Here, her knee is at the same level as the border between the *Book of Day* and the *Book of Night*, i.e., level with the horizon, so that the stars seem to fall down from the sky as far as the horizon. Also in the corridor version, the picture shows sand extending along its base upwards along her legs to about the level of the lowermost stars. It may likewise be significant that this group of stars represents one of three which adorn Nut's body and can therefore be interpreted as roughly representing *a third of the stars* on her body, i.e., in the sky – as in Rev. 12:4. Although the text in the *Books of the Heavens* does not explicitly state that these stars are falling to earth as described in Revelation, it can certainly be inferred from this picture.

Flight of the Mother (Rev. 12:6,14)

Revelation tells us that after the child is born "the woman fled into the wilderness, where she has a place prepared by God, in which to be nourished" (Rev. 12:6). Later, in Rev. 12:14, we are told that "*the woman was given the two wings of the great eagle that she might fly from the serpent into the wilderness, to the place where she is to be nourished.*" The *Books of the Heavens* make no reference to such an escape by Nut although the woman's flight into the wilderness clearly parallels a popular myth in which Isis has wings and can fly. One such myth was found on an Egyptian stele in Paris and involves the conception, birth and secluded early development of her son Horus:

> She [Isis] *flew round and round* ˙ over the earth uttering wailing cries of grief, and she did not alight on the ground until she had found him [Osiris]. She produced light from her feathers, *she made air to come into being by means of her two wings,*˙ and she cried the death cry for her brother. She made to rise up the inert members of him whose heart was at rest. She drew from him his essence, and she made therefrom an heir. *She suckled the child in solitariness*˙ [a wilderness], and none knew where his place was, and he grew in strength, and his arm increased in strength in the house of Gebb [Geb, the earth].[763]

This is but one variant of the many myths which parallel this passage in Revelation.

War in Heaven (Rev. 12:7-9)

Rev. 12 next shifts from the birth of the child to a war which breaks out in heaven: "Now *war arose in heaven*, Michael and his angels fighting against the dragon; and the dragon and his angels fought" (Rev. 12:7). As in Revelation, the first hint of war in heaven in the *Book of Day* appears almost immediately after the account of the birth of Re. Four jackals in the middle register make the prophetic announcement, "When thou [Re] hast overthrown Apophis, thy heart rejoices in thy mysterious regions."[764] Further along the same register the sun-god stands in his shrine while his soldiers stand near his barque, prepared for war. Two columns of text describe them: "As to these mysterious gods, *their function is to repulse Apophis*˙ and to lift up (the barque)."[765] The 17th Chapter of the *Book of the Dead* elaborates on the war "in which were destroyed the enemies of the Lord of All. ... As for that night of making war, it means that they entered into the east of the sky, *and war broke out in the entire sky*˙ and earth."[766] This quotation bears and uncanny resemblance to Rev. 12:7.

Along the 1st, 2nd and 4th registers of the *Book of Day* long rows of soldiers armed with swords and spears stand ready to fight the forces of Apophis; a portion of the 1st register is shown in Figure 84. Their magical names[a] endow them with the power to do valiant deeds.[b] We read of the deeds of "cobras, those who rapidly sting the enemy

---

[a] The names of some of the soldiers in the first and second registers of the First Hour (page numbers in Piankoff (1954) in brackets) are as follows: *She who brings Storms* (p. 395); *He kills with his Tongue* (p. 395); *He annihilates with his Speech* (p. 395); *The evil which overthrows* (p. 395); *Annihilation is before him* (p. 395); *He who eats up the bellies* (p. 395); *Earthquake* (p. 399). And in the fifth register of the Twelfth Hour: *The Fighter* (p. 405); *No Protection from him* (p. 405); *She who devours* (p. 405); *Her flames are on her knife* (p. 405); *Lord of Massacre* (p. 406); *Annihilation in the Heart and Eye* (p. 406).

[b] Concerning the importance of such names, Lurker (1980, p. 83) writes: "A name contained its owner's whole being. People and objects actually only had an existence from the moment that they bore a name, therefore the name was more than a mere means of identification, for it signified the manifestation of an entity or *the realization of a quality,*˙ hence the fact that it is said of Osiris, 'he purifies the lands in his name of Sokar; the fear of him is great in this

of the Flame [i.e., of the sun-god], when they swim in front of the Flame"[767] and "The Spirits of the North, these are the four gods among the followers. It is they who repulse the tempest of the sky on the day of the Great Contest [i.e., the war of the sun-god against the powers of darkness and chaos]."[768] In the sixth hour of the day, the war cry is given: "Rise, rise, let the gods [soldiers] who are in the barge rise in order to repulse Apophis!" Here, the powerful magic of Isis is invoked to cause Seth to go into battle against Apophis: "Let Seth stretch forth his arm to let Apopis fall! – says Isis in her incantation."[a, 769]

Figure 84. Prior to the war in heaven which parallels that described in Rev. 12:7-8, the army of the sun-god stands ready to fight Apophis and his army in the upper register of the 1st Hour of the *Book of Day*. Soldiers are equipped with swords and spears while fire-breathing cobras rear up in their baskets to destroy the enemy.

Michael, Leader of the Army (Rev. 12:7):- Revelation tells us that the name of the leader of the army of angels is Michael. There is no mention of a "Michael" among the Egyptian warriors' names provided by Piankoff (1954). In fact, the name of the leader of the Egyptian celestial army was *not* Michael; it was the god Thoth (or Horus in some versions) who led the army of the sun-god against Apophis (or Seth) and his followers (see Chapter 5, *"The Word of God"* for discussion on Thoth and Horus in this context). If there is a parallel between Revelation's Michael and Egypt's Horus, we must therefore look elsewhere for it.

Coogan (1993) tells us that Michael was "Israel's patron angel (Dan. 12.1), who fights for Israel against the angels of other nations (Dan. 10.13,21). Later tradition identifies him as the nameless divine messenger called 'the prince of the army of Yahweh in Joshua 5.13-15 (cf Exod. 23.23)." It is germane that Jesus the Christ was considered by at least some early Christians as being an incarnation of the angel Michael. This has been extensively explored by Hannah (1999) who reviews his main findings by saying that some,

---

name of Osiris, he endures unto the ends of eternity in the name of Wennefer'." In contrast, the names of soldiers in Apophis' army are not given in the Book of the Day although a few are found in the Book of the Night in the context of their punishment; their names are less descriptive: *The Utau* (an Egyptian term for a particular kind of enemy, Piankoff, 1954, p. 416) and *The Strangers* (Piankoff, p.418). The reason for not providing the names of enemy soldiers in the *Book of Day* is likely that to do so would have endowed them with powers implied by the names. See discussion on the power of names in section on the *Gift of a Stone with a Secret Name* in Chapter 8, *Egyptian Parallels in the Seven Letters*.

[a] In many ancient texts, Seth fought *with* the sun-god against Apophis, and he is frequently depicted standing guard at the bow of the solar barque. It was during the rule of the Hyksos (the 2nd Intermediate Period, 1640-1532 BCE) and especially during the New Kingdom (1550-1070) that Seth became a national enemy and a figure symbolic of evil.

early Christians understood the pre-incarnate Christ, ontologically, as an angel. This "true" angel Christology took many forms and may have appeared as early as the late first century ... Some Valentinian Gnostics supposed that Christ took on an angelic nature that he might be the Saviour of angels. ... The author of *De Centesima* and Epiphanius' "Ebionites" held Christ to have been the highest and most important of the first created archangels, a view similar in many respects to Hermas' equation *of* Christ with Michael.[770]

The equating of Christ, Christianity's son of God, and Michael is similar to the Egyptian belief that Horus, the son of Re was, as king of Egypt, an incarnation of "Horus of the Netherworld," the "fighter" who led the heavenly war against evil. But recall from Chapter 3, *The Preeminent Deities*, that Horus, the king of Egypt is a very close parallel with the Christ of the Book of Revelation. Thus, if the author of the Book of Revelation or a later redactor was a Christian who adhered to the belief that Jesus, the son of God, and Michael, leader of Yahweh's celestial army were one, a reference to Egypt's *christos*, the "anointed one," may have been interpreted as meaning Jesus Christ who, in his role as captain of Yahweh's celestial army, was called Michael.

A possible parallel to the name Michael in the Book of Revelation lies in the phonetic similarity of the original Greek to a *descriptive noun* used to describe the leader of any Egyptian army. The word used in Rev. 12:7 is Μιχαήλ (a name of Hebrew origin usually written as *Miykáel* and pronounced *Michaeél, mikh-al-ale'* or *me-kaw-alé*.[771] Phonetically similar words to Michael in the Egyptian tongue are associated with war, just as Michael is in Rev. 12:7. We note, for example, that the Egyptian word, *ma ḫȝy (ma khai)* means "to strike, to fight, to contend," while *ma ḫȝyw (ma khaiu)* means "fighters."[772] The pronunciation of the Egyptian *ma ḫȝy* or *ma ḫȝyw* thus compares reasonably well with that of the Greek for Michael. This parallel, coupled with the similarity between Egypt's (Horus) and Christianity's *christos* (Jesus), and the linking of Christianity's *christos* with the angel Michael, strengthens the parallel between Rev. 12:7 and Egyptian writings.

The inclusion of such parallels in the Book of Revelation could have occurred if the author of Revelation was either Hebrew or was at least acquainted with Hebrew traditions – and that he wrote the original draft in Greek. (These likely attributes of the author are well recognized among New Testament scholars). And if the author also had a basic understanding of Egyptian religious beliefs, he would also have known that the leader of the sun-god's heavenly army was Horus, whose earthly incarnation was Horus, the king of Egypt and the leader of the sun-god's armies on earth whom he identified as the christos. And on seeing or hearing the reference to the Egyptian words, *ma ḫȝy* or *ma ḫȝyw*, or some phonetically similar word used for the leader of the sun-god's army, he may even have concluded that Horus was the equivalent of Christ – and thus, Michael.

Defeat of the Dragon (Rev. 12:8-9):- The 1st Hour of the *Book of Day* identifies a group of four which is to defeat Apophis. As noted above, it says that "The Spirits [the four uraeus serpents] of the North ... . It is they who repulse the tempest in the sky on this day of the Great Contest."[773] This text is accompanied by a picture of Apophis being slain by three soldiers as he swims in the primeval waters toward the solar barque (Figure 85). The mood of the Egyptian text is not all together unlike that of Rev. 12:9 where we read, "And the great dragon was thrown down, that ancient serpent, who is called the Devil and Satan."[a] The main difference between this particular scene and that in Revelation is that Revelation describes one leader whereas the *Book of Day* describes a single group of four, a difference not particularly potent, especially if one considers that the Spirits of the North were themselves under the leadership of Horus. And later, in the 8th Hour, the mood is reinforced with, "the gods are in jubilation when Apopis is overthrown and when his majesty is justified."[774]

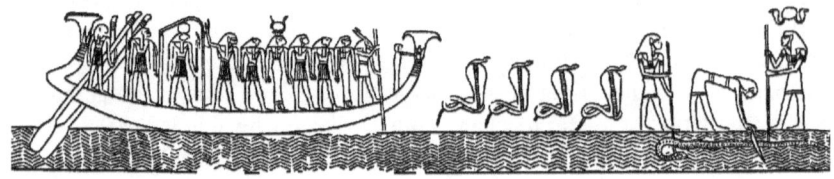

Figure 85. Scene showing battle with dragon (as in Rev. 12:8-9) in the 1st Hour (and which rages on until the 8th Hour) in the *Book of Day*. The sun-god Re stands in his shrine on the solar barque while his followers slay Apophis, the ancient dragon-serpent who would attack him.

The Kingdom of God (Rev. 12:10-11)

Immediately following the defeat of the dragon in Rev. 12:9, a loud voice is heard saying, "Now the salvation and the power and the kingdom of our God and the authority of his Christ [*the anointed one*] have come" (Rev. 12:10). The *Book of Day* has a similar abrupt change from its account of the celestial war in the 8th Hour to the land of the blessed in 9th Hour wherein we find the celestial Fields of Yaru (Figure 86).[b] It is in these fields that crops grew to fantastic sizes and giant "Spirits four cubits high" (more than 2 meters; almost 7 feet) mowed the fields in the presence of Horus. The text says, "the fields of Yaru, it is the city of Re."[775] The 110th Chapter of the *Book of the Dead* tells us that the Fields of Yaru are in the Field of Offerings, a place of "abundance to souls and spirits" where there is no mourning, turmoil, or any source of harm. The Osirian[776] believer yearned to go to this place after death. The text goes on to say,

> I eat and carouse in it, I drink and plow in it, I reap in it, I copulate in it, I make love in it, I do not perish in it ... I will not be aroused in it, my happy heart is not apprehensive in it. ... there is no shouting in it, there is nothing evil in it. ... I am one who recalls to

---

[a] Evidence was presented in Chapter 4, *Other Characters in Revelation,* that the Devil and Satan of the Book of Revelation very closely parallel ancient Egypt's Apophis.

[b] The Egyptian Fields of Yaru are mythologically equivalent to their Fields of Reeds and Fields of Rushes.

himself that of which I have been forgetful. I plow and I reap, and I am content in the *City of God*."⁷⁷⁷

Indeed, the Egyptian name *City of God* is similar to "the city of my God" in Rev. 3:12 which "comes down from my God out of heaven" and its attributes are similar to those described for the Holy City of Rev. 21-22.[a] And just as the Fields of Yaru are a part of the Field of Offerings, Revelation's City of God is a part of the "Kingdom of God." The abrupt change from the war in Rev. 12:8-9 to the kingdom of God in Rev. 12:10 thus parallels the abrupt change from the celestial war in the 8th Hour when "Apophis is overthrown" to the blessed Fields of Yaru in the 9th Hour in the *Book of Day*.

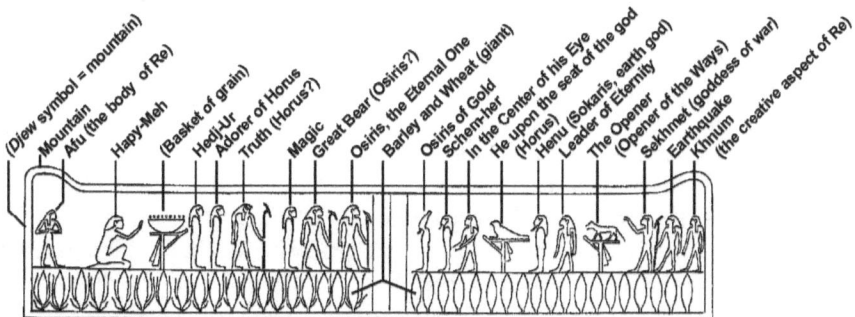

Figure 86. The Fields of Yaru – also called "the city of Re" and the "City of God"– as depicted in the 9th Hour of the *Book of Day*. This scene parallels the Kingdom of God referred to in Rev. 12:10. It is here that the blessed dead dwell throughout eternity in the presence of Re, Osiris and Horus, living in the midst of a plenteous supply of oversized grain and enjoying the pleasures of their renewed life in the hereafter. Two different manifestations of Osiris face each other and the central columns of text; at the right extremity of the figure is a manifestation of the sun-god, Re, while another manifestation of him is identifiable as the deity at the left extremity. At least one, or possibly two, manifestations of Horus are also present, situated as the forth deity from the center of each side of the figure. Bracketed names and comments are by JHCP.

Notice too that Rev. 12:10 links God with Christ: "the kingdom of our God *and* the authority of his Christ have come." From an Egyptian perspective, we should therefore determine if Horus (*the christos* of Revelation) is also mentioned in relation to the Field of Yaru. In fact, we do find such an association, as shown in Figure 86. This figure shows both Osiris and Horus ("He upon the seat of the god") in the fields of Yaru. The text says, "It [Horus] is the ... Son of the Sun [Re] ... the justified one, beloved of Osiris, He at the Head of the West, the Great God [Osiris], Lord of Abydos."⁷⁷⁸ The mention of both God (Osiris) and Christ (Horus) in Rev. 12:10 is similarly found in both pictures and text in this part of the *Book of Day*.

Rev. 12:11 says, "And they have conquered him by the blood of the Lamb and by the word of their testimony, for they loved not their lives even unto death." The reference in this verse to the blessed dead who died while fighting the dragon is also of interest from an Egyptian point of view. As we saw in Chapter 7, *The Great*

---

[a] See Chapter 27, *The Holy City*, for details.

Multitude, the soldiers who fought for their god against Apophis were counted among the groups of twelve who received special blessings from Re, including shelter, clothing, food and water – rewards essentially similar to many found in the Fields of Yaru. These soldiers are shown in a picture directly over the picture of Fields of Yaru and discussed above in relation to those with magical names of the fighters which endowed them with supernatural powers. The part of the *Book of Day* showing the Fields of Yaru next to the soldiers thus conforms with the juxtaposition of the coming of the Kingdom of God referred to in Rev. 12:10 and the reference to those who died in battle in Rev. 12:11.

Rev. 12:11 also says that the followers of God conquered the dragon "by the blood of the Lamb." This is also of interest from an Egyptian point of view. Recall from Chapter 3, *The Preeminent Deities*, that the "blood of the lamb" parallels the "efflux of Osiris." Nevertheless, most of the many references referring to the "efflux of Osiris" can also apply to the "efflux of Re" when the combined Osiris-Re form of the sun-god is meant. It was generally believed that this "water of life" had life-giving qualities. Lurker says that it was, "the primeval matter which 'brought forth all things' ... . In the mortuary cult the water used in libation was linked to the idea of reanimation. As the 'efflux' which issued from *Osiris' water liberated one from the paralysis of death*."[779] And it was the resurrected dead who fought for the sun-god in the heavenly war against Apophis. In this sense, Revelation's "*by* the blood of the Lamb" could readily be considered a parallel with the Egyptian belief that the dead could be resurrected "*by*" the efflux of Osiris" (or by the blood of "the Lamb").

Pursuit of the Woman (Rev. 12:15-16)

We are told in Rev. 12:15-16 that the ancient serpent poured "water like a river out of his mouth after the woman, to sweep her away with the flood. But the earth came to the help of the woman, and the earth opened its mouth and swallowed the river which the dragon had poured from his mouth." The use of the word "ancient" to describe the dragon in Rev. 12:9 suggests that this part of Rev. 12 emphasizes events at a very early point in time and that, if we are to understand the scene in an Egyptian context, we should examine it in this context.

Nowhere is the idea of an ancient serpent expressed so forcefully as in Chapter 175 of the *Book of the Dead*. Here, the deceased asks of the god Atum, "What will be the duration of my life?" Atum answers, "You shall be for millions on millions of years, a lifetime of millions of years." Atum then goes on to describe events at the end of time and the beginning of the next great cosmic circle. He says, "I ... will destroy all that I have made; the earth shall return to the Primordial Water, to the surging flood, as in its original state. But I will remain with Osiris, I will transform myself into something else, namely a serpent."[780] This passage goes on to speak of various aspects of the re-birth of the cosmos, complete with the familiar gods such as Osiris and Horus and the domains over which they rule. But the most relevant parts of Chapter 175 are how the sun-god describes himself as returning to the Primordial Water and his form as a serpent at the end of time and at the beginning of a new creation. Hornung (1983) highlights the metamorphosis of the sun-god into a primordial serpent with the following explanation:

17. The Woman in the Sky

> Only he [Atum, the creator god] and Osiris can change back into the enduring form of a snake, that is , into the same form – or rather formlessness – which the eternal enemy of the gods, Apopis, possesses as a power of chaos. It is also visible in the Ouroboros, the snake biting its own tail, as the regenerating nonexistence that encircles the world. The snake remains, but the world it encloses sinks away into the primeval water and vanishes with the gods and all living beings; the state of things before creations returns.[781]

In the mind of the Egyptians, the forces of chaos, personified as a serpentine deity, thus forever strove to disrupt the normal, orderly form of creation, including the very time of creation itself. It is against this background that the images found in Rev. 12:15-16 are best examined.

The Egyptians envisioned the interior of Nut's body as representing, or at least being the equivalent of, that place deep below the surface of the earth – the Netherworld, through which the primeval river flowed and emerged from Nut's vulva each morning at dawn. It then flowed along her back (the daytime sky) and completed its cyclical journey into the darkness of the Netherworld by passing into her mouth in the evening. This observation identifies the main, potential, parallel elements in the *Books of the Heavens* to this part of Revelation.

Since the interior of Nut's body was considered to be the equivalent of Egypt's Netherworld, i.e., it was situated inside a series of caverns deep in the earth, and the primeval river passed into her mouth from the sky, it may be said that *the river passed into the earth.* The name of the earth-god was Geb so that it may also be said that it is Geb who swallows the primeval waters each evening. This event strongly parallels Revelation's statement that "the earth (i.e., the earth-god Geb) opened its mouth and swallowed the river" (Rev. 12:15). This act of swallowing the river of water is clearly visible in Figure 81 where we see the primeval river flowing into Nut's mouth (or Geb's, as above), carrying with it the aged sun-god (represented by the solar disk).

While the above parallel is almost certainly valid, especially since it deals with the very general idea of water being poured against, or into, a woman which personifies the sky, a more pertinent parallel to the scene in Rev. 12:15-16 is found in Figure 87. In this scene, found in the 12th Hour of the *Book of Night*, we see a scarab beetle with something coming from its mouth; Piankoff (1954) describes it as "a stream of water issuing from its head and falling on the sign of heaven [⌐], supported by another beetle."[782] The scarab beetle, as discussed elsewhere, is the well-known "image of self-creation"[783] and the determinative of words like *ḫpr*, "become,"[784] so that the beetle holding the sky indicates this is a pre-dawn, or infantile sky in the process of being born. This interpretation is supported by the presence of the second beetle which holds up the sky symbol (⌐) from below in exactly the same way that a real scarab beetle would hold a ball of dung containing its single larva, it's next generation. The part of Figure 87 containing these two beetles thus conforms with both the primordial aspect of the scene and the flow of water toward the "woman in the sky" described in Rev. 12:15 and described above as a parallel to Egypt's sky-goddess, Nut.

The primordial nature of this scene is repeated in two deities, one which kneels before the upper two beetles and the other before a figure of the young sun-god; the male deity is Heh (*Ḥḥ* and the kneeling female is called Hehet (*Ḥḥt*).[a, 785] Clagett (1989) tells us that Heh and Hehet along with Nun and Nunet are the four primordial gods of the Ogdoad of Hermopolis[786] and Gardiner (1927) says that *Ḥḥ* was "one of the eight Ḥeḥ-gods who hold aloft the sky."[787] Meanwhile, Faulkner (1962) says that the word *ḥḥ* refers to a "million, a great number," a translation which conforms with the great number of years in the idea of a long primordial time implied in Figure 87. A second reference to the primordial nature of this scene is found in the name of the crocodile-headed god standing to the right of altar. His name is Pauty-Nenty, which means "*The Primeval*,' the One of the Nether Sky [i.e., the Netherworld's sky]."[788] Pauty-Nenty in this scene may therefore represent a form of the

Figure 87. In the 12th Hour of the *Book of Night*, primeval water floods the sky (⌒) the sky (the personification of which is the sky-goddess, *Nut*) from the and mouth of a beetle (●). To the left, two representations of the young sun-god (the lower ● and the ♙ symbol) are worshiped. This scene parallels portions of Rev. 12:13-16.

primeval serpent, Apophis, a suggestion which conforms with the popular belief that the crocodile was considered to be "Seth's henchman" and sometimes "the embodiment of Seth"[789] and often equated with Apophis himself. All of these factors speak to the primordial character of this particular scene in the *Books of the Heavens*.

We might argue, however, that the upper beetle in Figure 87 is neither a serpent nor a dragon so that this scene is not a perfect parallel with Rev. 12:15. We should therefore take a closer look at the Egyptian symbolism in this scene. According to Lurker (1980) Atum was not only "present in the image of the scarab," but that "The

---

[a] The actual hieroglyphs in the text spell the names as 𓎛𓎛𓃀 (*ḥḥw*) and 𓎛𓎛𓃀𓏏 (*ḥḥw-t*). Budge's dictionary tells us that *Ḥḥw* (Ḥeḥu) is "a dawn-god whose consort was 𓎛𓎛𓃀𓏏." A word phonetically similar to or identical with *ḥḥw* is *Ḥuḥu*, 𓎛𓎛𓃀𓈖𓈖𓈖, and this word is identified by Budge (1920) as "the primeval watery mass whence came everything." A second homophone, 𓎛𓎛𓃀𓈖𓈖𓈖𓊖, means "Eternity, one of the four elemental gods of the company of Thoth." Thus, both Heh and Hehet embody concepts of the primeval state of the cosmos. (These comments are based on the hieroglyphic text provided in Plate 196 of Piankoff (1954), *The Tomb of Ramesses VI*.)

serpent as a chthonic animal could also be a manifestation of the god [i.e., of Atum]."⁷⁹⁰ If we attribute this concept to Figure 87, the upper beetle could very well represent both Atum the creator god *and* the primeval serpent, Apophis. Indeed, according to Lurker (1980) Atum was not only "present in the image of the scarab," but that "The serpent as a chthonic animal could also be a manifestation of the god."⁷⁹¹ In other words, the upper beetle in Figure 87 could represent both Atum the creator god *and* the primeval serpent. In this manner, the flood of water from the upper beetle can be said to parallel that which is poured out by the serpent against the woman in Rev. 12:15. This, of course, conforms with the above discussion on events at the end in Chapter 175 of the *Book of the Dead* as discussed in the previous section.

The activity of the lower beetle pushing against the sky symbolizes the manner in which *ḫprr*, the dung beetle, in real life, pushes against a ball of dung containing its egg – the beginning of its next generation. This symbolism of the regeneration of life is consistent with the overall concept portrayed by the *Books of the Heavens* wherein the final scenes of the *Book of Night* represent the last hours of the night, i.e., the final hours of time prior to the beginning of a new creation; activities in the last hours of night feed naturally into the creation scenes in the first part of the *Book of Day* (see also Chapter 26, *A New Creation*). In this manner, the night-day cycle is completed. And the fetus of the yet-to-be-born sun-god is illustrated as a child sitting near the base of the altar where he is worshiped by a goddess.

The Egyptians believed these allusions to events at the beginning of primeval time were symbolically repeated each morning before dawn and that they were closely related to the scene in Figure 79 showing the fetal sun-god (O) in the 12th Hour of the *Book of Night* being raised toward the heavens by the two goddesses, Isis and Nephthys. Later, in the register directly above Figure 79 we find a picture (Figure 80) in the *Book of Day* showing the birth of the sun-god. The juxtaposition of the pictures of the young sun-god being cared for by Isis and her sister in Figure 80 and the pouring of the primeval waters onto the sky Figure 87 thus closely parallel the juxtaposition of the caring for the child in Rev. 12:14 and the outpouring of water in Rev. 12:15-16.

There is an apparent inconsistency in the events described in Rev. 12:14-16. In the first case, the woman is given "two wings of a great eagle that she might fly from the serpent into the wilderness." Next, the serpent pours water against the woman, to sweep her away with the flood. A flood of water is a very poor way to attack one who flies with the wings of an eagle. This dilemma is resolved when considered in the light of Egyptian parallels: the former refers to a common Isis myth while the latter parallels the Nut myth portrayed in the *Books of the Heavens*, a topic which will be further discussed near the end of this chapter.

War on the Woman's Offspring (Rev. 12:17)

Immediately after the flood of water, we are told that "the dragon was angry with the woman, and went off to make war on the *rest of her offspring*" (Rev. 12:17). If we assume this woman to be the sky-goddess, it is against Nut's children that the dragon takes action. Hornung (1983) provides us with a brief account of one of the early myths concerning her children, albeit a version which does not explicitly include Re among Nut's children.

The primeval being Atum engenders through self-impregnation the first sexually differentiated divine couple, Shu [the atmosphere] and Tefnut [moisture], and from them is born the next generation of gods, Geb [earth] and Nut [sky]; the union of this earth god and sky goddess produces the siblings Osiris, Seth, Isis, and Nephthys. ... From the New Kingdom on, Seth is often banished from the ennead and replaced by Horus, while other manifestations of the sun god [for example, Re] may substitute for Atum.[792]

Thus, Seth is replaced by Horus as one of the children of Nut so that this group of four children (Osiris, Isis, Nephthys *plus Horus*) parallels the "rest of her offspring" referred to in Rev. 12:17. Many books of the Egyptian afterlife for this period refer to Apophis and Seth as enemies of these deities and there is an abundance of myths telling of battles fought between them. Two of the main books pertaining to this work, the *Amduat* and the *Book of Gates*, have especially good examples (see BG8-9), especially where they mention the dragon's war on the woman's children, including Horus. In this manner Rev. 12:17 parallels the serpentine Apophis dragon who makes war on Horus and his siblings – Osiris, Isis and Nephthys. This is particularly significant because Horus was identified in Chapter 3, *The Preeminent Deities*, as a close parallel to the anointed one, the "Christ" of the Book of Revelation. Rev. 12:17 tells us that the dragon went off to make war "on *those* who keep the commandments of God and bear testimony to Jesus." In an Egyptian context, this parallels the followers of Re, Osiris and Horus who fought in the heavenly battle against Apophis and his followers in the *Book of Day*.

One Standing on the Sand (Rev. 12:17)

Rev. 12:17 ends with the statement, "And he stood on the sand of the sea." The exact meaning of this passage is ambiguous from an important point of view: Exactly *who* is being described as standing on the sand? Before comparing this text with parts of the Egyptian *Book of Day* we should briefly examine this ambiguity. The KJV (which designates this verse as Rev. 13:1) translates it in the first person, "*I* stood upon the sand," whereas the RSV and the ASV translate it as "*he* stood upon the sand." The NIV (also as Rev. 13:1) on the other hand, goes further by actually identifying who is standing; it say, "the *dragon* stood on the shore." The latter is more speculative on the part of the translator because the "dragon" (δράκων, *drakon*) is not mentioned in the original Greek text and other versions conform with the former mix of interpretations. If we discard the more speculative interpretations, we are left with the one standing on the sand being referred to as either *I* or *he*. If the former, it is the writer of Revelation himself who is standing on the sand. This choice of the first person is not likely correct because, as Marshall (1984) informs us, the phrase, "And I ...," is used only in the later manuscripts of the Book of Revelation.[793] On the other hand, if *he* is meant and we assume an Egyptian parallel is at play, the one spoken of here is either Apophis (the dragon as defined in Chapter 4, *Other Characters in Revelation*) or Horus (*the christos*, "the anointed one," as defined in Chapter 3, *The Preeminent Deities*). A parallel found in the Egyptian *Book of Day* would seem to clarify this issue.

17. The Woman in the Sky

The most prominent deity standing on sand in the entire *Books of the Heavens* is found in the 1st Hour of the night, an area viewed as an "interstitial area" prior to the actual events described in the *Book of Night*.[794] Here we see a picture (Figure 81) of the deceased king of Egypt standing between the arms of Nut.[795] The material on which he stands is unambiguously identifiable from the stippled pattern commonly used for sand by the Egyptian artists. Above him and to the left of Nut's head and upper arms are the primeval waters represented by densely drawn wavy lines. The text in the vicinity of the king supports the idea of the sand being on the bank of the primeval waters. It is located to the far left of figure standing on the sand in Figure 81 between the god, Mind, and nine mummies lying on their funeral biers. Mind is quoted as saying, "Measure your banks ..."[796] a statement obviously referring to sandbanks along the shore of a river. That this text refers to the king or is otherwise associated with him is evident in the version found in the tomb of Seti I where we find the king is in a different location, this time standing beside Mind[797] so it is obvious here that it is the king of Egypt to whom Mind is saying, "Measure your banks." Recall that Horus was one of the offspring of Nut and as such would parallel one of the children on which the dragon made war in Rev. 12:17. The king of Egypt, of course, was considered to be an incarnation of the god Horus[798] and the anointed one referred to as the *christos* in the Greek version of Revelation as discussed in Chapter 3, *The Preeminent Deities*. If one assumes an Egyptian connection with this scene, the preferred interpretation would read, "And *he* (i.e., Horus, the king, the *anointed one*) stood on the sand of the sea."[a]

Parallels in the *Book of Night* (Rev. 11:15-18)

As indicated in the introductory section to this chapter, Rev. 11:15-18 provides us with a brief account of the arrival of the "kingdom of our God" (Rev. 11:15-17) and the judgment of the dead and the rewarding of the saints (Rev. 11:18). This general scenario parallels events described in the *Book of Night* – the other half of the *Books of the Heavens*; more specifically, they parallel events found in the 1st through 8th Hours of the book.

Rev. 11:15-18 is not the only part of the Book of Revelation which discusses the judgment of the dead, rewards to the faithful and punishment of the damned. A more detailed account is provided in Rev. 20:11-15, a passage which, remarkably, contains even closer similarities to scenes in the *Book of Night* than Rev. 11:15-18. For this reason, details of the Egyptian parallels with Rev. 11:15-18 will be deferred to

---

[a] Another possible candidate for the "one standing on the sand" is found in the primordial waters just to the left of the large sun-disk near Nut's mouth in Figure 81. It is in the form of the head of a bubalis (𓃲), a desert antelope often associated with the evil god Seth (Lurker, 1980, p. 28) who, in the *Book of Night*, replaces the god Apophis. Next to it is the 🪨 symbol which can represent a mound or a bank of sand in the river. The bubalis may therefore be interpreted as representing Seth standing on "the sand of the sea," an interpretation which parallels the translation suggested in the NIV. There is no mention of this scene in the text of the *Book of Night* so that the evidence for Seth being the one standing on the sand in Rev. 12:17 is not as convincing as that for the king although the possibility warrants further investigation.

Chapter 25, *Resurrection and Judgment*, where the parallels will be discussed in a broader context. Chapter 25 presents them in the context of the overall fate of both the followers and the enemies of God. For our present purposes, it will suffice to provide here a brief summary of a limited number of parallels to Rev. 11:15-18. The important elements of the verses in Rev. 11:15-18 are not in the same order as they appear in Rev. 20:11-15 and will be discussed in the same order as they appear in the *Book of Night*.

Arrival of the Kingdom of God (Rev. 11:15)

Rev. 11:15 introduces a dramatic transition from the calamitous events which followed the ascension of the two witnesses in Rev. 11:12-13. The text declares, "The kingdom of the world has become the kingdom of our Lord and of his Christ, and he shall reign for ever and ever." The main point of this statement conforms with the movement of the sun-god from the daytime sky to the darkness of the Egyptian Netherworld – in other words, from the kingdom of Re (the sky) to the kingdom of Osiris (the Netherworld, underneath the earth). This scenario of events also conforms with evidence presented in Chapter 3, *The Preeminent Deities*, that Revelation's God on the Throne parallels Osiris who is quite often depicted as sitting on a throne. Like the "Lord" of Revelation who "shall reign for ever and ever," the *Book of the Dead* refers to Osiris as "King of Eternity, Lord of Everlasting, who passes millions of years in his lifetime ... sovereign of gods and men."[799]

But Rev. 11:15 also makes reference to "his Christ." Recall that, just as Pharaoh, the king of Egypt, was considered to be Horus, "the anointed one," *the christos* and the son of Re on earth, his manifestation in the Netherworld was called "Horus of the Netherworld." It was in the latter form that Horus played an important role in the judgment of the dead by Osiris. This is depicted in Figure 88 where hawk-headed Horus stands eye-to-eye in front of Osiris. Another notable aspect of this scene is that Horus' head is at the same level as that of Osiris. This position is by no means coincidence for it illustrates an Egyptian convention which has been classified by Egyptologists as *isocephaly* (from two Greek roots indicating heads drawn on

Figure 88. The judgment of the dead by Osiris in the 8th Hour of the *Book of Night*. This scene parallels the judgment of the dead in Rev. 11:18 and the presence of the Kingdom "of our Lord and his Christ in Rev. 11:15.

the same line). Isocephaly implies equality of authority and Wilkinson (1994) says that its representation is commonly employed in scenes involving the Egyptian king and the gods[800] – just as is implied in the description in Rev. 11:15 of "the kingdom of our Lord [Osiris] *and* of his Christ [Horus]."

The Resurrection (Rev. 11:18)

Shortly after Re enters the Netherworld, the dead of both the followers and the enemies of the sun-god are resurrected prior to their judgment before the throne of Osiris. This is illustrated in Figure 89 where we see a variety of stages of the resurrection process, from the blessed dead lying on their funeral biers with headboards consisting of lion heads (symbols of Re) in the 2nd and 3rd Hours to their rising up to a siting position in the 3rd and 5th Hours to standing upright over their biers in the 6th Hour (in the 5th Hour, they are shown with raised heads as well as in a sitting position away from their biers). This scene of the resurrection in Rev. 11:18 is, of course, necessary before the judgment of the dead.

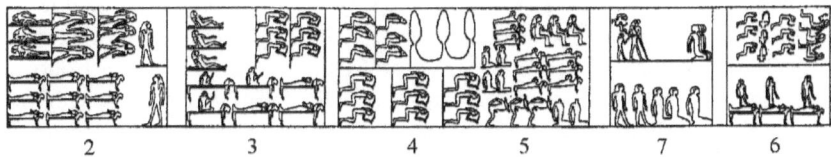

Figure 89. The resurrection scene in the third registers of the 2nd to 7th Hours of the *Book of Night* corresponds to that described in Rev. 11:18, and in greater detail, that in Rev. 20:13. The 6th and 7th Hours are interchanged in this version (from the ceiling of the corridor of the Tomb of Ramesses VI; BN2-7)

Figure 89 and its accompanying text also make it quite clear that the resurrected include both the sun-god's faithful followers and his enemies. The figures in the 2nd Hour may be classified as followers of the sun-god because the deity standing in front of the nine figures lying on their funeral biers says, "Count your hearts, receive your gifts."[801] In the 4th and 5th Hours, however, we find pictures of bound, wounded and decapitated enemies. The text in the 4th Hour makes reference to "One who chastises the enemies of Weary-Heart (Osiris)"[802] while that in the 5th Hour refers to the "followers of Seth" and the *Utau*,[803] a term used for some kind of enemy.[a] The upper part of the 6th Hour in Figure 89 shows several groups of enemies called "The Strangers" and "The Burned Ones."[804] In the 7th Hour we find one called "She who strikes the allies of Seth"[805] as well as a list of the various nations to which the enemies belong. This mix of *the faithful and the enemies* among the resurrected in Figure 89 conforms with Rev. 11:18 which announces "the time for the dead to be judged, *for rewarding thy servants*, the prophets and saints, and those who fear thy name, both small and great, and *for destroying the destroyers of the earth*."

---

[a] Also, see footnote referring to the *Utau* on page 348.

The Nations Rage (Rev. 11:18a)

The statement in Rev. 11:18 that "The nations raged, but thy wrath came" implies that enemy armies were to be punished for their evil deeds at judgment time. References to foreign nations and their evil deeds are implied in Figure 89 and its accompanying text. The foreign nature of the many enemies depicted in the 4th Hour is denoted by a hieroglyph with three mountains ⛰ (each surmounted by a tree, ♣), symbolizing "foreign countries."[806] Also, the associated text clearly identifies the group of three (= many) kneeling enemies before the hawk-headed figure of Horus in the upper part of the 7th Hour as being mostly foreigners. It identifies them as "The Asiatics, The Libyans, The Madjai, The Negroes, The Red Men, and The Egyptians."[a] Horus says to them, "You are the rebels, the male and female Ut, who have acted against my father Osiris .... Hence it is I who strikes you."[807]

The Judgment (Rev. 11:18c)

The judgment referred to in Rev. 11:18 is "for rewarding thy servants ... and for destroying the destroyers of the earth." As already mentioned, the deity standing in front of the nine figures lying on funeral biers in the 2nd Hour says, "Count your hearts, receive your gifts,"[808] a statement clearly compatible with "rewarding of thy servants." And the beheading and destruction by fire in the 5th and 6th Hours are compatible with "destroying the destroyers." Piankoff (1954) describes the judgment scene in the 8th Hour (Figure 88) as part of a representation of events in the Netherworld, "the kingdom of Osiris,"[809] a designation similar to that described in Rev. 15 when one considers that Osiris parallels Revelation's "God on the Throne." Furthermore, the reference to the judging of "the small and the great" in Rev. 11:18 (see also Rev. 20:11-15) also conforms with the fourteen praising deities in the upper two registers of Figure 88 and the ten with staffs of authority in the two lower registers respectively;[b] this will be discussed in detail in Chapter 25, *Resurrection and Judgment*.

Discussion

Merging of Egyptian Myths in Rev. 12:- Parallels to two different Egyptian myths have been identified in the text of Rev. 11:15 to Rev. 12:17. The main framework of this passage parallels the Apophis-Nut-Re myth while the two verses, Rev. 12:6 (where the woman escapes into the wilderness for a time) and Rev. 12:14 (where the woman is given wings to escape the serpent) parallel events in the Seth-Isis-Horus myth. The reason for this apparent mixing of myths could be related to the ever-changing nature of the role of Isis and Nut as mother of the sun-god on the one hand and the complex identity of the sun-god himself (Horus/Re/Osiris). The following shows how such intertwining of the two myths may be explained.

---

[a] Not all Egyptians were considered to be faithful to Osiris; some were rebellious and did not adhere to the principal of truth, order and justice, i.e., *maat*.

[b] It is not likely, however, that the twenty-four deities in these groups of followers form a reliable parallel with the twenty-four elders who sit on their thrones before God in Rev. 11:15; this will be discussed in Chapter 25, *Resurrection and Judgment*.

The earliest versions of the Seth-Isis-Horus myth appear in the *Pyramid Texts* which date back to Egypt's Old Kingdom (2575-2134 BCE) and variations of this myth abounded in the latter part of Egypt's dynastic period; Budge (1934) says that dramas of the "Mysteries of Isis" became very popular in Egypt.[810] The two *Books of the Heavens* which present the Apophis-Nut-Re myth, and apparently form the bulk of Rev. 11:15 to Rev. 12:17, were quite popular on the ceilings of tombs during the Middle Kingdom. Nevertheless, it does not replace the Seth-Isis-Horus myths but rather incorporates elements of it, placing them in the more complex cosmology of the day-night cycle and its cosmic twin, the cyclical beginning and end of creation. In the *Books of the Heavens* it is Nut who gives birth to the all-powerful god Re while Re, in turn, replaces Horus of the older myth. This switch was probably a logical step for, as Spence (1915) points out, "Horus ... was originally a sun-god, and as such was equivalent to Ra, but in time the two gods came to be regarded as separate and distinct personages, Ra being the highest, and Horus serving him as a sort of war-captain."[811] Furthermore, Hornung (1990) points out that Re was at times identified with "Horus of the Netherworld." He says that "Being dead, Osiris is always in danger and requires the aid of the sun-god on his nightly voyage. Re thus fulfills the role of the loyal son Horus, forcing his way against all odds to his father in the Netherworld, and the texts of the Beyond frequently identify him as 'Horus of the Netherworld.'"[812] Thus, while Re can be called the son of Nut, so too, as the equivalent of Re, can Horus be considered to be her son; remarkably, this belief could be maintained at the same time as another popular belief held Horus to be the son of Isis. And instead of battling with his brother Seth, Horus now fights the army of Apophis, the ancient god of chaos (who parallels Revelation's ancient serpent, the Devil and Satan) while during the day he presides over the judgment and punishment of Seth (here considered to be Apophis's equal) and his followers.

This is but an oversimplification of the complex development over time of the Seth-Isis-Horus and Apophis-Nut-Re myths as they relate to the *Books of the Heavens*. The evolution of these complicated changes in Egyptian mythology conforms with ancient Egypt's reluctance to discard any of its old myths when new ones came in vogue but rather at times incorporated new myths into the old ones. Segments of the Seth-Isis-Horus myth in Rev. 12:6 and Rev. 12:14 could in this manner have found their way into events normally associated with the Apophis-Nut-Re myth which parallels the bulk of Rev. 11:15-18 to Rev. 12:17.

The Cosmic Cycle:- Practically all modern students of the Book of Revelation consider Rev. 12 to be a stand-alone chapter dealing only with the woman in heaven. Such an assumption is considered inadvisable in a study such as this for it would close the door to consideration of broader and more meaningful parallels with Egyptian sources. For this reason, Rev. 12 was first examined in the context of its association with the latter part of Rev. 11 and the first part of Rev. 13. While the first part of Rev. 13 did not seem to be closely related to Rev. 12, the latter part of Rev. 11 seemed to be so. One of the more interesting aspects of the above findings is that the events which form the links between the *Book of Day* and the *Book of Night* parallel similar events at the end of Rev. 11 and the beginning of Rev. 12; they neatly conform with the natural flow of events between the two Egyptian books.

It is generally recognized that the *Books of the Heavens* form a single myth in which the story line cycles between the two; the end of the *Book of Day* feeds into the beginning of the *Book of Night* and the end of the *Book of Night* feeds into the beginning of the *Book of Day* and so on. This follows the normal day-to-night/night-to-day cycle experienced on earth. The near juxtaposition of the third last scene in Rev. 12:16, i.e., the swallowing of the water by the earth, and the scene referring to one standing on the sand in Rev. 12:17, so closely parallels the juxtaposition of the last scene in the *Book of Day* and the first in the *Book of Night* respectively that one readily sees the parallel with Rev. 11:15-18 (Figure 90). The complete story of the woman in the sky in the Book of Revelation, as seen from an Egyptian perspective, thus follows the cycle from Rev. 11:15 to Rev. 12:17 and then back to Rev. 11:15. When these observations are displayed graphically, as in Figure 90, they form an excellent picture of the cyclical series of scenes in Revelation which parallels a similar series in the Egyptian composition.

Of particular interest is how the falling stars and the flood waters relate, not only to the heralding of a new day, but the rebirth of creation itself. This will be discussed next.

Renewal of the Earth:- An interesting observation arises when the *Books of the Heavens* are examined in the context of both the Egyptian view of events at the end of time and the catastrophic events described in the Book of Revelation as discussed in Chapter 13, *Catastrophes*. As noted in that chapter, several important celestial events in Revelation's war in heaven parallel events associated with the volcanic

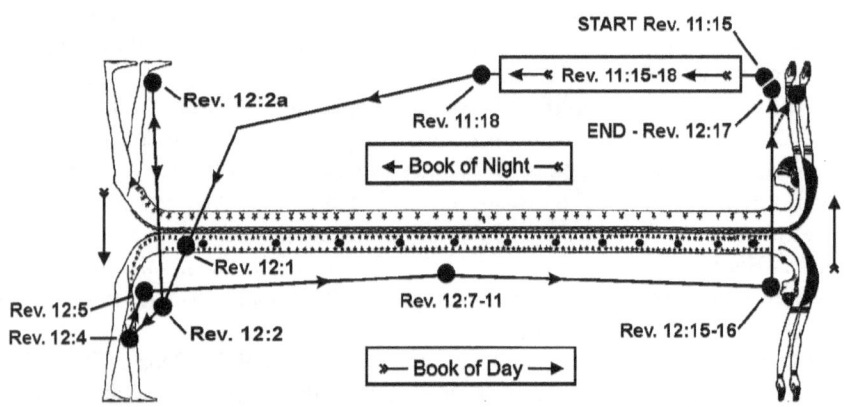

Figure 90. Locations in the *Books of the Heavens* of parallel scenes found in Rev. 11:15 to Rev. 12:16. Parallels in the upper right-hand corner and arrows within boxes indicate the direction of the flow of text and pictures in the two books. Note that, when looked at from an Egyptian perspective, the scenes in Rev. 11:15-18 (including point labeled START) naturally flow into Rev. 12:1 and Rev. 12 generally continues the counterclockwise flow from left to right. Finally, the scene in Rev. 12:17 (labeled END) feeds directly into Rev. 11:15 (labeled START). The cyclical nature of practically all the scenes in Rev. 11:15 to Rev. 12:17 thus parallels the cyclical nature of the scenes in the *Books of the Heavens*. (See text for explanation of line between Rev. 12:2a and Rev. 12:2.)

17. The Woman in the Sky 363

eruption in the Aegean Sea in c. 1628 BCE described in the *Book of the Dead* and other sources; these involve the falling of the stars from the sky (Rev. 12:4) and a great flood (Rev. 12:15-16). The falling of stars from the sky conforms with the blocking of light from the sun, moon and stars, a phenomenon caused by the plume of volcanic ash in the sky over the eastern and south-eastern Mediterranean Sea when the volcano erupted on the small island of Thera. And the great flood of water on the other hand, conforms with the unusually devastating tsunami which immediately followed the cataclysmic phase of the eruption and destroyed the low-lying coastal areas in the Nile Delta and the Levant. The story in Rev. 12 of the dragon pouring out water which is subsequently swallowed up by the earth could be a mythological allusion to flooding of the coastal areas and its ultimate absorption into the earth or drainage into the rivers from which it ultimately flowed back to the sea. If parts of the *Books of the Heavens* are indeed linked to these catastrophes, one would expect them to contain a reference to the event, or at least an allusion to one or more of the Egyptian sources described in Chapter 13, *Catastrophes*. As will be discussed next, this is indeed the case.

The opening scenes of the *Book of Night*, especially those in the second to fourth hours make reference to a goddess whose names recall a distant enemy which "no one can pass," who is "quick to kill" and "consumes with fire." The relevant texts are as follows:

> The Lady of Trembling, high of walls, the Chieftain, Mistress of Destruction who predicts the acts, who repulses the Furious One, who saves the robbed from the enemy who comes from afar, Mistress of Brilliance.[813] (First Gate (Second Hour)/second register)

> The majesty of this God sails and reaches the Second Gate [3rd Hour] She who lights the fire, She who consumes with pointed flames, without remainder, quick in killing. She from whom there is no protection, She by whom one cannot pass, She from whom there is no escape, the One who elevates her Lord, and unto the Third Hour, the One who slaughters the Souls.[814] (Second Gate (3rd Hour)/second register)

> ... the One with sharp knives, Mistress of the Two Lands, the One who chastises the enemies of Weary-Heart, who causes fear before the Sinless One, She who removes evil from the Lord of the Two Lands.[815] (Third Gate (4thHour)/Intro.)

These passages are remarkable in that most of the names found in them are similar or identical to some found in Chapter 146 of the *Book of the Dead*, the same chapter identified in *Catastrophes* as ancient Egypt's prime source of information on the eruption of Thera. A comparison of names from the two sources is provided in Table 17.2. It is obvious from the table that certain passages in the *Book of Night* allude to Egypt's mythologized accounts of the eruption of Thera described in *Catastrophes*. Recall that Chapter 146 contained numerous elements which included unusual darkness when the light of the sun and moon was blocked and most or all the stars disappeared from view. It was suggested that these events were very likely interpreted by the ancients as representing a great cosmic upheaval which affected both heaven and the earth, and on earth, signaled the end of the world (and its subsequent renewal). Similarly, Rev. 12 alludes to a war in heaven (Rev. 12:7) whose effects were felt on earth (Rev. 12:9).

Conclusion

Evidence presented here confirms and expands on the conclusion by Collins (1976) that significant parallels to elements in Rev. 12 can be found among ancient Egyptian myths. This evidence is summarized in Table 17:3 which gives a list of both previously recognized and some of the newly found parallel elements, and in Figure 90 which demonstrates how these elements follow the same sequence as elements in the Egyptian *Book of Day*. Additional newly-found parallels in the *Book of Night* (Rev. 11:15-18) conform with the cyclical nature of the *Book of Day* and the *Book of Night* (Figure 90) which make up the *Books of the Heavens*. The totality of these findings, including the composition dates of the Egyptian sources, and especially those findings related to events in the *Book of Day*, constitute an extremely good fit to Rev. 11:15-18 and the bulk of Rev. 12.

Table 17.2 Names of the goddesses found in both the *Book of Night* and the portals in Chapter 146 of the *Book of the Dead*. The similarities suggest that events in this part of the *Book of Night* are an allusion to events described in Chapter 146, events likely associated with the destruction, or cleansing, of the earth in preparation for its renewal at the beginning of the next great cosmic cycle.

Hour	Book of Night	Portal	Book of the Dead, Chapter 146
	—	2	Mistress of the Sky
2	Lady of Trembling	1	Mistress of trembling
2	who comes from afar	7	Far out of sight
2	Chieftain	1 9 9	Chieftainess Foremost One Mistress of Power
2	high of walls	1	lofty of enclosure wall
2	Mistress of Destruction	1	Mistress of Destruction
2	Mistress of Brilliance	12	Bright One
3	She who lights the fire	5 8 17	Fiery One, Misstress of Heat Heat of Flames, Sharp of Flames Mistress of Fire
3	She who consumes with pointed flames	5 8	One who Spears the Disaffected Heat of Flames, Sharp of Flames
3	quick in killing	8	who kills without warning
3	She from whom there is no protection	8	waves over the water in which none have power
3	She by whom one cannot pass	8	One whom no one passes
3	One who slaughters the Souls	16	Lady of Pestilence who casts away thousands of human souls.
3	One with sharp knives	4 11	Mighty of Knives She who bears knives
3	One who chastises the enemies of Weary-Heart	4	the one who smashes the enemies
3	She who removes evil from the Lord of the Two Lands	12	She who summons her Two Lands, who destroys those who come at dawn
4	Mistress of the Two Lands	1	Lady of the Two Lands
4	One who chastises the enemies	4	one who smashes the enemies
4	One who causes fear	8	One whom no one passes because of the fear of her pain
4	One who removes evil	3	one who refreshes every god

Table 17.3 Comparisons between (1) Rev. 12, (2) the Egyptian *Books of the Heavens* (plus segments of the Seth-Isis-Horus myth) and (3) the main themes of the Python-Leto-Apollo myth identified by Collins (1976, p. 66). This demonstrates the closer affinity of Rev. 12 to Egyptian myths than to the Greek myth. See Figure 90 for a pictorial presentation of the similarities between the sequence of parallel scenes in Rev. 11-12 and the *Books of the Heavens*. (Comments in square brackets by JHCP.)

Book of Revelation	Egyptian Sources N=*Book of Night*; D=*Book of Day*	Greek Python-Leto-Apollo myth (Collins' theme #)
Rev. 12:1 A woman in the sky	Nut, the sky-godess (D,N) and/or Isis myth	[Leto was is a sky-goddess]
Rev. 12:2 Woman in labor	Nut gives birth to Re (D)	2. Leto pregnant by Zeus [with twins, Apollo and Artemus]
Rev. 12:4a Dragon casts stars to earth	Stars flow down Nut's leg to earth (D)	—
Rev. 12:4b Dragon intends to kill child	Apophis, the primeval dragon, seeks to destroy child of Nut; D	1. Motivation of Python's attack (possession of the oracle) 3. Python pursues Leto with intent to kill her
Rev. 12:5a,c Child born and is caught (lifted) up to God and his throne	Re is born and flies up to heaven or is lifted up by Isis and Nephthys (D,N)	5. Birth of Apollo (and Artemis) [Apollo does not go heavenward]
Rev. 12:5b Kingship of child foretold	*Isis Myth*: Horus' kingship is foretold	—
Rev. 12:6 Woman flees to wilderness, where she is nourished by God	*Isis Myth*: Isis flees to wilderness where she is nourished by Re	[Hera pursues Leto before birth of twins]
Rev. 12:7a War in sky	Conflict with Apophis in the sky (D)	[Conflict on earth]
Rev. 12:7b Michael, leader of Army	"Michael" is a near homonym of the "Northern Leaders" of Re's army which fought in the sky (D)	[Lone Apollo fights Python]
Rev. 12:8-9 Dragon defeated by army	Apophis defeated by army (D)	6. Apollo defeats Python

17. The Woman in the Sky

Book of Revelation	Egyptian Sources N=*Book of Night*; D=*Book of Day*	Greek Python-Leto-Apollo myth (Collins' theme #)
Rev. 12:10-11 Arrival of the Kingdom of God/Christ	City of Re in sky with Osiris (God) and Horus (Christ) present (D)	—
Rev. 12:13 Dragon pursues woman	(Apophis: the perpetual enemy of Nut, D, N)	[Python pursues Leto and child at moment of Apollo's birth]
Rev. 12:14 Woman given wings and flies to wilderness.	*Isis Myth*: Isis given wings to fly to wilderness	4. By order of Zeus: North wind rescues Leto & Poseidon aids Leto
Rev. 12:16 Water is poured out against woman.	Water poured out upon sky, the personification of which is the sky-goddess, Nut (N)	—
Rev. 12:15-16 Pursuit of Woman	Apophis, enemy of Nut and her children; D, N	—
Rev. 12:17a War on woman's offspring	Apophis: the perpetual enemy of Nut's children, Osiris, Horus, Isis and Nephthys and their followers; D, N	—
Rev. 12:17b One standing on the sand by the sea	Horus (the king) stands on sand by the primeval waters (N)	—

Chapter 18. The Beasts of Rev. 13[816]

The 13th chapter of the Book of Revelation focuses on two creatures which it calls "beasts." The 1st beast comes out of the sea (Rev. 13:1-6) while the 2nd comes from the earth (Rev. 13:11-18). Both rule with the authority of the "dragon" (Rev. 13:2-4), a creature which, as discussed in Chapter 4, *Other Characters in Revelation*, parallels Egypt's Apophis, the primeval god of chaos.

It will be shown here that these beasts and events involving them parallel characters and events in the 4th Division of the *Amduat* (Figure 91). The first part (Rev. 13:1-6) deals with the beast from the sea and the set of parallel events found in the bottom register. The second set of parallels (Rev. 13:7-10) deals with the faithful and is confined to the middle register, while the third set (Rev. 13:11-18) is associated with the beast from the earth and is found in the upper register. The parallels flow from the bottom register, through the middle one, and conclude in the upper register, i.e., in the same order as in Revelation if one begins at the bottom rather than the top register. While the most obvious parallel is structural (both Revelation and the *Amduat* are divided into three parts), while the most important involves the 1st and 2nd beasts, the image of the 1st beast and the false prophet.

The structure of the 4th Division is different from any other in the *Amduat* in that a diagonal passageway zigzags from the upper left to the lower right corner (see Figure 91). The text tells us this entire area represents the *Imhat Necropolis* and forms the entrance to the large underground cavern of Sokaris (i.e., to the place represented in the next division (the 5th) which was discussed earlier in Chapter 15, *The Little Scroll,* in relation the events described in Rev. 10:1-7).

Traditional interpretations say it is in the depths of this cavern that the forces of evil conspire to impede or even stop the progress of the solar barque by reducing the flow of water in the primordial river. To circumvent this, the barque must crisscross through a maze of sandbanks and, for the first time in his travel through the Netherworld, must be towed over sand. Also unlike other divisions, the riverbanks are not lined with deities and spirits of the dead who shout praises as Re passes. Instead, the sun-god must pass serpents with legs or wings as well as what Budge (1934) calls "the monster two-headed and three-headed serpents which guarded the domain of Seker [Sokaris], and it is clear that both he and Osiris, are subordinate to Seker and his gods, who live on their sand, and are unseen and respond not to words of Afu

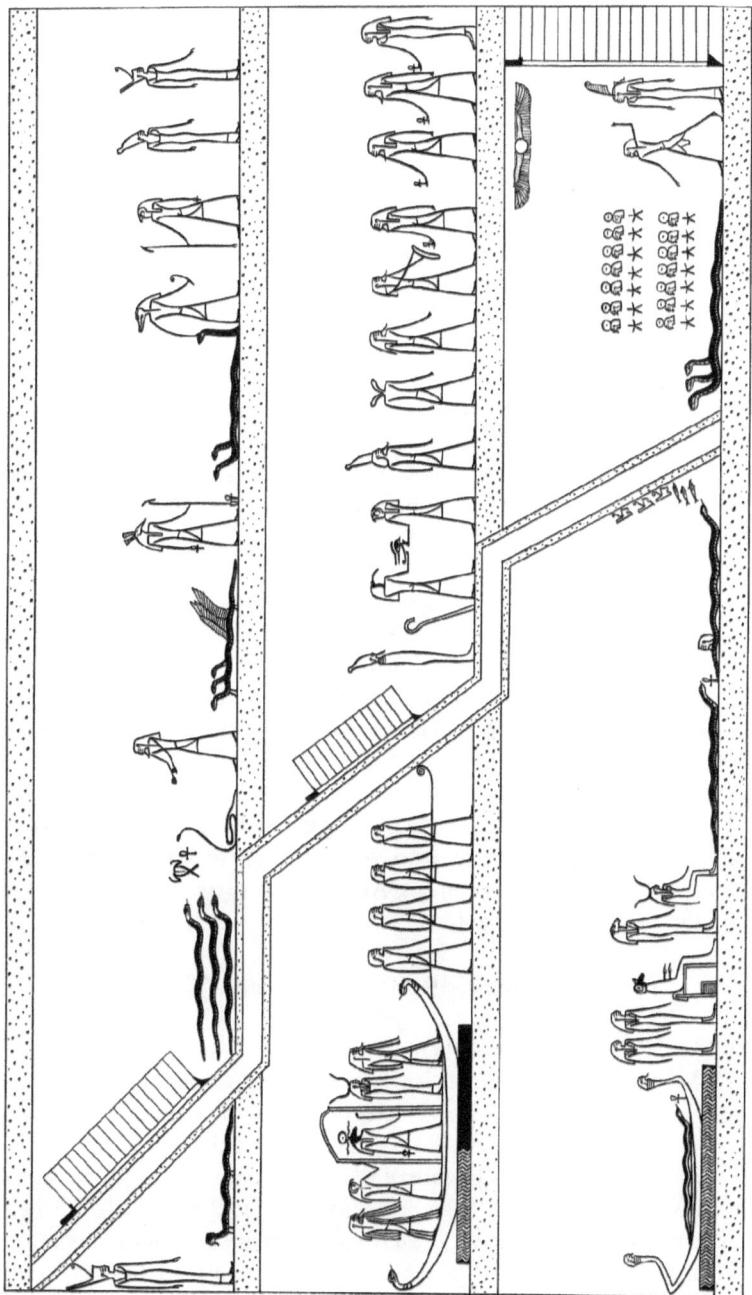

Figure 91. The 4th Division of the *Amduat* is replete with scenes parallel to those described in the 13th chapter of the Book of Revelation.

[the sun-god]."⁸¹⁷ Re's limited power and control in this area is expressed in the middle register with the granting of eternal life to only a portion of the residents of the place; these are his own faithful followers. There seems to be no clear understanding among Egyptologists as to the meanings of many of the details in this division. Thus, much of the following discussion uses Rev. 13 as a tentative basis for interpretation of its elements and scenes. This approach clearly illustrates the parallel nature of both the division's structure and its scenes.

Rev. 13 is one of the most difficult chapters in the Book of Revelation – and it is also the most difficult to understand from an Egyptian perspective. The difficulties in Revelation arise primarily from the introduction of three enigmatic characters which it associates with "beasts." The first is the "1st beast," the second is the "2nd beast" and the third is called "the image of the 1st beast made by the 2nd beast" which the subjects of the 2nd beast are to worship or be slain. These characters are situated in a complex mix of images and events. Because of its complexity, and to facilitate a thorough understanding of the many Egyptian parallels which have been found, there is perhaps an overly frequent use of explanatory notes (usually in brackets) included with most of the references to different beasts and other characters. Although this approach results in a more cumbersome reading experience, it should greatly reduce the chances of misunderstanding the arguments and conclusions presented.

Before going into details of the events outlined in Rev. 13, it is important to realize that these events all occur under the general direction of the dragon who appoints the 1st beast who then rules over the 2nd beast who then makes an image of the 1st beast for the people of the land to worship. In Rev. 13:2 we read that the 1st beast comes out of the water under the authority of the dragon; Revelation's dragon, of course, parallels Satan the devil. The verse says, "And to it [the 1st beast] the dragon gave his power and his throne and great authority" – a very clear statement that almost all the characters and events in Rev. 13 are controlled by the dragon.

The lower register of the 4th Division of the Amduat begins in basically the same manner as Rev. 13 except that there is no clear reference to Apophis. Nevertheless, that Apophis plays important roles in the events of this division will become amply clear during the course of this chapter.

The First Beast:- from the Sea (Rev. 13:1-8)

Arrival of the 1st Beast (Rev. 13:1)

Rev. 13:1-4 says that the 1st beast rises "out of the sea" and gets its authority from "the dragon" (Egypt's Apophis; see Chapter 4, *Other Characters in Revelation*). Similarly, the 4th Division begins with a scene found at the far left of the bottom register (Figure 92). It contains a picture of a serpent riding in a boat floating on the symbol for a body of water (▭)⁸¹⁸ – an obvious parallel to Revelation's link between the 1st beast and the sea. Also, the text above the serpent says that it "sets forth," a phrase which, when combined with the image of it sailing on the sea, conforms reasonably well with Revelation's beast actively *"rising* out of the sea."

The idea of the beast "rising out of the sea" implies motion, a notion consistent with the label over the serpent. The hieroglyphic text above the boat says, *ncw ḥd wbn dḫ* (Λ 〰〰 ⌣@ꜥ 𓏺𓂋●).⁸¹⁹ Piankoff translates this as "Moving Radiance"⁸²⁰ but does not provide the basis of his translation. Rev. 13:1, on the other hand, provides us with a basis for an alternative translation of the original text, as follows: The Λ symbol denotes "movement"[821] and 〰〰 ⌣@, *ncw*, means "serpent";[822] 𓏺 has the phonetic value of *ḥḏ*[823] which can mean, "set forth at dawn";[824] and 𓏺 is a determinative of "sunshine";[825] 𓂋● is pronounced *dḫ* and means, "pupil of the eye,"[826] which in the context of 𓏺, would mean the eye of Re, i.e., the sun, and is therefore related to sunshine or simply daylight. This text, *ncw ḥd wbn dḫ*, may thus, in the context of Rev. 13:1 be translated as, "the serpent sets forth at the dawn's light." The first part, "the serpent sets forth," agrees quite well with the idea of motion referred to in Revelation's description of a beast "rising out of the sea" in much the same way as the sun may appear to be rising out the sea at dawn.

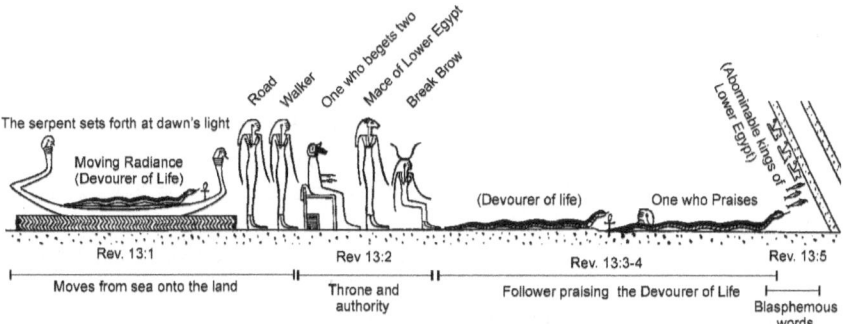

Figure 92. Egyptian parallels to the arrival of the 1ˢᵗ beast (the serpent in the boat on the far left) from the sea (▬), his subsequent enthronement (𓉼), demonic activities (destruction of life, ☥), and blasphemous words (⬅⬅⬅ ⸖⸖⸖) spoken of in Rev. 13:1-8. (AM4.3.1-7).

The great authority of the serpent in the boat is also demonstrated in this figure; the boat's bow and stern form bearded human heads (𓁷), symbols denoting authority which are frequently used as ideographs in words such as "head," "chief," or "first."[827] This, of course, parallels the "great authority" of the 1ˢᵗ beast mentioned in Rev. 13:2. Moreover, the serpent's nature is signified by the portrayal of it attacking an *ankh* symbol ☥, the symbol of life itself. We may infer from this arrangement of images that this serpent is a destroyer of life, or perhaps more appropriately, a "Devourer of Life"; in effect, it has control over life and death. This, of course, conforms with the beast's power to declare war as mentioned in Rev. 13:7 – "it was allowed to make war on the saints."

The next picture in this part of the lower register takes us from the sea to the land. This is at first indicated by the two goddesses who stand in front of the serpent's boat. Their names clearly indicate they are on land; the first is called "Road" while the second is called "Walker."[828] When this information is considered in the light of the serpent, we can envisage the serpent rising from the sea and walking on a road, i.e., rising from the sea and on to the land – as is clearly implied in the events which follow Rev. 13:1.

The beast's power and war (Rev. 13:2,7)

The part of the lower register from the two standing goddesses to the diagonal passageway on the right, contains a number of images consistent with events associated with Revelation's 1st beast. Rev. 13:2 says that "to it [the 1st beast] the dragon [Egypt's Apophis] gave his power and his throne and great authority." Reference to the serpent's authority is discussed in the previous section in relation to the heads at the stern and bow of his boat. The three figures in front of the two standing goddesses provide a graphic reference to a throne and give us some idea of the nature of the rule of the one seated on it, as follows.

The name of the baboon-headed figure on the throne (𓊁) is revealing. His name, *Bnny*, is not translated by Piankoff although it's English translation conforms with the action of the 1st beast. *Bnn* means "begets"[829] and *Bnny* ends with a *y* which identifies it as the dual form of *Bnn*. *Bnny* may therefore be translated as "One who begets *two*." In the context of Rev. 13, this name is consistent with the concept in Rev. 13 that the 1st beast gives his power to a 2nd beast who makes – or "begets" – an "image of the 1st beast" to be worshiped by the people.

In a very loose way, the word *bnn* may also be viewed as a simple mnemonic referring to certain activities of the one on the throne. For example, another word for *bnn*, (to beget) is *iri*."[830] It so happens that *iri* is also used to describe a host of situations pertaining to authoritative activities by a reigning person. For example, it can mean "exercise an office" or "make decrees or laws" as well as "act as" or "in the capacity of (an official)," or even "appoint officials."[831] The word is also used to express ideas such as "act" or "take action"[832] and even to "inflict (a wound)."[833] Note that all these associations conform with authority to govern implied by the throne on which *Bnny* sits.

Revelation also says that the beast made war. Rev. 13:7 says, "it was allowed to make war on the saints and to conquer them." Egyptian parallels to such a warlike ruler are also present in this part of the Amduat. This is evident in the names of the next two figures, the first of which is a lion-headed, standing goddess and the second a goddess with horns on her head and sitting on an invisible throne. The name of the lion-headed goddess is *Henget*,[834] which can be translated as "Mace of lower heaven."[a] The mace, of course, implies the power and authority of the one on the throne. Next, the name of the seated goddess can be translated as "Break Brow,"[b] a name which suggests a merciless rule, a feature of the rule of Revelation's 2nd beast, the effective servant of the 1st beast and one who is to later lead the people to worship the 1st beast (Rev. 8, 15).

---

[a] The Egyptian text, 𓌉𓏺𓏺𓂻, can be written as *ḥḏ nnt* where *ḥḏ* means "mace" (Faulkner, p. 181) and *nnt* "lower heaven" (Faulkner, p. 134). Hence, "Mace of Lower Heaven."

[b] The Egyptian text, 𓏴𓏺𓂻, begins with 𓏴, a determinative for "break" (Gardiner, p. 538) and ends with the word *wpt*, meaning "horn," "top of the head" or "brow" (Faulkner, p. 59). Piankoff (p. 259) translates this as "She who binds the Horns." In the context of the translation of the name of the goddess behind her, it seems more appropriate to translate the name as "Break Brow" or "She who breaks the brow."

Another interesting feature of the baboon-headed god is the form of his hands. While versions of the *Amduat* use the hand symbol we normally find at the end of the bent-arm symbol, ▬, as in Figure 92, others, such as the version found in the tomb of Ramesses VI, use the closed fist symbol, ▬. The latter is used as the determinative in words such as "to grasp" (*khefa*) and "to seize" (*amem*),[835] concepts which could indicate that the throne depicted in Figure 92 has been illegally taken. This will be discussed latter and shown to parallel historical events during Egypt's 2nd Intermediate Period.

It is apparent from the foregoing paragraphs that the serpentine figure in the boat and the one the throne in the lower register conforms with the 1st beast of Rev. 13. Not only does his entrance from the sea conform with that of the 1st beast but his ruling authority on a throne is also made clear.

Blasphemous words of the 1st beast (Rev. 13:5)

Rev. 13:5 says that the "beast was given a mouth uttering haughty and blasphemous words." This statement conforms with elements associated with the two-headed serpent called "The One who Praises"[836] just to the left of the v-shaped corner of the diagonal passageway in Figure 92. Its human head indicates it has a position of authority so that this serpent could actually be a second manifestation of the serpent on the boat at the far left, i.e., the 1st beast. Thus, anything its says can be construed as the words of the 1st beast.

Immediately in front of the mouth of the "One who Praises" are six hieroglyphic symbols indicating a phrase which is not translated by Piankoff (1994). It is written as ◄ ◄ ◄ ⴹ ⴹ ⴹ and the concept of at least the first three symbols conform with Rev. 13:5 which says that "the beast was given a mouth uttering haughty and blasphemous words." The fish hieroglyph, ◄, is typically used as the determinative in words such as *bw* or *bwt* meaning "detest, abominate" or "abomination"[837] (for example, *bwytyw*, ⌡▮▮▮◄▬ means "those who are abominated").[838] We may therefore conclude that the use of three fish (◄ ◄ ◄) suggests spoken phrases containing many "many abominations." The next three symbols, crowns of Lower Egypt (ⴹ ⴹ ⴹ), are a little more difficult to relate to the situation given in Revelation but it is clear that they suggest the abominable phrases are associated with the kings (or a king) of Lower Egypt who, as we will see later, parallel the idea of the Revelation's 2nd beast (this will be discussed later in the section on the 2nd beast and to a greater extent in the *Discussion* part of this chapter). This group of hieroglyphs suggesting abominable words from the mouth of the serpent – which seems to parallel Revelation's 1st beast – thus conforms with Rev. 13:5 which says that "the beast was given a mouth uttering haughty and blasphemous words."

Moreover, the idea that ⴹ ⴹ ⴹ may indicate a group of abominable kings in Lower Egypt conforms with Rev. 13:1 which indicates that Revelation's 1st beast is somehow related to a group of kings. This verse tells us that the 1st beast had "ten horns and seven heads, with ten diadems upon its horns and a blasphemous name upon its heads." This leads us to the possibility that the expression ◄ ◄ ◄ ⴹ ⴹ ⴹ may also be interpreted to mean something like "abominations on the heads of the kings of Lower Egypt," an expression conforming with the last part of Rev. 13:1. This would be especially true for Lower Egypt if it was related to a time when a group of non-native kings who ruled in Lower Egypt were considered to blaspheme Re in the sense that they each claimed to be, like most native kings of Egypt, the "son of Re." For not-Egyptians to wear the crown of Lower Egypt was an abomination to many Egyptians in Upper Egypt, and to a lesser extent, Lower Egypt. This topic will be elaborated on and discussed in some detail in the *Discussion* part of this chapter.

The Forty-two Month Reign (Rev. 13:5-6)

We now switch our attention to the picture to the immediate right of the sloping passageway in the lower register and to the part of Rev. 13:5 which says that the beast was "allowed to exercise authority for forty-two months." As will be shown next, this brief statement conforms with the scene to the immediate right of that shown in Figure 92 and enlarged in Figure 93.

The predominant action in this scene involves a man standing with legs apart and one arm held high in a threatening gesture. This stance is typical of that used in head-smiting scenes by pharaohs from the earliest dynasties and was later displayed as an expression of the king's power within his kingdom and his authority over the nations.[839] In this particular case, however, the domineering figure does not wear a crown so that his relationship to royalty, if any, is unclear; the text refers to him as "The One who is in Heaven" and the winged disk of

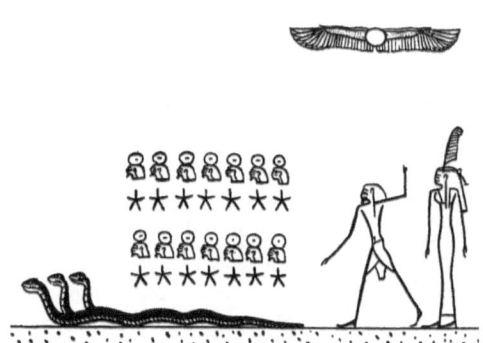

Figure 93. Scene showing array of symbols (☉, 🯅, ★) which together parallel the 42 time periods in Rev. 13:5 (which says that the 1ˢᵗ beast is allowed to exercise authority over the saints for 42 months). (AM4.3.7-10)

the young sun-god (here called, "Khepri") hovers in the sky above him. The text underneath the disk says, "He goes to rest in his forms, as *He of the Dappled Plumage*,"[840] a title typically used for the god Horus. In front of him, a three-headed serpent (suggesting many individuals) lies flat on the ground in a position indicative of submission. On the far right of the figure is the goddess *Maat* wearing her emblem, the feather of truth (↑); her presence at the extreme end of the register seems to emphasize the validity of the events depicted in this register – or at least, this scene..

The next significant aspect of Figure 93 is the group of the 14 heads (🯅), 14 solar disks (☉) and 14 stars (★). When added together, we have the number 42, the same number of months referred to in Rev. 13:5. We should therefore enquire if this number can be rationalized with the 42 month period of authoritative rule described in Rev. 13:5. A brief examination of the three symbols (☉, ★, 🯅) is thus warranted.

The solar disk (☉) is, among other things, an ideograph or determinative used in words for "period of time, or time in the general"[841] so that it can represent periods of time. The stars, can also denote time periods,[842] thus emphasizing this aspect of the scene. And finally, as noted above, head symbols denote the top of a command structure and are used in words such as "chief" or "first." We therefore find that this set of 42 symbols emphasizes time, and especially the idea of 42 periods involving a leader of a group of people represented here as the three-headed serpent. Although there seems to be no explicit reference to the 42 periods being months, this scene nevertheless parallels 42 periods of authoritative rule, as described in Rev. 13:5, especially when the domineering stance of the "The One who is in Heaven" is taken into consideration. We may, in fact, be reasonably certain that the periods alluded to here are either months or years, the only divisions of time which would make sense in the context of this scene.

The proximity of the symbols for 42 periods to those for blasphemous words (they lie opposite one another on opposing sides of the slanting passage) conforms with the adjacency of parallel elements in the same short verse in Revelation – Rev. 13:5.

Not all versions of the *Amduat* contain the same arrangement of the 42 symbols shown in Figure 93, however; the version in the tomb of Seti I, for example, contains fourteen sets of two heads with disks over them, and to these, stars are added to three.[843] But even in this version, 42 periods can still be accounted for by multiplying 14 by 3. This example shows that the parallel nature of Revelation's 42 month period can be readily identified in other versions of the *Amduat* which use a different set of symbols to express the same period.

Finally, and in addition to the above, the fourteen heads crowned with solar disks may be interpreted to mean a group, such as a dynasty, of kings.

•••

The above interpretation of texts and symbolism found in the lower register may be summarized as follows: The serpent (king) in the boat sails from the sea to the shore, seizes the throne, rules ruthlessly with great power and authority for 42 months or years and is somehow connected to abominable reputations of certain kings of Lower Egypt. This summary conforms with Rev. 13:1-6 where the author describes a beast with many crowns rising out of the sea who takes over the throne for 42 months with power and great authority and speaks with blasphemous words.

Egypt's parallel to Revelation's 1st beast

In this section we examine evidence of an Egyptian parallel to Revelation's 1st beast. As we shall see, several texts examined in this study suggest a likely Egyptian candidate for a parallel. A good starting point to discuss this is our knowledge of the god Apophis, the ancient serpent which, as stated in Chapter 4, *Other Characters in Revelation* parallels Revelation's "dragon," the character which Rev. 13:2 identifies as the source of the 1st beast's "power, throne, and great authority." This close association of the 1st beast with Apophis immediately brings to mind an Egyptian god which, like Apophis, was at certain times and places considered to be a god of evil. Indeed, at times he was even equated with or confused with Apophis. He name is Seth.

Apophis and Seth:- Seth had a distinctly dualistic nature. In Egypt's early days he was considered a benevolent god who defended the sun-god during his journey through the primordial river. Kings often referred to themselves as "beloved of Seth." But Seth was also regarded as lord of the desert and an opponent of Osiris. The cruel sea was also thought to be one of Seth's manifestations.[844] And Seth was responsible for murdering Osiris, hacking up his body and distributing the parts throughout Egypt. An ensuing tribunal condemned him to "dominion over his own proper region, the barren deserts and the foreign countries beyond the limits of the Creation, where he can reign freely."[845] Seth thus left the heavenly realm with its primordial river and came to earth, an observation which, in addition to the above reasons, conforms with Rev. 13:1 which describes a "beast rising out of the sea."[a]

Seth was a popular, benevolent deity before Osirian beliefs became dominant and especially prior to the arrival of the Hyksos to the Delta region. His popularity declined thereafter although it later resurfaced during the 19th and 20th Dynasties when he became important as the patron deity of the Ramesside kings. Nevertheless, the worship of Seth declined after the 20th Dynasty "and his role as god of the desert and foreign lands led to his association in the later periods with Egypt's hated foreign overlords. By the Twenty-fifth Dynasty, veneration of Seth had virtually ended."[846] Lurker (1980) points out that, "During the time of foreign rule, especially after the Assyrian invasion, he [Seth] ... became a national enemy and a figure symbolic of all evil."[847] As such, Seth was often confused with – even equated with – Apophis, the primeval serpent of evil[848] and Revelation's Satan, the devil.

Seth's mortal wound:- A more direct line of evidence supporting the idea of a parallel between Egypt's Seth and Revelation's 1st beast is based on Rev. 13:3 where we find the extraordinary statement that "One of its heads seemed to have a mortal wound, but its mortal wound was healed." This reference corresponds to events described in the well-known, very ancient Egyptian *Legend of Horus of Beḥuṭ-t and the Winged Disk* the hieroglyphic text of which was found carved on the stone walls of the temple of Horus of Edfû in Upper Egypt.[849] The use of stone to tell the story attests to its importance and ensured that it remained unchanged through Egypt's many dynasties and generations. The legend begins with Horus of Edfû and the sun-god, Re-Ḥarakhti (when he lived on earth), sailing downstream to fight the enemies of Re who "began to talk sedition (or conspire) against their lord"[850] and are later described as even "overthrowing the earth." Horus wages war against Seth and his followers and kills over 600 of them before reaching the Delta where he kills nearly 400 more. Seth is ultimately slain but miraculously, returns to once again oppose Horus and Re. Budge's (1934) translation provides us with the following details:

> Set [Seth] rose up and came forth raging horribly, and shouted out curses and revilings because of the deeds which Horus of Beḥuṭ-t had done whilst he was in the act of slaying him . ... And Horus of Beḥuṭ-t waged war against the Enemy for a long time. ... [Then] Horus of Beḥuṭ-t came back and brought the enemy in fetters. His spear was in his neck ... he took him before his father [Rā] ... . And Rā said unto Thoth, 'Let the enemies and Set be delivered over to Isis and her son Horus, so that they may work all their hearts' desires upon them'. ... [Then] *Horus, the son of Isis, cut off the head of the Enemy (Set)*' and the heads of his followers in the presence of his father Rā, and the Great Company of the Gods.[851]

---

[a] It is noteworthy that during the 2nd Intermediate Period a corrupted version of Seth was a counterpart of the Asiatic god Baal whom the Hyksos invaders worshiped. This will be discussed later.

And just as the 1st beast in Rev. 13:3 recovers from his mortal wound to the head, Seth is revived and returns to once again threaten the sun-god:

> Set took upon himself the form of a hissing serpent, and he entered into the earth at this place without being seen. Rā said, 'Set hath taken upon himself the form of a hissing serpent. Let Horus, the son of Isis, in the form of a hawk-headed staff, set himself over the place where he is so that he may never be able to come forth again."[852]

This is an especially striking parallel between the 1st beast of Rev. 13 and the Egyptian god Seth.

Seth as a pig:- Another somewhat less conspicuous piece of evidence for a parallel between the two is found in the hieroglyphics used to compose the names of the two goddesses standing in front of the boat in Figure 92. As noted, their names are "The Road" and "The Walker." Each of these names ends with a bird's claw phonogram, ⊥, $š_3$. It so happens that the $š_3$ sound is a homophone for "pig,"[a, 853] an animal which from time to time was used as a symbol of the god Seth. Lurker (1980) tells us that

> The ancient Egyptians regarded the pig as unclean as was later the case under Judaism and Islam. It was seen as the familiar of the evil god Seth. In the Book of the Dead (Chap. 112) the text states that Seth attacked the god Horus 'under the disguise of a black boar' and injured his eye or, according to another version, swallowed it. In the reliefs in the temple of Edfu Horus hunted Seth who was in the form of a pig. In the 'Book of Gates' the judgment scene [see Figure 109] shows a ship above the steps leading up to Osiris in which a monkey is driving a pig before it as a symbol of evil.[854]

For these reason, it is reasonable to assume that the names of the two figures, "The Road" and "The Walker," were meant refer to both the serpent in the boat and the baboon-headed god as Seth (the pig) and Egypt's parallel to Revelation's 1st beast.

Additional evidence:- Additional evidence for the parallel between Seth and the 1st beast will be discussed later in this chapter in the section on *The Beast from the Earth* where it will be shown that several attributes of the 1st beast described in Rev. 13:11-18 parallel those of Seth. The same section will discuss Seth's identification with the number, "666" (the now infamous "mark of the beast" of Rev. 13:18).

Fate of the Faithful (Rev. 13:7-10)

The central portion of Rev. 13 deals with the fate of those individuals who choose whether or not to follow the 1st beast. We first read in Rev. 13:7 that the beast was allowed to make war on the saints and to conquer them. Rev. 13:8 then divides the conquered troops into two groups – the followers of the Lamb and the followers of the beast – such that each follower of the beast is one *"whose name has not been written before the foundation of the world in the book of life of the Lamb."* The

---

[a] It is also interesting to note that $š_3$ is also a homophone for words such as "ordain, predestine and assign," words which have meaning in the context of the identification, separation and fate of followers of the beast in Rev. 13:15.

saints are encouraged to endure and have faith and "If any one is to be taken captive, to captivity he goes; if any one slays with the sword, with the sword must he be slain" (Rev. 13:10). Taken together, these verses imply that anyone captured or killed in the war against the beast is guaranteed the gift of eternal life if their names are written in the "Book of Life."

Perhaps the most prominent aspect of Rev. 13:7-10 is its sudden switch away from the forgoing characteristics of the 1st beast and his rise to power to an entirely different point of view – that of the Lamb and the ultimate fate of his followers (as opposed to those who did not follow him). We find this same shift in point of view when we go from the lower register of the 4th Division of the Amduat to the middle register, the realm of the sun-god. Here, to the left of the sloping corridor, we see the juvenile from of Re (his lamb form) standing in his barque as he passes through this part of the Netherworld (Figure 91). And to the immediate right of the corridor, we see Osiris who is ruler of the land of the dead (the Netherworld). In front of Osiris is a scene which, remarkably, corresponds to that outlined in Rev. 13:7-10 (Figure 94).

Details in Rev. 13:7-10 provide us with the basis for a comparison with the right side of the middle register (Figure 94). On the far left of this figure Osiris watches over events while a leaning crook (?) stands before him. The crook is typically used as a scepter by Egyptian gods and is the determinative or ideograph in words related to the "rule"[855] of kings and gods. Its leaning position in this figure likely signifies a reduction of his authority in this part of the Netherworld,[a] the region over which the

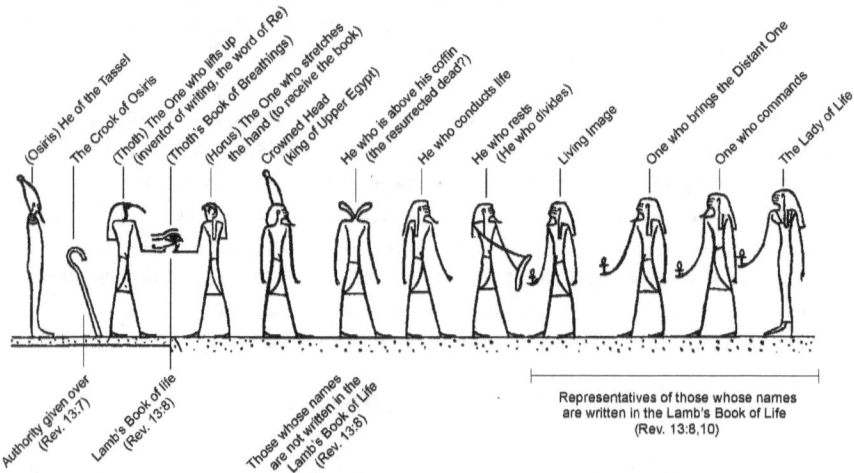

Figure 94. Events which parallel those in Rev. 13:7-10. Near the far left, the leaning crook signifies a reduction of Osiris's authority (vs. 7) in this part of the Netherworld. Meanwhile, the ibis-headed Thoth presents Horus with knowledge (vs. 8) of all who are to receive the gift of life (represented by the four deities on the right) for their faithfulness in the fight against Seth and his followers (vss. 8,10). (AM4.2.5-10)

---

[a] This same interpretation of the leaning crook is applied to the two leaning crooks in the picture of the ten kings in the upper register of the 9th Division of the *Book of Gates* (Figure 115); see the discussion on Rev. 17:12-13 in Chapter 23, *The Harlot and the Kings*.

god Sokaris presides. Indeed, Budge (1904) points out that, unlike most other areas in the Netherworld,

> Here there is no river with banks lined with gods and the souls of the dead, and here there are no fields to be distributed by Rā among the faithful followers of himself and Osiris; indeed there are so few beings to render him service that he is obliged to betake himself to another kind of boat, and the god of day is compelled to glide through the passages of the dark and gloomy land almost without a following of gods."[856]

This reduction in power thus parallels that described in Rev. 13:7-8 where we read that, "it [the 1st beast, Seth] was allowed to make war on the saints and to conquer them. *And authority was given it over every tribe and people and tongue and nation*, and all who dwell on earth [= the Netherworld in the sense used in the *Amduat*] will worship it." This peculiar situation in the Book of Revelation thus parallels a similar account in the Egyptian *Amduat*.

The Book of Life:- In front of the crook and facing away from it is the ibis-headed god Thoth, who is here called "The One who lifts up" and he passes a *wedjat*-eye (𓂀) to the falcon-headed god, Horus, called "The One who stretches out the hand."[857] The exact significance of the wedjat-eye in this setting is not readily apparent but is, nevertheless, generally understandable. W*edjat*-eyes were symbolic of the sun and moon; the right eye (𓂀) represented the sun and the left (𓂁) the moon. Note that the one portrayed in Figure 94 is the right eye and hence, the sun – the symbol of Re (Revelation's Lamb). This picture thus seems to show Thoth presenting to Horus something to do with the sun-god. Now since Thoth was believed to have been the inventor of writing and he is obviously presenting something physical to Horus, we may assume that Thoth is presenting Horus with a composition having something to do with Re, i.e., Revelation's Lamb.

Since a book, "the book of life of the Lamb," is mentioned in this part of Rev. 13:8-10, we should look more closely at some of the attributes of Thoth to determine the extent to which they conform with the overall sense of this part of Revelation. As the inventor of writing and the official recorder at the judgment of the dead by Osiris, Thoth would be the obvious deity to be in charge of writing down the names of the faithful in a book which, like that in Rev. 13:8, was "written before the foundation of the world." Since Thoth was one of the primeval gods, he could indeed be the author of such a book. Budge (1904) tells us that,

> In the late work called the "Book of Breathings" it is said, "Thoth, the most mighty god, the lord of Knemennu, cometh to thee, and *he writeth for thee the 'Book of Breathings'* with his own fingers. *Thus thy soul shall breathe for ever and ever*,' and thy form shall be endowed with life upon earth."[858]

Breathing is, of course, universally equated with life and all of Thoth's activities related to the giving of life were either directed by Re or were at times simply a manifestation of Re's wishes. It is therefore apparent that *Thoth's Book of Breathings* represents a strong parallel to "the book of life of the Lamb" referred to in Rev. 13:8. Furthermore, Egyptians believed that a person could live in the hereafter as long as his name was recorded somewhere. The contents of *Thoth's Book of Breathings* would obviously not have fulfilled its purpose if it did not contain the names of all those who were to "breathe for ever and ever," as stated in Rev. 13:8 where, if a person's name is found in the Book of Life, he or she will live forever.

But the *wedjat*-eye had yet another significance to the Egyptians, one which has further relevance to our discussion of Rev. 13. Wilkinson (1992) provides us with the following pertinent information:

> Despite the uncertainties surrounding the origin and significance of the sacred eye symbol, its use in Egyptian iconography is widespread and relatively clear. Above all, the eye was a *protective device*,' and this is seen in the countless representations of the *wedjat* which are found in amulets and jewelry and on the protective plaques which were placed over the embalming incision on mummies.[859]

The picture of Horus presenting the wedjat-eye in Figure 94 may therefore also represent the presentation of the gift of *protection* – including protection against death in the hereafter to the followers of the sun-god depicted on the far right of the figure. Such a gift would therefore emphasize the parallel pointed out above that eternal life is promised in Thoth's *Book of Breathings*. When combined with the earlier observation that Osiris' authority is diminished in this part of the *Amduat*, the assurance that the names of his followers were included in his *Book of Breathings* would be a logical safeguard. This interpretation thus parallels the message implied in Rev. 13:7-8 involving the *preservation* of the saints.

Separation of the faithful:- Two other relevant references to eternal life appear in this register. The first is found in the pictures of four deities on the far right of Figure 94; each holds the symbol of life (☥), suggesting they are the recipients of "eternal, existence,"[860] i.e., eternal life. The second may be inferred in the name of the bearded deity standing behind the one carrying a slightly curved object in the figure; he is appropriately called, "He who conducts Life,"[861] a possible reference to the conveying of eternal life to the four on the far right of the figure.

The name of the bearded deity carrying the curved object is translated by Piankoff (1954) as "He who Rests."[862] But his function in the scene may be deduced as "one who divides," a phrase conforming with the idea in Rev. 13:8 of the separation of the faithful from the unfaithful. This suggestion is based on the curved object which, in the tomb of Ramesses VI is c-shaped (see Figure 95) and bears a distinct similarity to the Egyptian ⊏ hieroglyph without its vertical line. That this object is indeed a representation of the ⊏ symbol is demonstrated in the tomb version where the bearer's entire left arm seems to be purposefully held straight against the back of the object to form the vertical stroke of the symbol.[863] Gardiner (1927) says the ⊏ symbol is the determinative of words such as "dam off," "restrain," or "split"[864] while Budge (1920) suggests it signifies "divide" or "cut."[865] The fact that this symbol is held out toward the four deities carrying the ☥ signs may therefore be interpreted to mean they are "divided," or separated, from those who do not receive the gift of life – as in Rev. 13:8.

By combining the above observations it is possible to interpret the presentation of *The Book of Breathings* to Horus, the son of Re, as a book listing the faithful followers of Osiris who are to receive the gift of eternal life by virtue of their

Figure 95. Symbolic separation of the saints from the followers of the 1st Beast in Rev. 13:7-10. The rounded, c-shaped object leaning against the straight left arm of its carrier conforms with an Egyptian hieroglyphic indicating "division" (⊂). (AM4.2.8-9).

separation from the enemies of Osiris. Osiris is, of course, the physical or bodily form of the sun-god (while Re is his spiritual aspect so that together they are called Osiris-Re). The *Book of Breathing* is thus, in effect, as much a part of Osiris as it is of Re, Revelation's Lamb, or as Revelation puts it, the Lamb's book of life.

(The next two verses, Rev. 13:9-10, will be examined later in the *Discussion* part of this chapter; meanwhile, we will proceed with the remaining verses in Rev. 13.)

The Second Beast:- from the Earth (Rev. 13:11-18)

The last eight verses of Rev. 13 deal with a 2nd beast which is said to rise out of the earth rather than the sea. Rev. 13:12 says it has all the authority of the 1st beast "in its presence." The phrase, "in its presence," unambiguously indicates it coexisted with the 1st beast, a fact which is relevant to our identification of the 2nd beast.

One of the more interesting aspects of this part of Revelation, however, is the emphasis placed on the 2nd beast making of an image of the 1st beast for people to worship and all who refuse to worship this image are to be killed (Rev. 13:14-15). Everyone else is to be branded with the mark, or name, of the 1st beast without which they can neither buy nor sell (Rev. 13:16-18). We are also told that the 2nd beast "works great signs, even making fire come down from heaven to earth in the sight of men" (Rev. 13:13). Parallels to all these events are present in the upper register of the 4th Division (Figure 96) and will be discussed next in the same order as they appear in Revelation.

Egypt's parallel to Revelation's 2nd beast (Rev. 13:11)

Revelation's 2nd beast is introduced in Rev. 13:11. The author writes, "Then I saw another beast which rose out of the earth." In Egyptian illustrations, the earth, or ground on which people stand is usually depicted as a stippled area; in texts, it is often referred to as "sand." It is therefore significant that the introductory text of the upper register of the 4th Division makes a specific reference to sand and even identifies the earthly location of the events it portrays. It describes the area as "The mysterious ways of Ro-Setau, the sacred roads of the Imhat Necropolis, the hidden gates which are in the earth of Sokaris, He on His Sand."[866] This reference to sand conforms with the scene on the far left of the upper register (Figure 96 and Figure 97) where we see a human-headed, four-legged serpent standing in the v-shaped corner of sand (the stippled area of the figure) to the immediate left of the sloping corridor. Note that the serpent's legs resemble the Λ hieroglyph typically used as a determinative for "movement" in words such as "go" (*šm*, 🞲 𝅃 Λ), "approach" (*tkn* – ⬬ ⬬ ⬞⬞⬞ Λ) and "hasten" (*ḥ₃ḥ*, 𝅃 𝅃 • Λ).[867] We may therefore conclude that the serpent is "moving" on the sand, i.e., on the earth, just as we may also infer about the beast in Rev. 13:11 which rises out of the earth. Furthermore, note the name of the serpent's guardian in Figure 97 – "She who guards the *Rising One*." This name, and the sand below and behind the serpent, therefore also conforms with the statement in Rev. 13:11 which tells us that the 2nd beast "*rose* out of the earth."

The Egyptian text describes the serpent as "The One of the Head," suggesting it exercises authority, an interpretation in keeping with the human-headed (◉) aspect of the serpent.[868] Meanwhile, the crown of Lower Egypt on the head of "She who guards the Rising One" suggests this authority is associated with Lower Egypt. Hence, it is quite possible that the serpent, "The Rising One," represents a king of Lower Egypt. (Additional supporting evidence that the king of Lower Egypt parallels (or represents) Revelation's 2nd beast will be presented later in this chapter).

Rev. 13:12 says that the 2nd beast "makes [i.e., forces] the earth and its inhabitants to worship the first beast [= Seth, as above]." This statement conforms with the action implied in Figure 98 located to the immediate right of the sloping corridor in the upper register (see Figure 96). In it we see three serpents facing a rearing serpent which the text refers to as being "at the head of this way," a phrase which suggests it is another manifestation of "The One of the Head" (near the register's far left), i.e., a parallel to one or more of the kings of Lower Egypt which, as suggested above, parallels the 2nd beast.

The following additional argument, albeit not a very strong one, is presented to support the identification of the rearing uraeus serpent in Figure 98 as a parallel to Revelation's 2nd beast. Note the scorpion in the center of the figure; Piankoff (1954) says it represents the scorpion goddess, Selkit[869] (*Srḳt*) and he assumes this is the name of the serpent. This is not necessarily the case, however. Consider this: The name Selkit means "she-who-relieves-the-wind-pipe"[870] a possible reference to respiratory distress brought on by the venom from a scorpion's sting. Thus, the scorpion in front of the rearing serpent may be a reference to the serpent's (2nd beast's) deadly *nature* rather than the *name* of the scorpion goddess. It could equally refer to the burning pain of its sting or even a metaphor for the flame believed to come from the uraeus serpent's mouth. In either case, the location of the ⚴ symbol near the serpent's mouth supports the idea of the uraeus being a devourer (or controller) of life. Danger, of course, was also often associated with the god Seth who was not only an opponent of the vegetation god Osiris and a god of the cruel seas, but was at times, also known as lord of all non-Egyptian lands (and hence, the enemies of Osiris). As pointed out earlier, Seth was at times a national enemy and a symbol of evil and danger.[871] Following this line of reasoning, we note that the rearing serpent seems to be threatening the three serpents which probably represent "many people" which lie on their bellies in subjugation on the ground before it, a position which parallels the statement in Rev. 13:12 saying that the 2nd beast (the king) "makes," or forces, the inhabitants to submit to its will and worship the 1st beast (Seth).

18. The Beasts of Rev. 13   383

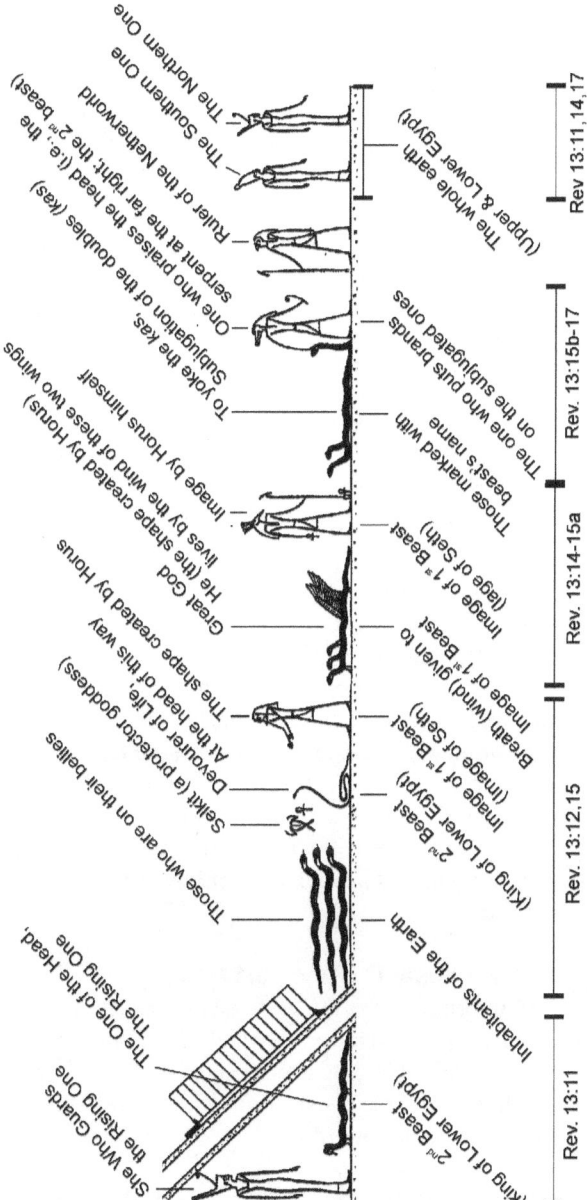

Figure 96. Sequence of scenes in Rev. 13:11-16 and their Egyptian parallels in AM4.1. Labels above the standing figures are translations of the Egyptian text by Piankoff (1954) except for the author's comments (which are in brackets) and the text, "To yoke the *ka*," above the three-headed serpent on the right side.

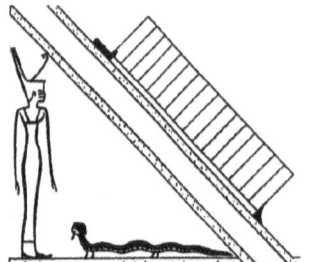 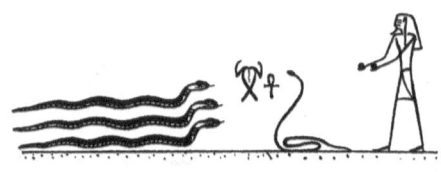

Figure 97. Scene from the *Amduat* (AM4.1.1-2) which parallels that describing the beast in Rev. 13:11 which "*rose* out of the earth." The crowned goddess guards the "Rising One," a human-headed serpent which emerges from a V-shaped intersection of sand (the earth).

Figure 98. Egyptian parallel to the worshiping of the image of the 1st beast in Rev. 13:12. The rearing serpent (which parallels Egypt's king of Lower Egypt and Revelation's 2nd beast) threatens the people (the three serpents, as in Rev. 13:12) while the "shape created by Horus" (Revelation's "image of the 1st beast") stands nearby carrying two offering pots suggesting the idea of worship, as in Rev. 13:12. (AM4.1.3-5)

We should also mention the reference to fire from heaven in Rev. 13:13. In ancient Egypt, the main fear of the uraeus serpent was related to the fire which it spewed from its mouth against its enemies. If we are to assume that the rearing serpent in Figure 98 indeed parallels Revelation's 2nd beast, its ability of spew fire would conform with Rev. 13:13 which states that he (the 2nd beast) "works great signs, *even making fire come down from heaven to earth in the sight of men.*"[a] Also note that the rearing serpent may also represent the king of Lower Egypt because the uraeus serpent "was associated from very early times with the kingdom of Lower Egypt," even with "the person of the king."[872] This conforms with the suggested identity of the rearing serpent in Figure 98 being a king of Lower Egypt as well as a parallel to Revelation's 2nd beast.

The "Image of the 1st beast" (Rev. 13:14-15)

Rev. 13:14-15 informs us that the 2nd beast (a king, as above) bids the people to "make an *image* for the [1st] beast [Seth], which was wounded by the sword and yet lived [discussed above]." This interpretation of these two verses of Revelation conforms with not less than three instances of Egyptian texts in the upper register of this division (Figure 96), as follows:

1. "He is like this in the *shape created by Horus*." (at AM4.1.5)[873]

2. "He is like this as an *image by Horus*' himself." (at AM4.1.7)[874]

3. "They are like this according to the *image made by Horus*." (at AM4.1.8-10)[875]

---

[a] This symbolism may also allude to the fire from heaven discussed in Chapter 13, *Catastrophes*.

The first two are clearly labeled characters which conform with the idea of a shape or image of someone or something. The third is a portion of text found on the far right of the register above the four standing gods and a three-headed serpent; it is ambiguous in the sense that, rather than forming a label for the group, it seems to refer to the two other shapes/images (#1 and #2 above) located on either side of the central winged serpent. We will next discuss each of these three references to images or shapes, beginning with the first two which seems to be separate manifestations of the same god.

1. The "shape created by Horus":- "Horus" was a name adopted by the kings of Egypt, each of whom was believed to be an earthly incarnation Horus, the divine son of the sun-god. "The shape created by Horus" in Figure 96 thus suggests a shape created by a king of Egypt. But as suggested above, the king of Egypt (in the context of the 4th Division of the *Amduat*) parallels Revelation's 2nd beast. We may therefore conclude that the "*shape* created by Horus" at AM4.1.4 parallels Revelation's *image* of the 1st beast (i.e., of Seth) made by the 2nd beast (i.e., Horus, an Egyptian king).

There is another reason for suggesting that this "shape created by Horus" parallels Revelation's image of the 1st beast – his stance. His stance conforms with the concept of worship mentioned in Rev. 13:15 in that it is similar to that found in the determinative, 𓀢, of words like "praise", "adore" or "extol."[876] This aspect alone of the "shape created by Horus" is suggestive of worship. But in addition, the two round objects in his hands are readily identifiable in some versions as offering or incense pots (●) which are used in worship and therefore imply worship. It is therefore reasonable to suggest that this "shape created by Horus" is somehow involved with worship, just as we read about the image of the 1st beast in Rev. 13:15.

Yet another parallel to Rev. 13:15 involves the three serpents which lie on the ground directly in front of the rearing serpent immediately in front of the "shape created by Horus." Recall that this rearing serpent was equated with Revelation's 2nd beast, a king of Lower Egypt, and that it was suggested the three serpents who are called "Those who are on their bellies," represent "many" subservient people, as implied in Rev. 13:14 which refers to "those who dwell on the earth" and Rev. 13:16 which refers to "all, both small and great, both rich and poor, both free and slave." The submissive posture of the three serpents could very well be in response to the danger represented by the rearing up of the deadly uraeus serpent, a danger which would conform with the statement in Rev. 13:15 that the 2nd beast causes "those who would not worship the image of the [1st] beast to be slain." Simply put, the three serpents (= many subjects) are submissive to the rearing serpent, Egypt's equivalent to Revelation's 2nd beast (Horus, a king of Lower Egypt, as above), because they feared for their lives if they did not worship the "shape created by Horus," i.e., the figure which stands directly behind him – or next to him in Figure 96 depending on how the reader might visualize the three dimensional equivalent of the picture. In this manner, the serpent (Revelation's 2nd beast) seems to be introducing the shape *he made* of Seth (Revelation's 1st beast) while the image itself seems to invite worship through his stance and his holding out of incense vessels toward the people ("Those who are on their bellies").

2. "Image by Horus himself":- Piankoff (1954) translates the name of the Seth-headed deity as "The Image *of* Horus Himself"; it is shown carrying a *was* scepter and an *ankh* sign.[877] We note here an important difference from the previous "shape" of Horus; this one describes an image *of* Horus while the other refers to an image *by* Horus. Furthermore, the "image *of* Horus himself" bears the head of Seth (Revelation's 1st beast) so that the picture seems to contradict the text – the text says it is Horus while the picture is of Seth.

The simplest solution to this apparent contradiction is that the figure in question is an image of both Horus and Seth, a solution which would suggest the dual god, Horus-Seth, who will be discussed later in this chapter. Suffice it to say here, however, that such an identification at this particular point in the sequence of events in the upper register does not entirely conform with the sequence of events expected if this entire register parallels in Rev. 13:14-15. Another possibility was therefore examined before further considering the Horus-Seth option.

We might well ask if Piankoff's name for this figure is an error in translation and enquire if the original text might be interpreted as the image "*by* Horus" rather than "*of* Horus." All that would be necessary to demonstrate such a misinterpretation would be to show that not all versions of the Amduat use the Egyptian equivalent of the preposition, *of* in this part of the text and that others may use the word *by*. In fact, the version in the tomb of Ramesses VI uses the preposition *by* ($ḥr$)[a, 878] rather than the more typical "of" (n, nt, or nw).[879] The likely reason for this difference is clear and it relates to the many mistakes made by the original artists or scribes who painted the text of this part of the Amduat on the walls of the tomb. Piankoff (1954) expresses his frustration for this and outlines his approach at arriving at an acceptable English version. He writes in italics:

> *In R VI [the tomb of Ramesses VI] the inscriptions and names are frequently mixed and are full of mistakes. We include, therefore, the translations according to the older versions.*[880]

This means there is some uncertainty about which English translation is correct; "Is it the image '*by* Horus' or '*of* Horus?'" This uncertainty and the above arguments in favor of an image "*by* Horus" may be used as the basis for assuming that, at least in some cases – the Seth-headed figure represents an image made *by* Horus rather than being an image *of* Horus. It may also be significant that Budge (1920) suggests that the preposition *mā* can mean either "by" or "of"[881] although neither Gardiner (1927) nor Faulkner (1962) mention such an equivalence. While more research is necessary on this matter and the current conclusion may be considered to be less than ideal, it is suggested here that there is sufficient evidence that the Seth figure does indeed parallel the "image *of* the [1st] beast," i.e., the image *of* Seth made *by* Horus.

In summary, and in the context of earlier arguments and conclusions, it is suggested that Rev. 13:14 can be interpreted to mean that the 2nd beast (Horus, a king

---

[a] See photo of hieroglyphics in Piankoff (1954), Plate 82; and Gardiner (1927), §39, p. 42.

of Lower Egypt) bids the people to "make an image for [of][a] the [1st] beast [Seth], which was wounded by the sword and yet lived [discussed earlier]." In view of the above, the preferred label for this figure should read "Image *by* Horus" rather than Piankoff's (1954) translation, "Image *of* Horus."

3. "Image made by Horus":- The conclusion reached in the previous two instances conforms with the text written above the four gods and the three-headed serpent located directly in front of the Seth-headed figure in Figure 96. The text says, "*They*˙ [presumably the two images of Seth in this register, as above] are like this according to the image made *by*˙ Horus."[882] This text therefore conforms with the conclusion reached above for the translation of an "image *by* Horus himself."

• • •

With these observations in mind, we may dismiss the possibility discussed above that the "image *by* Horus" represents the dual god Horus-Seth. Also, as we will see later in the *Discussion* part of this chapter, Horus-Seth may indeed play an important parallel role in events associated with the 2nd beast in Rev. 13.[b] We should note, however, that the two image/shapes by Horus in the upper register stand in front of and behind a winged, three-headed serpent. These preferred positions next to a set of beating wings lead us directly to the next parallel, the reference to giving "breath" to the image of the 1st beast in Rev. 13:15.

Breath to the Image of the 1st beast (Rev. 13:15)

Rev. 13:15 goes on to say that the 2nd beast [Horus, king of Lower Egypt] "was allowed to give breath to the image of the [1st] beast [the image (of Seth) created by Horus (the king of Lower Egypt) in Figure 96] so that the image of the [1st] beast should even speak." In an Egyptian context, then, it is Horus, the king of Lower Egypt who gives the breath of life to the *image* of the god Seth which he created.

---

[a] That Revelation's statement "make an image *for* the beast" actually means to "make an image *of* the beast" is demonstrated in Rev. 13:15 which says that "those who would not worship the image *of* the beast [were to be] slain."

[b] The possibility that the Seth-headed figure is in fact the god Horus-Seth should not be completely ruled out. It is entirely possible that the Hyksos kings who revered Seth saw themselves as representing both Horus (the son of Re) and Seth (their national god). In this scenario, the textual label "image of Horus" would conform with the appearance of the figure being that of Seth. An alternative is that writers in later dynasties simply assumed that the Hyksos king had set himself up to represent the traditional Horus-Seth image, an image which would conform with the Hyksos affirmation of Seth as their god. This alternative would mean that Horus-Seth could very well be a good parallel to a Hyksos King and hence also equivalent to Revelation's 2nd Beast; this possibility is discussed in detail under Historical Parallels in the Discussion part of this chapter. One or both these suggestions could explain the label for the Seth figure as "image *of* Horus." If the latter were to be considered the preferred explanation for the apparent error in translation, it would not significantly change the general conclusions concerning the parallel sequence of events found for this part of the *Amduat*.

This interpretation corresponds to similar events in the next picture in the series shown in Figure 96. Here, we find a centrally located, three-headed, winged serpent between the two images of Seth, i.e., between the "Shape [of Seth, the 1st beast] created by Horus" and the "Image [of Seth, the 1st beast] by Horus). The serpent's four legs suggest it is but another manifestation of the one portrayed on the far left-hand side of this register, the one identified earlier as the 2nd beast (the king) of Rev. 13:11. The text above the winged serpent says, "he [the image/shape created by Horus, Revelation's 2nd beast] lives by the wind of the two wings of his [the 2nd beast's] bodies and of his heads."[883] This is entirely consistent with Rev. 13:15 which says that the 2nd beast breathes the breath of life into the image of the 1st beast (Seth).

The symbolism of the breath of life being represented by wind created by flapping wings is well established in Egyptian mythology, perhaps the best known being found among the legends of Isis and Osiris. After the death of Osiris, Isis found his body and fanned it with her wings to revive him so that he might father her son Horus. Erman (1966) provides us with the pertinent portion of one version of the legend found in a New Kingdom Hymn to Osiris. Here it is obvious that the creation of life-giving air by the wings of Isis was pivotal in the resuscitation of his inert body.

> Beneficent Isis, that protected her brother, that sought for him without wearying,
>   that traversed this land mourning, and took no rest until she found him!
> She that afforded him shade with her feathers, and with her wings created air.
> *She that cried aloud for joy* ' and brought her brother to land.
> *She that revived the faintness of the Weary One*' ...[884]

Furthermore, the same Egyptian words were at times used for both wind and breath. For example, *t3w*[885] and *nft*[886] can each mean both wind and breath. It is therefore entirely appropriate to associate the wind made by the flapping wings of the serpent with the breath of life being breathed into the shape/image of Seth created by Horus who stands behind the winged serpent (see Figure 96). In this manner, the giving of the breath and life to the image of Seth thus closely parallels the giving of the breath of life to the image of the 1st beast in Rev. 13:15.

It should be pointed out here that Piankoff's (1954) translation of *"He lives by the wind of the two wings of his bodies and of his heads"*[887] seems to mean that the one spoken of is the winged serpent itself. The interpretation used here, however, splits this sentence and indicates that *he* – the one "who lives by the wind" – is not the serpent but rather the shape/image created by Horus which stands in front of and behind the serpent.

Authority of the Image of the 1st beast (Rev. 13:15)

The authority of this "image by Horus Himself" is revealed by the scepter in his left hand while the *ankh* sign in his right hand suggests he has power over life itself. These symbols conform with the reference in Rev. 13:15 that "those who would not worship the image of the (1st) beast (are) to be slain." Seth's subjects – or rather, the subjects of his image under the reign of the 2nd beast – can be seen in Figure 96 and Figure 99 as a three-headed serpent (one of its heads rears from its tail end) lying on its belly in the gesture of prostration and supplication. Near the serpent we find, the words, nhb-k_3w,[888] which Piankoff (1954) does not translate but which Budge (1920) defines as "to yoke the ka" or "to subjugate the double [i.e., the kas]."[889] Since the kas were understood to be the intellectual and spiritual powers of individuals,[890] we may interpret this to mean "to subjugate their spirits" (and/or intellectual powers). These subjugated kas clearly represent the subjects of "The image [of Seth, the 1st beast] by Horus [the 2nd beast]" who holds both the $ankh$ and scepter in his hands. A second $ankh$ symbol is set at the base of his scepter emphasizing that he has power over the life – and death – of the subjugated kas. This interpretation conforms with Rev. 13:15 when the 2nd beast gave breath to the image of the beast so that it "should ... cause those who would not worship the image of the [1st] beast to be slain."

Branding of the Beast's Followers (Rev. 13:16)

The next verse tells us the 2nd beast (a king of Lower Egypt) "causes all, both small and great, both rich and poor, both free and slave, to be marked on the right hand or the forehead" (Rev. 13:16). In this section we shall see how this description conforms with the apparent fate of the subjugated kas, especially those represented by the rear head of the three-headed serpent in Figure 99.[a]

The crocodile-headed figure which holds the rear head of the serpent in his right hand is called, "The One who praises the head," a name which likely refers to his allegiance to both the serpent on the far left of the register called "The One of the Head"[891] and identified earlier with Revelation's 2nd beast, and to the Seth-headed "Image by Horus" identified above as Revelation's image of the 1st beast. This clearly infers allegiance to Seth (as well as his image).

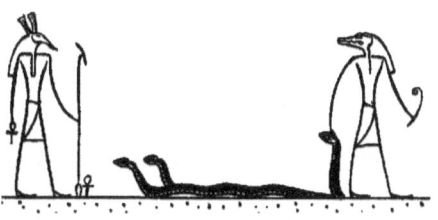

Note too the apparent action about to be taken against the serpent's head which the crocodile-headed god holds;[b] this clearly involves the ⸢ shaped object in his left hand. This hieroglyphic symbol usually means "rope" and is used as a determinative in words such as

Figure 99. The "image [of Seth] by Horus" (which parallels Revelation's "image of the 1st beast) on the left stands over the "subjugated ones" represented by a three-headed serpent. One of the serpent's heads is held in the right hand of the crocodile-headed figure which carries a branding iron in his left hand. This scene parallels that of the branding of the subjugated people in Rev. 13:16. (AM4.1.7-8)

---

[a] According to Piankoff (1954), the two heads facing the picture of the Seth-headed figure and the single head being held by the crocodile headed figure are from two *separate* serpents. The alternative interpretation used here follows that of Budge (1934, p360) who concludes that this serpent "has two heads at one end of his body and another head terminates at its tail." Budge's opinion conforms with many illustrations of this part of the *Amduat* which clearly show the third head emerging from the tail end of the *same* serpent, as shown in Figure 99.

[b] At least one version, that found in the tomb of Ramesses VI, does not show the crocodile-headed figure actually holding the serpent's head (see Plate 84 in Piankoff, (1954).

"rope," the "front-rope of a ship," "tie," "string," and others.[892] As a rope, it could be used as a symbol of bondage – or, for example, to restrain anyone who resisted being branded. At first glance, however, it seems there is no valid reason to suspect this particular object has anything to do with the branding of people referred to in Rev. 13:16. Nevertheless, it behooves us to further examine the possible significance of this object in light of the question, "Could this ᔕ device have been also used, not as a rope, but as branding instrument for livestock and slaves? And if so, why?"

We begin our consideration of these questions by pointing out that the ᔕ symbol, as the determinative for rope, is normally pronounced, *nwḥ,*[893] a word which is phonetically identical to a word referring to a "band (of metal)."[894] Furthermore, the idea of heating and branding with the ᔕ object is found in another phonetically similar word, *nwḫ,* which means to "heat" or "be scorched."[895] It is also significant that the hieroglyphic form of all of these words contains the ᔕ symbol. Finally, the ᔕ object resembles the spiral-shaped "bent appendage" ᔕ, or *ḥɜb* (🠴] ᔕ), on the Crown of the Lower Egypt 𓋔[896] (another link in this part of the *Amduat* to the king of Lower Egypt). The *ḥɜb* was possibly made of metal[897] and as such, may have been used for branding. These suggestions conform with the possibility that the presence of the ᔕ in the hand of this god is either a direct reference to a branding iron or acts as a mnemonic for one.

We may ask if there is any mention in the text of this division of the *Amduat* which would indicate the heating of the ᔕ object so it could be used as a branding iron? The answer is a qualified, "Yes." We find this in the name of the god holding the ᔕ object; Piankoff translates it as "The One who praises the head." The reference to "praises" (*àau* – praise, acclamation, adoration)[898] in his name could be a pun on the somewhat similar-sounding word, *àaā,* meaning "to burn."[899] Thus, by means of a near pun, the name of the one holding the ᔕ object could be a mnemonic suggesting a reading something like, "The One who *burns* the head." This interpretation would imply the use of the ᔕ object for branding the head of the serpent which he holds in his right hand. In this manner, an auditory pun coupled with the visual suggestion (ᔕ) in the picture represents a parallel to the reference in Rev. 13:16 to the faithful being marked, or branded, on the forehead.[a]

We next consider if there is any connection between the ᔕ symbol used here, and Seth, the name with which followers of the 2nd beast had to be branded. To answer this, a brief review of some of the material presented in Chapter 4, *Other Characters in Revelation* on how his name was written in ancient Egypt is in order. "Seth" was usually written with the determinative, 𓃩, commonly called the "Seth animal," but was also be written simply as either 𓃩 or 𓃩 or spelled phonetically with a wide variety of pronunciations, including *Set* (*St,* 𓊃𓏏𓃩),[900] Seth (*Stḥ,* 🠴 🠒 🠴 𓃩), and Setesh, (*Stš,* 𓊃𓏏🠒).[901] Now when ᔕ was combined with the sign for a door bolt, 🠒, it became 🠒, *stɜ* (the ideograph for words like "drag" and "draw").[902] When

---

[a] But note the previous comment on the name "The One who praises the head." It was suggested above that this phrase referred to the praising of the serpent called "The One of the Head" at the left end of the register. That the name could imply both meanings would certainly not be all that unusual in Egyptian religious literature where, as pointed out in Chapter 2, *New Approaches,* the use of puns, and hence, double meanings, abound.

18. The Beasts of Rev. 13

three ᶜ signs were placed on the door bolt to become the 𓊃𓊃𓊃 hieroglyph, it was pronounced *st̯* as in name *R-st̯ʒw* (Ro-se*t*au).[a, 903] In this manner, we can link the ᶜ sign in the hand of the figure in the upper register to sounds like *st*, *št*, and *sth*, any or all of which could act as mnemonics or puns for a reference to the god Seth, Revelation's 1st beast. Also, Budge (1920) suggests a variant of this hieroglyph, 𓋴𓋴𓋴, had the phonetic value of *st* (set, ⎯⚬).[904] It may also be significant that if all three heads (many) in Figure 99 are branded, the concept of three ᶜ symbols (𓊃𓊃𓊃, ᶜᶜᶜ or 𓋴𓋴𓋴) can be interpreted to mean Seth's name (as discussed in the next section).

Branding of livestock has been used to designate ownership since time immemorial. Not surprisingly then, that it was also used in the ancient Middle East as a means to identify ownership of slaves as well as animals for sacrifice. We find a possible use of the ᶜ in the ʏ emblem called the *ḥ₃b* which was used as an ideograph or determinative in words such as "office" and "rank."[905] In it the ᶜ sign is placed between the two horns of a bull mounted on top of a pole or mace, i.e., on or close to the animal's forehead. Recall that it was also present on the crown of Lower Egypt ⚘ which was, of course, also placed on the king's head. Thus, in both cases the ᶜ sign is associated with the head or forehead. Also note that a close homonym of *ḥ₃b*, *áab*, means "to burn or to brand"[906] as well as "an animal marked for sacrifice."[907] And quite significantly, at times the sign was even used as a mark on animals sacrificed to Seth![908] – the same god which parallels the 1st beast of Rev. 13. Here we find both conceptual and a linguistic parallels between the ᶜ sign and Rev. 13:16 where it says that everyone is "to be marked on the ... forehead" with "the name of the [1st] beast."

"666" – the Mark of the Beast (Rev. 13:17-18)

The writer of Revelation also indicates the name and the number of the 1st beast are essentially the same, "six hundred and sixty-six" (Rev. 13:17-18). This has already been discussed in Chapter 4, *Other Characters in Revelation*, where it was pointed out that the Egyptian ᶜ (or ℭ) sign was similar to the ancient Hebrew, Arabic and Syrian numbers "6" so that the triple use of the ᶜ sign in the hieroglyph, (𓊃𓊃𓊃, ᶜᶜᶜ or 𓋴𓋴𓋴) could represent, at least figuratively, the number 666 in these languages.[b] With this in mind, Rev. 13:16 might well be interpreted as "to be marked on the ... forehead" with "the name of the [1st] beast," Seth.

---

[a] The *r* sound (⚬) was combined with 𓊃𓊃𓊃 to create the word *R-st̯ʒw* (⚬ | 𓊃𓊃𓊃 ⎯), a word which meant "necropolis" – and in particular, the necropolis of the god Sokar whose realm is represented in the 4th Division of the *Amduat* – the one being discussed here.

[b] It seems unlikely, however, that Egyptian slaves would be marked with more than one ᶜ symbol where one would suffice; a single mark would have caused a lot less suffering to those being branded while at the same time identifying them just as well as three. This makes one wonder if a more reasonable parallel to Rev. 13:18 would be one in which three ᶜ symbols would simply refer to brand marks on the heads of *many* people (three = many).

Discussion

The above comparison of Rev. 13 with the 4th Division of the *Amduat* has revealed a number of intriguing parallels. These include not only parallels for Revelation's 1st and 2nd beasts and the image of the beast but also events in which they are involved – and significantly, the order in which they occur. All the Egyptian parallels to Rev. 13's characters and their interactions with one another could be readily identified with specific individuals and their activities in the *Amduat*. Important aspects of these parallels will be discussed next.

Parallels to the Main Characters

In this chapter, the 1st beast, which rises out of the sea in Rev. 13:1 was found to parallel the god Seth. Meanwhile, the image of the 1st beast in Rev. 13:15 paralleled two figures, the "Shape created by Horus" and the "Image by Horus himself" (= "the image of Seth made by Horus"). And the 2nd beast, the maker of the shape/image of the 1st beast was found to parallel Horus who is mentioned in the descriptive names of the two images (or shapes). Suggestions were made that the earthly manifestations of the Horus (i.e., the 2nd beast) found in the 4th Division of the *Amduat* represents a king (or kings) of Lower Egypt.

There is, however, one apparent difficulty with the suggestion that the Horus identified in the 4th Division is the maker of the "image of Seth" which, according to Revelation, everyone is ordered to worship. It seems that the typical pharaohs of Egypt were not apt to behave in such a restrictive manner as to limit beliefs in different gods;[a] the kings were usually quite tolerant of different beliefs about Egypt's many gods so it is extremely unlikely that any native Egyptian would have a portion of the populace slain if they did not follow a particular god, as we read about in Revelation. Nevertheless, as we will see in the following sections, there is one particular group of Egyptian kings whose activities conform quite well with this possibility and many of the events outlined here – the infamous Hyksos kings who reigned in Lower Egypt during the 2nd Intermediate Period (1640-1532 BCE).

Organizational Parallels

As indicated in the introduction to this chapter, Rev. 13 can be neatly broken down into three parts, the first (Rev. 13:1-6) specifically deals with the arrival of the 1st beast and his worship by the people for a period of 42 months; the second (Rev. 13:7-9) deals with the fate of those who choose to follow or not to follow him; and the third (Rev. 13:10-18) deals with the arrival of the 2nd beast who creates an image of the 1st beast for the people to worship and describes how these followers are to be marked to identify them as followers of the 1st beast. These same three parts were found to have readily recognizable parallels in the 4th Division of the *Amduat*; they are its lower, middle, and upper registers respectively. Furthermore, events portrayed in

---

[a] The best known exception is Akhenaten (1353-1335 BCE) who established the god Aten as the god of Thebes and did his best to make the whole of Egypt worship him as Egypt's supreme deity.

each register were shown to follow the same sequence as events described in Revelation.

Rev. 13:1-5 parallels the flow of images which begins in the lower left-hand corner of the lower register and proceeds all the way to the right-hand corner (Figure 91 to Figure 93); Rev. 13:7-8 parallels the flow of images which begins in the center of the middle register and proceeds to its far right (Figure 94); finally, parallels to events in Rev. 13:11-18 begin on the far left of the upper register and proceed to the register's far right (Figure 96). The location of the many parallels in the organization of the two sources are summarized graphically in Figure 100.

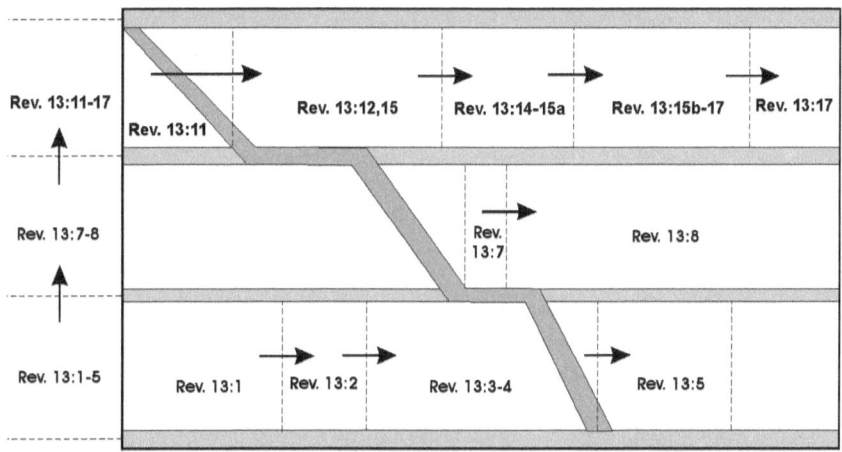

Figure 100. Arrangement in the 4th Division of the *Amduat* of parallel scenes from Rev. 13.

The only part of the 4th Division which does not have a parallel in the Book of Revelation is the left-hand side of the middle register which shows the passage of the barque of the sun-god through this division of the Netherworld. But this scene is a common element in all but the third division of the book so that a lack of a parallel in Rev. 13 does not stand out as being particularly significant; such scenes are only occasionally mentioned in other parts of the Book of Revelation. We may therefore be confident in concluding that the overall content and sequence of the scenes in Rev. 13 and the 4th Division are in good agreement and represent exceptionally well defined parallels.

There is, however, one rather peculiar difference in the flow of events in the two sources: the hieroglyphic text of the 4th Division flows from right to left in each of the registers whereas the parallel images in each register flow in the opposite direction – from left to right. Remarkably, this observation conforms with that by Rabinovich (2005) regarding the layout of this division. He notes that:

> All figures here are facing in the proper direction: as we enter into the realm of Sokar, the looking-glass world reversal that has so far characterized the world of the dead is itself reversed: this turn-around signifies that the grave is also the place of renewed life, where death itself is reversed.

But there is a further refinement: the logic of the procession, the way its themes are unfolded and developed, dictates that *we must read it in reverse, from bottom left to top right!* [909]

Thus, even this peculiar arrangement of the 4th Division parallels the account presented in Rev. 13.

Historical Parallels

Like so many other parallels between the Book of Revelation and Egyptian texts, Rev. 13 is by no means a translation – or even a crude translation – of the text of the 4th Division. If we were to assume that Rev. 13 is based on the 4th Division the most likely explanation for these differences would be that either Rev. 13 simply represents a broad overview of the division, or perhaps less likely, that a different version of the Egyptian text was involved. Nevertheless, we may hypothesize that, while the *Amduat* provides us with a better understanding of the Revelation account – the Book of Revelation may offer an even deeper understanding of the *Amduat* account.

Indeed, as we shall see next, the observed parallels suggest both Rev. 13 and the 4th Division of the *Amduat* may refer to historical events in the Nile Delta during Egypt's 2nd Intermediate Period. Thus, we begin a search for historical parallels by assuming Rev. 13 describes historical events in a rather simplistic manner whereas the text of the 4th Division is presented in the relatively complex symbolism and compositional structure typical of ancient Egyptian religious texts (see Chapter 2, *New Approaches*).

The current approach provides us with a unique opportunity to compare the idea of a parallel for this part of Revelation with actual historical events. It is possible that certain parts of Rev. 13 may in fact be treated as ready-made guides to explain aspects of the imagery and texts which have puzzled Egyptologists for decades. Such an approach would not be perfect and it would be far better if we could ask some ancient priestly guide to clarify difficult parts of the pictures and texts as we go. Nevertheless, the parallels found in Revelation offer quite reasonable interpretations of the Egyptian texts and permit at least a preliminary, more enlightened examination of their content. The only assumption we need make before going further is that the contents of the 4th Division represent a mythologization of actual events which happened in ancient Egypt some time before the writing of the *Amduat*, i.e., some time before *c.* 1507 BCE (when we find the oldest known fragments of the book).[910]

The Hyksos in the 2nd Intermediate Period:- According to the introductory comments in the 4th Division of the *Amduat*, the events described in this division are associated with the "Imhat Necropolis."[911] The location of this cemetery is in Lower Egypt about seven kilometers downstream of Avaris in the Nile Delta.[a] Avaris was the capital city of the Hyksos "invaders," an Asiatic group who settled in the Delta during or a little before the 2nd Intermediate Period. The dominant Hyksos king typically ruled over a number of sub-kingdoms in the Delta, each of which had its own

---

[a] Baines and Málek (1980, p.167) identify Imet (Imhat) with Tell Nabasha, Tell Bedawi, and Tell Farᶜun located in the eastern part of the Delta at 30° 51' E; 31° 55' N.

king. The power and influence of the Hyksos grew in time until, by the end of the 2nd Intermediate Period their principal king effectively ruled *all* of Egypt. It is prudent to keep this general overview in mind when we seek historical parallels to the interpretation of events described here.

One clue to the timing of events alluded to in the 4th Division is provided by the reference to "many abominable kings of Lower Egypt" (⬅⬅⬅ 𓋴𓋴𓋴). This suggests a time when the rulers of Lower Egypt were considered an abomination to the normal sense of order (*maat*) in Egypt. Another clue is the reference to the establishment of Seth as the chief god of the Hyksos kings. These two observations, along with the location of the Imhat Necropolis, correspond to only one era in the history of Egypt – the 2nd Intermediate Period which lasted from about 1640 to 1532 BCE.

At the height of their domination, all of Egypt, including Thebes, the capital of Upper Egypt, recognized (perhaps with some degree of reluctance) the ruling authority in Avaris. Nevertheless, a successful rebellion by two of Egypt's "legitimate rulers" in Thebes marked the end of the 2nd Intermediate Period and the beginning of Egypt's New Kingdom and ultimately the 18th Dynasty which began in 1550 BCE. During the 18th Dynasty the period of foreign rule was looked upon as one of national disgrace. (This dynasty is particularly relevant here because it coincides with the advent of the first appearance of certain parts of the *Amduat*, as mentioned above).

The Hyksos impacted significantly on the form of worship of the Egyptian god Seth. Grimal (1992) comments on this in his summary of their conquest of Egypt.

> In the sphere of religion, as in the political arena, *they instituted an official Egyptian-style cult based on Seth of Avaris,*' the enemy of Osiris; contenting themselves with the introduction of more Semitic features into his iconography; it was at this time that Seth was assimilated with Baal-Reshef and the Hittite god Teshub. The Hyksos also continued to worship the Syro-Palestinian goddess Anat-Astarte ... and [the Hyksos] kings continued to hold the title "son of Ra."[912]

Thus, in adopting the Egyptian god Seth, the Hyksos rulers embellished him with attributes of several non-Egyptian gods so that he in fact represented a newly fashioned version of Seth. Events associated with the worship of this corrupted version of Seth and the setting up of a national cult based on him almost certainly played a major role in the fabrication of the mythology expressed in this part of the *Amduat* – and possibly the composition of Rev. 13 as well.

Parallels with the Hyksos Rule:- If the observed parallels with Rev. 13 are based on historical events and do indeed relate to the Hyksos rule then the arrival of the 1st beast of Rev. 13 equates with the union in the delta of Egypt's Seth with Syrio-Palestinian gods. The arrival of Revelation's 2nd beast would then parallel the rise to power of the first Hyksos king (or kings) and the establishment of the official, corrupted version of Seth as their chief god. This, of course, would include an image (in personality, pictures and sculptures) of Seth, the 1st beast which people were obliged to worship. Upper Egypt, which originally capitulated to the Hyksos rulers, naturally resisted this switch away from the worship of Re as Egypt's supreme deity and from their traditional form of Seth. This interpretation would be consistent with Rev. 13:14 which describes the 2nd beast (a Hyksos king) as deceiving "those who dwell on earth [in this case, mostly Lower Egypt], bidding them make an image for [of] the [1st] beast [i.e., of Seth] which was wounded by the sword [according to Egypt's ancient writings and beliefs] and yet lived."

Signs from Heaven:- There is one seemingly incidental piece of information given in Rev. 13 which can now be examined from the point of view of the time of Hyksos rule. Rev. 13:13 says that the 2nd beast "works great signs, even making fire come down from heaven to earth in the sight of men." The whole matter of fire coming down from heaven has been discussed in Chapter 13, *Catastrophes*. Recall that the fire from heaven in Revelation parallels certain events during the eruption of Thera's volcano in *c.* 1628 BCE, i.e., during the early part of Egypt's 2nd Intermediate Period (1640-1532 BCE) and the rule of the Hyksos kings. It therefore seems reasonable to assume that the ruler at the time of the catastrophe (or some time thereafter) was the first Hyksos king, possibly Salitis (= Sheshi),[913] who ruled for the first twenty years or so of the 2nd Intermediate Period.[914] Like the Hyksos kings which followed him, Salitis took on the Egyptian title of the "son of Re," Re's representative on earth, and as such, had dominion over all things in the eyes of his people – including natural phenomena such as earthquakes and volcanoes. In this scenario, Salitis (or one of the later kings)[a] might well have claimed responsibility for the eruption of Thera and the subsequent fire from heaven which was visible from the Nile Delta (see Chapter 13, *Catastrophes*). This would conform with the statement in Rev. 13:13 that the 2nd beast (an "illegitimate king" of Egypt) made "fire come down from heaven to earth in the sight of men."[b]

The Two and Ten Kings:- In spite of the above parallels between Rev. 13 and the 4th Division of the *Amduat*, there is one nagging problem, albeit a minor one, which remains unresolved. Recall that in Rev. 13:1, the 1st beast (Seth) was envisioned as having "ten horns and seven heads, with ten diadems [crowns][c] upon its horns" while in Rev. 13:11 the 2nd beast (a Hyksos king) "had two horns." The parallel imagery in these passages suggests that Seth, the 1st beast, was somehow involved with ten kings while events surrounding the Hyksos rulers, the 2nd beast, involved only two kings. One might well speculate that the ten kings represent the ten kings of Thebes who ruled during the Hyksos period and effectively relinquished control over

---

[a] The correct identification of the king who ruled during Thera's eruption is dependant on two factors, both of which are disputed by modern scholars. The first is, as pointed out in Chapter 13, *Catastrophes,* the actual date of Thera's eruption. The second is the reliability of the chronology of events and kings during Egypt's 2nd Intermediate Period in Egypt. Differences in opinions among experts in these two fields could place the eruption during any of the Hyksos kings from Salitis, the first, to Apophis, the last (or conceivably, shortly after this period).

[b] It is immaterial whether the catastrophic events happened in the Delta or stories of them were brought to the Delta by survivors or traders from the Aegean Sea area; the Egyptian king could still claim credit for them.

[c] Horns were used as the head-dress of many Egyptian deities (Lurker, 1980, p. 65) and as such may be thought of as crowns or diadems of the gods.

Lower Egypt to the Hyksos while the 2nd beast represents either one or two of most prominent Hyksos kings – Salitis, who ruled for about twenty years and Apophis I, who ruled about forty-three years. There are, however, inconsistencies between this interpretation and the one given above, inconsistencies which could be related to our lack of reliable information on the chronology of the kings and dynasties in this period of Egypt's history. The suggestions here provide an additional avenue for further research on this period.

The Forty-two Month Period:- The 42 month period mentioned in Rev. 13:5 does not seem to parallel the entire Hyksos dynasty because the Hyksos reigned in Lower Egypt for about 100 years, not three and a half. If a period of 42 months is indeed correct, the period could represent the reign of one of the shorter ruling Hyksos kings. This would be an unlikely scenario because the Hyksos kings with shorter reigns did not achieve great notoriety or fame. But if 42 months is incorrect, we might consider that 42 "time periods" would be a better fit – as Figure 93 seems to suggest. For example, if the period was in *years* rather than months, we might well be looking at the reign of the longest ruling king – Apophis I, who reigned for either 43 years according to Baines and Malek (1980; see introductory table, *Chronology of Ancient Egypt*) or 40 years according to Grimal (1992)[915] – or somewhere in between, such as 42 years. Furthermore, it may be significant that this Hyksos king's name was "Apophis." Recall that the primordial god Apophis paralleled Revelation's dragon, the devil/Satan. It was the king Apophis who ruled in the Delta during the rebellion against the Hyksos by the last three Theban kings of the 17 Dynasty (Ta'a I, Seqenenre Ta'a II and Kamose) and the final expulsion by Ahmose, the first king of the 18th Dynasty.[916] Surely, in retrospect and at the time of writing of the *Amduat*, this king's name must have had some influence on the Theban view that the Hyksos' corrupted version of Seth was in some way linked to the god Apophis.

The False Prophet:- In addition to the 1st and 2nd beasts and the image of the 1st beast, there is yet another character, one who is also mentioned in other chapters of Revelation (Rev. 16:13, Rev. 19:20, and Rev. 20:10); he is called the "false prophet." Like the main characters in Rev. 13, the false prophet parallels an ancient Egyptian character. This conclusion is based on one passage in Rev. 13 and one in Rev. 19, as follows. In Rev. 13 we read that,

> It [the 2nd beast, a Hyksos king] *works great signs*, even making fire come down from heaven to earth in the sight of men; *and by the signs which it* [the Hyksos king] *is allowed to work* in the presence of the [1st] beast [the god Seth], *it* [the 2nd beast/king] *deceives those who dwell on earth* [Lower Egypt], bidding them *make an image* for the [1st] beast [Seth] which was [traditionally believed to have been] wounded by the sword and yet lived. (Rev. 13:13-14)

Note that it is the 2nd beast who works great signs and deceives the people. Also, note that this same combination of signs and deceit is found in Rev. 19 in reference to the "false prophet."

> And the [1st] beast [Seth] was captured, *and with it* [the 1st beast] *the false prophet who in its presence had worked the signs by which he deceived* those who had received the

mark of the [1st] beast [𓆄𓆄𓆄, 𓆄𓆄𓆄 or 𓆄] and those who worshiped its image [the image of 1st beast]. (Rev. 19:20)

It is obvious from this brief comparison of these two passages that the characteristics of the "false prophet" and the 2nd beast describe the same entity; the false prophet and the 2nd beast may be considered as one. And since Revelation's 2nd beast parallels an imposter Hyksos king(s) of Lower Egypt, so too does its false prophet.

Rev. 19:20 also leads to the identity of the beast mentioned in Rev. 19:19 which says that,

> the [2nd] beast [the imposter Hyksos king(s)] and the [subordinate] kings of the earth [Lower Egypt] with their armies gathered to make war against him [the Theban King] who sits upon the horse and against his army.

Later, in Rev. 20:10 we read that,

> the devil [Apophis] who [through the agency of the 2nd beast, the imposter king] had deceived them was thrown into the lake of fire and sulphur where the [1st] beast [the corrupted form of Seth] and the false prophet [the 2nd beast; the imposter king,] were, and they will be tormented day and night for ever and ever.

This rationale enables us to identify the parallel characters in Rev. 16:13 (to be discussed later in Chapter 22, *Armageddon*) where we read that the author of Revelation "saw, issuing from the mouth of the dragon [Apophis] and from the mouth of the [1st] beast [the corrupted form of Seth] and from the mouth of the false prophet [= the 2nd beast, the imposter king], three foul spirits like frogs." Again, like the king of Lower Egypt, Revelation's false prophet is seen to parallel Revelation's 2nd beast.

There is another parallel, albeit not a very strong one, between the 2nd beast/false prophet and a king of Egypt. It relates to homonyms of the Egyptian word for "prophet," ḥm-nṯr.[917] Literally, this word means "servant of god" where ḥm means "servant" and nṯr means "god."[918] But ḥm also means "majesty"[919] so that we end up with a phrase applying to the king himself. This suggests that ḥm-nṯr may be interpreted to mean that his majesty (ḥm) the king may also be looked upon as a prophet (ḥm-nṯr). From an etymological point of view, then, the Egyptian king may have been considered to have been a prophet in the minds of the people. Indeed, many of the Egyptian king's subjects believed this to be the case.

But what of a king being described as a *false* prophet as mentioned above? To examine this question it is instructive to go back to the descriptive word for "false" used in the original Greek text, *pseudoprofeétou*. Strong's Dictionary indicates that *pseudoprofeétou* refers to "a spurious prophet, i.e. pretended foreteller or religious impostor." Since Egypt was a theocracy, the idea of a "religious imposter" conforms quite well with the suggestion that the false prophet of Revelation was an "imposter king." It also conforms with the context of the above discussion on the possibility of "the imposter Hyksos king(s) of Lower Egypt" being Revelation's 2nd beast.

There is another Egyptian god in the *Amduat* (and elsewhere) which also conforms with Revelation's "false prophet." He is known to Egyptologists as "His

Two Faces," or "Horus-Seth" and is shown here in Figure 101. This deity has two heads, one belongs to the beloved, hawk-headed Horus while the other belongs to Seth. Chapter 17 of the *Book of the Dead* tells us that, "He is Horus [the king], he has two heads, one bearing right and one bearing wrong; he gives wrong to whoever does it and right to whoever comes with it."[920] Attributing these characteristics to Horus and Seth can be traced back as far as the *Pyramid* and *Coffin Texts* where, according to Breasted (1912), "Some of the oldest royal monuments of Egypt represent the falcon of Horus and the strange Seth animal side by side, as the symbol of the kingship of the two kingdoms now ruled by one Pharaoh."[921] This close association of the two deities probably served as the basis for

Figure 101. Egypt's parallel to the 2nd beast of Rev. 13; he is called "Horus-Seth" or "His Two Faces" and has two heads, "one bearing right and one bearing wrong."

the two-headed representations of the king of Egypt in the upper and lower registers of 2nd Division (Figure 103 and Figure 105) of the *Amduat* and the upper register of the 9th Division of *Book of Gates* (Figure 115). Furthermore, the conflict between right and wrong expressed in the *Book of the Dead* is particularly applicable to Egypt's opinion of the Hyksos kings of 2nd Intermediate Period.

With respect to a possible relationship between Horus-Seth and prophecy we also note that Horus-Seth conforms with the idea of the false prophet of the Book of Revelation. His picture, shown in Figure 101 is presented in such a way that the two heads point in opposite directions, an ideogram used by the Egyptians to indicate the dualistic nature of time; one head looks to the past and the other looks to the future.[a] If future time is indeed implied in one of these heads, one can readily understand how the double-headed figure might be considered to be looking into the future, as would a prophet. And if the time frame referred to in this part of the *Amduat* is indeed the 2nd Intermediate Period, it would be easy to understand how a non-native Egyptian and self-proclaimed, "imposter" king, who for a time ruled over not only Lower Egypt but Upper Egypt as well, would have been called a "false prophet" by native Egyptians (who later composed the *Amduat*).

This analysis of Egyptian parallels to Revelation's false prophet enables us to suggest the identities of possible parallels to the characters referred to in Rev. 20:10 which contains the third and final reference to the false prophet in the Book of Revelation. It reads, "and the devil [Apophis] who had deceived them was thrown into the lake of fire and sulphur where the beast [1st Beast, Seth] and the false prophet [2nd

---

[a] In some pictures of "His Two Faces," the two heads are human, but in this case they are different; one is that of hawk-headed Horus (representing good) while the other is the enigmatic head of the god Seth (representing evil).

beast/false prophet"; illegitimate Egyptian king(s)] "will be tormented day and night for ever and ever." These identifications suggest a logical way to better understand events described in Rev. 19:20, especially if we accept the above suggestion that the 2nd beast of Revelation represents a Hyksos king. As noted above, it would seem that the 2nd "*beast and the kings of the earth* [Lower Egypt] with their armies who gathered together to make war" (Rev. 19:19) against "The Word of God"[a] (Rev. 19:13) represents the chief Hyksos king (the 2nd beast) and his subordinate Hyksos kings who ruled in the Delta and fought with him in the fight against the armies of the "legitimate" Egyptian kings of Thebes (Kamose in the 2nd Intermediate Period and Ahmose in the early 18th Dynasty).

In later chapters, it will be shown that the relative location in the text of Revelation of references to the 2nd beast/false prophet also coincides with relative locations of pictures of Horus-Seth in the *Book of Gates*. These additional "in-context" parallels support the conclusion that Horus-Seth is indeed a good parallel to both Revelation's 2nd beast and false prophet.

Conclusion

We are now in a position to identify practically all references to the beasts and their associates mentioned in the Book of Revelation, including the "image of the beast" and the "false prophet." An interpretive listing of these identifications is provided in Table 18.1. This list will assist the reader in identifying, with a better understanding from an Egyptian perspective, an important selection of parallel events cited throughout the Book of Revelation.

In spite of the anti-sun-god theme of the 4th Division, the sun-god is present, as in other divisions, standing in his shrine on his holy barque on the left side of the middle register. But here, for the first time in the *Amduat*, his barque is in the form of a double-headed serpent, presumably to facilitate its navigation (by lighting the darkness with the fire from its two mouths), including the towing over sand bars which are everywhere in this land of Sokaris. Whereas the sun-god was praised and worshiped as he passed through the earlier divisions, here, for the first time since entering the Netherworld, there are no such activities. Budge (1934) describes this as a place where "there were no beings on whom he could confer estates, and no gods to offer loyal address."[922]

The findings presented in this chapter offer an entirely new perspective – perhaps a detailed elaboration – of the traditional interpretation of this part of the Amduat. We might say, for example, that it was in the Delta that native Egyptians who would had normally followed Re, are described as being recruited, marked (or branded) with the name of Seth and made to follow a corrupted version of him. Those who do not serve the corrupt version of Seth will be killed. This is suggested by the symbol of life and by extension, power over life and death, which is held by the image of Seth in the upper register. The central register, on the other hand, is dedicated to the faith of

---

[a] See Chapter 5, *"The Word of God"* for a discussion on the Egyptian parallel to the one called "The Word of God" who sits on a white horse and leads the army of the faithful in Rev. 19:11-21.

those Lower Egyptian followers of Re who are rewarded by the promise that their names will be written in the Book of Life, most likely Thoth's *Book of Breathings*.

We saw that this interpretation conforms with earthly events associated with the uprising started by the 17th Dynasty king Ta'o II of Thebes. This was expanded by the last king of the dynasty, Kamose of Thebes who fought against the Hyksos king Apophis I and his armies at the end the 2nd Intermediate Period. The final ousting of the Hyksos from Egypt was affected by King Ahmose of Thebes early in Egypt's 18th Dynasty and the New Kingdom. True-blooded Egyptians in the Delta who remained faithful to Re and the rulers in Thebes and died because of it, were granted eternal life in the hereafter by virtue of their names having been entered into Thoth's *Book of Breathings*.

The main body of this chapter illustrates a remarkable series of parallels between Rev. 13 and the 4th Division of the *Amduat*. Some of these (for example, the beast from the sea, the image of the beast, the forty-two time periods and the scene involving the Book of Life) are quite obvious and stand on their own merits. Others may be less convincing on their own but are strengthened when viewed in the context of the more convincing parallels and their specific positions in the sequence of events. Such less significant parallels are to be expected in a study of this nature simply because not all characters and events lend themselves to the same level of scrutiny.

While Table 18.1 summarizes Egyptian parallels to characters mentioned in Rev. 13, it also illustrates the confusing array of references to the dragon, the two beasts, the image of the beast and the false prophet in other chapters of Revelation, including references which are not clearly identified with the 1st or 2nd beasts. Nevertheless, the table will assist the reader in identifying "Who's Who" among the beasts in the Book of Revelation and the reader should find this table useful in following analyses of passages involving their presence in parts of other chapters of Revelation not discussed in this chapter.

It should be pointed out that no other segment of the ancient Egyptian literature examined in this study comes even close to the long series of parallel characters and events as that found in the 4th Division of the *Amduat*. Furthermore, as we will see in subsequent chapters, the identification of the characters in Rev. 13 continue to be valid when they are applied to instances of the same characters in events described in other chapters of Revelation. Some readers may agree that the combination of this many parallels is so remarkable as to indicate a reliance of this part of Revelation on the *Amduat* so that the observed parallels can be used as a source of enrichment of our understanding of both sources; others may disagree. Suffice it to say here that the parallels between Rev. 13 and the 4th Division of the *Amduat* – and historical events of the 2nd Intermediate Period – are quite striking. Nevertheless, more research is needed on all the above findings and how they might relate to this complex and little understood period in Egypt's history.

Table 18.1 Egyptian parallels to the Devil, Satan, the dragon, the 1st and 2nd beasts, the false prophet, and the image of the 1st beast in the Book of Revelation. These parallels are based on a critical comparison between the characters and sequences of scenes in the 4th Division of the *Amduat* and those of Rev. 13 (in bold print) as well as other chapters in Revelation. Most of the parallels in the other chapters are discussed in context elsewhere in this work (see the *Index to the Book of Revelation* near the back of this book for the locations of specific passages).

Book of Revelation	Identity in Revelation	Egyptian Parallel
Rev. 2:9, Rev. 2:10, Rev. 2:13, Rev. 2:21,Rev. 3:9, Rev. 11:7, Rev. 12:3, Rev. 12:4, Rev. 12:7a,b, Rev. 12:9,Rev. 12:12, Rev. 12:13, Rev. 12:16, Rev. 12:17, **Rev. 13:2, Rev. 13:3, Rev. 13:4,** Rev. 16:13, Rev. 17:3?, Rev. 17:7?, Rev. 17:8a?, Rev. 17:8b?, Rev. 17:11, Rev. 17:12, Rev. 17:13, Rev. 17:16, Rev. 17:17, Rev. 19:19, Rev. 19:20a,b,Rev. 20:2, Rev. 20:7, Rev. 20:10.	Devil, Satan, & the Dragon	Apophis
Rev. 13:1, Rev. 13:2, 13:5, 13:12a, Rev. 13:4a,b,c, Rev. 13:12b,c, Rev. 13:14a,b, Rev. 13:15a,b,c, Rev. 13:17, Rev. 13:18 Rev. 14:9, Rev. 14:11, Rev. 15:2, Rev. 16:2, Rev. 16:10 (?), Rev. 19:19, Rev. 19:20a,b, Rev. 20:4, Rev. 20:10.	1st beast	Seth
Rev. 13:14, Rev. 13:15a,b,c, Rev. 14:9, Rev. 14:11, Rev. 15:2, Rev. 16:2, Rev. 19:20, Rev. 20:4.	image of the 1st beast (made by 2nd beast)	the image of Seth
Rev 14:11 Rev. 15:2, Rev. 16:2, Rev 20:4	1st beast *and/or* its image	Seth *and/or* his image
Rev. 13:11, Rev. 13:12a ("it"), Rev. 13:13, Rev. 19:20, Rev. 20:10	2nd beast (= False Prophet)	Horus, Horus-Seth, His Two Faces (probably = an imposter, Hyksos king)
Rev. 16:13, Rev. 19:20, Rev. 20:10.	false prophet (= 2nd beast)	Horus (as in previous)

Chapter 19. Reaping of the Harvest (Rev. 14:6-20)[923]

The 14th Chapter of Revelation has three readily distinguishable parts. The first (Rev. 14:1-5) gives a description of the 144,000 faithful followers of the Lamb and has already been discussed in Chapter 7, *The Great Multitude*. The second (Rev. 14:6-13) informs the reader that the time of judgment and punishment of the followers of the beast has come. The speaker advises the faithful that many of them will die during this period but they will be rewarded for their labors; the third (Rev. 14:14-20) describes the harvest of grapes in which juice from the wine-press is likened unto blood which is to flow from the enemy.

The second part of the chapter begins with a proclamation by an angel to all who dwell on earth that they should "Fear God and give him glory, for the hour of his judgment has come; and worship him who made heaven and earth, the sea and the fountains of water" (Rev. 14:7). Later, in Rev. 14:9-10, another angel expands on the reference to "the hour of his judgment" with the words, "If anyone worships the [1st] beast and its image, and receives a mark on his forehead or on his hand, he also shall drink the wine of God's wrath ... he shall be tormented with fire and sulphur." It is clear in this statement that the punishment of the followers of the beast is to ultimately include burning with fire (a fate also described in Rev. 20:15).

In the third part of Rev. 14 we read that, "the angel swung his sickle on the earth and gathered the vintage of the earth, and threw it into the great wine-press of the wrath of God" (Rev. 14:19). We readily see here a powerful metaphor which links the harvest of the fields to the punishment of the followers of the 1st beast and its image.

While the general concept of harvest time is present in both Revelation and the 2nd Division of the *Amduat*, there is no mention here – or elsewhere in the *Amduat* – of the pressing of grapes; instead, the Egyptian text and associated pictures tell us it is grain which is to be harvested. Nevertheless, the similarity between the two sources suggests a detailed examination of the most obvious parallels is warranted. In this chapter we will first examine the Egyptian parallels which deal with the harvest of crops (in Rev. 14:14-18) and next, those which deal with the judgment and punishment of the followers of the beast (in Rev. 14:6-13 and Rev. 14:19-20).

The Harvest (Rev. 14:14-18)

Arrival of Harvest Time (Rev. 14:6-7,15)

In Rev 14:15 an angel is described as coming out of the temple and calling with a loud voice, "Put in your sickle, and reap, the hour to reap has come, for the harvest of the earth is fully ripe." Similarly, the text of the 2nd Division also signals the beginning of harvest. Here, the sun-god first assigns the fields to be harvested and then promises rewards to those who are to reap the harvest. We read in the middle register that, "This Great God makes grants of fields to the gods of the Netherworld, he takes care of those in this field. ... This Great God will grant him fields in their place among the fields of Urnes."[924]

The middle register also depicts the early stages of this harvest. It shows the arrival of four (= a multitude) of the sun-god's barges (Figure 102; see also Figure 66) which travel toward the fields ahead of his regal barque. The purpose of at least three of them is to collect the grain after it is harvested. The first boat, immediately in front of the solar barque bears the label "The Grain Gods," while the text above its armless passengers says that "They come while he [the sun-god] rows toward this field."[925]

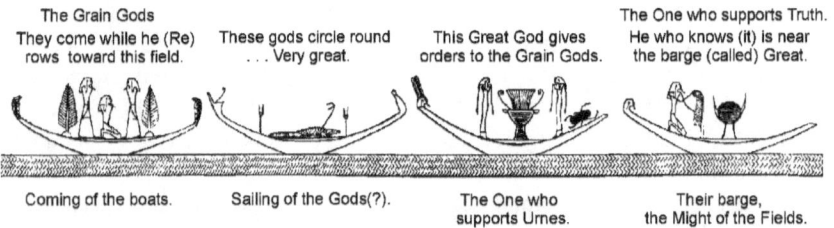

Figure 102. Procession of grain boats traveling toward the fields to reap the harvest in AM2.2.3-10. This scene parallels the main theme of Rev. 14 in that it sets the stage for the harvest of the fields and the judgment of the wicked. See also Figure 66. (All labels from Piankoff 1954, p. 243)

Under its prow is an explanatory note indicating this boat represents the "Coming of the boats."[926] Similarly, the label under the next boat which contains a crocodile with the spear in its back says, "Sailing of the Gods (?)."[927] Presumably, the spear in the crocodile's body promises protection from crocodiles as they sail toward the fields. Also, above the boat is the comment, "These barges circle round," an activity suggesting this group of boats serves a protective function for the others. Next, above the boat with the two goddesses and the scarab beetle, the text says that "This Great God gives orders to the Grain Gods." The name of the forward boat, the one containing the disk and crescent, is "The Might of the Fields", possibly suggesting that a large harvest from many fields is to take place. All these names and labels conform with the main theme of this division – the sailing of workers toward the fields to be harvested and their protection against crocodiles as they go. There is very little explanatory text in this register so we must assume that its pictures and brief explanatory notes acted as simple reminders to knowledgeable priests of the details of events portrayed.

19. Reaping the Harvest 405

The next stage of the harvest is shown in the lower register of the 2nd Division (Figure 103). On the left side are four figures, three of which carry ſ hieroglyphs. The message which these three bring is implicit in the hieroglyphs they carry (in some versions (as in Figure 103) they carry ſ signs while in others they carry the ☥ sign). (The ſ hieroglyph, a palm-branch stripped of leaves and notched to serve as a tally, typically means "year" while a similar sign, ſ, mounted on a ◉ symbol represents "season."[928]) The one on the far left is "The Carrier" who presumably carries the records of the harvest; in front of him is "The Opener of Time," who is likely the

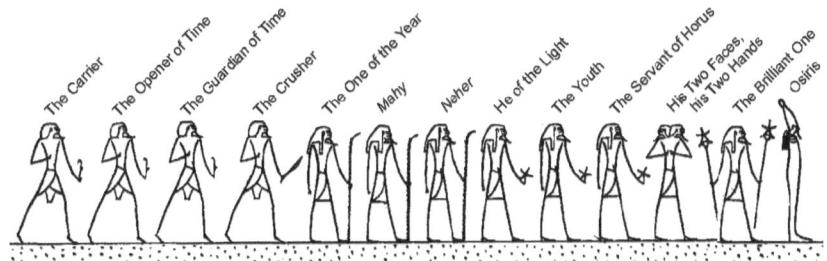

Figure 103. Left-hand side of the lower register of the 2nd Division of the *Amduat* which deals with the announcement of the arrival of harvest time. The three figures holding ſ signs announce the arrival, the three with measuring rods measure the yields of the fields, while those carrying stars (torches) stand ready to burn the chaff. This scene has several events which parallel those described in Rev. 14:14-18. (AM2.3.1-6)

organizer or overseer of the various stages of the harvest while "The Guardian of Time" is most likely the time-keeper of the activities of field crews. This interpretation conforms with the beginning of the harvest indicated in the middle register discussed above. The fourth character, "The Crusher," carries a knife, suggesting he represents either a foreman or an actual worker involved in the harvesting of the grain. The names of these four thus introduce the beginning of harvesting activities; the text above the first three also conforms with the harvesting theme: "These gods are like this, they acclaim this Great God with the symbols of the year. They acclaim him with [palm] branches which they hold in their hands, while this Great God gives them orders. ... He sends them toward the plants which are in the fields."[929]

The next three figures carry measuring rods,[930] presumably to measure and assign tracts of fields to be harvested. The name of the one in the center is "Mahy"[931] (*m₃hy*), meaning "one who burns,"[932] a name possibly related to the burning of the chaff in the fields, a function which would conform with that of the six figures who hold seven stars (including the two stars in Figure 104).[a] In the context of the burning of the chaff, these stars probably represent torches[b] either to light the chaff or illuminate the paths of workers returning from fields after dark, or both.

---

[a] In some versions, these figures hold *ankh* signs ☥ instead of stars (see Hornung, 1999, p.43).

[b] See the section on the *Seven Spirits of God* in Chapter 4, *Other Characters in Revelation*, for a discussion on the phonetic and conceptual relationships between stars and torches.

Recall from Chapter 4, *Other Characters in Revelation,* that the figures who hold the seven stars in this register were a part of the Egyptian parallel to the judgment scene in Rev. 4:5 which says that "before the throne burn seven torches of fire, which are the seven spirits of God" as suggested in Figure 21. Their positioning in this particular part of the *Amduat* suggests that they may not only be a part of the judgment of the enemies of the sun-god but also in the annual harvesting of the grain. This double function thus sets the stage for the harvesting scene as an ideal metaphor for the judgment.

The Harvest Begins (Rev. 14:14-18)

In Rev. 14:14-15 we read of the announcement to actually begin the harvesting of the crops. An angel comes out of the temple and calls with a loud voice to one seated on a "cloud," "Put in your sickle, and reap, for the hour to reap has come, for the harvest of the earth is fully ripe." The one seated on the cloud, wears a "golden crown" and holds a "sickle." The crown suggests authority to order harvest activities while being seated on a cloud could mean authority over weather conditions.

On the right side of the lower register, shown here as Figure 104, we find a distinct parallel to the actual beginning of the harvest. A seated god called "The Swallower of the Ass" holds a knife which, in the context of a harvest, can represent the cutting tools used in harvesting. Note that he has the head of a cow, an animal which was associated with the sky in the Delta region.[933] A cow's head was also a symbol of the goddess Hathor, a popular sky-goddess. We thus see in this horned deity a linked to both harvesting and the sky, just as we find in Rev. 14:15 (*cf.* the reference to the sickle and the cloud). In a later section dealing with the *Punishment of the followers of the Beast*, the "Swallower of the Ass is identified as Osiris while the "ass" referred to in his name almost certainly refers to Seth, his evil enemy.

Rev. 14:16 continues with the words that, "he who sat upon the cloud swung his sickle on the earth, and the earth was reaped." This "reaping of the earth" corresponds to the rest of the register, i.e., that part in front of the cow-headed deity. Rev. 14:17 then makes a brief reference to another angel who "came out of the temple in heaven, and he too had a sharp sickle." Similarly, the god directly in front of the horned deity

Figure 104. Parallel to the scene describing reaping of the harvest in Rev. 14:14-18. Osiris oversees the harvest while those with knives (sickles in Revelation) reap the crops. Six figures carrying grain collect and transport it to the boats. The figure standing on the far right is in charge of the burning of the chaff (in Rev. 14:18). (AM2.3.6-10)

also carries a sickle; his name is "The Keeper of the Divine Abode." Next, we see a row of six field workers. Three of them (= many) have grain symbols in their hands while three others carry similar but larger loads on their heads. The functions of the latter three (many) workers are evident in their names; the first is called "The One of the Head" (presumably foremen), the second is "Grain" (presumably those who do the actual reaping, and the third, "The Fiery One" (those who were likely involved with the burning of the chaff).

The last person described in Rev. 14:18 is an "angel who has power over fire." This angel parallels "One of the Two Flames" who stands at the far right of the register facing "The Fiery One."[934] This location at the far side of a register is frequently one of importance so that we may assume that "One of the Two Flames" is in charge of, or "has power over" the one who does the actual burning, namely, the "The Fiery One." In other words, like the angel in Rev. 14:18, he "has power over fire." Furthermore, when we assume that he also has power over the other five field workers we find that the latter part of Rev. 14:18, which says that "he called with a loud voice to him who had the sharp sickle (i.e., to The Keeper of the Divine Abode who stands in front of the horned deity in Figure 104), 'Put in your sickle, and gather the clusters of the vine of the earth.'" This gathering of the clusters of the vine parallels the harvesting of grain in the *Amduat*. And in the next verse we read, "So the angel swung his sickle on the earth and gathered the vintage of the earth" (Rev. 14:19). And so the harvest – and the judgment – begins.

The Judgment (Rev. 14:6-13,19-20)

Judgment against the followers of the beast and his image begins with an angelic proclamation warning all who dwell on earth to "Fear God and give him glory, for the hour of his judgment has come; and worship him who made heaven and earth, the sea and the fountains of water" (Rev. 14:7). A little later, another angel clarifies this announcement with an unambiguous statement of its intent: "If any one worships the [1st] beast [Seth] and its image, and receives a mark on his forehead or on his hand, he also shall drink the wine of God's wrath ... he shall be tormented with fire and sulphur" (Rev. 14:9-10). The capture of the enemies of God is likened to the swinging of the sickles and the gathering of the vintage of the earth (Rev. 14:19) while their punishment is likened to them going into a "great wine-press of the wrath of God" (Rev. 14:19-20) and their burning with fire and sulfur.

As pointed out above we find references to the punishment of the enemies of the sun-god in the 2nd Division of the *Amduat*. Indeed, judgment against the enemy is one of the themes of this division where the orders come directly from Osiris as is evident in the center of the register (on the far left of Figure 105); here we see three symbols – the "Orders of Osiris," the "Words of Osiris" and the "Crook of Osiris" (indicating his authority).

The fourth figure from the left side in Figure 105, i.e., at the center of the upper register, is "His Two Faces,"[a] also known as Horus-Seth, the two-headed god who, in Chapter 18, *The Beasts of Rev. 13,* is shown to parallel the 2nd beast and the false prophet of Revelation and may in fact represents one or more "illegitimate" Hyksos kings of Lower Egypt. Two baboons, typically associated with Thoth, the god of wisdom who presided over the judgment,[935] are seated in front of him, suggesting wisdom is especially needed in this particular judgment process. In front of them "One who cuts the shadows"[b] wields a knife or sword ready to do his part in the punishment of the guilty. Next to him stands "Horus of the Netherworld" who, by the authority of his father, Osiris, exercises great power in the Netherworld; his name in this scene indicates this judgment is conducted in the afterlife. Before Horus we see a group involved in the judgment and punishment of the enemy. One called "Powerful Arm, He who smites the enemies" stands behind six seated judges holding knives. Their names signify the main theme in this entire scene – the judgment of the enemies of the sun-god; three of them clearly reflect their function as assessors in a judgment process: "Thoth on his throne", "Khnum of the Judgment Place" and "Geb of the Judgment Place" while the enthroned, baboon-headed deity, who is called "The Flesh on his Throne," is likely another manifestation of Osiris. Also seated are "Isis the Protectoress," who protects Osiris, and "The One of the caldron [who] ... destroys the

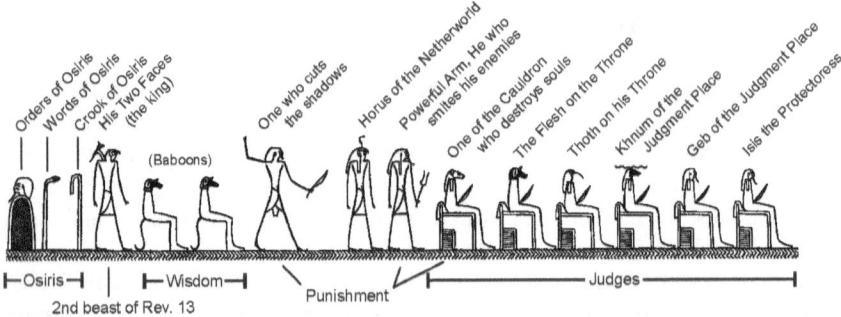

Figure 105. Parallel scene to the judgment and punishment of the enemies of God in Rev. 14:7-11. Under the orders of Osiris (the three figures on the far left) a tribunal of six judges (the six figures on the far right) determines the fate of the sun-god's enemies. The figure with a sword and raised arm stands ready to carry out the sentences. (AM2.1.4-10)

---

[a] Note that "His Two Faces" is again depicted in the lower register, and again, positioned at the center of the register. This positioning of "His Two Faces" at the center of the upper and lower registers suggests that he plays a major role in the events which take place in this division.

[b] Recall that the Egyptians considered the shadow to be an essential part of one's person. The destruction of the shadow by the gods effectively destroyed a person almost as surely as the destruction of his soul, spirit, etc.

souls" of those upon whom judgment is passed.[a,936] The presence and location of the latter figure emphasize the main theme of this part of the division, the punishment of the guilty. The main difference between this scene and that of the usual judgment of the dead[b] is that this judgment is specifically applied to enemies who have fought in battle against the sun-god and his followers. Also note that the "defendant" in the judgment process is "His Two Faces" (= Horus-Seth, located in the center of the register) parallels Revelation's 2nd beast (and Revelation's false prophet), who misleads the faithful in Rev. 14:11-17.

Punishment of the followers of the Beast (Rev. 14:7-11)

We earlier discussed the role of the one described in Rev. 14:14 as "seated on a cloud ... with a sharp sickle in his hand" and who was depicted as a horned deity sitting on a throne while holding a knife in the lower register in AM2.3.6-10 (Figure 104); the *Amduat* refers to him as "The Swallower of the Ass." The *Amduat* does not, however, expand on the functions of this "The Swallower of the Ass" so we must turn to other sources to make a positive determination of his identity, especially in the context of Rev. 14. This is by no means a simple matter.

There are two very different versions of the identity of "The Swallower of the Ass," each of which is broadly associated with a different time in the development of Egypt's religious thought. They involve important changes in the identity and character of the ass over time. The 40th chapter of the *Book of the Dead,* called *The Chapter of repelling him who swallowed an ass,* speaks of the swallower as an enemy of Osiris: the "Male whom Osiris detests, whose head Thoth has cut off! ... Get back, you whom Osiris ... detests. ... Purify yourselves all you gods, and fell with shouting the enemies of Osiris. ... *Get back you swallower of the ass*' ..."[937] It is obvious here that the "Swallower of the Ass" was considered to be an enemy of Osiris and that the ass was not an enemy. In contrast, part of the *Introductory Hymn to the Sun-God Re* in the *Book of the Dead* reads, "*May I smite the Ass,*' may I drive off the rebel-serpent, may I destroy Apophis when he acts."[938] Here we learn that it is the enemy Apophis who is an ass, an observation which conforms with Osiris (Revelation's God on the throne) being the "swallower of the ass" in Figure 104.

---

[a] It is interesting to note that six, the number of assessors in the upper register, is exactly the same as the number of angels who take an active part in announcing the various events described in Rev. 14. Their activities are described in (1) Rev. 14:6-7, (2) Rev. 14:8, (3) Rev. 14:9-12, (4) Rev. 14:15, (5) Rev. 14:17 and (6) Rev. 14:18. Note that these activities are spread throughout Rev. 14 which for the most part deals with the punishment of the followers of the beast; it is implied in the wording and imagery describing harvesting activities.

[b] As noted, this judgment scene should not be confused with the typical scene of the "judgment of the dead" as described in detail in the *Book of the Dead* where it is the souls of the dead, including those who did not worship Seth or his image, who stand before the throne of Osiris and a panel of assessors and are judged according to their deeds while on earth (as described in the so-called "negative confession"). This better-known judgment of the dead will be discussed in Chapter 25, *Resurrection and Judgment,* in relation to events described in Rev. 20.

Budge (1904) suggests that, "The probable explanation of the existence of these two opposite views about the ass is that Egyptian opinion changed about the animal, and that the later form of it held the ass to be a devil and not a god as in the oldest times."[939] Lurker (1980) discusses the development of the idea of the ass as a fiend:

> Already in the Middle Kingdom [2040-1640 BCE] the animals which bore the corn [grain] were regarded as Sethian entities who carried off Osiris who was present in it. Once Seth had been outlawed his animal became a scapegoat. After the New Kingdom the festival of Osiris included a rite in which the 'ass of Seth' was stabbed with a spear. ... the hieroglyph for 'ass' bore two knives stuck between the shoulder blades in order to render the animal's typhonic powers harmless.[940]

Since the *Amduat* was composed early in the New Kingdom [1550-1070 BCE], the texts which refers to the "Swallower" in the lower register most likely refers to Osiris while the ass represents Seth rather than Apophis. Thus, the "Swallower" in this setting – in the midst of the grainfields – is Osiris and it is the god Seth who is swallowed, an interpretation which conforms with the action taken against the followers of the 1st beast (Seth) and his image in Rev. 14: 9 and Rev. 14:11.

That Seth is indeed the object of the action of "The Swallower of the Ass" is supported by the presence of the two-headed figure in the very center of the lower register; he is called "His Two Faces."[941] "His Two Faces" is another name for Horus-Seth who in Chapter 18, *The Beasts of Revelation 13*, was identified as the 2nd beast of Rev. 13, and very likely an imposter king of Lower Egypt. His importance in this part of the 2nd Division is emphasized by his central location in both the upper and lower registers; both these registers have something important to say about Horus-Seth, especially his punishment.

Action against the enemies of the sun-god begins in the text of the upper register where we read that the followers of the sun-god "overthrow the enemies at their hour."[942] The text in the lower register, while emphasizing the harvesting of the fields, also says that the workers are involved in the war against evil; it says that "... you are the field workers of Urnes, whose souls live through me. You are those who fight for my limbs, who protect me against Apopis."[943] Elsewhere in the same register it is said that, "Their arms are firm when annihilating Apopis for thee at the Hour."[944] In this case, annihilating Apophis includes his followers and this would, of course, include Seth and his followers, as suggested above in parallels to the events of Rev. 14.

Rev. 14:10-11 says that part of the punishment of the followers of the (1st) beast (Seth) and his image involves burning with fire: "he shall be tormented with fire and sulphur. ... And the smoke of their torment goes up for ever and ever; and they have no rest, day or night, these worshipers of the beast and its image, and whoever receives the mark of its name." Furthermore, we find references to fire in this division being expressed in the names, "The Fiery One" and "The One of the Two Flames," and if one assumes that the "lights" held by several others are torches, we might include, "He of the Light," "The Brilliant One," "The Light," and "Hand of the Light."

Discussion

In spite of the undeniable reference to the harvest of crops in Rev. 14:14-18, the primary emphasis of Rev. 14 is on the punishment of the followers of the beast and its image. The main purpose for mentioning the harvest is to set the scene for use as a metaphor whereby the punishment of the followers of the beast is likened unto the harvesting and pressing of grapes. This is eminently clear in the last two verses of the chapter:

> So the angel swung his sickle on the earth and gathered the vintage of the earth, and threw it into the great wine-press of the wrath of God; [20]and the wine-press was trodden outside the city, and blood flowed from the wine-press, as high as a horse's bridle, for one thousand six hundred stadia." (Rev. 14:19-20)

On close inspection, a similar metaphor can be found in the 2nd Division of the *Amduat*. We find elements of it in all three registers. While the text in the upper register emphasizes the granting of the fields and other rewards to the faithful followers of the sun-god, mention is also made to the "overthrow of the enemies in their hour." This is coupled with a reference to punishment of the enemies in the presence of the panel of six judges and in the names of two standing deities, "Seben, the one who smites the enemies" and "Powerful Arm, He who smites his enemies." Similarly, in the lower register, which emphasizes the coming of the harvest, we find a picture of enthroned Osiris representing "The Swallower of the Ass," (i.e., the swallower of Seth, Revelation's 1st beast). Nearby, "His Two Faces," identified elsewhere as a parallel to Revelation's 2nd beast (the imposter king of Lower Egypt) stands in the midst of the field workers who carry torches (possibly to burn the chaff as possible allusion to the burning of Horus-Seth and his followers) to "revivify anew the fields." These same workers are also said to "fight for my [the sun-god's] limbs, who protect me against Apopis [most likely represented by Horus-Seth]." Later, they "rest in the field of the Grain Gods."[945] Similarly, in the middle register we find a very tight connection between the harvest of the fields and the burning of the enemies of the sun-god. The text says,

> He sends them toward the plants which are in the fields ... . It is they who give the green plants of Urnes to (eat) to the gods in the following of Re. It is they who bring water to the spirits according to the order of the Great God. It is they who light the flames to consume the enemies of Re, it is they who place the hearts in the fire.[946]

It is obvious that the text likens the harvest of the fields to the punishment of the enemies of the sun-god; the struggle between good and evil is incorporated into the very act of harvesting grain – just as we find when we compare action against the followers of the beast in Rev. 14.7-12 with the harvest of the vineyards in Rev. 14:14-16. The Egyptian text is more explicit, however, in that it describes how the evil-doers are punished by linking the harvesting of the grain to knives and the destruction of the chaff by fire to the fight against evil.

There is however, one obvious difference between the metaphors in the two sources: Revelation uses the imagery of the harvest of grapes while the *Amduat* uses the harvest of grain. Nevertheless, it is important to realize that the harvesting and pressing of the grapes metaphor is well within the scope of other potential metaphors in ancient Egypt. Like all ancient cultures in the Middle East, the Egyptians also harvested and pressed grapes to make wine. They even had a god over this activity; he was called the "wine-press god" and his main function was in complete agreement with the reference in Rev. 14:19 of the angel throwing the followers of the beast and its image into the "great wine-press of the wrath of God." His name was Shesmu and he was usually depicted in the form of a lion-headed man. Lurker (1980) says that, "The god of the wine-press Shesmu handed this life-giving drink to the deceased but he pulled the heads of sinners down and crushed them in his press. It was said of Horus that he drank blood of his enemies as he drank wine."[947] Budge (1934) informs us that Shesmu "was known to later theologians as the heads-man or executioner of Osiris, who hacked in pieces the bodies of the damned."[948] Hornung (1990), in particular, speaks of the wine-press god in much the same dramatic tone as we find in Rev. 14, as follows:

> The entire, uncontrollable rage of the deity is directed against those who have been condemned in the judgment after death, who fall from the ordered, existent world and then, tortured in every imaginable way and "destroyed," are consigned to nonexistence. They are deprived of their sense organs, must walk on their heads and eat their own excrement; they are burned in ovens and cauldrons and swim in their own blood, which Shezmu, the god of the wine-press, has squeezed out of them.[949]

Similarly, the idea of linking the punishment of the enemy to the pressing of grapes into wine and then to the drinking of blood and the torment of fire is also expressed in Rev. 14:10. It says, "he also shall drink the wine of God's wrath (blood), poured unmixed into the cup of his anger, and he shall be tormented with fire and sulphur." When considered in this light, the difference between grapes and grain in the two sources is not nearly as important as the presence in both sources of metaphors linking harvest of the fields to the punishment of the wicked. While the metaphors used in the 2nd Division of the *Amduat* and Rev. 14 may be different with respect to the type of harvest, the metaphor based on the harvest of grapes in Revelation is certainly in keeping with a known metaphor in ancient Egypt.

PART IV

THE BOOK OF GATES SERIES (Rev. 15-22)

The earliest extant copy (partial) of the *Book of Gates* dates from the reign of King Haremhab (1323-1295 BCE) and appears on the walls of his tomb; the first complete copy is on the sarcophagus of Sethos I (1294-1279 BCE) in the Valley of the Kings.[950] Like the *Amduat*, the *Book of Gates* is a funerary work describing the dangerous voyage of the sun-god through the Netherworld. It begins with him sailing along the primeval waters through the twin mountains at the western horizon and on into the depths of "The West." From there he passes on to his triumphant emergence into the eastern sky at dawn, accompanied by a great multitude of his faithful followers. As in the *Amduat*, the sun-god's safety is assured by those who travel with him and once again, he and his followers are typically found in the central register while the multitudes of deities on either side of the river are depicted in the upper and lower registers. Also like the *Amduat*, the *Book of Gates* is divided into twelve parts corresponding to the twelve hours of the night. Although most divisions of the *Book of Gates* are divided into three horizontal registers, the last one contains a single register with a picture of the renewal of creation. The book itself seems to have been based on the *Amduat* so that many of the scenes discussed may seem familiar to the reader. Nevertheless there are significant differences, some of which will be pointed out as we work through them. The version used in this study is found in the Tomb of Ramesses VI and the English translation used is by Piankoff (1954).

Like the *Amduat*, many parts of the *Book of Gates* are unusually difficult to understand. As pointed out in Chapter 2, *New Approaches,* ancient Egyptian texts and pictures were quite often intimately interdependent so that a full understanding of a given picture is often impossible without an equally good understanding of the text and how the two relate to one another. This is especially so in the *Book of Gates*; it is written in such a way that, for the most part, to properly read and understand a particular passage of text, the reader is meant to already have an informed understanding of the basic meanings of the pictures along with their explicit and hidden symbols, including visual puns. Modern scholars with their limited understanding can therefore only guess at the meanings of many of its passages and in some, it is practically impossible to even guess. Nevertheless, our most notable Egyptologists have persevered against these difficulties and successfully translated practically all of its text and interpreted many of the symbols in its pictures.

As will be shown here, just as the scenes in the *Amduat* and certain other Egyptian texts followed sequences of scenes in the 4th through 14th chapters of Revelation, parallel sequences in the *Book of Gates* will be identified with sequences in Revelation's 15th through 22nd chapters. And just as the sequences in the *Amduat* are interrupted by parallel scenes from other writings, parallel sequences in the Book of Revelation, especially in its latter chapters, are at times interrupted by parallel sequences from other Egyptian sources, two notable sources being the Egyptian *Books of the Heavens* and the *Victory Hymn of Thutmosis III*.

Chapter 20. The Song of Moses (Rev. 15:2-4)[951]

The Song of Moses (Rev. 15:2-4) has been recognized by many Bible scholars as problematic because no source has yet been identified for it in the Old Testament. Nevertheless, frequent annotations made by biblical scholars in modern bibles associate it with Exodus 15:1-18 and/or Deuteronomy 32.[952] The reference in Exodus begins with the phrase, "Then Moses and the Israelites sang this song to the Lord" and goes on to describe the triumphant passing of the Israelites across the Red Sea and their arrival in the lands of Philistia, Edom, Moab and Canaan. This "song to the Lord" has, however, very few if any elements in common with the Song of Moses in Revelation. The song in Deuteronomy, which contrasts God's faithfulness with Israel's faithlessness and contains elements of a "covenant lawsuit" or legal controversy, has some of the elements of Revelation's song but hardly enough to suggest even a moderately strong connection. Finally, there is no mention of singers of the song standing by a Lake of Fire in either of these two sources as in the Book of Revelation. Consequently, some biblical scholars doubt that there is a convincing relationship between these Old Testament songs and the one described in Revelation.

In this chapter, it will be demonstrated that this scene is a close parallel to one found in the 2nd Chapter of the *Book of Gates*. Here, in the upper register at BG2.1.6-10, we find a group of deities standing on the shore of the well-known Egyptian "Lake of Fire." Also, another scene involving a reference to justice similar to that found in Rev. 15:4 parallels a scene in the next division at BG3.3.1-4. And with respect to the song itself, it will be shown that its form and content closely parallels portions of the well-known, *Victory Hymn of Thutmosis III* written on a stele found in the temple of the god Amen at Karnak. Hence, the parallels in the *Book of Gates* will be supported by detailed comparisons of similar parallels in the writings of Thutmosis III.

Singers by the Lake of Fire (Rev. 15:2)

The author of Revelation dramatically introduces the singers of the Song of Moses with the words, "I saw what appeared to be a sea of glass mingled with fire, and those ... beside the sea of glass with harps of God in their hands" (Rev. 15:2). Those standing by the sea are obviously not adversely affected by the fire which is mingled with water (as clear as "glass") for we read in the following verse that they are singing. The Egyptian equivalent of this extraordinary scene is found in the upper register of the 2nd Division of the *Book of Gates* (Figure 106). In it, we see twelve deities positioned above a rectangle filled with vertical wavy lines (ⵏⵏⵏ) indicating a body of water. Significantly, the Egyptian text above this picture unambiguously conforms with the idea of Revelation's sea containing fire. It says, "This is the lake which is in the Netherworld, it is surrounded by these gods. ... the water of the lake is fire."

Figure 106. Twelve gods standing by a lake of fire and water wear clothing consisting of ceremonial collars and white robes, as do those surrounding the sea of glass and fire in Rev. 15:2. (BG2.1.6-10)

The choice of words used in the version of the Song of Moses in Rev. 15 is also worthy of comment in the context of the Egyptian sources. Almost all the key words in the description of singers around the lake appear to have Egyptian counterparts among words beginning with the *tcha* (*ḏ₃*) sound. For example, the word *tchatcha-t*[953] (*ḏ₃ḏ₃t*)[954] can mean harp, which the singers in Revelation are described as carrying, while the word *tchaḥaḥ* which means "rejoice."[955] Also, a close homophone, *tchatcha* (*ḏ₃ḏ₃t*), can mean "to water or to fill with water,"[956] a term consistent with the artificial sacred lakes near many Egyptian temples and which could be used as a model to describe the lake of fire and water around which the singers stood (especially at night when the sacred lake was surrounded by torches whose light reflected in calm *glassy* water). Yet another phonetically similar word related to the concept of a lake of fire is *tchatu* which means "fire," and "burn."[957] Finally, the word *tchatcha-t*[958] (and *dt*[959]) can also refer to "estate, domain, or landed property" on which the singers stood by the lake. This grouping of similar sounding words is applicable to the description of the scene in Rev. 15:2-3 and represents an additional and tantalizing parallel to Revelation's lake of fire.

Furthermore, like the Lake of Fire in Rev. 15:2, this fiery water in the Egyptian Netherworld does not harm the gods which surround it. In the register just below the picture, the ram-headed form of the sun-god (i.e., the "Lamb" of Revelation as described in Chapter 3, *The Preeminent Deities*) stands in his barque and assures them of their safety: "It's water is for you, its fire is not against you, its heat is not against your bodies!" Their response affirms their belief in its beneficial nature:

> Come thou to us, O thou who sailest in thy boat, whose Eye's fire consumes, whose Glorious Eye gives light to the inhabitants of the Netherworld. Hail! Thou approachest, beneficial (it) is to us, Great God, the fire of thy Eye.[960]

20. The Song of Moses

Rev. 15:2 also tells us that those who stand by the water are "those who had conquered the [1ˢᵗ] beast and its image and the number of its name [666]." In other words they had fought against the beast. While the *Book of Gates* makes no explicit claim that the deities in Figure 106 are "those who have *conquered*," this is obvious from the guarantee of their safety while standing so near the fiery lake. The text leaves no doubt about them being among the sun-god's blessed dead:

> Your portions, as those of the gods, consist of barley from your lake. (May) your heads be uncovered, your flesh be hidden! May there be air for your nostrils, and may there be offerings for you consisting of barley! And may there be oblations for you out of your lake.[961]

Furthermore, as has already been shown in Chapter 6, *The Twelve Tribes of Israel*, the twelve deities surrounding this lake belong to a much larger group which parallels the Twelve Tribes of Israel described in Rev. 7.

The Singers' Harps (Rev. 15:2)

Rev. 15:2 also tells us that those standing by the water had "harps of God in their hands." The *Book of Gates* makes no explicit mention of such harps in the hands of those standing by the lake of fire although harps seem to be implied in several symbols found on the clothing of the gods by the lake (Figure 106). These symbols are ſ-shaped hieroglyphs on two of the deities and a ╬-shaped hieroglyph on an adjacent deity; together, they form the word, ſſ╬. We know that the ſ symbol is the determinative in the word *ḵnbt* which means "corner" or "angle."[962] It is possible, however, that it was placed here as a mnemonic which at first glance does not seem to be related to the harps of Revelation. For example, two of these hieroglyphs combined would pronounce, *kenken* (*ḵnḵn*), meaning "to sing to a beaten drum, or to clap the hands rhythmically."[963] Moreover, the parallel between the harp in Rev. 15:2 and the *kn* sound is also apparent in the word *kennarut* which means "musical instruments or *harps*."[964] It is therefore evident that, while the exact translation of ſſ╬ may not be known, its meaning may have had something to do with musical instruments, most likely harps.

The ſ hieroglyphs in Figure 106 could also have been perceived by the Egyptians to represent harps in their own right, especially the ancient "angle harp" or "trigon." This harp, which did not appear in Egypt until the Semitisation of the 18th dynasty, was probably imported from Ur in Assyria.[965] It was made with two pieces of wood joined at an acute, or right angle. The *Encyclopædia Britannica* describes it as being similar to the traditional African bow harp except that "the bowlike support is replaced with two crosspieces at right angles to one another; the strings are stretched between these at an angle of 45°."[966]

The second type of hieroglyph in the word ſſ╬ is the ideograph, ╬, pronounced *'imy*.[967] The word *'imy* has the possessive connotation, "*of* (mine)" or "*belongs to* (me),"[968] a meaning which relates well to the phrase in Rev. 15:2, "harps *of* God" – or *of* the deities holding them. The possible association of ſſ with music, and more specifically, with harps and the possessive connotation of the ╬ symbol in Figure 106 supports the above-mentioned parallel of this scene describing the "sea of glass mingled with fire ... with harps of God in their hands" in Rev. 15:2.

The Song of Moses (Rev. 15:3-4)

We are told in Rev. 15:3 that those who stand by the fiery water "sing the Song of Moses." The song begins in the same verse with words of praise to the sovereign one: "Great and wonderful are thy deeds, O Lord God the Almighty! Just and true are thy ways, O King of the ages!" It continues in Rev. 15:4 where it says his name will be feared and glorified, that his ways are just and true, and his "judgments have been revealed."

The judgments of God, which are to take place in the form of seven plagues delivered by seven angels (Rev. 15:6) will be discussed in detail in the next chapter; a brief comment on them will be given later. They vary from "foul and evil sores upon the men who bore the mark of the beast and worshiped its image" (Rev. 16:2) to widespread environmental upheaval resulting in great loss of life – water pollution, fish kills, fierce heat, darkness, lightning, earthquakes, shifting river flows, and great hailstones (Rev. 16:3-21). The reader should recall that these plagues were discussed in Chapter 13, *Catastrophes*, where they were described as parallels to the effects of the volcanic eruption of the island of Thera in the Aegean Sea in *c.* 1628 BCE. Some of these plagues will be discussed in the next chapter, not in the context of the Theran eruption but in the context of the *Book of Gates*. Suffice it to say here that the function of the Song of Moses in Revelation is to briefly introduce these plagues as punishment of the unbelievers and to praise God for their place of bliss by the lake of fire.

A number of similarities to the song itself are present in both the next division of the *Book of Gates* and the *Victory Hymn of Thutmosis III;* these will be considered separately.

The Song in the *Book of Gates*

The song of Moses in Rev. 15:3-4 is basically a hymn of praise; the words are as follows:

> ³Great and wonderful are thy deeds, O Lord God the Almighty!
> Just and true are thy ways, O King of the ages!
> ⁴Who shall not fear and glorify thy name, O Lord? For thou alone art holy.
> All nations shall come and worship thee, for thy judgments have been revealed.

Similarities to this song are found in the text written over the heads of twelve walking deities on the far left of the upper register at BG3.1.1-4 while others are written over the god Horus at the extreme left of the lower register. Just as the singers in Revelation sing the song of Moses and the Lamb, these twelve deities *praise* the morning manifestation of the sun-god (the Lamb of Revelation; see Chapter 3, *The Preeminent Deities*) with the words, "Laudation to thee, Re of the Horizon , perfect soul upon earth! Hail to thee, Everlasting One, Lord of Years, Eternal One, who has no lessening!"[969]

Like the latter part of Rev. 15:4 which mentions God's judgment against the nations, the bottom register of the 3rd Division mentions the sun-god's judgments against his enemies. On the far right of this register we find four fire pits attended to by "Those who are over their pits."[970] Horus (the hawk-headed god on the far left) speaks to these gods with the words, *"Seize the enemies* of my father [Osiris], drag them to your nets because of this evil which they have done against the Great One." Next to the centrally located shrine containing Osiris stands a rearing cobra called "The Fiery One," ready to light the fire in the pits. Nearby, a group of eleven deities praises Osiris with the words, *"Thou art exalted.*' ... Thy son Horus restores thee thy diadem ... *he punishes thy enemies.*'" Horus adds, "The heart of my father is just! .... Thou art powerful, O Osiris, glory to thee, O He at the head of the Westerners! ... .

Table 20.1 Elements in the 3rd Division of the *Book of Gates* which parallel those found in the Song of Moses (Rev. 15:3-4). Quotations are from Piankoff (1954), pp. 159-163. Italicized text emphasizes the most similar components.

Book of Revelation	Book of Gates
Rev. 15:3a. And *they sing* the song of Moses, the servant of God, and *the song of the Lamb,*	They say to Re: *Laudation to thee, Re of the Horizon*' [*the Lamb of Revelation*], perfect soul upon earth! Hail to thee, (BG3.1.1-4)
Rev. 15:3b saying, "Great and wonderful are *thy deeds,* O Lord God the Almighty!	Your portions are yours, you gods, taken from your rightful offerings. Your *Kas* are yours. You are in peace while *your enemies are annihilated. They shall not exist.*' Your spirits are destined for their seats while your souls are to be sealed up. (BG3.1.1-4)
Rev. 15:3c *Just* and true are thy ways,	The heart of *my father*' [Horus' father, Re] *is just!* (BG3.3.1) (see also parallel to Rev. 15:4c below)
Rev. 15:3d *O King of the ages!*"	*Everlasting One, Lord of Years, Eternal One, who has no lessening!*' (BG3.1.1-4)
Rev. 15:4a *Who shall not fear and glorify thy name, O Lord?* For thou alone art holy.	Thou art powerful, *O Osiris, glory to thee,* O he at the Head of the Westerners! ... *The spirits are in fear of thee, the dead are in dread (before) thy dignity.*' (BG3.3.1)
Rev. 15:4b *All nations shall come and worship thee,*	*Thy portion is to rule the Netherlands, O thou whose forms are exalted in the mysterious region.*' (BG3.3.1)
Rev. 15:4c for *thy judgments have been revealed.*	My heart is glad before my father! *The heart of my father is just!* ' (BG3.3.1)

Thy diadem is restored! I am thy son Horus! I reckon [determine] the wrong done (to thee)."⁹⁷¹ The main similarities with Rev. 15:3-4 are highlighted in italics and are included in Table 20.1 along with several others to present a simplified comparison between the two sources. Note that, like the Song of Moses, the lower register basically deals with praise to the sun-god and the administration of justice against his enemies.

Although the above similarities may not be particularly convincing, when combined with their proximity in the 2ⁿᵈ Division to parallels with Revelation's song of Moses in the 3ʳᵈ Division, the similarities between scenes from the *Book of Gates* and those described in Rev. 15:2-4 are strengthened.

The Song in the Victory Hymn of Thutmosis III

Egyptian parallels between Rev. 15:1-4 and the 2ⁿᵈ and 3ʳᵈ Divisions of the *Book of Gates* are not the only ones we find among the Egyptian texts; far more remarkable parallels are present in the *Victory Hymn of Thutmosis III* which was quite famous in Egypt before and after his death. The hymn was composed to commemorate the military conquests by Thutmosis III (1479-1425 BCE) who was and still is considered to have been the greatest military leader in Egypt's history. His most famous battle was fought at Megiddo, a fortified city built to control the principal pass through the Carmel Range (which connects present-day Gaza and Damascus). The following paragraphs and sections explore Revelation's "Song of Moses" in the context of this hymn.

Translated by Breasted (1962), the original *Victory Hymn of Thutmosis III* consists of twenty five lines of hieroglyphics and emphasizes Thutmosis's battles and other events.⁹⁷² It can be divided into three basic parts. A prologue introduces Thutmosis III as Re's (divine) son and avenger who lives forever, whom he loves, and for whom he has worked marvels. The second part consists of eleven verses, each representing a distinct battle cry against a different enemy or group of enemies of Egypt.ᵃ The third part praises Thutmosis' accomplishments, confirms his authority to rule, and promises continued divine assistance from Amon-Re. Finally, it says that all nations come and worship Amon-Re.

The following selection of lines from the first and last parts of the hymn highlight those basic elements (in italics) also found in the Song of Moses in Rev. 15:3-4. References in square brackets will be discussed in the following paragraphs.

> *Utterance of Amon-Re*, [i.e., a song of the Lamb as in Rev. 15:3a] lord of Thebes:
> Thou comest to me, thou exultest, seeing my beauty,
> O my son, my avenger, Menkheperre [= Thutmosis III; in Rev. 15:3a], living forever.
> I shine for love of thee,

ᵃ The central portion of the *Hymn of Victory* which has a group of battle cries beginning with the phrase "I have come" parallels text in Rev. 6:1-8. The second portion seems to parallel part of the 8ᵗʰ Division of the *Amduat* (see Chapter 10, *Call to Arms*).

20. The Song of Moses

My heart is glad at thy beautiful comings into my temple;
(My) two hands furnish thy limbs with protection and life.
... .
I have worked a marvel for thee;
I have given to thee might and victory against all countries,
I have set thy fame (even) the fear of thee in all lands.
Thy terror as far as the four pillars of heaven,
I have magnified the dread of thee in all bodies, [Rev. 15:3b]
... .
The Northerners by hundreds of thousands of captives.
I have felled thine enemies beneath thy sandals,
thou hast smitten the hordes of rebels according as I have commanded thee.
The earth in its length and breadth, Westerners and Easterners are subject to thee [Rev. 15:4b]
Thou tramplest all countries, thy heart is glad.
None presents himself before thy majesty,
While I am thy leader, so that thou mayest reach them.
... .
There is no rebel of thine as far as the circuit of heaven;
they come, bearing tribute upon their backs,
bowing down to thy majesty according to my command. [Rev. 15:4b]
... .
[The next section of the hymn contains a group of *battle cries beginning with the phrase "I have come."* These were discussed in detail in Chapter 10, *Call to Arms.*]
... .
I have caused thee to reign, my beloved son,
Horus, Mighty Bull, Shining in Thebes, whom I have begotten, in uprightness of heart. *Thutmose, living forever, who hast done for me all that my ka desired;* [Rev. 15:3b]
... .
Thou has feted the beauty of Amon-Re,
Thy monuments are greater than (those) of any king who has been.
When I commanded thee to do it, I was satisfied therewith,[973] [Rev. 15:4c]

A Song of Moses *and* the Lamb (Rev. 15:3):- The first part of Rev. 15:3 clearly identifies the song as being that of both Moses *and* the Lamb: "And they sing the song of *Moses*, the servant of God, and the song of the *Lamb*." We find a similar association with two similar names also found in Thutmosis's victory hymn.

The name of *Moses* will be dealt with first. Note that Thutmosis's name can be expressed as a two-part name, Thut-mosis, the latter part of which sounds very much like "Moses." In Hebrew, the name Moses was not only pronounced as *moce-yoos'*, but also as *mo-sace'* and *mo-oo-sace'*[974] (i.e., close to the more familiar English pronunciation). Budge (1920) writes Thutmosis' name as Teḥuti-*mes'* III[975] while Breasted (1962) writes it as Thut*mose'*[976] and Grimal (1992) pronounces it as Tuth*mosis.'*[977] With all three endings being similar to the Hebrew pronunciation, some versions of the last part of Thutmosis' name very closely resemble the Hebrew pronunciation of Moses' name.

Next, with respect to the reference to the *Lamb* in Rev. 15:3, note that the first line of Thutmosis' victory hymn says that it is the "Utterance of Amon-Re, lord of Thebes." The god "Amon-Re" is the syncretic name for the two gods, Amon and Re. And, as discussed in Chapter 3, *The Preeminent Deities*, the ram-headed form of Re in the morning is an excellent parallel with the juvenile or "lamb" form of Re. Amon-Re may therefore be loosely considered to represent Re, the "Lamb" of Revelation and the *Victory Hymn of Thutmosis III* may be considered, in the context of events in the Book of Revelation, to be about both Moses (Thutmosis III) *and* the Lamb (Amon-Re), i.e., it may even be considered as being a song of both Thutmosis and of Re, or, as in Rev. 15:3, "Moses and the Lamb."

Moses, Servant of God (15:3):- We read in Rev. 15:3 that Moses was a "servant of God." If Egypt's Thutmosis III is indeed a good parallel with Revelation's Moses we might expect that he would have been considered, like Revelation, to be a "servant of Re," his god. With this in mind, we turn to Wilkinson (1994) who explains the attitude of servitude of the Egyptian kings:

> Because the king acted as an intermediary between the human and the divine, he was responsible for satisfying the gods in order to ensure the smooth functioning of the cosmos itself. Most of the work involved in this service was actually performed by the priest and temple personnel, of course, but it was nevertheless the king, in theory, who provided for the gods and supplied their physical needs in the various temple rituals.[978]

As both the pharaoh and "son of Re," Thutmosis III was considered to be a servant of Re. His servitude can be understood in the context of the *Victory Hymn of Thutmosis III*. In it, Amon-Re says, "O my son, my avenger, Menkheperre [Thutmosis III], living forever. I shine for love of thee." Details of this are emphasized in the hymn as a series of commands which Amon-Re begins with the phrase, "I have come,[a] causing thee to ...," as follows:

> I have come, as the instructions from causing thee to smite the
> princes of Zahi. ...
> I have come, causing thee to smite the Asiatics. ...
> I have come, causing thee to smite the eastern land. ...
> I have come, causing thee to smite the western land. ...
> I have come, causing thee to smite those who are in their marshes. ...
> I have come, causing thee to smite those who are in the isles [of
> the Mediterranean]. ...
> I have come, causing thee to smite the Tehenu (Libyans). ...
> I have come, causing thee to smite the uttermost ends of the lands. ...
> I have come, causing thee to smite those who are in front of their
> land [i.e., the nearest lands to Egypt]. ...
> I have come, causing thee to smite the Nubian Troglodytes. ...
> I have caused thee to reign, my beloved son ... living forever ... *who* [as my
> servant] *has done for me all that my* ka *desired.*[979]

---

[a] A very similar refrain to "I have come ..." is incorporated into the battle cries of the four living creatures directed at the four horsemen of Rev. 6:1-8 where each of the cries simply says, "Come!" See Chapter 10, *Call to Arms*.

Near the end of the hymn, Amon-Re acknowledges Thutmosis' response to his command to build him a monument with the words, "When I commanded thee to do it, I was satisfied therewith." Thus, the servitude of the pharaoh, and specifically that of Thutmosis III to the god Amon-Re, conforms with the idea in Rev. 15:3 of Moses being a "servant of God."[a]

King of the Ages (Rev. 15:3):- "Just and true are thy ways, *O King of the ages!*" says Rev. 15:3. Similarly, the third line of the *Victory Hymn* includes the phrase "*living forever*" albeit that it seems to refer to Thutmosis rather than Amon-Re.

Great and Wonderful Deeds (Rev. 15:3-4):- The statement in Rev. 15:3, – "*Great and wonderful* are thy *deeds,* O Lord God the Almighty, just and true are thy ways" – also conforms with Victory Hymn, especially where the sun-god says "*I have worked a marvel*' for thee [Thutmosis III]; I have given to thee might and victory against all countries." In fact, a large portion of this hymn is effectively a long list of the Thutmosis' deeds facilitated by Amon-Re where Amon-Re's more celebrated victories are inferred in the introductory statement, "I have caused thee to ..."

Rev. 15:4 then asks the question, "Who shall not *fear* and glorify thy name, O Lord?" The parallel to the great fear of the deeds of Amon-Re through the agency of Thutmosis III are obvious:

> I have set thy [Thutmosis'] fame (even) the *fear of thee*' in all lands.
> *Thy terror*' as far as the four pillars of heaven;
> I have magnified the *dread of thee*' in all bodies ...

Finally, the statement in Rev. 15:4 that "All nations shall come and worship thee" is alluded to in the hymn where it says,

> There is no rebel of thine *as far as the circuit of heaven;*
> *they come, bearing tribute*' upon their backs,
> *bowing down to thy majesty* ' according to my command.

Discussion

The above evidence suggests several parallels between the Song of Moses in Rev. 15 and Egypti's *Victory Hymn of Thutmosis III*, and perhaps to a lesser extent, the *Book of Gates*. This hymn was quite well known in ancient Egypt, not only because of its exceptional literary qualities, but because it was prominently displayed in at least one Egyptian temple. Breasted (1962) tells us that The *Victory Hymn of Thutmosis III,* the original of which was written on a black granite tablet 180cm. in height, was discovered by Mariette in a chamber northwest of the main sanctuary room of the temple at Karnak.

---

[a] In an Egyptian context, this reference to "God" in Rev. 15:3 should probably be interpreted to refer to Osiris rather than Re. This restriction disappears, however, when we consider that the concept of the sun-god which eventually developed in ancient Egypt involved Osiris being the body and Re being the spirit of the sun-god; the two combine at or before dawn to become "Osiris-Re." See Chapter 3, *The Preeminent Deities*.

At the top, occupying one-fourth of the stela, are two scenes of worship, in each of which Thutmosis III [1479-1425 BCE], accompanied by the goddess of the Theban necropolis, *Kḫaft't-ḥr-nbs*, with the ususal superscriptions. The hymn itself is twenty-lines occupying the remainder of the stela, is the best specimen of its class, and was later partly copied by scribes of Seti I [1294-1279 BCE] for the wall of the great Karnak temple in which this tablet was set up.[980]

When a king such as Thutmosis III died the new king took for himself many of his predecessors' attributes and claimed them for his own, a practice conforming with the belief that each new king was a reincarnation of the same Horus, the son of the sun-god; this often included the most notable accomplishments of his predecessors. Indeed, the hymn was so venerated that other Pharaohs used portions of it in their own hymns, especially those of Sethos I (1306-1290 BCE) and Ramesses II (1290-1224 BCE).[981] It is thus obvious that this hymn occupied a significant place in the function of the temple. In view of the many other parallels documented elsewhere in this work, it is by no means surprising that such a popular hymn could be alluded to in the Book of Revelation.

Chapter 21. Seven Angels with the Wrath of God
(Rev. 15:1,5-8; Rev. 16:1-12a, 17-21)[982]

Rev. 15:1 speaks of "another portent in heaven, great and wonderful, seven angels with seven plagues, which are the last, for with them the wrath of God is ended." Judgment against the enemies of God is thus announced and, as discussed in the previous chapter, those around the throne celebrate with praises to their sovereign and sing the song of Moses which ends with the unequivocal statement that, "All nations shall come and worship thee, for thy judgments have been revealed" (Rev. 15:2-4). At this point, the seven angels emerge from the temple and are given bowls filled with the wrath of God (Rev. 15:5-8). This chapter describes and compares the scene in the central register of the 2nd Division of the *Book of Gates* with that described in Rev. 15:1,5-8 and Rev. 16:1-12a,17-21.

The Egyptian Setting

At the very center of the 2nd Division of the *Book of Gates* is a picture (Figure 107) which is filled with Egyptian symbolism and forms the basis for our comparison of this division with Rev. 15:1,5-8; this figure provides an Egyptian context for all the events described in this passage.

We begin our description of the figure with the long horizontal rectangular component bearing a bull's head facing outwards on either end. The text labels it as "The Barge of the Earth." This name is entirely consistent with its nature and function. Firstly, its rectangular shape is reminiscent of a number of hieroglyphic symbols which are linked in one way or another to the earth. For example, the simple rectangular hieroglyph, ▬, is a determinative in words for both "irrigated land,"[983] and "stone."[984] The stylized version found in the figure is usually described as a "rod,"[985] perhaps because it seems to rest on the shoulders of eight gods; the text calls them the "The Carriers." A good analogy to the eight carriers bearing up The Barge of the Earth is the ancient Greek image of Atlas holding the earth up on his shoulders. The concept of the "Barge of the Earth" is also reminiscent of the modern phrase, "Spaceship Earth," which is often used by insightful writers to depict the finite limits of our earthly environment in space and time.

And the Barge of the earth is not empty. The proclamation above the eight carriers says, "Honor be to Re, may his soul rejoice with the earth god! ... The barge rejoices – *its Netherworld is in this barge!*"⁹⁸⁶ The image of the earth presented here is therefore more complicated than it first seems; the inside of the Barge of the Earth represents the Netherworld which the Egyptians believed lay deep beneath the earth, a fact which is immediately obvious from the brief introductory text which describes the sun-god's passage through it: "Behold, I pass through the mysterious region to take care of those who are in it!"⁹⁸⁷

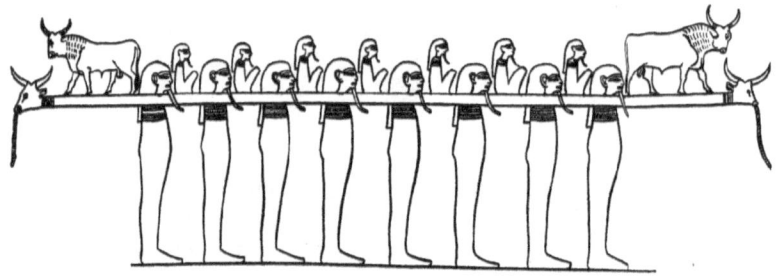

Figure 107. Details of the seven deities (the seven angels with the seven plagues of Rev. 15) seated between two bulls on a rod called the "Barge of the Earth." The standing bulls have the aggressive stance of guardians while the mouths of the bulls' heads mounted on either end of the rod represent the entrance and exit to the Netherworld, which itself, is represented by the rod supported on the shoulders of eight standing deities. (BG2.2.5-7)

The sun-god's journey into the Netherworld begins as he is towed into its entrance, as signified by the mouth of a bull whose head is mounted on one end of the barge, and it ends when it exits the mouth of a second head at the opposite end. The full range of this movement into, through, and out of the Netherworld is depicted along the entire length of the middle register (Figure 108). At the far left of this figure the sun-god stands in his shrine on his barque as it is towed into the mouth of the bull's head on the left and out through the opposite side by four towers called, "Those of the Netherworld."ᵃ Note that the sun-god's presence in the Netherworld is indicated by his absence behind the tow rope as it is being pulled from the bull's mouth. Hornung (1999) says the towing of the sun-god "along in the 'barque of the earth,' is symbolic condensation of his entire journey through the depths of the earth."⁹⁸⁸

The purpose of the sun-god's journey through the Netherworld is explicitly stated in the opening remarks in the upper register of the 1ˢᵗ Division; they refer to the judgment and punishment of the wicked:

ᵃ These are the same deities which parallel the four creatures before the throne of God described in Rev. 4 and elsewhere (see Chapter 4, *Other Characters in Revelation*). The Egyptians typically called them the four sons of Osiris or of Horus.

> The sailing of this Great God on the ways of the Netherworld. ... to make divisions of what is upon earth; to take care of those who are in it; *to judge in the West;*· to abolish all differences among the gods who are in the Netherworld; to place the spirits on their thrones; *to deliver the dead to their judgment* [or *"to deliver the damned to their judgment"*][a] *to annihilate the bodies of the wicked;*· to restrain the soul(s). (BG1.2.6-10)[989]

This statement is followed in the 3rd register with more details on the fate of the sun-god's enemies. Atum speaks to the condemned:

> Your evil deeds (turn) against you, your outrages (come) against you, your slander (recoils) upon you ... *you are examined before Re ... . you are those who did evil, who committed slaughter* in the Great Hall. *Your bodies are to be cut up, your souls are destined not to exist.*· And you shall not see Re in his forms while he travels in the mysterious region. Hail Re! Powerful is Re! *Thine enemies are (destined) for the Place of Destruction.*· (BG1.3)[990]

Details of the annihilation and destruction of the wicked are provided in subsequent divisions of the *Book of Gates* and some of these will be discussed in Chapter 22, *Armageddon*. Suffice it to say here that the purpose of the sun-god's journey through the Netherworld conforms with the mention of the wrath of God spoken of in Rev. 15.

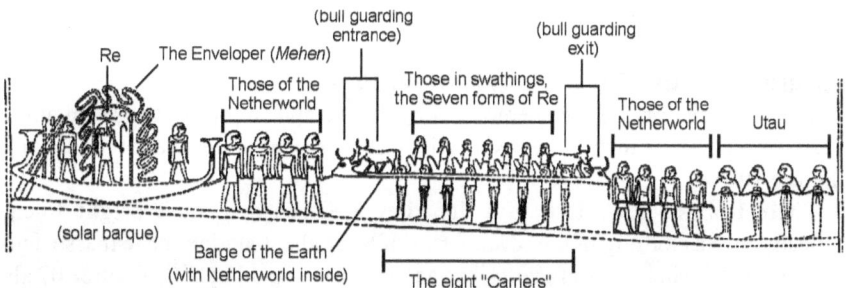

Figure 108. Middle register of the 2nd Division of the *Book of Gates*. The sun-god Re stands in his shrine (on the far left) as it is towed *through* the Netherworld represented here the interior of the long, rod-shaped rectangle with a bull's head mounted on either end (also see Figure 107). Seven forms of Re (the seven angels with seven plagues of Rev. 15:6) sit on the rod while at the far right, four figures (Revelation's four creatures of Rev. 15:7) stand with arms hidden. (BG2.2)

The two bull-heads emphasize the presence and function of the two standing bulls on the barge. Wilkinson (1992) informs us that, "As a cosmic animal, the powerful bovine appears as the 'Bull of Re' in the Pyramid Texts."[991] And it is the stance of these two bulls which reveals his wrath. The bull was typically represented

---

[a] This alternative translation is from Clagett (1989, p 481).

in either of two hieroglyphic forms, one showing a docile stance with its head held high [☥,🐃] and the other in a rampant stance with its head held low in a threatening posture [☥,🐃]. The latter posture (☥), which conforms with that of the two standing bulls in Figure 107, was considered so important by the Egyptians that it was used as the determinant for the word $\underline{d}nd$, or "rage,"⁹⁹² a concept which may be perceived as wrath. The two standing bulls and their heads may thus be said to represent the wrath of Re as he rages against his enemies in the Netherworld (i.e., inside the Barge of the Earth). On earth, it was Horus, the king of Egypt who took the form of a bull to trample the enemies of the sun-god.[a] Their location and orientation also suggest that they are guardians of the entrance and exit of the Netherworld.

Between the two standing bulls on the "Barge of the Earth" are seven deities which, as we shall see next, conform with the seven angels in Rev. 15.

The Seven Angels

Just as the seven angels are central to the announcement of events in Rev. 15, the seven deities seated on the Barge of the Earth occupy the important, central part of the middle register of the 2ⁿᵈ Division (Figure 108). They are seated between the two standing bulls on the barge. The Egyptian text tells us that "what is in it is holy!" and quotes Re as saying, "The Barge of the Earth gives way before me, *the barge of the Netherworld carries my forms.*"⁹⁹³ In other words, the seven deities seated on the rod represent seven forms of the sun-god, Re, presumably seven of his spirits (recall that Osiris also had seven spirits; see Chapter 3, *The Preeminent Deities*).

Appearance of the Seven Angels (Rev. 15:6)

The following paragraphs demonstrate how the appearance of the seven angels in Rev. 15:6 parallels that of the seven spirits of Re seated on the Barge of the Earth in Figure 107.

Their Robes:- Rev. 15:6 says that they are "robed in pure bright linen." Emphasis on the clothing of the seven forms of Re is also found in the text associated with Figure 107 where they are described as "Those in swathings."⁹⁹⁴ Figure 107 also shows the deities wearing white robes although this can hardly be regarded as good evidence for a parallel because white garments are typically worn by deities elsewhere in the *Book of Gates* (and in most other Egyptian religious compositions). Nevertheless, the accompanying text itself *emphasizes the brightness* of their clothes as in Revelation; it says, "Gifts are given to them of *light-colored garments.*"⁹⁹⁵ This reference to light-colored garments conforms with the description given in Revelation in a rather remarkable way. The Greek word used to describe the garments of the seven angels in Rev. 15:6 is *lampros*, a word which the King James version usually translates as "bright, clear or white." *Lampros* is based on the primary verb *lampo*, which means "to beam, i.e., radiate brilliantly (literally or figuratively)" and the KJV

---

[a] Lurker (1980, p. 36) says that "The kings of the New Kingdom often bore the epithet 'mighty bull' or 'strong bull of Horus,' whilst in the Archaic Period the ruler was regularly depicted as a bull, as on the Narmer pallette where the king pushes down the wall of a town with his horns and throws its protector to the ground with his hooves."

usually translates it to mean "give light or shine."[a, 996] The reference to "light-colored garments" of the seven forms of Re in the Egyptian text thus conforms quite well with the description in Rev. 15 of the seven angels being "robed in *pure bright* linen" and especially the Greek version which incorporates their brilliance.

Their Collars:- Rev. 15:6 also says that "their breasts [are] girded with golden girdles." As discussed in *Chapter 3. The Preeminent Deities*, the golden girdle of Revelation parallels the Egyptian broad collar worn by the Egyptians and many of their deities, including Osiris whose ceremonial collar is described in Rev. 1:13. The sizes of the collars differ in different versions of the *Book of Gates* as is evident when those in Figure 108 are compared with those in Figure 107; it is clear from Figure 108, however, that at times they were large enough to cover the entire chest area as described in Rev. 15:6.

Also, the material of which the collars of the seven angels were made conforms with the Egyptian tradition of collars of gold being worn by the most important officials and gods (see Chapter 3, *The Preeminent Deities*).

Opening of the Temple (Rev. 15:5-7)

Rev. 15:5-6 tells us that " the temple of the tent of witness in heaven was opened, and out of the temple came the seven angels." The temple referred to here conforms with the shrine over which the protective *Mehen* serpent (the "Enveloper") is draped. Re is quoted as saying, "The Barge of the Earth gives way before me, the barge of the Netherworld carries my forms."[997] It seems reasonable that the seven forms of Re must leave him in order for them to be seated on the "Barge of the Earth" before he enters the Netherworld. If so, this event would conform with Rev. 15:6 where it says that "out of the temple came the seven angels" thus representing another parallel among the seven angels of God in Rev. 15.

The Bowls of Wrath (Rev. 15:6-7)

Rev. 15:7 says that "one of the four living creatures gave the seven angels seven golden bowls full of the wrath of God." Recall from Chapter 4, *Other Characters in Revelation*, that the four living creatures of Revelation parallel the four sons of Osiris in ancient Egyptian beliefs. In Figure 108 there are two manifestations of the four sons, one shows them towing the sun-god into the Netherworld while the second shows them towing him out of it. A third group of four deities, who are not as readily identified as the other two groups, is located on the far right of the register; Piankoff (1954) does not translate its name but transliterates it as "Utau."[998]

We are told very little about the Utau although their preferred location on the far right of the register suggests an important role in the events of the register. The text above the seven forms of Re makes reference to their arms being hidden, a point which may mean they are hiding something in their garments. It also clearly indicates that these Utau are faithful followers of the sun-god:

---

[a] The Greek word, *lampros* is used in Rev. 19:8 as well as Rev. 15:6 but another word, *leukos*, is used in Rev. 1:14; 2:17; 3:4,5,18; 4:4; 6:2; 7:9,13,14; 14:14; 19:11; 19:14; and 20:11. In the second group, the Greek word translated to mean "white" is *leukos* so that the emphasis among these other incidents of usage is on the "white" color rather than its relation to "light."

> The gods of the Netherworld, in the glorious boat which is in the earth, utter words unto the Utau whose arms are hidden:
> Your portions are yours, O Utau of the earth, who roar: ... Uncover your heads, hide your arms! May there be air for your nostrils, may your swathings be unloosened, may you take your offerings, enjoy what I have created! Their offerings are bread, their beer is Djesert, their refreshment is water. Gifts are given to them of light-colored garments in the Netherworld.[999]

This statement outlining the Utau's rewards is quite remarkable in the light of a comment made by Piankoff (1954) concerning another group of Utau found in the 4th Hour of the *Book of Night*. In that location they are six in number and their picture shows them with arms tied and kneeling next to the "Followers of Seth." Three of them have been beheaded. Piankoff adds a footnote suggesting that Utau is "A term for some kind of enemy."[1000]

In order to reconcile this apparent difference in the meaning of the term Utau, we should look at the context in which we find them. In the *Book of Night*, as "followers of Seth" they are definitely enemies of Re while in the *Book of Gates*, they are clearly faithful followers of Re. The difference between the two disappears, however, if we consider the term Utau to simply mean "enemies" without reference to them being followers of either Seth or Re. Thus, in the *Book of Gates*, as the followers of Re, they are enemies of Apophis and/or Seth while in the *Book of Night*, as followers of Seth, they are enemies of Re. We may therefore conclude that the function of the Utau in this part of the *Book of Gates* is to act as enemies against those who do evil and to take appropriate actions against them.

Aggressive action by the four Utau against those who do evil certainly parallels the action taken by the four creatures outlined in Rev. 15:6 ("And one of the four living creatures gave the seven angels seven golden bowls full of the wrath of God who lives for ever and ever"). This parallel takes us to yet another one – the function of the four sons of Osiris in this part of the *Book of Gates* and that of the four creatures before the throne in Rev. 15:7, i.e., the destruction and annihilation of the wicked.

Although the four sons of Osiris were best known in their role as protectors of Osiris, and especially of the embalmed body parts of the dead, their potential for aggressive behavior was well known. Hornung (1990) points out that "they aid the sun god in his conflict with the Apophis serpent."[1001] Chapter 17 of the *Book of the Dead*, describes them as, "Lords of Justice, tribunal which is behind Osiris. Who put terror into the doers of wrong."[1002] And Budge (1934) provides us with a passage from a papyrus in the British Museum which says, "The Sons of Horus smash thee with their blows, thou art destroyed by their violence."[1003]

Even their name, "Utau" ( ), reflects the morbid aspect of their character. Consider, for example, the meanings of several short words which also begin with the *ut-* (*wt*) sound. Many of them are associated with death and destruction: Budge 1920 gives us *ut* (to mummify, to embalm), *uti* (and embalmed body), *utt* (to burn), *uti* (destruction), *utu* (death) and *utiu* (mummy, coffin).[1004] Faulkner (1926) provides us with the words *wt* (embalm, embalmer, bandage), *wtḫ* (flee), *wtḫw* (fugitive) and *wdi*(shoot an arrow, commit offence, stir up strife).[1005] Budge (1920) also refers to a similar word, *utiu* IV, as a name for the "the four embalmers, i.e., the four sons of Horus."[1006] Such near homonyms could very well have also played a role in the naming of a group of Utau gods.

To this list of characteristics we must add earthquakes because the text above the Barge of the Earth in Figure 107 quotes Re as saying to the Utau, "Your portions are yours, O Utau of the *earth who roar*."[1007] Earthquakes in this division are thus emphasized in the text above the middle register which also tells us that as the sun-god passes through this region: "The earth quakes, the earth quakes."[1008] Meanwhile, the four sons of Osiris were known to play an active role in the war against Apophis and his followers. Hornung (1990) tells us that in the Books of the Netherworld "they aid the sun god in his conflict with the Apophis serpent."[1009] For example, in the 11th Division of the *Book of Gates* Apophis is captured and his bonds are held by the "progeny of Horus while they [the followers of Apophis] flee before this god ... . The progeny of Horus take hold of him ... they put fetters on him. His coils are in the sky, his poison flows down in the west." It would therefore be quite within character for the sons of Osiris to deliver the bowls which contain the wrath of God in Rev. 15:7, and as we shall see later, this would almost certainly include earthquakes.

There is, however, no reference in the *Book of Gates* to the four *Utau* or the four sons giving bowls full of wrath to the seven forms of Re seated on the Barge of the Earth. Instead, it presents an opposite sequence of events: the seven spirits of Re speak to the four *Utau*. The Egyptian text says that "The [seven] gods of the Netherworld, in the glorious boat which is in the earth, utter words unto the [four] Utau whose arms are hidden... ."[1010] Thus, while a similar event seems to be described in both sources, the identity of the characters in the action is reversed. If one assumes an Egyptian background to this part of the Book of Revelation, it is the Egyptian version which seems more accurate because the *Utau* are associated with earthquakes. The next chapter of Revelation reveals the awful magnitude of the terrible wrath of God; Rev. 16, outlines a series of catastrophic events which concludes in what Rev. 16:18 describes as "a great earthquake such as had never been seen since men were on earth." (See *Chapter 13, Catastrophes*).

Judgment against the Nations

That the dispensing of judgment against the nations is indeed the main theme of Rev. 16 is emphasized in Rev. 16:4-7 where we read that after "the third angel poured his bowl "into the rivers and the fountains of water, and they became blood," an angel is quoted as saying, "Just art thou in these thy judgments, thou who art and wast, O Holy One." Shortly afterwards, we hear a cry form the altar saying, "Yea, Lord God the Almighty, true and just are thy judgments!"

The Egyptian counterpart of this scene is found in the *Book of Gates* in a special scene inserted between the 5th and 6th Divisions (Figure 109). Its solitary nature and central location emphasizes the judgmental nature of many of the events described in the *Book of Gates* and presents us with a brief overview of what Rev. 16:2 refers to as judgment against "the men [i.e., the followers of Seth] who bore the mark of the [1st] beast and worshiped its image."

Figure 109 shows a god carrying the balance of justice on his shoulders while standing before the throne of Osiris. Above and behind him, a baboon strikes the evil god Seth – Revelation's 1st beast who in this scene assumes the form of a fleeing pig.[1011] The followers of Seth are described as "The enemies of Osiris" who are "under his soles"[1012] (cf. Rev. 16:2). Hornung (1990) points out that "Osiris usually wears the double crown here, rather than his own; it symbolizes the pharaoh's role as sovereign of Upper and Lower Egypt."[1013] The scene therefore suggests that just as Osiris is the judge in the Netherworld, the king of Egypt has the same authority over earth and is responsible for judging the enemies of the sun-god on earth – and it is on earth that the plagues described in Rev. 16 are unleashed (see Chapter 13, *Catastrophes*).

Rev. 16 can be divided into two very different components. The main part represents the pouring of the wrath of God upon the wicked through a series of seven catastrophic events which cause great suffering on the earth. The second component involves the element of human intervention and is embedded in the sixth event in Rev. 16:12b-16 where we read of the amassing of many thousands of troops to do battle at a place called Armageddon. For a full discussion on Egyptian parallels to elements the main part of Rev. 16, the reader is referred back to Chapters 13 and 14, *Catastrophes* and *From Catastrophe to Myth*. Meanwhile, a very brief overview of the basic nature of the contents of each of the seven bowls of wrath poured onto the earth will suffice to focus the reader's mind on the series of events described in this chapter of Revelation.

Figure 109. The judgment scene in the *Book of Gates* showing Seth (Revelation's 1st beast) portrayed here as a pig being beaten by a baboon with a stick; the text tells us that his followers lie beneath the feet ("soles") of the enthroned Osiris. This scene conforms with the judgment scene in Rev. 15:4 which sets the stage for the dispensing of plagues on the earth in Rev. 16. (BG5/6)

Angel #1: Foul and evil sores break out among the people. (Rev. 16:2)
Angel #2: The sea becomes like blood and mass marine mortalities occur. (Rev. 16:3)
Angel #3: Fresh waters turn to blood and people must drink this water. (Rev. 16:4-6)
Angel #4: Men are scorched with fire. (Rev. 16:8-9)
Angel #5: Darkness covers the land. (Rev. 16:10)
Angel #6: The Euphrates River dries up. (Rev. 16:12a)[a]
Angel #7: Lightning, voices, thunder, and a great earthquake. (Rev. 16:18-21)

This dispensing of judgment against the nations is the main theme of Rev. 16 and is emphasized in a cry form the altar: "Yea, Lord God the Almighty, true and just are thy judgments!" (Rev. 16:7).

Waters turned to blood and consumed (Rev. 16:4-6)

Rev. 16:4 says, "The third angel poured his bowl into the rivers and the fountains of water, and they became blood" (Rev. 16:4). The Egyptian parallel to this scene in the upper register of the 3rd Division of the *Book of Gates* and shown in Figure 110.

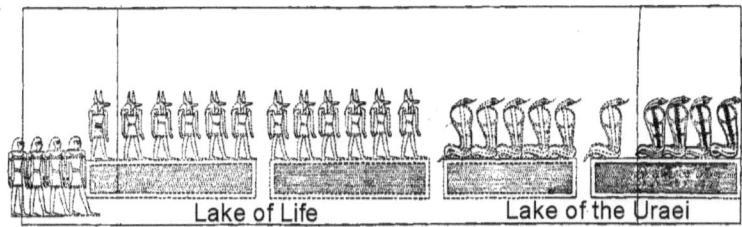

Figure 110. This picture shows four symbols of lakes of water, fire and blood. The first two and the second two actually each represent single lakes: the *Lake of Life* is surrounded by twelve jackal-headed deities while *The Lake of the Uraei* is surrounded by twelve uraeus serpents (ten are shown in this figure). On the far left stand four of twelve gods "who purify themselves by consuming the red stuff [blood] of the slaughtered enemies" an event similar to that described in Rev. 16:6. (BG3.1.3-10)

Here, the "rivers and fountains of water" are represented by the two bodies of water (shown as four rectangles in the figure) around which jackal-headed and serpentine Uraei stand. On the right side of the figure is a lake surrounded by Uraeus serpents; it is called *The Lake of the Uraei*. Uraeus serpents were fire-spitting cobras who represented the sun-god as well as the heat of the sun. Their presence here implies this lake is a lake of fire where the wicked were burned, an observation which conforms with Rev. 16:8 which says that "The fourth angel poured his bowl on the sun and it was allowed to scorch men with fire."

On the left side of the figure is a second body of water (also shown as two rectangles). It is called *The Lake of Life* and twelve dog-headed deities stand on its

---

[a] The reference to the gathering of troops at Armageddon, which is embedded in events associated with the sixth angel at Rev. 16:12b-16), and the Egyptian parallels to elements in this passage will be discussed in the next chapter, *Armageddon*.

shore. Re "purifies himself" in this lake and those who are not his followers "do not approach" it.[1014] The idea that this lake contains blood as in Rev. 16:4, is consistent with the red color with which it is usually painted; red was the symbolic color of both blood and fire.[1015] Twelve other deities around the *Lake of Life* in the 3rd Division (only four of the 12 are shown in Figure 110) are called "The gods who go to their Kas [spirits]"[a] and the text tells us they "purify themselves by consuming the red stuff [i.e., blood] of the slaughtered enemies to the end of their time."[1016] This statement parallels that of Rev. 16:6 which says, "thou hast given them blood to drink. It is their due!"

The drinking of the blood and eating of the flesh of vanquished foes is well documented in Egyptian religious texts. For example, in Chapter 179 of the *Book of the Dead*, Re threatens his enemies with the words, "an end will be put to him under me in the tribunal. I will eat him in the Great Field upon the altar of Wadjet."[1017] And in Chapter 134 of the same book we read that Re "will bathe in your blood, he will drink of your gore, O you who would do much harm to *N* in the Bark of his father Re."[1018] This aspect of cannibalism undoubtedly dates back to pre-historic times. It is already mentioned in the *Pyramid Texts*, the earliest known compilation of Egyptian texts. One such text reads,

> He has taken the hearts of the gods;
> He has eaten the Red,
> He has swallowed the Green
> King Unis is nourished on satisfied organs,
> He is satisfied, living on the hearts and their charms.
> ...
> Their charms are in his belly.
> The dignities of king Unis are not taken away from him;
> He hath swallowed the knowledge of every god.[1019]

Breasted (1912) comments on this subject, saying that it survives from

> vastly prehistoric days, in which we see the savage pharaoh ferociously preying upon the gods like a blood-thirsty hunter in the jungle. ...
> In this remarkable picture, the motive of the grotesque cannibalism is perfectly clear. The gods are hunted down, lassoed, bound, and slaughtered like wild cattle, that the king may devour their substance, and especially their internal organs, like the heart where the intelligence had its seat, in the belief that he might thus absorb and appropriate their qualities and powers. When "he has taken the hearts of the gods," "he has swallowed the knowledge of every god," and "their charms are in his belly'" and because the organs of the gods which he has devoured are plentifully satisfied with food, the king cannot hunger, for he has, as it were, eaten to compel satiety.[1020]

There is one obvious difference between the Revelation and *Book of Gates* accounts: Revelation says that it is the enemies who are given the blood to drink while the *Book of Gates* refers to the followers of the sun-god receiving the blood of their enemies. This discrepancy would not exist if the original text of Revelation had said, "and thou has given *their* blood to drink" rather than "and thou has given *them* blood

---

[a] Piankoff (1954, p 159 footnote) notes that this context of *kas* is "a usual term for the dead."

to drink." If we assume that this part of Revelation was in some way based on this part of the *Book of Gates*, two possibilities are readily apparent to explain the discrepancy. The first, which seems less likely, is that the Greek version of Revelation was originally written using the word for *their (auteés)* and early scribes changed this to the current version in which *them (autoís)* is used. Research on this possibility seems to be in order. The second possibility, which is simpler, involves the assumption that the original draft of Revelation was based on an Egyptian source to be later translated into Greek. In this case, confusion in the translation could have happened because the Egyptian word for both *them* and *their* is written as 𓊪𓏤𓏤𓏤 and pronounced the same way (·*sn*).[1021] In this scenario, the original text could have been written,"thou has given *their* (·*sn*) blood to drink" and this was later translated into the Greek to mean "thou has given *them* (·*sn*) blood to drink." This change in meaning could have been made by the author if the original draft was based on a verbal presentation which he wrote down in Greek, especially if he was unaware of the correct context at the time. Or it could have been done deliberately to create a pun to conceal the true meaning of the text from any reader who was not familiar with the *Book of Gates*. Alternately, some scribe other than the author made an error in judgment when an Egyptian version of the Book of Revelation was translated into Greek.

Praise for God's Judgment and his Eternal Nature (Rev. 16:5-7)

After the third angel causes the water to become blood in Rev. 16:4, an angel praises God by saying, "*Just art thou* in these thy judgments, *thou who art and wast*, O Holy One" (Rev. 16:5). And after the reference to blood being given for drink in Rev. 16:6b, a voice from the altar cries,"Yea, Lord God the Almighty, *true and just* are thy judgments!" (Rev. 16:7). Note that these quotations contain three distinct characteristics. The first is that they are words of praise, the second is that God's present and eternal nature is mentioned and the third refers to the correctness of his judgments.

Similarly, in the *Book of Gates*, after the victorious warriors are given the blood of their enemies to drink in BG3.3.3-10, they praise Re with the words, "*Laudation to thee*, Re of the Horizon. Hail, *perfect soul* upon earth! Hail to thee, *Everlasting One, Lord of Years, Eternal One, who has no lessening!*"[1022] In both Revelation and the *Book of Gates* a deity is praised and reference to his eternal nature is mentioned. Meanwhile, we may infer that the reference in the *Book of Gates* to Re being a "perfect soul" includes and conforms with the reference to "true and just" judgments of God in Rev. 16:6b.

With respect to the statement referring to the correctness of the judgments of the one on the throne in Revelation – "*true and just* are thy judgments!" – many scenes in the *Book of Gates* may be viewed as parallels in an Egyptian context. For example, in the 8th Division, Horus condemns twelve (three groups of four) enemies of the sun-god who stand before him (Figure 111). He says to them,

> O enemies of my father. ... O you evil ones! You are fettered from behind, *you are the evil ones to be decapitated* ' – you shall not exist! Your souls shall be annihilated and

shall not live because of what you have done to my father Osiris. ... My father *Osiris is justified against you, I am justified against you,'* for you have laid bare the mysteries which concern the peace of the Great One who begot me in the Netherworld. Hail! You have ceased to exist, you evil ones! (BG8.3.1-5)[1023]

Decapitation is, of course, but one of the numerous methods of punishment of the enemies of the sun-god described in the *Book of Gates*. Meanwhile, the fire-breathing serpent called the *Fiery One* in Figure 111 is called upon to "belch forth the flame among the enemies of my father, burn their bodies, consume their souls by this heat of thy mouth, by the fire which is in thy body!" The enemies here are referred to as "the burned ones."

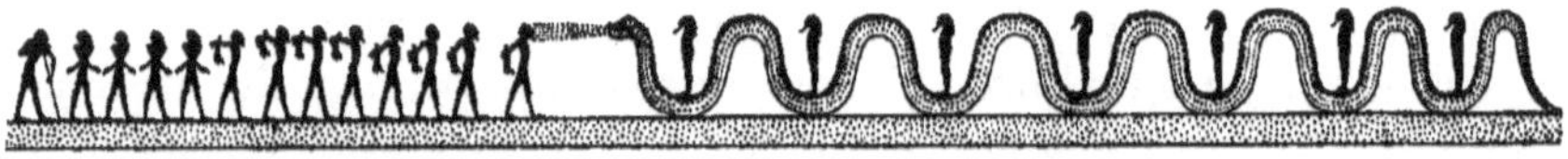

Figure 111. Seven deities called the *Gods upon the Fiery One* stand on the coils of a serpent called *The Fiery One* as they help guard the sun-god's enemies who stand before Horus at the far left of the scene. Parts of the text in this scene conforms with Rev. 16:5-7. (BG8.3)

Finally, just as Osiris rules over the powers of nature in the Netherworld, the Egyptian king, the earthly manifestation of his son Horus, was believed to have control over the powers of nature on earth so that he could execute his father's judgments on his enemies.

Natural Phenomena in the Wrath of God (Rev. 16)

In Chapter 13, *Catastrophes,* practically all natural catastrophes mentioned in the Book of Revelation were discussed from the point of view of them being caused either directly or indirectly by a volcanic eruption. In this chapter, only those phenomena referred to in Rev. 16 will be discussed and these will be dealt with only in reference to parallels found in the *Book of Gates*. With the exception of the drying up of the Euphrates River (Rev. 16:12) which will be discussed in the next chapter, *Armageddon,* they will be presented in the same order as they appear in the *Book of Gates*.

Earthquakes (Rev. 16:18-20):- Rev. 16:18 says that there was "a great earthquake such as had never been since men were on the earth, so great was that earthquake." Earthquakes are frequently mentioned in the *Book of Gates*. Perhaps the most relevant to the Book of Revelation is found in association with the bull-headed barge on which the seven deities are seated in the 2nd Division. The text over it says, "The earth quakes, the earth quakes, O thou whose soul is honored! The Double Bull rejoices, the god is satisfied with what he has created [earthquakes?]."[1024] Also, the seven deities who speak to the four *Utau* deities on the far right the register say, "Your portions are yours, *O Utau of the earth who roar*,'" words conforming with the rumbling from deep within the earth during an earthquake.

21. Seven Angels with the Wrath of God

This scene seems to be related to the opening scene of the next division where one of the guardians of the gate is called *Earthquake* and the other is called *Trembling of Earth*. The text above the ennead of nine deities at this gate makes a statement which may be interpreted as the tearing apart of the earth by an earthquake. It says, "Thou hast opened the earth, thou hast thrown open the door, O thou Heavenly One. Thou hast uncovered those who are in darkness."[1025] This could be related to graves opened during a strong earthquake.

There is, however, no mention in the *Book of Gates* to either the destruction of a "great city," the "cities of the nations," of entire mountains or the disappearance of islands described in Rev. 16:18-21 and discussed in Chapter 13, *Catastrophes;* these phenomena have parallels in of other Egyptian sources.

Poisonous Waters (Rev. 16:3-4):- Rev. 16:3-4 describes the sea becoming "like the blood of a dead man, and every living thing died that was in the sea." An allusion to poisonous waters is found in the 2nd Division of the *Book of Gates* in relation to the Lake of Fire discussed in Chapter 20, *The Song of Moses*. Remarkably, the water of that lake is not only described as being "fire" but also as being "filled with barley" and the "Birds fly away when they see the waters and smell the smell of what is in it."[1026] It is uncertain whether the mention of "fire in the lake" means that the lake is stagnant with "fermenting blood" and barley. Nevertheless, while the text does not explicitly state that the lake is poisonous, it strongly implies that it is dangerous to anyone or anything that might go near it (excepting, of course, the blessed dead).

The lake hieroglyphs (▭) in Figure 110 are painted red, a color which probably represents a visual pun. Such a pun, for example, might be based on words sounding like *tesher*, which means to be "red in color or reddish"[1027] or "to become red"[1028] and *tesher-t* which means a "red thing" or "red flame."[1029] But *tesher* also means "to terrify"[1030] and *tesher-ti* means "horrible."[1031] Meanwhile, the expression, "fountains of water" in Rev. 16:4 is akin to the meaning of *teshtesh*, "to flow out, to overspread (of water),"[1032] a concept consistent with the idea of a fountain. The water's red color could thus be interpreted as a sign of a fountain of terrifying and deadly substance.

But *tesh* ... words are not the only potentially relevant homonyms. Various Egyptian words for barley are also associated with fire or the color red. For example, one word for barley is *ser*[1033],[a] while *Serser* is "a fiery region of the of the Tuat."[1034] And *bet-t* means barley[1035] while *bet* means "to burn."[1036] Even *Ami*, a name of the eye of Horus and a fire-god[1037] is similar to another word for barley, *am*.[1038] It is even possible that the birds which "fly away when they see the waters and smell the smell of what is in it" are *ba*-birds (souls) of the wicked dead who would be harmed by the fire or blood if they approached too close. For the above reasons, we may conclude that the poisonous nature of the bodies of water in Figure 110 parallel those of the waters in Rev. 16:3-4.

---

[a] Note that the word *ser* also meant "drum" or "tambourine" (Budge, 1920, p.610b), musical instruments which reminds one of those who sing the song of Moses as they stand by the Lake of Fire in Rev. 15:2.

Fire from the Sun (Rev. 16:8-9):- Fiery heat is one of the most common and feared modes of torment and destruction described in the ancient Egyptian records. It should not be surprising to read in Revelation that when the fourth angel poured out his bowl, the *sun "scorched men with fire"* (Rev. 16:8). This image is entirely consistent with a common symbolism of rearing cobras. Wilkinson tells us that, "The cobra [*uraeus*] was held to represent *the fiery "eye" of the sun god Re*,' and twin uraei ... [were] represented on either side of the solar disk [☩]."[1039] In the upper register of the 3rd Division of the *Book of Gates* we read of flames breathed against the enemies of the sun-god. Here, ten *uraei* representing the sun-god's eye are seen sitting over a lake of fire, called the *Lake of the Uraei*; the text over them says, "O serpents of this lake. You guard your flame which you breathe against my enemies. Your fire (is) directed against those who acted evilly toward me. Hail to you, O serpents!"[1040] Furthermore, the text above the circular pool of fire at BG5.3.10 says that Re orders the twelve guardians of the pool to take action against the enemies of Osiris: "Ho you gods, who guard this holy pool ... . The flame of your fiery breath and your fire (?) are directed against the souls who might come near to Osiris with bad intent."[1041]

A close parallel to the verse in Revelation is also found in the 8th Division where we find a picture showing seven deities called the *Gods upon the Fiery One* who stand on the back a giant serpent called the *Fiery One* (BG8.3.5-10; Figure 111). This serpent spits fire against the enemies of sun-god and the text tells us that the mouth of the serpent is but a vehicle through *which the fire from the sun (the eye of Re) rains upon the enemies*:

> O mighty fire, *O this great flame of my eye*' [the sun] which comes out of this mouth, he whose coils are guarded by my children! Open thy mouth! Distend thy jaws, *belch forth the flame among the enemies of my father, burn their bodies*,' consume their souls by this heat of thy mouth, by the fire which is in thy body! My children are against them, they annihilate (their) souls, and those who have come forth from me are against them. They shall not exist! May the fire which is in this serpent come forth! (BG8.3.5-10)[1042]

Discussion

Piankoff's portrayal of the middle register of the 2nd Division shows that the solar barque is actually being towed *through* the Barge of the Earth. The towrope passes into the mouth of one of the bull-heads and out through the mouth of the other. The actual passage of the solar barque through the barge is depicted in two steps, the first shows it being towed into the barge while the second emphasizes its exit from it. Note that just as the last of the four towers exits the barge, the sun-god's barque is figuratively, still inside it, as indicated by the barque's invisibility behind the towers.

A similar concept is found 12th Division of the *Amduat* where more detail of the overall meaning of the event is presented. In that scene, the solar barque is towed through the body of a giant serpent rather than a bull-headed barge as in the *Book of Gates*. Again, the solar barque is described as being towed through the Netherworld and the text tells us that Re and his celestial followers are born anew as they emerge from the mouth of the serpent (AM12.2.1-3): "This god travels like this in the city[a] along the backbone of this hidden image of the serpent, Life of the Gods. His gods tow him while he enters into the tail and comes out of its mouth, being born, in his forms of Khepri of the gods who are in his barge."[1043] As the sun-god and his followers pass through both the bull-headed barge in the *Book of Gates* and the serpent in the *Amduat,* all travelers are rejuvenated – first, the sun-god's followers from the Netherworld and then Re himself. Hornung (1990) suggests these transformations actually represent an important aspect of the renewal of creation:

> ... immediately before dawn, the solar bark with all its gods and an incredible number of the blessed dead enters into the serpent's tail. The text notes that they all enter ... [and] travel along its backbone, and step forth from its mouth as small children. The inverse route, traveling from the tip of the tail to the mouth, plays on the marvelous reversal of time, which is possible only in the Beyond – from old man to child, from death to birth.[1044]

Such renewal, of course, results in the closing of time past, i.e., the end of time, which makes way for its renewal. And the faithful followers of the sun-god reach the end of mortality and the beginning of eternal life in the heavens.

But for the enemies of the sun-god who propagated evil deeds on earth or in the Netherworld, passage of the sun-god through the Netherworld meant their judgment, damnation, destruction, and total annihilation from the most horrible forms of death – dismemberment, cooking in cauldrons of boiling water, and a second death in the Lake of Fire or in the flames of the fire pits. The dispensing of this judgment is often supervised by "Horus of the Netherworld." On earth it is done by Horus, the king of Egypt and divine son of the sun-god,. The pharaoh imposed this judgment on the enemies of the sun-god within Egypt and on all nations who threatened Egypt's sovereignty or failed to do his bidding.

These judgments were waged as wars during which enemy soldiers and civilians alike were punished, taken as prisoners or slaves or killed. At times, the king's military activities coincided with natural phenomena such as thunder, lightning, earthquakes and possibly, at times, volcanic eruptions (see Chapter 12, *Catastrophes*). When such things happened, he, being the sun-god's representative on earth, undoubtedly claimed them as manifestations of his own great power and authority. The sun-god's judgments against evil were thus not only manifest in the afterlife but also through his divine son on earth. The ultimate demonstration of his power on earth was not death and destruction associated with wars but through catastrophic natural phenomena. This included phenomena such as those described as being poured onto the earth by the seven angels in Rev. 16 and discussed in the next chapter, *Armageddon.*

The journey through the Barge of the Earth not only involves the rebirth of the sun-god and his faithful followers but also the cleansing of all who pass through it.

---

[a] Note that here the serpent is called a "city," a term often applied to the Egyptian "holy city," a part of the Netherworld. The Egyptian concept of the holy city is discussed in detail in Chapter 27, *The Holy City.*

Thus, Re's judgment against the nations may be viewed as happening inside the barge (the Netherworld) – and on earth (see Chapter 13, *Catastrophes*) where they represent actual events. Figure 107 thus represents both the setting and the summary of things to come, including the wrath of Re when all evil is destroyed and the earth is renewed; only that which is pure can pass from the mouth of the bull into a new life. It is in this context that we find an important parallel between this scene and the statement in Rev. 5:1, "with them [the seven angels] the wrath of God is ended."

Chapter 22. Armageddon (Rev 16:12b-16)[1045]

Rev. 16 begins with the following statement: "Then I heard a loud voice from the temple telling the seven angels, 'Go and pour out on the earth the seven bowls of the wrath of God'" (Rev 16:1). From there it goes on to describe seven catastrophes unleashed upon the world. These are discussed in detail in Chapter 13, *Catastrophes*. The sixth plague is different from the others, however, in that it contains not only natural catastrophes, but also the drying up of a river and the gathering for war of hundreds of thousands of troops at a place called Armageddon.

Other than in Rev. 16:16, the name "Armageddon" does not appear anywhere else in early Hebrew or Christian literature. Barnes (1993) notes that,

> Scholars generally explain the name Armageddon (NRSV: 'Harmagedon') as a Greek transliteration of the Hebrew phrase *har měgiddô* ('the mountain of Megiddo'). The city of Megiddo, strategically located in the western part of the Esdraelon valley at the crossroads of two trade routes, was the site of several important battles in ancient times.[1046]

Judges 5:19-20 speaks of a victory song sung there by Deborah and Barak when Gidion defeated Midian (Judges 6:33) and it was at Megiddo that Saul fought a battle with the Philistines (I Samuel 31:1-6) and Josiah was slain in a battle with the Egyptian Pharaoh Necho (II Kings 23:39,30) during Egypt's 26th Dynasty. Zondervan emphasizes Megiddo's strategic importance with the comment that the low mountains in the area "were silent witnesses of perhaps more bloody encounters than any other spot on earth, continuing down to recent times."[1047] And Megiddo was the site of many of Egypt's greatest battles.

In this chapter we compare two well-known Egyptian sources to Revelation's account of events at Armageddon. We begin with what is perhaps the best documented of all Egyptian battles – an assault on the fortified city of Megiddo by an Egyptian king as documented in *The Annals of Thutmosis III*[1048] which describes events during the twenty-third year of the reign of Thutmosis III (1479-1425 BCE), the fifth king of Egypt's 18th dynasty. We will conclude with several parallel scenes found in the *Book of Gates*.

Breasted (1962) points out that the *Annals of Thutmosis III* were found on the inside of the walls enclosing the corridor which surrounds the granite holy of holies of the great Karnak temple of Amon. These walls were built by Thutmosis III.[1049] For relevant information on the *Book of Gates* we turn to Hornung (1999) who says its first exemplar, which is itself incomplete, was found in the sarcophagus chamber of Haremhab (1319-1307 BCE), the last king of the same dynasty. The later date of the *Book of Gates* enables the suggestion that parts of it may actually represent mythologizations of events described in the *Annals*, including the description of events at Megiddo. This allows both sources to be legitimately compared with scenes from the Book of Revelation which was presumably written long after Haremhab's rule.

Armageddon in the *Annals of Thutmosis III*

Cities of the Nations Fall (Rev. 16:19)

The sequence of events leading up to Thutmosis' battle at Megiddo is discussed by Grimal (1992):

> After the death of Queen Hatshepsut, Thutmosis III found himself confronted by a revolt of the main Asiatic peoples, united around the prince of Qadesh with the support of the Mitanni. ... Its empire, made up of the remains of the domain of the Babylonian king Hammurapi, reached its peak in the fifteenth century BC. ... [it] stretched across Syria and Kurdistan as far as the Palestinian region. This was the geographical area of their conflict with Egypt from the time of Ahmose [1550-1525 BCE] onwards, because the Egyptians' aim was to push back as far as possible the 'Asiatics' who threatened their borders. Mitanni, on the other hand, attempted to embroil its Egyptian rivals in local struggles among the Syrian city-states, thus ensuring that the Mitannian empire itself was not directly threatened. The Mitannians achieved this aim by exacerbating the constant rivalries between each of the city-states through a subtle game of switching alliances.[1050]

So it was that in the twenty-second to twenty-third years of his reign, Thutmosis III launched a major campaign into the area. According to his *Annals*, a coalition of enemy forces under the Prince of Kadesh (Qadesh) had taken Megiddo and were amassed in the area. His *Annals* tell us that as he approached Megiddo, Thutmosis called a council of war.

> His majesty ordered a consultation with his valiant troops, saying as follows: "That wretched enemy, the chief of Kadesh has come and entered into Megiddo; he is there at this moment. He has gathered to himself the chiefs of all the countries which are on the water of Egypt, and as far as Naharin [the area between the upper Tigris and Euphrates River and likely including that beyond the Euphrates] consisting of the countries of Kharu, the Kode, their horses, their troops, – thus he speaks. 'I have arisen to fight against his majesty in Megiddo.[1051]

The reference to the chief of Kadesh gathering "to himself the chiefs of all the countries" is surely consistent with the Revelation account where we read that the spirits "are demonic spirits ... who go abroad to the kings of the whole world, to assemble them for battle [at Armageddon]" (Rev. 16:14). When viewed in the light of the effective geographical extent of Thutmosis' victory at Megiddo, the parallel to the phrase in Rev. 16:19 that "the cities of the nations fell," is obvious.

22. Armageddon

There are at least three other parallels found in the *Annals of Thutmosis III*, each of which conforms with elements in the text of Rev. 16:15 – "Lo, I am coming like a thief! Blessed is he who is awake, keeping his garments that he may not go naked and be seen exposed!" The three main elements in this verse – coming like a thief, a reference to being awake, and nakedness – will be dealt with separately.

"Coming like a thief"(Rev. 16:15a)

This element is found in the description of a surprise attack by the Egyptian army. It was led by Thutmosis III against the multinational assembly of troops encamped around the fortified city of Megiddo, Revelation's Armageddon. The Annals tell us that Thutmosis secretly led his army toward Megiddo through a narrow mountainous road:

> ... the majesty commanded the entire army to march ... upon that road which threatened to be narrow. His majesty saying: "None shall go forth in the way before my majesty ..." He went forth at the head of his army showing the way by his own footsteps; horse behind horse, his majesty being at the head of the army.[1052]

The armies protecting Megiddo had been expecting the attack to come from a different direction and the bulk of their forces was deployed such that the approach from the mountain pass was left unguarded. On emerging from this narrow way, Thutmosis' army re-grouped and prepared to attack. This stealthy approach to Megiddo conforms quite well with Revelation's statement, "Lo, I am coming like a thief!" This is especially so when it is interpreted in the context of the gathering of troops at Armageddon, as it most certainly does, being couched in the midst of the other verses between Rev. 16:11 and Rev. 16:17 which deal with the battle.

Before the attack, "the king rested in the royal tent."[1053] The *Annals* tell us that the army set up camp and prepared themselves for the coming battle on the plains surrounding Megiddo. In them we hear echoes of "pep" talks to the soldiers: "... command was given to the whole army, saying: 'Equip yourselves! Prepare your weapons! For we shall advance to fight that wretched foe in the morning.' ... The watch of the army went about saying, 'Steady of heart! Steady of heart! *Watchful! Watchful!*'"[1054] Bravery and alertness were obviously necessary as the troops waited to attack; Thutmosis did not want his troops to engage in battle unless they were psychologically prepared and well rested, factors which improved their chances of survival in the battle – and of victory.

Naked Enemy Soldiers (Rev. 16:15c)

Since the attack was sudden, the enemy encampment was caught off guard and at least some of the soldiers must have been caught naked (as in Rev. 16:15) as they rested in their tents and had no time to fully prepare themselves for battle. Rev. 16:15 says, "Blessed is he who is awake," an apparent reference to an enemy coming under attack while they were resting.

> Then his majesty prevailed against them at the head of his army, and when they saw his majesty prevailing against them they fled headlong to Megiddo (*My-k-ty*) in fear,

abandoning their horses and chariots of gold and silver. The people hauled them (up), pulling (them) by their clothing, into this city; the people of this city having closed (it) against them and lowered clothing to pull them up into this city. ... The fear of his majesty had entered their hearts, their arms were powerless, his serpent diadem was victorious among them.[1055]

There can be little doubt that in the ensuing panic, both the rescuers inside the city walls and the soldiers outside stripped off what clothing they had on to contribute to the construction of ropes on which more soldiers could climb to safety. Many or all of those captured in the act of trying to climb up the hurriedly prepared ropes would have been found naked as described in Rev. 16:15. Further parallels on the nakedness of captured enemy soldiers will be discussed shortly in relation to a parallel scene found in the *Book of Gates*.

Armageddon in the *Book of Gates*

The *Book of Gates* does not specifically identify the battle of Megiddo in any of its battle scenes. Nevertheless, a passage in the 6th Division bears several similarities to the account in Revelation. Here we see an army of soldiers represented by twelve deities at BG6.1.5-10 who carry feathers of truth on their heads (Figure 30).[a] The text tells us that these are "Those who have acted according to justice while on earth, who fight for their god, who are convoked to the place (called) the *Gladness of Earth*."[1056] Similarly, Rev. 16:14 refers to those who are "assembled ... for battle. ... at the place which is called ..." When we compare these two sources we find two similar concepts – troops being assembled, and "a place called ..." These elements appear in juxtaposition in both sources; both refer to a group of soldiers assembled for battle at a place which is identified by name; the only difference between the two sources is in the name of the place.

The apparent difference between the name Megiddo and "place of Gladness," however, disappears if the name, "place of Gladness," is considered as a descriptive term for a place rather than the actual name of the place itself. For example, the "place of Gladness" mentioned in the *Book of Gates* could be any area where a great battle was fought and won. The joy of winning undoubtedly would warrant a special descriptive name for those who survived the battle and reaped the spoils.[b] Also, "Gladness" may have been a euphemism for those who died in battle and passed on to the glorious Fields of the Blessed in the Egyptian afterlife.

---

[a] This is the same group of twelve which parallels "those who live on truth" mentioned in Chapter 7, *The Great Multitude*."

[b] The spoils from the Battle of Armageddon (Megiddo) will be dealt with later in this chapter in relation to Rev. 16:19.

22. Armageddon

Another parallel is found in the text of Rev. 16:17 where a voice from the throne says, "It is done!" Similarly, in the *Book of Gates*, Osiris[a] says to the twelve who carry the feathers of truth, "May you be satisfied with *what you have done.*"[1057]

This series of three parallels – the troops being assembled, the reference to "a place called ..." and the parallel to Revelation's statement "It is done!" – conforms with this part of the *Book of Gates* and can be said to parallel this part of Rev. 16:13-17.

Events at the Euphrates River (Rev. 16:12-16)

The plague delivered by the sixth angel is described as the drying up of the Euphrates River. As discussed in the previous chapter, this conforms with a well-known phenomenon involving changes to the courses of rivers caused by strong earthquakes. But Rev. 16:12-16 adds an unusual element. It links the event with the assemblage of a great army: "... its water was dried up ... And I saw, issuing from the mouth of the dragon [serpent] ... foul spirits like frogs ... who go abroad to the kings of the whole world, to assemble them for battle ... at a place called Armaged'don." The unusual nature of this description presents us with an ideal opportunity to make a reasonably good identification of its parallel in the 3rd Division of the *Book of Gates*.

Elements of the Revelation account will be shown to have counterparts in the *Book of Gates* as follows: (1) a river whose stream-bed has dried up (Rev. 16:12), (2) evil spirits emerge from a serpent/dragon (Rev. 16:13) and (3) spirits organize different armies (Rev. 16:14) to go to war (Rev. 16:15). Each of these elements are present in Figure 112 and will be dealt with separately.

A River Dries up (Rev. 16:12):-The parallel to this scene is found in the middle register of the 3rd Division. Here we see six goddesses (some versions show male deities) standing on each side of a dried-up riverbed. Some stand on overhanging riverbanks painted with vertical water symbols inside the triangular form of the river's over-hanging banks. Between the two banks is a large multi-coiled serpent. In

Figure 112 Twelve goddesses stand guard over a multi-coiled serpent lying in the center of a dried-up river bed. As in Rev. 16:12-14, evil entities emerge from the serpent and must to be destroyed. (BG3.2.7-10)

---

[a] In Chapter 3, *The Preeminent Deities*, it was shown that the one on the throne in Revelation closely parallels the Egyptian god Osiris.

hieroglyphic symbolism, the coils of a serpent may represent sandbanks,[a] and thus serve to emphasize the idea of a dried-up river.

There is also what seems to be a hidden reason for the drying up of the riverbed in this scene. Recall that the text introducing this Division refers to one of its guardians as *Earthquake* and another as *Trembling of Earth*.[1058] We may therefore conclude that earthquakes are a feature of this division. The shifting of the earth during earthquakes, of course, is renowned for changing the courses of rivers where old ones run dry and water follows new courses. The dried-up riverbed in Figure 112 thus conforms with the known effects of earthquakes as well as the river scene described in Rev. 16:12, especially in light of the series of events in the rest of Rev. 16, which concludes with a great earthquake in Rev. 16:18-19.

The Dragon in the River (Rev. 16:13):- As noted above, immediately after mentioning the drying up of the Euphrates River in Rev. 16:13 a dragon is described. As pointed out in Chapter 4, *Other Characters in Revelation*, Revelation's dragon parallels Apophis, Egypt's primordial serpent. Its large size and multi-coiled form in Figure 112 suggests the serpent is Apophis although the text says its name is Hereret (or Herit, *Hrrt*), a name with a female ending (*-t*) suggesting it is female. This apparent contradiction in gender serves as a clue to how Hereret might be related to Apophis and, as will be discussed next, this will serve as the basis for a comparison with the evil spirits which Rev. 16:13-14 says come out of the dragon.

Grimal (1992) tells of a well-known Hyksos woman called Hereret, the daughter of the second Hyksos king of the 15th Dynasty. Apophis I was the most long lived of the 15th Dynasty and reigned from Avaris for forty years.[1059] He was also the most peaceful Hyksos king and very likely formed an alliance with Thebes (of Upper Egypt); there is evidence that during this more peaceful time and in the early years of his reign, Apophis' daughter, Hereret, married someone in the Theban royal family. Remarkably, as Grimal points out, this marriage "would have made Herit [Hereret] one of the ancestors of the Eighteenth Dynasty"[1060] in Thebes. Offspring of Hereret (and hence Apophis) were thus related to later kings of the Hyksos dynasty. This of course, may well have eventually further embittered the memories of Hyksos rule, memories which were undoubtedly nurtured by many Middle Egyptian kings. What seems most significant here is that the last (important) Hyksos king also bore the name of Apophis (Apophis II) and could have been one of Hereret's children or grandchildren.

The next step in developing a possible link between Hereret's children and the evil god Apophis is to consider the scenario developed in Chapter 18, *The Beasts of Rev. 13*. Recall that the Hyksos adopted the Egyptian god Seth, albeit in a corrupted form resembling the Palestinian god Baal. Also, recall that Seth and Apophis were at times considered to be very similar and sometimes even equated with one another. Finally, recall from the same chapter that the Hyksos kings of Lower Egypt effectively ruled over Upper Egyptian kings and thus, could be designated as "illegitimate" kings from the point of view of the Theban kings. The early Hyksos kings may well parallel

---

[a] Lurker (1980, p. 29) points out that Apophis "tried to hinder the sun-god's journey with its coils, described as 'sandbanks.'" Hornung (1990, p. 84-85), in dealing with the concept of time, suggests that "each coil forms an hour that slips away devoured and then is re-formed."

Revelation's 2nd beast who made an image of the 1st beast (Seth) who received its power from the dragon as stated in Rev. 13. This could be the reason why the serpent, Hereret, in the dried-up river in Figure 112 has the same many-coiled form typical of illustrations of the serpent/dragon Apophis; the serpent probably represents the power of the god Apophis expressed through the corrupted version of Seth, the god of Hereret's children and/or grandchildren who became Hyksos kings, one or more of whom were parallels to the 2nd beast of Rev. 13.

The False Prophet (Rev. 16:13):- Rev. 16:13 says that evil spirits came out of the mouths of not only the dragon and the beast, but *also* the "false prophet." Before discussing the emergence of the spirits themselves, it is advisable that we review an Egyptian parallel with the false prophet since this is the first time he appears in the Book of Revelation.

Rev. 16 gives us practically no information about the false prophet which might enable his identification with a particular Egyptian. In order to identify him, we must look ahead to Rev. 19 where he is mentioned for the second time; here we find some useful information – we are told that he is the one who worked signs in the presence of the beast:

> And I saw the (2nd) beast and the kings of the earth with their armies gathered to make war against him who sits upon the horse and against his army. And the [2nd] beast was captured, and with it *the false prophet who in its presence had worked the signs by which he deceived* those who had received the mark of the [1st] beast and those who worshiped its image. (Rev. 19:19-20, RSV)

But earlier, in Rev. 12, we read of the one who also works signs (miracles) in the presence of the 1st beast:

> And [the 2nd beast] *deceiveth them that dwell on the earth by the means of those miracles which* he had power to do in the sight of the [1st] beast; saying to them that dwell on the earth, that they should make an image to the [1st] beast." (Rev. 13:14, KJV)

We thus see from these two verses that the "false prophet" and the 2nd beast of Revelation are clearly one and the same person by virtue of them both having made miracles, or signs, before the people; both are clearly linked to the image of the 1st beast (see Chapter 18, *The Beasts of Rev. 13*).

Evil Spirits from the Dragon (Rev. 16:13-14):- We next leave the drying up of the Euphrates River in Rev. 16:12 to go on to Rev. 16:13-14 which describes the foul spirits issuing out of the mouth of the "dragon, the beast and the false prophet."

In view of the above paragraphs, and in consideration of the findings in Chapter 18, we may conclude from Rev. 16:13 that the authority of the 2nd beast (an illegitimate king of Egypt)) who made an image of the 1st beast (Seth) for the people to worship, came under the same authority, i.e., of Apophis, the dragon. In other words, the evil spirits issuing "from the mouth of the dragon [Egypt's Apophis] and from the mouth of the [1st] beast [Seth] and from the mouth of the false prophet [the 2nd beast/illegitimate king of Egypt]" in Rev. 16:13 may be envisaged as having all issued from Apophis himself. And if we assume that the apparent reference to

Apophis is in fact a reference to *king* Apophis II rather than the god Apophis, an assumption which makes sense in consideration of the line of command from king Apophis II to the corrupted god Seth and from there to the god Apophis, we have a basis for considering the reference to the dragon of Rev. 16:13 to be a parallel to Apophis II; this would suggest a play on the name Apophis, the primordial serpent, and that of the earthly king, Apophis II.

Rev. 16:13-14 tells us that the spirits which came out of the dragon were "foul" and "demonic spirits." Similarly, enemies of the sun-god emerge from the multi-coiled serpent which lies in the dried up center of the riverbed in Figure 112; the Egyptian text refers to the serpent as "Hereret"[1061] and describes it as "He who should be removed,"[1062] indicating he is an enemy of the sun-god. The text also gives instructions concerning the entities to which Hereret gives birth: "Twelve ones to be destroyed are being born before her."[1063] A little later Re says to the twelve goddesses:

> "Harken, you goddesses of the Hours. The appeals are addressed to you – act for yourselves among you. ... Stop you the serpent Hereret! Live you by what comes out of him. Your portions are in the Netherworld, you swallow what Hereret gives birth to, you annihilate what comes out of him."[1064]

Thus, like the foul and demonic nature of the spirits which issues from the mouth of the dragon and his followers in Revelation, enemies of the sun-god are born of the serpent Hereret, who, in effect, represents Apophis the dragon.

Revelation says that "three foul spirits like frogs" emerge from the serpent. In an Egyptian sense, "three" can mean "many" so this may be interpreted to mean more than three. This interpretation would conform with the Egyptian text which says that the serpent gives birth to twelve entities so that the difference in the number of entities emerging from the two serpents is not significant. Also note that, from an Egyptian perspective, the number twelve can be represented as 3 x 4 so that twelve can mean "many multitudes," which also conforms with the sense of "many."

Also, Revelation's reference to the foul spirits being "like frogs" is entirely consistent with the idea of "many multitudes" of spirits. The *Book of Gates* does not, it seems, explicitly suggest their form but simply refers to them as "twelve *ones*."[a] The image of frogs "issuing from" the serpent in Revelation is, however, consistent with Egypt's use of hieroglyphic symbolism for the word "birth." Wilkinson (1992) informs us that the idea of being born and giving birth was intimately associated with the image of a frog (🐸, *kerer, krr*): "Because of its prodigious reproductive capacity the frog was a symbol of creation, fertility, birth, and regeneration. As an underworld animal it was associated with the forces which initially brought life into being. Most important, however, the frog was sacred to Heket, the goddess of childbirth who was venerated as the female complement of the creator-god Khnum."[1065] In this way, the idea of Hereret giving birth to a great number of entities conforms with the *issuing of frogs* from the dragon in Rev. 16:13.

---

[a] Budge (1934, p.370) says that Hereret "spawns twelve serpents" but the basis of this statement is unclear.

The name of the group of twelve goddesses who stand on the banks of the river is "The Hours of the Netherworld,"[1066] i.e., they are time goddesses. This is also instructive, particularly because their title seems to contain puns related to the wrath of God. There are several Egyptian homonyms or near homonyms related to time which may be used as puns to refer to their delivery of the "wrath of God." Consider, for example, the following: *At* and *at* can mean "a small portion of time, moment, minute, hour, a time of culmination of some act or *emotion*."[1067] Meanwhile, *at-t* can mean "wrath"[1068] and *at* can mean an "evil doer"[1069] while *at* can refer to emotions such as "angry" or "to rage at"[1070] or possibly even refer to a natural catastrophe where *at* and *atch* can both have the same mean meaning, i.e., "calamity."[1071] Thus, the meaning of the name given to the twelve deities (they are time goddesses) could conceivably be interpreted as "The *Wrath* of the Netherworld" as well as "The Hours of the Netherworld." Meanwhile, in this context even the preposition "of" in the name "The Hours of the Netherworld" is subject to scrutiny since the Egyptian word, *m*, the word for "of," can also mean "in."[1072] Thus, the name of the goddesses could also mean "The Wrath in the Netherworld," a phrase which would also be in keeping with the catastrophes outlined in Rev. 16.

The statement in Rev. 16:13 that the birth of frog-like spirits should occur through the *mouth* of the dragon conforms with a number of mythological instances of birth in the Egyptian Netherworld. One prominent example is the birth of the sun-god and his followers from the mouth of a bull (see Chapter 21, *Seven Angels with the Wrath of God* and Figure 107). The idea of demonic spirits like frogs which issued from the mouth of the dragon in Revelation does not conflict with Egyptian imagery.

The Battle of Armageddon

It may well be significant that the Egyptian words for "battlefield," *per-t*[1073] and *prỉ*,[1074] are phonetically similar to *Perath*, a Hebrew name for the Euphrates River. These Egyptian words would thus be associated in the mind of a Hebrew scribe with the word for the Euphrates River and in this way could form a link to the Euphrates River which had to be crossed by armies en route to Armageddon from the east.[a] The choice of the name "Euphrates" for the river described in Rev. 16:12 is thus interesting from the point of view of events attributed to the sixth angel. The dried up river obviously intersects the route to be taken by "the kings of the east" to join the kings from other parts of the world for we read in Rev. 16:14 that the demonic spirits "go abroad to the kings of the whole world, to assemble them for battle on the great day of God the Almighty" and in Rev. 16:16 we are told that "they assembled ... at the place which is called in Hebrew Armaged'don," i.e., Megiddo. In this manner, this reference to the Euphrates would, from an Egyptian perspective, conjure memories of past battles with enemy forces from the east.

The *Book of Gates* does not mention the stealthy trek by Thutmosis III through a mountain pass. But it does make reference to affairs being put in order,

---

[a] This possible connection would be even more plausible if this part of Revelation was based on Egyptian texts and the author of Revelation was a Hebrew whose interpretation of Egyptian was influenced by his knowledge of the Hebrew language.

presumably prior to the surprise attack. The text in the 6th division says, "*Re has taken possession of the Silent Region. This Great God puts your affairs in order.*"[1075] Note that the first part of this passage can be interpreted as referring to the stealthy march of his army through a narrow mountain pass, a part of which took place in the silence of the night as outlined in the *Annals*. The next day, the last of Thutmosis' army arrived on the plain south of Megiddo in a strategically advantageous position against the enemy troops. The *Annals* tell us that "On emerging from this narrow way, Thutmosis' army re-grouped and prepared for the attack. Then "the king rested in the royal tent" and "the *affairs of the chiefs were arranged.*"[1076] The reference to putting affairs in order in both the *Annals* and *the Book of Gates* suggest a link between the two scenes; both seem to refer to events at Megiddo. And this similarity between the two Egyptian sources supports the view that the events described in this part of the *Book of Gates* parallel the "coming like a thief" described in Rev. 16:15.

An allusion to the large number of troops gathered for battle at Armageddon is found in Rev. 16:14-16; its says that *spirits like frogs* "go abroad to the kings of the whole world, to assemble them for battle." As noted above, references to frogs may, from an Egyptian perspective, suggest an approximate number of soldiers involved. Also, the "spirits like frogs" which came from the mouth of the dragon may refer to the *birth* of the spirits, as suggested above. To carry this analogy with frogs even further, we examine another symbol associated with frogs – the one illustrating their juvenile form, i.e., tadpoles. Wilkinson (1992) informs us that, "Like the mature animal, the swarming tadpole *(hefner)* was a symbol of abundance and was represented in the hieroglyphic script as the symbol [ʖ] for 100,000."[1077] And since Revelation points out that there were *three* frogs involved, we might infer from an Egyptian perspective that the total number of troops involved was 3 x 100,000 = 300,000 – or "many" hundreds of thousands if we emphasize the fact that the number 3 can mean "many." The characterization of the three foul spirits being "like frogs" conforms with and parallels the large number of troops of "the kings of the whole world" which gathered for the battle at Armageddon.[a]

Nakedness of the Enemy (Rev. 16:15):- Rev. 16:15 says, "Lo, I am coming like a thief! Blessed is he who is awake, *keeping his garments that he may not go naked and be seen exposed!*" This conforms with Egyptian pictures of naked enemy soldiers captured in battle; such pictures are not uncommon among secular and religious scenes showing captives being led back to Egypt at the end of military campaigns. In religious texts studied here we find such pictures in the upper register of the 7th Division of the *Amduat* and the lower register of the 1st Division of the *Book of Gates* – and, more significantly, in the middle register of the 6th Division. Here, and

---

[a] This large number of 300,000 troops, while not as great as the number assembled for battle in Rev. 9:16 ("The number of the troops of cavalry was twice ten thousand times ten thousand," i.e., 200 million) and in Rev. 20:8 ("their number is like the sand of the sea"), it falls in the same category of very large number which the Egyptians tended to express in general terms rather than absolute numbers. For example, in an inscription on a monument behind the Memnon colossi, Amenhotep III refers to the cattle of captive enemies of Egypt as being "like the sand of the shore, they make up millions." (Breasted, 1962. *Ancient Records of Egypt, Historical Documents, Vol. 2, The Eighteenth Dynasty.* p.357, section 884.)

immediately below the picture of the sun-god's massive army (carrying the feather of *maat* in Figure 30)[a] is a group of fourteen naked enemies tied to seven poles and shown here as Figure 113.

Figure 113. Representatives of the enemies of the sun-god tied to seven *Useru* poles of Geb (an earth god) are guarded by seven gods who are "in the following of the *Useru* poles ... who are in the following of Geb, the Prince." The nakedness of the enemy soldiers conforms with Rev. 16:15. (BG6.2.4-10)

Furthermore, the text associated with the naked soldiers in Figure 113 conforms with the diverse origins of the armies mentioned in Rev. 16:14 which are gathered at Armageddon. In the first place, the text in the 6th Division tells us that these are the *"Useru* poles of Geb, to which the enemies are assigned after the judgment has been pronounced in the West."[1078] Next, it divides them into seven different groups, as follows: (1) The enemies of the Neck of Re, (2) The enemies of Atum, (3) The enemies of Khepri, (4) The enemies of Shu, (5) The enemies of Geb, (6) The enemies of Osiris, and (7) The enemies of (Horus).[1079] It may be significant that this is the same number of groups as there were angels who poured their bowls of wrath on the followers of the beast in Rev. 16. The scene may also suggests they have seven different origins, possibly different nationalities, since they are grouped according to the names of different Egyptian gods which guard them, an observation that conforms with the mix of armies from the "kings of the whole world" mentioned in Rev. 16:14.

Each of the seven groups of naked enemies has a guard standing over them; they are given instructions, as follows:

> Guard you the enemies, take hold of the rebels! O you gods who are in the following of the *Useru* poles, you who are in the following of Geb, the Prince! Seize you the enemies, guard you the rebels that they may not come out of your arms, nor escape through your fingers! O you enemies, you are assigned to be beheaded according to what Re has decreed against you in his plans. ... He has decreed your massacre.[1080]

Except for a reference to them being beheaded, the text over this scene does not provide us with many details of the actions to be taken against them. Nevertheless, the similarity between the seven groups of enemies, each of which is guarded by a single deity, conforms with the idea of the involvement of seven angels with the seven bowls of the wrath of God which released their plagues in Rev. 16.

---

[a] Note that the soldiers in Figure 30 carry feathers of *maat* on the heads to represent the truth and proper order of things in the sun-god's massive army.

Cities of the nations fall (Rev. 16:19):- The battle of Armageddon ended when "the cities of the nations fell, and God remembered great Babylon, to make her drain the cup of the fury of his wrath" (Rev. 16:19).

In the *Book of Gates*, the international nature of many of its characters, at least in the early divisions, is portrayed visually in the lower register of the 4th Division. Here, four groups of four deities are shown, each representing a different race; they are designated as Libyans, Asiatics, Negros – and men. Each group is assigned a reigning deity: the goddess of the Libyans and the Asiatics (considered enemies at the time of Thutmosis III) was Sekhmet while Horus ruled over the Negroes (allies during the same time). The sun-god Re was the great god of the Egyptians, who called themselves "men" and who, because of their special relationship with him, called themselves the "cattle of Re." The text refers to men with the words:

> You are happy, cattle of Re who are in the Netherworld, Egypt, and the red country: You are happy, cattle of Re, who were created from the Great One who is in heaven. Let there be breath for your nostrils and let your bandages be loosened. For you are the tears of my Glorious Eye[a] in your name of Men."[1081]

And of the Negroes, it says, "you are those I struck against, and I was pleased with the multitude which came out of me in your name of Negroes. You [the faithful ones] have been created for Horus, for it is he who protects your souls."[1082] There is no mention of whether the Asiatics and Libyans are considered enemies in the context of events in the 4th Division although the name of the deity who is "created for them" is Sekhmet, the same goddess who in the *Book of the Divine Cow* was instructed by the sun-god to destroy all of mankind; her rule over Libyans and Asiatics might therefore allude to this act of aggression against them, and thus complete Revelation's concept of "all the nations." Also, the Egyptians very likely considered the Babylonians to be among the "Asiatics," in conformity with the reference to Babylon in Rev. 16:19.

The purpose of the council of eight on the far right of the lower register of the 4th Division of the *Book of Gates* is to destroy enemies of the sun-god; the text says,

> This council annihilates the enemies. ... For they are those who give orders (in) the Place of Destruction and who assign the duration of life to the souls in the West. (Re speaks to them:) May your destruction be against my enemies, assign them to the Place of Destruction. I have come here in order to reckon my bodies to cause my enemies to suffer! (BG4.3.9-10).[1083]

In a situation similar to that described in Rev. 16:19, a group involving the Libyans and many soldiers from Asiatic countries constituted an international coalition of enemies of the sun-god who became the recipients of his wrath in the place called the "Place of Destruction" referred to in BG4.3.9-10. This documentation in the *Book of Gates* very likely represents a reflection of actual events on earth.

---

[a] This refers to the Egyptian belief that "men," i.e., Egyptians, were created from the tears of the sun-god.

Discussion

It has already been suggested in Chapter 13, *Catastrophes,* that the many catastrophic events described in Rev. 16 closely parallel, either directly or indirectly, those associated with a powerful volcanic eruption, and in particular, one which occurred in the Aegean Sea in about 1628 BCE. This eruption, and its associated events which parallel Revelation's seven plagues, occurred some 150 years before the reign of Thutmosis III. Nevertheless, the Armageddon account in Rev. 16 is couched in the midst of these plagues, a situation which does not conform with the chronology of the two separate events.

This apparent conflict can be rationalized, however, if we assume a telescoping of accounts of the different events so that their dates coincide; such linking of the two separate events could have been used to construct a plausible story in which the already 150 year-old story of past natural catastrophes was used to dramatize the Thutmosis account of his attack on Megiddo. Such an approach would seem quite natural to the Egyptian way of thinking because of the eternal nature of Horus, the Son of Re, who was incarnate in each successive king (the king may die, but Horus, the Son of Re lives on in the new king). For this reason it was not uncommon for one pharaoh to claim events in the reign of an earlier pharaoh as his own by incorporating them into accounts of events during his own reign. A prime example of this is sited by Erman (1966) who points out that several of the valiant activities described in the *Victory Hymn of Thutmosis III* were claimed by later pharaohs such as Sethos I and Ramesses II.[1084] Therefore, mixing in the Book of Revelation of apparently unrelated, parallel events in Egyptian sources would, from an Egyptian perspective, not be surprising. And the account in Rev. 16:12 of the Euphrates River drying up, and the account in Rev. 16:18-19 of the great earthquake, and all the other geophysical events mentioned in Rev. 16, could very well have happened many years before the actual battle of Megiddo.

One might well ask *why*, if Rev. 16 were based on the *Annals of Thutmosis III*, would Thutmosis' account of the battle of Megiddo include the catastrophic events from 150 years earlier? A likely answer to this question is that it was a means of reminding Thutmosis' soldiers of the king's awesome power which could control even nature itself. Such an announcement given to his troops before leaving on the campaign could very well be to lift the spirits of the soldiers by suggesting that he could, as the son of the almighty god Re, call down devastating natural forces on the enemy whenever necessary – just as another Egyptian king of Upper Egypt did against the Hyksos kings and their armies in the Nile Delta during Egypt's 2nd Intermediate Period.

The scene in Rev. 16:12-14 describing events leading up to the great battle is interesting from the point of view of a somewhat similar series of events during the nearly one hundred year reign in the Nile Delta of the Hyksos kings during the 2nd Intermediate Period. When we consider that Apophis II might well have been a descendant or at least a relative of Apophis I (through his daughter, Hereret), additional parallels come into focus. It was during the reign of Apophis II that relations with Thebes turned from bad to worse. The growing hatred for the Hyksos was undoubtedly influenced by the fact that the Hyksos king claimed to be a son or Re even though he and his people worshiped a form of Seth corrupted by beliefs in the Palestinian god Baal. After Seqenenre II, who waged war with the Hyksos as far north as Cusee,[1085] died, Kamose came to the throne of Thebes and continued the fighting. After he died, Ahmose rose to power and all-out war with the Hyksos ensued. Apophis II reacted to this threat by sending an emissary to plead for help from the king of Kush (Sudan), Egypt's southern neighbor, against Ahmose and his army. This event is well documented in an Egyptian account of the capture of Apophis' messenger while he was en route to Kush to seek assistance.[1086] We therefore have evidence that Apophis sent out messengers for military assistance against Thebes and there is no reason to believe that he did not do the same with Syria-Palestine. If so, the dispatching of such emissaries would conform with the statement in Rev. 16:13-14 that three foul spirits, or emissaries, issued "from the mouth of the dragon [Apophis] and the mouth of the [2nd] beast [Apophis II, the illegitimate king in Avaris] and [i.e.,] the mouth of the false prophet [Apophis II]" and went "abroad to the kings of the whole world [from Kush in the south to beyond the Euphrates River in the north], to assemble them for battle on the great day of God the Almighty." Grimal (1992) says that Apophis and his army was chased by Ahmose of Thebes well into "Syria-Palestine and perhaps even up to the Euphrates."[1087] If Ahmose did, in fact, chase the Hyksos as far as the Euphrates, and if Figure 112 actually represents the drying up of that river at that time, then Figure 112 may be said to parallel events associated with the Northern-most part of Ahmose's push against the Hyksos and these events later found their way into the *Book of Gates*.

It is possible that the Egyptian word used for what Piankoff translates as "gladness" in Thutmosis' "place of *gladness*" was used in a play on words which would effectively link the *Book of Gates* account to the one in the *Annals of Thutmosis III*. The word used in the Tomb of Ramesses VI and which Piankoff translates as "gladness" in the phrase "the place (called) the Gladness of Earth," is ⟨hieroglyphs⟩[1088] or *rs ḥnt*. Now the word *rs* means "wake" or "be watchful"[1089] while *ḥnt* can mean "festival."[a, 1090] *Rs ḥnt* can therefore mean "watchful festival,"[b] "festival of being watchful," or simply, "festival of watchfulness." Piankoff's "of gladness" seems a rather liberal translation of *rs ḥnt* based on the word for "festival." When the state of watchfulness among the troops of Thutmosis III mentioned above is taken into account, *rs ḥnt* in the *Book of Gates* might better be translated as a "festival of watchfulness." And when the location of this festival is taken into account, it could mean the "*place* of the festival of watchfulness." There was undoubtedly much feasting during the night before the battle as the troops prepared for their surprise attack on the next day; many must have believed they would die during the coming

---

[a] Interestingly, *ḥnt* can also refer to an "act of rebellion," a concept which would apply to the actions of the once allied nations which gathered at Megiddo against Thutmosis III.

[b] The word *rs* in Faulkner (1962, p.152) means "wake" or "be watchful" while the word *ḥnt* (p. 192) can mean "festival" – or an "act of rebellion," a meaning which might also apply to the enemy encountered at Megiddo.

22. Armageddon

battle and reveled the longer because of it. And there was certainly great joy when Megiddo finally fell.

The occupants of the fortified city of Megiddo remained steadfast against Thutmosis' successful surprise attack on the enemy troops camped outside its walls and it was only after seven months of siege that Megiddo finally surrendered.[1091] Grimal (1992) says that on his return to Thebes, Thutmosis introduced a series of feasts and offerings in remembrance of his successful campaign. According to the Papyrus Harris (IV, 182-412), Thutmosis instituted a special "Feast of Victory." The papyrus reads,

> Behold, he landed at Thebes ... My majesty established for him [Amon] a "Feast of Victory" for the first time, when my majesty arrived from the first victorious expedition, overthrowing the wretched Retenu (*rtnw*) and widening the borders of Egypt.[1092]

In view of this suggestion and the suggested rationale for the parallel arrangement of the upper and middle registers of the 6th Division in the *Book of Gates* (the troops and the drying up of a river), a critical review of the translation by qualified Egyptologists of this portion of the original Egyptian text is appropriate, especially in relation to ▬ ⓪ 〰 ◉ in the *Book of Gates*. The results of such a review are not, however, critical to the above conclusion that this part of the *Book of Gates* parallels scenes in the *Annals of Thutmosis III*, which itself contains other significant parallels to Revelation's account of the battle of Armageddon.

Chapter 23. The Harlot and the Kings (Rev. 17)[1093]

At this point in the Book of Revelation, the scene changes abruptly from the seven plagues and the Battle of Armageddon to an entirely different setting; the reader's attention is captured by a command from an angel who instructs the author to "Come, I will show you the judgment of the great harlot who is seated upon many waters (Rev. 17:1)." The author then describes a harlot (Rev. 17:3-6) seated on a beast (Rev. 17:7-8). She is said to represent a city which has dominion over the kings of the earth (Rev. 17:18) and is involved in a conflict with a group of kings (Rev. 17:7-14). The beast is described as having horns which represent groups of kings some of which are to make war on the Lamb.

Rev. 17 is especially remarkable in that it is presented in the form of a riddle in which the reader is supposed to guess the name of the city, the people, and the various kings with which the woman is associated; "This calls for a mind of wisdom," the writer says in Rev. 17:9. It will be demonstrated in this chapter that the imagery presented in Rev. 17 accurately describes a series of scenes found in the *Book of Gates*, a parallel which suggests the identity of the woman, the city, the people and the beast on which the woman sits.

As indicated in the previous two chapters, the description of the seven angels and their action in Rev. 15-16 parallel certain events in the 2nd through 8th Divisions of the *Book of Gates*. Evidence will be presented in this chapter to show that Rev. 17, in turn, parallels the next division, the 9th, of the *Book of Gates*.

The Great Harlot

The story of the harlot and the kings begins with a physical description of the harlot. She is described in Rev. 17:4-5 as "a woman ... arrayed in purple and scarlet, and bedecked with gold and jewels and pearls, holding in her hand a golden cup full of abominations and the impurities of her fornication; and on her forehead was written a name of mystery." This description conforms with the picture of the woman located in the *Book of Gates* at BG9.2.8-10 and shown here as Figure 114. In fact, as we shall soon see, the woman is depicted twice in this picture, once in the form of the forward-leaning woman and the other in the form of the crocodile seated on a multi-coiled serpent. Both manifestations of the woman will be compared separately with the

23. The Harlot and the Kings

Revelation account, dealing first with the picture of the leaning woman and showing how her textual and pictorial attributes parallel those in the Revelation account.

The woman in Figure 114 holds a rope in her hand and wears the divine royal beard usually reserved for pharaohs and certain gods. She wears an elaborately decorated dress and above her head, a disk surmounted with ears of an ass. Her name, written above her in hieroglyphics, is *Iai*. We begin our comparison with a brief examination of her name and the ass-eared symbol above her head.

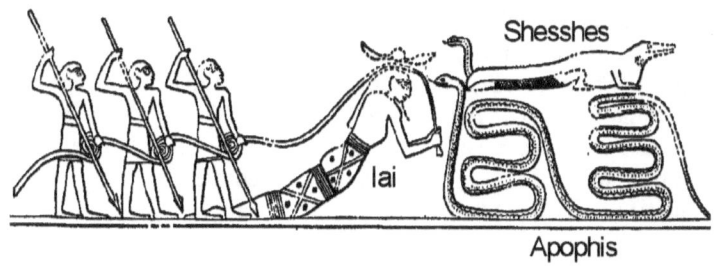

Figure 114. Like the woman of Rev. 17, the gaudily dressed woman called Iai in this scene bears derogatory names and is under attack by the sun-god's troops. In this same picture, she is also depicted as the crocodile Sheshes who sits on the multi-coiled, evil serpent Apophis. This scene contains many of the elements described in Rev. 17. See also Figure 116. (BG9.2.8-10)

While Piankoff (1953) tentatively translates *Iai* as "the Old One,"[1094] a not very flattering name, the phonetics of her name suggests other attributes which an Egyptian reader might readily assume about her. The sound of the name *Iai* has the ring of several derogatory Egyptian homophones or near homophones. For example, *āa* can mean "ass" and *āa-t,* "she-ass,"[1095] either of which conforms with the ass-eared symbol over her head. Associating anyone with an ass was, as in most ancient and modern cultures, a derogatory connotation. Furthermore, and perhaps more relevant to the woman in Rev. 17, several close homophones of *Iai* evoke images of the word "harlot." For example, *āa* can also mean "pubic hair"[1096] or a "disease of the genital organs"[1097] while *àa-t* means not only "old woman"[1098] but also "she who embraces."[1099] Finally, *iā* can mean an "unwashed or impure"[1100] woman in the same sense as "harlot" is used in Rev. 17:4. In this manner, *Iai,* the name of the woman in the *Book of Gates,* conforms with the unsavory reference to the woman in Rev. 17:1 and Rev. 17:15-16.

The woman in Revelation is also described as being "arrayed in purple and scarlet, and bedecked with gold and jewels and pearls" (Rev. 17:4). Such images of colorful, rich apparel are so unusual in the Egyptian religious literature as to be practically absent. There is, nevertheless, the suggestion of sumptuous apparel in Figure 114. Finally, *Iai* is not only the most elaborately decorated figure in the entire *Book of Gates* but is possibly the most richly decorated female figure in mainstream Egyptian religious literature. Her topless dress is bedecked with small round objects (pearls?) and horizontal bands (of gold?) and is cris-crossed with ribbons which we may presume are colorful. This special mention of her dress accentuates the parallel between her and the woman in Rev. 17:4.

In spite of the above similarities between the women in the two sources, there is an important *apparent* difference between them; the woman in Rev. 17:4 holds a cup in her hand while the one in the *Book of Gates* holds a rope. This difference is so obvious as to lead one to suspect a visual pun based on a possible perceived relationship between the Egyptian words for "cup" and "rope." We therefore consider the following remarkable series of phonetically similar words: *āb-t* can mean "a vessel"[1101] while a similar word, *ābut*, can mean "ropes, bonds, or fetters;"[1102] *ȧnh-t* can refer to "a vase or vessel"[1103] while *ȧnth-t* can mean "fetter, cord, cordage, or rope;"[1104] *m'hanu* can be used for "pot, vessel, or milk-can"[1105] while *mānnu* can mean a "cord or rope;"[1106] *hesa* can mean both "milk vessel"[1107] and a "cord, rope, string, or thread;"[1108] and finally, *hen* can mean "cord or rope"[1109] while the female form of the same word, *hen-t*, means "pot, vase or vessel."[1110] With so many homonyms or near homonyms, a rope would be an ideal visual pun to represent the word "cup."[a] The "rope" in Figure 114 can thus be seen as a pun for a "cup" which parallels the "cup" in Rev. 17:4.

Another parallel may be found in Rev. 17:6 where we read that "the woman, [was] drunk with the blood of the saints and the blood of the martyrs of Jesus." This statement conforms with the woman in Figure 114 in the following way: she is depicted as lying on her belly while holding a cup (i.e., the rope, as above) in her hand. We can assume it is filled with wine. If one accepts this interpretation, she may be seen as lying in a drunken state with a cup of wine in her hand. Meanwhile, the three soldiers holding spears behind her suggest she has something to do with warfare (this will be discussed later) so that the scene may include a reference to the blood of the slain (symbolized by red wine, the assumed content of the cup); hence, she could very well be said to be drunk with the blood of her victims.

But Rev. 17:3 says that the woman *sits* on a beast. This position is not consistent with that of the woman in Figure 114. Close inspection of other aspects of Figure 114, however, provides us with a straightforward parallel to this statement. Immediately in front of the woman we see a crocodile seated on the back of a multi-coiled serpent. Now the hieroglyphic symbol for a crocodile (➤) is also the determinative of the word *seken* which means to "lust after"[1111] so there is at least a conceptual link between the crocodile and the harlot described in Revelation. Meanwhile, the crocodile's name, *Shesshes,* can mean "to hide,"[1112] a concept which embodies the idea of "mystery" just as we find in Rev. 17:5, "and on her forehead was written a name of *mystery*." Also, the female equivalent of the crocodile's name, *Shesshes-t,* means "evil," or "misfortune,"[1113] while the similar sounding word, *shesa-t,* means "night" or "darkness,"[1114] all terms which one might associate with prostitution and mystery. Finally, *Shesshes* can be broken down into two identical sounds, *shes*, each of which can mean "cord or rope" as well as "vase or vessel,"[1115] a linkage which seems to refer

---

[a] This apparent play on the words, "cup" and "rope" is an excellent example of how, if the Book of Revelation is in some way related to Egyptian texts, it can assist in the identification of visual and auditory puns in Egyptian texts. It would be impossible to make such an inference without reference to an outside source such as Rev. 17:4.

to the rope/cup held by *Iai* (as discussed above). We might therefore conclude that *Shesshes*, the crocodile, is but a second manifestation of the same woman, *Iai*, and that the meaning of both her names are consistent with the immorality of a harlot. The picture of the woman and the crocodile in the 9th Division of the *Book of Gates* thus parallels the description of the woman of Rev. 17. Additional evidence for this conclusion will be discussed next in relation to the multi-coiled serpent which lies beneath the crocodile in Figure 114.

The Beast Beneath the Woman (Rev. 17:3)

The author of Revelation goes on to say that the woman was seated "on a scarlet beast which was full of blasphemous names" (Rev. 17:3) and represented "many waters" (Rev. 17:1). This beast "is to ascend from the bottomless pit and go to perdition" (Rev. 17:8), an aspect of the Egyptian god *Apophis*, earlier identified in Chapter 4, *Other Characters in Revelation*, as a parallel to the Dragon, Satan and the Devil of Revelation.

We begin our discussion on the beast with a brief comment on its color. Like the god Seth, Apophis was associated with the color red. This is alluded to in two areas: his battle with the protectors of Re's solar barque at sunset and dawn, and his character. Lurker (1980) tells us that "Each morning, when the sun emerged from the netherworld, and each evening at the beginning of its nightly voyage, the sun barque was attacked by the serpent. This caused the sky to be dyed red with the blood of the defeated and wounded Apophis."[1116] With respect to his the character, Wilkinson (1994) tells us that,

> Red could ... be used to signify anger, destruction, and death, and expressions such as *desher ieb* "furious" (literally red of heart), and *desheru* "wrath," are formed from the basic word for this color. Egyptian scribes used red ink rather than the usual black to write the hieroglyph for "evil" and for unlucky days of the year, as well as the names of hostile monsters and gods such as Apophis (the cosmic serpent) and Seth.[1117]

Scarlet, the color of the beast on which the woman sits, is very similar to red, the color of Apophis, who like Seth who was often equated with him, was the "personification of evil."[1118] And like Seth, Apophis was a figurative expression of anger, danger, and fire. This is evidence that the color of beast on which the woman sits in Rev. 17:3 parallels that of Apophis in Figure 114.

Furthermore, just as the beast in Rev. 17:3 was "full of blasphemous names" Apophis was known by "77 accursed names."[1119] Indeed, Hornung (1990) was so impressed with the large number of names of Apophis that he describes some them in a manner similar to that used in Revelation; he refers to them as "a whole series of contemptuous names for the enemy of the sun: Raw Face, Evil Lizard, Bad, Sneaky, Rebel, Enemy."[1120] Revelation's "scarlet beast which was full of blasphemous names" is thus an excellent description of Apophis, the ancient Egyptian god of chaos and evil.

And the similarities continue. The reference to the beast representing "many waters" conforms with beliefs about Apophis. He was believed to have already inhabited the primeval waters at the time of creation and Hornung (1983) tells us that the temple of Esna contains a late reference to his origin. "He is interpreted etymologically as the 'one who was spat out,' the product of the goddess Neith's saliva in the primeval water. Thus, certain aspects of Apophis' background conform with the notion in Rev. 17:1 of him representing "many waters." Interestingly, if the serpent Apophis represents waters, it seems natural that the woman should be represented in the picture as a crocodile (which lives in water).

"Many waters" also brings to mind the Syrian god known to the Hebrews as Baal[1121] who the Egyptians despised and equated with Seth (who, as noted above, was also at times equated with Apophis). It so happens that Baal's Egyptian name was *Bār*, a word which meant "a mass of water."[1122] Note too that the phonetically similar Egyptian word *bāḥ* meant "an abundance of water."[1123]

In addition to the above, identification of the beast beneath the woman as Apophis also conforms with the characteristic of the beast in Rev. 17:8 which says, "The beast that you saw was, and is not, and is to ascend from the bottomless pit and go to perdition." The hieroglyphic text over the picture in Figure 114 gives us some idea of the punishment received in Apophis' state of perdition:

> Hail, rebel! Apopis is bound, the evil doer! Thy face is destroyed, O Apopis! Get thee to the slaughtering block, knives are against thee, thou art hacked to pieces. ... Those of the spears throw their magic against thee, thou art in our midst. Hail! The annihilated one is repulsed, the serpent to be chastised is punished.[1124]

Finally, the phrase stating that the beast "was and is not and is to come" conforms quite well with the ever recurring death and reappearance of the evil Apophis who repeatedly dies, is reanimated, and lives to once again endanger and foil the sun-god's journey through the Netherworld.[1125] The reference to the beast ascending from the bottomless pit and going into perdition in Rev. 17:8 will be discussed later in some detail in Chapter 24, *The Millennium*.

The Kings (Rev. 17:9-13)

In the latter part of Rev. 17 we are introduced to two distinct groups of kings. The first consists of seven kings, five of whom are dead, the sixth is alive, and the seventh has not yet come to power (Rev. 17:10). The second group contains ten kings who have yet to come to power (Rev. 17:12). The phrasing of the description of the two groups as well as certain events in Rev. 17 thus reveal a dynamic situation involving changes in kingship. Evidence for two groups of kings and discord among them is found in the 9th Division of the *Book of Gates* in the register below the one represented in Figure 114. The group of ten kings will be discussed first to facilitate a better understanding of the ideas to be discussed about the group of seven.

The Ten Kings (Rev. 17:12-13)

Rev. 17:3,7 tells us that the scarlet beast upon which the woman sat "had seven heads and ten horns." The symbolism of the horns is explained in Rev. 17:12 where we read that "the ten horns ... you saw are ten kings who have not yet received royal power, but they are to receive authority as kings for one hour, together with the beast."

Remarkably, a reference to ten kings is also apparent in the 9th Division of the *Book of Gates*. It is found in the scene containing a central, reclining lion with ten crowned figures (five on each side) and presented here as Figure 115. Six of the ten crowns belong to Upper Egypt (l) while four represent Lower Egypt (S).

The reclining, falcon-headed lion in the same figure typically represents Horus, son of Re and king of Egypt.[1126] This lion is unusual in that it has a second head on its rump; like the falcon head in front, this one also wears a crown. Standing on the back of the lion with legs apart and one hand on each of the lion's crowns, is a two-headed human figure. One of his heads is that of the Seth animal while the other is

Figure 115. The ten kings of Rev. 17:12 parallel six kings wearing the crown of Upper Egypt (l) plus the four wearing the crown of Lower Egypt (S). These kings are apparently subservient to the centrally located figure, "His Two Faces," who stands on the back of a two-headed lion. The names and arrangements of figures in this picture impart it with a dynamic action in which kings rise and fall under the authority of "His Two Faces," a situation which conforms with the text of Rev. 17. (BG9.1.1-5)

that of a falcon (cf. Figure 101); his name is "His Two Faces."[a] Chapter 17 of the *Book of the Dead*, refers to "His Two Faces" by asking a question and giving several possible answers concerning his identity. *"Who is he?"* it says. Then comes the answer: "He is Shesmu [Seth], he is the mutilator of Osiris. *Otherwise said:* He is Apophis." The text goes on to say that "he has only one head which bears righteousness. *Otherwise said:* He is Horus, he has two heads, one bearing right and one bearing wrong; he gives wrong to whoever does it and right to whoever comes with it."[1127] As a bearer of both good and evil, "His Two Faces" epitomizes, in a single drawing, the conflict between good and evil. His central position and the way he holds his hands suggest a conflict among the kings in which some of them are considered to be on the side of good (to the left) and the others on the side of evil (to the right).[b]

---

[a] "His Two Faces" is introduced in Chapter 4, *Other Characters in Revelation* and discussed more fully in Chapter 18, *The Beasts of Rev. 13*.

[b] Since "His Two Faces" can represent the combined forces of good and evil, he takes on the characteristics befitting a monster – or "beast" – as described in the latter part of Rev. 17:12.

The lion is called "Horus in the boat," its reclining posture representing a boat in which Horus travels. It is in terms of a boat that the lion is described. The text says that the two ropes in the picture are attached to the boat's front and rear; the single uncrowned deity in front of the lion is called "He who presides over the fore rope" while the one behind it is called "He who presides over the aft rope." This arrangement of towers tells us that Horus's boat is traveling from right to left in the figure, i.e., the direction in which the hawk's head on the lion faces.

The key to understanding the dynamics of this scene lies in the implied movement represented by the leaning of the crowned staves, one located in front and the other behind the "boat." As the boat moves forward in time, the king on the left (the king of upper Egypt, ⟨⟩) falls back, i.e., dies or loses authority, while the king on the right rises, or comes into power. As the boat continues to move forward, the next king in the procession would rise, only to later fall and be replaced by still another. This dynamic relationship between the "boat," ropes, towers, and kings in this picture conforms with the statement in Rev. 17:12 that "they [the ten kings] are to receive authority as kings for one hour," i.e., for a short time.

The reigns of each of the kings in Figure 115 seems to be represented by the central reclining lion ("Horus in the boat") behind which another king stands in line for power. Phonetic evidence to support this view is based on a perceived relationship between "boat" and "throne." *Tcha āa-t,*[1128] is a word for "the great sailing" or "the Great Boat" while another phonetically similar word, *tchaāut,* means "throne or throne-chamber."[1129] The phrase, "Horus in his boat," may be thought of as a play on the word for throne so that the phrase may actually (or also) mean something like "Horus on his throne." The dominant position of "His Two Faces" (Horus-Seth, Revelation's 2nd beast) on the back of the lion implies control over the lion who wears the ⟨⟩ crown – and hence over the king of Upper Egypt – a suggestion supported in the text above the lion which says that "His Two Faces" enters "into this god [Horus, the current king] after Re has passed by him." Note that the head of Horus (the "good side") on "His Two Faces" looks toward the kings of upper Egypt while the head of Seth (the "evil side") looks toward the kings of lower Egypt. These various symbols may be interpreted to mean that this figure refers to a time in Egypt's history when the kings of Lower Egypt were considered to be evil and had dominance over the kings of Upper Egypt. For now, suffice it to say that various elements of Figure 115 conform with the idea of the ten kings of Rev. 17:12 and with Rev. 17:13 which says that the reigning kings (of Upper Egypt at Thebes) "are of one mind and give their power and authority to the [2nd] beast" (the kings of Lower Egypt). This will be discussed in some detail in the Discussion at the end of this chapter.

The Seven Kings (Rev. 17:9-10)

Rev. 17:1 not only mentions that the beast has ten horns which are identified as kings in Rev. 17:12, but that it also has seven heads. Rev. 17:10 identifies these heads as "seven kings, five of whom have fallen, one is, the other has not yet come, and when he comes he must remain only a little while." The reference to these kings remaining for only a little while is remarkably similar to the comment on the ten kings in Rev. 17:12 who "are to receive authority as kings for one hour." The similarity makes one wonder if these seven kings are but a sub-set of the ten kings

23. The Harlot and the Kings

discussed above. To explore this and a possible Egyptian parallel to this situation we return to Figure 115 and examine it in the light Rev. 17:10.

A sub-set of seven kings is readily apparent in Figure 115; these are the seven figures wearing the crown of Upper Egypt ( ). The "five of whom have fallen" (Rev. 13:10) are all accounted for on the left-hand side of the recumbent lion (one of these is represented by a crowned staff). The sixth is represented by the recumbent lion which wears two such crowns. And the seventh king is represented by the crowned staff in front of the lion. As "Horus in his boat" moves to the left, the sixth (the current) king will "fall" and the seventh will come to the throne. This interpretation of Figure 115 is consistent with Rev. 17:10 which says, "they are also seven kings, five of whom have fallen, one is, the other has not yet come, and when he comes he must remain only a little while." Also, this interpretation makes it just barely possible to visualize references to both seven *and* ten kings in Figure 115, just as is indicated in Rev. 17:3.

The Eighth King (Rev. 17:11)

Rev. 17:11 speaks of an eighth king in a rather confusing way. It says that "the beast that was and is not, it is an eighth but it belongs to the seven, and it goes to perdition." The "beast that was and is not" and "goes to perdition" corresponds, as discussed earlier, to Apophis, Egypt's primeval god of evil and chaos. How then can he be an eighth king, especially one that belongs to a group of seven, a subset of the group of ten kings? How exactly do we make sense of this statement?

One possible explanation may relate to the presence in a picture to the immediate right of ten kings. Here we find two serpents, a smaller one with eight human heads which lies between the heads of a larger two-headed serpent. The two heads of the larger serpent bear crowns of Upper Egypt ( ) suggesting that, like the two headed lion on its left (as discussed above), this serpent represents a ruling king. Thus, we find in this picture a reference to the number eight and a king, just as we find in Rev. 17:11. Unfortunately, the difficulty in understanding Rev. 17:11 remains and is difficult to understand exactly how this picture might parallel the details provided in Rev. 17:11.

The Egyptian text found over the serpents provides us with some evidence, albeit very weak, which may link one or both these serpents to Apophis, and hence to a parallel with the "eighth" king of Rev. 17. Part of the text over the two-headed serpent reads, "to him are reckoned the souls of the evil ones in the Netherworld,"[1130] while a part of that over the eight-headed serpent reads, "He is like this. He passes through the mysterious region and goes back to the place where knives are raised."[1131] We thus find in this part of the *Book of Gates* the possibility of an association between an eight-headed serpent and a going into perdition (i.e., into "the place where knives are raised"), as in Rev. 17:11. Even with this additional information, a possible similarity to an eighth king belonging to the seven is still quite unsatisfactory and we might be well advised to look elsewhere for a more suitable one.

If we are to assume an Egyptian link with the Book of Revelation, the reference to an "eighth king" belonging to the seven could involve a known difficulty in interpreting Egyptian passages dealing with one individual (in this case, the "eighth king") in a set of several individuals (in Rev. 17:11, the seven kings). The difficulty involves the confusing use of cardinal numbers with ordinal meanings in some Egyptian texts. Gardiner (1927) outlines the problem in the following example:

> We shall see below, in dealing with the fractions, that there too the cardinal numbers have ordinal meaning. Much more doubtful is the following:
> ⸺ *aḥa·n·i ḥd·kwi ḥr šms m 6 n ḥnw* I sailed downstream in the escort (lit. in following) with five others of the Residence. Lit. perhaps 'as six', the text seeming to say he was six or represented them; hardly 'with six (others)' as has recently been suggested.[1132]

In this example, Gardiner dismisses the idea of a group of seven with the individual as the seventh and prefers to interpret the text as meaning that the speaker is one of six who sailed downstream. If we were to assume an Egyptian connection to Rev. 17:11, it is possible that the original expression encountered by the author of the Book of Revelation was either verbally, pictorially or in written form, similarly confusing. It would then seem likely that what was actually meant in Rev. 17:11 is that the "eighth" king should have been designated as one of the seven kings, i.e., the "seventh" rather than the "eighth" king. This explanation not only makes more sense than the suggestion that the "eighth belongs to the seven" but it also conforms with the diagram presented in Figure 115 and its presentation of the idea of seven kings as discussed above.

War with the Lamb (Rev. 17:13-14)

After the description of the woman and the kings in Rev. 17:3-12 we are told in Rev. 17:13-14 that "These [kings] are of one mind and give over their power and authority to the beast; they will make war on the Lamb, and the Lamb will conquer them, for he is Lord of lords and King of kings, and those with him are called and chosen and faithful." In Figure 116, which constitutes the middle register of the same division, we find the picture of the woman (*Iai*) and the scarlet beast (Apophis) which are obviously enemies of the groups of figures behind them. On the far left we see the ram-headed form of the sun-god standing in his shrine aboard his barque which is being towed by four towers. In front of the four towers are fourteen soldiers wielding magic nets and three with spears aimed toward the woman and the Apophis serpent. The number of the spear-holding figures (three) is the sign for "many," and this number in combination with the adjacent groups of six (men), four (baboons), and four (women) indicates the presence of a very large army. This arrangement of the sun-god and his amassed armed followers against the woman and Apophis conform

Figure 116. The military forces of the ram-headed sun-god (the Lamb standing in his shrine on the barque) fight with magic nets and spears against the forces of evil led by the multi-coiled serpent Apophis. The relative location of this scene in Revelation conforms with its relative location in the Book of Gates. See also Figure 114. (BG9.2)

with the overall sense of the description given in Rev. 17:13-14, and will be discussed next.

Recall that the ram-headed form of Re in the Netherworld parallels Revelation's Lamb and that the Egyptian texts, like Rev. 17:14, frequently refer to Re as the "King of kings and Lord of lords." We may therefore conclude that components of the juvenile form of the ram-headed Re in Figure 116 parallels the Lamb, the "Lord of lords and King of kings" while the seventeen soldiers which lead him parallel the statement that "those with him are called and chosen and faithful." In Revelation, the Lamb's army fights against ten kings and the beast while in the *Book of Gates* Re's army fights against the woman and the followers of Apophis (who was often equated with Seth who parallels the 1st beast). Furthermore, the statement in Rev. 17:14, "the Lamb will conquer them," is consistent with the Egyptian text just above the army:

> They are like this: they proceed from Re [the Lamb], they enchant Apopis for him. ...
> They say their magic words:
> Hail rebel! Apopis is bound, the evil doer! Thy face is destroyed, O Apopis! Get thee to the slaughtering block, knives are against thee, thou art hacked to pieces. The Iaiu are against thee, thou art annihilated! Those of the spears throw their magic against thee, thou art in our midst. Hail! The annihilated one is repulsed, the serpent to be chastised is punished![1133]

Revelation's "chosen and faithful" who rally with the Lamb against the beast and his army also conform with the three soldiers shown immediately behind the woman. The text tells us that "They are like this carrying their spears. They guard the ropes of the Old One (?) [*Iai*]. They do not let the serpent approach to the barge of the Great God."[1134] The presence in this part of the *Book of Gates* of a large army of soldiers bearing spears and magic nets to protect the ram-headed sun-god against his enemies parallels the war described in Rev. 17:12-14.

Opposition to the Harlot and the Beast (Rev. 17:15-18)

Before discussing the opposition to the harlot and the beast we should note that Rev. 17:18 defines the harlot as "the great city which has dominion over the kings of the earth." Also, Rev. 17:15 says that "The waters ... where the harlot is seated, are peoples and multitudes and nations and tongues." Recall from the discussions above that these same waters were identified with the serpent Apophis in the *Book of Gates*. These observations, from an Egyptian perspective, would lead us to the conclusion that Revelation's "peoples and multitudes and nations and tongues" represent parallels to practically all foreigners in Egypt; all foreigners were, at times, considered to be enemies of Osiris and hence, followers of Apophis.

Rev. 17:16-17 describes a remarkable set of events: a revolt occurs in which *the ten kings and the beast* rise up against the woman and destroy her. The text says that,

> [16]... they and the beast will hate the harlot [the great city]; they will make her desolate and naked, and devour her flesh and burn her up with fire, [17]for God has put it into their hearts to carry out his purpose by being of one mind and giving over their royal power to the [2nd] beast, until the words of God shall be fulfilled." (Rev. 17:16-17)

This rebellion against the woman (the city) conforms with the stance of the three gods who hold spears against the woman's (*Iai's*) back. While there is no mention of the burning of enemies of the sun-god in this division as there is in Rev. 17:16 ("they will ... burn her up with fire"), similar action against the sun-god's enemies is described in the lower register of the previous (8th) division (i.e., the adjacent division when the *Book of Gates* is read from a continuous scroll). In that scene, the bound enemies of Osiris are burned by "The Fiery One," the giant undulating serpent which is guarded by seven gods.[1135] Horus of the Netherworld (who in this scene is the Netherworld's counterpart of Horus, the pharaoh of Egypt on Earth) stands with his staff to the left of the enemies and says to the fiery serpent:

> O mighty fire, O this great flame of my eye which comes out of this mouth, he whose coils are guarded by my children! Open thy mouth! Distend thy jaws, belch forth the flame among the enemies of my father [Revelation's Lamb], burn their bodies, consume their souls by this heat of thy mouth, by the fire of thy body! ... May the fire which is in this serpent come forth! ... Then these enemies are burned down after Horus has called him (the serpent).[1136] (BG8.3)

Discussion

The above analyses suggest several parallels between the events described in Rev. 17 and the 9th Division of the *Book of Gates*; some are more evident than others. The two most obvious are the physical descriptions of the harlot and the dynamics of the succession of kings. Highlights of these and the other parallels will be discussed next.

The Woman:- Practically all the essential elements of the passage in Revelation dealing with the woman seated on the beast conform with those of the scene on the far right of the middle register of the 9th Division. These include at least the following: her remarkable apparel, the cup (= rope) in her hand, the derogatory sign over her head (ears of an ass) and her manifestation as a crocodile seated on the serpent Apophis (many waters). These most obvious elements serve to make this scene one of the key markers in the series of parallel scenes in the Book of Revelation. Other elements support this view although it may be argued that less obvious and less important elements would not be very convincing on their own. When viewed as mere details in the overall picture, however, they provide a degree of comfort in the conclusion that this scene in Rev. 17 conforms with the one in the *Book of Gates*.

A similar argument might be put forward to support the conclusion that the story of the kings in Rev. 17 parallels the story in the register above the woman and the beast. This remarkable and unusual scene parallels the dynamics implicit in the succession of the ten kings in Rev. 17:12 and seven described in Rev. 17:10. It also clearly identifies "His Two Faces" (the 2nd beast of Revelation discussed in Chapter 4, *Other Characters in Revelation*, and Chapter 18, *The Beasts of Rev. 13*) standing on the back of the lion (the current king) directing the actions of several kings, just as described in Rev. 17:12. By themselves, these images may be considered to be only mildly convincing parallels supported by tenuous arguments made to relate the details of events associated with the seven kings. But when they are placed in juxtaposition to the picture of the woman and the war against her, they contribute to a convincing argument for a strong parallel between the story in Rev. 17 and this scene in the 9th Division.

Finally, note that the scene with the woman and the one with the kings in the 9th Division lie in the same relative position as their counterparts in Revelation; they refers to events *after* the catastrophic events described in Rev. 16 (Chapter 13, *Catastrophes* and Chapter 21, *The Seven Angels with the Wrath of God*) and, as will be pointed out in Chapter 24, *The Millennium, before* the prominent events described in Rev. 20 and the 10th Division of the *Book of Gates*.

The Woman as a "Great City":- Rev. 17:18 says that "the woman ... is a great city which has dominion over the kings of the earth." Parallels with the "great city" mentioned in Rev. 17:18 are obviously open to speculation and at least two possibilities quickly present themselves. The first is that "the great city" parallels Egypt itself. A second is that it parallels some nation or empire distant from Egypt. The first is more likely because the entire country of Egypt was at times considered to be the earthly counterpart of the great celestial city. In this suggestion, the "mountains" or "hills" of Egypt would represent the mounds on which many of Egypt's cities were built (a geographic necessity in a country formed along a river which annually flooded its banks). This possibility is supported by the fact that several Egyptian and Greek words can be used for both mountains (or mounds) and hills, mounds and hills being conceptually similar. For example, the Egyptian words *ṭu*[1137] and *ṭuá*[1138] can mean both hill and mountain while *her* can mean "a high hill"[1139] and *har* a "mountain"[1140] (similarly, the Greek word, *óree*, which is translated as "mountains" in Rev. 17:9, can mean both "hills" and "mountains"[1141]). In a general sense, however, it fails to address many of the physical and political details alluded to in Rev. 17.

A second parallel with the text of Revelation relates to the Nile Delta with its numerous waterways and tributaries; this area in particular conforms with the notion of the "many waters" on which the woman in Revelation is located. But perhaps more interesting than the physical characteristics are the politics referred to in Rev. 17. The ten and seven kings of Rev. 17 and the kings in Figure 115 strongly parallel aspects of the succession of kings in Upper and Lower Egypt. Also, the war between the Lamb and the followers of the beast in Revelation is consistent with the scene in Figure 116. Similar outcomes of the conflicts are obvious in the two sources – the forces of good prevail over those of evil with fire being an important instrument of destruction in both. It therefore seems that both Rev. 17 and the 9th Division (and a part of the 10th Division) of the *Book of Gates* describe political strife and warfare. The *Book of Gates* therefore seems to refer to a conflict between Upper and Lower Egypt, the latter region paralleling the "multitudes and nations and tongues" of Rev. 17:15 and "the kings of the earth" in Rev. 17:18.

Many Nations:- There is only one era in ancient Egypt which conforms with the various elements described in the two sources – the 2nd Intermediate Period which spanned the years from about 1640 to 1532 BCE.[1142] This was a period of great political upheaval and social turmoil caused in part by the movement into the Delta of groups of foreigners whose kings for a time dominated all of Egypt. Ultimately, these kings were driven from Egypt primarily through the efforts of two Egyptian kings who ruled from Thebes.

Many of the events which occurred during this period are similar to those described in Rev. 17. The following discussion relies heavily on Grimal's (1992) *History of Ancient Egypt* and assumes that the harlot of Rev. 17 represents the Hyksos domain with its capital city Avaris in the delta during the XVth and XVIth Dynasties.

As far as we know, the Hyksos were of diverse origin and seem to have been made up of many 'Asiatic' peoples with whom the Egyptians had fought for centuries. Grimal tells us that,

> Their name is the debased Greek version of the Egyptian term: *hekaw-khasut* ('the chiefs of foreign lands'). This name gives no indication of race or any clearly defined homeland: it was a term applied to all foreigners in Nubia and Syria-Palestine during the Old and Middle Kingdoms. The Hyksos seem to have approximated the 'Asiatic' peoples whom the Egyptians had previously fought: the Aamu, Setjetiu and Mentjiu of Asia or Retjenu.[1143]

Such diversity of peoples parallels the description in Rev. 17:15 of the "multitudes and nations and tongues." And "the kings of the earth" in Rev. 17:18 parallel the "Chiefs of foreign lands" in the Delta region. Furthermore, their spread throughout the Delta conforms with Rev. 17:9 which says that they, as symbolized by a woman, live on seven hills; Grimal also informs us that,

> Hyksos control over northen Egypt evolved in a number of stages. Starting from [1] Avaris they gradually moved towards Memphis, following the eastern edge of the Delta. They established centers at [2] Farasha, [3] Tel el-Sahaba (at the mouth of Wadi Tumilat), [4] Bubastis, [5] Inshas and [6] Tel el Yahudiya (about 20 kilometers north of Heliopolis)."[1144]

Grimal's estimate of six centers could, of course, be an underestimate and the actual number could easily have been the seven, the same as stated in Revelation, or even more than seven. In any event, by the end of the 2nd Intermediate Period, the Hyksos had expanded to likely more than six control centers, so that seven centers would have been known at some point during the Hyksos occupation.

It has already been suggested that the corrupted Egyptian god Seth parallels the (1st) "beast" of Rev. 13 so it is not surprising to find in Rev. 17:3 a reference to a "woman sitting on a scarlet beast which was full of blasphemous names." And since the Hyksos had great influence over, and for a time even ruled the kings of Upper Egypt, so did Seth. It is therefore not surprising to see a king of Upper Egypt (who usually represents Horus, the son of Re) being shown in the form of "His Two Faces," Horus and Seth, standing on the back of the regal lion in the upper register of the 9th Division. Recall too, from Chapter 18, *The Beasts of Rev. 13,* that "His Two Faces," in the context of the Book of Revelation, represents a religious imposter, one who claimed to be the "son of Re" but who was not; he was therefore not considered to be a legitimate king over all of Egypt. Also recall from our interpretation in the same chapter that, according to Rev. 13:2, it was Apophis who gave Seth his power. It is therefore not surprising to find that the serpentine form of Apophis at the far right of the middle register of the 9th Division parallels a "beast" in Rev. 17. If the Book of Revelation is somehow dependant on ancient Egyptian texts, it would seem that its author, in order to simplify the account of the harlot and the kings, elected to refer to the Apophis/Seth/Horus-Seth amalgam as a "beast."

The Harlot:- The association of the woman of Revelation with the beast also conforms with the religious beliefs of the Hyksos rulers. Grimal says that,

> In the sphere of religion, as in the political arena, they instituted an official Egyptian-style cult based on Seth of Avaris, the enemy of Osiris; contenting themselves with the introduction of more Semitic features into his iconography; it was at this time that Seth was assimilated with Baal-Reshef and the Hittite god Teshub. The Hyksos also continued to worship the Syro-Palestinian goddess Anat-Astarte ... and kings continued to hold the title "son of Ra."[1145]

Anat-Astarte is of particular interest because she was believed to be the consort of Baal whom the Egyptians identified with their god Seth.[1146] The Babylonians and the Assyrians knew Astarte by the name of *Ishtar*, goddess of fertility and love[1147] while the Egyptians knew her as a goddess of war.[1148] She is usually represented as a naked woman holding her breasts in her hands.[1149] Because of her association with the Hyksos, the Egyptians developed a special hatred for her after the Hyksos were expelled.[a]

Larousse's Encyclopedia informs us that Ishtar was the "courtesan of the gods" and describes her in terms befitting of the harlot of Rev. 17.

> Sacred prostitution formed part of her cult and when she descended to earth she was accompanied by 'courtesans, harlots and strumpets'. ... Ishtar herself, moreover, was the 'courtesan of the gods' and she was the first to experience the desire which she inspired. Her lovers were legion and she called them from all walks of life. But woe to him whom Ishtar had honoured! The fickle goddess treated her passing lovers cruelly, and the unhappy wretches usually paid dearly for the favours heaped on them.[1150]

This description certainly conforms with the idea of the harlot portrayed in Rev. 17:4. "The woman was arrayed in purple and scarlet, and bedecked with gold and jewels and pearls, holding in her hand a golden cup full of abominations and the impurities of her fornication." And if the kings of Rev. 17 parallel those of the 2nd Intermediate period as suggested above, the harlot of Revelation may be said to parallel Astarte/Ishtar, the Hyksos goddess – or was inspired by her. As a consort of Baal/Seth and chief goddess of the Hyksos, her capital city in Egypt would have been Avaris, the city which controlled practically all of Egypt for most of the 2nd Intermediate Period. We may conclude that the city of Avaris parallels the one destroyed in Rev. 17:16 whom "the ten horns ... hate ... will make her desolate and naked, and devour her flesh and burn her up with fire." This concept may even be expanded to include all the cities of Egypt under Hyksos control, especially those in the Delta.

---

[a] Nevertheless, (according to the Encylcopædia Britannica, p. 473) by the reign of Amenophis II (1425-1401 BCE) she became revered for her reputed potence in warfare, was honored in connection with medicine, love, and fertility, and was finally combined with Sekhmet, the Egyptian goddess of pestilence.

The Egyptian texts yield other evidence for a parallel between the woman of Rev. 17 and the Hyksos reign. This evidence is in the form of the names of the crocodile and serpent in the middle register of the 9th Division (Figure 114). The crocodile seated on the serpent is called Shesshes, a name phonetically close to that of the first Hyksos king, Sheshi.[1151] Furthermore, the name of the serpent on which Shesshes sits, Apophis, is the same as that Apophis I, the longest ruling king Hyksos king of XVIth Dynasty. Through this line of reasoning, the crocodile Shesshes, (the woman of Rev. 17) could represent the first king of the Hyksos dynasty and might therefore be thought of as the "mother" of the dynasty – and thus, the Hyksos dynasty itself. The Hyksos regime ultimately extended its authority from Avaris in the Delta along the Nile valley to Gebelein, a little south of Thebes, and even out into the desert trade routes which paralleled the west side of the Nile.[1152] If one accepts that the woman and the "great city" are the same in that they both parallel Avaris, it follows that she also parallels the Hyksos dynasty which ruled from it. This suggestion parallels Rev. 17:18 which says that the woman is "the great city which has dominion over the kings of the earth [i.e., Lower Egypt or even all of Egypt]."

The Seven Kings of Avaris:- One naturally wonders if the number of Hyksos kings of the XVth and XVIth Dynasties equaled the seven referred to in Rev. 17 but it is as yet practically impossible to provide a definitive statement to this effect. The problem lies in the poor quality of our knowledge of the chronology of the Hyksos kings (and indeed, of all the dynasties during the 2nd Intermediate Period). This problem has resulted in the publication of a variety of different king lists for this period. For example, Baines and Málek (1980) list five kings "and others,"[1153] Clagett (1989) says the dynasty "included" six kings,[1154] Hornung (1999) lists seven in his chronology but refers to "only six" in his text, and Shaw (2000) lists only four Hyksos kings.[1155] After listing five kings in his chronology (Salitis (Sheshi), Yaqub-Har, Khyan, Apophis I and Apophis II) Hornung (1999B) extends the number to seven in his text.[1156] Grimal (1992) lists five in his chronology but refers to seven in his text;[1157] his discussion of the names of the kings provides us with an idea of scope of the problem.

> The chronology of the last two Hyksos kings is somewhat confused. They ruled between the tenth and fifteenth years of Ahmose's reign [the first king of the XVIIIth Dynasty]. The name of one of them, Aazehre, the 1st king of the Fifteenth Dynasty, appears on an obelisk at Tanis – he probably correspondes to Manetho's Asseth and Turin Canon's Khamundy. The other, Apophis III, was the last of the Sixteenth Dynasty Hyksos vassal kings, and his name appears on several monuments, including a dagger from Saqqara. No textual source can supply the least detail on the final phase of Hyksos rule. They were obviously no longer posing a real threat to the Thebans when Ahmose undertook a campaign in the twenty-second year of his reign, in which he advanced at least into the Djahy region of Syria-Palestine and perhaps even up to the Euphrates.[1158]

Other authorities suggest other numbers. Because of the variation in numbers proposed by different authorities, it is not possible to say with any certainty that seven, the number of kings of Rev. 17, agrees with the actual number of Hyksos Kings – nor is it possible to say that they disagree. We may say, however, that the number conforms with the opinions of at least some modern scholars and is certainly

The Ten Kings of Thebes:- If the seven kings of Rev. 17 belong to the XVth Hyksos dynasty then we must turn our attention to the contemporary XVIIth Dynasty at Thebes. This dynasty is of particular interest because it was during its latter years that its native-born Egyptian kings rose up in arms against the Hyksos; this marks the XVIIth Dynasty as an ideal candidate for a parallel to the 10 kings of Rev. 17. Unfortunately, as with the number of Hyksos kings, the number of Theban kings in this dynasty is almost as difficult to determine. For example, Baines and Málek (1980)[1159] list fifteen kings, Hornung (1999)[1160] gives a partial list of four kings, Shaw (2000)[1161] lists nine kings, Calgett (1989)[1162] does not provide an estimate, and Grimal (1992)[1163] lists ten. Grimal's suggestion of ten kings is rather intriguing and especially applicable. He begins by saying that,

> According to the Turin Canon there were fifteen kings in the Seventeenth Dynasty, but according to the Karnak Table of Kings (now in the Louvre) there were nine. *The Theban monuments bear the names of ten Seventeenth Dynasty kings,*' and the tombs of seven of the listed kings have also been found at Thebes, as well as an eighth tomb of a king whose name does not appear in either of the lists.[1164]

For this reason, and the parallel with the seven kings of Avaris described above, it is reasonable to suggest that the ten kings of Rev. 17 parallel the popular view of the number of kings recognized in the practically immortal stone monuments of Egypt.

But not all kings of the XVIIth Dynasty were against the Hyksos. Indeed, most of the dynasty's early kings feared and supported their overlords to the north. Grimal explains their cooperation with the Hyksos rulers as follows:

> At the time of Rahotep's reign [the first king of the XVIIth Dynasty in Thebes], the Hyksos king was Yaqub-Har (or Yaqub-Baal), Salitis' [Sheshi's] successor. Yaqub-Har reigned for eighteen years and seals bearing his name have been found from Gaza to Kerma. He remained on good terms with the three Theban kings who succeeded Rahotep. The first was Inyotef 'the Old' .... He reigned for three years and was buried by his young brother and short-lived successor Inyotef VI at Dra Abu el-Naga.ᵃ, [1165]

Grimal later describes how Inyotef VII, the seventh king of the Theban dynasty, was especially friendly to the Hyksos regime, even to the point of marrying the daughter of its king:

> During Inyotef VII's reign Thebes was at peace with the Hyksos king Apophis I, who ruled for forty years according to the Turin Canon. There were numerous contacts between the two kingdoms. ... [Apophis I] may even have been related by marriage to the Theban royal family; the tomb of Amenophis I contained a vase bearing the name of Apophis I's daughter *Herit*.' This object was probably passed on through successive

---

ᵃ See also page 392 of Grimal's (1992) appendix entitled *Chronology of Ancient Egypt* (pp. 391-395).

generations, commemorating a marriage that would have made her one of the ancestors of the Eighteenth Dynasty. This is clearly a long way from the mutual hatred described in later texts. In Addition, Apophis I is called 'King of Upper and Lower Egypt' on a scribe's palette from the Faiyum and on several scarabs.[1166]

Nevertheless, toward the end of the reign of Apophis I, relationships between the two dynasties deteriorated to the point of open conflict.[1167] Later, Seqenenre Ta'a II of Thebes waged war with the Hyksos as far north as Cusae, a little north of Asyut.[1168] His son Kamose, the last king of the XVIIth Dynasty, continued with the war and set the stage for the final expulsion of the Hyksos by Ahmose, the first king of the XVIIIth Dynasty.[1169]

In an intercepted message sent to his ally, the king of Kush at Egypt's southern border, Apophis I sought help in the fight against King Kamos of Thebes who had caused widespread destruction to his land in the Delta.

> Have you (not) beheld what Egypt has done against me, the chieftain who is in it, Kamose the Mighty, ousting me from my soil and I have not reached him – after the manner of all that he has done against you, he choosing the two lands to devastate them, my land and yours, and he has destroyed them. Come, fare north at once, do not be timid.[1170]

The military actions taken by Kamose against the Hyksos-held territory had thus caused much devastation to the land. This was not very unlike the passage in Rev. 17:16 which reads, "And the ten horns [the kings of Thebes] ... will make her desolate and naked, and devour her flesh and burn her up with fire."

Rev. 17:16 has one critical difference from the situation described above. The relevant text says that "the ten horns [the ten kings] ... *they and the beast* will hate the harlot. If we are to accept this passage as written, then the reference to the ten kings laying waste to the harlot (the great city) with the help of "the beast" does *not* agree with available historical records of the 2nd Intermediate Period. Recall from Chapter 18, *The Beasts of Rev. 13*, that the beast with ten horns parallels the kings of Thebes, the last two of which declared war on the Hyksos kings in the Delta during Egypt's 2nd Intermediate period. It makes *no* sense that the Theban kings would form an alliance with the Hyksos king (the 2nd beast) to make war on Avaris, the Hyksos capital and Revelation's Harlot. This difference is of special interest because it is one of the very few statements in the Book of Revelation which do not conform with the great abundance of parallels in the Egyptian texts. A close examination of this difference is therefore warranted.

This inconsistency with historical evidence is likely related to differences among translators as well as different ancient sources of Revelation. For example, the RSV (used throughout this work), the NIV and the ASV conform closely with one another. The NIV says, "*The beast and the ten horns* you saw will hate the prostitute. They will bring her to ruin." The ASV says, "*the ten horns* which thou sawest, *and the beast, these* shall hate the harlot, and shall make her desolate." And the KJV says, "the ten horns *which thou sawest upon the beast*, these shall hate the whore, and shall make her desolate and naked." Each of these translations are, for the most part in agreement with one another. Nevertheless, they do not agree with the above conclusion that the group of ten horns parallel ten kings of Thebes during the 17th Dynasty (recall that the seven heads parallel seven Hyksos kings at Avaris during the same period). There is evidence, however, that this interpretation of Rev. 17:16 was not used in all Greek versions of the Book of Revelation. For example, Conybeare (1974) translates this verse from of a "Codex preserved in the Armenian Convent of St. James in Jerusalem" to mean a follows:

> And the *ten horns, which thou sawest, they shall judge the strumpet* [harlot], and desolate and naked they shall make her; and her flesh they shall eat, and her shall they burn with fire.[1171]

This Armenian version thus conforms with the parallels to the ten horns and seven kings suggested above, an observation which suggests that more in-depth comparison should be conducted of a wider range of ancient manuscripts of the Book of Revelation to clarify this issue.

The parallel with Rev. 17:16 also leads to another intriguing historical parallel; this is especially true if the verse in the Armenian version of the Book of Revelation is closest to the meaning in the original version. The relevant text in the RSV says,

> And the ten horns that you saw are ten kings who have not yet received royal power, but they are to receive authority as kings for one hour, together with the beast. These are of one mind and give over their power and authority to the beast; they will make war on the Lamb, and the Lamb will conquer them." (Rev. 17:12-14).

The reference to the ten (Theban) kings who are of one mind and give over their power and authority to the (2nd) beast may well refer to the capitulation to Hyksos rule by the kings of the first part of the 17th Dynasty in Thebes. The late kings of this dynasty, as pointed out earlier, rose up against the Hyksos and war ensued. Naturally, the Hyksos fought back so that it may be said that the Hyksos made "war on the Lamb [i.e., on Re's followers in the latter part of the Theban dynasty], and the Lamb ... conquered them [the Hyksos]" (Rev. 17:14). This parallel with Rev. 17:12-14 represents a simple refinement of the earlier parallels found in the *Book of Gates*.[a]

Egypt's 2nd Intermediate Period:- As noted above, several important events during Egypt's 2nd Intermediate Period parallel those outlined in Rev. 17. These center around the war which broke out between the native Egyptian kings of the 17the Dynasty in Thebes in Upper Egypt and the kings of the 15th (Hyksos) Dynasty and 16th Dynasty (minor Hyksos rulers contemporary with the 15th Dynasty) in the Nile Delta. Unfortunately, uncertainties in the number of kings in the two areas and in the details of political and military events of the period make it difficult to accurately

---

[a] It should be noted here that the final expulsion of the Hyksos from the Delta was not actually accomplished until after the death of both king Kamose and Apophis I, i.e., when Ahmose, the first king of the XVIIth Dynasty came into power. Nevertheless, in a practical sense, we may say that while Ahmose may have driven the Hyksos north into Palestine, it was Kamose, the last king who effectively defeated them in Egypt.

describe the full extent of the similarities. Nevertheless, the available information suggests significant parallels with this period.

The *Book of Gates* was composed by the priests of the next dynasty, the XVIIIth, – the same dynasty which, under its first king, Ahmose, was responsible for concluding the expulsion of the Hyksos. It is therefore not surprising that the most memorable events in the 2nd Intermediate Period later found their way into the *Book of Gates* which is a later composition than the *Amduat*.

Meanwhile, and in apparent contradiction to the parallel that the woman of Revelation represents Avaris, it also seems possible that the "great city" of Rev. 17 parallels the ancient Minoan empire which ruled much the Mediterranean Sea during 2nd Intermediate Period and this should not be overlooked, especially since that empire was viewed as an enemy of Egypt during much of this period. As discussed in Chapter 13, *Catastrophes*, this empire was centered in the Aegean Sea, most likely on the island of Crete, and included many islands (paralleling the many waters and seven mountains of Rev. 17:9) populated by representatives from its many trading partners and nations. Much of it was destroyed by the cataclysmic eruption of Thera in *c.* 1628 BCE., i.e., during the early years of Hyksos rule in Egypt. As pointed out in Chapter 13, *Catastrophes* this event involved fire (Rev. 16:8-9), a hail of rocks falling from the sky (Rev. 16:21), darkness (Rev. 16:10), lightning (Rev. 16:18), earthquakes (Rev. 16:18-20), rivers drying up (Rev. 16:18-20), poisoned water (Rev. 16:3-4), social upheaval (Rev. 16:13-19) and many deaths. These same phenomena are described in greater detail in Revelation Chapters 18 and 19 so that the story of the harlot and the kings in Rev. 17 is closely associated with this mixture of accounts of natural disasters. Nevertheless, in trying to associate Revelation's "city" with the Minoan empire we are encumbered by an even greater lack of information than we have about Egypt's 2nd Intermediate Period. It is entirely possible that what we are experiencing here is a telescoping in time of two major events in the 2nd Intermediate Period – catastrophes associated with the eruption of Thera and the ousting of the Hyksos. More research is needed in these areas.

Chapter 24. The Millennium (Rev. 20:1-10)[1172]

The 20th chapter of Revelation covers an array of diverse and unusual scenes, a characteristic which, as we shall see in this chapter, makes it readily identifiable with certain scenes in the 10th Division of the *Book of Gates*. The first scene (Rev. 20:1-3) describes the capture and imprisonment of "the dragon, that ancient serpent, who is the Devil and Satan," a creature identified in Chapter 4, *Other Characters in Revelation*, as Apophis, Egypt's primeval god of chaos and evil; we are told that he was bound in chains and shut in "the bottomless pit" for a thousand years. The next scene (Rev. 20:4-6) describes how those who had been killed for supporting their god came to life and reigned with him for a thousand years. Following the thousand years, the serpent is released from prison and leads a large army made up of many nations against the "camp of the saints and the beloved city" (Rev. 20:7-9). The army is destroyed by fire and the Devil thrown into a lake of fire (Rev. 20:10). This chapter will show how practically all these scenes as well as various images within these scenes parallel pictures and text of the 10th Division of the *Book of Gates*.

Capture of the Ancient Serpent (Rev. 20:1-4)

The story of the one thousand year reign begins with the capture of the ancient serpent: "Then I saw an *angel* coming down from heaven, holding in his *hand* the key of the bottomless pit and a *great chain*. And he seized the dragon, that *ancient serpent*, who is the Devil and Satan, and *bound him* for a thousand years, and threw him into the *pit*, and shut it and sealed it over him" (Rev. 20:1-2). There is also an indirect reference is also made to the followers of the beast, "*who ... worshiped the beast or its image*" (Rev. 20:4). There are seven notable elements in these brief passages, as follows: the ancient serpent, an angel, a hand, a great chain, the binding of the ancient serpent, the pit and finally, the beast's followers. Close scrutiny of the upper register of the 10th Division (Figure 117) reveals that these seven elements play important roles in the action implicit in the scene. Details of the elements will be considered separately (although in a different order).

The Ancient Serpent:- The Egyptian text identifies the serpent lying on its belly near the far left of Figure 117 as Apophis who, as described in Chapter 4, *Other Characters in Revelation,* represents the "the dragon, that ancient serpent, who is the Devil and Satan" of Rev. 20:2. The Egyptian text describes him as "The Burned One,"[1173] an obvious parallel with Rev. 20:10 where we read that "the devil who had deceived them was thrown into the lake of fire and sulphur ... and ... will be tormented day and night for ever and ever."

The Angel:- Immediately above the Apophis serpent is a goddess with outstretched arms (arms not visible in Figure 117), lying on her belly holding a chain attached behind Apophis' head. The Egyptian text identifies her as the goddess *Selkit* (one of the four protector goddesses of coffins and canopic jars). This figure thus conforms with the description in Rev. 20:1 of an "an angel ... holding in his[a] hand ... a great chain." Lurker tells us that Selkit was endowed with authority over the sun's scorching heat,[1174] a characteristic in keeping with the text of Rev. 20:10 which says that the devil (Apophis) was thrown into a lake of fire (as above). Rev. 20:1 tells us that the angel carried "the key of the bottomless pit," a possible reference to her role in the protection of the canopic jars in which the mummified internal organs of the deceased were stored until the resurrection when they would be reunited with the body (reunion with these organs was an important aspect to the resurrection of the body). Her function as a protectress of the dead is evident in Figure 117 where we see that she presides over the chain holding the ever-threatening Apophis.

The text accompanying the scene in Figure 117 also conforms with that of Rev. 20:1 where the angel is described as coming down from heaven. The middle register indicates that the events which are described in this division are closely associated with heavenly events. The deities who tow the solar barque in this register say "We tow Re toward heaven, we tow toward heaven. We accompany Re toward Nut [the sky-goddess]."[1175] Elsewhere in the same register, the text over three deities singing praises to Re says, "They are like this. They salute with their stars, they take hold of the fore rope of this barge, they enter Nut."[1176] Further to the right a group of deities call to Re when he enters the heavens, "Hail! Come, Child! Hail! Come, Creator of the Netherworld! Come, thou who settest foot on the heights of heaven. Hail, appearance of Re!"[1177] The welcoming sentiment is echoed in the upper register where the text over the five deities who hold the other end of the chain on the far right of Figure 117 says, "Re rises, the One of the Horizon is powerful, behold, we have overthrown the chained Apopis. Thou dost not approach thy enemies, O Re. ... Re comes into his hour of rest."[1178] Note that Selkit's role in the fight against Apophis in this part of heaven conforms with the idea of an angel "coming down from heaven" in Rev. 20:1.

Figure 117. Apophis, the "ancient serpent," is held in chains by the reclining god Selkit who is assisted by a group of sixteen deities and a giant hand. On the far right, the chain is linked to the followers of Apophis and held by the Four Sons of Horus and another deity. Several significant elements in this scene conform with Rev. 20:2-3. (BG10.1.3-10)

---

[a] While Selkit is a female deity, this text and Rev. 20:1 refer to her as being male.

24. The Millennium

The Hand:- The clenched hand symbol (🖝) was used to denote a closed fist; it was used in words such as 'to grasp' (*khefa*) and 'to seize' (*amem*),[1179] concepts which conform with the idea expressed Revelation. The presence of and the relatively large size of this symbol in Figure 117 emphasizes the "holding in his hand ... a *great*· chain" in Rev. 20:1 and the "*seizing*· of the dragon" in Rev. 20:2.

The Great Chain:- Rev. 20:1 describes the chain in the angel's hand as being a *great* chain. The Greek word used here for "great" is *megas,* a word which may also mean "large, mighty, or strong,"[1180] or even "long."[1181] That the chain shown in Figure 117 is all of large, mighty, strong – and long (it extends to a significant portion of the length of the upper register) is shown by the relatively small size of the figure of Selkit and the over-sized clenched hand shown pulling the chain down toward the earth in front of the group of sixteen deities which hold it.

In Egyptian drawings, larger figures were typically interpreted as being relatively more important parts of scenes. In pictures showing royalty, the pharaoh is almost always shown larger (or taller, or at a higher level) than his subjects – as well as other members of the royal family.[a] Similarly, the importance of the chain in Figure 117 is accentuated by the small size of Selkit and the large size of the hand which holds it. Their relative sizes also act as mnemonics for a knowledgeable person such as a priest to remember that the chain it grasps is indeed a "great" and "long" – as described in Rev. 20:1.

The Binding of the Serpent:- Rev. 20:2 tells us that the angel "seized ... that ancient serpent, ... and bound him." Figure 117 clearly shows that the serpent Apophis is not only "seized," as denoted by the hand symbol, but also that he is bound by the great chain attached behind his head.

The Pit:- While there are no explicit statements in the Egyptian text that the deities who chained Apophis "threw him into the pit, and shut it and sealed it over him," there are a number of pictorial allusions to it. One is found in the makeup of the five deities holding the chain on the right side of Figure 117. The text identifies the first four as the Sons of Horus while the fifth, on the far right, is Geb, the earth god who can be said to be a reference to "the pit" as in Rev. 20:1. Also, note that the conspicuously solitary, giant hand causes the chain to bend as Apophis is pulled down into the earth (Geb). The text above the five says that "They keep guard over the chains of the punished one which are in the Hand of the Hidden Body."[1182] It is interesting to note that Rev. 20:3 tells us that the serpent was thrown into the pit so "that he should deceive the nations no more." This comment conforms with a comment made next to Apophis's name in Figure 117: "His voice [cries?] goes round the Netherworld" where the Netherworld may be interpreted to mean the pit, i.e., the depths below the earth. The action implicit in this figure is therefore consistent with that described in Rev. 20:2-3 where the ancient serpent was not only bound by a chain held by a hand of an angel, but was also thrown into the depths of the earth.

---

[a] See Chapter 2 entitled *Measure and Meaning, the Symbolism of Size* in *Symbol and Magic in Egyptian Art* by Wilkinson (1994), pp. 38-51.

Judgment of the Serpent and his Followers (Rev. 20:4): The first part of Rev. 20:4 refers to "thrones, and seated on them were those to whom judgment was committed." Except for four seated deities shown in the middle register (at BG10.2.3-4), immediately below the picture of Apophis, there are no other seated individuals in this Division; neither does the Egyptian text accompanying them refer to judges *per se*. Nor does Revelation say exactly who is to be judged although we might infer from the latter part of the verse that it refers to those who had "worshiped the [1st] beast or its image" and had "received its mark on their foreheads or their hands" (Rev. 20:4). From an Egyptian perspective, the ones to be judged are those who worshiped Seth or his image who, according to Rev. 13:2 received power from the dragon (Apophis) and thus, were followers of Apophis as well. Although there is no clear reference to judges, *per se*, in the 10th Division, a textual reference to the judgment of the followers of Apophis is found above the five deities (the four sons of Horus and the earth-god, Geb) holding the chain on the far right of Figure 117. Below them are five serpents representing the followers of Apophis. These are also in chains, each attached to the same chain which holds Apophis. The text pertaining to them says,

> They are like this, guarding the issue of the helpless one. They keep guard over the chains of the punished one which are in the Hand of the Hidden Body, *placed to be judged* before the gates of He at the Head of the Westerners."
> These gods say:
> Let darkness be upon thy face [in the pit], O (serpent) Burned One. Offspring of the Helpless One, you shall be annihilated, you are in the Hidden Hand which causes evil to the chained evil ones [the followers of Apophis]. Geb guards your chains, the sons of the bonds fit them for you, O chained evil ones [followers of Apophis], who are guarded as those assigned to He at the Head of the Westerners [Osiris]. They are like this, they make heavy the bonds of the offspring of the Helpless One, while the barge of the Good God [Re] passes by.[1183]

The text above the upper register refers to a period during which Re rests after the capture of Apophis and his followers:

> He rises, the One of the Horizon [Re] is powerful, behold, we have overthrown the chained Apophis. Thou dost not approach thy enemies, O Re. Thy enemies do not come near thee, O Re. Thy sanctity has come into being in the coils of the Enveloper, while *Apopis is slain lying in his blood*, being executed. Re comes into his *hour of rest*.
> Then this Great God passes on after his fetters (on Apopis) have been tightened.[1184]

Considering that the "hour of rest" for Re referred to here could represent any period of time, it is not unrealistic to suggest that this period could be one thousand years. The "hour of rest" would then parallel the one thousand-year period referred to in Rev. 20:2-3 when the serpent "should deceive the nations no more." The period of one thousand years during which the serpent of Revelation is sealed in the pit will therefore be discussed next in relation to the thousand-year reign of the martyrs.

The 1,000 Year Period (Rev. 20:2-7)

There are six references to a thousand-year period in this chapter of Revelation (all in Rev. 20:2-7). For example, Rev. 20:4 says that "They came to life, and reigned with Christ *a thousand years*." There are, however, no explicit references to a thousand-year period in the text of the *Book of Gates* although there seem to be allusions to a long period embedded in the pictures. Before examining these possible allusions, a brief examination of the use of the number 1,000 in Egyptian mythology will be presented to help orient the reader to Egyptian thoughts on this subject.

1,000 as a very large number

Perhaps the simplest use of the number 1,000 is in reference to the age-old practice of using it as a means of expressing any very large number. For example, one very ancient use in a mythological context is found in the *Pyramid Texts* which not only use it to express large numbers but, like Rev. 20, combine it with many of the same rewards we read about in Revelation. The relevant text, a spell originally written to apply to the dead king, was in later years accorded to all Osirian believers. It reads as follows:

> *Raise yourself,* O King, [a reference to the resurrection of the king] to *your thousand of bread, your thousand of beer, your thousand of oxen, your thousand of poultry, your thousand of clothing, your thousand of alabaster.* I have gone forth for you from the house, O King, that you may inherit the leadership of the lord of the Gods and give orders to the Westerners, because you are a great and mighty spirit, and those who have suffered death(?) are united for you wherever you wish to be. O King, may you have power thereby, for the gods have commanded that you guard yourself from those who speak against you, O King, because you are he whom Osiris installed on his throne that you may lead the Westerners and be a spirit at the head of the gods. (Pyramid Text 665A)[1185]

Significantly, Faulkner (1969) refers to this utterance as a *resurrection text*. Note that in addition to rewards being expressed in their thousands, this passage, when applied to all Osirian believers, includes reference to the resurrection of the faithful ("Raise yourself ..."), those who die (as martyrs?) will inherit leadership over the people ("inherit the leadership of the lord of the Gods [as priests?] and give orders to the Westerners"), and will reign with Osiris on his throne ("your are he whom Osiris installed on his throne that you may lead the Westerners and be a spirit at the head of the gods"). We may therefore conclude that many of the rewards described in Rev. 20:2-7 (resurrection, leadership and co-reigning with a deity) were already well known to the ancient Egyptians for at least as far back as the pyramid era. In Utterance 665A, above, they were understood in the context of 1,000's.

The 1,000 year link with a lifetime

A second possible association with the number 1,000 is based on an unusual perceived distortion of time among the resurrected dead in the Egyptian afterlife. In his discussion on this topic, Hornung (1990) points out that "The Egyptians suspected the sun covered 'millions of miles' on its daily journey through the heavens and the Netherworld. We also learn that even time had other dimensions in the Beyond, an hour of the nightly voyage corresponding to an entire lifetime on earth."[1186] Hornung (1983) points out that "In the next world, time is ... measured on a different scale, so that the judges of the dead 'regard a lifetime as an hour' but without stepping outside the categories of time and space."[1187] Budge (1934) provides us with a relevant extract from the *Teaching of King Khati:*

> Fill not thy heart (or mind) {with the thought of} the length of {thy} years, for the *djadjau* [the judges of the dead] look upon the whole lifetime as an hour, their opportunity {for doing this is} after death, and they set his (i.e. a man's) qualities before him like a wall (?). Moreover, existence there is for ever. If the man who attaineth to this hath committed no sins his existence there is like that of *Neter* (i.e., God, or the God), and he marcheth on like the Lords who are everlasting.[1188]

Hornung (1990) suggests that "The awakening to rejuvenated life never lasts more than an hour after which life and light pass on with the sun god, even though an hour of the Beyond is adjusted to that world's monstrous dimensions and corresponds to an entire lifetime here on earth."[1189] Elsewhere, he says that "The sun god ... spends an entire 'lifetime' in each hour, deciding on the fate of the blessed and the damned. His presence awakens the departed from their deathly sleep, and as souls join bodies, life blooms everywhere."[1190] There can be little doubt that, to those who are victorious in the judgment, the concept of an hour in the hereafter being equal to a lifetime here on earth is associated with the judgment of the dead and a continued existence with their god. It remains then to show how this concept might parallel the idea of the thousand-year reign of the faithful as expressed in Rev. 20.

We begin with the likely average life span of the ancient Egyptians. According to Numbers 32:13 in the Old Testament, the average life span of the Hebrews just prior to their exodus from Egypt was forty years: "And the Lord's anger was kindled against Israel, and he made them wander in the wilderness *forty years*, until all the generation that had done evil in the sight of the Lord was consumed." We should expect that the *average* life span of the native Egyptians, who lived at a higher standard of living (better food, living conditions and health care, etc.), would be somewhat greater than forty years and a number of about 42 years seems reasonable – i.e., one hour in the hereafter would represent about 42 years, or a lifetime, on earth. Now since there are 24 hours in a day, we may conclude that 24 hours in the hereafter (the time, in celestial units, required for the sun-god to make a complete circuit through the daytime sky and the depths of the Netherworld) would represent about 24 hours x 42 years/hour which amounts to 1008 years, a figure which is close to the 1,000 years required for complete agreement with Revelation. Considering the inherent error in the estimate of 42 years, this agreement is quite remarkable (an estimate of 41.7 years is what is required to arrive at the practically identical figure of 1,000 years). It therefore seems that even the Egyptians' seemingly metaphorical reference to one hour in the beyond being equal to a lifetime on earth conforms with the concept of the thousand year reign of the resurrected dead referred to in the Book of Revelation.

The 1,000 year Phoenix Period

The third possible parallel to the number 1,000 involves the so-called Phoenix Period. This period is important, not only because it is related to the rebirth of creation but also because of its length. Budge (1904) tells us this period was related to the

> Bennu, 𓅽, a bird of the heron species which was identified with the Phoenix. This bird is said to have created itself, and to have come into being out of the fire which burned on the top of the sacred Percea Tree of Heliopolis; it was essentially a Sun-bird, and was a symbol both of the rising sun and of the dead Sun-god Osiris, from whom it sprang, and to whom it was sacred. The Bennu not only typified the new birth of the sun each morning, but in the earliest period of dynastic history it became the symbol of the resurrection of mankind, for a man's spiritual body was believed to spring from the dead physical body, just as the living sun of to-day had its origin in the dead sun of yesterday.[1191]

Elsewhere, Budge (1893) provides us with various documented lengths of the Phoenix period – 500, 540, 1,000 and 7006 years.[1192] Note that these periods include the 1,000 year period of Rev. 20, so that we might very well make note of this numerical parallel and move on to the next topic. Herodotus, however, claims the phoenix made its appearance once in 500 years,[1193] a figure most commonly referred to today. Research on reasons why we might find the 1,000 as well as the 500 year period in Egyptian mythology is therefore warranted.

Support for the idea of a 1,000 year period of the sun-god, may also be found in Utterance 600 of the *Pyramid Texts* which contains an association of the phoenix and a pun on the number 1,000. In it we read that Atum, here affiliated with the Mansion of the Phoenix, created the atmosphere (Shu) and the earth (Tefenet) and endowed them with his *ka* – a word which, as noted above, can mean 1,000 as well as the more traditional "spirit" or "soul." "O Atum-Khoprer, you became high on the Height. You rose up as the *bnbn*-stone in the Mansion of the Phoenix in On [i.e., Heliopolis]. You spat out Shu, you expectorated Tefenet and set your arms about them like a *ka*-symbol, that your *ka* might be in them."[1194] If we assume a pun on the word *ka,* the final phrase in the utterance may be interpreted as "that your *one thousand* (years) might be in them." In this context, the 1,000 year period is associated with the cyclical nature of creation, and in particular, the rebirth into the sky of the young sun-god (as Atum-Khepri) – and thus, the juvenile Re which parallels the Lamb of Revelation as discussed in Chapter 3, *The Preeminent Deities*.

As already pointed out, the Egyptians envisioned their righteous dead as rising with the sun-god each morning at dawn and reigning with him throughout the day. But, given their belief in the cyclical nature of the daily birth and death of the sun-god, they undoubtedly assumed that the twelve daylight hours on earth represented a five hundred years reign of the sun-god in the heavens, that is, five hundred years from his birth (or rebirth) in the morning to his death in the evening. It is therefore logical to assume that they also envisioned that the twelve hours of night during which the sun-god remained in the dark timeless depths of the Netherworld represented an additional five hundred years. In other words, a complete cycle of the sun-god through the daytime sky and the darkness of the Netherworld would take twenty-four hours on earth. For the faithful dead with the sun-god, this would mean one thousand years in his holy presence. This time frame is consistent with the Egyptian belief that a day on earth was equivalent to a thousand years in the beyond, a period which is also consistent with the 1,000 year period referred to in Revelation.

1,000 Year Periods in the *Book of Gates*

The first obvious reference to a lengthy period of time in the 10th Division of the *Book of Gates* is found in the symbolism of the two-headed serpent rearing up behind the priest to the right of center in the middle register (Figure 118). Clagett (1989) informs us that the heads of this serpent demonstrate "the Egyptian image of the two-headed nature of time, one head looking toward the past and the other toward the future."[1195] Meanwhile, the text above this scene makes an unequivocal link to a time period. Piankoff (1954) translates it as "She who establishes *Time*,' who writes it down in *years*' on the serpent,[a] and who raises it before him to the heights of heaven."[1196] As pointed out above, a 500 year period for each celestial day and each night in the Netherworld is not an unreasonable estimate of the time frame involved, especially in light of the belief that 1,000 years on earth was considered equal to a day in the afterlife. It is therefore reasonable to assume that one head may be considered to be represent one time period and the other, another; more specifically, one represents a total of 500 years in the light of the celestial day while the other represents a total 500 years in the darkness of night in the Netherworld, a total of 1,000 years and a period which parallels that mentioned in Rev. 20.

Figure 118. Pictorial representation of the rewards to those killed in fighting for their god, including resurrection, reigning with their god for 1,000 years, and the privilege of serving as priests as in Rev. 20. See text for explanation of the symbolism found in this scene. (BG10.2.8-9)

On close inspection of Figure 118, we find what may well be several other visual puns conforming with the suggestion that a 1,000 year period is implied in the scene. The first is found in the upper *part of the altar on which the priest pours fire*, i.e., that part of the altar formed by the head of a bull. The Egyptian word for "bull" is *ka*, or k_3,[1197] a word phonetically similar to or even identical with a word meaning "one thousand," h_3[1198] (*kha*).[1199] A second pun is not as obvious but is probably significant nonetheless; it is associated with the long vertical, columnar base of the "altar" which holds up the bull's head. *Kha* is also an Egyptian word for a column[1200] so that the shape of the base of this altar serves to emphasize the number 1,000. When these puns are considered in the context of the two-headed serpent called "She who established

---

[a] Clagett (1989, p. 482) refers to the name of this serpent as "The One Who Establishes Lifespans and writes them down as years on this Uraeus"

time, who writes it down in *years*,'" this scene seems to emphasize a period of 1,000 years during which the priest serves, as in Rev. 20:6. Reinforcement of the idea of a one thousand year period is also found in puns associated with the use of the bull-headed altar upon on which fire is poured. Again, words sounding like *kha*, 1,000, are encountered. Alternative words for altar are *khai-t*,[1201] *khau-t*,[1202] *ḥꜣy*,[1203] or *ḫꜣw*[1204] while words for fire can be *khu*[1205] and *kheb*.[1206] A fire-place can be a *khā*[1207] while the burning of incense may be referred to as *kꜣp*.[1208] Also, the offering bowl from which the fire flows in Figure 118 may be called a *ḥꜣw* (a small bowl),[1209] a *kḥ* (a jar),[1210] or a *khau* (a pot or altar vessel).[1211] When all these visual puns are considered together, the inference is the same as that outlined in Rev. 20:6, *"they shall be priests ... a thousand years."*

The First Resurrection

Reign of the Lamb (Rev. 20:4-5)

Other elements in Rev. 20:4-5 are found in the *Book of Gates* which parallel Revelation's statement that, "They came to life, and reigned with Christ a thousand years" (Rev. 20:4). We first encounter an Egyptian parallel to the reign of those who have been resurrected in the middle register of the 10th Division where several deities emerge from the underworld into the morning sky with the sun-god. Three (many) of them at BG10.2.4-5 are deities who tow the sun-god's barque with one hand and carry stars in the other; the text tells us these are *The Praisers*. It also says that *they enter the sky with Re*. "They are like this. They salute with their stars, they take hold of the fore-rope of this barge, they enter Nut [the sky]."[1212]

The scene which alludes to the rising of the sun (the sun-god) into the morning sky is found at the right-hand side of the same register and shown here as a winged serpent in Figure 118. The symbolism inherent in this serpent relates well to this part of Revelation, especially that aspect which involves the renewal of the reign of the sun-god in the heavens; to the Egyptians the winged serpent alluded to regeneration and resurrection[1213] and in Chapter 87 of the *Book of the Dead*, which is devoted entirely to this aspect of the serpent, we find the remark, "I am a long-lived snake; I pass the night and am reborn every day. I am a snake which is in the limits of the earth; I pass the night and am reborn, renewed, and rejuvenated every day."[1214] Lurker (1980) who says that "the snake, because it sloughs its skin, became a symbol of survival after death.

Also, note that the wings of the serpent have their own symbolism. Wilkinson (1992) describes an early understanding of them:

> According to a very ancient Egyptian conception of the cosmos, the heavens were the wings of a great falcon whose eyes were the sun and moon, and the speckled underside was the starry sky. This deity was the falcon-shaped god Horus, and the conception of the heavens as his wings may be seen in the First Dynasty tomb of King Djet where the wings are attached to the solar barque on which the falcon rides.[1215]

This natural association of wings with the heavens finds support in the text which accompanies Figure 118. It informs us that the serpent's name is, "The Leader ...

[who] rises before Re. ... who leads the Great God [Re, Revelation's Lamb] to the Gate of the Eastern Horizon." Meanwhile, the four female deities on the right, who are "The Callers," raise their hands toward a two headed serpent, or the winged serpent, or both, and herald the appearance of Re in the heavens with the words, "Hail! Come, Child![a] Come, Creator of the Netherworld! Come, thou who settest foot on the heights of heaven. Hail, appearance of Re!"[1216] The scene thus depicts the newly born sun-god, led by the winged-serpent ("The Leader") into the morning sky in the midst of praises sung by the four (a multitude of goddesses).

Similarly, Rev. 20:4 tells us that those who participated in the first resurrection are described as

> the souls of those who had been beheaded for their testimony to Jesus and for the word of God, and who had not worshiped the beast or its image and had not received its mark[b] on their foreheads or their hands. *They came to life* ... This is the first resurrection.

In the context of the events we have been discussing in the *Book of Gates*, these martyrs would represent those followers of the sun-god who fought and died to protect Re from the assaults of Apophis and his army as he made his hazardous journey through the Netherworld (see the section on the *War with the Lamb* in Chapter 23, *The Harlot and the Kings*). These martyrs thus parallel those in Rev. 20:4-5 who came to life and reigned with their sovereign, who, in Egyptian terms would be the young sun-god, the lamb of the ram-headed form of Re.

Reign of the Martyrs (Rev. 20:4)

The 3rd register of 10th Division of the *Book of Gates* (Figure 119) deals with the faithful followers of the sun-god rising with him into the heavens as in Rev. 20:4. We find here two groups of twelve deities, the first of which have paddles and are called the "Gods of the stars which do not perish." The other group consists of time goddesses called "The Hours who Tow." The text over this register tells us:

> They are like this. They cause to rise before Re, they take hold of their paddles (going) toward this cavern while the One of the Hours causes them to come (into) being when Re is born in Nut. They come into being at the birth of Re and they come out of the Abyss

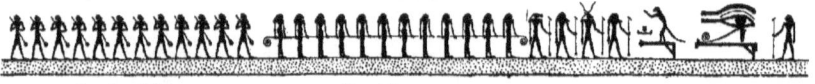

| Gods of the | Goddesses |
| imperishable stars | of the hours |

Figure 119. Two groups of twelve deities represent the followers of the sun-god who are born with him into the morning sky, a scene which conforms with Rev. 20:4. (BG10.3)

---

[a] The juvenile form of the ram-headed sun-god, i.e., the Lamb of Revelation.

[b] The mark, defined as "666" in Rev. 13:18, is discussed in Chapter 4, *Other Characters in Revelation*, where it is shown to represent the name of Seth, a deity who during much of the Middle Kingdom was effectively synonymous with Apophis, the god of chaos and evil.

24. The Millennium

along with him. It is they who row this Great God after he has taken a seat [throne] in the Eastern Horizon of Heaven [at dawn]. (BG10.3)

Re says to these twelve goddesses of The Hours who Tow,

> Take hold of the Nefert-rope, be content while you tow my followers toward the heights of heaven and lead me toward your ways. When I am born [i.e., reborn, resurrected] you are born [reborn, resurrected] when I come into being you come into being! Hail! You establish the periods of life and the years of those among whom you are. (BG10.3.1-4)[1217]

And to the twelve who stand behind them, he says, "Take your paddles, your stars are your abodes. When you come into being [i.e., reborn, resurrected] then I also come into being; when you are born [again] I am also born [again]. Row me, you will not go under [the horizon], you gods who are the Imperishable Stars!" (BG10.3.1-4)[1218]

Revelation's likely parallel to the two groups of twelve in this register was discussed in detail in Chapter 7, *The Great Multitude*, where it was shown that most groups of twelve in the *Book of Gates* parallel aspects of the faithful dead in Rev. 7 who once lived on earth. Recall that these followers included those who had fought and died for their god in the war against evil; they included the martyrs who had been faithful to their god. In this part of the 10th Division we find these faithful followers, after receiving new life, rising into the sky with Re at dawn. As representatives of those who once died fighting for their god, this scene is consistent with the resurrection of the martyrs in Rev. 20:4 who had been slain (beheaded) for their God and came to life and reigned with him.

Rev. 20:4 also tells us that the martyrs were resurrected and "reigned with Christ a thousand years." This parallels the quotation found at BG10.3.1-4 where we read that a group of twelve followers are told they "will not go *under*, you are the Imperishable Stars!" "Imperishable Stars" was a name given to a group of northern, circumpolar stars because only they remained above the horizon each night throughout the entire year.[1219] But it was during the night that the sun-god passed through the darkness of the Egyptian Netherworld. Their perpetual presence in the night sky thus accentuated the fact that, in spite of the location of the sun-god in the Netherworld, he was still their supreme god, who now ruled the underworld and he would not let his faithful martyrs be subject to its dangers.

The reference to the faithful "reigning *with Christ*," however, is more difficult to explain in terms of Egyptian beliefs; as noted above, they believed the martyrs reigned with the sun-god, i.e., Re or Osiris-Re, not Horus the anointed one who parallels Revelation's Christ. It seems the only way we can draw a parallel here is to point out that "Horus of the Netherworld" also reigned with the sun-god in the Netherworld. We may say that since Horus, the king of Egypt was, as pointed out elsewhere, the earthly manifestation of Horus of the Netherworld, those martyrs who died for their king continued to be with him in the afterlife where they reigned with him *and* the sun-god Re (or Osiris-Re). One might argue that this rationale for a parallel to the martyrs who reign *with Christ* in Rev. 20:4 is indirect and therefore not a very strong one. Nevertheless, if we were to demand a parallel at this point in the study, as the various parallels surrounding this statement in Revelation seem to suggest, this explanation may be appropriate. Obviously, more research is needed in this area.

This fellowship of the faithful with the sun-god is perhaps nowhere more graphically portrayed than in a scene found in Hornung (1990) and shown here as Figure 120. Here, the sun-god is represented in his unified, Osiris-Re form which was in Chapter 3, *The Preeminent Deities*, identified with Revelation's "God and the Lamb." Hornung says that "the god who emerges triumphantly before our eyes from the gates of the eastern horizon is in fact the *ba* [soul] of Osiris, which traverses the arc of heaven with Re, and with Re the souls of the deceased remain eternally in the light of the sun."[1220] These souls of the faithful are depicted in Figure 120 as stars[a] who travel with the sun-god across the sky from horizon to horizon (shown in the figure as two outstretched arms). Furthermore, as indicated elsewhere, the star hieroglyph also represents the concept of "praise," so that these stars can not only be seen as the souls of the faithful followers of the sun-god, but also of their praises to him as they rise into the heights of heaven with him. The Egyptian concept of the resurrected followers rising with Osiris-Re (Osiris is Revelation's "God" while the combined, Osiris-Re, is his one of his juvenile form especially at dawn) into the heavens and reigning with their god as in Figure 120 is, of course, consistent with the statement in Rev. 20:6 that the followers of "God (Osiris) and Christ (Re), *they shall reign with him* for a thousand years.[b]

Phonetic analysis on Egyptian equivalents of important words used in Revelation also support the idea of a parallel with the souls of the resurrected Egyptian dead reigning with their god. Consider, for example, *Ḥeqit*, the well-known goddess of the resurrection.[1221] Her name is phonetically similar to *ḥeq-t,* meaning "rule, authority, sovereignty, dominion, or government"[1222] while the words *ḥeq, ḥeqa,* and *ḥeqi* meant "power, to rule or to govern"[1223] and *ḥekau* was a name of a diadem or crown.[1224] Similar sounding words also had conceptual links with the idea of praise which the resurrected faithful made to the sun-god as discussed above. For example, *ḥekai,* meant "enchanter,"[1225] *ḥekniu,* "singers,"[1226] and *ḥeken* meant "to praise, adore, sing, or acclaim."[1227] *Ḥeka* could also mean "incantation or charm,"[1228] suggesting a link between the faithful followers (the stars) and their protective encircling of the sun-god in the heavens which is emphasized by the dotted circle surrounding the sun-god in Figure 120. Also significant is another phonetically similar word, *ḥeki*, which meant "to fight,"[1229] a word which reminds the knowledgeable reader that the group of praising stars includes those who had fought for their god, as indicated above. Finally, another somewhat similar word is *ḥeḥ*, meaning "a period of unlimited time,"[1230] "a great number"[1231] or "eternity,"[1232] time-frames is consistent with a thousand year period in the minds of many Egyptians – as in Revelation. We thus have a group

---

[a] The status of the faithful as stars in the sky conforms with the ancient Egyptian hope to one day become a star in the heavens, as discussed in the section entitled the *Gift of the Morning Star* in Chapter 7, *Egyptian Beliefs in the Seven Letters*.

[b] Note that the reference to "reigning with God" seems to be implied in Rev. 20:4, especially since it is included in Rev. 20:6 which says that "they (the followers of Christ) shall be priests of God and of Christ, and they shall reign with him."

of phonetically similar words with meanings that embody resurrection (*Heqit*), reigning power (*heq-t*), praise (*heka*), conflict (*heki*), and a long period of time (*heh*), all of which are either explicitly stated or strongly implied in Rev. 20:4.

In addition to the possible reference to a 1,000 year period in the *Book of Gates*, there is a potential visual pun for this period embedded in Figure 120. It is found in the hieroglyphic symbol ◯ (*'nk*) which cradles the sun-god at its center, its arms extending horizontally from the left hand side of the figure. This symbol is the determinative for the words "envelop and embrace"[1233] and is similar to the *ka* symbol, ⊔, the ideograph of "soul and spirit."[1234] The two symbols are clearly related, not only in form, but by virtue of the use of the *'nk*, ◯, in another symbol, ⊕, which means "servant of the *ka*" or "*ka*-priest, (a symbol incorporating the ▌ symbol, the ideogram for a "club used by fullers in washing"[1235]). Furthermore, the horizontal bar underneath the solar barque in Figure 120 may represent the club or stick symbol[a] found in ⊕ so that its use and orientation in the picture could represent a stylized ⊕. In either case, we may interpret the ◯ as being a stylized ⊔, or *ka*, so that we find three embedded symbols in this figure – the first is ⊔ (or ◯), referring to the souls or spirits (*kas*) of the dead which are shown in the picture as stars; the second is ⊕ which identifies the stars (souls) as being "*ka*-priests;" and the third is *kha*, the number 1,000 expressed as a visual pun in the ⊔ (or ◯) symbol. And since the ◯ symbol is shown enfolding the many stars (the *kas*) it may be seen as endowing them with at least one attribute of the word *ka* – the number 1,000. In this way the stars which reign in the sky with their god have the number 1,000 associated with them – as in Rev. 20:2. Finally, there is the parallel concept of them being priests ("*ka*-priests") – as in Rev. 20:6. We will next discuss the latter parallel further in relation to Figure 118 (from the *Book of Gates*).

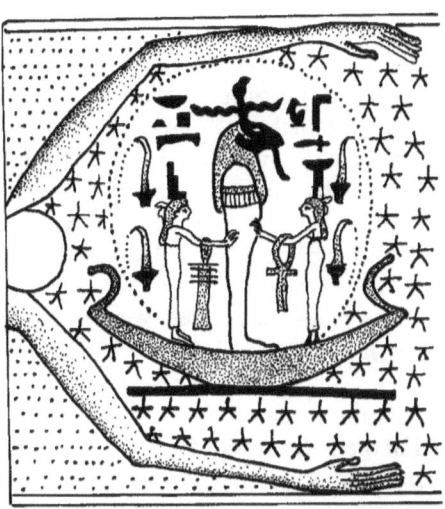

Figure 120. The resurrected faithful are depicted as stars who reign with the ram-headed sun-god (the Lamb of Rev. 20:4) as he stands in his bark while traveling across the day-time sky from one horizon to the other.

The Resurrected Made Priests (Rev. 20:6)

Rev. 20:6 says, "Blessed and holy is he who shares in the first resurrection! ... they shall be priests of God and of Christ." Although there are no explicit references to "priests" of the sun-god in the text of this part of the *Book of Gates*, they are either

---

[a] Note that this symbol does not contain the wavy lines indicative of water (▬) as we usually see when the solar barque is shown sailing on the primordial sea.

implied or are depicted in pictures. For example, Figure 118 contains a picture of a single priest making an offering on a bull-headed altar. And in the lower register, directly below this scene and facing the monkey in Figure 119 are four figures holding *was* scepters (𓌀) performing duties normally associated with priests. The first figure is identified with the one who "orders the gate to be open before Re," the second "calls to the stars at the moment when this Great God is born," the third "calls the gods in the barge of Re," and the fourth "places the stars in their abodes," and "praises Re." Furthermore, all four of these deities pass "on before this Great God" into the morning sky[1236] and can therefore to be included among the resurrected faithful discussed above.

There is also a parallel between the priest in Figure 118 and the resurrected faithful of Rev. 20:4, "those who had been beheaded for their testimony to Jesus and for the word of God." We find it in the text near the knife placed across the pole which forms the base of the bull-headed altar. It refers to "the knife ... which is in the hand of the fighters who are in the following of this god,"[1237] and thus connects the priest with those who fought for Re.

Another possible parallel is related to the part of Rev. 20:4 which says that these are they who "had not received its [the 1st beast's] mark on their foreheads." The priest in Figure 118 is seen pouring fire from an offering pot onto the forehead of the bull while the text tells us that "He places the fire between the horns"[1238] of the bull. This action, in conjunction with the presence of the knife and its association with "the fighters who are in the following of this god" may be interpreted as being a symbolic gesture referring to destruction of those enemy troops who bore the brand mark of their leader (i.e., 𓊃𓊃𓊃, a "phonetic symbol" of Seth, Revelation's 1st beast) on their foreheads as discussed in Chapter 4, *Other Characters in Revelation* and Chapter 18, *The Beasts of Rev. 13*. The absence of a textual reference to such a brand mark on the followers of Apophis in this scene, however, makes this suggestion somewhat tenuous at best and is thus a candidate for further research. Nevertheless, the pictorial reference to the priest, the bull's forehead, and the text concerning the resurrected followers who fought and died for their god is quite evident and suggests parallels to the scene in Rev. 20:4.

But Rev. 20:6 adds that they "shall be priests of *God and of Christ,*" a statement which differs from this part of the *Book of Gates* which mentions neither Osiris (= Revelation's God) nor Horus (= Revelation's Christ, the anointed one). The reader will note, however, that the first part of this discrepancy, the reference to God, disappears when one takes into consideration Egyptian beliefs which evolved over time to take into account the combined supremacy of Re and Osiris in which the two deities are simply viewed as if one was contained within the other. Hornung (1990) discusses the idea of this unified view Re-Osiris and points out that,

> as early as the Middle Kingdom Coffin Texts it is remarked that the one god "appears" as the other, and the New Kingdom considered that the union of their souls begat the "united ba" which speaks with "a single mouth," according to the Abydos stela of Ramesses IV.

The concept of "unification" [of Osiris and Re] can be traced back to the Litany of Re and the early New Kingdom, where the deceased pharaoh aspired to be identified as Re and Osiris. The unions of these two gods is simply formulated:

> A shout of joy is in the Realm of the Dead:
> "Re it is, who has gone into Osiris,
> Osiris reposes in Re." [1239]

With this in mind we can tenuously propose a parallel between the "God" (Osiris) of Rev. 20:6 and Re as he rose in his Osiris-Re form into the morning sky with his entourage of resurrected faithful servants; God, or Osiris, could be seen as the equivalent of Re and the sun-god could be considered to be either Re or Re-Osiris.

The second part of this apparent discrepancy concerns the statement that the resurrected will become "priests of God *and his Christ*" (Rev. 20:6). A possible parallel to this concept may exist, as follows: In Chapter 3, *The Preeminent Deities*, we saw that the Pharaoh of Egypt parallels Horus, the son of Re (or Re-Osiris). The Pharaoh, of course, was the chief priest and the *christos*, "the anointed one," and the sun-god's representative on earth. The king thus parallels the Christ of Revelation.

From an Egyptian context, then, Rev. 20:6 may be interpreted as referring to the priests of both Osiris and the king. This interpretation applies to the 10th Division where, as seen in Figure 119, twenty-four faithful followers face both the Udjat-eye (☥, a symbol of the sun-god) and, at the far right, a bearded "porter"[1240] standing with a *was* scepter (𓌂, a symbol of "power" and "dominion"[1241]) in his hand. Since the lower register effectively introduces those who are to rule with the sun-god in the heights of heaven, we may conclude that the function of the "porter" is to guide the faithful into their proper places as stars in the heavens. On earth, this person would be Horus of the Netherworld, or from an earthly point of view, Horus the son of Re on earth, the king. This authority would be expressed in the theocratic regime of ancient Egypt in terms of priests who held important administrative positions in temples and government offices to assist in the king's rule over earth as his heavenly father's representative. In this way, the followers of the king and his father Re would have been considered as priests of both Pharaoh and Re (or Re-Osiris, or both) as in Rev. 20:6. And just as the living priests served, worshiped, and ruled with their Pharaoh on earth, the resurrected dead did the same in Egypt's mirror image in the afterlife, rising into the morning sky with their god.

Yet another possibility remains to explain the reference to Christ in Rev. 20:6. To understand this one, we must again assume that the original version of the Book of Revelation was based on Egyptian beliefs. Note that the Christ of Christianity was at times referred to as "the Lamb" (see John 1:29,36, Acts 8:32 and I Peter 1:19) and Christian scribes and redactors of early copies of the Book of Revelation may have incorrectly identified references to the ram-headed form of Re (his juvenile ram, or lamb form) as Christianity's Christ in a sincere attempt to interpret and clarify the text of the Book of Revelation in the context of their own beliefs. In such a scenario, the original text of Revelation could have meant something like "they shall be priests of God and of *the juvenile form of Re*" rather than "they shall be priests of God and of *Christ*," i.e., the Lamb of God described in the New Testament.

The Second Resurrection (Rev. 20:5)

Rev. 20:5 tells us that not all of the dead were resurrected at the same time as the martyrs: "The rest of the dead did not come to life until the thousand years were ended." In the last section, we took note of a special group of faithful followers, the martyrs of Re, who were resurrected, became stars, and rose into the morning sky with him. But, like Rev. 20:5, these did not represent all those who had been faithful to Re. Indeed, there are many more references to Re's followers who, in spite of their faithfulness to him, remain in the Netherworld rather than join him as stars in the sky. For example, it is written above a deity at BG10.3.10 in Figure 119 that he "remains in his place and does not pass [into the sky] before Re."[1242] Similarly, in the bottom register of the 11th Division, three of the seven groups of four deities remain in the Netherworld. The first group (at BG11.3.1-2) represents those who follow Re and establish the White Crown on the gods; "their souls go forward and stand at (this) gate." The second (at BG11.3.7-8) are those who loosen their hair before the Great God in West; "They turn back to this gate, they do not enter the sky." The third (at BG11.3.8-10) represents the gate keepers who worship, praise, and honor Re; "They remain in their places."[1243] The fate of these other four groups is different still; their souls go into the following of Re but their bodies remain in their places in the Netherworld.[1244]

As noted above, there are numerous references to those who remain in their places in the Netherworld after the sun-god passes by; these are normally identified as those who are left behind in the gateways after the Great God leaves one division to go on to the next. One passage reads "They wail for Re and they lament for the Great God after he has passed by them. As the god passes, darkness envelops all this, and their cavern is sealed upon them."[1245] Most references to them, however, simply say that "Those who are in this gate wail on hearing the closing of the door."[a] Hornung (1990) provides a vivid description of the transition between the joy of being with their god and the desperate cries of the dead when he leaves them in the silence of the Netherworld.

> Universal rejoicing becomes a wail as the luminous bark [of the sun-god] moves on, passing through another well-guarded gate. Darkness drops over the region and the doors clang to a last wail before all the creatures resume the sleep of the dead. The jubilation and a dialogue with the god are followed by silence, another symbol of the Realm of the Dead.[1246]

But even this is not the end for the faithful who do not follow their god into the sky. A brief glance at the characteristics and references to their rewards (Table 24.1) suggests otherwise. It is obvious that these individuals represent faithful followers of the sun-god who, while not destined to follow him into the brilliance of the morning sky to rule over the earth during the coming day, must stay behind in the Netherworld.

---

[a] For example, on p.144 of Piankoff (1954): the gates at BG1; BG4, p. 165; BG7, p.185; BG8, p. 191; BG9, p. 196; and BG11, p. 215.

24. The Millennium

If they are to eventually join him, they must await his return to the Netherworld in the next solar cycle when, presumably, they would then have the privilege of fighting for him against Apophis and his followers to die as martyrs and join the ranks of the those resurrected at an earlier dawn; this was the second resurrection.

Table 24.1 Characteristics of, and rewards to the dead who rejoice on the arrival of the sun-god in different parts of the Netherworld; many who wail after being shut up in darkness after Re has passed by. Locations of the deities in the Divisions and page numbers in Piankoff (1954) are given in the last two columns.

Characteristics	Reward	Location	Page
Repulse and enchant Apophis	Live on offerings, oblations	BG2.3.2-10	155
Purify themselves and direct offerings	Peace, offerings, water	BG3.1.1-4	159
Guard life in their lake	Bread, beer, wine	BG3.1.4-10	160
Guard the souls and raise disk of Re	Meat, beer, water	BG3.2.4-7	161
a. Follow Re and establish White Crown on gods	Souls go forward and stand at the gate	BG11.3	220
b. Lament for Osiris	Remain in train of Osiris, but souls go forward in Re's train	BG11.3	220
c. Cause birth of Re to appear on earth	Bodies remain in their places, but souls go in following of Re	BG11.3	220
d. They who rear Re, make great names of all his forms	Bodies remain in their places, but souls go in following of Re	BG11.3	220
e. Elevate truth and establish it in shrine of Re	Bodies remain in their places, but souls go in following of Re	BG11.3	221
f. Establish duration of life and create years for guardians	In the train of this god	BG11.3	221
g. Loosen their hair before the Great God	Turn back at this gate, they do not enter the sky.	BG11.3	221
h. Worship, praise, honor Re: gate keepers	Remain in their places	BG11.3	221

Satan's Release from Prison (Rev. 20:7-10)

Rev. 20:7 says that "When the thousand years are ended, Satan will be loosed from his prison and will come out to deceive the nations." This statement is not surprising if one accepts that Satan represents the Egyptian god Apophis as discussed in Chapter 3, *Other Characters in Revelation*. Apophis regularly, even perpetually, returned to fight again against the forces of good; regardless of the severity of his punishment, he always returned to menace the sun-god again, and again, and yet again. Hornung, after discussing the chaining of Apophis in the 10th Division of the

Book of Gates, brings our attention to this remarkably persistent aspect of Apophis's character. He summarizes it as follows:

> The crippled enemy [Apophis] remains behind, his body cut into pieces, the head detached, each coil carefully sliced. The flame of the eye of Horus burns him, and exposed to the unbearable heat of the Netherworld, he is reduced to ashes and ceases to exist.
>
> It might appear that the triumph of order is final. But the struggle is renewed, and *Apophis reappears.* The *threat to the creation* has been overcome only temporarily. In the temples of the Late Period, a ritual book against the solar enemy and his gang was read daily, to save the world from paralysis and catastrophe, thus striking at all of the enemies of Creation as well as the archenemy. The ritual[a] included a wax imitation of the serpentine fiend, which was to be *dismembered and burned* in place of Apophis.[1247]

Hornung's summary conforms closely with the events described in Rev. 20:7-10. The struggle with Apophis is renewed 1,000 years after his defeat (as in Rev. 20:7). Apophis and his followers are again viewed as a threat against creation (i.e., the *world* in Rev. 20:8) and is again defeated (as in Rev. 20:9). Finally, Apophis is (ritually) tried (Rev. 20:11-13), tormented, burned and dismembered (Rev. 20:10,14-15).

Another belief held that, at the end of the day when the sun-god grew old and weak, he lost his brilliance and passed into the Netherworld beyond the western horizon. It was in this weakened stated that Apophis and his followers re-emerge to once again try to kill him. As will be demonstrated next, this pattern is similar to that found in the latter half of Rev. 20 where Satan or the Devil (Apophis) returns to renew the war against the forces of good and is defeated, judged, and destroyed (yet again).

Battle of Magog (Rev. 20:7-10)

Rev. 20:8-9 tells us that immediately after Satan's release from his prison he

> [8]will come out to deceive the nations which are at the *four corners of the earth*, that is, Gog and Magog, to gather them for battle; their number is like the sand of the sea. [9]And they *marched up over the broad earth* and surrounded the camp of the saints and *the beloved city*; but *fire came down from heaven* and consumed them. (Rev. 20:8-9).

An examination of the text of the 10th Division of the *Book of Gates* to the immediate right of the scene showing the winged serpent and the two-headed serpent (Figure 118) is another a scene (Figure 121) with associated text containing at least two components which are remarkably similar to Rev. 20:8-9; the text states:

> This Enveloper of the cobras *strides through the Netherworld*.
> The bows support His Two Faces in the mysteries.
> It is they who announce *Re in the Eastern Horizon of Heaven*,
> *they traverse heaven* in his train. [1248]

---

[a] The ritual referred to here is described in *The Book of the Overthrowning of Āpepi* and is discussed along with relevant extracts by Budge (1934, pp. 516-521).

The most obvious parallel between this text and Rev. 20:7-10 involves the reference to a group of individuals *marching* through an area. In Revelation we read of an army which "*marched* up over the broad earth" while in the *Book of Gates* we read that the "Enveloper of the cobras *strides through the Netherworld.*"[1249] In an apparent contrast, the last line in the above quotation says that "*they traverse heaven...* ." This conflict may be resolved if we consider certain early Egyptian concepts of the spiritual realm. During the Old Kingdom (2575-2134 BCE) it was held that the deceased lived on in two celestial realms, together called the *Tuat*. One was located in the sky above while the other was found in the "counter-sky," called the *Netherworld*.[a] The two realms were apparently extensions of one another. Thus, if we assume that the ancient idea of the Tuat was employed in the two parts of the above quotation, the reference to His Two Faces "striding through the Netherworld" and "traversing heaven" are indeed consistent with one another.

This background enables an explanation of the linkage in Rev. 20:8-9 between the three elements, "the earth," "the beloved city" and "heaven." Firstly, the earth may be considered to represent the Netherworld part of the Tuat while heaven represents the celestial part so that the war raged between these two realms with fire coming down from the heavenly part to destroy enemies of the sun-god in the Netherworld. And in agreement with Revelation's reference to the "beloved city," and as will be demonstrated in Chapter 27, *The Holy City*, the sky was the site of Egypt's own celestial city, the "City of Re" and the heavenly abode of the blessed dead.

We should also bear in mind that the Egyptians believed their own Holy City to be a mirror image of the earthly realm in terms of both geography and important events. With this in mind, the marching of Gog and his army over the earth can be understood as also happening in the heavenly realm so that a reference to the holy city in the heavens would also apply to Egypt's holy city, the "City of Re," i.e., Heliopolis.

Revelation tells us that Satan gathered the nations together for battle. The reader may recall from Chapter 18, *The Beasts of Rev. 13,* that Revelation's Satan (Egypt's Apophis) had assigned all his power and authority to the 1st beast, who was identified as the equivalent of Egypt's god Seth, and hence incorporated in "His Two Faces," Horus-Seth, Revelation's 2nd beast. References to war may also be seen in Figure 121 where Horus-Seth stands in the midst of eight symbols – symbols often associated with war. Six are rearing cobras (uraeus serpents, fire-breathing servants of the sun-god) and two are bows. The sense of war in this scene is obvious. Furthermore, Apophis (Satan) is indirectly associated with this war through his representatives Seth (Revelation's 1st beast) and Horus-Seth (Revelation's 2nd beast), so that we find here three essential elements described in Rev. 20:7-9 – Horus-Seth (Apophis'/Satan's representative), war (bows) and fire (uraeus serpents), all of which are linked to a beloved city, Heliopolis and/or the Heavenly City.

But the parallels do not end here. In Figure 121, His Two Faces bears the descriptive name, "The Enveloper of the Uraei."[1250] As "The Enveloper," Horus-Seth is described as one who envelopes, or encircles, the uraei in a manner reminiscent of

---

[a] Clagett (1989) feels that the Tuat consisted primarily of the celestial region because its name was written as a star enclosed in a circle (✱). For brief discussions of this see Budge (1934, p. 270) and Clagett (p. 359).

that of *Mehen,* the serpent-god which protectively envelopes the sun-god as he travels through the Netherworld. It does not necessarily mean, however, that Horus-Seth plays the same "protective" role in this picture as the *Mehen* serpent who remains faithfully coiled around Re in his travels. Indeed, this particular "enveloping" by Horus-Seth may in fact mean that he *actually encircles* or surrounds the sun-god's Uraei. A possible hidden allusion to such a war-time tactic may be present in the extension of Horus-Seth's four hands which can symbolize an encircling formation defined by the "four corners of the earth" mentioned in Rev. 20:8. Furthermore, since Horus-Seth is seen standing on two bows it is likely that this is an act of aggression rather than protection. This interpretation parallels Rev. 20:9 where it says that Satan's armies [those of Apophis's under Horus-Seth] "surrounded [encircled] the camp [the beloved city] of the saints" and it is especially applicable if the reference to "saints" parallels the faithful soldiers of the sun-god.

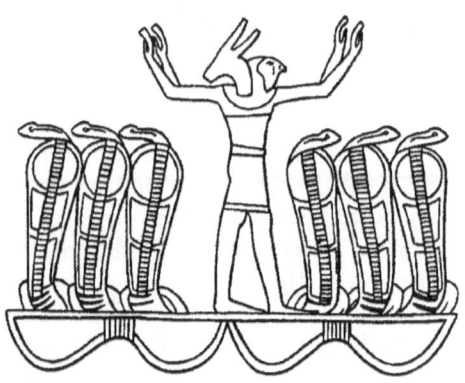

Figure 121. Pictorial representation of a military scene in the *Book of Gates* which parallels the Battle of Gog and Magog in Rev. 20:7-10. (BG10.2.9-10)

Rev. 20:9 ends with a reference to the type of defense mounted against Satan's army; it says that "fire came down from heaven and consumed them." This action is entirely consistent with the protective function of uraeus serpents which represent the destruction power of the sun-god's eyes and spews fire against any enemies who threaten him or his son Horus with malevolent intent. With this in mind, note in Figure 121 that the two groups of serpents face away from His Two Faces in a position effectively looking away from and down from each other (when the drawing is considered in isolation of nearby drawings) to facilitate the destruction by fire of the two armies (bows) below them. This interpretation is consistent with the events in Rev. 20:9.

The Egyptian text thus tells us that "The [two] bows [the armies of Horus-Seth and his allies?] support His Two Faces in the mysteries [the war against the sun-god]," a statement consistent with the reference to the army of Magog and its neighbors supporting the followers of Satan in his march over the earth described in Rev. 20:8-9.

One final parallel between the two sources which should not be overlooked is simply that the scene in Figure 121 is immediately adjacent to the altar scene (Figure 118) containing the reference to the 1,000 year reign of the faithful described in Rev. 20:3-6 just a few verses earlier and discussed above.

Many of the above interpretations of the Egyptian source are based on the text of Rev. 20 and would be impossible without reference to it. Ancient Egyptian priests trained in interpreting the Book of Gates would not need such assistance; the cryptic text and mnemonics implicit in the drawings would be sufficient.

Re-capture of the Ancient Serpent (Rev. 20:10)

As discussed above, after a period of a thousand years Satan was released from prison (Rev. 20:7) and Gog's ensuing battle (Rev. 20:8-9) paralleled a scene in the 10th Division of the *Book of Gates*. Shortly afterwards, in Rev. 20:10 we read that "the devil [Satan] who had deceived them was thrown into the lake of fire and sulphur where the [1st] beast [Seth] and the false prophet [the 2nd beast, Horus-Seth] were, and they will be tormented day and night for ever and ever." Satan, the devil, and his followers are recaptured.

Egypt's counterpart to Satan's recapture is found in the 11th Division of the *Book of Gates* (Figure 122) where, once again, the followers of the sun-god punish him. The text tells us that "Their sticks are in their hands, they take hold of their knives, they chastise Apopis. It is they who cut him to pieces, they cause pain to the worm in the heights of heaven."[1251] And in a scene reminiscent of his capture in the previous division (Figure 117), Apophis is again placed in bonds. The text above Figure 122 and immediately in front of the sun-god's warriors says that "The bonds of this rebel are in the hands of the progeny of Horus while they [the followers of Apophis] flee before this god, the rope being in their fingers. ... This serpent is like this. The progeny of Horus take hold of him. His coils are in the sky, his poison flows down in the West."[1252]

As the blood of Apophis flows once more, his followers are again captured, bound and chastised. We see them in Figure 122 represented by five sets of chains portrayed in a manner similar to that in Figure 117 in the 10th Division. This graphic similarity suggests that the composer(s) of the *Book of Gates* meant for the reader to interpret these two scenes in relation to one another, just as presented in Rev. 20.

Figure 122. The warriors of Horus recapture Apophis and put fetters upon him a second time – just as Satan is recaptured in Rev. 20:7-10. (BG11.2.4-8)

Discussion

In this chapter it was demonstrated how the events of Rev. 20:1-10 correspond to several of the more important events portrayed in the 10th and 11th Divisions of the *Book of Gates*. We saw how the description of the first capture of the ancient serpent in Rev. 20:1-3a was in excellent agreement with the capture of Apophis in the upper register of the 10th Division (Figure 117). The next scene, the resurrection of the faithful and their 1,000 year reign as priests described in Rev. 20:3b-6, conformed with the altar scene showing priestly followers of the sun-god closely associated with symbols for a 1,000 year period (Figure 118). And like those who reigned with Christ for a thousand years in Rev. 20:6, the gods of the "Imperishable Stars" (Figure 119) reign in heaven with Re along with the martyrs (Figure 120). King Gog's battle described in Rev. 20:8-9 was identified in a scene adjacent to the altar scene in the 10th Division (Figure 121). Finally, the serpent's recapture and punishment, along with his followers described in Rev. 20:9-10, was similar to events described in the 11th Division (Figure 122). These similarities between the two sources, including their parallel sequence, support the idea of a parallel between the various elements in this Rev. 20:1-10 and those of the 10th and 11th Divisions of the *Book of Gates*.

In spite of the above parallels, there is no mention of either of the names Gog or Magog in any of the mainstream Egyptian religious texts surveyed here, including the *Book of Gates*. Nevertheless, there is at least one possible parallel between this battle and battles fought by the Egyptians. Barnes (1993), in discussing Ezekiel 38-39 in the Bible's Old Testament, describes details of what is probably this same battle. He says that Gog was the "ruler of the land of Magog. As such, he is 'chief prince' of the lands of two tribes of Asia Minor, Meshech and Tubal; the specific location of Magog is unknown."[1253] Meanwhile, "Josephus and Greek writers generally applied this name [Magog] to the Scythians."[1254] a people known to have been enemies of the Egyptians during the 26th Dynasty (664-525 BCE).[1255] The *Book of Gates* was, however, written long before the 26th Dynasty so that it is not possible that its text alludes to a battle involving the king Gog of Magog – unless it is related to an as yet much earlier, unidentified battle with a Scythian king. In this scenario, the battle with the Scythians and the name "Gog of Magog" would have had to be projected in time in the Book of Revelation to apply to the battles during the 26th Dynasty in that particular part of Asia Minor (see Map 2) — a possible clue for the latest composition date for the Book of Revelation?

There is one aspect of the text in the *Book of Gates*, however, which seems to directly conflict with the account of the battle of Gog and Magog in the Book of Revelation. It involves the last sentence in the above mentioned quotation from the Book of Gates: "It is they who announce Re in the Eastern Horizon of Heaven, they traverse heaven in his train." If we assume that "they" in this sentence refers to the "bows who support His Two Faces" as suggested earlier, it would seem that it is the *enemies* of the sun-god "who ... traverse heaven in his train." This is, of course, inconsistent with the interpretation of the scene in Figure 121. Further research on this inconsistency is needed, including consideration of the question: "Could the text of the *Book of Gates* mean that the enemies of the sun-god *followed Re and his train* with ill intent as they traversed heaven, and *not* that they *followed in the train of Re* of his devoted followers?

Regardless of the few inconsistencies, the most important parallels remain between this part of the *Book of Gates* (Figure 121) and the scene described in Rev. 20:8-10. Firstly, there is the reference to the False Prophet (the 2nd beast, His Two Faces); secondly, to the armies (the two bows) which support him; and thirdly, the fire from heaven (the six uraei). And finally, the important parallel between the Egyptian text referring to those who "stride through the Netherworld" and surround and traverse heaven's city in the *Book of Gates* and that in Revelation which describes those who "march up over the broad earth" and surround the beloved city. These parallels are strengthened when one considers the relative placement of the Egyptian parallel elements found in the text of Rev. 20:1-10; the sequence is similar in both sources.

Chapter 25. Resurrection and Judgment
(Rev. 20:11-15)[1256]

The Book of Revelation mentions God's judgment in various contexts (for example, Rev. 14:7; Rev. 17:1; Rev. 18:10 and Rev. 20:4). Similarly, ancient Egyptian texts provide us with many different versions of the judgments and punishments meted against the wicked. Judgment scenes which involve Osiris seated on his throne, although less frequent, are usually more prominent when they do occur, the most prominent being those found in the *Book of the Dead* (Chapter 30B), the *Book of Gates* (4th/5th Divisions), and the *Book of Night* (8th Hour). The versions found in the first two sources do not conform well with the description given in Rev. 20:11-15 while the version in the *Book of Night* is the closest parallel of all Egyptian accounts of the judgment process studied here, especially in regard to Rev. 20:12 which says that "the dead, great and small ... were judged ... by what they had done."

The *Book of Night* forms one half of the *Books of the Heavens*, the other half being the *Book of Day*.[a] As the reader may recall from Chapter 17, *The Woman in the Sky*, certain scenes in the *Book of Day* strongly parallel those of Rev. 12, especially those of the appearance in heaven of a woman who is "clothed with the sun" (Rev. 12:1) and a "great war which arose in heaven" (Rev. 12:7). While the *Book of Day* deals with events which happen in the day-time sky, the *Book of Night* deals mostly with events deep within the Egyptian Netherworld during the night. It is here that the dead await the arrival of their god, some in dread of the resurrection and punishment, others in the hope of resurrection and great rewards.

---

[a] The relative positions of the two books are not the same in all versions. For example, in the sarcophagus chamber of the Tomb of Ramesses VI the two are placed back to back so that they are separated by the body of the sky-goddess Nut (see Figure 78) with which the events are intimately connected; the orientation of the two books is such that the pictures and text of one are vertically inverted so that the top of the text faces the body of Nut in each of its two parts. In the corridor of the same tomb, they appear together, the *Book of Day* being situated immediately above the *Book of Night*, the two being similarly oriented and separated by a single row of stars; also, the pictures and text are similarly oriented.

Like the *Book of Day*, the series of events described in the *Book of Night* is divided into twelve Hours. The first Hour, which deals with the sun-god's entry into the Netherworld just before sunset, has already been discussed in Chapter 17 *The Woman in the Sky*. We now look at the remaining eleven hours from the point of view of the following operative categories:

1	Hours 2-7	*Resurrection* of the dead and *punishment* of those who had been enemies of the sun-god.
2	Hour 8	*Judgment* of the followers of the sun-god.
3	Hours 9-12	*Rewards* to the resurrected who are victorious in the judgment, and *punishment* to those who are not victorious.

At first glance, this structure does not seem to follow that of Rev. 20; the judgment of the dead (Hour 8) in Rev. 20 happens *before* they are resurrected (Hours 2-7). Thus, in Rev. 20:11-12 we find a reference to the dead standing before the judgment throne but it is only later, in Rev. 20:13-15, that the resurrection of the dead and the judgment is described. Our comparison with the Book of Revelation will use the more logical sequence found in the *Book of Night* rather than that in Revelation (possible reasons for this difference in the order of events will be discussed later); this approach provides a better understanding of the parallels between sources.

The Resurrection (Rev. 20:13)

Revelation provides us with only a very brief description of the resurrection. It simply says, "And the sea gave up the dead in it, Death and Hades[a] gave up the dead in them" (Rev. 20:13). The reference to Death and Hades giving up their dead is rather difficult to understand and requires some comment before proceeding further. Commentary in "The New Oxford Annotated Bible" suggests that the phrase "Death and Hades" represents a *personification* of the "temporary abode of the dead."[1257] While this interpretation may be correct, it does not assist us much in our attempts to examine it from an Egyptian perspective. To do this, the term used for "Hades" requires a brief explanation. The original text uses the Greek word *Hádees* which refers to the Greek concept of the Underworld. Budge (1934) compares the Greek Underworld with the Egyptian Netherworld, as follows:

Ṭuat is the name which the Egyptians gave to the abode of the spirits and souls of the dead; it is a very old word and .... is commonly rendered 'Other World', or 'Underworld' .... it was regarded as the region through which the sun passed after he set, and where

---

[a] Some translations of the Book of Revelation, such as the King James Version, use the word Hell.

spirits and souls of the dead lived. The Egyptians divided the world into three parts, Heaven ... Earth ... and Ṭuat; many of them thought that the Ṭuat was below the earth just as the heaven was above it. To translate the word by 'Hell' is incorrect, for that conveys to modern peoples ideas which were wholly foreign to schools of ancient Egyptian thought. The enemies of Osiris and Rā suffered punishment in the Ṭuat, but the various Books of the Dead show that there was a portion of it wherein the beatified lived happily and enjoyed immortality.[1258]

It is only natural that, since our oldest copies of the Book of Revelation are in Greek, descriptions of places, events and concepts would be strongly biased by the availability of suitable Greek words. If the Book of Revelation is linked to Egyptian beliefs, we might assume that the reference to the Greek Hades is at best an attempt to relay a meaningful description of the Egyptian Netherworld, a concept which was an obscure or even unknown concept to the vast majority of Greek speaking readers two or more thousand years ago. Nevertheless, a reasonable English translation of *Hádees* might still be the Egyptian "Netherworld," "Tuat" or "Duat." If this were the case, the reference to the resurrection in Rev. 20:13 would be more accurately stated as: "And the sea gave up the dead in it, Death and *the Netherworld* gave up the dead in them." As we shall see next, this interpretation results in a number of important parallels to scenes in the *Book of Night* and Rev. 20.

Rev. 20:13 provides us with two categories of the dead: (1) those who died at sea and (2) those who died on land and whose bodies were interred in graves or tombs. The Egyptians, on the other hand, placed their dead into three categories: (1) those who died on land were mummified (to protect the bodies against decomposition so that they might be suitable to rejoin their souls at the resurrection), (2) those who died by drowning and whose bodies were not recovered (probably eaten by creatures such as crocodiles) and therefore not available for embalming, and (3) foreigners and other enemies of Osiris (who were not judged by trial as were the Osirian believers but were punished immediately after being resurrected).[a] For a better understanding of the potential parallels with Rev. 20:11-15 we will first consider the resurrection in terms of the original three Egyptian groupings.

A brief introduction to the Egyptian resurrection scene extending from the 2nd to 7th Hours of the *Book of Night* was discussed in Chapter 17, *The Woman in the Sky*, in relation to Rev. 11:18 and illustrated in Figure 89. There is little commentary associated with this scene so that we must rely on the illustration's visual symbolism, the names of the individuals portrayed, and a few cryptic references to some of them. To identify the Osirian believers we rely on their names or the limited amount of text for identification. The drowned ones are easily recognized by their swimming posture and their treatment in the text. The resurrected enemies of the sun-god are recognizable in that they are typically shown with their hands tied behind their backs, beheaded, burning with fire, or leaning face-down in a seated position. We will deal with each of the three Egyptian groupings separately, beginning with the resurrection of the believers.

---

[a] In effect, the three Egyptian categories can be reduced to two (as described in Revelation) if we simply combine the first two categories, i.e., (1) those who died on land (foreigners (#3) being added to this group) and (2) those who died at sea.

Resurrection of the Believers

At least a portion of Osirian believers in Figure 89 can be positively identified from the type of funeral biers depicted in most of the 2nd, 5th and 6th Hours. Each of these is decorated with the head of a lion, a symbol of the sun-god (Re) and of rebirth. Lurker (1980) tells us that in the *Book of the Dead* (Chap. 62) the text says,

> "I am the Lion, Re." In the New Kingdom the lion was regularly regarded as a manifestation of the sun-god ... . Since it was a solar animal the lion could symbolize not only destruction and death at night but also rebirth in the morning, hence the bier on which the mummy was laid was often given leonine form or feline feet.[1259]

The mummies of the dead lying on such biers may thus be identified as the followers of Re, and hence, of Osiris as well. Furthermore, they are shown in various stages of resurrection, from lying prostrate on the biers (as in the 2nd, 3rd and 5th Hours) to sitting (in the 3rd Hour) and finally, even standing on their biers (in the 6th).

The names and sometimes descriptive text associated with those on the lion-headed biers also suggest affiliation with the sun-god. The names of those in the 2nd Hour are "Spirits," " Nobles," or simply, "The dead." Nearby, the god Mind says, "Count your hearts, receive your gifts."[1260] In the 3rd Hour, there are two groups of three mummies on lion biers. In one group, they are reclining on their biers while in others they are sitting upright in the process of receiving new life. The reclining mummies are labeled with the words, "The sleeping Ones" and "The awakened ones"[1261] while the seated figures are called "Those of the Silent Region." In the 5th Hour, the names above the nine reclining mummies with raised heads are untranslated by Piankoff.[a] In the 6th Hour there are three reclining corpses in the process of receiving their souls as they rise; the text above them simply says they are "The living souls," and "the corpses sail in their places."[1262] Except for a reference to the risen ones counting their hearts and receiving gifts in the 2nd Hour, there are no references to rewards or punishments of any of those lying on biers. In general, such actions must await the final judgment before Osiris. That judgment is depicted later, in the 8th Hour, while the mention of gifts in the 2nd Hour suggests that some of the risen ones receive gifts even before their judgment. The resurrected dead among these groups parallel those in Rev. 20:12 which are resurrected prior to that of the remaining dead in Rev. 20:13.

Resurrection of the Drowned (Rev. 20:13)

As mentioned above, not all Osirian believers have the privilege of being embalmed after they die; the bodies of many who drowned were lost. How then were these to be resurrected when their bodies no longer existed? Many prominent Egyptologists have already addressed this issue and the following review by Hornung

---

[a] Piankoff (1954, p. 416) gives their names as follows: *Hau, Bautiu,* and *Negaiu*. Because of their upright position, it seems likely that the three seated figures next to them may also be followers of the sun-god. The enemies sit face down or face up or are bound in some way and their names are not translated by Piankoff but given as *Uash, Djamu,* and *Detdjeru*.

(1990) provides us with a reasonable understanding of the Egyptian answer to the dilemma:

> Several passages in the Books of the Netherworld show that the drowned reached the shores of the Beyond directly from the Nile, arriving from the primeval waters and thus into the depths of the world. ... Parts of the tenth hour of the *Amduat* and the ninth hour of the *Book of Gates* resemble one another in their detailed treatment of this theme. In a large rectangular pool – representing the primaeval water, Nun – swim several groups of naked drowned, in quite different positions: some on their backs, others on their bellies, still others on their sides. In the *Amduat*, Horus calls to them from the riverbank, while in the *Book of Gates* it is the passing sun god himself who promises that they will be able to breathe in the water and that their bodies will not decompose: "Your members are not putrefied, your flesh is not decomposed!" Their souls are also provided for, and their bodies can land uninjured on the shores of the Netherworld, where they may benefit from all the Beyond has to offer, even without the ritual burial ceremonies.[1263]

A brief look at the *Book of Night* also reveals special attention to those who died at sea. Indeed, the drowned are the very first figures to be shown in the 2nd Hour. Here they are shown as three swimming figures in the upper left-hand corner of Figure 89; the text calls them "The weary ones."[a, 1264] The god Sia, or Mind, who stands nearby tells them to "Measure your banks, lift up [i.e., move] your legs." This instruction seems to imply that the resurrected dead should begin their new life by walking the riverbank to measure land allocated to them. They are mentioned again in the 3rd Hour where they are shown as three half-reclining figures in the upper left-hand corner and are called "The drowned ones."[1265] Again, these are associated with those who work in the fields along the irrigation canals; the text over the two nearby groups in sitting position, facing downward and holding a lock of hair reads, "Those of the fields" and "Those of the channels (?)."[1266] Groups of "spirits" and "shadows" are located in the vicinity, possibly belonging to victims of drowning. The next time the drowned are mentioned in the *Book of Night* is in the 8th Hour where "The drowned ones"[1267] appear among those before the throne of Osiris to be judged; their rewards will be discussed later in relation to the judgment. Meanwhile, it is sufficient to conclude here that the Egyptian faithful who died by drowning were given special consideration after their resurrection and in preparation for the judgment – just as described in Rev. 20:13, "And the sea gave up the dead in it."

Resurrection of the Enemies (Rev. 20:13)

Resurrection of the enemies of Osiris is first evident in the 4th Hour and references to them continue to be made through to the 7th Hour. Unlike the followers of the sun-god, the enemies are not shown lying on funeral biers; representation of their resurrection is different. Although sometimes shown standing, most are shown face-up or face down in a seated position, typically with their hands tied behind them.

---

[a] In the context of the dead, the term "weary" (or "tired") is usually interpreted to mean that the dead are simply sleeping in a deep, tired, deathly sleep. Nevertheless, we should not rule out the possibility that they may also be considered to "weary" of waiting for the arrival of the sun-god as they sleep (in wait) for their resurrection into a new life.

Also different is the swiftness with which judgment is unceremoniously and immediately imposed on them; they seem to be resurrected, condemned, and punished forthwith. Their resurrection and punishment are thus almost simultaneous, just as we read in the last part of Rev. 20:1, "Death and Hades gave up the dead ... *and all were judged by what they had done.*"

The introductory text of the 4th Hour describes the arrival of the sun-god and identifies this Hour as one in which the enemies are chastised. The text in the 2nd register says, "The sailing of the majesty of this God [Re], approaching the Third Gate [i.e., the 4th Hour], the One with the sharp knives, Mistress of the Two Lands, the One who chastises the enemies of Weary-Heart [Osiris], who causes fear before the Sinless One [Osiris]."[1268] Pictorial aspects of the scene provide us with a rough idea of their nature. In the upper right of the 4th Hour in Figure 89 is a large hieroglyph meaning foreign land (a mountain with three peaks, ⩳[1269] with a tree (♦) on each peak) suggesting the figures portrayed here are foreigners, possibly from an area famous for its trees such as the Lebanon, Egypt's source of cedars. The upper left-hand corner shows two groups of three figures bearing heads of fish, an animal generally regarded as unclean, and in Osirian beliefs, associated with the god Seth.[1270] It is entirely possible that all the figures in this register are followers of Seth, a possibility supported by the events in the next, the 5th Hour, where Seth is specifically mentioned in relation to his followers.

Also, in the lower part of the third register, three figures identified as "The followers of Seth" are shown as bent-over and decapitated, each with a knife placed in the neck. Nearby, are three decapitated figures called "The Rementiou" (meaning = ?) and "The Utau,"[1271] a term which, according to Piankoff (1954), refers to "some kind of enemies."[1272]

The 6th hour is particularly interesting because it unequivocally demonstrates the punishment by fire of the sun-god's enemies. Here we see three bound figures face down in the sitting position; they are "The Strangers," a term which gives them practically the same status as the foreigners referred to in the 4th Hour. Nearby are three flames of fire, each containing an inverted figure of an enemy with his hands tied behind his back and enclosed in a circle (Figure 123). The symbolism of this figure (the fire symbol (🜂) containing an oversized circular base) indicates punishment by being cast into a circular lake of fire.[a] The text tells us that these are "The burned Ones."[1273]

Finally, in the 7th Hour, the standing or kneeling enemies of the sun-god are identified as either foreign nationals or Egyptians, the latter being traitors to Osiris

---

[a] While most lakes of fire were depicted as being rectangular in shape, some were circular. One such circular lake is shown in the lower register of the 5th Division of the *Book of Gates* (at BG5.3.10).

(and hence to Egypt). The text identifies them as "The Asiatics, The Libyans, The Madjai, The Negroes, The Red Men, [and] The Egyptians." They appear before Horus who leans on his staff behind them and informs them he is punishing them on behalf of Osiris. He says, "You are the rebels, the male and female Ut, who acted against my father Osiris. What was granted to my father Osiris is that I ... should strike your (?) Enemies. Hence it is he who strikes you."[1274] These enemies are also allied with Seth because in this Hour we also read of "She who strikes the allies of Seth."[a, 1275]

It is obvious from the above, that in each of the cases from the 3rd through 7th Hours, wherever punishment is depicted, it is incorporated into scenes which do not show the judgment throne of Osiris (which is shown in the 8th Hour). This may mean that the resurrected enemies of the sun-god are not necessarily afforded the privilege of a formal judgment process as ordinary Osirian believers. Instead, they are punished immediately after their resurrection.

The Judgment (Rev. 20:12-13)

The judgment of the dead was one of the best-known and most feared rituals of the Egyptian afterlife. For the resurrected Osirian believer to pass on into the realm of eternal bliss with Osiris (or in the more general sense, the sun-god, Re, who parallels Revelation's Lamb) each believer had to stand before the throne of Osiris and prove his or her worthiness. The importance of this ritual to the Egyptian is outlined in Goelet's (1994) introduction to the subject:

> Egyptian biographies contained fulsome praise of the dead and proclaimed their charitable deeds on behalf of the poor and weak. Underlying all such protestation of virtue was a strong and consistent belief that people would be judged after death according to their deeds in this life. This meant that the Egyptian concepts of the afterlife were deeply imbued with a moral sense. The fear of that final judgment haunted Egyptian mortuary literature. Since probably no Egyptian entered the next world entirely spotless, one of the BD's [*Book of the Dead*] purposes was to magically purge the deceased of sin. ... At the time the BD became the chief mortuary text, the judgment was seen as the key event of the passage into the next existence. ... the most important scene in the majority of BD papyri was the Weighting of the Heart before Osiris and the Great Council of Gods 'who hear cases.'"[1276]

In Chapter 7, *Egyptian Beliefs in the Seven Letters,* it was shown that details of many aspects of the final judgment described in the *Book of the Dead* parallel those of the second and third chapters of the Book of Revelation. Among the Egyptian beliefs were the authority and power of the judge (Osiris) who stated, "I know your works." Rewards and punishment were allotted according to deeds committed on earth. Those "victorious" at the judgment, i.e., those who "conquered," were provided with an abundance of gifts including: new white garments, hidden manna, eating in the presence of Osiris, the morning star, a stone with a secret name, the tree of life, no second death, being made a pillar (priest) in the temple and the maintenance of their

---

[a] I.e., the followers of Seth (who parallels the 1st beast of Revelation); see Chapter 18, *The Beasts of Rev. 13*.

names in the Book of Life. In contrast, apart from a picture of a judgment scene, a sparse introductory comment, and few labels accompanying the lineups of the "great and the small" (Rev. 20:12), there is practically nothing said of the judgment process *per se* in the 8th Hour of the *Book of Night*. Apparently, the reader of the *Book of Night* was expected to already have had such knowledge from other sources such as the *Book of the Dead*. Meanwhile, the judgment scene in the *Book of Night* adds a number of new elements which are not described in the *Book of the Dead* and, as we shall see next, these elements are mirrored in Rev. 20.

The Great White Throne (Rev. 20:11)

We begin our discussion of these elements with events in the 8th Hour, events which immediately follow the resurrection scenes depicted in Figure 89. The judgment scene in this Hour (Figure 124) parallels that described in Rev 20:11. The most prominent figure in this picture is Osiris who sits on his throne (𓊹) holding a *was* scepter of power and authority (𓌀). Note that Osiris and his throne are drawn to a much larger scale than the other figures, a tradition used to express his superior power and importance.[a] With this in mind, the phrase "*great* white throne" expressed in Revelation takes on a potentially new meaning – that of power and authority. The "great" throne of Rev. 20 can therefore be easily seen to parallel this part of the *Book of Night*.

Figure 123. The judgment scene in the 8th Hour of the *Book of Night* showing Osiris seated on his "great white throne" in the midst of two groups of followers, the "great and small" as well as visual puns suggesting a parallel to the opening of the books in Rev. 20:11-12. Underneath his throne the evil Seth lies in bonds. (BN8)

But whence came the reference to a great "white" throne? There is no obvious reference to the throne in this scene being white, or any other color. Nevertheless, the reference to a color in Revelation begs a closer examination because Wilkinson (1994) says that in Egyptian art,

> Color becomes an important way of adding life and individuality to an image, so that it is perhaps not surprising that the color of an object was regarded by the Egyptians as an integral part of its nature or being, just as a man's shadow was

---

[a] For an excellent discussion on the meaning of relative sizes in Egyptian art, see the chapter on *Measure and Meaning, the Symbolism of Size* in Wilkinson's (1994) book on *Symbol & Magic in Egyptian Art*, pp. 38-59.

viewed as part of his total personality. In this sense, color was virtually synonymous with "substance."[1277]

We should therefore examine how the word "white" was used in ancient Egypt and how it might have been applied to the throne of Osiris if we are to complete the comparison of the throne found in the *Book of Night* and the "great *white* throne" in the Book of Revelation. For this, we turn to phonetic analyses.

A close look at the Egyptian word for "white," *hedj* (*ḥḏ*),[1278] provides us with evidence for an Egyptian parallel to the expression. Wilkinson (1994) points out that *hedj* was also "used to denote the metal silver."[1279] Meanwhile, Spence (1915) indicates that the throne of the sun-god was believed to be made of metal.[1280] Bearing in mind that Re was the spiritual form of the sun-god while Osiris represented his physical body, Osiris was considered to be an alternative form of the sun-god so that the throne of Osiris may be considered to have been made of the same, white metallic material as that of Re. This observation strengthens the previously noted parallel with the "great *white* throne" in Rev. 20:11.

Wilkinson (1994) also informs us that Egyptians considered the color "white" to be "best suited to denote cleanliness and thus ritual purity and sacredness, white was almost invariably used to depict the clothing of most Egyptians and was especially symbolic in regard to the priesthood."[1281] It is no surprise that Osiris, who acted as the final arbitrator of deeds in the judgment scene, is often dressed in white from his "White Crown" to his feet.

The Great and the Small (Rev. 20:12)

The next verse describes "the dead, *great and small*, standing before the throne." A parallel to this aspect of the throne scene can also be readily identified in Figure 124. On close inspection of this figure we see that there are two distinct groups of followers before the throne of Osiris – those who hold *was* scepters () of power and authority and those without them with their arms raised in adoration; scepters, symbols of power and authority, are absent in the second group. The slightly larger size of the figures bearing the scepters confirms their higher social standing.[a] Classification of these two groups as being socially "great" and "small" is also confirmed by the names of the individuals in them; these are listed in Table 25.1. The first group, "the great ones," contains well-known Egyptian deities while the second group, "the small ones," contains anonymous individuals of lesser importance. These two groups of deities thus conform in three ways with the "the great and small, standing before the throne" in Rev. 20:12 – the symbols they carry, their relative sizes and their names.

The Beast and his Followers (Rev. 20:10)

Beneath the throne of Osiris in Figure 124 is a "seated" figure lying face down and bound with ropes held by the deities standing in front of and behind (i.e., around) the throne. The name of this figure is not given in early versions of the *Book*

---

[a] For a review of the symbolism of relative sizes of images in Egyptian art, see Wilkinson (1994, pp. 38-59)

Table 25.1 The names of those before the judgment throne of Osiris in the 8th Hour of the *Book of Night*[1282] in Figure 124. This scene includes "the dead, *great* and *small*" referred to in Rev. 20:12. The last two (identified by italics) are found in a second manifestation of the same groups in the 9th Hour.

The "Great Ones"		The "Small Ones"	
Neith	Kebeh-senuf	The spirits	The watchful ones
Anubis	Nephthys	The souls	Those of the opposite sky
Shu	Selkit	The mummies	The awakened ones
Hepuy	Hapy	The dead	The sleeping ones
Mind	Imesty	The tired ones	The silent ones
Dua-Mutef	Tefnut	The punished ones	*The shadows*
Isis	Sendet	The drowned ones	*Those of the fields*

of Night, such as that found in the Tomb of Ramesses VI, although Piankoff (1954) suggests it represents the evil god Seth who, as discussed in Chapter 18, *The Beasts of Rev. 13*, parallels the 1st beast of Revelation. Hornung (1999) interprets this scene to show Osiris "triumphing over a well-fettered enemy, here anonymous but whom the versions of the Late Period [712-332 BCE] address directly as Seth."[1283] There is, however, no mention of Seth being "in the lake of fire" as in Rev. 20:10. We must therefore draw on our prior knowledge of his destruction by fire discussed in relation to his punishment in Rev. 19:20 which says that the 1st beast (Seth) was "thrown alive into the lake of fire." Also, note that the resurrection scene described above in relation to Rev. 20:13 and the (earlier) 6th Hour, as shown in Figure 123, includes the punishment by fire of the enemies of the sun-god. Regardless of such minor temporal problems, the presence of a bound form of Seth under the throne parallels the defeat of the 1st beast and his followers described in Rev. 20:10.

Opening of the Books (Rev. 20:12)

The latter part of Rev. 20:12 says that, "books were opened. Also another book was opened, which is the book of life. And the dead were judged by what was written in the books, by what they had done." In spite of the obvious parallels to elements in Rev. 20 as described above, there are no explicit references to any books (scrolls) in the *Book of Night*. There are, however, at least two hidden or implied references to them in Figure 124. These are located on the far left and right-hand sides of the figure where they are indicated by a single leaf of a door (⇌). The door-leaf on the left-hand side is surmounted by a lion and one or five uraeus serpents (only the largest serpent is shown in Figure 124). The door-leaf on the far right is unadorned. As will be demonstrated next, these doors can symbolize books (scrolls).

The Egyptian word, *ārit*, (*ārrit* or *arrryt*) can mean "door or gate"[1284] as well as a "leaf of a double door"[1285] and *ār* (*ar*) can simply mean the "two leaves of a door."[1286] Meanwhile, a common Egyptian word for scroll is *ār-t*[1287] (*art* or *art*)[1288] which typically refers to a register, document, a writing, a leather scroll or roll, or simply

25. Resurrection and Judgment

parchment. Thus, when Figure 124 is viewed in the context of Rev. 20:12 the two doors to the judgment chamber may be interpreted as visual puns referring to books used in the judgment process.

If the two door-leaves do indeed represent books, we might be tempted to assume that a total of two books is used in the process, one for each leaf of a door. This interpretation, however, is at odds with Rev. 20:12 where at least three are mentioned: "and *books* were opened. Also *another book* was opened." How then might this apparent discrepancy be resolved? The answer is found next to the door-leaf found on the left-hand side where we see a uraeus serpent (*āār-t, i'rt* or *aryt*) which again, is phonetically similar to the word for book. The uraeus may therefore represent yet another visual pun indicating the presence of a second book on the left side of the figure, a possibility which does indeed conform with the number of books described in Rev. 20:12.

It is also possible that even more books may be implied here; in some versions of the *Book of Night* there are four additional uraeus serpents nearby, a number indicating that a multitude of books may be implied in this judgment process. Such a conclusion would conform with the apparently large number of individuals which are to appear before the throne of Osiris as well as the scene in Rev. 20:12-13 which says that "the dead were judged by what was written in the books, by what they had done. ... and all were judged by what they had done." It seems that, in the context of Rev. 20:12, the presence of the one or more uraeus serpents near the door on the left-hand side represents a mnemonic for the knowledgeable reader to infer the use of at least two and possibly several to even a multitude of books in this scene.

Rev. 20:12 also explicitly identifies one of the books used in the process; it says that a "book was opened, which is *the book of life*." And again, this book is not clearly identified in Figure 124 so we must look deeper still into the figure's symbolism if we are to find evidence of such a book. And as before, we find yet another potential visual pun. This time it is found in the form of the recumbent lion lying on the top of the left door-leaf. While the Egyptians typically referred to the lion as a *rw*, it was also known as an *ār* (*ar*),[1289] a word which, like that for door-leaves mentioned above, is phonetically close to a similar word for book, *ār-t* (*art* or *art*) – and phonetically similar to *ār* (*ar*), a word for "a writing tablet with two leaves,"[1290] a word conceptually related to a book. Furthermore, the lion can also symbolize the sun-god himself. Recall from the above discussion on the lion-headed funeral biers that the lion was regularly regarded as a manifestation of the sun-god. The nearby cobras (fiery uraeus serpents) also point to the sun-god because, as Wilkinson (1992) points out, the cobra "was held to represent the fiery eye of the sun god Re."[1291] The presence of the lion on the book (i.e., door-leaf) and the nearby cobras seem to indicate that this book, or books, represent the well known "Book(s) of Re."

This combination of phonetic similarities among various Egyptian nouns suggests the use of puns intended for the reader to interpret the two door-leaves as representing, not only the doors to the judgment chamber of Osiris, but also the books used in the judgment. This interpretation parallels the use of books in the judgment scene in Rev. 20:12.

Next, we note that Rev. 20:12 implies that records of deeds were maintained in the books. Egyptian writings also mention such records. For example, one ancient

Pyramid Text (§1160), although it relates primarily to the deeds of a king, informs us that the sun-god "put his annals (the record of the king's deeds) among his people, and his love among the gods."[1292] Meanwhile, Budge (1934) refers to the writing of Lanzone[1293] who points out that, Seshat (Figure 125) "was the celestial librarian and is called the 'lady of books.' She dwelt by the Tree of Heaven, and as the Rembrancer of the gods wrote down on the leaves of the tree *the deeds'* and duration of life of every man and every god."[1294] Budge also says that, "The *Pyramid Text* (§954) show that this Just God [Osiris] possessed registers of the deeds of men which were carefully kept by Thoth and Sesheta (= Seshat), and according to these records the hearts of men were judged."[1295] This information parallels the latter half of Rev. 20:12 that "the dead were judged by what was written in the books, by what they had done."[a]

Figure 124. *Seshat*, the goddess of writing who maintained a record of the deeds of every person, a record which parallels the Book of Life in Rev. 20:12.

Judgment of the Believers and the Drowned (Rev. 20:13,15)

Believers appearing before the throne of Osiris in the 8th Hour of the *Book of Night* were identified above in Figure 124 as belonging to either of two large groups, one bearing scepters of authority and one of commoners showing hands raised in adoration. It was shown that these two groups parallel the "great and small" mentioned in Rev. 20:12. But they also included "the drowned ones" who were to receive special attention in the judgment (see Table 25.1). Now, in the 9th Hour, we are provided with evidence of just how well separated the victims of drowning were from the rest of the believers. In this Hour, the god *Mind* at the far right of Figure 126 addresses the group of commoners who were successful in the judgment. He pays special attention of the drowned ones, even though they represent only one of the fourteen "small ones" in Table 25.1. Mind says to them, "(O you) the weary ones and the drowned ones."[1296] The two groups (or possibly one group if we consider the weary and the drowned as one group) are "submerged together with the Nile god, ... [to]

---

[a] In spite of this obvious reference to the early Egyptian belief that records were kept of one's deeds, use of such records was not an overwhelming feature of the Osirian judgment in later dynasties. These later versions of the judgment depended to a large extent on the testimony of a person's heart and a judicial assessment by a panel of judges presided over by the god Thoth. Furthermore, not everyone in Egypt, and especially immigrants from foreign lands, were Osirian believers with knowledge of the many critical, magical spells found in the *Book of the Dead* and would not be acquainted with the vast array of magical spells and rituals necessary to be victorious in the final judgment. It was therefore practically impossible for non-native Egyptians (i.e., non-Osirian believers) to be victorious in the final judgment.

reach the land together with the god of food, the offering given to you are princely rents."[1297] There, they are further rewarded, some of them remaining "in the place where he [Osiris] resides eternally. The justified among you are in the following of Osiris and in front of him as ancestors. It is he who grants you offerings. The sun is before your eyes, the wind is in your nostrils." Special, selected individuals among the justified are depicted in the 10th Hour (three of them are shown at the far left in Figure 126) and the 11th Hour.

Figure 125. The 9th Hour of the *Book of Night* shows fifteen groups of three figures in the center of this figure. Two categories, the "weary ones" and the "drowned Ones," parallel those in Rev. 20:13 who were "given up by the sea" and whose names were written in the Book of Life. On the far right, the god Sia (Mind) advises them of their rewards. (BN9-10)

One group of the fourteen "small ones" depicted in the 9th Hour (Table 25.1) is peculiar and deserves mention here. These are called "The punished ones." The reason for their presence in this list is not clear so one might legitimately wonder how they made it through the final judgment and why they are included here? The answer to this question seems to be related firstly to events which occur immediately after the resurrection and secondly, to the nature of the rituals conducted in the judgment process itself.

In the first case, as indicated in the above discussion on the resurrection, many enemies of Osiris were punished immediately after their resurrection. Others, who had been Osirian believers, had, despite their faith, committed a punishable offence. Having already received their just punishment according to Osirian beliefs, they must ultimately appear before Osiris and the final judgment. Remarkably, it was possible for even the worst Egyptian offenders to pass the judgment and be saved from eternal damnation and punishment if they were suitably versed in the protocols and spells provided in the *Book of the Dead*. The well known "negative confession" or "statement of innocense" of Chapter 125, for example, provided the deceased with a list of deeds which he must deny at the tribunal. Having successfully repeated the words of this spell, the stated innocense became reality through the magic inherent in the "creative word" of the spell. Clagett (1989) outlines this phenomenon as follows:

> It would of course be surprising if very many people of power could truly assert that they had led the blameless life outlined in Spell 125. Indeed there is evident recognition among the Egyptians of the fact that men will often say anything to achieve resurrection in the Netherworld for there exists a spell whose purpose is to make sure that the deceased's heart does not speak out against him in the god's domain. But perhaps the thought that if the statements of innocence were solemnly and formally spoken as a spell, then by the

doctrine of the creative word, i.e., the bringing into existence of something by magical word, the assertion could somehow produce the truth.[1298]

By means of such magic and in spite of one's evil deeds done during his lifetime, the Osirian believer could ensure success in the judgment and avail of an abundance of rewards in the afterlife. This did not mean that the guilty avoided punishment in the Netherworld. Indeed, as we saw in the 2nd to 7th Hours of the *Book of Night* they were apparently punished for their evil deeds in the 8th Hour, along with non-Egyptian enemies of the sun-god, *before* the final judgment process. In this context, it is easy to understand the presence of "the punished ones" among those who are successful in final judgment (as listed in Table 25.1).

This development of religious thought among the Egyptians had severe, negative, moral consequences. Breasted (1912) emphasizes this point:

> The general reliance upon such devices for escaping ultimate responsibility for an unworthy life must have seriously poisoned the life of the people. While the Book of the Dead discloses to us more fully than ever before in the history of Egypt the character of the moral judgment in the hereafter, and the reality with which the Egyptian clothed his conception of moral responsibility, it is likewise a revelation of ethical decadence. In so far as the Book of the Dead had become a magical agency for securing moral vindication in the hereafter, irrespective of character, it had become a positive force for evil.[1299]

As in Rev. 20:13,15, both the small and the great Egyptians, and especially those who had drowned, could be vindicated – or be called "conquerors" in the judgment of the dead. Furthermore, in Egypt even those who had committed sins listed in the "negative confession" could be conquerors.

Discussion

Several basic elements stand out as significant parallels between Rev. 20:11-15 and the Egyptian *Book of Night*. The most prominent of those discussed above include the division of the resurrected dead into the "great and small" before the judgment throne in Rev. 20:12 and the emphasis on victims of drowning among the resurrected dead in Rev. 20:13. Next, the coupling of a reference to *several books* to one of a *single book* in Rev. 20:12 conforms with visual puns involving pictures of doors, serpents and a lion in the Egyptian judgment scene. These parallels are accentuated by the agreement between the white color of the judgment throne in Rev. 20:11 and traditional belief that the sun-god's throne was believed to have been made of the white metal, silver. Finally, emphasis is placed on the use of fire as punishment in both sources. These multiple parallels combine to demonstrate that even the details of the two main themes of Rev. 20:11-15, namely the resurrection and the judgment of the dead, closely parallel the main series of events described in the *Book of Night*.

The main difference between the two sources is the specific order in which the various parallels appear. As noted in the introductory paragraphs to this chapter, the Book of Revelation begins with a description of the judgment scene and goes from there to the resurrection, a sequence which does not logically flow one from the other.

One might well expect that the resurrection would happen before the judgment – as it does in the *Book of Night* so one wonders why these important scenes appear in different orders if this part of the Book of Revelation so closely parallels the *Book of Night*. If one assumes a dependance of this part of Revelation on the *Book of Night*, three of the more obvious reasons immediately come to mind. The first is that the author of the book simply got the two scenes out of order at some point in the preparation of his text. The second is that he worked from a copy of the *Book of Night* in which the scenes were reversed. Unfortunately, there no way of testing the first suggestion and the absence of any knowledge of such a version of the *Book of Night* makes the second suggestion difficult to accept. A third possibility might be that the author of Revelation for some reason simply reversed the reading of the relevant parts of the *Book of Night*. These possibilities require further study.

The placement of the resurrection-judgment scene in Rev. 20:11-15 immediately after a similar scene described in Rev. 20:1-6 is also worthy of comment. As pointed out in Chapter 24, *The Millennium*, Rev. 20:1-6 parallels events described in the 10th and 11th Divisions of the *Book of Gates*, events associated with the pre-dawn period in the Netherworld. Now, in this chapter, we find that Rev. 20:11-15 also conforms with the same predawn period even though they are presented in the context of the *Book of Night* rather that the *Book of Gates*. Both texts thus describe events occurring during the night and leading up to dawn and the rising of the newly born sun-god into the morning sky. Other parallels between these two sources are apparent and these will be discussed later.

The *Book of Night* ends with a comment on the exiting of the sun-god from the Netherworld and his re-birth in the morning sky at dawn:

> To come out of the Netherworld, to rest in the Morning Barge, to navigate the Abyss until the Hour of Re, She [Nut, the sky-goddess] who sees the beauty of her Lord, to make transformations in Khepri [the juvenile form of the sun-god], to rise to the horizon, to enter the [Nut's] mouth, to come out of the vulva, to burst forth out of the Gate of the Horizon at the Hour. She who lifts up the Beauty of Re in order to make live men, all cattle, all worms he has created.[1300]

This final scene in the *Book of Night* does not have a parallel in Rev. 20. Nevertheless, it leads us directly to the main theme of Rev. 21– the creation of a new heaven and a new earth, and the main topic of the next chapter.

Chapter 26. A New Creation (Rev. 21:1-8)[1301]

The 21st Chapter of the Book of Revelation is special in that it presents a dramatic culmination of a long series of events which began in Rev. 2 with God's warning of his coming to judge those who did not follow him. From there it goes through a long series of sometimes cataclysmic events leading up to the judgment of the dead and ends with Rev. 21:1-8 and the renewal of all of creation.

Rev. 21 begins with the author's declaration that he "saw a new heaven and a new earth; for the first heaven and the first earth had passed away, and the sea was no more." He next describes a Holy City "coming down out of heaven from God, prepared as a bride adorned for her husband" (Rev 21:2). Life in this city is described as a paradise in which "death shall be no more, neither shall there be mourning nor crying nor pain any more" (Rev 21:4) and from which the "cowardly, the faithless, the polluted ... murderers, fornicators, sorcerers, idolaters, and all liars" are barred and cast into "the lake that burns with fire and sulphur" (Rev 21:8). (The rest of the verses in Rev. 21 and the first five of Rev. 22 provide us with a detailed description of the Holy City itself and will be discussed in the next chapter).

The Egyptians believed in a cyclical cosmos in which the world was created, existed for a time, then destroyed, re-created, and so on. There was, of course, a "first time." And each subsequent creation was similar to the one which preceded it. The beginning of each new day symbolized events which happened at the "first time." Hornung says that, "Rebirth in the morning is ... a renewal of creation, and is achieved with the help of the primeval gods, who sent the sun forth from their midst on the 'first occasion' at the beginning of creation; like the creation of the world, sunrise can thus be called the 'first occasion.'"[1302]

We begin our comparison of the sources by pointing out that the events from Rev. 21:1-8 are similar to those illustrated or implied in the 11th and 12th Divisions of the *Book of Gates*. As we shall see, while this parallel is one of the last, important scenes in the Book of Revelation, it also corresponds with the highest spiritual point in the day of the pious Egyptian sun-worshiper – the arrival of the sun-god into sky at dawn. These events were so important that they constituted the finale of each of the most influential of the religious writings of the New Kingdom, including the *Amduat*, the *Book of Gates*, *Book of Caverns*, and the *Book of Night*. Each of these sources uses pictures and text to present different aspects and versions of the event, some of which

26. A New Creation

are very similar to those described in this part of Revelation. In this chapter we will focus our discussion on a comparison of Revelation's "new creation" (including references to a new earth, heavens and the Holy City) with Egyptian texts, and especially those found in the closing scene of the *Book of Gates*.

Most of the parallel texts concerning the new creation in the *Book of Gates* are found in the 11th Division while the 12th Division contains an all-encompassing interpretive picture shown here as Figure 127.[a] Perhaps the most straightforward interpretation of this picture is one in which the totality of creation is lifted out of the primordial waters (the Abyss) on the arms of Nun (the personification of the Abyss). Figure 127 can also be visualized as a sequence of events beginning with the appearance of the earth and sky from the Abyss in the upper one third of the picture and concluding with the rising of the sun into the heavens in the lower two thirds.

The first elements to emerge from the waters are Osiris (at times known as an earth-god), whose body forms a circle with his feet touching his head, thus enclosing the Netherworld inside the circle of his body. (In other contexts – and possibly in this one

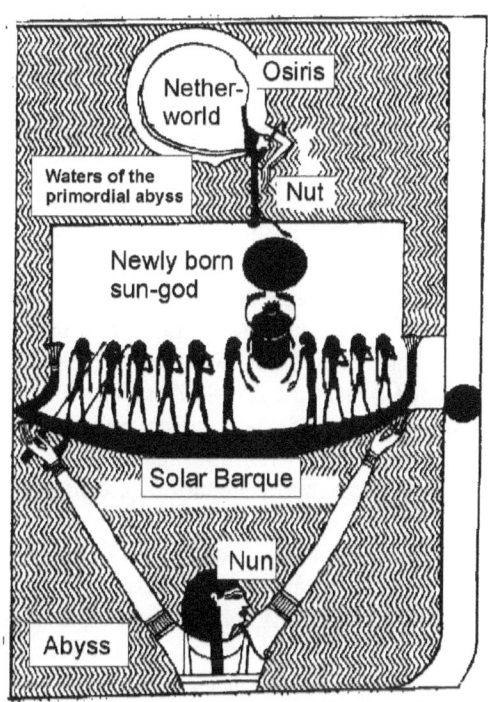

Figure 126. Visual representation of the daily re-enactment of creation portrayed in the 12th and final Division of the *Book of Gates*. The main elements in this scene conform with those in the description of the new creation presented in Rev. 21:1-8.

as well – the Netherworld was believed to be inside the body of Nut). The next element to come forth is Nut, the goddess and personification of the sky. She stands upside down with her feet resting on Osiris's head and her arms stretched out to receive the disk of the newly born sun-god (O●). The sun-god's birth from the Abyss is assisted by two goddesses and witnessed by a group of elders standing on the deck of his newly created solar barque.

---

[a] Piankoff's (1954) 11th and 12th Divisions of the *Book of Gates* are considered by Hornung (1999, pp. 55-77) to represent a single division, the 12th. Hornung's arrangement of the *Book of Gates* still has twelve divisions, however, because he refers to Piankoff's "Prologue" as his 1st Division and Piankoff's 1st Division as the 2nd, and so on. Piankoff's numbering system is used here simply because his translation is the primary source used throughout the rest of this study.

Finally, the celestial barque itself is lifted from the Abyss by Nun to carry the young sun-god on his journey across the newly created sky, across the very body of Nut.[a] Figure 127 thus shows that the underworld and the earth were created first from the primordial abyss, next came the sky and finally the sun.

It will be shown in this chapter that these events are similar to those described in Rev. 21:1-8, including the reference in Rev. 21:2 to the Holy City being "prepared as a bride adorned for her husband." Details of the events will be discussed separately in the same order as they appear in the Book of Revelation.

A New Heaven (Rev. 21:1)

In Rev. 21:1 the author of Revelation says that he "saw *a new heaven* and a new earth, for the first heaven and the first earth had passed away." The Greek word used for heaven in this text is *ouranón*, which is based on the word *ouranos*, meaning "sky,"[1303] or "the vaulted expanse of the sky with all things visible in it."[1304] New Testament translators almost universally translate it as "heaven." It is therefore reasonable to assume that the original reference to "heaven" in this verse can legitimately be interpreted to mean "sky" as well as "heaven" or "the heavens" so that we are justified in examining Egyptian beliefs from either perspective.

Hornung (1983) informs us that in the *Pyramid Texts* "the sky, in which the gods live and the domains of the blessed are situated, is evidently the goal of the king's journey into the next world."[1305] He says that the "sky" was "the earliest home of the gods that we can discern" and points out that we have an example of a deity traveling across the sky in a bark, a scene that is repeated countless times in later iconography, for example, on an ivory comb of the early dynastic King Djet (*c.* 2840 BCE). Clagett (1989) tells us that "In the course of the [deceased] king's celestial travels he visits many ill-defined regions, such as the High Mounds, the Mounds of Seth, and above all, the Field of Rushes and the Field of Offerings.[b, 1306] Also,

> There was a rather vaguely expressed belief in the Old Kingdom that the Dat or Duat [Tuat] (the land where the deceased lived in company with the gods) had an upper part in the skies and a lower counter-sky in the Netherworld, though surely the term Dat originally must have been principally used in connection with the celestial regions, since it was written with a star enclosed by a circle [✷] .... the doctrine of the death and birth of the sun each day exerted enormous influence on funerary practice in the Middle and New Kingdoms.[1307]

It is therefore clear that the sky (or the heavens) and the Netherworld (a term often restricted to the Tuat) were at times believed to be different parts of the dwelling place of the blessed dead. In other words, depending on the age or context of a given

---

[a] See Chapter 17, *The Woman in the Sky* for a discussion of the most important events which occur during the sun-god's crossing.

[b] Clagett (1989, p.356 and Note 108 on p. 402) draws the reader's attention to the suggestion by Kees and several other authors that the Field of Offerings may be the prototype of the Greek Elysian Fields.

document, the Tuat could represent either the heavens (sky), the Netherworld, or both. Many of the physical characteristics of heaven and the Netherworld, especially the domains of the blessed dead, therefore applied to both. For these reasons, we may assume that certain references to the Tuat or Netherworld in the *Book of Gates* may refer to the sky or heavens. One which seems to imply both regions is found in the upper register of the 11th Division where we read of four gods "who make new the Netherworld ... so that Re may rest in the body of Nut."[1308] The association of the Netherworld with the body of Nut in this statement suggests a combined nature of the Netherworld and the sky in this part of the *Book of Gates*. This results in a close parallel between the *newly created heaven* in Rev. 21:1 and the *renewal of the Netherworld* (in this case, a part of the *Tuat*) in the Egyptian text.

A New Earth (Rev. 21:1)

At first glance, we find no reference to a *new earth* in the Figure 127; on close examination, however, we encounter a distinct reference to one. This is found in the person of Osiris whose body forms a circle in the picture. The Egyptians believed that the body of Osiris was intimately connected with the earth and indeed, represented the very substance from which all vegetation arose, a concept shown graphically in Figure 128. At times, Osiris was a god of vegetation and Breasted (1912) believes that this "view of Osiris is carried so far in a hymn of the twelfth century BCE as to identify Osiris, not only with the soil but even with the earth itself." Osiris is described as one

> with outspread arms, sleeping upon his side upon the sand,
> lord of the soil, mummy with long phallus. ...
> Re-Khepri shines on thy body, when thou liest as Sokar [Sokaris],
> and he drives away the darkness which is upon thee,
> that he may bring light to thy eyes.
> For a time he shines upon thy body mourning for thee. ...
>
> The soil is on thy arm, its corners are upon thee as far as the four pillars of the sky.
> When thou movest, the earth trembles. ...
> As for thee, the Nile comes forth from the sweat of thy hands.
> Thou spewest out the wind that is in thy throat into the nostrils of men,
>   and that whereon men live is divine.
> It is alike in thy nostrils, the tree and its verdure,
>   reeds – plants, barley, wheat, and the tree of life.
> When canals are dug ... [when] houses and temples are built,
>   when monuments are transported and fields are cultivated,
>   when tomb-chapels and tombs are excavated, they rest on thee,
>   it is thou who makest them.
> They are on thy back, although they are more than can be put into writing.[1309]

The body of Osiris therefore at times represented the earth itself on whose back the plants grew, canals ran, houses and temples were built, and monuments constructed. With this in mind, the creation of the curved body of Osiris at the top of Figure 127 conforms quite well with the description in Rev. 21:1 of the creation of "a new earth." Furthermore, the intimate association of Osiris as a personification of the earth, and Nut as a personification of the sky who stands on the Osiris's head in Figure 127 conforms quite well with the juxtaposition of references to both the earth and sky in Rev. 21:1, "Then I saw a new heaven *and* a new earth; for the first heaven and the first earth had passed away, and the sea was no more."

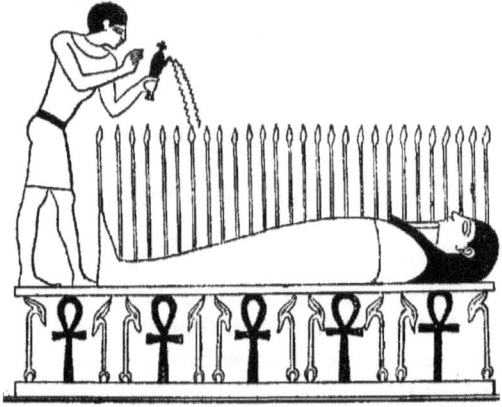

Figure 127. Osiris is shown here as the earth from which plants grow when they receive life-giving water of the Nile. In this picture, Osiris plays the role of an earth-god.

The Sea is No More (Rev. 21:1)

The last part of Rev. 21:1 is peculiar for a scene which is obviously meant to describe the renewal of the cosmos; it refers to a new heaven and a new earth but not a new sea. Indeed, it suggests the opposite – that "the sea was no more." The statement seems to contradict Figure 127 where the entire background of the picture consists of wavy lines which represent water, or the sea. This water does not represent the earthly ocean, however, but the primordial waters from which all of creation is formed. Close examination of the picture reveals that these waters do not extend into the circle formed by the curved body of Osiris. It is as if, in order to be created, the earth (Osiris) had to push aside the primordial waters identified in the figure as the "Abyss." This aspect of creation, or re-creation, of the earth in Figure 127 is thus consistent with that of the last part of the Rev. 21:1 which states that "the sea [the primeval water] was no more." From an Egyptian perspective, it is the primordial sea which no longer exits on earth; the primeval waters no longer occupy the space taken by the newly created earth.

The Egyptians considered that the primordial sea as a whole always existed and without it, no creation or regeneration could ever happen. Hornung (1983) points out that,

> Regeneration is impossible in the ordered and defined world. It can happen only if what is old and worn becomes immersed in the boundless regions that surround creation – in the healing and dissolving powers of the primeval ocean, Nun. The sun god in his bark is

raised from Nun every morning, as is shown in the concluding picture in the Book of Gates [Figure 127].[1310]

Arrival of the Holy City (Rev. 21:2-4)

Hornung (1990) tells us that "Egyptian belief placed the gods beyond the confines of this earth. Our reality can know them only in picture and parable, never directly; their apartments are in the heavens and the Netherworld, the two spheres of the beyond."[1311] It is in these two parts of the Beyond that we must seek the city referred to in Rev. 21:2 as a "holy city ... coming down out of heaven from God."

The most straight-forward means of identifying the location of Egypt's Holy City is based on the traditional name of the sky-goddess, Nut. Her name was pronounced *Nu-t, Nuit,*[1312] or *Nwt,*[1313] which was identical or phonetically similar to *nu-t*[1314] or *niwt*,[1315] common Egyptian names for "a city, town, village or hamlet." In this manner the sky-goddess and the sky which she personified are conceptually related to the idea of a *celestial city*. Thus, just as we see the newly created Nut reaching down from the head of the earth-god form of Osiris in Figure 127, Rev. 21:2 tells us that the author saw "the holy city [Nut] ... coming down ... from God [Osiris]." The picture of Nut in Figure 127 may thus be interpreted as a visual pun in which the ancient Egyptians saw the heavenly city emerging from the abyss each morning at dawn. Just as the sky-goddess was visualized as a woman's body stretching from horizon to horizon,[a] she could also be visualized as an immense heavenly city (*nut*) stretched across the center of sky like a giant metropolis where the gods and the souls of the blessed dead resided.

The celestial city of the ancient Egyptians was complete with streets for walking, canals for transportation and irrigation, fields for produce, and a great deal more. It was, in effect, the celestial equivalent of Egypt, the mirror image of its provinces, towns, cities, and suburbs in the form of a celestial mega-city, stretching from horizon to horizon. Chapter 169 of the *Book of the Dead* promises the deceased a special place in this city:

> Your soul is bound for the sky, your corpse is beneath the ground; there is bread for your belly, water for your throat and sweet air for your nose. Those who are in their tombs will be kindly to you, those who are in their coffins will be open to you, they will bring to you your members [body parts] when you are reestablished in your original shape. You shall go up to the sky, the cord shall be knotted for you in the presence of Re, you shall close the net in the river, you shall drink water from it, you shall walk on your feet, you shall not walk upside down. You shall ascend to those who are above the earth, you shall not go out to those who are under the walls; your walls which belong to you, *being what your city god made* for you, will not be thrown down.[1316]

Egyptian texts contain many other details concerning the physical appearance and other characteristics of their celestial city and these will be compared with those of Revelation's Holy City in the next chapter, *The Holy City*.

Since the idea of a celestial city was clearly well known to the ancient Egyptians it is only fitting that it should be described as one of the earliest components of

---

[a] See Chapter 17, *The Woman in the Sky*.

creation. And just as Nut is viewed as coming from the abyss, Rev. 21:2 describes a Holy City as coming down from heaven.

A City Prepared as a Bride (Rev. 21:2,9-10)

Rev. 21:2 also likens the Holy City to one "prepared as a bride adorned for her husband." Later, in Rev. 21:9-10 it is even described as "the Bride, the wife of the Lamb." These statements clearly indicate the Holy City can be thought of as a woman, just as the Egyptians thought of it in terms of a woman – Nut, the sky-goddess. Meanwhile, in Chapter 3, *The Preeminent Deities*, the Lamb was identified with the juvenile form of the ram-headed sun-god, Re. If there is a parallel here, we may say that, from an Egyptian perspective, Revelation's bride is Nut and her husband is Re. Remarkably, this statement is entirely consistent with a popular ancient belief that the pharaoh of Egypt was the son of Re and Nut, a belief frequently reinforced in the titles of kings written on the walls of the tombs in the Valley of the Kings. Breasted (1912) says that "As the son of Re, born of the Sky-goddess, he [the king] is frequently represented as suckled by one of the Sky-goddesses or some other divinity connected with Re."[1317] Meanwhile, the final scene in the *Book of Gates* shows an intimate relationship between Nut and Re. Nut is shown lifting, or perhaps even reaching for, the newly born sun-god (the Lamb). The reference in Rev. 21:2 and Rev. 21:9-10 to the Holy City being the wife of the Lamb thus conforms quite well with the ancient Egyptian beliefs that Nut was the wife of Re.

While this is perhaps the most simplistic approach to explaining how Egypt's heavenly city may be described as a bride, it is not the only one. An alternative explanation is based on another, more popular ancient belief that Nut was the wife of the earth-god Geb rather than Re. Most versions of this myth say that four children were born of this union – Osiris, Isis, Seth, and Nephthys while some included Re himself. For example, one hymn to Amon-Re says, "Hail to thee, Amen-Re, ... lord of the sky, eldest son of the earth [Geb]."[1318] In this manner, just as Nut was prepared to unite with Geb (the earth) each morning at dawn, Revelation's Holy City was "prepared as a bride adorned for her husband." This scenario is also applicable to the final scene in the *Book of Gates* when one considers the proximity of Nut (the sky) to Osiris (the earth) in Figure 127. While it suggests a parallel between Osiris and the "husband" of Rev. 21:2, it fails to explain Osiris' link with Re, the Lamb and husband of the bride in Rev. 21:9 – unless one assumes that Osiris-Re is referred to as the Lamb, an assumption which may well be valid, as discussed in Chapter 3, *The Preeminent Deities*. If the latter case is true then both these versions of the myth conform with Rev. 21 although the one in the previous paragraph is a better fit.

Dwelling Place of God and Men (Rev. 21:3)

The next verse in Revelation makes a rather remarkable statement: "Behold, the dwelling of God is with men. He will dwell with them, and they shall be his people, and God himself will be with them." A parallel to this text is also found in the picture in the final division of *Book of Gates* where the newly born sun-god (O☉) is lifted up out of the abyss to be received by Nut. The scene reflects the sun-god's arrival into earth's morning sky where it is visible to everyone. In this sense the scene is like that in Revelation where the writer is instructed to "Behold, the dwelling of God [Osiris-Re, as above] is with men." The sun-god literally "dwells with" his people during the day as he sheds his light upon earth and they worship him and call themselves "his people" (or more specifically and in Egyptian terms, "his cattle"). This simple arrival of the sun-god from beneath the eastern horizon and his glorious entrance into the daytime sky in full view of all who dwell on earth is thus an obvious parallel to Rev. 21:3.

According to the *Pyramid Texts*, after the young sun-god emerges from the Netherworld into the morning sky he assumes his seat on the heavenly throne. A reference to the deity's throne in Rev. 21:5 at this point in Revelation thus conforms with long-held Egyptian beliefs about celestial events at dawn – except for one possible difference: the one seated on the throne in Revelation corresponds to Osiris rather than Re, as discussed in Chapter 3, *The Preeminent Deities*,. This discrepancy disappears, however, when one assumes that firstly, it is Osiris whose voice it is which parallels the text of Rev. 21:5 – "I heard a *voice* from the throne saying ..." and secondly, that the person spoken of in the statement, "*he* will dwell with them" and "*he* will wipe away every tear" (Rev. 21:3-4) parallels the sun-god, Re. Together they form Osiris-Re, the unified form of Osiris and Re. This is especially applicable in the early morning hours when the sun-god was looked upon in his unified form, a form which parallels "God and the Lamb" in the Book of Revelation.

There is another parallel to Rev. 21:3. This one is found in the opening scene of the *Amduat*. Here, the scene involves the arrival of the sun-god, not into the morning sky but rather as he sails from the evening sky down into the Netherworld at sunset. The aged sun-god enters the Netherworld's counterpart of the Great City; Hornung (1990) describes events on his arrival:

> Jubilation resounds as the sun god appears; .... baboons acclaim the sun god in the name of all the creatures of the Beyond, making music and dancing before him, and in the scenes of the sun's path, the exultant apes represent all creation. "The gates of the great city are opened for you," they sing while pushing open the Gate of the Netherworld, that the solar bark may enter the Great or Eternal City, the Realm of the Dead with its millions.[1319]

Elsewhere, Hornung (1992) explains that

> Life after death does not mean the resumption of life on earth; this new life is in the sky and the underworld. Having become a god, the deceased resides where the gods reside and may encounter them face to face. While still on earth the gods are approached only indirectly, through images and symbols. One such symbol is the sun, but only in the depths of the underworld can humans actually meet the sun in person.[1320]

Their new lives are lived in the presence of their god, either in his train as he travels through the sacred regions, or in the heavenly towns, suburbs, and cities of "the great city." These suburbs are, as pointed out earlier, otherworldly images of earthly counterparts situated in the Beyond, the supernal image of earthly Egypt. Hornung (1990) describes the arrival of the deceased into his city/suburb of choice:

Rosetau is the blessed place where the dead desire to share the lively and happy company of Osiris. In the Beyond, it is the sister city of Abydos, the goal of earthly pilgrims, where the living erected tombs, chapels, or small stelae in the vicinity of Osiris's temples, in order to be present at the gods's mysteries, the yearly festival at which mythical events were recounted, re-enacting the death and revival. In spell 138 of the Book of the Dead, the deceased arrives at an otherworldly Abydos, where the gods greet him with acclaim as son of Osiris, but he is in general more concerned with attaining access to Rosetau (spells 117-119), where the enlightened receive their bread and beer in the company of Osiris.[1321]

It is obvious that Revelation's concept of God (Osiris) or the Lamb (Re) living with his people was present among the Osirian believers. Indeed, this belief was one of the most profound desires of the Osirian penitent. Its conformity with Rev. 21:3 indicates yet another strong parallel between ancient Egyptian beliefs and the Book of Revelation.

The End of Mourning (Rev. 21:4)

The theme of Rev. 21:4 is the end of sorrow: "he will wipe away every tear from their eyes, and death shall be no more, neither shall there be mourning nor crying, for the former things have passed away." While there are no explicit references to the "wiping away of tears" or to the end of "mourning or crying" in the *Book of Gates*, there are references to mourning. Four male "Mourners" located at BG11.3.2-3 "make lamentations for Osiris after Re has come out of the West."[1322] Nearby, at BG11.3.7-8, four female deities stand behind four inclining gods; they are called "Female Mourners"[1323] and the text over them says that "They loosen their hair [typical of mourning traditions in the Middle East] before the Great God in the West." But the text also says "They turn back to this gate, they do not enter the sky." The mourning of these beings is apparently caused by their being forbidden to follow the sun-god into his celestial domain. It is significant, however, that it is their "bodies" which remain behind, not their souls, for the text then tells us that "Their souls go forward in his (Re's) train [in the sky] while they themselves (remain) in the train of Osiris."[1324] It is inconceivable that their souls would be mourning at this point; their souls would be delighted and happy with their new circumstance. We therefore have in this scene a switch from mourning in the their bodies to joy of their souls. Their new life with the sun-god is emphasized by one group of female deities (at BG11.3.6-7) who "establish the duration of life ... for those who live in the sky. They are in the train of this god."[1325]

The fight against Apophis has been won and Apophis has been destroyed and his followers punished. Those who died in the service of the sun-god are resurrected to new life and the mourning for the separation of their bodies from Re as he leaves the Netherworld is overwhelmed by the triumphant entry of their souls into the morning sky with him. The numerous dangers they faced in the Netherworld, including the fight with Apophis, are passed; or as Rev. 21:4 puts it, "the former things have passed away." And they are to reign with this god in the sky for an entire earth-day – i.e., 1,000 years in the presence of Re.

The dramatic change from the vicissitudes of earthly life to a blessed existence in the afterlife is perhaps nowhere more concisely put than the summary by Budge (1895):

> He [the deceased] sits on a great throne by the side of God. ... He receives the *urerit* crown from the gods. ... He thirsts not, nor hungers, *nor is sad;* he eats the bread of Ra: and drinks what he drinks daily, and his bread also is that which ... comes forth from the mouth of the gods. ... all the gods give him their food that *he may not die.* ... he is clothed in white ... and these great and never failing gods give unto him *{to eat} of the tree of life* of which they themselves do eat ... that he likewise may live. ... He eats of the *"bread of eternity"* and drinks of the *"beer of everlastingness."* ... He suffers neither hunger nor thirst ... He is washed clean, and his *ka* [spirit] is washed clean.[1326]

Notice that the blessed dead are neither sad nor do they die. Indeed, there are at least five references to the joys of eternal existence (italicized) in this brief quotation. This brief vision of everlasting life implies the absence of mourning after death – as stated in Rev. 21:4.

Renewal (Rev. 21:5-22:5)

All Things Made New (Rev. 21:5)

The next portion of text begins with a reference to the throne: "And he who sat upon the throne said ..." (Rev. 21:5). The text near the end of the *Book of Gates* contains at least one allusion to such a throne. It is found in the 11th Division over four hawk-headed deities on the upper register and says, "They are like this. Scepters are in their hands. *It is they who establish the shrine* and who give a hand to the crew of the divine double barge after its coming out of the Uniter (the gate)"[1327] Note the reference to the "shrine" of the sun-god. As pointed out in Chapter 3, *The Preeminent Deities*, the Egyptian word *khent* means both "shrine" and "throne" so that this statement in the *Book of Gates* can represent either an explicit reference to a throne or one which may be interpreted to mean, "It is they who establish the *throne* ..." Furthermore, in the middle the same division the physical location of this throne is described as being on the "two banks of the Abyss" in "the heights of heaven."

> (*Behold*) the coming forth from the West [the Netherworld], taking a place on *the two banks* of the Abyss, making transformations on the arms of the Abyss, (in peace).
> This god enters the heights of heaven, he opens the Netherworld toward the heights of heaven by his forms which are in the Abyss. ... He is in complete darkness when Re enters it (the heights of heaven) at dawn.[1328] (BG11.2.1-3)

Note the use of the first word, "Behold," in this passage from the *Book of Gates*. Piankoff's (1989) use of brackets here implies it is his best guess at an accurate translation of the text. This suggestion conforms with the use of the word in Rev. 21:5, "*Behold*, I make all things new." The Egyptian text thus implies instruction to the reader to look to the east where the newly born sun-god is emerging from the darkness of the Netherworld between the two banks of the abyss, a reference to the mythological mountains on the earth's eastern horizon through which the sun rises at dawn[1329] and to the two out-stretched arms depicted in Figure 120.

And just as Revelation makes reference to "making all things new," Re's purpose for entering the sky was to "make new the Netherworld," the complete text of the relevant passage being:

> They are like this [= "*Behold* the picture"]. They carry the disk of Re. It is they who *make new the Netherworld*˙ with this image [the sun-disk] which they carry in their hands, the soul which speaks to the Pylon of the Silent Region, so that Re may rest within the body of Nut.[1330] (BG11.1.1-2)

In this part of the text, the expression, "They are like this ..." is obviously meant to direct the reader's attention to the illustration at the end of the *Book of Gates* (Figure 127). Therefore, it too has a meaning which is similar to the expression "behold" used in Rev. 21:5. Such a reference to "Behold" in conjunction with the reference to "making new the Netherworld" in the same paragraph conforms with the use of the word "Behold" in conjunction with the words "I make all things new" in Rev. 20:5. The structure of this phrase is also comparable to that in the previously quoted passage immediately above this one (at BG11.2.1-3) which describes the sun-god's entrance into morning sky with the words, "(Behold) the coming forth from the West ..."

Truth of the Claim (Rev. 21:5)

The concluding comment in Rev. 21:5 has a distinctively Egyptian ring to it. It says, "Write this for these words are trustworthy and true." This phrase is similar to one over the four goddesses wearing the crowns of the South at BG11.3.5-6; it reads, "They are like this [Behold]. *They elevate Truth*˙ and they establish it in the shrine of Re when Re takes a rest in Nut."[1331] Other Egyptian sources bear even more marked similarities to the words of Revelation, especially when one considers the complete phrase, "*Write this*, for these words are trustworthy and true." Revelation's explicit instruction to write about the truth of what is being said is also found at the end of the rubric to 72nd chapter of the *Book of the Dead*: "As for him who *knows*˙ this book on earth and *it is put in writing*˙ .... A matter of a million times *true*.'" Note that the phrase, "A matter of a million times true," expresses the same sentiment as the phrase, "these words are trustworthy and true." The juxtaposition of the concepts of "truth" and the putting something "in writing" conforms with the juxtaposition of the same concepts in Revelation; they both relate to the validity of something written down. This parallel to the statement in Rev. 21:5 therefore echoes a common belief held by Egyptian priests that great truths should be recorded in writing.

Alpha and the Omega (Rev. 21:6a)

Rev. 21:6 opens with the statement, "It is done!" We may assume from Rev. 21:1-5 that this refers to the act of creating a new heaven and earth, and from Rev. 21:2-3, to the arrival of God to dwell with his people. From an Egyptian perspective, the statement conforms with the creation scene at the end of the *Book of Gates* wherein the universe is renewed (at the "first time," and each morning at dawn) as it emerges from the primeval waters and the sun-god rises into the morning sky to shed his glory (light) on the people his earth.

26. A New Creation

The next part of Rev. 21:6 requires more in-depth consideration. In it, the speaker says, "I am the Alpha and the Omega, the beginning and the end." The words *Alpha* and the *Omega*, of course, refer to the first and last letters of the Greek alphabet, letters not found in Egyptian writings but which, to a person writing the Book of Revelation in Greek, conceptually conform with the idea of "the beginning and the end," just as Revelation's author interprets it. *Alpha* conforms with the beginning or renewal of heaven and earth as well as the arrival of the Holy City in Rev. 21:1-5. The reference to *Omega* as "the end," however, requires slightly more thought to be interpreted from an Egyptian perspective. The Egyptian concept of the beginning and the end was, in a philosophical sense, far more complicated than this and has been a subject of much debate among modern Egyptologists.

Of course the most obvious aspect of the phrase "the beginning and the end" is that it refers to the general concept of *time*. Time was an essential element of many Egyptian religious concepts and a great deal of thought was given to its nature. Perhaps the most important attribute of time involved the two expressions, *neheh* and *djet* (*nḥḥ* and *ḏt*). The exact meanings of *neheh* and *djet* have been the subject of scholarly debate since the late nineteenth century probably because of their esoteric and apparently inconsistent usage by Egyptian priests. When used in relation to the nature of the time and of material existence within it, Hornung (1983) suggests that,

> Since the created world is bounded and ordered in time and space, it follows that it has an end and must disappear; it is an island or an 'episode' (Thomas Mann) 'between nothingness and nothingness.' It has duration, but there is no such thing as eternal existence, which would be a contradiction in terms. The pair of Egyptian words we translate 'eternity' (*nḥḥ* and *ḏt*) in fact means 'time.' "[1332]

Clagett (1989) expands on this, suggesting that *neheh* means "the long stretch of past time" and *djet* "the indefinitely long future," which, when combined in the expression, *"neheh* and *djet,"* represents "all time."[a] *Neheh* and *djet* thus implies the complete time period from the *beginning* of all past time to the *end* of all future time. Hornung (1992) expresses this vastness of time in terms of the afterlife where, "The duration of existence in the afterlife is *neheh* and *djet*. In comparison, the duration of earthly existence is hardly worth consideration."[1333] He further explains that,

> While the two terms do not signify eternity in an absolute sense, they do come as close as possible to meaning 'eternity' without actually being synonymous with it, since they represent the sum of all conceivable units of time. ... This Egyptian 'eternity' has both a beginning and an end, and it consists of years and days.[1334]

He goes on to quantify this time as it may have been perceived by priests and Osirian believers:

---

[a] See Note 3 on pp. 445-446 in Clagett (1989) referring to *The Book of the Divine Cow*.

According to the Book of the Dead, Osiris 'lives a lifetime of millions of years' (spell 175). Each person becomes an Osiris after death, and as a result the hope for 'millions of years' – which suggests something of the duration of *neheh* and *djet* – is not the privilege of the god alone, but extends to include all humanity."[1335]

It seems that believers saw in Osiris the hope of an eternal existence which lasted from a fixed beginning to a fixed end, a period which lasted millions of years. This hope conforms quite well with the words from the throne in Rev. 21:5-6 – "Behold, ... I am ... the beginning and the end." It is in no way surprising to read that this statement comes from the throne of God, for the opening statement of the *Introductory Hymn to Osiris* in the *Book of the Dead* describes Osiris as the "King of Eternity, Lord of Everlasting," in other words, the "King of *Neheh*, Lord of *Djet*" a title equivalent to the "King of the *Beginning*, Lord of the *End*." Osiris's title of "King of *Neheh*, Lord of *Djet*" is thus in complete agreement with the sense of Revelation's God on the throne: "I am ... the beginning and the end."

It remains to tie this parallel to the last scene of the *Book of Gates*. How does Osiris and the idea of the "beginning and the end," of *neheh* and *djet*, conform with this scene? The answer is in the shape of the body of Osiris as he emerges out of the primordial abyss in Figure 127. Recall that Osiris's body forms a circle so that his feet touched the top of his head. This form is reminiscent of the so-called "tail-in-his-mouth" motif formed by the body of the primordial serpent; like Osiris, the serpent's body is bent into a circle so that its tail touches its head. The symbol thus created was well-known to the ancient Greeks as the *ouroboros* and was held to be a symbol of the *renewal of time* itself.

In Egyptian mythology, the *ouroboros* symbolized the cyclical nature of time. Figure 129 shows the ouroboros serpent encircling the young sun-god, Re, as he is passes through the two arms of Geb (the earth) into the morning sky (shown as a cow's head) from between two mountains (the two lions of Acker the earth god). In addition to the nature of time, the picture highlights the importance of the birth of the sun-god, especially as it applies to his arrival each morning over the eastern horizon.

Note the similarity between this picture and that of the last scene in the *Book of Gates* (Figure 127). The relative position of head and feet of the bent body of Osiris illustrates the same cyclical nature of the head to tail aspect of the serpent as in Figure 129.

Figure 128. The young sun-god, depicted here as a child with a finger in his mouth, is encompassed by a serpent with its tail in its mouth, the ouroboros symbol representing the ever continuing cycle of the beginning and end of time.

26. A New Creation

This suggests that the circular form of Osiris in Figure 127 symbolizes eternity and its cyclical nature, including the beginning and end of time. In this manner, the very shape of Osiris' body illustrates the words of the *Introductory Hymn to Osiris* where he is described as the "King of *Neheh* and Lord of *Djet.*"

There is another Egyptian myth worthy of consideration in relation to the expression, "I am ... the beginning and the end." It involves the unified form of the sun-god, *Osiris-Re* (see Chapter 3, *The Preeminent Deities*). As discussed in Chapter 3, Osiris-Re, otherwise known as the "Joint God" or "The One Joined Together," was considered to represent a special kind of union of Re and Osiris, and as such, the ultimate expression of the nature of the sun-god. This dichotomy is mentioned in Chapter 17 of the *Book of the Dead* where we find references to the different aspects of Osiris and Re simultaneously appearing as one sun-god, thereby providing us with a definition which alludes to the complete time period from the *beginning* of all past time past to the *end* of all future time, as discussed above. In it, the deceased is asked the meaning of the expression, "To me belongs yesterday, I know tomorrow." The deceased answers, "As for yesterday, that is Osiris. As for tomorrow, that is Re on the day in which the foes of the Lord of All were destroyed."[1336] "Yesterday," of course, can represent the past, that long stretch of time all the way back to the beginning; similarly, "tomorrow" can express the future, the indefinitely long future all the way to the end when all the sun-god's foes are vanquished and creation is renewed. The two concepts, that of the "Osiris ouroboros" at the end of the *Book of Gates* and the well-known concept of Osiris-Re, the unified sun-god, therefore complement each other. And together, they strengthen the idea that the one described as "the beginning and the end" on the throne in Rev. 21:6 parallels the belief in the dual nature of time expressed in pictures and text describing the sun-god.

Reward of the Water of Life (Rev. 21:6b-7)

In the latter part of Rev. 21:6, the writer of Revelation is told by the one who sits on the throne, "To the thirsty I will give from the fountain of the *water of life* without payment." But delivery of this water of life was not, however, limited to the fountains of the earth and sky; water also came from the "tree of life" and has already been discussed in the section on the *Gift of the Tree of Life* in Chapter 7, *Egyptian Beliefs in the Seven Letters*. There, a different kind of fountain was presented – one in the form of a vase held by the tree goddess and from which the life giving fluid flows into the outstretched hands of the blessed dead who kneels nearby; lotus blossoms, signifying the renewal of life[1337] decorate the bread of life on the tray held in her other hand. Indeed, it was this particular water, i.e., that from the Tree of Life, which was granted to those Egyptians triumphant in the final judgment.

Lurker (1980) tells us that "The notion of the water of life was shown in the symbolism of purification, thought of not only in a superficial sense but also as supposed to provide divine grace."[1338] An ancient writing dedicated to the god Thoth emphasizes the importance of water to the pious Egyptian scribe and Frankfort (1948) refers to it as the basis for his comments on the importance of water in meditation. While the entire poem is provided to us by Frankfort, the last verse only is reproduced here because of its similarity to the latter part of Rev. 21:6.

> Thou who bringest water to a distant place, come deliver me, the silent man,
> Thoth, thou sweet well for one who thirsts in the desert;
> It is closed for one who argues but open for him who keeps silence.
> The silent one comes and finds the well.[1339]

Frankfort says,

> This last verse shows that the elaborate imagery of the poem serves to bring the opposition of the passionate and the silent man in relation with the god to whom the scribe is particularly attached. His feelings evoke images of the greatest delights, the shade of the palm and the cool water from the well. Hence the associative progression of the images: the dom palm of great height; the fruit; the moisture-filled kernels in the fruit; the moisture that refreshes the thirsting; the well from which the "right," the "silent" man draws strength and consolation.[1340]

The importance of water to the Egyptians cannot be overemphasized. It is no wonder that it was deeply rooted in their religious beliefs.

Water from the Nile was treated with special dignity by those living in Egypt. Lurker (1980) says that the "sacred lake at Heracleopolis was supposed to have come into being from the blood and discharges of Osiris."[1341] Beyond death, the water of life provided by Osiris had life-giving qualities. He goes on to say that it was,

> the primeval matter which 'brought forth all things.' ... As a god of vegetation *Osiris was himself regarded as lord of the waters of the Nile'* ... . In the mortuary cult the water used in libation was linked to the idea of reanimation [resurrection]. As the 'efflux which issued from *Osiris' water liberated one from the paralysis of death*.'[1342]

Not surprisingly then, this water of life played an important ceremonial role in the coronation of the king. Lurker (1980) says, "The rites performed at the king's accession were full of symbolism. First, the candidate for the throne was purified with the water of life, 'that he might become young like Re,' who also cleansed himself before he embarked on his journey across the heavens."[1343] Meanwhile, a priestly explanation in the *Pyramid Texts* says that the annual inundation of the Nile is of sacred origin with Osiris being its source: "The lakes fill, the canals are inundated, by the purification that came forth from Osiris";[1344] Also, "Ho this Osiris, King *N!* Thy water, thy libation is the great inundation that came forth from thee (as Osiris)."[1345]

The *Amduat* also refers to the importance of water in the hereafter and, like Rev. 21:6, mentions its status as a special gift:

> This Great God takes care of the gods who are in the following of Osiris. He grants them portions in this field. (This is) to know the souls. As to one who knows their names, he will reach the place where Osiris is. Water of the field will be given him at this bank. Water of the Unique Lord which creates Offerings is the name of this field.[1346] (AM3.1)

The 149th Chapter of the *Book of the Dead* also expresses the exceptional importance of the water of life to the Osirian believer: "I shall be provided with the efflux which issued from Osiris, and I will never let go of it,"[1347] the believer says. Furthermore, the blessed dead who identified themselves with Osiris even associated it with the Lake of Fire: "My hand shall not be thrust aside in the tribunal of all gods, for I [the deceased] am Osiris, Lord of Rosetjau. I will share with this one who is on the dias, for I have come for what my heart desires into the Lake of Fire which is quenched for me."[1348]

Egyptians even believed that all water everywhere, even that outside Egypt, was sacred. The holy waters of the earthly domain were believed to well up as a fountain from the primeval abyss below the earth into the First Cataract in the vicinity of Elephantine.[1349] From there, it flowed through Egypt proper and into the Mediterranean Sea. Breasted (1912) comments on this flow of sacred life-giving water.

> While the great fountains of waters are thus identified with Osiris, it [the Nile] is evidently a particular function of the waters with which he was associated. It was water as a source of fertility, *water as a life-giving agency with which Osiris was identified.*' It is water which brings life to the soil, and when the inundation comes the Earth-god Geb says to Osiris: "The divine fluid that is in thee cries out, thy heart lives, thy divine limbs move, thy joints are loosed," in which we discern the water bringing life and causing the resurrection of Osiris, the soil. In the same way in a folk-tale thirteen or fourteen hundred years later than the *Pyramid Texts*, the heart of a dead hero, who is really Osiris, is placed in water, and *when he has drunk the water containing his heart, he revives and comes to life.*'[1350]

Rain too was recognized for its life-giving properties and brought the hope of purification, rebirth and regeneration. This view forms the basis of a passage in the *Pyramid Texts* which says that "The waters of life that are in the sky come; the waters of life that are in the earth come. The sky burns for thee, the earth trembles for thee, before thy [Osiris'] divine birth."[1351]

In view of the above evidence, it is quite easy to see the parallel with the words of Rev. 21:6, "I will give from the fountain of the water of life." The reference to the gift of water in Rev. 21:7 with the judgment ("He who conquerors shall have this heritage") at this point in the Book of Revelation seems to hark back to the rewards mentioned in Rev. 2-3 (see Chapter 7, *Egyptian Beliefs in the Seven Letters*) which those successful in the last judgment will enjoy in their newly created holy city.

Punishment of the Unrighteous (Rev. 21:8)

Those who were not victorious in the final judgment were condemned to a fiery second death: "But as for the cowardly, the faithless, the polluted, as for murderers, fornicators, sorcerers, idolaters, and all liars, their lot shall be in the lake that burns with fire and sulphur, which is the second death" (Rev. 21:8). This topic was covered in Chapter 7, *Egyptian Beliefs in the Seven Letters* and needs little elaboration here except to say that those not victorious in the judgment were often condemned to be burned in the lake of fire normally seen near the throne of Osiris in many judgment scenes. (Conversely, and as noted elsewhere, while the lake of burning fire brought a dreadful death to the unfaithful and the enemies of Osiris, it contained desirable, refreshing water for those victorious at the judgment).

Discussion

In this chapter, we have seen how the dramatic appearance of a new heaven and earth in Rev. 21:1-3a parallels an equally dramatic creation scene at the end of the *Book of Gates*, a scene in which the creation of the sky-goddess, the wife of Re, may be interpreted as the arrival in the sky (part of ancient Egypt's *Tuat*) at dawn of a great celestial city. Furthermore, we have seen how the blessings of the people described in Rev. 21:3b-8 conform with Egyptian texts describing the good fortune of the blessed dead who dwell in this city. The idea of Revelation's Holy City coming down from heaven is in excellent agreement with Egyptian beliefs in the arrival of a celestial city at dawn and its identification as their final abode of eternal peace and contentment of the followers of the sun-god who have been successful in the final judgment; those found to be unworthy in the judgment had been relegated to the tortures of the lake of fire as part of the purification of all aspects of the previous great cycle of time, a cycle personified by Osiris, Revelation's God on the Throne, and the *"neheh* and *djet."* It is obvious that elements of beliefs in the daily re-enactment of the original creation of the universe portrayed in the final scene of the *Book of Gates* are similar to elements of the new creation described in Rev. 21:1-8.

The reference in Rev. 21:2 to the celestial city being called "new Jerusalem" beseeches comment. This name does not conform with the name of any earthly or celestial cities directly associated with ancient Egypt and reference to it here is one of the very few parts of the Book of Revelation which cannot be readily explained in terms of ancient Egyptian beliefs. If we assume an Egyptian connection with the Book of Revelation, one possible explanation for the reference to the name of "Jerusalem" is that it suggests early Hebrew or Christian scribes incorporated the name as glosses in early versions Greek versions of Book of Revelation. If so, it might be possible that the reference may indicate an approximate time for the original writing of the book (during the time of one of the destructions of Jerusalem by enemy forces?) and research on this and other possibilities may be helpful in solving its appearance in the book.

Meanwhile, the next part of Rev. 21 (Rev. 21:9-27) and the first five verses of Rev. 22 continues with the theme of a holy city and provides us with a very detailed description of it. And as we shall see in the next chapter, *The Holy City*, this description also conforms with the appearance, structural details and physical dimensions of ancient Egypt's own heavenly city.

Chapter 27. The Holy City (Rev. 21:10 - Rev. 22:5)[1352]

In the previous chapter, *A New Creation*, it was concluded that Egyptian beliefs about the sky-goddess Nut and her association with a great celestial city conformed with the description of the Holy City coming down out of heaven in Rev. 21:1-10. From the next part of Revelation (Rev. 21:11-27) to the first part of the following chapter (Rev. 22:1-5) we find a detailed, physical description of this city: the decorations on the foundations of its walls; its shape, size and number of gates (Rev. 21:9-17); the names and appearance of its gates (Rev. 21:18-22); its source of light; the river which runs through it; restrictions on entrance; and finally, the practices of its residents (Rev. 21:23-27 to Rev. 22:5). These elements are well defined and therefore enable a fairly detailed comparison with Egyptian equivalents in the heavenly abode of Egypt's blessed dead.

The Egyptian sky was at times envisioned as a vast heavenly vault of metal held aloft by high mountains on the horizons of each of its cardinal points. We may infer that it was seen as being not only square, but (obviously) very high as well. This sense of shape and height is accentuated by the portrayal of Nut, the personification of the sky in the *Books of the Heavens*, especially as she is presented on the ceilings of the sarcophagus chambers of several tombs in the Valley of the Kings. As outlined in Chapter 17, *The Woman in the Sky*, Nut was visualized as bending over the celestial sphere with her hands and feet resting on each of the four corners of the earth, her arms and legs forming tall pillars extending down to meet the ground. The most distant horizons formed the foundations of this celestial *nut*, or city. Typically, Nut's body was decorated with twelve sun-disks said to represent the twelve hours of the day and, like the Holy City in Rev. 21-22, they also served basically the same function – gates through which the deceased pass. These and other similarities will serve as the basis for development of a better understanding of the parallels between Egypt's heavenly city and the Holy City in the Book of Revelation.

One striking aspect of Revelation's Holy City is its immense size (Rev. 21:16) which will be discussed shortly. Meanwhile, we should bear in mind that this aspect of the city should not surprise us if we are to view the description in Revelation in the light of ancient Egyptian beliefs in the hereafter. Hornung (1990) emphasizes that things in the hereafter were generally much larger than on earth:

> The Beyond is also a distorted mirror of the here and now. Everything there is larger than life; measurements are made with "divine cubits" far larger than the earthly royal ones, and the grain grows far better than here, being reaped by the "enlightened," themselves real giants of 7 or even 9 cubits (over 12 and 15 feet respectively). The dimensions of the Beyond given in the Amduat overshadow any earthly measures. The length of the mere buffer zone leading to the real Netherworld is greater than the entire length of the Nile Valley to a point below the second cataract, and the length of the region passed in the second hour is almost three times as great, 309 Egyptian miles, being exceeded only by the expanse of the "offering fields" in the Coffin Texts, which measured 1,000 Egyptian miles across and the same in length.[1353]

Such huge dimensions are, as we soon shall see, entirely consistent with those of the Holy City described in Revelation.

These and other characteristics of the Holy City will be discussed in a different order than that found in the Book of Revelation because they tend to be fragmented and scattered throughout Revelation. In order to facilitate our understanding of the description of the city and how its attributes compare with those of the holy city of the ancient Egyptians, they will be discussed in a logical order, beginning with its size and shape and from there on to its walls and gates and finally, its contents and residents.

The City's Shape and Size (Rev. 21:16)

Rev. 21:16 says that "The city lies foursquare, its length the same as its breadth." Recall that Nut was visualized as bent over the celestial sphere with her hands and feet resting on each of the four corners of the earth; this attitude obviously provides us with the first parallel, a square. Note from the above quotation from Hornung that the "offering fields" are also square, being 1,000 by 1000 Egyptian miles. This shape thus conforms with the overall "ground plan" of Revelation's Holy City – they are both square. The 70th Chapter of the *Book of the Dead* describes Egypt's celestial city with a comment on its shape: "I am happy and pleased... I travel about on its riverbanks, I breathe the east wind because of its tresses, I grasp the north wind by its braided lock, I grip the south wind by its plaits, I grasp the west wind by its nape. *I travel around the sky on its four sides.*"[1354] So large was the celestial city of the Egyptians that, like large cities on earth, it had subdivisions. In the 99th Chapter of the *Book of the Dead* the deceased is confronted with the statement, "Take Care! Do you say that you would cross to the east side of the sky? If you cross, what will you do?" His answer implies its enormity: "I will govern the towns, I will rule the villages, I will know the rich and give to the poor, I will prepare cakes for you when going downstream and bread when going upstream."[1355]

Rev. 21:16 also says that "its length and breadth *and height* are equal." In other words, Revelation's Holy City has the shape of a cube. From an Egyptian point of view, this would mean that Nut, as a celestial city, would have to be as high above the earth as it is from horizon to horizon, a reasonable assumption considering the apparent height of the sky above the Earth. Rev. 21:16 also provides us with the actual dimensions of Revelation's Holy City; it is 12,000 stadia square: The author "measured the city with his rod, twelve thousand stadia; its length and breadth and height are equal." This description is almost universally interpreted by biblical scholars to mean that the city is cube-shaped[1356] with each horizontal and vertical side measuring 12,000 stadia. It would be ideal to compare these dimensions with the size of the actual Egyptian celestial city but comparable measurements are not readily available in the Egyptian literature. We may, however, infer its size from the fact that the Egyptians viewed the celestial city to be a mirror image of their earthly Egypt. Thus, if we know the *perceived shape and size* of ancient Egypt, we can infer the same for its heavenly city. In the absence of reliable information on Egyptian perceptions of the overall shape and size of ancient Egypt, we turn to ancient Hebrew knowledge on the subject mentioned by Budge (1904). Budge compares *Gehenna,* the Hebrew equivalent of the Egyptian Ṭuat (which as noted elsewhere was in the early dynasties equivalent to Egypt's celestial city) to determine the size and shape of Egypt as perceived by the ancients themselves. He writes as follows:

> Reference has already been made to the influence upon the hell of the Copts of the old Egyptian mythology about the Ṭuat, and it is right here to point out that the Hebrews appear to have borrowed from it many of their ideas concerning the abodes of the dead in the Underworld. ... According to the Rabbis "Gehenna" was created on the second day of creation, with the firmament and the angels, and just as there were an Upper and Lower Paradise so there were two Gehennas, one in the heavens and one on the earth. As to the size of Gehenna we read that Egypt was 400 parassangs long and 400 parassangs wide.[1357]

If we assume that the Hebrew dimensions of the size of ancient Egypt echo the early Egyptian view, we may convert these measurements into Greek stadia to directly compare them with those in Rev. 21:16. Budge tells us that one parassang is equal to 30 stadia.[1358] The perceived length and breath of Egypt was therefore 12,000 stadia (from 400 parassangs x 30 stadia per parassang) on each side. Since the Tuat was visualized by the Egyptians to be a virtual duplicate of the terrestrial Egypt, the heavenly Egypt was very likely deemed to measure 12,000 by 12,000 stadia – the same area described for the Holy City in Rev. 21:16.

With respect to the height of the Holy City a similarly excellent match for the 12,000 stadia in height does not seem to exist in either Egyptian or Hebrew writings. Nevertheless, given the Egyptian belief that the sky was very high indeed, it is not inconceivable that the same number of stadia would be considered as its height, especially if one considers the relative length of Nut's arms and legs which determine her height above the earth in paintings on the ceilings of New Kingdom sarcophagus chambers. Suffice it to say here that the area of the Holy City given in Rev. 21:16 is in excellent agreement with what the ancient Egyptians probably believed for their celestial city; the height given in Revelation is reasonable from an Egyptian perspective.

Material Composition of the City (Rev. 21:18)

With respect to the material composition of the city, Rev. 21:18 describes it as being "pure gold." Gold, of course, is yellow, a color which had special mythological significance for the Egyptians. Wilkinson (1994) says color was considered to be

> virtually synonymous with "substance." In fact, the word *iwen* used to signify the concept of "color" in the Egyptian language can be translated as not only "external appearance," but also "nature," "being," "character," or even "disposition;" and the determinative used to write the word in the hieroglyphic script were either an animal pelt ⚵ or a lock of human hair ⚶ – showing the connection in the minds of the Egyptians between color and individual appearance and being.[1359]

With respect to the specific color, yellow, Wilkinson says,

> The color of the sun, yellow (and thus gold) was seen as symbolic of that which was eternal and imperishable. The flesh and bones of the gods were held to be of pure gold, and thus the yellow metal was the natural material for the construction of images of deities as much from a symbolic perspective as from considerations of the inherent worth of the precious substance. Two-dimensional representations of deities are also often given yellow skin tones to reflect the mythologically golden nature of their bodies.[1360]

Revelation's statement that "the city was pure gold" can thus be interpreted as being yellow in color in addition to its being made of gold. And just as the flesh and bones of the gods in general were considered to be made of gold, so too was that of the sky-goddess Nut. Indeed, when Nut was presented in color, as on the ceilings of some of the tombs in the Valley of the Kings, her flesh was painted yellow, the color of gold. But as pointed out above, Nut is the personification, not only of the sky, but of the celestial city of the ancient Egyptians. Since her body was visualized as being made of gold we may conclude Egypt's celestial city was also deemed to be made of gold. This, of course, conforms with the nature of the Holy City in Rev. 21:18.

But Rev. 21:18 also says the city was as "clear as glass." By this we may assume that the Holy City was transparent like glass. Transparency is, of course one of the most obvious attributes of the sky so that a reference to the celestial city being as "clear as glass" in this context is quite understandable.

The City's Walls and Gates (Rev. 21:12-14,16-21)

We are told in Rev. 21:12 that the Holy City is surrounded by "a great, high wall, with twelve gates, and at the gates twelve angels, and on the gates the names of the twelve tribes of the sons of Israel were inscribed." These and other attributes of the walls and gates will now be compared with traditional Egyptian beliefs.

Wall's Material and Foundation (Rev. 21:18-21)

Rev. 21:18 says that the wall surrounding the city is made of jasper while Rev. 21:19-20 says that its twelve foundations are beautified with every jewel: (1) jasper, (2) sapphire (3) agate, (4) emerald, (5) onyx, (6) carnelian, (7) chrysolite, (8) beryl, (9)

27. The Holy City

topaz, (10) chrysoprase, (11) jacinth and (12) amethyst. Such elaborately constructed and decorated city walls and foundations could not be found in the Egyptian religious literature. One possible secular parallel, however, may relate to the blaze of different colors which the wall of the city might be imagined to have in the array of bright colors displayed in the sky at dawn.

There is, however, an alternative Egyptian parallel for the jewels described in the walls of the Holy City – one which is not mutually exclusive to the sunset analogy. If the body of the sky-goddess when represented as the celestial city and her arms and legs acting as pillars on which it rested, then we may assume the part of the earth on which she rested represents the foundations. This possibility is of particular interest because it is in the ground and its rocks that we find precious stones in their natural state. We may therefore legitimately ask the question, "Is there is anything in the literature of ancient Egypt which might link the presence of jewels with that part of the earth believed to be physically connected to the celestial city?" The answer to this question is "Yes." It is in the vicinity of the most sacred area of the Nile River, *Abu* (known as Elephantine to the Greeks), and it was believed to contain many precious stones. We are therefore justified in closely examining this area.

The Egyptians believed it was in the vicinity of the first cataract near Abu (Elephantine) that the primordial waters of the Nile flowed up through two caverns from the Netherworld into this world; the area was therefore considered to be an important earthly boundary between the Netherworld, the earth and the sky. It would be here that the primordial river metaphorically flowed up to pass between the left and right representations of the body of the sky-goddess as painted on the ceilings of some sarcophagus chambers. We may therefore reasonably assume that the Egyptians believed the rocks in this area represented the very foundation of the sky and of the celestial city. And it is here we look for evidence of an abundance of precious stones.

With this in mind, we turn to an ancient Egyptian legend which refers to rich mineral deposits in this area. It is called, *The Legend of the God Khnemu and of a Seven Years' Famine*[1361] which tells of an Egyptian priest who journeys upstream on the Nile to the "city of Abu" to seek help; he is told of

> all things which men had written concerning it, and he [his guide] revealed to me the secret doors (?) whereto my ancestors had betaken themselves quickly, the like of which has never been to {any} king since the time of Rā(?). ... There is a city in the middle of the stream wherefrom Ḥāpi [the Nile god] maketh his appearance; "Abu" was its name in the beginning; it is the City of the Beginning.[1362]

While there he learns of three parts of the surrounding area which have many valuable stones, such as "iron ore, alabaster for statues ... antimony." One of the areas has what he describes as thirteen "precious stones." He lists them as follows: "gold, silver, copper, iron, lapis-lazuli, emerald, *Thehen* (crystal?), *Khenem* (Ruby), *Ḳāi, Mennu, Betḳā* (?), *Temi, Nà* (?)."[1363] It is possible to identify only one of these (emerald) with the list provided Rev. 21:19-20 although there may well be others; it is impossible to say with certainty because we lack reliable knowledge of the ancient Egyptian names for practically all of those provided in Revelation. The same may be said of the other two lists of seven stones provided in the legend, except possibly for Budge's "mother-of-emerald." For these reasons, it is impossible to say at this time if there is much agreement between the names of the precious stones listed in Rev. 21:19-20 and those listed in the Egyptian legend.

Nevertheless, this legend contains at least two parallels to Holy City in Revelation 21. The first is its basic association with the primordial river, the waters which parallel the river passing through the city. The second is found in the area associated with the point where a river emerges from below the earth (Abu) toward the sky; here, we find one of Nut's hands or a foot planted on the earth forming part of the foundation of the sky. And this area was said to contain many precious stones although the number of types of stones found is thirteen rather than twelve in Revelation 21; the difference here may or may not be significant.

It is entirely possible, of course, that with more complete knowledge of the precious stones mentioned in the two sources, agreement with the identity of all twelve might be found. Suffice it to say here, however, that parallels can be identified between the description of the foundation of Holy City described in Rev. 21:19-21 and the ancient mythology surrounding of Egypt's city of Abu.

Height of the Walls (Rev. 21:17)

Rev. 21:17 gives the height of the walls as "a hundred and forty-four cubits by a man's measure, that is, an angel's." Before discussing their height, it is important to note the reference to the standard of measurement used. The text refers to "a man's measure, that is, an angel's," a statement which implies the existence of more than one standard for the length of a cubit. Similarly, the existence of different standard lengths for the Egyptian cubit is well documented. The Egyptians recognized three standard cubits; two were used on earth, one being the common cubit of about 47 centimeters (18 inches) while the other was the royal cubit which measured about 57 centimeters (22 inches). The third standard cubit was the divine cubit used to measure things in the hereafter and for which we have no definite length. In the absence of the knowledge of which standard cubit was used in the Book of Revelation to define the height of the walls, the ambiguity of the description which equates the "man's measure" with that of "an angel's" does not enable us to grasp the actual height of the walls. If we assume that the divine cubit was reasonably close to the two known cubits, however, we may conclude that the wall was at roughly 65 to 80 meters high – higher than the Great Pyramid at Giza! Earthly walls of such great height were unknown in ancient times although such a height would be consistent with the gigantic sizes envisaged for things in the Egyptian afterlife (as discussed elsewhere). Suffice it to say here that the mere reference in Revelation to special measuring standards such as man's cubit and an angel's cubit parallels known ancient Egyptian uses of several measurement standards – in addition to the reference to the fantastic height of the city wall.

Function of the Walls

The walls of Revelation's Holy City kept out undesirable evils and maintained the city's purity. Rev. 21:27 says that "nothing unclean shall enter it" and Rev. 22:3 says that "There shall no more be anything accursed" inside it. This brings into focus the functional aspect of the gigantic height of the wall. Such high walls around earthly cities would, in reality, be impossible. In the Egyptian afterlife, however, both good and bad spirits were believed to be extraordinarily tall and Egyptian logic demanded an extraordinarily high wall surrounding their celestial city. A relevant sentiment is implied in the 169th Chapter of the *Book of the Dead* where promises are made to keep the deceased eternally separated from the evils believed to lurk outside the walls.

> Your soul is bound for the sky ... You shall go up to the sky, the cord shall be knotted for you in the presence of Re, you shall close the net in the river, you shall drink water from it, you shall walk on your feet, you shall not walk upside down. You shall ascend to those who are above the earth, *you shall not go out to those who are under* [outside] *the walls; your walls which belong to you, being what your city god made for you, will not be thrown down.'* [1364]

Rev. 22:3 also says that "the throne of God and of the Lamb shall be in it [the city], and his servants shall worship him." The wall of the Holy City thus forms the same basic function as that of an ancient, traditional temple wall. Egypt's temples were surrounded by walls to protect it and its occupants against outside evils. Wilkinson (1994) explains how their walls conformed with this need.

> From the time of the New Kingdom, the exterior walls of most Egyptian temples (including those of the pylon and first court) show scenes depicting the destruction of the enemies. Although these scenes may depict actual enemies, the motif is symbolic in that it represents the much broader chaos and disorder which threatened Egyptian society – and the balance of the very cosmos itself. The depicted destruction of these enemies is no mere military boasting, therefore, but the symbolic containment of chaos and the establishment of order and harmony, with the scenes creating by their very location a magical guarantee of security and calm for the gods's home which lay within their parameters. [1365]

Indeed, Egyptian texts flanking the doors and entrances to the central areas of temples required that those who entered "be purified four times." Wilkinson (1994) tells us that these notices "either served as a reminder that those who entered must be ritually purified or, since they already certainly were, perhaps magically conferred purification upon all who passed."[1366] It is obvious from the above that the walls of Egyptian temples served the same function as the walls of Revelation's Holy City.

Number and Form of its Gates (Rev. 21:12,21)

Twelve gates in the walls of the Holy City are described in Rev. 21:12. The *Book of Day* outlines events during the sun-god's journey through the sky which, like the *Amduat* and the *Book of Gates*, can be divided into twelve separate parts. These two books describe twelve "gates" through which the sun-god must pass on his nightly journey through the Netherworld. There is no such distinguishing term, however, for each of the divisions of the *Book of Day*. Indeed, only five of the divisions have names, and of these, four are called "Hours" while the other (the 6th Hour) is called a "Portal."[a] Egyptologists typically refer to each of the twelve divisions as Hours. It is possible that the name of the 6th division, "Portal who seizes" reflects an early time when more than one, or even all, of the divisions were called gates although the sometimes nebulous divisions within the *Book of Day* are by no means clear in drawings from the book examined here.

In spite of the absence of the explicit mention of "gates" in the *Books of the Heavens*, gates were certainly associated with Egypt's heavenly city. This belief was especially prominent in the Old Kingdom where we find several passages referring to them. Breasted (1912) refers to one group of texts which describes "A favorite means of ascension, of opening the sky-gates, of ferrying over, of purification and the like."[1367] Also, he quotes one of the *Pyramid Texts* which describes the deceased ascending to heaven: "Thou ascendest to thy mother Nut; she seizes thy arm. She gives to thee the way to the horizon, to the place where Re is. The double *doors of the sky*' are opened for thee, the double doors of Kebehu (the sky) are opened for thee."[1368] Such beliefs persisted on into later periods of Egypt's history, even though they are not mentioned in the *Book of Day*. This is obvious in several passages from the *Book of the Dead*. For example, in Chapter 68, the deceased says, "The *doors* of the sky are opened for me ..."[1369] And in Chapter 127 the deceased expresses the belief in the presence of gates in the sky in the same way as they exist in the Netherworld. He says, "Open for me *the gates of the sky*,' earth, and the Duat, for I am the soul of Osiris, and I am at peace thereby."[1370]

Egyptians thus imagined their celestial city (and the Netherworld in general) to have gates. In the *Book of Day* the twelve hours are depicted as twelve solar disks decorating the body of the sky-goddess Nut (the personification of the celestial city). The idea of twelve divisions in ancient Egypt's celestial city is thus entirely consistent with the number of gates in the walls of the Holy City in the Book of Revelation.

The form of each of the gates in Revelation's Holy City is especially relevant. We are told that "the twelve gates were twelve pearls, each of the gates made of a single pearl" (Rev. 21:12). We can assume from this that each gate was either round or spherical, either of which would be highly unusual for a gate leading into a city. From the point of view of the *Book of Day*, however, such a description is entirely understandable, as described above. The twelve "gates" in this book can be viewed as twelve circular solar-disks evenly spaced along Nut's body (see Figure 78), each disk representing the time and location of the sun-god as he traveled through the heavens. One can therefore readily imagine how such a picture of the solar disk shining in the heavens might be described as a pearl glistening brightly in the sky. Indeed, describing the solar disk as a sphere like a pearl be entirely consistent with some Egyptian portrayals of the disk in statues and statuettes. For example, some statuettes of Amen bear a solar disk with a convex surface like that of a pearl. Spherical

---

[a] Piankoff (1954, pp. 389-403) translates the five names as follows: 1st Hour, *She who lifts up;* 6th Hour, *Portal who seizes;* 10th Hour, *She who lights the sky;* 11th Hour, *Beautiful of Sight;* 12th Hour, *She who gives light in the Island of Life.*

representations of the solar disk in burnished metal figurines like this can thus be easily thought of as having the shape and glistening appearance of pearls. The appearance of the twelve solar disks in the *Books of the Heavens*, thus parallels the description of the twelve gates of Revelation's Holy City which says that each was "made of a single pearl" (Rev. 21:12).

There are, nevertheless, few if any distinct references to the gates of Egypt's heavenly city being called "pearls." One possibility, albeit remote, is based on phonetics. According to Budge (1920), the word *àri-t peḥui* (𓂝𓏏𓊪𓎛𓈊)[1371] means"fil de perles" in French and "a thread of pearls" or "a pearl necklace" in English, But note that *àri-t* is phonetically not very different from *ārit* which can mean a "door or a gate.[1372] Àri-t peḥui* could therefore be used as a pun for the word "pearl gate" or, as modern Christians might say, "pearly gate." Indeed, the row of twelve solar disks adorning Nut's body in Figure 78 is reminiscent of a row of pearls, and hence, "a pearl necklace." More research is needed on the origin and meaning of *àri-t peḥui* before anything definite can be said about this possible parallel.

In view of the identification of the 6th Hour with a "portal," (gate) the phonetic evidence linking pearls with gates – and to simplify our comparison of Revelation's Holy City with Egypt's celestial city – we will use the term "gates" rather than the traditional "hours" in the remainder of our comparisons of this aspect of the two sources.

Names of the Twelve Gates (Rev. 21:12)

Rev. 21:12 says that each of the twelve gates bore a name of one of the tribes of Israel. Given that the meanings of the names of most of the twelve tribes of Israel in Revelation parallel the names found in a group of twelve gods and twelve goddesses in the *Book of Gates* (see Chapter 6, *The Twelve Tribes of Israel*), it would not be surprising to find them applied to the twelve gates of Revelation's Holy City. Nevertheless, as discussed above, only five of the gates in Egypt's celestial city have names. And only one of these, that of the 1st Hour, *She who lifts up* (*cf.* Table 6.2) can be said to be conform with only one the names of the tribes: Gad.

Notwithstanding this discrepancy, the assignment of specific gates to individuals, or groups of individuals as we find in Revelation, would not be entirely foreign to ancient Egyptian thinking. As pointed out in the above quotation from the 169th Chapter of the *Book of the Dead*, the walls of the city were considered to belong to its residents. It says, "your walls which belong to you, being what your city god made for you, will not be thrown down."[1373] This is consistent with the idea that the walls of the Egyptian heavenly city were identified according to its inhabitants although there is little or no evidence that certain parts of the walls belonged to one or more family line as we read in Rev. 21:12. Nevertheless, these walls would almost certainly have gates and the reference to the walls being assigned to specific groups living in different parts of the city seems quite reasonable. This would parallel the assignment of particular gates to the twelve tribes of Israel in Revelation's Holy City.

The Angels at the Gates (Rev. 21:12)

Rev. 21:12 also describes an angel at each of the gates. As discussed in Chapter 4, *Other Characters in Revelation*, "angels" in the Book of Revelation may signify any of a broad range of "deities" depicted in the religious literature of the ancient Egyptians. Descriptions and pictures of the gates in the *Book of Gates* contain powerful, protective guardians typically depicted as intimidating serpents rearing up on their tails. These gates usually have five such guardians, one of which has a special status and is named separately from the others[a] and may thus parallel the single angel at each gate in Revelation.

As noted above, while the gates in the *Amduat* and the *Book of Gates*[b] had guardians, the *Book of Day* does not. If we were to assume that this part of the Book of Revelation is somehow linked to the Egyptian *Book of Day*, the resulting inconsistency with the Revelation account of the Holy City would suggest the author may indeed have identified the Egyptian sun disks with gates, gates which were typically guarded in Egypt's Tuat. Such extrapolation would be a reasonable assumption when one considers the other parallels with the walls and gates, as discussed above.

Location of the Twelve Gates (Rev. 21:13)

Rev. 21:13 says that three of the twelve gates were located in each of its four walls so that three pointed to the east, three to the north, three to the south, and three to the west. There does not seem to be any reference to a similar arrangement of gates in the Egyptian Netherworld or in the celestial sphere, although it is possible such a symmetrical arrangement might have been envisioned. One can easily understand how the deceased might have imagined the arrangement of the twelve gates in the walls of the heavenly city because, as noted in the 70th Chapter of the *Book of the Dead*, the deceased travels "around the sky on its four sides"[1374]

The River (Rev. 22:1-2)

An important Egyptian parallel in Revelation's Holy City is its "river of the water of life, bright as crystal, flowing from the throne of God and of the Lamb through the middle of the street of the city" (Rev. 22:1). We have already discussed this verse in Chapter 3, *The Preeminent Deities* where water is described as flowing from the throne of Osiris, water called the "Efflux of Osiris." We saw this in a picture from the 110th Chapter of the *Book of the Dead* (Figure 8) showing water flowing from the throne of Osiris in the Egyptian paradise, the Field of Offerings. It was also noted that

---

[a] The names of the special serpents at the gates of ten of the twelve gates in the *Book of Gates* are as follows: (gate #2) The Encircler, (3) Stinging One, (4) Flame Face, (6) He whose eye roves about, (7) Closed Eye, (8) Flame Face, (9) Horn of the Earth, (10) The Uniter, (11) The One of his discharge, and (12) The One of the Morning. The names of some of the other serpent guardians of the gates are as follows: (gate #2) He who swallows the sinful ones and He who laps blood, (3) Earthquake, Trembling of Earth and Stinging One, (4) The Swallower and The Near One, (5) True Heart and Mysterious Heart, (6) He who unites and He who stands, (7) The Lacking One and The Blind, (8) Overflow and Embracer, (9) He who encompasses the earth and He who supports the earth, (10) The Executioner and The Uncoverer, (11) The Knife and The Cutting One, and (12) The Flier and He of the Dawn. (from Piankoff, 1954)

[b] The *Book of Gates* provides elaborate pictures and names of each of the gates. For details, see Figures 34, 39, 42, 53, 54, 68 and 73 of Piankoff (1954).

in many versions of the throne scene in the *Book of the Dead* Osiris is seated on a body of water indicated by the ▭ hieroglyph (Figure 7). The association of water with the throne of Osiris is therefore well established conforms with the notion of a river flowing from the throne of God in Revelation. That the water is described as flowing from the throne of the Lamb in Revelation (= Egypt's young sun-god, Re; see Chapter 3, *The Preeminent Deities*) is consistent with the concept of the united form of Osiris and Re, i.e., Osiris-Re.

While the Nile River was viewed as the efflux of Osiris, it was also viewed as a part of the primordial waters which flowed through the Netherworld, the heavens, and hence, the celestial city. Rev. 22:1-2 places its river in the middle of the Holy City, a position in complete agreement with the location of the river of primordial water envisioned as flowing through the heavens, the embodiment of the sky-goddess. Its location is obvious in a painting of Nut on the ceiling of the sarcophagus chamber of the Tomb of Ramesses VI in the Valley of the Kings. In this case, it is shown flowing between the right and left halves (i.e., on the inside) of her body (see Figure 78).

Another parallel with the river in Revelation's Holy City may be found through a brief phonetic analysis of *Nut*, the name of the Egyptian sky-goddess. The phonetically similar word *nt* means "water;"[1375] *nu-t* can mean "a mass of water, lake, pool, stream, or canal";[1376] *nwyt* can mean "waters of a canal";[1377] and *Nu,* "the mass of water which existed in primeval times."[1378] Meanwhile, *Net* was "a form of the Nile god"[1379] and *Net Ásár* was the "stream of Osiris in the Tuat" while *Net-Rā* was "a river or canal in the tuat."[1380] Given this remarkable cluster of potential puns based on the name of the sky-goddess and the presence of other parallels to the Revelation's Holy City, and the obsession of ancient Egyptian priests with word play, it is not surprising to find, from an Egyptian perspective, emphasis on a river running through the Revelation's Holy City.

The Tree of Life (Rev. 22:2)

We are also told that "on either side of the river, the tree of life grew with its twelve kinds of fruit, yielding its fruit each month" (Rev. 22:2). Since the tree of life is described as being on both sides of the river we may assume that this statement refers to more than one tree – or more than one type of tree because these trees are described as bearing "twelve kinds of fruit." We may conclude that at least twelve types of trees contribute to the concept of the "tree of life." We find a reasonably accurate parallel to this scene in the *Book of Day* where it shows the "Yaru Fields of the Blessed" on the banks of the primordial river which runs through Nut's body (Figure 130). Here, between the blessed dead and the river lies a long row of plants, nineteen trees to the left and nineteen heads of grain (barley and wheat) to the right. The entire scene is framed by a *ḏw* hieroglyph, ⌒, meaning "mountain," suggesting a river flowing through a valley, as implied in the scene in Rev. 22:2.

Deities are present on either side of the central part of the Yaru Fields in Figure 130. Central columns of text contain the names of these deities and vertically split the scene, suggesting a mechanism whereby the picture of the Yaru Fields can interpreted as showing its contents as being distributed along *both* sides of the river: the scene may be folded upon itself so that the celestial river is viewed as flowing through the center of the fields, as shown graphically in Figure 131. This interpretation of the

Figure 129. The Yaru Fields in the *Book of Day*. These fields are situated beside the primordial river which flows through the body of Nut (the sky). The solar barque in which the sun-god stands in his shrine is moored at the Yaru Fields while the residents of the field worship different aspects of his being. And like Rev. 21:3, the dwelling place of Osiris (Revelation's God) is nearby.

Figure 130. The picture of the Yaru Fields from another version of the *Book of Day* showing its appearance when folded to represent fields spread across both sides of the primordial river.

figure clearly demonstrates how each of the major elements, the central river, the rows of plants and the blessed dead on each side can be visualized as an excellent parallel to the scene described in Rev. 22:2.

The latter part of Rev. 22:2 says that "the leaves of the tree were for the healing of the nations." A parallel to this statement may be found through a more thorough examination of some of the pictorial versions of the Yaru Fields; some contain possible references to healing or medicine. For example, in Figure 131 there are nine ● symbols (●●●●●●●●●) on top of a ⌣ symbol. The ⌣ hieroglyph represents a "wickerwork basket"[1381] so we may assume that the ●●●●●●●●● symbols on top of it represent it contents. Gardiner (1927) tells us that the ● symbol represents a "grain of sand, pellet or the like"[1382] while Budge (1920) suggests it means "grain or powder."[1383] In the context of the rows of grain growing along the riverbank, we may interpret the combination of the ⌣ and ●●●●●●●●● symbols as meaning a basket full of grain, or in more general terms, food. This interpretation conforms with Rev. 22:2 where we read of the "tree of life with its twelve kinds of fruit," especially if we interpret the twelve kinds of fruits to represent (as the Egyptians would), many multitudes (recall: 3 x 4 is equivalent to many multitudes) of food types. But Rev. 22:2 also suggests another parallel involving the ● symbol; it relates to the last part of the verse which refers to the "leaves of the trees ... for the *healing* the nations." Not only is ● used as a determinant in *š ay,* the word for "sand," it is also used as a determinant in *msdmt,* the word for "medicaments," and in *ph̭rt,* the word for medicine or prescription.[1384] A scribe knowledgeable about Egyptian religious texts might well interpret this picture as showing, not only a basket full of food, but of medicinal plants as well – or even a basket of medicinal plants for healing the sick, as in Rev. 22:2.

Light in the City (Rev. 21:11,23; Rev. 22:5)

The Holy City is said to be illuminated by the "glory of God, its radiance like a most rare jewel, like a jasper, clear as crystal" (Rev. 21:11). If the Holy City of Revelation parallels the sky personified by the sky-goddess, we may consider this statement as meaning that it is the *sky* which is illuminated by the glory of God. And since, as also pointed out above, God in this part of Revelation can be seen to represent the newly born sun-god (i.e., the juvenile form of the ram-headed Re, a lamb), Revelation's Lamb. We may therefore suggest that from an Egyptian perspective, Rev. 21:11 describes the *sky* being illuminated by the light from the young sun-god, Re (and/or Osiris-Re). This theme parallels Rev. 21:23 and Rev. 22:5 which says that, "the glory of God [Osiris] is its light, and its lamp is the Lamb [Re]," or in Egyptian terms, "the glory of Osiris-Re is its light." The reference to the city being like a jewel, and its appearance as transparent, gold-colored glass (Rev. 21:11) is consistent with the dramatic, ever-shifting colors of the sky as the sun rises from below the horizon to its full glory in the morning sky. And just as sky is illuminated by the sun, the body of Nut is clothed with twelve solar disks so that *Nut*, Egypt's celestial city, is illuminated by the light of the sun-god throughout the day.

City's Temple is God (Rev. 21:22)

Rev. 21:22 makes a rather unusual statement. It says, "And I saw no temple in the city, for its temple is the Lord God the Almighty and the Lamb." (= the unified form of Osiris and Re, Osiris-Re). We might legitimately ask, "How could a temple *be* a god?" The answer to this question may be found in an equally peculiar belief of the ancient Egyptians pertaining to their temples. Hornung (1992) explains it this way:

> The Egyptians undoubtedly viewed not only religious images but the entire temple building as a physical body that could unite with the psychic *ba* of the god, just as each night the *ba* united with its real body in the underworld. Especially in the Ramesside Period we find temples personified as divine creatures with human forms. The Corporeality of the temple is emphasized by the use of gold, bronze, and semi-precious stones such as are recorded in the building inscriptions of Amenophis III.[1385]

Thus, a building can not only *be a temple* within which to worship a god such as Osiris or Re, but it can actually *be that god*. In this sense, the reference in Rev. 21:22 that the city's "temple is ... God and the Lamb" parallels Egyptian beliefs. Since Revelation's God on the throne parallels Osiris, who can also be represented by the unified god, Osiris-Re, the complete parallel to Rev. 21:22 is apparent: "its temple is the Lord God the Almighty [i.e., Osiris] ... and the Lamb [i.e., the juvenile form of Re]. In this case, God and the Lamb are referred to together as if they represented Egypt's "Osiris-Re" so that it might equally read, "its 'temple' is Osiris-Re, and Osiris-Re is the 'temple.'"

We should also consider that the absence of a temple in Revelation's Holy City also conforms with pictures of the Egyptian lands of the blessed. Although almost all show the blessed dead worshiping before altars, none show temples.

The Dwelling Place of God (Rev. 21:3)

In the last chapter, we showed how Rev. 21:3 could be looked upon from the point of view of the Holy City representing earth's sky in which the sun-god dwelled: "Behold, the dwelling of God is with men."

An equally valid interpretation of the same verse conforms with the almost universal belief that temples were the dwelling places of the gods. Hornung (1990) points out that the Egyptian word for "temple" meant literally "god's house."[1386] David (1980) says that "The cultus temple was designed to house the statue of the god, as the earliest shrines had done, and to provide a center where worship rituals could be carried out."[1387] Also, "All temples shared a common role: each was a place of sanctity and rest for the resident deity, a place where the god's cult-statue could receive attention from his priest and where the divinity could be approached by man, through the person of the king."[1388] A small, portable statue of the chief god of the temple was placed in the inner sanctuary, a small, dark rectangular room on the main axis of the temple near the rear. Each of the sun-god's temples was believed to be the very dwelling place of Re while the most sacred part of the temple, the holy of holies, was his resting place. Thus, the idea that a representation of a god in a temple is synonymous with his presence parallels Revelation's statement that "the dwelling of God [in the broadest sense, the heavens] is with men"

Discussion

An interesting aspect of Revelation's Holy City is its close association with creation; the announcement of its "coming down out of heaven" in Rev. 21:1 immediately follows the reference to the creation of a new heaven and new earth and can therefore be readily identified as an integral part of this creation. In the last chapter, we concluded that Rev. 21:1-9 parallels Egypt's creation of a new heaven and a new earth, as presented in the last two divisions of the *Book of Gates*. A part of Egypt's new creation was the sky-goddess Nut shown in the *Book of Gates* (Figure 127) standing on the head of Osiris while she greets Re as he emerges from the primordial waters. In this chapter, Nut was further identified with the personification of the sky, the location of Egypt's heavenly abode (*nut*) of the blessed dead.[a] Physical aspects of the Holy City given in Rev. 21:10-22:5 were readily identifiable with the attributes of the great celestial city of the Egyptians. The most notable parallels were the city's brightness, its twelve pearl-like gates, it shape and size, its high walls and the presence of precious stones in their foundations, and the element of purity required of

---

[a] This aspect of Nut was well established in the Old Kingdom but in later dynasties was combined with the Underworld to become, conceptually at least, one with the Netherworld, i.e., the Tuat. In those latter times, references to the early concept were frequently mixed with those of earlier times.

all who entered it. Finally, and in agreement with Egyptian beliefs that earthly temples to their gods can be described as a manifestation of God himself.

The explicit reference to the temple in Rev. 21:22 is accompanied by several other allusions to temples in Rev. 21-22. For example, Rev. 21:15 relates an event which at first glance seems a little strange. The author of Revelation is given "a measuring rod of gold to measure the city and its gates and walls." Since each of the four walls measured 12,000 stadia in length, the circumference of the city would be 48,000 stadia, or 8,880 kilometers (5506 miles), this task would take many months to accomplish on foot and is therefore an impractical task, especially in light of the sense of immediacy apparent in the scene. We may therefore conclude that this measuring of the city was a symbolic event which was very likely a part of a ceremony.

Ceremonies involving the measurement of the distance around cities were rare, especially when one realizes that not all towns and cities were surrounded by well defined borders or walls and there appears to be no such ceremonies documented in the main-stream religious literature of ancient Egypt. This was not so for temples, however; ceremonies involving the measuring of temples were commonplace and especially important at the start of construction activities. According to Lurker (1980), the goddess who presided over these ceremonies was Seshat (Figure 125), the goddess of writing who was venerated under the epithet "she who is foremost in the house of books," i.e., the temple. "On the founding of a temple either she or her priest established the ground-plan with a measuring cord, hence she was also the 'lady of builders.'"[1389] Also, Wilkinson (1994) informs us that "Representations show the king involved in a foundation ritual known as 'stretching the cord' which probably took place before work began on the construction of a temple or of any addition."[1390] This ceremony was often later repeated during special events to commemorate the completion of a temple. The ceremony of the measuring of the Holy City in Rev. 21:15 parallels the Egyptian ceremony of measuring the temple, especially since the city in Revelation was itself considered to be a temple in which God dwelled.

If the celestial city itself could be described as a temple, it follows that temples on earth could be viewed as representing the celestial realm, including the heavenly abode. In discussing the cosmological symbolism of the Egyptian temple, Hornung (1992) says that "By ceremonially establishing a temple the Egyptians reenacted creation."[1391] Elsewhere, he expands on this idea:

> The Egyptians celebrated the renewal of creation in a particularly ceremonious way when they founded a new temple. In their eyes, such an event brought an entire cosmos into being and established a new residence for the gods on earth. Whether in the daily sunrise or in the pharaoh's deeds, at the beginning of a new year or a new king's reign, the Egyptians felt the breath of the creator god upon them and experienced the living renewal of his work; hence their confidence to make pronouncements about the beginning of the world.[1392]

The founding of a new temple was thus closely linked to the idea of a new creation, or as Rev. 21:1 puts it, the arrival of "a new heaven and a new earth." But this was not only symbolic of the "first beginning" to the Egyptians, it was also symbolic in the daily renewal of the cosmos as graphically shown in the last Division of the *Book of Gates* and discussed in the previous chapter.

Another aspect of Revelation's Holy City which is reminiscent of Egyptian temples is the reference to the construction material and its decorations and the magic associated with them. Rev. 21:18 purposely brings our attention to a difference between the building material of the walls and the rest of the temple; it says that, "The wall was built of jasper, while the city was pure gold." Of course neither the surrounding walls nor the inner walls of Egyptian temples were made of such precious materials – but, like those in Revelation, they were made of two different kinds of material. Wilkinson (1994) brings our attention to this aspect of the Egyptian temple. He says that, "The developed, axial temple consisted of an encircling *temenos* or precinct wall of mud brick, within which was situated the temple proper, of stone."[1393]

Hornung (1992) says that, "the Egyptians believed that helpful, healing powers were at work even in ordinary stone."[1394] In discussing the main gate, or pylon, of the temple and its external walls, he adds that, "On both the pylon and the external walls of the temple, *the decoration*' served an exclusively apotropaic function, that is, it was designed to ward off evil and in particular to frighten enemy forces away from the temple area."[1395] Both Revelation and Egyptian traditions therefore distinguish between the material composition of the inner and outer walls of the temple; in Revelation, the city itself is the temple and the walls of the temple/city are decorated with precious stones. Thus, at least some of the Egyptian traditions concerning the functions of the different decorations and structures of the city conform with Rev. 21.

It is apparent from the above discussion that the Holy City of Rev. 21-22 is a metaphor for a temple. This is especially evident in its designation as a dwelling place of God, its overall shape and geographic orientation, the need for some light inside its dark interior, and the construction of its protective walls and gates which restricted entry to only the righteous. We also find another important attribute of Egyptian temples here: the water of life, either real or symbolic, which flows through it. In Revelation, it is described as the "river of the water of life" while in the *Books of the Heavens* it is the primordial river, in the *Book of the Dead*, the "efflux of Osiris," and in the temples of earthly Egypt it was represented by either the (primordial) groundwater from underneath the temples or the flow of water from the annual flooding of the Nile between their pillars and through doorways. It is evident that, in addition to its design, the Holy City of Revelation may be viewed from an Egyptian perspective as a great celestial temple – as well as a celestial city in which the blessed dead lived.

PART V. CONSPECTUS

As pointed out at the beginning of this work, of all the books of the New Testament, the Book of Revelation has been the most controversial, especially with respect to the meanings embodied in its complex symbolism and the long delay before it was finally accepted as a genuine Christian document by all the churches. It seems that a significant part of the reason for much of this controversy was the scarcity or absence of non-Christian documents which might be used to provide alternative interpretations to its symbolism, structure, and extraordinary imagery. This situation, along with Revelation's many apparent allusions to events described in the Old Testament – and some in the New Testament – led early church leaders to conclude that the book was primarily, or even completely, of Judaeo-Christian origin. Through the centuries, numerous searches for unambiguous Christian and Jewish explanations for many of the enigmatic images in the book have been fruitless and many different interpretations have been proposed by both eminent Christian scholars, church leaders and laymen. Meanwhile, Revelation's references to Jesus Christ, the Lamb, the twelve tribes of Israel, the New Jerusalem, Satan and the judgment have cemented the idea of a Christian origin of the book into the very fabric of modern Christianity.

Some of the images which remained unexplained in either Jewish or Christian contexts include the story of the great harlot and the kings (Rev. 17), parts of the chapter on the woman in the sky (Rev. 12), the four horsemen of the apocalypse (Rev. 6), many of the unusual apocalyptic events, and a multitude of less prominent texts and images. The absence of comparable events in the Judeo-Christian literature has contributed to the wide range of diverging interpretations of practically all its scenes and imagery. This study, however, has critically examined the Book of Revelation from a purely Egyptian perspective and the results have been enlightening: the Book of Revelation contains at least as many parallels with Egyptian texts and beliefs as with texts of known Christian origin. Indeed, it may even be soundly argued that there are many, many more parallels in ancient Egyptian literature than in Christian literature. Some the most notable similarities involve readily identifiable sequences of scene elements, scenes and sequences of scenes – features not found in either Judaic or Christian sources.

The approach taken to identify the Egyptian parallels in the Book of Revelation was, generally, to first compare and identify the main characters in Revelation with prominent Egyptian gods and then identify parallel scenes, many of which contained references to the same characters identified earlier. Finally, parallel sequences (and sub-sequences) in which the characters and the scenes appeared in both sources were compared. Observations and conclusions in these areas were at times supported by brief studies based primarily on the likely use of Egyptian homophones and puns in the selection of words used to describe characters, scenes and events; these studies frequently strengthened conclusions based on other criteria. It became readily apparent that, while the *Amduat* and the *Book of Gates* followed sequences of the scenes similar to those found in Revelation, scenes and sequences from other books, such as the *Books of the Heavens*, the *Book of Aker*, the *Book of the Dead*, and other mainstream Egyptian religious and secular texts could also be identified within these sequences. As a result, and from an Egyptian perspective, many of the previously enigmatic characters, images, scenes, sequences of scenes and symbolism in the Book of Revelation took on clear, understandable and at times rather simple meanings.

Part V provides summaries and commentaries on Egyptian parallels involving the more prominent characters, scenes, events, and sequences of scenes and events in the Book of Revelation. To this is added a brief literary analysis of the book and finally, some general comments on this research and its possible value in further studies on the Book of Revelation and the study of the religion and history of the ancient Egypt.

Chapter 28
Egyptian Deities in the Book of Revelation

Parallels to least eighteen important deities in the Egyptian pantheon were found in the Book of Revelation (Figure 132 and Figure 133). Since, with the exception of Satan, Christ and the Amen, none of the deities are specifically named in Revelation, their Egyptian parallels were deduced from their physical attributes, activities and contexts within scenes and series of scenes. This absence of names is in itself consistent with ancient Egyptian traditions in which the most important names of powerful deities were not spoken except in special circumstances, and then only by priests; the names of some were known only by the highest priests. In a general sense, parallels to angels in the Book of Revelation could be identified by their actions or physical characteristics in comparison with particular deities in the Egyptian pantheon. These parallels are listed in summary form in Table 28.1 and Table 28.2. Finally, Table 28.3 provides the reader with a brief comparison of the current results with those of Massey (1907), a work introduced in Chapter2, *New Approaches* where it was identified as the only previous study to attempt a broad, in-depth comparison of the Book of Revelation with the religious beliefs and gods of the ancient Egyptians.

A few brief comments will refresh the reader's memory on some of the more notable parallels. The first and most striking scene found in the Book of Revelation which parallels ancient Egyptian beliefs is the throne scene described mainly in Rev. 1 and Rev. 4. We find this dramatic and all-inclusive parallel in Chapter 30B of the *Book of the Dead*. Both sources describe a deity sitting on a throne surrounded by many followers. In the *Book of the Dead*, the scene is described in text and pictures showing an enthroned Osiris who passes judgment on his followers and enemies by rewarding the faithful and punishing his enemies. The physical description of Osiris conforms quite well with that of Revelation's "God on the throne" described in Rev. 1:13-14, especially in regard to the collar which covers his chest, a long white robe reaching to his feet, eyes like fire, and a white crown upon his head; and, just as God on the throne is described in Rev 1:4 as having seven spirits, Osiris also has seven spirits. The reference to a "sharp two-edged sword" which issues from the mouth of God in

Rev. 1:16 is of particular interest from an Egyptological point of view because it parallels the hieroglyph showing a picture of a person pointing to his mouth and kneeling next to a hieroglyphic symbol of a weapon resembling a two-edged sword – a determinative for the word, "word."

The slain "Lamb of God" described in Rev. 5:6 is similar to the juvenile form of the ram-headed form of the sun-god, Re, including Re's slain body (the equivalent of Revelation's slain lamb) portrayed and described in the 6th Division of the *Amduat*. The same division also contains a picture of the "Lion of Re" which parallels the Lion of Judah in Rev. 5:5. Furthermore, other contexts of references to the Lamb in Revelation are similar to the contexts of references to the sun-god Re in Egyptian texts such as the *Amduat* and the *Book of Gates*. And references to "God and the Lamb" conform with scenes involving Osiris-Re, *the united one*, a transitory, but important deity formed by the intermingling of Osiris and Re at dawn.[a]

Revelation's Christ, in an Egyptian context, has been shown to be a descriptive term ("the anointed one") rather than a name *per se*; Jesus, the other part of the name in some verses of Revelation, was considered from an Egyptian perspective as being a corruption of the original text by Christian redactors (less convincingly, it was also viewed as a close homonym for an Egyptian name for Horus, king of Egypt). Meanwhile, the description of events involving the "Christ" in Revelation conforms quite well with those of Egypt's Horus, "the anointed one," the Son of the sun-god. Closely related is another deity whose name is only rarely mentioned in Revelation. He is called "The Word of God" and he leads the armies of God in a heavenly war against the forces of evil (Rev. 19:13-15). Both Thoth and Horus are both close parallels to Christ although, in this particular case, Horus is marginally closer.

Parallels to other deities in the Egyptian texts include Revelation's "Amen" (Rev. 3:14) who parallels the primeval god, Amen, "the hidden one," also known as Amen-Re. Also, the "mighty angel" who comes down from heaven and presents the little scroll to Revelation's author in Rev. 10 parallels the mortuary god, Sokaris while the scroll he carries tells the story of the two witnesses in Rev. 11 which contains events paralleling a remarkable series of events in the *Book of Aker*, an Egyptian earth god. Finally, the woman which appears in heaven in Rev. 12 is a close parallel to Nut, the sky-goddess whose story is told in the Egyptian *Books of the Heavens*, a story whose sequence of events conforms with that in Revelation.

Among the "evil" deities of the Egyptian pantheon, Apophis, the preeminent Egyptian god of evil and chaos, parallels Revelation's Devil, Satan and ancient serpent. Also, Revelation's two beasts, the image of the beast, the false prophet and their activities all parallel the various characters and events described in the *Amduat*. The 1st beast of Rev. 13 was found to parallel the evil god Seth while the 2nd beast and the false prophet are recognizable as Horus-Seth, the dual god of good and evil. Also, Revelation's "image of the beast" parallels the "the image of Seth" in the *Amduat*.

---

[a] The importance of this deity (Osiris-Re) is accentuated by the fact that a major book on the subject was published in 2004 by Egyptologist John Darnell entitled, *The Enigmatic Netherworld Books of the Solar-Osirian Unity*. Also, see discussions on this topic in Clagett (1989) and Horning (1990).

28. Egyptian Deities in Revelation

The great harlot who is full of blasphemous names and associated with seven and ten kings in Rev. 17 was found to be similar to the Egyptian goddess, Sheshes and the Syro-Palestinian goddess Anat-Astarte, a goddess worshiped by the Hyksos in the Egyptian Delta during the 2nd Intermediate Period; she personified Avaris, the chief city of the Hyksos invaders in Lower Egypt during that Period.

In addition to the above characters the Book of Revelation contains references to several *groups* of deities (Table 28.2). And like the individual deities which paralleled those in Egyptian texts, these groups were shown to have attributes similar to groups of deities in the Egyptian texts; they generally fall into four size categories – four, seven, twelve and twenty-four. The first category includes the four creatures in Rev. 4:7 who bear the heads of a lion, an ox, a man and an eagle; these parallel the four deities usually associated with the throne of Osiris where they are referred to as the "four sons of Osiris." Also, the description of their wings and numerous eyes conform with descriptions of Egyptian "All-Gods." In the second category, the "seven spirits of God" in Revelation corresponded with the "seven spirits of Osiris," or of Re; their physical descriptions and functions are similar in Revelation and Egyptian sources. The twelve tribes of Israel were readily identified with many groups of twelve faithful followers of the sun-god depicted throughout the *Book of Gates* and, to a lesser degree, the *Amduat*. Sometimes, the attributes of two adjacent groups of twelve corresponded with the twenty-four elders described in various locations in the Book of Revelation as bowing their heads to the ground before the throne of God. And finally, the great multitudes of angels in Revelation were observed to have attributes similar to those of the great multitudes of deities found in the *Book of the Dead*, the *Amduat*, and the *Book of Gates* who were usually associated with either Re or Osiris or both.

This chapter would be incomplete without some comparison of the parallels drawn here with those inferred by Massey (1907). As mentioned in Chapter 1, *The Enigmatic Book of Revelation*, Massey suggests parallel identities to several characters in the Book of Revelation although it is difficult to follow his logic for some of his conclusions. Also, he does not give details on how the various characters conform with events in Revelation's many scenes. Nor does he follow Revelation's characters through any sequences of parallel Egyptian scenes with those of characters and scenes and sequences of scenes found in the Book of Revelation. Table 28.3 provides a concise comparison of the identification of characters made by Massey with parallels found in this study. It is obvious from this table that none of Massey's parallels agree completely with those found in this study. There is, however, partial agreement between the parallels for Christ, the woman in the sky and the Bride of the Lamb (the goddess Hathor was in very ancient times a sky-goddess). Unfortunately Massey's literary style, current difficulties in accessing published literature to which he makes reference, and a wide variety of now obsolete names of deities does not readily lend his work to a critical comparisons with the results of this study.

Figure 131. Egyptian deities with attributes similar to characters portrayed in the Book of Revelation (see also Figure 133). These parallels are based on comparisons of the physical characteristics, activities or functions and the order of their appearance in sequences of events in the Book of Revelation. They appear primarily in the *Book of the Dead*, the *Amduat* and the *Book of Gates*. Egyptian names are given at the top of each frame while relevant names in Revelation are located at the bottom. The reason for uncertainty of the parallel between Horus and Revelation's "Word of God" is given in Chapter 5, *The Word of God*.

28. Egyptian Deities in Revelation 551

Figure 132. More Egyptian deities portrayed in the Book of Revelation (see also Figure 132).

Table 28.1 Names of characters or deities in the Book of Revelation and their Egyptian parallels. References to Revelation and Egyptian sources are representative examples.

Name in Book of Revelation	Verse(s)	Egyptian Equivalent	Egypt. Source	Comment
God (on the throne)	Rev. 4	Osiris	BD30B	God of the Netherworld
Lamb in midst of throne	Rev. 7:17	Re	AM11.2.2-3	Egyptian sun-god in shrine
Lamb which was slain	Rev. 5:6,12	Re	AM6.2.9-10	The body of dead sun-god
God and the Lamb	Rev. 21:1,3	Osiris-Re	Litany of Re	"The Unified One"
Christ	Rev. 1:5	Horus	many sources	Son of Osiris and/or Re, Pharaoh, "the anointed one," ruler of earth
Lion of Judah	Rev. 5:5	Lion of Re	AM6.1.6-7	Corrupted name of the sun-god
Word of God	Rev. 19:13	Thoth/Horus	BD18	Leader of the army of God (context sensitive)
Angel holding the little scroll	Rev. 10:1-6	Sokar	AM5	Arch over head of Sokaris in AM5, face like sun, legs of fire; Sokaris holds *Book of Aker* in hands
Woman in heaven/sky	Rev. 12	Nut	Books of Night and Day	Sky-goddess
Child of woman	Rev. 12	Re		Newly born sun-god
Satan, Devil, the ancient Serpent	Rev. 12:2-3	Apophis	many sources	Primeval serpent, god of evil
1st Beast	Rev. 13:1-8	Seth	AM4.3.1-2	Beast from the sea, "666"
2nd Beast, False Prophet	Rev. 13:14-15	Horus-Seth	AM4.1.6	"His Two Faces," good and evil; illegitimate king of Egypt
The Great Harlot	Rev. 17:1-6,18	Iai and Sheshes	BG9.3.8-10	Characteristics Similar to Syro-Palastinian goddess Anat-Astarte and Babylon's, Istar

Table 28.2 Names of groups of beings in the Book of Revelation and their Egyptian parallels. References to Revelation and Egyptian sources are representative examples.

Name of Group in Book of Revelation	Verse(s)	Egyptian Equivalent	Egypt. Source	Comment
4 creatures before throne	Rev. 4:6-9	4 sons of Osiris; Egyptian All-Gods	BD30B	Belong to the seven spirits of Osiris (BD17); have many characteristics of Egyptian "All-Gods."
7 Spirits of God	Rev. 1:12-20	7 Spirits of Osiris	BD17	Includes the 4 sons of Osiris; "Those who put terror into the doers of wrong" (BD17)
12 tribes of Israel	Rev. 7:4-8	groups of 12 faithful	AM7.3.1-9	Meanings of names of individuals in both groups agree.
24 elders	Rev. 4:4	groups of 9, 12, or 24 assessors	AM9.1&3.1-6	Also found in other sources, such as BD30b
The Multitudes	Rev. 7:9-17	Blessed dead	AM9.1.1-5 BD130	Similar characteristics in both Revelation and Egyptian sources

Table 28.3 Comparison between parallel characters by Massey (1907) and those found in this study. Note that none of the parallels in the two works are in complete agreement with one another. This study identifies at least eighteen deities or groups of deities (see Figure 132 and Figure 133); Massey identifies only nine deities, at least one (Nut) of which, according to this study (*cf.* Table 23.1), possibly agree. (Page numbers for references to Massey's parallels are based on his original 1904 publication.)

Passage in Revelation	Character in Revelation	Massey (1907) Egyptian Parallel	This Study Egyptian Parallel
Rev. 4:2-3	God the Father	Atum (p. 717), Horus as the Human form of his father, Osiris (p. 723)	Osiris
Rev. 5:5	Christ, Jesus	Osiris, Horus (971), Sebek (p. 723)	Horus (only)
Rev. 5:6	The Lamb, Jesus	Horus (pp. 716, 718, 723)	Re, especially his juvenile form
Rev. 12:1-2	Woman in the sky	Apt, Hathor (p. 715)	Nut
Rev. 12:7	Michael	Atum-Huhi in the person of Horus (p. 711)	Horus and/or Thoth
Rev. 12:9	Satan, Dragon	Apophis, Sut/Seth (p. 712)	Apophis
Rev. 19:13	The Word of God	John, the author (p. 691)	Thoth, Horus
Rev. 20:1-2	Angel with chain	Aker (p. 713)	Selkit
Rev. 21:2	Bride	Hathor (pp. 717, 721)	Nut

Chapter 29. Parallel Series of Scenes

The previous chapter outlined Egyptian parallels to characters and groups of characters found in the Book of Revelation. An important aspect of many of these characters is that they frequently appear in similar sequences of scenes in both sources. These types of parallels are themselves enhanced by their relative positions within even longer series. In this chapter, relatively long sequences of scenes in the *Amduat Series* and the *Book of Gates Series* will be examined to determine how well their overall position and organization in the Book of Revelation corresponds to that of a single Egyptian source, a tomb in the Valley of the Kings.

We first focus on the arrangement of the best and most prominent parallels, an approach involving a procedure which requires at least a crude rating system to ensure inclusion of the most relevant and important scenes. We begin by dividing parallel scenes into two general categories, those which contain a grouping of predominantly commonplace elements and those which contain peculiar elements; the latter requires some explanation. Similar scenes with peculiar elements in both Revelation and Egyptian sources are by far the most reliable indication of parallels. For example, water which quenches thirst would be normal but water from a lake of fire would be peculiar. We also include unusually large clusters of similar elements or unusually long parallel series of parallel elements. Scenes with an abundance of parallel elements or containing peculiar elements are classified as *landmark scenes*. A detailed account of all categories of parallel scenes is given in Appendix 5 while a brief listing of the more notable ones is presented in Table 29.1.

The sequence of landmark scenes in the *Book of Gates* is shown in Table 29.1, follow the same direction and order as in the Book of Revelation. The situation with the *Amduat* is a little different and an understanding of it is best approached from the point of view of the longer listing in Appendix 5; they can be divided into two groups with decidedly different directions. As in the *Book of Gates*, the direction and order of scenes in the first group (Divisions 6 through 11) coincides with the sequence of similar scenes in Revelation, except for one – that which corresponds to the tribes of Israel in Rev. 7:4-8, which is only slightly out of place. In the second group (Divisions 2 through 5), however, scenes flow in the direction opposite to those in Revelation; instead of flowing from the 2nd to 5th Divisions, they flow from the 5th to the 2nd, i.e., the flow is *reversed* in the Book of Revelation.

Table 29.1 Comparison of the order of the landmark scenes in the *Amduat* and the *Book of Gates* Series with their counterparts in the Book of Revelation. A more inclusive distribution of parallels in the two series is presented in Appendix 5.

The Amduat Series			The Book of Gates		
Rev.	Parallel scene	Div.	Rev.	Parallel scene	Div.
5:1-7	Opening of the scroll	6	15:2-4	12 by lake of fire	2
5:6-9	The slain lamb	6	16:12-14	River dries up	3
6:9-11	Cries of the slain	8	17:1-9	The harlot	9
7:4-8	Tribes of Israel	7	17:10-18	Rise & fall of kings	9
7:9-10	Many with palm branches	9	20:1-4	Capture of Satan	10
7:15	The sheltered ones	11	20:7-10	Gog and Magog	10
			20:10	Recapture of Satan	11
----	--------------	-----			
10:1-3	The little scroll	5	21:1-8	A new creation	11-12
13	1st and 2nd beasts, 666	4	21:2,9-10	City as a bride	11-12
13:7-8	Names in Book of Life	4			
14:14-18	Harvest time	2			

This reversal naturally leads to a line of questions: How and why, if the Book of Revelation is so similar in so many ways to the Egyptian sources, such an anomaly might occur only in the *Amduat Series*? Was the mix-up brought about by scribal error? Or was it a deliberate rearrangement of the text of Revelation to fit some notion of legitimacy? Or was it because the particular version of the *Amduat* used as the basis for the writing of this part of Revelation was corrupt? Or maybe the author worked with a source which for some reason had been organized differently from standard versions. A possible solution to the reversal will be addressed next.

We begin with a simple, apparently unrelated observation on the landmark scene which deals with the holding back of the four winds in Rev. 7:1-3 and its Egyptian parallel, the *Schutzbild* scene (Figure 55) discussed in Chapter 11, *Prelude to War*. It so happens that the only extant copy of this particular scene is found in the tomb of Ramesses VI in the Valley of the kings. This tomb is also unusual because it contains on its walls and ceilings almost complete copies of most of the main Egyptian texts dealt with in this study. We may therefore hypothesize (for the moment) that the Book of Revelation was based at least in part on text and paintings found in the Tomb of Ramesses VI. A closer look at this particular tomb the is therefore warranted.

Figure 134 shows the layout of the tomb and groups of scenes which parallel those described in the Book of Revelation. To compare the relative arrangements of the various scenes in the two sources we first examine the general floor plan and the locations of the most prominent blocks of parallel texts and scenes. We note that the arrangement of practically all the tomb's parallels conform with that of similar scenes in the Book of Revelation. This includes not only the general sequential arrangement of scenes belonging to both the *Amduat* and *Book of Gates Series*, but also those found in the *Book of Aker* and the *Books of the Heavens*. Indeed, we may say that the overall similarity of the arrangements of these parallels in the two sources conform with the hypothesis that this tomb is the likely original source of most of the Book of Revelation.

Before addressing the specifics of the reversal of parallel scenes found in the *Amduat*, however, we should first take note of the details of the *Amduat's* organization and location in the tomb. We find the *Amduat* on the left and right walls of Halls E to G, (excluding the walls of the four chambered part of Hall E). Divisions 1 through 5 are on the left walls and are in ascending order going into the tomb while Divisions 6 through 11 are located on the right side and are also in ascending order. Presumably, this means that the *Amduat* is supposed to read beginning at the inner part of the left wall of Hall E and including scenes from the 1st to the 5th Divisions. Next, one would proceed to the inner part of the right wall of Hall E to read the rest of the book, from the 6th to the 11th Divisions (the 12th Division is not present in the tomb).

It is obvious that this reading order does not agree with that of parallel scenes found in the Book of Revelation. Instead, scenes corresponding to those in Revelation begin at the outer, right side rather than the left so that the latter half of the *Amduat* (from the 6th to the 11th Divisions) is read first. Furthermore, and instead of proceeding from the 1st to 5th Divisions, parallel scenes in Revelation run in *reverse* – from the 5th to 2nd Divisions (parallels were not found in the 1st Division). In other words, the text flow in Revelation is as one would expect if the writer followed the *Amduat* through the three halls, E, F and G in a counterclockwise direction. Finally, note that the *Schutzbild* scene is set between the two halves of the *Amduat* (between the right and left walls of Hall G) – in concert with a counterclockwise reading which includes this scene. This counterclockwise direction of the writer's apparent movements through this part of the tomb is probably the simplest explanation for this reversal of the parallel scenes in Revelation.

One possible reason for the positioning of the 5th Division at this particular point in the tomb is its contextual relationship to two major books found further into the tomb, on the walls and ceiling of the sarcophagus chamber (Hall I). Recall from Chapter 15, *The Little Scroll*, that the main function of the 5th Division, which parallels Rev. 10, was to introduce the *Book of Aker*. Here we find that, just as the next grouping of parallel scenes to those in Rev. 11 is found in the *Book of Aker*, we find this same book just a little beyond Hall E, on the walls of the sarcophagus chamber (Hall I, see Chapter 16, *The Two Witnesses*). Recall that the *Book of Aker* concludes with an account of what the Egyptians likely referred to as "events at the end of time." Meanwhile, the concept of the "end of time" is also found in the *Books of the Heavens* which are painted on the ceiling above the *Book of Aker* on the vaulted ceiling over the place where king's sarcophagus once lay. In the Books of the Heavens, the end of time is associated with the beginning of an all-together new

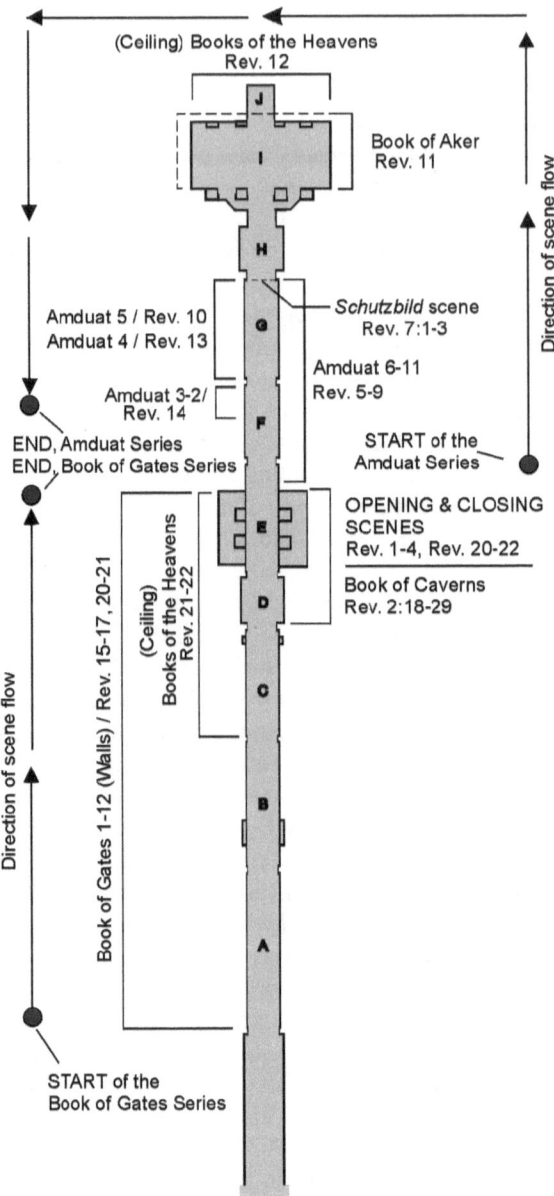

Figure 133. Arrangement in the tomb of Ramesses VI of parallels to scenes found the Book of Revelation. Note that the organization of texts in the tomb conforms with the overall organization of chapters and scenes in the Book of Revelation. It also explains the reference to the blowing of the four winds in Rev. 7:1-3 and the otherwise inexplicable reversal of a section of the *Amduat's* parallel scenes in the Rev. 10-14.

29. Parallel Series of Scenes

creation expressed as part of the cyclical nature of time (see Chapter 17, *The Woman in the Sky*). Finally, from the sarcophagus chamber, Revelation's text take us back to Hall G and the 4th Division of the *Amduat* where we begin the outward, *reverse* journey through the remaining scenes through to the 2nd Divisions of the *Amduat*.

The *Book of Gates* is also represented in the tomb. Confined to the left walls of Halls A to E, its organization corresponds to the sequence of parallel scenes found in Rev. 15 in Hall A to the first part of Rev. 21 found on the inner left wall of the four-pillared Hall E where we find the book's creation scene. Note that, in contrast to the reversal of scenes in the *Amduat Series*, parallel scenes in the *Book of Gates Series* flow in a single direction, passing inwards from Hall A to Hall E.

In Hall E, the flow of parallel scenes give way to the tomb's second version of the *Books of the Heaven*s painted on its ceiling and extending out to include that of Hall C. The part of the book found in Hall E contains a number of scenes related to the resurrection and judgment of the dead which parallel scenes in latter part of Rev. 21 to Rev. 22:5.

The most notable exceptions to the smooth flow of sequences of parallel scenes in the Revelation are associated with the volcanic eruption of Thera (Santorini) described in Chapter 13, *Catastrophes*. Parallel catastrophic events are described in different parts of Revelation, mainly in Rev. 8-9, 15-16, and Rev. 18-19 where we find allusions to ancient Egypt's written and verbal accounts describing the near and distant effects of the eruption of Thera in the mid 17th century BCE. Many accounts, both verbal and written, would have been brought to Egypt from the Aegean area by survivors of the catastrophe. The wide geographic origin of different accounts of entirely different experiences undoubtedly added greatly to the variety of apocalyptic events available for inclusion in Egypt's religious and secular writings – and their seemingly random occurrence in the Egyptian sources (and hence, in the Book of Revelation). The Egyptians had no way of knowing the actual order in which the various related events (eg., earthquakes, tsunamis and daytime darkness) occurred over such a broad region so there would be no obvious reason to arrange them in the same logical manner we expect today in reports of major volcanic eruptions with widespread impacts. The importance of the event to the Egyptians is evident in their many and varied descriptions of dramatic images as well as in the identity of certain gods in certain religious documents.

The author apparently began writing the Book of Revelation with the throne scene in the 4-pillared Hall E and from there walked along the right side of Halls F and G (AM6-11) before crossing to the left side of Hall G (AM5) and thence further into the tomb, circling around Hall I (BA + BH) before moving outwards along the left side of Halls G-F (AM4-2), and from there, back to the tomb entrance (for an intermission?). He then reenters the tomb and describes scenes on the left sides of Halls A-E (BG) and concludes Revelation with scenes from the ceiling of Hall E (BH). Sequences are punctuated by significant scenes from other sources in the tomb, the locations of which conform with the overall organizational similarities described here. This general pattern of movement supports the idea that the tomb of Ramesses VI is the birthplace of the Book of Revelation. Detailed study of the proposed route has revealed new – and at times dramatic – supporting evidence for the observed organizational similarities; these will be published in a separate volume.

Chapter 30. Literary Analyses[1396]

Similarities between the sounds of Egyptian words and phrases used in descriptions of deities and scenes in the Book of Revelation were examined at various points in this work and many supported the observed Egyptian parallels. Also, several types of literary parallels were found scattered throughout the texts, including possible transliterations of Egyptian texts, a practice which sometimes resulted in unusual imagery of the type which could have contributed to the enigmatic nature of the book. At times, Egyptian words seemed to be translations of Hebrew equivalents before being translated into Greek. Evidence was also found for the extensive use of alliteration and Egyptian puns when Revelation was viewed in an Egyptian context; on rare occasions sometimes this became evident only when the Greek text of Revelation was compared with Egyptian sources. The following paragraphs provide examples of some of the more obvious types of parallels found.

Egyptian-Greek Substitutions

An example of a substitution of an Egyptian name or title into Greek (and from there into an English word or phrase) is that of the Egyptian city of *Kheraha* located in the Nile Delta; the Greeks called it "Babylon." *Kheraha* is phonetically similar to the old name of the Greek island of Thera (modern-day Santorini) where a volcanic eruption destroyed or devastated many cities and towns in the area in *c.* 1628 BCE. This eruption was very likely the source of many of the apocalyptic images in Egyptian writings and likely in the Book of Revelation as well, especially the images presented in Rev. 16 and Rev. 18. A final example is the name "Christ," the Greek *christos,* which meant "the anointed one" and involved a concept which applied to Egyptian pharaohs as well as many other kings, including the Christ of Christianity.

Egyptian-Hebrew Translations

Several words in the Book of Revelation did not follow the straightforward pattern of word substitution just mentioned; others appear to have been translated first into Hebrew and then into Greek. One example is the name Michael, or *Michaeél,* the name of the leader of the army which fought the dragon and his angels in Rev. 12:7-9. It was observed that similar sounding Egyptian words, *ma khai* (*ma ḫȝy*), which means "to strike, to fight, to contend," or *ma khaiu* (*ma ḫȝ yw*), which means "fighters,"

30. Literary Analyses

could have been an Egyptian reference to an army general. We can add to these parallels the meanings of the Hebrew names for the twelve tribes of Israel and those of the Egypt's descriptive names of deities found among groups of twelve in the *Amduat* and the *Book of Gates*.

If we assume a link between the Egyptian texts and the Book of Revelation, it is interesting to speculate on the manner in which Egyptian words might be interpreted as Hebrew equivalents. For example, words such as *ma khai* could have found their way into Revelation, especially if the mother tongue of the author of the book was Hebrew. If the author's mother tongue had been Greek, it is unlikely that he would have first translated the Egyptian *ma khai* into Hebrew before expressing it in his own language. On the other hand, if his mother tongue was indeed Hebrew, he may well have used homophones found in that language to express Egyptian ideas or names; hence, the Egyptian *ma khai* became the name "Michael." This substitution would be especially likely if the homophones involved conformed with Hebrew beliefs or traditions as seems to be the case here. Another example of an Egyptian word being phonetically similar is the Hebrew word "Amen" found in Rev. 3:14 (and possibly elsewhere in the text). *Amen (Amun, Amon,* and others) was the name of one of the most powerful Egyptian gods. But it was also a descriptive name of the ancient Hebrew God Jehovah (or Yahweh). Such associations as these conform with the commonly held notion that the author of the Book of Revelation was a Hebrew scribe (see Chapter 1, *The Enigmatic Book of Revelation*). Sweet (1993) says that "John's language is indeed extraordinary, breaking all sorts of grammatical rules – but not out of incompetence; he can write correct and powerful Greek. He seems to be echoing Hebrew construction, perhaps to give a biblical feel to the book."[a, 1397]

Another straightforward example involves the enigmatic number, "666." It was shown in Chapter 4, *Other Characters in Revelation* that the Egyptian syllable, *set,* was often written with three ⟨ symbols (⟨⟨⟨, ⟨⟨⟨ or ⟨⟨⟨), symbols which were visually similar to three Hebrew (or Arabic or Syriac) sixes. This Egyptian sound was similar or identical to the name of the Egyptian god of evil, *Seth*. This suggestion conforms with events and series of events involving *Seth,* the deity which parallels the "1st beast" of Rev. 13. The number 666 in the Book of Revelation may thus be understood to represent a simple Hebrew assignment of the number 6 to an Egyptian hieroglyph (⟨=100) which originally had nothing to do with the number 6.

Closely related to straightforward descriptions of hieroglyphic symbols is the transliteration of Egyptian words or phrases into the Greek text of Revelation. In such cases, some Greek renditions of hieroglyphic words become approximations of the original Egyptian. One such word, for example, is *Khepri-Re,* ●O which literally means "becoming (●) Re (O)" or simply, "juvenile Re." Another form of the same name is ●🐏 which can mean "one who is *becoming* the ram of Re," the "juvenile ram of Re," or "the lamb of Re" – or simply, "the Lamb," a descriptive name conforming with that of Jesus Christ in the New Testament which, of course, was compiled during the days of early Christianity.

---

[a] See also Phillip's (1957) preface to his English translation of the Book of Revelation, p. xiii.

Use of Word Play

The use of word play in Egyptian religious writings is apparent in many parts of the Book of Revelation. In Chapter 2, *New Approaches,* several examples of Egyptian word play were presented to introduce the reader to the age-old practice of *paronomasia* where identical or similar sounding words were used to endow the speech of the speaker with great power. Magical deeds and powerful influences over others – especially enemies – could be wrought through the appropriate use of word play. We especially noted that this technique was used in the very act of creation by the creator god himself and from there, found its way into practically every religious document composed by Egyptian priests.[a] It is therefore not surprising that, since the Book of Revelation has several different types of parallels with ancient Egyptian beliefs and traditions, we find abundant cases where the choice of words, phrases and individual elements of passages appear to be based on Egyptian word play. Evidence for this was, of course, impossible to recognize when the possibility of Egyptian was not included in previous studies, for example, when only Greek and later, modern languages such as English were used. It is only when we actively pursue evidence of Egyptian word play in the text of Revelation that we find this phenomenon.

Many instances of Egyptian word play in the Book of Revelation involve texts containing just a few identical or similar sounding Egyptian words. These tend to be brief and to the point. Practically all of them follow patterns typical of those found in Egyptian texts (as outlined in Chapter 2, *New Approaches*). During the course of this study, however, it became obvious that the use of word play in the composition of Revelation went far beyond the simple two, three, or even four word sets of similar sounding words; when passages with obvious word play were identified, word play in some tended to continue for some distance before or after its use to highlight a critical component of the text. For example, in the scene in Rev. 10:1-3, involving a *mighty angel* carrying a *book* is described coming down from *heaven*, we find an unusually high concentration of words with the Egyptian *tch* prefix; the words shown in bold in the following quotation from Revelation are based on possible near homonyms found in Budge, 1920:

> ¹Then I saw another mighty (***tchara***) angel (***tchatcha-t***) coming down from heaven (***tche-t***), wrapped (***tcheb***) in a cloud, with a rainbow (***tcheser***) over his head, and his face was like the sun (***tcheserit***), and his legs like pillars (***tchetu***) of fire (***tchatu***). ²He (***tchatcha-t***) had a little (***tcham***) scroll (***tchamaa***) open in his hand (***tcher-t***). And he set (***tchabagi***) his right foot on the sea (***tcha***), and his left foot on the land (***tchama***), ³and called out

---

[a] Clagett (1989, pp. 276-277) refers to the use of word play in the act of creation as "the doctrine of the creative word." He says that "various cosmogonic systems may be alluded to, namely the use of the doctrine of the creative word, that is, the view that to name something and then to pronounce the name can bring it into existence. This was the central view of creation in the *Memphite Theology* but it played at least some role in other systems. Indeed *this doctrine accounts for the extraordinary use of punning in almost all Egyptian theological accounts,*' as is evident for example in the statements by which Re creates the sky, the Field of Offering, the Field of Rushes, and the ever shining stars in the Book of the Divine Cow."

30. Literary Analyses

(*tchaaa*) with a loud voice, like a lion roaring; when he called out (*tchaaa*), the seven thunders (*tchaasu*) sounded (*tchanna*). (Rev. 10:1-3)[a]

Another, more extensive example was found for Rev 19:10-21 where, in the following paragraph, an abundance of words with the prefixes *qen, khen, qem* and *khem* are emphasized (in bold) and additional words provided (not in bold) may also apply. Egyptian translations of the English words are from Budge (1920):

> [10]Then I fell down (***khemb***) at his feet to worship him, but he said to me, "You must not do that! (***khen***) I am a fellow servant (***khem***) with you and your brethren who hold the testimony of Jesus. Worship God." For the testimony of Jesus is the spirit of prophecy. [11]Then I saw (***qemh***) heaven (***khem***; *khenti; khen; khemen-t*) opened, and behold, a white horse (***qenu***)! He who sat upon it is called Faithful and True, and in righteousness he judges and makes war (***qenu***; *qen, qeni; qenqenau*). [12]His eyes are like a flame of fire (***kem-t***; *kem, khem; qenu*), and on his head (***qemhu***) are (***khema***) many diadems; and he has a name inscribed which no one knows but himself (***khem***). [13]He is clad in a robe (***qenà-t***, *qena; qeni; khemen-t; khemt*) dipped in blood (***khenti; qena***), and the name by which he is called is The Word of God. [14]And the armies (***qeni-t***) of heaven, arrayed in fine linen (***khemt***; *qeni; khemen-t*), white and pure, followed him on white horses (***qen***). [15]From his mouth (***qema***) issues a sharp sword (***qemau***) with which to smite (***qenqen***) the nations (***khemi***), and he will rule (khent; qeni) them with a rod (***qema***; *qenn, qenna*) of iron; (***qemamu***; qema) he will tread the wine (***khemkhem***) press (***qenqenu***; *qenfi; khent*)

---

[a] The following more extensive assessment of Rev. 10:1-3. Best matches are in bold while less applicable but possible matches are in regular print (page numbers refer to Budge, 1920):

> [1]Then I saw another mighty (***tchara*** = strong, mighty, 899b) angel (*tchau* = official, 893; ***tchatcha-t*** = a high official, chief of a company of priests, 901a; *tchert* = a powerful bird, 910a) coming down from heaven (*tche-t* = divine abode, 893a), wrapped (*tcheb* = to clothe, to dress, to dress up, 904b) in a cloud, with a rainbow (*tcheser* = splendors of the sun, 917a; *tchet* = to shine, light, brilliance, radiance, 914a) over his head, and his face was like the sun (***Tcheserit*** = a name of the Eye of Horus, 912b), and his legs like pillars (***tchetu*** = pillars, 914a; *tchet* = a sacred pillar, 914a) of fire (***tchatu*** = fire, 900b; *tchafu* = flame, fire, 897b) of fire (***tchatu*** = fire, 900b; *tchafu* = flame, fire, 897b). [2]He (*tchau* = official, 893; ***tchatcha-t*** = a high official, chief of a company of priests, 901a; *tchert* = a powerful bird, 910a) had a little (***tcham*** = young, 898a) scroll (***tchamaa*** = book, 898a) open in his hand (*tcha-t*, ***tcher-t*** = hollow of his hand, 894a,908b). And he set (***tchabagi*** = to dip, to immerse, 897b) his right foot on the sea (***tcha*** = lake, 896b; *tchau* = a rectangular lake of pool, 897a; *tchetku* = a kind of a lake, 915b; *tchaau* = sailors, 895a; *Tcheta-t* = a lake in the Tuat, 914a), and his left foot on the land (***tchama*** = dry land, 898a; *tchaiu* = a kind of ground or land, 896b), [3]and called out (***tchaaa***, *tchaaq, tchaaqta* = to cry out, 896b), with a loud voice, like a lion roaring; when he called out (*tchaaa, tchaaq, tchaaqta* = to cry out, 896b), the seven thunders (***Tchaasu*** = the Seven Divine Masters of Wisdom, 896a; *Tchaas* = the seven wise gods who presided over painting and writing, 896a; *Tchatiu* = a group of gods in the Tuat, 900b; *tchat* = wind storm, tempest, 903b; *tcha* = violent storm, 902a) sounded (***tchanna*** = to shake, to shiver through fear, 898b).

564   *Egyptian Origin of the Book of Revelation*

of the fury of the wrath (***qent-t***; *qent*) of God the Almighty (***qen-t***; *qeni*). ¹⁶On his robe (***qenà-t;*** *qeni*; *khemen-t*; *khemt*) and on his thigh (***Khent***; *khent*) he has a name inscribed, King of kings and Lord of lords. ¹⁷Then I saw (***qemh***) an angel (***khen***) standing in the sun, and with a loud voice he called (***khen***; *khenu*) to all the birds (***khemi***) that fly (***khens***) in midheaven (***khenn***; *khen-t*), "Come (***khen***), gather for the great supper of God, ¹⁸to eat (***qenqen***; *khenp*) the flesh (***qens;*** *qen-ti*; *qena*) of kings, the flesh (***qens***) of captains, the flesh (***qens***) of mighty (***qen-t;***) men, the flesh (***qens***) of horses and their riders (***qen***), and the flesh (***qens***) of all men, both free and slave (***khem***), both small (***khem***; *khemi*) and great (***qen-t***; *qeni*). ¹⁹And I saw the beast (***khenti***; *Khenti*) and the kings of the earth with their armies (***qeni-t***) gathered to make war (***qenu***; *qen,qeni*; *qenqenau*) against him who sits upon the horse (***qenu***) and against his army (***qeni-t***). ²⁰And the beast (***khenti***; *Khenti*) was captured, (***khena***) and with it the false prophet (***Khentui***) who in its presence had worked the signs by which he deceived those who had received the mark of the beast (***khenti***; *Khenti*) and those who worshiped its image (***khenti***; *qema-ti*; *qema-t*; *qemt*). These two were thrown alive into (***khent***; *khena*; *khenr, khenra*) the lake of fire (***kem-t***) that burns (***qenu***) with sulphur. ²¹And the rest were slain by the sword of him who sits upon the horse (***qenu***), the sword that issues from his mouth (***qema***); and all the birds were gorged (***qenau***; *khenup*) with their flesh (***qens***; *qen-ti*; *qena*). (Rev 19:10-21)

Still other examples might be given. For example, one is found in Rev. 17:3-6 where a grouping of puns seems to be based on the name of *Shesshes*, the crocodile goddess at BG9.2.10 (Figure 114); it contains an assortment of words with prefixes such as *ses*, *sesh*, and *shes*. Another is found in Rev. 20:1-3 which has a concentration of *sh* sounding words (for example, *shen, shenu, shnep* and *Shtat*). The full extent of the use of possible Egyptian word play in the Book of Revelation has not been determined and more research is suggested for this area using more modern dictionaries.

Concentrations of potential Egyptian words in the text of the Book of Revelation do not necessarily mean that these exact or similar words were used in the original hypothetical Egyptian text or any of the early versions of it. Also, one wonders if such words may have been used in verbal readings of the book. In such cases, word play used by a speaker would have been hidden, thus bestowing the text with especially potent magic. Recitation of passages in which alliteration abounded and many homonyms were used to replace certain words would make a presentation totally unintelligible to an untrained person but could have formed the basis of powerful, magical incantations. It is even possible that this type of recitation constituted what the Egyptians called "skilled of tongue" or even the "creative word." More research on this possibility is suggested, especially from the point of view of Egyptian hieroglyphic texts and since parts of this work are primarily based on comparisons of English versions of the Book of Revelation and English versions of the Egyptian texts, a fact which undoubtedly biased to some degree the approach and hence, results. Such research would best be done by qualified linguists specializing in ancient Egyptian.

Use of Metaphors

It was assumed from the start of this study that none of the apparent metaphors found in Revelation should initially be accepted as such; to accept them without question could very well close doors to alternative, possibly relevant interpretations when a passage was viewed from an Egyptian perspective. This approach reduced the tendency to find metaphors where none were meant and thus increased awareness of possible alternative interpretations of the Egyptian text. For example, this was the basis for rejecting the apparent metaphor in Rev. 2:16, which says that the one on the throne will fight his enemies with the "sword of his mouth." This was first rejected as a metaphor and later accepted as a simple physical description of the hieroglyphic word for "word." But it was not always this easy to identify such parallels. For example, the scene describing the judgment of the dead in Rev. 14:8-11(Egyptian parallel: the judgment scene in AM2.1) was likened to the harvesting of the vines in Rev. 14:14-20 (Egyptian parallel: the harvest scene in AM2.3). Was a metaphor really meant in this and certain other occasions, just as they seem to be in Revelation? Or does this and the many other apparent metaphors in Revelation simply represent literal references to Egyptian texts or drawings?

Special Numbers

The use of numbers in the Book of Revelation is by no means random in nature. This is most obvious in the emphasis on the number seven in events concerning the seven angels with seven bowls and the seven angels with seven trumpets. To these should be added the seven spirits of God and a few other instances of its usage. Indeed, if we look at the overall use of primary integers and their ordinals in the Book of Revelation, we find that the numbers 2, 3, 4 and 7 are by far the most frequently used. Of a total of 153 references to the numbers from 2 to 9, 135 or 88% belonged to this set of four numbers. Of these 135 occurrences, the number 7 was by far the most frequently used; this was followed by 3, 4, and finally 2, as shown in Table 30.1.

Table 30.1 Number of occurrences and proportionate usage of numerals and ordinals 2, 3, 4, and 7 in the Book of Revelation. (The following occurrences are omitted from this table: 5 appears 9 times; 6 appears 6 times; 8 appears twice; and 9 is absent.)

Number or its Ordinal	Occurrences	Proportion %
2 or 2nd	17	12.6
3 or 3rd	33	24.4
4 or 4th	26	19.3
7 or 7th	59	43.7
	135	100

These observations conform with the use of numbers in Egyptian religious documents. In his chapter on the *Symbolism of Numbers*, Wilkinson (1994) writes that,

> In the early part of the twentieth century, the great German Egyptologist Kurt Sethe showed that quite a few numbers were regarded as sacred or "holy" by the Egyptians, but

this element of sanctity and significance was accorded the numbers themselves only inasmuch as abstract principles had become associated with them. This is especially true of some of the primary integers which serve as the basic building blocks of most computation and numerical description – *especially 2, 3, and 4 (and also 7) and their direct multiples,'* for most other numbers with symbolic significance for the Egyptians were simply multiples or combinations of these.[1398]

The following examples are indicative of how the numbers 2, 3, 4 and 7 are used in the Book of Revelation: in Rev. 2:12 we find reference to a sword with *2 edges, 2 witnesses* are referred to in Rev. 11:3, and *2 olive trees* and *2 candlesticks* are before the throne of God in Rev. 11:4. There are *3 unclean spirits* like frogs (Rev. 16:13); *3 gates* on each of the *4 sides* of the holy city (Rev. 21:13); *4 angels* loosed to slay a *3rd part of men* (Rev. 9:15); *4 creatures* before the throne (Rev. 4:6); *4 quarters* of the earth (Rev. 20:8); *7 churches* in Asia (Rev. 1:4); *7 spirits of God* (Rev. 3:1); *7 thunders* (Rev. 10:3); *7 trumpets* (Rev. 8:6) and *7 plagues* (Rev. 15:1). Furthermore, as in ancient Egypt, multiples of these numbers are also common in the Book of Revelation. For example there are *12 (from 3 x 4) Tribes of Israel; 12 gates* in the walls of the holy city (Rev. 21:12); *12 types of fruit* growing on the tree of life (Rev. 22:2); *24 (from 3 x 4 x 2) elders* (Rev. 4:4); and the holy city was to be trod for *42 (from 3 x 7 x 2) months* (Rev. 11:2). Also, numbers in the 1,000's are, as in Egyptian works, presented in terms of the four basic numbers and the number 1,000. For example, *7,000 (from 7 x 1,000) men died* in a great earthquake (Rev. 11:13); the length and breath of the city was *12,000 (from 3x4x1,000) stadia* (Rev. 21:16); and each of the *12 tribes* referred to in Rev. 14:1 consisted of *12,000 individuals* for a total of *144,000 (from (3 x 4 x 3 x 4 x 1,000)*. All of these numbers have been identified here as having parallels in the religious literature of the ancient Egyptians.

Wilkinson describes why such numbers and combinations of them received so much attention by the Egyptians:

> Of fundamental importance in understanding ancient Egyptian culture is the fact that Egyptian scholars and theologians saw the relationships between similar words or objects as more than mere "coincidental," and as a reflection of order, design, and meaning in the world. Just as verbal and "visual" puns were felt to reflect an important aspect of reality, the relationships between the abstract numbers found in myth and in nature were also seen as meaningful patterns reflecting divine planning and cosmic harmony.[1399]

It is apparent from the above that the author of the Book of Revelation incorporated a similar approach to the use of numbers as did the ancient Egyptians in many of their religious documents.

Discussion

The preceding comments on parallel aspects of the text and literary style of the Book of Revelation represent a modest first step toward future studies in this area; they suggest the beginning of just a few of many avenues of potentially fruitful directions of research. Such studies should only follow acceptance by Egyptologists of the most significant Egyptian parallels identified in this study (i.e., their true significance should be determined by further, more critical research). It is to be hoped that such studies will set in motion the establishment of a far more detailed and structured approach to the language and style of the Book of Revelation. Also, it is to be hoped that future research will lead to a better understanding of which language was used to compile the original version of the book. Was it originally written in Greek? Was it in Egyptian? Or Hebrew or some other language? And what influence did the original author's mother tongue have on the apparent widespread allusions to typically Hebrew events, customs and beliefs? For example: allusions such as those to Jezebel, the New Jerusalem, the battle of Gog and Magog, the twelve tribes of Israel, the Devil and Satan, "the anointed one," the judgment of the dead, Babylon the enemy, and others. Were these allusions inherent in the original version of Revelation or were they added by scribes intent on interpreting it (or later versions of it) from a Hebrew and/or a Judaeo-Christian perspective? Or were they simply a product of the time in which they were written? Nor are such questions and observations likely to point to the only avenues of fruitful research.

The critical reader should by no means accept without question many of the weak interpretations of the symbolism, imagery, and possible religious and historic settings presented here as evidence of a dependance of the Book of Revelation on Egyptian beliefs; while many of the strongest parallels identified in this work will undoubtedly be supported by future studies, some of the weak ones may not. Hopefully, a comprehensive compilation of acceptable parallels will be developed over time which can serve as a more reliable basis for a better comparison of the whole of the Book of Revelation with a wider range of Egyptian sources. We might also expect improvements to come from studies involving more detailed comparisons of Egyptian, Greek and Hebrew sources as well as possible influences from related Semitic languages in the Levant; a likely weakness in some of the interpretations of potential puns in this study may be that the approaches taken did not consider possible influences on interpretations of similar or related words in other Semitic languages. Critical refinements and further research in all of these areas will undoubtedly provide additional background to evaluate the status of the Book of Revelation in the corpus Christian literature – as well as that of ancient Egypt.

Chapter 31. Perspectives[1400]

The almost overwhelming number of parallels between the Book of Revelation and ancient Egyptian writings, beliefs and traditions suggest that practically all of the book can be understood within the context of Egyptian sources. For example, Revelation's opening scene and the letters to the seven churches closely resemble the opening scene of the *Book of the Divine Cow* wherein the sun-god calls together his high-ranking deities to discuss what should be done about mankind's rebellious activities. Similarly, Revelation begins with a throne scene in which a central deity dictates a series of ultimatums to the inhabitants of seven localities, advising several of them to cease their rebellious ways or face severe punishment, even war. The structure of these ultimatums is similar to certain chapters in the *Book of the Dead* and the *Book of Caverns* while their details parallel a variety of commonly held Osirian beliefs, most of which are recorded in the *Book of the Dead*.

With the opening of the scroll in Rev. 5, the reader is introduced to a group of scenes which follow the same general sequence as similar scenes near the middle of Egypt's *Amduat Series* of scenes. Next, scenes which parallel events in Rev. 6-7 are found in the 6th through 11th Divisions of the *Amduat* and, as in Revelation, end with a scene in which a great multitude carrying palm branches stand before a deity's throne. After several accounts of manifestations of the wrath of God in Rev. 8-9, which parallel events in several Egyptian sources, the scenes switch back in Rev. 10 to parallels in the 5th Division of the *Amduat*. Parallels then temporarily switch from the *Amduat* to scenes in two other Egyptian texts. Firstly, the *Book of Aker* parallels Rev. 11 and presents a story about two "witnesses" which culminates in a great earthquake and the death of 7,000 people. Next, in scenes in the *Books of the Heavens* which parallel those found in Rev. 12, we read of the birth of a god-child and conflict with a dragon. From there, Egyptian parallels to events in Rev. 13-14 switch back to the remaining parts of the *Amduat* where the sequence of parallel events reverse, flowing backwards from the 4th through 2nd Divisions and culminating in the destruction of evil doers on the earth in the well-known metaphor of the reaping of the harvests of the fields of the earth described in Rev. 14. Meanwhile, parts of the *Amduat Series* are frequently augmented by brief scenes and passages from other Egyptian sources such as the *Book of the Dead*, the *Victory Hymn of Thutmosis III* and the *Annals of Thutmosis III*.

The second series of scenes, the *Book of Gates Series,* covers most of the remaining chapters (Rev. 15-22) which contain scenes and sequences of scenes resembling those found primarily in the *Book of Gates* and the *Books of the Heavens.* In the 2nd Division of the *Book of Gates* we find seven deities who dispense the fiery wrath of the sun-god while a nearby group of twelve singers stand by a lake of fire. Similarly, in Rev. 15, seven angels dispense the wrath of God while singers by a lake of fire sing the "Song of Moses" which itself parallels a section of the well-known Egyptian *Victory Hymn of Thutmosis* (Thut-*moses*) *III*. Next, the description of the drying up of the Euphrates River in Rev. 16 paints a picture similar to a dried-up riverbed scene in the 3rd Division of the Book of Gates. And the battle of Armageddon in the same chapter of Revelation contains significant similarities to events portrayed in both the 6th Division of the *Amduat* and the *Annals of Thutmosis III*. The story of the conflict between the harlot and the kings in Rev. 17 parallels events shown graphically in the 9th Division. Then, events associated with the wrath of God described in Rev. 18-19 parallel Egyptian descriptions of catastrophes caused by the eruption of a volcano in the Aegean Sea in *c*. 1628 BCE. And just as the capture and chaining of the ancient serpent is followed by a 1,000 year reign of the faithful in Rev. 20, Egypt's ancient serpentine enemy of the sun-god is captured and bound with a chain in the 10th Division where reference is also made to a 1,000 year period. Furthermore, in both sources the serpent is described as once again being free and then recaptured and punished yet again. Rev. 20 then switches to resurrection and judgment scenes which have significant parallels in the *Books of the Heavens*. Finally, the arrival of a new heaven and earth in Rev. 21 leads us to the conclusion of the *Book of Gates* in its 11th and 12th Divisions where we find a dramatic picture depicting the re-creation of the cosmos and a new celestial city whose physical characteristics conform with Revelation's Holy City in Rev. 21-22.

Significantly, evidence for these and many other parallels includes not only scenes and sequences of scenes but also the identities of individual characters. Exquisite details of the physical attributes of many of these characters and groups of characters in scenes and sequences of scenes conform so well with those in Egyptian texts and pictures as to render them unequivocal parallels.

Individual parallels and the sum total of all the various types of parallels found in this study represent strong evidence for an Egyptian link to the Book of Revelation; the crowning piece of evidence is the similarity between the overall organization of the Book of Revelation and that of parallel compositions and scenes painted on the walls and ceilings of the tomb of Ramesses VI. When confronted with this remarkable volume of parallels, from the minutiae of possible Egyptian homonyms to the overall organization of scenes and chapters, it is practically impossible to conclude anything other than that the Book of Revelation is of Egyptian origin.

In spite of this conclusion, no part of the Book of Revelation is an obvious translation of any of the Egyptian texts examined. Instead, the book seems to merely allude to Egyptian sources. This is not necessarily an abnormal weakness when considering ancient manuscripts; biblical scholars have come to the same conclusion about references in Revelation to events described in the Old Testament. For example, Sweet (1993) tells us that,

Biblical metaphors and images – dragon, lamb, harlot, bride – come to new life in his [John's] imagination. There are allusions to or echos of practically every book in the Hebrew Bible. Daniel and Ezekiel are particularly formative; Isaiah, Jeremiah, Zechariah, and Psalms are pervasive influences; so too are the stories of creation and Exodus, and of the return from Babylon and rebuilding of Jerusalem, which Isaiah depicted as a new Exodus and act of creation. ... though no doubt Jewish, the author is also a citizen of Greco-Roman world and knows its myths and astrology.[1401]

The main difference between Sweet's conclusion and the current one is that the parallels observed here not only appear to be allusions to Egyptian texts, but they are almost all found in discrete, parallel series of events which themselves fit within larger sequences of events (the *Amduat Series* and the *Book of Gates Series*). The same is not true of Revelation's apparent allusions to events in the Old Testament where they do not follow the same order. This difference is quite significant and weighs in favor of an Egyptian rather than a Jewish connection.

The current findings do not, however, negate Sweet's comment that the author of Revelation is Jewish; a Jewish background could indeed account for many of the apparent allusions to Old Testament "metaphors and images" (for example, Jezebel, Gog and Magog, Megiddo, and the New Jerusalem) even if their primary sources were Egyptian. Their presence in the Book of Revelation may even suggest a Jewish author who lived in Old Testament times, centuries before early Christian scholars discovered the book's existence; the original version could even have existed for hundreds of years in an Egyptian library until its discovery by early Christian or Greek scholars.

Of course the reader may ask, "If so many Egyptian parallels are so obvious in the Book of Revelation, why have they not been noticed before? How is it that they remained unnoticed for so many centuries?" One possible reason is that the book also contains many allusions to what seem at first glance to be New Testament images and themes. But if early Christian scribes sincerely believed their Greek versions of the book to be a genuinely Christian document, they might very likely have interpreted the word *christos* ("the anointed one") to refer to Jesus the Christ of Christianity and hence, used this as a basis for translating and interpreting certain passages in early redactions of the book. Also, references to Horus the king and son of god Re could have been interpreted to refer to Jesus the Christ, Christianity's son of God. For example, we have seen how both Horus and Christ were referred to as "the anointed one," "the first born of the dead," "the ruler of the kings of the earth" and each acted as "a faithful witness" and advocate for the individual in the final judgment. Furthermore, the overall acceptance of the book by early Christian scribes and scholars could have been influenced by the similarity between expressions such as "the lamb of Re" (i.e., the juvenile form of the well-known, ram-headed representation of the sun-god) in Egyptian beliefs and "the Lamb of God" used for Jesus by the apostle John (1John 1:29, 36); the Egyptian "lamb of Re" was, as in Rev. 5:12, believed to have been worthy, died, reanimated (resurrected) and subsequently received "power and wealth and wisdom and might and honor and glory and blessing!" Other similarities between the "lamb of Re" and the Christ of Christianity are equally relevant, not the least of which are the contexts of scenes and events in which they are portrayed.

As pointed out in Chapter 1, *The Enigmatic Book of Revelation*, the controversy surrounding the acceptance of the Book of Revelation by the early Christian churches waged on until 508 CE when it was finally accepted by both the western and eastern Christian churches of the day. Ever since those early years, interpretations of the book's many passages have been based almost entirely on Judaeo-Christian beliefs and traditions along with a modest sprinkling of references to other Middle Eastern beliefs and mythologies. The intervening centuries have witnessed inordinately large numbers of conflicting treatises and commentaries on the origins and meanings of its symbolism by both early and modern Christian scholars. Indeed, as discussed earlier, Christian giants such as Luther, Zwingli, and Erasmus felt the book was not of Christian origin. The results of the current research suggest a reason for this opinion: the Book of Revelation should, instead, be interpreted from a non-Christian perspective – an ancient Egyptian rather than a Christian one.

Prophesy concerning the end times has been traditionally considered the main theme of Book of Revelation. The book contains visions of political unrest and confusion, war, and dramatic destruction by, among other things, earthquakes and fire, all of which contribute to its placement in the genre of apocalyptic literature. Christians have typically associated these images with the end of the world, the second coming of Christ and the final judgment when His followers are rewarded for their faithfulness and sinners are punished. In the end, a New Jerusalem, the celestial city of the blessed appears in the sky where the faithful live and reign with Christ for a thousand years. A purely Egyptian perspective on these same themes provides us with a dramatic set of parallels to all these and many more events, an observation which may suggest the Egyptians had a basically similar view of events at the end of time.

With respect to the arrival of the holy city in the sky, it should be pointed out that the Egyptians considered their celestial city to have a river running through it – to be a heavenly counterpart of their own Nile River valley with its own cities, towns, villages, waterways, fields and farms; it was considered to be the very abode of the blessed dead. This equivalence included a belief that events in the heavenly sphere had counterparts on earth with many earthly events being more or less mere reflections of realities playing out in the spiritual world. This view of the cosmos leads us to look closely at seemingly prophetic events in the Book of Revelation which could span two interacting worlds – heavenly and earthly conflicts, wars, catastrophes and judgments.

It should be noted that the cyclical appearance of the sun in the morning sky, its voyage across the heavens and its final demise in the evening forms a context for interpreting what appear to be visions of the future in the Book of Revelation. The sun-god daily entered the morning sky to bless and reward his earthly followers and to punish his enemies. Later, he and his followers fought a celestial war with the forces of evil before his body died (his soul did not die) and he passed into the Netherworld at sunset. The great cosmic cycle was completed with his rejuvenation through the re-uniting of his soul with his dead body (i.e., Osiris, thus affecting his reanimation/resurrection), and his triumphant appearance with his faithful, celestial followers in the morning sky to once again rule over the earth.

It is within this broad context that we take note of the opening theme of Revelation which conforms with events during the early days of the sun-god's reign on earth as described in the *Book of the Divine Cow*. Just as Revelation opens with orders from the throne of God for letters to be sent to groups of rebellious followers warning them to change their ways or face war, the sun-god's first action is to announce from the throne that he will destroy those who had rebelled against him. Meanwhile, in the *Book of Gates*, with multitudes of the faithful looking on, a scroll is opened and a detailed account of all that is to happen during the sun-god's journey through the sky is revealed. The great celestial war to be fought against Apophis and his followers is to be reenacted on earth where soldiers are to be recruited from among the faithful and promised great rewards in the hereafter if killed in battle. To this is added the promise that the sun-god's full power will be brought to bear on the enemy by the release from the very depths of the earth the most powerful natural forces of the then-known cosmos: volcanic eruptions, powerful earthquakes, fire, floods and tsunamis. His wrath will ultimately destroy not only all evil, but all of creation as well; the destruction of evil is likened to the harvest of grain and the cosmos is thoroughly cleansed of all evil before being renewed. Those of the faithful who die from the release of these terrible forces are promised bodily resurrection and privileged positions in the heavenly abode where they will live and rule in bliss with their partners, friends, relatives, servants – and their sun-god – as he traverses the next, newly created sky over his newly created kingdom, the earth. Modern Christians consider many of the events in the Book of Revelation to be prophetic while Egyptians considered similar events to be part of the natural unfolding of each great cosmic cycle of time.

On earth, the king's throne was thought of as being representative of the sun-god's heavenly throne while the king, the son of Re, was the sun-god's representative on earth. And just as heavenly wars were declared against Apophis and his followers, earthly wars were declared against the sun-god's enemy and his followers on earth. Hence, Revelation's seven letters are identifiable as "military dispatches" or even "declarations of war" against the king's rebellious subjects or suzerainties. Evil doers are accused of being the followers of Seth, who at times was considered to be the equivalent of Baal the chief god of the Palestine area. Egyptian recruits and seasoned soldiers are assured that the sun-god's full power will be brought to bear on the enemy, including the release of the most powerful forces of the cosmos, just as outlined for the hereafter in books such as the *Amduat*, the *Book of Gates* and the *Book of Aker*. Veterans of the coming war are promised plots of productive farmland and a plentiful food supply for themselves and their families as they live in peace along the Nile with their beloved protector, Horus, the son of Re. Those who die in battle are promised bodily resurrection and privileged situations in the celestial abode where they will rule with their sun-god for 1,000 celestial-years (equivalent to one day on earth) as he passes through his newly created city in the sky.

We may well ask, "Where do the current findings leave the debate on the provenance of the Book of Revelation?" When answering this question we should bear in mind that the debate began during the days of the early Christian church when the book first came to the attention of Christian scholars; it ended in about 500 CE when the western churches finally capitulated to a Christian origin. But about a thousand years later, the leaders of the Reformation followed the lead of Jerome, an early Christian theologian, that the book should not be held as canonical because it was not of apostolic origin and "lacked the heart and spirit of John the Divine" (see Chapter 1, *The Enigmatic Book of Revelation*,). Nevertheless, meaningful debate on the issue of the book's provenance effectively stalled after the Reformation when the church settled back into an attitude of a general acceptance of a Christian origin (in spite of the opinions of Luther and others). Perhaps the most important contributing factor to this acceptance was the complete absence of an alternative context for interpreting its many enigmatic passages. The results of this study fill this void and enable a new round of meaningful debate on the subject to be considered in the 21st century.

The main reason for the delay in the recognition of Revelation's likely association with ancient Egyptian beliefs and texts is the long time it took for Egypt's hieroglyphic texts to be deciphered. After they were first translated in the early 1800's and slowly gave up their secrets during the rest of the century, a vast body of knowledge about Egyptian beliefs finally came into focus. Nevertheless, it was not until 1907 that a possible relationship between the Book of Revelation and ancient Egyptian beliefs was first suggested in a publication by Gerald Massey. The style and/or the level of scholarship of Massey's publication did not resonate with Egyptologists, however, and his basic conclusions remained largely untapped and fallow throughout the twentieth century. The results of the current research adds many new and significant findings to Massey's work; they suggest the time has come for Christian theologians to seriously examine the very real possibility that the Book of Revelation is, in fact, not of Christian origin.

A relatively simple and straightforward starting point for such a review would be a critical comparison of the parallels found in this study with generally accepted parallels suggested in footnotes on the pages of many modern versions of the Book of Revelation. A valid question to pursue may well be, "Does the substance and the sum total of Egyptian parallels found in the current study carry more – or less – weight to the argument than Old Testament parallels identified by biblical scholars in Judaeo-Christian texts?" A cursory look at many of these footnotes suggests the answer will likely be that the nature and full spectrum of types of Egyptian parallels found here are more relevant than the results of previous work by ancient to modern Christian theologians. Very likely, the final outcome of such a study will suggest the need for more in-depth analyses which will, in turn, ultimately support the conclusion of this work and confirm an Egyptian origin of the book.

Of course, concurrent studies should certainly be conducted by scholars specializing in ancient Egyptian beliefs. These should include critical examinations of the evidence presented here along with reexamination and reinterpretation of certain passages found in the *Book of the Dead*, the *Amduat* and other relevant sources. It is to be expected that many parts of the Book of Revelation will shed new light on the meaning of certain Egyptian texts and how the Egyptians may have understood their already ancient texts as well as how these interpretations were expressed in their day-to-day lives. For example, it may well be found that they interpreted parts of the texts as being, not only religious and historical in nature, but also prophetic in the same sense as Christians currently view the Book of Revelation, especially as it relates to political and apocalyptic events and the judgment of the dead at the end of time. Other studies may well reveal even more convincing evidence for an Egyptian origin. This last suggestion is based on the sometimes almost daily discoveries of new parallels encountered throughout this study. Such discoveries seemed to emerge like bright beacons from the Egyptian texts; very likely, there are many more to be identified.

In the opening paragraph of Chapter 1 of this book, the reader's attention was brought to a statement by Fiorenza (1985) that "Despite all scholarly efforts, no generally recognized or accepted consensus has been reached in regard to the composition and the theological interpretation of the book." She added that,

> While serious scholarly works are rare, popular and fundamentalist writings abound. No wonder that Rev. is still considered to be the most difficult book in the NT [New Testament]. Scholars seem to have arrived at a consensus that the book does not provide us with any details of church – or world-history nor give us a calendar of future events, while popular interest still focuses on such information.

On the same page, she opens her introductory section on "Historical-Critical Analyses" with the comment, "It is universally acknowledged that Rev. has to be understood in its historical-cultural and religious context." Of course this statement was made in the context of an assumed Judaeo-Christian origin. The results of this study strongly suggest that the book be re-examined from an Egyptian and possibly an Egyptian-Judaeo origin.

If future research and learned and considered opinions conclude that the Book of Revelation is indeed based on Egyptian rather than Christian or other Middle Eastern beliefs, it should best be assigned to the corpus of literature from ancient Egypt, albeit a corrupted version of a now-lost, earlier work possibly written in Greek. Such research would broaden our understanding of the religious beliefs and traditions of the ancient Egyptians, including the influence on their world view of major natural catastrophes. It should also be useful in garnering a greater depth of knowledge about the role religious beliefs played in Egypt's political affairs and military exploits, both internally and internationally. At the same time, acceptance of the current results will offer an alternative basis for the understanding of what has been for many centuries the most enigmatic book in the annals of Christian literature.

BIBLIOGRAPHY
(List of Documents Cited in *REFERENCES*)

Allen, T.G., 1969. *The Book of the Dead. Documents in the Oriental Institute Museum at the University of Chicago,* The University of Chicago Oriental Institute Publications, Chicago, Vol 82.

Anthes, R., 1954. *The Original Meaning of* M3a ḪRW. *Journal of Near Eastern Studies,* Vol. XIII, pp. 21-51.

Baines, J. and J. Málek, 1980. *Atlas of Ancient Egypt,* Facts on File Inc., New York, 240 pp.

Barnes, W.H., 1993. In *The Oxford Companion to the Bible,* Metzger, Bruce M. and Michael D. Coogan, editors, p. 56.

Bible: *The New Oxford Annotated Bible, New Revised Standard Version,* 1991. Oxford University Press.

Borghouts J. F., 1978. *Ancient Magical Texts* (Leiden, 1978), p. 2.

Bourriau, J., 2000. *The Second Intermediate Period* in *The Oxford History of Ancient Egypt,* p. 195.

Boylan, P., 1922. *Thoth: the Hermes of Egypt*, Oxford, (Quoted by Clagett, 1989, p. 644).

Breasted, J.H., 1912. *Development of Religion and Thought in Ancient Egypt.* University of Pennsylvania Press, Philadelphia, 379 pp. (Pennsylvania Paperback Edition, 1972, 379 pp.)

Breasted, J.H., 1962. *Records of Ancient Egypt. Historical Documents from the Earliest Times to the Persion conquest, Collected, Edited and Translated with Commentary.* Russell & Russel Inc., New York. Volume II.

Bright, J., 1959. *A History of Israel,* Westminster Press, Philadelphia, 501 pp. + Map Plates I to XVI.

Budge, E.A.W., 1893. *The Mummy. A Handbook of Egyptian Funerary Archaeology,* reprinted by KPI Limited, London and New York, 513 pp.Budge, E.A.W., 1894. *The Egyptian Book of the Dead. Papyrus of Ani — The Egyptian*

Text with Interlinear Transliteration and Translations, a Running Translation, Introduction, etc. Original published by Trustees of the British Museum, 1895; Dover edition by Dover Publications Inc. New York, 1967, 377 pp. + Introduction, i-clv pp.

Budge, E.A.W., 1900. *Egyptian Religion*. Republished by Carol Publishing Group, New York, with new introduction and additional illustrations, New York, 1987, 224.

Budge, E.A.W., 1904. *The Gods of the Egyptians*. Volume I, (Dover Publications Inc., New York, 1969, 525 pp.)

Budge, E.A.W., 1904. *The Gods of the Egyptians*. Volume II, (Dover Publications Inc., New York, 1969, 431 pp.)

Budge, E.A.W., 1912. *Legends of the Egyptian Gods, Hieroglyphic Texts and Translations.* London: Kegan Paul, Trench, Trübner, 1912. Republished by Dover Publications Inc., New York, 1994, 248 pp.

Budge, E.A.W,. 1920. *An Egyptian Hieroglyphic Dictionary.* Vols I and II, 1314 pages. Republished by Dover Publications, Inc. New York. 1978.

Budge, E.A.W., 1934. *From Fetish to God in Ancient Egypt.* Originally published by Oxford University Press, London, 1934. Version used here published by Dover Publications Inc., New York, 1988, 545 pp.

Clagett, M., 1989. *Ancient Egyptian Science, A Source Book.* American Philosophical Society, Independence Square, Philadelphia, Volume I, 863 pp.

Collins, A.Y., 1976. *The Combat Myth in the Book of Revelation.* (Ph.D. Thesis, Harvard University, Scholars Press, University of Montana, 292 pp.

Collins, A. Y., 1984. *Crisis and Catharsis: The Power of the Apocalypse.* The Westminster Press, Philadelphia, 179 pp.

Coogan, M.D., 1993. In *Oxford Companion to the Bible*. 1993. Edited by Bruce M. Metzger, and Michael D. Coogan, 1993. Oxford University Press, Oxford, 874 pp. + maps.

Bruce M. M. and M.D. Coogan, 2001. *The Oxford Guide to People & Places of the Bible*. Edited by. Oxford University Press, xxii, 374 pp., [28] p. of plates.

Conybeare, F.C., 1907. *The Armenian Version of Revelation, Apocalypse of John* edited and translated by Fred C. Conybeare. Philo Press, Amsterdam, 1974. Reprint of the Edition London 1907, Printed in the Netherlands. ISBN 90 6022 305 5, pp. 1-163.

Daniel J. S. and H. Sheng (1986). *Volcanic shards from Santorini (Upper Minoan ash) in the Nile Delta, Egypt.* Nature 320, 733 - 735.

Dassow, E. von, 1994. *The Egyptian Book of the Dead, The Book of Going Forth by Day*, with Translation by Raymond O. Faulkner and Ogden Goelet, illustrations by E.A. Wallis Budge, and commentary by Ogden Goelet. 175 pp.

Darnell, J.C., *The Enigmatic Netherworld Books of the Solar-Osirian Unity, Cryptographic Compositions in the Tombs of Tutankhamun, Ramesses VI and Ramesses IX.* Academic Press Fribourg, Vandenhoeck & Ruprecht Göttingen, 640 pp. + 43 Plates.

David, R., 1980. *The Cult of the Sun, Myth and Magic in Ancient Egypt*, J.M. Dent & Sons Ltd, Toronto, 207 pp.

Derchain, P., (1965). *Lower Egypt Papyrus Salt 825 (B.M. 10051), ritual pour la conservation de la vie en Egypt,* Académie Royale de Belgique, Classe des Lettres, Mémoires, Vol 58 (Brussels, 1965) pp. 139-40; Part III, pp. 7-10. Referred to by Clagett (1989), pp. 30-32.

Du Tooit, A.B., 1993. In *The Oxford Companion to the Bible*, Edited by Bruce M. Metzger, and Michael D. Coogan, 1993. Oxford University Press, Oxford, 874 pp. + maps. pp. 98-104.

Encyclopedia Britannica, 15th Edition, 1976, Macropædia

Erman, A., 1927. See English edition (1966) and the original German, 1926 edition entitled, *Die Literatur der Aegypter.*

Erman, A., 1966. *The Ancient Egyptians, A Sourcebook of their Writings*, translated by Aylward M. Blackman, Harper Torchbooks, The Acadamy Library, Harper and Row, NY. 318 pp. (Originally published under the title *The Literature of the Ancient Egyptians*, Methuen & Col, Ltd., London. 1927).

Faulkner, R.O., 1962. *A Concise Dictionary of Middle Egyptian.* Griffith Institute, Ashmolean Museum, Oxford, 327 pp. (Reprinted 1996).

Faulkner, R.O. 1969. *The Ancient Egyptian Pyramid Texts.* Oxford at the Clarendon Press, 330 pp.

Faulkner, R.O. 1973. *The Ancient Egyptian Coffin Texts.* Aris & Phillips Ltd, Warminster, England, Volume I, Spells 1-354, 285 pp.

Faulkner, R.O. 1973. *The Ancient Egyptian Coffin Texts.* Aris & Phillips Ltd, Warminster, England, Volume II, Spells 355-787, 308 pp.

Faulkner, R.O. 1973. *The Ancient Egyptian Coffin Texts.* Aris & Phillips Ltd, Warminster, England, Volume III, Spells 788-1185, 204 pp.

Faulkner, R.O., 1994. In *The Egyptian Book of the Dead, The Book of Going Forth By Day.* Edited by E. Von Dassow, First Edition, 1994, Chronicle Books, San Fancisco, 175 pages. (See Von Dassow, 1994)

Fiorenza, Elizabeth S. 1985, *The Book of Revelation - Justice and Judgment.* Fortress Press, Philadelphia, 211 pp.

Ford, J.M., 1975. *Revelation, Introduction, Translation and Commentary, The Anchor Bible,* Dubbleday & Company Inc. Garden City, New York.

Frankfort, H., 1948. *Ancient Egyptian Religion, An Interpretation,* Harper and Row, New York, 181 pages.

Gardiner, A., 1927. *Egyptian Grammar, Being an Introduction to the Study of Hieroglyphics.* Griffith Institute, Ashmolean Museum, Oxford, 646 pp.

Gardiner, A., 1938. *House of Life,* referred to by Clagett (1989), p. 768.

Gardiner, P.B., 1995. *The Complete Who's Who of the Bible,* published by Marshall Pickering, xiii, 688 pp.

Glasson, T.F., 1965. *The Cambridge Bible Commentary on the New English Bible: The Revelation of John,* Cambridge University Press, 128 pp.

Goelet, O., 1994. *A Commentary on the Corpus of Literature and Tradition Which Constitutes the Book of Going Forth by Day.* In *The Egyptian Book of the Dead, The Book of Going Forth By Day,* Edited by E. Von Dassow et al, First Edition, 1994. (See Von Dassow, 1994)

Grimal, N., 1992. *A History of Ancient Egypt.* (Translation by Ian Shaw) Blackwell, Oxford, 518 pp.

Guichard, F., S. Carey, M. A. Arthur, H. Sigurdsson & M. Arnold 1993. *Tephra from the Minoan eruption of Santorini in sediments of the Black Sea.* Nature 363, 610 - 612.

Gyles, M. F., 1959. *Pharaonic Policies and Administration,* 663 to 323 B.C., The James Sprunt studies in history and political science; Vol. 41, University of North Carolina Press, vi, 120 pp.

Hackett, J.A., 1993. "Jezebel" in *The Oxford Companion to the Bible,* p.368. Hannah, D.D., 1999, *Michael and Christ: Michael traditions and Angel Christology in Early*

Christianity. – Tübingen: Mohr Seibeck, (Wissenchaftliche Untersuchungen zum Neuen Testament 2. Reihe 109), 289 pp.

Harper Study Bible, NRSV, 1991. Zondervan Publishing House, Grand Rapids, Michigan, 1,914 pp. + Concordance, 183 pp. + Maps.

Hayes, J., 1993. In *The Oxford Companion to the Bible,* Metzger, Bruce M. and Michael D. Coogan, editors, p. 729.

Henry, M., 1964. *Commentary on the Whole Bible,* Zondervan Publishing House, Michigan, 1986 pp.

Hill, D. *Prophecy and Prophets in the Revelation of St. John*, New Testament Studies, 20 (1973-1974), p. 417. Referred to in Fiorenza (1985), p. 135.

Hornung, E., 1983. *Conceptions of God in Ancient Egypt, the one and the many.* Routledge & Kegan Paul, London. 295 pp.

Hornung, E., 1990. *The Valley of the Kings; Horizon of Eternity.* Timkin Publishers Inc., New York, 221 pp.

Hornung, E., 1992. *Idea Into Image: Essays on Ancient Egyptian Thought.* Timkin Publishers Inc., New York, 209 pp.

Hornung, E., 1999A. *The Ancient Egyptian Books of the Afterlife.* Cornell University Press, 188 pp.

Hornung, E., 1999B. *History of Ancient Egypt.* Cornell University Press, 185 pp.

James, E.O., 1960, *The Ancient Gods: The History and Diffusion of Religion in the Ancient Near East and the Eastern Mediterranean,* G.P. Putnam's Sons, New York, 359 pp.

Kuniholm, P. I., B. Kromer, S. W. Manning, M. Newton, C. E. Latini and M. J. Bruce, 1996. *Anatolian tree rings and the absolute chronology of the eastern Mediterranean, 2220-718 BC.* Nature 381, 780 - 783.

Lasor, W.S., D.A. Hubbard and F.W. Bush, 1982. *Old Testament Survey: The Message, Form, and Background of the Old Testament.* Eerdmans Publishing Company, Grand Rapids, Michigan, 696 pp.

Lee, D.P., (1971). *Plato, Timaeus and Critias,* Penguin Books, Middlesex, England, 165 pp.

Lentz (1999), *The Volcano Registry,* McFarland, p. ix, 190.

Lohmeyer, E., 1934. *Die Offenbarung des Johannes 1920-1934*, TRu NF 6 (1934) 270. Referred to by Fiorenza (1985, p.35)

Luce, J.V., 1969. *The End of Atlantis,* Granada Publishing Ltd, London, 187 pp.

Lurker, M., 1980. *An Illustrated Dictionary of the Gods and Symbols of Ancient Egypt.* Thames and Hudson Ltd., London, 142 pages.

Manning, S.W., 1999. *A Test of Time. The Volcano of Thera and the chronology and history of the Aegean and east Mediterranean in the mid second millennium BC.* Oxbow Books, Oxford and Oakville, 494 pp.

Marshall, A., 1984. *The Interlinear Greek-English New Testament, The Nestle Greek Text with a Literal English Translation* by A. Marshall. In *The Greek-English New Testament*, Zondervan Publishing House, Grand Rapids, Michigan,xxiii, 1027 pp. (Book of Revelation on pp. 724-777).

Massey, G., 1907. *Ancient Egypt, the Light of the World: Book XI: Egyptian Wisdom in the Revelation of John the Divine.* T.Fisher Unwin, Adelphi Terrace, London, 1907.

Metzger, B.M. and M.D. Coogan, editors, 1993. *The Oxford Companion to the Bible*, Oxford University Press, Oxford, 874 pp. + maps.

Negev, A. (Editor), 1986. *The Archological Encylopedia of the Holy Land,* Prentice Hall Press, New York, 419 pp.

New Oxford Annotated Bible, New Revised Standard Version, 1991. Oxford University Press, New York.

Odelain, O. and R. Séguineau, 1981. *Dictionary of Proper Names and Places of the Bible,* Doubleday, xl, 479 p. [6] leaves of plates.

Osman, Ahmed, 1990. *Moses, Pharaoh of Egypt - The Mystery of Akhenaten Resolved*, Collins Publishing Co., London, Toronto, 262 pp., [8] p. of plates: ill., maps.

Oxford Companion to the Bible. 1993. Edited by Bruce M. Metzger, and Michael D. Coogan, 1993. Oxford University Press, Oxford, 874 pp. + maps.

Oxford Encyclopedic English Dictionary, 1991. Edited by J.M. Hawkins and Rev.. Allen, Clarendon Press, Oxford, 1684 pp. plus appendices.

PC Study Bible, Version 1.7, *(1994)*, Biblesoft, Seattle, WA, USA.

Plato: See translation by Lee (1971).

Phillips, J.B., 1957. *The Book of Revelation – A new translation of the Apocalypse.* Wyman & Sons, Ltd, London. Preface + 55 pp.

Piankoff, A., 1954. *The Tomb of Ramesses VI, Translations with Introductions by A.P. and Photographic plates by L.F. Husson.* 441 pp. + Figures 143-157 + 196 Plates. Pantheon Books Inc. For Bollingen Foundation Inc., Princeton University.

Piankoff, A., 1955. *The Shrine of Tutankamon.* Bollingen Series XL.2, published by Pantheon Books Inc. For Bollingen Foundation Inc., xii, 139 pp, 33 leaves of plates.

Piankoff, A., 1974. *The Wandering of the Soul,* Bollingen Series XL.6, Princeton University Press, xviii, 124 pp., 47 pp. of illus.

Rabinovich, Y., 2005. *Isle of Fire.* Vol. 5, *The Book of What's in Hell* , Invisible Books (invisiblebooks.com), 278 pp.

Rebbi, C., 1979. *Solitons in particle physics,* Scientific American, Vol. 240, No. 2, Feb. 1979 pp. 92-116.

Petrie, F., 1940. *Wisdom of the Egyptians,* British school of archaeology in Egypt and B. Quaritch Ltd., xvi, 162 pp.

Sawyer, John F.A., 1993. In *The Oxford Companion to the Bible,* p. 514.

Sauneron S., 1957. *Les prêtres de l'ancienne Egypte,* (Paris, 1967); referred to by Clagett, M., (1989). *Ancient Egyptian Science,* Note 14, p. 378.

Shanks, H. (editor), 1992. *Understanding the Dead Sea Scrolls.* Random House, New York, 336 pp.

Shaw, I. (editor), 2000. *The Oxford History of Ancient Egypt,* Oxford University Press, Oxford, pp. 512.

Simpson, Wm. K., 1965. *The Study of Egyptian Literature, 1925-1965,* an Introduction to the Torchbook edition of Erman, A., 1926, *The Ancient Egyptians,* p. xxix.

Spence, L., 1915. Ancient Egyptian Myths and Legends. Originally published in 1915 by George G. Harrap & Company, London, under the name Myths and Legends of Ancient Egypt. Edition used here is that by Dover Publications, Mineola, N.Y., 1990, 370 pp.

Strong's Electronic Concordance (KJV), 1989.

Sullivan, D. G., 1988. *The discovery of Santorini Minoan tephra in western Turkey.* Nature 333, 552 - 554.

Sweet, J., 1993. *The Book of Revelation.* In *The Oxford Companion to the Bible*, pp. 651-655.

Van Seters, J., 1966. *The Hyksos; a new investigation.* New Haven and London, Yale University Press, xix, 220 pp. Illus., maps.

Vine's Expository Dictionary of Biblical Words, 1985. Thomas Nelson Publishers

Webster's Third New International Dictionary of the English language, Unabridged, 1993, Editor in Chief, Philip B. Grove and the Merrian-Webster editorial staff, Merriam-Webster, Inc., Publisher, 1662p.

Whybray, R.N., 1993. In *The Oxford Companion to the Bible,* p. 778.

Wilkinson, R.H., 1992. *Reading Egyptian Art, A hieroglyphic Guide to Ancient Egyptian Painting and Sculpture,* Thames and Hudson Ltd, London, 224 pp.

Wilkinson, R.H., 1994. *Symbol & Magic in Egyptian Art.* Thames and Hudson Ltd., London, 224 pages.

Wilson, I., 1985. *Exodus, the True Story Behind the Biblical Account,* Harper & Row, San Francisco, 208 pp.

Yadin, Y., 1992. *The Temple Scroll – the Longest Dead Sea Scroll.* In *Understanding the Dead Sea Scrolls,* edited by Shanks, 1992, pp. 88-112.

Von Dassow, E., 1994. *The Egyptian Book of the Dead.* Translated by Raymond O. Faulkner with additional translations and a commentary by Ogden Goelet. Introduction by Carol A. R. Andrews; edited by Eva Von Dassaw. Chronicle Books, San Francisco, 175 pp.

Young, Y., 1982. *Young's Analytical Concordance to the Bible,* Thomas Nelson Publishers, Nashville, 1090 pp. + *Index-Lexicon to the Old Testament,* 56 pp. + *Index-Lexicon to the New Testament,* 93 pp. + *Scripture Proper Names,* 22 pp.

Zeller, O., 1969. *Coptic Version of the New Testament in the Southern Dialect, Volume VII, The Catholic Epistles and the Apocalypse,* Osnabruck, 565 pp.

Zondervan Pictorial Bible Dictionary, 1963. Editor M.C. Tenney, Zondervan Publishing House, Grand Rapids, Michigan, 927 pages + maps with index.

REFERENCES

1. **Chapter 1.**
The Enigmatic Book of Revelation

2. Fiorenza (1985), p.35; quoted from Lohmeyer (1934) in *Die Offenbarung des Johannes*

1920-1934, TRu NF 6 (1934).

3. Fiorenza (1985), p. 35.

4. Fiorenza (1985), p. 15.

5. Du Tooit, (1993), p. 104.

6. Fiorenza, 1983, p. 86.

7. Fiorenza, 1983, p. 198.

8. Fiorenza (1983), pp. 85-113.

9. *Unger's Bible Handbook*, p. 838.

10. Collins, 1984, pp. 25-53.

11. Collins, 1984, p. 34.

12. Collins, (1976), p. 25.

13. Sweet (1993), p. 653

14. Hill (1985), p. 417; quoted by Fiorenza (1985), p. 135.

15. Fiorenza, 1983, pp. 133-134.

16. Fiorenza, 1983, p. 134.

17. Budge (1904), Vol. I, page 279.

18. Budge (1904), Vol. I, p. 279.

19. **Chapter 2.**
New Approaches

20. Goelet (1994), p. 148.

21. Clagett (1989), p. 241.

22. Gardiner (1927), p. 26-28.

23. Lurker (1980), p. 121.

24. Sauneron (1957), pp. 123-125; quoted by Clagett (1989), p. 277-279.

25. Goelet (1994), p. 146.

26. Goelet (1994), p. 147.

27. Goelet (1994), p. 146.

28. Budge (1904), Vol. 1 p. 370.

29. Budge (1904), Vol. 1, p. 402.

30. Budge (1904), Vol 2, p. 169.

31. Budge (1904), Vol 2, p. 298.

32. Clagett (1989), p. 346-347.

33. Fiorenza (1985), p. 35.

34. **Chapter 3.**
The Preeminent Deities

35. Budge (1934), p. 190.

36. Budge (1895), p. 274.

37. Budge (1934), p. 424.

38. Hornung (1983), p. 134-135.

39. Faulkner (1994), BD90, p. 109.

40. Budge (1895), p. cviii.

41. Breasted (1912), p. 33.

42. Budge(1904), Vol. 2, p. 113.

43. Hornung (1983), p. 134.

44. Budge (1934), p. 424.

45. Wilkinson (1992), p. 103.

46. Breasted (1912), p. 175.

47. Clagett (1989), p. 304.

48. Faulkner (1962), p. 122.

49. Budge (1920), p. 336.

50. Budge (1920), p. 334.

51. Faulkner (1962), p. 122.

52. Budge (1920), p. 334a.

53. Gardiner (1927), T8 on p. 511.

54. Gardiner (1927), p. 511.

55. Faulkner (1994), Plate BD110, Plate 34B.

56. Gardiner (1927), p. 491.

57. Wilkinson (1992), p. 85.

58. Clagett (1989), p. 520.

59. Gardiner (1927), p.459.

60. Faulkner (1962), p. 188.

61. Faulkner (1962), p. 189.

62. Gardiner (1927), p. 442.

63. Faulkner (1962), p. 189.

64. Lurker (1980), p. 55.

65. Piankoff (1954), p. 133.

66. Piankoff (1954), p. 134.

67. Marshall (1984), p. 735.

68. Budge (1920), p. 559b.

69. Budge (1920), p. 557b.

70. Hornung (1990), p. 88.

71. Hornung (1983), p. 93.

72. Hornung (1990), p. 88.

73. Hornung (1990), p. 122.

74. Hornung (1990), p. 122-124.

75. Hornung (1983), p. 95.

76. Budge (1920), p. 51a; Faulkner (1962), p. 21.

77. Budge (1920), p. 51b.

78. Hornung (1983), p. 274.

79. Lurker (1980), p. 26.

80. David (1980), p. 98.

81. Clagett (1989), p. 565.

82. Clagett (1989), p. 318.

83. Clagett (1989), p. 558.

84. *Zondervan's Pictorial Dictionary* (1963), p. 159.

85. *Vine's Expository Dictionary*.

86. Conybeare (1907), Note 1, p.3.

87. Ford (1975), p. 18.

88. Breasted (1912), p. 15.

89. Lurker (1980), p. 10, 100.

90. Lurker (1980), p. 66.

91. Hornung, (1990), p. 115.

92. Budge (1934), p. 202.

93. Piankoff (1954), p. 365.

94. Hornung (1990), p. 116.

95. Faulkner (1973), p. 125.

96. Budge (1934), p. 427.

97. Faulkner (1994), , p. 133-134.

98. *Encyclopædia Britannica, Micropædia (1976)*, Vol. I, p. 398.

99. *Vine's Articles*.

REFERENCES

100. Sawyer (1993), p. 514.
101. Faulkner (1994), BD122, p. 115c.
102. Faulkner (1969), p. 192.
103. Clagett (1989), p. 427, note 15.
104. Faulkner (1994), BD130, p. 117.
105. Faulkner (1 994), BD30A, Plate 3A.
106. Faulkner (1994), BD30B; Plate 4.
107. Faulkner (1994), BD30A; Plate 3A.
108. Budge, E.A.W., , 1934, p. 121.
109. Budge, E.A.W., , 1934, p. 181.
110. Faulkner (1994), BD17, Plate 8B.
111. Breasted (1912), p. 31.
112. Conybeare (1907)
113. Budge (1920), p. 504b.
114. *Zondervan's Pictorial Dictionary* (1963), p. 156.
115. Budge (1920), p. 508a.
116. Budge (1920), p. 509a.
117. **Chapter 4.
Other Characters in Revelation**
118. *Strong's Definitions.*
119. Budge (1904), Vol 1, pp. 157- 158.
120. Lurker (1980), p.66.
121. Piankoff (1954), p. 206.
122. Budge (1934), p. 518.
123. Faulkner (1994), Plate 9A.
124. Budge (1920), p. 32a.
125. Budge (1920), p. 31b.
126. Budge (1920), p. 645a.
127. Budge (1920), p. 636a.
128. Budge (1934), p. 132.
129. Budge (1904), Vol. 1, p, 492.
130. Faulkner (1962), p. 283.
131. Goelet (1994), p. 152.
132. Faulkner (1962), p. 5.
133. Budge (1920), p. 530b.
134. Budge (1920), p. 540b.
135. Faulkner (1962), p. 253.
136. Lurker (1980), p. 54.
137. Spence (1915), p. 53.
138. Clagett (1989), p.554.
139. Breasted (1912), p. 138.
140. Piankoff (1954), p. 188-190.
141. *Vine's Expository Dictionary.*
142. *Encyclopædia Britannica, Macropædia,* Vol. 1, p. 874g.
143. *Thayer's Definition*
144. *Encyclopædia Britannica, Macropædia,* Vol. 1, p. 875c.
145. Budge (1904), Vol. 1, p. 4-5.
146. Budge (1904), Vol. I. pp. 4-7.
147. *Vine's Expository Dictionary.*
148. *Strong's Definitions.*
149. *Brown-Driver-Briggs Definitions.*
150. *Strong's Definitions.*
151. *Encyclopædia Britannica, Micropædia,* Vol. III, 1976, p. 652-653.
152. Clagett (1989), Vol. I, p.291.

153. Hornung (1983), p. 163-164.

154. Gardiner (1927), p. 537.

155. Gardiner (1927), p. 521.

156. Gardiner (1927), p. 522.

157. Piankoff (1954), Plate 80 and p. 255.

158. Budge (1920), p. cxli.

159. Gardiner (1927), pp. 449, 593.

160. Lurker (1980), p. 29.

161. Wilkinson (1992), p. 67.

162. Wilkinson (1992), p. 67.

163. **Chapter 5.**
"The Word of God"

164. Clagett (1989), p. 304.

165. Budge (1904), Vol. I pp. 407.

166. Budge (1934), p. 121.

167. Clagett (1989) p. 390.

168. Lurker (1980), p. 120.

169. Faulkner (1994), p. 134.

170. Faulkner (1994), BD182, p. 133.

171. Faulkner (1994), BD123, p. 115,.

172. Budge (1934), p. 157.

173. Budge (1934), p. 307.

174. Breasted (1912), p. 304-305.

175. Budge (1934), p. 305

176. Budge (1934), p. 157.

177. Faulkner (1994), Plate 4.

178. Faulkner (1994), BD30B, Plate 3.

179. Faulkner (1994), BD183, p. 134,.

180. Budge (1934), p. 307.

181. Faulkner (1994), p. 102, BD17.

182. Faulkner (1994), Plate 12b, BD18.

183. Faulkner (1994), Plate 14a, BD18.

184. Breasted (1912), pp. 29-30.

185. Faulkner (1994), Plate 5, BD1.

186. Clagett (1989), p. 581.

187. Faulkner (1994), BD95, p. 109.

188. Frankfort (1948), p. 133.

189. Clagett (1989), p. 336.

190. Borghouts (1978); quoted by Clagett (1989), p. 337.

191. Faulkner (1994), BD182, p.133.

192. David (1980), p. 84.

193. David (1980), p. 83.

194. David (1980), p. 84.

195. David (1980), p. 85.

196. Erman (1927), pp.116-131.

197. Spence (1915), p. 92.

198. Clagett (1989), p. 415.

199. Budge (1904), Vol 1, p. 473.

200. Budge (1934), p. 208.

201. Wilkinson (1994), p. 109.

202. Wilkinson (1994), p. 106-107.

203. Lurker (1980), p. 100.

204. Breasted (1962), p. 178.

205. Erman (1927), p.95.

206. Budge (1904), Vol. I, p. 402.

207. Budge (1934), p. 152.

208. Budge (1904), Vol. I, p. 402.

209. Lurker (1980), p. 121.

210. **Chapter 6.
The Twelve Tribes of Israel**

211. Whybray (1993), p. 778.

212. Glasson (1965), p. 52.

213. Goelet (1994), p. 169.

214. Piankoff (1954), p. 169.

215. Piankoff (1954), p. 141.

216. Piankoff (1954), p. 141.

217. Piankoff (1954), p. 144.

218. Piankoff (1954), p. 180.

219. Piankoff (1954), p. 189.

220. Piankoff (1954), p. 188.

221. Piankoff (1954), p. 205.

222. Piankoff (1954), p. 180.

223. Piankoff (1954), p. 166.

224. Piankoff (1954), p. 144.

225. Piankoff (1954), p. 166.

226. Piankoff (1954), p. 173.

227. Piankoff (1954), p. 187.

228. Piankoff (1954), p. 187.

229. Piankoff (1954), p. 173.

230. Piankoff (1954), p. 176.

231. Glasson (1965), p. 52.

232. Gardiner (1927), p. 445.

233. Budge (1934), p. 456.

234. Breasted (1912), p. 146.

235. Piankoff (1954), pp. 313-314.

236. Piankoff (1954), pp. 316.

237. Piankoff (1954), pp. 314-315.

238. Piankoff (1954), p.145.

239. Piankoff (1954), p. 166.

240. BG4.2.7-10, A. Piankoff (1954), p. 168.

241. Piankoff (1954), p 180.

242. Piankoff (1954), p. 145.

243. Piankoff (1954), p. 180-189.

244. Piankoff (1954), p. 145.

245. Faulkner (1994), p. 106.

246. Piankoff (1954), p. 164.

247. Piankoff (1954), pp. 313.

248. Piankoff (1954), p. 164.

249. Piankoff (1954), p. 159.

250. Clagett (1989), pp. 556-559.

251. Faulkner (1994), BD64, p.106e.

252. Hornung (1999), p. 27–28.

253. Hornung (1983), pp. 66–99.

254. Budge (1934), pp. 12-17; 380-381.

255. Budge (1934), p. 16.

256. **Chapter 7. The Great Multitude**

257. Lurker (1980), p. 62.

258. Breasted, 1912, p. 336.

259. Lurker (1980), p. 62.

260. Hornung (1990), p. 139.

588   *Egyptian Origin of the Book of Revelation*

261. Hornung (1990), p. 139.

262. Gardiner (1927), p. 479.

263. Gardiner (1927), p. 479.

264. Lurker (1980), p.94.

265. Gardiner (1927), p. 479.

266. Piankoff (1954), p. 243.

267. Piankoff (1954), p. 298.

268. Piankoff (1954), p. 298.

269. Faulkner (1994), p. 128 .

270. Faulkner (1994), p.128

271. Wilkinson (1992), p. 175.

272. Piankoff (1954), p. 294-295.

273. Piankoff (1954), p. 190.

274. Spence, (1915), p. 134.

275. Piankoff (1954), p. 189.

276. Piankoff (1954), p. 188.

277. *New Oxford Annotated Bible*, p. 372 NT.

278. Hayes (1993), p. 729.

279. Piankoff (1954), p. 189.

280. Piankoff (1954), p. 308.

281. Budge (1920), p. 112a.

282. Faulkner (1962), p. 39.

283. Budge (1920), p. 114a.

284. Budge (1920), p. 776.

285. Budge (1920), p. 777.

286. Budge (1920), pp. 522a, 523a.

287. Budge (1920), p. 522b.

288. Budge, (1920), p. 909b.

289. Budge (1920), p. 909b.

290. Budge (1920), 914b.

291. Faulkner (1994), Plate 2.

292. Piankoff (1954), p. 168.

293. Piankoff (1954), p.177.

294. Piankoff (1954), p 189-190.

295. Piankoff (1954), p. 175.

296. Piankoff (1954), p. 189.

297. Piankoff (1954), p. 180.

298. Piankoff (1954), p. 144.

299. Piankoff (1954), p. 297.

300. Faulkner (1994), BD17, p. 102.

301. Faulkner (1994), BD17, p. 102.

302. Piankoff (1954), p. 141.

303. **Chapter 8. Egyptian Parallels in the Seven Letters**

304. Fiorenza (1985), p. 164.

305. Budge (1895), pp. xxxix to xl.

306. Piankoff (1954), p.49.

307. Faulkner, R., 1954, p. 103.

308. Faulkner, 1994, p. 114-115.

309. Piankoff (1954), p. 49.

310. Piankoff (1954), p. 49.

311. Piankoff (1954), p. 75.

312. Piankoff (1954), p. 53.

313. Piankoff (1954), p. 53.

314. Faulkner (1994), BD175, Plate 29.

REFERENCES

315. Faulkner (1994), BD125p. 115.

316. Anthes (1954), p. 44.

317. Anthes (1954), p. 21.

318. Clagett (1989), p 355.

319. Clagett (1989), p 428.

320. Anthes (1954), p. 21.

321. Zeller (1969), p. 276.

322. Breasted (1912), p. 33-34.

323. Breasted (1912), p. 33-34.

324. Breasted (1912), p. 36-37.

325. Faulkner (1994), Plate 3.

326. Faulkner (1994), Plate 4.

327. Faulkner (1994), Plate 22.

328. Faulkner (1994), Plates 12-14.

329. Faulkner (1994), Plate 4.

330. Faulkner (1994), Plate 4.

331. Budge (1895), p. lv.

332. Wallis (1895), p. lxxvii.

333. Budge (1895), p. 300.

334. Hornung (1990), p. 156.

335. Hornung (1990), p. 77.

336. Faulkner (1994), BD135, p. 118e.

337. Lurker (1980), p.123.

338. Lurker (1980), p.124.

339. Faulkner (1994), p. 107f.

340. Faulkner (1994), BD189. p. 134g-135e.

341. Hornung (1990), p. 55.

342. Budge (1895), p. lxxvi (quoting from the *Recueil de Travaux*, t. v., p. 10, l. 54ff).

343. Faulkner (1994), BD171, p. 128.

344. Faulkner (1994), BD172, p. 129e-f.

345. Faulkner (1994), Plate 1.

346. Piankoff (1954), p. 93-94.

347. Piankoff (1954), p. 100.

348. Hornung, (1990), p. 205

349. Faulkner (1994), BD18, Plate 12.

350. Lurker (1980), p. 47

351. David (1980), p. 75.

352. Faulkner (1994), p. 115a.

353. Faulkner (1994), BD136A, p. 118h.

354. Faulkner (1994), BD117, p. 114-115

355. Faulkner (1994), BD30B, Plate4Ag

356. Faulkner (1994), BD153B, p. 124d

357. *Interlinear Bible.*

358. Goelet (1994), p. 153.

359. Faulkner (1994), Plate 2Bh.

360. Budge (1904), Vol. 1. p. 301.

361. Budge (1904), Vol. 1. p. 301.

362. Lurker1980, p.25.

363. Goulet (1994), p.146.

364. Goulet (1994), p.146.

365. Budge (1912), pp. 42-55.

366. Budge (1893), p. 294.

367. Budge (1893), p. 295.

368. Faulkner (1994), BD30B, p. 103.

369. Budge (1893), p. 281.

370. Budge (1893), p. 295.

371. Lurker (1980), p. 129.

372. Faulkner (1994), BD164, p. 126a.

373. Faulkner (1994), BD122, p. 115.

374. Pyr. §1219a. Quoted by Breasted (1912), p. 173.

375. Faulkner (1969), PT §1207.

376. Budge (1934), p. 244.

377. Clagett (1989), p. 427, note 15.

378. Budge (1934), p. 244.

379. Budge (1904), Vol.2, p. 156.

380. Breasted (1912), p. 284; quote from Lacau, LXXXV, *Rec.* 32, 78.

381. Faulkner (1994), p.106e.

382. Faulkner (1994), p.106e.

383. Lurker (1980), p. 48.

384. Lurker (1980), p. 48.

385. After Erman, *Literature*, p. 64, and A. de Buck, in *Nieuw theologisch Tydschrift*, p. 337.

Quoted by Frankfort (1948, *Ancient Egyptian Religion*), p. 74.

386. Piankoff (1954), p. 49.

387. Piankoff (1954), p. 73.

388. Piankoff (1954), p. 129.

389. Faulkner (1994), p. 114-115.

390. Faulkner (1994), BD110, p. 113.

391. Budge (1904), , Vol. I. p. 328.

392. Budge (1904), Vol. II, p. 95-96.

393. Budge (1904), Vol. II, p. 97.

394. Budge (1920), p. 833a.

395. Hornung, (1990), Fig. 48, p. 83; Piankoff (1954), p. 87.

396. Hornung, (1990), p.83, Figure 48.

397. Piankoff (1954), p. 94.

398. Piankoff (1954), p. 97.

399. Piankoff (1954), p. 97.

400. Piankoff (1954), p. 93.

401. Piankoff, A., 1954, p. 98.

402. Piankoff (1954), p. 114.

403. Piankoff (1954), p. 115-116.

404. Piankoff (1954), p. 107.

405. Piankoff (1954), p. 116.

406. Piankoff (1954), p. 115-116.

407. Piankoff (1954), p. 107.

408. Piankoff (1954), p. 107.

409. *Thayer's Definition.*

410. *Strong's Definition.*

411. *The Zondervan Pictorial Bible Dictionary,* 1963., p. 711.

412. *The Zondervan Pictorial Bible Dictionary,* 1963., p. 711.

413. Piankoff (1954), p. 100.

414. Piankoff (1954), p. 45.

415. Piankoff (1954), p. 100.

416. Piankoff (1954), p. 96.

417. Piankoff (1954), p. 96.

418. Piankoff (1954), p. 97.

REFERENCES

419. Piankoff (1954), p. 97.

420. Wilkinson (1992), p. 183.

421. Piankoff (1954), p. 96.

422. Lurker (1980), p. 31.

423. Piankoff (1954), p. 90.

424. Piankoff (1994), p. 47.

425. *Zondervan Pictorial Bible Dictionary* (1963), Maps XIII to XVI.

426. Bourriau (2000), p. 194.

427. Bourriau (2000), p. 187.

428. Bourriau (2000), p. 195.

429. Bourriau (2000), p. 201.

430. Bourriau (2000), p. 195.

431. Grimal (1992), p. 186.

432. Bourriau (2000), p. 214.

433. Bourriau (2000), p. 195.

434. Grimal (1992), p. 392.

435. Baines and Malek (1980), p. 174.

436. Hornung (1999), p. 27.

437. Hornung (1999), p. 28.

438. Clagett (1989), p. 472.

439. **Chapter 9. Opening of the Scroll**

440. Piankoff (1954), p. 274.

441. Wilkinson (1992), p. 89.

442. Lurker (1980) p. 121.

443. Clagett (1989), pp. 371-372.

444. Faulkner, 1994, p. 107.

445. Faulkner, 1994, p. 109.

446. Gardiner (1927), p. 445.

447. Budge (1920), pp. 349-352; Gardiner (1927), pp. 572-573.

448. Gardiner (1927), p. 572.

449. Budge (1920), p. 348b.

450. Budge (1920), p. 349a, 376b.

451. Faulkner (1962), p. 134.

452. Piankoff (1954), p. 274.

453. Budge (1920), pp. 424b, 424a.

454. Faulkner, (1994), BD62, p. 106.

455. Lurker, 1980, p. 77.

456. *Zondervan Pictorial Bible Dictionary,* 1963, p. 484.

457. *Brown-Driver-Brigg's Definition.*

458. Piankoff (1954), p. 272.

459. Piankoff (1954), p. 273.

460. Piankoff (1954), p. 273.

461. Piankoff (1954), p. 274.

462. Clagett (1989), p. 30-32.

463. Budge (1904), Vol. 1, pp. 414-415.

464. **Chapter 10. Call to Arms**

465. Piankoff (1954), pp. 179-180.

466. Piankoff (1954), p. 144.

467. Piankoff (1954), p. 173.

468. Piankoff (1954), p. 297.

469. Wilkinson (1994), p. 144.

470. Gardiner (1927), p. 464.

471. *Oxford Encyclopedic English Dictionary,* (1991).

472. *Thayer's Definitions*.

473. *Webster's Third New International Dictionary of the English Language* (1993).

474. Piankoff (1954), p. 169.

475. Breasted (1962), p. 262.

476. Breasted (1962), p. 264.

477. Breasted (1962), p. 263.

478. Breasted, (1962), #418, p.180.

479. Breasted (1962), #416, p.179.

480. Breasted (1962), §435-436, pp. 187-188,

481. Breasted (1962), §437, p. 188-189.

482. Faulkner (1962), p. 14.

483. Faulkner (1962), p. 14.

484. Piankoff (1954), p. 281-282.

485. Piankoff (1954), p. 279.

486. Gardiner (1927), p. 513.

487. Piankoff (1954), p. 289.

488. Clagett (1989), p. 306.

489. Piankoff (1954), p. 286.

490. Piankoff (1954), p. 290.

491. Piankoff (1954), p. 290.

492. Piankoff (1954), p. 287.

493. Piankoff (1954), p. 286-292.

494. Breasted (1962), #657, p. 264.

495. **Chapter 11. Prelude to War**

496. Darnell (2004), p. 231.

497. Darnell (2004), p. 267.

498. Darnell (2004), p. 270.

499. Darnell (2004), p. 245.

500. Darnell (2004), p. 389.

501. Darnell (2004), p. 242.

502. Darnell (2004), p. 268.

503. Gardiner (1927), p. 443.

504. Gardiner (1927), p. 512.

505. Gardiner (1927), p. 443.

506. Wilkinson (1992), p. 135.

507. Darnell (2004), p. 275.

508. Darnell (2004), p. 274.

509. Darnell (2004), p. 275.

510. Wilkinson (1992), p. 135.

511. Budge (1920), p. 13b.

512. Budge (1920), p. 12b.

513. Darnell (2004), p. 270-272.

514. Faulkner (1994), p. 103.

515. Faulkner (1962), p. 112.

516. Faulkner (1962), p. 114.

517. Budge (1920), p. 346b.

518. Budge (1920), p. 344b.

519. Piankoff (1954), p. 295.

520. Piankoff (1954), p. 297.

521. Piankoff (1954), p. 308.

522. Budge (1920), p. 319b.

523. Budge (1920), p. 319b.

524. **Chapter 12. Silence in Heaven (Rev. 8:1)**

REFERENCES 593

525. Glasson (1965), p.55.

526. Unger (1967), p. 855.

527. Henry (1960), p. 1977.

528. *New Oxford Annotated Bible NRSV* (1989), p. 372NT.

529. Lurker (1980), p. 80.

530. Frankfort (1948), p. 65.

531. Frankfort (1948), p. 66.

532. Frankfort (1948), p. 69-70.

533. Frankfort (1948), p. 67-68; after A. de Buck, in *Nieuw theologisch Tydschrift,* XXI (Haarlem, 1932), 339.

534. Frankfort (1948), p. 78; quoted from Gunn, in *Journal of Egyptian Archaeology,* III (1916), 84.

535. Breasted (1912), p. 355-356.

536. Budge (1934), p. 317.

537. Budge (1934), p. 516.

538. Faulkner, 1994. , p. 116.

539. Faulkner, 1994. , p. 132.

540. Faulkner (1994), Plate 2B.

541. Faulkner, 1994. , p. 113.

542. Piankoff (1954), p.189-190.

543. Hornung (1990), p. 76.

544. Clagett (1989), p. 317.

545. Hornung (1990), p. 103.

546. Faulkner (1994), Plate 29B.

547. Faulkner (1994), Plate 29B.

548. Budge (1920), p. 810a.

549. Budge (1920), p. 800b.

550. Budge (1920), p. 810a.

551. Budge (1920), p. 800b.

552. Piankoff (1954), p. 310.

553. Piankoff (1954), p. 307.

554. Piankoff (1954), p. 310.

555. Faulkner (1994), p. 102.

556. **Chapter 13. Catastrophes**

557. *Thayer's Definitions* .

558. *Strong's Definitions.*

559. Wilson (1985), p. 122.

560. Wilson (1985), pp. 120-122.

561. Wilson (1985), p. 112.

562. Wilson (1985), p. 123.

563. Luce (1969), p. 84.

564. Luce (1969), p. 84.

565. Wilson (1985), p. 123.

566. Clagett (1989). p.372.

567. Clagett (1989), p. 247.

568. Faulkner (1994), pp. 121-123.

569. Faulkner (1994), p. 121.

570. Faulkner (1994), pp. 121-123.

571. Budge (1934), pp. 463-467.

572. Piankoff (1955), pp. 27-34.

573. Erman (1927), p.112-115.

574. Erman (1927), p.113.

575. Erman (1927), p.113.

576. Erman (1927), p.113.

577. Erman (1927), p.113.

578. Erman (1927), p.113.

579. Erman (1927), p.113.

580. Erman (1927), p.113-114.

581. Erman (1927), p.115.

582. Erman (1927), p.113.

583. Erman (1927), p.94-104.

584. Plato, *Timaeus*, Lee (1965), p. 34c.

585. Plato, *Timaeus*, Lee (1965), p. 33c.

586. Plato, *Timaeus*, Lee (1965), p. 35.

587. Plato, *Timaeus*, Lee (1965), p. 39b.

588. Plato, *Timaeus*, Lee (1965), p. 36a.

589. Plato, *Critias*. Lee, p.130c.

590. Plato, *Critias*. Lee, p. 134a.

591. Plato, *Critias*., Lee, p. 143.

592. Lentz (1999), p.138.

593. *Encyclopædia Britannica*, Macropaedia Vol. I, p. 119.

594. Wilson (1985), p. 112.

595. Wilson (1985), p. 122-123.

596. Wilson (1985), p. 122-123.

597. Wilson (1985), p. 119-120.

598. Sullivan (1988), Nature 333, 552 - 554.

599. Guichard *et al* (1993), Nature, 363, p. 610 - 612.

600. Daniel and Sheng (1986), Nature 320, pp. 733 - 735.

601. Kuniholm *et al* (1996), Nature 381, pp. 780 - 783.

602. Wilson (1985), p. 119.

603. Luce (1969), p. 71.

604. Wilson (1985), p. 135.

605. Rebbi (1979), Naturepp. 92-116.

606. Plato's *Timaeus*, Lee (1965), p. 34.

607. **Chapter 14.**
From Catastrophe to Myth

608. Simpson (1965) in Erman (1926), p. xxix.

609. Allen (1969), pp. 235-237.

610. Goelet (1994), p. 140.

611. Goelet (1994), p. 140.

612. Clagett, (1989), p. 492

613. Clagett (1989), p. 493.

614. Clagett (1989), p. 494.

615. Clagett, (1989), Note 1, p. 507.

616. Hornung (1999), p. 34.

617. Faulkner (1962), p. 63.

618. Gardiner (1927), p. 561.

619. Faulkner (1962), *ns* on p. 139.

620. Hornung (1990), p. 77.

621. Piankoff (1954), p. 177.

622. Hornung (1990), p. 156.

623. Collins (1984), p. 57-58.

624. Clagett (1989), p. 141.

625. Faulkner (1993), BD 17, Plates 9&10; also p. 102.

626. Budge (1920), p. 1030a.

627. Budge (1920), p 582a

628. Budge (1920), p. 132a.

629. Gardiner (1927), p. 455.

630. Gardiner (1927), p. 498; Faulkner (1962), p. 125.

631. Budge (1920), 796a.

632. Budge (1920), 775b.

633. Budge (1920), 775b.

634. Budge (1920), 796a.

635. Budge (1920), 439b.

636. Budge (1920), 439b.

637. Budge (1920), 439b.

638. Faulkner (1962), p. 160.

639. Grimal (1992), pp. 192-194.

640. **Chapter 15. The Little Scroll**

641. Piankoff (1954), p. 267.

642. Gardiner (1927), p. 474.

643. Piankoff (1954), p. 267.

644. Gardiner (1927), (see both N2 & N3), p. 485.

645. Budge (1920), p. 96a.

646. Faulkner (1962), p. 32.

647. Piankoff (1954), p. 267.

648. Piankoff (1954), p. 267.

649. Gardiner (1927), p. 533.

650. Budge (1920), p. 129b.

651. Budge (1934), p. 22.

652. Piankoff (1954), p. 263.

653. Piankoff (1954), p. 267.

654. Faulkner (1962), p. 256.

655. Budge (1920), p. 714b.

656. Faulkner (1962), p. 255.

657. Piankoff (1954), p. 265.

658. Piankoff (1954), p. 262.

659. Piankoff (1954), p. 262.

660. Piankoff (1954), p. 262.

661. Piankoff (1954), p. 267.

662. Hornung (1990), p. 122.

663. Clagett (1989), p. 541.

664. Piankoff (1955), note 97, p. 32.

665. Goelet (1994), p. 165.

666. Goelet, (1994), p. 147.

667. Wilkinson (1994), p. 157.

668. Lurker (1980), p. 26.

669. Piankoff (1954), p. 268.

670. Faulkner (1994), Plate 24B.

671. Piankoff (1954), p. 320.

672. Piankoff (1954), p. 320.

673. Budge (1912), p. 39.

674. Budge (1920), p. 38b.

675. Budge (1920), p. 39a.

676. Budge (1920), p. 209a.

677. Faulkner (1962), p. 79.

678. Budge (1920), p. 209a.

679. Faulkner (1962), p. 79.

680. Budge (1912), p. 39.

681. Conybeare (1974), p. 28.

682. Budge (1920), p. c.

683. Gardiner (1927), p. 443.

684. **Chapter 16.
Two Witnesses**

685. Hornung (1999), p. 96.

686. Hornung (1999), p. 97.

687. Hornung (1999), p. 97.

688. Hornung (1999), p. 102.

689. Gardiner (1927), p. 494.

690. Piankoff (1954), p. 357.

691. Faulkner (1962), p. 146.

692. Faulkner (1962), p. 165.

693. Piankoff (1954), p. 357.

694. Piankoff (1954), p. 359.

695. Gardiner (1927), p. 443.

696. Faulkner (1962), p. 208.

697. Faulkner (1962), p. 207.

698. Piankoff (1954), p. 331.

699. Piankoff (1954), p. 362.

700. Piankoff (1954), p. 362.

701. Gardiner (1927), p. 453.

702. Faulkner (1962), p. 160.

703. Faulkner (1962), p. 161.

704. Faulkner (1962), p. 183.

705. Gardiner (1927), p. 467.

706. Gardiner (1927), p. 451.

707. Gardiner (1927), p. 442.

708. Lurker (1980), p. 125.

709. Piankoff (1954), p. 348.

710. Faulkner (1962), p. 53.

711. Gardiner (1927), pp. 58-60.

712. Gardiner (1927), p.543.

713. Hornung (1990), p. 77.

714. Piankoff (1954), p. 256.

715. Piankoff (1954), p. 374.

716. Faulkner (1962), p. 123.

717. Faulkner (1962), p. 121.

718. Piankoff (1954), p. 359.

719. Piankoff (1974), p. 7.

720. Piankoff (1954), p. 376.

721. Piankoff (1954), p. 349.

722. Budge (1920), p. 891a.

723. Budge (1920), p. 891a.

724. Piankoff (1974), p. 14.

725. Faulkner (1962), p. 288.

726. Faulkner (1962), p. 289.

727. Faulkner (1962), p. 280.

728. Gardiner (1927), p. 485.

729. Piankoff (1954), p. 352.

730. Faulkner (1962), p. 280.

731. Piankoff (1954), pp. 340, 344, 349.

732. Faulkner (1962), p. 135.

733. Faulkner (1962), p. 7.

734. Gardiner (1927), p. 524.

REFERENCES 597

735. Gardiner (1927), p. 508.
736. Piankoff (1954), p. 343-344.
737. Budge (1920), p. 462a.
738. Piankoff (1954), p. 350.
739. Budge (1904), Vol. 2, p. 370.
740. Lurker (1980), p. 28.
741. Budge (1904), Vol 2, p. 369-370.
742. Lurker (1980), p. 49.
743. Hornung (1999), p. 97.
744. Hornung (1999), p. 102.
745. Hornung (1999), p. 97.
746. **Chapter 17.
The Woman in the Sky**
747. Collins (1976), p. 67.
748. Faulkner (1962), p. 87.
749. Faulkner (1962), p. 127.
750. Budge (1904), Vol 2, p. 104.
751. Hornung (1983), pp. 121-122.
752. Gardiner (1927), p. 486.
753. Hornung (1990), p. 90.
754. Piankoff (1954), p. 428.
755. Piankoff (1954), p. 390.
756. Piankoff (1954), p. 390.
757. Piankoff (1954), p. 391.
758. Piankoff (1954), p. 94.
759. Piankoff (1954), p. 391.
760. Budge (1900), p. 47.
761. Budge (1934), p. 491.
762. Budge (1934), p. 503.
763. Budge (1934), p. 202.
764. Piankoff (1954), p. 391.
765. Piankoff (1954), p. 392.
766. Faulkner (1994), p. 102.
767. Piankoff (1954), p. 398.
768. Piankoff (1954), p. 400.
769. Piankoff (1954), p. 401.
770. Hannah (1999), pp. 214-215.
771. *Strong's Definitions*.
772. Budge (1920), p. 285a.
773. Piankoff (1954), p. 400.
774. Piankoff (1954), p. 401.
775. Piankoff (1954), p. 402.
776. Faulkner (1994), Plate 34A.
777. Faulkner (1994), p. 113.
778. Piankoff (1954), p. 402.
779. Lurker (1980), p. 127-128.
780. Faulkner (1994), Plate 29B.
781. Hornung (1983), p. 164.
782. Piankoff (1954), p. 427.
783. Lurker (1980), p. 104.
784. Gardiner (1927), p. 477.
785. Piankoff (1954), p. 427.
786. Clagett (1989), p. 368.
787. Gardiner (1927), p. 582.
788. Piankoff, (1954), Note 37, p. 404.
789. Lurker (1980), p. 43.

790. Lurker (1980), p. 31.

791. Lurker (1980), p. 31.

792. Hornung (1983), p. 222.

793. Marshall (1984), pp. 750.

794. Hornung (1999), p. 124.

795. Piankoff (1954), p. 409.

796. Piankoff (1954), p. 411.

797. Piankoff (1954), p. 412.

798. Clagett (1989), p. 279.

799. Piankoff (1954), Plate 2.

800. Wilkinson (1994), p. 46.

801. Piankoff (1954), p. 411.

802. Piankoff (1954), p. 415.

803. Piankoff (1954), p. 416.

804. Piankoff (1954), p. 418.

805. Piankoff (1954), p. 419.

806. Gardiner (1927), p. 488.

807. Piankoff (1954), p. 420.

808. Piankoff (1954), p. 411.

809. Piankoff (1954), p. 421.

810. Budge (1934), p. 202.

811. Spence (1915), p. 92.

812. Hornung (1990), p. 117.

813. Piankoff (1954), p. 411.

814. Piankoff (1954), p. 412-413.

815. Piankoff (1954), p. 413.

816. **Chapter 18.
The Beasts of Rev. 13**

817. Budge (1934), p. 360.

818. Gardiner (1927), p. 545.

819. Piankoff (1954), Plate 80.

820. Piankoff (1954), p. 269.

821. Gardiner (1927), p. 457.

822. Faulkner (1962), p. 126.

823. Gardiner (1927), p. 510.

824. Faulkner (1962), p. 181.

825. Gardiner (1927), p. 486.

826. Budge (1920), p. 893a.

827. See Gardiner (1927), p. 449.

828. Piankoff (1954), p. 259.

829. Faulkner (1962), p. 82.

830. Faulkner (1962), p. 25.

831. Faulkner (1962), p. 26.

832. Faulkner (1962), p. 26.

833. Faulkner (1962), p. 27.

834. Piankoff (1954), p. 259.

835. Wilkinson (1992), p. 54-55.

836. Piankoff (1954), p. 259.

837. Faulkner (1962), p. 82; Gardiner (1927), p. 476.

838. Faulkner (1962), p. 82; Gardiner (1927), p. 476.

839. Wilkinson (1994), p. 189.

840. Piankoff (1954), p. 259.

841. Gardiner (1927), p. 485.

842. Gardiner (1927), p. 487.

843. Budge (1904), Vol I, figure on p. 219.

REFERENCES

844. Lurker (1980), p. 109.
845. Hornung (1990), p. 115.
846. Wilkinson (1992), p. 67.
847. Lurker (1980), p. 110.
848. Lurker (1980), p. 29.
849. Budge (1934), p. 467.
850. Budge (1934), p. 469.
851. Budge (1934), p. 473.
852. Budge (1934), p. 474.
853. Faulkner (1962), p. 260.
854. Lurker (1980), p. 95-96.
855. Gardiner (1927), p. 508.
856. Budge (1904), Vol. I, p. 217-218.
857. Piankoff (1954), p. 257.
858. Budge (1904), Vol I, p. 409.
859. Wilkinson (1992), p. 43.
860. Lurker (1980), p. 26.
861. Piankoff (1954), Note 87, p. 258.
862. Piankoff (1954), p. 258.
863. Piankoff (1954), Plate 83.
864. Gardiner (1927), p. 523.
865. Budge (1920), p. cxivii.
866. Piankoff (1954), p. 255.
867. Gardiner (1927), p. 457.
868. Gardiner (1927), p. 449.
869. Piankoff (1954), p. 255.
870. Gardiner (1927), p. 478.
871. Lurker (1980), p. 119-110.
872. Wilkinson (1992), p. 109.
873. Piankoff (1954), p. 255.
874. Piankoff (1954), p. 256.
875. Piankoff (1954), p. 256.
876. Gardiner (1927), p. 445.
877. Piankoff (1954), p. 256.
878. Gardiner (1927), §39, p. 42.
879. Gardiner (1927), §86, p. 66.
880. Piankoff (1954), p. 255
881. Budge (1920), p. 279b.
882. Piankoff (1954), p. 256.
883. Piankoff (1954), p. 256.
884. Erman (1927), p. 143.
885. Faulkner (1962), p. 303.
886. Faulkner (1962), p. 131.
887. Piankoff (1954), p. 256.
888. Piankoff (1954), p. 256.
889. Budge (1920), p. 384a.
890. Lurker (1980), p. 73.
891. Piankoff (1954), p. 255.
892. Gardiner (1927), p. 521.
893. Gardiner (1927), p. 521.
894. Faulkner (1962), p. 128.
895. Faulkner (1962), p. 128.
896. Gardiner (1927), p. 521.
897. Gardiner (1927), p. 521.
898. Budge (1920), p. 17a.
899. Budge (1920), p. 17a.

900. Budge (1920), p. 706b.
901. Budge (1920), p. 706b.
902. Gardiner (1927), p. 521.
903. Gardiner (1927), p. 522.
904. Budge (1920), p. cxli.
905. Gardiner (1927), p. 497.
906. Budge (1920), p. 19a.
907. Budge (1920), p. 19b.
908. Budge (1920), p. 19b.
909. Rabinovich (2005), p. 148.
910. Hornung (1999), p. 27.
911. Piankoff (1954), p. 255.
912. Grimal (1992), p. 186.
913. Grimal (1992), p. 187.
914. Grimal (1992), p. 187.
915. Grimal (1992), p. 189.
916. Grimal (1992), pp. 189-193.
917. Faulkner (1962), p. 169.
918. Faulkner (1962), p. 142.
919. Faulkner (1962), p. 169.
920. Faulkner (1994), BD17, p. 102.
921. Breasted (1912), p. 40.
922. Budge (1934), p. 360.

923. **Chapter 19.**
Reaping of the Harvest

924. Piankoff (1954), p. 241.
925. Piankoff (1954), p. 242.
926. Piankoff (1954), p. 243.
927. Piankoff (1954), p. 243.
928. Gardiner (1927), p. 479.
929. Piankoff (1954), p. 244.
930. Piankoff (1954), p. 240.
931. Piankoff (1954), p. 244.
932. Faulkner (1962), p. 103.
933. Lurker (1980), p.58.
934. Piankoff (1954), p. 245.
935. Wilkinson (1992), p. 73.
936. Piankoff (1954), p. 242.
937. Faulkner (1994), p. 104.
938. Faulkner (1994), Plate 1A.
939. Budge (1904), Vol 2, pp. 367-368.
940. Lurker (1980), pp. 30-31.
941. Piankoff (1954), p. 244.
942. Piankoff (1954), p. 241.
943. Piankoff (1954), p. 245.
944. Piankoff (1954), p. 245.
945. Piankoff (1954), p. 246.
946. Piankoff (1954), p. 243-244.
947. Lurker (1980), p. 130.
948. Budge (1934), p. 243.
949. Hornung (1983), p. 206.
950. Clagett (1989), Vol. 1, p. 479.

951. **Chapter 20.**
The Song of Moses

952. Fiorenza (1985), p. 135.
953. Budge (1920), p. 902a.

REFERENCES

954. Faulkner (1962), p. 320.

955. Budge (1920), p. 900a.

956. Budge (1920), p. 902a.

957. Budge (1920), p. 900b.

958. Budge (1920), p. 900b.

959. Faulkner (1962), p. 318

960. Piankoff (1954), p. 152.

961. Piankoff (1954), p. 152.

962. Gardiner (1927), p. 497.

963. Budge (1920), p. 795a.

964. Budge (1920), p. 795a.

965. Petrie (1940), p.61.

966. *Encyclopædia Britannica* (1976), *Macropædia,* Vol. 17, p. 742.

967. Gardiner (1927), p. 539.

968. Faulkner (1962), p. 19.

969. Piankoff (1954), p. 159.

970. Piankoff (1954), p. 163.

971. Piankoff (1954), p. 163.

972. Breasted (1962), §655, p. 262.

973. Breasted (1962), pp. 263-266.

974. *Strong's Definitions* .

975. Budge (1920), p. 932.

976. Breasted (1962), p. 262.

977. Grmial (1992), p. 392.

978. Wilkinson (1994). p. 173.

979. Breasted (1962), §657-658, pp. 264-266.

980. Breasted (1962), p. 262.

981. Erman (1927), p. 254.

982. **Chapter 21.
Seven Angels with the Wrath of God**

983. Gardiner (1927), p. 491.

984. Gardiner (1927), p.497.

985. Piankoff (1954), p. 153.

986. Piankoff (1954), p. 154.

987. Piankoff (1994), p. 153-154.

988. Hornung (1999), p. 60.

989. Piankoff (1954), p. 146.

990. Piankoff (1954), pp. 147-148.

991. Wilkinson (1992), p. 57.

992. Gardiner (1927), p. 461.

993. Piankoff (1954), p. 153.

994. Piankoff (1954), p. 153.

995. Piankoff (1954), p. 154.

996. *Strong's Definitions* .

997. Piankoff (1954), p. 153.

998. Piankoff (1954), p. 153.

999. Piankoff (1954), p. 154.

1000. Piankoff (1954), Note 15, p. 416.

1001. Hornung (1990), p. 59.

1002. Faulkner (1994), Plate 9B.

1003. Budge (1934), p. 518.

1004. Budge (1920), p. 188-189.

1005. Faulkner (1962), pp. 71-72.

1006. Budge (1920), p. 188a.

1007. Piankoff (1954), p. 154.

1008. Piankoff (1954), p. 154.

1009. Hornung (1990), p. 59.

1010. Piankoff (1954), p. 154.

1011. Hornung (1990), p. 151.

1012. Piankoff (1954), p. 172.

1013. Hornung (1990), p. 151-152.

1014. Piankoff (1954), p. 159.

1015. Wilkinson (1994), p. 106.

1016. Piankoff (1954), p. 159.

1017. Faulkner (1994), p. 131.

1018. Faulkner (1994), BD134, Plate 22B.

1019. Breasted (1912), p. 128.

1020. Breasted (1912), p. 129.

1021. Faulkner (1927), §34, p. 39.

1022. Piankoff (1954), p. 159.

1023. Piankoff (1954), p. 195.

1024. Piankoff (1954), p. 154.

1025. Piankoff (1954), p. 157.

1026. Piankoff (1954), p. 152.

1027. Budge (1920), p. 889a.

1028. Budge (1920), p. 889a.

1029. Budge (1920), p. 889b.

1030. Budge (1920), p. 889b.

1031. Budge (1920), p. 889b.

1032. Budge (1920), p. 889a.

1033. Budge (1920), p. 611a.

1034. Budge (1920), p. 611a.

1035. Budge (1920), p. 227b.

1036. Budge (1920), p. 227b.

1037. Budge (1920), p. 50b.

1038. Budge (1920), p. 50b.

1039. Wilkinson (1992), p. 109.

1040. Piankoff (1954), p. 160.

1041. Piankoff (1954), p. 177.

1042. Piankoff (1954), p. 195.

1043. Piankoff (1954), p. 314.

1044. Hornung (1990), p. 91.

1045. **Chapter 22. Armageddon**

1046. Barnes (1993), p. 56.

1047. *Zondervan's Pictorial Bible Dictionary*, 1963. p. 71

1048. Breasted (1962), pp. 163(§391) - 266(§662)

1049. Breasted (1962), Note *a*, p. 163.

1050. Grimal (1992), p.213.

1051. Breasted (1962), p. 180, §420.

1052. Breasted (1962), p. 181, §424.

1053. Breasted (1962), p. 183, §429.

1054. Breasted (1962), p. 183, §429.

1055. Breasted (1962), p. 184, §430.

1056. Piankoff (1954), p. 180.

1057. Piankoff (1954), p. 180-181.

1058. Piankoff (1954), p. 157.

1059. Grimal (1992), p. 189.

1060. Grimal (1992), p. 189.

1061. Piankoff (1954), p. 162.

REFERENCES

1062. Piankoff (1954), p. 161.

1063. Piankoff (1954), p. 161.

1064. Piankoff (1954), p. 162.

1065. Wilkinson (1992), p. 107.

1066. Piankoff (1954), p. 161.

1067. Budge (1920), p. 12b.

1068. Budge (1920), p. 14a.

1069. Budge (1920), p. 12b.

1070. Budge (1920), p. 14a.

1071. Budge (1920), p. 14a.

1072. Faulkner (1962), p. 99.

1073. Budge (1920), p. 240b.

1074. Faulkner (1962), p. 91.

1075. Piankoff (1954), p. 182.

1076. Breasted (1962), §429, p. 183.

1077. Wilkinson (1992), p. 107.

1078. Piankoff (1954), p. 182.

1079. Piankoff (1954), p. 181.

1080. Piankoff (1954), p. 183.

1081. Piankoff (1954), p. 169.

1082. Piankoff (1954), p. 169.

1083. Piankoff (1954), p. 170.

1084. Erman (1966), p. 254.

1085. Grimal (1992), p. 191.

1086. Grimal (1992), p. 192.

1087. Grimal (1992), p. 194.

1088. Piankoff (1954), Plate 50 and p.180.

1089. Faulkner (1962), p.152.

1090. Faulkner (1962), p. 192.

1091. Grimal (1992), p. 213.

1092. Breasted (1962), §549, p. 221.

1093. **Chapter 23.**
The Harlot and the Kings

1094. Piankoff (1954), p. 200.

1095. Budge (1920), p. 109b.

1096. Budge (1920), p. 109b.

1097. Budge (1920), p. 109b.

1098. Budge (1920), p. 15a.

1099. Budge (1920), p. 15b.

1100. Budge (1920), p. 142a.

1101. Budge (1920), p. 117a.

1102. Budge (1920), p. 118a.

1103. Budge (1920), p. 63a.

1104. Budge (1920), p. 64b.

1105. Budge (1920), p. 284a.

1106. Budge (1920), p. 282a.

1107. Budge (1920), p. 510a.

1108. Budge (1920), p. 510a.

1109. Budge (1920), p. 486b.

1110. Budge (1920), p. 486b.

1111. Wilkinson (1992), p. 105.

1112. Budge (1920), p. 751a.

1113. Budge (1920), p. 751a.

1114. Budge (1920), p. 751b.

1115. Budge (1920), pp. 751a,b.

1116. Lurker (1980), p. 29.

1117. Wilkinson (1994), pp. 106-107.

1118. Budge (1920), p. 111a.

1119. Budge (1920), p. 111a.

1120. Hornung (1990), p. 104.

1121. Budge (1920), p. 213a.

1122. Budge (1920), p. 231a.

1123. Budge (1920), p. 213a.

1124. Piankoff (1954), p.200.

1125. Hornung (1990), p. 104.

1126. Wilkinson (1992), p. 69.

1127. Faulkner (1994), p. 102.

1128. Budge (1920), p. 895a

1129. Budge (1920), p. 896a.

1130. Piankoff (1954), p. 199.

1131. Piankoff (1954), p. 198.

1132. Gardiner (1927), p. 196.

1133. Piankoff (1954), p. 200.

1134. Piankoff (1954), p. 201.

1135. Piankoff (1954), p. 195.

1136. Piankoff (1954), p. 195.

1137. Budge (1920), p. 869a.

1138. Budge (1920), p. 872b.

1139. Budge (1920), p. 449b.

1140. Budge (1920), p. 442a.

1141. *Strong's Definitions* .

1142. Baines and Malak (1980), p.36.

1143. Grimal (1992), p. 185-186.

1144. Grimal (1992), p. 185.

1145. Grimal (1992), p. 186.

1146. Hornung (1999), p. 71.

1147. Negev (1986), p. 45.

1148. Lurker (1980), pp. 26, 31.

1149. Negev (1986), p. 45.

1150. *New Larousse Encylopedia of Mythology*, p. 58.

1151. Grimal (1992), p. 185.

1152. Grimal (1992), p. 187.

1153. Baines and Málek (1980), p.36.

1154. Clagett (1989), p. 632.

1155. Shaw (2000), p. 481.

1156. Hornung (1999B), pp. xvi, 72.

1157. Grimal (1992), pp. 194, 392.

1158. Grimal (1992), p. 194.

1159. Baines and Málek (1980), p.36.

1160. Hornung (1999), pp. xvi, 72.

1161. Shaw(2000), p. 481.

1162. Clagett (1989). p. 632.

1163. Grimal (1992), pp. 194, 392.

1164. Grimal (1992), p. 187.

1165. Grimal (1992), pp. 187-188.

1166. Grimal (1992), p. 189.

1167. Grimal (1992), p. 189.

1168. Grimal (1992), p. 191.

1169. Grimal (1992), p. 191-193.

1170. Grimal (1992), p. 192.

1171. Conybeare (1974), p. 45.

1172. **Chapter 24.**
The Millennium

1173. Piankoff (1954), p. 205.

1174. Lurker (1980), p. 106.

1175. Piankoff (1954), p. 208.

1176. Piankoff (1954), p. 209.

1177. Piankoff (1954), p. 209.

1178. Piankoff (1954), p. 206.

1179. Wilkinson (1992), p. 54-55.

1180. *Strong's Definitions*.

1181. *Thayer's Definitions*.

1182. Piankoff (1954), p. 206.

1183. Piankoff (1954), p. 206-207.

1184. Piankoff (1954), p. 206.

1185. Faulkner (1969), PT Utterance 665A, §1910-1912, p. 276.

1186. Hornung (1990), p. 74.

1187. Hornung (1983), p. 168.

1188. Budge (1934), p. 286.

1189. Hornung (1990), p. 142.

1190. Hornung (1990), p. 80.

1191. Budge (1904), Vol. 2, p. 371-372.

1192. Budge (1893), p. 479.

1193. Budge (1904), Vol. 2, p. 371-372.

1194. Clagett (1989), p. 423.

1195. Clagett (1989), p. 482.

1196. Piankoff (1954), p. 208.

1197. Faulkner (1962), p. 283.

1198. Faulkner (1962), p. 183.

1199. Budge (1920), p. 526a.

1200. Budge (1920), p. 526b.

1201. Budge (1920), p. 529a.

1202. Budge (1920), p. 529b.

1203. Faulkner (1962), p. 183.

1204. Faulkner (1962), p. 183.

1205. Budge (1920), p. 538a.

1206. Budge (1920), p. 539a.

1207. Budge (1920), p. 535b.

1208. Faulkner (1962), p. 284.

1209. Faulkner (1962), p. 184.

1210. Faulkner (1962), p. 281.

1211. Budge (1920), p. 529b.

1212. Piankoff (1954), p. 209.

1213. Lurker (1980), p. 108.

1214. Faulkner (1994), BD87, Plate 27A.

1215. Wilkinson (1992), p. 101.

1216. Piankoff (1954), p. 209.

1217. Piankoff (1954), p. 211.

1218. Piankoff (1954), p. 211.

1219. Wilkinson (1992), p. 131.

1220. Hornung (1990), p. 123-124.

1221. Budge (1920), p. 514a.

1222. Budge (1920), p. 512b.

1223. Budge (1920), p. 512b.

1224. Budge (1920), p. 515a.

1225. Budge (1920), p. 514b.

1226. Budge (1920), p. 515b.

1227. Budge (1920), p. 515b.

1228. Budge (1920), p. 514b.

1229. Budge (1920), p. 515b.

1230. Budge (1893), p. 478.

1231. Faulkner (1962), p. 176.

1232. Faulkner (1962), p. 176.

1233. Gardiner (1927), p. 453.

1234. Gardiner (1927), p. 453.

1235. Gardiner (1927), p. 453.

1236. Piankoff (1954), p. 211-212.

1237. Piankoff (1954), p. 209.

1238. Piankoff (1954), p. 209.

1239. Hornung (1990), p. 121.

1240. Piankoff (1954), p. 210.

1241. Wilkinson (1992), p. 181.

1242. Piankoff (1954), p. 212.

1243. Piankoff (1954), pp. 220-221.

1244. Piankoff (1954), p. 220-221.

1245. Piankoff (1954), p. 156.

1246. Hornung (1990), p. 76.

1247. Hornung (1990), p. 106-107.

1248. Piankoff (1954), p. 210.

1249. Piankoff (1954), p. 210.

1250. Piankoff (1954), p. 208.

1251. Piankoff (1954), p. 218.

1252. Piankoff (1954), p. 218-219.

1253. Barnes (1993), p. 256.

1254. *Zondervan Pictorial Bible Dictionary* (1963), p. 502.

1255. Grimal (1992), pp. 350, 358-359.

1256. **Chapter 25.
Resurrection and the Judgment**

1257. *The New Oxford Annotated Bible*, RSV, 1991, p. 385NT.

1258. Budge (1934), p. 351.

1259. Lurker (1980), p. 77.

1260. Piankoff (1954), p. 411.

1261. Piankoff (1954), p. 413.

1262. Piankoff (1954), p. 417.

1263. Hornung (1990), p. 138.

1264. Piankoff (1954), p. 411.

1265. Piankoff (1954), p. 413.

1266. Piankoff (1954), p. 413.

1267. Piankoff (1954), p. 422.

1268. Piankoff (1954), p. 414-415.

1269. Gardiner (1927), p. 488.

1270. Lurker (1980), p. 51.

1271. Piankoff (1954), p. 416.

1272. Piankoff (1954), note 15, p. 416.

1273. Piankoff (1954), p. 418.

1274. Piankoff (1954), p. 420.

1275. Piankoff (1954), p. 419.

1276. Goelet (1994), p. 153.

1277. Wilkinson (1994), p. 104.

1278. Faulkner (1962), p. 181.

1279. Wilkinson (1994), p. 109.

1280. Spence (1915), p. 125.

1281. Wilkinson (1994), p. 109.

1282. Piankoff (1954), p. 422.

1283. Hornung (1999), p. 125.

1284. Budge (1920), p. 130b.

1285. Faulkner (1962), p. 45.

1286. Budge (1920), p. 129b.

1287. Budge (1920), p. 129a.

1288. Faulkner (1962), p. 45.

1289. Budge (1920), p. 129a.

1290. Budge (1920), p. 129b.

1291. Wilkinson (1992), p. 109.

1292. Breasted (1912), p. 136.

1293. Lanzone, op. cit., pl. 360, p. 1068; quoted by Budge (1934), p. 61.

1294. Budge (1934), p. 61.

1295. Budge (1934), p. 287.

1296. Piankoff (1954), p. 424.

1297. Piankoff (1954), p. 424.

1298. Clagett, M., (1989). , p. 455.

1299. Breasted (1912), p. 309.

1300. Piankoff (1954), p. 428.

1301. **Chapter 26.
A New Creation**

1302. Hornung (1983), p. 161-162.

1303. *Strong's Definitions* .

1304. *Thayer's Definitions* .

1305. Hornung (1983), p. 227.

1306. Clagett (1989), p. 356.

1307. Clagett (1989), p. 359-360.

1308. Piankoff (1954), pp. 215-216.

1309. Breasted (1912), p. 21-22 (reformatted).

1310. Hornung (1983), p. 161.

1311. Hornung (1990), p. 56.

1312. Budge (1920), p. 350a.

1313. Faulkner (1962), p. 127.

1314. Budge (1920), p. 350b.

1315. Faulkner (1962), p. 125.

1316. Faulkner (1994), BD169, p. 128.

1317. Breasted (1912), p. 130.

1318. Budge (1934), p. 409.

1319. Hornung (1990), p. 75.

1320. Hornung (1992), p. 110.

1321. Hornung (1990), p. 122.

1322. Piankoff (1954), p. 220.

1323. Piankoff (1954), p. 220.

1324. Piankoff (1954), p. 220-221.

1325. Piankoff (1954), p. 221.

1326. Budge (1895), pp. lxxv-lxxvi.

1327. Piankoff (1954), p. 216.

1328. Piankoff (1954), p. 217-218.

1329. Wilkinson (1992), p.135.

1330. Piankoff (1954), p. 215-216.

1331. Piankoff (1954), p. 221.

1332. Hornung (1983), p. 183.

1333. Hornung (1992), p. 65.

1334. Hornung (1992), p. 64-65.

1335. Hornung (1992), p. 65.

1336. Piankoff (1954), Plate 7A.

1337. Hornung (1990), figure on p. 55.

1338. Lurker (1980), p. 127.

1339. Frankfort, (1948), p. 80.

1340. Frankfort, (1948), p. 80.

1341. Lurker (1980), p. 102.

1342. Lurker (1980), p. 127-128.

1343. Lurker (1980), p. 11.

1344. *Pyramid Text* §848 quoted by Breasted (1912), p. 19.

1345. Pyramid Text §848 quoted by Breasted (1912), p. 19.

1346. Piankoff (1954), p. 248.

1347. Faulkner (1994), p. 122.

1348. Faulkner (1994), Plate 6.

1349. Clagett (1989), p. 325.

1350. Breasted (1912), p. 20-21.

1351. Breasted (1912), *Pyramid Text* §2063-8, p. 19.

1352. **Chapter 27. The Holy City**

1353. Hornung (1990), p. 74.

1354. Faulkner (1994), BD70, p. 108.

1355. Faulkner (1994), BD99, p. 110.

1356. Glasson (1965), p. 118.

1357. Budge (1904), Vol I, pp. 273-274.

1358. Budge (1904), Vol I, note 1, p. 274,.

1359. Wilkinson (1994), p. 104.

1360. Wilkinson (1994), p. 108.

1361. Budge (1912), pp. 121-141.

1362. Budge (1912), pp. 123-125.

1363. Budge (1912), p. 131.

1364. Faulkner (1994), BD169, p. 128.

1365. Wilkinson (1994), p. 67.

1366. Wilkinson (1994), p. 174.

1367. Breasted (1912), p. 154-155.

1368. Breasted (1912), p. 162.

1369. Faulkner (1994), BD68, p. 107.

1370. Faulkner (1994), BD127, p. 117.

1371. Budge (1920), p. 70b.

1372. Budge (1920), p. 130b.

1373. Faulkner (1994), BD169, p. 128.

1374. Faulkner (1994), BD70, p. 108.

1375. Faulkner (1962), p. 125.

1376. Budge (1920), p. 349b.

1377. Faulkner (1962), p. 127.

1378. Budge (1920), p. 349b.

1379. Budge (1920), p. 400a.

1380. Budge (1920), p. 400a.

1381. Gardiner (1927), p. 525.

1382. Gardiner (1927), p.490.

1383. Budge (1920), p. cxxvi.

1384. Gardiner (1927), p. 490.

1385. Hornung (1992), p. 127-128.

1386. Hornung (1992), p. 116.

1387. David (1980) p. 62.

1388. David (1980) p. 70.

1389. Lurker (1980), p. 109.

1390. Wilkinson (1994), p. 174.

1391. Hornung (1992), p. 118.

1392. Hornung (1992), p. 54.

1393. Wilkinson (1994), p. 27.

1394. Hornung (1992), p. 128.

1395. Hornung (1992), p. 119.

1396. **Chapter 30.
Literary Analyses**

1397. Sweet (1993), p. 654.

1398. Wilkinson (1994) p. 127.

1399. Wilkinson (1994), p. 126.

1400. **Chapter 31.
Perspectives**

1401. Sweet (1993), p. 654.

LIST OF APPENDICES

1. Names of the Tribes of Israel in the *Book of Gates* 611

2. Names of the Tribes of Israel in the *Amduat* 612

3. Attributes of the Multitudes in the Book of Revelation 614

4. *Book of Aker*, Part B 616

5. List of Selected Parallels 617

6. Glossary
   Egyptian Gods and Goddesses 620
   Egyptian Terms 622

APPENDIX 1

Names of the Tribes of Israel in the *Book of Gates*

English translations of the names of 33 of the 34 groups of 12 in the Book of Gates showing names matched (group #17 is unnamed) with those of the tribes of Israel referred to in Rev. 7:4-8. Those labeled "Good matches" in Table 6.1 are in bold.

1. BG-prologue/upper Those who came into being from Re 141
2. BG-prologue/lower (Those who came into being from Re ....) 143
3. **BG1.1.1-6 Those who are in** *peace* **who** *worship* **Re (Asher, Judah) 44**
4. BG1.1.6-10 The Just who are in the Netherworld 145
5. BG2.1a The Holy Ones in the Netherworld 151
6. BG2.1b The gods in the Lake of Fire 152
7. BG3.1a The gods who go to their *Kas* 159
8. BG3.1b The Jackals in the Lake of Life 159
9. BG3.1c The Living Uraie 160
10. BG3.2 They who stand upon their land 162
11. BG3.3 Gods behind the shrine 163
12. **BG4.1.1-4 Those who** *Acclaim* **in the Netherworld (Judah) 166**
13. **BG4.1.4-8 Those who carry the** *cord* **in the fields of the Netherworld (Levi) 166**
14. BG4.2a The souls of men in the Netherworld 167
15. BG4.2b Those who have spoken truth upon earth, those who worshiped the form of the god 168
16. BG4.3 They establish the duration of life and they appoint the days for the souls in the West, destined for the Place of Destruction 170
17. BG5.1a ———— 173
18. BG5.1.4-7 Gods who carry the Swallower, from whose coils issue heads [people](Joseph) 173
19. **BG5.1.7-10 Those who carry the** *twisted cord* **from which come out stars (Levi) 173**
20. BG5.2 Those whose arms are hidden, who carry the mysteries 175
21. BG5.3a Those who are about Osiris, the sleeping ones, the sleepy ones 176
22. **BG5.3.7-10 (Those of the) hole in the hard (?) earth (Zebulum) 176**
23. **BG6.1.1-5 Those who are in** *peace*. **Those who create (?)** *the gifts* **of the Just (Asher, Issachar) 180**
24. BG6.1b Those who carry Truth 180
25. BG6.3 Those who make grain in the fields of the Netherworld 183
26. **BG7.1.1-5 Those who carry the** *rope* **and create the mysteries (Levi) 187**
27. **BG7.1.6-10 Those who carry the** *coiled serpent rope* **and create the hours (Levi) 187**
28. **BG7.2.4-8 Lords of Provisions of the West,** *judge* **me your judgment (Dan) 188**
29. BG7.3a Perfect spirits, accomplished spirits 189
30. **BG7.3.7-10 The Council who** *judges* **(Dan) 189**
31. BG8.1 The Council who gives bread to the just and herbs to the souls in the Island of Flame 192
32. **BG10.1.5-7 (The gods who cut the throats [and** *overthrow* **the evil god Apophis] Gad) 205**
33. BG10.3a The gods of the stars which do not perish 210
34. BG10.3b The Hours who tow 210

APPENDIX 2

Names of the Tribes of Israel in the *Amduat*

English translations of the names of the 111 deities in 10 groups of 12 in the Amduat. Names matched with those of the tribes of Israel (in brackets) in Rev. 7:4-8 and Table 6.2 are given in bold. Numbers in brackets indicate page numbers for English translations given by Piankoff (1954).

A7.3a (group of twelve standing gods with stars on heads has no name) (p. 283): (1) Great of the Lower Region, (2) Lord of the Lower Region, (3) Lord of the provisions of Earth, (4) The One of the Netherworld, (5) **Hey of the stars (Simeon)**, (6) **Hay of the spirits (Simeon)**, (7) **He who lifts his arm (Gad)**, (8) **He whose arm is holy (Judah)**, (9) **He who is powerful of arm (Naphtali)**, (10) Knife in his tongue, (11) Knife in his eye, (12) He who allows the heads to breathe.

A7.3b (group of twelve standing goddesses with stars on heads has no name) (p. 283): (1) **The Adorer (Judah)**, (2) **Lady of the Land (Zebulin?)**, (3) Lady of Ladies, (4) The One of the Netherworld, (5) **The One of the Right Hand (Bengamin)**, (6) The Leader, (7) **The Bringer (Issachar)**, (8) **The Opener (Dan (= Manasseh, see text)**, (9) **The Weaver (Levi)**, (10) She who makes brightness, (11) **She who makes the forms (Joseph)**, (12) **She who presents evil (Asher)**.

A9.1a The Council of the Gods who avenge Osiris every day (p. 295): (1) ——, (2) **The enveloper (Zebulum?)**, (3) Blue Stuff, (4) The one of the Bandelets, (5) The Clothed One, (6) The Lordly One, (7) Divine Deputy, (8) The Deputy of the Nine, (9) The Soul of the Spirits, (10) Lord of the People, (11) The Uniter, (12) The One with the Hidden Arm.

A9.1b (group of twelve standing goddesses has no name) (pp.295-296): (1) She who comes out, (2) The Wanderer (?) Of the Spirits, (3) Mistress of Slaughter, (4) Mistress of Dignity, (5) Great of Due, (6) Mistress of Trembling, (7) She who puts her city in order, (8) Mistress of the Cities, (9) Holy One of the Valley, (10) Great of Brilliance, (11) Powerful of Speech, (12) The Dancer of Re.

A9.2 (group of twelve gods with paddles has no name) (p. 296): (1) The Rower, (2) He who ignores his annihilation, (3) He who ignores his weariness, (4) He who ignores retreat, (5) He who ignores the return, (6) He who ignores his decay, (7) The One who rows in his Hour, (8) The Oar of the Earth, (9) **Peace of the Boat (Asher)**, (10) God of the Gods, (11) The One who crosses the Netherworld, (12) The One of the Boat.

Appendix 2 (Continued)

A9.3 (group of twelve cobras on clothing signs has no name) (pp. 297-298): (1)Her tongue causes pain, (2) The Fiery One, (3) The Flaming One, (4) She who protects the Netherworld, (5) She who repulses the Storm, (6) She who scatters Stars, (7) The One with the Living Face, (8) The One who lifts her side, (9)Beautiful of Appearances, (10) Great of Form, (11) Lady of the Fiery Glow, (12) —— .

A11.2 (group of twelve gods who carry the serpent has no name) (pp. 308-309): (1) **The Carrier (Issachar**, (2) **The Bearer (Issachar)**, (3) The Loader, (4) The One who seizes, (5) The One who grasps, (6) **Strong of Arm (Naphthali)**, (7) The One who takes hold, (8) —— , (9) The One who drags, (10) The Companion, (11) The One who conducts the Image, (12) **The One belonging to the Enveloper (Zebulum)**.

A12.1a (group of twelve standing goddesses has no name) (p. 313): (1) The Beautiful Emergence of Light, (2) She who prepares the way for Re, (3) Mistress of the Power of Earth, (4) Uadjet the Leader, (5) She who unites the Two Banks of the Sky, (6) She who Exalts in her Two Lands, (7) She who is exalted in her Works, (8) She who has power over her Spirits, (9) She who exults of his Enemies, (10) **She who creates the body, the Power of his Barge (Joseph)**, (11) She who appears on the crown of the Head of Re, (12) Mistress of the Uraei in the Barge of Millions (of years).

*A12.1b (group of twelve **adoring gods** has no name) (Judah) (p. 314):* (1) Lord of Life, (2) **Hail (Judah?)**, (3) **Lord of Praise (Judah)**, (4) **Lord of Praising (Judah)**, (5) Sweet of Heart, (6) **The One who Praises Re (Judah)**, (7) Noble of Heart, (8) The Youth, (9) The One who adores the East, (10) The One who renews the Heads of the Gods, (11) **The One who gives praise to Kheper (Judah)**, (12) —— .

A12.2 (group of twelve gods who tow the barge has no name) (p. 315): (1) The Great One, (2) The Elder, (3) ——, (4) ——, (5) ——, (6) —— , (7) Power of Time, (8) The Honorable One, (9) The Lord of Honor, (10) —— , (11) ——, (12) Life.

APPENDIX 3

Distribution of Attributes of the Multitudes in the Book of Revelation

Underlined characters (X̲) indicate uncertainty; M and F indicate male and female; "Prol." refers to the Prologue. Several attributes of the groups of twelve are not included in this table; these include "followers of the Lamb" which apply to all the groups, and "wearing of white clothing" which is assumed to apply to all the ...

Attributes	Location of attributes in groups of 12 in the Book of Gates (See key below table for meanings of letters)													
	Prol.		1st Div.		2nd Div.		3rd Div.				4th Div.			
	A	B	C	D	E	F	G	H	I	J	K	L	M	N
Tribes of Israel (Rev. 7:4-8, Rev. 14:1-5)														
Once lived on earth			X	X							X		X	
Owned by God									X					
Followers of Lamb									X					
First Fruits for God														
Truthfulness				X									X	
Sealed with name							X̲							
Praise / Worship			X	X			X	X			X		X	
The Great Multitude (Rev. 7:9-17)														
Serve as priests														
Sheltered ones					X						X̲			
Resting ones			X̲				X̲							
Receive food/water			X	X	X	X	X	X		X	X		X	
Happiness														
Unassigned Multitudes (Rev. 6:9,11; Rev. 11:18; Rev. 12:7,11; Rev. 19:19)														
Fight for their god				X				X						
	A	B	C	D	E	F	G	H	I	J	K	L	M	N

A. BGPro.1.1-10
B. BGPro.2.1-10
C. BG1.1.1-6
D. BG1.1.6-10
E. BG2.1.1-5
F. BG2.1.6-10
G. BG3.1.1-4
H. BG3.1.5-7
I. BG3.1.7-10
J. BG3.3.5-8
K. BG4.1.1-4
L. BG4.1.4-9
M. BG4.2.7-10
N. BG4.3.5-7
O. BG5.1.1-4
P. BG5.1.4-7 ...

APPENDIX 3 (Continued)

... groups because the drawings suggest white clothing. Also, references to their multiracial composition and those holding palm branches are omitted here because they are only accounted for in the Amduat, not in the Book of Gates. (See Chapters 5 and 6 for a discussion on this appendix.

Location of attributes in groups of 12 in the Book of Gates (See key below table for meanings of letters)																	
5th Div.						6th Div.			7th Div.					8th	10th Div.		
O	P	Q	R	S	T	U	V	W	X	Y	Z	a	b	c	d	e	f
Tribe Tribes of Israel (Rev. 7:4-8, Rev. 14:1-5)																	
							X										
							X										
																X	X
							X										
							X										
														X			
The Great Multitude (Rev. 7:9-17)																	
										X							
										X							
				X		X̲				X							
X	X		X	X	X		X	X	X	X	X	X	X				
	X					X̲	X			X							
Unassigned Multitudes (Rev. 6:9,11; Rev. 11:18; Rev. 12:7,11; Rev. 19:19)																	
X	X			X		X̲			X					X			
O	P	Q	R	S	T	U	V	W	X	Y	Z	a	b	c	d	e	f

Q. BG5.1.7-10
R. BG5.2.4-8
S. BG5.3.1-6
T. BG5.3.7-10

U. BG6.1.1-5
V. BG6.1.6-10
W. BG6.3.2-7
X. BG7.1.1-5

Y. BG7.1.6-10
Z. BG7.2.5-9
a. BG7.3.2-7
b. BG7.3.7-10

c. BG8.1.2-4
d. BG10.1.5-7
e. BG10.3.1-5
f. BG10.3.5-7

APPENDIX 4

Book of Aker, Part B

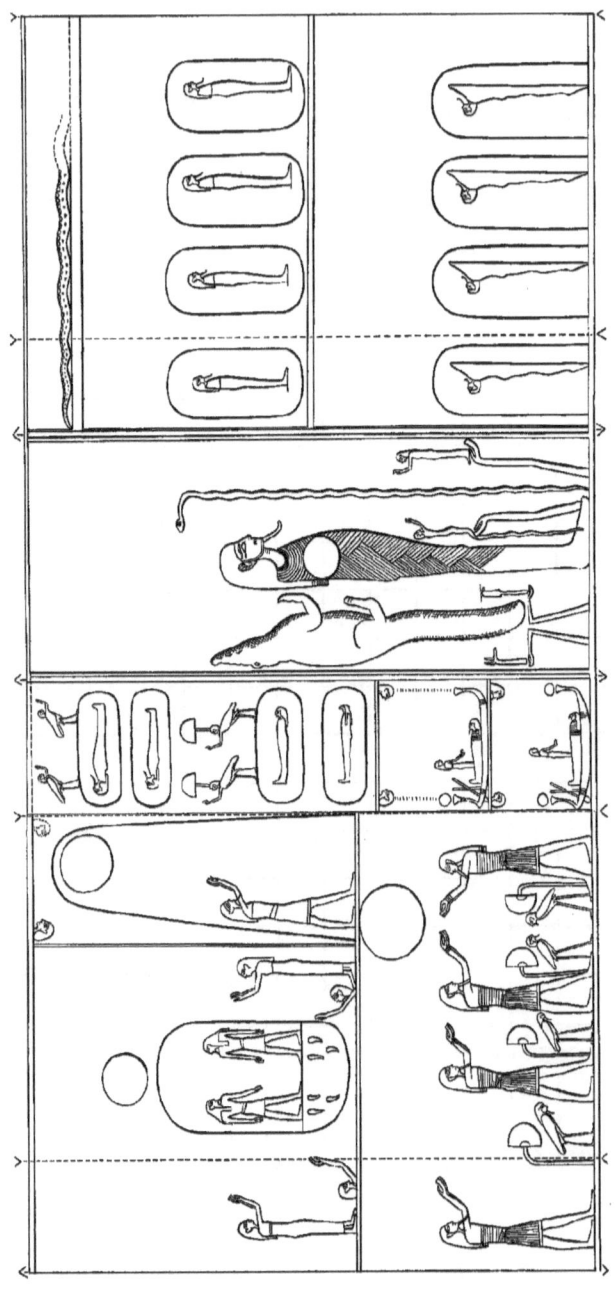

APPENDIX 5

List of Selected Parallels

List of the more prominent parallels to scenes in the Book of Revelation; numerous additional parallel scenes and elements are frequently present between and within these parallels. The last column gives the figure numbers of the most representative Egyptian illustrations. See Chapter 1, *The Enigmatic Book of Revelation* for abbreviations used for the Egyptian sources AM, BC and BD. *Landmark scenes* in the Amduat and Book of Gates Series are underlined and sources of concentrations of parallel apocalyptic scenes are in **bold print**. The numbers, 1-3 in the "Degree" column correspond to the following degrees of similarity with #1 being the highest:

1. Scenes with one or more "peculiar" elements — Example: Slain lamb standing in Rev. 5:6 and AM6.2 (Figure 46); singers standing by a lake of fire in Rev. 15:2 (Figure 106).

2. Scenes with linear arrangements of parallel elements in the same order as they appear in passages in Revelation, i.e., as parallel series of scenes. — Example: Rev. 12 and the Books of the Heavens (Figure 90); the 2nd beast of Rev. 13 and AM4.1 (Figure 92).

3. Scenes with parallel elements grouped, but not in a linear manner as in similar scenes in Revelation. — Example: Capture of the serpent in Rev. 20:1-3 and BG10.1 (Figure 117) and the letter to Thyatira in Rev. 2:11-28 and 5th Division of the Book of Caverns (*Figure 40*).

Revelation	Parallel	Egyptian Source	Degree	Figure
		THE THRONE SCENE		
Misc.	Characters in Revelation	Misc. sources	1	Figure 132
			3	Figure 133
1, 4	Throne Scene	BD125, Misc.	1,3	Figure 6
2-3	Egyptian beliefs in seven letters	Misc. sources	3	—
2:12-16	Letter to Pergamum	BD108 (?)	?	—
2:18-28	Letter to Thyatira	BC5	3	Figure 40
3:7-12	Letter to Philadelphia	BD115	2	—

Revelation	Parallel	Egyptian Source	Degree	Figure
		THE AMDUAT SERIES		
5:1-7	Opening of the scroll	AM6.2	1	Figure 46
5:6	The slain lamb	AM6.2	1	Figure 46
		House of Life	3	Figure 48
5.5	Lion of Judah	AM6.1.6-10	3	Figure 47
6:1-8	The four horsemen	*Hymn of Thutmosis III*	3	—
6:9-11	Cries of the slain	AM8.1; AM8.3	1,1	Figure 54
7:1-3	4 angels & winds	*Schutzbild scene* in Tomb of Ramesses VI	1	Figure 55
7:4-8	Tribes of Israel	AM7.3	1	Figure 28
7:9-17	Great Multitude	AM9.1,3	3	—
7:9	Many with palm branches	AM9.3	1	—
		BG Misc.	3	—
7:15	The sheltered ones	AM11.2.1-8	1	Figure 34
8:1	Silence in Heaven	*Hymn to Amen-Re*	3	—
8:6-11:19	**Apocalyptic Events**	BD146	3	—
		BD149	3	—
		-Admon. of Egyptian Sage	3	—
		-Prophesy of Neferrohu	3	—
		- Misc. sources	3	
10:1-3	The little scroll	AM5	1	Figure 58
11:3-18	The two witnesses	BA	2	Figure 76
11:19	Catastrophic events	BA	3	Figure 75
12	Woman in the sky	-*Books of the Heavens*	1	Figure 90
12:6,14	Flight of the woman	-*Isis myths*	2,3	—
13	1st beast & 2nd beast	AM4.3.1	2	Figure 96
			1	Figure 92
13:7-8	Names in Book of Life	AM4.2.6-10	2	Figure 94
13:18	Beast's Mark: "666"	AM4.1.8	1	Figure 96
14:6-20	Harvest time	AM2	1	Figure 102
			3	Figure 103
			3	Figure 104
			3	Figure 105

Appendix 5. List of Selected Parallels

Revelation	Parallel	Egyptian Source	Degree	Figure
		THE BOOK OF GATES SERIES		
15:2-4	Twelve by lake of fire	BG2.1.6-10	3	Figure 106
15:3	Song of Moses	-Victory Hymn of Thutmosis III	3	—
15:1, 2-8	The Seven angels	BG2.2.6-7	3	Figure 107
15:6-16:21	Apocalyptic events	AM12	3	—
		BD149	3	—
		-Annals Thutmosis III	3	—
		-Admon. of Egn. sage	3	—
16:4-7	Judgment scene	BG5/6	3	Figure 109
		BG Misc.	3	—
16:12-14	River dries up	BG3.2.7-10	1	Figure 112
16:13-16	Battle of Armageddon	BG6	3	Figure 113
		-Annals Thutmosis III	3	—
17:1-9	The harlot	BG9.2.10-8	1	Figure 114
17:10-18	Rise & fall of kings	BG9.1,2	1	Figure 115
18:1-19:4	Apocalyptic Events	BD149	3	—
		-Annals Thutmosis III	3	—
		Admon. of Egtn. Sage	3	—
19:11-21	The Word of God	Misc. sources	3	Figure 25
20:1-4	Capture of Satan	BG10.1.3-10	1	Figure 117
20:1-4	Resurrected made priests	BG10.2.8-9	3	Figure 118
20:2-7	The Millennium	BG10.2.8-9	3	Figure 118
20:4	Reign of Martyrs	BG10:3	3	Figure 119
20:7-10	Gog and Magog	BG10.2.9-10	1	Figure 121
20:10	Recapture of Satan	BG11.2.7-8	1,3	Figure 122
20:12-13	Resurrection & Judgment	BN2 - BN7	3	Figure 124
20:12	The "great and the small"	BN8-9	3	Figure 124
20:13,15	Judgment of the drowned	BN9-10	3	Figure 126
21:1-8	A new creation	BG11-BG12	1	Figure 127
21:6	Alpha & Omega	BD-Intro Hymn	3	—
21:2-9-10	City as a bride	BG11	1	—
		BG12	1	Figure 127
21:10 ff.	Holy City characteristics	Misc. sources	3	—
21:22	City's Temple = God	Misc. sources	3	—
22:1-2	River of water of life	Book of Day	3	Figure 131
			3	Figure 8

APPENDIX 6. Glossary

Egyptian Gods and Goddesses

Aker, ancient personification of the earth. He is prominent in the 5th Division of the Amduat and the *Book of Aker*.

Amun, (also: *Amen, Amon, Amana, Amon, Ammon, Amun, Amūn*), an ancient god, "the hidden one," who became prominent in Thebes during the 11th Dynasty. Usually depicted as a ram with curved horns. See also *Amun-Re*.

Amun-Re, see *Re*.

Anat-Astarte, Syro-Palestinian consort of *Baal*. She was introduced into the Delta by the Hyksos during the 2nd Intermediate Period. The Babylonians and the Assyrians knew *Astarte* by the name of *Ishtar*, a goddess of fertility and love, while the Egyptians knew her as a goddess of war.

Apophis, a huge primordial, serpentine deity and the embodiment of the powers of evil and darkness; he was the sun-god's arch-enemy and a constant threat to his passage through the sky and the Netherworld. In later times, he was frequently equated the god *Seth*.

Atum, primeval creator and god of Heliopolis; represented by a sun-disk. He was worshiped as the evening manifestation of the sun-god.

Baal (Baal-Reshef), a Syro-Palestinian storm-god which the Hyksos rulers of the 2nd Intermediate Period combined with the Egyptian god, Seth, thus introducing elements of Baal worship into Egypt.

Duamutef, see Sons of Osiris.

Geb, the most common earth god (also, see Aker) who was the wife of the sky-goddess Nut.

Hapi, a personification of the Nile's life-giving inundation; a fecundity god.

Hapy, see *Sons of Osiris*.

Harakhty, (Harakhte), otherwise known as "Horus of the Horizon," was the daytime form of the sun-god. He was envisaged as falcon or a human with a falcon's head.

Hathor, an ancient sky-goddess envisaged as having the form of a cow. In later times, she merged with the most popular goddess, Isis, the sister/wife of *Osiris*, mother and protector of *Horus*.

Heh, personification of a very long period of time; his name means a million years.

Horus, usually depicted with the head of falcon, he was the son of *Isis* and the sun-god. He was known as Horus of the Netherworld in the afterlife and as the pharaoh, the son of the sun-god on earth.

Horus-Seth, an amalgamation of the two gods, *Horus* and *Seth*, usually depicted as a human with two heads, one of *Horus* representing good and looking in one direction while the other is *Seth*, representing evil and looking in the opposite direction.

Imsety, see Sons of Osiris.

Isis, the sister/wife of *Osiris*, mother and protector of *Horus*. She is usually shown with the sign of a throne on her head and was associated with numerous other benevolent goddesses. She used her magic to breath new life into the slain body of Horus. (Also, see *Hathor*)

Khepri, Kheper, a primeval god depicted as a scarab beetle. In early times, a manifestation of Atum but later of Re, especially as the morning sun. Linked with the symbol of resurrection, youth, and new beginnings.

Khmun, a ram-headed god who was the guardian of the source of the Nile River. He was also well known as a creator-god who fashioned the bodies of both children and gods.

Maat, goddess who personified the basic laws of the universe, representing law, truth and world order. As the goddess of truth, she played an important roll in the judgment of the dead where her symbol, a feather, was placed on one side of a balance and the heart of the deceased was placed on the other.

Mehen: A protective deity usually depicted as a serpent whose body forms a protective shield over the sun-god, and at times, his followers.

Mertseger, a goddess especially revered in Thebes where she was worshiped as the goddess of silence, especially the necropolis on the west bank of the Nile.

Neith, an important Egyptian goddess of war. Also, see *Sekhmet*.

Nephthys, mythologically, the sister/wife of *Seth*, murderer of Osiris. She is the sister of Isis and a protector and servant of the sun-god. She and *Isis* attended *Nut* during the birth of *Re*.

Nun, the personification of the primeval waters from which all of creation arose.

Nut, ancient sky-goddess usually depicted as a woman arched over the earth with each of her limbs resting on one of the four corners of the earth. As the wife of *Geb*, the earth-god, she gave birth to the sun-god, *Re*. The primordial river was envisioned as passing over and through her body and *Re* sailed in his barque over her body during the day and inside her body at night. Also, see *Hathor, Isis an*ℨ*hetait*.

Osiris-Re, an impermanent god created in the Netherworld by the union of Osiris and Re; his existence extends until shortly after the juvenile sun-god enters the eastern sky at dawn.

Ptah, an ancient god of Memphis, he was regarded as the god of craftsmanship and the inventor of the arts. He was also known as the creator of the world which was made manifest by the power of his word. He was the husband of *Sekhmet*.

Qebehsenuef, see *Sons of Osiris*.

Re, the sun-god who enters the sky at dawn and crosses the daytime sky in his barque to enter the Netherworld at sunset. As the chief god of Heliopolis he was worshiped as the creator and sustainer of the world. He was typically represented with the head of a mature ram while in his juvenile form, the ram's head was accompanied by a beetle; his juvenile form was dominant in the Netherworld and in the sky at dawn where he may be referred to as that of a lamb. He was sometimes combined with other Egyptian gods, such as *Re-Atum* and *Amun-Re*.

Sekhmet, wife of Ptah, she was a powerful Egyptian goddess of war who subdued *Apophis* as well as *Seth* and his followers. She was associated with the fiery breath of uraeus serpents, hot desert winds, and arrows which pierced the hearts of her enemies.

Selkit (= Selket), one of the four protectress of coffins and canopic jars.

Seshat (Sesheta), as the goddess of writing and learning, she acted as a sort of librarian and was closely associated with the god *Thoth*. As such, she was one of the two deities who kept records of the deeds of men by which they were judged in the final judgment.

Sheshes, a crocodile deity (= Apophis) in the 9th Division of the Book of Gates.

Shetait, a manifestation of Nut in the Book of Caverns C5.1.1st picture.

Seth (Set), the uncle/brother of Horus. At times he was considered an ally and protector of the sun-god, a benevolent deity and beloved of the pharaoh. Many important myths describe him as the murderer of Osiris. At other times his domain was the desert and he was considered to represent storms and the cruel sea and was an enemy of *Osiris*. He was usually depicted as a human with the head of an unidentified creature, typically called the *Seth*-animal. Also, see *Horus-Seth*.

Shesmu (Shezmu), god of the wine-press. Shesmu handed this life-giving drink to the deceased but he pulled the heads of sinners down and crushed them in his press.

Shu, a child of the sun-god, he was the god of the air and sister of *Tefnut*, the god of moisture, and at times, the sun. He was depicted as a man with a feather on his head. His offspring were the sun-god *Nut* and the earth-god *Geb*.

***Sokaris** (Sokar)*, originally an earth and fertility god whose sledge was used to symbolically till the soil. His earthly domain is accentuated in the 5th Division of the Amduat where he is called "he who is upon his sand."

***Sons of Osiris** (or of Horus)*, four deities who typically stand before the throne of Osiris. Each is depicted with a different head, *Imsety* with the head of a man, *Hapy* with that of a baboon, *Duanmutef* had the head of a jackel, and *Qebehsenuef* the head of a hawk. They represent the four corners of the earth, were protectors of the bodily remains of the dead, and played a role in enforcing the divine will of the one on the throne.

Tatenen, personification of the depths of the earth. The name means "risen land."

***Tefnut** (**Tefenet**)*, sister of *Shu* and sometimes appeared as the eye of the sun. She was envisaged as a pair of lions.

Thoth, the moon god and inventor and patron of writing as well as keeper of records. He was typically associated with knowledge and wisdom and was depicted in human form with the head of an ibis, and at times a baboon. He was also the "lord of time" and the "tongue and heart of Re," the "word of God"). He was believed to be the author of a now lost set of secret books containing the entire history of the world. He played an important role in the judgment of the dead where he was keeper of the scales of justice.

Selected Egyptian Terms

afterlife: A person's continued existence after death involved several parts of his or her's person. For example, a person's *ba* (soul) left the dead person's body and flew as a bird in the sky between heaven and earth. A person's *ka* (spirit) left the body and and became a part of heavenly spirit world. These and other aspects of a person (such as the shadow, heart and name could be destroyed by harsh judgments meted out by the sun-god (typically Osiris or Re) in the afterlife.

akh: This part of a person manifests itself in the afterlife as one of the "blessed dead." It was that part which, after death of the body, took the form of a solar or stellar being, and became one of the "blessed dead." The *akh* was closely related to the *soul* which was at times also believed to be represented by a star; sometimes they *were* stars. (See *ka* for the additional six parts of a person).

ba: The *ba* was similar or identical to the Christian concept of the "soul" and typically manifested itself only when the body died; at death, it was depicted as a bird with a human head, a *ba*-bird, which was free to fly wherever it pleased, including flights back to earth to receive offerings from the living. (See *ka* for the additional six parts of a person).

body: The most obvious part of a person, the physical *body* not only served a person on earth, but in the afterlife as well. After it was resurrected and prior to the judgment of the dead, it was joined by the person's *ka*. (See *ka* for the additional six parts of a person).

creation legends: These varied considerably from one part of Egypt to another as well as from one time to another. Different legends involved and emphasized different creation deities and events.

ennead(s): These were groups of nine gods consisting of a creator god at the head and three generations of lesser deities. The most popular was the ennead of Heliopolis with the god Atum at its head.

heart: This part of a person was considered to be the seat of emotions and the intellect. (See *ka* for the additional six parts of a person). It played a key role in the judgment of the dead.

isocephaly: A modern term, based on Greek roots, used to describe that aspect of Egyptian art in which more important individuals were depicted in illustrations as being larger or taller with their heads placed higher in a composition than the less powerful.

ka: Thought to be similar to modern Christian beliefs about the "spirit," the *ka* represented the "vital energy" of a person's existence; it could exist separately from a person's body while he or she was still alive and played active roles in events in the afterlife. It was one of the seven parts of a person, and rejoined the *body* at the resurrection of the dead. The *ka* is one of the seven parts of a person; the other six being the *body, shadow, heart, name, ba, akh*. Powerful deities such as Re, Osiris or Hathor who could have many *kas*.

maat: This term, which embodies the concepts of truth, justice, law and world order, is personified by the goddess *Maat* and judges were considered to be her priests. From an ethical perspective, *maat* resembled straightforwardness, honesty and uprightness. *Maat* was symbolized by a feather worn on the head or carried in the goddess' hand or on many of her followers.

ma'a-kheru, (Greek, *nikao*): This term is usually applied to individuals who were successful in a judgment process, including the final judgment before Osiris. It was a legal term meaning something like, "the acclamation given to him is 'right,'" "he is called right," "he is acknowledged as right by means of acclamation," "he is acknowledged as right(eous)," "vindicated" or "acclaimed right" by a judge. In later times, the Egyptian Coptic Christians translated *ma'a-kheru*, as "victorious" or "conquerors."

name: A person's *name* was considered to be so vital a part of a person that its loss in time or the physical destruction of all written records containing it could annihilate the entire person. Power over another person or malevolent being could be gained through the mere knowledge of that name. For their own protection, Egyptians had secret names which only they knew.

neter: Modern translators typically translated this rather vague term as meaning a "god," usually in a very general sense. While *neter* could refer to any Egyptian god worshiped by the Egyptians, it could also apply to the after-death existence of a person or deity, or groups of people or "deities," described in texts such as the *Amduat* and *The Book of Gates*. It's plural form was *neteru*.

Netherworld: That part of the Tuat/Duat/Dat which lay deep beneath the earth where the sun-god and his followers traveled each night. Many dangerous and evil beings resided there and threatened the sun-god and his followers.

ogdoad(s): These were groups of eight primitive gods representing four generations of personifications of the primeval forces of chaos. The head of each ogdoad was usually a creator god whose identity varied among different groupings. The most popular the ogdoad was established in Hermopolis.

ouroboros: This is a Greek term typically applied to the Egyptian serpent "tail-in-mouth" or "tail-swallower" which was depicted as a serpent with its tail in its mouth so that its body formed a circle. Time (typically, each hour) was mysteriously born of the ouroboros and then swallowed. It effectively represented the cyclical aspect of the past-present-future nature of time.

shadow: This part of a person had an intimate connection with the sun and was a constant reminder of the presence and personal care by Re the sun-god. It was associated with a person being able to move "with the swiftness of a shadow." (See *ka* for the additional six parts of a person).

Tuat/Duat/Dat: An ancient Egyptian word for that part of creation where the sun traveled during the day (the heavens) and the night (the Netherworld deep beneath the earth). During the New Kingdom, the term most often referred to the Netherworld.

INDEX TO BOOK OF REVELATION

Chapter 1

Rev. 1	547
Rev. 1:1	73, 74, 77, 94, 278
Rev. 1,4	212
Rev. 1:1,2,5,9	73, 74
Rev. 1:1-2	94
Rev. 1:1-7	278
Rev. 1:4	57, 88, 566
Rev. 1:4; 3:1; 4:5 5:6	88
Rev. 1:5	22, 74-78, 80, 146, 552
Rev. 1:5a	79, 82
Rev. 1:5b	80, 82
Rev. 1:5-6	146
Rev. 1:6	73, 146
Rev. 1:7	73
Rev. 1:9b	81
Rev. 1:11	165
Rev. 1:12	57, 553
Rev. 1:12-16	57
Rev. 1:12-20	553
Rev. 1:13	60, 429, 547
Rev. 1:13-14	547
Rev. 1:14	60, 61, 111, 429
Rev. 1:15	61
Rev. 1:16	60, 62, 63, 105, 548
Rev. 1:16, 21:10-11,23	60
Rev. 1:17	94, 155
Rev. 1:17-18	155
Rev. 1:18	73
Rev. 1:19	280
Rev. 1:20	94

Chapter 2

Rev. 2	58, 512
Rev. 2-3	89, 154-155, 156, 162, 170, 171, 187, 188, 190, 192, 195, 211, 212, 278, 280
Rev. 2:1	23, 89, 94
Rev. 2:2	154-156, 171
Rev. 2:2,9	156
Rev. 2:2,9,13,19	155
Rev. 2:2,19	156
Rev. 2:3	156
Rev. 2:4	156, 192
Rev. 2:5	90, 156, 157
Rev. 2:7	24, 155-157, 159, 163, 164, 170, 192
Rev. 2:7,11,17,26	159
Rev. 2:7,11,17,29	170
Rev. 2:8	94, 165
Rev. 2:8-10	165
Rev. 2:9	154, 156, 171, 192, 402
Rev. 2.9a	157
Rev. 2:9b	157
Rev. 2:9-10	156, 192
Rev. 2:10	90, 157, 158, 192, 402
Rev. 2:11	24, 90, 155, 156, 162, 163, 192, 617
Rev. 2:12	94, 154, 566
Rev. 2:13	154-157, 171, 402
Rev. 2:14	154, 156, 158, 159, 192
Rev. 2:14, 20	158
Rev. 2:15	187
Rev. 2:15-16	187
Rev. 2:16	62, 90, 105, 156, 157, 192, 211, 565
Rev. 2:17	111, 155-157, 167-169, 192
Rev. 2:18	24, 61, 94, 111, 177-179, 184
Rev. 2:18-27	179
Rev. 2:18-28	177, 184
Rev. 2:19	154, 171
Rev. 2:20	24, 154, 157-159, 177, 179, 187, 192
Rev. 2:20-22	157
Rev. 2:20-23	177, 179, 192
Rev. 2:21	179, 402
Rev. 2:21-22	179
Rev 2:21-23	187
Rev. 2:22	90, 156, 179, 180, 192
Rev. 2:22-23	156, 192
Rev. 2:23	90, 182
Rev. 2:23a	180

INDEX TO BOOK OF REVELATION

Rev. 2:23b 180
Rev. 2:24 .... 24, 90, 154, 181, 182
Rev. 2:25 .... 157, 182
Rev. 2:26 ..... 24, 155-157, 182, 183, 192
Rev. 2:26-27 .... 157, 182
Rev. 2:27 183
Rev. 2:28 .... 169, 170
Rev. 2:29 183

Chapter 3

Rev. 3:1 .... 94, 154-157, 171, 566
Rev. 3:1,8,15 .... 155, 156
Rev. 3:2 .... 187, 211
Rev. 3:2-3 .... 187, 211
Rev. 3:3 .... 156, 192
Rev. 3:4 .... 156, 192
Rev. 3:5 . 57, 155-157, 159, 161, 164, 165, 192
Rev. 3:5,12,21 159
Rev. 3:5a 164
Rev. 3:5b 165
Rev. 3:6,13,22 170
Rev. 3:7 .... 61, 94, 154, 172
Rev. 3:7,8 172
Rev. 3:7-12 172
Rev. 3:8 .... 154, 156, 170, 171
Rev. 3:8a 172
Rev. 3:8b 172
Rev. 3:9 .... 154, 156, 173, 174, 192, 193, 402
Rev. 3:9-10 156
Rev. 3:9a 173
Rev. 3:9b 173, 193
Rev. 3:10 .... 174, 193
Rev. 3:11 174
Rev. 3:12 ..... 24, 155, 156, 165-167, 173, 175, 176, 192, 351
Rev. 3:12a 174, 175
Rev. 3:12b 175, 176, 193
Rev. 3:12c 176
Rev. 3:14 .... 71-73, 94, 548, 561
Rev. 3:15 .... 154, 156, 171
Rev. 3:15-16 156
Rev. 3:16 156
Rev. 3:18 156
Rev. 3:20 167
Rev. 3:21 .... 155-157, 161, 162, 182, 192

Chapter 4

Rev. 4 547
Rev. 4-5 57
Rev. 4:1-8 116
Rev. 4:2 .... 280, 554
Rev. 4:2-3 554
Rev. 4:2-11 280
Rev. 4:4 .... 23, 90-93, 553, 566
Rev. 4:5 .... 88, 406
Rev. 4:6 .. 22, 57, 84, 85, 87, 206, 553, 566
Rev. 4:6, 8 87
Rev. 4:6-9 .... 84, 206 553
Rev. 4:7 .... 85, 86, 549
Rev. 4:8 .... 23, 85, 87
Rev. 4:9 197
Rev. 4:10 92

Chapter 5

Rev. 5 568
Rev. 5-9 557
Rev. 5:1 .... 137, 165, 197-199, 440
Rev. 5:1,6 197
Rev. 5:1-2 197
Rev. 5:1-4 .... 137, 199
Rev. 5:1-7 556
Rev. 5:2 .... 94, 165, 199, 206, 297
Rev. 5:2-3 199
Rev. 5:2-4 199
Rev. 5:3 .... 165, 198, 199, 203-207
Rev. 5:3-4 206
Rev. 5:3-11 204
Rev. 5:4 .... 165, 199, 205, 206
Rev. 5:5 . 24, 165, 197, 200, 202, 204, 548, 552, 554
Rev. 5:6 ... 22, 24, 57, 66, 67, 69, 85, 198, 203-205, 548, 552, 554
Rev. 5:6a 205, 206
Rev. 5:6a,c 205
Rev. 5:6b 205
Rev. 5:6,12 552
Rev. 5:6-9 203
Rev. 5:7 165
Rev. 5:8 .... 92, 94, 165
Rev. 5:9 .... 165, 197, 204
Rev. 5:9a 206, 207
Rev. 5:9b 206, 207
Rev. 5:10 .... 146, 202, 207, 208
Rev. 5:10a 206
Rev. 5:10b 206

Rev. 5:11 .... 93, 94, 197	Rev. 6:14 .... 229, 231
Rev. 5:11a 205	Rev. 6:14,17 231
Rev. 5:12 570	Rev. 6:15 .... 228, 268
Rev. 5:14 .... 73, 92, 94, 195	Rev. 6:16 268
	Rev. 6:17 228

Chapter 6

Rev. 6:1-8 212
Rev. 6.1-17 211
Rev. 6,8,9,14,16,18,19 250
Rev. 6:1 . 25, 212-215, 217, 220, 221, 227,
228, 231, 420, 422
Rev. 6:1-2 .... 215, 221
Rev. 6:1-8 ... 212, 215, 217, 222, 420, 422
Rev. 6:1-11 .... 227, 228
Rev. 6:1-8 .... 214, 215, 221, 231
Rev. 6:2 ...... 25, 161, 212, 216, 217, 222
Rev. 6:2a 221
Rev. 6:2b 221
Rev. 6:2c 221
Rev. 6:2-4 220
Rev. 6:2-8 222
Rev. 6:3 215
Rev. 6:3-4 215
Rev. 6:4 .... 25, 212, 217, 218, 223
Rev. 6:4-8 223
Rev. 6:5 .... 215, 218, 219
Rev. 6:5-6 .... 212, 215, 218-220
Rev. 6:6 .... 88, 219, 220
Rev. 6:7 .... 213, 215, 220
Rev. 6:7-8 .... 213, 215, 220
Rev. 6:8 .... 220, 223, 272
Rev. 6:9 . 25, 110, 150, 211, 212, 223-226,
231, 614, 615
Rev. 6:9,11 .... 150, 211, 614, 615
Rev. 6:9-10 226
Rev. 6:9-11 . 150, 211, 212, 222, 223, 225,
.... 231
Rev. 6-7 568
Rev. 6-7 568
Rev. 6:9-11 556
Rev. 6:10 .... 223, 225-227
Rev. 6:11 .... 110, 225-227, 231, 239
Rev. 6:12 ... 194, 212, 227, 228, 231, 249,
250, 252, 253, 256
Rev. 6:12,13 .... 250, 256
Rev. 6:12-13 252
Rev. 6:12,14 .... 250, 256
Rev. 6:12-15 250
Rev. 6:12-17 ..... 194, 212, 227, 228, 249
Rev. 6:13 253

Chapter 7

Rev. 7:1 . 3, 25, 94, 231-236, 239, 249, 557
Rev. 7:1,3 231
Rev. 7:1-15 231
Rev. 7:1-3 ...... 231, 232, 235, 236, 239,
249, 556 557
Rev. 7:2 .... 94, 233, 234, 239
Rev. 7:2-3 233
Rev. 7:3 ...... 94, 134, 233, 236, 237, 240
Rev. 7:3-8 236
Rev. 7:4 . 3, 23, 57, 116-119, 121-123, 126,
127, 136, 137, 141, 142, 231, 236,
239, 240, 553, 556, 611, 612, 614,
615
Rev. 7:4-8 ... 116, 119, 121-123, 126, 127,
137, 231, 236, 141, 239, 553 556
Rev. 7:4-8,14:1-5 57
Rev. 7:5 .... 117, 136
Rev. 7:5-8 .... 117, 136
Rev. 7:9 .... 3, 23, 116, 136, 137, 142-146,
237, 239, 553, 614, 615
Rev. 7:9-10 237
Rev. 7:9-13 146
Rev. 7:9-17 .... 142, 553
Rev. 7:10 .... 69, 231
Rev. 7:10-17 231
Rev. 7:11 92-94
Rev. 7:12 73
Rev. 7:13 238
Rev. 7:15 .... 23, 146-148, 238, 239
Rev. 7:15-16 239
Rev. 7:15-17 148
Rev. 7:17 ...... 68, 69, 142, 143, 149, 552

Chapter 8

Rev. 8-9 .... 559, 568
Rev. 8-11 235
Rev. 8:1 .... 3, 90, 241-243, 245, 246, 248,
249
Rev. 8:1 - Rev. 11:19 90
Rev. 8:1-5 246
Rev. 8:2 .... 235, 246
Rev. 8:2-6 249

INDEX TO BOOK OF REVELATION 627

Rev. 8:4 .... 250, 256, 257
Rev. 8:4,7 250
Rev. 8:4,7,8 256
Rev. 8:4-13 250
Rev. 8:5 . 94, 246, 247, 250, 252, 256, 262
Rev. 8:5,8 252
Rev. 8:6 .... 246, 268, 566
Rev. 8:7 ... 90, 93, 94, 246-250, 253, 256, 262, 268, 320
Rev. 8:7-9 .... 247, 320
Rev. 8:7-13 248
Rev. 8:8 .. 90, 94, 246, 250, 252, 263, 266, 268
Rev. 8:8-9 90
Rev. 8:9 .... 250, 255, 256, 266
Rev. 8:9,10,11 250
Rev. 8:9-11 .... 255, 256, 266
Rev. 8:10 .... 90, 94
Rev. 8:10-11 .... 90, 532
Rev. 8:11 .... 255, 272
Rev. 8:12 ..... 90, 94, 246, 250, 252, 253, 256, 269
Rev. 8:13 .... 64, 94

Chapter 9

Rev. 9:1 90
Rev. 9:1-12 90
Rev. 9:2-11 262
Rev. 9:2 .... 246, 250, 252, 253, 256, 257, 262
Rev. 9:2-10 253
Rev. 9:2,17 .... 250, 256
Rev. 9:2-18 250
Rev. 9:3 .... 250, 254, 256, 272
Rev. 9:3-4 272
Rev. 9:3-6 .... 254, 256
Rev. 9:3-8 256
Rev. 9:4 .... 246, 255
Rev. 9:4-6 246
Rev. 9:5 269
Rev. 9:6 269
Rev. 9:9 .... 250, 254, 256
Rev. 9:11 264
Rev. 9:13 90
Rev. 9:13-18 90
Rev. 9:15 .... 94, 566
Rev. 9:16 450
Rev. 9:17 .... 40, 255
Rev. 9:17-19 40
Rev. 9:18 .... 254, 263

Rev. 9:19 254
Rev. 9:20 90
Rev. 9:20-21 90

Chapter 10

Rev. 10 ...... 306, 309, 311, 548, 557, 568
Rev. 10:1 ..... 25, 297-300, 310, 311, 326, 368, 552, 562, 563
Rev. 10:1-3 .... 297, 556, 562-563
Rev. 10:1-4 .... 297, 299, 311
Rev. 10:1-6 552
Rev. 10:1-7 368
Rev. 10:2 .... 165, 300, 301
Rev. 10:3 .... 301, 566
Rev. 10:4 .... 302, 303
Rev. 10:5 ..... 31, 267, 297, 303-305, 310, 311
Rev. 10:5-6 .... 31, 267, 304, 310, 311
Rev. 10:5-6a 305
Rev. 10:5-7 .... 297, 303
Rev. 10:6 94
Rev. 10:6a 304
Rev 10:6b 304
Rev 10:6b-c 304
Rev 10:6d 304, 305
Rev. 10:8 .. 25, 94, 297, 306-308, 310-312
Rev. 10:8-10 .... 310, 312
Rev. 10:8-11 .... 297, 306-307, 311
Rev. 10:9 .... 306, 308
Rev. 10:10 .... 305, 308, 309
Rev. 10-14 .... 557, 559
Rev. 10:11 307-311

Chapter 11

Rev. 11 .... 54, 295, 312-314, 328, 557, 361, 568
Rev. 11:1 .... 3, 26, 94, 267, 306, 312-315, 335, 336
Rev. 11:1-2 312-315
Rev. 11:1-13 .... 267, 306, 312
Rev. 11:2 .... 314, 566
Rev. 11:3 ..... 26, 312, 315-317, 323, 333, 557, 566
Rev. 11:3,6 323
Rev. 11:3-13 333
Rev. 11:3-14 315
Rev. 11:4 .... 26, 312, 319, 321, 566
Rev. 11:4a 318, 321
Rev. 11:4b 317, 318

Rev. 11:4-6 312	Rev. 12:2,5 341
Rev. 11:5 . . . . 26, 317-320, 332	Rev. 12:2-3 552
Rev. 11:6 . . . . 317, 319, 320, 326, 332	Rev. 12:2-5 344
Rev. 11:7 . 26, 85, 161, 312, 318, 321-323,	Rev. 12:2a 340
329, 332, 402	Rev. 12:3 . . . . 40, 96, 343, 345, 402
Rev. 11:7-8 312	Rev. 12:3-4 345
Rev. 11:7-11 321	Rev. 12:3-6 343
Rev. 11:7-12 312	Rev. 12:3-9 96
Rev. 11:8 . . . . 26, 323, 324	Rev. 12:3-9 96
Rev. 11:8-12 323	Rev. 12:4 . . . . 345, 346, 363, 402
Rev. 11:9 . . . . 26, 323-325	Rev. 12:4a 366
Rev. 11:11 . . . . 26, 312, 324-327, 329, 330,	Rev. 12:4b 366
332, 334	Rev. 12:5 . . . . 27, 68, 341, 344-346
Rev. 11:11-12 . . . . 324-327, 332	Rev. 12.5a 337
Rev. 11:12 . . . . 27, 323, 325, 326, 337, 358	Rev. 12.5b . . . .
Rev. 11:12-13 . . . . 325, 358	Rev. 12:5b 337, 366
Rev. 11:13 . . . 26, 246, 265, 267, 268, 312,	Rev. 12:5a,c 366
325, 327-330, 332, 333, 336, 566	Rev. 12:6 . . . . 346, 360, 361, 366
Rev. 11:13a 268	Rev. 12:6,14 346
Rev. 11:13-13 312	Rev. 12:7 . . 27, 93, 94, 150, 151, 211, 292,
Rev. 11:15 . . . . . 3, 27, 73, 78, 90, 336-338,	343, 345, 347-349, 364, 497, 554,
357-362, 364, 557	560, 614, 615
Rev. 11:15-17 . . . . 336, 357	Rev. 12:7a 366
Rev. 11:15-18 . . . . . 90, 336-338, 357, 358,	Rev. 12:7b 366
361, 362, 364	Rev. 12:7, 9 93
Rev. 11:16 92	Rev. 12:7,11 . . . . 150, 211, 614, 615
Rev. 11:18 . . . 27, 150, 211, 235, 336, 357-	Rev. 12:7-8 94
360, 499, 614, 615	Rev. 12:7-9 . . . . 337, 347, 560
Rev. 11:18a 360	Rev. 12:7-11 343
Rev. 11:18c 360	Rev. 12:8 . . . . 27, 349-351, 366
Rev. 11:19 90	Rev. 12:8-9 . . . . 349, 351, 366
Rev. 11:19c 268	Rev. 12:8-10 350
Rev. 11-12 366	Rev. 12:9 . . . . 350, 352, 364, 402, 554
Rev. 11:3-14 557	Rev. 12:10 . . . 27, 73, 77, 78, 325, 350-352,
Rev. 11:15-18 557	367
Rev. 13:11-18 377	Rev. 12:10-11 . . . . 350, 367
Rev. 16:12b-16 432	Rev. 12:11 . . . . 351, 352
	Rev. 12:12 402

Chapter 12

Rev. 12 . 334, 336-339, 343, 347, 352, 361-	Rev. 12:13 . . . . 27, 325, 343, 354, 367, 402
364, 366, 497, 548, 568	Rev. 12:13-16 343
Rev. 12; 13:2-4; 20:2-3 95	Rev. 12:14 . . . . 346, 355, 360, 361, 367
Rev. 12:1 . . . . . 27, 343, 362, 366, 497, 554	Rev. 12:14-16 355
Rev. 12:1-2 343	Rev. 12:15 . . . . 352-355, 363, 367
Rev. 12:1a 339	Rev. 12:15-16 . . . . 352, 353, 355, 363, 367
Rev. 12:1b 339	Rev. 12:16 . . . . 27, 362, 367, 402
Rev. 12:1c 343	Rev. 12:17 . . . . 27, 74, 211, 342, 343, 355-
Rev. 12:1d 343	357, 360-362, 402
Rev. 12:1-2 554	Rev. 12:17a 367
Rev. 12:2 . . . . 341, 344, 362, 366, 552	Rev. 12:17b 367

Chapter 13

Rev. 13 . 100, 361, 370, 377, 381, 392-397, 401, 402, 468, 548, 557
Rev. 13:1 . 27, 40, 356, 368, 370, 371, 373, 375, 376, 392, 393, 396, 402, 552
Rev. 13:1-2 375
Rev. 13:1-6 .... 368, 392, 393
Rev. 13:1-8 .... 370, 552
Rev. 13:1-4 370
Rev. 13:1-8 375
Rev. 13:2 ..... 99, 368, 370-372, 375, 402, 468, 478
Rev. 13:3 .... 376, 377, 402
Rev. 13:4 402
Rev. 13:5 .... 28, 373-375, 397
Rev. 13:5-6 374
Rev. 13:5-6 375
Rev. 13:7 .... 28, 161, 368, 371, 372, 377-381, 392, 393
Rev. 13:7-8 ...... 379-380, 383, 556, 618
Rev. 13:7-9 .... 392, 393
Rev. 13:7-10 .... 368, 377, 378, 380
Rev. 13:8 .... 165, 377, 379, 380
Rev. 13:8-10 .... 378, 379
Rev. 13:9 .... 170, 381
Rev. 13:10 .... 378, 392, 463
Rev. 13:10-18 .... 392, 393
Rev. 13:11 .... 28, 54, 100, 368, 377, 381-384, 388, 393, 396, 402
Rev. 13:11-16 381
Rev. 13:11-17 100
Rev. 13:11-18 368
Rev. 13:12 .... 28, 381, 382, 384
Rev. 13:13 .... 381, 384, 396, 397, 402
Rev. 13:13-14 .... 397, 398
Rev. 13:14 .. 100, 381, 384-386, 396, 402, 447, 552
Rev. 13:14-15 .... 381, 384, 552
Rev. 13:15 .... 377, 385, 387-389, 392
Rev. 13:16 .... 28, 381, 385, 389-391
Rev. 13:16-18 381
Rev. 13:17 .... 31, 98, 391, 402
Rev. 13:17-18 .... 98, 391
Rev. 13:18 .. 23, 97, 99, 377, 391, 402, 484
Rev. 13-14 568

Chapter 14

Rev. 14, 16 249
Rev. 14 ..... 326, 403, 404, 409, 411, 412, 559, 568
Rev. 14:1 ... 3, 69, 116, 134-136, 240, 403, 566, 614, 615
Rev. 14:1-5 .... 116, 403
Rev. 14:2 .... 135, 136
Rev. 14:2-3 136
Rev. 14:2-3 .... 135, 136
Rev. 14:3 .... 85, 131, 133, 240
Rev. 14:3-4 .... 131, 133, 240
Rev. 14:4 .... 130-133, 240
Rev. 14:4-5 133
Rev. 14:5 .... 23, 131, 132, 135
Rev. 14:6 .... 3, 64, 66, 94, 403, 404, 407, 409
Rev. 14:6-7 .... 64, 66, 409
Rev. 14:6-13 403
Rev. 14:6-13,19-20 407
Rev. 14:6-18 403
Rev. 14:6-20 403
Rev. 14:6-7,15 404
Rev. 14:7 ..... 28, 251, 403, 407-409, 497
Rev. 14:7-11 409
Rev. 14:7-12 .... 411, 251
Rev. 14:8 .... 409, 565
Rev. 14:8-11 565
Rev. 14:9 .... 402, 403, 407, 409
Rev. 14:9-10 .... 403, 407
Rev. 14:9-12 409
Rev. 14:10 .... 250, 272, 410, 412
Rev. 14:10,11 250
Rev. 14:10-1 272
Rev. 14:10-11 410
Rev. 14:11 .... 402, 409, 410
Rev. 14:11-17 409
Rev. 14:13 .... 24, 148
Rev. 14:14 .... 28, 403-406, 409, 411, 565
Rev. 14:14-16 411
Rev. 14:14-18 .... 404, 406, 411, 556
Rev. 14:14-20 403
Rev. 14:15 .... 406, 409
Rev. 14:15-16 406
Rev. 14:16 406
Rev. 14:17 .... 406, 409
Rev. 14:18 .... 406, 407, 409
Rev. 14:19 .... 403, 407, 411, 412
Rev. 14:19-20 .... 403, 407, 411
Rev. 14:14-20 565
Rev. 14:20 268

Chapter 15

Rev. 15 ...... 360, 416, 423, 429, 559, 569
Rev. 15-16 456
Rev. 15-21 569
Rev. 15-22 413
Rev. 15:1 .... 3, 268, 420, 425, 566
Rev. 15:1,5-6 428
Rev. 15:1,5-8 425
Rev. 15:1,5-8 425
Rev. 15:1-4 420
Rev. 15:2 .. 3, 28, 402, 415-418, 420, 425,
                                437, 617
Rev. 15:2-3 416
Rev. 15:2-4 .... 415, 420, 425, 556
Rev. 15:3 .... 32, 418-423
Rev. 15:3a 419, 420
Rev. 15:3b 419, 421
Rev. 15:3c 419
Rev. 15:3d 419
Rev. 15:3-4 .... 32, 418, 419, 420, 423
Rev. 15:4 ..... 29, 415, 418, 419, 423, 432
Rev. 15:4a 419
Rev. 15:4b 419, 421
Rev. 15:4c 419, 421
Rev. 15:5 .... 425, 429
Rev. 15:5-6 429
Rev. 15:5-7 429
Rev. 15:5-8 425
Rev. 15:6 .... 418, 427-430
Rev. 15:6-7 429
Rev. 15:7 .... 86, 427, 429-431
Rev. 15:7-8 86
Rev. 15:8 60

Chapter 16

Rev. 16 ..... 254, 431-433, 436, 439, 441,
                      447, 453, 467, 560, 569
Rev. 16:1 .... 251, 425
Rev. 16:1-10 251
Rev. 16:1-12a, 17-21 425
Rev. 16:2 .... 254, 255, 402, 418, 431-433
Rev. 16:3 ...... 94, 250, 255-257, 265, 266,
                      320, 418, 433, 437, 474
Rev. 16:3,4 250
Rev. 16:3,4,13 .... 255, 266
Rev. 16:3-21 418
Rev. 16:3-4 .... 255, 256, 437, 474
Rev. 16:3-6 320
Rev. 16:4 .. 29, 94, 268, 431, 433-435, 437
Rev. 16:4-7 431
Rev. 16:4-6 433
Rev. 16:5 435
Rev. 16:5-7 435
Rev. 16:6 .... 433, 434
Rev. 16:6b 435
Rev. 16:7 .... 62, 433, 435
Rev. 16:8 .... 94, 433, 438, 474
Rev. 16:8-9 .... 438, 474
Rev. 16:8-9 433
Rev. 16:9 .... 250, 256
Rev. 16:10 .... 94, 250, 252-254, 256, 262,
                      268, 269, 402, 433, 474
Rev. 16:10,11,21 .... 253, 262
Rev. 16:10-11 254
Rev. 16:11 .... 269, 443
Rev. 16:12 ..... 29, 94, 270, 436, 445-447,
                                449, 453
Rev. 16:12a 433
Rev. 16:12-14 .... 445, 453, 556
Rev. 16:12-16 445
Rev. 16:13 .... 39, 397, 398, 402, 445-449,
                                454, 474, 566
Rev. 16:13-14 .... 398, 447, 448
Rev. 16:13-19 474
Rev. 16:13-14 .... 446, 447, 454
Rev. 16:13-17 445
Rev. 16:14 .... 442, 444, 445, 449-451
Rev. 16:14-16 450
Rev. 16:15 .... 29, 443-445, 450, 451
Rev. 16:15a 443
Rev. 16:15c 443
Rev. 16:16 .... 292, 441, 449
Rev. 16:17 .... 94, 443, 445
Rev. 16:18 .. 250, 252, 256, 262, 264, 431,
                      433, 436, 437, 446, 453, 474
Rev. 16:18,19 .... 250, 252, 256
Rev. 16:18-19 .... 262, 446, 453
Rev. 16:18-20 .... 436, 474
Rev. 16:18-21 .... 433, 437
Rev. 16:19 .. 250, 252, 256, 442, 444, 452
Rev. 16:20 .... 250, 252, 256
Rev. 16:21 ... 250, 253, 256, 264, 265, 474

Chapter 17

Rev. 17 .. 456, 460, 466-471, 474, 549, 569
Rev. 17:1 . 93, 94, 456, 457, 459, 460, 462,
                                474, 497, 552
Rev. 17:1,9 474

INDEX TO BOOK OF REVELATION

Rev. 17:1-6,18 552
Rev. 17:1-9 556
Rev. 17:3 .... 29, 402, 456, 458, 459, 461, 463, 464, 468, 564
Rev. 17:3,7 461
Rev. 17:3-6 .... 456, 564
Rev. 17:3-12 464
Rev. 17:4 .... 456-458, 469
Rev. 17:4-5 456
Rev. 17:5 458
Rev. 17:6 .... 39, 458
Rev. 17:7 .... 39, 94, 402, 456
Rev. 17:7-8 456
Rev. 17:7-14 456
Rev. 17:8 .... 165, 459, 460
Rev. 17:9 ..... 29, 456, 460, 462, 467, 468
Rev. 17:9-10 462
Rev. 17:9-13 460
Rev. 17:10 .... 460, 462, 463, 466
Rev. 17:10-18 556
Rev. 17:11 .... 402, 463, 464
Rev. 17:12 ... 378, 402, 460-462, 464-466, 473
Rev. 17:12-13 .... 378, 461
Rev. 17:12-14 473
Rev. 17:12-18 464
Rev. 17:13 .... 402, 462, 464, 465
Rev. 17:13-14 .... 464, 465
Rev. 17:14 .... 29, 161, 465, 473
Rev. 17:15 .... 457, 465, 467, 468
Rev. 17:15-16 457
Rev. 17:16 ... 402, 465, 466, 469, 472, 473
Rev. 17:16-17 465
Rev. 17:16-18 465
Rev. 17:17 402
Rev. 17:18 .... 456, 465, 467, 468, 470
Rev. 17:21 251

Chapter 18

Rev. 18 .... 249, 266
Rev. 18:1 .... 93, 94
Rev. 18:2 .... 94, 292
Rev. 18:3 .... 250, 292
Rev. 18:3,19 250
Rev. 18:4 .... 251, 252, 256, 258, 270, 272
Rev. 18:5 .... 250, 251, 256, 262, 263, 275
Rev. 18:5,9 256
Rev. 18:8 .... 250, 255, 256, 263, 272
Rev. 18:8,10 250
Rev. 18:9 .... 250, 256

Rev. 19:10 .... 81, 94
Rev. 18:10 ... 250, 252, 256, 264, 266, 497
Rev. 18:10,15 256
Rev. 18:10,15,17 .... 250, 256, 266
Rev. 18:11 .... 250, 272
Rev. 18:11-14 250
Rev. 18:14 250
Rev. 18:15 .... 252, 256
Rev. 18:16 250
Rev. 18:17 .... 250, 252, 256, 264, 266
Rev. 18:17,19 250
Rev. 18:17,20,21 .... 250, 256
Rev. 18:17-18 .... 264, 266
Rev. 18-19 .... 559, 569
Rev. 18:21 .... 94, 250, 256, 264, 266
Rev. 18:24 .... 39, 265, 266

Chapter 19

Rev. 19 111
Rev. 19:2 40
Rev. 19:4 .... 73, 85, 92, 94
Rev. 19:8 429
Rev. 19:11-21 101
Rev. 19:11, 14 115
Rev. 19:11, 14-15 104
Rev. 19:11, 14-16 103
Rev. 19:11-16 .... 31, 102, 115
Rev. 19:11-21 .... 57, 101, 111, 114
Rev. 19:12 .... 102, 110-112, 115
Rev. 19:12,16 115
Rev. 19:13 ... 23, 101, 102, 109, 115, 400, 548, 552, 554
Rev. 19:13-15 548
Rev. 19:14 .... 103, 108, 110, 115
Rev. 19:14-15 103
Rev. 19:15 ..... 52, 62, 101, 104-106, 108, 115
Rev. 19:16 .... 106-108, 113
Rev. 19:17 94
Rev. 19:19 .. 101, 150, 152, 211, 398, 400, 402, 447, 614, 615
Rev. 19:19-20 447
Rev. 19:20 ... 39, 163, 397, 398, 400, 402, 506
Rev. 19:21 .... 62, 101

Chapter 20

Rev. 20 .... 159, 467, 492, 498, 504, 506, 557, 569

Rev. 20:1 . . . . . 3, 29, 94, 97, 475-477, 495, 496, 502, 511, 554, 564, 617	**Chapter 21**
Rev. 20:1-2 . . . . 475, 554	Rev. 21 . . . . 159, 512, 528, 569
Rev. 20:1-3 . . . . 97, 475, 564	Rev. 21-22 . . . . 249, 559
Rev. 20:1-3a 495	Rev. 21:1 . . . 3, 30, 512-516, 522, 523, 528, 529, 542, 543, 552
Rev. 20:1-4 556	
Rev. 20:1-6 511	Rev. 21:1,3 552
Rev. 20:1-10 . . . . 475, 495-496	Rev. 21:1-3 514
Rev. 20:2 . . . 29, 95, 97, 402, 475-479, 487	Rev. 21:1-3a 528
Rev. 20:2-3 . . . . 477, 478	Rev. 21:1-5 523
Rev. 20:2-7 479	Rev. 21:1-8 . . . . 512, 513, 528, 556
Rev. 20:3 . . . . 96, 477, 494	Rev. 21:1-9 542
Rev. 20:3-6 494	Rev. 21:1-10 529
Rev. 20:3b-6 495	Rev. 21:1-8 512
Rev. 20:4 . 29, 57, 73, 78, 92, 93, 147, 402, 475, 478, 479, 483-488, 497	Rev. 21:2 . . . . 514, 517, 518, 522, 528, 554
	Rev. 21:2,9-10 556
Rev. 20:4,6 . . . . 73, 486	Rev. 21:2,9-10 518
Rev. 20:4-5 . . . . 483, 484	Rev. 21:2-3 522
Rev. 20:4-6 475	Rev. 21:2-4 517
Rev. 20:5 . . . . 490, 522	Rev. 21:3 . . . . 518-520, 540, 542
Rev. 20:6 . . . . . 78, 146, 483, 486-489, 495	Rev. 21:3-4 519
Rev. 20:7 . . . . . . 29, 30, 402, 475, 491-495	Rev. 21:3b-8 528
Rev. 20:7,10 495	Rev. 21:4 . . . . 520, 521
Rev. 20:7-8 . . . . 491, 493	Rev. 21:5 . . . . 519, 521, 522, 524
Rev. 20:7-9 475	Rev. 21:5-6 524
Rev. 20:7-10 . . . . 492, 493, 495, 556	Rev. 21:5-22:5 521
Rev. 20:8 . . . . 450, 492-496, 566	Rev. 21:6 . . . . 522, 523, 525-527
Rev. 20:8-9 . . . . 492, 494-496	Rev. 21:6a 522
Rev. 20:9 . . . . 492, 494, 496	Rev. 21:6b-7 525
Rev. 20:9b-10 496	Rev. 21:7 . . . . 159, 527
Rev. 20:10 . . . . 39, 163, 397-399, 402, 475, 476, 492, 495, 505, 506	Rev. 21:7-8 159
	Rev. 21:8 527
Rev. 20:10,14-15 492	Rev. 21:9 . . . . 94, 518, 528, 529
Rev. 20:11 . 3, 30, 357, 358, 360, 492, 497-499, 504, 505, 510, 511	Rev. 21:9-10 518
	Rev. 21:9-17 529
Rev. 20:11-12 498	Rev. 21:9-10 518
Rev. 20:11-13 492	Rev. 21:10 . . . . 3, 60, 529, 542
Rev. 20:11-15 . . . 357, 358, 360, 497, 499, 510, 511	Rev. 21:10-22:5 542
	Rev. 21:10-11 60
Rev. 20:12 . . . . 30, 32, 165, 497, 500, 503-508, 510	Rev. 21:10-27 512
	Rev. 21:11 . . . . 529, 541
Rev. 20:12-13 . . . . 503, 507	Rev. 21:11,23 541
Rev. 20:13 . . . . . 27, 30, 359, 498-501, 506, 508-510	Rev. 21:11-27 529
	Rev. 21:12 . . . . 94, 532, 535-537, 566
Rev. 20:13,15 . . . . 508, 510	Rev. 21:12,21 535
Rev. 20:13-15 498	Rev. 21:12-14,16-21 532
Rev. 20:14 . . . . 24, 57, 162	Rev. 21:13 . . . . 538, 566
Rev. 20:14-15 162	Rev. 21:15 543
Rev. 20:15 . . . . 165, 403	Rev. 21:16 . . . . 529-531, 566
	Rev. 21:17 534
	Rev. 21:18 . . . . 529, 532, 544

INDEX TO BOOK OF REVELATION

Rev. 21:18-21 532
Rev. 21:18-22 529
Rev. 21:19 532-534
Rev. 21:19-20 .... 533, 534
Rev. 21:19-21 534
Rev. 21:22 .... 69, 541, 543
Rev. 21:22-23 69
Rev. 21:23 .... 60, 68, 69, 529, 541
Rev. 21:23-27 529
Rev. 21:27 .... 131, 165, 534
Rev. 21-22 ... 249, 351, 529, 543, 544, 569

Chapter 22

Rev. 22 .... 512, 528, 559
Rev. 22:1 . 22, 30, 63-65, 69, 70, 324, 529, 538, 539
Rev. 22:1-2 .... 63, 324, 539
Rev. 22:1-3 .... 69, 70, 538
Rev. 22:1-5 529

Rev. 22:3 .... 534, 535
Rev. 22:5 .... 3, 529, 541
Rev. 22:6 .... 93, 94
Rev. 22:7 165
Rev. 22:8 94
Rev. 22:9 165
Rev. 22:10 165
Rev. 22:15 131
Rev. 22:16 .... 57, 78, 94
Rev. 22:18 165
Rev. 22:19 165
Rev. 22:1-2 63
Rev. 22:1-3 69
Rev. 22:2 .... 539-541, 566
Rev. 22:20 .... 73, 81
Rev. 22:20-22 81
Rev. 22:21 .... 73, 74

GENERAL INDEX

1,000 year period 478-479, 481, 481-482, 487, 495, 569
1,260 days 312
12 gates 566
12 tribes of Israel 23, 553
144,000 . 69, 116-118, 136, 142, 152, 236, 237, 239, 240, 403, 566
1st beast 27, 28, 31, 97-100, 322, 368, 370-379, 381, 382, 384-389, 391, 392, 395-397, 402, 403, 432, 447, 465, 469, 493, 503, 506, 548, 552, 618
1st Intermediate Period 18
2 Counselors 318
2 lampstands 312, 317, 321
2 Lands 72, 76, 220, 346, 363, 365, 472, 502, 613
2 trees 312, 319, 321
2 witnesses 3, 26, 267, 301, 306, 310-312, 315-319, 321, 323-327, 329, 330, 332-334, 336, 358, 548, 566, 596, 618

2nd beast 28, 100, 322, 370, 372, 373, 381, 382, 384-390, 392, 395-400, 402, 408-411, 447, 462, 466, 472, 493, 495, 496, 548, 552, 617, 618
2nd Intermediate Period . 18, 108, 138, 139, 188, 189, 193, 260, 282-285, 287, 295, 348, 373, 376, 392, 394-396, 399-401, 420, 453, 467-470, 472-474, 549, 620
4 creatures ... 22, 40, 84-87, 205, 206, 426, 427, 430, 549, 553, 566
4 sons of Horus 85, 431, 476, 478
4 sons of Osiris 22, 85-87, 100, 205, 206, 208, 426, 429-431, 553
four winds 25, 231, 232, 234-236, 557
7 angels 3, 28, 90, 150, 235, 246, 249, 268, 418, 425-430, 439, 441, 449, 451, 456, 467, 565, 569, 602, 619
7 churches 24, 42, 89, 90, 154, 171, 184, 187-192, 194, 195, 212, 568
7 deities 311, 426, 428, 436, 438, 569

7 golden lampstands 89
7 kings 460, 462-464, 466, 467, 470, 471, 473
7 letters 3, 24, 34, 91, 110, 154-158, 160, 170, 171, 181, 185-188, 190, 192, 211, 280, 348, 486, 503, 525, 527, 572, 588, 590, 617
7 male towers 302
7 plagues 28, 165, 268, 418, 425-427, 453, 456
7 spirits 57, 84, 88-90, 100, 280, 405, 406, 428, 431, 547, 553, 565
7 spirits of God 88-90, 280, 405, 565
7 stars 89, 405, 406
7 torches of fire 88, 280, 406
7 trumpets 246, 268, 565
12 deities 23, 67, 100, 116-119, 131, 132, 135, 139, 145, 146, 149, 150, 152, 239, 240, 244, 416-418, 444, 449, 484
12 gates 532, 535-538
12 goddesses . 132, 445, 448, 449, 485, 537
12 hours of night 481
12 kinds of fruit 539, 540
12 tribes 3, 23, 31, 42, 57, 114, 116-120, 122, 123, 127, 130-134, 136, 137, 141, 142, 201, 230, 239, 240, 417, 532, 537, 545, 549, 561, 567, 587
12 tribes of Israel 3, 23, 31, 42, 57, 114, 116, 118-120, 123, 127, 130-133, 137, 141, 142, 230, 239, 240, 417, 537, 545, 549, 561, 567, 587
24 deities 127
24 deities ... 23, 90-93, 118,122, 125-126, 128, 360
42 months 28, 312, 315, 374, 375, 392, 397
666 .... 31, 97-99, 391, 556, 561
Aamu 188, 190, 193, 468
abomination 131, 244,373-374, 395, 456, 469
Abu 135, 471, 533, 534
Abydos ... 24, 71, 177, 181, 203-205, 351, 488, 520
abyss 97, 104, 243, 245, 280, 322, 344,

GENERAL INDEX 635

484, 511, 513, 514, 517, 518, 521, 524, 527
acacia tree 163
Admonitions of an Egyptian Sage ... 31, 42, 110, 260, 271, 272, 279, 281-286, 294
adultery 177, 179, 180, 184, 187
Aegean Sea .. 255, 267, 270, 274, 275, 277, 279, 281, 282, 288, 295, 305, 306, 363, 396, 418, 453, 474, 559, 569
Aepep (see also, Apophis) 96
afterlife . 61, 77, 79, 88, 103, 145, 146, 148, 149, 170, 182, 195, 199, 244, 245, 286, 288, 356, 408, 439, 444, 479, 482, 485, 489, 503, 510, 521, 523, 534, 535, 579, 620
agate 532
Ahmose . 19, 139, 190, 192, 193, 286, 295, 397, 400, 401, 442, 454, 470, 472-474
air 75, 90, 96, 143, 228, 229, 252, 254, 257, 258, 262, 267, 331, 332, 341, 344, 347, 388, 417, 430, 517, 622
Aker . 26, 33, 42, 44, 54, 75, 163, 196, 208, 267, 279, 283-286, 295, 298-301, 303, 306, 307, 310-313, 315-318, 321-325, 327-335, 546, 548, 552, 554, 555, 557, 568, 572, 610, 616, 620
Akrotiri 274
Alexandria 38, 39
All-god 87, 553
Almighty . 62, 69, 140, 418, 419, 423, 431, 433, 435, 453, 454, 541, 564
Alpha and the Omega 522-523
altar 62, 150, 201, 246, 247, 313, 314, 354, 355, 431, 433-435, 482, 483, 488, 494-496, 542
Amana 71, 620
Amduat 3, 21-25, 27, 28, 31-33, 42, 44, 47, 48, 54, 55, 66, 67, 69, 71, 89-93, 116-125, 127, 129, 130, 133, 135-141, 144-147, 149, 151, 163, 195-198, 200-203, 208, 212, 222-224, 226, 229, 238-240, 247, 283-289, 294, 295, 297-303, 307, 308, 310, 311, 317, 318, 326, 356, 368-370, 372, 373, 375, 378-380, 384-387, 389-403, 405-407, 409-414, 420, 438, 439, 450, 501, 512, 519, 526, 530, 535, 538, 546, 548-550, 555-557, 559, 561, 568-570, 572, 573, 610, 612, 615, 617, 618, 620, 622

Amduat Series . 3, 137, 141, 195, 197, 208, 556, 557, 559, 568, 570
Amen . 22, 67, 71-74, 82-84, 128, 134, 205, 216, 225, 243-245, 289, 415, 518, 536, 547, 548, 561, 618, 620
Amenemhet I 283, 284
Amenhotep III 450
Amenope 198, 259
Amentet 155
Amen-Re ... 67, 72, 82, 83, 134, 205, 216, 245, 289, 518, 548, 618
amethyst 533
Ammon 71, 187, 620
Amon 71-73, 134, 142, 216, 217, 220, 244, 245, 420-423, 442, 518, 561, 620
Amon-Re . 72, 73, 134, 217, 220, 420-423, 518
Amon-Re-Atum-Harakhti 73
amulets 168, 169, 380
Amun 71, 144, 213, 221, 561, 620, 621
Amūn 71, 620
Anat-Astarte 395, 469, 549, 552, 620
ancient serpent 23, 26, 95-97, 100, 290, 322, 350, 352, 361, 375, 475, 477, 495, 548, 552, 569
Anedjti 143
angels 3, 25, 28, 31, 42, 61, 64, 66, 72, 93, 84, 89, 90, 93-96, 100, 150,151, 161, 173, 197, 231-235, 246-247, 249-250, 253, 264, 266, 268, 298-301, 303-305, 308, 310-312, 326, 347-349, 403, 404, 406, 407, 409, 411-412, 418, 425-431, 433, 435, 438-439, 441, 445, 449, 451, 456, 467, 475-477, 531-532, 537, 538, 547, 549, 552, 554, 560, 562-564, 566, 569, 578, 602, 618, 619
Ani 161, 244, 265, 575
ankh ... 127, 168, 307, 332, 371, 386, 388, 389, 405
Annals of Thutmosis III 38, 109, 215, 217-220, 260, 441-443, 450, 453-455, 508, 568, 569, 619
anointed 22, 73-75, 77-79, 82-84, 350, 356-358, 485, 488, 489, 508, 548, 552, 560, 567, 570
anointed one ... 73, 74, 77, 79, 82, 356-358, 485, 488, 489, 548, 552, 560, 567, 570
anointing 77, 78
antelope 99, 357
Antipas 156
Apep (see also Apophis) .. 96, 97, 104, 235

Apepi (see also Apophis) 96
apocalypse 34, 212, 290, 545, 576, 581, 582
Apophis . 18, 19, 23, 25-27, 29, 30, 85, 96-
100, 104, 105, 112, 114, 173, 174,
178, 190, 192, 212, 222, 235, 285,
287, 290, 291, 293, 294, 322, 323,
339, 345, 347-350, 352, 354-357,
360, 361, 366-368, 370, 375, 376,
396, 397, 401, 402, 409, 410, 430,
431, 446-448, 453, 454, 457, 459-
461, 463-466, 468-473, 475-478,
484, 488, 491-493, 495, 520, 548,
552, 554, 572, 620, 621
Apopis (see also Apophis) 96, 150, 178,
212, 222, 348, 350, 353, 410, 411,
460, 465, 476, 478, 495
arch 285, 299, 552, 620
archangels 93, 349
Armageddon . 3, 29, 34, 398, 427, 432, 433,
436, 439, 441-444, 449-453, 455,
456, 569, 603, 619
Armenian Version of Revelation 576
Arms of Geb 325, 524
armies . 27, 57, 101, 103-104, 105, 108-115,
117, 150-152, 190, 192-193, 208,
211-216, 219, 220, 223, 229, 231,
236, 237, 239, 348, 349, 352, 361,
366, 398, 400-401, 443-445, 447,
449, 450, 451, 453-454, 464-465,
475, 484, 493, 494, 496, 548,
552, 560, 561, 563, 564
ascension 358, 536
ash 104, 228, 251-258, 262, 266, 269,
272, 274-277, 282, 286, 294, 332,
363, 577
Asher 116, 119, 120, 125, 611, 612
Asia Minor ... 154, 171, 187, 188, 192, 496
Asiatic peoples 442
Asiatics . 189, 216, 218, 221, 228, 271, 360,
422, 452, 503
ass 99, 406, 409-411, 457, 466
assessors 92, 408, 409, 553
Assyria 417
Atlantis 271, 273, 274, 580
Atum ... 52, 61, 73, 76, 82, 102, 160, 183,
236, 352, 354-356, 427, 451, 481,
554, 620
Atum-Khoprer 481
avenge . 108, 150, 223, 225, 227, 237, 346,
612
awe 60, 242

ba 22, 26, 54, 66, 71, 76, 88, 103, 164,
95, 304 309, 314-324, 326, 330,
331, 333-335, 437, 486, 541, 618
Baal . 18, 90, 188, 190, 192, 376, 395, 446,
454, 460, 469, 471, 572, 620
Baal-Reshef 190, 395, 469, 620
baboons ... 25, 85, 86, 113, 197, 198, 307,
308, 372, 373, 377, 408, 432, 622
464, 519
Babylon 39, 42, 54, 249-252, 255, 264,
266, 281, 290-292, 452, 567, 570
Baines and Málek (1980) ... 470, 471, 605
Balaam 154, 156, 187
balance .. 79, 103, 160, 162, 215, 218, 219,
244, 432, 535, 621
bandages 149, 214, 452
Barak 441
Barge of the Earth 425, 426, 428, 429,
431, 438, 439
bark ... 143, 233, 434, 439, 487, 490, 514,
516, 519
barley .. 149, 215, 218-220, 229, 417, 437,
515, 539
Barnes (1993) 441, 496, 603, 607
barque 55, 63, 64, 67, 85, 91, 99, 117,
118, 132, 147, 195, 223, 225, 297,
299, 302, 308, 311, 315, 316, 318,
319, 321, 323, 347, 348, 350, 368,
378, 393, 400, 404, 416, 426, 438,
459, 464, 476, 483, 487, 513, 514,
540, 621
battles ... 29, 41, 76, 80, 82, 103, 108-110,
129, 133, 137, 150-151, 160, 211,
212, 214-220, 222, 223, 225, 226,
229, 231, 237, 239, 240, 257, 285,
291-294, 345, 348, 351, 352, 356,
409, 420-422, 432, 441-445, 449,
450, 452-456, 459, 492-496, 567,
569, 572, 619
Battle of Armageddon . 444, 449, 452, 455,
456, 569, 619
battle of Horus and Seth 80, 292
ba-bird 88, 164
beast from the earth 368, 377
beast from the sea 368, 401, 552
beasts . 3, 23, 27-29, 31, 32, 39, 40, 42, 54,
84, 85, 97-101, 134, 150, 162, 163,
170, 211, 215, 220, 253, 268, 270,
321-323, 329, 332, 368, 370-379,
381, 382, 384-392, 395-403, 406-

412, 417, 418, 432, 446-447, 451, 454, 456, 458-469, 472, 473, 478, 484, 488, 493, 495, 496, 503,505-506, 548, 552, 556, 598, 564, 617, 618
beer 79, 103, 145, 149, 162, 167, 268, 306, 430, 479, 491, 520
bees 227
beetles .. 66-68, 70, 87, 118, 169, 203, 298, 332, 341, 344, 353-355, 404, 620, 621
beginning and the end 74, 523-525
beheaded 25, 158, 225, 314, 430, 451, 484, 485, 488, 499
Benjamin 116, 119, 120, 122, 125
bennu 481
benu bird 170
beryl 532
Beu-t 376
Beyond . 51, 69, 75, 86, 105, 110, 127, 143, 164, 187, 252, 260, 275, 286, 287, 289, 306, 309, 361, 376, 439, 442, 454, 480, 482, 492, 501, 517, 519, 520, 526, 530, 559, 562
Bible 2, 37-39, 43, 44, 81, 94, 96, 116, 117, 121, 130, 139, 140, 147, 152, 154, 167, 174, 181, 184, 187, 201, 242, 290, 415, 441, 496, 498, 570, 575-583, 588, 589, 591-593, 603, 607
biers 24, 51, 147, 148, 244, 357, 359, 360, 500, 501, 507
birds 51, 64, 66, 79, 87, 88, 110, 164, 170, 199, 227, 246, 247, 270, 272, 298-299, 437, 481, 563-564
blessed 22, 30, 42, 61, 64, 65, 74, 120, 125, 133, 136, 145, 146, 148, 149, 164, 169, 170, 175, 245, 289, 331, 350, 351, 359, 417, 437, 439, 443, 444, 450, 480, 493, 514, 515, 517, 520, 521, 525, 527-529, 539, 540, 542, 544, 553, 571
blessed dead ... 30, 42, 133, 136, 145, 146, 148, 149, 164, 170, 175, 245, 289, 331, 351, 359, 417, 437, 439, 493, 514, 515, 517, 521, 525, 527-529, 539, 540, 542, 544, 553, 571
Blind Horus 331
blood 29, 57, 74, 80, 82, 90, 103, 104, 109, 110, 150, 180, 194, 206, 223, 225, 227, 228, 234, 236, 238, 246, 247, 249, 253, 255, 257, 259, 263, 265-268, 270, 272, 293, 312, 314, 315, 319, 320, 351, 352, 403, 411, 412, 431, 433-435, 437, 458, 459, 478, 495, 526, 538, 563
blood of the lamb 351, 352
blue 169, 612
boat 26, 28, 105, 117, 251, 256, 274, 287, 301, 302, 319, 321, 323, 324, 370-373, 375, 377, 379, 404,4 06 416, 430, 431, 462, 612
body . 22, 26, 27, 40, 48, 51, 60, 61, 70, 71, 74-76, 78, 80, 87, 88, 96, 105, 107, 131, 148, 152, 163, 168, 170, 178, 183, 185, 198, 202-205, 222, 233, 237, 239, 240, 291, 303, 308, 311, 314, 316, 317, 319, 320, 322, 327, 329, 331, 337-339, 342-346, 353, 370, 376, 388, 389, 401, 404, 416, 423, 430, 433, 436, 438, 466, 476-478, 481, 492, 497, 505, 513-517, 522, 524, 525, 529, 532, 533, 536, 537, 539-541, 548, 552, 571, 573, 613, 620, 621
body parts 183, 185, 202, 319
bombs ... 252, 254, 256-258, 262, 264, 265
bondage 243, 390
Book of Aker . 26, 33, 42, 44, 54, 196, 208, 267, 279, 283-286, 295, 299, 301, 303, 306, 307, 310-313, 315-318, 321-325, 327-335, 546, 548, 552, 555, 557, 568, 572, 610, 616, 620
Book of Breathings 379, 380, 401
Book of Caverns ... 24, 31, 33, 54, 55, 67, 155, 157, 158, 165, 171, 177-184, 186, 286, 345, 512, 568, 617, 621
Book of Day 27, 30, 54, 286, 337, 338, 341-352, 355, 356, 361, 362, 364, 366, 497, 498, 535, 536, 538-540, 619
Book of Gates . 3, 21, 28-33, 42, 44, 48, 54, 55, 66, 69, 85, 91-93, 116-121, 129, 131-140, 143, 144, 146-152, 196, 211, 212, 214, 240, 244, 283, 285, 286, 288, 289, 294, 295, 356, 378, 399, 400, 413-420, 423, 425, 427-439, 441, 442, 444, 445, 448-450, 452, 454-461, 463-467, 473-475, 479, 482-485, 487, 488, 492-497, 501, 502, 511-513, 515, 517, 518, 520-522, 524, 525, 528, 535,

638   *Egyptian Origin of the Book of Revelation*

537, 538, 542, 544, 546, 548-550,
  555-557, 559, 561, 569, 570, 572,
  610, 611, 614, 615, 617, 621
Book of Gates Series . 3, 32, 196, 413, 555-
  557, 559, 569, 570, 617
Book of Genesis 116
Book of Life .. 30, 162, 165, 171, 185, 377,
  379-381, 401, 504, 506-509, 556, 618
Book of Night . 27, 30, 32, 54, 55, 337, 338,
  340, 342, 344, 346, 348, 353-355,
  357-359, 361-366, 430, 497-499,
  501, 502, 504-512
Book of the Dead 22, 31-33, 36, 42, 44,
  46, 54, 56-61, 63, 71, 76, 78-80,
  85, 100, 102-106, 132, 136, 143,
  145, 149, 151, 155, 156, 158-167,
  169-176, 186, 188, 196, 198, 200,
  208, 235, 236, 244-246, 248, 259-
  261, 263, 265-267, 275, 279, 281-
  285, 288, 291-294, 297, 306-308,
  310, 336, 345, 347, 350, 352, 355,
  358, 363, 365, 377, 399, 409, 430,
  434, 461, 483, 497, 500, 503, 504,
  508-510, 517, 520, 522, 524-526,
  530, 535-539, 544, 546, 547, 549,
  550, 557, 568, 573, 575, 577, 578,
  582, 584
Book of the Divine Cow . 31, 44, 51, 54, 85,
  135, 259, 267, 268, 278-281, 283-
  286, 294, 297, 303-306, 309-311,
  452, 523, 562, 568, 572
Book of Two Ways 245, 321, 323
books . 27, 32-34, 38, 42-45, 54, 68, 69, 77,
  111, 117, 118, 144, 165, 196, 206-
  209, 259, 296, 311, 313, 336-338,
  342, 346, 353-357, 361-364, 366,
  414, 431, 497, 499, 501, 504, 506-
  508, 510, 529, 535-537, 543-546,
  548, 552, 555, 557, 559, 568, 569,
  572, 577-582, 617, 618, 622
Books of the Heavens ... 27, 32, 33, 42, 54,
  68, 196, 208, 296, 336-338, 342,
  346, 353-355, 357, 361-364, 366,
  414, 497, 529, 536, 537, 544, 546,
  548, 555, 557, 559, 568, 569, 617,
  618
bottomless pit . 26, 257, 321, 322, 329, 332,
  459, 460, 475, 476
bowing down 92, 173, 193 421, 423
bow harp 417
bowl 253, 268, 431, 433, 438, 483
bows ... 48, 53, 92, 99, 162, 173, 193, 213,
  215-218, 221, 291, 300, 318, 321,
  348, 371, 372, 492-494, 496, 417
braided lock 172, 173, 530
brand ....
branding 28, 389-391, 488
bread 52, 79, 103, 131, 149, 162, 167,
  270, 294, 308, 430, 479, 491, 517,
  520, 521, 525, 530, 611
bread of life 525
breast 60
breath .. 106, 126, 152, 171, 214, 217, 228,
  243, 255, 261-264, 266, 275, 289,
  293, 324-327, 387-389, 438, 452,
  531, 543, 566, 620, 621
brick 107, 544
bride .. 40, 43, 69, 259, 512, 514, 518, 549,
  554, 556, 570, 619
Brilliant One 410
broad collar 60, 429
broad earth 492-493, 496
bronze 57, 61, 218, 250, 258, 274, 541
Bubastis 468
bulls ... 104, 108, 216, 221, 391, 421, 227,
  426-428, 436, 438-440, 449, 482,
  483, 488
Burned One 475, 478
Busiris 104
Byblos 272, 275, 288
cackler 245, 246
Cairo 80, 177, 188, 260, 291
caldrons 180,181, 184, 247, 289, 314,
  319, 408
call . 3, 25, 38, 95, 110, 120, 125, 144, 154,
  156, 157, 165, 171, 182, 185, 193,
  210-212, 218, 221, 223, 228, 229,
  231, 233, 240, 242, 243, 251, 252,
  280, 303, 420-422, 453, 476, 519,
  591
calm 242, 243, 416, 535
calves 25, 213, 214
Canaan(ites) 116, 141, 139, 415
canal 539
candlesticks 566
canon 33, 37, 39, 471
canopic jars 476, 621
canopy 147, 239
cardinal points 85, 204, 234, 338, 529
carnelian 532
cataclysmic events 54, 241, 249, 252,
  256, 258, 281, 287, 305, 311, 363,

GENERAL INDEX

474, 512
catastrophic events ... 3, 25, 31, 34, 80, 90, 93, 193, 194, 210, 227-231, 243, 246, 248, 249- 250, 255-256, 259, 266-267, 271,274, 277-278, 279, 281-283,285-286, 287, 295, 302-303, 305, 320, 328, 330, 332, 334, 362, 363, 384, 396,418, 431-432, 436, 437, 439-441, 449, 453, 467, 474, 492, 557, 559, 569, 571, 574, 594-595, 618
cats 227
cattle of Re 214, 229, 452
cauldrons 181-183, 185, 319, 412, 439
cavalry 450
caverns . 24-25, 31, 33, 54, 55, 67, 155-158, 165, 171, 177-186, 227, 233, 286, 297, 298, 302-303, 311, 316, 345, 353, 368, 484, 490,512, 533, 568, 617, 621
celestial city .. 50, 176, 202, 323, 467, 493, 517, 528-533, 535-537, 539, 541-544, 569, 571
celestial fruits 164
celestial river 286, 539
censer 89, 246, 247
ceremonial collars 416, 429
ceremonies 78, 79, 94, 165, 197, 208, 212, 221, 244, 306-310,312, 501, 543
chains 29, 291, 475-478, 495, 554, 569
chambers ... 180, 184, 204, 215, 226, 227, 238, 313, 314, 321, 337, 338, 423, 442, 462, 497, 507, 539
Champollion 184, 271
chaos 96, 97, 100, 104, 173, 254, 277, 294, 295, 322, 345, 353, 361, 368, 459, 463, 475, 484, 535, 548
chariots .. 108-110, 190, 216-218, 220-221, 250, 254, 257, 258, 444
chastiser 222, 223
chastity 132, 133
Cheops 18, 106
cherubim 93
chest 86, 201, 298, 314, 429, 547
child .. 27, 68, 75, 107, 273, 337, 341, 343-347, 355, 366, 367, 439, 476, 484, 524, 552, 568, 622
children of Nut 158, 356
Chinese dragon 96
Christ . 2, 22, 33, 34, 40, 42, 43, 54, 57, 73-84, 94, 135, 146, 209, 348-351, 358, 359, 367, 479, 483, 485-489, 495, 545, 547-549, 552, 554, 560, 561, 570, 571, 578
Christian ... 2, 33-41, 43, 44, 53, 54, 73, 74, 77, 80-82, 84, 88, 93, 94, 140, 154, 159, 190, 209, 281, 290, 349, 441, 489, 528, 545, 548, 567, 570-574
Christian mystical theology 93
Christianity .. 38, 54, 74, 78, 81, 82, 93, 94, 154, 192, 209, 489, 545, 560, 561, 570, 579
christos .. 73-78, 80-82, 146, 170, 349, 351, 356-358, 489, 560, 570
chrysolite 532
chrysoprase 533
churches 2, 24, 33-34, 37-39, 41-42, 62, 72, 89, 90, 154, 155, 157-158, 158, 168, 170-173, 183, 184,186-187, 192, 194, 195, 209, 211, 212, 280, 545, 566, 568, 571-574, 572
cinnamon 250
circle of darkness 172
city .. 3, 22, 27, 30, 50, 54, 60, 64, 69, 128, 129, 131, 144, 147, 154, 175, 176, 187-189, 193, 202, 218, 225, 238, 239, 245, 250, 252, 256, 258, 260, 264-268, 272-274, 281, 287, 290-292, 295, 312, 313, 323, 324, 327-329, 350, 351, 367, 394, 411, 420, 437, 439, 441-444, 455, 456, 465-470, 472, 492, 493, 496, 512-514, 517-520, 523, 527-539, 541-544, 549, 556, 560, 566, 569, 571, 572, 578, 609, 612, 619
City of God 175, 351
city of my God 175-176, 193
City of Re 193, 350, 367
clothed in white ... 84, 132, 142, 145, 146, 151, 237, 521
clothing . 23, 25, 90, 91, 93, 109, 110, 113, 115, 145, 146, 151, 152, 195, 212, 218, 223, 225-227, 237, 238, 352, 416, 417, 428, 444, 479, 505, 613, 615
clouds .. 253, 254, 256, 258, 262, 275-277, 298-301, 310, 312, 320, 321, 324-327, 232, 252, 256, 406, 409, 562, 563
cobras 111, 325, 348, 151, 212, 419, 433, 438, 492, 493, 507, 613
Codex 74
Coffin Texts 44, 45, 54, 283-285, 399, 488, 530, 577, 578

coffins .. 26, 44, 45, 54, 85, 283-285, 321, 331, 323, 330, 399, 430, 476, 488, 517, 530, 577, 578, 621
collars 57, 60, 416, 429, 547
colors . 25, 41, 61, 108-110, 113, 151, 169, 213-215, 229, 253, 257, 272, 320, 429, 434, 437, 459, 504, 505, 510, 532-533, 541
combat myth 41, 336, 576
"Come!" 212, 213, 215, 217, 221, 229, 422
coming like a thief 443, 450
coming soon 174
commandments 150, 211, 356
conception 184, 347, 483, 510
conqueror(s) 24, 159-160, 162-163, 165-167, 169, 173, 174, 182, 193, 202, 216, 510, 527
conscripts 229, 230, 236
consecration 77
Constantinople 39, 209
copper 61, 270, 533
Coptic(s) 159, 582
corn 326, 410
coronation 77, 78, 526
corpse of Osiris 71
cosmic upheaval 248, 363
cosmic war 248
cosmogony 50, 77, 248
council(s) 2, 57, 92, 120, 146, 160, 161, 166, 237, 442, 452, 503, 611, 612
Council of Judges 57, 92
covenant 128, 129
cowardly 527
creation 3, 23, 30, 50, 52, 61, 71-73, 77, 96, 100, 135, 175, 218, 243, 245, 246, 248, 249, 259, 267, 268, 270, 279, 289, 293, 296, 302, 303, 305, 310, 331, 332, 338, 339, 352, 353, 355, 361, 362, 376, 388, 413, 439, 448, 460, 481, 492, 511-513, 515, 516, 518, 519, 522, 528, 529, 531, 542, 543, 556, 562, 569, 570, 572, 608, 619, 621
creative activity 285-287, 295
creative power 62
creative word 73, 510, 562
creatures . 22, 40, 42, 57, 66, 68, 73, 84-87, 93, 135, 197, 205, 206, 215, 245, 247, 257, 287, 368, 422, 426, 427, 429, 430, 490, 499, 519, 541, 549, 553, 566

Crete 215, 274, 277, 282, 288, 474
Critias 273, 579, 594
crocodile(s) 40, 156, 178, 221, 234-236, 243, 272, 287, 345, 354, 389, 404, 499, 456-460, 466, 470, 564, 621
crops ... 212, 218-220, 258, 270, 271, 276, 277, 283, 294, 323, 350, 403, 406, 411
crown (s) ... 22, 27, 48, 53, 57, 61, 62, 68, 71, 72, 90-91, 93, 102, 111, 112, 115, 127, 131, 162, 168, 174, 199, 202, 215, 216, 221, 225, 339, 343-344, 373-375, , 382, 390, 391, 396, 406, 432, 461-463, 486, 490, 491, 521-522, 547, 613
crystal 60, 63, 533, 538
cube 530, 531
cubit 534
cubit(s) 97, 104, 107, 117, 302, 350, 530, 534
Cusae 189, 472
cycle of time 61, 528, 572
cyclical nature of time 296, 334, 524
Cyprus 188, 215, 216
Damascus 420
damned 179, 234, 289, 357, 412, 427, 480
Dan 116, 117, 119, 120, 122, 125, 348, 611, 612
darkness 25, 71, 90, 96, 102, 108, 156, 172, 182, 184, 238, 245, 246, 250, 252, 253, 256, 258, 260, 262, 263, 268, 269, 275, 276, 285, 286, 289, 290, 294, 298-300, 318-321, 331, 332, 334, 339, 348, 353, 358, 363, 400, 418, 433, 437, 474, 478, 481, 482, 485, 490, 491, 515, 521, 620
Dat (see also Tuat) 92, 514
David . 36, 72, 77, 106, 107, 166, 200, 542, 577, 584, 586, 589, 609
dawn ... 22, 67, 68, 82, 104, 105, 130, 232-234, 247, 248, 262-265, 268, 291, 293, 303, 338, 353-355, 365, 371, 413, 439, 459, 481, 485, 491, 511, 512, 517-519, 521, 522, 528, 533, 538, 548, 621
death . 24, 26, 69, 75, 88, 90, 109, 112, 146, 150, 151, 156, 157, 160, 162-164, 170, 171, 180, 184, 185, 211, 215, 220, 223, 226, 227, 231, 234, 244, 248, 249, 253, 254, 256, 257, 260-262, 265, 267, 269, 272, 277, 286, 287, 290, 298, 299, 321, 322, 327,

329-332, 334, 347, 350-352, 371,
380, 388, 389, 393, 400, 412, 430,
439, 442, 459, 460, 473, 479-481,
483, 498-500, 503, 514, 519-521,
524, 526-528, 568
Deborah 441
deceased . 59, 61, 62, 70, 71, 78, 79, 82, 92,
103, 132, 145, 149, 159-169, 185,
198, 200, 231, 244, 306-309, 321,
352, 357, 412, 476, 486, 488, 493,
503, 509, 514, 517, 519, 520, 525,
529, 530, 535, 536, 538, 621, 622
deeds . 30, 57, 90, 133, 148, 156, 157, 159,
160, 165, 171, 173, 184, 188, 210,
225, 231, 251, 280, 347, 360, 376,
409, 418, 419, 423, 427, 439, 503,
505, 507-510, 543, 562, 621
demonic spirits 442, 449
demons 77, 93, 105, 232, 292
denarius 215, 218, 219
desert ... 99, 118, 129, 134, 152, 153, 246,
267, 268, 270, 291, 357, 375, 376,
470, 526, 621, 622
desolation 332
destroyer 265, 266, 371
Destroyer of Souls 265, 266
destruction 24, 40, 42, 88, 90, 94, 103,
109, 153, 158, 163, 177, 179-181,
184, 193, 220, 245, 246, 248, 249,
252, 256, 258, 261, 264, 267, 270,
273, 281, 283, 285, 291-293, 297,
299, 305, 306, 311, 324, 325, 330,
331, 338, 360, 363, 365, 371, 408,
411, 427, 430, 437-439, 452, 459,
467, 472, 488, 494, 500, 506, 535,
568, 571, 572, 611
Detdjeru 500
Deuteronomy 415
diadem(s) 53, 91, 111, 112, 153, 228,
373, 396, 419-420, 444, 486, 563
Dionysius 39
disaster 110, 229, 250, 271, 289, 305
discord 157, 158, 460
disease 220, 256, 317, 320
disk(s) .. 22, 48, 53, 61, 67, 68, 70, 76, 108,
111, 118, 177, 198, 206, 207, 232-
234, 284, 289, 321, 325, 326, 331,
332, 237, 324-326, 339, 343, 345,
353, 357, 374-375, 376, 404, 438,
457, 491, 513, 522, 529, 536-538,
541, 620

dispatch(es) 211, 245
divine beings 95, 280
divine grace 525
divine hawk 227
Djamu 500
djebat-nefret tree 164
djed 49, 166, 168
djet 483, 514, 523-525, 528
door(s) 33, 50, 98, 143, 170, 172, 204-
205, 206, 208, 226, 245, 300-301,
321, 345, 361, 390-391, 437, 490,
506, 507, 510, 533, 535, 536, 564
double ... 72, 163, 184, 199, 298, 301, 306,
316, 323, 389, 390, 399, 400, 406,
432, 436, 506, 521, 536
double-headed lion 301, 316
dragon (s) ... 27, 29, 32, 40, 41, 93, 96, 97,
99, 150, 151, 211, 337, 343, 345,
347, 349-352, 354-357, 363, 366,
367, 370, 372, 397, 398, 401, 402,
445-450, 454, 459, 475, 478, 554,
560, 568, 570
drama 242, 256
driving of the calves 213, 214
drum 244, 417
Duamutef 85, 86, 206, 620
Duat 136, 170, 286, 514, 536
dust 110, 228, 246, 254-258, 272, 276,
277, 294
dying a second time (see second death) . 163
dynasty .. 18, 19, 72, 74, 99, 106, 107, 134,
135, 143, 162, 182, 189, 190, 192,
213, 283-286, 288, 291, 295, 337,
375, 376, 395, 397, 400, 401, 417,
441, 442, 446, 450, 470-474, 483,
496, 620
eagle 64, 66, 85, 86, 337, 346, 355, 549
ear(s) 99, 170, 171, 183, 273, 457, 466
earthquakes ... 26, 90, 193-194, , 210, 227-
228, 246-253, 256-258, 260, 262,
264-269, 270, 272, 274, 276, 277,
279, 286, 291, 292, 294-295, 301-
302, 303, 306, 312, 315, 325, 327-
330, 332-334, 336, 347, 396, 418,
431, 433, 436-437, 439, 445, 446,
453, 474, 538, 566, 568, 571, 572
earth-god 30, 135, 160, 175, 178, 225,
251, 292, 298, 316, 325, 353, 478,
513, 516-518, 527, 621, 622
eastern horizon of heaven ... 345, 485, 492,
496

Edfu 377
Edom 415
efflux 288, 352, 526, 539
efflux of Osiris 288, 539
egg .. 67, 76, 175, 204, 205, 298, 300, 301, 355
elder(s) 23, 66, 68, 73, 84, 90-93, 135, 197, 200, 204, 205, 208, 245, 248, 280, 360, 513, 549, 553, 566, 613
eldest son of the earth 518
Elephantine 527, 533
emerald 532-534
enchant 465, 491
encircling .. 92, 94, 203, 486, 494, 524, 544
end of time .. 267, 279, 296, 305, 352, 355, 362, 439, 525, 571, 574
ennead(s) .. 48, 76, 79, 103, 132, 160, 162, 164, 245, 308, 356, 437
enveloper ... 147, 148, 238, 239, 294, 478, 492, 493, 612, 613
Ephesus . 39, 154, 156, 157, 171, 188, 192
eruptions .. 31, 43, 228, 250-255, 257, 259, 263, 266, 274, 275, 282, 291, 293, 295, 439, 572
Esdraelon 441
eternity . 104, 140, 144, 160, 167, 238, 304, 305, 346, 348, 351, 358, 521, 523-525, 579
Euphrates River ... 54, 187, 218, 258, 270, 281, 290, 291, 433, 436, 442, 445-447,449, 453, 454, 470, 569
everlasting .. 164, 358, 418, 419, 435, 480, 521, 524
everlastingness 304, 305, 521
evil .. 29, 57, 61, 74, 80, 82, 84-86, 93, 95-100, 105, 108, 111, 114, 120, 125, 131, 145, 146, 150, 151, 155, 157, 158, 162, 164, 168, 171, 173, 175, 177, 178, 180, 184, 188, 211, 212, 233-235, 238-240, 244, 246, 248, 251, 254, 262, 267, 280, 285, 287, 291-293, 308, 310, 331, 339, 346-350, 357, 360, 363, 365, 368, 375-377, 382, 399, 410, 411, 418, 419, 427, 430, 432, 433, 435, 436, 439, 440, 445-447, 457, 459-465, 467, 475, 478, 480, 484, 485, 504, 506, 510, 544, 548, 552, 561, 568, 571, 572, 611, 612, 620
Evil Face 85
executioner(s) 319, 412, 538

existence 40, 48, 50, 54, 88, 99, 101, 131, 163, 168, 169, 203, 245,259, 273, 307, 308, 347, 380, 409, 412, 480, 503, 510, 521, 523, 524, 534, 562, 570, 621
Exodus . 128, 129, 138, 139, 141, 153, 276, 415, 480, 570, 582
eye of Horus 61, 437, 492, 563
eyebrow 326
eye(s) 22, 57, 60-61, 48, 61, 71, 80, 82, 85, 87-89, 97, 104, 111, 113, 115, 118, 126, 149, 152, 166, 168, 172, 178, 200, 203, 214, 245, 267, 268, 273, 269, 280, 291, 292, 294, 298, 300, 317, 321, 326, 345, 347, 358, 371, 377, 379-380, 396, 416, 437-438, 452, 466, 483, 486, 489, 492, 494, 507, 509, 515, 520, 538, 543, 547, 549, 563, 612, 622
eyes of fire 57
Ezekiel 201, 496, 570
faithful .. 28, 29, 42, 71, 72, 78, 79, 84, 90, 101, 103, 112, 115, 117, 128, 132, 145-148, 154-158, 167, 170, 171, 173-175, 182-184, 186, 187, 192, 193, 195, 211, 222, 230, 237, 238, 240, 287, 299, 337, 339, 357, 359, 360, 368, 370, 377, 379, 380, 390, 400, 401, 403, 409, 411, 413, 429, 430, 439, 452, 464, 465, 479-481, 484-490, 494, 495, 501, 547, 549, 553, 563, 569-572
faithfulness ... 162, 192, 378, 415, 490, 571
faithless 512, 527
falcon .. 22, 70, 75, 79, 113, 221, 298, 332, 379, 399, 461, 483, 620
falling stars 346
fall on faces 92, 161
falling down 93, 197
false credentials 156, 173, 174, 185
false prophet . 32, 39, 42, 84, 163, 368, 397-402, 408, 409, 447, 454, 495, 496, 548, 552, 564
falsehood 103, 308
famine . 193, 215, 220, 250, 256, 258, 271, 276, 295, 533
Farasha 189, 468
fear . 60, 217, 220, 221, 243, 251, 258, 263, 264, 266, 345, 347, 359, 363, 365, 384, 418, 419, 421, 423, 443, 444, 502, 503, 563

GENERAL INDEX 643

feather(s) .. 53, 62, 79, 103, 131, 132, 160, 374, 451, 621, 622
feet 57, 61, 68, 77, 112, 173, 178, 179, 193, 216, 223, 274, 277, 301, 302, 315, 324, 325, 338, 339, 343, 344, 350, 432, 500, 505, 513, 517, 524, 529, 530, 535, 547, 563
Feller of Fish 265
festival of watchfulness 454
Field of Offerings 58, 64, 79, 103, 175, 350, 351, 514, 538
Field of Peace 164
Field of Reeds 169
Field of Rushes 514, 562
Fields of the Blessed 444
Fields of Yaru 27, 58, 149, 350-352
fiery eye(s) 61, 111, 267, 507
fiery eye of the sun god 507
Fiery One ... 263, 365, 407, 419, 436, 438, 466, 613
fiery serpent 466
fig tree 194
fight ... 27, 29, 80, 93, 113, 114, 128, 129, 138, 142, 150, 152, 211, 212, 229, 236, 239, 242, 292, 347-349, 376, 378, 400, 410, 411, 442-444, 464, 472, 476, 486, 491, 520, 560, 565, 614
final judgment .. 78, 79, 82, 102, 112, 159, 160, 162, 164, 165, 169, 185, 307, 500, 503, 508-510, 525, 527, 528, 570, 571, 621
fire 24-26, 28-30, 40, 57, 58, 60, 61, 88, 90, 96, 97, 101, 109, 111, 115, 151, 159, 162, 163, 171, 173, 180, 181, 183, 184, 212, 216, 232, 234, 235, 244, 246-250, 252-258, 261-264, 266, 268, 269, 272, 275, 277, 280, 284, 286, 289, 291-294, 298, 300, 312, 315, 317-321, 330, 332, 348, 360, 363, 365, 381, 384, 396-400, 403, 406, 407, 410-412, 415-419, 433, 434, 436-439, 459, 465-467, 469, 472-476, 481-483, 488, 492-496, 499, 502, 506, 510, 512, 527, 528, 547, 552, 555, 556, 562-564, 569, 571, 572, 581, 611, 617, 619
firmament 531
first and last 225, 334, 420, 523
first beast (see 1st beast)

first-born of the dead 74-75, 78, 570
First Cataract 527, 533
first fruits 130, 614
first time . 72, 140, 144, 245, 368, 400, 447, 455
fish . 60, 249, 255, 257, 265, 266, 270, 276, 277, 373, 418, 502
fish kills 255, 265, 418
flame(s) 60, 61, 89, 109, 111, 115, 151, 163, 180, 181, 184, 212, 216, 223, 226, 228, 233, 234-236, 238, 247, 249, 261, 262-264, 289, 291, 292, 318, 321, 326, 347-348, 382, 436-438, 363-365, 410, 411, 438, 439, 466, 492, 502, 538, 563, 611
Flaming One 317, 318, 613
flesh 61, 128, 149, 169, 181, 203, 223, 238, 254, 298, 300, 408, 417, 434, 465, 469, 472, 473, 501, 532, 564
flood . 27, 61, 198, 214, 227, 246, 259, 264, 266, 301, 352, 355, 362, 363
flour 250, 258
flowers 60
flute 244, 259
follower(s) ... 23-25, 28, 29, 42, 57, 69, 79, 84, 85, 90, 93, 101, 103-105, 117, 128, 130-137, 140-142, 144-152, 155-158, 160, 162, 167, 171, 173, 175, 177-180, 182, 185, 186, 192, 202, 207, 211, 212, 222, 223, 225, 227, 235, 239, 240, 285, 287, 290, 294, 299, 308, 321, 322, 343, 346, 348, 350, 352, 356, 358-361, 367, 370, 376-381, 389, 390, 392, 401, 403, 406, 407, 409-413, 429-432, 434, 438, 439, 448, 449, 451, 464, 465, 467, 473, 478, 484-486, 488-492, 494-496, 498, 500-506, 520, 528, 547, 549, 571, 572, 614, 621
followers of Horus 79, 103, 160, 162, 167, 202
followers of Osiris 42, 380
followers of Re ... 135, 141, 202, 239, 356, 401, 430, 500
food . 24, 51, 142, 146, 148, 149, 152, 157-159, 163, 164, 177, 186, 195, 214, 258, 270, 306, 308, 352, 434, 480, 509, 521, 540, 541, 572, 614
food and water 142, 148, 149, 152, 352
forehead(s) ... 92, 134, 135, 237, 232, 240, 254, 390, 391, 403, 407, 456,

foreign land(s) 77, 99, 112, 295, 376, 458, 478, 484, 488, 502, 508
foreigner(s) .. 206-207, 271, 313, 314, 360, 465, 467, 468, 499, 502
fornicators 512, 527
forty-two months (see 42 months)
forty-two month reign 374
foundation(s) 377, 379, 529, 532-534, 542-543, 581
fountain(s) .. 257, 268, 403, 407, 431, 433, 437, 525, 527
fountains of the earth and sky 525
fountains of water . 527, 257, 268, 431, 433
four corners of the earth 231, 234-236, 239, 492, 529, 530, 621, 622
four creatures 22, 40, 84-87, 205, 206, 426, 427, 430, 549
four horsemen 212-214, 216, 222, 223, 229, 231, 422, 545, 618
four living creatures ... 42, 66, 68, 73, 135, 197, 205, 215, 422, 429, 430
four pillars of heaven 85, 421, 423
four pillars of the sky 515
four sons ... 22, 85-87, 100, 205, 206, 208, 426, 429-431, 476, 478
four sons of Horus .. (see 4 sons of Horus)
four sons of Osiris .... (see 4 sons of Osiris)
four winds .... (see 4 winds)
fowl 145, 270
fragrance 60
frankincense 250, 258
frog(s) 398, 445, 448-450, 566
fruit 130-131, 134, 163, 164, 194, 258, 272, 526, 539, 540, 566, 614
Furious One 363
furnace 90, 105, 252, 257
future .. 34, 38, 50, 94, 102, 174, 209, 210, 220, 295, 308, 309, 334, 344, 399, 482, 523, 525, 566, 567, 571, 574
Gad 116, 119, 120, 122, 125, 137, 537, 611, 612
garment 57, 60, 110, 145, 164, 165
garments .. 28, 90, 110, 145, 146, 151, 164, 171, 185, 229, 237, 244, 428-430, 443, 450, 503
gas(es) 251-252, 252, 256-258
gate 155, 245, 344, 363, 437, 484, 488, 490, 491, 502, 511, 519-521, 536-538, 544
gates .. 3, 21, 28-33, 42, 44, 48, 54, 55, 66, 69, 71, 85, 91-93, 116-121, 129, 131-140, 143, 144, 146-152, 160, 196, 211, 212, 214, 240, 244, 272, 283-286, 288, 289, 294, 295, 345, 356, 378, 381, 399, 400, 413-420, 423, 425, 427-439, 441, 442, 444, 445, 448-450, 452, 454-461, 463-467, 473-475, 478, 479, 482-488, 490, 492-497, 501, 502, 511-513, 515, 517-522, 524, 525, 528-530, 532, 535-538, 542-544, 546, 548-550, 555-557, 559, 561, 566, 569, 570, 572, 610, 611, 614, 615, 617, 619, 621
gates of heaven 345
Gaza 420, 471
Geb . 76, 135, 159-161, 175, 178, 204, 205, 280, 316, 325, 331, 343, 345, 353, 356, 451, 477, 478, 518, 524, 527, 620-622
Gebelein 470
Gehenna 531
gigantic sizes 534
Giza 534
Gladness of Earth .. 149, 150, 211, 444, 454
glass 28, 393, 415, 416, 418, 532, 541
glory ... 60, 64, 66, 69, 130, 140, 145, 162, 202, 233, 237, 267, 280, 327, 329, 403, 407, 419, 523, 541, 570
glory of God 60, 66, 69, 541
gnostics 349
God 3, 22-30, 32, 39, 41, 42, 50-54, 58, 60-74, 76-80, 82-123, 125-138, 140-152, 155-158, 160, 162-168, 170, 171, 173-176, 178-185, 187, 189, 190, 192-195, 197, 198, 200-212, 214, 215, 222, 223, 225-227, 231-240, 242-249, 251, 254, 258, 263-269, 273, 280, 284, 286-295, 297-305, 307-319, 321-327, 329-332, 336-361, 363, 365-368, 373-382, 385-387, 389-393, 395, 397-400, 403-413, 415-440, 444-454, 459, 460, 462-469, 475-478, 480-503, 505-528, 533, 535-544, 547-550, 552-554, 561-566, 568-572, 576, 579, 602, 611, 612, 614, 619-622
God and the Lamb ... 64, 69, 93, 130, 131, 541, 543, 552
God on the Throne ... 23, 42, 58, 60-62, 65,

GENERAL INDEX

82, 85, 89, 90, 93, 105, 111, 126, 127, 183, 197, 198, 208, 358, 377, 524, 528, 541, 547
goddess of moisture 331
god-child 568
God's domain 163, 166, 263, 509
God's wrath 412
Gog and Magog 29, 492-494, 496, 556, 567, 570, 619
gold .. 60, 61, 107, 109, 145, 169, 218, 250, 258, 429, 444, 456, 457, 469, 532, 541, 543, 544
golden collar 57, 60
golden crown 90
golden girdle 60, 429
goodwill of the gods 170
grace 525
grain . 28, 91, 134, 219, 351, 403-407, 411, 412, 530, 539, 540, 572, 611
grain gods 404, 411
grapes 219, 403, 411, 412
grass 247, 254, 255, 257, 268
Great Bear 108
great cackler 245, 246
Great Circle 217
great city 250, 252, 258, 264, 266, 323, 324, 465, 467, 470, 472, 519
great councilors 166
great earthquake .. 194, 227, 246, 256, 258, 264, 265, 267, 268, 306, 312, 325, 327, 336, 431, 433, 436, 446, 453, 566, 568
great egg 175
Great Ennead 103
great flood 301, 363
great furnace 90, 252, 257
great god ... 72, 76, 79, 104, 118, 128-130, 144, 147, 167, 171, 180, 183, 202, 205, 225, 238, 287, 298-301, 307, 318, 319, 329, 330, 351, 404, 405, 411, 416, 427, 450, 452, 465, 478, 484, 485, 488, 490, 491, 520, 526
great mountain 90, 247, 252, 257, 263, 266, 286
great multitude .. 3, 23, 110, 114, 116, 136, 137, 142, 143, 145-152, 212, 237, 344, 352, 403, 413, 444, 485, 568, 588, 614, 615, 618
Great of Forms 66
Great Pyramid 534
great red dragon 96, 343

great revision 165
great sword 215
great, high wall 532
Greece 250, 336
Greek 41, 43-45, 48, 49, 51, 52, 68, 73, 77, 80-82, 84, 85, 93, 96, 147, 159, 167, 174, 180, 181, 189, 209, 214, 238, 239, 249, 251, 259, 273, 281, 282, 304, 305, 336, 349, 356-358, 366, 398, 425, 428, 429, 435, 441, 467, 468, 477, 496, 498, 499, 514, 523, 528, 531, 560-562, 567, 570, 574, 580, 587
green ... 169, 214, 247, 254, 255, 257, 268, 411, 434
griffon 99
groups of twelve .. 31, 90, 92, 100, 116-123, 129-141, 143, 145, 146, 149, 151, 152, 201, 240, 352, 484, 485, 549, 561, 614
guard 85, 86, 105, 158, 289, 298, 316, 322, 348, 436, 438, 443, 445, 451, 465, 477-479, 491
guardian(s) ... 26, 85, 93-94, 182, 314-319, 321-327, 329, 330, 382, 405, 426, 428, 437, 438, 446, 491, 538, 621
guards ... 94, 110, 149, 264, 331, 382, 384, 478
guide(s) . 37, 41, 43, 93-94, 121, 142, 148, 271, 315-316, 318, 329, 394, 489, 576, 582
Hades 215, 498, 499, 502
Hahotep 260, 264
hail 71, 79, 86, 90, 104, 130, 134, 148, 244, 246, 247, 249, 250, 253, 254, 256-258, 262, 264-266, 268, 305, 345, 416, 418, 419, 427, 435, 436, 438, 460, 465, 474, 476, 484, 485, 613
hailstones 253, 258, 264, 265, 418
hair ... 51, 57, 61, 172, 174, 214, 228, 490, 491, 501, 520
hand ... 35, 41, 48, 54, 56, 89, 91, 92, 103-105, 117, 120, 122, 125, 127, 144, 162, 168, 172, 177, 197, 198, 203, 204, 215, 218, 219, 232, 233, 235, 236, 247, 261, 272, 275, 283, 297, 298, 300, 301, 303-305, 308, 310, 312, 313, 316, 327, 345, 356, 362, 363, 371, 373, 379, 388-391, 393, 400, 403, 405, 407, 410, 442, 456-

	458, 461, 463, 466, 469, 475-478, 483, 487-489, 499, 501, 502, 506, 507, 521, 525, 527, 561-563, 612
Hapi	206, 620
happiness	148-150, 168, 614
Harakhty (Harakhte)	620
harlot	3, 29, 42, 378, 456, 458, 459, 465, 466, 468, 469, 472, 474, 484, 545, 549, 552, 556, 569, 570, 604, 619
harp(s)	135, 244, 415-416, 417
harpers	135, 259
harvest	3, 28, 219, 403-407, 411, 412, 556, 565, 572, 600, 618
harvest time	403-405, 556, 618
Hathor	53, 88, 163, 164, 198, 267, 268, 339, 406, 549, 554, 620, 621
Hatshepsut	19, 139, 195, 218, 442
Haunebu	306
hawk	76, 85, 86, 227, 299, 358, 360, 377, 399, 419, 521, 622
He at the Head of the West	158, 351
He of the Dappled Plumage	299, 374
He on his Sand	381
Head of the Westerners	133, 419, 478
healing	77, 516, 540, 541, 544
hearing	74, 154, 157, 170, 171, 183, 185, 228, 244, 431, 443, 503
hear my voice	157, 171
hear the words	171
heart(s)	39, 51, 62, 60, 75, 76, 79, 88, 97, 101-104, 160, 162, 163, 169-171, 180-183, 185, 181, 187, 211, 216, 217, 221, 228, 244, 268-269, 280, 289, 314, 319, 346, 347, 350, 359, 360, 363, 365, 411, 419, 421, 434, 443-444, 459, 465, 480, 500, 502, 503, 508, 509, 527, 538, 573, 613, 621, 622
heaven	3, 26, 27, 41, 61, 71, 85, 87, 93, 103, 110, 128, 129, 132, 135, 146, 150, 151, 155, 162, 175, 183, 198, 199, 205-207, 211, 214, 217, 218, 228, 242, 246, 249, 251, 253, 254, 257-259, 262-265, 267-269, 280, 293, 297-301, 303-305, 310, 312, 323-326, 329, 341, 343, 345-348, 353, 361-364, 366, 372, 381, 384, 396, 397, 403, 406, 407, 421, 423, 425, 429, 452, 475, 476, 482, 484-486, 489, 492-497, 499, 508, 511, 512, 514-518, 521-523, 528, 529, 536, 542, 543, 548, 552, 562, 563,
	569, 593, 618
heavenly city	69, 175, 517, 518, 528, 529, 531, 536-538
heavens	26, 27, 32, 33, 42, 54, 57, 68, 69, 71, 85, 108, 196, 208, 209, 286, 292-294, 296, 299, 304, 325, 326, 336-338, 342, 344, 346, 353-355, 357, 361-364, 366, 414, 439, 476, 480, 481, 483, 484, 486, 489, 493, 497, 513-515, 517, 526, 529, 531, 536, 537, 539, 544, 546, 548, 555, 557, 559, 568, 569, 571, 617, 618
Hebrew	31, 44, 73, 81, 95, 97, 98, 116, 119-122, 124-127, 129, 138, 141, 147, 153, 181, 193, 240, 349, 391, 421, 441, 449, 528, 531, 560, 561, 567, 570, 587
Hebrew beliefs	561
Hebrew mythology	95
Hebrew scribe(s)	81, 193, 561
Hebrews	78, 128, 129, 138, 140, 460, 480, 531
Heh	144, 238, 354, 620
heir	70, 75, 167, 222, 226, 246, 347
Heir of Osiris	70, 226
Hekau	189
heket	219, 448
Heliopolis	72, 75, 80, 96, 104, 149, 156, 159, 163, 167, 172-176, 183, 188-190, 193, 198, 260, 291, 468, 481, 493, 620, 621
Helpless One	478
Heracleopolis	526
herald(s)	90, 94 484
Heralds of Destruction	94
Hereret	132, 446-448, 453
Herit	446, 471
Hermopolis	103, 111, 155, 189, 245, 354
Herodotus	336, 481
heron	481
Hidden Chamber	314, 321
hidden hand	478
hidden manna	167, 185, 503
hidden one	205, 548, 620
His Two Faces	402, 492-494, 496
holiness	133, 140, 146
holy city	3, 22, 30, 60, 64, 69, 131, 175, 176, 193, 225, 312, 313, 351, 439, 493, 512-514, 517, 518, 523, 527-539, 541-544, 566, 569, 571, 609, 619

holy of holies 441, 542
Holy Place 77, 201, 303
holy shore 64
homage 136
homonym(s) 35, 50, 56, 63, 68, 86, 89,
    127, 148, 235, 236, 246, 247, 264,
    292, 317, 354, 366, 377, 391, 398,
    416, 431, 437, 449, 458, 546-548,
            561-562, 564, 569
honey 305, 306, 308, 309
honor 238, 280, 490, 491, 570, 613
Horite regions 160
horizon ... 29, 71, 128-130, 135, 147, 160,
    233, 234, 247, 275, 277, 287, 302,
    309, 315, 332, 338, 344-346, 413,
    418, 419, 435, 476, 478, 484-487,
    492, 496, 511, 517, 519, 522, 524,
            531, 536, 541, 579, 620
horn(s) 39, 53, 66, 111, 341, 344,
    345, 372, 373, 391, 396, 428, 456,
    461, 462, 469, 472, 473, 538, 620
horse(s) 25, 40, 108-109, 110, 113,115,
    150, 211-214, 216, 220, 221-222, 229,
    250,254, 255, 257, 258, 398, 400,
            442, 444, 447,563, 564
horseman 217
Horus ... 22, 31, 34, 41, 53, 59, 61, 74-86,
    91, 99-115, 126-128, 133-135,
    143-145, 160-163, 167, 169, 170,
    193, 200-202, 204-207, 210, 226,
    227, 237, 244, 246, 247, 291-293,
    302, 326, 331, 336, 337, 342, 346-
    352, 356-358, 360, 361, 366, 367,
    374, 376-380, 384-389, 392, 399,
    400, 402, 408-412, 418-421, 424,
    426, 428, 430, 431, 435-437, 439,
    451-453, 461, 462, 466, 468, 469,
    476-478, 483, 485, 488, 489, 492-
    495, 501, 503, 548, 550, 552, 554,
            563, 570, 572, 620-622
Horus of Edfû 376
Horus of the Netherworld .. 74, 79, 91, 106,
    109, 112, 127, 247, 331, 466, 485,
            489, 620
House of Cool Water 149, 167
house of life 24, 31, 203-210, 259, 578,
            618
hunger 148, 164, 272, 434, 521
husband 75, 514, 518, 621
Hyksos . 18, 19, 24, 99, 139, 141, 186, 189-
    193, 260, 283, 285, 286, 295, 322, 348,
    376, 387, 392, 394-402, 408, 446,
    447, 453, 454, 468-474, 549, 582,
            620
Hymn of Praise 418
Hymn to Osiris 51, 60, 61, 76, 92, 149,
            165, 167, 244, 388, 524, 525
"I know" 136, 155-157, 170, 172,
            173, 175, 525
Iai 457, 459, 464, 466, 552
ibis ... 51, 53, 113, 197-199, 378, 379, 622
Idaho 253, 275
idol(s) 90, 157, 158, 177
idolaters 512, 527
Idu 260
image of Seth 386, 388, 392, 400, 402
image of the beast .. 32, 42, 387, 389, 392,
            401, 548
immorality 177, 188, 459
imperishable stars 485
impurities 109, 456, 469
Imsety 85, 206, 620, 622
incense 246, 250, 258, 385, 483
Indonesia 275
inferno 256
iniquities 251, 263
Inshas 468
intellect 88, 160
Introductory Hymn to Osiris . 149, 165, 167,
            244, 524, 525
inundation 190, 526, 527, 620
Inyotef 19, 471
Inyotef VII 471
Irenaeus 38, 39
iron 182, 185, 250, 258, 389, 390,
            533, 563
Ises 260, 275
ished-tree 163
Ishtar 469, 620
Isis .. 31, 41, 51, 53, 70, 75, 76, 79, 80, 85,
    105, 107, 168, 174, 204, 205, 226,
    232-234, 289, 299, 324, 329, 331,
    336, 337, 339, 340, 344, 346-348,
    355, 356, 360, 361, 366, 367, 376,
    377, 388, 506, 518, 618, 620, 621
Islam 93, 377
island of fire 244, 246
isocephaly 358, 359
Israel .. 3, 23, 31, 42, 57, 77, 114, 116-124,
    126-133, 136-142, 150-152, 201,
    230, 231, 236, 239, 240, 277, 348,
    417, 480, 532, 537, 545, 549, 553,

556, 561, 566, 567, 575, 587, 610-612, 614, 615, 618
Israelites . 94, 128, 129, 136, 137, 139-141, 181, 415
Issachar 611-613
Italy........................... 282
iunmutef priest 165, 166, 173, 174
ivory 250, 258, 514
jacinth.......................... 533
jackal 85, 86, 99, 220, 433
Jacob 116
Japanese dragon 96
jasper 60, 532, 541, 544
javelins 24, 150, 151, 212
Jerusalem ... 176, 190, 193, 290, 528, 545, 567, 570, 571
Jesus . 40, 43, 73, 74, 78-81, 348, 349, 356, 458, 484, 488, 545, 548, 554, 561, 563, 570
Jesus Christ 43, 74, 349, 545, 561
jewel 60, 532, 541
jewels 250, 258, 456, 457, 469, 533
Jews ... 74, 78, 95, 152-154, 156, 173, 193
Jezebel .. 24, 154, 157, 177, 179, 180, 187, 188, 567, 570
John . 1, 2, 36, 39, 40, 43, 74, 82, 489, 548, 554, 570, 573, 576, 578-581
John the Evangelist 74
Joint God 83, 205
Joseph 116, 119, 121, 125, 611-613
Joshua 348
Josiah 441
joy...... 135, 388, 444, 455, 489, 490, 520
Judah ... 24, 116, 119, 120, 122, 123, 125, 126, 137, 149, 197, 200-202, 548, 552, 611-613, 618
Judaism 93, 377
judge 92, 102, 103, 107, 112, 113, 119, 120, 122, 125, 146, 150, 160, 161, 223, 225, 227, 427, 432, 473, 503, 512, 611
judges ... 57-59, 84, 92, 93, 102, 103, 107, 115, 120, 132, 146, 161, 165, 408, 411, 441, 478, 480, 508, 563, 611
judgment .. 3, 22, 24, 27-30, 32, 39, 40, 42, 54, 57, 58, 61, 62, 64, 66, 71, 78, 79, 82, 92, 93, 97, 100, 102-104, 112, 113, 120, 132, 146, 159-167, 169, 172, 181, 185, 211, 252, 258, 289, 307, 336, 339, 357-361, 377, 379, 403, 404, 406-409, 412, 419, 425-427, 431-433, 435, 439, 440, 451, 456, 478, 480, 497, 498, 500-512, 525, 527, 528, 545, 547, 565, 567, 569-571, 573, 578, 607, 611, 619, 621, 622
justice 62, 86, 102, 107, 131, 134, 140, 150, 211, 360, 415, 420, 430, 432, 444, 578, 622
ka .. 88, 130, 131, 149, 383, 421, 422, 481, 482, 487, 521
kas 88, 95, 389, 419, 434, 487, 611
Kameni Islands 255
Kamose . 19, 189, 190, 192, 286, 295, 397, 400, 401, 454, 472, 473
Karnak ... 72, 215, 415, 423, 424, 442, 471
Karnak temple of Amon 442
Keeper of the Balance 79
Keeper of the Divine Abode 407
Keftyew 216
Kerma......................... 471
Kharu 442
Khati.......................... 480
Khemennu 155
Khepera 345
kheprer 66
Khepri ... 66, 67, 172, 203, 235, 302, 303, 322, 331, 344, 439, 451, 481, 511, 515, 561, 620
Kheraha 80, 260, 291-293, 560
Khnum 107, 448
Khu 483
King Djet 483, 514
king of kings 202, 244, 464, 564
king of the ages 418, 419, 423
King of the Gods 345
kingdom . 18, 19, 27, 45, 46, 48, 61, 71, 77-79, 99, 129, 139, 146, 159, 160, 162, 166, 188-190, 193, 202, 206, 207, 213, 253, 258, 263, 268, 283, 285, 336, 348, 350-352, 356, 358-361, 367, 374, 384, 388, 395, 401, 410, 428, 484, 488, 493, 500, 512, 514, 531, 535, 536, 542, 572
Kingdom of God ... 27, 350-352, 358, 367
kissing the ground 92
knife(s) . 104, 126, 127, 222-223, 225-226, 264, 265, 319, 347, 363, 365, 405, 406, 408, 409-411, 460, 463, 465, 488, 495, 502, 538, 612
Knossos 274
knowing the souls 155, 172

GENERAL INDEX 649

knowledge ... 25, 33, 35-37, 41, 45, 51, 58, 88, 97, 127, 138, 155-157, 171, 173, 181, 185, 188, 197, 198, 201, 203, 209, 212, 259, 283, 288, 289, 294, 297, 306-311, 321, 375, 378, 434, 449, 470, 504, 506, 508, 511, 531, 534, 573, 574, 622
Kode 228, 442
Krakatau 253, 275, 277
Kurdistan 442
Lady of Pestilence 261, 264, 265, 365
lake of fire ... 24, 28, 30, 57, 97, 101, 162, 163, 171, 289, 292, 294, 398, 399, 415-418, 433, 437-439, 475, 476, 495, 502, 506, 527, 528, 555, 556, 564, 569, 611, 617, 619
Lake of Life 433, 434, 611
Lake of the Uraei 433, 438
lamb .. 22-24, 29, 40, 42-43, 57, 64, 66-69, 71, 82, 84, 93, 130-131, 133, 135, 137, 142, 146, 151, 194-195, 197-198, 201, 203-208, 221, 227, 231, 233, 237, 239, 240, 242, 246-247, 268, 341, 344, 351, 352, 377-379, 381, 403, 418-422, 456, 464-465, 467, 473, 481, 483, 484, 486, 487, 489, 503, 518, 520, 535, 538, 539, 541, 543, 545, 548-549, 552, 554-556, 561, 570, 614, 617-618, 621
Lamb of God 489
Lamb of Re 66, 67
lament(ing) 227, 252, 316, 490, 491
lamentations 520
lamp 66, 68, 69, 89, 259, 541
lamps 89
lampstands 23, 89, 171, 312, 315, 317-319, 321
Land of Sokaris 302, 303, 400
landmark scenes 32, 555, 556, 617
Laodicea 72, 154, 156, 187, 188
Late Kingdom 285
Late Period 19, 177, 285, 492, 506
lava 251, 252, 254, 256, 257, 262, 264, 265, 289, 294
lava bombs .. 252, 254, 256, 257, 262, 264, 265
leaves .. 143, 144, 282, 300, 405, 417, 490, 506-508, 520, 540, 580, 581
Legend of Horus of Beu-t and the Winged Disk 376
leg(s) . 87, 178, 203, 232-234, 298-300, 310, 322, 338, 346, 366, 368, 374, 382, 388, 461, 501, 529, 531, 533, 552, 562, 563
Leiden Papyrus 245
Leto 31, 32, 336, 337, 366, 367
letters to the seven churches 42, 184, 195, 568
Levant . 107-109, 138, 187, 188, 201, 210, 211, 215, 216, 218, 220, 229, 270, 275, 279, 287, 288, 294, 295, 363, 567
Levi ... 116, 119, 121, 122, 125, 201, 202, 611, 612
liars 173-174, 527
libation(s) 63, 149-352, 526
libation vessels 63
library 31, 203, 205, 207, 208, 570, 577
Libya 215
Libyans 360, 422, 452, 503
lie(s) .... 26, 131, 162, 163, 173, 179, 186, 201, 260, 267, 274,-275, 289, 309, -323, 324, 343, 349, 374-375, 382, 385, 432, 448, 459, 462, 463, 467, 470, 504, 530, 539, 555
life span 480
lifetime 352, 358, 479, 480, 510, 524
light . 34, 36, 40, 41, 43, 51, 57, 60, 61, 66, 68, 69, 71, 94, 108, 138, 146, 152, 169, 180, 182, 195, 228, 233, 234, 238, 244, 252, 253, 257, 259, 269-271, 277, 288-291, 318, 319, 321, 330, 344, 345, 347, 355, 363, 371, 390, 405, 410-412, 416, 419, 428-430, 442, 446, 463, 480, 482, 486, 515, 519, 523, 529, 530, 536, 541, 543, 544, 563, 573, 580, 613
lightning .. 76, 90, 246, 247, 249, 250, 252, 256-258, 262, 264, 268, 418, 433, 439, 474
light-colored garments 428, 430
limbs 61, 106-108, 113, 114, 228, 233, 410, 411, 421, 527, 621
linen ... 103, 110, 145, 165, 237, 250, 258, 428, 563
lion(s) . 24, 85, 86, 137, 149, 168, 197, 200-202, 221, 298-299, 301, 307, 315, 316, 359, 372, 412, 461-463, 466, 468, 500, 506, 507, 510, 524, 548, 549, 552, 563, 618, 622
Lion of Egypt 202
Lion of Judah 137, 149, 200, 548, 552,

Litany of Re 66, 69, 176, 488, 552, 618
little scroll .. 3, 25, 267, 297, 298, 300, 301, 305, 306, 308-312, 368, 548, 552, 556, 595, 618
lock 166, 172, 173, 501, 530, 532
Lord 51, 60, 62, 69, 72, 73, 78, 79, 85, 102-104, 106, 111, 113, 126, 128, 130, 134, 150, 160, 167, 180, 184, 197, 216, 221, 223, 226, 227, 237, 243, 263, 264, 280, 291, 302, 304, 305, 318, 319, 321, 336, 344, 347, 351, 358, 359, 363, 365, 375, 379, 382, 418-420, 422, 423, 431, 433, 435, 464, 465, 479, 480, 511, 515, 518, 524-527, 541, 564, 612, 613
Lord God the Almighty ... 62, 69, 418, 419, 423, 431, 433, 435, 541
lord of brightness 60
Lord of Eternity 167, 304, 305
Lord of Knemennu 379
Lord of Lords 106, 464, 465, 564
Lord of Maat 134
Lord of Rosetjau 527
Lord of Shouting 263, 264
Lord of the earth 318, 319, 321
Lord of the East 321
Lord of the Thrones 72
Lord of the Thrones of the Two Lands .. 72
Lord of the Two Lands 363, 365
Lord of the West 160, 167
Lord of Truth 102
love .. 39, 60, 156, 170, 217, 350, 420, 422, 469, 508, 620
Lower Egypt . 48, 175, 189, 190, 199, 202, 209, 225, 295, 373-375, 382, 384, 385, 387, 389-392, 394, 395, 397-399, 408, 410, 411, 432, 446, 461, 462, 467, 470, 549, 577
lower sky 161
lunar disk 111, 343
Luther..................... 39, 571, 573
maat .. 53, 62, 79, 103, 132, 134, 135, 160, 162, 294, 360, 374, 395, 451, 621
Machir 117
magic ... 43, 105, 108, 111, 156, 168, 195, 236, 348, 460, 464, 465, 477, 504, 509, 510, 544, 564, 565, 577, 582, 620
magical spells 58, 306, 508
Magog 29, 492, 494, 496, 556, 567, 570, 619
Mamu 151, 212
Manasseh 612
manna.................. 167, 185, 503
mansion 104, 165, 481
Mansion of the Phoenix 481
marble 250, 258
mark(s) 36, 54, 134, 236, 237, 42, 307, 334, 381, 391, 398, 403, 407, 410, 418, 432, 447, 478, 484, 488, 564, 618
mark of the beast 391, 418, 564
marriage 446, 471, 472
Maxims of Ani 244
measure(ed) ..... 219, 253, 275, 312, 313, 326, 405, 477, 480, 501, Å 504, 530-531, 534, 543
Medamud 143
Medinet Habu 144
Mediterranean Sea .. 43, 97, 187, 209, 250, 259, 274-276, 287-289, 293, 363, 474, 527, 579, 580
mega-tsunamis 266
Megiddo 218, 219, 420, 441-444, 449, 450, 453-455, 570
Memnon Colossi 450
Memphis 140, 166, 190, 468, 621
Memphite theology 562
Menkheperre 420, 422
Mentjiu....................... 468
Merneptah 19, 139, 177, 181, 285
Mertseger 243, 621
Mesekhent 107
Meshech 496
messenger(s) .. 51, 79, 90, 93-95, 154, 171, 348, 454
messiah........................78
metal..... 61, 390, 505, 510, 529, 532, 537
metallic flesh 61
metaphor(s) 45, 52-53, 54, 62-63, 109, 209, 214, 234, 240, 307, 382, 403, 406, 411, 412, 544, 564- 566, 568, 570
Metternich Stele 336
Michael 94, 151, 337, 347-349, 366, 554, 560, 575-580
Middle East .. 17, 21, 78, 94, 96, 194, 213, 316, 391, 412
Middle Kingdom .. 18, 46, 48, 61, 99, 139, 159, 188, 189, 193, 283, 361, 410, 484, 488
mighty angel .. 250, 264, 266, 298, 326, 562

GENERAL INDEX

Mighty of Knives 264, 365
Min 71
Minoan empire 274, 474
miracle(s) 75, 447
mirror image 287, 489, 493, 517, 531
Mistress of Destruction 264, 363, 365
Mistress of Heat 262
Mistress of Power 263, 365
Mistress of Trembling 264, 365, 612
Mistress of Wrath 265
Mitanni 218, 442
Moab 415
moisture 164, 331, 332, 526, 622
monotheistic cultures 168
Montana 253, 275, 576
months ... 28, 90, 166, 190, 217, 254, 255,
  257, 269, 274, 276, 312, 315, 374,
  375, 392, 397, 455, 543, 566
moon ... 27, 53, 66, 69, 90, 111, 113, 194,
  227, 228, 249, 253, 257, 269, 274,
  276, 277, 294, 308, 331, 332, 339,
  343, 363, 379, 483, 622
morning sky .. 22, 29, 68, 82, 83, 130, 195,
  284, 289, 340, 344, 483, 484, 488-
  490, 511, 519, 520, 522-524, 541,
  571
morning star 78, 79, 92, 169, 170, 185,
  486, 503
mortal wound 376, 377
Mosaic legislation 201
Moses .. 3, 28, 32, 147, 415, 416, 418-423,
  425, 437, 569, 580, 601, 619
Mound of Spirits 263
Mound of Water 264, 266
Mount Etna 254
Mount St. Helens 253, 255, 275
mountain . 69, 90, 194, 227, 246, 247, 250-
  252, 257, 260-263, 266, 269, 273,
  274, 277, 284, 286, 289, 291, 293,
  294, 345, 441, 443, 449, 450,
  467, 502
mountain of fire ... 90, 250, 261, 269, 291,
  293, 294
mountainous waves 266
mourners 25, 299, 316, 317
mourning ... 250, 256, 258, 315-317, 350,
  388, 512, 515, 520, 521
mouth .. 29, 30, 52, 57, 62, 63, 73, 97, 103-
  106, 115, 131, 158, 172, 173, 206,
  247, 260, 272, 291, 292, 305-309,
  317-319, 338, 344, 352-354, 357,
  373, 382, 384, 398, 426, 436, 438-
  440, 445, 447-450, 454, 466, 468,
  488, 511, 521, 524, 547, 548, 563-
  565
multitude . 3, 23, 24, 37, 57, 110, 114, 116-
  118, 136, 137, 142-152, 197, 212,
  226, 227, 237, 261, 344, 352, 403,
  404, 413, 444, 452, 484, 485, 507,
  545, 568, 588, 614, 615, 618
mummy(ies) 55, 70, 85, 166, 272, 316,
  318, 328, 330-332, 357, 380, 430, 506,
  500, 515, 575
mummification 317
murderer(s) 99, 512, 527, 621
myrrh 250, 258
Mysterious One 177, 178, 180, 345
mythologization 250, 394
mythology .. 41, 51, 66, 68, 76, 87, 91, 95,
  282, 284, 285, 323, 361, 388, 395,
  469, 479, 481, 524, 531, 534, 605
nakedness 29, 202, 443, 444, 450, 451
Naneferkaptah 306
Naphtali 612
nation(s) 62, 63, 94, 95, 103, 105, 113,
  115-116, 129, 136, 143, 182, 185, 193,
  194, 201, 206, 218, 229, 258, 306-
  307, 309-311, 313, 314, 324, 345,
  237, 290, 348, 359, 360, 374, 379,
  418-420, 423, 425, 431, 433, 437,
  439, 440, 442, 452, 454, 465, 467,
  468, 474, 475, 477, 478, 491-493,
  540, 563
Nebmaat 134, 135
Necho 288, 441
necropolis ... 118, 243, 248, 368, 381, 391,
  394, 395, 424, 621
negative confession 409-410
negation of existence 163
Negroes 117, 360, 452, 503
neheh 523-525
Nehep 148, 149
Neith 96, 97, 104, 506, 621
Nekhbet 64
Nekhen 155
Nephthys . 70, 76, 105, 174, 204, 205, 232-
  234, 299, 324, 329, 340, 344, 355,
  356, 366, 367, 506, 518, 621
net.................... 517, 535, 539
Netchemet 177
neter(u)...................... 95, 480
Netherworld .. 32, 57, 58, 67-69, 71, 74, 76,

79, 82, 83, 85, 87, 88, 91, 92, 95,
106, 108, 109, 112, 118, 120, 121,
126-128, 132, 133, 139, 143-149,
151, 152, 155-158, 162, 163, 167,
170, 171, 180, 181, 195, 197, 198,
202, 210-212, 214, 222, 223, 232,
234, 237-239, 244, 245, 247, 248,
284-290, 293, 299, 303, 306, 311,
316, 318, 319, 322, 331, 338, 339,
344, 349, 353, 358-361, 368, 378,
379, 393, 400, 404, 408, 413, 416,
423, 426-432, 436, 438-440, 448,
449, 452, 459, 460, 463, 465, 466,
476, 477, 480-482, 484, 485, 489-
494, 497-499, 501, 509-511, 513-
515, 517, 519-522, 530, 533, 535,
536, 538, 539, 542, 548, 552, 571,
577, 611-613, 620, 621

new creation 3, 30, 267, 268, 293, 302,
305, 339, 352, 355, 512, 513, 528,
529, 542, 543, 556, 608, 619
new earth 511-516, 542, 543
new heaven . 249, 511, 512, 514, 516, 522,
528, 542, 543, 569
new Jerusalem 545, 567, 570, 571
New Kingdom . 19, 71, 139, 190, 213, 283,
285, 336, 348, 356, 388, 395, 401,
410, 428, 488, 500, 512, 531, 535
New Testament 33, 37, 39, 40, 44, 93,
154, 188, 240, 349, 514, 545, 561,
570, 579, 580, 582
newly born sun-god ... 247, 293, 303, 484,
511, 513, 518, 521, 541, 552
night ... 27, 30, 32, 44, 54, 55, 70, 71, 103,
132, 136, 146, 151, 163, 195, 228,
239, 242, 246, 253, 257, 271, 273,
275, 276, 286, 290, 291, 299, 331,
337-340, 342, 344, 346-348, 353-
355, 357-359, 361-366, 398, 400,
410, 413, 416, 430, 450, 454, 476,
481-483, 485, 495, 497-502, 504-
512, 541, 552, 621
Nile River 43, 64, 65, 141, 176, 211,
282, 288, 533, 539, 571, 621
Nile Valley 163, 470, 530
Nilometer of Rodah 177
nnu 155
noise ... 228, 244-246, 252, 254, 257, 262,
264, 272, 298, 332
Nubia 215, 468
Nubian 217, 422
Nun ... 304, 354, 501, 513, 514, 516, 517,
621
Nut 24, 27, 50, 85, 158, 163, 175-178,
204, 205, 268, 280, 323, 331, 336,
338, 339, 341-346, 353-357, 360,
361, 366, 367, 476, 483, 484, 497,
513-518, 522, 529, 530, 532, 536,
539-542, 548, 552, 554, 620-622
oblations 417, 491
ocean .. 245, 252, 255, 260, 276, 289, 516
Ogdoad 354
oil ... 78, 145, 215, 218-220, 229, 250, 258
oil and wine 215, 218-220, 229
Okeanos 217
Old Kingdom . 45, 139, 166, 283, 336, 361,
493, 514, 536, 542
Old One 317, 457, 465
Old Testament . 33, 40, 44, 77, 78, 93, 122,
129, 137, 153, 188, 415, 480, 496,
545, 569, 570, 579, 582
olive(s) 219, 220, 229, 315, 321, 566
olive trees 220, 315, 321, 566
One of the Horizon 147, 315, 476, 478
One of the Nether Sky 354
One of the Two Flames 410
one thousand years .. (see 1,000 year period)
One who Praises 389, 390, 613
Onomasticon of Amenope 198, 259
onyx 532
Orders of Osiris 408
ordination 77
Orion 21, 136, 170
Osirian penitent 79, 520
Osiris   22, 23, 25-27, 30, 32, 34, 42, 43, 51,
53, 57-65, 69-71, 74-80, 82-90, 92,
93, 95, 100-106, 108, 111-114,
126, 127, 130-133, 143, 146, 149,
151, 155, 157-163, 165-171, 176,
180-183, 185, 197-199, 204-206,
208, 210, 222, 223, 226, 233-239,
244, 246, 287-289, 291, 302, 303,
308, 309, 313, 314, 317, 321, 322,
324, 329, 331, 333, 337, 347, 348,
351-353, 356, 358-361, 367, 368,
375-382, 388, 395, 406-410, 412,
419, 423, 426, 428-432, 436, 438,
445, 451, 461, 465, 466, 469, 479,
481, 485, 486, 488, 489, 491, 497,
499-509, 513, 515-520, 524-528,
536, 538-542, 544, 547-549, 552-
554, 571, 611, 612, 620-622

GENERAL INDEX

Osiris-Re 64, 69, 70, 83, 84, 131, 133, 205, 233, 235, 239, 288, 303, 381, 485, 486, 489, 518, 519, 525, 539, 541, 548, 552, 621
ouroboros 353, 524
overseer(s) 94, 102, 165, 226, 405
ox 85, 86, 108, 549
oxen 145, 479
pain 151, 254, 262, 263, 266, 269, 365, 382, 495, 512, 613
Palestine 188, 190, 193, 218, 295, 454, 468, 470, 473, 572
palm 23, 137, 142-145, 164, 237, 238, 405, 526, 556, 568, 615, 618
palm branches . 23, 137, 142-145, 237, 238, 556, 568, 615, 618
Papias 39
Papyrus Carlsberg 48
Papyrus Harris 455
Papyrus of Ani 265, 575
Papyrus Salt 203, 577
paradise ... 58, 63, 64, 163, 164, 175, 512, 531, 538
parassang(s) 531
past .. 34, 37, 119, 174, 209, 210, 229, 245, 251, 273, 334, 399, 439, 449, 453, 482, 523, 525
Pe 155
pearl(s) 250, 258, 456, 457, 469, 536, 537 542
Pedemenopet 181
penitent....................... 79, 520
Pepi 162
percea tree of Heliopolis 481
Pergamum 154-156, 158, 186, 617
pestilence ... 193, 215, 220, 249, 250, 256, 258, 261, 264, 265, 365, 469
pharaoh ... 70, 75, 77, 139, 142, 146, 190, 193, 201, 210, 287, 358, 399, 422, 423, 434, 439, 441, 453, 466, 477, 488, 489, 518, 552, 580, 620, 621
Philadelphia .. 62, 154, 156, 171-173, 175-177, 186-188, 193, 575, 576, 578, 617
Philistia 415
Philistines 441
Phoenix period 481
physical body .. 88, 233, 303, 481, 505, 541
pillar(s) 24, 77, 85, 112, 165-166, 168, 173, 174, 217, 298, 300, 310, 313, 338, 421, 423, 503, 515, 529, 533, 544, 562, 563
pillar in the temple .. 24, 165, 166, 173, 174
pillars of fire 298, 300
pillars of heaven 85, 217, 421, 423
pit ... 26, 95, 247, 252, 257, 321, 322, 329, 332, 459, 460, 475-478
place of destruction ... 158, 179, 180, 184, 324, 325, 427, 452, 611
plague(s) 28, 264-165, 210, 246, 249, 250, 252, 254, 256-258, 263, 268, 312, 315, 317, 319, 320, 332, 418, 425-427, 432, 445451, 453, 456, 566
Plato ... 271, 273, 274, 278, 579, 580, 594
play on words 34, 37, 42, 45, 49-52, 73, 89, 220, 244, 247, 316, 321, 356, 387, 431, 448, 454, 458, 462, 475, 539, 562-564
plumage 299, 374
poison 80, 105, 236, 431, 495
poisonous gases 251
poisonous water 255, 266
pool(s) ...64, 175, 289, 438, 501, 539, 563
powder 246, 540
power 24, 48, 50-52, 54, 60, 62, 66, 71, 72, 76, 77, 88, 90, 97, 99, 105-108, 112, 122, 128, 146, 149, 157, 162, 168, 173, 174, 181-183, 185, 186, 189, 192, 193, 198, 210, 215, 217, 218, 228, 229, 232, 235, 236, 243, 254, 257, 261-266, 268, 274, 277, 280, 289, 290, 294, 295, 305, 306, 309, 317, 319-321, 326, 332, 345-348, 350, 353, 365, 370-372, 374, 375, 378, 379, 388, 389, 394, 395, 400, 407, 408, 439, 447, 453, 454, 460-462, 464, 465, 468, 473, 478, 479, 487, 493, 494, 503-505, 509, 562, 572, 576, 613, 621
praise .. 81, 84, 91, 93, 120, 123, 125, 135, 136, 152, 202, 237, 304, 315, 329, 345, 390, 418, 420, 435, 486, 487, 490, 491, 503, 613, 614
precious materials 61, 544
priest(s)...... 24, 29, 42, 46, 50, 74, 77-78, 92, 107, 109, 129, 132, 138-140,146, 147, 156, 165-167, 169, 172-175, 189, 190, 199-202, 204, 206-209, 242, 245, 261, 266, 272, 273, 286, 294, 328, 404, 422, 474, 477, 479, 482, 483, 486-489, 494, 495, 503, 522, 523, 533, 539, 542-

543, 547, 562, 563, 614, 619
priesthood ... 109, 128, 129, 146, 166, 167, 198, 505
primeval serpent 354, 355, 376, 552
primeval water(s) 350, 353-355, 357, 367, 413, 460, 501, 516, 523, 621
primordial river ... 30, 132, 368, 375, 376, 533, 534, 539, 540, 544, 621
primordial sea 487, 516
primordial water(s) 61, 65, 246, 342, 352, 357, 513, 516, 533, 539, 542
principalities 93
prisoners 25, 218, 439
prophesies 33, 165
prophesy 42, 260, 269, 271, 279, 281-286, 294, 306-308, 310, 345, 346, 571, 618
prophet(s) 32, 39, 40, 42, 74, 77, 84, 93-94, 100, 163, 259, 265-266, 269, 270, 323, 329, 359, 368, 397-402, 408, 409, 447, 454, 579, 495, 496, 548, 552, 564
prophetess 177, 179, 187
protection . 85, 87, 104, 111, 170, 193, 231, 233, 237-239, 242, 252, 257, 305, 309, 339, 347, 363, 365, 380, 404, 421, 476, 494
protective serpent(s) 68, 118, 147, 148, 234, 239, 325
protector(s) 85, 94, 104-105, 111, 149, 319, 329, 331, 428, 430, 459, 476, 572, 620, 62, 622
Psalms 77, 570
Ptah . 61, 77, 101, 128, 140, 166, 198, 213, 259, 621
Ptahotep 170
Ptah-Tatenen 77
Ptolemaic Period 203
pun(s) .. 35, 45, 48, 50-54, 62, 86, 98, 108, 128, 199, 234-236, 265, 300, 302, 309, 325-326, 390-391, 413, 435, 437, 449, 458, 481-482, 483, 487, 504, 507, 510, 517, 537 539, 546, 560, 564, 566, 567
punishment ... 25, 28, 156, 157, 159, 163, 171, 177, 180, 184, 222, 223, 248, 289, 330, 336, 339, 348, 357, 361, 403, 406-412, 418, 426, 436, 460, 491, 496-500, 502, 503, 506, 509,

510, 527, 568
pure garment 145, 164, 165
purification 78, 202, 525-528, 535, 536
purify 409, 433, 491
purple 250, 258, 456, 457, 469
pylon(s) .. 40, 144, 308, 309, 522, 535, 544
pyramid . 40, 44, 45, 54, 61, 62, 79, 80, 92, 104, 108, 127, 148, 160, 162, 283, 284, 336, 361, 399, 427, 434, 479, 481, 508, 514, 519, 526, 527, 534, 536, 577, 608
Pyramid Age 148
Pyramid Texts .. 40, 44, 45, 54, 61, 62, 92, 104, 108, 160, 283, 284, 336, 361, 427, 434, 479, 481, 514, 519, 526, 527, 536, 577
Python-Leto-Apollo myth 32
Qadesh 218, 442
Qahu 260
Quebsennuef 206
Ra (also see Re) ... 101, 108, 310, 337, 361, 395, 469, 521
Rā (also see Re) 101, 305, 346, 499, 533, 539
races 142, 143, 210
radiance 60, 216, 541, 563
radiant substance 61, 201, 202
rage(d) 275, 360, 412, 449, 493
Rahotep 471
rainbow 298, 300, 301, 310, 562, 563
ram . 22, 23, 29, 53, 66-71, 82, 91, 92, 130, 131, 133, 135, 143, 147, 168, 177, 195, 207, 225, 226, 232, 321, 322, 331, 332, 341, 344, 345, 416, 422, 464, 465, 484, 487, 489, 518, 541, 548, 561, 570, 620, 621
Ram, Great of Forms 66
Ramesses II 19, 139, 213, 424, 453
Ramesses IV 488
Ramesses V 19
Ramesses VI 2, 19, 27, 30, 44, 77, 91, 112, 177, 232, 235, 300, 313, 336-338, 346, 354, 359, 373, 380, 386, 389, 413, 454, 497, 506, 539, 557-559, 569, 577, 581, 618
Ramesside Period 142, 541
ram-headed sun-god 22, 29, 67, 92, 147, 207, 345, 464, 465, 484, 487, 518
Re ... 22, 30, 34, 37, 48, 50, 51, 53, 62, 64, 66-73, 75-78, 82-84, 88, 90-93, 95, 97, 100, 101, 104-109, 112-114,

GENERAL INDEX 655

118, 120, 127-131, 133-135, 140-143, 145, 150-152, 156, 160, 163, 168, 171, 172, 174-176, 179-181, 184, 185, 189, 190, 192, 193, 195, 198, 200-202, 204-208, 210-214, 216, 217, 220-222, 225, 227, 229, 230, 233-235, 237, 239, 245, 246, 248, 259, 267-270, 279, 280, 287-289, 291-293, 295, 302, 303, 314-316, 321, 322, 324-327, 330-332, 338, 339, 341, 344-347, 349-352, 355, 356, 358-361, 366-368, 371, 374, 376, 378-381, 387, 395, 396, 400, 401, 409, 411, 418-423, 426-431, 434, 435, 438-440, 443, 446, 448, 450-454, 461, 462, 465, 468, 476, 478, 481, 483-486, 488-496, 500, 503, 505, 507, 511-513, 515-522, 524-526, 528, 535, 536, 539, 541, 542, 548, 549, 552, 554, 561, 562, 569-572, 574, 611-613, 618, 620-622

Realm of the Dead . 70, 143, 163, 245, 333, 489, 490, 519
reanimation 352, 526, 571
reap 28, 175, 219, 350, 351, 404, 406
rebel(s) 104, 136, 156, 181, 185, 206, 208, 212, 217, 218, 228, 267,280, 291, 314, 360, 409, 421, 423, 451, 459-460, 503, 465, 495
rebellion 157, 158, 192, 218, 267, 395, 397, 454, 466

rebirth .. 130, 195, 293, 332, 362, 439, 481, 500, 527
red .. 41, 96, 109, 110, 113, 115, 163, 172, 174, 213-215, 228, 253-255, 257, 258, 265, 266, 268, 272, 288, 289, 293, 320, 343, 360, 415, 433, 434, 437, 452, 458, 459, 503
red dragon 96, 343
Red Sea 288, 415
redeemed 131, 133, 135
refreshment 149, 163, 430
Region of Silence 146, 244
reign on earth 146, 206, 207, 572
religious texts ... 2, 33, 34, 37, 48, 51, 112, 135, 394, 434, 450, 496, 541, 546
renewal ... 26, 32, 245, 246, 248, 268, 283, 303, 310, 331, 332, 362, 364, 365, 413, 439, 483, 512, 515, 516, 521,
523-525, 543, 544
renewal of creation 245, 246, 310, 413, 439, 512, 543
renewal of time 524
repent ... 90, 157, 171, 177, 179, 184, 187, 211
rest 24, 70, 75, 81, 130, 142, 147, 148, 150, 175, 182, 186, 209, 223, 229, 231, 265, 267, 287, 315, 327, 329, 338, 344, 347, 355, 374, 388, 406, 410, 425, 446, 476, 478, 490, 508, 511-513, 515, 522, 542, 544, 564, 573
resting ones 148, 614
resurrected dead .. 352, 479, 480, 489, 500, 501, 510
resurrection ... 3, 26, 27, 29, 30, 165, 170, 203, 225, 324-326, 330, 332, 339, 358-360, 409, 476, 479, 481-487, 490, 491, 495, 497-504, 506, 509-511, 527, 569, 571, 572, 607, 619, 620
Retenu 109, 216, 217, 221, 455
Reuben 116, 119, 120, 125
revolt 97, 104, 218, 442, 465
Re-Atum 73
re-creation .. 246, 248, 267, 270, 279, 293, 303, 332, 338, 516, 569
Re-Khepri........................ 515
Re-Osiris 69, 488, 489
rising of the sun 232-234, 483, 513
ritually purified 535
river(s) ... 22, 27, 29, 30, 43, 54, 57,63-65, 132,133, 169, 176, 187, 189, 195, 211, 214, 227, 251, 257-258, 262, 268-270, 272, 281, 282, 286, 288, 290, 291, 293, 301, 323, 324, 352, 353, 357, 363, 368, 375, 376, 379, 413, 418, 431, 433, 436, 441, 442, 445-447, 449, 453-455, 467, 474 517, 529, 533-535, 538-540, 544, 556, 569, 571, 619, 621
Rodah 177
Rosetau 71, 98, 324, 520
royalty 92, 374, 477
Ro-Setau 308, 309, 381, 391
ruby 533
ruler of kings 74, 78, 82
ruler of kings on earth 74, 78, 82
ruler of rulers 244
ruler of the earth 76, 112

sackcloth ... 194, 227, 228, 253, 256, 312, 315, 317
Sacred Eye 291, 380
sacred lake 416
saints ... 28, 170, 246, 259, 265, 266, 336, 357, 359, 371, 372, 374, 377-381, 458, 475, 492
Salatis (Salitis) 18, 396, 397, 470
Samuel 77, 441
sand ... 205, 300-302, 342, 346, 356, 357, 362, 367, 368, 381, 382, 384, 400, 450, 492, 515, 540, 622
sandals 217, 421
Santorini 281, 282, 577, 578, 581
sapphire 532
sarcophagus . 177, 290, 312, 313, 337, 338, 413, 442, 497, 529, 531, 533, 539
sarcophagus chamber .. 313, 337, 338, 442, 497, 539
Sardis 154, 156, 171, 187, 193
Satan . 23, 25, 30, 32, 40, 42, 90, 93, 95-97, 154, 156, 173, 175, 177, 181, 185, 192, 212, 350, 361, 370, 376, 397, 402, 459, 475, 491-495, 545, 547, 548, 552, 554, 556, 567, 619
savior 78
scarab(s) 66-68, 168, 169, 298, 344, 353-355, 404, 472 620
scarlet .. 250, 258, 456, 457, 459, 461, 464, 468, 469
Schutzbild scene 25, 232-235, 249, 557, 618
scorpion 80, 236, 254, 257, 269, 382
scribe(s) ... 46, 47, 74, 80, 81, 95, 98, 103, 111, 146, 166, 188, 190, 193, 197, 206, 207, 259, 286, 306, 386, 424, 435, 459, 489, 525-526, 528, 541, 561, 567, 570
scroll . 3, 24, 25, 34, 69, 137, 194, 197-200, 203-209, 212, 242, 267, 297-301, 303, 305-312, 368, 466, 506, 548, 552, 556, 562, 563, 568, 572, 582, 591, 595, 618
Scythian 496
sea ... 28, 30, 43, 54, 80, 90, 96, 229, 231-234, 246, 247, 249, 250, 252, 253, 255-258, 261, 263-267, 270, 273-277, 279, 281, 282, 286-289, 293-295, 298, 301, 304-306, 356, 357, 363, 367, 368, 370, 371, 373, 375, 376, 381, 392, 396, 401, 403, 407, 415, 416, 418, 433, 437, 453, 474, 487, 492, 498, 499, 501, 512, 516, 527, 552, 559, 562, 563, 569, 578, 581, 582, 622
sea of glass 28, 415, 416
sea of glass mingled with fire 415
seal(s) 134, 165, 200, 206, 207, 221, 232, 233, 237, 246, 254, 297, 300, 471
seal of the living God 232
sealed ... 96, 134, 197, 231, 232, 240, 253, 419, 475, 477, 478, 490, 614
seat 79, 88, 118, 134, 145, 149, 160, 181, 419, 485, 351, 434, 519
sea-monster 96
second beast .... (see 2nd beast)
second death .. 24, 146, 162, 163, 171, 185, 439, 503, 527
secret gates 160
seer(s) 323
Sekhmet 53, 452, 469, 621
Selkit (= Selket) 382, 476, 477, 506, 554, 621
Senusret III 143
Seqenenre 19, 397, 454, 472
Seqenenre Ta'a II................. 472
sequence(s) . 26, 28, 31, 35, 42, 58, 69, 71, 83-84, 100, 137, 170, 176, 177, 186, 196, 208, 267, 307, 313, 332-334, 336, 337, 364, 366, 383, 386, 387, 393, 401, 402, 414, 431, 442, 496, 498, 510, 513, 548, 545-546, 549-550, 555-557, 559, 568, 569, 570
seraphim 93
serpent(s) 23, 25-26, 29, 30, 40, 68, 85, 90-91, 95-97, 99, 100, 104-105, 117, 118, 121, 130-132, 137, 145, 147-151, 172, 173, 178, 183, 203, 212, 223, 226, 228, 232, 234-236, 238-239, 240, 247, 290, 294, 298, 299, 307, 314, 316-319, 321-322, 325, 329, 346, 350, 352, 354, 355, 360, 361, 368, 370, 371, 373-377, 381-385, 387-390, 400, 409, 429-431, 433, 436, 438, 439, 444-448, 456-460, 463-466, 470, 475-478, 482-484, 492, 493-494, 495, 506-507, 510, 524,538, 548, 552, 569, 611, 613, 617, 621
serpent of evil 376
servant of Re 422
servants .. 74, 95, 134, 146, 150, 157, 158, 177, 187, 189, 211, 226, 231, 232,

236, 359, 360, 489, 493, 535, 572
Seshat 30, 53, 508, 543, 621
Sesheta 508, 621
Seth 23, 29, 31, 34, 41, 53, 75, 76,
  78, 80, 82, 98, 98-100, 102-104, 108,
  113, 114, 127, 143, 159-161, 187,
  189, 190, 192, 213, 235, 291-294,
  322, 326, 336, 337, 339, 348, 354,
  356, 357, 360, 361, 366, 375-378,
  382, 385-392, 395-397, 399, 400,
  402, 406, 408-411, 430, 432, 446-
  448, 454, 459-462, 465, 468, 469,
  478, 484, 488, 493, 494, 502-504,
  506, 514, 518, 548, 552, 554, 561,
  572, 620-622
Sethos I 19, 213, 336, 413, 424, 453
Seti I 22, 78, 304, 305, 357, 375, 424
Setite regions 160
Setjetiu 468
Setne Khauemwas and Naneferkaptah . 306
seven . 3, 23, 24, 28, 29, 34, 39, 40, 42, 53,
  57, 84, 88-91, 93, 100, 110, 150,
  154-158, 160, 165, 170, 171, 181,
  184-195, 200, 211, 212, 221, 235,
  246, 249, 265, 267, 268, 273, 280,
  297, 298, 301-303, 311, 327, 328,
  331, 333, 348, 373, 394, 396, 405,
  406, 418, 425-432, 436, 438-441,
  449, 451, 453, 455, 456, 460-464,
  466-468, 470, 471, 473, 474, 486,
  490, 503, 525, 527, 533, 547, 549,
  553, 563, 565, 568, 569, 572, 588,
  590, 602, 617, 619
shadow(s) 88, 149, 180, 181, 185, 223,
  247, 252, 269, 314, 329, 408, 504, 506
sharp knife 104
sharp sword 62, 105, 563
Sharuhen 190, 218, 295
she who loves silence 243
sheep 66, 209, 250, 258
shelter 238, 239, 254, 255, 262, 352
sheltered ones 147, 556, 614, 618
shepherd 142, 143
Sheshi 18, 396, 470
Shesmu 412, 461, 622
shesshes 458, 459, 470, 564
Shetait 24, 177, 178, 621
ship(s) 247, 250, 253, 256-258, 270,
  276, 288, 294, 377, 390
shipmasters 250, 258, 266
shrine .. 22, 23, 29, 44, 67, 68, 79, 90, 131,
  134, 143, 146-148, 195, 198, 204,
  206-208, 239, 246, 313, 314, 321,
  322, 347, 350, 400, 419, 426, 427,
  429, 464, 491, 522, 540, 552, 581,
  611
shrine of Osiris 321
Shu . 53, 136, 170, 172, 176, 206, 207, 280,
  331, 341, 344, 356, 451, 481, 506,
  622
sickbed 177, 180, 184, 187
sickle(s) 403, 404, 406, 407, 409, 411
Sidon 188, 275
sign(s) 20, 51, 63, 90, 97, 144, 145,
  151, 163, 200, 203, 212, 237-238,
  243, 251, 256, 270, 277, 307, 318,
  353, 380-381, 384, 386, 388, 390,
  391, 396, 397, 405, 447, 464, 466,
  564, 613, 620
signet ring 237
silence 3, 146, 241-249, 450, 490, 526,
  593, 618, 621
silent communion 244
silent land 244
silent man 243, 526
silent region 181, 450, 500, 522
silk 250, 258
silver ... 218, 250, 258, 444, 505, 510, 533
Simeon . 116, 119, 120, 122, 125, 126, 612
sin(s) 74, 80, 103, 160, 251, 258, 262,
  263, 275, 308, 480, 503, 510
sing 135, 244, 417-419, 421, 425, 437,
  486, 519, 569
Sinless One 363, 502
sisters 172, 174, 233, 329
skies 514
sky ... 3, 22, 27, 29, 40, 50, 67, 68, 71, 79,
  82, 83, 85, 103, 108, 113, 130,
  133, 136, 151, 152, 160, 161, 163,
  166, 169, 172, 174, 175, 177, 178,
  180, 194, 195, 200, 204, 212, 227,
  228, 234, 240, 246, 248, 251, 253,
  257, 262, 263, 267-269, 274, 275,
  282, 284, 285, 287, 289-294, 296,
  298, 299, 301, 304, 320, 321, 324,
  326, 327, 331, 332, 334, 336-349,
  353-356, 358, 362, 363, 365-367,
  374, 406, 413, 431, 459, 474, 476,
  480, 481, 483-491, 493, 495, 497-
  499, 506, 511-520, 522-525, 527-
  536, 538-542, 545, 548, 549, 552,
  554, 562, 571, 572, 597, 613, 618,

sky-goddess 27, 50, 85, 163, 175, 177, 178, 204, 331, 339, 341, 342, 353, 354, 356, 406, 497, 517, 518, 528, 529, 532, 533, 536, 539, 541, 542, 548, 549, 552, 620, 621
slain 62, 105, 110, 137, 150, 198, 202, 203, 205, 206, 222, 223, 225-227, 259, 265, 266, 293, 322, 323, 350, 370, 376, 385, 387-389, 392, 441, 443, 458, 478, 485, 548, 552, 556, 564, 617, 618, 620
slain lamb ... 137, 198, 203, 548, 556, 617, 618
slaughtering 247, 460, 465
slave(s) 194, 218, 228, 257-258, 268, 385, 389-391, 439, 564
sleep 148, 245, 480, 490, 501
smoke ... 90, 228, 236, 246, 250-258, 262-264, 266, 275-277, 284, 286, 294, 332, 410
Smyrna 38, 154, 156, 187, 192
snake(s) 96, 104, 233-236, 275, 287, 318, 353, 483
Snefru 283
social upheaval 270, 271, 277, 474
Sokar(is) 25, 163, 297-303, 310, 311, 326, 347, 368, 379, 381, 391, 393, 400, 515, 548, 552, 622
solar barque (or bark) 55, 67, 118, 132, 143, 147, 195, 302, 308, 315, 316, 318, 319, 348, 350, 368, 404, 438-439, 459, 476, 483, 487, 513, 519, 540
solar disk(s) .. 53, 67, 68, 70, 76, 111, 177, 198, 206, 207, 232-234, 237, 289, 331, 332, 343, 353, 374-375, 438, 536, 537 541
soldier(s) 24, 25, 93, 94, 108, 110, 113, 115, 117, 132, 133, 138, 151, 189, 190, 192, 202, 212, 213, 219, 222, 223 225, 226, 229, 231, 236-240, 347-348, 350, 352, 439, 443, 444, 450- 453, 458, 464, 465, 494, 572
solitons 277, 581
Solon 271, 273, 278
son of Osiris ... 22, 74-78, 82, 84, 113, 520, 552
son of Re ... 70, 75, 77, 106-108, 112-114, 207, 227, 346, 349, 358, 380, 387, 453, 461, 468, 489, 518, 570, 572

son of the sun 79, 107, 113, 138, 146, 210, 225, 351, 385, 424, 439, 548, 620
song of Moses ... 3, 28, 32, 415, 416, 418-421, 423, 425, 437, 601, 619
Sopd 236
sorcerers 512, 527
sores 254, 269, 418, 433
Sothis 170
soul (s) .... 25, 57, 71-72 , 88, 92, 103, 116, 117, 128, 129, 130, 134, 136, 148-150, 155-158, 163-164, 170-173, 180-182, 184, 185, 188, 202, 211, 223, 225-227, 231, 233, 242, 244, 247, 258, 261, 264-266, 286, 287, 289, 294, 303, 304, 316, 322, 323, 330, 350, 363, 365, 379, 408-409, 410, 418-419, 426-427, 435-438, 452, 463, 466, 480, 484, 486-488, 490, 491, 498- 501, 506, 517, 520, 522, 526, 611, 535-536, 571, 581, 612
spear(s) 24, 96, 151, 212, 291, 347, 348, 365, 376, 404, 410, 458, 460, 464-466
spew 151, 234, 251, 315, 318, 384
sphinx 163
spice 250, 258
spirit ... 39, 88, 89, 94, 145, 147, 148, 163, 164, 170, 175, 183, 185, 408, 423, 479, 487, 563, 573
Spirits of the East 345
spiritual beings 88, 94, 95
spiritual body 481
spoils (of war) 190, 218 444
spotless 131, 133, 503
stadia 268, 411, 531, 543, 566
star(s) .... 27, 53, 57, 78-79, , 88-90, 92 121, 125, 126, 128, 135, 136, 169-170, 185, 194, 216, 227, 228, 235, 236, 249, 253, 257, 269, 274, 286, 287, 294, 339, 343, 344, 346, 362, 363, 366, 374, 375, 405, 406, 476, 483-490, 493, 497, 503, 514, 562, 611-613
steatite 168, 169
Stele of Paris 75
stones ... 60, 169, 254, 264, 265, 282, 332, 533, 534, 541, 542, 544
storm(s) 102, 190, 193, 210, 227, 242, 269, 298, 299, 301, 321, 347, 563, 613, 620, 622

street(s) 26, 64-65, 323, 324, 517, 538
strife 218, 272, 431, 467
sulphur . 163, 255, 257, 263, 398, 399, 403, 410, 412, 476, 495, 527, 564
sun .. 22-24, 26, 27, 29, 30, 32, 48, 50, 57, 60-62, 65-69, 71, 72, 77-79, 82-85, 87, 88, 90-93, 99, 100, 104-109, 112-114, 117, 118, 127, 130-138, 140, 142, 144-148, 150-152, 155-158, 165, 171, 174-176, 178-185, 192-195, 200-205, 207, 209-212, 214, 215, 222, 223, 225, 227, 228, 232-235, 237, 239, 240, 245, 247-249, 252, 253, 256, 257, 262, 268, 269, 274, 276, 277, 283-295, 297-300, 302, 303, 308, 310, 311, 313-319, 321-327, 330-333, 338-345, 347-361, 363, 368, 370, 371, 374-381, 385, 393, 400, 404, 406-411, 413, 416-420, 423, 424, 426-436, 438, 439, 446, 448, 449, 451, 452, 457, 459, 460, 464-466, 479-481, 483-487, 489-496, 498-503, 505-514, 516, 518-525, 528, 532, 535, 536, 538-542, 548, 549, 552, 562-564, 568-572, 577, 620-622
Sunda Straits 253, 276
sun-bird 481
sun-disk 48, 68, 232, 357, 620
sun-god .. 22-24, 26, 27, 29, 30, 32, 50, 61, 62, 65-69, 72, 77, 79, 82, 83, 85, 87, 88, 90-93, 100, 104-109, 112-114, 117, 118, 127, 130-138, 140, 142, 144-148, 150-152, 155-158, 165, 171, 174-176, 178-185, 192, 193, 195, 200, 201, 203, 204, 207, 209-212, 214, 215, 222, 223, 225, 227, 232-235, 237, 239, 240, 245, 247-249, 268, 284, 286-290, 292-295, 297, 299, 302, 303, 310, 314-319, 321-327, 330-332, 338, 340-342, 345, 348, 350-352, 354, 368, 374-381, 385, 393, 400, 404, 406-411, 413, 416, 418, 420, 423, 424, 426-429, 431-436, 438, 439, 448, 449, 451, 452, 464-466, 480, 481, 483-487, 489-496, 498-503, 505-508, 510-514, 518-521, 523-525, 528, 535, 536, 539-542, 548, 549, 552, 568-572, 620-622
Swallower of the Ass 406, 409-411

sword .. 52, 57, 62, 63, 104-106, 109, 115, 201, 211, 213, 215, 220, 222, 223, 225, 378, 384, 387, 396, 397, 408, 548, 563-566
sword of my mouth 62
sycamore 163, 164
sycamores 321
synagogue(s) 154, 156, 173, 192
Syria ... 189, 218, 295, 442, 454, 468, 470
Syrian National Church 39
tabernacle 147, 148, 238, 239
table of offerings 149
tadpoles 144, 450
tale known as Setne Khauemwas and Naneferkaptah 306
tamarisk 163
Tambora 275, 276
tambourine 244
Taoism 96
Taster 307
Taweret 168
Teaching of King Khati 480
Teachings of Amen-em-apt 244
Tefenet, Tefnut 481, 622
Tefnut, Tefenet 172, 176, 280, 331, 356, 506, 622
Tehenu 422
Tel el Yahudiya 468
Tel el-Sahaba 468
temenos 544
tempest 242, 292, 348, 349, 563
temple(s) ... 24, 26, 46, 60, 66, 69, 96, 97, 104, 109, 135, 139, 143, 146, 159, 163, 165-167, 172-175, 185, 186, 190, 203, 204, 207-208, 213, 215, 217, 242, 244, 260, 271, 290, 311-315, 333, 376, 377, 404, 406, 415-416, 421-425, 429, 441, 442, 460, 489, 492, 503, 515, 520, 535, 541-544, 582, 619
Temple of Esna 96, 97, 104, 460
temple of God 26, 312-315, 543
ten kings . 29, 378, 396, 460-463, 465, 466, 471-473, 549
tent 23, 147, 148, 238, 239, 429, 443
tephra 254, 257, 578, 581
terror . 60, 86, 216, 217, 264-266, 421, 430, 553
Teshub 190, 395, 469
testimony ... 147, 321, 351, 356, 484, 488, 508, 563

Teti 18, 92
Thasos 288
The Wanderings of Isis in the Delta and the Birth of Horus 346
Theban kings . 19, 189, 190, 192, 397, 446, 471, 472
Theban necropolis 424
Thebes . . 72, 138, 189, 192, 392, 395, 396, 400, 401, 420-422, 446, 454, 455, 462, 467, 470-473, 620, 621
theocracy 79, 129, 237, 398
theocratic system 207
theology 93, 99, 562
Thera 25, 255, 267, 274-279, 281-291, 295, 305, 334, 363, 396, 418, 474, 559, 560, 580
thigh 57, 106, 108, 113, 564
thirst 148, 164, 263, 264, 521, 555
Thoth . 23, 31, 50, 51, 53, 79, 80, 101-106, 108, 110-115, 158, 160-162, 165, 197-199, 204-210, 212, 259, 307, 337, 346, 348, 354, 376, 378, 379, 408, 409, 508, 525, 526, 548, 552, 554, 575, 621, 622
Thoth's Book of Breathings . 379, 380, 401
thousand years 78, 243, 293, 475, 478, 479, 481-483, 485, 486, 490, 491, 495, 499, 571, 572
thousands of thousands 93, 227
throne 3, 22, 23, 25, 32, 34, 40, 42, 53, 57-63, 65, 69, 72-73, 76-78, 82-93, 99, 100, 105, 107, 111, 126-128, 132, 135, 142, 143, 145-147, 155, 156, 159-162, 165, 167, 180, 182, 183, 185-187, 194, 195, 197-199, 201, 204-206, 208, 212, 218, 222, 223, 237-239, 242, 246, 253, 268, 278, 280, 291, 344, 346, 358-360, 366, 370, 372, 373, 375, 377, 406, 408, 409, 425, 426-427, 430, 432, 435, 445, 454, 462, 463, 479, 497, 498, 501, 503-508, 510, 519, 521, 524-528, 535, 538, 539, 541, 547, 549, 552, 553, 555, 565, 566, 568, 572, 617, 620, 622
throne of God 63, 64, 69, 92, 142, 146, 206, 238, 426, 524, 535, 538, 539, 549, 566, 572
throne of Osiris . 22, 25, 32, 57, 63, 64, 85, 86, 127, 132, 160-162, 182, 199, 222, 223, 359, 409, 432, 501, 503, 505-508, 527, 538, 539, 549, 622
throne scene . . . 3, 22, 57-59, 64, 66, 82-84, 89, 92, 194, 195, 206, 212, 242, 505, 539, 547, 555, 568, 617
thunder . . 90, 135, 221, 246, 247, 250, 252, 257, 258, 264, 268, 301, 302, 433, 439
Thutmosis I 195, 285
Thutmosis III . 44, 109, 113, 139, 195, 215-220, 228, 229, 283-285, 414, 415, 418, 420, 422-424, 441-443, 449, 452-455, 568, 569, 618, 619
Thyatira . . 24, 31, 154, 157, 158, 170, 171, 177-179, 181, 183, 184, 186-188, 617
Tigris River 442
Timaeus . . 31, 273, 278, 280, 579, 594, 595
time . . 28-30, 33-36, 39, 48, 50, 53, 54, 61, 67, 71, 72, 74, 88, 91, 102, 106, 108, 111-113, 132, 133, 139-141, 143, 144, 150, 152, 155, 163, 165, 166, 168, 177, 187, 189, 192, 199, 209, 211, 218-220, 227, 229, 232, 233, 238, 242, 245, 246, 249, 251, 253, 262, 263, 267, 269, 271, 273, 274, 278, 279, 281-284, 290, 291, 293-296, 299, 303-305, 310, 324, 326, 330, 334, 338, 339, 352-355, 357, 359-362, 368, 373-377, 391, 394-397, 399-401, 403-405, 409, 425, 434, 435, 439, 442, 443, 446, 447, 449, 452, 455, 460, 462, 467-469, 471, 474, 478-480, 482-484, 486-488, 490, 494-497, 501, 503, 507, 512, 515, 523-525, 528, 533-536, 556, 567, 571-574, 580, 613, 618, 620
Titans 80
Tomb of Ramesses VI 2, 27, 30, 44, 77, 91, 112, 177, 232, 235, 300, 337, 338, 346, 354, 359, 373, 380, 386, 389, 413, 454, 497, 506, 539, 557-559, 569, 581, 618
tongue . . 45, 101, 112, 126, 127, 206, 347, 349, 379, 561, 567, 612, 613
tongue of Re 112
topaz 533
torch 90, 257
torches 23, 88, 89, 280, 318, 405, 406, 410, 411, 416
torment 90, 257, 258, 264, 410, 438

GENERAL INDEX

torture 254, 257, 269
towrope 302, 438
trample 312, 313, 428
transformations . 66, 67, 344, 439, 511, 521
tree goddess 164, 525
Tree of Heaven 508
tree of life 24, 163, 164, 185, 503, 515, 525, 539, 566
tree spirits 163
trees ... 163, 219, 220, 232-234, 247, 257, 268, 269, 312, 315, 319, 321, 502, 539, 540, 566
trial . 79, 103, 112, 127, 159-161, 174, 193, 194, 499
tribes of Israel .. 3, 23, 31, 42, 57, 114, 116-124, 126-133, 136-142, 150-152, 230, 231, 236, 239, 240, 417, 537, 545, 549, 553, 556, 561, 566, 567, 587, 610-612, 614, 615, 618
tribulation(s) .. 33, 34, 85, 90, 154, 156-158, 171, 177, 179, 180, 184, 187, 193
tribunal(s) 79, 86, 104, 159, 161, 162, 165, 180, 376, 408, 430, 434, 509, 527
triumphant 24, 76, 106, 160, 164, 413, 415, 520, 525, 571
Troglodytes 217, 422
troops .. 110, 122, 125, 190, 213, 219, 229, 231, 239, 291, 377, 432, 433, 441-445, 450, 453-455, 457, 488
trumpet(s) 246, 249, 268, 565, 566
truth 23, 33, 61, 62, 72, 73, 79, 91-93, 102, 103, 131, 132, 134, 146, 150, 160, 211, 244, 273, 287, 294, 308, 360, 374, 444, 445, 451, 491, 510, 522, 611, 621
truth symbols 91
truthfulness 131, 135, 137, 160, 614
tsunamis 252, 266, 294, 332
Tuat 77, 246, 437, 493, 514, 515, 528, 531, 538, 539, 542, 563
Tubal 496
Turin Canon 471
Turkey 276, 581
turquoise 60, 61, 321, 345
turquoise country 345
Tutankhamun 285, 577
two-edged sword 62, 63
two-headed nature of time 482
two-headed serpent ... 299, 307, 463, 482, 492
Typhon 41, 108, 337, 494, 506-507, 621
Typhonic 410
Tyre 177, 187, 188, 275
Tyrrhenian Sea 282
Uash 500
Udjat-eye 489
unfaithful 90, 156, 157, 182, 195, 210, 380, 528
unguent 149, 246
Unique One 72
Uniter (gate) 521
universe . 50, 273, 280, 294, 331, 338, 522, 528, 621
upheaval, social 270, 271, 277, 474
Upper Egypt ... 61, 64, 189, 199, 202, 295, 374, 376, 395, 399, 446, 453, 461-463, 468, 473
upper sky 161
Ur 169, 289, 302, 417
uraei 433, 438, 493, 494, 496, 613
uraeus 26, 48, 105, 145, 151, 238, 316-319, 329, 349, 382, 384, 385, 433, 493, 494, 506, 507, 621
uraeus serpent(s) .. 26, 105, 145, 151, 238, 316-319, 329, 382, 384-385, 433, 493
Urnes 288, 404, 410, 411
Useru poles 451
Utau 348, 359, 429-431, 436, 437, 502
Valley of the Kings ... 243, 290, 413, 518, 529, 532, 539, 579
veiled ones 165
Vesuvius 253, 254, 282, 293
victorious 76, 108, 159, 161, 164, 165, 167, 307, 435, 444, 455, 480, 498, 508, 527, 528
victory ... 75, 80, 104, 108, 109, 139, 160, 162, 174, 215, 217, 218, 220, 228, 414, 415, 418, 420-423, 441-443, 453, 455, 568, 569, 619
Victory Hymn of Thutmosis III ... 215, 217, 218, 228, 414, 415, 418, 420, 422, 423, 453, 568
vindicate(d) 59, 76, 103, 104, 136, 159-162, 510
vizier 146
voice(s) 62, 64, 90, 93, 102, 103, 135, 144, 150, 157, 159, 171, 215, 219,

221, 226, 227, 232, 234, 237, 243-247, 249, 252, 257-258, 259, 264, 268, 298, 302, 307, 316, 326, 330, 350, 404, 406, 407, 433, 435, 441, 445, 477, 519, 563, 564
volcanic dome   251, 256-258, 262, 266, 289
volcanic eruption ... 31, 228, 229, 249-252, 254-256, 266-269, 271-273, 276, 279, 281-285, 292, 294, 295, 305, 330, 332, 418, 436, 453, 559, 560
volcanic eruptions .. 31, 43, 228, 250, 252, 259, 263, 266, 291, 293, 295, 439, 572
volcano .. 25, 251, 253, 255, 257, 259-262, 270, 272, 274, 279, 281, 282, 289, 330, 363, 396, 569, 579, 580
vulture 48, 64, 66
Wadi Tumilat 468
Wahaf........................... 96
wail(ing) 245, 255, 258, 278, 347, 490, 491
Wanderings of Isis in the Delta and the Birth of Horus 346
war . 3, 25, 27, 90, 101, 103, 104, 108, 115, 138, 150, 151, 158, 170, 176, 186, 187, 190, 192, 193, 195, 211-213, 215-218, 220-223, 226, 227, 229, 231, 237-239, 242, 248, 249, 270, 291, 294, 295, 321, 322, 336, 343, 345, 347-352, 355-357, 361, 362, 364, 366, 367, 371, 372, 376-379, 398, 410, 431, 441, 442, 445, 447, 454, 456, 464-467, 469, 472, 473, 484, 485, 492-494, 497, 548, 557, 563, 564, 568, 571, 572, 592, 620, 621
war cries 213, 215, 216, 218, 220, 221, 223, 227, 229, 231
war cry 216, 218, 220, 221, 348
war in heaven .. 27, 345, 347, 348, 362, 364
warrior(s) .. 29, 85, 93, 117, 102-104, 108, 151, 226-227, 229, 435,495
Washington 253, 255, 275
water . 22, 24, 27, 29, 30, 61, 63-65, 78, 80, 142, 143, 148, 149, 152, 163, 164, 167, 169, 176, 190, 221, 246, 254-258, 260-264, 266-272, 283, 287, 289, 291, 294, 301, 306, 315, 320, 324, 331, 332, 352-355, 362, 363, 365, 367, 368, 370, 411, 415-418, 430, 431, 433, 435, 437, 439, 442, 445, 446, 460, 474, 487, 491, 501, 516, 517, 525-528, 535, 538, 539, 544, 555, 614, 619
water of life 63, 64, 164, 525-527, 538, 544, 619
water of Osiris 176, 287
Weary-Heart 502
weaver 122, 125, 201, 202, 612
wedjat-eye 168, 379, 380
weep(ing) 200, 255, 258, 317
welcome 166
Wennefer 79, 161
Wepwawet 163
West .. 77, 79, 92, 104, 112, 120, 128, 129, 146, 155, 157, 158, 160, 167, 169, 183, 202, 205, 212, 215, 235, 244, 245, 282, 287, 288, 303, 308, 309, 316, 338, 351, 413, 427, 431, 451, 452, 470, 490, 495, 520-522, 530, 538, 611, 621
Westerners ... 133, 217, 419, 421, 478, 479
whale 96
wheat .. 215, 218, 219, 229, 250, 258, 515, 539
white 23, 30, 53, 57, 60, 61, 84, 90, 91, 93, 103, 108-110, 113, 115, 127, 132, 142, 145, 146, 151, 152, 164, 168, 169, 171, 185, 195, 199, 202, 213, 215, 221, 223, 231, 237, 255, 272, 326, 400, 416, 428, 490, 503-505, 510, 521, 547, 563, 614, 615
white crown 53, 61, 127, 199, 490, 547
white garment(s) 57, 60, 90, 110, 164, 171, 185, 428, 503
white hair 57, 61
white horse ... 108, 115, 215, 221, 400, 563
white linen 110, 237
white robes 23, 91, 110, 142, 145, 146, 151, 223, 237, 416, 428
white throne 504
widow 76
wife 36, 75, 107, 518, 528, 620, 621
wind(s) 25, 51, 149, 231-232, 234-236, 239, 255, 337, 367,382, 388, 509, 515, 530, 563, 557, 618, 621
wine ... 215, 218-220, 229, 237, 250, 258, 268, 292, 403, 407, 411, 412, 458, 491, 563, 622
wine-press ... 268, 403, 407, 411, 412, 622
wine-press god 412
Winged Disk 108, 374, 376
winged serpent 385, 388, 483, 484, 492
wings 23, 51, 66, 75, 85, 87, 113, 298,

GENERAL INDEX 663

299, 341, 346, 347, 355, 360, 367, 368, 387, 388, 483, 549
wisdom . 25, 40, 43, 97, 140, 170, 197-199, 209, 243, 307, 308, 310, 311, 408, 456, 563, 570, 580, 581, 622
witness(es) 3, 71-72, 74, 79, 26, 103, 107, 112, 150, 160-161, 174, 223-244, 267, 294, 301, 306, 310-312, 315-319, 321, 323-327, 329, 330, 332-334, 336, 358, 429, 441, 548, 566, 570, 596, 618
woman ... 3, 27, 29, 40, 68, 172, 174, 177, 179, 184, 199, 244, 262, 296, 316, 334, 336-339, 343-346, 352, 353, 355, 360-362, 366, 367, 446, 456-461, 464-470, 474, 497-499, 514, 517, 518, 529, 545, 548, 549, 552, 554, 597, 618, 621
wood 218, 219, 250, 258, 417
word of God .. 3, 23, 39, 42, 101, 102, 104, 110, 112, 150, 197, 484, 488, 550, 552, 554, 563, 619
Word of Power 305, 309
word play . 37, 42, 45, 49-52, 89, 539, 562-564
wormwood 255, 257
worship 71, 85, 90, 94, 120, 125, 136, 169, 175, 190, 209, 244, 312-314, 345, 370, 372, 376, 379, 381, 382, 384, 385, 387-389, 392, 395, 403, 407, 409, 418-420, 423-425, 447, 469, 490, 491, 519, 535, 540-542, 563, 611, 614, 620
wound 80, 372, 376, 377
wrath .. 3, 28, 86, 101, 150, 170, 193, 194, 227, 230, 231, 242, 247-249, 251, 261, 265-268, 289, 295, 403, 407, 411, 412, 425, 427-432, 436, 440, 441, 449, 451, 452, 467, 564, 568, 569, 572, 602
wrath of God ... 3, 28, 101, 150, 193, 194, 249, 251, 268, 411, 412, 425, 427, 429-432, 436, 440, 449, 451, 467, 568, 569, 602
Yaru Fields 30, 539, 540
Yeraza 218
young sun-god 30, 354, 374, 481, 484, 514, 519, 524, 539, 541
Zahi 216, 422
Zeller (1969) 159, 589
Zeus 273, 280, 337, 366, 367

www.ingramcontent.com/pod-product-compliance
Lightning Source LLC
Chambersburg PA
CBHW031659230426
43668CB00006B/49